PEARSON.

ALWAYS LEAR...

 W9-CNV-032

Welcome to the History portal for Grand Rapids Community College

Your class will be using a custom-built online educational resource. Once you register, you will have easy access to all your materials with just a few clicks!

To register for your course, you will need:
☐ A **Student Access Code** (This code can be found on your Online Access card. Example: SIMPLE-FRILL-TONLE-WEIRS-CHOIR-FLEES)
☐ Your school's zip code: 49503
☐ A valid email address

How to Register for and Access Your Course or MyLab

1) Please go to: http://www.pearsoncustom.com/mi/grcc_history. The URL can also be found on the Online Access card that came with your textbook.
2) Please choose your section HST 249 or HST 250
2) Click **Register**.
3) Read the License Agreement and Privacy Policy and click **I Accept**.
4) Do you have a Pearson account?
   a. Select **Yes** if you already have a Pearson account
   b. Select **No** if you do NOT have a Pearson Account.
   c. Select **Not Sure** if you do not know if you have a Pearson Account. Enter your email address and if you had a Pearson account an email will be sent with your login information.
5) Type in your Student Access Code in the fields provided and click **Next**.
6) Fill out the fields on the Account Information screen and click **Next**.
7) When successful, you will see a Confirmation & Summary page with your account information. This information will also be emailed to you – be sure to keep this email for future reference.
8) Click the **Log In Now** button on the Confirmation & Summary page to view your course or MyLab.

Important Note: Each time you access your course or MyLab, you will need to log in with your Login Name and Password.

Need Help?
Assistance is available at
http://www.pearsoncustom.com/_global/productinfo/websites/_24_7/

Good luck in your course!

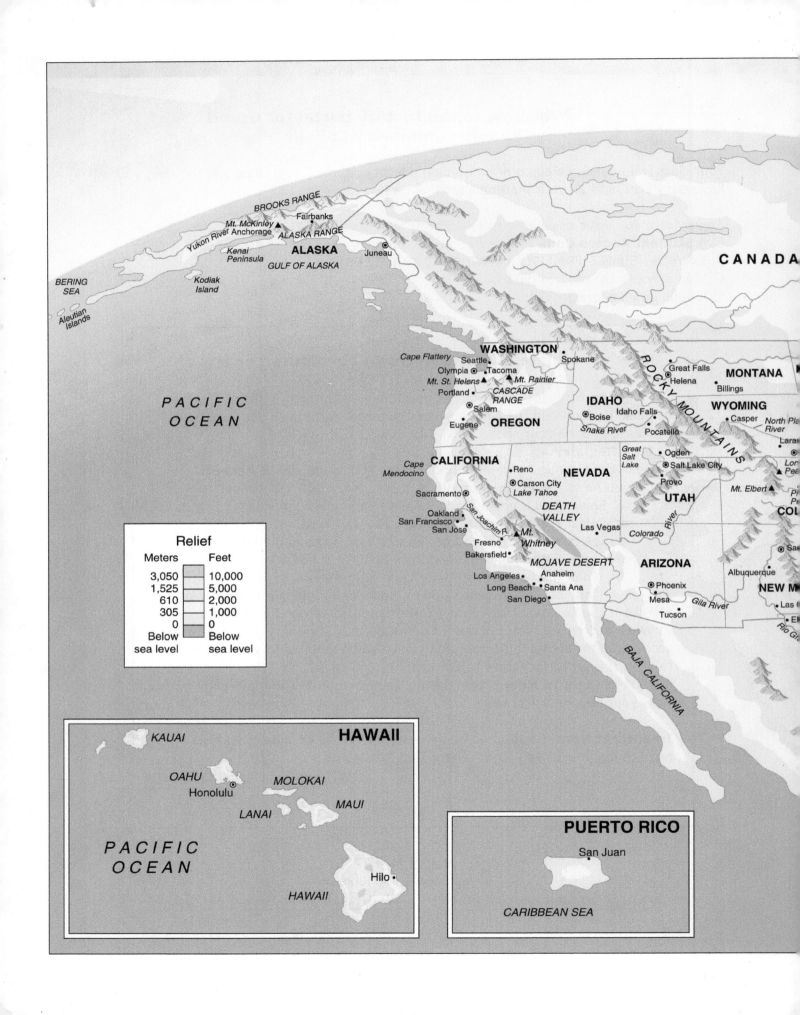

PACIFIC
OCEAN

BERING
SEA

Aleutian
Islands

BROOKS RANGE

Mt. McKinley ▲ Fairbanks
Yukon River Anchorage
ALASKA RANGE
Kenai
Peninsula   ALASKA   Juneau ⊙
GULF OF ALASKA
Kodiak
Island

CANADA

ROCKY MOUNTAINS

Cape Flattery
WASHINGTON   Spokane   Great Falls   MONTANA
Seattle   Helena
Olympia ⊙ Tacoma   Billings
Mt. St. Helens ▲ Mt. Rainier ▲
Portland   CASCADE   IDAHO   WYOMING
RANGE
⊙ Salem   ⊙ Boise Idaho Falls   Casper North Platte
Eugene   OREGON   River
Snake River   Pocatello   Lara

Cape   Great
Mendocino   CALIFORNIA   Salt   ⊙ Ogden
Reno   Lake   ⊙ Salt Lake City
⊙ Carson City   Provo   Lon
Sacramento ⊙   Lake Tahoe   NEVADA   Pe
Oakland   San Joaquin R.   DEATH   Mt. Elbert ▲   Pi
San Francisco   VALLEY   Pe
San Jose   ▲ Mt.   Las Vegas   River   COL
Fresno   Whitney   UTAH
Bakersfield   MOJAVE DESERT   Colorado   ⊙ Sar
Los Angeles   Anaheim   ARIZONA   Albuquerque
Long Beach Santa Ana   ⊙ Phoenix   NEW M
San Diego   Mesa   Gila River   Las
Tucson   E
Rio Gr

BAJA CALIFORNIA

Relief

Meters	Feet
3,050	10,000
1,525	5,000
610	2,000
305	1,000
0	0
Below sea level	Below sea level

HAWAII

KAUAI

OAHU   MOLOKAI
Honolulu ⊙
LANAI   MAUI

PACIFIC
OCEAN

Hilo •
HAWAII

PUERTO RICO

San Juan •

CARIBBEAN SEA

Out of Many

Out of Many
A History of the American People

Custom Edition for Grand Rapids Community College

HST 250

Taken from:
Out of Many: A History of the American People,
Volume 2, Seventh Edition
by John Mack Faragher, Mari Jo Buhle,
Daniel Czitrom, Susan H. Armitage

Cover Art: "Soviet Jewish Refugees" courtesy of Nathan Benn/Corbis; "Italian Arrivals at Ellis Island" courtesy of Bettmann/Corbis; "Afghan refugees pray on the day of Korban-Eid Ul Adha" courtesy of epoca libera/Corbis

Taken from:

Out of Many: A History of the American People, Volume 2, Seventh Edition
by John Mack Faragher, Mari Jo Buhle, Daniel Czitrom, Susan H. Armitage
Copyright © 2012, 2009, 2006 by Pearson Education, Inc.
Published by Prentice Hall
Upper Saddle River, New Jersey 07458

This special edition published in cooperation with Pearson Learning Solutions.

All trademarks, service marks, registered trademarks, and registered service marks are the property of their respective owners and are used herein for identification purposes only.

Pearson Learning Solutions, 501 Boylston Street, Suite 900, Boston, MA 02116
A Pearson Education Company
www.pearsoned.com

Printed in the United States of America

3 4 5 6 7 8 9 10 V092 17 16 15 14 13

000200010271302991

MT/CM

ISBN 10: 1-256-72465-3
ISBN 13: 978-1-256-72465-0

Brief Contents

17   Reconstruction, 1863–1877   458

18   Conquest and Survival: The Trans-Mississippi West, 1860–1900   490

19   Production and Consumption in the Gilded Age, 1865–1900   524

20   Democracy and Empire, 1870–1900   554

21   Urban America and the Progressive Era, 1900–1917   584

22   A Global Power: The United States in the Era of the Great War, 1901–1920   620

23   The Twenties, 1920–1929   652

24   The Great Depression and the New Deal, 1929–1940   688

25   World War II, 1941–1945   720

26   The Cold War Begins, 1945–1952   754

27   America at Midcentury, 1952–1963   786

28   The Civil Rights Movement, 1945–1966   816

29   War Abroad, War at Home, 1965–1974   850

30   The Conservative Ascendancy, 1974–1991   884

31   The United States in a Global Age, 1992–2010   916

CONTENTS

Communities in Conflict   xxv
Maps   xxvii
Charts, Graphs & Tables   xxix
Preface   xxxi
About the Authors   xlii
Community & Diversity   xliii

17

RECONSTRUCTION, 1863–1877   458

AMERICAN COMMUNITIES:
Hale County, Alabama: From Slavery to Freedom in a Black Belt Community   459
The Politics of Reconstruction 461
    The Defeated South 461
    Abraham Lincoln's Plan 462
    Andrew Johnson and Presidential Reconstruction 464
    Free Labor and the Radical Republican Vision 464
    Congressional Reconstruction and the Impeachment Crisis 466
    The Election of 1868 467
    Woman Suffrage and Reconstruction 468
The Meaning of Freedom 469
    Moving About 470
    African American Families, Churches, and Schools 470
    Land and Labor After Slavery 472
    The Origins of African American Politics 473

SEEING HISTORY   Changing Images of Reconstruction 474
Southern Politics and Society 476
    Southern Republicans 476
    Reconstructing the States: A Mixed Record 476
    White Resistance and "Redemption" 477
    King Cotton: Sharecroppers, Tenants, and the Southern Environment 479

COMMUNITIES IN CONFLICT   The Ku Klux Klan in Alabama 480
Reconstructing the North 482
    The Age of Capital 482
    Liberal Republicans and the Election of 1872 484
    The Depression of 1873 484
    The Electoral Crisis of 1876 485

Conclusion 486   Chronology 487   Review Questions 487   Recommended Reading 488

18

CONQUEST AND SURVIVAL: THE TRANS-MISSISSIPPI WEST, 1860–1900   490

AMERICAN COMMUNITIES:
The Oklahoma Land Rush   491

Indian Peoples Under Siege 493
    Indian Territory 493
    The Reservation Policy and the Slaughter of the Buffalo 494
    The Indian Wars 494
    The Nez Perces 496

The Internal Empire 497
    Mining Towns 497
    Mormon Settlements 500
    Mexican Borderland Communities 500

The Open Range 502
    The Long Drives 502

SEEING HISTORY   The Legendary Cowboy: Nat Love, Deadwood Dick 503
    The Sporting Life 504
    Frontier Violence and Range Wars 504

Farming Communities on the Plains 505
    The Homestead Act 505
    Populating the Plains 505
    Work, Dawn to Dusk 506

The World's Breadbasket 507
    New Production Technologies 507
    California Agribusiness 509
    The Toll on the Environment 510

The Western Landscape 510
    Nature's Majesty 510
    The Legendary Wild West 512
    The "American Primitive" 513

The Transformation of Indian Societies 514
    Reform Policy and Politics 515

COMMUNITIES IN CONFLICT   The Carlisle Indian Industrial School 516
    The Ghost Dance 518
    Endurance and Rejuvenation 519

Conclusion 520   Chronology 521   Review Questions 521   Recommended Reading 521

19

PRODUCTION AND CONSUMPTION
IN THE GILDED AGE, 1865–1900

524

AMERICAN COMMUNITIES:
Haymarket Square, Chicago, May 4, 1886   525
The Rise of Industry, the Triumph of Business 527
    Mechanization Takes Command 527
    Expanding the Market for Goods 528
    Integration, Combination, and Merger 529

SEEING HISTORY   The Standard Oil Company 531
    The Gospel of Wealth 532
Labor in the Age of Big Business 533
    The Wage System 533
    The Knights of Labor 534
    The American Federation of Labor 535
The New South 536
    An Internal Colony 536
    Southern Labor 536
    The Transformation of Piedmont Communities 537
COMMUNITIES IN CONFLICT   Regulating the Conditions and Limiting the Hours of Labor in the State
    of Illinois 538
The Industrial City 540
    Populating the City 540
    The Urban Landscape 541
    The City and the Environment 542
The Rise of Consumer Society 543
    "Conspicuous Consumption" 543
    Self-Improvement and the Middle Class 544
    Life in the Streets 545
Cultures in Conflict, Culture in Common 546
    Education 547
    Leisure and Public Space 548
    National Pastimes 549

Chronology 550   Conclusion 551   Review Questions 551   Recommended Reading 552

20

DEMOCRACY AND EMPIRE, 1870–1900   554

AMERICAN COMMUNITIES:

The Annexation of Hawai'i   555
Toward a National Governing Class 557
The Growth of Government 557
The Machinery of Politics 558
The Spoils System and Civil Service Reform 559

Farmers and Workers Organize Their Communities 560
The Grange 560
The Farmers' Alliance 561
Workers Search for Power 562
Women Build Alliances 563
Populism and the People's Party 563

The Crisis of the 1890s 564
Financial Collapse and Depression 564
Strikes: Coeur d'Alene, Homestead, and Pullman 565
The Social Gospel 567

Politics of Reform, Politics of Order 567
The Free Silver Issue 567
Populism's Last Campaigns 568
The Republican Triumph 568
Nativism and Jim Crow 569

The Path to Imperialism 571
All the World's a Fair 571
The "Imperialism of Righteousness" 571

SEEING HISTORY   The White Man's Burden 572
The Quest for Empire 574

Onto a Global Stage 574
A "Splendid Little War" in Cuba 575
War in the Philippines 577

COMMUNITIES IN CONFLICT   Two Sides of Anti-Imperialism 578
Critics of Empire 580

Conclusion 580   Chronology 581   Review Questions 581   Recommended Reading 582

21

URBAN AMERICA AND THE PROGRESSIVE ERA, 1900–1917

584

AMERICAN COMMUNITIES:
The Henry Street Settlement House: Women Settlement House Workers Create a Community
of Reform   585
The Origins of Progressivism 587
   Unifying Themes 588
   New Journalism: Muckraking 588
   Intellectual Trends Promoting Reform 589

SEEING HISTORY Photographing Poverty in the Slums of New York 590
   The Female Dominion 591
Progressive Politics in Cities and States 593
   The Urban Machine 593
   Progressives and Urban Reform 594
   Statehouse Progressives 595
Social Control and Its Limits 596
   The Prohibition Movement 596
   The Social Evil 597
   The Redemption of Leisure 597
   Standardizing Education 597

COMMUNITIES IN CONFLICT Debating Prohibition in Progressive-Era Ohio 598
Challenges to Progressivism 601
   The New Global Immigration 601
   Urban Ghettos 603
   Company Towns 604
   Competing Visions of Unionism: The AFL and the IWW 605
   Rebels in Bohemia 606
Women's Movements and Black Activism 607
   The New Woman 607
   Birth Control 608
   Racism and Accommodation 609
   Racial Justice, the NAACP, and Black Women's Activism 610
National Progressivism 611
   Theodore Roosevelt and Presidential Activism 611
   Trust-Busting and Regulation 611
   The Birth of Environmentalism 612
   The Election of 1912: A Four-Way Race 614
   Woodrow Wilson's First Term 615

Conclusion 616   Chronology 617   Review Questions 617   Recommended Reading 618

22

A GLOBAL POWER: THE UNITED STATES IN THE ERA OF THE GREAT WAR, 1901–1920   620

AMERICAN COMMUNITIES:
The American Expeditionary Force in France   621
Becoming a World Power 623
    Roosevelt: The Big Stick 624
    Taft: Dollar Diplomacy 625
    Wilson: Moralism and Intervention in Mexico 625
The Great War 628
    The Guns of August 628
    American Neutrality 628
    Preparedness and Peace 629
    Safe for Democracy 630
American Mobilization 631
    Selling the War 631
    Fading Opposition to War 631
    "You're in the Army Now" 631

    SEEING HISTORY Selling War 632
    Racism in the Military 633
    Americans in Battle 634
    The Russian Revolution, the Fourteen Points, and Allied Victory 635
Over Here 635
    Organizing the Economy 636
    The Government–Business Partnership 636
    Labor and the War 637
    Women at Work 638
    Woman Suffrage 638
    Prohibition 640
    Public Health and the Influenza Pandemic 640
Repression and Reaction 641
    Muzzling Dissent: The Espionage and Sedition Acts 641

COMMUNITIES IN CONFLICT   The War at Home in Wisconsin 642
    The Great Migration and Racial Tensions 644
    Labor Strife 645
An Uneasy Peace 646
    Peacemaking and the Specter of Bolshevism 646
    Wilson in Paris 647
    The Treaty Fight 647
    The Red Scare 648
    The Election of 1920 648

Chronology 649   Conclusion 649   Review Questions 650   Recommended Reading 650

23

THE TWENTIES, 1920–1929   652

AMERICAN COMMUNITIES:
The Movie Audience and Hollywood: Mass Culture Creates a New National Community   653
Postwar Prosperity and Its Price 655
    The Second Industrial Revolution 655
    The Modern Corporation 656
    Welfare Capitalism 657
    The Auto Age 658
    Cities and Suburbs 660
The State, the Economy, and Business 660
    Harding and Coolidge 661
    Herbert Hoover and the "Associative State" 661
    War Debts, Reparations, Keeping the Peace 662
    Global Commerce and U.S. Foreign Policy 662
    Weakened Agriculture, Ailing Industries 663
The New Mass Culture 664
    Movie-Made America 664

SEEING HISTORY   Creating Celebrity 665
    Radio Broadcasting 666
    New Forms of Journalism 666
    Advertising Modernity 667
    The Phonograph and the Recording Industry 668
    Sports and Celebrity 668
    A New Morality? 670
Modernity and Traditionalism 672
    Prohibition 672
    Immigration Restriction 672
    The Ku Klux Klan 674
    Fundamentalism in Religion 675
Promises Postponed 675
    Feminism in Transition 675

COMMUNITIES IN CONFLICT   The Scopes Trial in Dayton, Tennessee 676
    Mexican Immigration 678
    The "New Negro" 679
    Alienated Intellectuals 682
    The Election of 1928 683

Conclusion 684   Chronology 685   Review Questions 685   Recommended Reading 686

24

THE GREAT DEPRESSION AND THE NEW DEAL, 1929–1940

688

AMERICAN COMMUNITIES:
Sit-Down Strike at Flint: Automobile Workers Organize a New Union   689

Hard Times 691
Underlying Weaknesses of the 1920s' Economy 691
The Bull Market and the Crash 692
Mass Unemployment 693
Hoover's Failure 694
A Global Crisis and the Election of 1932 695

FDR and the First New Deal 696
FDR the Man 696
"The Only Thing We Have to Fear": Restoring Confidence 696
The Hundred Days 697
Roosevelt's Critics, Right and Left 698

Left Turn and the Second New Deal 700
The Second Hundred Days 700
Labor's Upsurge: Rise of the CIO 701
The New Deal Coalition at High Tide 702

The New Deal in the South and West 702
Modernizing Southern Farming and Landholding 703
An Environmental Disaster: The Dust Bowl 703
Water Policy 705

COMMUNITIES IN CONFLICT   Californians Face the Influx of "Dust Bowl" Migrants 706
A New Deal for Indians 708

The Limits of Reform 709
Court Packing 709
The Women's Network 709
A New Deal for Minorities? 710
The Roosevelt Recession and the Ebbing of the New Deal 711

Depression-Era Culture 711
A New Deal for the Arts 711
The Documentary Impulse 712
Waiting for Lefty 713
Raising Spirits: Film, Radio, and the Swing Era 713

SEEING HISTORY   Documenting Hard Times in Black and White and Color 714

Conclusion 716   Chronology 717   Review Questions 717   Recommended Reading 717

25

WORLD WAR II, 1941–1945   720

AMERICAN COMMUNITIES:
Los Alamos, New Mexico   721
The Coming of World War II 723
    The Shadows of War across the Globe 723
    Roosevelt Readies for War 724
    Pearl Harbor 725
The Great Arsenal of Democracy 726
    Mobilizing for War 726
    Organizing the War Economy 727
    New Workers 728

SEEING HISTORY   Norman Rockwell's "Rosie, the Riveter" 729
The Home Front 730
    Families in Wartime 730
    The Internment of Japanese Americans 732
    "Double V": Victory at Home and Abroad 733
    Zoot Suit Riots 734
    Popular Culture and "The Good War" 734
Men and Women in Uniform 735
    Creating the Armed Forces 735
    Women Enter the Military 736
    Old Practices and New Horizons 736
    The Medical Corps 737
The World at War 738
    Soviets Halt Nazi Drive 738
    Planning and Initiating the Allied Offensive 740
    The Allied Invasion of Europe 741
    The High Cost of European Victory 743
    The War in Asia and the Pacific 743
The Last Stages of War 745
    The Holocaust 745

COMMUNITIES IN CONFLICT   On Deploying the Atomic Bomb 746
    The Yalta Conference 748
    The Atomic Bomb 749

Chronology 750   Conclusion 751   Review Questions 751   Recommended Reading 751

26

THE COLD WAR BEGINS, 1945–1952   754

AMERICAN COMMUNITIES:
University of Washington, Seattle: Students and Faculty Face the Cold War   755

Global Insecurities at War's End 757
    Financing the Future 757
    The Division of Europe 758
    The United Nations and Hopes for Collective Security 759

The Policy of Containment 760
    The Truman Doctrine 760
    The Marshall Plan 760
    The Berlin Crisis and the Formation of NATO 762
    Atomic Diplomacy 763

Cold War Liberalism 763
    "To Err Is Truman" 763
    The 1948 Election 764
    The Fair Deal 765

The Cold War at Home 766
    The National Security Act of 1947 766
    The Loyalty-Security Program 767
    The Second Red Scare 767
    Spy Cases 769
    McCarthyism 769

COMMUNITIES IN CONFLICT   Congress and the Red Scare 770

Cold War Culture 772
    An Anxious Mood 772
    The Family As Bulwark 773

SEEING HISTORY   The Hollywood Film *Invasion, U.S.A* 774
    Military-Industrial Communities in the American West 776
    "The American Way" 777

Stalemate for the Democrats 777
    Democratizing Japan and "Losing" China 777
    The Korean War 778
    The Price of National Security 779
    "I like Ike": The Election of 1952 780

Conclusion 782   Review Questions 782   Recommended Reading 782   Chronology 783

27

AMERICA AT MIDCENTURY, 1952–1963   786

AMERICAN COMMUNITIES:
Popular Music in Memphis   787
Under the Cold War's Shadow 789
　　The Eisenhower Presidency 789
　　The "New Look" in Foreign Affairs 791
　　Covert Action 792
　　Global Interventions 792
The Affluent Society 794
　　Subsidizing Prosperity 794
COMMUNITIES IN CONFLICT　Integrating Levittown, Pennsylvania 796
　　Suburban Life 798
　　Organized Labor and the AFL-CIO 799
　　Lonely Crowds and Organization Men 800
　　The Expansion of Higher Education 800
　　Health and Medicine 801
Youth Culture 801
　　The Youth Market 801
　　"Hail! Hail! Rock 'n' Roll!" 802
　　Almost Grown 803
　　Deviance and Delinquency 803
Mass Culture and Its Discontents 804
　　Television: Tube of Plenty 804
　　Television and Politics 805
　　Culture Critics 806
The Coming of the New Frontier 806
　　The Election of 1960 807
　　New Frontier Liberalism 808
　　Kennedy and the Cold War 809
　　The Cuban Revolution and the Bay of Pigs 810
　　The 1962 Missile Crisis 810
　　The Assassination of President Kennedy 811

SEEING HISTORY　Televising a National Tragedy 812

Chronology 813　Conclusion 813　Review Questions 814　Recommended Reading 814

28

THE CIVIL RIGHTS MOVEMENT, 1945–1966　　　816

AMERICAN COMMUNITIES:
The Montgomery Bus Boycott: An African American Community Challenges Segregation　　817
Origins of the Movement　819
　　Civil Rights after World War II　819
　　The Segregated South　821
　　Brown v. Board of Education　822

SEEING HISTORY　Visualizing Civil Rights　824
　　Crisis in Little Rock　825
No Easy Road to Freedom, 1957–62　825
　　Martin Luther King Jr. and the SCLC　825
　　Sit-Ins: Greensboro, Nashville, Atlanta　826
　　SNCC and the "Beloved Community"　828
　　The Election of 1960 and Civil Rights　828
　　Freedom Rides　830
　　The Albany Movement: The Limits of Protest　831
The Movement at High Tide, 1963–65　831
　　Birmingham　831
　　JFK and the March on Washington　832

COMMUNITIES IN CONFLICT　Showdown at Oxford: Integrating Ole Miss, 1962　834
　　LBJ and the Civil Rights Act of 1964　836
　　Mississippi Freedom Summer　837
　　Malcolm X and Black Consciousness　838
　　Selma and the Voting Rights Act of 1965　839
Civil Rights Beyond Black and White　842
　　Mexican Americans and Mexican Immigrants　842
　　Puerto Ricans　843
　　Japanese Americans　844
　　Indian Peoples　844
　　Remaking the Golden Door: The Immigration and Nationality Act of 1965　845

Conclusion 846　Review Questions 846　Chronology 847　Recommended Reading 848

29

WAR ABROAD, WAR AT HOME, 1965–1974 850

AMERICAN COMMUNITIES:
Uptown, Chicago, Illinois   851
The Vietnam War 853
    Johnson's War 853
    Deeper into the Quagmire 854
    The Credibility Gap 855
A Generation in Conflict 855
    "The Times They Are A-Changin'" 855
    From Campus Protest to Mass Mobilization 857
COMMUNITIES IN CONFLICT The Prospects for Peace in Vietnam, April 1965 858
    Teenage Soldiers 860
Wars on Poverty 861
    The Great Society 861
    Crisis in the Cities 862
    Urban Uprisings 862
1968: Year of Turmoil 865
    The Tet Offensive 865
    King, the War, and the Assassination 865
    The Democrats in Disarray 865
    "The Whole World Is Watching!" 867
    The Republican Victory 867
The Politics of Identity 868
    Black Power 868
    Sisterhood Is Powerful 869
    Gay Liberation 872
    The Chicano Rebellion 872
    Red Power 873
    The Asian American Movement 873
The Nixon Presidency 874
    Domestic Policy 875
    Nixon's War 875
    Nixon's Foreign Policy 877

SEEING HISTORY Kim Phuc, Fleeing a Napalm Attack near Trang Bang 878
    Dirty Tricks and the 1972 Election 879
    Watergate: Nixon's Downfall 879

Conclusion 880   **Chronology 881**   **Review Questions 882**   **Recommended Reading 882**

30

THE CONSERVATIVE ASCENDANCY, 1974–1991   884

AMERICAN COMMUNITIES:
Grassroots Conservatism in Orange County, California   885
The Overextended Society 887
   A Troubled Economy 887
   The Endangered Environment 889

COMMUNITIES IN CONFLICT   Three Mile Island, Pennsylvania 890
   "Lean Years Presidents": Ford and Carter 892
   The Limits of Global Power 893
   The Iran Hostage Crisis 894
The New Right 895
   Neoconservatism 895
   The Religious Right 895
   The Pro-Family Movement 896
   The 1980 Election 896

SEEING HISTORY   The Inaugurations of Carter and Reagan 897
The Reagan Revolution 898
   The Great Communicator 898
   Reaganomics 899
   The Election of 1984 900
   Recession, Recovery, and Fiscal Crisis 900
Best of Times, Worst of Times 901
   A Two-Tiered Society 901
   The Feminization of Poverty 903
   Sunbelt/Rustbelt Communities 903
   Epidemics: Drugs, AIDS, Homelessness 904
Toward a New World Order 905
   The Evil Empire 906
   The Reagan Doctrine 906
   The Middle East and the Iran-Contra Scandal 907
   The Collapse of Communism 909
"A Kinder, Gentler Nation" 909
   Reagan's Successor: George H. W. Bush 910
   The Persian Gulf War 911
   The Economy and the Election of 1992 911

Conclusion 912   Review Questions 912   Chronology 913   Recommended Reading 914

31

THE UNITED STATES IN A GLOBAL AGE, 1992–2010 916

AMERICAN COMMUNITIES:
Transnational Communities in San Diego and Tijuana 917
The Presidency of Bill Clinton 919
 A "New Democrat" in the White House 919
 The "Globalization" President 920
 Presiding Over the Boom 922
 High Crimes and Misdemeanors 922
Changing American Communities 923
 Silicon Valley 923
 New Media and Virtual Communities 923
 The New Immigrants 924
 Growing Social Disparities 926
 The Culture Wars 926

COMMUNITIES IN CONFLICT Illegal Immigrants and the Border Fence 928
President George W. Bush and the War on Terror 930
 The Election of 2000 930
 Terrorist Attack on America 931

SEEING HISTORY The 9/11 Attacks 932
 Reshaping U.S. Foreign Policy 933
 Invasion of Iraq 934
 Bush's "Compassionate Conservatism" 936
 Divided Government, Divided Nation 938
Barack Obama and the Audacity of Hope 938
 The Election of 2008 939
 The Great Recession 940
 Obama in Office 941

Chronology 943 Review Questions 943 Recommended Reading 944

Appendix A-1
Bibliography B-1
Credits C-1
Index I-1

COMMUNITIES IN CONFLICT

Chapter 17: The Ku Klux Klan in Alabama **480**

Movements of the Mystic Klan, from the *Shelby County Guide*, December 3, 1868

George Houston's Testimony, Montgomery, October 17, 1871

Chapter 18: The Carlisle Indian Industrial School **516**

Richard Henry Pratt Explains How He Made Indian Children "White"

Luther Standing Bear Remembers Being Made "White"

Chapter 19: Regulating the Conditions and Limiting the Hours of Labor in the State of Illinois **538**

Florence Kelley's proposal for the Illinois Factory and Workshop Inspection Act, 1893

Factory Act Declared Unconstitutional: Opinion of Supreme Court of Illinois, March 18, 1895

Chapter 20: Two Sides of Anti-Imperialism **578**

Andrew Carnegie, Anti-Imperialist: America Cannot Absorb Alien Populations (August 1898)

Josephine Shaw Lowell, Anti-Imperialist: America Must Not Wage Unjust Wars (ca. 1900)

Chapter 21: Debating Prohibition in Progressive-Era Ohio **598**

Percy Andreae: "Behind the Mask of Prohibition" (1915)

Prohibitionist James A. White: "Give Me Your Boy" (1918)

Chapter 22: The War at Home in Wisconsin **642**

Professor E.A. Schimler Is Tarred and Feathered (April 1, 1918)

Victor Berger: "In the Land of the Free and the Home of the Brave" (October 19, 1918)

Chapter 23: The Scopes Trial in Dayton, Tennessee **676**

William Jennings Bryan's Undelivered Speech to the Jury

H. L. Mencken in the *Baltimore Evening Sun* (July 27, 1925)

Chapter 24: Californians Face the Influx of "Dust Bowl" Migrants **706**

Los Angeles Times, July 21, 1937: "Squatter Army Wages Grim Battle for Life"

Thomas McManus, California Citizens' Associations: California "Indigents Peril"

Chapter 25: On Deploying the Atomic Bomb **746**

July 3, 1945: A Petition to the President of the United States

Teller's Response to Szilard

Chapter 26: Congress and the Red Scare **770**

Senator Joseph McCarthy Charges That Communists Riddle the State Department, Wheeling, West Virginia (February 9, 1950)

Senator Margaret Chase Smith Announces Her Declaration of Conscience (June 1, 1950)

Chapter 27: Integrating Levittown, Pennsylvania **796**

"Police Rout 400 at Negro's Home" (August 20, 1957)

Reactions: "When a Negro Family Moved into a White Community" (August 30, 1957)

Chapter 28: Showdown at Oxford: Integrating Ole Miss, 1962 **834**

Document 1: Letter from James Meredith to Thurgood Marshall, NAACP Legal Defense and Educational Fund, January 29, 1961

Document 2: Governor Ross Barnett, Proclamation to the People of Mississippi, TV and Radio broadcast, September 12, 1962

Chapter 29: The Prospects for Peace in Vietnam, April 1965 **858**

President Lyndon Johnson Calls for "Peace without Conquest" (April 7, 1965)

SDS President Paul Potter, "Naming the System" (April 17, 1965)

Chapter 30: Three Mile Island, Pennsylvania **890**

Environmental Activist Jane Lee Opposes Nuclear Power (1980)

Pennsylvania Governor Richard Thornburgh Recalls the Three Mile Island Accident (2003)

Chapter 31: Illegal Immigrants and the Border Fence **928**

Governor Bill Richardson Urges Comprehensive Immigration Reform (December 7, 2006)

Law Professor Jan C. Ting Considers "Immigration, National Security, and the Need for a Border Fence" (2005)

MAPS

Reconstruction of the South, 1866–77 **466**

The Barrow Plantation, Oglethorpe County, Georgia, 1860 and 1861 (approx. 2,000 acres) **473**

Southern Sharecropping and the Cotton Belt, 1880 **479**

The Election of 1876 **486**

Oklahoma Territory **492**

Major Indian Battles and Indian Reservations, 1860–1900 **495**

Railroad Routes, Cattle Trails, Gold and Silver Rushes, 1860–1900 **498**

Mormon Cultural Diffusion, ca. 1883 **500**

The Establishment of National Parks and Forests **511**

Patterns of Industry, 1900 **529**

Population of Foreign Birth by Region, 1880 **541**

Strikes by State, 1880 **562**

Election of 1896 **569**

The American Domain, ca. 1900 **575**

The Spanish-American War **576**

Immigration to the United States, 1901–1920 **602**

The Election of 1912 **615**

The United States in the Caribbean, 1865–1933 **626**

The Western Front, 1918 **634**

Black Population, 1920 **681**

The Election of 1928 **683**

The Election of 1932 **696**

The Dust Bowl, 1935–40 **704**

The New Deal and Water **705**

The War in Europe **739**

War in the Pacific **744**

Divided Europe **759**

The Election of 1948 **765**

The Korean War **779**

The United States in the Caribbean, 1948–66 **793**

The Election of 1960 **808**

The Civil Rights Movement **829**

Impact of the Voting Rights Act of 1965 **840**

Urban Uprisings, 1965–1968 **864**

The Southeast Asian War **866**

The Election of 1968 **868**

Major Indian Reservations, 1976 **874**

World's Leading Oil Producers **888**

The Election of 1976 **892**

The Election of 1980 **898**

Population Shifts, 1970–80 **903**

The United States in Central America, 1978–90 **907**

The United States in the Middle East in the 1980s **908**

The Election of 2000 **931**

Invasion in Iraq **935**

CHARTS, GRAPHS & TABLES

Machine Labor on the Farm, ca. 1880   **508**

A Growing Urban Population   **540**

School Enrollment of 5- to 19-Year-Olds, 1870–1900   **547**

Falling Price of Wheat Flour, 1865–1900   **561**

African American Representation in Congress, 1867–1900   **570**

The Great Migration: Black Population Growth in Selected Northern Cities, 1910–20   **644**

Stock Market Prices 1921–1932   **656**

Consumer Debt 1920–31   **656**

Immigration Trends to the United States by Continent/Region, 1880–1930   **673**

Mexican Immigration to the United States in 1920s   **679**

Distribution of Total Family Income Among Various Segments of the Population, 1929–44 (in Percentages)   **692**

Strikes and Lockouts in the United States, 1940–45   **730**

Distribution of Total Personal Income among Various Segments of the Population, 1947–70 (in Percentages)★   **775**

U.S. Birthrate, 1930–80   **775**

The Growth of the Suburbs, 1950–70   **798**

L.A. County Population 1920–80   **799**

Comparative Figures on Life Expectancy at Birth by Race and Sex 1950–70   **861**

Comparative Figures on Infant Mortality by Race, 1940–1970   **861**

Percent of Population Below Poverty Level, by Race, 1959–69   **862**

Women in the Workforce, 1940–80   **871**

U.S. Military Forces in Vietnam and Casualties, 1961–81   **875**

Public Opinion on the War in Vietnam   **876**

Decline of U.S. Oil Consumption, 1975–81   **888**

Union Membership, 1940–90   **889**

Percentage Share of Aggregate Family Income, 1980–92   **901**

Federal Budget Deficit and National Debt, 1970–98   **901**

Share of Total Net Worth of American Families   **902**

Measures of Average Earnings, 1980–92 (In 1990 Dollars)   **902**

Number of Poor, Rate of Poverty, and Poverty Line, 1979–92   **902**

Net New Job Creation by Wage Level, 1979–87   **902**

Median Family Income and Ratio to White, by Race, and Hispanic Origin, 1980–92 (in 1992 Dollars)   **903**

Growth of Sunbelt Cities, 1940–80   **904**

Continent of Birth for Immigrants, 1990–2000   **924**

OVERVIEW TABLES

Reconstruction Amendments to the Constitution, 1865–1870   **469**

Major Indian Treaties and Legislation of the Late Nineteenth Century   **514**

Currents of Progressivism   **592**

Key Legislation of the First New Deal ("Hundred Days," March 9–June 16, 1933)   **699**

Key Legislation of the Second New Deal (1935–38)   **701**

Major Cold War Policies   **761**

Landmark Civil Rights Legislation, Supreme Court Decisions, and Executive Orders   **836**

The Great Society   **863**

Protest Movements of the 1960s   **870**

PREFACE

Out of Many: A History of the American People, seventh edition, offers a distinctive and timely approach to American history, highlighting the experiences of diverse communities of Americans in the unfolding story of our country. The stories of these communities offer a way of examining the complex historical forces shaping people's lives at various moments in our past. The debates and conflicts surrounding the most momentous issues in our national life—independence, emerging democracy, slavery, westward settlement, imperial expansion, economic depression, war, technological change—were largely worked out in the context of local communities. Through communities we focus on the persistent tensions between everyday life and those larger decisions and events that continually reshape the circumstances of local life. Each chapter opens with a description of a representative community. Some of these portraits feature American communities struggling with one another: African slaves and English masters on the rice plantations of colonial Georgia, or *Tejanos* and Americans during the Texas war of independence. Other chapters feature portraits of communities facing social change: the feminists of Seneca Falls, New York, in 1848, or the African Americans of Montgomery, Alabama, in 1955. As the story unfolds we find communities growing to include ever larger groups of Americans: the soldiers from every colony who forged the Continental Army into a patriotic national force at Valley Forge during the American Revolution, or the moviegoers who aspired to a collective dream of material prosperity and upward mobility during the 1920s.

Out of Many is also the only American history text with a truly continental perspective. With community vignettes from New England to the South, the Midwest to the far West, we encourage students to appreciate the great expanse of our nation. For example, a vignette of seventeenth century Santa Fé, New Mexico, illustrates the founding of the first European settlements in the New World. We present territorial expansion into the American West from the viewpoint of the Mandan villagers of the upper Missouri River of North Dakota. We introduce the policies of the Reconstruction era through the experience of African Americans in Hale County, Alabama. A continental perspective drives home to students that American history has never been the preserve of any particular region.

Out of Many includes extensive coverage of our diverse heritage. Our country is appropriately known as "a nation of immigrants," and the history of immigration to America, from the seventeenth to the twenty-first centuries, is fully integrated into the text. There is sustained and close attention to our place in the world, with special emphasis on our relations with the nations of the Western Hemisphere, especially our near neighbors, Canada and Mexico. The statistical data in the final chapter has been completely updated with the results of the 2000 census.

In these ways *Out of Many* breaks new ground, but without compromising its coverage of the traditional turning points that we believe are critically important to an understanding of the American past. Among these watershed events are the Revolution and the struggle over the Constitution, the Civil War and Reconstruction, and the Great Depression and World War II. In *Out of Many*, however, we seek to integrate the narrative of national history with the story of the nation's many diverse communities. The Revolutionary and Constitutional period tested the ability of local communities to forge a new unity, and success depended on their ability to build a nation without compromising local identity. The Civil War and Reconstruction formed a second great test of the balance between the national ideas of the Revolution and the power of local and sectional communities. The depression and the New Deal demonstrated the importance of local communities and the growing power of national institutions during the greatest economic challenge in our history. *Out of Many* also looks back in a new and comprehensive way—from the vantage point of the beginning of a new century and the end of the Cold War—at the salient events of the last fifty years and their impact on American communities. The community focus of *Out of Many* weaves the stories of the people and the nation into a single compelling narrative.

Out of Many, seventh edition, is completely updated with the most recent scholarship on the history of America and the United States. All the chapters have been extensively reviewed, revised, and rewritten. The final chapter details the tumultuous events of the new century, including a completely new section on the "war on terror," and concluding with the national election of 2008. Throughout the book the text and graphics are presented in a stunning new design. Moreover, this edition incorporates two important new features. The seventh edition offers two features in each chapter designed to bring history vividly alive for students: *Communities in Conflict*, featuring two primary sources that offer opposing voices on a controversial historical issue and *Seeing History*, carefully chosen images that show how visual sources can illuminate their understanding of American history.

WHAT'S NEW TO THIS EDITION

With each edition of *Out of Many* we have sought to strengthen its unique integration of the best of traditional American history with its innovative community-based focus and strong continental perspective. This new version is no exception.

- New and expanded coverage on topics such as native religious practices, the position of women in New England, class and ethnicity in the Revolution, the Spanish and the American Revolution, Southern Republicans in the reconstruction era, and the role of moderate white Southerners in the civil rights struggle.
- New coverage of the election of 2008 and Barack Obama's first year as president as well as extensive treatment of the Great Recession.
- New topics in the special features, *Communities and Conflict* and *Seeing History*, include Indian Removal, P.T. Barnum's "curiosities," civility and democracy, working conditions and labor in Illinois, race riots in Tulsa, and visualizing civil rights.
- Extensive updating of numerous topics within the text make the seventh edition up-to-date with the most recent scholarship in the discipline.
- New references identified by icons cite specific documents, audio, video, maps, and images available on the MyHistoryLab website that enhance topics discussed in the chapters. A description of MyHistorylab appears on page xxxix.
- The bibliography has been extensively updated with recent scholarly works to provide students and instructors with a complete reference resource within the text.

Chapter-by-Chapter Changes

Chapter 1 There is more discussion of native religious practices. The chapter now incorporates new theories of migration from Asia.

Chapter 2 Expanded discussions are included on the "Merchant Class and the Renaissance" and the "Columbian Exchange," and the newest material on the demographic consequences of the conquest.

Chapter 3 There is new coverage of the position of women in New England, the Salem Witch Trials, and Bacon's Rebellion.

Chapter 4 The sections on slavery in the Spanish and French colonies have been thoroughly revised.

Chapter 5 Sections within the chapter have been revised for better narrative flow, and there is increased emphasis on the importance of religion.

Chapter 6 New emphasis on the importance of the Seven Years War has been included as well as more explicit coverage of class and ethnicity in the Revolution and of soldiers in the early fighting.

Chapter 7 There are two new sections in this chapter on "The Toll of War" and "Women and the War" and new material on the Spanish and the Revolution.

Chapter 8 The discussions of American culture and on the writing and ratification of the Constitution have been extensively revised, and a new discussion of republicanism has been added.

Chapter 9 Two new historical views of the capitol building underline the point that the nation's new capital city had small and undistinguished beginnings. The updated bibliography describes the Missouri Compromise to make the point that differing views on slavery were a political danger as early as 1820.

Chapter 10 This chapter Incorporates the newest scholarship to deepen student appreciation of the human costs of the slave system.

Chapter 11 There is a new **Communities in Conflict** feature on Indian Removal and extensive updating of the chapter bibliography.

Chapter 12 A new set of maps emphasize the importance of transportation in the rapid development of the Yankee West and commercial agriculture and new detail has been added in readings on early factory conditions.

Chapter 13 A new **Seeing History** analyzes the popular appeal of PT Barnum's "curiosities."

Chapter 15 A revised **Seeing History** feature includes a new picture and poses a question about civility and democracy.

Chapter 16 There is a use of new scholarship to increase understanding of the impact of the Civil War on soldiers and civilians.

Chapter 17 The expanded discussion of Southern Republicans in the Reconstruction era emphasizes regional differences within the South.

Chapter 18 The section on "Producing for the Global Market" has been dropped, with the material integrated into "New Production Technologies," to streamline the outline.

Chapter 19 There is a new **Communities in Conflict: Regulating the Conditions and Limiting the Hours of Labor in the State of Illinois.**

Chapter 21 A new section discusses immigration from the Carriibean basin in the early twentieth century and includes a revised map of Immigration to the U.S., 1900–1920.

Chapter 22 A new **Communities in Conflict** explores the race riot in Tulsa, 1921, and the coverage of women's experiences during WW I has been revised.

Chapter 23 The coverage of the relationship between global commerce and U.S. foreign policy has been strengthened. The extensively revised bibliographies reflect a large amount of new scholarship on the 1920s.

Chapter 24 There are revised and updated statistics and analysis of "Underlying Weaknesses of the 1920s Economy."

Chapter 25 Much of the Isolationism section has been streamlined and merged into the section "Roosevelt Readies for War" to streamline the chapter outline.

Chapter 26 The section "Zeal for Democracy" is replaced by "The American Way," which is a phrase that comes up in the most recent scholarship on Cold War culture.

Chapter 27 Clarified are the major goals—and tensions within—Eisenhower's foreign policy.

Chapter 28 A new **Seeing History** explores visualizing Civil Rights. There is new material on the role of moderate white Southerners in the civil rights struggle. The extensively revised bibliographies reflect a large amount of new scholarship on the civil rights movement.

Chapter 29 The chapter outline has been streamlined by grouping the sections "Playing the China Card" and "Foreign Policy as Conspiracy" under a new section, "Nixon's Foreign Policy." The section on Johnson and the Vietnam War has been revised to reflect recent historiographical tendency to characterize Johnson as more hesitant about escalating the war than earlier scholars contended and to assign more responsibility to his advisors.

A discussion of the founding of *Ms. Magazine* has been added.

Chapter 30 The **Seeing History** feature has been revised to compare the Reagan and Carter inaugurations.

Chapter 31 A new section, "Barack Obama and the Audacity of Hope," covers the election of 2008 and Obama's first year as president. Extensive treatment of the Great Recession examines its causes and its impact on American life. The chapter has been reorganized to more fully integrate political and economic developments in the Clinton/Bush/Obama years.

SPECIAL FEATURES

Out of Many offers a wealth of special features and peda-gogical aids that reinforce our narrative and helps students grasp key topics and concepts.

- **Community and Diversity.** This special introduc-tory essay begins students' journey into the narrative history that unfolds in *Out of Many*. The essay acquaints students with the major themes of the book and provides them with a framework for understand-ing American History. (pp. xliii–xlvi)

COMMUNITY & DIVERSITY

One of the most characteristic features of our country is its astounding variety. The American people include the descendants of native Indians; colonial Europeans of British, French, and Spanish background; Africans; and

Every human society is made up of communities. A community is a set of relationships linking men, women, and their families to a coherent social whole that is more than the sum of its parts. In a community

- **American Communities.** Each chapter opens with a story that highlights the experiences of diverse com-munities of Americans as a way of examining the complex historical forces shaping people's lives at var-ious moments in our past.

Women Reformers of Seneca Falls Respond to the Market Revolution

AMERICAN Communities

In the summer of 1848, Charlotte Woodward, a nineteen-year-old glove maker who did outwork in her rural home, saw a small advertisement in an upstate New York newspaper announcing a "conven-tion to discuss the social, civil, and religious condition and rights of woman," to be held at Seneca Falls on July 19 and 20. Woodward persuaded six friends to join her in the forty-mile journey to the convention. "At first we travelled quite alone," she recalled. "But before we had gone many miles we came on other wagon-loads of women, bound in the same direction. As we reached different crossroad we saw wagons coming from every part of the country, and long before we reached Seneca Falls we were a procession."

To the surprise of the convention organizers, almost 300 people—men as well as women—attended the two-day meeting, which focused on the Declaration of Sentiments, a peti-tion for women's rights modeled on the Declaration of Independence. "We hold these truths to be self-evident," it announced: "That all men and women are created equal." As the Declaration of Independence detailed the oppressions King George III had imposed on the colonists, the Declaration of Sentiments detailed, in a series of resolutions, the oppressions men had imposed on women. Men had deprived women of legal rights, of

335

- **Communities in Conflict.** This special feature highlights two primary sources that offer opposing voices on a controversial historical issue. With intro-ductory source notes and critical thinking ques-tions, "Communities in Conflict" offers students and instructors the opportunity to discuss how Americans have struggled to resolve their differences at every point in our past.

COMMUNITIES *in* CONFLICT

The Debate over Immigration

Briefly, in the early 1850s, the Know-Nothing Party rode the wave of widespread public apprehension about the new immigrants to political success. The following expression of views, first from a nativist, I. Wayne Laurens, and second from Senator William H. Seward, a leader of the new Republican Party, debated the nature of American citizenship.

- Debates over immigration continue to this day, in much the same terms that Laurens and Seward argued in the 1850s. What does this continuing debate suggest about the nature of Americanism?

From The Crisis, or, the Enemies of America Unmasked

Many of our leading statesmen have recently declared that no foreigner should be naturalized till he has resided in this country twenty-one years. But we care for no man's authority in so plain a case. The thing is self-evident. Americans should rule America; and the voters are really the rulers. None but a native born American would ever have been allowed to vote, if justice had been done, from the beginning. The fran-chise should have been held sacred. Let those vote, whose vote is already legalized. But when we come to revise the naturalization laws, . . . let us make thorough work of it, and in future grant the privilege of voting to no man who was not born on the American soil. We have had enough of artificial naturalizing. In all future time, let nature do the naturalizing herself. Then there will be no mistake, and no false swearing. Foreigners will cease to perjure themselves in order to acquire the privilege of fighting at the polls, and the interests of peace and good morals will be promoted . . . Let no American born citizen vote for a foreigner or for a man who will appoint foreigners to office, and the thing is done. We shall thus rid our-selves of the greatest evil with which this country was ever cursed.

> "We have had enough of artificial naturalizing . . ."

- **Seeing History.** This feature helps students use visual culture for making sense of the past. These carefully chosen images, with critical thinking questions for interpretation, include a broad array of fine art, drawings, political cartoons, advertisements, and photographs. Encouraged to look at the image with an analytical eye, students will think critically about how visual sources can illuminate their understanding of American history and the important role visuals play in our knowledge of the past.

- **Focus Questions.** These critical thinking questions are located at the beginning of each chapter. They focus on the content of each main section within the chapters and allow students to consider carefully the main issues addressed in the narrative.

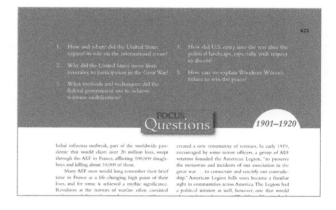

- **Overview tables.** Overview tables provide students with a summary of complex issues.

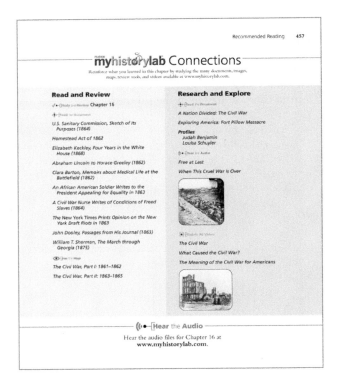

- **NEW Myhistorylab Icons.** Throughout each chapter, icons refer students to primary source documents, maps, videos, and activities from the MyHistoryLab website that relate directly to specific topics within the chapter.

- **NEW MyHistoryLab Connections.** A list of documents, images, maps, activities, and videos available online at **www.myhistorylab.com** that relate to the specific content in each chapter. For a full description of the MyHistoryLab website for *Out of Many*, see page xxxix.

- **Photos and Illustrations.** The abundant illustrations in *Out of Many* include extensive captions that treat the images as visual primary source documents from the American past, describing their source and explaining their significance. In addition, the **Seeing History** feature in each chapter highlights a stunning visual and introduces students to the importance of visual documents in the study of history.

Joseph Brant, the brilliant chief of the Mohawks who sided with Great Britain during the Revolution, in a 1786 painting by the American artist Gilbert Stuart. After the Treaty of Paris, Brant led a large faction of Iroquois people north into British Canada, where they established a separate Iroquois Confederacy.

MAP 24.2 The Dust Bowl, 1935–40 This map shows the extent of the Dust Bowl in the southern Great Plains. Federal programs designed to improve soil conservation, water management, and farming practices could not prevent a mass exodus of hundreds of thousands out of the Great Plains.

- **Chronologies, Review Questions, and Recommended Readings.** A chronology at the end of each chapter helps students build a framework of key events. Review questions at the end of chapters help students review, reinforce, and retain the material in each chapter and encourage them to relate the material to broader issues in American history. The works in the short, annotated Recommended Reading list at the end of each chapter have been selected with the interested introductory student in mind.

CHRONOLOGY

1441	African slaves first brought to Portugal	1712	Slave uprising in New York City
1619	First Africans brought to Virginia	1713	Peace of Utrecht
1655	English seize Jamaica	1721–48	Robert Walpole leads British cabinet
1662	Virginia law makes slavery hereditary	1729	Natchez Rebellion in French Louisiana
1672	Royal African Company organized	1739	Stono Rebellion in South Carolina
1691	Virginia prohibits interracial sexual contact	1739–43	War of Jenkins' Ear
1698	Britain opens the slave trade to all its merchants	1741	Africans executed in New York for conspiracy
1699	Spanish declare Florida a refuge for escaped slaves	1744–48	King George's War
		1752	Georgia officially opened to slavery
1702	South Carolinians burn St. Augustine	1770s	Peak period of the English colonies' slave trade
1705	Virginia Slave Code established	1808	Importation of slaves into the United States ends
1706	French and Spanish navies bombard Charles Town		
1710	English capture Port Royal in Acadia		

"ten thousand recollections, by the blacks, of the injuries they have sustained." Perhaps he knew of these feelings from his long relationship with Sally Hemings. "I tremble for my country when I reflect that God is just," Jefferson concluded in a deservedly famous discussion of slavery and "that his justice cannot sleep forever."

Conclusion

During the eighteenth century, hundreds of thousands of Africans were kidnapped from their homes, marched to the African coast, and packed into ships for up to three months before arriving in British North America. They provided the labor that made colonialism profitable. Southern planters, northern merchants, and especially British traders and capitalists benefited greatly from the commerce in slave-produced crops. That prosperity trickled down to the ordinary white colonists of British North America. Mercantilism was a system designed to channel colonial wealth produced by slaves to the nation-state, but as long as profits remained high, the British tended to wink at colonists' violations of mercantilist regulations. In short, slavery was fundamental to the operation of the British empire in North America.

Review Questions

1. Trace the development of the system of slavery and discuss the way it became entrenched in the Americas.

2. Describe the effects of the slave trade both on enslaved Africans and on the economic and political life of Africa.

3. Describe the process of acculturation involved in becoming an African American. In what ways did slaves "Africanize" the South?

4. Explain the connection between the institution of slavery and the building of a commercial empire.

5. In what ways did colonial policy encourage the growth of racism?

Recommended Reading

Ira Berlin, *Many Thousands Gone: The First Two Centuries of Slavery in North America* (1998). A history of colonial slavery with attention to the differences between the regions of the Chesapeake, the Lower South,

FOR INSTRUCTORS AND STUDENTS

Supplements for Instructors	Supplements for Students
myhistorylab www.myhistorylab.com Save TIME. Improve Results. MyHistoryLab provides a wealth of resources geared to meet the diverse teaching and learning needs of today's instructors and students. (See page xxxix for a description of the MyHistoryLab features.)	**myhistorylab** www.myhistorylab.com Save TIME. Improve Results. MyHistoryLab's many accessible tools will encourage you to read your text and help you improve your grade in your course. (See page xxxix for a description of the MyHistoryLab features.)
Instructor's Resource Center www.pearsonhighered.com/irc This website provides instructors with additional text-specific resources that can be downloaded for classroom use. Resources include the Instructor's Resource Manual, PowerPoint presentations and the test item file. Register online for access to the resources for *Out of Many*.	***American Stories: Biographies in United States History*** This collection of sixty-two biographies provides insight into the lives and contributions of key figures as well as ordinary citizens to American history. Introductions, pre-reading questions, and suggested resources helps students connect the relevance of these individuals to historical events. Volume 1 **ISBN-10: 0131826549 ISBN-13: 9780131826540** Volume 2 **ISBN-10: 0131826530 ISBN-13: 9780131826533**
Instructor's Resource Manual Available at the Instructor's Resource Center for download, www.pearsonhighered.com/irc, the Instructor's Resource Manual contains chapter outlines, detailed chapter overviews, lecture outlines, topics for discussion, and information about audio-visual resources.	**Library of American Biography Series** www.pearsonhighered .com/educator/series/Library-of-American-Biography/10493.page Pearson's renowned series of biographies spotlighting figures who had a significant impact on American history. Included in the series are Edmund Morgan's *The Puritan Dilemma: The Story of John Winthrop*, B. Davis Edmund's *Tecumseh and the Quest for Indian Leadership*, J. William T. Youngs, *Eleanor Roosevelt: A Personal and Public Life*, and John R. M. Wilson's *Jackie Robinson and the American Dilemma*.
Test Item File Available at the Instructor's Resource Center for download, www.pearsonhighered.com/irc, the Test Item File contains more than 2,000 multiple-choice, identification, matching, true-false, and essay test questions.	**Penguin Valuepacks** www.pearsonhighered.com/penguin A variety of Penguin-Putnam texts is available at discounted prices when bundled with *Out of Many, 7/e*. Texts include Benjamin Franklin's *Autobiography and Other Writings*, Nathaniel Hawthorne's *The Scarlet Letter*, Thomas Jefferson's *Notes on the State of Virginia*, and George Orwell's *1984*.
PowerPoint Presentations Available at the Instructor's Resource Center for download, www.pearsonhighered.com/irc, the PowerPoints contain chapter outlines and full-color images of maps and art.	***A Short Guide to Writing About History, 7/e*** Written by Richard Marius, late of Harvard University, and Melvin E. Page, Eastern Tennessee State University, this engaging and practical text explores the writing and researching processes, identifies different modes of historical writing, including argument, and concludes with guidelines for improving style. **ISBN-10: 0205673708; ISBN-13: 9780205673704**
MyTest Available at www.pearsonmytest.com, MyTest is a powerful assessment generation program that helps instructors easily create and print quizzes and exams. Questions and tests can be authored online, allowing instructors ultimate flexibility and the ability to efficiently manage assessments anytime, anywhere! Instructors can easily access existing questions and edit, create, and store using simple drag-and-drop and Word-like controls.	***Longman American History Atlas*** This full-color historical atlas designed especially for college students is a valuable reference tool and visual guide to American history. This atlas includes maps covering the scope of American history from the lives of the Native Americans to the 1990s. Produced by a renowned cartographic firm and a team of respected historians, the Longman American History Atlas will enhance any American history survey course. **ISBN: 0321004868; ISBN-13: 9780321004864**
Retrieving the American Past Reader Program Available through the Pearson Custom Library (www.pearsoncustom.com, keyword search | rtap), the *Retrieving the American Past* (RTAP) program lets you create a textbook or reader that meets your needs and the needs of your course. RTAP gives you the freedom and flexibility to add chapters from several best-selling Pearson textbooks, in addition to *The American Journey, 5/e* and/or 100 topical reading units written by the History Department of Ohio State University, all under one cover. Choose the content you want to teach in depth, in the sequence you want, at the price you want your students to pay.	

PEARSON myhistorylab™

For Instructors and Students

Save TIME. Improve Results.

MyHistoryLab is a dynamic website that provides a wealth of resources geared to meet the diverse teaching and learning needs of today's instructors and students. MyHistoryLab's many accessible tools will encourage students to read their text and help them improve their grade in their course.

Features of Myhistorylab

- **Pearson eText**—An e-book version of *Out of Many* is included in MyHistorylab. Just like the printed text, students can highlight and add their own notes as they read the book online.
- **Audio Files**—Full audio of the entire text is included to suit the varied learning styles of today's students. In addition there are audio clips of speeches, readings, and music that provide another engaging way to experience history.
- **Pre-test, Post-tests, and Chapter Reviews**—Students can take quizzes to test their knowledge of chapter content and to review for exams.
- **Text and Visual Documents**—Over 1,500 primary source documents, images, and maps available organized by chapter in the text. Primary source documents are also available in the MyHistoryLibrary and can be searched by author, title, theme, and topic. Many of these documents include critical thinking questions.
- **History Bookshelf**—Students may read, download, or print 100 of the most commonly assigned history works like Homer's *The Iliad* or Machiavelli's *The Prince*.
- **Lecture and Archival Videos**—Lectures by leading scholars on provocative topics give students a critical look at key points in history. Videos of speeches, news footage, key historical events, and other archival video take students back to the moment in history.
- **MySearchLab**—This website provides students access to a number of reliable sources for online research, as well as clear guidance on the research and writing process.
- **Gradebook**—Students can follow their own progress and instructors can monitor the work of the entire class. Automated grading of quizzes and assignments helps both instructors and students save time and monitor their results throughout the course.

NEW In-text References to MyHistorylab Resources

Read, View, See, Watch, Hear, Study, and Review Icons integrated in the text connect resources on MyHistorylab to specific topics within the chapters. The

icons are not exhaustive; many more resources are available than those highlighted in the book, but the icons draw attention to some of the most high-interest resources available on MyHistorylab.

Read the **Document** Primary and secondary source documents on compelling topics such as *Brown v. Board of Education of Topeka, Kansas* and Engel, Address by a Haymarket Anarchist enhance topics discussed in each chapter.

View the **Image** Photographs, fine art, and artifacts, provide students with a visual perspective on topics within the chapters, underscoring the role of visuals in understanding the past.

See the **Map** Atlas and interactive maps present both a broad overview and a detailed examination of historical developments.

Watch the **Video** Video lectures highlight topics ranging from Columbus to Lincoln to Obama, engaging students on both historical and contemporary topics. Also included are archival videos, such as footage of Ellis Island immigrants in 1903 and the Kennedy-Nixon debate.

Hear the **Audio** For each chapter there are audio files of the text, speeches, readings, and other audio material, such as "Battle Hymn of the Republic" and "The Star Spangled Banner" that will enrich students' experience of social and cultural history.

Study and **Review** MyhistoryLab provides a wealth of practice quizzes, tests, flashcards, and other study resources available to students online.

NEW MyHistorylab Connections

At the end of each chapter, a new section, MyHistorylab Connections, provides a list of the references within the chapter and additional documents, maps, videos, or additional resources that relate to the content of the chapter.

ACKNOWLEDGMENTS

In the years it has taken to bring *Out of Many* from idea to reality and to improve it in successive editions, we have often been reminded that although writing history sometimes feels like isolated work, it actually involves a collective effort. We want to thank the dozens of people whose efforts have made the publication of this book possible.

We wish to thank our many friends at Prentice Hall for their efforts in creating the seventh edition of *Out of Many*: Yolanda de Rooy, President; Craig Campanella, Editorial Director; Charlyce Jones Owen, Publisher; Maureen Prado Roberts, Senior Marketing Manager; Brandy Dawson, Director of Marketing; Cheryl Keenan, Project Manager; Ann Marie McCarthy, Senior Managing Editor; Maria Lange, Art Director; from GEX Publishing Services: Micah Petillo, Production Editor.

Although we share joint responsibility for the entire book, the chapters were individually authored: John Mack Faragher wrote chapters 1–8; Susan Armitage wrote chapters 9–16; Mari Jo Buhle wrote chapters 18–20, 25–26, 29; and Daniel Czitrom wrote chapters 17, 21–24, 27–28. For this edition Buhle and Czitrom co-authored Chapters 30–31.

Each of us depended on a great deal of support and assistance with the research and writing that went into this book. We want to thank: Kathryn Abbott, Nan Boyd, Krista Comer, Jennifer Cote, Crista DeLuzio, Keith Edgerton, Carol Frost, Jesse Hoffnung Garskof, Pailin Gaither, Jane Gerhard, Todd Gernes, Mark Krasovic, Daniel Lanpher, Melani McAlister, Rebecca McKenna, Cristiane Mitchell, J. C. Mutchler, Keith Peterson, Alan Pinkham, Tricia Rose, Gina Rourke, Jessica Shubow, Gordon P. Utz Jr., Maura Young, Teresa Bill, Gill Frank, and Naoko Shibusawa. Our families and close friends have been supportive and ever so patient over the many years we have devoted to this project. But we want especially to thank Paul Buhle, Meryl Fingrutd, Bob Greene, and Michele Hoffnung.

REVIEWERS AND CONSULTANTS

Historians around the country greatly assisted us by reading and commenting on chapters for this and previous editions. Their many insightful suggestions, encouragement, and dedication have been a tremendous help to us and to the textbook. We want to thank each of them for the commitment of their valuable time and for sharing their experience and ideas on previous editions as well as this new seventh edition.

Seventh Edition:

Daniel M. Anderson, *Cincinnati State Technical and Community College*
TJ Boisseau, *University of Akron*
Cynthia Carter, *Florida Community College, Jacksonville*
Thomas Clarkin, *San Antonio College*
Dr. John S. Leiby, *Paradise Valley Community College*
Richard H. Owens, *West Liberty University*
Burton Peretti, *Western Connecticut State University*
Michael J. Pfeifer, *John Jay College of Criminal Justice*
Jeffrey M. Schulze, *University of Texas, Dallas*
Deborah Welch, *Longwood University*

Previous Editions:

Jeffrey. S. Adler, *University of Florida*
Jennifer L. Altenhofel, *Taft College*
Lee Annis, *Montgomery College*
Caroline Barton, *Holmes Community College*
Jon S. Blackman, *University of Oklahoma*
James Bradford, *Texas A&M University*
Fran Campbell, *College of Southern Nevada*
Frank Chartrand, *Los Angeles Pierce College*
Robert E. Cray, *Montclair State University*
Lawrence Culver, *Utah State University*
Amy Curry, *Montgomery College*
Alan Downs, *Georgia Southern University*
John T. Duke, *Alvin Community College*
Keith Edgerton, *Montana State University, Billings*
Greg Ference, *Salisbury University*
Kate Foss-Mollan, *University of Wisconsin, Milwaukee*
Jennifer Fry, *King's College*
Michael Gabriel, *Kutztown University*
Jessica Gerard, *Ozarks Technical College*
George Gerdow, *Northeastern Illinois University*
Jerry Gershenhorn, *North Carolina Central University*
Jolyon P. Girard, *Cabrini College*
Wendy Gordon, *SUNY Plattsburgh*
Kathleen Gorman, *Minnesota State University, Mankato*
W. Scott Haine, *College of San Mateo*
Gordon Harvey, *The University of Louisiana, Monroe*
Leslie Heaphy, *Kent State University*
Rebecca Hill, *CUNY, Borough of Manhattan Community College*
Don Jacobson, *Oakton Community College*
Jeff Janowick, *Lansing Community College*

Hasan Jeffries, *Ohio State University*

Jeanette Keith, *Bloomsburg University*

Kathleen Kennedy, *Western Washington University*

William Kerrigan, *Muskingum College*

Jonathan Mercantini, *Canisius College*

Peter Messer, *Mississippi State University*

James Mills, *University of Texas, Brownsville*

Joseph P. Moore III, *University of Vermont*

James Owens, *Oakton Community College*

Ken Poston, *Beaumont Independent School District*

G. David Price, *University of Florida*

Caroline Pruden, *North Carolina State University*

Carol Quirke, *SUNY Old Westbury*

Kathleen L. Riley, *Ohio Dominican University*

James R. Rohrer, *University of Nebraska, Kearney*

Joshua P. Schier, *Western Michigan University*

Melissane Schrems, *St. Lawrence University*

Jeffrey Shepherd, *University of Texas, El Paso*

Jean Stuntz, *West Texas A&M*

Karen R. Utz, *University of Alabama, Birmingham*

James Williams, *Middle Tennessee State University*

Larry Wilson, *San Jacinto College*

James Wolfinger, *DePaul University*

Jason Young, *SUNY Buffalo*

Charles A. Zappia, *San Diego Mesa College*

ABOUT THE AUTHORS

John Mack Faragher

John Mack Faragher is Arthur Unobskey Professor of American History and director of the Howard R. Lamar Center for the Study of Frontiers and Borders at Yale University. Born in Arizona and raised in southern California, he received his B.A. at the University of California, Riverside, and his Ph.D. at Yale University. He is the author of *Women and Men on the Overland Trail* (1979), *Sugar Creek: Life on the Illinois Prairie* (1986), *Daniel Boone: The Life and Legend of an American Pioneer* (1992), *The American West: A New Interpretive History* (2000), and *A Great and Noble Scheme: The Tragic Story of the Expulsion of the French Acadians from their American Homeland* (2005).

Daniel Czitrom

Daniel Czitrom is Professor of History at Mount Holyoke College. Born and raised in New York City, he received his B.A. from the State University of New York at Binghamton and his M.A. and Ph.D. from the University of Wisconsin, Madison. He is the author of *Media and the American Mind: From Morse to McLuhan* (1982), which won the First Books Award of the American Historical Association and has been translated into Spanish and Chinese. He is co-author of *Rediscovering Jacob Riis: Exposure Journalism and Photography in Turn of the Century New York* (2008). He has served as a historical consultant and featured on-camera commentator for several documentary film projects, including the PBS productions *New York: A Documentary Film; American Photography: A Century of Images*; and *The Great Transatlantic Cable*. He currently serves as a Distinguished Lecturer for the Organization of American Historians.

Mari Jo Buhle

Mari Jo Buhle is William R. Kenan, Jr. University Professor *Emerita* of American Civilization and History at Brown University, specializing in American women's history. She received her B.A. from the University of Illinois, Urbana-Champaign, and her Ph.D. from the University of Wisconsin, Madison. She is the author of *Women and American Socialism, 1870–1920* (1981) and *Feminism and Its Discontents: A Century of Struggle with Psychoanalysis* (1998). She is also coeditor of the *Encyclopedia of the American Left*, (second edition, 1998). Professor Buhle held a fellowship (1991-1996) from the John D. and Catherine T. MacArthur Foundation. She is currently an Honorary Fellow of the History Department at the University of Wisconsin, Madison.

Susan H. Armitage

Susan H. Armitage is Professor of History and Women's Studies, *Emerita*, at Washington State University, where she was a Claudius O. and Mary R. Johnson Distinguished Professor. She earned her Ph.D. from the London School of Economics and Political Science. Among her many publications on western women's history are three coedited books, *The Women's West* (1987), *So Much To Be Done: Women on the Mining and Ranching Frontier* (1991), and *Writing the Range: Race, Class, and Culture in the Women's West* (1997). She served as editor of the feminist journal *Frontiers* from 1996 to 2002. Her most recent publication, coedited with Laurie Mercier, is *Speaking History: Oral Histories of the American Past, 1865–Present* (2009).

COMMUNITY & DIVERSITY

One of the most characteristic features of our country is its astounding variety. The American people include the descendants of native Indians; colonial Europeans of British, French, and Spanish background; Africans; and migrants from virtually every country and continent. Indeed, at the beginning of the new century the United States is absorbing a flood of immigrants from Latin America and Asia that rivals the great tide of people from eastern and southern Europe one hundred years before. What's more, our country is one of the world's most spacious, sprawling across than 3.6 million square miles of territory. The struggle to meld a single nation out of our many far-flung communities is what much of American history is all about. That is the story told in this book.

Every human society is made up of communities. A community is a set of relationships linking men, women, and their families to a coherent social whole that is more than the sum of its parts. In a community people develop the capacity for unified action. In a community people learn, often through trial and error, how to transform and adapt to their environment.

The sentiment that binds the members of a community together is the mother of group consciousness and ethnic identity. In the making of history, communities are far more important than even the greatest of leaders, for the community is the institution most capable of passing a distinctive historical tradition to future generations.

William Sidney Mount (1807–1868) *California News* 1850. Oil on canvas. The Long Island Museum of American Art, History and Carriages.

Gift of Mr. and Mrs. Ward Melville, 1955.

Harvey Dinnerstein, *Underground, Together* 1996, oil on canvas, 90" × 107".

Photograph courtesy of Gerold Wunderlich & Co., New York, NY.

Communities bind people together in multiple ways. They can be as small as local neighborhoods, in which people maintain face-to-face relations, or as large as the nation itself. This book examines American history from the perspective of community life—an ever-widening frame that has included larger and larger groups of Americans.

Networks of kinship and friendship, and connections across generations and among families, establish the bonds essential to community life. Shared feelings about values and history establish the basis for common identity. In communities, people find the power to act collectively in their own interest. But American communities frequently took shape as a result of serious conflicts among groups, and within communities there was often significant fighting among competing groups or classes. Thus the term *community,* as we use it here, includes conflict and discord as well as harmony and agreement.

For decades Americans have complained about the "loss of community." But community has not disappeared—it has been continuously reinvented. Until the late eighteenth century, community was defined primarily by space and local geography. But in the nineteenth century communities were reshaped by new and powerful historical forces such as the marketplace, industrialization,

the corporation, mass immigration, mass media, and the growth of the nation-state. In the twentieth century, Americans struggled to balance commitments to multiple communities. These were defined not simply by local spatial arrangements, but by categories as varied as race and ethnicity, occupation, political affiliation, and consumer preference.

The "American Communities" vignettes that open each chapter reflect these transformations. Most of the vignettes in the pre–Civil War chapters focus on geographically defined communities, such as the ancient Indian city at Cahokia, or the experiment in industrial urban planning in early nineteenth-century Lowell, Massachusetts. Post–Civil War chapters explore different and more modern kinds of communities. In the 1920s, movies and radio offered communities of identification with dreams of freedom, material success, upward mobility, youth and beauty. In the 1950s, rock 'n' roll music helped germinate a new national community of teenagers, with profound effects on the culture of the entire country in the second half of the twentieth century. In the late 1970s, fear of nuclear accidents like the one at Three Mile Island brought concerned citizens together in communities around the country and encouraged a national movement opposing nuclear power.

The title for our book was suggested by the Latin phrase selected by John Adams, Benjamin Franklin, and Thomas Jefferson for the Great Seal of the United States: *E Pluribus Unum*—"Out of Many Comes Unity." These men understood that unity could not be imposed by a powerful central authority but had to develop out of mutual respect among Americans of different backgrounds. The revolutionary leadership expressed the hope that such respect could grow on the basis of a remarkable proposition: "We hold these truths to be self-evident, that all men are created equal; that they are endowed by their Creator with certain unalienable rights; that among these are life, liberty, and the pursuit of happiness." The national government of the United States would preserve local and state authority but would guarantee individual rights. The nation would be strengthened by guarantees of difference.

"Out of Many" comes strength. That is the promise of America and the premise of this book. The underlying dialectic of American history, we believe, is that as a people we must locate our national unity in the celebration of the differences that exist among us; these differences can be our strength, as long as we affirm the promise of the Declaration. Protecting the "right to be different," in other words, is absolutely fundamental to the continued existence of democracy, and that right is best protected by the existence of strong and vital communities. We are bound together as a nation by the ideal of local and cultural differences protected by our common commitment to the values of the American Revolution.

Today those values are endangered by those who use the tactics of mass terror. In the wake of the September 11, 2001 attack on the United States, and with the continuing threat of biological, chemical, or even nuclear assaults, Americans can not afford to lose faith in our historic vision. The thousands of victims buried in the smoking ruins of the World Trade Center included people from dozens of different ethnic and national groups. The United States is a multicultural and transnational society. We must rededicate ourselves to the protection and defense of the promise of diversity and unity.

Our history demonstrates that the promise has always been problematic. Centrifugal forces have been powerful in the American past, and at times the country seemed about to fracture into its component parts. Our transformation from a collection of groups and regions into a nation was marked by painful and often violent struggles. Our past is filled with conflicts between Indians and colonists, masters and slaves, Patriots and Loyalists, Northerners and Southerners, Easterners and Westerners, capitalists and workers, and sometimes the government and the people. War can bring out our best, but it can also bring out our worst. During World War II thousands of Japanese American citizens were deprived of their rights and locked up in isolated detention centers because of their ethnic background. Americans often appear to be

Thomas Satterwhite Noble, Last Sale of Slaves on the *Courthouse Steps*, 1860, oil on canvas, Missouri Historical Society.

little more than a contentious collection of peoples with conflicting interests, divided by region and background, race and class.

Our most influential leaders have also sometimes suffered a crisis of faith in the American project of "liberty and justice for all." Thomas Jefferson not only believed in the inferiority of African Americans but feared that immigrants from outside the Anglo-American tradition might "warp and bias" the development of the nation "and render it a heterogeneous, incoherent, distracted mass." We have not always lived up to the American promise and there is a dark side to our history. It took the bloodiest war in American history to secure the human rights of African Americans, and the struggle for full equality for all our citizens has yet to be won. During the great influx of immigrants in the early twentieth century, fears much like Jefferson's led to movements to Americanize the foreign born by forcing them, in the words of one leader, "to give up the languages, customs, and methods of life which they have brought with them across the ocean, and adopt instead the language, habits, and customs of this country, and the general standards and ways of American living." Similar thinking motivated Congress at various times to bar the immigration of Africans, Asians, and other people of color into the country, and to force assimilation on American Indians by denying them the freedom to practice their religion or even to speak their own language. Such calls for restrictive unity resound in our own day.

But other Americans have argued for a more fulsome version of Americanization. "What is the American, this new man?" asked the French immigrant Michel Crévecoeur in 1782. "A strange mixture of blood which you will find in no other country." In America, he wrote, "individuals of all nations are melted into a new race of men." A century later Crévecoeur was echoed by historian Frederick Jackson Turner, who believed that "in the crucible of the frontier, the immigrants were Americanized, liberated, and fused into a mixed race, English in neither nationality nor characteristics. The process has gone on from the early days to our own."

The process by which diverse communities have come to share a set of common American values is one of the most fundamental aspects of our history. It did not occur, however, because of compulsory Americanization programs, but because of free public education, popular participation in democratic politics, and the impact of popular culture. Contemporary America does have a common culture: we share a commitment to freedom of thought and expression, we join in the aspirations to own our own homes and send our children to college, we laugh at the same television programs or video clips on You Tube.

To a degree that too few Americans appreciate, this common culture resulted from a complicated process of mutual discovery that took place when different ethnic and regional groups encountered one another. Consider just one small and unique aspect of our culture: the barbecue. Americans have been barbecuing since before the beginning of written history. Early settlers adopted this technique of cooking from the Indians—the word itself comes from a native term for a framework of sticks over a fire on which meat was slowly cooked. Colonists typically barbecued pork, fed on Indian corn. African slaves lent their own touch by introducing the use of spicy sauces. The ritual that is a part of nearly every American family's Fourth of July silently celebrates the heritage of diversity that went into making our common culture.

The American educator John Dewey recognized this diversity early in the last century. "The genuine American, the typical American, is himself a hyphenated character," he declared, "international and interracial in his make-up." It was up to all Americans, Dewey argued, "to see to it that the hyphen connects instead of separates." We, the authors of *Out of Many*, endorse Dewey's perspective. "Creation comes from the impact of diversity," the American philosopher Horace Kallen wrote about the same time. We also endorse Kallen's vision of the American promise: "A democracy of nationalities, cooperating voluntarily and autonomously through common institutions, . . . a multiplicity in a unity, an orchestration of mankind." And now, let the music begin.

Out of Many

Chapter 17 at www.myhistorylab.com

((•• Hear the Audio

Reconstruction

1863–1877

CHAPTER OUTLINE

American Communities 459
Hale County, Alabama: From Slavery to Freedom in a Black Belt Community

The Politics of Reconstruction 461
The Defeated South
Abraham Lincoln's Plan
Andrew Johnson and Presidential Reconstruction
Free Labor and the Radical Republican Vision
Congressional Reconstruction and the Impeachment Crisis

The Election of 1868
Woman Suffrage and Reconstruction

The Meaning of Freedom 469
Moving About
African American Families, Churches, and Schools
Land and Labor After Slavery
The Origins of African American Politics

Southern Politics and Society 476
Southern Republicans
Reconstructing the States: A Mixed Record

White Resistance and "Redemption"
King Cotton: Sharecroppers, Tenants, and the Southern Environment

Reconstructing the North 482
The Age of Capital
Liberal Republicans and the Election of 1872
The Depression of 1873
The Electoral Crisis of 1876

Theodor Kaufmann (1814–1896), *On to Liberty*, 1867. Oil on canvas, 36 × 56 in (91.4 × 142.2 cm). Runaway slaves escaping through the woods. Art Resource/Metropolitan Museum of Art.

Hale County, Alabama: From Slavery to Freedom in a Black Belt Community

On a bright Saturday morning in May 1867, 4,000 former slaves streamed into the town of Greensboro, bustling seat of Hale County in west-central Alabama. They came to hear speeches from two delegates to a recent freedmen's convention in Mobile and to find out about the political status of black people under the Reconstruction Act just passed by Congress. Tensions mounted in the days following this unprecedented gathering, as military authorities began supervising voter registration for elections to the upcoming constitutional convention that would rewrite the laws of Alabama. On June 13, John Orrick, a local white, confronted Alex Webb, a politically active freedman, on the streets of Greensboro. Webb had recently been appointed a voter registrar for the district. Orrick swore he would never be registered by a black man and shot Webb dead. Hundreds of armed and angry freedmen formed a posse to search for Orrick but failed to find him. Galvanized by Webb's murder, 500 local freedmen formed a chapter of the Union League, the Republican Party's organizational arm in the South. The chapter functioned as both a militia company and a forum to agitate for political rights.

Violent political encounters between black people and white people were common in southern communities in the wake of the Civil War. Communities throughout the South struggled over the meaning of freedom in ways that reflected their particular circumstances. The 4 million freed people constituted roughly one-third of the total southern population, but the black–white ratio in individual communities varied enormously. In some places, the Union army had been a strong presence during the war, hastening the collapse of the slave system and encouraging experiments in free labor. Other areas had remained relatively untouched by the fighting. In some areas, small farms prevailed; in others, including Hale County, large plantations dominated economic and political life.

West-central Alabama had emerged as a fertile center of cotton production just two decades before the Civil War. There, African Americans, as throughout the South's black belt, constituted more than three-quarters of the population. With the arrival of federal troops in the spring of 1865, African Americans in Hale County, like their counterparts elsewhere, began to challenge the traditional organization of plantation labor.

One owner, Henry Watson, found that his entire workforce had deserted him at the end of 1865. "I am in the midst of a large and fertile cotton growing country," Watson wrote to a partner. "Many plantations are entirely without labor, many plantations have insufficient labor, and upon none are the laborers doing their former accustomed work." Black women refused to work in the fields, preferring to stay home with their children and tend garden plots. Nor would male field hands do any work, such as caring for hogs, that did not directly increase their share of the cotton crop.

Above all, freed people wanted more autonomy. Overseers and owners grudgingly allowed them to work the land "in families," letting them choose their own supervisors and find their own provisions. The result was a shift from the gang labor characteristic of the antebellum period, in which large groups of slaves worked under the harsh and constant supervision of white overseers, to the sharecropping system, in which African American families worked small plots of land in exchange for a small share of the crop. This shift represented less of a victory for newly freed African Americans than a defeat for plantation owners, who resented even the limited economic independence it forced them to concede to their black workforce.

Only a small fraction—perhaps 15 percent—of African American families were fortunate enough to be able to buy land. The majority settled for some version of sharecropping, while others managed to rent land from owners, becoming tenant farmers. Still, planters throughout Hale County had to change the old routines of plantation labor. Local African Americans also organized politically. In 1866, Congress had passed the Civil Rights Act and sent the Fourteenth Amendment to the Constitution to the states for ratification; both promised full citizenship rights to former slaves. Hale County freedmen joined the Republican Party and local Union League chapters. They used their new political power to press for better labor contracts, demand greater autonomy for the black workforce, and agitate for the more radical goal of land confiscation and redistribution. "The colored people are very anxious to get land of their own to live upon independently; and they want money to buy stock to make crops," reported one black Union League organizer. "The only way to get these necessaries is to give our votes to the [Republican] party." Two Hale County former slaves, Brister Reese and James K. Green, won election to the Alabama state legislature in 1869.

It was not long before these economic and political gains prompted a white counterattack. In the spring of 1868, the Ku Klux Klan—a secret organization devoted to terrorizing and intimidating African Americans and their white Republican allies—came to Hale County. Disguised in white sheets, armed with guns and whips, and making nighttime raids on horseback, Klansmen flogged, beat, and murdered freed people. They intimidated voters and silenced political activists. Planters used Klan terror to dissuade former slaves from leaving plantations or organizing for higher wages. With the passage of the Ku Klux Klan Act in 1871, the federal government cracked down on the Klan, breaking its power temporarily in parts of the former Confederacy. But no serious effort was made to stop Klan terror in the west Alabama black belt, and planters there succeeded in reestablishing much of their social and political control.

The events in Hale County illustrate the struggles that beset communities throughout the South during the Reconstruction era after the Civil War. The destruction of slavery and the Confederacy forced African Americans and white people to renegotiate their old roles. These community battles both shaped and were shaped by the

1. What were the competing political plans for reconstructing the defeated Confederacy?

2. How did African Americans negotiate the difficult transition from slavery to freedom?

3. What were the most important political and social legacies of Reconstruction in the southern states?

4. How did economic and political transformations in the North reflect another side of Reconstruction?

FOCUS Questions

1863–1877

victorious and newly expansive federal government in Washington. But the new arrangements of both political power sharing and the organization of labor had to be worked out within local communities. In the end, Reconstruction was only

Greensboro

partially successful. Not until the "Second Reconstruction" of the twentieth-century civil rights movement would the descendants of Hale County's African Americans begin to enjoy the full fruits of freedom—and even then not without challenge.

AMERICAN Communities

The Politics of Reconstruction

When General Robert E. Lee's men stacked their guns at Appomattox, the bloodiest war in American history ended. More than 600,000 soldiers had died during the four years of fighting, 360,000 Union and 260,000 Confederate. Another 275,000 Union and 190,000 Confederate troops had been wounded. Although President Abraham Lincoln insisted early on that the purpose of the war was to preserve the Union, by 1863 it had evolved as well into a struggle for African American liberation. Indeed, the political, economic, and moral issues posed by slavery were the root cause of the Civil War, and the war ultimately destroyed slavery, although not racism, once and for all.

The Civil War also settled the constitutional crisis provoked by the secession of the Confederacy and its justification in appeals to states' rights. The name "United States" would from then on be understood as a singular rather than a plural noun, signaling an important change in the meaning of American nationality. The old notion of the United States as a voluntary union of sovereign states gave way to the new reality of a single nation, in

which the federal government took precedence over the individual states. The key historical developments of the Reconstruction era revolved around precisely how the newly strengthened national government would define its relationship with the defeated Confederate states and the 4 million newly freed slaves.

The Defeated South

The white South paid an extremely high price for secession, war, and defeat. In addition to the battlefield casualties, the Confederate states sustained deep material and psychological wounds. Much of the best agricultural land was laid waste, including the rich fields of northern Virginia, the Shenandoah Valley, and large sections of Tennessee, Mississippi, Georgia, and South Carolina. Many towns and cities—including Richmond, Atlanta, and Columbia, South Carolina—were in ruins. By 1865, the South's most precious commodities, cotton and African American slaves, no longer were measures of wealth and prestige. Retreating Confederates destroyed most of the South's cotton to prevent its capture by federal troops. What remained was confiscated by Union agents as contraband of war. The former slaves, many of whom had fled to Union lines during the latter stages of the war, were determined to chart their own course in the reconstructed South as free men and women.

Emancipation proved the bitterest pill for white Southerners to swallow, especially the planter elite. Conquered and degraded, and in their view robbed of their slave property, white people responded by regarding African Americans, more than ever, as inferior to themselves. In the antebellum South, white skin had defined a social bond that transcended economic class. It gave even the poorest white a badge of superiority over even the most skilled slave or prosperous free African American. Emancipation, however, forced white people to redefine their world. The specter of political power and social equality for African Americans made racial order the consuming passion of most white Southerners during the Reconstruction years. In fact, racism can be seen as

Read the Document

Confederate Song, "I'm a Good Old Rebel" (1866) at **www.myhistorylab.com**

one of the major forces driving Reconstruction and, ultimately, undermining it.

Abraham Lincoln's Plan

By late 1863, Union military victories had convinced President Lincoln of the need to fashion a plan for the reconstruction of the South (see Chapter 16). Lincoln based his reconstruction program on bringing the seceded states back into the Union as quickly as possible. His Proclamation of Amnesty and Reconstruction of December 1863 offered "full pardon" and the restoration of property, not including slaves, to white Southerners willing to swear an oath of allegiance to the United States and its laws, including the Emancipation Proclamation. Prominent Confederate military and civil leaders were excluded from Lincoln's offer, though he indicated that he would freely pardon them.

The president also proposed that when the number of any Confederate state's voters who took the oath of allegiance reached 10 percent of the number who had voted

"Decorating the Graves of Rebel Soldiers," *Harper's Weekly,* August 17, 1867. After the Civil War, both Southerners and Northerners created public mourning ceremonies honoring fallen soldiers. Women led the memorial movement in the South that, by establishing cemeteries and erecting monuments, offered the first cultural expression of the Confederate tradition. This engraving depicts citizens of Richmond, Virginia, decorating thousands of Confederate graves with flowers at the Hollywood Memorial Cemetery on the James River. A local women's group raised enough funds to transfer over 16,000 Confederate dead from northern cemeteries for reburial in Richmond.

in the election of 1860, this group could establish a state government that Lincoln would recognize as legitimate. Fundamental to this Ten Percent Plan was that the reconstructed governments accept the abolition of slavery. Lincoln's plan was designed less as a blueprint for reconstruction than as a way to shorten the war and gain white people's support for emancipation.

Lincoln's amnesty proclamation angered those Republicans—known as Radical Republicans—who advocated not only equal rights for the freedmen but also a tougher stance toward the white South. In July 1864, Senator Benjamin F. Wade of Ohio and Congressman Henry W. Davis of Maryland, both Radicals, proposed a harsher alternative to the Ten Percent Plan. The Wade–Davis bill required 50 percent of a seceding state's white male citizens to take a loyalty oath before elections could be held for a convention to rewrite the state's constitution. The Radical Republicans saw reconstruction as a chance to effect a fundamental transformation of southern society. They thus wanted to delay the process until war's end and to limit participation to a small number of southern Unionists. Lincoln viewed Reconstruction as part of the larger effort to win the war and abolish slavery. He wanted to weaken the Confederacy by creating new state governments that could win broad support from southern white people. The Wade–Davis bill threatened his efforts to build political consensus within the southern states. Lincoln, therefore, pocket-vetoed the bill by refusing to sign it within ten days of the adjournment of Congress.

As Union armies occupied parts of the South, commanders improvised a variety of arrangements involving confiscated plantations and the African American labor force. For example, in 1862 General Benjamin F. Butler began a policy of transforming slaves on Louisiana sugar plantations into wage laborers under the close supervision of occupying federal troops. Butler's policy required slaves to remain on the estates of loyal planters, where they would receive wages according to a fixed schedule, as well as food and medical care for the aged and sick. Abandoned plantations would be leased to northern investors.

In January 1865, General William T. Sherman issued Special Field Order 15, setting aside the Sea Islands off the Georgia coast and a portion of the South Carolina Lowcountry rice fields for the exclusive settlement of freed people. Each family would receive forty acres of land and the loan of mules from the army—the origin, perhaps, of the famous call for "forty acres and a mule" that would soon capture the imagination of African Americans throughout the South. Sherman's intent was not to revolutionize southern society but to relieve the demands placed on his army by the thousands of impoverished African Americans who followed his march to the sea. By the summer of 1865 some 40,000 freed people, eager to take advantage of the general's order, had been settled on 400,000 acres of "Sherman land."

Photography pioneer Timothy O'Sullivan took this portrait of a multigenerational African American family on the J. J. Smith plantation in Beaufort, South Carolina, in 1862. Many white plantation owners in the area had fled, allowing slaves like these to begin an early transition to freedom before the end of the Civil War.

Conflicts within the Republican Party prevented the development of a systematic land distribution program. Still, Lincoln and the Republican Congress supported other measures to aid the emancipated slaves. In March 1865 Congress established the Freedmen's Bureau. Along with providing food, clothing, and fuel to destitute former slaves, the bureau was charged with supervising and managing "all the abandoned lands in the South and the control of all subjects relating to refugees and freedmen." The act that established the bureau also stated that forty acres of abandoned or confiscated land could be leased to freed slaves or white Unionists, who would have an option to purchase after three years and "such title thereto as the United States can convey."

On the evening of April 14, 1865, while attending the theater in Washington, President Lincoln was shot by John Wilkes Booth and died of his wounds several hours later. At the time of his assassination, Lincoln's reconstruction policy remained unsettled and incomplete. In its broad outlines, the president's plans had seemed to favor a speedy restoration of the southern states to the Union and a minimum of federal intervention in their affairs. But with his death the specifics of postwar Reconstruction had to be hammered out by a new president, Andrew Johnson of Tennessee, a man whose personality, political background,

●●●⌐**Read** the Document

Carl Schurz, Report on the Condition of the South (1865) at **www.myhistorylab.com**

and racist leanings put him at odds with the Republican-controlled Congress.

Andrew Johnson and Presidential Reconstruction

Andrew Johnson, a Democrat and former slaveholder, was a most unlikely successor to the martyred Lincoln. Throughout his career, Johnson had championed yeoman farmers and viewed the South's plantation aristocrats with contempt. He was the only southern member of the U.S. Senate to remain loyal to the Union, and he held the planter elite responsible for secession and defeat. In 1862, Lincoln appointed Johnson to the difficult post of military governor of Tennessee. There he successfully began wartime Reconstruction and cultivated Unionist support in the mountainous eastern districts of that state.

In 1864, the Republicans, in an appeal to northern and border state "War Democrats," nominated Johnson for vice president. But despite Johnson's success in Tennessee and in the 1864 campaign, many Radical Republicans distrusted him, and the hardscrabble Tennessean remained a political outsider in Republican circles. In the immediate aftermath of Lincoln's murder, however, Johnson appeared to side with those Radical Republicans who sought to treat the South as a conquered territory. Any support for Johnson quickly faded as the new president's policies unfolded. Johnson defined Reconstruction as the province of the executive, not the legislative branch, and he planned to restore the Union as quickly as possible. He blamed individual Southerners—the planter elite—rather than entire states for leading the South down the disastrous road to secession. In line with this philosophy, Johnson outlined mild terms for reentry to the Union.

In the spring of 1865, Johnson granted amnesty and pardon, including restoration of property rights except slaves, to all Confederates who pledged loyalty to the Union and support for emancipation. Fourteen classes of Southerners, mostly major Confederate officials and wealthy landowners, were excluded. But these men could apply individually for presidential pardons. (During his tenure Johnson pardoned roughly 90 percent of those who applied.) Significantly, Johnson instituted this plan while Congress was not in session.

By the autumn of 1865, ten of the eleven Confederate states claimed to have met Johnson's requirements to reenter the Union. On December 6, 1865, in his first annual message to Congress, the president declared the "restoration" of the Union virtually complete. But a serious division within the federal government was taking shape, for the Congress was not about to allow the president free rein in determining the conditions of southern readmission.

Andrew Johnson used the term "restoration" rather than "reconstruction." A lifelong Democrat with ambitions to be elected president on his own in 1868, Johnson hoped to build a new political coalition composed of northern Democrats, conservative Republicans, and southern Unionists. Firmly committed to white supremacy, he opposed political rights for the freedmen. Johnson's open sympathy for his fellow white Southerners, his antiblack bias, and his determination to control the course of Reconstruction placed him on a collision course with the powerful Radical wing of the Republican Party.

Free Labor and the Radical Republican Vision

Most Radicals were men whose careers had been shaped by the slavery controversy. One of the most effective rhetorical weapons used against slavery and its spread had been the ideal of a society based upon free labor. The model of free individuals, competing equally in the labor market and enjoying equal political rights, formed the core of this worldview. Equality of opportunity created a more fluid social structure where, as Abraham Lincoln had noted, "There is not of necessity any such thing as a free hired laborer being fixed in that condition."

Radicals now looked to reconstruct southern society along these same lines, backed by the power of the national government. They argued that once free labor, universal education, and equal rights were implanted in the South, that region would be able to share in the North's material wealth, progress, and social mobility. Representative George W. Julian of Indiana typified the Radical vision for the South. He called for elimination of the region's large plantations, arguing that the South needed to develop "small farms, thrifty tillage, free schools, social independence, flourishing manufactures and the arts, respect for honest labor, and equality of political rights." In the most far-reaching proposal, Representative Thaddeus Stevens of Pennsylvania called for the confiscation of 400 million acres belonging to the wealthiest 10 percent of Southerners to be redistributed to black and white yeomen and northern land buyers. "The whole fabric of Southern society must be changed," Stevens told Pennsylvania Republicans in September 1865, "and never can it be done if this opportunity is lost. How can republican institutions, free schools, free churches, free social intercourse exist in a mingled community of nabobs and serfs?"

Northern Republicans were especially outraged by the stringent "black codes" passed by South Carolina, Mississippi, Louisiana, and other states. These were designed to restrict the freedom of the black labor force and keep freed people as close to slave status as possible. Laborers who left their jobs before contracts expired would forfeit wages already earned and be subject to arrest by any white citizen. Vagrancy, very broadly defined, was punishable by fines and

Read the Document

Mississippi Black Code (1865) at **www.myhistorylab.com**

"Office of the Freedmen's Bureau, Memphis, Tennessee," *Harper's Weekly*, June 2, 1866. Established by Congress in 1865, the Freedmen's Bureau provided economic, educational, and legal assistance to former slaves in the post–Civil War years. Bureau agents were often called on to settle disputes between black and white Southerners over wages, labor contracts, political rights, and violence. Although most southern whites only grudgingly acknowledged the bureau's legitimacy, freed people gained important legal and psychological support through testimony at public hearings like this one.

involuntary plantation labor. Apprenticeship clauses obliged black children to work without pay for employers. Some states attempted to bar African Americans from land ownership. Other laws specifically denied African Americans equality with white people in civil rights, excluding them from juries and prohibiting interracial marriages. The black codes underscored the unwillingness of white Southerners to accept freedom for African Americans

The Radicals, although not a majority of their party, were joined by moderate Republicans as growing numbers of Northerners grew suspicious of white southern intransigence and the denial of political rights to freedmen. When the Thirty-ninth Congress convened in December 1865, the large Republican majority prevented the seating of the white Southerners elected to Congress under President Johnson's provisional state governments. Republicans also established the Joint Committee on Reconstruction. After hearing extensive testimony from a broad range of witnesses, it concluded that not only were old Confederates back in power in the South but also that black codes and racial violence required increased protection for African Americans.

In the spring of 1866, Congress passed two important bills designed to aid African Americans. The landmark Civil Rights bill, which bestowed full citizenship on African Americans, overturned the 1857 *Dred Scott* decision and the black codes. It defined all persons born in the United States (except Indian peoples) as national citizens, and it enumerated various rights, including the rights to make and enforce contracts, to sue, to give evidence, and

to buy and sell property. Under this bill, African Americans acquired "full and equal benefit of all laws and proceedings for the security of person and property as is enjoyed by white citizens."

Congress also voted to enlarge the scope of the Freedmen's Bureau, empowering it to build schools and pay teachers, and also to establish courts to prosecute those charged with depriving African Americans of their civil rights. The bureau achieved important, if limited, success in aiding African Americans. Bureau-run schools helped lay the foundation for southern public education. The bureau's network of courts allowed freed people to bring suits against white people in disputes involving violence, nonpayment of wages, or unfair division of crops. The very existence of courts hearing public testimony by African Americans provided an important psychological challenge to traditional notions of white racial domination.

But an angry President Johnson vetoed both of these bills. In opposing the Civil Rights bill, Johnson denounced the assertion of national power to protect African American civil rights, claiming it was a "stride toward centralization, and the concentration of all legislative powers in the national Government." But Johnson's intemperate attacks on the Radicals—he damned them as traitors unwilling to restore the Union—united moderate and Radical Republicans and they succeeded in overriding the vetoes. Congressional Republicans, led by the Radical faction, were now unified in challenging the president's power to direct Reconstruction and in using national authority to define and protect the rights of citizens.

In June 1866, fearful that the Civil Rights Act might be declared unconstitutional, and eager to settle the basis for the seating of southern representatives, Congress passed the Fourteenth Amendment. The amendment defined national citizenship to include former slaves ("all persons born or naturalized in the United States") and prohibited the states from violating the privileges of citizens without due process of law. It also empowered Congress to reduce the representation of any state that denied suffrage to males over twenty-one. Republicans adopted the Fourteenth Amendment as their platform for the 1866 congressional elections and suggested that southern states would have to ratify it as a condition of readmission. President Johnson, meanwhile, took to the stump in August to support conservative Democratic and Republican candidates. His unrestrained speeches often degenerated into harangues, alienating many voters and aiding the Republican cause.

For their part, the Republicans skillfully portrayed Johnson and northern Democrats as disloyal and white Southerners as unregenerate. Republicans began an effective campaign tradition known as "waving the bloody shirt"—reminding northern voters of the hundreds of thousands of Yankee soldiers left dead or maimed by the war. In the November 1866 elections, the Republicans increased their majority in both the House and the Senate and gained control of all the northern states. The stage was now set for a battle between the president and Congress. Was it to be Johnson's "restoration" or Congressional Reconstruction?

Congressional Reconstruction and the Impeachment Crisis

United against Johnson, moderate and Radical Republicans took control of Reconstruction early in 1867. In March, Congress passed the First Reconstruction Act over Johnson's veto. This act divided the South into five military districts subject to martial law. To achieve restoration, southern states were first required to call new constitutional conventions, elected by universal manhood suffrage. Once these states had drafted new constitutions, guaranteed African American voting rights, and ratified the Fourteenth Amendment, they were eligible for readmission to the Union. Supplementary legislation, also passed over the president's veto, invalidated the provisional governments established by Johnson, empowered the military to administer voter registration, and required an oath of loyalty to the United States (see Map 17.1).

See the Map
Reconstruction at
www.myhistorylab.com

Congress also passed several laws aimed at limiting Johnson's power. One of these, the Tenure of Office Act, stipulated that any officeholder appointed by the president with the Senate's advice and consent could not be removed until the Senate had approved a successor. In

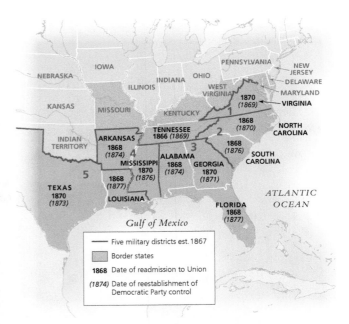

MAP 17.1 Reconstruction of the South, 1866–77 Dates for the readmission of former Confederate states to the Union and the return of Democrats to power varied according to the specific political situations in those states.

this way, congressional leaders could protect Republicans, such as Secretary of War Edwin M. Stanton, entrusted with implementing Congressional Reconstruction. In August 1867, with Congress adjourned, Johnson suspended Stanton and appointed General Ulysses S. Grant interim secretary of war. This move enabled the president to remove generals in the field that he judged to be too radical and replace them with men who were sympathetic to his own views. It also served as a challenge to the Tenure of Office Act. In January 1868, when the Senate overruled Stanton's suspension, Grant broke openly with Johnson and vacated the office. Stanton resumed his position and barricaded himself in his office when Johnson attempted to remove him once again.

Outraged by Johnson's relentless obstructionism, and seizing upon his violation of the Tenure of Office Act as a pretext, moderate and Radical Republicans in the House of Representatives again joined forces and voted to impeach the president by a vote of 126 to 47 on February 24, 1868, charging him with eleven counts of high crimes and misdemeanors. To ensure the support of moderate Republicans, the articles of impeachment focused on violations of the Tenure of Office Act. The case against Johnson would have to be made on the basis of willful violation of the law. Left unstated were the Republicans' real reasons for wanting the president removed: Johnson's political views and his opposition to the Reconstruction Acts.

An influential group of moderate Senate Republicans feared the damage a conviction might do to the constitutional separation of powers. They also worried about the political and economic policies that might be pursued by Benjamin Wade, the president pro tem of the Senate and a leader of the Radical Republicans, who, because there was no vice president, would succeed to the presidency if Johnson were removed from office. Behind the scenes during his Senate trial, Johnson agreed to abide by the Reconstruction Acts. In May, the Senate voted 35 for conviction, 19 for acquittal—one vote shy of the two-thirds necessary for removal from office. Johnson's narrow acquittal established the precedent that only criminal actions by a president—not political disagreements—warranted removal from office.

The Election of 1868

By the summer of 1868, seven former Confederate states (Alabama, Arkansas, Florida, Louisiana, North Carolina, South Carolina, and Tennessee) had ratified the revised constitutions, elected Republican governments, and ratified the Fourteenth Amendment. They had thereby earned readmission to the Union. In 1868 Republicans nominated Ulysses S. Grant, the North's foremost military hero, as their nominee for President. Grant enjoyed tremendous popularity after the war, especially when he broke with Johnson. Totally lacking in political experience, Grant admitted, after receiving the nomination, that he had been forced into it in spite of himself.

Significantly, at the very moment that the South was being forced to enfranchise former slaves as a prerequisite for readmission to the Union, the Republicans rejected a campaign plank endorsing black suffrage in the North. State referendums calling for black suffrage failed in eight northern states between 1865 and 1868, succeeding only in Iowa and Minnesota. The Democrats, determined to reverse Congressional Reconstruction, nominated Horatio Seymour, former governor of New York and a longtime foe of emancipation and supporter of states' rights.

Read the Document

History Bookshelf: Ulysses S. Grant, Memoirs (1886) at **www.myhistorylab.com**

The Fifteenth Amendment, ratified in 1870, stipulated that the right to vote could not be denied "on account of race, color, or previous condition of servitude." This illustration expressed the optimism and hopes of African Americans generated by this consitutional landmark aimed at protecting black political rights. Note the various political figures (Abraham Lincoln, John Brown, Frederick Douglass) and movements (abolitionism, black education) invoked here, providing a sense of how the amendment ended a long historical struggle.

The Ku Klux Klan emerged as a potent instrument of terror (see the opening of this chapter). In Louisiana, Arkansas, Georgia, and South Carolina, the Klan threatened, whipped, and murdered black and white Republicans to prevent them from voting. This terrorism enabled the Democrats to carry Georgia and Louisiana, but it ultimately cost the Democrats votes in the North. In the final tally, Grant carried twenty-six of the thirty-four states for an Electoral College victory of 214 to 80. Significantly, more than 500,000 African American voters cast their ballots for Grant, demonstrating their overwhelming support for the Republican Party. The Republicans also retained large majorities in both houses of Congress.

In February 1869, Congress passed the Fifteenth Amendment, providing that "the right of citizens of the United States to vote shall not be denied or abridged on account of race, color, or previous condition of servitude." To enhance the chances of ratification, Congress required the four remaining unreconstructed states—Mississippi, Georgia, Texas, and Virginia—to ratify both the Fourteenth and Fifteenth Amendments before readmission. They did so

and rejoined the Union in early 1870. The Fifteenth Amendment was ratified in February 1870. In the narrow sense of simply readmitting the former Confederate states to the Union, Reconstruction was complete.

Woman Suffrage and Reconstruction

Many women's rights advocates had long been active in the abolitionist movement. The Fourteenth and Fifteenth Amendments, which granted citizenship and the vote to freedmen, both inspired and frustrated these activists. Insisting that the causes of the African American vote and the women's vote were linked, Elizabeth Cady Stanton, Susan B. Anthony, and Lucy Stone founded the American Equal Rights Association in 1866. The group launched a series of lobbying and petition campaigns to remove racial and sexual restrictions on voting from state constitutions. Throughout the nation, the old abolitionist organizations and the Republican Party emphasized passage of the Fourteenth and Fifteenth Amendments and withdrew funds and support from the cause of woman suffrage. Disagreements over these amendments divided suffragists for decades.

This contemporary colored engraving depicts a meeting of the National Woman Suffrage Association in Chicago, c.1870. The suffrage campaign attracted many middle class women into political activism for the first time.

OVERVIEW | Reconstruction Amendments to the Constitution, 1865–1870

Amendment and Date Passed by Congress	Main Provisions	Ratification Process (3/4 of all States Including Ex-Confederate States Required)
13 (January 1865)	• Prohibited slavery in the United States	December 1865 (27 states, including 8 southern states)
14 (June 1866)	• Conferred national citizenship on all persons born or naturalized in the United States • Reduced state representation in Congress proportionally for any state disfranchising male citizens • Denied former Confederates the right to hold state or national office • Repudiated Confederate debt	July 1868 (after Congress made ratification a prerequisite for readmission of ex-Confederate states to the Union)
15 (February 1869)	• Prohibited denial of suffrage because of race, color, or previous condition of servitude	March 1870 (ratification required for readmission of Virginia, Texas, Mississippi, and Georgia)

The radical wing, led by Stanton and Anthony, opposed the Fifteenth Amendment, arguing that ratification would establish an "aristocracy of sex," enfranchising all men while leaving women without political privileges. They argued for a Sixteenth Amendment that would secure the vote for women. Other women's rights activists, including Lucy Stone and Frederick Douglass, asserted that "this hour belongs to the Negro." They feared a debate over woman suffrage at the national level would jeopardize passage of the two amendments.

By 1869 woman suffragists had split into two competing organizations: the moderate American Woman Suffrage Association (AWSA), which sought the support of men, and the more radical all-female National Woman Suffrage Association (NWSA). For the NWSA, the vote represented only one part of a broad spectrum of goals inherited from the Declaration of Sentiments manifesto adopted at the first women's rights convention held in 1848 at Seneca Falls, New York (see Chapter 13).

Although women did not win the vote in this period, they did establish an independent suffrage movement that eventually drew millions of women into political life. The NWSA in particular demonstrated that self-government and democratic participation in the public sphere were crucial for women's emancipation. The failure of woman suffrage after the Civil War was less a result of factional fighting than of the larger defeat of Radical Reconstruction and the ideal of expanded citizenship.

The Meaning of Freedom

For nearly 4 million slaves, freedom arrived in various ways in different parts of the South. In many areas, slavery had collapsed long before Lee's surrender at Appomattox. In regions far removed from the presence of federal troops, African Americans did not learn of slavery's end until the spring of 1865. There were thousands of sharply contrasting stories, many of which revealed the need for freed slaves to confront their owners. One Virginia slave, hired out to another family during the war, had been working in the fields when a friend told her she was now free. "Is dat so?" she exclaimed. Dropping her hoe, she ran the seven miles to her old place, confronted her former mistress, and shouted, "I'se free! Yes, I'se free! Ain't got to work fo' you no mo'." But regardless of specific regional circumstances, the meaning of "freedom" would be contested for years to come. The deep desire for independence from white control formed the underlying aspiration of newly freed slaves. For their part, most southern white people sought to restrict the boundaries of that independence. As individuals and as members of communities transformed by emancipation, former slaves struggled to establish economic, political, and cultural autonomy. They built on the twin pillars of slave culture—the family and the church—to consolidate and expand African American institutions and thereby laid the foundation for the modern African American community.

Moving About

The first impulse of many emancipated slaves was to test their freedom. The simplest, most obvious way to do this

•••[Read the Document
Jourdon Anderson to His Former Master (1865) at
www.myhistorylab.com

involved leaving home. Throughout the summer and fall of 1865, observers in the South noted enormous numbers of freed people on the move. One former slave squatting in an abandoned tent outside Selma, Alabama, explained his feeling to a northern journalist: "I's want to be free man, cum when I please, and nobody say nuffin to me, nor order me roun'." When urged to stay on with the South Carolina family she had served for years as a cook, a slave woman replied firmly: "No, Miss, I must go. If I stay here I'll never know I am free."

Yet many who left their old neighborhoods returned soon afterward to seek work in the general vicinity or even on the plantation they had left. Many wanted to separate themselves from former owners, but not from familial ties and friendships. Others moved away altogether, seeking jobs in nearby towns and cities. Many former slaves left predominantly white counties, where they felt more vulnerable and isolated, for new lives in the relative comfort of predominantly black communities. In most southern states, there was a significant population shift toward black belt plantation counties and towns after the war. Many African Americans, attracted by schools, churches, and fraternal societies as well as the army, preferred the city. Between 1865 and 1870, the African American population of the South's ten largest cities doubled, while the white population increased by only 10 percent.

Disgruntled planters had difficulty accepting African American independence. During slavery, they had expected obedience, submission, and loyalty from African Americans. Now many could not understand why so many former slaves wanted to leave, despite urgent pleas to continue working at the old place. The deference and humility white people expected from African Americans could no longer be taken for granted. Indeed, many freed people went out of their way to reject the old subservience. Moving about freely was one way of doing this, as was refusing to tip one's hat to white people, ignoring former masters or mistresses in the streets, and refusing to step aside on sidewalks. When freed people staged parades, dances, and picnics to celebrate their new freedom, as they did, for example, when commemorating the Emancipation Proclamation, white people invariably condemned them angrily for "insolence," "outrageous spectacles," or "putting on airs."

African American Families, Churches, and Schools

Emancipation allowed freed people to strengthen family ties. For many former slaves, freedom meant the opportunity to find long-lost family members. To track down these relatives, freed people trekked to faraway places, put ads in newspapers, sought the help of Freedmen's Bureau agents, and questioned anyone who might have information about loved ones. Many thousands of family reunions, each with its own story, took place after the war. One North Carolina slave, who had seen his parents separated by sale, recalled many years later what for him had been the most significant aspect of freedom. "I has got thirteen great-gran' chilluns an' I know whar dey ever'one am. In slavery times dey'd have been on de block long time ago." Thousands of African American couples who had lived together under slavery streamed to military and civilian authorities and demanded to be legally married. By 1870, the two-parent household was the norm for a large majority of African Americans.

For many freed people, the attempt to find lost relatives dragged on for years. Searches often proved frustrating, exhausting, and ultimately disappointing. Some "reunions" ended painfully with the discovery that spouses had found new partners and started new families.

Emancipation brought changes to gender roles within the African American family as well. By serving in the Union army, African American men played a more direct role than women in the fight for freedom. In the political sphere, black men could now serve on juries, vote, and hold office; black women, like their white counterparts, could not. Freedmen's Bureau agents designated the husband as household head and established lower wage scales for women laborers. African American editors, preachers, and politicians regularly quoted the biblical injunction that wives submit to their husbands.

African American men asserted their male authority, denied under slavery, by insisting their wives work at home instead of in the fields. African American women generally wanted to devote more time than they had under slavery to caring for their children and to performing such domestic chores as cooking, sewing, gardening, and laundering. Yet African American women continued to work outside the home, engaging in seasonal field labor for wages or working a family's rented plot. Most rural black families barely eked out a living and, thus, the labor of every family member was essential to survival. The key difference from slave times was that African American families themselves, not white masters and overseers, decided when and where women and children worked.

The creation of separate African American churches proved the most lasting and important element of the energetic institution building that went on in postemancipation

An overflow congregation crowds into Richmond's First African Baptist Church in 1874. Despite their poverty, freed people struggled to save money, buy land, and erect new buildings as they organized hundreds of new black churches during Reconstruction. As the most important African American institution outside the family, the black church, in addition to tending to spiritual needs, played a key role in the educational and political life of the community.

years. Before the Civil War, southern Protestant churches had relegated slaves and free African Americans to second-class membership. Black worshipers were required to sit in the back during services, they were denied any role in church governance, and they were excluded from Sunday schools. Even in larger cities, where all-black congregations sometimes built their own churches, the law required white pastors.

In communities around the South, African Americans now pooled their resources to buy land and build their own churches. Before these structures were completed, they might hold services in a railroad boxcar, where Atlanta's First Baptist Church began, or in an outdoor arbor, the original site of the First Baptist Church of Memphis. Churches became the center not only for religious life but also for many other activities that defined the African American community: schools, picnics, festivals, and political meetings. The church became the first social institution fully controlled by African Americans. In nearly every community, ministers, respected for their speaking and organizational skills, were among the most

influential leaders. By 1877, the great majority of black Southerners had withdrawn from white-dominated churches. In South Carolina, for example, only a few hundred black Methodists attended biracial churches, down from over 40,000 in 1865. Black Baptist churches, with their decentralized and democratic structure and more emotional services, attracted the greatest number of freed people. By the end of Reconstruction, the vast majority of African American Christians belonged to black Baptist or Methodist churches.

The rapid spread of schools reflected African Americans' thirst for self-improvement. Southern states had prohibited education for slaves. But many free black people managed to attend school, and a few slaves had been able to educate themselves. Still, over 90 percent of the South's adult African American population was illiterate in 1860. Access to education thus became a central part of the meaning of freedom. Freedmen's Bureau agents repeatedly expressed amazement at the number of makeshift classrooms organized by African Americans in rural areas. A bureau officer described these "wayside schools": "A negro riding on a loaded wagon, or sitting on a hack waiting for a train, or by the cabin door, is often seen, book in hand delving after the rudiments of knowledge. A group on the platform of a depot, after carefully conning an old spelling book, resolves itself into a class."

African American communities received important educational aid from outside organizations. By 1869, the Freedmen's Bureau was supervising nearly 3,000 schools serving over 150,000 students throughout the South. Over half of the roughly 3,300 teachers in these schools were African Americans, many of whom had been free before the Civil War. Other teachers included dedicated northern white women, volunteers sponsored by the American Missionary Association (AMA). The bureau and the AMA also assisted in the founding of several black colleges, including Tougaloo, Hampton, and Fisk, designed to train black teachers. Black self-help proved crucial to the education effort. Throughout the South in 1865 and 1866, African Americans raised money to build schoolhouses, buy supplies, and pay teachers. Black artisans donated labor for construction, and black families offered room and board to teachers.

Land and Labor After Slavery

Most newly emancipated African Americans aspired to quit the plantations and to make new lives for themselves. Some freed people did find jobs in railroad building, mining, ranching, or construction work. Others raised subsistence crops and tended vegetable gardens as squatters. White planters, however, tried to retain African Americans as permanent agricultural laborers. Restricting the employment of former slaves was an important goal of the black codes. For example, South Carolina legislation in 1865 provided that "no person of color shall pursue or practice the art, trade, or business of an artisan, mechanic, or shopkeeper, or any other trade employment, or business, besides that of husbandry, or that of a servant under contract for service or labor" without a special and costly permit.

The majority of African Americans hoped to become self-sufficient farmers. Many former slaves believed they were entitled to the land they had worked throughout their lives. General Oliver O. Howard, chief commissioner of the Freedmen's Bureau, observed that many "supposed that the Government [would] divide among them the lands of the conquered owners, and furnish them with all that might be necessary to begin life as an independent farmer." This perception was not merely a wishful fantasy. Frequent reference in the Congress and the press to the question of land distribution made the idea of "forty acres and a mule" not just a pipe dream but a matter of serious public debate. But by 1866, the federal government had already pulled back from the various wartime experiments involving the breaking up of large plantations and the leasing of small plots to individual families. President Johnson directed General Howard of the Freedmen's Bureau to evict tens of thousands of freed people settled on confiscated and abandoned land in southeastern Virginia, southern Louisiana, and the Georgia and South Carolina Lowcountry.

In communities throughout the South, freed people and their former masters negotiated new arrangements for organizing agricultural labor. In Hale County, Alabama, for example, local black farmhands contracted to work on Henry Watson's plantation in 1866 deserted him when they angrily discovered that their small share of the crop left them in debt. Local Union League activists encouraged newly freed slaves to remain independent of white farmers, and political agitation for freedmen's rights encouraged them to push for better working conditions as well. Yet few owners would sell or even rent land to blacks. Watson, desperate for field hands, finally agreed to subdivide his plantation and rent it to freedmen, who would work under their own supervision without overseers. Black families left the old slave quarters and began building cabins scattered around the plantation. By 1868, Watson was convinced that black farmers made good tenants; like many other landowners, he grudgingly accepted greater independence for black families in exchange for a more stable labor force. By 1869, as one Hale County correspondent reported, "Many planters have turned their stock, teams, and every facility to farming, over to the negroes, and only require an amount of toll for the use of the land" (see Map 17.2).

By the late 1860s, sharecropping and tenant farming had emerged as the dominant form of working the land. Sharecropping represented a compromise between planters and former slaves. Under sharecropping arrangements that were usually very detailed, individual families contracted with landowners to be responsible for a specific plot. Large plantations were thus broken into family-sized farms. Generally, sharecropper families received one-third of the year's crop if the owner furnished implements, seed, and draft animals or one-half if they provided their own supplies. African Americans preferred sharecropping to gang labor, as it allowed families to set their own hours and tasks and offered freedom from white supervision and control. For planters, the system stabilized the workforce by requiring sharecroppers to remain until the harvest and to employ all family members. It also offered a way around the chronic shortage of cash and credit that plagued the postwar South. Freed people did not aspire to sharecropping. Owning land outright or tenant farming (renting land) were both more desirable. But though black sharecroppers clearly enjoyed more autonomy than in the past, the vast

●●—Read the Document
A Sharecrop Contract (1882) at **www.myhistorylab.com**

MAP 17.2 The Barrow Plantation, Oglethorpe County, Georgia, 1860 and 1881 (approx. 2,000 acres) These two maps, based on drawings from *Scribner's Monthly*, April 1881, show some of the changes brought by emancipation. In 1860, the plantation's entire black population lived in the communal slave quarters, right next to the white master's house. In 1881, black sharecropper and tenant families lived on individual plots, spread out across the land. The former slaves had also built their own school and church.

majority never achieved economic independence or land ownership. They remained a largely subordinate agricultural labor force.

The Origins of African American Politics

Hundreds of African American delegates, selected by local meetings or churches, attended statewide political conventions held throughout the South in 1865 and 1866. Previously free African Americans, as well as black ministers, artisans, and veterans of the Union army, tended to dominate these proceedings, setting a pattern that would

hold throughout Reconstruction. Convention debates sometimes reflected the tensions within African American communities, such as friction between poorer former slaves and better-off free black people, or between lighter- and darker-skinned African Americans. But most of these state gatherings concentrated on passing resolutions on issues that united all African Americans. The central concerns were suffrage and equality before the law.

The passage of the First Reconstruction Act in 1867 encouraged even more political activity among African Americans. The military started registering the South's electorate, ultimately enrolling approximately 735,000 black

Changing Images of Reconstruction

After the Civil War, northern journalists and illustrators went south to describe Reconstruction in action. They took a keen interest in how the newly freed slaves were reshaping local and national politics. A drawing by *Harper's Weekly* illustrator William L. Sheppard titled "Electioneering in the South" clearly approved of the freedmen's exercise of their new citizenship rights. "Does any man seriously doubt," the caption asked, "whether it is better for this vast population to be sinking deeper and deeper in ignorance and servility, or rising into general intelligence and self-respect? They can not be pariahs; they can not be peons; they must be slaves or citizens."

Thomas Nast was the nation's best-known political cartoonist during the 1860s and 1870s. During the Civil War he strongly supported the Union cause and the aspirations of the newly freed slaves. But by 1876, like many Northerners originally sympathetic to guaranteeing blacks full political and civil rights, Nast had turned away from the early ideals of Reconstruction. Nast used grotesque racial caricature to depict southern African Americans and northern Irish immigrants as undeserving of the right to vote. The aftermath of the disputed 1876 presidential election included charges of widespread vote fraud from both Republicans and Democrats. Nast's view—published in *Harper's Weekly* in December 1876, while the election's outcome was still in doubt—reflected concerns among many middle-class Northerners that the nation's political system was tainted by the manipulation of "ignorant" voters in both the South and the North.

• **How does the portrayal of the larger African American community in "Electioneering in the South" reflect the political point being made?**

• **What do the caricatures in "The Ignorant Vote" suggest about Reconstruction era ideas about the meaning of "whiteness"?**

and 635,000 white voters in the ten unreconstructed states. Five states—Alabama, Florida, Louisiana, Mississippi, and South Carolina—had black electoral majorities. Fewer than half the registered white voters participated in the elections for state constitutional conventions in 1867 and 1868. In contrast, four-fifths of the registered black voters cast ballots in these elections. Much of this new African American political activism was channeled through local Union League chapters throughout the South. However, as the fate of Alex Webb in Hale County, Alabama, again makes clear, few whites welcomed this activism.

Begun during the war as a northern, largely white middle-class patriotic club, the Union League now became the political voice of the former slaves. Union League chapters brought together local African Americans, soldiers, and Freedmen's Bureau agents to demand the vote and an end to legal discrimination against African Americans. It brought out African American voters, instructed freedmen in the rights and duties of citizenship, and promoted Republican candidates. Not surprisingly, newly enfranchised freedmen voted Republican and formed the core of the Republican Party in the South. For most ordinary African Americans, politics was inseparable from economic issues, especially the land question. Grassroots political organizations frequently intervened in local disputes with planters over the terms of labor contracts. African American political groups closely followed the congressional debates over Reconstruction policy and agitated for land confiscation and distribution. Perhaps most important, politics was the only arena where black and white Southerners might engage each other on an equal basis.

◄●─ Read the Document

Address from the Colored Citizens of Norfolk, VA (1865) at **www.myhistorylab.com**

"The First Vote," *Harper's Weekly*, November 16, 1867, reflected the optimism felt by much of the northern public as former slaves began to vote for the first time. The caption noted that freedmen went to the ballot box "not with expressions of exultation or of defiance of their old masters and present opponents depicted on their countenances, but looking serious and solemn and determined."

Southern Politics and Society

By the summer of 1868, when the South had returned to the Union, the majority of Republicans believed the task of Reconstruction to be finished. Ultimately, they put their faith in a political solution to the problems facing the vanquished South. That meant nurturing a viable two-party system in the southern states, where no Republican Party had ever existed. If that could be accomplished, Republicans and Democrats would compete for votes, offices, and influence, just as they did in northern states. Most Republican congressmen were moderates, conceiving Reconstruction in limited terms. They rejected radical calls for confiscation and redistribution of land, as well as permanent military rule of the South. The Reconstruction Acts of 1867 and 1868 laid out the requirements for the readmission of southern states, along with the procedures for forming and electing new governments.

Yet over the next decade, the political structure created in the southern states proved too restricted and fragile to sustain itself. To most southern whites, the active participation of African Americans in politics seemed extremely dangerous. Federal troops were needed to protect Republican governments and their supporters from violent opposition. Congressional action to monitor southern elections and protect black voting rights became routine. Despite initial successes, southern Republicanism proved an unstable coalition of often conflicting elements, unable to sustain effective power for very long. By 1877, Democrats had regained political control of all the former Confederate states.

Southern Republicans

Three major groups composed the fledgling Republican coalition in the postwar South. African American voters made up a large majority of southern Republicans throughout the Reconstruction era. Yet African Americans outnumbered whites in only three southern states; Republicans would have to attract white support to win elections and sustain power.

A second group consisted of white Northerners, derisively called "carpetbaggers" by native white Southerners. Most carpetbaggers combined a desire for personal gain with a commitment to reform the "unprogressive" South by developing its material resources and introducing Yankee institutions, such as free labor and free public schools. Most were veterans of the Union army who stayed in the South after the war. Others included Freedmen's Bureau agents and businessmen who had invested capital in cotton plantations and other enterprises.

Carpetbaggers tended to be well educated and from the middle class. Albert Morgan, for example, was an army veteran from Ohio who settled in Mississippi after the war. When he and his brother failed at running a cotton plantation and sawmill, Morgan became active in Republican politics as a way to earn a living. He won election to the state constitutional convention, became a power in the state legislature, and risked his life to keep the Republican organization alive in the Mississippi Delta region. Although they made up a tiny percentage of the population, carpetbaggers played a disproportionately large role in southern politics. They won a large share of Reconstruction offices, particularly in Florida, South Carolina, and Louisiana and in areas with large African American constituencies.

The third major group of southern Republicans was the native whites pejoratively termed "scalawags." They had even more diverse backgrounds and motives than the northern-born Republicans. Some were prominent prewar Whigs who saw the Republican Party as their best chance to regain political influence. Others viewed the party as an agent of modernization and economic expansion. "Yankees and Yankee notions are just what we want in this country," argued Thomas Settle of North Carolina. "We want their capital to build factories and workshops. We want their intelligence, their energy and enterprise." Loyalists during the war and traditional enemies of the planter elite (most were small farmers), these white Southerners looked to the Republican Party for help in settling old scores and relief from debt and wartime devastation.

Southern Republicanism also reflected prewar political divisions. Its influence was greatest in those regions that had long resisted the political and economic power of the plantation elite. Thus, southern Republicans could dominate the mountainous areas of western North Carolina, eastern Tennessee, northern Georgia, and southwestern Virginia as much as Democrats controlled other areas. Yet few white Southerners identified with the political and economic aspirations of African Americans. Moderate elements more concerned with maintaining white control of the party, and encouraging economic investment in the region, outnumbered and defeated "confiscation radicals" who focused on obtaining land for African Americans.

Reconstructing the States: A Mixed Record

With the old Confederate leaders barred from political participation, and with carpetbaggers and newly enfranchised African Americans representing many of the plantation districts, Republicans managed to dominate the ten southern constitutional conventions from 1867 to 1869. Most of these conventions produced constitutions that expanded democracy and the public role of the state. The new documents guaranteed the political and civil rights of African Americans, and they abolished property qualifications for officeholding and jury service as well as imprisonment for debt. They created the first state-funded systems of education in the South to be administered by state commissioners. The new constitutions also mandated establishment of orphanages, penitentiaries, and homes for the insane. In 1868, only three years after the end of the war, Republicans came to power in most of the southern states. By 1869, new constitutions had been ratified in all the old Confederate states.

Republican governments in the South faced a continual crisis of legitimacy that limited their ability to legislate change. They had to balance reform against the need to gain acceptance, especially by white Southerners. Their achievements were thus mixed. In the realm of race relations there was a clear thrust toward equal rights and against discrimination. Republican legislatures followed up the federal Civil Rights Act of 1866 with various antidiscrimination clauses in new constitutions and laws prescribing harsh penalties for civil rights violations.

Segregation, though, became the norm in public school systems. African American leaders often accepted segregation because they feared that insistence on integrated education would jeopardize funding for the new school systems. Segregation in railroad cars and other public places was more objectionable. By the early 1870s, as black influence and assertiveness grew, laws guaranteeing equal access to transportation and public accommodation were passed in many states. By and large, though, such civil rights laws were difficult to enforce in local communities.

In economic matters, Republican governments failed to fulfill African Americans' hopes of obtaining land. Few former slaves possessed the cash to buy land in the open market, and they looked to the state for help. Republicans tried to weaken the plantation system and promote black ownership by raising taxes on land. Yet even when state governments seized land for nonpayment of taxes, the property was never used to help create black homesteads.

Republican leaders envisioned promoting northern-style capitalist development—factories, large towns, and diversified agriculture—through state aid. Much Republican state lawmaking was devoted to encouraging railroad construction. But in spite of all the new laws, it proved impossible to attract significant amounts of northern and European investment capital. The obsession with railroads withdrew resources from education and other programs. As in the North, it also opened the doors to widespread corruption and bribery of public officials. Railroad failures eroded public confidence in the Republicans' ability to govern.

White Resistance and "Redemption"

The emergence of a Republican Party in the reconstructed South brought two parties, but not a two-party system, to the region. The opponents of Reconstruction,

The Ku Klux Klan emerged as a potent political and social force during Reconstruction, terrorizing freed people and their white allies. An 1868 Klan warning threatens Louisiana governor Henry C. Warmoth with death. Warmoth, an Illinois-born "carpetbagger," was the state's first Republican governor. Two Alabama Klansmen, photographed in 1868, wear white hoods to hide their identities.

the Democrats, refused to acknowledge Republicans' right to participate in southern political life. Republicans were split between those who urged conciliation in an effort to gain white acceptance and those who emphasized consolidating the party under the protection of the military.

From its founding in 1868 through the early 1870s, the Ku Klux Klan waged an ongoing terrorist campaign against Reconstruction governments and local leaders. Just as the institution of slavery had depended on violence and the threat of violence, the Klan acted as a kind of guerrilla military force in the service of the Democratic Party, the planter class, and all those who sought the restoration of white supremacy. It employed a wide array of terror tactics: destroying ballot boxes, issuing death threats, beating and murdering politically active blacks and their white allies. Freedmen and their allies sometimes resisted the Klan. In Hale County, Alabama, Union Leaguers set up a warning system using buglers to signal the activities of Klan raiders. But violence and intimidation decimated Union League leadership in the countryside by 1869.

In October 1870, after Republicans carried Laurens County in South Carolina, bands of white people drove 150 African Americans from their homes and murdered thirteen white and black Republican activists. In March 1871, three African Americans were arrested in Meridian, Mississippi, for giving "incendiary" speeches. At their court hearing, Klansmen killed two of the defendants and the Republican judge, and thirty more African Americans were murdered in a day of rioting. The single bloodiest episode of Reconstruction era violence took place in Colfax, Louisiana, on Easter Sunday 1873. Nearly 100 African Americans were murdered after they failed to hold a besieged courthouse during a contested election.

Southern Republicans looked to Washington for help. In 1870 and 1871, Congress passed three Enforcement Acts designed to counter racial terrorism. These declared that interference with voting was a federal offense. The acts provided for federal supervision of voting and authorized the president to send the army and to suspend the writ of habeas corpus in districts declared to be in a state of insurrection. The most sweeping measure was the Ku Klux Klan Act of April 1871, which made the violent infringement of civil and political rights a federal crime punishable by the national government. By the election of 1872, the federal government's intervention had helped break the Klan and restore a semblance of law and order.

The Civil Rights Act of 1875 outlawed racial discrimination in theaters, hotels, railroads, and other public places. But the law proved more an assertion of principle than a direct federal intervention in southern affairs. Enforcement required African Americans to take their cases to the federal courts, a costly and time-consuming procedure.

As wartime idealism faded, northern Republicans became less inclined toward direct intervention in southern

affairs. They had enough trouble retaining political control in the North. In 1874, the Democrats gained a majority in the House of Representatives for the first time since 1856. Key northern states also began to fall to the Democrats. Northern Republicans slowly abandoned the freedmen and their white allies in the South. Southern Democrats were also able to exploit a deepening fiscal crisis by blaming Republicans for excessive extension of public credit and the sharp increase in tax rates.

Gradually, conservative Democrats "redeemed" one state after another. Virginia and Tennessee led the way in 1869, North Carolina in 1870, Georgia in 1871, Texas in 1873, and Alabama and Arkansas in 1874. In Mississippi, white conservatives employed violence and intimidation to wrest control in 1875 and "redeemed" the state the following year. Republican infighting in Louisiana in 1873 and 1874 led to a series of contested election results, including bloody clashes between black militia and armed whites, and finally to "redemption" by the Democrats in 1877.

Several Supreme Court rulings involving the Fourteenth and Fifteenth Amendments effectively constrained federal protection of African American civil rights. In the so-called Slaughterhouse cases of 1873, the Court issued its first ruling on the Fourteenth Amendment. The cases involved a Louisiana charter that gave a New Orleans meatpacking company a monopoly over the city's butchering business on the grounds of protecting public health. A rival group of butchers had sued, claiming the law violated the Fourteenth Amendment, which prohibited states from depriving any person of life, liberty, or property without due process of law. The Court held that the Fourteenth Amendment protected only the former slaves, not butchers, and that it protected only national citizenship rights, not the regulatory powers of states. It separated national citizenship from state citizenship and declared that most of the rights that Americans enjoyed on a daily basis—freedom of speech, fair trials, the right to sit on juries, protection from unreasonable searches, and the right to vote—were under the control of state law. The ruling in effect denied the original intent of the Fourteenth Amendment—to protect against state infringement of national citizenship rights as spelled out in the Bill of Rights.

Three other decisions curtailed federal protection of black civil rights. In *United States* v. *Reese* (1876) and *United States* v. *Cruikshank* (1876), the Court restricted congressional power to enforce the Ku Klux Klan Act. Future prosecution would depend on the states rather than on federal authorities. In these rulings, the Court held that the Fourteenth Amendment extended the federal power to protect civil rights only in cases involving discrimination by states; discrimination by individuals or groups was not covered. The Court also ruled that the Fifteenth Amendment did not guarantee a citizen's right to vote; it only barred certain specific grounds for denying suffrage—"race, color, or previous condition of servitude." This interpretation opened the door for southern states to disenfranchise African Americans for allegedly nonracial reasons. States back under Democratic control began to limit African American voting by passing laws restricting voter eligibility through poll taxes and property requirements.

Finally, in the 1883 Civil Rights Cases decision, the Court declared the Civil Rights Act of 1875 unconstitutional, holding that the Fourteenth Amendment gave Congress the power to outlaw discrimination by states but not by private individuals. The majority opinion held that black people must no longer "be the special favorite of the laws." Together, these Supreme Court decisions marked the end of federal attempts to protect African American rights until well into the next century.

King Cotton: Sharecroppers, Tenants, and the Southern Environment

The Republicans' vision of a "New South" remade along the lines of the northern economy failed to materialize. Instead, the South declined into the country's poorest agricultural region. Unlike midwestern and western farm towns burgeoning from trade in wheat, corn, and livestock, Southern communities found themselves almost entirely dependent on the price of one commodity. In the post–Civil War years, "King Cotton" expanded its realm, as greater numbers of small white farmers found themselves forced to switch from subsistence crops to growing cotton for the market (see Map 17.3).

A chronic shortage of capital and banking institutions made local merchants and planters the sole source of credit. They advanced loans and supplies to small owners, tenant farmers, and sharecroppers in exchange for a lien, or claim, on the year's cotton crop. They often charged extremely high interest rates on advances, while marking up the prices of the goods sold in their stores. Taking advantage of the high illiteracy rates among poor Southerners, landlords and merchants easily altered their books to inflate the figures. At the end of the year, sharecroppers and tenants found themselves deep in debt to stores for seed, supplies, and clothing. Despite hard work and even bountiful harvests, few small farmers could escape from heavy debt. The spread of the "crop lien" system as the South's main form of agricultural credit forced more and more farmers into cotton growing.

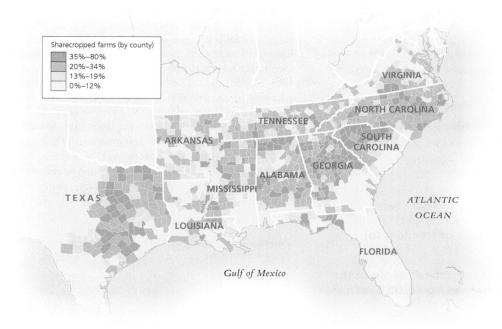

MAP 17.3 Southern Sharecropping and the Cotton Belt, 1880 The economic depression of the 1870s forced increasing numbers of southern farmers, both white and black, into sharecropping arrangements. Sharecropping was most pervasive in the cotton belt regions of South Carolina, Georgia, Alabama, Mississippi, and eastern Texas.

The Ku Klux Klan in Alabama

During Reconstruction the Ku Klux Klan (KKK) claimed as many as 12,000 members in Alabama, or about one in every nine white male voters. The KKK enjoyed deep and widespread support from many whites, including women and children, who viewed the Klan as the protector of white supremacy and a weapon against the Republican Party. Democratic newspapers routinely printed favorable accounts of Klan activities, as well as pro-Klan advertisements, songs, and jokes—and threats directed at intended Klan victims. The following excerpt from a sympathetic newspaper report of Klan activities in the central Alabama town of Florence was published in the *Shelby County Guide* on December 3, 1868.

African Americans and their Republican allies, however, experienced the Klan as a terrorist organization responsible for murder, beatings, arson, and violent intimidation aimed at preventing African American political organizing and economic advancement. This view is vividly presented in a first-person account of Klan terror given by George Houston, an ex-slave and tailor, who had been elected to represent Sumter County in the Alabama state legislature. Houston had helped organize a Union League chapter and actively registered black voters. After local Klansmen wounded his son and broke down the door to his house, Houston grabbed his gun and shot back. In this testimony to a congressional committee investigating the KKK's terrorist campaign, he describes the immediate scene and the campaign to intimidate him.

- **How do the documents reveal profoundly different understandings of the consequences of freedom for African Americans?**

- **What do the sources tell us about the connections between political dominance and economic power in the Reconstruction era South?**

Movements of the Mystic Klan, from the *Shelby County Guide*, December 3, 1868

About a week ago Saturday night the Ku Klux came into town to regulate matters. They were here from eleven p.m. to three o'clock a.m.—five hundred in all. They shot one very bad Negro, putting six balls through his head. Many heard the noise, but did not know what was going on. They also hung three or four Negroes nearly dead, and whipped others severely in order to make them tell them about their nightly meetings, and what their object was in holding the same; also, as to who their leaders were. They made a clean breast of the whole matter, telling everything. The strongest thing about these Ku Klux was that they did not hesitate to unmask themselves when asked to do so; and out of the whole party none were identified.— Every one who saw them says their horses were more beautiful than, and far superior to, any in the country round about. They spoke but little but always to a purpose. They went to several stores and knocked; the doors were opened at once. They then called for rope, and at each place a coil was rolled out to them. They cut it in suitable length to hang a man with. No one asked for money and they offered none. They did not disturb any one else, nor did they take any thing except some few Enfield rifles which were found in possession of some very bad Negroes.—They called on the revenue officer and passed a few remarks with him. What transpired is not known, but it has made a great improvement in his conversation. The visitants advent has been productive of much good and benefit to the community, though all regret such steps should have to be resorted to, every one says "give us peace," and really I believe them to be truly sincere.

> "They shot one very bad Negro. . . . [T]hey also hung three or four . . . nearly dead. . . ."

SOURCE: Reprinted with permission from the Alabama Department of Archives and History, Montgomery, Alabama

George Houston's Testimony, Montgomery, October 17, 1871

Q: How many were there in the crowd that attacked your house?

A. I can't tell. It looked like a great many men. It was starlight and before day. There was a good deal of cursing after they got shot and broke down my door. The reason they were afraid to come in was, I think, because that shot was fired. They didn't come back.

Q: Did you notice whether they were disguised?

A. Only the one that I shot at. He looked like he was wrapped up in some white cloth; it looked so by starlight. That is all I could see.

Q: Had you any trouble with your neighbors?

A. Nothing more than some talk that I didn't like from some wealthy men of the county. One of them had come to me, and told me if I turned against them they would turn against me. They looked upon me as being the prominent Negro of the county. I know the men that told me that thing very well. It was in a dry goods store in that town.

Q: What did they want you to do?

A. They wanted me to deny what was called the Union League. They had understood I belonged to it. The reason they took a great fancy to me was, I was a tailor in that place. My master had learned me this trade on account of my health and crippleness when I was a slave. I had run a shop for sixteen years there. They came to me, and said I made my living off of them and not off of the damned niggers, and if I turned against them they would turn against me. I said my belonging to the Union League didn't do them any harm. They said, 'Yes, it does.' I said, 'It's only to teach our ignorant colored men.' This was our talk privately, and this was only a few months before I was shot. That is all I could assign for the cause of it, and taking the fact that the other colored men were shot down just before, and I was a representative of that county. There was a public meeting; we had made some public speeches, some white and some black men, and I told them I was opposed to this.

Q: Opposed to what?

A. Opposed to colored men being shot down like dogs, when I knew that the officers of the county could stop it. I told the sheriff that to his face. If they took exceptions to me on that account, that is all I can tell, for I was raised there, and they never could put a scratch of a pen against me before, and nothing else could they have taken from it except that I tried

> "[I was] opposed to colored men being shot down like dogs."

to hold up the men that had been shot down by violence; some at night, some by daylight; some were found in the stock pools with their guts cut out. All this came to my ears and the other men's ears.

Q: How many colored men were assassinated in that county?

A. I think eight or nine, before I was shot, were killed dead, according to the accounts of the white men and black men I got through the county. I stop at eight or nine, but I really think there were a few more.

Q: Is the bullet there now in the leg?

A. Yes sir; and it will stay there until God Almighty takes it out. I had a doctor fifteen minutes probing to get that out. The ball went through my child's flesh, too. My child had to go fifteen miles to his grandfather and I had to suffer and go off. I had to sacrifice my property. And yet I am a Republican, and I will die one. I say the Republican Party freed me, and I will die on top of it. I don't care who is pleased. I vote every time. I was register of my county, and my master sent in and lent me his pistols to carry around my waist when I was register, to protect myself against my enemies. I am a Republican today, and if the Republican Party can't do me any good, I will never turn against it. I can work in the cotton patch and work at my trade, and get along without any benefit from my party, and so I will stick to the Republican Party and die in it.

SOURCE: "Affairs in Insurrectionary States: Report and Minority Reviews, Alabama, vol. 2," *Senate Reports*, 42nd Congress, 2nd Session, vol. 2, pt. 9, no. 41.

As the "crop lien" system spread, and as more and more farmers turned to cotton growing as the only way to obtain credit, expanding production depressed prices. Competition from new cotton centers in the world market, such as Egypt and India, accelerated the downward spiral. As cotton prices declined alarmingly, to roughly eleven cents per pound in 1875 to five cents by the early 1890s, per capita wealth in the South fell steadily, equaling only one-third that of the East, Midwest, or West by the 1890s. Small farmers caught up in a vicious cycle of low cotton prices, debt, and dwindling food crops found their old ideal of independence sacrificed to the cruel logic of the cotton market.

To obtain precious credit, most southern farmers, both black and white, found themselves forced to produce cotton for market and, thus, became enmeshed in the debt-ridden crop lien system. In traditional cotton-producing areas, especially the black belt, landless farmers growing cotton had replaced slaves growing cotton. In the Upcountry and newer areas of cultivation, cotton-dominated commercial agriculture, with landless tenants and sharecroppers as the main workforce, had replaced the more diversified subsistence economy of the antebellum era. These patterns hardened throughout the late nineteenth century. By 1900, roughly half of the South's 2,620,000 farms were operated by tenants, who rented land, or sharecroppers, who pledged a portion of the crop to owners in exchange for some combination of work animals, seed, and tools. Over one-third of the white farmers and nearly three-quarters of the African American farmers in the cotton states were tenants or sharecroppers. Large parts of the southern landscape would remain defined by this system well into the twentieth century: small farms operated by families who did not own their land, mired in desperate poverty and debt.

Read the Document

*James T. Rapier,
Testimony Before U.S.
Senate (1880)* at
www.myhistorylab.com

Reconstructing the North

Abraham Lincoln liked to cite his own rise as proof of the superiority of the northern system of "free labor" over slavery. "There is no permanent class of hired laborers amongst us," Lincoln asserted. "Twenty-five years ago, I was a hired laborer. The hired laborer of yesterday, labors on his own account today; and will hire others to labor for him tomorrow. Advancement—improvement in condition—is the order of things in a society of equals." But the triumph of the North brought with it fundamental changes in the economy, labor relations, and politics that brought Lincoln's ideal vision into question. The spread of the factory system, the growth of large and powerful corporations, and the rapid expansion of capitalist enterprise all hastened the development of a large unskilled and routinized workforce. Rather than becoming independent producers, more and more workers found themselves consigned permanently to wage labor.

The old Republican ideal of a society bound by a harmony of interests had become overshadowed by a grimmer reality of class conflict. A violent national railroad strike in 1877 was broken only with the direct intervention of federal troops. That conflict struck many Americans as a turning point. Northern society, like the society of the South, appeared more hierarchical than equal.

The Age of Capital

In the decade following Appomattox, the North's economy continued the industrial boom begun during the Civil War. By 1873, America's industrial production had grown 75 percent over the 1865 level. By that time, too, the number of nonagricultural workers in the North had surpassed the number of farmers. Between 1860 and 1880, the number of wage earners in manufacturing and construction more than doubled, from 2 million to over 4 million. Only Great Britain boasted a larger manufacturing economy than the United States. During the same period, nearly 3 million immigrants arrived in America, almost all of whom settled in the North and West.

The railroad business both symbolized and advanced the new industrial order. Shortly before the Civil War, enthusiasm mounted for a transcontinental line. Private companies took on the huge and expensive job of construction, but the federal government funded the project, providing the largest subsidy in American history. The Pacific Railway Act of 1862 granted the Union Pacific and the Central Pacific rights to a broad swath of land extending from Omaha, Nebraska, to Sacramento, California. An 1864 act bestowed a subsidy of $15,000 per mile of track laid over smooth plains country and varying larger amounts up to $48,000 per mile in the foothills and mountains of the Far West. The Union Pacific employed gangs of Irish American and African American workers to lay track heading west from Omaha.

Meanwhile the Central Pacific, pushing east from California, had a tougher time finding workers, and began recruiting thousands of men from China. In 1868, the Senate ratified the Burlingame Treaty, giving Chinese the right to emigrate to the United States, while specifying that "nothing contained herein shall be held to confer naturalization." The right to work in America, in other words, did not bestow any right to citizenship. Some 12,000 Chinese laborers (about 90 percent of the workforce) bore the brunt of the difficult conditions in the Sierra Nevada where blizzards, landslides, and steep rock faces took an awful toll. Chinese workers earned a reputation for toughness and efficiency. "If we found we were in a hurry for a job of work," wrote one of the Central Pacific's superintendents, "it was better to put on Chinese at once." Working in baskets suspended by ropes, Chinese laborers chipped away at solid granite walls and became

Chinese immigrants, like these section gang workers, provided labor and skills critical to the successful completion of the first transcontinental railroad. This photo was taken in Promontory Point, Utah Territory, in 1869.

expert in the use of nitroglycerin for blasting through the mountains. But after completion of the transcontinental line threw thousands of Chinese railroad workers onto the California labor market, the open-door immigration pledge in the Burlingame Treaty would soon be eclipsed by a virulent tide of anti-Chinese agitation among western politicians and labor unions. In 1882, Congress passed the Chinese Exclusion Act, suspending any further Chinese immigration for ten years.

On May 10, 1869, Leland Stanford, the former governor of California and president of the Central Pacific Railroad, traveled to Promontory Point in Utah Territory to hammer a ceremonial golden spike, marking the finish of the first transcontinental line. Other railroads went up with less fanfare. The Southern Pacific, chartered by the state of California, stretched from San Francisco to Los Angeles, and on through Arizona and New Mexico to connections with New Orleans. The Atchison, Topeka, and Santa Fe reached the Pacific in 1887 by way of a southerly route across the Rocky Mountains. The Great

Northern, one of the few lines financed by private capital, extended west from St. Paul, Minnesota, to Washington's Puget Sound.

Railroad corporations became America's first big businesses. Railroads required huge outlays of investment capital, and their growth increased the economic power of banks and investment houses centered in Wall Street. Bankers often gained seats on the boards of directors of railroad companies, and their access to capital sometimes gave them the real control of the corporations. By the early 1870s the Pennsylvania Railroad was the nation's largest single company with more than 20,000 employees. A small group of railroad executives, including Cornelius Vanderbilt, Jay Gould, Collis P. Huntington, and James J. Hill, amassed unheard-of fortunes. When he died in 1877, Vanderbilt left his son $100 million. By comparison, a decent annual wage for working a six-day week was around $350.

Some of the nation's most prominent politicians routinely accepted railroad largesse. Republican Senator

William M. Stewart of Nevada, a member of the Committee on Pacific Railroads, received a gift of 50,000 acres of land from the Central Pacific for his services. The worst scandal of the Grant administration grew out of corruption involving railroad promotion. As a way of diverting funds for the building of the Union Pacific Railroad, an inner circle of Union Pacific stockholders created the dummy Crédit Mobilier construction company. In return for political favors, a group of prominent Republicans received stock in the company. When the scandal broke in 1872, it politically ruined Vice President Schuyler Colfax and led to the censure of two congressmen.

Other industries also boomed in this period, especially those engaged in extracting minerals and processing natural resources. Railroad growth stimulated expansion in the production of coal, iron, stone, and lumber, and these also received significant government aid. For example, under the National Mineral Act of 1866, mining companies received millions of acres of free public land. Oil refining enjoyed a huge expansion in the 1860s and 1870s. As with railroads, an early period of fierce competition soon gave way to concentration. By the late 1870s, John D. Rockefeller's Standard Oil Company controlled almost 90 percent of the nation's oil-refining capacity.

Liberal Republicans and the Election of 1872

With the rapid growth of large-scale, capital-intensive enterprises, Republicans increasingly identified with the interests of business rather than the rights of freedmen or the antebellum ideology of "free labor." State Republican parties now organized themselves around the spoils of federal patronage rather than grand causes such as preserving the Union or ending slavery. Republicans had no monopoly on political scandal. In 1871 New York City newspapers reported the shocking story of how Democratic Party boss William M. Tweed and his friends had systematically stolen tens of millions from the city treasury. But to many the scandal represented only the most extreme case of the routine corruption that now plagued American political life.

By the end of President Grant's first term, a large number of disaffected Republicans sought an alternative. The Liberal Republicans, as they called themselves, emphasized the doctrines of classical economics. They called for a return to limited government, arguing that bribery, scandal, and high taxes all flowed from excessive state interference in the economy.

Liberal Republicans were also suspicious of expanding democracy. They believed that politics ought to be the province of "the best men"—educated and well-to-do men like themselves, devoted to the "science of government."

They proposed civil service reform as the best way to break the hold of party machines on patronage.

Although most Liberal Republicans had enthusiastically supported abolition, the Union cause, and equal rights for freedmen, they now opposed continued federal intervention in the South. The national government had done all it could for the former slaves; they must now take care of themselves. In the spring of 1872, a diverse collection of Liberal Republicans nominated Horace Greeley to run for president. A longtime foe of the Democratic Party, Greeley nonetheless won that party's presidential nomination as well. All Americans, Greeley urged, must put the Civil War behind them and "clasp hands across the bloody chasm."

Grant easily defeated Greeley, carrying every state in the North and winning 56 percent of the popular vote. But the 1872 election accelerated the trend toward federal abandonment of African American citizenship rights. The Liberal Republicans quickly faded as an organized political force. But their ideas helped define a growing conservative consciousness among the northern public. Their agenda included retreat from the ideal of racial justice, hostility toward trade unions, suspicion of immigrant and working-class political power, celebration of competitive individualism, and opposition to government intervention in economic affairs.

The Depression of 1873

In the fall of 1873, the postwar boom came to an abrupt halt as a severe financial panic triggered a deep economic depression. The collapse resulted from commercial overexpansion, especially speculative investing in the nation's railroad system. By 1876, half the nation's railroads had defaulted on their bonds. Over the next two years more than 100 banks folded and 18,000 businesses shut their doors. The depression that began in 1873 lasted sixty-five months—the longest economic contraction in the nation's history until then.

The human toll was enormous. As factories began to close across the nation, the unemployment rate soared to about 15 percent. In many cities the jobless rate was much higher; roughly one-quarter of New York City workers were unemployed in 1874. Many thousands of men took to the road in search of work, and the "tramp" emerged as a new and menacing figure on the social landscape. The Pennsylvania Bureau of Labor Statistics noted that never before had "so many of the working classes, skilled and unskilled been moving from place to place seeking employment that was not to be had." Farmers were also hard hit by the depression. Agricultural output continued to grow, but prices and land values fell sharply. As prices for their crops fell, farmers had a more difficult time repaying their fixed loan obligations; many sank deeper into debt.

"The Tramp," *Harper's Weekly*, September 2, 1876. The depression that began in 1873 forced many thousands of unemployed workers to go "on the tramp" in search of jobs. Men wandered from town to town, walking or riding railroad cars, desperate for a chance to work for wages or simply for room and board. The "tramp" became a powerful symbol of the misery caused by industrial depression and, as in this drawing, an image that evoked fear and nervousness among the nation's middle class.

Mass meetings of workers in New York and other cities issued calls to government officials to create jobs through public works. But these appeals were rejected. Indeed, many business leaders and political figures denounced even meager efforts at charity. They saw the depression as a natural, if painful, part of the business cycle, one that would allow only the strongest enterprises (and workers) to survive. The depression of the 1870s prompted workers and farmers to question the old free-labor ideology that celebrated a harmony of interests in northern society. More people voiced anger at and distrust of large corporations that exercised great economic power from outside their communities

The Electoral Crisis of 1876

With the economy mired in depression, Democrats looked forward to capturing the White House in 1876. New scandals plaguing the Grant administration also weakened the Republican Party. In 1875, a conspiracy surfaced between distillers and U.S. revenue agents to cheat the government out of millions in tax revenues. The government secured indictments against more than

200 members of this "Whiskey Ring," including Orville E. Babcock, Grant's private secretary. Though acquitted, thanks to Grant's intervention, Babcock resigned in disgrace. In 1876, Secretary of War William W. Belknap was impeached for receiving bribes for the sale of trading posts in Indian Territory, and he resigned to avoid conviction.

Democrats nominated Governor Samuel J. Tilden of New York, who brought impeccable reform credentials to his candidacy. In 1871 he had helped expose and prosecute the "Tweed Ring" in New York City. As governor he had toppled the "Canal Ring," a graft-ridden scheme involving inflated contracts for repairs on the Erie Canal. In their platform, the Democrats linked the issue of corruption to an attack on Reconstruction policies. They blamed the Republicans for instituting "a corrupt centralism."

Republican nominee Rutherford B. Hayes, governor of Ohio, also sought the high ground. As a lawyer in Cincinnati he had defended runaway slaves. Later he had distinguished himself as a general in the Union army. Hayes promised, if elected, to support an efficient civil service system, to vigorously prosecute officials who betrayed the public trust, and to introduce a system of free universal education.

On an election day marred by widespread vote fraud and violent intimidation, Tilden received 250,000 more popular votes than Hayes. But Republicans refused to concede victory, challenging the vote totals in the electoral college. Tilden garnered 184 uncontested electoral votes, one shy of the majority required to win, while Hayes received 165 (see Map 17.4).

The problem centered on twenty disputed votes from Florida, Louisiana, South Carolina, and Oregon. In each of the three southern states two sets of electoral votes were returned. In Oregon, which Hayes had unquestionably carried, the Democratic governor nevertheless replaced a disputed Republican elector with a Democrat.

The crisis was unprecedented. In January 1877, Congress moved to settle the deadlock, establishing an Electoral Commission composed of five senators, five representatives, and five Supreme Court justices; eight were Republicans and seven were Democrats. The commission voted along strict partisan lines to award all the contested electoral votes to Hayes. Outraged by this decision, Democratic congressmen threatened a filibuster to block Hayes's inauguration. Violence and stalemate were avoided when Democrats and Republicans struck a compromise in February. In return for Hayes's ascendance to the presidency, the Republicans promised to appropriate more money for southern internal improvements, to appoint a Southerner to Hayes's cabinet, and to pursue a policy of noninterference ("home rule") in southern affairs.

Shortly after assuming office, Hayes ordered removal of the remaining federal troops in Louisiana and South Carolina. Without this military presence to sustain them, the Republican governors of those two states quickly lost power to Democrats. "Home rule" meant Republican abandonment of freed people, Radicals, carpetbaggers, and scalawags. It also effectively nullified the Fourteenth and Fifteenth Amendments and the Civil Rights Act of 1866. The Compromise of 1877 completed repudiation of the idea, born during the Civil War and pursued during Congressional Reconstruction, of a powerful federal government protecting the rights of all American citizens.

Conclusion

Reconstruction succeeded in the limited political sense of reuniting a nation torn apart by the Civil War. The Radical Republican vision, emphasizing racial justice, equal civil and political rights guaranteed by the Fourteenth and Fifteenth Amendments, and a new southern economy organized around independent small farmers, never enjoyed the support of the majority of its party or the northern public. By 1877, the political force of these ideals was spent and the national retreat from them nearly complete.

The end of Reconstruction left the way open for the return of white domination in the South. The freed people's political and civil equality proved only temporary. It would take a "Second Reconstruction," the civil rights movement of the next century, to establish full black citizenship rights once and for all. The federal government's failure to pursue land reform left former slaves without the economic independence needed for full emancipation. Yet the newly autonomous black family, along with black-controlled churches, schools, and other social institutions, provided the foundations for the modern African American community. If the federal government was not yet fully committed to protecting equal rights in local communities, the Reconstruction Era at least pointed to how that goal might be achieved. Even as the federal government retreated from the defense of equal rights for black people, it took a more aggressive stance as the protector of business interests. The Hayes administration responded decisively to one of the worst outbreaks of class violence in American history by dispatching federal troops to several northern cities to break the Great Railroad Strike of 1877. In the aftermath of Reconstruction, the struggle between capital and labor had clearly replaced "the southern question" as the number one political issue of the day. "The overwhelming labor question has dwarfed all other questions into nothing," wrote an Ohio Republican. "We have home questions enough to occupy attention now."

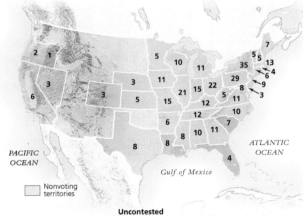

	Uncontested Electoral Vote (%)	Electoral Vote (%)	Popular Vote (%)
RUTHERFORD B. HAYES (Republican)	165 (47)	185 (50)	4,034,311 (48)
Samuel J. Tilden (Democrat)	184 (53)	184 (50)	4,288,546 (51)
Peter Cooper (Greenback)	—	—	75,973 (1)
Disputed			

MAP 17.4 The Election of 1876 The presidential election of 1876 left the nation without a clear-cut winner.

CHRONOLOGY

1865	Freedmen's Bureau established
	Abraham Lincoln assassinated
	Andrew Johnson begins Presidential Reconstruction
	Black codes begin to be enacted in southern states
	Thirteenth Amendment ratified
1866	Civil Rights Act passed
	Congress approves Fourteenth Amendment
	Ku Klux Klan founded
1867	Reconstruction Acts, passed over President Johnson's veto, begin
	Congressional Reconstruction
	Tenure of Office Act
	Southern states call constitutional conventions
1868	President Johnson impeached by the House but acquitted in Senate trial
	Fourteenth Amendment ratified
	Most Southern states readmitted to the Union
	Ulysses S. Grant elected president
1869	Congress approves Fifteenth Amendment
	Union Pacific and Central Pacific tracks meet at Promontory Point in Utah Territory
	Suffragists split into National Woman Suffrage Association and American Woman Suffrage Association
1870	Fifteenth Amendment ratified
1871	Ku Klux Klan Act passed
	"Tweed Ring" in New York City exposed
1872	Liberal Republicans break with Grant and Radicals, nominate Horace Greeley for president
	Crédit Mobilier scandal
	Grant reelected president
1873	Financial panic and beginning of economic depression
	Slaughterhouse Cases
1874	Democrats gain control of House for first time since 1856
1875	Civil Rights Act
1876	Disputed election between Samuel Tilden and Rutherford B. Hayes
1877	Electoral Commission elects Hayes president
	President Hayes dispatches federal troops to break Great Railroad Strike and withdraws last remaining federal troops from the South

Review Questions

I. How did various visions of a "reconstructed" South differ? How did these visions reflect the old political and social divisions that had led to the Civil War?

2. What key changes did emancipation make in the political and economic status of African Americans? Discuss the expansion of citizenship rights in the post–Civil War years. To what extent did women share in the gains made by African Americans?

3. What role did such institutions as the family, the church, the schools, and the political parties play in the African American transition to freedom?

4. How did white Southerners attempt to limit the freedom of former slaves? How did these efforts succeed, and how did they fail?

5. Evaluate the achievements and failures of Reconstruction governments in the southern states.

6. What were the crucial economic changes occurring in the North and South during the Reconstruction era?

Recommended Reading

David W. Blight, *Race and Reunion: The Civil War in American Memory* (2001). An elegantly written and deeply researched inquiry into how Americans "remembered" the Civil War in the half-century after Appomattox, arguing that sectional reconciliation came at the cost of racial division.

Thomas J. Brown, ed., *Reconstructions: New Perspectives on the Postbellum United States* (2006). A wide-ranging collection of essays that explores Reconstruction from a broadly national perspective, including economic, political, and cultural impacts.

Jane Dailey, *Before Jim Crow: The Politics of Race in Postemancipation Virginia* (2000). A fine study that focuses on the tension between the drive to establish white supremacy and the struggle for biracial coalitions in post–Civil War Virginia politics.

Michael W. Fitzgerald, *Splendid Failure: Postwar Reconstruction in the American South* (2007). A beautifully written one-volume overview of Reconstruction, focusing on national politics and the slow but steady capitulation of Republican leaders to white supremacist public opinion in the North and South.

Eric Foner, *Forever Free: The Story of Emancipation and Reconstruction* (2005). An excellent, brief, one-volume overview that condenses Foner's more comprehensive work on Reconstruction. It also includes several striking "visual essays" by Joshua Brown, documenting the changes in visual representations of African Americans in popular media of the era.

Eric Foner, *Reconstruction: America's Unfinished Revolution, 1863–1877* (1988). The most comprehensive and thoroughly researched overview of the Reconstruction era.

Steven Hahn, *A Nation Under Our Feet: Black Political Struggles in the Rural South from Slavery to the Great Migration* (2003). This Pulitzer Prize–winning history includes excellent chapters detailing the political activism of recently freed slaves and the violent resistance they encountered throughout the rural South.

Charles Lane, *The Day Freedom Died: The Colfax Massacre, the Supreme Court, and the Betrayal of Reconstruction* (2008). A riveting narrative account of the era's single worst incident of racist violence, along with its legal and political aftermath.

Elizabeth Regosin, *Freedom's Promise: Ex-Slave Families and Citizenship in the Age of Emancipation* (2002). A thoughtful analysis of how freedmen and freedwomen asserted familial relationships as a means to claiming citizenship rights after emancipation, based on research into federal pension applications made by dependent survivors of Civil War soldiers.

Scott Reynolds Nelson, *Iron Confederacies: Southern Railways, Klan Violence, and Reconstruction* (1999). Pathbreaking analysis of how conservative southern and northern business interests rebuilt the South's railroad system and also achieved enormous political power within individual states.

Mark Wahlgren Summers, *A Dangerous Stir: Fear, Paranoia, and the Making of Reconstruction* (2009). A thoughtful new interpretation by a leading scholar of nineteenth-century politics, emphasizing how deep-seated, often unreasonable fears of conspiracy and revolution dominated much of the era's political discourse.

PEARSON myhistorylab™ Connections

Reinforce what you learned in this chapter by studying the many documents, images, maps, review tools, and videos available at www.myhistorylab.com.

Read and Review

✔● Study and Review Chapter 17

●●● Read the Document

Confederate Song, "I'm a Good Old Rebel" (1866)

Carl Schurz, Report on the Condition of the South (1865)

Mississippi Black Code (1865)

Jourdon Anderson to His Former Master (1865)

A Sharecrop Contract (1882)

Address from the Colored Citizens of Norfolk, VA (1865)

James T. Rapier, Testimony Before U.S. Senate (1880)

👁 See the Map Reconstruction

Research and Explore

●●● Read the Document

Exploring America: Did Reconstruction Work for the Freed People?

Profiles
Tunis Campbell
Nathan Bedford Forrest

History Bookshelf: Ulysses S. Grant, Memoirs (1886)

Whose History Is it?: Flying the Stars and Bars: The Contested Meaning of the Confederate Flag

▶● Watch the Video

Reconstruction in Texas

The Promise and Failure of Reconstruction

Trials of Racial Identity in Nineteenth-Century America

((●● Hear the Audio

Hear the audio files for Chapter 17 at
www.myhistorylab.com.

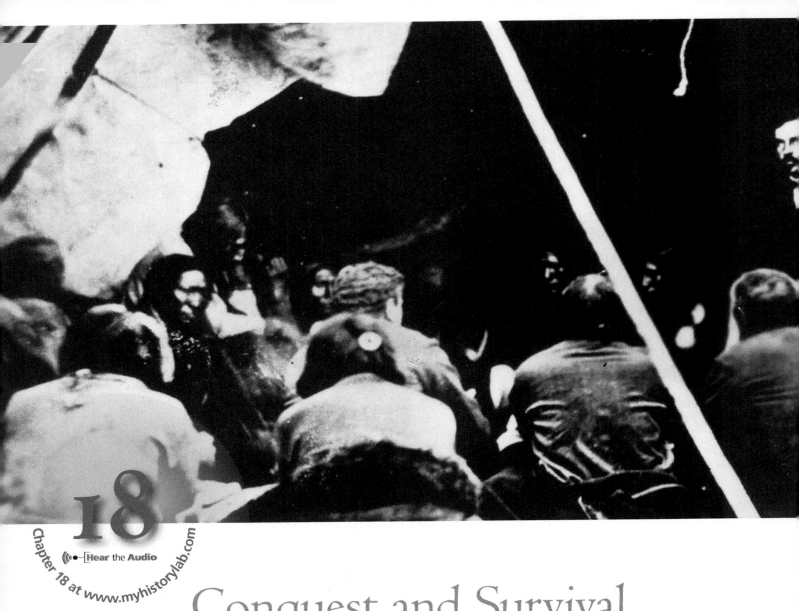

Conquest and Survival
The Trans–Mississippi West 1860–1900

CHAPTER OUTLINE

American Communities 491
The Oklahoma Land Rush

Indian Peoples Under Siege 493
Indian Territory
The Reservation Policy and the Slaughter
   of the Buffalo
The Indian Wars
The Nez Perces

The Internal Empire 497
Mining Towns
Mormon Settlements
Mexican Borderland Communities

The Open Range 502
The Long Drives
The Sporting Life
Frontier Violence and Range Wars

Farming Communities on the Plains 505
The Homestead Act
Populating the Plains
Work, Dawn to Dusk

The World's Breadbasket 507
New Production Technologies
California Agribusiness
The Toll on the Environment

The Western Landscape 510
Nature's Majesty
The Legendary Wild West
The "American Primitive"

The Transformation of Indian
Societies 514
Reform Policy and Politics
The Ghost Dance
Endurance and Rejuvenation

General William T. Sherman and the Peace Commission negotiate the 1868 Fort Laramie Treaty during the Great Sioux War. Getty Images, Inc./Hulton Archive Photos.

The Oklahoma Land Rush

Décades after the event, cowboy Evan G. Barnard vividly recalled the preparations settlers made when Oklahoma territorial officials announced the biggest "land rush" in American history. "Thousands of people gathered along the border. . . . As the day for the race drew near, the settlers practiced running their horses and driving carts." Finally, the morning of April 22, 1889, arrived. "At ten o'clock people lined up . . . ready for the great race of their lives." Like many others, Barnard displayed his guns prominently on his hips, determined to discourage competitors from claiming the 160 acres of prime land that he intended to grab for himself.

Evan Barnard's story was one strand in the larger tale of the destruction and

AMERICAN Communities

creation of communities in the trans–Mississippi West. In the 1830s, the federal government designated what was to become the state of Oklahoma as Indian Territory, reserved for the Five Civilized Tribes (Cherokees, Chickasaws, Choctaws, Creeks, and Seminoles) who had been forcibly removed from their eastern lands. All five tribes had reestablished themselves as sovereign republics in Indian Territory. The Cherokees and Choctaws became prosperous cotton growers. The Creeks managed large herds of hogs and cattle, and the Chickasaws grazed not only cattle but also sheep and goats on their open fields. The Five Tribes also ran sawmills, gristmills, and cotton gins. Indian merchants were soon dealing with other tribespeople as well as licensed white traders and even contracting with the federal government.

The Civil War, however, took a heavy toll on their success. Some tribes, slaveholders themselves, sided with the Confederacy; others with the Union. When the war ended, more than 10,000 people—nearly one-fifth of the population of Indian Territory—had died. To make matters worse, new treaties required the Five Civilized Tribes to cede the entire western half of the territory, including the former northern Indian territory of Nebraska and Kansas, for the resettlement of tribes from other regions.

Western Oklahoma thereby became home to thousands of newly displaced peoples, including the Pawnees, Peorias, Ottawas, Wyandots, and Miamis. Many small tribes readily took to farming and rebuilt their communities. But the nomadic, buffalo-hunting Kiowas, Cheyennes, Comanches, and Arapahoes did not settle so peacefully. They continued to traverse the plains until the U.S. Army finally forced them onto reservations. Eventually, more than 80,000 tribespeople were living on twenty-one separate reservations in western Oklahoma, all governed by agents appointed by the federal government.

The opening of the unassigned far western district of Oklahoma, however, signaled the impending end of Indian sovereignty. Many non-Indians saw this almost 2-million-acre strip as a Promised Land, perfect for dividing into thousands of small farms. African Americans, many of whom were former slaves of Indian planters, appealed to the federal government for the right to stake claims there. Another group of would-be homesteaders, known as "Boomers," quickly tired of petitioning and invaded the district in 1880, only to be booted out by the Tenth Cavalry. Meanwhile, the railroads, seeing the potential for lucrative commerce, put constant pressure on

the federal government to open No Man's Land for settlement. In 1889, the U.S. Congress finally gave in.

Cowboy Barnard was just one of thousands to pour into No Man's Land on April 22, 1889. Many homesteaders simply crossed the border from Kansas. Southerners, dispossessed by warfare and economic ruin in their own region, were also well represented. Market-minded settlers claimed the land nearest the railroads, and by nightfall of April 22, they had set up tent cities along the tracks. In a little over two months, after 6,000 homestead claims had been filed, the first sod houses appeared, sheltering growing communities of non-Indian farmers, ranchers, and other entrepreneurs. Some Indian leaders petitioned the federal government for the right to resettle on new land distant from white settlers, but nothing came from their efforts.

Dramatic as it was, the land rush of 1889 was only one in a series of events that soon dispossessed Oklahoma's Indians of their remaining lands. First, the federal government broke up the estates held collectively by various tribes in western Oklahoma, assigning to individuals the standard 160-acre allotment and allowing non-Indian homesteaders to claim the rest. Then, in 1898, Congress passed the Curtis Act, which abolished tribal jurisdiction over all Indian Territory. Members of the former Indian nations were directed to dismantle their governments and abandon their estates (see Map 18.1). Before a decade had

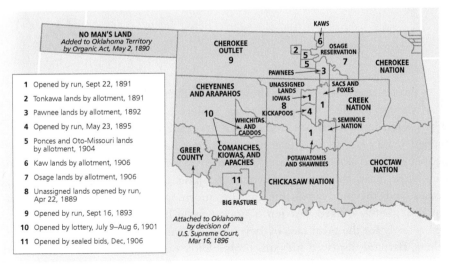

MAP 18.1 Oklahoma Territory Land openings to settlers came at different times, making new land available through various means.

SOURCE: From *Historical Atlas of Oklahoma* by Morris, Goins, McReynolds. Copyright © 1965 University of Oklahoma Press. Reprinted by permission.

1. What was the impact of U.S. western expansion on Indian societies?

2. In what ways was the post–Civil War West an "internal empire," and how did its development depend on the emergence of new technologies and new industries?

3. How did the open range offer different opportunities to men and to women?

4. How did agribusiness differ from forms of family farming?

5. What place did the West hold in the national imagination?

FOCUS Questions

1860–1900

passed, tribespeople in Oklahoma were outnumbered by ten to one. In 1907, at the festivities marking statehood, a huge crowd witnessed a mock wedding ceremony uniting a white man representing Oklahoma Territory and a demure part Cherokee bride representing Indian Territory.

By this time, nearly one-quarter of the entire population of the United States lived west of the Mississippi River. Hundreds of new communities, supported primarily by cattle ranching, agriculture,

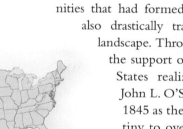
Indian Territory (Oklahoma)

mining, or other industries, had not only grown with the emerging national economy but also helped to shape it in the process. The newcomers had displaced communities that had formed centuries earlier. They also drastically transformed the physical landscape. Through their activities and the support of Easterners, the United States realized an ambition that John L. O'Sullivan had described in 1845 as the nation's "manifest destiny to overspread the continent" and remake it in a new image.

AMERICAN Communities

Indian Peoples Under Siege

The Indians living west of the Mississippi River keenly felt the pressure of the gradual incorporation of the West into the American nation. California became a state in 1850, Oregon in 1859. In the next decades, Congress granted territorial status to Utah, New Mexico, Washington, Dakota, Colorado, Nevada, Arizona, Idaho, Montana, and Wyoming. The purchase of Alaska in 1867 added an area twice the size of Texas. The federal government made itself the custodian of these thinly settled regions, with appointed white governors supervising the transition from territorial status to statehood.

A series of events brought large numbers of white settlers into these new states and territories: the discovery of gold in California in 1848, the opening of western lands to homesteaders in 1862, and the completion of the transcontinental railroad in 1869. With competition for the land and its resources escalating into violent skirmishes and small wars, federal officials became

determined to end tribal rule and bring Indians into the American mainstream.

Indian Territory

Before the European colonists reached the New World, hundreds of tribes, totaling perhaps a million members, had occupied western lands for more than 20,000 years. Invasion by the English, Spanish, and other Europeans brought disease, religious conversion, and new patterns of commerce. But geographic isolation still gave many tribes a margin of survival unknown in the East. At the close of the Civil War, approximately 360,000 Indian peoples still lived in the trans–Mississippi West, the majority of them in the Great Plains.

The surviving tribes adapted to changing conditions. The Plains Indians learned to ride the horses and shoot the guns introduced by Spanish and British traders. The Pawnees migrated farther westward to evade encroaching non-Indian settlers, while the Sioux and the Comanches fought neighboring tribes to gain control of large stretches of the Great Plains. The southwestern Hopis and Zunis, conquered earlier by the Spanish, continued to trade with the Mexicans who lived near them. Some tribes took dramatic steps toward accommodation with white ways. Even before they were uprooted and moved across the Mississippi River, the Cherokees had learned English, converted to Christianity, established a constitutional republic, and become a nation of farmers.

Legally, the federal government had long regarded Indian tribes as autonomous nations residing within American boundaries and had negotiated numerous treaties with them over land rights and commerce. But pressured by land-hungry whites, several states had violated these federal treaties so often that the U.S. Congress passed the Indian Removal Act of 1830 (see Chapter 10), which provided funds to relocate all eastern tribes by force if necessary. The Cherokees challenged this legislation by claiming to be, legally, a foreign nation and therefore not subject to such jurisdiction. The U.S. Supreme Court in *Cherokee Nation* v. *Georgia* (1831) denied the right of the Cherokee people to sue in court and defined their status as that of a "domestic dependent nation." President Andrew Jackson, known as a hardened Indian fighter, forced many tribes to cede their land and remove to Indian Territory. There, it was believed, they might live undisturbed by whites and gradually adjust to "civilized" ways. But soon, the onslaught of white settlers, railroad entrepreneurs, and Gold Rush prospectors pressured tribes to cede millions of their acres to the United States. As demand for resources and land accelerated, the entire plan for a permanent Indian Territory fell apart.

The Reservation Policy and the Slaughter of the Buffalo

As early as the 1840s, highly placed officials had outlined a plan to subdue the intensifying rivalry over natural resources and land. Under the terms of their proposal, individual tribes would agree to live within clearly defined zones—reservations. In exchange, the Bureau of Indian Affairs would provide guidance, while U.S. military forces ensured protection. By the end of the 1850s, eight western reservations had been established where Indian peoples were induced to speak English, take up farming, and convert to Christianity (see Map 18.2).

Several tribes signed treaties, although often under duress. High-handed officials, such as Isaac Stevens, the first governor of Washington Territory, intimidated and deceived the tribal chiefs into signing away their lands. Government officials moved the Indians onto three reservations after their leaders ceded 45,000 square miles of tribal land. The Suquamish leader Seattle admitted defeat, but warned the governor: "Your time of decay may be distant, but it will surely come."

Those tribes that moved to reservations often found provisions inadequate to their needs. The Medicine Lodge Treaty of 1867 assigned reservations in existing Indian Territory to Comanches, Plains (Kiowa) Apaches, Kiowas, Cheyennes, and Arapahoes, bringing these tribes together with Sioux, Shoshones, and Bannocks. All told, more than 100,000 people found themselves competing intensely for survival. Over the next decade, a group of Quakers appointed by President Ulysses S. Grant attempted to mediate differences among the tribes and to supply the starving peoples with food and seed. Corrupt officials of the Bureau of Indian Affairs routinely diverted funds for their own use and reduced food supplies, a policy promoting malnutrition, demoralization, and desperation.

Nomadic tribes that had hunted buffalo, or bison, for centuries saw their freedom sharply curtailed. The Lakotas, or Western Sioux, a loose confederation of bands scattered across the northern Great Plains, were one of the largest and most adaptive of all Indian nations. Seizing buffalo-hunting territory from their rivals, the Pawnees and the Crows, the Sioux had learned to follow the herds on horseback. Buffalo meat and hides fed and clothed the Sioux and satisfied many of their other needs as well. But, as Luther Standing Bear of the Lakota tribe remarked, "The Indian was frugal in the midst of plenty. When the buffalo roamed the plains in multitudes, he slaughtered only what he could eat and these he used to the hair and bones."

The mass slaughter of the buffalo undermined a way of life centuries old. As gunpowder and the railroad moved west, the herds that once darkened the western skies fell rapidly. Non-Indian traders avidly sought fur for coats, hide for leather, bones for fertilizer, and heads for trophies. New rifles by Sharps and Remington could kill at 600 feet; one sharpshooter bragged of single-handedly killing 3,000 buffalo. Army commanders encouraged the slaughter, accurately predicting that starvation would break tribal resistance to the reservation system. With their food sources practically destroyed, and diseases such as smallpox and cholera (brought by fur traders) sweeping through their villages, many Great Plains tribes, including several Sioux, concluded that they could only fight or die.

The Indian Wars

In 1864, large-scale war erupted. Having decided to terminate all treaties with tribes in eastern Colorado, territorial governor John Evans encouraged a group of white civilians, the Colorado Volunteers, to stage raids through Cheyenne campgrounds. Seeking peace and protection, Chief Black Kettle brought a band of 800 Cheyennes to U.S. Fort Lyon and received orders to set up camp at Sand Creek. Feeling secure in this arrangement, Black Kettle sent out most of his young warriors to hunt. Several weeks later, on November 29, 1864, the Colorado Volunteers and soldiers attacked. While Black Kettle held up a U.S. flag and a white truce banner, a disorderly group of 700 men, many of them drunk, slaughtered as many as 200 Cheyennes, the majority elderly men, women, and children. They mutilated the

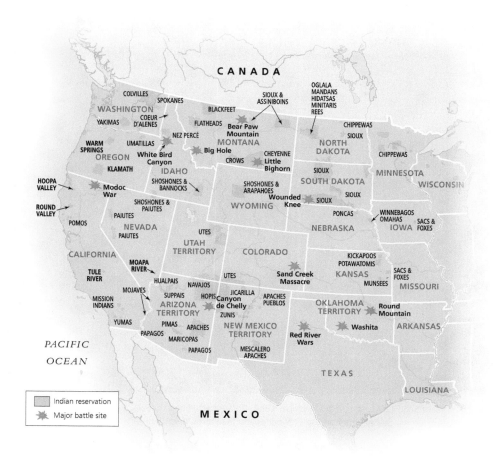

MAP 18.2 Major Indian Battles and Indian Reservations, 1860–1900
As commercial routes and white populations passed through and occupied Indian lands, warfare inevitably erupted. The displacement of Indians to reservations opened access by farmers, ranchers, and investors to natural resources and to markets.

corpses and took scalps back to Denver to exhibit as trophies. Iron Teeth, who survived, remembered seeing a

Read the Document

Congressional Report on Sand Creek Massacre (1867) at **www.myhistorylab.com**

woman "crawling along on the ground, shot, scalped, crazy, but not yet dead." Months after the Sand Creek Massacre, bands of Cheyennes, Sioux, and Arapahoes were still retaliating, burning civilian outposts and sometimes killing whole families.

The Sioux played the most dramatic roles in the Indian Wars. In 1851, believing the U.S. government would recognize their own rights of conquest over other Indian tribes, the Sioux relinquished large tracts of land as a demonstration of good faith. But within a decade, a mass invasion of miners and the construction of military forts along the Bozeman Trail in Wyoming, the Sioux's principal buffalo range, threw the tribe's future into doubt. During the Great Sioux War of 1865–67, the Oglala Sioux

warrior Red Cloud fought the U.S. Army to a stalemate and forced the government to abandon its forts, which the Sioux then burned to the ground. The Treaty of Fort Laramie, signed in 1868, restored only a temporary peace to the region.

The Treaty of Fort Laramie granted the Sioux the right to occupy the Black Hills, or Paha Sapa, their sacred land, "as long as the grass shall grow," but the discovery of gold soon undermined this guarantee. Directed to map a site for a new fort and to quietly look for gold, Lieutenant Colonel George Armstrong Custer led an expedition to the Black Hills during the summer of 1874. Contrary to the plan, the Civil War hero broadcast his discovery of the precious ore. White prospectors soon overran the territory. Determined to fight for the right to this land, thousands of Sioux, Cheyenne, and Arapaho warriors moved into war camps during the summer of 1876 and prepared for battle (see Map 18.2).

This painting depicts the Battle of Sand Creek, fought in November 1864. Colorado militia volunteers, under Colonel John Chivington, led the deadly attack on the Cheyennes and their allies in southeastern Colorado Territory.

After several months of skirmishes between the U.S. Army and Indian warriors, Lieutenant Colonel Custer decided to rush ahead to a site in Montana known to white soldiers as Little Bighorn and to Lakotas as Greasy Grass. This foolhardy move offered the allied Cheyenne and Sioux warriors a perfect opportunity to cut off Custer's logistical and military support. On June 25, 1876, one of the largest Indian contingents ever assembled, an estimated 2,000 to 4,000 warriors, wiped out Custer and his ill-trained troops.

"Custer's Last Stand" gave Indian-haters the emotional ammunition to whip up public sentiment against the Indians. After Custer's defeat, Sitting Bull reportedly said, "Now they will never let us rest." The U.S. Army tracked down the disbanded Indian contingents one by one and forced them to surrender. In February 1877, Sioux leadership in the Indian Wars ended.

Among the last to strike out against the reservation system were the Apaches in the Southwest. Unable to tolerate the harsh conditions on the reservation, and angered by the encroachment of whites, some of the Apache bands returned to their old ways of seizing territory and stealing cattle. Pursued by the U.S. Army, the Apaches earned a reputation as intrepid warriors. Brilliant strategists like Geronimo and skilled horse-riding braves became legendary for lightning-swift raids against the white outposts in the rugged Arizona terrain.

In 1874–75, the Kiowas and the Comanches, both powerful tribes, joined the Apaches in one of the bloodiest conflicts of the era, the Red River War. The U.S. Army ultimately prevailed, although less by military strategy than by new technologies of warfare and by denying Indians access to food. Small-scale warfare sputtered on until September 1886, when Geronimo, his band reduced to only ten people, finally surrendered, thereby ending the Indian Wars.

The Nez Perces

For generations, the Nez Perces (Nimiipuu) had regarded themselves as good friends to white traders and settlers. Living in the plateau where Idaho, Washington, and Oregon now meet, they had saved the Lewis and Clark expedition from starvation in 1806. The Nez Perces had occasionally assisted American armies against hostile tribes, and many of them converted to Christianity.

The discovery of gold on Nez Perce land in 1860 changed their relations with whites for the worse and also challenged their tribal identity. Pressed by prospectors and mining companies, U.S. government officials demanded, in the treaty of 1863, that the Nez Perces cede about nine-tenths of their holdings, at less than ten cents per acre. Some of the Nez Perce leaders agreed to the terms of the treaty, which had been fraudulently signed on behalf of the entire tribe, but others refused. Joseph, who became chief of the Wallowa band in 1871, held out. He kept his faith in the teachings of his ancestors and refused join other Nez Perces in their conversion to Christianity. Only to avoid warfare did he agree to move his band to the small Lapwai Reservation in Idaho.

In 1877, Chief Joseph's band reluctantly set out from the Wallowa Valley with their livestock and all the possessions they could carry. Along the way, some young members of another Indian band traveling with them rode away from camp to avenge the death of one of their own by killing several white settlers. Hoping to explain the situation, a Nez Perce truce team approached U.S. troops. The troops opened fire, and the Indian riders fired back, killing one-third of the soldiers. Brilliantly outmaneuvering vengeful U.S. troops sent to intercept them, the 750 Nez Perce retreated for some 1,400 miles into Montana and Wyoming through mountains and prairies and across the Bitterroot Range. Over the three-and-a-half months of their journey, Nez Perce braves fought 2,000 regular U.S. troops and eighteen Indian auxiliary detachments in eighteen separate engagements and two major battles. U.S. troops finally trapped the Nez Perces in the Bear Paw Mountains of northern Montana, just thirty miles from the Canadian border. Suffering from hunger and cold, they surrendered.

The Nez Perces were sent to disease-ridden bottomland near Fort Leavenworth in Kansas and then to Oklahoma. Arguing for the right of his people to return to their ancestral land, Joseph spoke eloquently, through an interpreter: "Treat all men alike. Give them all the same law. Give them all an even chance to live and grow. All men were made by the same Great Spirit Chief." The last remnants of Joseph's band were eventually deported to a non–Nez Perce reservation in Washington, where Chief Joseph died in 1904 of a broken heart, according to a reservation doctor, and where his descendants continue to live in exile to this day.

Kiowa Preparing for a War Expedition, ca. 1887. This sketch on paper was made by an Indian artist, Silverhorn, who had himself taken part in the final revolt of the Kiowas in 1874. He later became a medicine man and then served as a private in the U.S. Cavalry at Fort Sill, Oklahoma Territory.

SOURCE: Silverhorn (Native American), "Kiowa Preparing for a War Expedition." From "Sketchbook," 1887. Graphite, ink, and crayon on paper. Collection of the McNay Art Museum, Gift of Mrs. Terrell Bartlett.

The Internal Empire

Since the time of Christopher Columbus, the Americas had inspired in Europeans visions of a land of incredible wealth, free for the taking. In the nineteenth century, the North American continent, stretching across sparsely populated territories toward the Pacific Ocean, rekindled this fantasy. Determined to make their fortunes from the abundant natural resources, be it from copper in Arizona, timber in Washington, wheat in Montana, or oranges in California, numerous adventurers traveled west. As a group, they carried out the largest migration and greatest commercial expansion in American history.

But the settlers themselves also became the subjects of a huge "internal empire" whose financial, political, and industrial centers of power remained in the East. Only a small number of settlers actually struck it rich in the great extractive industries—mining, lumbering, ranching, and farming—that ruled the western economy and supported industrial development in the east. Meanwhile, older populations—Indian peoples, Hispanic peoples, and more recently settled communities like the Mormons—struggled to create places for themselves in this new expansionist order.

Mining Towns

The discovery of gold in California in 1848 attracted fortune seekers from across the United States, from Europe, and from as far away as Chile and China; just ten years later, approximately 35,000 Chinese men were working in western mines. Meanwhile, prospecting parties overran the territories, setting a pattern for intermittent rushes for gold, silver, and copper that extended from the Colorado mountains to the Arizona deserts, from California to Oregon and Washington, and from Alaska to the Black Hills of South Dakota. Mining camps and boomtowns soon dotted what had once been thinly

See the Map
Resources and Conflict in the West at **www.myhistorylab.com**

settled regions and speeded the urban development of the West. The population of California alone jumped from 14,000 in 1848 to 223,856 just four years later. Mining soon brought the West into a vast global market for capital, commodities, and labor (see Map 18.3).

Watch the Video
The Real West Is an Urban West at **www.myhistorylab.com**

The mining industry quickly grew from its treasure-hunt origins into a grand corporate enterprise. The most

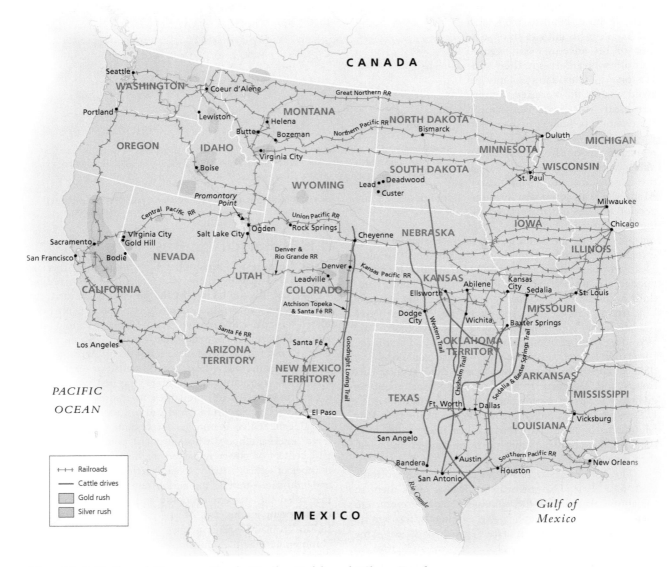

Map 18.3 Railroad Routes, Cattle Trails, Gold and Silver Rushes, 1860–1900 By the end of the nineteenth century, the vast region of the West was crosscut by hundreds of lines of transportation and communication. The trade in precious metals and in cattle helped build a population almost constantly on the move, following the rushes for gold or the herds of cattle.

SOURCE: *Encyclopedia of American Social History.*

successful mine owners bought out the smaller claims and built an entire industry around their stakes. They found investors to finance their expansion and used the borrowed capital to purchase the latest in extractive technology, such as new explosives, compressed-air or diamond-headed rotary drills, and wire cable. They gained access to timber to fortify their underground structures and water to feed the hydraulic pumps that washed down mountains. They built smelters to refine the crude ore into ingots and often financed railroads to transport the product to distant markets. The Anaconda Copper Mining Company, which had mining interests throughout the West, soon became one of the most powerful corporations in the nation.

Read the Document

John Lester, Hydraulic Mining (1873) at www.myhistorylab.com

The mining corporations laid the basis for a new economy as well as an interim government and established many of the region's first white settlements. Before the advent of railroads, ore had to be brought out of, and supplies brought into, mining areas by boats, wagons, and mules traveling hundreds of miles over rough territory. The railroad made transportation of supplies and products easier and faster. The shipping trade meanwhile grew into an important industry of its own, employing thousands of merchants, peddlers, and sailors.

Gold Hill and nearby Virginia City, Nevada, began as a cluster of small mining camps and by the early 1860s became a thriving urban community of nearly 6,000 people. A decade later, the population had quadrupled, but it subsequently fell sharply as the mines gave out. Occasionally, ore veins lasted long enough—as in Butte, Montana, center of the copper-mining district—to create permanent cities.

The many boomtowns, known as "Helldorados," flourished, if only temporarily, as ethnically diverse communities. Men outnumbered women by as much as ten to one, and very few lived with families or stayed very long. The Chinese men, the sojourners who hoped to find riches in the "Gold Mountain" of America before returning home, created their own institutions such as social clubs, temples, and fraternal societies known as tongs. Some miners lived unusually well, feasting on oysters trucked in at great expense. The town center was usually the saloon, where, as one observer complained, men "without the restraint of law, indifferent to public opinion, and unburdened by families, drink whenever they feel like it, whenever they have the money to pay for it, and whenever there is nothing else to do."

The western labor movement began in these camps, partly as a response to dangerous working conditions. In the hardrock mines of the 1870s, one of every thirty workers was disabled, and one of every eighty killed. Balladeers back in Ireland sang of Butte as the town "where the streets were paved with Irish bones." Miners began to organize in the 1860s, demanding good pay for dangerous and life-shortening work.

By the end of the century, miners had established the strongest unions in the West. They helped to secure legislation mandating a maximum eight-hour day for certain jobs and compensation for injuries. Such laws were enacted in Idaho, Arizona, and New Mexico by the 1910s, long before similar laws in most Eastern states.

The unions fought hard, but they did so exclusively for the benefit of white workers. The native-born and the Irish and Cornish immigrants (from Cornwall, England) far outnumbered other groups before the turn of the century, when Italians, Slavs, and Greeks began to replace them. Labor unions

After news of the discovery of gold in the Klondike reached the United States in July 1897, tens of thousands of "stampeders," hoping to strike it rich, rushed to the Yukon Territory. Among them were more than twenty commercial photographers who made good livings selling photographs, such as this image of prospectors weighing gold nuggets. Many prospectors themselves also used roll film cameras and contributed to the production of thousands of photographs of their adventures.

eventually admitted these new immigrants but drove away Chinese, Mexican, Indian, and African American workers.

When prices and ore production fell sharply, not even unions could stop the owners from shutting down the mines and leaving ghost towns in their wake. Often they also left behind an environmental disaster. Hydraulic mining, which used water cannons to blast hillsides and expose gold deposits, drove tons of rock and earth into the rivers and canyons. By the late 1860s, California's rivers were clogged, producing floods that wiped out towns and farms. In 1893, Congress finally passed the Caminetti Act, giving states the power to regulate the mines. Underground mining continued unregulated, using up whole forests for timbers and filling the air with dangerous, sulfurous smoke.

Mormon Settlements

Led by their new prophet, Brigham Young, a group of Mormons, or Latter-day Saints, migrated in 1846–47 from the Midwest to the Great Salt Lake Basin to form an independent theocratic state called Deseret and to affirm the sanctity of plural marriage, or polygamy. By 1870, more than 87,000 Mormons lived in Utah Territory, creating relatively sizable communities complemented by satellite villages joined to communal farmlands and a common pasture. Relying on agricultural techniques learned from local Indian tribes, they built dams for irrigation and harvested a variety of crops from desert soil. Eventually, nearly 500 Mormon communities spread from Oregon to Idaho to northern Mexico (see Map 18.4).

As territorial rule tightened, the Mormons saw their unique and tightly organized way of life threatened. The newspapers and the courts repeatedly assailed the Mormons, often condemning them as heathens and savages. Preceded by prohibitory federal laws enacted in 1862 and 1874, the Supreme Court finally ruled against polygamy in the 1879 case of *United States* v. *Reynolds*, which granted the freedom of belief but not the freedom of practice. In 1882, Congress passed the Edmunds Act, which disfranchised those who believed in or practiced polygamy and threatened them with fines and imprisonment. More devastating was the Edmunds-Tucker Act, passed five years later, which effectively destroyed the temporal power of the Mormon Church by confiscating all assets over $50,000 and establishing a federal commission to oversee all elections in the territory. By the early 1890s, Mormon leaders officially renounced the practice of plural marriage.

◆◆◆[Read the Document

Elizabeth Cady Stanton Speaks to Mormon Women in Utah (1871) at **www.myhistorylab.com**

Although Brigham Young wed as many as fifty-six women and fathered fifty-seven children by sixteen of them, no more than 25 percent of Mormon men practiced polygamy, and even then two wives was the norm. Still, the "celestial" law of plural marriage had been central to the Mormons' messianic mission. Forced to abandon the practice, they gave up many other aspects of their distinctive

MAP 18.4 Mormon Cultural Diffusion, ca. 1883
Mormon settlements permeated many sparsely populated sections of Idaho, Nevada, Arizona, Wyoming, Colorado, and New Mexico. Built with church backing and the strong commitment of community members, they survived and even prospered in adverse climates.

SOURCE: "THE MORMON CULTURE REGION: STRATEGIES AND PATTERNS IN THE GEOGRAPHY OF THE AMERICAN WEST, 1847–1964" by Donald W. Meinig, from *The Annals of the Association of American Geographers* 55, no. 2, June 1965, reprinted by permission of the publisher (Taylor & Francis Group, http://www.informaworld.com).

communal life, including the common ownership of land. By the time Utah became a state in 1896, Mormon communities resembled in some ways the society that the original settlers had sought to escape. Nevertheless, they combined their religious cohesion with leadership in the expanding regional economy to become a major political force in the West.

Mexican Borderland Communities

The Treaty of Guadalupe Hidalgo, which ended the Mexican-American War in 1848, allowed the Hispanic people north of the Rio Grande to choose between immigrating to Mexico or staying in what was now the United States. But the new Mexican-American border, one of the longest unguarded boundaries in the world, did not sever communities that had been connected for centuries. What gradually emerged was an economically and socially interdependent zone, the Anglo-Hispanic borderlands linking the United States and Mexico.

For a time, the borderlands held out hope for a mutually beneficial interaction between Mexicanos and Anglos (as Mexicans called white Americans). A prosperous class of Hispanic landowners, with long-standing ties to Anglos through marriage, had established itself in cities like Albuquerque and Tucson, old Spanish towns that had been founded in the seventeenth and eighteenth centuries. Estevan Ochoa, merchant, philanthropist, and the first Mexican to serve as mayor of Tucson following the Gadsden Purchase in 1853–54, managed to build one of the largest business empires in the West. In Las Cruces, New Mexico, an exceptional family such as the wealthy Amadors could shop Bloomingdale's by mail, travel to the World's Fair in Chicago, and send their children to English-language Catholic schools. Even the small and struggling Mexicano middle class could afford such modern conveniences as kitchen stoves and sewing machines. These Mexican elites, well integrated into the emerging national economy, continued to wield political power as ranchers, landlords, and real estate developers until the end of the century. They secured passage of bills for education in their regions and often served as superintendents of local schools. Several prominent merchants became territorial delegates to Congress.

The majority of Mexicans who had lived in the mountains and deserts of the Southwest for more than two centuries were less prepared for these changes. Most had worked outside the commercial economy, farming and herding sheep for their own subsistence. With the Anglos came land closures as well as commercial expansion, prompted by railroad, mining, and timber industries. Many poor families found themselves crowded onto plots of land too small for subsistence farming. Many men turned to seasonal labor on the new Anglo-owned commercial farms, where they became the first of many generations of poorly paid migratory workers. Others took jobs on the railroad or in the mines. Meanwhile, their wives and daughters moved to the new towns and cities in such numbers that by the end of the century Mexicanos had become a predominantly urban population, dependent on wages for survival.

Women were quickly drawn into the expanding network of market relations. They tried to make ends meet by selling produce from their backyard gardens; more often they worked as seamstresses or laundresses. Formerly at the center of a communal society, Mexicanas found themselves with fewer options in the cash economy. What wages they could earn fell below even the low sums paid to their husbands, and women lost status within both the family and community.

Commercial expansion occasionally strained relations between Mexicanos and Anglos to the breaking point. Although the Treaty of Guadalupe Hidalgo formally guaranteed Mexicanos the rights of citizenship, including the "free enjoyment of their liberty and property,"

Mexican Americans in San Antonio continued to conduct their traditional market bazaar well after the incorporation of this region into the United States. Forced off the land and excluded from the better-paying jobs in the emerging regional economy, many Mexicanos, and especially women, sought to sell the products of their own handiwork for cash or for bartered food and clothing.

SOURCE: Thomas Allen, *Market Plaza*, 1878–1879. Oil on canvas, 26 × 39 ½. Witte Museum, San Antonio, Texas.

local Anglos often violated these provisions and, through fraud or coercion, took control of the land. The Sante Fe Ring, a group of lawyers, politicians, and land speculators, stole millions of acres from the public domain and grabbed over 80 percent of the Mexicano landholdings in New Mexico alone.

Mexicanos organized to reverse these trends or at least to limit the damage done to their communities. In the late 1880s, Las Gorras Blancas, a band of agrarian rebels in northern New Mexico, destroyed railroad ties and farm machinery and posted demands for justice on new fences enclosing Anglo farms and ranches that shut off grazing land. In 1890, Las Gorras turned from social banditry to political organization, forming *El Partido del Pueblo Unido* (The People's Party). Organized along similar lines, *El Alianzo Hispano-Americano* (The Hispanic-American Alliance) was formed "to protect and fight for the rights of Spanish Americans" through political action.

Despite many pressures, Mexicanos preserved much of their cultural heritage, often because they had few choices. In addition, the influx of new immigrants from Mexico helped to reinforce older ways. Beginning in the late 1870s, the modernizing policies of Porfirio Diaz, the president of Mexico from 1876 to 1911, brought deteriorating living conditions to the masses of poor people and prompted a migration northward that accelerated through the first decades of the twentieth century. These newcomers revitalized old customs and rituals associated with family and religion. The Roman Catholic Church retained its influence in the community, and most Mexicans continued to turn to the church to baptize infants, to celebrate the feast days of their patron saints, to marry, and to bury their dead. Special saints like the Virgin of Guadalupe and distinctive holy days like the Day of the Dead survived, along with fiestas celebrating the change of seasons. Many communities continued to commemorate Mexican national holidays, such as *Cinco de Mayo* (the Fifth of May), marking the Mexican victory over French invaders in the battle of Puebla in 1862. Spanish language and Spanish place names continued to distinguish the Southwest.

The Open Range

The borderlands, especially the Mexican territory that became Texas in 1836, gave birth to the enormously profitable cattle industry. Texas longhorns, introduced by the Spanish in the late fifteenth century, numbered more than 5 million at the close of the Civil War and represented a potentially plentiful supply of beef for eastern consumers. Entrepreneurs such as Joseph G. McCoy began to build a spectacular cattle market in the eastern part of Kansas, where the Kansas Pacific Railroad provided crucial transportation links to slaughtering and packinghouses and commercial distributors in Kansas City, St. Louis, and Chicago. By 1880, nearly 2 million cattle were slaughtered in Chicago alone, and cattle reigned as the West's bonanza industry.

The Long Drives

The great cattle drives depended on the cowboy, a seasonal or migrant worker. After the Civil War, cowboys—one for every 300–500 head of cattle on the trail—rounded up herds of Texas cattle and drove them as much as 1,500 miles north to grazing ranches or to the stockyards where they were readied for shipping by rail to eastern markets. The boss supplied the horses, the cowboy his own bedroll, saddle, and spurs. The workday lasted from sunup to sundown, with short night shifts for guarding the cattle. Scurvy, a widespread ailment, could be traced to the basic chuck-wagon menu of sowbelly, beans, and coffee, a diet bereft of fruits and vegetables. The cowboy worked without protection from rain or hail, and severe dust storms could cause temporary blindness.

In return for his labor, the cowboy received at the best of times about $30 per month. Wages were usually paid in one lump sum at the end of a drive, a policy that encouraged cowboys to spend their money quickly and recklessly in the booming cattle towns. In the 1880s, when wages began to fall along with the price of beef, cowboys fought back by stealing cattle or by forming unions. In 1883, many Texas cowboys struck for higher wages; nearly all Wyoming cowboys struck in 1886. Aided by the legendary camaraderie fostered in the otherwise desolate conditions of the long drive, cowboys, along with miners, were among the first western workers to organize against employers.

Like other parts of the West, the cattle range was ethnically diverse. Mexican cowboys, or *vaqueros*, had worked the great herds before Texas became a state in 1845, and they passed on their skills to Americans. During the peak of the cattle drives, between one-fifth and one-third of all workers were Indian, Mexican, or African American. Indian cowboys worked mainly on the northern plains and in Indian Territory; the *vaqueros* continued to work in the borderlands. African American cowboys worked primarily in Texas (see Seeing History). The majority of cowboys were white, and often former soldiers hoping to avoid the indoor work that prevailed in the cities.

Like the *vaqueros*, African American cowboys were highly skilled managers of cattle. Some were sons of former slaves who had been captured from the African territory of Gambia, where cattle raising was an age-old art. Unlike Mexicans, they earned wages comparable to those paid to Anglos and, especially during the early years, worked in integrated drover parties. By the 1880s, as the center of the cattle industry shifted to the more settled regions around the northern ranches, African Americans were forced out, and they turned to other kinds of work.

●●─Read the Document

Perspectives on the American Cowboy (1884, 1886) at **www.myhistorylab.com**

The Legendary Cowboy: Nat Love, Deadwood Dick

SEEING History

Nat Love was born a slave in 1854 and spent his childhood on a plantation in Tennessee. In 1907 he published a short autobiography, *The Life and Adventures of Nat Love, Better Known in the Cattle Country as "Deadwood Dick,"* recounting his "unusually adventurous" life during the decades after emancipation. He worked as a cowboy, a ranch hand, an Indian fighter, and a rodeo performer. His most famous episode occurred in the boomtown of Deadwood, South Dakota, where in 1876 he won a cowboy tournament. It began with a roping contest, in which Love roped, saddled, and mounted a mustang in just nine minutes, winning the almost unbelievably large prize of $200. In the second part of this competition, a shooting contest, Love once again came out on top, hitting the bull's-eye in ten out of twelve shots. He boasted that the miners and gamblers who had gathered for the tournament were so awed that they called him "Deadwood Dick," a name he proudly claimed until his death in 1921.

That name became familiar to the many readers of Edward Wheeler's *Deadwood Dick* dime novels, and at least five of Love's contemporaries claimed to be that character. Wheeler published the first installment in this popular series in 1877 as *Deadwood Dick, the Prince of the Road, or, The Black Rider of the Black Hills.* It is said that Love's autobiography reads like a dime novel, packed with adventures that no historian has yet been able to authenticate.

The photograph illustrating Love's popular autobiography captures the standard image of the cowboy of the legendary Wild West—the chaps, firearm, and ammunition in the cartridge belt circling his waist, the tack on the floor (saddle, harness, rope), and the assertive body language. But in Love's case, the cowboy is a black man.

• How does Nat Love fit into the legendary Wild West? How readily would you expect nineteenth-century readers of the *Deadwood Dick* dime novels to accept the hero's identity as a black man?

• How does Nat Love's identity as an African American line up with the image of the heroic cowboy in modern American popular culture?

Very few women participated in the long drives. Sally Redus, wife of an early Texas cattleman, once accompanied her husband on the trip from Texas to Kansas. Carrying her baby on her lap, she most likely rode the enormous distance sidesaddle, with both legs on one side of the horse. Most women stayed back at the ranch. Occasionally, a husband and wife worked as partners, sharing even the labor of wrangling cattle, and following her husband's death, a woman might take over altogether. Elizabeth Collins, for example, turned her husband's large ranch into an extraordinarily prosperous business, earning for herself the title "Cattle Queen of Montana." The majority of wives attended to domestic chores, caring for children and maintaining the household. Their daughters, however, often tagged along after their fathers and learned to love outdoor work. They were soon riding astride, clothespin style, roping calves, branding cattle or cutting their ears to mark them, and castrating bulls. But not until 1901 did a woman dare to enter an official rodeo contest.

The Sporting Life

In cattle towns as well as mining camps, saloons, gambling establishments, and dance halls were regular features. The hurdy-gurdy, a form of hand organ, supplied raucous music for cowboys eager to spend their money and blow off steam after the long drive. Here they found dancing partners, often called hurdy-girls or hurdies. If they wanted to do more than dance, the cowboy and his partner could retreat to one of the small rooms for rent, which were often located at the rear of the building.

During the first cattle drive to Abilene in 1867, only a few women worked as prostitutes; but by the following spring, McCoy's assistant recalled, "they came in swarms, & as the weather was warm 4 or 5 girls could huddle together in a tent very comfortably." Although some women worked in trailside "hoghouses," the best-paid prostitutes congregated in the brothel districts. Most cattle towns boasted at least one bawdy house. Dodge City had two: one with white prostitutes for white patrons; another with black prostitutes for both white and black men. Although prostitution was illegal in most towns, the laws were rarely enforced until the end of the century, when reformers led campaigns to shut down the red-light districts. Until then, prostitution supplied these women with the largest source of employment outside the home.

Like the cowboys who bought their services, most prostitutes were unmarried and in their teens or twenties. Often fed up with underpaid jobs in dressmaking or domestic service, they found few alternatives to prostitution in the cattle towns, where the cost of food and lodging was notoriously high. Still, earnings in prostitution were slim, except during the cattle-shipping season when young men outnumbered women by as much as three to one. Injury or even death from violent clients, addiction to narcotics such as cocaine or morphine, and venereal disease were workaday dangers.

Frontier Violence and Range Wars

The combination of prostitution, gambling, and drinking discouraged the formation of stable communities. Personal violence was notoriously commonplace on the streets and in the barrooms of cattle towns and mining camps populated mainly by young, single men. Many western towns such as Wichita outlawed the carrying of handguns, but enforcement usually lagged. Local specialty shops and mail-order catalogs continued to sell weapons with little regulation. But contrary to popular belief, gunfights were relatively rare. Local marshals, such as Wyatt Earp and James Butler "Wild Bill" Hickok, worked mainly to break up fights among drunken cowboys.

After the Civil War, violent crime, assault, and robbery rose sharply throughout the United States. In the West, the most prevalent crimes were horse theft and cattle rustling, which peaked during the height of the open range period and then fell back by the 1890s. Death by legal hanging or illegal lynching—at "necktie parties" in which the victims were "jerked to Jesus"—was the usual sentence. On occasion, attacks were racially motivated. In the 1880s, white groups attacked Chinese workers in several communities in the Northwest.

As early as 1879, the local newspaper described Leadville, Colorado, as a town that never sleeps: "The dancing houses and liquoring shops are never shut. . . . The streets are full of drunken carousers taking the town." This photograph of a typical saloon was taken shortly before the silver mining town reached its peak, with a population topping 60,000 in 1893. That year, the repeal of the Sherman Silver Act forced thousands of out-of-work miners to search for jobs elsewhere in the West.

The "range wars" of the 1880s and 1890s produced violent conflicts. By this time, both farmers and sheepherders were encroaching on the fields where cattle had once grazed freely. Sheep chew grass down to its roots, making it practically impossible to raise cattle on the same land. Farmers built fences to protect their crops and domestic livestock. Great cattle barons fought back by ordering cowboys to cut the new barbed-wire fences.

The cattle barons helped to bring about their own demise, but they did not go down quietly. Eager for greater profits, and often backed by foreign capital, they overstocked their herds, and eventually the cattle began to deplete the limited supply of grass. Finally, during 1885–87, a combination of summer drought and winter blizzards killed 90 percent of the cattle in the northern Plains. Many ranchers went bankrupt. Along the way, they often took out their grievances against the former cowboys who had gathered small herds for themselves. They charged these small ranchers with cattle rustling, taking them to court or, in some cases, rounding up lynching parties. As one historian has written, violence was "not a mere sideshow" but "an intrinsic part of western society."

Farming Communities on the Plains

The vision of a huge fertile garden extending from the Appalachians to the Pacific Ocean had inspired Americans since the early days of the republic. But the first explorers who traveled through the Great Plains quashed this dream. "The Great Desert" was the name they gave to the region stretching west from Kansas and Nebraska, north to Montana and the Dakotas, and south again to Oklahoma and Texas. Few trees blocked the blazing sun of summer or promised a supply of lumber for homes and fences. The occasional river or stream flowed with "muddy gruel" rather than pure, sweet water. Economically, the entire region appeared as hopelessly barren as it was vast. It took massive improvements in both transportation and farm technology—as well as unrelenting advertising and promotional campaigns—to open the Great Plains to widescale agriculture.

The Homestead Act

The Homestead Act of 1862 offered the first incentive to prospective farmers. This act granted a quarter section (160 acres) of the public domain free to any settler who lived on the land for at least five years and improved it; or who could buy the land for $1.25 per acre after only six months' residence. Unmarried women filed between 5 and 15 percent of the claims.

Homesteaders achieved their greatest success in the central and upper Midwest, where the soil was rich and weather relatively moderate. But those settlers lured to the Great Plains by descriptions of land "carpeted with soft grass—a sylvan paradise" found themselves locked in a fierce struggle with the harsh climate and arid soil.

The dream of a homestead nevertheless died hard. Five years after the passage of the Homestead Act, *New York Tribune* editor Horace Greeley still advised his readers to strike off "into the broad, free West" and "make yourself a farm from Uncle Sam's generous domain, you will crowd nobody, starve nobody, and . . . neither you nor your children need evermore beg for Something to Do." He was wrong. Although the Homestead Act did spark the largest migration in American history, only 10 percent of all farmers got their start under its terms, and nearly half of all homesteaders lost their claims.

Rather than filing a homestead claim with the federal government, most settlers acquired their land outright. State governments and land companies usually held the most valuable land near transportation and markets, and the majority of farmers were willing to pay a hefty price for those benefits. The big-time land speculators did even better, plucking choice locations at bargain prices and selling high. And the railroads, which received land grants from the federal government, did best, selling off the holdings near their routes at top dollar.

Populating the Plains

The rapid settlement of the West could not have taken place without the railroad. Although the Homestead Act offered prospective farmers free land, it was the railroad that promoted settlement, brought people to their new homes, and carried crops and cattle to eastern markets. Railroad agents—reputed to know every cow in the district—therefore wielded tremendous economic and political power. In designing routes and locating depots, they put whole communities "on the map," or left them behind.

Unlike the railroads built before the Civil War, which followed the path of villages and towns, the western lines preceded settlement. Bringing people west became their top priority, and the railroad companies conducted aggressive promotional and marketing campaigns. Agents enticed Easterners and Europeans alike with long-term loans and free transportation by rail to distant points in the West. The Santa Fe Railroad sent agent C. B. Schmidt to Germany, where he managed to entice nearly 60,000 Germans to settle along the rail line. The railroads also sponsored land companies to sell parcels of their own huge allotments from the federal government. The National Land Company, founded in Chicago in 1869, alone organized sixteen colonies of mainly European immigrants in parts of Kansas and Colorado.

More than 2 million Europeans, many recruited by professional promoters, settled the Great Plains between

1870 and 1900. Some districts in Minnesota seemed to be virtual colonies of Sweden; others housed the largest number of Finns in the New World. Nebraska, whose population as early as 1870 was 25 percent foreign-born, concentrated Germans, Swedes, Danes, and Czechs. But Germans outnumbered all other immigrants by far. A smaller portion of European immigrants reached Kansas, still fewer reached the territories to the south where Indian and Hispanic peoples and African Americans remained the major ethnic groups.

Many immigrants found life on the Great Plains difficult but endurable. "Living in Nebraska," the locals joked, "is a lot like being hanged; the initial shock is a bit abrupt, but once you hang there for awhile you sort of get used to it." The German-speaking Russians who settled the Dakotas discovered soil similar to that of their homeland but weather that was even more severe. Having earlier fled religious persecution in Germany for Russia, they brought with them heavy coats and the technique of using sun-dried bricks to build houses in areas where lumber was scarce.

Traveling the huge distance with kin or members of their Old World villages meant immigrants formed tight-knit communities of their fellow travelers on the Great Plains. Many married only within their own group. For example, only 3 percent of Norwegian men married women of a different ethnic background. Like many Mexicanos in the Southwest, several immigrant groups retained their languages well into the twentieth century, usually by sponsoring parochial school systems and publishing their own newspapers. A few groups closed their communities to outsiders. The Poles who migrated to central Nebraska in the 1880s, for example, formed an exclusive settlement; and the German Hutterites, who disavowed private property, lived in seclusion as much as possible in the Bon Homme colony of South Dakota, established in 1874.

Among the native-born settlers of the Great Plains, the largest number had migrated from states bordering the Mississippi River. Settling as individual families rather than as whole communities, they faced an exceptionally solitary life on the Great Plains. To stave off isolation, homesteaders sometimes built their homes on the adjoining corners of their homestead plots. Still, the prospect of improving their lives, which brought most homesteaders to the Great Plains in the first place, caused many families to keep seeking greener pastures. Mobility was so high that between one-third and one-half of all households pulled up stakes within a decade.

Communities eventually flourished in prosperous towns like Grand Island, Nebraska; Coffeyville, Kansas; and Fargo, North Dakota, that served the larger agricultural region. Built alongside the railroad, they grew into commercial centers, home to banking, medical, legal, and retail services. Town life fostered a special intimacy; even in the county graveyard, it was said, a town resident remained among neighbors. Closeness did not necessarily promote social equality or even friendship. A social hierarchy based on education (for the handful of doctors and lawyers) and, more important, investment property (held mainly by railroad agents and bankers) governed relationships between individuals and families. Reinforced by family ties and religious and ethnic differences, this hierarchy often persisted across generations.

Work, Dawn to Dusk

By the 1870s, the Great Plains, once the home of buffalo and Indian hunters, was becoming a vast farming region populated mainly by immigrants from Europe and white Americans from east of the Mississippi. In place of the first one-room shanties, sod houses, and log cabins stood substantial frame farmhouses, along with a variety of other buildings like barns, smokehouses, and stables. The built environment took nothing away from the predominating vista—the expansive fields of grain. "You have no idea, Beulah," wrote a Dakota farmer to his wife, "of what [the wheat farms] are like until you see them. For mile after mile there is not a sign of a tree or stone and just as level as the floor of your house. . . . Wheat never looked better and it is nothing but wheat, wheat, wheat."

Most farm families survived, and prospered if they could, through hard work, often from dawn to dusk. Men's activities in the fields tended to be seasonal, with heavy work during planting and harvest. At other times, their labor centered on construction or repair of buildings and on taking care of livestock. Women's activities were usually far more routine, week in and week out: cooking and canning of seasonal fruit and vegetables, washing, ironing, churning cream for butter, and keeping chickens for their eggs. Women tended to the young children, and they might occasionally take in boarders, usually young men working temporarily in railroad construction. Many women complained about the ceaseless drudgery, especially when they watched their husbands invest in farm equipment rather than in domestic appliances. Others relished the challenge.

Milking the cows, hauling water, and running errands to neighboring farms could be done by the children, once they had reached the age of nine or so. The "one-room school," where all grades learned together, taught the basics of literacy and arithmetic that a future farmer or commercial employee would require.

The harsh climate and unyielding soil nevertheless forced all but the most reclusive families to seek out friends and neighbors. Many hands were needed to clear the land for cultivation or for roadbeds, to raise houses and barns, or to bring in a harvest before a threatening storm. Neighbors might agree to work together haying, harvesting, and threshing grain. A well-to-do farmer

In 1887, Lizzie Chrisman filed the first homestead claim on Lieban Creek in Custer County, Nebraska. Joined by her three sisters, she is shown here standing in front of her sod cabin. "Soddies," as these small houses were called, were constructed of stacked layers of cut prairie turf, which were eventually fortified by a thick network of roots. The roofs, often supported by timber, were usually covered with more sod, straw, and small branches.

might "rent" his threshing machine in exchange for a small cash fee and, for instance, three days' labor. His wife might barter her garden produce for her neighbor's bread and milk or for help during childbirth or illness. Women often combined work and leisure in quilting bees and sewing circles, where they made friends while sharing scraps of material and technical information. Whole communities turned out for special events, such as the seasonal husking bees, which were organized mainly by women.

Much of this informal barter, however, resulted from lack of cash rather than from a lasting desire to cooperate. When annual harvests were bountiful, even the farm woman's custom of bartering goods with neighbors and local merchants—butter and eggs in return for yard goods or seed—diminished sharply, replaced by cash transactions.

For many farmers, the soil simply would not yield a livelihood, and they often owed more money than they took in. Start-up costs, including the purchase of land and equipment, put many farmers deep in debt. Some lost their land altogether. By the turn of the century, more than one-third of all farmers in the United States were tenants on someone else's land.

The Garden of Eden was not to be found on the prairies or on the plains, no matter how hard the average farm family worked. Again and again, foreclosures wiped out the small landowner through dips in commodity prices, bad decisions, natural disasters, or illness. The swift growth of rural population soon ended. Although writers and orators alike continued to celebrate the family farm as the source of virtue and economic well being, the hard reality of big money and political power told a far different story.

The World's Breadbasket

During the second half of the nineteenth century, commercial farmers employed the most advanced methods of agricultural production in the world. They brought huge numbers of acres under cultivation and used new technologies to achieve unprecedented levels of efficiency in the planting and harvesting of crops. As a result, farming became increasingly tied to international trade, and modern capitalism soon ruled western agriculture, as it did the mining and cattle industries.

New Production Technologies

Only after the brush had been cleared and grasslands cut free of roots could the soil be prepared for planting. Farmers on the Great Plains knew quite well, however, that the sod west of the Mississippi did not yield readily to cultivation and often broke the cast-iron plows typically used by eastern farmers. Farther west, some farmers resorted to drills to plant seeds for crops such as wheat and oats. Even in the best locations, where loamy, fertile ground had built up over centuries into eight or more inches of decayed vegetation, the preliminary breaking, or "busting," of the sod required hard labor.

Agricultural productivity depended as much on new technology as on the farmers' hard labor. In 1837, John Deere designed his famous "singing plow," which easily turned prairie grasses under and turned up even highly compacted soils. Around the same time, Cyrus McCormick's reaper began to be used for cutting grain; by the 1850s, his factories were turning out reapers in mass quantities. The harvester, invented in the 1870s, drew the cut stalks upward to a platform where two men could bind them into sheaves; by the 1880s, an

This "thirty-three horse team harvester" was photographed at the turn of the century in Walla Walla, Washington. Binding the grain into sheaves before it could hit the ground, the "harvester" cut, threshed, and stacked wheat in one single motion.

automatic knotter tied them together. By drastically reducing the number of people traditionally required for this work, the harvester increased the pace many times over. The introduction of mechanized corn planters and mowing or raking machines for hay all but completed the technological arsenal (see Table 18.1). The improvements in the last half of the century allowed an average farmer to produce up to ten times more than was possible with the old implements.

Scientific study of soil, grain, and climate conditions was another factor in the record output. Beginning in the mid-nineteenth century, federal and state governments added inducements to the growing body of expertise, scientific information, and hands-on advice. Through the Morrill Act of 1862, "land-grant" colleges acquired space for campuses in return for promising to institute agricultural programs. The Department of Agriculture, which attained cabinet-level status in 1889, and the Weather Bureau (transferred from the War Department in 1891) also made considerable contributions to farmers' knowledge. The federal Hatch Act of 1887, which created a series of state experimental stations, provided for basic agricultural

research, especially in the areas of soil minerals and plant growth. Many states added their own agricultural stations, usually connected with state colleges and universities.

The technologies of production did not necessarily guarantee success. Land, draft animals, and equipment remained very expensive, and start-up costs could keep a family in debt for decades. A year of good returns often preceded a year of financial disaster.

Nature often reigned over technological innovation and seemed in places to take revenge against these early successes. West of the 98th meridian—a north–south line extending through western Oklahoma, central Kansas and Nebraska, and eastern Dakota—perennial dryness due to an annual rainfall of less than twenty inches constantly threatened to turn soil into dust and to break plows on the hardened ground. Summer heat burned out crops and ignited grass fires. Mountains of winter snows turned rivers into spring torrents that flooded fields; heavy fall rains washed crops away. Even good weather invited worms and flying insects to infest the crops. During the 1870s, grasshoppers in clouds a mile long ate everything organic, including tree bark and clothes.

TABLE 18.1

	Machine Labor on the Farm, ca. 1880			
	Time Worked		Labor Cost	
Crop	Hand	Machine	Hand	Machine
Wheat	61 hours	3 hours	$3.55	$0.66
Corn	39 hours	15 hours	3.62	1.51
Oats	66 hours	7 hours	3.73	1.07
Loose Hay	21 hours	4 hours	1.75	0.42
Baled Hay	35 hours	12 hours	3.06	1.29

Civil War veteran John Wesley Powell explored much of this region and concluded that the shortage of water would remain a huge problem unless the federal government intervened to develop plans for the region. His *Report on the Lands of the Arid Region of the United States,* published in 1878, advised agricultural settlements near watersheds and the construction, where necessary, of irrigation systems. Prompted by the railroads, Congress ignored his suggestions, fearing that such planning would inhibit free enterprise.

California Agribusiness

The new technology and scientific expertise favored the large, well-capitalized farmer over the small one. The majority of farmers with fewer resources continued to plant vegetable gardens and usually kept fowl or livestock for the family's consumption, but they understood that their success depended on raising crops for a market that stretched across the world. To keep pace, farmers in the seven leading grain-growing states increased their individual holdings from approximately 64 acres in 1880 to more than 100 acres in 1900.

The trend toward large-scale or bonanza farming reached an apex in California, where farming as a business surpassed farming as a way of life. Bankers, railroad magnates, and other Anglos made rich by the gold rush took possession of the best farming land in the state. They introduced the latest technologies, built dams and canals, and invested huge amounts of capital, setting the pattern for the state's prosperous agribusiness. Farms of nearly 500 acres dominated the California landscape in 1870; by the turn of the century, two-thirds of the state's arable land was in 1,000-acre farms.

This scale of production made California the national leader in wheat production by the mid-1880s.

But the state also produced tons of fruits and vegetables. Large- and medium-sized growers, shrewdly combined in cooperative marketing associations during the 1870s and 1880s, used the new refrigerator cars to ship produce in large quantities to the East and to Europe. By 1890, cherries, apricots, and oranges, packed in mountains of ice, made their way into homes across the United States.

California growers learned quickly that they could satisfy consumer appetites and even create new ones. Orange producers packed their products individually in tissue paper, a technique designed to convince eastern consumers that they were about to eat a luxury fruit. By the turn of the century, advertisers for the California Citrus Growers' Association described oranges as a necessity for good health, inventing the "Sunkist" trademark, which they stamped on each orange. Meanwhile grape growing grew into a big business. Long considered inferior to French wines, California wines found a ready market at lower prices. Other grape growers made their fortunes in raisins. One company trademarked its raisins as "Sun Maid" and packaged them in small boxes for schoolchildren.

By 1900, California had become the model for American agribusiness—not the home of self-sufficient homesteaders, but the showcase of heavily capitalized farm factories that employed a huge tenant and migrant workforce, including many Chinese. After the mines gave out and work on the transcontinental railroad ended, thousands of Chinese helped to bring new lands under cultivation. Chinese tenant farmers specialized in labor-intensive crops, such as vegetables and fruits, and peddled their crops door-to-door or sold them in roadside stands. Others worked in packing and preserving in all the major agricultural regions of the state. However, the Chinese,

This painting by the British-born artist Thomas Hill (1829–1908) depicts workers tending strawberry fields in the great agricultural valley of northern California. Chinese field hands, such as the two men shown here, supplied not only cheap labor but also invaluable knowledge of specialized fruit and vegetable crops.

SOURCE: Thomas Hill, *Irrigating at Strawberry Farm, Santa Clara,* 1888. Courtesy of the Bancroft Library, University of California, Berkeley.

like the majority of field hands, rarely rose to the ranks of agricultural entrepreneurs. By the turn of the century, amid intense legislative battles over land and irrigation rights, it was clear that the rich and powerful dominated California agribusiness.

The Toll on the Environment

Viewing the land as a resource to command, the new inhabitants often looked past the existing flora and fauna toward a landscape remade strictly for commercial purposes. The changes they produced in some areas were nearly as cataclysmic as those that occurred during the Ice Age.

Farmers "improved" the land by introducing exotic plants and animals—that is, biological colonies indigenous to other regions and continents. Farmers also unintentionally introduced new varieties of weeds, insect pests, and rats. Surviving portions of older grasslands and meadows eventually could be found only alongside railroad tracks, in graveyards, or inside national parks.

Numerous species disappeared altogether or suffered drastic reduction. The grizzly bear, for example, an animal exclusive to the West, once could be found in large numbers from the Great Plains to California and throughout much of Alaska; by the early decades of the twentieth century, one nature writer estimated that only 800 survived, mostly in Yellowstone National Park. At the same time, the number of wolves declined from perhaps as many as 2 million to just 200,000. By the mid-1880s, no more than 5,000 buffalo survived in the entire United States, and little remained of the once vast herds except great heaps of bones sold for $7.50 per ton.

The slaughter of the buffalo had a dramatic impact, not only on the fate of the species, but also on the grasslands of the Great Plains. Overall, the biological diversity of the region had been drastically reduced. Having killed off the giant herds, ranchers and farmers quickly shifted to cattle and sheep production. Unlike the roaming buffalo, these livestock did not range widely and soon devoured the native grasses down to their roots. With the ground cover destroyed, the soil eroded and became barren. By the end of the century, huge dust storms swept across the plains.

Large-scale commercial agriculture also took a heavy toll on inland waters. Before white settlement, rainfall had drained naturally into lakes and underground aquifers, and watering spots were abundant throughout the Great Plains. Farmers mechanically rerouted and dammed water to irrigate their crops, causing many bodies of water to disappear and the water table to drop significantly. In the 1870s, successful ranchers in California pressed for ever greater supplies of water and contracted Chinese work gangs to build the largest irrigation canal in the West. In 1887, the state of California formed irrigation districts, securing bond issues for the construction of canals, and other western states followed. But by the 1890s, irrigation had seemed to reach its limit without federal support. The Newlands or National Reclamation Act of 1902 added 1 million acres of irrigated land, and state irrigation districts added more than 10 million acres. Expensive to taxpayers, and ultimately benefiting corporate farmers rather than small landowners, these projects further diverted water and totally transformed the landscape.

Although western state politicians and federal officials debated water rights for decades, they rarely considered the impact of water policies on the environment. Lake Tulare in California's Central Valley, for example, had occupied up to 760 square miles. After farmers began to irrigate their land by tapping the rivers that fed Tulare, the lake shrank dramatically, covering a mere 36 square miles by the early twentieth century. Finally the lake, which had supported rich aquatic and avian life for thousands of years, disappeared entirely. The land left behind, now wholly dependent on irrigation, grew so alkaline in spots that it could no longer be used for agricultural purposes.

The need to maintain the water supply indirectly led to the creation of national forests and the Forest Service. Western farmers supported the General Land Revision Act of 1891, which gave the president the power to establish forest reserves to protect watersheds against the threats posed by lumbering, overgrazing, and forest fires. In the years that followed, President Benjamin Harrison established fifteen forest reserves exceeding 16 million acres, and President Grover Cleveland added more than 21 million acres. Only in 1897 did the secretary of the interior finally gain the authority to regulate the use of these reserves.

The Forest Management Act of 1897 and the National Reclamation Act of 1902 set the federal government on the path of large-scale regulatory activities. The Forest Service was established in 1905, and in 1907, forest reserves were transferred from the Department of the Interior to the Department of Agriculture. The federal government began to play an even larger role in economic development of the West, dealing mainly with corporate farmers and ranchers eager for improvements.

The Western Landscape

Throughout the nineteenth century, many Americans viewed western expansion as the nation's "manifest destiny," and just as many marveled at the region's natural and cultural wonders. The public east of the Mississippi craved stories about the West and visual images of its sweeping vistas. The region and its peoples came to represent what was both unique and magnificent about the American landscape.

Nature's Majesty

Artists, writers, and scientists soon built their reputations on what they saw and imagined. Scores of writers described spectacular, breathtaking natural sites like the

Grand Tetons and High Sierras, vast meadows of waving grasses and beautiful flowers, expansive canyons and rushing white rivers, and exquisite deserts covered with sagebrush or dotted with flowering cacti, stark yet enticing. Geologists, botanists, historians, and anthropologists toured the trans–Mississippi West in pursuit of new data.

Landscape painters, particularly the group that became known as the Rocky Mountain School, also piqued the public's interest in western scenery. In the 1860s, German-born Albert Bierstadt, equipped with a camera, traveled the Oregon Trail. Using his photographs as inspiration, Bierstadt painted mountains so wondrous that they seemed nearly surreal, projecting a divine aura behind the majesty of nature. His "earthscapes"—huge canvases with exacting details of animals and plants—thrilled viewers and sold for tens of thousands of dollars.

Moved by the depictions of the West's natural beauty, the federal government set aside huge tracts of land as nature reserves. In 1864, Congress passed the Yosemite Act, which placed the spectacular cliffs and giant sequoias under the management of the State of California. Meanwhile, explorers returned to the East awestruck by the varied terrain of the Rocky Mountains, the largest mountain chain in North America, and described huge sky-high lakes, boiling mud, and spectacular waterfalls. In 1872, Congress named Yellowstone the first national park. Yosemite and Sequoia in California, Crater Lake in Oregon, Mount Rainier in Washington, and Glacier in Montana all became national parks between 1890 and 1910 (see Map 18.5).

Read the Document
History Bookshelf: Muir, The Yosemite at www.myhistorylab.com

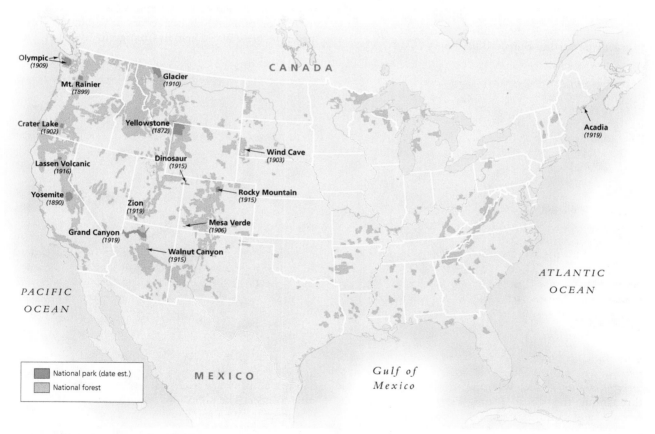

MAP 18.5 The Establishment of National Parks and Forests The setting aside of land for national parks saved large districts of the West from early commercial development and industrial degradation, setting a precedent for the later establishment of additional parks in economically marginal, but scenic, territory. The West, home to the vast majority of park space, became a principal site of tourism by the end of the nineteenth century.

The Legendary Wild West

By the end of the century, many Americans, rich and poor alike, imagined the West as a land of promise and opportunity and, above all, of excitement and adventure. Later President Theodore Roosevelt helped to promote this view. Soon after his election to the New York State Assembly in 1882, Roosevelt was horrified to see himself lampooned in the newspapers as a dandy and a weakling. A year later, after buying a ranch in North Dakota, he began to reconstruct his public image. He wrote three books recounting his adventures in the West, claiming that they had instilled in him not only personal bravery and "hardihood" but also self-reliance. The West, Roosevelt insisted, meant "vigorous manhood."

The first "westerns," the "dime novels" that sold in the 1860s in editions of 50,000 or more, reflected the myths about the West. Competing against stories about pirates, wars, crime, and sea adventures, westerns outsold all other genres. Edward Zane Carroll Judson's *Buffalo Bill, the King of the Border Men,* first published in 1869, spawned hundreds of other novels, thousands of stories, and an entire magazine devoted to Buffalo Bill.

Cowman Joseph McCoy staged Wild West shows in St. Louis and Chicago, where Texas cowboys entertained prospective buyers by roping calves and breaking horses. Many cowboys played up this imaginary role, dressing and talking to match the stories told about them. The first professional photographers often made their living touring the West, setting up studios where cowboys and prostitutes posed in elaborate costumes.

In 1883, the former army scout and famed buffalo hunter William F. Cody hit upon the idea of an extravaganza that would bring the legendary West to those who could never experience it in person. "Buffalo Bill" Cody made sharpshooter Annie Oakley a star performer. Entrancing crowds with her stunning accuracy with pistol or rifle, Oakley shot dimes in midair and cigarettes from her husband's mouth. Cody also hired chief Sitting Bull and other Sioux Indians and hundreds of cowboys to perform in mock stagecoach robberies and battles.

Cody's Wild West Show attracted masses of fairgoers at the World's Columbian Exposition, the spectacular celebration of the 400th anniversary of Columbus's landing in the New World held in Chicago in 1893. Less well

Albert Bierstadt became one of the first artists to capture on enormous canvases the legendary vastness and rugged terrain of western mountains and wilderness. Many other artists joined Bierstadt to form the Rocky Mountain School. In time, the camera largely replaced the paintbrush, and most Americans formed an image of these majestic peaks from postcards and magazine illustrations.

SOURCE: Albert Bierstadt (1830–1902), *Among the Sierra Nevada Mountains, California,* 1868. Oil on canvas, 71 × 120 in. (183 × 305 cm). © Smithsonian American Art Museum, Washington, DC/Art Resource, Ny.

Born Phoebe Ann Moses in 1860, Annie Oakley was a star attraction in Buffalo Bill's Wild West show. Dubbed "Little Sure Shot" by Chief Sitting Bull, Oakley traveled with Cody's show for seventeen years. This poster from 1901 advertises her sharp-shooting talents.

attended but nonetheless significant was the annual meeting of the American Historical Association, the leading professional society of historians, and the presentation of an essay that one historian has deemed "the single most influential piece of writing in the history of American history."

At this meeting, Frederick Jackson Turner, a young historian at the University of Wisconsin, read a paper that, like Cody's Wild West Show, celebrated the West. "The Significance of the Frontier in American History" made a compelling argument that the continuous westward movement of settlement allowed Americans to develop new standards for democracy. Turner reasoned that each generation, in its move westward, mastered the "primitive conditions" and thereby developed a distinctive American character—"that coarseness and strength combined with acuteness and acquisitiveness; that practical inventive turn of mind, quick to find expedients; that masterful grasp of material things . . . that restless, nervous energy; that dominant individualism"—all of which encouraged democracy. "The true point of view in the history of this nation," Turner concluded, "is not the Atlantic coast, it is the Great West."

What became known as the "frontier thesis" also sounded a warning bell. The 1890 federal census revealed that the "free land" had been depleted, prompting Turner to conclude that the "closing" of the frontier marked the end of the formative period of American history. The "frontier thesis" lived on, although most historians no longer consider the frontier as the key to all American history. Many have pointed out that the concept of "the frontier" has meaning only to Euro-Americans and not to the tribal people who had occupied this land for centuries. Nevertheless, many of Turner's contemporaries found in his argument the rationale for seeking new "frontiers" through overseas expansion.

The "American Primitive"

New technologies of graphic reproduction encouraged painters and photographers to circulate new images of Indian peoples. A young German American artist, Charles Schreyvogel, saw Buffalo Bill's tent show and decided to make the West his life's work. His canvases depicted Indian warriors and U.S. cavalry fighting furiously but without blood and gore. Charles Russell, a genuine cowboy, painted the life he knew but also indulged in imaginary scenarios, producing paintings of buffalo hunts and first encounters between Indian peoples and white explorers.

Frederic Remington, the most famous of all the western artists, left Yale Art School to visit Montana in 1881, became a Kansas sheepherder and tavern owner, and then returned to painting. Inspired by newspaper stories of the army's campaign against the Apaches, he made himself into a war correspondent and captured vivid scenes of battle in his sketches. Painstakingly accurate in physical details, especially of horses, his paintings and popular magazine illustrations celebrated the "winning of the West" from the Indian peoples.

Remington joined hundreds of other painters and engravers in reproducing the most popular historic event: Custer's Last Stand. Totally fictionalized by white artists to show a heroic Custer personally holding off advancing Indian warriors, these renditions dramatized the romance and tragedy of conquest. Indian artists recorded Custer's defeat in far less noble fashion.

Photographers often produced highly nuanced portraits of Indian peoples. Dozens of early photographers from the Bureau of American Ethnology captured the gaze of noble tribespeople or showed them hard at work digging clams or grinding corn. President Theodore Roosevelt praised Edward Sheriff Curtis for vividly conveying tribal virtue. Generations later, in the 1960s and 1970s, Curtis's photographs again captured the imagination of western enthusiasts, who were unaware or unconcerned that this sympathetic artist had often posed his subjects or retouched his photos to blur out any artifacts of white society.

OVERVIEW │ Major Indian Treaties and Legislation of the Late Nineteenth Century

1863	**Nez Perce Treaty**	Signed illegally on behalf of the entire tribe, in which the Nez Perces abandoned 6 million acres of land in return for a small reservation in northeastern Oregon. Led to Nez Perce wars, which ended in 1877 with the surrender of Chief Joseph.
1867	**Medicine Lodge Treaty**	Assigned reservations in existing Indian Territory to Comanches, Plains (Kiowa), Apaches, Kiowas, Cheyennes, and Arapahoes, bringing these tribes together with Sioux, Shoshones, Bannocks, and Navajos.
1868	**Treaty of Fort Laramie**	Successfully ended Red Cloud's war by evacuating federal troops from Sioux Territory along the Bozeman Trail; additionally granted Sioux ownership of the western half of South Dakota and rights to use Powder River country in Wyoming and Montana.
1871		Congress declares end to treaty system.
1887	**Dawes Severalty Act**	Divided communal tribal land, granting the right to petition for citizenship to those Indians who accepted the individual land allotment of 160 acres. Successfully undermined sovereignty.

Painters and photographers led the way for scholarly research on the various Indian societies. The early ethnographer and pioneer of fieldwork in anthropology Lewis Henry Morgan devoted his life to the study of Indian family or kinship patterns, mostly of eastern tribes such as the Iroquois, who adopted him into their Hawk Clan. In 1851, he published *League of the Ho-de-no-sau-nee, or Iroquois,* considered the first scientific account of an Indian tribe. A decade later, Morgan ventured into Cheyenne country to examine the naming patterns of that tribe. In his major work, *Ancient Society,* published in 1877, he posited a universal process of social evolution leading from savagery to barbarism to civilization.

One of the most influential interpreters of the cultures of living tribespeople was the pioneering ethnographer Alice Cunningham Fletcher. In 1879, Fletcher met Susette (Bright Eyes) La Flesche of the Omaha tribe, who was on a speaking tour to gain support for her people, primarily to prevent their removal from tribal lands. Fletcher, then forty-two years old, accompanied La Flesche to Nebraska, telling the Omahas that she had come "to learn, if you will let me, something about your tribal organization, social customs, tribal rites, traditions and songs. Also to see if I can help you in any way." After transcribing hundreds of songs, Fletcher became well known as an expert on Omaha music. She also promoted assimilation through the allotment of individual claims to

160-acre homesteads, eked out of tribal lands, and helped to draft the model legislation that was enacted by Congress as the Omaha Act of 1882. In 1885, Fletcher produced for the U.S. Senate a report titled *Indian Education and Civilization,* one of the first general statements on the status of Indian peoples. As a founder of the American Anthropological Society and president of the American Folklore Society, she encouraged further study of Indian societies.

While white settlers and the federal government threatened the survival of tribal life, Indian lore became a major pursuit of scholars and amateurs alike. Adults and children delighted in discovering arrowheads. Fraternal organizations such as the Elks and Eagles borrowed tribal terminology. The Boy Scouts and Girl Scouts, the nation's premier youth organizations, used tribal lore to instill strength of character. The U.S. Treasury stamped images of tribal chiefs and buffalo on the nation's most frequently used coins.

The Transformation of Indian Societies

In 1871, the U.S. government formally ended the treaty system, eclipsing but not completely abolishing the sovereignty of Indian nations. Still, the tribes persisted. Using a mixture of survival strategies from farming and trade to the leasing of reservation lands, they both adapted to changing conditions and maintained old traditions.

Reform Policy and Politics

By 1880, many Indian tribes had been forcibly resettled on reservations, but few had adapted to white ways. For decades, reformers, mainly from the Protestant churches, had lobbied Congress for a program of salvation through assimilation, and they looked to the Board of Indian Commissioners, created in 1869, to carry out this mission. The board often succeeded in mediating conflicts among the various tribes crowded onto reservations but made far less headway in converting them to Christianity or transforming them into prosperous farming communities.

The majority of Indian peoples lived in poverty and misery, deprived of their traditional means of survival and, more often than not, subjected to fraud by corrupt government officials and private suppliers. Reformers who observed these conditions firsthand nevertheless remained unshaken in their belief that tribespeople must be raised out of the darkness of ignorance into the light of civilization. Some conceded, however, that the reservation system might not be the best means to this end.

Unlike most Americans, who saw the conquest of the West as a means to national glory, some reformers were genuinely outraged by the government's continuous violation of treaty obligations and the military enforcement of the reservation policy. One of the most influential was Helen Hunt Jackson, a noted poet and author of children's stories. In 1879, Jackson had attended a lecture in Hartford, Connecticut, by a chief of the Ponca tribe whose destitute people had been forced from their Dakota homeland. Heartstruck, Jackson lobbied former abolitionists such as Wendell Phillips to work for Indians' rights and she herself began to write against government policy. Her book-length exposé, *A Century of Dishonor,* published in 1881, detailed the plight of Indian peoples.

Read the Document

Helen Hunt Jackson, from A Century of Dishonor (1881) at **www.myhistorylab.com**

Jackson threw herself into the Indian Rights Association, an offshoot of the Women's National Indian Association (WNIA), which had been formed in 1874 to rally public support for a program of assimilation. The two organizations helped to place Protestant missionaries in the West to work to eradicate tribal customs as well as to convert Indian peoples to Christianity. According to the reformers' plans, men would now farm as well as hunt, while women would leave the fields to take care of home and children. Likewise, all communal practices would be abandoned in favor of individually owned homesteads, where families could develop in the "American" manner and even celebrate proper holidays such as the Fourth of July. Children, hair trimmed short, would be placed in boarding schools where, removed from their parents' influence, they would shed traditional values and cultural practices. By 1882, the WNIA had gathered 100,000 signatures on petitions urging Congress to phase out the reservation system, to establish universal education for Indian children, and to award title to 160 acres to any Indian individual willing to work the land.

The Dawes Severalty Act, passed by Congress in 1887, incorporated many of these measures and established federal Indian policy for decades to come. The act allowed the president to distribute land, not to tribes, but to individuals legally "severed" from their tribes. The commissioner of Indian affairs rendered the popular interpretation that "tribal relations should be broken up, socialism destroyed and the family and autonomy of the individual substituted. The allotment of land in severalty, the establishment of local courts and police, the development of a personal sense of independence and the universal adoption of the English language are means to this end."

Those individuals who accepted the land allotment of 160 acres and agreed to allow the government to sell unallotted tribal lands (with some funds set aside for education) could petition to become citizens of the United States. A little over a decade after its enactment, many reformers believed that the Dawes Act had resolved the basis of the "Indian problem." Hollow Horn Bear, a Sioux chief, offered a different opinion, judging the Dawes Act to be "only another trick of the whites."

The Dawes Act successfully undermined tribal sovereignty but offered little compensation. Indian religions and sacred ceremonies were banned, the telling of legends and myths forbidden, and shaman and medicine men imprisoned or exiled for continuing their traditional practices. "Indian schools" forbade Indian languages, clothing styles, and even hair fashions (see Communities in Conflict).

These and other measures did little to integrate Indians into white society. Treated as savages, Indian children fled most white schools. Nor did adults receive much encouragement to become property holders. Government agencies allotted them inferior farmland, inadequate tools, and little training for agricultural self-sufficiency. Seeing scant advantage in assimilating, only a minority of adults dropped their tribal religion for Christianity or their communal ways for the accumulation of private property. Within the next forty years, the Indian peoples lost 60 percent of the reservation land remaining in 1887 and 66 percent of the land allotted to them as homesteaders. The tenets of the Dawes Act were not reversed until 1934. In that year, Congress passed the Indian Reorganization Act, which affirmed the integrity of Indian cultural institutions and returned some land to tribal ownership (see Chapter 24).

The Carlisle Indian Industrial School

Richard Henry Pratt (1840–1924) founded the Indian school in Carlisle, Pennsylvania, in 1879 with the approval of the Department of the Interior and the War Department. He had served in a volunteer regiment during the Civil War and then continued his military assignment in the Indian Territory, where he began to develop ideas of "civilizing" Native Americans. Before his first encounter he had anticipated meeting "atrocious aborigines," but he soon came to believe that, if given sufficient opportunities and guidance, Indian peoples could thrive and become equal citizens of the United States.

Pratt headed the Carlisle Indian School for twenty-five years, until he retired from military service in 1904. Together with his wife, Anna Mason Pratt, he supervised every aspect of the Indian children's life, including language, dress, and deportment. Sharing with many well-intentioned white reformers the conviction that Christianity provided the best moral guidance, the Pratts forbade the children to practice their native religion. Pratt's motto, "Kill the Indian, but save the man," aptly expressed his belief that the salvation of the Indians depended on the sacrifice of their culture.

Luther Standing Bear (1868–1939), the son of the Oglala Sioux chief Standing Bear, was born on the Sioux Pine Ridge reservation in South Dakota and educated at the Carlisle Indian School. He was a member of the first class to graduate. In 1898, he joined Buffalo Bill's Wild West Show as an interpreter and chaperon for Indian performers and also performed, along with his wife. In 1912, he moved on to the motion picture industry in California, where he became an actor and consultant on movies about Indians. He wrote several books about his experiences; an excerpt from one of them appears here.

• **Why did Richard Henry Pratt choose haircuts and new clothing as important measures in training Indian children for citizenship?**

• **How did Luther Standing Bear interpret this act?**

Richard Henry Pratt Explains How He Made Indian Children "White"

Just before starting for the Indian Territory party, I employed a couple of barbers to cut the hair of the boys. This work was scarcely begun when I had to leave and the barbers were to finish the work under Mrs. Pratt's oversight. Upon my return Mrs. Pratt gave me this experience: The interpreter came to her saying all the boys had their hair cut except two of the older ones who refused to part with their long braids. She went at once to the room where the hair cutting was being done and asked these big boys why they refused to carry out the Captain's order. "Well," said one, "we were told we would have new clothes like the white men. We have none so we keep our long hair." "All right," said Mrs. Pratt, "the clothes will come later, and if you do not want to have your hair cut now, I must send away these barbers and then you must wait until the Captain returns." The spokesman relented and said that if she would stand by, he would let the man cut his hair, which she willingly did. The other, however, stubbornly held to his decision. Later that night she was aroused by a very discordant wailing, which grew in volume. Mrs. Pratt sent a boy for the interpreter. When the interpreter came, he gave the explanation that the young man who had refused to have his hair cut afterwards relented and did the job himself with a knife. He then said his people always wailed after cutting their hair, as it was an evidence of mourning, and he had come onto the parade ground to show his grief. His voice had awakened the girls, who joined with their shrill voices, then other boys joined and hence the commotion. . . .

There was a very considerable delay in the arrival of clothing, and when it finally came it was delivered under a Bureau contract with one of our great American merchants. It was the shoddiest of shoddy clothing. As the price was insignificant, the worth was the same, but it illustrated the ill-considered system of buying the cheapest materials. Agent Miles stopped off on his way to Washington. I made a bundle of a cloth cap, through which I could push my finger, a coat out at the elbows and ripped, and trousers torn and worn out at the knees and seat, all in use less than a month . . .

We were scarcely underway when I received a letter from the Commissioner of Indian Affairs, enclosing a printed table of the per capita allowance of food for Indian schools. Experience in army service

> # "Kill the Indian, but save the man."

showed that children living on that ration would be hungry all the time. . . .

The next time I visited Washington, the Commissioner, Mr. Hayt, laughingly told me that he wanted me to see how that table came to be adopted by the Bureau and sent for the chief of the division in the Indian Office having the matter in charge. When he came in, the Commissioner said, "I want you to tell Captain Pratt how you came to make up that school food supply table." The man said: "We had a rational allowance considerably more liberal than that for several years, and as nobody complained about it I thought there could be a reduction."

"I accordingly made up that table and have been waiting for complaints." I said, "You did that, without investigating allowances at boarding schools for young people or making inquiries of people who know about such things, and pushed it on the Indians as the conclusion of this Bureau?" "Well," he said, "I knew no other way. No one complained and I thought it right to economize."

SOURCE: Excerpt from *Battlefield and Classroom: Four Decades with the American Indian*. By Pratt and Utley. Pp. 232–234. Copyright © 2003 University of Oklahoma Press. Reprinted by permission.

Luther Standing Bear Remembers Being Made "White"

. . . At the age of eleven years, ancestral life for me and my people was most abruptly ended without regard for our wishes, comforts, or rights in the matter. At once I was thrust into an alien world, into an environment as different from the one into which I had been born as it is possible to imagine, to remake myself, if I could into the likeness of the invader.

By 1879, my people were no longer free, but were subjects confined on reservations under the rule of agents. One day there came to the agency a party of white people from the East. Their presence aroused considerable excitement when it became known that these people were school teachers who wanted some Indian boys and girls to take away with them to train as were white boys and girls. . . .

I could think of no reason why white people wanted Indian boys and girls except to kill them, and not having the remotest idea of what a school was, I thought we were going East to die. . . . In my decision to go, I gave up many things dear to the heart of a little Indian boy, and one of the things over which my child mind grieved was the thought of saying good-bye to my pony. I rode him as far as I could on the journey, which was to the Missouri River, where we took the boat. There we parted from our parents, and it was a heart-breaking scene, women and children weeping. Some of the children changed their minds and were unable to go on the boat, but for many who did go it was a final parting. . . .

At last at Carlisle the transforming, the "civilizing" process began. It began with clothes. Never, not matter what our philosophy or spiritual quality, could we be civilized while wearing the moccasin and blanket. The task before us was not only that of accepting new ideas and adopting new manners, but actual physical changes and discomfort had to be borne uncomplainingly until the body adjusted itself to new tastes and habits. Our accustomed dress was taken and replaced with clothing that felt cumbersome and awkward. Against trousers and handkerchiefs we had a distinct feeling—they were unsanitary and the trousers kept us from breathing well. High collars, stiff-bosomed shirts, and suspenders fully three inches in width were uncomfortable, while leather boots caused actual suffering. We longed to go barefoot, but were told that dew on the grass would give us colds. That was a new warning for us, for our mothers had never told us to beware of colds, and I remember as a child coming

"... the 'civilizing' process began ... with clothes. Never ... could we be civilized while wearing the moccasin and blanket."

into the tipi with moccasins full of snow. . . . My niece once asked me what it was that I disliked the most during those first bewildering days, and I said, "red flannel." Not knowing what I meant, she laughed, but I still remember those horrid, sticky garments which we had to wear next to the skin, and I still squirm and itch when I think of them.

SOURCE: Reproduced from *Land of the Spotted Eagle* by Luther Standing Bear by permission of the University of Nebraska Press. Copyright © 1933 by Luther Standing Bear. Copyright renewed 1960 by May Jones.

The Ghost Dance

After the passage of the Dawes Severalty Act, one more cycle of rebellion remained for the Sioux. In 1889, the Northern Paiute Wovoka had a vision during a total eclipse of the sun. In his vision, the Creator told him that if the Indian peoples learned to love each other, they would be granted a special place in the afterlife. The Creator also gave him the Ghost Dance, which the shaman performed for others and soon spread to other tribes. The Sioux, among others, elaborated Wovoka's prophecy into a religion of resistance. They came to believe that when the day of judgment came, all Indian peoples who had ever lived would return to their lost world and white peoples would vanish from the earth. The chant sounded:

> *The whole world is coming.*
> *A nation is coming, a nation is coming.*
> *The eagle has brought the message to the tribe.*
> *The father says so, the father says so.*
> *Over the whole earth they are coming.*
> *The buffalo are coming, the buffalo are coming.*
> *The crow has brought the message to the tribe,*
> *The father says so, the father says so.*

Many white settlers and federal officials feared the Ghost Dancers, even though belief in a sudden divine judgment was common among Christians and Jews. Before the Civil War, Protestant groups such as the Millerites, who had renounced personal property and prepared themselves for the millennium, were tolerated by other Americans. After decades of Indian warfare, however, white Americans took the Ghost Dance as a warning of tribal retribution rather than a religious ceremony. As thousands of Sioux danced to exhaustion, local whites intolerantly demanded the practice be stopped. The U.S. Seventh Cavalry, led in part by survivors of the Battle of Little Bighorn, rushed to the Pine Ridge Reservation, and a group of the Sioux led by Big Foot, fearing mass murder, moved into hiding in the Badlands of South Dakota. After a skirmish, the great leader Sitting Bull and his young son lay dead.

The Seventh Cavalry pursued the Sioux Ghost Dancers and 300 undernourished Sioux, freezing and without horses, to Wounded Knee Creek on the Pine Ridge Reservation. There, on December 29, 1890,

while the peace-seeking Big Foot, who had personally raised a white flag of surrender, lay dying of pneumonia, they were surrounded by soldiers armed with automatic guns. The U.S. troops expected the Sioux to surrender their few remaining weapons, but an accidental gunshot from one deaf brave who misunderstood the command caused panic on both sides.

Within minutes, 200 Sioux had been cut down and dozens of soldiers wounded, mostly by their own crossfire. For two hours soldiers continued to shoot at anything that moved—mostly women and children straggling away. Many of the injured froze to death in the snow; others were transported in open wagons and finally laid out on beds of hay under Christmas decorations at the Pine Ridge Episcopal Church. The massacre, which took

The explorer John Wesley Powell led an expedition of ten men in 1869 to map the Colorado River, its tributaries, and its canyons. He became fascinated with the culture of the tribespeople he encountered and learned to speak the Ute language. In 1871–1872 Powell, accompanied by a photographer, remade the trip to the Grand Canyon, which he named. In this image, Powell appears alongside Tau-gue, Chief of the Paiutes, overlooking the Virgin River.

place almost exactly 400 years after Columbus "discovered" the New World for Christian civilization, seemed to mark the final conquest of the continent's indigenous peoples.

Endurance and Rejuvenation

The most tenacious tribes were those occupying land rejected by white settlers or those distant from their new communities. Still, not even an insular, peaceful agricultural existence on semiarid, treeless terrain necessarily provided protection. Nor did a total willingness to peacefully accept white offers prevent attack.

The Pimas of Arizona, for instance, had a well-developed agricultural system adapted to a scarce supply of water, and they rarely warred with other tribes. After the arrival of white settlers, they integrated Christian symbolism into their religion, learned to speak English, and even fought with the U.S. cavalry against the Apaches. Still, the Pimas saw their lands stolen, their precious waterways diverted, and their families impoverished.

The similarly peaceful Yana tribes of California, hunters and gatherers rather than farmers, were even less fortunate. Suffering enslavement, prostitution, and multiple new diseases from white settlers, they faced near extinction within a generation. One Yana tribe, the Yahi, chose simply to disappear. For more than a decade, they lived in caves and avoided all contact with white settlers.

Many tribes found it difficult to survive in the proximity of white settlers. The Flatheads, for example, seemed to Indian commissioners in the Bitterroot region of Montana to be destined for quick assimilation. They had refused to join the Ghost Dance and had agreed to sell their rich tribal land and move to a new reservation. While waiting to be moved, however, the dispossessed Flatheads nearly starved. When they finally reached the new reservation in October 1891, the remaining 250 Flatheads put on their finest war paint and whooped and galloped their horses, firing guns in the air in celebration. Disappointment and tragedy lay ahead. The federal government drastically reduced the size of the reservation, using a large part of it to provide a national reserve for buffalo. Only handfuls of Flatheads, mostly elderly, continued to live together in pockets of rural poverty.

A majority of tribes, especially smaller ones, sooner or later reached numbers too low to maintain their collective existence. Intermarriage, although widely condemned by the white community, drew many young people outside their Indian communities. Some tribal leaders also deliberately chose a path toward assimilation. The Quapaws, for example, formally disbanded in the aftermath of the Dawes Severalty Act. The minority that

managed to prosper in white society as tradespeople or farmers abandoned their language, religious customs, and traditional ways of life. Later generations petitioned the federal government and regained tribal status, established ceremonial grounds and cultural centers (or bingo halls), and built up one of the most durable powwows in the state. Even so, much of the tribal lore that had underpinned distinct identity had simply vanished.

For those tribes who remained on reservations, the aggressively assimilationist policies of the Office of Indian Affairs (OIA) challenged their traditional ways. The Southern Ute, for example, at one time hunted, fished, and gathered throughout a huge region spanning the Rocky Mountains and the Great Basin. In 1848, they began to sign a series of treaties in accord with the reservation policy of the U.S. government. Twenty years later, their territory had been reduced to approximately one-quarter of Colorado Territory, and in 1873, they had further relinquished about one-quarter of this land. After the passage of the Dawes Act, the U.S. government, pressured by white settlers, gave the tribe two choices: they could break up their communal land holdings and accept the 160 acres granted to the male heads of families, or they could maintain their tribal status and move to a reservation in Utah. The Utes were divided over the issue, but a considerable number chose to live on reservations under the administration of the OIA.

Under the terms of the Dawes Act, Southern Ute men and women endured continuous challenges to their egalitarian practices. The OIA assumed, for example, that Ute men would represent the tribe in all official matters, a policy that forced Ute women to petition the U.S. government to recognize their rights and concerns. Similarly, Ute women struggled to hold on to their roles as producers within the subsistence family economy against the efforts of the OIA agents to train them for homemaking alone. In the 1880s, the OIA established a matrons program to teach Ute women to create a "civilizing" home, which included new lessons about sanitation, home furnishings, and health care. But even fifty years later, some Ute preferred to live at least part of the year in a teepee in a multigenerational family, rather than in a private residence designed for a single married couple and their children.

A small minority of tribes, grown skillful in adapting to dramatically changing circumstances, managed to persist and even grow. Never numbering more than a few thousand people, during the late eighteenth century the Cheyennes found themselves caught geographically between aggressive tribes in the Great Lakes region and had migrated into the Missouri area, where they split into small village-sized communities. By the mid-nineteenth century, they had become expert horse traders on the Great Plains, well prepared to meet the massive influx of white settlers by shifting their location frequently. They avoided the worst of the pestilence that spread from the diseases white people carried and likewise survived widespread intermarriage with the Sioux in the 1860s and 1870s. Instructed to settle, many Cheyennes took up elements of the Christian religion and became farmers, also without losing their tribal identity. Punished by revenge-hungry soldiers after the battle of Little Bighorn, their lands repeatedly taken away, they still held on. The Cheyennes were survivors.

The Navajos experienced an extraordinary renewal, largely because they built a life in territory considered worthless by whites. Having migrated to the Southwest from the northwestern part of the continent perhaps 700 years earlier, the Diné ("the People"), as they called themselves, had already survived earlier invasions by the Spanish. In 1863, they had been conquered again through the cooperation of hostile tribes led by the famous Colonel Kit Carson. Their crops burned, their fruit trees destroyed, 8,000 Navajos were forced in the 300-mile "Long Walk" to the desolate Bosque Redondo reservation, where they nearly starved. Four years later, the Indian Bureau allowed the severely reduced tribe to return to a fraction of its former lands.

By 1880, the Navajos' population had returned to nearly what it had been before their conquest by white Americans. Quickly depleting the deer and antelope on their hemmed-in reservation, they had to rely on sheep alone as a food reserve during years of bad crops. With their wool rugs and blankets much in demand in the East, the Navajos increasingly turned to crafts, eventually including silver jewelry as well as weaving, to survive. Although living on the economic margin, they persevered to become the largest Indian nation in the United States.

The nearby Hopis, like the Navajos, survived by stubbornly clinging to lands unwanted by white settlers, and by adapting to drastically changing conditions. A famous tribe of "desert people," the Hopis had lived for centuries in their cliff cities. Their highly developed theological beliefs, peaceful social system, sand paintings, and kachina dolls interested many educated and influential whites. The resulting publicity helped them gather the public supporters and financial resources needed to fend off further threats to their reservations.

Fortunate northwestern tribes remained relatively isolated from white settlers until the early twentieth century, although they had begun trading with white visitors centuries earlier. Northwestern peoples relied largely on salmon and other resources of the region's rivers and bays. In potlatch ceremonies, leaders redistributed tribal wealth and maintained their personal status and the status of their tribe by giving lavish gifts to invited guests. Northwestern peoples also made intricate wood carvings, including commemorative "totem" poles that recorded their history and identified their regional status. Northwestern peoples maintained their cultural integrity in part through connections with kin in Canada, as did southern tribes with kin in Mexico. In Canada and Mexico, native populations suffered less pressure from new populations and retained more tribal authority than in the United States.

Indian nations approached their nadir as the nineteenth century came to a close. The descendants of the great pre-Columbian civilizations had been conquered by foreigners, their population reduced to fewer than 250,000. Under the pressure of assimilation, the remaining tribespeople became known to non-Indians as "the vanishing Americans." It would take several generations before Indian sovereignty experienced a resurgence.

Conclusion

Amid the land rush of April 22, 1889, the town of Guthrie, Oklahoma, was built, contemporaries liked to brag, not in a day but in a single afternoon, its population leaping from a dozen or so to 10,000 by sundown. Throughout the territory, new communities formed almost as rapidly and often displaced old ones. Farms and ranches owned by white settlers soon spread out across the vast countryside that earlier had been Indian Territory. This spectacular development of Oklahoma was, however, but one chapter in the history of the trans–Mississippi West as an internal empire.

The West, rich in natural resources, soon served the nation in supplying ore and timber for its expanding industries and agricultural products for the growing urban populations. Envisioning the West as a cornucopia whose boundless treasures would offer themselves to the willing pioneer, most of the new residents failed to calculate the odds against their making a prosperous livelihood as miners, farmers, or petty merchants. Nor could they appreciate the long-term consequences of the violence they brought with them from the battlefields of the Civil War to the far reaches of the West.

The new settlers adapted their political and legal systems, as well as many of their economic and cultural institutions, to western circumstances. Ironically though, even after statehood, they would still be only distant representatives of an empire whose financial, political, and industrial centers remained in the Northeast. They were often frustrated by their isolation and enraged at the federal regulations that governed them and at the eastern investors and lawyers who seemed poised on all sides to rob them of the fruits of their labor. Embittered Westerners, along with Southerners, would form the core of a nationwide discontent that would soon threaten to uproot the American political system.

CHRONOLOGY

1848	Treaty of Guadalupe Hidalgo		**1876**	Custer's Last Stand
1853	Gadsden Purchase		**1877**	Defeat of the Nez Perces
1862	Homestead Act makes free land available		**1878**	John Wesley Powell published *Report on the Lands of the Arid Region*
	Morrill Act authorizes "land-grant" colleges		**1881**	Helen Hunt Jackson, *A Century of Dishonor*
1865–67	Great Sioux War		**1882**	Edmunds Act outlaws polygamy
1866	Texas cattle drives begin		**1885–87**	Droughts and severe winters cause the collapse of the cattle boom
1867	Medicine Lodge Treaty established reservation system		**1887**	Dawes Severalty Act
	Alaska purchased		**1890**	Sioux Ghost Dance movement
1869	Board of Indian Commissioners created			Massacre of Lakota Sioux at Wounded Knee
	Buffalo Bill, the King of the Border Men sets off "Wild West" publishing craze			Census Bureau announces the end of the frontier line
1870s	Grasshopper attacks on the Great Plains		**1893**	Frederick Jackson Turner presents his "frontier thesis"
1872	Yellowstone National Park created		**1897**	Forest Management Act gives the federal government authority over forest reserves
1874–75	Sioux battles in Black Hills of Dakotas			
	Red River War			

Review Questions

1. Discuss the role of federal legislation in accelerating and shaping the course of westward expansion.

2. How did the incorporation of western territories into the United States affect Indian nations such as the Sioux or the Nez Perce? Discuss the causes and consequences of the Indian Wars. Discuss the significance of reservation policy and the Dawes Severalty Act for tribal life.

3. What were some of the major technological advances in mining and in agriculture that promoted the development of the western economy?

4. Describe the unique features of Mexicano communities in the Southwest before and after the mass immigration of Anglos. How did changes in the economy affect the patterns of labor and the status of women in these communities?

5. What role did the Homestead Act play in western expansion? How did farm families on the Great Plains divide chores among their members? What

factors determined the likelihood of economic success or failure?

6. Describe the responses of artists, naturalists, and conservationists to the western landscape. How did their photographs, paintings, and stories shape perceptions of the West in the East?

7. How can the history of the American West be told as the creation of new communities and the displacement of old communities?

Recommended Reading

James Donovan, *A Terrible Glory: Custer and the Little Bighorn* (2008) puts this famous battle within the context of the Indian Wars and argues that the famed leader woefully underestimated the ability of his troops to carry it out. Donovan builds his case on ample sources.

Jon Gjerde, *The Minds of the West: Ethnocultural Evolution in the Rural Middle West, 1830–1917* (1997). A combination cultural and economic history that weighs the importance of ethnicity in the shaping of American identities in the farming regions of the Middle West.

Gjerde pays close attention to the religious institutions and systems of belief of European immigrants as the basis of community formation.

Robert V. Hine and John Mack Faragher, *The American West: A New Interpretive History* (2000). A sweeping, amply illustrated survey of western history with reference to recent scholarship. The authors emphasize Native Americans and include rich material on ethnicity, the environment, and the role of women.

John C. Hudson, *Making the Corn Belt: A Geographical History of Middle-Western Agriculture* (1994). An ecologically oriented study of corn growing that traces its development from Indians to Southerners moving westward.

Andrew C. Isenberg, *The Destruction of the Bison: An Environmental History, 1750–1920* (2000). A rich study of the forces behind the near-extinction of the bison, with special attention to the interplay among Indians, Euroamericans, and the environment of the Great Plains. Isenberg constructs a narrative that is as much cultural as economic in framing the environmental problems.

Karl Jacoby, *Shadows at Dawn: A Borderland Massacre and the Violence of History* (2009). An engaging, well-researched, and multi-perspective examination of the brutal Camp Grand Massacre of Apaches, which took place on April 30, 1875.

Elizabeth Jameson and Susan Armitage, eds., *Writing the Range* (1997). A collection of essays on women in the West that presents an inclusive historical narrative based on the experiences of women of differing backgrounds, races, and ethnic groups.

Valerie Sherer Mathes and Richard Lowitt, *The Standing Bear Controversy: Prelude to Indian Reform* (2003). A fascinating account of the Ponca chief's efforts to bring attention to the injustices surrounding the forced removal of the Poncas from their tribal lands.

Katherine M. B. Osburn, *Southern Ute Women: Autonomy and Assimilation on the Reservation, 1887–1934* (1998). Presents a careful analysis of the impact of the Dawes Act on the role and status of women among the Southern Ute. Osburn acknowledges the changes brought by the Office of Indian Affairs programs on the reservations but emphasizes the resistance of the Ute and the retention of old ways.

Glenda Riley, *Building and Breaking Families in the American West* (1996). Essays covering the variety of cultures in the American West, organized topically to highlight courtship, marriage and intermarriage, and separation and divorce.

Thomas E. Sheridan, *Los Tucsonenses: The Mexican Community in Tucson, 1854–1941* (1986). A highly readable account of Mexican American communities in the Southwest. Sheridan shows how a midcentury accommodation of Anglos and Mexicanos faded with the absorption of the region into the national economy and with the steady displacement of the Mexicano community from its agricultural landholdings.

Louis S. Warren, *Buffalo Bill's America: William Cody and the Wild West Show* (2005). Deals with many of the legends Cody created about himself and his performers and relates his celebrity at the turn of the twentieth century to continuing forms of mass entertainment.

Elliott West, *The Last Indian War: The Nez Perce Story* (2009). Engaging narrative by one of the leading historians of the American West. West treats the war of 1877 in careful detail and follows the Nez Perces into the subsequent decades of defeat.

Liping Zhu, *A Chinaman's Chance: The Chinese on the Rocky Mountain Mining Frontier* (1997). Studies the mining communities of Chinese in the Boise Basin of Idaho. Zhu emphasizes the success the Chinese enjoyed not only as miners but also as merchants in the face of discriminatory practices and laws.

myhistórylab Connections
PEARSON

Reinforce what you learned in this chapter by studying the many documents,
images, maps, review tools, and videos available at www.myhistorylab.com

Read and Review

✓● Study and Review **Chapter 18**

●●● Read the Document

*Congressional Report on Sand Creek
Massacre (1867)*

John Lester, Hydraulic Mining (1873)

*Elizabeth Cady Stanton Speaks to Mormon
Women in Utah (1871)*

*Perspectives on the American Cowboy
(1884, 1886)*

*Helen Hunt Jackson, from A Century of
Dishonor (1881)*

◉ See the Map *Resources and Conflict in the West*

Research and Explore

●●● Read the Document

Exploring America: Dakota Sioux Conflict

History Bookshelf: Muir, The Yosemite

Profiles
  George Armstrong Custer
  Helen Hunt Jackson

((●● Hear the Audio *Omaha Funeral Song*

●● Watch the Video

The Real West Is an Urban West

The Plains

((●● **Hear the Audio**

Hear the audio files for Chapter 18 at
www.myhistorylab.com.

19

Chapter 19 at www.myhistorylab.com

((●●—[Hear the Audio

Production and Consumption in the Gilded Age

1865–1900

CHAPTER OUTLINE

American Communities 525
Haymarket Square, Chicago, May 4, 1886

The Rise of Industry, the Triumph of
Business 527
Mechanization Takes Command
Expanding the Market for Goods
Integration, Combination, and Merger
The Gospel of Wealth

Labor in the Age of Big Business 533
The Wage System

The Knights of Labor
The American Federation of Labor

The New South 536
An Internal Colony
Southern Labor
The Transformation of Piedmont
    Communities

The Industrial City 540
Populating the City
The Urban Landscape
The City and the Environment

The Rise of Consumer Society 543
"Conspicuous Consumption"
Self-Improvement and the Middle Class
Life in the Streets

Cultures in Conflict, Culture
in Common 546
Education
Leisure and Public Space
National Pastimes

The Anarchist Riot in Chicago. Illustration from Harper's Weekly, Volume 30, May 15, 1886. Courtesy of the Library of Congress.

Haymarket Square, Chicago, May 4, 1886

As rain approached the city, approximately 1,500 people gathered for a mass meeting in Haymarket Square to protest the brutality of the previous day, when Chicago police killed four strikers at the fiercely antiunion McCormick Reaper Works. The crowd listened peacefully as several speakers denounced the violence. Around 10:00 P.M., when the winds picked up, most headed for home, including the city's longtime mayor, Democrat Carter Harrison. According to newspaper reports, the crowd quickly dwindled to only 600 people. The final speaker, stone hauler Samuel Fielden, jumped up on the hay wagon that served as a makeshift stage and concluded on an ominous note. He warned that "war

has been declared on us" and advised the crowd "to get hold of anything that will help you to resist the onslaught of the enemy and the usurper."

Within minutes, a column of 176 police marched down the street, pushing what remained of the crowd onto the wooden sidewalks and commanding them to disperse. Then, according to the city's leading newspaper, the *Tribune*, "something like a miniature rocket suddenly rose out of the crowd on the east sidewalk." The bomb exploded "with terrific force, shaking buildings on the street and creating havoc among the police."

AMERICAN · · Communities

One policeman died immediately, provoking others to open fire into the scattering crowd. At the end of just a few minutes of chaos, seven policemen had received mortal wounds and as many as sixty more were injured, many in their own crossfire. Several civilians were killed, and dozens were injured.

Those who attended the rally were mainly disgruntled workers, recent immigrants from central and eastern Europe who had come to Chicago to take advantage of the city's growing industries. Grateful for employment in the "city of smoke," they nevertheless balked at the pace of the newly mechanized production lines that sapped their life's blood and returned wages barely enough to support a family. At this moment, though, they were primarily determined to establish unions and a workday shorter than the customary ten or twelve hours.

Since early in the year, an eight-hour campaign had been sweeping the nation, with its center in Chicago. Workers and sympathetic consumers alike boycotted brands of beer, tobacco, bread, and other products made in longer-hour shops. They expressed their aspirations in their anthem, the "Eight-Hour Song."

> *We want to feel the sunshine;*
> *We want to smell the flowers;*
> *We're sure God has willed it.*
> *And we mean to have eight hours.*
>
> *We're summoning our forces from*
> *Shipyard, shop and mill;*
> *Eight hours for work, eight hours for rest,*
> *Eight hours for what we will.*

With more than wages at stake, workers were joining unions and striking so often that the era became known as the "Great Upheaval." Their leaders responded to this upsurge by calling for a general strike across all industries on May 1, 1886.

A community of radical workers who had emigrated from Germany and settled in Chicago's near North Side made up the most militant contingent of the movement. They called themselves "revolutionary socialists," and sought a government of working people in place of politicians and corporate power. Writing in the *Arbeiter-Zeitung* (*Workers' Newspaper*), the local German-language newspaper, editor August Spies greeted May 1, hailed as "Emancipation Day,"

calling: "Workmen, let your watchword be: No compromise! Cowards to the Rear! Men to the front!"

On May Day, Spies renewed the cry of "eight for ten" and helped to lead the spectacular parade of 80,000 men, women, and children up Michigan Avenue, Chicago's main street. A Saturday, the day passed peacefully. However, when the workweek resumed on Monday, May 3, the deadly confrontation of strikers and police at the McCormick Reaper Works set the stage for virtual class warfare.

Feelings of animosity on all sides intensified. In the days following the tragedy at Haymarket Square, Chicago police arrested hundreds of working people, rounded up known leaders, and searched their homes and detained them without warrants. Meanwhile, newspapers denounced them as "enemy forces" and the "scum" of Europe. Sentiment swung sharply against immigrants. Many prominent citizens called for a ban on "foreign savages who might come to America with their dynamite bombs and anarchic purposes."

Ultimately, eight men were charged with incitement to murder. In the most celebrated trial of the nineteenth century, a jury of middle-class men pronounced all eight guilty despite the lack of evidence linking the defendants to the bombing. Three of the eight had not even been at Haymarket Square on the evening of May 4. The judge sentenced them to death by hanging.

At the other end of the social scale, the 1880s for middle- and upper-class Chicagoans was an era of unprecedented prosperity. Incorporated in 1837, the city boasted a population of 200,000—second only to New York—and dozens of new mass industries and vibrant new classes of consumers. Thousands of large and small businesses produced goods ranging from ball bearings to baseballs to luxury passenger cars for travel by rail. Many of the workers in these industries, especially immigrants, could barely make ends meet. But thousands of better-off Chicagoans, foreign- and native-born alike, rushed to Marshall Field & Company to survey the ever-expanding range of goods in one of the finest department stores in the nation and a major source of pride for the city. If prices at Field's were beyond the capacity of their pocketbooks, aspiring consumers could turn to less expensive goods offered by Chicago-based Montgomery Ward, the nation's first large-scale mail-order business.

1. What was the effect of the expansion in the production of both capital goods and consumer goods?

2. What were the sources of the new labor being recruited for factory work in Gilded Age America?

3. How did industrial development affect African Americans living in the South?

4. How did populations change and grow in Gilded Age cities?

5. What accounts for the rise of a consumer society, and how did various groups participate in its development?

6. What role did public spaces play in late nineteenth-century popular culture?

FOCUS Questions

1865–1900

By the final decades of the nineteenth century, the nation's eyes were fixed on Chicago because the city was marking the steps being taken by the nation as a whole. If class differences sharpened and led

Chicago

to violence, the rise in living standards provided a different, more appealing focus. The city with the most technologically advanced industries in the world seemed to be leading the way—but to what?

AMERICAN·
Communities

The Rise of Industry, the Triumph of Business

At the time of the Civil War, the typical American business firm was a small enterprise, owned and managed by a single family, and producing goods for a local or regional market. By the turn of the century, businesses depending on large-scale investments had organized as corporations and grown to unforeseen size. These mammoth firms could afford to mass-produce goods for national and even international markets. At the helm stood unimaginably wealthy men, powerful representatives of a new national business community, who led in the transformation of the United States from a rural to an urban industrial nation.

Mechanization Takes Command

The Centennial Exposition of 1876, held in Philadelphia, celebrated not so much the American Revolution 100 years earlier as the industrial and technological promise of the century to come. The visiting emperor of Brazil spoke into an unfamiliar device on display and gasped, "My God, it talks!" The telephone, patented that year by Alexander Graham Bell, signaled the rise of the United States to world leadership in industrial technology.

The year 1876 also marked the opening of Thomas Alva Edison's laboratory in Menlo Park, New Jersey, one of the first devoted to industrial research. Three years later, his team produced an incandescent lamp that burned for thirteen hours. By 1882, the Edison Electric Light Company had launched its service in New York City's financial district. Electricity revolutionized both urban life and industry.

Read the Document

Thomas Edison, The Success of the Electric Light (1880) at **www.myhistorylab.com**

The second industrial revolution (1871–1914) proceeded at a pace that was not only unprecedented but also previously unimaginable. In 1865, the annual production of goods was estimated at $2 billion; by 1900, it stood at $13 billion, transforming the United States from fourth to first in the world in terms of productivity. American industry had outstripped its European rivals, Germany and Great Britain, and manufactured one-third of the world's goods.

A major force behind economic growth was the vast transcontinental railroad, completed in 1869. The addition of three more major rail lines (the Southern Pacific, the Northern Pacific, and the Atchison, Topeka, and Santa Fe) in the early 1880s, and the Great Northern, a

In 1887, Thomas Alva Edison (1847–1931), shown here with the phonograph, moved his laboratory from Menlo Park to West Orange, New Jersey. There, he invented the alkaline storage battery, the phonograph, and the kinetoscope, the first machine to allow one person at a time to view motion pictures.

decade later, completed the most extensive transportation network in the world. As the nation's first big business and recipient of generous government subsidies, railroads linked cities in every state and served as nationwide distributors of goods. Freight trains carried the bountiful natural resources, such as iron, coal, and minerals, that supplied the raw materials for industry, as well as food and other commodities for the growing urban populations (see Map 19.1).

No factor was more important in promoting economic growth than the application of new technologies to increase the productivity of labor and the volume of goods. Machines, factory managers, and workers together created a system of continuous production by which more could be made—and faster—than anywhere else on earth. Higher productivity depended not only on machinery and technology but also on economies of scale and speed, reorganization of factory labor and business management, and the unparalleled growth of a market for goods of all kinds.

New systems of mass production replaced wasteful and often chaotic practices and speeded up the delivery of finished goods. In the 1860s, meatpackers set up one of the earliest production lines. The process of converting livestock into meat began with a live animal. A chain around the hind leg whirled the body to an overhead rail, which carried it to slaughter—all in barely half a minute's time. Next, a scraping machine removed hair

and bristles, the carcass was shifted to a conveyer belt where the chest was split and the organs removed, and then the body was placed in a cooler. This "disassembly line" displaced patterns of hand labor that were centuries old.

Sometimes the invention of a single machine could instantly transform production, mechanizing every stage from processing the raw material to packaging the product. The cigarette-making machine, patented in 1881, shaped the tobacco, encased it in an endless paper tube, and snipped off the tube at cigarette-length intervals. This machine could produce more than 7,000 cigarettes per hour, replacing the worker who at best made 3,000 per day. After a few more improvements, fifteen machines could meet the total demand for American cigarettes. Within a generation, continuous production— the assembly line—became standard in most areas of manufacturing, thus revolutionizing the making of furniture, cloth, grain products, soap, and canned goods; the refining, distilling, and processing of animal and vegetable fats; and eventually, the manufacture of automobiles.

Expanding the Market for Goods

To distribute the growing volume of goods and to create a dependable market, businesses demanded new techniques of merchandising on a national and, in some cases, international scale. For generations, legions of sellers, or "drummers," had worked their routes, pushing goods, especially hardware and patent medicines, to individual buyers and local retail stores. After the Civil War, the appearance of mail-order houses, which accompanied the consolidation of the railroad lines and the expansion of the postal system, helped to get new products to consumers.

Growing directly out of these services, the successful Chicago-based mail-order houses drew rural and urban consumers into a common marketplace. Sears, Roebuck and Company and Montgomery Ward offered an enormous variety of goods, from shoes to buggies to gasoline stoves and cream separators. The mail-order catalog also returned to rural folks the fruits of their own labor, now processed and packaged for easy use. The Sears catalog offered Armour's summer sausage as well as Aunt Jemima's Pancake Flour and Queen Mary Scotch Oatmeal, both made of grains that came from the agricultural heartland. In turn, the purchases made by farm families through the Sears catalog sent cash flowing into Chicago.

Chain stores achieved similar economies of scale. By 1900, a half-dozen grocery chains had sprung up. Frank and Charles Woolworth, for example, offered inexpensive variety goods in five-and-ten-cent stores. Other chains selling drugs, costume jewelry, shoes, cigars, and furniture soon appeared, offering a greater selection of goods and lower prices than the small, independent stores.

MAP 19.1 Patterns of Industry, 1900 Industrial manufacturing concentrated in the Northeast and Midwest, whereas the raw materials for production came mostly from other parts of the nation.

Opening shortly after the Civil War, department stores began to take up much of the business formerly enjoyed by specialty shops, offering a spectrum of services that included restaurants, restrooms, ticket agencies, nurseries, reading rooms, and post offices. Elegantly appointed with imported carpets, sweeping marble staircases, and crystal chandeliers, the department store raised retailing to new heights. By the close of the century, the names of Marshall Field of Chicago, Filene's of Boston, The Emporium of San Francisco, Wanamaker's of Philadelphia, and Macy's of New York came to represent the splendors of those great cities as well as the apex of mass retailing.

Advertising lured customers to the department stores, the chains, and the independent neighborhood stores. The advertising revolution began in 1869, when Francis Wayland Ayer founded the earliest advertising agency. Ayer's managed the accounts of such companies as Montgomery Ward, Wanamaker's Department Store, Singer Sewing Machines, and the National Biscuit

Company. With the help of this new sales tool, gross revenues of retailers raced upward from $8 million in 1860 to $102 million in 1900.

Integration, Combination, and Merger

The business community aspired to exercise greater control of the economy and to enlarge the commercial empire. From the source of raw materials to the organization of production, from the conditions of labor to the climate of public opinion, business leaders acted shrewdly. Economic cycles alternating between rapid growth and sharp decline also promoted the rise of big business. Major economic setbacks in 1873 and 1893 wiped out weaker competitors, allowing the strongest firms to rebound swiftly and to expand their sales and scale of operation during the recovery period.

Businesses grew in two distinct, if overlapping, ways. Through *vertical integration*, a firm gained control of production at every step of the way—from raw materials

The famed American architect Louis Sullivan designed the building that became the flagship of Carson Pirie Scott & Co., one of the leading department stores in Chicago. Sullivan, who studied at the Ecole des Beaux-Arts in Paris, incorporated geometrical and botanical elements, such as vines and leaves, into the design of the entrance and windows to create a distinctive architectural style that expressed both modernity and nature.

through processing to the transporting and merchandising of the finished items. In 1899, the United Fruit Company began to build a network of wholesale houses in the United States, and within two years it had opened distribution centers in twenty-one major cities. Eventually, it controlled an elaborate system of Central American plantations and temperature-controlled shipping and storage facilities for its highly perishable bananas.

The second means of growth, *horizontal combination*, entailed gaining control of the market for a single product. The most famous case was the Standard Oil Company, founded by John D. Rockefeller in 1870. Operating out of Cleveland in a highly competitive but lucrative field, Rockefeller first secured preferential rates from railroads eager to ensure a steady supply of oil. He then convinced or coerced other local oil operators to sell their stock to him. The Standard Oil Trust, established in 1882, controlled over 90 percent of the nation's oil-refining industry (see Seeing History).

In 1890, Congress passed the Sherman Antitrust Act to restore competition by encouraging small business and outlawing "every . . . combination . . . in restraint of trade or commerce." Ironically, the courts interpreted the law in ways that inhibited the organization of trade unions (on the grounds that they restricted the free flow of labor) and actually helped the consolidation of business. More than 2,600 firms vanished between 1898 and 1902 alone. By 1910, the industrial giants that would dominate the American economy until the last half of the twentieth century—U.S. Rubber, Goodyear, American Smelting and Refining, Anaconda Copper, General Electric, Westinghouse, Nabisco, Swift and Company, Armour, International Harvester, Eastman Kodak, and American Can—had already formed.

The Standard Oil Company

John D. Rockefeller, who formed the Standard Oil Company in 1870, sought to control all aspects of the industry, from the transportation of crude oil to the marketing and distribution of the final products. By the end of the decade, after making shrewd deals with the railroads and underselling his rivals, he managed to control 90 percent of the oil-refining industry. To further consolidate his interests, in 1882 Rockefeller created the Standard Oil Trust, which, by integrating both vertically and horizontally, became a model for other corporations and an inspiration for critical commentary and antitrust legislation.

Rockefeller's best-known critic was Ida Tarbell. In 1904 she published *The History of the Standard Oil Company*, first in serial form in the popular *McClure's*

Magazine and later as a book. Tarbell's muckraking exposé attracted a great deal of attention. Even more popular were political cartoons depicting Rockefeller's stranglehold on the entire oil industry. *Puck* magazine, which was founded in 1871 by Joseph Keppler, an immigrant from Austria, held up Rockefeller and his company to ridicule. This cartoon, published in *Puck* in 1904, shows Standard Oil as a sinister octopus, wrapping its arms around the White House and Congress as well as workers and even the denizens of Wall Street. In 1911, in response to an antitrust suit, the Supreme Court ordered the company to break up. The modern corporations Exxon, Mobil, Chevron, Amoco, and Sohio (some of which have merged) all descended from Rockefeller's Standard Oil.

• **What does this cartoon tell us about Rockefeller's reputation at the turn of the twentieth century?**

• **What does it suggest about Americans' feelings about the trusts?**

The Gospel of Wealth

Ninety percent of the nation's business leaders were Protestant, and the majority attended church services regularly. They attributed their personal achievement to hard work and perseverance and made these the principal tenets of a new faith that imbued the pursuit of wealth with old-time religious zeal.

One version of this "gospel of wealth" justified the ruthless behavior of the entrepreneurs who accumulated unprecedented wealth and power through shady deals and conspiracies. Speculator Jay Gould, known in the popular press as the "Worst Man in the World," wrung his fortune, it was widely believed, from the labor of others. He rose quickly from his modest origins through a series of unsavory financial maneuvers.

Speculation in railroads proved to be Gould's forte. He took over the Erie Railroad, paying off New York legislators to get the state to finance its expansion, and he acquired the U.S. Express Company by pressuring and tricking its stockholders. When threatened with arrest, Gould sold off his shares for $9 million and moved on to the Union Pacific, where he cut wages, precipitated strikes, and manipulated elections in the western and Plains states. Tired of being caricatured in the press as a great swindler, he bought the leading newspapers. At his death, one obituary described Jay Gould as "an incarnation of cupidity and sordidness," whose life symbolized "idolatrous homage [to] the golden calf."

This engraving of steel manufacturing at Andrew Carnegie's plant in 1886 features a Bessemer Converter, which converts molten pig iron into steel. The process was named after Sir Henry Bessemer of Sheffield, England, who first patented the process in 1855.

Andrew Carnegie—the "Richest Man in the World"—offered a strikingly different model. A poor immigrant from Scotland, Carnegie spent his boyhood studying bookkeeping at night while working days in a textile mill. In 1852, he became the personal secretary of the superintendent of the Pennsylvania Railroad's Western division. He learned quickly and soon stepped into the superintendent's job. While improving passenger train service, he invested brilliantly to build funds for his next venture.

Carnegie built an empire in steel. A genius at vertical integration, he undercut his competitors by using the latest technology and designing his own system of cost analysis. By 1900, Carnegie managed the most efficient steel mills in the world, which accounted for one-third of the nation's output. When he sold out to J. P. Morgan's new United States Steel Corporation in 1901, his personal share of the proceeds came to $225 million.

Carnegie was well known as a civic leader. From one point of view, he was a factory despot who underpaid his employees and ruthlessly managed their working conditions. But to the patrons of the public libraries, art museums, concert halls, colleges, and universities that he funded,

Carnegie appeared to be the single greatest philanthropist of the age. Late in his life, he outlined his personal philosophy in a popular essay, *The Gospel of Wealth* (1889), explaining that "there is no genuine, praiseworthy success in life if you are not honest, truthful, and fair-dealing." By the time he died, he had given away his massive personal fortune.

Whether following the rough road of Gould or the smooth path of Carnegie, the business community worked together to fashion the new conservative ideology of social Darwinism, which purportedly explained, and justified, why some Americans grew rich while others remained poor. Grafted on the biological theory of evolution propounded by the famed British naturalist Charles Darwin, social Darwinism raised the principle of the "survival of the fittest" as an ideal for modern society. In 1883, the Yale professor William Graham Sumner published an essay entitled *What Social Classes Owe to Each Other*, wherein he argued that only a few individuals were capable of putting aside selfish pleasures to produce the capital needed to drive the emerging industrial economy and, moreover, they were fully deserving of their great fortunes. In contrast, the vast majority, too lazy or profligate to rise above poverty, deserved their own miserable fates. To tamper with this "natural" order by establishing welfare programs to help the poor or redistributing wealth in any way would be hazardous to society. Meanwhile, the popular writer Horatio Alger produced a more temperate version of this credo. Publishing more than 100 rags-to-riches novels, he created heroes who manage to rise out of poverty by both hard work and luck and ultimately acquire, if not vast wealth, middle-class respectability and comfort.

Labor in the Age of Big Business

Like the gospel of wealth, the "gospel of work" affirmed the dignity of production and the importance of individual initiative. But unlike business leaders, the philosophers of American working people did not believe in riches as the proof of civic virtue or in the lust for power as the driving force of progress. On the contrary, they contended that a hard day's work should be the badge of all responsible citizens.

Behind the "gospel of work" stood the reality of the rising industrial order, especially its new systems of production that were, in turn, enabled by new technologies. The impact of the new order on the lives of working people would be nothing less than revolutionary. Increasingly, Americans made their livelihoods by producing, not for their own subsistence, but exclusively for the market, and they earned wages in return for their labor. Big business thus found its mirror image in the labor movement spawned by the consolidation of the wage system.

The Wage System

The accelerating growth of industry, especially the steady mechanization of production, dramatically changed employer–employee relations and created new categories of workers. Both in turn fostered competition among workers, particularly between native-born workers and the growing number from outside the United States. Immigrants from Europe and Asia took many of the new unskilled jobs in flourishing industries such as meat processing, clothing and textile manufacturing, cigar making, and mining.

For most craft workers, the new system destroyed long-standing practices and chipped away at their customary autonomy. Frederick Winslow Taylor, the pioneer of scientific management, explained that managers must "take all the important decisions . . . out of the hands of workmen." Teams of ironworkers, for example, had previously set the rules of production as well as their wages, while the company supplied equipment and raw materials. Once steel replaced iron, most companies gradually introduced a new system. Managers constantly supervised workers and set the pace of production and rate of payment. In addition, new, faster machinery made many skills obsolete. In the woodworking trades, highly skilled cabinetmakers, who for generations had brought their own tools to the factory, were largely replaced with "green hands"—immigrants, including many women—who with only minimal training and close supervision could operate new woodworking machines at the cheaper rates of pay.

Not all trades conformed to this pattern. The garment industry, for example, grew at a very fast pace in New York, Boston, Chicago, Philadelphia, Cleveland, and St. Louis, but retained older systems of labor along with the new. The highly mechanized factories employed hundreds of thousands of young immigrant women, while the outwork system, established well before the Civil War, contracted ever-larger numbers of families to work in their homes on sewing machines or by hand. Paid by the piece—a seam stitched, a collar turned, a button attached—workers in this "sweating" system labored faster and longer at home or in the factory to forestall a dip in wages.

Industrial expansion also offered new opportunities for women to work outside the home, and many young women fled the family farm for the factory. African American and immigrant women found employment in trades least affected by technological advances, such as domestic service. In contrast, English-speaking white women moved into the better-paying clerical and sales positions in the rapidly expanding business sector. After the typewriter and telephone came into widespread use in the 1890s, the number of women employed in office work rose even faster. At the turn of the century, 8.6 million women worked outside their homes—nearly triple the number in 1870.

E PLURIBUS UNUM (EXCEPT THE CHINESE).

Thomas Nast (1840–1902), the most famous political cartoonist of the late nineteenth century, used his art to comment on pressing political issues, such as the plight of former slaves during Reconstruction, the evils of machine politics, and the rivalry between the national political parties. His drawings were made into wood engravings that were then printed in newspapers and popular magazines. In this cartoon, published in *Harper's Weekly*, April 1, 1882, Nast shows America welcoming all immigrants except Chinese.

In contrast, African American men found themselves excluded from many fields. In Cleveland, for example, the number of black carpenters declined after 1870, just as the number of construction jobs grew. African American men were also systematically driven from restaurant service and barred from newer trades such as boilermaking, plumbing, electrical work, and paperhanging, which European immigrants secured for themselves.

Discriminatory or exclusionary practices fell hardest on workers recruited earlier from China. From the 1860s on, many Chinese established laundries and restaurants in West Coast cities where they were viewed as potential competitors by both white workers and proprietors of small businesses. A potent and racist anti-Chinese movement organized to protest "cheap" Chinese labor and to demand a halt to Chinese immigration. During the nationwide depression of the 1870s, white rioters insistently called for deportation measures and razed

●●◦ Read the Document

Chinese Exclusion Act (1882) at
www.myhistorylab.com

Chinese neighborhoods. In 1882, Congress passed the Chinese Exclusion Act, which restricted Chinese immigration by barring laborers, limited the civil rights of resident Chinese, and forbade their naturalization.

For even the best-placed wage earners, the new workplace could be unhealthy, even dangerous. Meatpacking produced its own hazards—the dampness of the pickling room, the sharp blade of the slaughtering knife, and the noxious odors of the fertilizer department. Factory owners often failed to mark high-voltage wires, locked fire doors, and allowed the emission of toxic fumes. Moreover, machines ran faster in American factories than anywhere else in the world, and workers who could not keep up or suffered serious injury found themselves without a job.

Even under less hazardous conditions, workers complained about the tedium of performing repetitive tasks for many hours each day. Although federal employees had been granted the eight-hour day in 1868, most workers still toiled upward of ten to twelve hours. "Life in a factory," one textile operative grumbled, "is perhaps, with the exception of prison life, the most monotonous life a human being can live." Nor could glamour be found in the work of saleswomen in the elegant department stores. Clerks could not sit down, despite workdays as long as sixteen hours in the busy season, or hold "unnecessary conversations" with customers or other clerks. Despite these disadvantages, most women preferred sales and manufacturing jobs to domestic service, which required live-in servants to be on call seven days a week, enjoying at best an occasional afternoon off.

Moreover, steady employment was rare. Between 1866 and 1897, fourteen years of prosperity stood against seventeen years of hard times. The major depressions of 1873–79 and 1893–97 were the worst in the nation's history up to that time. Three "minor" recessions (1866–67, 1883–85, and 1890–91) did not seem insignificant to the millions who lost their jobs.

The Knights of Labor

The Noble and Holy Order of the Knights of Labor, founded by a group of Philadelphia garment cutters in 1869, grew to become the largest labor organization in the nineteenth century. Led by Grand Master Workman Terence V. Powderly, the order sought to bring together wage earners, regardless of skill. The Knights endorsed a variety of reform measures—the restriction of child labor, a graduated income tax, more land set aside for homesteading, the abolition of contract labor, and monetary reform—to offset the power of the industrialists. They believed that the "producing classes," once freed from the grip of corporate monopoly and the curses of ignorance and alcohol, would transform the United States into a genuinely democratic society. The Knights insisted that "labor creates all wealth" and all wealth "belongs to those who create it."

The Knights sought to overturn the wage system and, as an alternative, they promoted producers' cooperatives. In these factories, workers collectively made all decisions on prices charged for goods and shared all the profits. Local assemblies launched thousands of small coops, such as the Our Girls Co-operative Manufacturing Company, which a group of Chicago seamstresses established in the 1880s. The Knights also ran small cooperative cigar shops and grocery stores, often housed in their own assembly buildings. Successful for a time, most cooperatives could not compete against the heavily capitalized enterprises and ultimately failed.

For women, the Knights of Labor created a special department within the organization "to investigate the abuses to which our sex is subjected by unscrupulous employers, to agitate the principles which our Order teaches of equal pay for equal work and the abolition of child labor." At the 1886 convention, delegates approved this plan, and Grand Master Powderly appointed knit-goods worker Leonora M. Barry general investigator. With perhaps 65,000 women members at its peak, the Knights ran daycare centers and occasionally even set up coopera-tive kitchens to reduce the drudgery of cooking.

The Knights reached their peak in 1886 during the great campaign for a shorter workday. The organization grew from a few thousand in 1880 to more than 700,000 six years later. The Knights welcomed workers usually excluded by other unions. Nearly 3,000 women formed their own "ladies assemblies" or joined mixed locals. The Knights also organized African American workers—20,000 to 30,000 nationally—mainly in sepa-rate assemblies within the organization. Chinese work-ers, however, were barred from membership.

The Haymarket affair in Chicago, where the Knights were headquartered, virtually crushed the organization. Local employers' associations successfully pooled funds to rid their factories of troublesome organizers. By 1890, membership had declined to less than 100,000. The wage system had triumphed.

The American Federation of Labor

The events of 1886 also signaled the rise of a very different kind of organization, the American Federation of Labor (AFL). Unlike the Knights, the AFL accepted the wage system. Following a strategy of "pure and simple union-ism," the AFL sought recognition of its union status to bar-gain with employers for better working conditions, higher wages, and shorter hours. In return, it offered compliant firms the benefit of amenable day-to-day relations with the most highly skilled wage earners. Only if companies refused to bargain in good faith would union members resort to strikes.

The new federation, with twelve national unions and 140,000 affiliated members in 1886, rapidly pushed ahead of the rival Knights by organizing craft workers. AFL pres-ident Samuel Gompers disregarded unskilled workers, racial minorities, and immigrants, believing they were impossible to organize and even unworthy of member-ship. He also believed in the "family wage," a wage paid to a male household head that would keep women and chil-dren at home and out of the factories. Women, Gompers insisted, did not belong in the workforce, where they would serve only to lower wages.

While Gompers advanced the interests of the "aristo-crats of labor," the rank-and-file often pursued broader

At the 1886 General Assembly of the Knights of Labor, which met in Richmond, Virginia, sixteen women attended as delegates. Elizabeth Rodgers, the first woman in Chicago to join the Knights and the first woman to serve as a master workman in a district assembly, attended with her two-week-old daughter. The convention established a Department of Women's Work and appointed Leonora M. Barry, a hosiery worker, as general investigator.

aims. Chicago's Central Labor Federation, for example, worked closely with urban reformers. Finding allies among women's clubs and church groups, within the state legislature, and even among some socially minded members of the business community, they cultivated an atmosphere of civic responsibility. The Illinois Factory Investigation Act of 1893 offered evidence of their hard work and patience: under its terms, unionists secured funds from the state legislature to monitor working conditions and, particularly, to improve the terrible conditions under which women and children worked in sweatshops.

Although the AFL represented only a small minority of working Americans—about 10 percent at the end of the century—local unions often played important roles in their communities. They may not have been able to slow the steady advance of mass production, which diminished the craft worker's autonomy and eliminated some of the most desirable jobs, but AFL members managed to make their presence felt. Local politicians courted their votes, and Labor Day, first celebrated in the 1880s, became a national holiday in 1894.

The New South

"Fifteen years have gone over" since the Civil War, journalist Whitelaw Reid complained, yet the South "still sits crushed, wretched, busy displaying and bemoaning her wounds." Physically and financially devastated by the war, the South remained economically stagnant, its per capita wealth only 27 percent of that of the northeastern states. While a few urban centers moved very slowly into the era of modern industry, the countryside receded into greater isolation and poverty. The southern economy in general was held back by dependence on northern finance capital, continued reliance on cotton production, and the legacy of slavery.

An Internal Colony

In the 1870s, a vocal and powerful new group of Southerners headed by Henry Woodfin Grady, editor of the *Atlanta Constitution*, insisted that the region enjoyed a great potential in its abundant natural resources of coal, iron, turpentine, tobacco, and lumber. Grady and his peers envisioned a "New South" where modern textile mills operated efficiently and profitably, close to the sources of raw goods, the expansive fields of cotton, and a plentiful and cheap supply of labor, unrestricted by unions or by legal limitations on the employment of children. Arguing against those planters who hoped to rejuvenate the agricultural economy by cultivating a few staple crops, this group forcefully promoted industrial development and welcomed northern investors.

Read the Document
William D. Grady, The New South (1887) at **www.myhistorylab.com**

Northern investors secured huge concessions from southern state legislatures, including land, forest, and mineral rights and large tax exemptions. Exploiting the incentives,

railroad companies laid more than 22,000 miles of new track, connecting the region to national markets and creating new cities. By 1890, a score of large railroad companies, centered mainly in New York, owned more than half of all the track in the South.

Northerners also employed various means to protect their investments from southern competition. By the late 1870s, southern merchants, with help from foreign investors, had begun to run iron factories around Birmingham, Alabama. Southern iron production was soon encroaching on the northeastern market. To stave off this competition, Andrew Carnegie ordered the railroads to charge higher freight fees to Birmingham's iron producers. After the turn of the century, the U.S. Steel Corporation simply bought out the local merchants and took over much of Birmingham's production.

The production of cotton textiles followed a similar course. Powerful merchants and large landowners, realizing that they could make high profits by controlling the cotton crop from field to factory, promoted the vertical integration of the cotton industry. The number of mills in the South grew from 161 in 1880 to 400 in 1900. Southern investors supplied large amounts of the capital for the industrial expansion and technological improvements. The latest machines ran the new mills, and the South boasted the first factory fully equipped with electricity. Production in the four leading cotton-manufacturing states—North Carolina, South Carolina, Georgia, and Alabama—skyrocketed, far outpacing the New England mills.

Recognizing the potential for great profit, many New England mill owners moved their operations to the South. By the 1920s, northern investors held much of the South's wealth, including the major textile mills, but returned through employment or social services only a small share of the profits to the region's people.

Beyond iron or steel and textiles, southern industry remained largely extractive and, like the South itself, rural. Turpentine and lumbering businesses pushed ever farther into diminishing pine forests, the sawmills and distilleries moving with them. Toward the end of the century, fruit canning and sugar refining flourished. For the most part, southern enterprises mainly produced raw materials for consumption or use in the North, thereby perpetuating the economic imbalance between the sections.

The governing role of capital investments from outside the region reinforced long-standing relationships. Even rapid industrialization—in iron, railroads, and textiles—did not carry the same consequences engendered in the North. The rise of the New South reinforced, rather than diminished, the region's status as the nation's internal colony.

Southern Labor

The advance of southern industry did little to improve the working lives of most African Americans, who made up more than one-third of the region's population. Although the majority continued to work in agriculture, large numbers found jobs in industries such as the railroad. In booming cities like Atlanta, they even gained skilled positions as bricklayers, carpenters, and painters. For the most part, however, African Americans were limited to unskilled, low-paying jobs. In the textile mills and cigarette factories, which employed both black and white workers, the workforce was rigidly segregated. African Americans were assigned mainly to janitorial jobs and rarely worked alongside the white workers who tended the machines. Nearly all African American women who earned wages did so as household workers; girls as young as ten worked as domestics or as nurses for white children.

Most trade unions refused membership to black workers. Locals of the all-white carpenters' union maintained a segregation policy so absolute that if too few members were available for a job, the union would send for out-of-town white workers rather than employ local members of the black carpenters' union. In an Atlanta mill in 1897, 1,400 white women operatives went on strike when the company proposed to hire two black spinners.

Only at rare moments did southern workers unite across racial lines. In the 1880s, the Knights of Labor briefly organized both black and white workers. But when white politicians and local newspapers began to raise the specter of black domination, the Knights were forced to retreat. Across the region, their assemblies collapsed. Other unions remained the exclusive preserve of white skilled workers.

Wages throughout the South were low for both black and white workers. Southern textile workers' wages were barely half those of New Englanders. In the 1880s, when investors enjoyed profits ranging from 30 percent to 75 percent, southern mill workers earned as little as twelve cents per hour. Black men earned at or below the poverty line of $300 per year, while black women rarely earned more than $120 and white women about $220 annually. The poorest paid workers were children, the mainstay of southern mill labor.

As industry expanded throughout the nation, so, too, did the number of children earning wages. This was especially so in the South. In 1896, only one in twenty Massachusetts mill workers was younger than sixteen, but one in four North Carolina cotton mill operatives was that age or younger. Traditions rooted in the agricultural economy reinforced the practice of using the labor of all family members, even the very young. Seasonal labor, such as picking crops or grinding sugarcane, put families on the move, making formal education all but impossible. Not until well into the twentieth century did compulsory school attendance laws effectively restrict child labor in the South.

A system of convict labor also thrived in the South. Bituminous coal mines and public work projects of all kinds, especially in remote areas, employed disciplinary

The processing of raw tobacco employed thousands of African American women, who sorted, stripped, stemmed, and hung tobacco leaves as part of the redrying process. After mechanization was introduced, white women took jobs as cigarette rollers, but black women kept the worst, most monotonous jobs in the tobacco factories. The women shown in this photograph are stemming tobacco in a Virginia factory while their white male supervisor oversees their labor.

methods and provided living and working conditions reminiscent of slavery. African Americans constituted up to 90 percent of the convict workforce. Transported and housed like animals—chained together by day and confined in portable cages at night—these workers suffered high mortality rates. White politicians expressed pride in what they called the "good roads movement"—the chief use of convict labor—as proof of regional progress.

The Transformation of Piedmont Communities

The impact of modern industry was nowhere greater than in the Piedmont, the region extending from southern Virginia and the central Carolinas into northern Alabama and Georgia. After 1870, long-established farms and plantations gave way to railroad tracks, textile factories, numerous mill villages, and a few sizable cities. Once the South's backcountry, the Piedmont surpassed New England in the production of yarn and cloth to stand first in the world.

Regulating the Conditions and Limiting the Hours of Labor in the State of Illinois

In the late 1880s, labor unions continued the shorter-hours movement spearheaded by the Knights of Labor and campaigned for legislation to limit hours and regulate working conditions. Reformer Florence Kelley drafted legislation that focused on the women and children who worked in sweatshops throughout Chicago. The state legislature passed this bill over the strong opposition of employers and appointed Kelley the first factory inspector in the state of Illinois. However, by 1895 the Illinois Supreme Court declared the eight-hour provision of the law unconstitutional.

• **Why did the Illinois Supreme Court reject Kelley's argument for limiting the hours of work for women?**

Florence Kelley's proposal for the Illinois Factory and Workshop Inspection Act, 1893

AN ACT to regulate the employment of women and children in manufacturing establishments, factories and work-shops, and to provide for the appointment of inspectors to enforce the same.

SECTION 1. No minor under eighteen years of age, and no woman shall be employed in any factory or work-shop more than eight hours in any one day or forty-eight hours in any one week.

SEC. 2. No process of making or finishing, altering or repairing for sale any coats, vests, trousers, overcoats, or any wearing apparel of any description whatsoever, intended for sale, shall be carried on in any dwelling by any woman or by any child under sixteen years of age.

SEC. 3. No child under fourteen years of age shall be employed in any manufacturing establishment, factory or work-shop within this state. It shall be the duty of every person, firm, corporation, agent or manager of any corporation employing children to keep a register in which shall be recorded the name, birthplace, age and place of residence of every person employed by him, her or them, under the age of sixteen years; and it shall be unlawful for any person, firm or corporation to hire or employ in any manufacturing establishment, factory or work-shop any child over the age of fourteen years and under the age of sixteen years, unless there is first provided and placed on file an affidavit made by the parent or guardian stating the age, date and place of birth of said child: if said child have no parent or guardian, then such affidavit shall be made by the child, which affidavit shall be kept on file by the employer

> "No child under fourteen years of age shall be employed in any manufacturing establishment . . ."

Rural poverty and the appeal of a new life encouraged many farm families to strike out for a mill town. Those with the least access to land and credit—mainly widows and their children and single women—were the first to go into the mills. Then families sent their children. Some families worked in the mills on a seasonal basis, between planting and harvesting. But more and more people abandoned the countryside entirely for what they called "public work."

A typical mill community was made up of rows of single-family houses, a small school, several churches, a company-owned store, and the home of the superintendent, who governed everyone's affairs. The manager of the King Cotton Mill in Burlington, North Carolina, not only kept the company's accounts in order, purchased raw material, and sold the finished yarn, but also bought Christmas presents for the workers' children. It was not unknown for a superintendent to prowl the and which said register and affidavit shall be produced for inspection on demand by the inspector, assistant inspector or any of the deputies appointed under this act. The factory inspector, assistant inspector and deputy inspectors shall have power to demand a certificate of physical fitness from some regular physician of good standing in the case of children who may appear to him or her physically unable to perform the labor at which they may be engaged, and shall have power to prohibit the employment of any minor that cannot obtain such a certificate.

SEC. 4. Every person, firm, or corporation, agent or manager of a corporation employing any woman or minor under the age of eighteen years in any manufacturing establishment, factory or work-shop, shall post, and keep posted, in a conspicuous place in every room where such help is employed, a printed notice stating the hours for each day of the week between which work is required of such persons, and in every room where children under sixteen years of age are employed, a list of their names with their ages.

SEC. 5 No child, under the age of sixteen years and over fourteen years of age, shall be employed in any manufacturing establishment, factory or workshop, who cannot read or write simple sentences in the English language, except during the vacation of the public schools in the city where such minor lives. . . .

SOURCE: *Report and Findings of the Joint Committee to Investigate the "Sweat Shop" System* (1893), pp. 139–40.

Factory Act Declared Unconstitutional: Opinion of Supreme Court of Illinois, March 18, 1895

It is not the nature of the things done, but the sex of the person doing then, which is made the basis of the claim that the act is a measure for the promotion of the public health. It is sought to sustain the act as an exercise of the police power upon the alleged ground that it is designed to protect woman on account of her sex and physique. It will not be denied that woman is entitled to the same rights, under the Constitution, to make contracts with reference to her labor as are secured thereby to men. The first section of the fourteenth amendment to the Constitution of the United States provides: "No State shall make or enforce any law which shall abridge the privileges or immunities of citizens of the United States, nor shall any State deprive *any person* of life, liberty or property without due process of law, nor deny to any persona within its jurisdiction the equal protection of the law."

It has been held that a woman is both a "citizen" and a "person" within the meaning of this section. . . . The privileges and immunities here referred to are in general, Protection by the government, with the right to acquire and possess property of every kind, and to pursue and obtain happiness and safety, subject, nevertheless, to such restraints as the government may prescribe for the general good of the whole. . . ." As a citizen, woman has the right to acquire and possess property of every kind. As a "person" she has the right to claim the benefit of the constitutional provision that she shall not be deprived of life, liberty or property without due process of law. Involved in these rights thus guaranteed to her is the right to make and enforce contracts. The law accords to her, as to every other citizen, the right to gain a livelihood by intelligence, honesty and industry in the arts, the sciences, the professions, or other vocations. Before the law, her right to a choice of vocations cannot be said to be denied or abridged on account of sex. . . .

SOURCE: *Third Annual Report of the Factory Inspectors of the State of Illinois for the Year Ending, December 15, 1895* (1896), Appendix A.

" . . . a woman is both a 'citizen' and a 'person' . . ."

neighborhood to see which families burned their lanterns past nine o'clock at night and, finding a violator, to knock on the door and tell the offenders to go to bed. Millworkers frequently complained that they had no private life at all. A federal report published shortly after the turn of the century concluded that "all the affairs of the village and the conditions of living of all the people are regulated entirely by the mill company. Practically speaking, the company owns everything and controls everything, and to a large extent controls everybody in the mill village."

Mill superintendents also relied on schoolteachers and clergy to set the tone of community life. They hired and paid the salaries of Baptist and Methodist ministers to preach a faith encouraging workers to be thrifty, orderly, temperate, and hardworking. The schools, similarly subsidized by the company, reinforced the lesson of moral and social discipline required of industrial life and encouraged students to follow their parents into the mill. It was mainly young children between six and eight years old who attended school. When more hands were needed in the mill, superintendents plucked out those youngsters and sent them to join their older brothers and sisters who were already at work.

Piedmont mill villages like Greenville, South Carolina, and Burlington, Charlotte, and Franklinville, North Carolina, nevertheless developed a cohesive character typical of isolated rural communities. The new residents maintained many aspects of their agricultural pasts, tilling small gardens and keeping chickens, pigs, and cows in their yards. Factory owners rarely paved roads or sidewalks or provided adequate sanitation. Mud, flies, and diseases such as typhoid fever flourished. Millworkers endured poverty and health hazards by strengthening community ties through intermarriage. Within a few generations, most of the village residents had, according to one study, "some connection to each other, however distant, by marriage," blood, or both.

The Industrial City

Before the Civil War, manufacturing had centered in the countryside, in new factory towns such as Lowell, Massachusetts, and Troy, New York. By the end of the nineteenth century, 90 percent of all manufacturing took place in cities. The metropolis stood at the center of the growing industrial economy, a magnet drawing raw material, capital, and labor, and a key distribution point for manufactured goods throughout the nation and worldwide. The industrial city became the home of nearly 20 million immigrants, mainly the so-called "new immigrants" from southern and eastern Europe, who hoped to escape famine, political upheaval, or religious persecution in their homelands or simply make a better life for themselves and their families.

Populating the City

The population of cities grew at double the rate of the nation's population as a whole. In 1860, only sixteen cities had more than 50,000 residents. By 1890, one-third of all Americans were city dwellers. Eleven cities claimed more than 250,000 people (see Table 19.1).

The nation's largest cities—New York, Chicago, Philadelphia, St. Louis, Boston, and Baltimore—achieved international fame for the size and diversity of their populations. Many of their new residents had migrated from rural communities within the United States. Between 1870 and 1910, an average of nearly 7,000 African Americans moved north each year, hoping to escape the poverty and oppression in the South and to find better-paying jobs. By the end of the century, nearly 80 percent of African Americans in the North lived in urban areas.

The major source of urban growth in the late nineteenth century were immigrants and their children. Most of those in the first wave of immigration, before the Civil War, had settled in the countryside. In contrast, the so-called new immigrants, who came primarily from eastern and southern Europe, populated the industrial cities. In 1880, San Francisco claimed the highest proportion of foreign born (45 percent), although not the largest number. By the turn of the century, Chicago had more Germans than all but a few German cities and more Poles than most Polish cities; New York had more Italians than a handful of the largest Italian cities, and Boston had nearly as many Irish as Dublin. In almost every group except the Irish, men outnumbered women (see Map 19.2).

Like rural migrants, immigrants headed for the American city to take advantage of the expanding opportunities for employment. While many hoped to build a new home in the land of plenty, many others intended to work hard, save money, and return to their families in the Old Country. In the 1880s, for example, nearly half of all Italian, Greek, and Serbian men returned to their native lands. Others could not return to their homelands or did not wish to. Jews, for instance, had emigrated to escape persecution in Russia and Russian-dominated Polish and Romanian lands. A Yiddish writer later called this generation the "Jews without Jewish memories. . . . They shook them off in the boat when they came across the seas. They emptied out their memories."

Of all groups, Jews had the most experience with urban life. Forbidden to own land in most parts of Europe and boxed into *shtetls* (villages), Jews had also formed thriving urban communities in Vilna, Berlin, London, and Vienna. Many had worked in garment manufacturing, in

TABLE 19.1

A Growing Urban Population				
	1870	1880	1890	1900
U.S. population	35,558,000	50,156,000	62,947,000	75,995,000
Urban population	9,902,000	14,130,000	22,106,000	30,160,000
Percent urban	25.7	28.2	35.1	39.7
Percent rural	74.3	71.8	64.9	60.3

Note that during each decade, the U.S. population as a whole grew between 20 and 30 percent. Figures in the table have been rounded to the nearest thousand.

SOURCE: From *The Gilded Age* edited by Charles W. Calhown. © 1996. Reprinted by permission of Rowman & Littlefield.

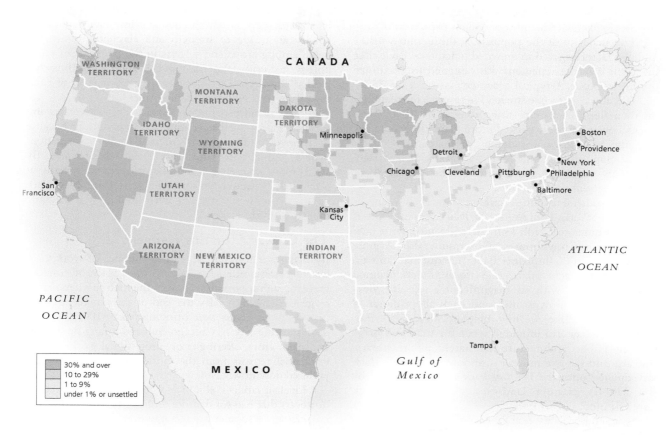

MAP 19.2 Population of Foreign Birth by Region, 1880 European immigrants after the Civil War settled primarily in the industrial districts of the northern Midwest and parts of the Northeast. French Canadians continued to settle in Maine, Cubans in Florida, and Mexicans in the Southwest, where earlier immigrants had established thriving communities.

SOURCE: From LORD. *Historical Atlas of the United States,* 1E. © 1962 Wadsworth, a part of Cengage Learning, Inc. Reproduced by permission. www.cengage.com/permission.

London's East End, for example, and followed a path to American cities like New York, Rochester, Philadelphia, or Chicago where the needle trades flourished.

Other groups, the majority coming from rural parts of Europe, sought out their kinfolk in American cities, where they could most easily find housing and employment. Bohemians settled largely in Chicago, Pittsburgh, and Cleveland. French Canadians emigrated from Quebec and settled almost exclusively in New England and upper New York State. Cubans, themselves often first- or second-generation immigrants from Spain, moved to Ybor City, a section of Tampa, Florida, to work in cigar factories. Still other groups tended toward cities dominated by fishing, shoemaking, or even glassblowing, a craft carried directly from the Old Country. Italians, the most numerous among the new immigrants, settled mainly in northeastern cities, laying railroad track, excavating subways, and erecting buildings.

Resettlement in an American city did not necessarily mark the end of the immigrants' travels. Newcomers, both native-born and immigrants, moved frequently from one neighborhood to another and from one city to another. As manufacturing advanced outward from the city center, working populations followed. American cities experienced a total population turnover three or four times during each decade of the last half of the century.

The Urban Landscape

Faced with a population explosion and an unprecedented building boom, the cities encouraged the creation of many beautiful and useful structures, including commercial offices, sumptuous homes, and efficient public services. At the same time, open space decreased as builders leveled hills, filled ponds, and pulled down any farms or houses in the way. Factories often occupied the best sites, typically near waterways, where goods could be easily transported and chemical wastes dumped. City officials usually lacked any master plan, save the idea of endless expansion.

The majority of the population, those who worked in dingy factories, lived in crowded tenements. Built after the Civil War, the tenement was designed to maximize the use of space. A typical tenement sat on a lot 25 by 100 feet and rose to five stories. There were four families on each floor, each with three rooms. By 1890, New York's Lower East Side packed more than 700 people per acre into back-to-back buildings, producing one of the highest population densities in the world. In Chicago, tenements were scattered, typically located near work sites throughout the city.

At the other end of the social scale, Chicago's Michigan Avenue, New York's Fifth Avenue, St. Paul's Summit Avenue, and San Francisco's Nob Hill fairly gleamed with new mansions and townhouses. Commonwealth Avenue marked Boston's fashionable Back Bay district, built on a filled-in 450-acre tidal flat. State engineers planned this community, with its magnificent boulevard, uniform five-story brownstones, and back alleys designed for deliveries. Like wealthy neighborhoods in other cities, Back Bay also provided space for the city's magnificent public architecture: its stately public library, fine arts and science museums, and orchestra hall. Back Bay opened onto the Fenway Park system designed by the nation's premier landscape architect, Frederick Law Olmsted.

The industrial city established a new style of commercial and civic architecture. Using fireproof materials, expanded foundations, and internal metal construction, the era's talented architects focused on the factory, office building, and department store. They fashioned hundreds of buildings from steel, sometimes decorating them with elaborate wrought-iron facades. The office building could rise seven, ten, even twenty stories high, and with the invention of the safety elevator, people and goods could easily be moved vertically.

Architects played a key role in the late nineteenth-century City Beautiful movement. Influenced by American wealth and its enhanced role in the global economy, they turned to the monumental or imperial style common in European cities, laying grand concrete boulevards at enormous public cost. New sports amphitheaters spread pride in a city's accomplishments. New schools, courthouses, capitol buildings, hospitals, museums, and huge new art galleries, museums, and concert halls promoted urban excitement as well as cultural uplift. The Art Institute of Chicago, for example, moved into its neoclassical Beaux-Arts building on Michigan Avenue in 1893.

The city inspired other architectural marvels. Opened in 1883, the Brooklyn Bridge won wide acclaim as the most original American construction. Designed by John Roebling and his son Washington Roebling, the bridge was considered an aesthetic and practical wonder. Its soaring piers, elegant arches, and intricate steel cables convey an image of strength and elasticity, inspiring a belief among artists and writers in the potential of technology to unite function and beauty. The Brooklyn Bridge also helped to speed the transformation of rural townships into suburban communities.

Like the railroad, but on a smaller scale, streetcars and elevated railroads changed business dramatically, because they moved traffic of many different kinds—information, people, and goods—faster and farther than before. By 1895, more than 800 communities operated systems of electrically powered cars or trolleys. In 1902, New York opened its subway system, which would grow to become the largest in the nation.

The City and the Environment

By making it possible for a great number of workers to live in communities distant from their place of employment, mass transportation allowed the metropolitan region to grow dramatically. By the end of the nineteenth century, suburban trains were bringing nearly 100,000 riders daily into the city of Chicago. Suburbs sprang up outside the major cities, offering many professional workers quiet residential retreats from the city's busy and increasingly polluted downtown.

Electric trolleys eliminated the tons of waste from horsecars that had for decades fouled city streets. The new rail systems also increased congestion and created new safety hazards for pedestrians. During the 1890s, 600 people were killed each year by Chicago's trains. Elevated trains, designed to avoid these problems, placed entire communities under the shadow of noisy and rickety wooden platforms.

Modern water and sewer systems constituted a hidden city of pipes and wires, mirroring the growth of the visible city above ground. These advances, which brought indoor plumbing to most homes, did not, however, eradicate serious environmental or health problems. Most cities continued to dump sewage into nearby bodies of water. Moreover, most municipal governments established separate clean-water systems through the use of reservoirs rather than outlawing upriver dumping by factories. Downriver communities began to complain about the unendurable stench from polluted rivers and streams.

The unrestricted burning of coal to fuel the railroads and to heat factories and homes after 1880 greatly intensified urban air pollution. Noise levels continued to rise in the most compacted living and industrial areas. Overcrowded conditions and inadequate sanitary facilities bred tuberculosis, smallpox, and scarlet fever, among other contagious diseases. Children's diseases like whooping cough and measles spread rapidly through poor neighborhoods. Only after the turn of the century, amid an intensive campaign against municipal corruption, did laws and

In his watercolor *The Bowery at Night*, painted in 1885, W. Louis Sonntag Jr. shows a New York City scene transformed by electric light. Electricity transformed the city in other ways as well, as seen in the electric streetcars and elevated railroad.

administrative practices address the serious problems of public health (see Chapter 21).

Meanwhile, the distance between the city and the countryside narrowed. Naturalists had hoped for large open spaces—a buffer zone—to preserve farmland and wild areas, protect future water supplies, and diminish regional air pollution. But soon the industrial landscape invaded the countryside. Nearby rural lands not destined for private housing or commercial development became sites for water treatment and sewage plants, garbage dumps, and graveyards—services essential to the city's growing population.

The Rise of Consumer Society

The growth of industry and the spread of cities promoted—and depended on—the consumption of mass-produced goods. During the final third of the nineteenth century, the standard of living climbed, although unevenly and erratically. Real wages (pay in relation to the cost of living) rose, fostering improvements in nutrition, clothing, and housing. Meanwhile, prices dropped. More and cheaper products came into the reach of all but the very poor. Food from the farms became more abundant and varied—grains for bread or beer; poultry, pork, and beef; fresh fruits and vegetables from California. Although many Americans continued to acknowledge the moral value of hard work, thrift, and self-sacrifice, the explosion of consumer goods and services promoted sweeping changes in behavior and beliefs, although in vastly and increasingly different ways.

"Conspicuous Consumption"

Labeled the "Gilded Age" by humorist and social critic Mark Twain, the era following the Civil War favored the growth of a new business class that pursued both money and leisure and formed national networks to consolidate their power. Business leaders built diverse stock portfolios and often served simultaneously on the boards of several corporations. Similarly, they intertwined their interests by joining the same religious, charitable, athletic, and professional societies. Their wives and children vacationed together in the sumptuous new seashore and mountain resorts, while they themselves made deals in the exclusive social clubs and on the golf links of suburban country clubs. Just as Dun and Bradstreet ranked the leading corporations, the Social Register identified the 500 families that controlled most of the nation's wealth.

According to economist and social critic Thorstein Veblen, the rich had created a new style of "conspicuous consumption." The Chicago mansion of real estate tycoon Potter Palmer, for example, was constructed without exterior doorknobs. Not only could no one enter uninvited, but a visitor's calling card supposedly passed through the hands of twenty-seven servants before admittance was allowed. A vice president of the Chicago & Northwestern Railroad, Perry H. Smith built his marble palace in the style of the Greek Renaissance. Its ebony staircase was trimmed in gold, its butler's pantry equipped with faucets not only for hot and cold water but also for iced champagne. The women who oversaw these

View the Image
Residence of Andrew Carnegie at **www.myhistorylab.com**

elaborate households served as measures of their husbands' status, according to Veblen, by adorning themselves in jewels, furs, and dresses of the latest Paris design.

Conspicuous consumption reached new heights of extravagance. In New York, wealthy families hosted dinner parties for their dogs or pet monkeys, dressing the animals in fancy outfits for the occasion. Railroad magnate "Diamond Jim" Brady commonly enjoyed after-theater snacks at the city's "lobster palaces," where he consumed vast quantities of food—oysters for an appetizer, two soups, fish, a main dinner of beef and vegetables, punches and sherbet on the side, dessert, coffee, and quarts of orange juice.

Toward the end of the century, the wealthy added a dramatic public dimension to the "high life." New York's Waldorf-Astoria hotel, which opened in 1897, incorporated the grandeur of European royalty but with an important difference. Because rich Americans wanted to be watched, the elegantly appointed corridors and restaurants were visible to the public through huge windows. The New York rich also established a unique custom to welcome the New Year: they opened wide the curtains of their Fifth Avenue mansions so that passersby could marvel at the elegant decor.

The wealthy became the leading patrons of the arts as well as the chief procurers of art treasures from Europe and Asia. They provided the bulk of funds for the new symphonies, operas, and ballet companies, which soon rivaled those of Continental Europe. An acoustical marvel and the largest building in the nation at the time, the Chicago Auditorium Building, built in 1888, served as home to the symphony orchestra and civic opera.

●●—[Read the Document
History Bookshelf: Veblen, Theory of the Leisure Class at
www.myhistorylab.com

Self-Improvement and the Middle Class

A new middle class, very different from its predecessor, formed during the last half of the century. The older middle class comprised the owners or superintendents of small businesses, doctors, lawyers, teachers, and ministers and their families. The new middle class included these professionals but also the growing number of salaried employees—the managers, technicians, clerks, and engineers who worked in the complex web of corporations and government. Long hours of labor earned their families a modest status and sufficient income to live securely in style and comfort.

By the end of the century, many middle-class families were nestled in suburban retreats far from the noise, filth, and dangers of the city. This peaceful domestic setting, with its manicured lawns and well-placed shrubs, afforded both privacy and rejuvenation as well as the separation of business from leisure and the breadwinner from his family for most of the day. Assisted by modern transportation systems, men often traveled one to two hours each day, five or six days a week, to their city offices and back again. Women and children stayed behind.

Middle-class women devoted a large part of their day to care of the home. They frequently employed one or two servants, but relied increasingly on the many new appliances to get their work done. Improvements in the kitchen stove, such as the conversion from wood fuel to gas, saved a lot of time. Yet, simultaneously, with the widespread circulation of cookbooks and recipes in newspapers and magazines, as well as the availability of new foods, the preparation of meals became more complex and time-consuming. New devices such as the egg-beater speeded some familiar tasks, but the era's fancy culinary practices offset any gains in saving time. Similarly, the new carpet sweepers surpassed the broom in efficiency, but the fashionable high-napped carpeting demanded more care. Thus, rather than diminishing with

Taken from J. B. Legg's architecture book, this page illustrates the ideal suburban home. His book, published in 1876, was aimed at the prospering middle class.

technological innovation, household work expanded to fill the time available.

By the end of the century, though, middle-class women had added shopping to their list of household chores. They took charge of the household budget and purchased an ever-expanding range of machine-made goods, packaged foods, manufactured clothing, and personal luxuries. With the rise of department stores, which catered specifically to them, shopping combined work and pleasure and became a major pastime for women.

Almost exclusively white, Anglo-Saxon, and Protestant, the new middle class embraced "culture" not for purposes of conspicuous consumption but as a means of self-improvement. Whole families visited the new museums and art galleries. One of the most cherished institutions, the annual season of lectures at the Chautauqua campgrounds in upstate New York, brought thousands of families together in pursuit of knowledge of literature and the fine arts. The middle class also provided the bulk of patrons for the new public libraries.

Middle-class families applied the same standards to their leisure activities. What one sporting-goods entrepreneur rightly called the "gospel of exercise" involved men

●● Read the Document
Frances E. Willard, On Riding the Bicycle (1895) at **www.myhistorylab.com**

and women in calisthenics and outdoor activities, not so much for pleasure as for physical and mental discipline. Hiking was a favorite among both men and women and required entirely new outfits: for women, loose upper garments and skirts short enough to prevent dragging; for men, rugged outerwear and jaunty hats. Soon men and women began camping out, with almost enough amenities to re-create a middle-class home in the woods. Roller-skating and ice-skating, which became crazes shortly after the Civil War, took place in specially designed rinks in almost every major town. By the 1890s, the "safety" bicycle had also been marketed. It replaced the large-wheel variety, which was difficult to keep upright. A good-quality "bike" cost $100 and, like the piano, was a symbol of middle-class status. In 1895, Chicago hosted thirty-three cycle clubs comprising nearly 10,000 members.

Leisure became the special province of middle-class childhood. Removed from factories and shops and freed from many domestic chores, children enjoyed creative play and physical activity. The toy market boomed, and lower printing prices helped children's literature flourish. Uplifting classics such as *Little Women* and *Black Beauty* were popular.

Life in the Streets

Immigrants often weighed the material abundance they found in the United States against their memories of the Old Country. One could "live better" here, but only by working much harder. In letters home, immigrants described the riches of the new country but warned

friends and relatives not to send weaklings, who would surely die of stress and strain amid the alien and intense commercialism of American society. Embittered German immigrants called their new land *Malhuerica*, "misfortune"; Jews called it *Ama Reka*, Hebrew for "without soul"; and Slavs referred to it as *Dollaryka*.

Many newcomers, having little choice about their place of residence, were concentrated in urban districts marked off by racial or ethnic lines. In San Francisco, city ordinances prevented Chinese from operating laundries in most of the city's neighborhoods, and the city's schools excluded their children. In the 1880s, Chinese San Franciscans, representing 10 percent of the city's population, crowded into a dozen blocks of restaurants, shops, and small factories known as Chinatown. In Los Angeles and San Antonio, Mexicans lived in distinctive barrios. In most cities, African American families were similarly compelled to remain in the dingiest, most crime-ridden, and dangerous sections of town.

The working-class home did not necessarily ensure privacy or offer protection from the dangers of the outside world. In the tenements, families often shared their rooms with other families or paying boarders. During the summer heat, adults, children, and boarders alike competed for a sleeping place on the fire escape or roof, and throughout the year, noise resounded through paper-thin walls. But so complex and varied were income levels and social customs that no single pattern emerged. Chicago's Slovaks, Lithuanians, and Poles, for example, frequently took in boarders, yet Bohemians rarely did. Neither did the skilled iron rollers who worked at the Carnegie Steel Company in Homestead, Pennsylvania. These well-paid craft workers often owned their own homes, boasting parlors and even imported Belgian carpets. At the other extreme, Italian immigrants, who considered themselves fortunate to get work with a shovel, usually lived in overcrowded rented apartments, just a paycheck away from eviction.

Whether it was a small cottage or a tenement flat, the working-class home involved women and children in routines of household labor without the aid of new mechanical devices. In addition to cooking and cleaning, women used their cramped domestic space for work that provided a small income. They gathered their children—and their husbands after a hard day's labor—to sew garments, wrap cigars, string beads, or paint vases for a contractor who paid them by the piece. And they cooked and cleaned for the boarders whose rent supplemented the family income.

Despite working people's slim resources, their combined buying power created new and important markets for consumer goods. Often they bought shoddy replicas of products sold to the middle class: cheaper canned goods, inferior cuts of meat, and partially spoiled fruit. Several leading clothing manufacturers specialized in inexpensive ready-to-wear items, usually copied from patterns designed for wealthier consumers but constructed hastily

The intersection of Orchard and Hester Streets on New York's Lower East Side, photographed ca. 1905. Unlike the middle classes, who worked and played hidden away in offices and private homes, the Jewish lower-class immigrants who lived and worked in this neighborhood spent the greater part of their lives on the streets.

from flimsy materials. Patent medicines for ailments caused by working long periods in cramped conditions sold well in working-class communities, where money for doctors was scarce.

The close quarters of the urban neighborhood allowed immigrants to preserve many Old World customs. In immigrant communities such as Chicago's German North Side, Pittsburgh's Poletown, New York's Lower East Side, or San Francisco's Chinatown, people usually spoke their native language while visiting friends and relatives. The men might play cards while women and children gathered in the stairwell or on the front stoop to trade stories. In good weather, they walked and talked, an inexpensive pastime common in European cities. No organization was as important as the fraternal society, which sponsored social clubs and provided insurance benefits. Social organizations, known as *huiguan*, were especially important in preserving clan and dialect among the largely male unmarried population of Chinese San Francisco. Immigrants also re-created Old World religious institutions such as the temple, church, or synagogue, or secular institutions such as German family-style saloons or Russian Jewish tearooms. Chinese theaters, in inexpensive daily and nightly performances, presented dramas depicting historical events or explicating moral teachings and thereby preserved much of Chinese native culture. Immigrants also replicated their native cuisine and married, baptized children, and buried their dead according to Old World customs.

In the cosmopolitan cities, immigrants, by being innovative entrepreneurs as well as the best customers, helped to shape the emerging popular culture. German

immigrants, for example, created Tin Pan Alley, the center of the popular music industry. They also became the first promoters of ragtime, which found its way north from Storyville, the red-light district of New Orleans. Created by African American and Creole bands, ragtime captivated the teenage offspring of immigrants who rushed to the new dance halls.

When developers realized that "wholesome fun" for the masses could pay better than upper-class leisure or lower-class vice, in 1895 they decided to transform Coney Island into a magnificent seaside park filled with ingenious amusements such as water slides, mechanized horse races, carousels, roller coasters, and fun houses. On the rides or at the nearby beach, young men and women could easily meet apart from their parents, cast off their inhibitions, and enjoy a hug or kiss. Or they could simply stroll through the grounds, looking at exotic performers, enjoying make-believe trips to the Far East or even the moon, entranced by fantastic towers, columns, minarets, and lagoons lit up at night to resemble dreams rather than reality. At Coney Island or at Riverview, Chicago's oldest amusement park, located on the city's North Side, millions of working-class people enjoyed cheap thrills that offset the hardships of their working lives.

Cultures in Conflict, Culture in Common

The new commercial entertainments gave Americans from various backgrounds more in common than they would otherwise have had. On New York's Lower East Side, for instance, theaters blossomed with dramas that

Broadway would adopt years later, while children dreamed of going "uptown" where the popular songs they heard on the streets were transcribed onto sheet music and sold in stores throughout the city. Even so, just as the changes in production fostered conflict in the forms of strikes and workers' protests, so, too, did the accompanying changes in the daily life of the community. Competing claims to the resources of the new urban, industrial society, such as public schools and urban parks, became more intense as the century moved to a close.

Education

Business and civic leaders realized that the welfare of society depended on an educated population, one possessing the skills and knowledge required to keep both industry and government running. In the last three decades of the nineteenth century, the idea of universal free schooling, at least for white children, took hold. Kindergartens in particular flourished. St. Louis, Missouri, opened the first public school kindergarten in 1873, and by the turn of the century, more than 4,000 similar programs throughout the country enrolled children between the ages of three and seven.

Public high schools, which were rare before the Civil War, also increased in number, from 160 in 1870 to 6,000 by the end of the century. In Chicago alone, average daily attendance multiplied sixfold. Despite this spectacular growth, which was concentrated in urban industrial areas, as late as 1890 only 4 percent of children between the ages of fourteen and seventeen were enrolled in school, the majority of them girls planning to become teachers or office workers (see Figure 19.1). Most high schools continued to serve mainly the middle class. In 1893, the National Education Association reaffirmed the major purpose of the nation's high schools as preparation for college, rather than for work in trades or industry, and endorsed a curriculum of rigorous training in the classics, such as Latin, Greek, and ancient history. The expected benefits of this kind of education rarely outweighed the immediate needs of working-class families who depended on their children's wages. At the end of the century, 50 percent of the children in Chicago between the ages of ten and twelve were working for wages.

Higher education also expanded along several lines. Agricultural colleges formed earlier in the century developed into institutes of technology and took their places alongside the prestigious liberal arts colleges. To extend learning to the "industrial classes," Representative

●•▶[Read the Document
Morrill Act (1862) at
www.myhistorylab.com

Justin Morrill (R., Vermont) sponsored the Morrill Federal Land Grant Act of 1862, which funded a system of state colleges and universities for teaching agriculture and mechanics "without excluding other scientific and classic studies."

Meanwhile, established private institutions like Harvard, Yale, Princeton, and Columbia grew with the

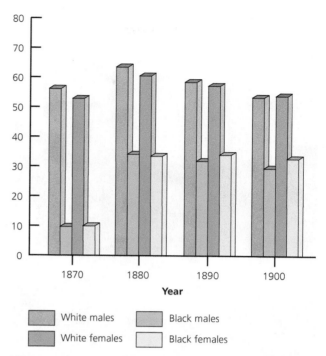

FIGURE 19.1 School Enrollment of 5- to 19-Year-Olds, 1870–1900 In the final decades of the nineteenth century, elementary and high school enrollments grew across the board, but especially so for children of color and for girls.

SOURCE: U.S. Department of Commerce, Bureau of the Census, *Historical Statistics of the United States, Colonial Times to 1970.* U.S. Department of Education, Office of Educational Research and Improvement.

help of huge endowments from business leaders. By 1900, sixty-three Catholic colleges were serving mainly the children of immigrants from Ireland and eastern and southern Europe. Still, while the overall number of colleges and universities grew from 563 in 1870 to nearly 1,000 by 1910, only 3 percent of the college-age population took advantage of these new opportunities. One of the most important developments occurred in the area of research and graduate studies, pioneered in this country in 1876 by the Johns Hopkins University. By the end of the century, several American universities, including Stanford University and the University of Chicago, offered advanced degrees in the arts and sciences.

This expansion benefited women, who previously had little access to higher education. After the Civil War, a number of women's colleges were founded, beginning in 1865 with Vassar, which set the academic standard for the remainder of the century. Smith and Wellesley followed in 1875 and Bryn Mawr in 1885. By the end of the century, 125 women's colleges offered a first-rate education comparable to that given to men at Harvard, Yale, or Princeton. Meanwhile, coeducation grew at an even faster rate; by 1890, 47 percent of the nation's colleges and universities admitted women. The proportion of women

George Washington Carver (1864–1943), who was born into slavery, had been invited by Booker T. Washington to direct agricultural research at the Tuskegee Institute in Alabama. A leader in development of agriculture in the New South, Carver promoted crop diversification to rejuvenate soil that was depleted by the continuous planting of cotton. He also encouraged the cultivation of alternative, high-protein crops such as peanuts and soybeans. He designed his programs in sustainable agriculture mainly for African American farmers and sharecroppers rather than for commercial purposes.

college students changed dramatically. Women constituted 21 percent of undergraduate enrollments in 1870, 32 percent in 1880, and 40 percent in 1910.

An even greater number of women enrolled in vocational courses. Normal schools, which offered one- or two-year programs for women who planned to become elementary school teachers, developed a collegiate character after the Civil War and had become accredited state teachers' colleges by the end of the century. Other institutions, many founded by middle-class philanthropists, also prepared women for vocations. For example, the first training school for nurses opened in Boston in 1873, followed in 1879 by a diet kitchen that taught women to become cooks in the city's hospitals. Founded in 1877, the Women's Educational and Industrial Union offered a multitude of classes to Boston's wage-earning women, ranging from elementary French and German to drawing, watercolor, and oil and china paintings; to dressmaking and millinery,

stenography and typing; as well as crafts less familiar to women, such as upholstering, cabinetmaking, and carpentry. In the early 1890s, when the entering class at a large women's college like Vassar still averaged fewer than 100, the Boston Women's Educational and Industrial Union reported that its staff of 83 served an estimated 1,500 clients per day. By that time, one of its most well-funded programs was a training school for domestic servants.

The leaders of the business community had also begun to promote manual training for working-class and immigrant boys. Trade unionists often opposed this development, preferring their own methods of apprenticeship to training programs they could not control. But local associations of merchants and manufacturers lobbied hard for "industrial education" and raised funds to supplement the public school budget. In 1884, the Chicago Manual Training School opened, teaching "shop work" along with a few academic subjects, and by 1895, all elementary and high schools in the city offered courses that trained boys for future jobs in industry and business.

The expansion of education did not benefit all Americans or benefit them all in the same way. Because African Americans were often excluded from colleges attended by white students, special colleges were founded shortly after the Civil War. All-black Atlanta and Fisk Universities both soon offered rigorous curricula in the liberal arts. Other institutions, such as Hampton, founded in 1868, specialized in vocational training, mainly in manual trades. Educator Booker T. Washington encouraged African Americans to resist "the craze for Greek and Latin learning" and to strive for practical instruction. In 1881, he founded the Tuskegee Institute in Alabama to provide industrial education and moral uplift. By the turn of the century, Tuskegee enrolled 1,400 men and women in more than thirty different vocational courses, including special cooking classes for homemakers and domestic servants. Black colleges, including Tuskegee, trained so many teachers that by the century's end, the majority of black schools were staffed by African Americans.

The nation's educational system was becoming more inclusive and yet more differentiated. The majority of children attended school for several years or more. At the same time, students were tracked—by race, gender, and class—to fill particular roles in an industrial society.

Leisure and Public Space

Most large cities set aside open land for leisure-time use by residents. New York's Central Park opened for ice-skating in 1858, providing a model for urban park systems across the United States. In 1869, planners in Chicago secured funds to create a citywide system comprising six interconnected large parks, and within a few years, Lincoln Park, on the city's north side, was attracting crowds of nearly 30,000 on Sundays. These parks were rolling expanses, cut across by streams and pathways and footbridges and set off by groves of trees, ornamental shrubs, and neat flower gardens. According to the designers' vision, the urban middle class might find here a respite from the stresses of modern life. To ensure this possibility, posted regulations forbade many activities, ranging from walking on the grass to gambling, picnicking, or ball playing without permission, to speeding in carriages.

The working classes had their own ideas about the use of parks and open land in their communities. Trapped in overcrowded tenements or congested neighborhoods, they wanted space for sports, picnics, and lovers' trysts. Young people openly defied ordinances that prohibited play on the grassy knolls, while their elders routinely voted against municipal bonds that did not include funds for more recreational space. Immigrant ward representatives on the Pittsburgh City Council, for instance, argued that band shells for classical music meant little to their constituents, while spaces suitable for sports meant much.

Eventually, most park administrators set aside some sections for playgrounds and athletic fields and others for public gardens and band shells. Yet intermittent conflicts erupted. The Worcester, Massachusetts, park system, for example, allowed sports leagues to schedule events but prohibited pickup games. This policy gave city officials more control over the use of the park for outdoor recreation but at the same time forced many ball-playing boys into the streets. When working-class parents protested, city officials responded by instituting programs of supervised play to the further dismay of the children.

Public drinking of alcoholic beverages, especially on Sunday, provoked similar disputes. "Blue laws," forbidding businesses to open on Sunday, were rigidly enforced when it came to neighborhood taverns, while large firms like the railroads enjoyed exemptions. Although civil leaders hoped to discourage Sunday drinking by sponsoring alternative events, such as free organ recitals and other concerts, many working people, especially beer-loving German immigrants, continued to treat Sunday as their one day of relaxation. In Chicago, when not riding the streetcars to the many beer gardens and taverns that thrived on the outskirts, Germans gathered in large numbers for picnics in the city's parks.

Toward the end of the century, many park administrators relaxed the rules and expanded the range of permitted activities. By that time, large numbers of the middle class had become sports enthusiasts and pressured municipal governments to turn meadowlands into tennis courts and golfing greens. In the 1890s, bicycling brought many women into the parks. Still, not all city residents enjoyed these facilities. Officials in St. Louis, for example, barred African Americans from the city's grand Forest Park and set aside the smaller Tandy Park for their use. After challenging this policy in court, African Americans won a few concessions, such as the right to picnic at any time in Forest Park and to use the golf course on Monday mornings.

National Pastimes

Toward the end of the century, the younger members of the urban middle class had begun to find common ground in lower-class pastimes, especially ragtime music. Introduced to many Northerners by the African American composer Scott Joplin at the Chicago World's Fair of 1893, "rag" quickly became the staple of entertainment in the new cabarets and nightclubs. Middle-class urban dwellers began to seek out ragtime bands and congregated in nightclubs and even on the rooftops of posh hotels to listen and dance and even to drink.

Vaudeville, the most popular form of commercial entertainment since the 1880s, also bridged middle- and working-class tastes. Drawing on a variety-show tradition of singers, dancers, comedians, jugglers, and acrobats, who had entertained Americans since colonial days, "vaude" became a big business that made ethnic and racial stereotypes and the daily frustrations of city life into major topics of amusement. Vaudeville palaces—ten in New York, six in Philadelphia, five in Chicago, and at least one in every other large city—attracted huge, "respectable" crowds that sampled between twenty and thirty dramatic, musical, and comedy acts averaging fifteen minutes each. Sunday matinees were especially popular with women and children.

Sports, however, outdistanced all other commercial entertainments in appealing to all kinds of fans and managing to create a sense of national community. No doubt the most popular parks in the United States were the expanses of green surrounded by grandstands and marked by their unique diamond shape—the baseball fields. Baseball clubs formed in many cities, and shortly after the Civil War, traveling teams with regular schedules made baseball a professional sport. The formation of the National League in 1876 encouraged other spectator sports, but for generations baseball remained the most popular.

Rowdy behavior gave the game a working-class ambience. Team owners, themselves often proprietors of local breweries, counted heavily on beer sales in the parks. Having to contend with hundreds of drunken fans, officials maintained order only with great difficulty. To attract more subdued middle-class fans, the National League raised admission prices, banned the sale of alcohol, and observed Sunday blue laws. Catering to a working-class audience, the American Association kept the price of admission low, sold liquor, and played ball on Sunday.

Baseball, like many other sports, soon became incorporated into the larger business economy. In Chicago, local merchants, such as Marshall Field, supported teams, and by the end of the 1860s there were more than fifty company-sponsored teams playing in the local leagues. By

BOSTON NATIONAL BLOOMER GIRL'S BASE BALL CLUB. L. J. GALBREATH, Originator and Owner.

By the 1890s, Bloomer Girls baseball teams had organized in many parts of the country. To fill out a season, many of these clubs played against men's teams. To fill out a lineup, many of these women's clubs included male players, who at first wore wigs and women's clothing. By the early twentieth century, when this photograph was taken, men played openly in regulation uniforms. The last Bloomer Girl club disbanded in the 1930s. This photograph shows the Boston club with owner L. J. Galbreath.

1870, a Chicago Board of Trade team emerged as the city's first professional club, the White Stockings. Capitalized as a joint stock company, the White Stockings soon succeeded in recruiting a star pitcher from the Boston Red Stockings, Albert Spalding, who eventually became manager and then president of the team. Spalding also came to see baseball as a source of multiple profits. He procured the exclusive rights to manufacture the official ball and the rule book, while producing large varieties of other sporting equipment. Meanwhile, he built impressive baseball parks in Chicago, with seating for 10,000 and special private boxes above the grandstands for the wealthy.

Spalding also succeeded in tightening the rules of participation in the sport. In 1879, he dictated the "reserve clause," which prevented players from negotiating a better deal and leaving the team that originally signed them. He encouraged his player-manager "Cap" Anson to forbid the White Stockings from playing against any team with an African American member. The firing of Moses "Fleet" Walker, an African American, from the Cincinnati Red Stockings in 1884 marked the first time

the color line had been drawn in a major professional sport. Effectively excluded, African Americans organized their own traveling teams. In the 1920s, they formed the Negro Leagues, which produced some of the nation's finest ball players.

Players occasionally organized to regain control over their sport. They frequently complained about low wages and arbitrary rules, and like the Knights of Labor in the 1880s, they formed their own league, the Brotherhood of Professional Base Ball Players, with profits divided between participants and investors. This effort failed, partly because fans would not desert the established leagues, but mostly because successful baseball franchises demanded large quantities of capital. American sports had become big business.

As attendance continued to grow, the enthusiasm for baseball straddled major social divisions, bringing together Americans of many backgrounds, if only on a limited basis. By the end of the century, no section of the daily newspaper drew more readers than the sports pages. Although it interested relatively few women, sports news

CHRONOLOGY

1862	Morrill Act authorizes "land-grant" colleges
1869	Knights of Labor founded
1870	Standard Oil founded
1873	Financial panic brings severe depression
1876	Baseball's National League founded
	Alexander Graham Bell patents the telephone
1879	Thomas Edison invents the incandescent bulb
	Depression ends
1881	Tuskegee Institute founded
1882	Peak of immigration to the United States (1.2 million) in the nineteenth century
	Chinese Exclusion Act passed
	Standard Oil Trust founded

1883	William Graham Sumner published the social Darwinist classic *What Social Classes Owe to Each Other*
1886	Campaigns for eight-hour workday peak
	Haymarket riot and massacre discredit the Knights of Labor
	American Federation of Labor founded
1889	Andrew Carnegie's *The Gospel of Wealth* recommends honesty and fair dealing
1890	Sherman Antitrust Act passed
1893	Stock market panic precipitates severe depression
1895	Coney Island opens
1901	U.S. Steel Corporation formed

riveted the attention of men from all social classes. Loyalty to the "home team" helped to create an urban identity, while individual players became national heroes.

Conclusion

By the end of the nineteenth century, industry and the growing cities had opened a new world for Americans. Fresh from Europe or from the native countryside, ordinary urban dwellers struggled to form communities of fellow newcomers through both work and leisure, in the factory, the neighborhood, the ballpark, and the public school. Meanwhile, their "betters," the wealthy and the new middle class, made and executed the decisions of industry and marketing, established the era's grand civic institutions, and set the tone for high fashion and art. Rich and poor alike shared many aspects of the new order. Yet inequality not only persisted but also increased and prompted new antagonisms.

The Haymarket tragedy highlighted the often strained relationships between Chicago's immigrant working population and civic leaders, precipitating violence, which included the public hanging of four of the eight men brought to trial, including August Spies. Although the new governor of Illinois, Peter Altgeld, pardoned the three who had their sentences commuted to life in prison, his attempt at amelioration did not signal a shift in the political climate. In the 1890s, hopes for a peaceful reconciliation of these tensions had worn thin, and the lure of an overseas empire appeared as one of the few goals that held together a suffering and divided nation.

Review Questions

1. Discuss the sources of economic growth in the decades after the Civil War. Historians often refer to this period as the era of the "second industrial revolution." Do you agree with this description?

2. Describe the impact of new technologies and new forms of production on the routines of industrial workers. How did these changes affect African American and women workers in particular? What role did trade unions play in this process?

3. Discuss the role of northern capital in the development of the New South. How did the rise of industry affect the lives of rural Southerners? Analyze these changes from the point of view of African Americans.

4. How did urban life change during the Gilded Age? How did economic development affect residential patterns? How did the middle class aspire to live during the Gilded Age? How did their lifestyles compare with those of working-class urbanites?

5. How did the American educational system change to prepare children for their adult roles in the new industrial economy?

6. How did the rise of organized sports and commercial amusements reflect and shape social divisions at the end of the century? Which groups were affected most (or least) by new leisure activities?

Recommended Reading

Cindy S. Aron, *Working at Play: A History of Vacations in the United States* (1999). Covers the expansion of vacations from wealthy families to the middle class in the nineteenth century. Aron examines several types of settings, ranging from the grand summer hotels and posh resorts to camping vacations in the new national parks.

Sven Beckert, *The Monied Metropolis: New York City and the Consolidation of the American Bourgeoisie, 1850–1896* (2001). A highly informative study of the rise of the industrial elite, their business strategies, political advances, and engagements with consumer culture. This book examines the formation of a distinct social class and assesses the power it amassed during the Gilded Age.

Jack S. Blocker, *A Little More Freedom: African Americans Enter the Urban Midwest, 1860–1930* (2008). Examines the movement of African Americans from small towns to major urban areas such as Chicago, Indianapolis, and Cleveland. Blocker emphasizes the positive attractions of these cities as well as the danger and oppression that marked the lives of small-town African Americans.

William Cronon, *Nature's Metropolis: Chicago and the Great West* (1991). Analyzes the changing economic and political relationship between the city of Chicago and the surrounding countryside. Cronon demonstrates, through a variety of evidence, the tight interdependence of urban and rural regions.

Sarah Deutsch, *Women and the City: Gender, Space, and Power in Boston, 1870–1940* (2000). A close study of women's struggle to define the shape of the modern city and to ease the oppressive quality of spacial divisions along lines of gender, race, and class. Deutsch illustrates the efforts of women to exert their own principles of "moral geography" in shaping Boston's urban landscape.

Rebecca Edwards, *New Spirits: Americans in the Gilded Age, 1865–1905* (2006). A synthesis of recent scholarship with a thematic arrangement that takes the shape of an engaging essay. Edwards provides regional coverage and links domestic events—political, cultural, and social—to overseas expansion.

James Green, *Death in the Haymarket* (2006). Examines the Haymarket event within the context of changing class relations in Chicago and explores its significance as the first act of bombing for political purposes.

Tera W. Hunter, *To 'Joy My Freedom: Southern Black Women's Lives and Labors after the Civil War* (1997). A careful study of African American workingwomen in the New South city of Atlanta. Hunter covers their various occupations in the modern urban economy without sacrificing attention to their pursuits of pleasure in the emerging world of mass entertainments and leisure.

Maury Klein, *The Genesis of Industrial America, 1870–1920* (2007). A succinct survey of business and economic history that centers on the sweeping developments in power, transportation, communication, and organization.

Susan Strasser, *Satisfaction Guaranteed: The Making of the American Mass Market* (1989). A clear and concise explanation of marketing and distribution during the rise of consumer society. Illustrated with examples of early advertising.

Alan Trachtenberg, *The Incorporation of America: Culture and Society in the Gilded Age*, Twenty-Fifth Anniversary ed. (2007). One of the best and most readable overviews of the post–Civil War era. Trachtenberg devotes great care to describing the rise of the corporation to the defining institution of national life and the reorientation of culture to reflect the new middle classes employed by the corporation.

PEARSON
myhistorylab Connections

Reinforce what you learned in this chapter by studying the many documents, images, maps, review tools, and videos available at www.myhistorylab.com.

Read and Review

✓●─Study and Review **Chapter 19**

●●●─Read the Document

Thomas Edison, The Success of the Electric Light (1880)

Andrew Carnegie, Wealth

Chinese Exclusion Act (1882)

William D. Grady, The New South (1887)

Frances E. Willard, On Riding the Bicycle (1895)

Morrill Act (1862)

☀─View the Image **Residence of Andrew Carnegie**

Research and Explore

●●●─Read the Document

Exploring America: French Canadian Controversy

Industrializing America: Life and Labor in Smokestack America

History Bookshelf: Veblen, Theory of the Leisure Class

Profiles
Samuel Gompers
Thomas Edison

──(((●─Hear the Audio──

Hear the audio files for Chapter 19 at
www.myhistorylab.com.

20

Chapter 20 at www.myhistorylab.com

((•—[Hear the Audio

Democracy and Empire
1870–1900

CHAPTER OUTLINE

American Communities 555
The Annexation of Hawai'i

Toward a National Governing Class 557
The Growth of Government
The Machinery of Politics
The Spoils System and Civil Service
  Reform

Farmers and Workers Organize Their
Communities 560
The Grange
The Farmers' Alliance

Workers Search for Power
Women Build Alliances
Populism and the People's Party

The Crisis of the 1890s 564
Financial Collapse and Depression
Strikes: Coeur d'Alene, Homestead, and
  Pullman
The Social Gospel

Politics of Reform, Politics of Order 567
The Free Silver Issue
Populism's Last Campaigns

The Republican Triumph
Nativism and Jim Crow

The Path to Imperialism 571
All the World's a Fair
The "Imperialism of Righteousness"
The Quest for Empire

Onto a Global Stage 574
A "Splendid Little War" in Cuba
War in the Philippines
Critics of Empire

Destruction of the battleship *Maine* in Havana harbor, 1898. Creator: Kurz & Allison. Chicago History Museum.

The Annexation of Hawai'i

On January 17, 1891, Lili'uokalani succeeded her brother, King Kalakaua, to become the queen of Hawai'i. Raised a Christian and fluent in English, the fifty-two-year-old monarch was nevertheless intensely loyal to the Hawaiian people and to their language and customs. This allegiance—and her strong opposition to a movement to annex Hawai'i to the United States—brought her downfall. On January 17, 1893, the queen was deposed in a plot carried out by an American diplomat and his coconspirators.

This event followed more than a half century of intense economic and diplomatic maneuvering by the United States and other nations. Both American and British missionaries, who had arrived in the 1820s to convert Hawaiians to Christianity, had bought up huge parcels of land, and they and their children—known as the *haole* to native Hawaiians—had grown into a large and

AMERICAN Communities

powerful community of planters. The missionaries in turn encouraged American businesses to buy into the sugar plantations, and by 1875, U.S. corporations dominated the sugar trade. Within a year, Hawaiian sugar was entering the United States duty free. Hawai'i was beginning to appear, in the opinion of Secretary of State James G. Blaine, to be "an outlying district of the state of California," and he pushed for formal annexation.

In 1888, American planters forced on the weak King Kalakaua a new constitution that severely limited his power and established wealth and property qualifications for voting. This so-called Bayonet Constitution, because it implied the use of U.S. arms to implement it, allowed noncitizens, Europeans as well as Americans, to vote, but denied the right of suffrage to poor native Hawaiians and the Chinese and Japanese who had come to work in the sugar fields.

In the name of democracy, the haole planters had secured a constitutional government that was closely allied to their economic interests—until King Kalakaua died in 1891. After ascending to the throne, Queen Lili'uokalani struck back. She decided she must empower native Hawaiians and limit the political influence of the haole elite and noncitizens.

The U.S.-led annexation forces first denounced the queen for attempting to abrogate the Bayonet Constitution and then welcomed Blaine's decision to send in U.S. troops to protect American lives and property. With no shots fired or documents signed, Lili was deposed and a new provisional government installed. Sanford B. Dole, Honolulu-born son of Protestant missionaries, stepped in as the president of the new provisional government of Hawai'i, now a protectorate of the United States.

Lili'uokalani immediately protested to President Grover Cleveland, explaining that she had yielded "to the superior force of the United States of America" only to avoid a serious armed confrontation and the loss of life. She called on President Cleveland to recognize her authority as "the constitutional sovereign of the Hawaiian Islands" and to reinstate her as queen. After investigating the situation, Cleveland agreed and ordered Lili'uokalani's reinstatement as queen. Ironically, Dole, who had been a major force for annexation, countered by refusing to recognize the right of the U.S. president "to interfere in our domestic affairs."

On July 3, 1894, he proclaimed Hawai'i an independent republic, with himself retaining the office of president.

After Lili'uokalani's supporters attempted an unsuccessful military uprising in 1895, the deposed queen was arrested, tried by a military tribunal, and convicted of misprision of treason (having knowledge of treason but not informing the authorities). She was fined and sentenced to a five-year term in prison at hard labor, although Dole allowed her to serve a shorter sentence under "house arrest."

President Cleveland later declared privately that he was "ashamed of the whole affair" and stubbornly refused to listen to arguments for annexation. But he was powerless to stop the process before William McKinley succeeded him as president in 1896. Although more than a hundred members of Congress voted against annexation, an improper joint resolution passed to annex Hawai'i. In 1900, at McKinley's urging, Hawai'i became a territory. The people of Hawai'i were never consulted about this momentous change in their national identity.

Many Americans had long viewed Hawai'i as a stepping-stone to vast Asian markets, and by the 1890s they were determined to acquire the island nation to extend the reach of the United States beyond the continent. Business leaders, among others, reasoned that new foreign markets for goods might serve as a safety valve for domestic pressures. Such a safety valve seemed much in need: the 1890s was turning out to be a decade of the most severe social conflict and economic crisis in American history. Domestic unrest increased pressures for overseas expansion. "American factories are making more than the American people can use; American soil is producing more than they can consume," declared Senator Albert J. Beveridge, Republican from Indiana. "[T]he trade of the world must and shall be ours." Others had different reasons for expanding the national boundaries, and a sizable number of Americans strongly opposed all such ventures. Nevertheless, the century closed on the heels of a war with Spain that won for the United States a swatch of new possessions that extended halfway around the world, from Puerto Rico to the Philippines.

The path to empire was paved with major changes in government and the party system. As the 1890s culminated in the acquisition of new territories, the

1. What factors contributed to the growth of government in the late nineteenth century?

2. How and why did workers and farmers organize to participate in politics during this era?

3. In what ways did the election of 1896 represent a turning point in U.S. political history?

4. Why did the United States take on imperialist ventures in the late nineteenth century?

5. Why did the United States go to war with Spain in 1898, and with what results?

FOCUS
Questions

1870–1900

United States also witnessed a decisive realignment of the party system. Voters not only changed affiliations that had been in place since the Civil War, but also waged significant challenges to the two-party system at the local,

Oahu

regional, and national levels. While Queen Lili'uokalani was trying to regain control of her government, a mass political movement was forming in the United States to revive the nation's own democratic impulse.

AMERICAN
Communities

Toward a National Governing Class

The basic structure of government changed dramatically in the last quarter of the nineteenth century. Mirroring the fast-growing economy, public administration expanded at all levels—municipal, county, state, and federal—and took on greater responsibility for regulating society, especially market and property relations. Growing numbers of citizens for the first time looked to the government, from the local level upward, for public education, military veterans' pensions, and other social services. The leaders of the business community looked just as eagerly, and with far more influence, for protection of their property and sometimes for personal gain. Moreover, the expansion of government at home, particularly its increasing oversight of commerce, laid the foundation for economic and territorial expansion abroad.

Reformers mobilized to rein in corruption and to promote both efficiency and professionalism in the multiplying structures of government. Meanwhile, some notable politicians acted to benefit directly, competing with one another for control of the new mechanisms of power. A lot was at stake.

The Growth of Government

Before the Civil War, local governments attended mainly to the promotion and regulation of trade and relied on private enterprise to supply vital services such as fire protection and public access to water. Cities gradually introduced professional police and firefighting forces and began to finance expanding school systems, public libraries, roads, and parks, an expansion requiring huge increases in local taxation. State governments grew in tandem, consolidating oversight of banking, transportation systems such as the railroads, and major enterprises such as the construction of dams and canals. By the end of the nineteenth century, city halls and state capitols had become beehives of activity.

At the national level, mobilization for the Civil War and Reconstruction had demanded an unprecedented degree of resources and their coordination, as both revenues and administrative bureaucracy grew quickly. At the end of Reconstruction, various aspects of federal government were trimmed by Congressional order, and the army was reduced to a fraction of its swollen size. Despite these particular reductions, the federal government as a whole continued to expand under the weight of new tasks and responsibilities. The federal bureaucracy soon doubled, from about 50,000 employees in 1871 to 100,000 only a decade later.

The modern apparatus of departments, bureaus, and cabinets took shape amid this upswing. The Department of the Interior, created in 1849, grew into the largest and most important federal office other than the Post Office. It consisted of some twenty agencies, including the Bureau of Indian Affairs and the U.S. Geological Survey. Through its authority, the federal government was the chief landowner in the West. The Department of the Treasury, responsible for collecting federal taxes and customs as well as printing money and stamps, quadrupled in size from 1873 to 1900, to nearly 25,000 employees. The Pension Office, pressured by a powerful veterans' lobby, accounted for a quarter to a third of all federal expenditures.

Regulatory agencies sprung up: foremost was the Interstate Commerce Commission (ICC). The ICC was created in 1887 to bring order to the growing patchwork of state laws concerning railroads. The five-member commission appointed by the president approved freight and passenger rates set by the railroads. The ICC remained weak during that period, its rate-setting policies usually voided by the Supreme Court. But ICC commissioners could take public testimony on possible violations, examine company records, and generally oversee enforcement of the law. This set a precedent for future regulation of trade as well as for positive government, making rules for business while superseding state laws with federal power—that is, for the intervention of the federal government into the affairs of private enterprise.

The Machinery of Politics

Only gradually did Republicans and Democrats adapt to the demands of government expansion. The Republican Party continued to run on its Civil War record, pointing to its achievements in reuniting the nation and in passing new reform legislation. Democrats, by contrast, sought to reduce the influence of the federal government, slash expenditures, repeal legislation, and protect states' rights. While Republicans held on to their longtime constituencies, Democrats gathered support from southern white voters and immigrants newly naturalized in the North. Neither party commanded a clear majority of votes until the century drew to a close.

Presidents in the last quarter of the century— Rutherford B. Hayes (1877–81), James A. Garfield (1881), Chester A. Arthur (1881–85), Grover Cleveland (1885–89), Benjamin Harrison (1889–93), and Cleveland again (1893–97)—lacked luster. Only 1 percent of the popular vote separated the presidential candidates in three of five elections between 1876 and 1892. Congressional races were equally tight, less than two percentage points

separating total votes for Democratic and Republican candidates in all but one election in the decade before 1888. Democrats usually held a majority in the House and Republicans a majority in the Senate. With neither party sufficiently strong to govern effectively, Congress passed little legislation before 1890.

One major political issue that separated the two parties was the tariff. Manufacturing regions, especially the Northeast, favored a protective policy, while the southern and western agricultural regions opposed high tariffs as unfair to farmers and ranchers who had to pay the steep fees on imported necessities. Democrats, with a stronghold among southern voters, argued for sharp reductions in the tariff as a way to save the rural economy and to give a boost to workers. Republicans, who represented mainly business interests, raised tariffs to new levels on a wide array of goods during the Civil War and retained high tariffs as long as they held power. The so-called McKinley Tariff of 1890, introduced by Representative William McKinley (R–Ohio), further increased the tax rate on imported goods, including sugar from Hawai'i, thus provoking haole planters to push even more strongly for annexation to the United States and thereby avoid all tariffs on their products.

Despite differences over the tariff, the Democratic and Republican parties both operated mainly as state or local organizations, and by the 1870s, partisan politics had become a full-time occupation, with local elections usually held every two years. "We work through one campaign," quipped one candidate, "take a bath and start in on the next." Election paraphernalia—leaflets or pamphlets, banners, hats, flags, buttons, inscribed playing cards, or clay pipes featuring a likeness of a candidate's face or the party symbol—became a major expense for both parties. And voters did turn out. During the last quarter of the century, participation in presidential elections peaked at nearly 80 percent of those eligible to vote. Thousands, in fact, voted several times on any given election day; voters who had died, or had never lived, also miraculously cast ballots.

The rising costs of maintaining local organizations and orchestrating mammoth campaigns drove party leaders to seek ever-larger sources of revenue. Winners often seized and added to the "spoils" of office through an elaborate system of payoffs and patronage. Legislators who supported government subsidies for railroad corporations, for instance, commonly received stock and sometimes cash bribes in return. At the time, few politicians or business leaders regarded these practices as unethical.

At the local level, where a combination of ethnicity, race, and religion determined party loyalty, powerful bosses and political machines dominated both parties. Democrats William Marcy Tweed of New York's powerful political organization, Tammany Hall, and Michael "Hinky Dink" Kenna of Chicago, specialized in giving municipal jobs to loyal voters and holiday food baskets to their

🔘 View the Image

Nast Cartoon: Boss Tweed at **www.myhistorylab.com**

families. Hundreds of smaller political machines ruled cities and rural courthouses through a combination of "boodle" (bribe money) and personal favors. As Democrat George Plunkitt of New York once remarked, "Men ain't in politics for nothin'."

A large number of federal jobs, meanwhile, changed hands each time the presidency passed from one party to another. More than 50 percent of all federal jobs were patronage positions—nearly 56,000 in 1881—jobs that could be awarded to loyal supporters as part of the "spoils" of the "victor."

Upon taking office, President James Garfield encountered loyal Republicans "lying in wait" for him "like vultures for a wounded bison." His colleagues in Congress were no less besieged. Observers estimated that decisions about patronage filled one-third of their time. Garfield himself served as president for only four months before being mortally wounded by a disappointed office seeker, an event that prompted his successor, Chester A. Arthur, to encourage reform of the civil service system.

The Spoils System and Civil Service Reform

As early as 1865, Republican representative Thomas A. Jenckes of Rhode Island proposed a bill for civil service reform, but the majority in Congress, fearing that such a measure would hamper candidates in their relentless pursuit of votes, refused to pass legislation. Finally, a group comprising mainly professors, newspaper editors, lawyers,

In 1888, Grover Cleveland, with his running mate, Allen G. Thurman, led a spirited campaign for reelection to the presidency. Although he played up his strong record on civil service reform and tariff reduction, Cleveland, an incumbent, lost the election to his Republican challenger, Benjamin Harrison. Cleveland tallied the greatest number of popular votes, but Harrison easily won in the Electoral College by a margin of 233 to 168. In this lithograph campaign poster, the Democratic ticket invokes the legacy of Thomas Jefferson and the patriotism of Uncle Sam.

and ministers organized the Civil Service Reform Association and enlisted Ohio Democratic senator George H. Pendleton to sponsor reform legislation.

In January 1883, a bipartisan congressional majority passed the Pendleton Civil Service Reform Act. This measure allowed the president to create, with Senate approval, a three-person commission to draw up a set of guidelines for executive and legislative appointments. The commission established a system of standards for various federal jobs and instituted "open, competitive examinations for testing the fitness of applicants for public service." The Pendleton Act also barred political candidates from funding their campaigns by assessing a "tax" on the salaries of holders of party-sponsored government jobs.

Although patronage did not disappear entirely, many departments of the federal government took on a professional character similar to that which doctors, lawyers, and scholars were imposing on their fields through regulatory societies such as the American Medical Association and the American Historical Association. At the same time, the federal judiciary began to act more aggressively to establish the parameters of government. With the Circuit Courts of Appeals Act of 1891, Congress granted the U.S. Supreme Court the right to review all cases at will. Despite these reforms, many observers still viewed government as a sinkhole of self-interest and corruption.

Farmers and Workers Organize Their Communities

Farmers and workers began to build regional as well as national organizations to oppose, as a Nebraska newspaper put it, "the wealthy and powerful classes who want the control of government to plunder the people." Over the course of the last quarter of the nineteenth century, they gradually developed a distinctively radical agenda that spoke directly to the increasing power of elected officials and government. By the 1890s, farmers and workers had formed a mass movement that presented the most significant challenge to the two-party system since the Civil War—Populism—and pledged themselves to restore the reins of government to "the hands of the people."

The Grange

In 1867, white farmers in the Midwest formed the Patrons of Husbandry for their own "social, intellectual, and moral improvement." Led by Oliver H. Kelley, this fraternal society resembled the secretive Masonic order but admitted women. Whole families staffed a complex array of offices and engaged in mysterious rituals involving passwords, flags, songs, and costumes. In many farming communities, the headquarters of the local chapter, known as the Grange (a word for "farm"), became the main social center, the site of summer dinners and winter dances.

The Granger movement spread rapidly, especially in areas where farmers were experiencing their greatest hardships. Great Plains farmers barely survived the blizzards, grasshopper infestations, and droughts of the early 1870s. Meanwhile, farmers throughout the trans–Mississippi West

The symbols chosen by Grange artists represented their faith that all social value could be traced to honest labor and most of all to the work of the entire farm family. The hardworking American required only the enlightenment offered by the Grange to build a better community.

and the South watched the prices for grains and cotton fall year by year in the face of growing competition from producers in Canada, Australia, Argentina, Russia, and India (see Figure 20.1). Membership soon swelled to more than 775,000 in a network of 20,000 local chapters.

Grangers blamed hard times on a band of "thieves in the night"—especially railroads and banks—that charged exorbitant fees for service. They fumed at American manufacturers, such as Cyrus McCormick, who sold farm equipment more cheaply in Europe than in the United States. They raged at the banks that charged high interest rates for the money farmers had to borrow to pay the steep prices for equipment and raw materials.

Grangers mounted their greatest assault on the railroad corporations. By bribing state legislators, railroads enjoyed a highly discriminatory rate policy, commonly charging farmers more to ship their crops short distances than over long hauls. In 1874, several midwestern states responded to pressure and passed a series of so-called Granger laws establishing maximum shipping rates. Grangers also complained to their lawmakers about the price-fixing policies of grain wholesalers and operators of grain elevators. In 1873, the Illinois legislature passed a Warehouse Act establishing maximum rates for storing grains. Chicago firms challenged the legality of this measure, but in *Munn* v. *Illinois* (1877), the Supreme Court upheld the law, ruling that states had the

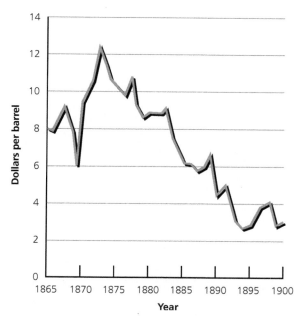

FIGURE 20.1 Falling Price of Wheat Flour, 1865–1900 The falling price of wheat was often offset by increased productivity, giving farmers a steady, if not higher, income. Nevertheless, in the short term, farmers often carried more debt and faced greater risk, both of which were factors in sparking the populists' protest by the end of the century.

power to regulate privately owned businesses like the railroads in the public interest.

Determined to buy less and produce more, Grangers created a vast array of cooperative enterprises for both the purchase of supplies and the marketing of crops. They established local grain elevators, set up retail stores, and even manufactured some of their own farm machinery. Grangers ran banks as well as fraternal life and fire insurance companies.

The deepening depression of the late 1870s wiped out most of these cooperative programs, and Grange membership soon fell. In the mid-1880s, the Supreme Court overturned most of the key legislation regulating railroads. Despite these setbacks, the Patrons of Husbandry had nonetheless effectively promoted the idea of an activist government with primary responsibility to its producer-citizens. This idea would remain at the heart of farmer-worker protest movements until the end of the century.

The Farmers' Alliance

Agrarian unrest did not end with the downward turn of the Grange, but instead moved south. The falling price of cotton underscored the need for action, and farmers organized in communities where both poverty and the crop-lien system prevailed. In the 1880s, the Southern Farmers' Alliance, with more than 500 chapters in Texas alone, established cooperative stores complemented by the cooperative merchandising of crops. Adopting as their motto, "Equal Rights to All, Special Privileges to None," the Southern Farmers' Alliance became a viable alternative to the capitalist marketplace—if only temporarily.

The Northern Farmers' Alliance took shape in the Great Plains states, drawing on larger organizations in Minnesota, Nebraska, Iowa, Kansas, and the Dakota Territory. During 1886 and 1887, summer drought followed winter blizzards and ice storms, reducing wheat harvests by one-third on the plains. Locusts and chinch bugs ate much of the rest. As if this were not enough, prices for wheat on the world market fell sharply for what little remained.

In 1889, the regional organizations joined forces to create the National Farmers' Alliance and Industrial Union. Within a year, the combined movement claimed 3 million white members. Excluded from the all-white chapters, the Colored Farmers' Alliance and Cooperative Union organized separately and quickly spread across the South; from its beginnings in Texas and Arkansas, it grew to more than a million members.

Grangers had pushed legislation that would limit the salaries of public officials, provide public school students with books at little or no cost, establish a program of teacher certification, and widen the admissions policies of the new state colleges. Only rarely, however, did they put up candidates for office. In comparison, the Farmers' Alliance had few reservations about entering electoral races. At the end of the 1880s, regional alliances put up candidates on platforms demanding state ownership of the railroads, a graduated income tax, lower tariffs, restriction of land ownership to citizens, and easier access to money through "the free and unlimited coinage of silver." By 1890, the alliances had won several local and state elections, gained control of the Nebraska legislature, and held the balance of power in Minnesota and South Dakota.

Workers Search for Power

Before the end of the century, more than 6 million workers would strike in industries ranging from New England textiles to southern tobacco factories to western mines. Some of the largest strikes were against the corporations targeted by farmers: the railroads. Although most of these strikes ended in failure, they showed that workers were ready to spell out their grievances in a direct and dramatic manner. They also suggested how strongly many townspeople, including merchants who depended on workers' wages, would support local strikes and turn them into community uprisings (see Map 20.1).

While the Farmers' Alliance put up candidates in the South and Plains states, workers launched labor parties in dozens of industrial towns and cities. In New York City, popular economist and land reformer Henry George, with the ardent support of the city's Central Labor Council, the Knights of Labor, and the Irish community, put himself

forward in 1886 as candidate for mayor on the United Labor Party ticket. In his best-selling book *Progress and Poverty* (1879), George advocated a sweeping "single tax" on all property to generate enough revenue to allow all Americans to live in comfort. He called on "all honest citizens" to join in independent political action as "the only hope of exposing and breaking up the extortion and speculation by which a standing army of professional politicians corrupt the people whom they plunder."

Tammany Hall delivered many thousands of the ballots cast for George straight into the Hudson River. Nevertheless, George managed to finish a respectable second with 31 percent of the vote. Although his campaign ended in defeat, his impressive showing encouraged labor groups in other cities to form their own parties.

In the late 1880s, labor parties won seats on many city councils and state legislatures. The Milwaukee People's Party elected the mayor, a state senator, six assemblymen, and one member of Congress. In smaller industrial towns where workers outnumbered the middle classes, labor parties did especially well. Rochester, New Hampshire, with a population of only 7,000, workers, mainly shoemakers, elected a majority slate from city council to mayor.

The victories of local labor parties caught the attention of farmers, who began to weigh their prospects for a political alliance with discontented urban workers. For the 1888 presidential election, they formed a coalition to

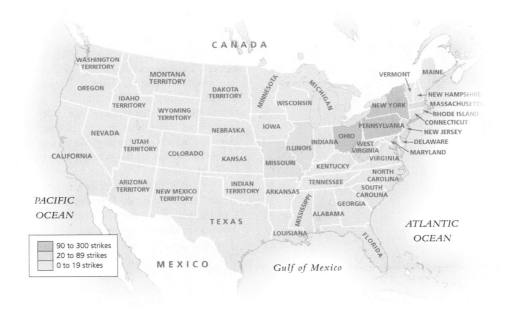

MAP 20.1 Strikes by State, 1880 Most strikes after the Uprising of 1877 could be traced to organized trades, concentrated in the manufacturing districts of the Northeast and Midwest.

SOURCE: From *Geographical Inquiry and American Historical Problems*, edited by Earl Carville. (Stanford, CA: Stanford University Press, 1992). Originally published in the *Third Annual Report of the Commissioner of Labor*, 1887.

sponsor the Union Labor Party, which ran on a plank of government ownership of the railroads. The new party made no headway against the two-party system, polling little more than 1 percent of the vote. Still, the successes in local communities nurtured hopes for a viable political alliance of the "producing classes," rural as well as urban.

Women Build Alliances

Women activists helped build both the labor and agrarian protest movements while campaigning for their own rights as citizens.

The Grangers issued a charter to a local chapter only when women were well represented on its rolls, and in the 1870s, delegates to its conventions routinely gave speeches endorsing woman suffrage and even dress reform. In both the Northern and Southern Farmers' Alliances, women made up perhaps one-quarter of the membership, and several advanced through the ranks to become leading speakers and organizers. A Kansas newspaper editor claimed that orator Mary E. Lease "could recite the multiplication table and set a crowd hooting and harrahing at her will." Lease achieved lasting fame purportedly for advising farmers to raise less corn and more hell.

Women in both the Knights of Labor and the Farmers' Alliance found their greatest leader in Frances E. Willard, the most famous woman of the nineteenth century and a shrewd politician in her own right. Willard argued that women, who guarded their families' physical and spiritual welfare, should play a similar role outside their homes. From 1878 until her death in 1897, she presided over the Woman's Christian Temperance Union (WCTU). Most numerous in the Midwest, WCTU members preached total abstinence from the consumption of alcohol, but ultimately endorsed Willard's "do everything" agenda. By the 1880s, the most militant branches were campaigning for an activist government and demanding an overhaul of the prison system, the eradication of prostitution, changes in the age of consent, and even the elimination of the wage system. Willard went so far as to draw up plans for a new system of government whereby all offices, right up to the presidency, would be shared jointly by men and women. By 1890, she had mobilized nearly 200,000 paid members into the largest organization of women in the world.

●●─┤**Read** the **Document**

Frances E. Willard on the Reorganization of Government (1891) at **www.myhistorylab.com**

Willard understood that for women to participate in politics they needed the right to vote. Under her leadership, the WCTU grew into the major force for woman suffrage, far surpassing the American Woman Suffrage Association and the National Woman Suffrage Association. By 1890, when the two rival suffrage associations merged to form the National American Woman Suffrage Association, the WCTU had already pushed the heart of the suffrage campaign into the Great Plains states and the West. In Iowa, Nebraska, Colorado, and especially Kansas, agitation for the right to vote provided a political bridge among women in the WCTU, Farmers' Alliance, Knights of Labor, and various local suffrage societies. The most active members—like Willard and Lease, who were both members of the Knights of Labor—were affiliated with several organizations or, in some cases, with all.

Populism and the People's Party

In December 1890, the Farmers' Alliance called a meeting at Ocala, Florida, to press for the creation of a national third party. This was a risky proposition because the Southern Alliance hoped to capture control of the Democratic Party, whereas many farmers in the Plains states and African Americans nearly everywhere voted Republican. In some

The Great Uprising of 1877, which began as a strike of railroad workers, spread rapidly to communities along the railroad routes. Angry crowds defied the armed militia and the vigilantes hired to disperse them. In Philadelphia, for example, strikers set fire to the downtown, destroying many buildings before federal troops were brought in to stop them. More than a hundred people died before the strike ended, and the railroad corporations suffered a $10 million loss in property.

areas, however, the Farmers' Alliance established an independent third party, put up full slates of candidates for local elections, won majorities in state legislatures, and even sent a representative to Congress. Reviewing these successes, delegates at Ocala decided to push ahead and form a national party, and they appealed to other farm, labor, and reform organizations to join them.

In February 1892, 1,300 representatives from the Farmers' Alliance, the Knights of Labor, and the Colored Farmers' Alliance, among others, met in St. Louis under a broad banner that read: "We do not ask for sympathy or pity. We ask for justice." The new People's Party called for government ownership of railroads, banks, and telegraph lines, prohibition of large landholding companies, a graduated income tax, an eight-hour workday, and restriction of immigration. The most ambitious plan called for the national government to build local warehouses—"subtreasuries"—where farmers could store their crops until prices reached acceptable levels. A universal suffrage plank drafted by Frances Willard, who

served on the platform committee, failed to pass. The People's Party convened again in Omaha in July 1892 and nominated James Baird Weaver of Iowa for president and, to please the South, the Confederate veteran James G. Field from Virginia for vice president.

▪▶ Read the Document

The People's Party Platform (1892) at **www.myhistorylab.com**

The Populists, as supporters of the People's Party styled themselves, quickly became a major factor in American politics. Although Democrat Grover Cleveland regained the presidency in 1892 (he had previously served from 1885 to 1889), Populists scored a string of local victories. They elected three governors, ten representatives to Congress, and five senators. Despite poor showings among urban workers east of the Mississippi, Populists looked forward to the next round of state elections in 1894. But the great test would come with the presidential election in 1896.

The Crisis of the 1890s

Populist Ignatius Donnelly wrote in the preface to his pessimistic novel *Caesar's Column* (1891) that industrial society appears to be a "wretched failure" to "the great mass of mankind." On the road to disaster rather than to a truly democratic community, "the rich, as a rule, hate the poor; and the poor are coming to hate the rich . . . society divides itself into two hostile camps . . . They wait only for the drum beat and the trumpet to summon them to armed conflict."

A series of events in the 1890s shook the confidence of many citizens in the reigning political system. But nothing was more unsettling than the severe economic depression that consumed the nation and lasted for five years. Many feared—while others hoped—that the entire political system would topple.

Financial Collapse and Depression

By the spring of 1893, the nation was drawn into a depression that had been plaguing European nations since the late 1880s. The European market for imported goods, including those manufactured in the United States, sharply contracted. Financial panic in England spread across the Atlantic, as British investors began to sell off their American stocks to obtain funds. Other factors—tight credit, falling agricultural prices, a weak banking system, and overexpansion, especially in railroad construction—all helped to bring about the collapse of the U.S. economy. In May and June, a crash in the stock market sent waves of panic splashing over business and financial institutions across the country. Agricultural prices meanwhile continued to plummet until they reached new lows. The business boom of nearly two decades ended, and the entire economy ground to a halt. The new century arrived before prosperity returned.

In many cities, unemployment rates reached 25 percent; Samuel Gompers, head of the American Federation of Labor (AFL), estimated nationwide unemployment at

Frances E. Willard (1839–1898) became a full-time activist for the national Woman's Christian Temperance Union (WCTU) in 1874. From 1879 until her death, she served as president, pushing the organization to expand its interests beyond temperance under the rubric of her "do-everything" policy. Under her leadership, the WCTU established 39 departments promoting a wide array of reform causes ranging from the establishment of free kindergartens to the prohibition of the manufacture of cigarettes.

3 million. Tens of thousands "rode the rails" or went "on the tramp" to look for work, hoping that their luck might change in a new city or town. Some panhandled for the nickel that could buy a mug of beer and a free lunch at a saloon. By night they slept in parks. Vagrancy laws (enacted during the 1870s) forced many without homes into prison. Inadequate diets prompted a rise in communicable diseases, such as tuberculosis and pellagra. Unable to buy food, clothes, or household items, many families learned to survive with the barest minimum.

As the depression deepened, so did demands on the federal government for positive action. Populist Jacob Sechler Coxey decided to gather the masses of unemployed into a huge army and then to march to Washington, DC. Far in advance of the New Deal, Coxey proposed that Congress fund a public works program to give jobs to the unemployed. On Easter Sunday, 1894, Coxey left Massillon, Ohio, with several hundred followers. Meanwhile, brigades from across the country joined his "petition in boots." Only 600 men and women reached the nation's capital, where the police first clubbed and then arrested the leaders for trespassing on the grass. "Coxey's Army" quickly disbanded, but not before voicing the public's expectation of federal responsibility for the welfare of its citizens, especially in times of crisis.

Read the Document
Jacob Coxey, Address of Protest (1894) at **www.myhistorylab.com**

Strikes: Coeur d'Alene, Homestead, and Pullman

Even before the onset of the depression, the conflict between labor and capital had escalated to the brink of civil war. In the 1890s, three major strikes dramatized the

extent of collusion between the corporations and government. In each case, state or federal troops were deployed to crush the labor uprising, providing a vivid lesson to workers on the growing role of government in this era.

Wage cuts in the silver and lead mines of northern Idaho led to one of the most bitter conflicts of the decade. To put a brake on organized labor, mine owners had formed a "protective association," and in March 1892, they announced a wage cut throughout the Coeur d'Alene district. After the miners' union refused to accept the cut, the owners locked out all union members and brought in strikebreakers ("scab" laborers) by the trainload. Unionists tried peaceful methods of protest. But after three months of stalemate, they loaded a railcar with explosives and blew up a mine. The governor proclaimed martial law and dispatched a combined state-federal force of about 1,500 troops, who broke the strike. Ore production resumed with "scab" labor, and by November, when the troops were withdrawn, the mine owners declared a victory. But the miners' union survived, and most members became active in the Populist Party, which at the next session of the Idaho legislature allied with Democrats to cut back all appropriations to the National Guard.

At Homestead, Pennsylvania, members of the Amalgamated Iron, Steel and Tin Workers, the most powerful union of the AFL, had carved out an admirable position for themselves in the Carnegie Steel Company. Well paid and proud of their skills, the unionists customarily directed their unskilled helpers without undue influence of company supervisors. Determined to gain control over every stage of production, however, Carnegie and his partner, Henry C. Frick, decided not only to lower wages but also to break the union.

After five weeks, the main body of Coxey's Army reached Washington, DC, where on May 1, 1894, the leaders were immediately arrested for trespassing on government property. Fifty years later, on May 1, 1944, the ninety-year-old Coxey finally gave his speech advocating public works programs on the steps of the nation's capitol.

In 1892, when Amalgamated's contract expired, Frick announced a drastic wage cut. He also ordered a wooden stockade built around the factory, with grooves for rifles and barbed wire on top. When Homestead's city government—the mayor and police chief were both union members—refused to assign police to disperse the strikers, Frick dispatched a barge carrying a private army armed to the teeth. Gunfire broke out and continued throughout the day. Finally, the governor stepped in and sent the Pennsylvania National Guard, 8,000 strong, to restore order, and Carnegie's factory reopened with strikebreakers doing the work.

After four months, the union was forced to concede a crushing defeat, not only for itself, but, in effect, for all steelworkers. The Carnegie Company reduced its workforce by 25 percent, lengthened the workday, and cut wages 25 percent for those who remained on the job. If the Amalgamated Iron, Steel and Tin Workers, known throughout the industry as the "aristocrats of labor," could be brought down, less skilled workers could expect little from the corporate giants. Within a decade, every major steel company operated without union interference.

View the Image
Homestead Strikers Surrendering at **www.myhistorylab.com**

Pullman, Illinois, just south of Chicago, had been constructed as a model industrial community. Its creator and proprietor, George M. Pullman, had manufactured luxurious "sleeping cars" for railroads since 1881. He built his company as a self-contained community, with the factory at the center, surrounded by modern cottages, a library, churches, parks, an independent water supply, even its own cemetery, but no saloons. The Pullman Palace Car Company deducted rent, library fees, and grocery bills from each worker's weekly wages. In good times, workers enjoyed a decent livelihood, although many resented Pullman's autocratic control of their daily affairs.

When times grew hard, the company cut wages by as much as one-half, in some cases down to less than $1 a day. Charges for food and rent remained unchanged. Furthermore, factory supervisors sought to make up for declining profits by driving workers to produce more. In May 1894, after Pullman fired members of a committee that had drawn up a list of grievances, workers voted to strike.

Pullman workers found their champion in Eugene V. Debs, who had recently formed the American Railway Union (ARU) to bring railroad workers across the vast continent into one organization. Debs, the architect of the ARU's victory over the Great Northern rail line just one month earlier, advised caution, but delegates to an ARU convention voted to support a nationwide boycott of all Pullman cars. This action soon turned into a sympathy strike by railroad workers across the country.

Compared to the Great Uprising of 1877, the orderly Pullman strike at first produced little violence. ARU officials urged strikers to ignore all provocations and hold

The popular magazine *Frank Leslie's* published this illustration of workers and their families confronting the private security force brought in to break the strike at the Carnegie Steel Company in Homestead, Pennsylvania, in July 1892.

their ground peacefully. But Richard C. Olney, a former railroad lawyer, used his current office as attorney general, claiming that the ARU was disrupting mail shipments (actually Debs had banned such interference), to issue a blanket injunction against the strike. On July 4, President Cleveland sent army units to Chicago, over the objections of pro-labor Illinois governor John Peter Altgeld. After a bitter confrontation that left thirteen people dead and more than fifty wounded, the army dispersed the strikers. For the next week, railroad workers in twenty-six other states resisted federal troops, and a dozen more people were killed. On July 17, the strike finally ended when federal marshals arrested Debs and other leaders.

Assailing the arrogance of class privilege that encouraged the government to use brute force against its citizens, Debs concluded that the labor movement could not regain its dignity without seizing the reigns of government. He came out of jail committed to the ideals of socialism, and in 1898 helped to form a political party dedicated to its principles.

The Social Gospel

"What is socialism?" Debs once asked. "Merely Christianity in action. It recognizes the equality in men." During the 1890s, especially as hard times spread across the nation, a growing number of Protestants and Catholics came close to sharing Debs's perspective.

Read the Document
Eugene V. Debs, The Outlook for Socialism in America (1900) at **www.myhistorylab.com**

Social gospel ministers called on the government to be more responsible toward its most impoverished and unprotected citizens. Supporting labor's right to organize and, if necessary, to strike, they petitioned government officials to regulate corporations and place a limit on profits. Washington Gladden, a Congregationalist minister, warned that if churches continued to ignore pressing social problems, they would devolve into institutions whose sole purpose was to preserve obscure rituals and superstitions. He addressed his most important book, *Applied Christianity* (1886), to the nation's business leaders, imploring them to return to Christ's teachings.

The depression of the 1890s produced an outpouring of similar treatises. The very popular *If Christ Came to Chicago* (1894), by British journalist W. T. Stead, forced readers to confront the "ugly sight" of a city with 200 millionaires and 200,000 unemployed men. It inspired Edward Everett Hale's *If Jesus Came to Boston* (1894), which similarly questioned social inequalities. The most famous tract, *In His Steps* (1896), by Methodist minister Charles M. Sheldon of Topeka, Kansas, urged middle-class readers to rethink their actions in the light of the simple question "What would Jesus do?"

Catholic clergy, doctrinally more inclined than Protestants to accept poverty as a natural condition, joined the social gospel movement in smaller numbers. Many of their parishioners, especially Polish and Irish Americans, however, allied with the labor movement, finding solace in Pope Leo XIII's encyclical *Rerum Novarum* (1891), which endorsed the right of workers to form trade unions.

Women guided the social gospel movement in their communities. Since the early part of the nineteenth century, middle-class women in northern cities had formed numerous voluntary associations to improve the conditions of the poor and destitute. They founded orphanages and hospitals and shelters for the homeless. In the 1890s, women activists revived this legacy and responded to the plight of the poor and dispossessed. In nearly every sizable city, groups of white women affiliated with various evangelical Protestant sects raised money to establish inexpensive residential hotels for working women, whose low wages rarely covered the price of safe, comfortable shelter. At the forefront of this movement was the Young Women's Christian Association (YWCA),

which by 1900 had more than 600 local chapters. The "Y" sponsored a range of services for needy Christian women, ranging from homes for the elderly and for unmarried mothers to elaborate programs of vocational instruction and physical fitness. Meanwhile, Catholic laywomen and nuns served the poor women of their faith, operating numerous schools, hospitals, and orphanages.

Affiliated principally with the Baptist Church, African American women sponsored dozens of self-help programs and, in addition, emphasized the importance of education to racial uplift. Excluded by the whites-only policy of the YWCA in most localities, they organized their own chapters and branched out to form nurseries, orphanages, hospitals, and nursing homes. In Chicago, for example, African American women established the Phyllis Wheatley Home, which opened in 1908 to provide, in the founders' words, a "Christian influence" for the working women and college students who boarded there.

Politics of Reform, Politics of Order

The severe hardships of the 1890s, following a quarter century of popular unrest, pushed economic issues to the forefront of politics. Voters were more than ready for a change. As a consequence, the presidential election of 1896, considered a turning point in American politics, marked a dramatic realignment. The election also sanctioned the popular call for a stronger government and, ultimately, established a clear link between domestic problems and overseas markets.

The Free Silver Issue

For generations, farmers had advocated "soft" currency, that is, an increase in the money supply that would loosen credit. During the Civil War, the federal government took decisive action, replacing state bank notes with a national paper currency popularly called "greenbacks" (from the color of the bills). Then in 1873, the Coinage Act tightened the money supply by eliminating silver from circulation, prompting farmers who depended on credit to call it "the Crime of '73." This measure actually had little real impact on the economy but opened the door to yet more tinkering.

Farmers readily approved the Sherman Silver Purchase Act of 1890, which directed the Treasury to increase the amount of currency coined from silver mined in the West and also permitted the U.S. government to print paper currency backed by silver. In turn, Westerners, who stood to benefit most from this reform, agreed to support the McKinley Tariff of 1890, which, by establishing the highest import duties yet on foreign goods, pleased the business community.

Following the crash of 1893, President Cleveland concluded that the economic crisis was "largely the result of financial policy . . . embodied in unwise laws" and insisted that only the gold standard could pull the nation out of the depression. By exerting intense pressure on congressional Democrats, Cleveland succeeded in repealing the Sherman Act in October 1893, but not without ruining his chances for renomination.

The midterm elections of 1894 brought the largest shift in congressional power in American history: the Republicans gained 117 seats, while the Democrats lost 113. The "Silver Democrats" of Cleveland's own party vowed revenge and began to look to the Populists, mainly Westerners and farmers who favored "free silver," that is, the unlimited coinage of silver. Republicans confidently began to prepare for the presidential election of 1896, warming to what they called the "battle of the standards."

Populism's Last Campaigns

Populists had been buoyed by the 1894 elections, which delivered to their candidates nearly 1.5 million votes—a gain of 42 percent over their 1892 totals. They made impressive inroads into several southern states and raised expectations west of the Mississippi. Still, even in the Midwest, where Populists doubled their vote, they managed to win less than 7 percent of the total, and, overall, they lost two seats in Congress.

As Populists prepared for the 1896 presidential campaign, they found themselves at a crossroad: what were they to do with the growing popularity of the Democratic candidate, William Jennings Bryan? A spellbinding orator, Bryan won a congressional seat in 1890. After seizing the Populist slogan "Equal Rights to All, Special Privilege to None," the thirty-six-year-old lawyer from Nebraska became a major contender for president of the United States.

Bryan won back many disaffected Democrats by championing free silver. For two years before the 1896 election, he wooed potential voters in a speaking tour that took him to every state in the nation. Pouring new life into his divided party, Bryan pushed Silver Democrats to the forefront.

At the 1896 party convention, Bryan thrilled delegates with his evocation of agrarian ideals. "Burn down your cities and leave our farms," Bryan preached, "and your cities will spring up again as if by magic; but destroy our farms and the grass will grow in the streets of every city in the country." What became one of the most famous speeches in American

●●⊢Read the Document

William Jennings Bryan, "Cross of Gold" Speech (1896) at **www.myhistorylab.com**

political history closed on a yet more dramatic note. Spreading his arms to suggest the crucified Christ figure, he pledged to resist all demands for a gold standard by saying, "You shall not press down upon the brow of labor this crown of thorns, you shall not crucify mankind upon a cross of gold." The next day, Bryan carried the Democratic presidential nomination.

The Populists realized that by nominating Bryan, the Democrats had stolen their thunder. They also feared that the growing emphasis on currency would overshadow their more important planks calling for government ownership

of the nation's railroads and communications systems. As the date of their own convention approached, delegates divided over strategy: they could endorse Bryan and give up their independent status, or they could run an independent campaign and risk splitting the silver vote.

In the end, Populists nominated Bryan for president and one of their own, Georgian Tom Watson, for vice president. Most of the state Democratic Party organizations, however, refused to put the "fusion" ticket on the ballot, and Bryan and his Democratic running mate Arthur Sewall simply ignored the Populist campaign.

The Republican Triumph

After Cleveland's blunders, Republicans anticipated an easy victory in 1896, but Bryan's nomination, as party stalwart Mark Hanna warned, "changed everything." Luckily, they had their own handsome, knowledgeable, courteous, and ruthless candidate, Civil War veteran William McKinley.

This Republican campaign poster of 1896 depicts William McKinley standing on sound money and promising a revival of prosperity. The depression of the 1890s shifted the electorate into the Republican column.

The Republican campaign, in terms of sheer expense and skill of coordination, outdid all previous campaigns and established a precedent for future presidential elections. Hanna guided a strategy that outspent Bryan more than ten to one. Using innumerable pamphlets, placards, hats, and parades, Republicans advertised their promise to "rebuild out of the ruins of the last four years the stately mansions of national happiness, prosperity and self-respect." McKinley even invited voters to his home, managing to attract as many as 750,000 people to his famous "Front Porch." Fearful that the silver issue would divide their own ranks, Republicans stepped around it while emphasizing the tariff. Delivering a hard-hitting negative campaign, they consistently cast Bryan as a naysayer.

McKinley triumphed in the most important presidential election since Reconstruction. Bryan managed to win 46 percent of the popular vote, but failed to carry the Midwest, West Coast, or Upper South (see Map 20.2). Moreover, the free silver campaign rebuffed traditionally Democratic urban voters who feared that soft money would bring higher prices. Many Catholics uncomfortable with Bryan's Protestant moral piety also deserted the Democrats. Finally, neither the reform-minded middle classes nor impoverished blue-collar workers were convinced that Bryan's grand reform vision really included them. The Populist following, already divided and now further disillusioned, dwindled away.

Once in office, McKinley strengthened the executive branch and actively promoted a mixture of probusiness and expansionist measures. He supported the Dingley Tariff of 1897, which raised import duties to an all-time high. In 1897, McKinley also encouraged Congress to create the United States Industrial Commission, which would plan business regulation; in 1898, he promoted a bankruptcy act that eased the financial situation of small businesses; and he proposed the Erdman Act of the same year, which established a system of arbitration to avoid rail strikes. The Supreme Court ruled in concert with the president, finding eighteen railways in violation of antitrust laws, and granting states the right to regulate hours of labor under certain circumstances. In 1900, McKinley settled the currency issue by overseeing the passage of the Gold Standard Act.

McKinley's triumphs ended the popular challenge to the nation's governing system. With prosperity returning by the end of the century and nationalism rising swiftly, McKinley encouraged Americans to go for "a full dinner pail," the winning Republican slogan of the 1900 presidential campaign. With news of his second triumph, stock prices on Wall Street skyrocketed.

Nativism and Jim Crow

Campaign rhetoric aside, McKinley and Bryan had differed only slightly on the major problems facing the nation in the 1890s. Neither Bryan, the reformer, nor

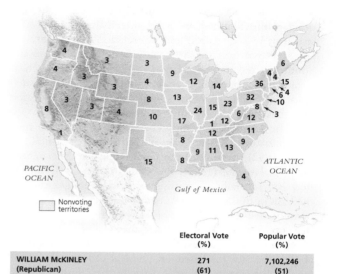

	Electoral Vote (%)	Popular Vote (%)
WILLIAM McKINLEY (Republican)	271 (61)	7,102,246 (51)
William J. Bryan (Democrat)	176 (39)	6,492,559 (47)
Minor parties	—	315,398 (2)

MAP 20.2 Election of 1896 Democratic candidate William Jennings Bryan carried most of rural America but could not overcome Republican William McKinley's stronghold in the populous industrial states.

McKinley, the prophet of prosperity, addressed the escalation of racism and nativism (anti-immigrant feeling) throughout the nation.

Toward the end of the century, many political observers noted, the nation's patriotic fervor took on a strongly nationalistic and antiforeign tone. Striking workers and their employers alike tended to blame "foreigners" for the hard times. Semisecret organizations such as the American Protective Association sprang up to defend American institutions. Fourth of July orators continued to celebrate freedom and liberty, but more often boasted about the might and power of their nation.

In the South, local and state governments codified racist ideology by passing discriminatory and segregationist legislation, which became known as Jim Crow laws. The phrase, dating from the early decades of the nineteenth century, was made popular by a white minstrel in blackface who used the name "Jim Crow" to demean all African Americans. By the end of the century, "Jim Crow" referred to the customs of segregation that were becoming secured by legislation throughout the South. With nine of every ten black Americans living in this region, the significance of this development was sweeping.

"The supremacy of the white race of the South," New South promoter Henry W. Grady declared in 1887, "must be maintained forever . . . because the white race is the superior race." To secure their privileges, Grady and other white Southerners acted directly to impose firm standards of segregation and domination and to forestall any appearance of social equality. State after state in the South enacted new legislation to cover facilities such as restaurants, public transportation, and even drinking fountains. Signs reading "White Only" and "Colored" appeared over theaters, parks, rooming houses, and toilets.

The United States Supreme Court upheld the new discriminatory legislation. Its decisions in the *Civil Rights Cases* (1883) overturned the Civil Rights Act of 1875; in *Plessy* v. *Ferguson* (1896), the Court upheld a Louisiana state law formally segregating railroad passenger cars on the basis of the "separate but equal" doctrine. The majority opinion, delivered by Justice Henry Billings Brown, stated that political equality and social equality are distinct: "Legislation is powerless to eradicate racial instincts or to abolish distinctions based on physical differences. If one race be inferior to the other socially, the Constitution of the United States cannot put them on the same plane."

This ruling established the legal rationale for segregation, in the North as well as the South, for the next fifty years. In *Cumming* v. *Richmond County Board of Education* (1899), the Court allowed separate schools for blacks and whites, even where facilities for African American children did not exist. This ruling reverberated in other parts of the country. For example, a year later, in 1900, the New Orleans school board decided to eliminate all schools for black children beyond the fifth grade, reasoning that African Americans needed only minimal education to fit them for menial jobs "to which they are best suited and seem ordained by the proper fitness of things."

Southern states enacted new literacy tests and property qualifications for voting. Loopholes permitted poor whites to vote even under these conditions, except where they threatened the Democratic Party's rule. "Grandfather clauses," invented in Louisiana, exempted from all restrictions those who had been entitled to vote on January 1, 1867, together with their sons and grandsons, a measure that effectively enfranchised whites while barring African Americans. In 1898, the Supreme Court ruled that poll taxes and literacy requirements enacted to prevent blacks (and some poor whites) from voting were a proper means of restricting the ballot to "qualified" voters. By this time, only 5 percent of the southern black electorate voted, and African Americans were barred from public office and jury service (see Figure 20.2).

Racial violence escalated. Race riots, which took the lives of hundreds of African Americans, broke out in small towns like Rosewood, Florida, and Phoenix, South Carolina, and in large cities like New Orleans and Tulsa. In November 1898, in Wilmington, North Carolina, where a dozen African Americans had ridden out the last waves of the Populist insurgency to win appointments to minor political offices, a group of white opponents organized to

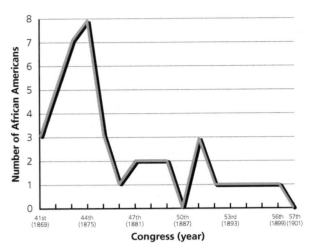

FIGURE 20.2 African American Representation in Congress, 1867–1900 Black men served in the U.S. Congress from 1870 until 1900. All were Republicans.

root them out and ultimately staged a violent coup, restoring white rule and forcing black leaders to leave town. "It come so," a black woman explained, "that we in this town is afraid of a white face." As many as 100 African Americans were killed in what came to be known as the Wilmington massacre.

Not only race riots, but also thousands of lynchings took place. Between 1882 and the turn of the century, the number of lynchings usually exceeded 100 each year; 1892 produced a record 230 deaths (161 black, 69 white). Mobs often burned or dismembered victims to drag out their agony and entertain the crowd of onlookers. Announced in local newspapers, lynchings in the 1890s became public spectacles for entire white families, and railroads sometimes offered special excursion rates for travel to these events.

Antilynching became the one-woman crusade of Ida B. Wells, the young editor of a black newspaper in Memphis. After three local black businessmen were lynched in 1892, Wells vigorously denounced the outrage, blaming the white business competitors of the victims. Her stand fanned the tempers of local whites, who destroyed her press and forced the outspoken editor to leave the city. She then launched an international movement against lynching, lecturing across the country and in Europe, demanding an end to the silence about this barbaric crime. Her work also inspired the growth of a black women's club movement. The National Association of Colored Women, founded in 1896, took up the antilynching cause and also fought to protect black women from sexual exploitation by white men.

Few white reformers rallied to defend African Americans. Even the National American Woman Suffrage Association, in an attempt to appease its southern members at its 1899 convention, voted down a resolution condemning racial segregation in public facilities. More than a few Americans had come to believe that their future welfare hinged on white supremacy, not only in their own country but across the globe as well.

The Path to Imperialism

Many Americans attributed the economic crisis of 1893–97 not simply to the collapse of the railroads and banks but also to basic structural problems: an overbuilt economy and an insufficient market for goods. Profits from total sales of manufactured and agricultural products had grown substantially over levels achieved in the 1880s, but output increased even more rapidly. Although the number of millionaires shot up from 500 in 1860 to more than 4,000 in 1892, the majority of Americans did not have enough money to buy a significant portion of what they produced. To find new markets for American goods, many Americans looked abroad.

All the World's a Fair

The World's Columbian Exposition, held in Chicago, commemorated the four hundredth anniversary of Columbus's landing and answered Congress's call for "an exhibition of the progress of civilization in the New World." On May Day 1893, less than two months after the nation's economy had collapsed, crowds began to flock to the fair, a complex of more than 400 buildings newly constructed in beaux arts design.

The section known as "The White City" celebrated the achievements of American business in the global economy. Agriculture Hall showcased the production of corn, wheat, and other crops and featured a gigantic globe encircled by samples of American-manufactured farm machinery. Another building housed a model of a canal cut across Nicaragua, suggesting the ease with which American traders might reach Asian markets if transport ships could travel directly from the Caribbean to the Pacific. One of the most popular exhibits, attracting 20,000 people a day, featured a mock ocean liner built to scale by the International Navigation Company, where fairgoers could imagine themselves as "tourists," sailing in luxury to distant parts of the world. The symbolism was evident: all eyes were on international trade as a marker of American prowess.

In contrast to the White City was the Midway, a strip nearly a mile long and more than 600 feet wide that offered entertainment. The new, spectacular Ferris wheel, designed to rival the Eiffel Tower of Paris, was the largest attraction. But the Midway also offered amusement in the form of "displays" of "uncivilized" people from foreign lands.

One enormous sideshow re-created Turkish bazaars and South Sea island huts. There were Javanese carpenters,

Dahomean drummers, Egyptian swordsmen, and Hungarian Gypsies, as well as Eskimos, Syrians, Samoans, and Chinese. Hawaiians were represented by a cyclorama of the Kilauea volcano, billed as the "Inferno of the Pacific" and guarded by the figure advertised as the "awful divinity" Pele, goddess of fire. The World Congress of Beauty, parading "40 Ladies from 40 Nations" dressed in native costume also was popular. Another favorite attraction was "Little Egypt," who performed at the Persian Palace of Eros; her *danse du ventre* became better known as the hootchy-kootchy. According to the guidebook, all these peoples had come "from the nightsome North and the splendid South, from the wasty West and the effete East, bringing their manners, customs, dress, religions, legends, amusements, that we might know them better."

By celebrating the brilliance of American industry and simultaneously presenting the "uncivilized" people of the world as a source of exotic entertainment, the planners of the fair delivered a powerful message. Former abolitionist Frederick Douglass, who attended the fair on "Colored People's Day," recognized it immediately. He noted that the physical layout of the fair, by carefully grouping exhibits, sharply divided the United States and Europe from the rest of the world, namely, from the nations of Africa, Asia, and the Middle East. Douglass objected to the stark contrast setting off Anglo-Saxons from people of color, an opposition between "civilization" and "savagery." He and Ida B. Wells also objected to the exclusion of African Americans from representation among the exhibits at the White City. Wells boycotted the special day set aside for African Americans, while Douglass attended, using the occasion to deliver a speech upbraiding white Americans for their racism.

Frederick Jackson Turner also spoke at the fair and read his famous essay about the disappearance of the frontier. Having passed "from the task of filling up the vacant spaces of the continent," the young historian warned, the nation is now "thrown back upon itself." His message was clear: if democracy were to survive, Americans required a new "frontier."

The Chicago World's Fair, which attracted 27 million visitors from all over the world, reassured Turner by marking the coming of age of the United States as a global power and by making a deliberate case for commercial expansion abroad. The exposition also gave material shape to prevalent ideas about the preeminence of American civilization as well as the superiority of the Anglo-Saxon race (see Seeing History).

The "Imperialism of Righteousness"

Social gospeler Josiah Strong, a Congregational minister who had begun his career hoping to "civilize" the Indians by converting them to Christianity, provided a prescient commentary in 1885. Linking economic and spiritual expansion, he advocated an "imperialism of righteousness."

The White Man's Burden

In 1899, the British poet Rudyard Kipling published "The White Man's Burden" in the American magazine *McClure's* with the subtitle "The United States and the Philippine Islands." Some interpreted the poem as an endorsement of the U.S. imperialist ventures in the Pacific; others read it as a cautionary note warning against taking on colonies. Those who favored expansion embraced the notion of the "white man's burden" as means to justify their position as a noble enterprise, that is, in "uplifting" those people of color who had not yet enjoyed the benefits of "civilization."

The concept even made its way into advertising for soap. In 1789, London soapmaster Andrew Pears began producing a distinctive oval bar of transparent amber glycerin and marketing it as a luxury item under the name Pears Soap. He found a talented promoter in Thomas J. Barratt, considered a pioneer of modern advertising, who built an international market for the product. By the end of the nineteenth century, Pears Soap had achieved brand-name status among middle- and upper-class Americans.

Barratt's advertising presented Pears Soap as safe and beneficial but suitable only for discerning consumers. Among its many other advantages, Pears Soap promised a smooth, white complexion, underscoring this message by associating dark skins with "uncivilized" people. The man pictured in this ad is probably a colonial official. The advertisement appeared first in 1899 in *McClure's*—the same magazine in which Kipling's poetic exhortation was published.

The first step towards lightening

The White Man's Burden

is through teaching the virtues of cleanliness.

Pears' Soap

is a potent factor in brightening the dark corners of the earth as civilization advances, while amongst the cultured of all nations it holds the highest place—it is the ideal toilet soap.

Take up the White Man's burden—
Send forth the best ye breed—
Go bind your sons to exile
To serve your captives' need;
To wait in heavy harness,
On fluttered folk and wild—

Your new-caught, sullen peoples,
Half-devil and half-child.
Take up the White Man's burden—
In patience to abide,
To veil the threat of terror
And check the show of pride . . .

• **What did the readers of *McClure's* magazine understand as "the white man's burden"? How did this responsibility relate to the belief in a hierarchy of races and civilizations expressed in Kipling's poem?**

◆◉◆ Read the Document

Josiah Strong, from Our Country (1885) at
www.myhistorylab.com

He identified white Americans as the best agents for "Christianizing" and "civilizing" the people of Africa and the Pacific and beyond. It was the white American, Strong argued, who had been "divinely commissioned to be . . . his brother's keeper."

The push for overseas expansion coincided with a major wave of religious evangelism and foreign missions. Early in the nineteenth century, Protestant missionaries, hoping to fulfill what they believed to be a divine command to carry God's message to all peoples and to win converts for their church, had focused on North America. Many disciples, like Josiah Strong himself, headed west and stationed themselves on Indian reservations. Others worked among the immigrant populations of the nation's growing cities. As early as the 1820s, however, a few missionaries had traveled to the Sandwich Islands (Hawai'i) in an effort to supplant the indigenous religion with Christianity. After the Civil War, the major evangelical Protestant denominations all sponsored missions directed at foreign lands.

By the 1890s, college campuses blazed with missionary excitement, and the intercollegiate Student Volunteers for Foreign Missions spread rapidly under the slogan "The Evangelicization of the World in This Generation." Magazines bristled with essays such as "The Anglo-Saxon and the World's Redemption." By the turn of the century, some 23 American Protestant churches had established missions in China, the majority staffed by women.

Young Protestant women rushed to join foreign missionary societies. Since the early part of the nineteenth century, Protestant women had headed "cent" and "mite" societies, which gathered money to support overseas missionaries. By 1820, women were accompanying their minister husbands to distant parts to convert the "heathens" to Christianity. After the Civil War, in tandem with the expansion of higher-education opportunities, unmarried women petitioned church leaders to request their own missionary assignments. By 1900, the various Protestant denominations were supporting forty-one women's missionary boards; several years later more than 3 million women had enrolled in societies to support this work, together surpassing in size all other women's organizations in the United States.

Outside the churches, the YMCA and YWCA, which had set up nondenominational missions for the working poor in many American cities, also embarked on a worldwide crusade to reach non-Christians. As foreign branches multiplied, a close observer ironically suggested that the

By the end of the nineteenth century, women represented 60 percent of the American missionary force in foreign lands. This photograph shows two Methodist women using "back chairs," a traditional form of transportation, at Mount Omei in Szechwan, China.

United States had three great occupying forces: the army, the navy, and the "Y." He was not far from wrong.

The missionaries did more than spread the gospel. They taught school, provided rudimentary medical care, offered vocational training programs, and sometimes encouraged young men and women to pursue a college education in preparation for careers in their homelands. They also played an important role in preparing the way for American economic expansion. As Josiah Strong aptly put it, "Commerce follows the missionary."

The Quest for Empire

Not only missionaries but also business and political leaders had set their sights on distant lands, which in turn meant new markets. In the 1860s, Secretary of State William Henry Seward, under Abraham Lincoln and then under Andrew Johnson, correctly predicted that foreign trade would play an increasingly important part in the American economy. Between 1870 and 1900, exports more than tripled, from about $400 million to over $1.5 billion, with textiles and agricultural products leading the way. But as European markets for American goods began to contract, business and political leaders, of necessity, looked more eagerly to Asia as well as to lands closer by.

Since the American Revolution, many Americans had regarded all nearby nations as falling naturally within their own territorial realm, destined to be acquired when opportunity allowed. Seward advanced these imperialist principles in 1867 by negotiating the purchase of Alaska (known at the time as Seward's Icebox) from Russia, and he hoped someday to see the American flag flying over Canada and Mexico. Meanwhile, with European nations launched on their own imperialist missions in Asia and Africa, the United States increasingly viewed the Caribbean as an "American lake" and all of Latin America as a vast potential market for U.S. goods. The crisis of the 1890s transformed this long-standing desire into a perceived economic necessity.

Americans focused their expansionist plans on the Western Hemisphere, determined to dislodge the dominant power, Great Britain. In 1867, when Canada became a self-governing dominion, American diplomats hoped to annex their northern neighbor, believing that Great Britain would gladly accede in order to concentrate its imperial interests in Asia. But Great Britain refused to give up Canada, and the United States backed away. Central and South America proved more accommodating to American designs (see Map 20.3).

Republican stalwart James G. Blaine, secretary of state under presidents Garfield and Harrison, determined to work out a Good Neighbor policy (a phrase coined by Henry Clay in 1820). Bilateral treaties with Mexico, Colombia, the British West Indies, El Salvador, and the Dominican Republic allowed American businesses to dominate local economies, importing their raw materials at low prices and flooding their local markets with goods manufactured in the United States. Often, American investors simply took over the principal industries of these small nations, undercutting national business classes. The first Pan-American Conference, held in 1889–90, marked a turning point in hemispheric relations.

The Good Neighbor policy depended, Blaine knew, on peace and order in the Latin American states. As early as 1875, when revolt shook Venezuela, the Department of State warned European powers not to meddle. If popular uprisings proved too much for local officials, the U.S. Navy would intervene and return American allies to power.

In 1883, wishing to enforce treaties and protect overseas investments, Congress appropriated funds to build up American sea power and in 1884 established the Naval War College in Newport, Rhode Island, to train the officer corps. Beginning with ninety small ships, over one-third of them wooden, the navy grew quickly to include modern steel fighting ships. The hulls of these ships were painted a gleaming white, and the armada was known as the Great White Fleet. The force behind this build-up of the U.S. Navy was Captain Alfred Thayer Mahan, one of the first presidents of the Naval War College.

Mahan achieved international fame for outlining an imperialist strategy based on command of the seas. His book, *The Influence of Sea Power upon History, 1660–1873* (1890), helped to define foreign policy not only for the United States, but also for Great Britain, Japan, and Germany by identifying sea power as the key to world dominance. For the United States to achieve global preeminence, he prescribed not only open markets but also the control of colonies. Viewing the U.S. Navy as the "handmaid of expansion," Mahan advocated the creation of bases in the Caribbean and the Pacific. In 1893, he came out for the annexation of Hawai'i, claiming the United States, with its continental border extending to the Pacific Ocean, was "the proper guardian for this most important position." The Hawai'ian archipelago, he insisted, held key strategic value as stepping-stone to Asia and beyond.

Onto a Global Stage

Influenced by Alfred Thayer Mahan, McKinley became an advocate of expansion as a means to make the United States first in international commerce and as a means to implement its humanitarian and democratic goals. He also hoped to achieve these ends peacefully. In taking office, the new president specified: "We want no wars of conquest; we must avoid the temptation of territorial aggression." He was pleased, therefore, to grease the wheels for the annexation of Hawai'i and in June 1898 agreed with representatives from the Republic on a treaty of annexation. Soon, however, McKinley found himself embroiled

MAP 20.3 The American Domain, ca. 1900 The United States claimed
numerous islands in the South Pacific and intervened repeatedly in Latin America to secure its own
economic interests.

in a war with Spain that would establish the United States
as a strong player in global imperialism (see Map 20.4).
McKinley had to admit: "Isolation is no longer possible or
desirable." By the end of the century, the United States had
joined Europe and Japan in the quest for empire and
claimed territories spread out from the Caribbean Sea
across the Pacific.

A "Splendid Little War" in Cuba

Before the Civil War, Southerners pushed for the acquisition
of Cuba, a possession of Spain, for the expansion of slavery
into its sugar mills, tobacco plantations, and mines. After failing several times to buy the island outright, the United States
settled for the continuation of the status quo and resolved to
protect Spain's sovereignty over Cuba against the encroachment of other powers, including Cuba itself.

In the mid-1860s, a movement for independence
began in Cuba when Spain, its empire in ruins, began to
impose stiff taxes on the island. After a series of defeats,
insurgents rallied in the 1890s under the nationalist leadership of José Martí. In May 1895, Spanish troops ambushed
and killed Martí, turning him into a martyr and fanning
the flames of rebellion. In February 1896, Spain appointed
General Valeriano Weyler as governor and gave him full
authority to crush the rebellion. Weyler instituted a policy
of *reconcentrado*, forcing civilians from the countryside into
concentration camps so they could not aid the rebels.
Thousands starved or died from the diseases that swept
these crowded, dirty camps.

In the United States, the popular press whipped up
support for the movement for *Cuba Libre*, circulating sensationalistic and even false stories of the atrocities that

MAP 20.4 The Spanish–American War In two theaters of action, the United States used its naval power adeptly against a weak foe.

Weyler, "the butcher," perpetrated against the insurgents. Newspapers ran stories on mass executions in the "death camps" and featured drawings of emaciated children. This so-called "yellow journalism," practiced brilliantly by publishers Joseph Pulitzer and William Randolph Hearst, boosted circulation and simultaneously aroused sympathy for the Cubans and abundant patriotic fervor.

Public sympathy, again whipped up by the press, turned into frenzy on February 15, 1898, when an explosion ripped through the battleship USS *Maine*, stationed in Havana harbor to protect American interests. The newspapers ran banner headlines charging a Spanish conspiracy, although there was no proof. The impatient public, meanwhile, demanded revenge for the death of 266 American sailors. Within days, a new slogan appeared: "Remember the Maine! To Hell with Spain!"

Finally, on April 11, President McKinley asked Congress for a declaration of war against Spain. Congress barely passed the war resolution on April 25, and only with the inclusion of an amendment by Senator Henry Teller (R-Colorado) that disclaimed "any disposition or intention

to exercise sovereignty, jurisdiction or control over said island, except for the pacification thereof." McKinley called for volunteers, and by the end of April, the fighting had begun.

Ten weeks later, the war was all but over. On land, Lieutenant Colonel Theodore Roosevelt—who boasted of killing Spaniards "like jackrabbits"—led his Rough Riders to victory. On July 3, the main Spanish fleet near Santiago Bay was destroyed; two weeks later Santiago itself surrendered, and the war drew to a close. Although poorly trained and lacking supplies, fewer than 400 Americans died in battle. Disease and the inept treatment of the wounded created a medical disaster, however, spreading sickness and disease to more than 20,000 in the regiments. Roosevelt nevertheless felt invigorated by the conflict, agreeing with McKinley's Secretary of State John Hay that it had been a "splendid little war."

On August 12, at a small ceremony in McKinley's office marking Spain's surrender, the United States secured Cuba's independence from Spain, but not its own sovereignty.

View the Image
African American Troops in the Spanish-American War at **www.myhistorylab.com**

Brought to power with the assistance of American businessmen, Queen Lili'uokalani sought to limit outsider influence. American Marines, Christian missionaries, and sugar planters joined in 1893 to drive her from her throne. A century later, the U.S. government apologized to native Hawaiians for this illegal act.

American businesses proceeded to tighten their hold on Cuban sugar plantations, while U.S. military forces oversaw the formation of a constitutional convention that made Cuba a protectorate of the United States. Under the Platt Amendment, sponsored by Republican senator Orville H. Platt of Connecticut in 1901, Cuba was required to provide land for American bases, including a navy base at Guantanomo Bay; to devote national revenues to pay back debts to the United States; to sign no treaty that would be detrimental to American interests; and to acknowledge the right of the United States to intervene at any time to protect its interests in Cuba. After the U.S. withdrawal of troops, the terms of the Platt Amendment were incorporated into the Cuban-American Treaty of 1903. This treaty, which remained in place until 1934, paved the way for American domination of the island's sugar industry and contributed to anti-American sentiment among Cuban nationalists.

War in the Philippines

The Philippines, another of Spain's colonies, seemed an especially attractive prospect, its 7,000 islands a natural way station to the markets of mainland Asia. In 1897, Assistant

Secretary of the Navy Theodore Roosevelt and President McKinley had discussed the merits of taking the Pacific colony in the event of war with Spain. At the first opportunity, McKinley acted to bring these islands into the U.S. strategic orbit. On May 4, shortly after Congress declared war on Spain, the president dispatched 5,000 troops to occupy the Philippines. George Dewey, a Civil War veteran who commanded the American Asiatic Squadron, was ordered to "start offensive action." During the first week of the conflict, he demolished the Spanish fleet in Manila Bay through seven hours of unimpeded target practice. Once the war ended, McKinley refused to sign the armistice unless Spain relinquished all claims to its Pacific islands. When Spain conceded, McKinley quickly drew up plans for colonial administration. He pledged "to educate the Filipinos, and to uplift and civilize and Christianize them." After centuries of Spanish rule, however, the majority of islanders—already Christians—were eager to create their own nation.

The Filipino rebels, like the Cubans, at first welcomed American troops and fought with them against Spain. But when the Spanish-American War ended and they perceived that American troops were not preparing to leave, the rebels, led by Emilio Aguinaldo, turned against their former allies and attacked the

View the **Image**
Filipino Guerillas at **www.myhistorylab.com**

American base of operations in Manila in February 1899. Predicting a brief skirmish, American commanders seriously underestimated the population's capacity to endure great suffering for the sake of independence.

U.S. troops had provoked this conflict in various ways. Military leaders, the majority veterans of the Indian Wars, commonly described the natives as "gugus," and reported themselves, as one said, as "just itching to get at the niggers." While awaiting action, American soldiers repeatedly insulted or physically abused civilians, raped Filipino women, and otherwise whipped up resentment.

The resulting conflict took the form of modern guerrilla warfare, with brutalities on both sides. By the time the fighting slowed down in 1902, 4,300 American lives had been lost, and one of every five Filipinos had died in battle or from starvation or disease. On some of the Philippine islands, intermittent fighting lasted until 1935. In 1901, William Howard Taft headed a commission that established a special apparatus to rule in the Philippines; after 1905, the president appointed a Filipino governor general to maintain the provincial government. Meanwhile, Americans bought up the best land and invested heavily in the island's sugar economy.

The conquest of the Philippines, which remained a U.S. colony until 1946, evoked for its proponents the vision of empire. The Philippines joined Hawai'i as yet another stepping-stone for U.S. merchants en route to China. At the end of the Spanish-American War, the United States advanced its interests in the Caribbean to include Puerto Rico, ceded by Spain, and eventually the

COMMUNITIES *in* CONFLICT

Two Sides of Anti-Imperialism

Industrialist Andrew Carnegie (1835–1919) gave generously to help finance the Anti-Imperialist League from its formation until his death. He also served as a vice president of the league. His position on American expansion was complex, arising out of his opinion that some peoples were incapable of assimilation into a democratic society. For example, Carnegie reluctantly agreed with the annexation of Hawai'i, in part because the islands were only thinly settled and, therefore, could absorb more advanced "races," including American immigrants. Strongly opposed to acquiring the Philippines, he made an offer to President McKinley to purchase the islands from the United States, after which he would restore governance to the Filipinos. McKinley rejected this offer, ensuring Carnegie's alliance with the anti-imperialists. His statement was originally published in August 1898, when U.S. forces were invading the Philippines and Americans were debating what to do with the Spanish colonies.

The widow of a prominent businessman and throughout her life a committed reformer, Josephine Shaw Lowell (1843–1905) also opposed the Spanish-American War. Like Carnegie, she denounced the annexation of the Philippines and likewise was a leader of the Anti-Imperialist League, serving as a vice president from 1901 to 1905. Lowell wrote her impassioned protest after the outbreak of Filipino resistance against American rule, but before the U.S. Army completed its bloody subjugation of the islands.

- **Are these two arguments contradictory or complementary? Is there more to Carnegie's objection to imperialism than racism? Is Lowell correct in arguing that some wars can be not only just but also morally elevating?**

Andrew Carnegie, Anti-Imperialist: America Cannot Absorb Alien Populations (August 1898)

Is the Republic, the apostle of Triumphant Democracy, of the rule of the people, to abandon her political creed and endeavor to establish in other lands the rule of the foreigner over the people, Triumphant Despotism?

Is the Republic to remain one homogeneous whole, one united people, or to become a scattered and disjointed aggregate of widely separated and alien races?

Is she to continue the task of developing her vast continent until it holds a population as great as that of Europe, all Americans, or to abandon that destiny to annex, and to attempt to govern, other far distant parts of the world as outlying possessions, which can never be integral parts of the Republic? . . .

There are two kinds of national possessions, one colonies, the other dependencies. In the former we establish and reproduce our own race. Thus Britain has peopled Canada and Australia with English-speaking people, who have naturally adopted our ideas of self-government.

> "[T]he question [is] whether we should embark upon the difficult and dangerous policy of undertaking the government of alien races. . . ."

With dependencies it is otherwise. The most grievous burden which Britain has upon her shoulders is that of India, for there it is impossible for our race to grow. The child of English-speaking parents must be removed and reared in Britain. The British Indian official must have long respites in his native land. India means death to our race. The characteristic feature of a dependency is that the acquiring power cannot reproduce its own race there.

If we could establish colonies of Americans, and grow Americans in any part of the world now unpopulated and unclaimed by any of the great powers, and thus follow the example of Britain, heart and mind might tell us that we should have to think twice, yea, thrice, before deciding adversely. Even then our decision should be adverse; but there is at present no such question before us. What we have to face is the question whether we should embark upon the difficult and dangerous policy of undertaking the government of alien races in lands where it is impossible for our own race to be produced. . . .

I am no "Little" American, afraid of growth, either in population or territory, provided always that the new territory be American, and that it will produce Americans, and not foreign races bound in time to be false to the Republic in order to be true to themselves. . . . The Philippines have about seven and a half millions of people, composed of races bitterly hostile to one another, alien races, ignorant of our language and institutions. Americans cannot be grown there. . . .

SOURCE: Andrew Carnegie, "Distant Possessions: The Parting of the Ways," in *The Gospel of Wealth* (New York: Century Company, 1901), p. 151. Originally published in the *North American Review* (August. 1898).

Josephine Shaw Lowell, Anti-Imperialist: America Must Not Wage Unjust Wars (ca. 1900)

I cannot speak on this subject without making a distinction between different kinds of wars.

A war which requires personal sacrifice, a war which makes a whole people place patriotism and public duty above private comfort and ease, which forces men and women out of self-indulgence, devotion to material wealth—such a war does not as a whole cause moral deterioration—but on the contrary, moral development in a nation.

Such a war was the Civil War in this country, forty years ago. . . .

The history of the introduction of the United States to the Philippine Islands is a disgraceful one. . . . In December, 1898 . . . the President of the United States proclaimed sovereignty over the Philippine Archipelago, this naturally aroused the anger of the Filipinos, who had been treasuring for six months or more the hope that the United States intended to help and protect their young republic against the attacks of other nations, and the feelings became more and more bitter, and finally culminated in a fight between the outposts of the two armies on February 4, 1899; and from that time, the United States devoted itself to the task of crushing out what was called the insurrection of the Filipinos.

That is, the United States, having obtained a foothold in a foreign country by professing friendship for the inhabitants, calls those inhabitants rebels because the people resist the invasion and try to defend their country. We direct our army to crush out all resistance. The Filipino people prefer death to subjugation, saying, as did Patrick Henry, the American patriot, "Give me liberty or give me death." Our unhappy army set to do such an un-American, such a wicked task, tried to obey orders, becomes gradually more and more cruel. . . .

It is incredible that the American people should have been so ignorant and so careless in regard to the great wrong which has been done in their name; but now at last we are awakening, we are beginning to realize the facts. . . . I said, that the liberties of the United States are at stake equally with the liberties of the Filipino people, for it is inevitable that should we willingly become the tyrant of these helpless millions, should we turn our backs so completely upon the principles which have made this country a world power, molding and influencing the character of all governments of the world during the past hundred and twenty-five years, as to make it possible for us to do such a

> "[T]he United States, having obtained a foothold in a foreign country by professing friendship for the inhabitants, calls those inhabitants rebels because [they] resist the invasion. . . ."

thing our moral deterioration is so rapid, our conscience must become so hardened in the process, our love of liberty so absolutely dead, that, we should become fit subjects for a tyranny ourselves.

SOURCE: "Moral Deterioration Following War," ca. 1900, reprinted in *The Philanthropic Work of Josephine Shaw Lowell: Containing a Biographical Sketch of Her Life,* collected by William Rhinelander Stewart (New York: Macmillan Co., 1911), pp. 466–470.

Virgin Islands of St. Thomas, St. John, and St. Croix, purchased from Denmark in 1917. The acquisition of Pacific territories, including Guam, marked the emergence of the United States as a global colonial power.

Once again, Josiah Strong proclaimed judgment over an era. His famous treatise *Expansion* (1900) roundly defended American overseas involvements by carefully distinguishing between freedom and independence. People could achieve freedom, he argued, only under the rule of law. Because white Americans had proven themselves superior in the realm of government, they could best bring "freedom" to nonwhite peoples by setting aside the ideal of national independence for a period of enforced guidance. Many began to wonder, however, whether the United States could become an empire without sacrificing its democratic spirit and to ask whether the subjugated people were really so fortunate under the rule of the United States (see Communities in Conflict).

Critics of Empire

No mass movement formed to forestall U.S. expansion, but distinguished figures like Mark Twain, Andrew Carnegie, William Jennings Bryan, and Harvard philosopher William James voiced their opposition strongly. To protest military action in the Philippines, a small group of prominent Bostonians organized the Anti-Imperialist League. They staged a mass meeting in June 1898 in historic Faneuil Hall, which had witnessed the birth of both the American Revolution and the antislavery movement. Those in attendance protested the "insane and wicked ambition which is driving the nation to ruin." Most supported American economic expansion, but advocated free trade rather than political domination as the means to reach this goal. All strongly opposed the annexation of new territories, including Hawai'i.

The *National Labor Standard* expressed its common hope that all those "who believe in the Republic against Empire should join." By 1899, the league claimed a half-million members. A few outspoken anti-imperialists, such as former Illinois governor John Peter Altgeld, openly toasted Filipino rebels as heroes. Morrison Swift, leader of the Coxey's Army contingent from Massachusetts, formed a Filipino Liberation Society and sent antiwar materials to American troops. Others, such as Samuel Gompers, a league vice president, felt no sympathy for conquered peoples and simply wanted to prevent colonized nonwhites from immigrating into the United States and "inundating" American labor.

Military leaders and staunch imperialists did not distinguish between racist and nonracist anti-imperialists. They called all dissenters "unhung traitors" and demanded their arrest. Newspaper editors accused universities of harboring antiwar professors, although college students as a group were enthusiastic supporters of the war.

Within the press, which overwhelmingly supported the Spanish-American War, the voices of opposition

"Uncle Sam Teaches the Art of Self-Government," editorial cartoon, 1898. Expressing a popular sentiment of the time, a newspaper cartoonist shows the rebels as raucous children who constantly fight among themselves and need to be brought into line by Uncle Sam. The Filipino leader, Emilio Aguinaldo, appears as a dunce for failing to learn properly from the teacher. The two major islands where no uprising took place, Puerto Rico and Hawai'i, appear as passive but exotically dressed women, ready to learn their lessons.

appeared primarily in African American and labor papers. The *Indianapolis Recorder* asked rhetorically in 1899, "Are the tender-hearted expansionists in the United States Congress really actuated by the desire to save the Filipinos from self-destruction or is it the worldly greed for gain?" The *Railroad Telegrapher* similarly commented, "The wonder of it all is that the working people are willing to lose blood and treasure in fighting another man's battle."

Most Americans put aside their doubts and welcomed the new era of imperialism. Untouched by the private tragedies of dead or wounded American soldiers and the mass destruction of civilian society in the Philippines, the vast majority could approve Theodore Roosevelt's defense of armed conflict: "No triumph of peace is quite so great as the supreme triumphs of war."

Conclusion

The conflicts marking the last quarter of the nineteenth century that pitted farmers, workers, and the proprietors of small businesses against powerful national interests had offered Americans an important moment of democratic promise. By the end of the century, however, the rural and working-class

CHRONOLOGY

1867	Grange founded
	Secretary of State Seward negotiates the purchase of Alaska
1874	Granger laws begin to regulate railroad shipping rates
1877	Rutherford B. Hayes elected president
	Great Uprising of 1877
1879	Henry George publishes *Progress and Poverty*
1881	President James A. Garfield assassinated; Chester A. Arthur becomes president
1882	Chinese Exclusion Act
1883	Pendleton Act passed
1884	Grover Cleveland elected president
1887	Interstate Commerce Act creates the Interstate Commerce Commission
1888	Colored Farmers' Alliance formed
	Benjamin Harrison elected president
1889	National Farmers' Alliance formed
1890	Sherman Silver Purchase Act
	McKinley Tariff enacted
	National American Woman Suffrage Association formed
1892	Populist (People's) Party formed
	Coeur d'Alene miners' strike

	Homestead strike
	Ida B. Wells begins crusade against lynching
1893	Western Federation of Miners formed
	Financial panic and depression
	World's Columbian Exhibition opens in Chicago
1894	"Coxey's Army" marches on Washington, DC
	Pullman strike and boycott
1896	*Plessy* v. *Ferguson* upholds segregation
	William McKinley defeats William Jennings Bryan for president
1897	Dingley Tariff again raises import duties to an all-time high
1898	Eugene V. Debs helps found Social Democratic Party
	Hawai'i is annexed
	Spanish-American War begins
	Anti-Imperialist League formed
	Wilmington, North Carolina, massacre
1899	*Cumming* v. *Richmond County Board of Education* sanctions segregated education
	Guerrilla war begins in the Philippines
1900	Gold Standard Act
	Josiah Strong publishes *Expansion*

campaigns to retain a large degree of self-government in their communities had been defeated, their organizations destroyed, their autonomy eroded. The rise of a national governing class and its counterpart, the large bureaucratic state, established new rules of behavior, new sources of prestige, and new rewards for the most successful citizens.

The nation would eventually pay a steep price for the failure of democratic reform. Regional antagonisms, nativist movements against the foreign-born, and, above all, deepening racial tensions blighted American society. As the new century opened, progressive reformers moved to correct flaws in government while accepting the framework of a corporate society and its overseas empire. So, too, did the majority of citizens who shared their president's pride in expansion.

William Jennings Bryan made another bid for the presidency in 1900 on a strong anti-imperialist platform and was roundly defeated at the polls. The dream of Queen Lili'iokalani for an independent Hawai'i was likewise crushed, although in 1993, a century after her overthrow, President William Clinton signed a joint congressional resolution apologizing for the "alleged role the United States had played" in her deposing. But in 1900, Americans would find the widening divisions in their own society difficult—if not impossible—to overcome.

Review Questions

I.   Discuss some of the problems accompanying the expansion of government during the late nineteenth century. What role did political parties play in this process? Explain how a prominent reformer such as James Garfield might become a leading "machine" politician.

2. What were the major causes and consequences of the Populist movement of the 1880s and 1890s? Why did the election of 1896 prove so important to the future of American politics?

3. Discuss the role of women in both the Grange and the People's Party. What were their specific goals?

4. Discuss the causes and consequences of the financial crisis of the 1890s. How did various reformers and politicians respond to the event? What kinds of programs did they offer to restore the economy or reduce poverty?

5. How did the exclusion of African Americans affect the outcome of populism? Explain the rise of Jim Crow legislation in the South and discuss its impact on the status of African Americans.

6. Describe American foreign policy during the 1890s. Why did the United States intervene in Cuba and the Philippines? What were some of the leading arguments for and against overseas expansion?

Recommended Reading

Steven Hahn, *A Nation Under Our Feet: Black Political Struggles in the Rural South from Slavery to the Great Migration* (2003). A sweeping history of African American politics with a focus on its influence in shaping the South and the nation in the last half of the nineteenth century. Hahn emphasizes the emergence of political communities and highlights the 1880s as a period of exceptional assertiveness on the part of southern African Americans.

Evelyn Brooks Higginbotham, *Righteous Discontent: The Women's Movement in the Black Baptist Church, 1880–1920* (1993). Documents the central role of women in shaping the theology and racial uplift programs of the National Baptist Convention, the largest denomination of African Americans at the end of the nineteenth century.

Matthew Frye Jacobson, *Barbarian Virtues: The United States Encounters Foreign Peoples at Home and Abroad, 1876–1917* (2000). Links the histories of immigration and empire-building to examine public discussions about foreign people, especially their "fitness"

for self-government. Jacobson casts the search for markets as a backdrop for cultural history.

Michael Kazin, *A Godly Hero: The Life of William Jennings Bryan* (2006). Makes a strong case for the relevance of Bryan to the history of American liberalism. Kazin explores the sources of Bryan's popularity among the nation's poor and working classes.

Walter LaFeber, *The New Empire: An Interpretation of American Expansion, 1860–1898* (1963, 1998). The best overview of U.S. imperial involvement in the late nineteenth century. LaFeber shows how overseas commitments grew out of the economic expansionist assumptions of American leaders and expanded continuously, if often chaotically, with the opportunities presented by the crises experienced by the older imperial powers.

Leon F. Litwack, *Trouble in Mind: Black Southerners in the Age of Jim Crow* (1998). An expansive social history of the first generation of African Americans born in freedom and surviving a period of extraordinary violent and repressive race relations in the South. Litwack examines the retrenchment of their political and civil rights but emphasizes their resourcefulness and resistance.

Eric T. L. Love, *Race over Empire and U.S. Imperialism, 1865–1900* (2004). An engaging narrative of expansion in the late nineteenth century and a keen analysis of the policies supporting and opposing annexation of territories and the assimilation of new populations.

Charles Postel, *The Populist Vision* (2007). A prize-winning book, Postel's intellectual and political history presents the populists as a forward-looking reform coalition committed to modernity, efficiency, and business-like models of government.

Noenoe K. Silva, *Aloha Betrayed: Native Hawaiian Resistance to American Colonialism* (2004). Highlights the active role native Hawaiians played in the face of U.S. annexation pressures. Silva breaks ground by using Hawaiian-language newspapers and sources.

John Lawrence Tone, *War and Genocide in Cuba, 1895–1898* (2006). Provides a new perspective on the Cuban rebellion from Spain and a careful study of Spanish policy in the hands of General Varleriano Weyler.

William Appleman Williams, *Empire as a Way of Life: An Essay on the Causes and Character of America's Present Predicament* (1982). A lucid general exploration of American views of empire. Williams shows that Americans allowed the idea of empire and, more generally, economic expansion to dominate their concept of democracy, especially in the last half of the nineteenth century.

myhistorylab Connections

Reinforce what you learned in this chapter by studying the many documents, images, maps, review tools, and videos available at www.myhistorylab.com.

Read and Review

✓• Study and Review **Chapter 20**

•••• Read the Document

Frances E. Willard on the Reorganization of Government (1891)

The People's Party Platform (1892)

Jacob Coxey, Address of Protest (1894)

Eugene V. Debs, The Outlook for Socialism in America (1900)

William Jennings Bryan, "Cross of Gold" Speech (1896)

Josiah Strong, from Our Country (1885)

•• View the Image

Nast Cartoon: Boss Tweed

Homestead Strikers Surrendering

African American Troops in the Spanish-American War

Filipino Guerillas

Research and Explore

•••• Read the Document

Exploring America: White Man's Burden

Exploring America: Homestead Strike of 1892

Profiles
Queen Liliuokalani
Williams Jennings Bryan

((•• Hear the Audio

Hear the audio files for Chapter 20 at
www.myhistorylab.com.

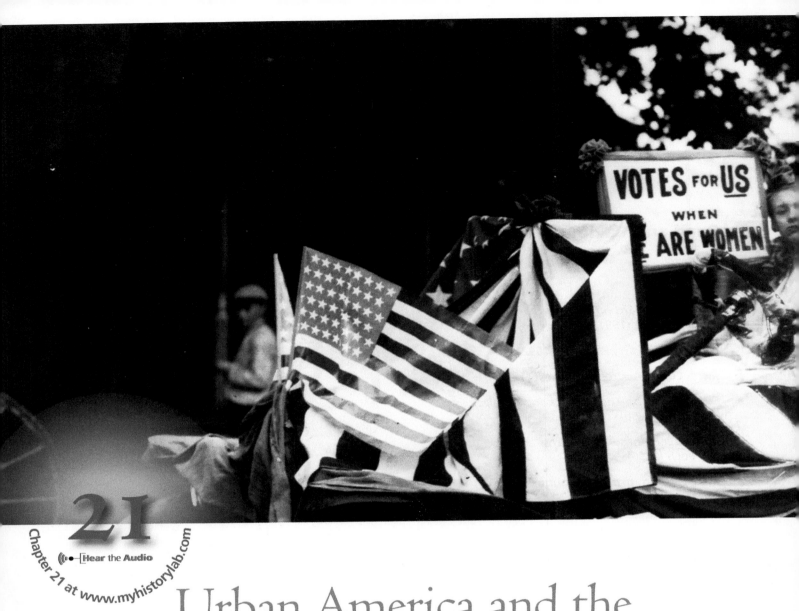

21

Chapter 21 at www.myhistorylab.com

((●●[Hear the Audio

Urban America and the Progressive Era 1900–1917

CHAPTER OUTLINE

American Communities 585
The Henry Street Settlement House: Women Settlement House Workers Create a Community of Reform

The Origins of Progressivism 587
Unifying Themes
New Journalism: Muckraking
Intellectual Trends Promoting Reform
The Female Dominion

Progressive Politics in Cities and States 593
The Urban Machine
Progressives and Urban Reform
Statehouse Progressives

Social Control and Its Limits 596
The Prohibition Movement
The Social Evil
The Redemption of Leisure
Standardizing Education

Challenges to Progressivism 601
The New Global Immigration
Urban Ghettos
Company Towns
Competing Visions of Unionism: AFL and IWW
Rebels in Bohemia

Women's Movements and Black Activism 607
The New Woman
Birth Control
Racism and Accommodation
Racial Justice, the NAACP, and Black Women's Activism

National Progressivism 611
Theodore Roosevelt and Presidential Activism
Trust-Busting and Regulation
The Birth of Environmentalism
The Election of 1912: A Four-Way Race
Woodrow Wilson's First Term

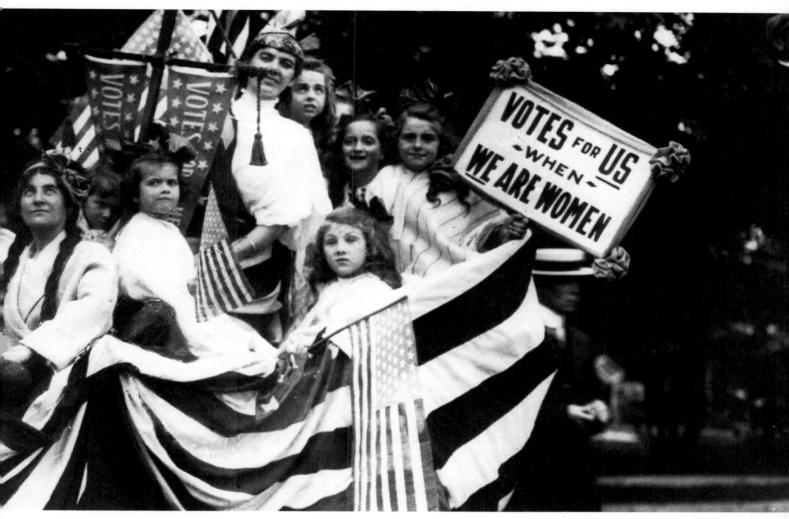

Suffragettes hold a victory jubilee, 1920. Elated women wave American flags and blow noisemakers. Courtesy of Library of Congress.

The Henry Street Settlement House: Women Settlement House Workers Create a Community of Reform

A shy and frightened young girl appeared in the doorway of a weekly home-nursing class for women on Manhattan's Lower East Side. The teacher beckoned her to come forward. Tugging on the teacher's skirt, the girl pleaded in broken English for the teacher to come home with her. "Mother," "baby," "blood," she kept repeating. The teacher gathered up the sheets that were part of the interrupted lesson in bed making. The two hurried through narrow, garbage-strewn, foul-smelling streets, then groped their way up a pitch-dark, rickety staircase. They reached a cramped, two-room apartment, home to an immigrant family of seven and several boarders. There, in a vermin-infested bed, encrusted with dried blood, lay a mother and her newborn baby. The mother had been abandoned by a doctor because she could not afford his fee.

The teacher, Lillian Wald, was a twenty-five-year-old nurse at New York Hospital. Years later, she recalled this scene as her baptism by fire and the turning point in her life. Born in 1867, Wald had enjoyed a comfortable upbringing in a middle-class German Jewish family in Rochester. Despite her parents'

**AMERICAN·•·
Communities**

585

objections, she moved to New York City to become a professional nurse. Resentful of the disdainful treatment nurses received from doctors, and horrified by the inhumane conditions at a juvenile asylum where she worked, Wald determined to find a way of caring for the sick in their neighborhoods and homes. With nursing school classmate Mary Brewster, Wald rented a fifth-floor walk-up apartment on the Lower East Side and established a visiting nurse service. The two provided professional care in the home to hundreds of families for a nominal fee of ten to twenty-five cents. They also offered each family they visited information on basic health care, sanitation, and disease prevention. In 1895, philanthropist Jacob Schiff generously donated a red brick Georgian house on Henry Street as a new base of operation.

The Henry Street Settlement stood in the center of perhaps the most overcrowded neighborhood in the world, New York's Lower East Side. Roughly 500,000 people were packed into an area only as large as a midsized Kansas farm. Population density was about 500 per acre, roughly four times the figure for the rest of New York City, and far more concentrated than even the worst slums of London or Calcutta. A single city block might have as many as 3,000 residents. Home for most Lower East Siders was a small tenement apartment that might include paying boarders squeezed in alongside the immediate family. Residents were mostly recent immigrants from southern and eastern Europe: Jews, Italians, Germans, Greeks, Hungarians, Slavs. Men, women, and children toiled in the garment shops, small factories, retail stores, breweries, and warehouses that were found on nearly every street.

The Henry Street Settlement became a model for a new kind of reform community composed essentially of college-educated women who encouraged and supported one another in a wide variety of humanitarian, civic, and political activities. These included support for organized labor, campaigns for better sanitation and more parks, lobbying state legislatures for tougher laws regulating tenement construction and factory safety, and pushing for women's right to vote. Settlement house living arrangements closely resembled those in the dormitories of such new women's colleges as Smith, Wellesley, and Vassar. Like these colleges, the settlement house was an "experiment," but one designed,

in settlement house pioneer Jane Addams's words, "to aid in the solution of the social and industrial problems which are engendered by the modern conditions of urban life." Unlike earlier moral reformers, who tried to impose their ideas from outside, settlement house residents lived in poor communities and worked for immediate improvements in the health and welfare of those communities. Yet, as Addams and others repeatedly stressed, the college-educated women were beneficiaries as well. The settlement house allowed them to preserve a collegial spirit, satisfy the desire for service, and apply their academic training.

With its combined moral and social appeal, the settlement house movement attracted many educated young women and grew rapidly. There were 6 settlement houses in the United States in 1891, some 74 in 1897, more than 200 by 1900, and more than 400 by 1910. Few women made settlement work a career, but those who did typically chose not to marry, and most lived together with female companions. As the movement flourished, settlement house residents called attention to the plight of the poor and fostered respect for different cultural heritages in countless articles and lectures. Leaders of the movement, including Jane Addams, Lillian Wald, and Florence Kelley, emerged as influential political figures during the progressive era.

The settlement house movement embodied the impulses toward social justice and civic engagement that were hallmarks of the progressive movement. But in a broader sense, the progressive era was defined by struggles over the true meaning of American democracy. If there was growing agreement that Americans needed to address the excesses of industrial growth and rapid urbanization, there was less consensus over precisely how. As progressive activism spread from reform communities like settlement houses, to city halls and statehouses, and finally to the national stage of the White House and Congress, Americans experimented with new approaches to urgent problems. How might the power of government be used to restrain corporate excess and improve the lives of children, industrial laborers, and others in need of protection? Could the machinery of democracy be reformed to make politics less corrupt and more responsive to the needs of ordinary citizens? Did the calls to social action mean that full citizenship rights

1. What were the social and intellectual roots of progressive reform?

2. How did tensions between social justice and social control divide progressives?

3. How did the impact of new immigration from southern and eastern Europe transform American cities?

4. What new forms of activism emerged among the working class, women, and African Americans?

5. How did progressivism become a central force in national politics?

FOCUS Questions

1900–1917

would be extended to African Americans, women, and new immigrants? What were the most effective ways to expose social problems and appeal to the public conscience?

During the first two decades of the twentieth century, millions of Americans identified themeselves as "progressives" and most, like Lillian Wald, were first drawn to causes and campaigns rooted in their local communities. But many

New York City

soon saw that confronting the grim realities of an urban and industrial society required national and even global strategies for pursuing reform. It was no cliché for Wald to say, as she did on many occasions, "The whole world is my neighborhood." By the time America entered World War I in 1917, despite its contradictions, the progressive movement had reshaped the political and social landscape of the entire nation.

AMERICAN Communities

The Origins of Progressivism

Between the 1890s and World War I, a large and diverse number of Americans claimed the political label "progressive." Progressives could be found in all classes, regions, and races. They shared a fundamental belief that America needed a new social consciousness to cope with the problems brought on by the enormous rush of economic and social change in the post–Civil War decades. The devastating depression of the 1890s, the often bloody labor conflicts of that decade, and the populist revolt caused many Americans to look for a stronger government response to economic and social ills. Yet progressivism was no unified movement with a single set of principles. It is best understood as a varied collection of reform communities, often fleeting, uniting citizens in a host of political, professional, and religious organizations, some of which were national in scope.

As a political movement, progressivism flowered in the soil of several key issues: ending political corruption,

bringing more businesslike methods to governing, and offering a more compassionate legislative response to the excesses of industrialism. As a national movement, progressivism reached its peak in 1912, when the four major presidential candidates all ran on some version of a progressive platform. This last development was an important measure of the extent to which local reform movements, like the Henry Street Settlement, and new intellectual currents had captured the political imagination of the nation.

Some progressives focused on expanding state and federal regulation of private interests for the public welfare. Others viewed the rapid influx of additional immigrants and the explosive growth of large cities as requiring more stringent social controls. Another variant emphasized eliminating corruption in the political system as the key to righting society's wrongs. In the South, progressivism was for white people only. Progressives could be forward-looking in their vision or nostalgic for a rapidly disappearing nineteenth-century world. Self-styled progressives often found themselves facing each other from opposite sides of an issue.

Unifying Themes

Three basic attitudes underlay the various progressive crusades and movements. The first was anger over the excesses of industrial capitalism and urban growth. Unlike Populist-era reformers, who were largely rural and small-town oriented, progressives focused their energies on the social and political ills experienced by Americans in factories and mines and in dreary city tenements or filthy streets. At the same time, progressives shared an essential optimism about the ability of citizens to improve social and economic conditions. They were reformers, not revolutionaries, who believed in using the democratic institutions available to them—the vote, the courts, the legislature—to address social problems. If those political processes were found to be corrupt or undemocratic, they would have to be reformed as well. Second, progressives emphasized social cohesion and common bonds as a way to understand how modern society and economics actually worked. They largely rejected the ideal of individualism that had informed nineteenth-century economic and political theory. For progressives, poverty and success hinged on more than simply individual character; the economy was more than merely a sum of individual calculations. Society's problems, in this view, were structural rather than just the result of individual failures. Third, progressives believed in the need for citizens to intervene actively, both politically and morally, to improve social conditions. They looked to convert personal outrage into civic activism and to mobilize public opinion in new ways. Progressives thus called for expansion of the legislative and regulatory powers of the state. They moved away from the nineteenth-century celebration of minimal government as the surest way to allow all Americans to thrive.

Progressive rhetoric and methods drew on two distinct sources of inspiration. One was evangelical Protestantism, particularly the late nineteenth-century social gospel movement. Social gospelers rejected the idea of original sin as the cause of human suffering. They emphasized both the capacity and the duty of Christians to purge the world of poverty, inequality, and economic greed. Many progressive activists with roots in the evangelical tradition adapted the old emphasis on individual salvation into a new social activism more focused on finding the common good. A second strain of progressive thought looked to natural and social scientists to develop rational measures for improving the human condition. They believed that experts trained in statistical analysis, engineering, and the sciences could make government and industry more efficient and set new standards for

personal behavior. Progressivism thus offered an uneasy combination of social justice and social control, a tension that would characterize American reform for the rest of the twentieth century.

New Journalism: Muckraking

Changes in journalism helped fuel a new reform consciousness by drawing the attention of millions to urban poverty, political corruption, the plight of industrial workers, and immoral business practices. As early as 1890, journalist Jacob Riis had shocked the nation with his landmark book *How the Other Half Lives*, a portrait of New York City's poor. Riis's book included a remarkable series of photographs he had taken in tenements, lodging houses, sweatshops, and saloons. These striking pictures, combined with Riis's analysis of housing patterns in the slums, had a powerful impact on a whole generation of urban reformers (see Seeing History).

Within a few years, magazine journalists turned to uncovering the seamier side of American life. The key innovator was S. S. McClure, a young midwestern editor who in 1893 started America's first large-circulation magazine, *McClure's*. Charging only a dime for his monthly, McClure effectively combined popular fiction

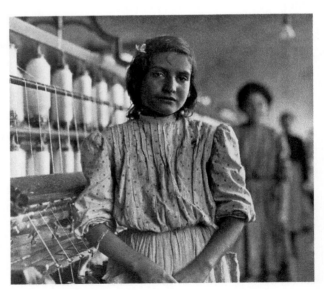

Lewis Hine, one of the pioneers of social documentary photography, made this evocative 1908 portrait of "Mamie," a typical young spinner working at a cotton mill in Lancaster, South Carolina. The National Child Labor Committee hired Hine to help document, publicize, and curb the widespread employment of children in industrial occupations. "These pictures," Hine wrote, "speak for themselves and prove that the law is being violated."

SOURCE: Lewis Hine (American, 1874–1940), "A Carolina Spinner," 1908. Gelatin silver print, 4 ¾ × 7 in. Milwaukee Art Museum, Gift of the Sheldon M. Barnett Family. M1973.83.

with articles on science, technology, travel, and recent history. He attracted a new readership among the urban middle class through aggressive subscription and promotional campaigns, as well as newsstand sales. By the turn of the century, *McClure's* and several imitators—*Munsey's, Cosmopolitan, Collier's, Everybody's*, and the *Saturday Evening Post*—had circulations in the hundreds of thousands. Making extensive use of photographs and illustrations, these cheap upstarts soon far surpassed older, more staid and expensive magazines such as the *Atlantic Monthly* and *Harper's* in circulation.

In 1902, McClure began hiring talented reporters to write detailed accounts of the nation's social problems. Lincoln Steffens's series *The Shame of the Cities* (1903) revealed the widespread graft at the center of American urban politics. He showed how big-city bosses routinely worked hand in glove with businessmen seeking lucrative municipal contracts for gas, water, electricity, and mass transit. Ida Tarbell, in her *History of the Standard Oil Company* (1904), thoroughly documented how John D. Rockefeller ruthlessly squeezed out competitors with unfair business practices. Ray Stannard Baker wrote detailed portraits of life and labor in Pennsylvania coal towns.

McClure's and other magazines discovered that "exposure journalism" paid off handsomely in terms of increased circulation. The middle-class public responded to this new combination of factual reporting and moral exhortation. A series such as Steffens's fueled reform campaigns that swept individual communities. Between 1902 and 1908, magazines were full of articles exposing insurance scandals, patent medicine frauds, and stock market swindles. Upton Sinclair's 1906 novel *The Jungle*, a socialist tract set among Chicago packinghouse workers, exposed the filthy sanitation and abysmal working conditions in the stockyards and the meatpacking industry. In an effort to boost sales, Sinclair's publisher devoted an entire issue of a monthly magazine it owned, *World's Work*, to articles and photographs that substantiated Sinclair's devastating portrait.

Muckraking crusades could take many forms. In the 1890s, the young African American newspaper editor Ida B. Wells set out to investigate an upsurge in lynchings around the city of Memphis. She paid special attention to the common white defense of lynching—that it was a necessary response to attempts by black men to rape white women. Her 1895 pamphlet *The Red Record* showed that the vast majority of black lynching victims had not even been accused of sexual transgression. Instead, Wells found that lynching was primarily a brutal device to eliminate African Americans who competed with white businesses or who had become too prosperous or powerful.

Read the Document
History Bookshelf: Upton Sinclair, The Jungle (1906) at **www.myhistorylab.com**

In 1906, David Graham Phillips, in a series for *Cosmopolitan* called "The Treason of the Senate," argued that many conservative U.S. senators were no more than mouthpieces for big business. President Theodore Roosevelt, upset by Phillips's attack on several of his friends and supporters, coined a new term when he angrily denounced Phillips and his colleagues as "muckrakers" who "raked the mud of society and never looked up." Partly due to Roosevelt's outburst, the muckraking vogue began to wane. But muckraking had demonstrated the potential for mobilizing public opinion on a national scale.

Intellectual Trends Promoting Reform

On a deeper level than muckraking, early twentieth-century thinkers challenged several core ideas in American intellectual life. Their new theories of education, law, economics, and society provided effective tools for reformers. The emergent fields of the social sciences—sociology, psychology, anthropology, and economics—emphasized observation of how people actually lived and behaved in their communities. Progressive reformers linked the systematic analysis of society and the individual characteristics of these new fields of inquiry to the project of improving the material conditions of Americans. Significantly, many of these intellectual currents transcended national boundaries. American progressives engaged in running dialogues with European counterparts who also contended with crafting effective and rational responses to the needs of overcrowded cities, impoverished industrial workers, and unresponsive political systems. Jane Addams's original inspiration for the Hull House settlement in Chicago had come when she visited Toynbee Hall in London. Housing reformers in Glasgow and Manchester, as well as workmen's compensation reformers in Berlin, and old-age insurance experts in Copenhagen provided important international forums for progressives here and around the world. Despite their national differences, progressives around the world searched for new ways to reinforce social bonds in the modern era.

Read the Document
History Bookshelf: Ida B. Wells-Barnett, The Red Record (1895) at **www.myhistorylab.com**

Sociologist Lester Frank Ward, in his pioneering work *Dynamic Sociology* (1883), offered an important critique of social Darwinism, the orthodox theory that attributed social inequality to natural selection and the "survival of the fittest." Ward argued that the conservative social theorists responsible for social Darwinism, such as Herbert Spencer and William Graham Sumner, had wrongly applied evolutionary theory to human affairs. They had confused organic evolution with social evolution. Nature's method was genetic: unplanned, involuntary, automatic, and mechanical. By contrast, civilization had been built on successful human intervention in the natural processes of organic evolution.

Photographing Poverty in the Slums of New York

SEEING
History

Jacob A. Riis was a twenty-year-old Danish immigrant when he arrived in New York City in 1870. After several years wandering the country as a casual laborer, he returned to New York and began a career as a reporter covering the police beat. By the early 1880s, Riis found himself drawn to report on perhaps the most overwhelming and rapidly worsening problem in the city: the deteriorating conditions of tenement house life. As he accompanied city police and Board of Health employees in their inspections of sanitary conditions, Riis's reports on the tenement districts reflected a keen outrage and new sense of purpose. Part of the story could be reduced to staggering statistics. By 1880, more than 600,000 New Yorkers lived in 24,000 tenements, each of which housed anywhere from four to several score families. Overcrowding kept getting worse, as in one Mulberry Street tenement that housed nearly two hundred people in small apartments meant for twenty families. Thousands of buildings had terrible sanitary conditions, with seriously defective plumbing, and often no ventilation or sewer connections. "It was upon my midnight

trips with the sanitary police," he recalled, "that the wish kept cropping up in me that there were some way of putting before the people what I saw there."

In 1888, Riis taught himself the rudiments of photography, using the new "flash powder" technology to take pictures where there was no natural light. He shot many of these photographs in the dead of the night, taking his subjects by surprise. Other photographs were carefully staged to ensure maximum emotional impact on the middle- and upper-class audience Riis was trying to reach. Riis converted his photographs into "lantern slides," which could be projected as large images before audiences. He spent two years touring the country, presenting an illustrated lecture called "The Other Half: How It Lives and Dies in New York" to churches and reform groups, appealing to the conscience and Christian sympathy of his listeners. Newspapers reviewed Riis's slide lecture as both an "entertainment" and a new philanthropic campaign. In 1890, he published his landmark book, *How the Other Half Lives: Studies Among the Tenements*, illustrated with his photographs. The use of photography would become a key element for reform crusades in the progressive era and beyond.

• **Here are two Riis photographs, "Five Cents a Spot" and "Home of an Italian Ragpicker." What visual information does each communicate about tenement life? How do they differ in their depiction of New York City's immigrant poor? How do you imagine Riis set up the scene for each of these photographs?**

Philosopher John Dewey criticized the excessively rigid and formal approach to education found in most American schools. In books such as *The School and Society* (1899) and *Democracy and Education* (1916), Dewey advocated developing what he called "creative intelligence" in students, which could then be put to use in improving society. Schools ought to be "embryonic communities," miniatures of society, where children were encouraged to participate actively in different types of experiences. By cultivating imagination and openness to new experiences, schools could develop creativity and the habits required for systematic inquiry. Dewey's belief that education was the "fundamental method of social progress and reform" inspired generations of progressive educators.

At the University of Wisconsin, John R. Commons founded the new field of industrial relations and organized a state industrial commission that became a model for other states. Working closely with Governor Robert M. La Follette, Commons and his students helped draft pioneering laws in worker compensation and public utility regulation. Another Wisconsin faculty member, economist Richard Ely, argued that the state was "an educational and ethical agency whose positive aim is an indispensable condition of human progress." Ely believed the state must intervene directly to help solve public problems. He rejected the doctrine of laissez-faire as merely "a tool in the hands of the greedy." Like Commons, Ely worked with Wisconsin lawmakers to apply his expertise in economics to reforming the state's labor laws.

Progressive legal theorists began challenging the conservative view of constitutional law that had dominated American courts. Since the 1870s, the Supreme Court had interpreted the Fourteenth Amendment (1868) as a guarantee of broad rights for corporations. That amendment, which prevented states from depriving "any person of life, liberty, or property, without due process of law," had been designed to protect the civil rights of African Americans against violations by the states. But the Court, led by Justice Stephen J. Field, used the due process clause to strike down state laws regulating business and labor conditions. The Supreme Court and state courts had thus made the Fourteenth Amendment a bulwark for big business and a foe of social welfare measures.

The most important dissenter from this view was Oliver Wendell Holmes Jr. A scholar and Massachusetts judge, Holmes believed the law had to take into account changing social conditions. And courts should take care not to invalidate social legislation enacted democratically. After his appointment to the Supreme Court in 1902, Holmes wrote a number of notable dissents to conservative court decisions overturning progressive legislation. Criticizing the majority opinion in *Lochner* v. *New York* (1905), in which the Court struck down a state law setting a ten-hour day for bakers, Holmes insisted that the Constitution "is not intended to embody a particular theory."

Before the late 1930s, Holmes's pragmatic views of the law seldom convinced a majority of the Court. But his views influenced a generation of lawyers who began practicing what came to be called sociological jurisprudence. In *Muller* v. *Oregon* (1908), the Court upheld an Oregon law limiting the maximum hours for working women, finding that the liberty of contract "is not absolute." Noting that "woman's physical structure and the performance of maternal functions place her at a disadvantage," the Court found that "the physical well-being of woman becomes an object of public interest and care." Louis Brandeis, the state's attorney, amassed statistical, sociological, and economic data, rather than traditional legal arguments, to support his arguments. The "Brandeis Brief" became a common strategy for lawyers defending the constitutionality of progressive legislation.

The Female Dominion

In the 1890s, the settlement house movement had begun to provide an alternative to traditional concepts of private charity and humanitarian reform. Settlement workers found they could not transform their neighborhoods without confronting a host of broad social questions: chronic poverty, overcrowded tenement houses, child

A portrait of the young Jane Addams, probably taken around the time she founded Hull House in Chicago, in 1889.

OVERVIEW | Currents of Progressivism

	Key Figures	Issues
Local Communities	Jane Addams, Lillian Wald, Florence Kelley, Frederic C. Howe, Samuel Jones	• Improving health, education, welfare in urban immigrant neighborhoods • Child labor, eight-hour day • Celebrating immigrant cultures • Reforming urban politics • Municipal ownership/regulation of utilities
State	Robert M. La Follette, Hiram Johnson, Al Smith	• Limiting power of railroads, other corporations • Improving civil service • Direct democracy • Applying academic scholarship to human needs
National	James K. Vardaman, Hoke Smith, Theodore Roosevelt, Woodrow Wilson	• Disfranchisement of African Americans • Trust-busting • Conservation and western development • National regulation of corporate and financial excesses • Reform of national banking
Intellectual/Cultural	Jacob Riis, Lincoln Steffens, Ida Tarbell, Upton Sinclair, S. S. McClure John Dewey, Louis Brandeis, Edwin A. Ross	• Muckraking • Education reform • Sociological jurisprudence • Empowering "ethical elite"

labor, industrial accidents, public health. They soon discovered the need to engage the political and cultural life of the larger community. As on Henry Street, college-educated, middle-class women were a key vanguard in the crusade for social justice.

Jane Addams founded one of the first settlement houses, Hull House, in Chicago in 1889, after years of struggling to find work and a social identity equal to her talents. A member of one of the first generations of American women to attend college, Addams was a graduate of Rockford College. Many educated women were dissatisfied with the life choices conventionally available to them: early marriage or the traditional female professions of

●●●—[Read the Document

History Bookshelf: Jane Addams, The Spirit of Youth and City Streets *(1909);* Twenty Years at Hull House *(1910) at* **www.myhistorylab.com**

teaching, nursing, and library work. Settlement work provided an attractive alternative. Hull House was located in a run-down slum area of Chicago. It had a day nursery, a dispensary for medicines and medical advice, a boarding-house, an art gallery, and a music school. Addams often spoke of the "subjective necessity" of settlement houses. By this she meant that they gave young, educated women a way to satisfy their powerful desire to connect with the real world. "There is nothing after disease, indigence and guilt," she wrote, "so fatal to life itself as the want of a proper outlet for active faculties."

Lillian Wald and her allies convinced the New York Board of Health to assign a nurse to every public school in the city. They lobbied the board of education to create the first school lunch programs. They persuaded the city to set up municipal milk stations to ensure the purity of milk. Henry Street also pioneered tuberculosis treatment and prevention. Its leaders became powerful advocates for playground construction, improved street cleaning, and tougher housing inspection. The settlement's Neighborhood Playhouse became an internationally acclaimed center for innovative theater, music, and dance. Lillian Wald became a national figure—an outspoken advocate of child labor legislation and woman suffrage and a vigorous opponent of American involvement in World War I. She offered Henry Street as a meeting place to the National Negro Conference in 1909, out of which emerged the National Association for the Advancement of Colored People (NAACP).

Social reformer Florence Kelley helped direct the support of the settlement house movement behind groundbreaking state and federal labor legislation. Arriving at Hull House in 1891, Kelley found what she described as a "colony of efficient and intelligent women." In 1893, she wrote a report detailing the dismal conditions in sweatshops and the effects of long hours on the women and children who worked in them. This report became the basis for landmark legislation in Illinois that limited women to an eight-hour workday, barred children under fourteen from working, and abolished tenement labor. Illinois governor John Peter Altgeld appointed Kelley as chief inspector for the new law. In 1895, Kelley published *Hull House Maps and Papers*, the first scientific study of urban poverty in America. Moving to the Henry Street Settlement in 1898, Kelley served as general secretary of the new National Consumers' League. With Lillian Wald, she established the New York Child Labor Committee and pushed for the creation of the U.S. Children's Bureau, established in 1912. Its director, the first woman to head a federal bureau, was Julia Lathrop, another alumna of Hull House.

New female-dominated occupations, such as social work, public health nursing, and home economics, allowed women to combine professional aspirations with the older traditions of moral reform, especially those centered on child welfare. The new professionalism, in turn, sustained reform commitments and a female dominion that simultaneously expanded the social welfare function of the state and increased women's public authority and influence.

Kelley, Addams, Wald, Lathrop, and their circle consciously used their power as women to reshape politics in the progressive era. Electoral politics and the state were historically male preserves, but female social progressives turned their gender into an advantage. Activists like Kelley used their influence in civil society to create new state powers in the service of social justice. "Women's place is Home," wrote reformer Rheta Childe Dorr, "but Home is not contained within the four walls of an individual home. Home is the community."

Progressive Politics in Cities and States

Progressive reformers poured much of their zeal and energy into local political battles. In cities and states across the nation, progressive politicians became a powerful force, often balancing the practical need for partisan support with nonpartisan appeals to the larger citizenry. Although their motives and achievements were mixed, progressives were united in their attacks on corruption in government, the need to reign in corporate power, and calls for more activist city and state governments.

The Urban Machine

By the turn of the century, Democratic Party machines, usually dominated by first- and second-generation Irish, controlled the political life of most large American cities. The keys to machine strength were disciplined organization and the delivery of essential services to both immigrant communities and business elites. The successful machine politician viewed his work as a business, and he accumulated his capital by serving people who needed assistance. Recent immigrants in particular faced frequent unemployment, sickness, and discrimination. In exchange for votes, machine politicians offered their constituents a variety of services. These included municipal jobs in the police and fire departments, work at city construction sites, intervention with legal problems, and food and coal during hard times.

For those who did business with the city—construction companies, road builders, realtors—staying on the machine's good side was simply another business expense. In exchange for valuable franchises and city contracts, businessmen routinely bribed machine politicians and contributed liberally to their campaign funds. George Washington Plunkitt, a stalwart of New York's Tammany Hall machine, good-naturedly defended what he called "honest graft": making money from inside information on public improvements. "It's just like lookin' ahead in Wall Street or in the coffee or cotton market. . . . I seen my opportunities and I took 'em."

Read the Document
George W. Plunkitt, "Honest Graft" (1905) at
www.myhistorylab.com

The machines usually had close ties to organized prostitution and gambling, as well as more legitimate commercial entertainments. Many machine figures began as saloonkeepers, and liquor dealers and beer brewers provided important financial support for organizations. Vaudeville and burlesque theater, boxing, horse racing, and professional baseball were other urban enterprises with economic and political links to machines. On New York City's Lower East Side, where the Henry Street Settlement was located, Timothy D.

Timothy D. "Big Tim" Sullivan, the popular and influential Democratic Party machine boss of the Bowery and Lower East Side districts of New York City, ca. 1901.

"Big Tim" Sullivan embodied the popular machine style. Big Tim, who had risen from desperate poverty, remained enormously popular with his constituents until his death in 1913. Critics charged that Sullivan controlled the city's gambling and made money from prostitution. His real fortune came through his investments in vaudeville and the early movie business. Sullivan, whose district included the largest number of immigrants and transients in the city, provided shoe giveaways and free Christmas dinners to thousands every winter. To help pay for these and other charitable activities, he informally taxed the saloons, theaters, and restaurants in the district.

In the early twentieth century, to expand their base of support, political machines in the Northeast began concentrating more on passing welfare legislation beneficial to working-class and immigrant constituencies. In this way, machine politicians often allied themselves with progressive reformers in state legislatures. In New York, for example, Tammany Hall figures such as Robert Wagner, Al Smith, and Big Tim Sullivan worked with middle-class progressive groups to pass child labor laws, factory safety regulations, worker compensation plans, and other efforts to make government more responsive to social needs. As Jewish and Catholic immigrants expanded in number and proportion in the city population, urban machines also began to champion cultural pluralism, opposing prohibition and immigration restrictions and defending the contributions made by new ethnic groups in the cities.

Progressives and Urban Reform

Political progressivism originated in the cities. It was both a challenge to the power of machine politics and a response to deteriorating urban conditions. City governments, especially in the Northeast and industrial Midwest, seemed hardly capable of providing the basic services needed to sustain large populations. For example, an impure water supply left Pittsburgh with one of the world's highest rates of death from typhoid, dysentery, and cholera. Most New York City neighborhoods rarely enjoyed street cleaning, and playgrounds were nonexistent. "The challenge of the city," Cleveland progressive Frederic C. Howe wrote in 1906, "has become one of decent human existence."

Reformers placed much of the blame for urban ills on the machines and looked for ways to restructure city government. The "good government" movement, led by the National Municipal League, fought to make city management a nonpartisan, even nonpolitical, process by bringing the administrative techniques of large corporations to cities. Reformers revised city charters in favor of stronger mayoral power and expanded use of appointed administrators and career civil servants. They drew up blueprints for model charters, ordinances, and zoning plans designed by experts trained in public administration.

Business and professional elites became the biggest boosters of structural reforms in urban government. In the summer of 1900, a hurricane in the Gulf of Mexico unleashed a tidal wave on Galveston, Texas. To cope with this disaster, leading businessmen convinced the state legislature to replace the mayor-council government with a small board of commissioners. Each commissioner was elected at large, and each was responsible for a different city department. Under this plan, voters could more easily identify and hold accountable those responsible for city services. The city commission, enjoying both policymaking and administrative powers, proved very effective in rebuilding Galveston. By 1917, nearly 500 cities, including Houston, Oakland, Kansas City, Denver, and Buffalo, had adopted the commission form of government.

Progressive politicians who focused on the human problems of the industrial city championed a different kind of reform, one based on changing policies rather than the political structure. In Cleveland, for example, wealthy businessman Thomas L. Johnson served as mayor from 1901 to 1909. He emphasized both efficiency and social welfare. His popular program included lower streetcar fares, public baths, milk and meat inspection, and an expanded park and playground system.

Statehouse Progressives

On the state level, progressives focused on two major reform themes that sometimes coexisted uneasily. On the one hand, they looked to make politics more open and accessible by pushing through procedural reforms. The *direct primary*, for example, promised to take the selection of electoral candidates out of the smoke-filled backrooms of party bosses and into the hands of party voters. In 1902, Oregon was the first state to adopt two other reforms: the *initiative*, the popular power to initiate legislation, and the *referendum*, the right to a popular vote on proposed legislation. Several states also adopted a related reform, the "Australian," or secret ballot, which took the mechanics of ballot printing and distribution from the parties and made it the responsibility of the government. California and other states also established the *recall*: the power to remove elected officials from office. And in 1913, the states and Congress ratified the Seventeenth Amendment, shifting the selection of U.S. senators from the state legislatures to direct election by voters. On the other hand, progressive activists sought to remove some decisions from the electoral process entirely. They believed that judgments about railroad regulations, improving a city's sewer system, or establishing tax rates might best be made by informed, unbiased experts appointed to boards and commissions charged with setting policy. Many progressive states became political laboratories that tested more-democratic procedures as well as a greater reliance on professional expertise.

In Wisconsin, Republican dissident Robert M. La Follette forged a coalition of angry farmers, small businessmen, and workers with his fiery attacks on railroads and other large corporations. Leader of the progressive faction of the state Republicans, "Fighting Bob" won three terms as governor (1900–06), and then served as a U.S. senator until his death in 1925. As governor, he pushed through tougher corporate tax rates, a direct primary, an improved civil service code, and a railroad commission designed to regulate freight charges. La Follette used faculty experts at the University of Wisconsin to help research and write his bills. Other states began copying the "Wisconsin Idea," the application of academic scholarship and theory to the needs of the people. In practice, La Follette's railroad commission accomplished far less than progressive rhetoric claimed. It essentially represented special interests—commercial farmers and businessmen seeking reduced shipping rates. Ordinary

consumers did not see lower passenger fares or reduced food prices. And, as commissioners began to realize, the national reach of the railroads limited the effectiveness of state regulation.

In New York, Theodore Roosevelt won the governor's race in 1898, propelled by his fame as a Spanish-American War hero. Although supported by the Republican Party machine, Roosevelt embraced the progressive view that the people's interest ought to be above partisan politics, and he used his personal popularity with voters to assert independence from party leaders. As governor, he held frequent press conferences to communicate more directly with voters and gain support for progressive legislation. Roosevelt's administration strengthened the state's civil service system, set wage and hour standards for state employees, raised teachers' salaries, and placed a franchise tax on corporations controlling public utilities. Roosevelt also championed progressive conservation measures by expanding New York's forest preserves and reforming the fish and game service, thus anticipating his strong support of environmental regulation as president.

Western progressives targeted railroads, mining and timber companies, and public utilities for reform. Large corporations such as Pacific Gas and Electric and the Southern Pacific Railroad had amassed enormous wealth and political influence. They were able to corrupt state legislatures and charge consumers exorbitant rates. An alliance between middle-class progressives and working-class voters reflected growing disillusionment with the ideology of individualism that had helped pave the way for the rise of the big corporation. In 1910, California elected progressive attorney Hiram Johnson governor, and he then pushed through laws regulating utilities and child labor, mandating an eight-hour day for workingwomen, and providing a state-worker compensation plan.

In the South, progressives organized to control both greedy corporations and "unruly" citizens. Citizen groups, city boards of trade, and newspapers pressed reluctant legislators to use state power to regulate big business. Between 1905 and 1909, nearly every southern state moved to regulate railroads by mandating lower passenger and freight rates. Southern progressives also directed their energies at the related problems of child labor and educational reform. In 1900, at least one-quarter of all southern cotton mill workers were between the ages of ten and sixteen, and many worked over sixty hours per week. Led by reform-minded ministers Edgar Gardner Murphy and Alexander McKelway and drawing on the activism of white club women, reformers attacked child labor by focusing on the welfare of children and their mothers and emphasizing the degradation of "Anglo Saxons." In 1903, Alabama and North Carolina enacted the first state child labor laws, setting twelve as a minimum age for employment. But the laws were weakened by many exemptions and no provisions for enforcement, as lawmakers also heard the loud complaints from parents and mill owners who resented the efforts of reformers to limit their choices.

But southern progressivism was for white people only. Indeed, southern progressives believed that the disenfranchisement of black voters and the creation of a legally segregated public sphere were necessary preconditions for political and social reform. With African Americans removed from political life, white southern progressives argued, the direct primary system of nominating candidates would give white voters more influence. Between 1890 and 1910, southern states passed a welter of statutes specifying poll taxes, literacy tests, and property qualifications with the explicit goal of preventing voting by blacks. This systematic disenfranchisement of African American voters stripped black communities of any political power. To prevent the disenfranchisement of poor white voters under these laws, states established so-called understanding and grandfather clauses. Election officials had discretionary power to decide whether an illiterate person could understand and reasonably interpret the Constitution when read to him. Unqualified white men were also registered if they could show that their grandfathers had voted.

Southern progressives also supported the push toward a fully segregated public sphere. Between 1900 and 1910, southern states strengthened Jim Crow laws requiring separation of races in restaurants, streetcars, beaches, and theaters. Schools were separate but hardly equal. A 1916 Bureau of Education study found that per capita expenditures for education in southern states averaged $10.32 a year for white children and $2.89 for black children. And African American teachers received far lower salaries than their white counterparts. The legacy of southern progressivism was thus closely linked to the strengthening of the legal and institutional guarantees of white supremacy.

Contradictions in the progressive approach to political reform were not limited to the South. Undermining party control of voting and elections may have also weakened politicians' incentives to get out the vote. Greater reliance on city commissions and other experts meant less in the way of promised favors for voters, which may have also made voters less interested in elections. Tightening up on residency requirements and voter registration rules in the cities cut into turnout in immigrant and ethnic neighborhoods. The effort to make politics more open, nonpartisan, and voter friendly also led, ironically, to a decline in voter participation and interest around the country. Whereas in the 1890s, voter participation in national elections was routinely close to 90 percent, by World War I that figure had fallen to barely 60 percent, where it would stay for most of the rest of the century.

Social Control and Its Limits

Many middle- and upper-class Protestant progressives feared that immigrants and large cities threatened the stability of American democracy. They worried that alien cultural practices were disrupting what they viewed as traditional American morality. Edward A. Ross's landmark work *Social Control* (1901), a book whose title became a key phrase in progressive thought, argued that society needed an "ethical elite" of citizens "who have at heart the general welfare and know what kinds of conduct will promote this welfare." Progressives often believed they had a mission to frame laws and regulations for the "benefit" of immigrants, industrial workers, and African Americans. These efforts at social control usually required some form of coercion. This was the moralistic and frequently xenophobic side of progressivism, and it provided a powerful source of support for the regulation of drinking, prostitution, leisure activities, and schooling.

The Prohibition Movement

During the last two decades of the nineteenth century, the Woman's Christian Temperance Union (WCTU) had grown into a powerful mass organization. The WCTU appealed especially to women angered by men who used alcohol and then abused their wives and children. It directed most of its work toward ending the production, sale, and consumption of alcohol. Local WCTU chapters put their energy into nontemperance activities as well, including homeless shelters, Sunday schools, prison reform, child nurseries, and woman suffrage. The WCTU thus provided women with a political forum in which they could fuse their traditional moral posture as guardians of the home with broader public concerns. By 1911, the WCTU, with a quarter million members, was the largest women's organization in American history.

Other temperance groups had a narrower focus. The Anti-Saloon League, founded in 1893, began by organizing local-option campaigns in which rural counties and small towns banned liquor within their geographical limits. It drew much of its financial support from local businessmen, who saw a link between closing a community's saloons and increasing the productivity of workers. The league was a one-issue pressure group that played effectively on antiurban and anti-immigrant prejudice. League lobbyists hammered away at the close connections among saloon culture, liquor dealers, brewers, and big-city political machines.

The battle to ban alcohol revealed deep ethnic and cultural divides within America's urban communities. Opponents of alcohol were generally "pietists," who viewed the world from a position of moral absolutism. These included native-born, middle-class Protestants associated with evangelical churches, along with some old-stock Protestant immigrant denominations. Opponents of prohibition were generally "ritualists" with less arbitrary notions of personal morality. These were largely new-stock, working-class Catholic and Jewish immigrants, along with some Protestants, such as German Lutherans (see Communities in Conflict).

The Social Evil

Many of the same reformers who battled the saloon and drinking also engaged in efforts to eradicate prostitution. Crusades against "the social evil" had appeared at intervals throughout the nineteenth century, but they reached a new

Read the Document

Report of the Vice Commission, Louisville, Kentucky (1915) at **www.myhistorylab.com**

level of intensity between 1895 and 1920. In part, this new sense of urgency stemmed from the sheer growth of cities and the greater visibility of prostitution in red-light districts and neighborhoods. Antiprostitution campaigns epitomized the diverse makeup and mixed motives of so much progressive reform. Male business and civic leaders joined forces with feminists, social workers, and clergy to eradicate "commercialized vice."

Between 1908 and 1914, exposés of the "white slave traffic" became a national sensation. Dozens of books, articles, and motion pictures alleged an international conspiracy to seduce and sell girls into prostitution. Most of these materials exaggerated the practices they attacked. They also made foreigners, especially Jews and southern Europeans, scapegoats for the sexual anxieties of native-born whites. In 1910, Congress passed legislation that permitted the deportation of foreign-born prostitutes or any foreigner convicted of procuring or employing them. That same year, the Mann Act made it a federal offense to transport women across state lines for "immoral purposes."

Reformers had trouble believing that any woman would freely choose to be a prostitute; such a choice was antithetical to conventional notions of female purity and sexuality. But for wage-earning women, prostitution was a rational choice in a world of limited opportunities. Maimie Pinzer, a prostitute, summed up her feelings in a letter to a wealthy female reformer: "I don't propose to get up at 6:30 to be at work at 8 and work in a close, stuffy room with people I despise, until dark, for $6 or $7 a week! When I could, just by phoning, spend an afternoon with some congenial person and in the end have more than a week's work could pay me." The anti-vice crusades succeeded in closing down many urban red-light districts and larger brothels, but the streetwalker and call girl, who were more vulnerable to harassment and control by policemen and pimps, replaced them. Rather than eliminating prostitution, reform efforts transformed the organization of the sex trade.

The Redemption of Leisure

Progressives faced a thorny issue in the growing popularity of commercial entertainment. For large numbers of working-class adults and children, leisure meant time and money spent at vaudeville and burlesque theaters, amusement parks, dance halls, and motion picture houses. These competed with municipal parks, libraries, museums, YMCAs, and school recreation centers. For many cultural traditionalists, the flood of new urban commercial amusements posed a grave threat. As with prostitution, urban progressives sponsored a host of recreation and amusement surveys detailing the situation in their individual cities. One distinctively progressive response was the Playgrounds Movement. Los Angeles created the nation's first urban Department of Playgrounds in 1904, and proponents nationwide saw municipal playgrounds as a way to offer free, healthy, outdoor recreation for city children.

By 1908, movies had become the most popular form of cheap entertainment in America. One survey estimated that 11,500 movie theaters attracted 5 million patrons each day. For five or ten cents, "nickelodeon" theaters offered programs that might include a slapstick comedy, a western, a travelogue, and a melodrama. Early movies were most popular in the tenement and immigrant districts of big cities and with children. As the films themselves became more sophisticated and as "movie palaces" began to replace cheap storefront theaters, the new medium attracted a large middle-class clientele as well.

Progressive reformers seized the chance to help regulate the new medium as a way of improving the commercial recreation of the urban poor. In 1909, New York City movie producers and exhibitors joined with the reform-minded People's Institute to establish the voluntary National Board of Censorship (NBC). A revolving group of civic activists reviewed new movies, passed them, suggested changes, or condemned them. Local censoring committees all over the nation subscribed to the board's weekly bulletin. They aimed at achieving what John Collier of the NBC called "the redemption of leisure." By 1914, the NBC was reviewing 95 percent of the nation's film output.

Standardizing Education

Along with reading, writing, and mathematics, schools inculcated patriotism, piety, and respect for authority. Progressive educators looked to the public school primarily as an agent of "Americanization." Elwood Cubberley, a leading educational reformer, expressed the view that schools could be the vehicle by which immigrant children could

Watch the Video

What Was the Progressive Education Movement? at **www.myhistorylab.com**

COMMUNITIES *in* CONFLICT

Debating Prohibition in Progressive-Era Ohio

Should the manufacture and sale of alcoholic beverages be made illegal? The State of Ohio had long been one of the most intense battlegrounds over this controversial issue. The Women's Christian Temperance Union had been founded in Cleveland in 1874, and the Anti-Saloon League was organized in Oberlin in 1893. Both groups quickly gained a national following. In 1909, the League established new national headquarters in Westerville, Ohio, a small city that strongly supported prohibition. But Ohio also had a large and well-organized brewery industry. Beer was by far the most popular alcoholic beverage among Americans, and the brewery industry was the most profitable sector of the alcohol business. German Americans dominated among brewers and maintained close ties to the large German American communities in cities like Cincinnati.

In 1908, the Anti-Saloon League and its allies succeeded in getting a law passed by the Ohio legislature granting counties a "local option" to ban the alcohol trade. As the "drys" set their sights on a statewide prohibition law, the brewers, working closely with German American community groups, organized a counterattack that featured lobbyists and a sophisticated propaganda campaign to mobilize the influence and votes of "wets." The brewers also tried to reform their industry by reducing the number of saloons and ensuring that saloonkeepers were citizens of "good character." With Ohioans closely divided between "wet" and "dry" views, both sides put an enormous amount of money into campaigns aimed at influencing public opinion. Well-financed interest group campaigns of this type were a distinctively new feature of progressive era politics. After losing statewide referendums in 1915 and 1917, the Anti-Saloon League spearheaded a narrow victory in 1918, finally achieving statewide prohibition in Ohio. National prohibition would follow in 1920 with the ratification of the Eighteenth Amendment to the Constitution.

Percy Andreae was a leading lobbyist for the brewery industry. James A. White was the head of the Ohio Anti-Saloon League and organizer of the Ohio Dry Federation, an umbrella group of prohibitionist forces. Here are their arguments.

Percy Andreae: "Behind the Mask of Prohibition" (1915)

I have met many active prohibitionists, both in this and in other countries, all of them thoroughly in earnest. In some instances I have found that their allegiance to the cause of prohibition took its origin in the fact that some near relative or friend had succumbed to over-indulgence in liquor. In one or two cases the man himself had been a victim of this weakness, and had come to the conclusion, firstly that every one else was constituted as he was, and, therefore, liable to the same danger; and secondly, that unless every one were prevented from drinking, he would not be secure from the temptation to do so himself.

This is one class of prohibitionists. The other, and by far the larger class, is made up of religious zealots, to whom prohibition is a word having at bottom a far wider application than that which is generally attributed to it. The liquor question, if there really is such a question per se, is merely put forth by them as a means to an end, an incidental factor in a fight which has for its object the supremacy of a certain form of religious faith. The belief of many of these people is that the Creator frowns upon enjoyment of any and every kind, and that he has merely endowed us with certain desires and capacities for pleasure in order to give us an opportunity to please Him by resisting them. They are, of course, perfectly entitled to this belief, though some of us may consider it eccentric and somewhat in the nature of a libel on the Almighty. But are they privileged to force that belief on all their fellow beings? That, in substance, is the question that is involved in the present-day prohibition movement. . . .

If there is any one who doubts the truth of this statement, let me put this to him: How many Roman Catholics are prohibitionists? How many Jews, the most temperate race on earth, are to be found in the ranks of prohibition? Or Lutherans? Or German Protestants generally? What is

> "The liquor question . . . is merely put forth . . . as a means to an end, an incidental factor in a fight which has for its object the supremacy of a certain form of religious faith."

• **What arguments does Andreae use to undermine the prohibitionist appeal, particularly with respect to religious belief? How does the Ohio Dry Federation make its case in this ad? Why do you think it emphasized this strategy over other prohibitionist objections to the alcohol trade?**

the proportion of Episcopalians to that of Methodists, Baptists and Presbyterians, and the like, in the active prohibition army? The answers to these questions will, I venture to say, prove conclusively the assertion that the fight for prohibition is synonymous with the fight of a certain religious sect, or group of religious sects, for the supremacy of its ideas.

Temperance and self-control are convertible terms. Prohibition, or that which it implies, is the direct negation of the term self-control. In order to save the small percentage of men who are too weak to resist their animal desires, it aims to put chains on every man, the weak and the strong alike. And if this is proper in one respect, why not in all respects? Yet, what would one think of a proposition to keep all men locked up because a certain number have a propensity to steal? Theoretically, perhaps, all crime or vice could be stopped by chaining us all up as we chain up a wild animal, and only allowing us to take exercise under proper supervision and control. But while such a measure would check crime, it would not eliminate the criminal. . . .

Prohibition, though it must cause, and is already causing, incalculable damage, may never succeed in this country; but that which is behind it, as the catapults and the cannon were behind the battering rams in the battles of olden days, is certain to succeed unless timely measures of prevention are resorted to; and if it does succeed, we shall witness the enthronement of a monarch in this land of liberty compared with whose autocracy the autocracy of the Russian Czar is a mere trifle. The name of this monarch is Religious Intolerance.

SOURCE: Percy Andreae, *The Prohibition Movement in Its Broader Bearings upon Our Social, Commercial, and Religious Liberties* (1915); http://www.druglibrary.org/schaffer/alcohol.

Prohibitionist James A. White: "Give Me Your Boy" (1918)

Take away the "camouflage" with which the Liquor Traffic tries to disguise itself and [a] sinister figure . . . stands revealed.

Take away the smooth phrases and cunning twists of the Liquor Traffic's appeal For Permission to continue its career—get right down to naked truth and you will see that the liquor traffic is asking fathers of Ohio to "give me your boys."

WHAT WILL THE SALOON DO FOR THE BOYS?

Is its purpose to inspire them with greater ambitions; to teach them clean morals, to avoid bad habits, to become better men and citizens, better husbands and fathers?

You know the saloon does nothing FOR boys, but appalling harm TO them.

Its prosperity depends on the number of VICTIMS it entraps.

Men in the liquor traffic are not blind to its evils.

Many distillers will not allow THEIR OWN SON to drink intoxicants; many brewers forbid the use of intoxicants to their sons; many saloonists don't drink the stuff they sell; they won't hire drinking bartenders and they bar their sons from the saloons.

Still, they ask you to give YOUR son for the sake of the money they can make out of him. They ask you to approve temptation of your son to become a drunkard.

They ask you to vote to MAKE DRUNKARDS out of thousands of Ohio's boys.

Are you with them? Are YOU for the Booze Huns or for the boys?

There can be no neutrality in this fight. Failure to vote "yes" on prohibition on November 5th is silent approval of the liquor traffic's record and misdeeds.

You must be either for the BEST INTERESTS of your state, your nation and humanity—or you must be for the ENEMY liquor traffic, which works AGAINST the best interest of the state, the nation and humanity.

Vote "Yes" for Prohibition November 5th

SOURCE: Ohio Dry Federation, 1918, http://ehistory.osu.edu/osu/sources.

"Take away the smooth phrases and cunning twists of the Liquor Traffic's appeal For Permission to continue its career—get right down to naked truth and you will see that the liquor traffic is asking fathers of Ohio to 'give me your boys.'"

Movies, by John Sloan, 1913, the most talented artist among the so-called Ashcan realist school of painting. Active in socialist and bohemian circles, Sloan served as art editor for *The Masses* magazine for several years. His work celebrated the vitality and diversity of urban working-class life and leisure, including the new commercial culture represented by the motion picture.

SOURCE: John Sloan, *Movies*, 1913. Oil painting. The Toledo Museum of Art.

break free of the parochial ethnic neighborhood. "Our task," he argued in *Changing Conceptions of Education* (1909), "is to break up these groups or settlements, to assimilate and amalgamate these people as a part of our American race, and to implant in their children, so far as can be done, the Anglo-Saxon conception of righteousness, law and order, and popular government."

The most important educational trends in these years were the expansion and bureaucratization of the nation's public school systems. In most cities, centralization served to consolidate the power of older urban elites who felt threatened by the large influx of immigrants. Children began school earlier and stayed there longer.

Kindergartens spread rapidly in large cities. They presented, as one writer put it in 1903, "the earliest opportunity to catch the little Russian, the little Italian, the little German, Pole, Syrian, and the rest and begin to make good American citizens of them." By 1918, every state had some form of compulsory school attendance. High schools also multiplied, extending the school's influence beyond the traditional grammar school curriculum. In 1890, only 4 percent of the nation's youth between fourteen and seventeen were enrolled in school; by 1930, the figure was 47 percent.

High schools multiplied, reflecting a growing belief that schools should be comprehensive, multifunctional institutions. To support vocational training in high schools, the Smith-Hughes Act of 1917 provided federal grants and set up a Federal Board for Vocational Education.

Challenges to Progressivism

While most progressive reformers had roots in Protestantism and the middle-class professions, other Americans vigorously challenged their political vision. Organized workers often invoked progressive rhetoric and ideals but for quite different, sometimes radical, ends. The Industrial Revolution, which had begun transforming American life and labor in the nineteenth century, reached maturity in the early twentieth century. The world of the industrial worker included large manufacturing towns in New England; barren mining settlements in the West; primitive lumber and turpentine camps in the South; steelmaking and coal-mining cities in Pennsylvania and Ohio; and densely packed immigrant ghettos from New York to San Francisco, where workers toiled in garment-trade sweatshops.

All these industrial workers shared the need to sell their labor for wages in order to survive. At the same time, differences in skill, ethnicity, and race proved powerful barriers to efforts at organizing trade unions that could bargain for improved wages and working conditions. So, too, did the economic and political power of the large corporations that dominated much of American industry. Yet there were small, closely knit groups of skilled workers, such as printers and brewers, who exercised real control over their lives and labors. These years also saw many labor struggles that created effective trade unions or laid the groundwork for others. Industrial workers also became a force in local and national politics, adding a chorus of insistent voices to the calls for social justice.

The New Global Immigration

The first two decades of the twentieth century saw a profound transformation in both the size and scope of immigration, as over 14.5 million people from all over the world made their way to the United States. In the nineteenth century, much of the overseas migration had come from the industrial districts of northern and western Europe, as English, Welsh, and German artisans had brought with them skills critical for emerging industries such as steelmaking and coal mining. By contrast, roughly 60 percent of early twentieth century immigrants came from southern and eastern Europe. Unlike their predecessors, nearly all the new Italian, Polish, Hungarian, Jewish, and Greek immigrants lacked industrial skills. They thus

Newly landed European immigrant families on the dock at Ellis Island in New York Harbor, 1900. Originally a black-and-white photograph, this image was later color tinted for reproduction as a postcard or book illustration.

entered the bottom ranks of factories, mines, mills, and sweatshops; by the eve of World War I, close to 60 percent of the industrial labor force was foreign-born (see Map 21.1).

These new immigrants had been driven from their European farms and towns by several forces, including the undermining of subsistence farming by commercial agriculture; a falling death rate that brought a shortage of land; and religious and political persecution. American corpora-

Read the Document

Lee Chew, "Life of a Chinese Immigrant" (1903) at **www.myhistorylab.com**

tions also sent agents to recruit cheap labor. Except for Jewish immigrants, a majority of whom fled virulent anti-Semitism in Russia and Poland, most newcomers planned on earning a stake and then returning home. Hard times in America forced many back to Europe. In the depression year of 1908, for example, more Austro-Hungarians and Italians left than entered the United States.

The decision to emigrate usually occurred through social networks—people linked by kinship, personal acquaintance, and work experience. These "chains," extending from places of origin to specific destinations in the United States, helped immigrants cope with the considerable risks entailed by the long and difficult journey. A study conducted by the U.S. Immigration Commission in 1909 found that about 60 percent of the immigrants of that time had their passage arranged by immigrants already in America.

Immigrant communities used ethnicity as a collective resource for gaining employment in factories, mills, and mines. One Polish steelworker recalled how the process operated in the Pittsburgh mills: "Now if a Russian got his job in a shear department, he's looking for a buddy, a Russian buddy. He's not going to look for a Croatian buddy. And if he sees the boss looking for a man he says, 'Look, I have a good man,' and he's picking out his friends." Specialization of work by ethnic origin was quite common throughout America's industrial communities.

The low-paid, backbreaking work in basic industry became nearly the exclusive preserve of the new immigrants.

MAP 21.1 Immigration to the United States, 1901–1920

SOURCE: Adapted from Historical Statistics of the United States, Volume 1, Part A Population, Chapter Ad, International Migration (NY, 2006, Millennial Edition).

In 1907, of the 14,359 common laborers employed at Pittsburgh's U.S. Steel mills, 11,694 were eastern Europeans. For twelve-hour days and seven-day weeks, two-thirds of these workers made less than $12.50 a week; one-third made less than $10.00. One-third of the immigrant steelworkers were single, and among married men who had been in the country less than five years, about two-thirds reported that their wives were still in Europe. Workers with families generally supplemented their incomes by taking in single men as boarders.

Not all of the recent immigrants came from Europe, as hemispheric migration increased sharply as well. Over 900,000 came from Canada between 1900 and 1920, including some 300,000 French Canadians, settling mostly in New England. The pull of jobs in New England's textile industry, along with its physical proximity, attracted male farmers and laborers unable to make a living in the rural districts of Quebec. Roughly one-third of female immigrants were domestic servants looking for the higher pay and greater independence associated with factory labor. The significant French Canadian presence often made them the largest single ethnic group in New England communities. French-language churches, newspapers, private schools, and mutual-benefit societies reinforced the distinctive cultural milieu, and the presence of kin or fellow villagers facilitated the arrival of largely rural migrants into these new, highly industrialized, and urbanized settings.

Mexican immigration also grew in these years, providing a critical source of labor for the West's farms, railroads, and mines. Between 1900 and 1920, the number of people of Mexican descent living and working in the United States nearly quadrupled from about 100,000 to 400,000. Economic and political crises spurred tens of thousands of Mexico's rural and urban poor to emigrate north. Large numbers of seasonal agricultural workers regularly came up from Mexico to work in the expanding sugar beet industry and then returned. But a number of substantial resident Mexican communities also emerged in the early twentieth century.

Throughout Texas, California, New Mexico, Arizona, and Colorado, western cities developed *barrios*, distinct communities of Mexicans. Mexican immigrants attracted by jobs in the smelting industry made El Paso the most thoroughly Mexican city in the United States. In San Antonio, Mexicans worked at shelling pecans, becoming perhaps the most underpaid and exploited group of workers in the country. By 1910, San Antonio contained the largest number of Mexican immigrants of any city. In southern California, labor agents for railroads recruited Mexicans to work on building new interurban lines around Los Angeles.

The Caribbean-born population of the United States grew significantly as well; approximately 230,000 immigrants from that region arrived between 1900 and 1920.

Bahamian farm laborers and Cuban cigar workers, for example, established small but permanent communities in South Florida in the early 1900s. New York City soon became the most popular destination for Caribbean immigrants, attracting tens of thousands who passed through Ellis Island in search of better paying jobs and career opportunities. By 1930, almost one-quarter of black Harlem was of Caribbean origin, and as many as one-third of all of New York's black professionals and business owners came from the ranks of Caribbean immigrants. These early Caribbean immigrants brought with them notably higher levels of literacy, formal education, and occupational skills, compared to European immigrants. Professionals and entrepreneurs from Barbados, Jamaica, Trinidad, and other islands flocked to New York. Such figures as the Pan Africanist leader Marcus Garvey (Jamaica) and the scholar Arturo Schomburg (Puerto Rico) would come to play a disproportionately large role in African American political life and the Harlem Renaissance of the 1920s. Yet, like native-born African Americans, Caribbean immigrants and their children often endured racial discrimination in their efforts to join craft unions, establish credit with banks, or integrate neighborhoods. Caribbean migration to the United States would not reach mass levels until after World War II, but the first wave of early twentieth-century immigrants laid the foundation for Afro-Caribbean communities in New York and elsewhere.

Over 200,000 Japanese also entered the United States during these decades. The vast majority were young men working as contract laborers in the West, mainly in California. American law prevented Japanese immigrants (the *Issei*) from obtaining American citizenship because they were not white. This legal discrimination, along with informal exclusion from many occupations, forced the Japanese to create niches for themselves within local economies. Most Japanese settled near Los Angeles, where they established small communities centered on fishing, truck farming, and the flower and nursery business. In 1920, Japanese farmers produced 10 percent of the dollar volume of California agriculture on 1 percent of the farm acreage. By 1930, over 35,000 *Issei* and their children (the *Nisei*) lived in Los Angeles.

Urban Ghettos

In large cities, new immigrant communities took the form of densely packed ghettos. By 1920, immigrants and their children constituted almost 60 percent of the population of cities over 100,000. They were an even larger percentage in major industrial centers such as Chicago, Pittsburgh, Philadelphia, and New York. The sheer size and dynamism of these cities made the immigrant experience more complex than in smaller cities and more isolated communities. Workers in the urban garment trades toiled for low wages and suffered layoffs, unemployment, and poor health. But conditions in the small, labor-intensive shops of the clothing industry differed significantly from those in the large-scale, capital-intensive industries like steel.

New York City had become the center of both Jewish immigration and America's huge ready-to-wear clothing industry. The city's Jewish population was 1.4 million in 1915, almost 30 percent of its inhabitants. In small factories, lofts, and tenement apartments, some 200,000 people, most of them Jews, some of them Italians, worked in the clothing trades. Most of the industry operated on the grueling piece-rate, or task, system, in which manufacturers and subcontractors paid individuals or teams of workers to complete a certain quota of labor within a specific time.

Read the Document

Letters to the Jewish Daily Forward (1906–1907) at **www.myhistorylab.com**

The garment industry was highly seasonal. A typical workweek was sixty hours, with seventy common during the busy season. But there were long stretches of unemployment in slack times. Often forced to work in cramped, dirty, and badly lit rooms, garment workers strained under a system in which time equaled money. Morris Rosenfeld, a presser of men's clothing who wrote Yiddish poetry, captured the feeling:

> *The tick of the clock is the boss in his anger*
> *The face of the clock has the eye of a foe*
> *The clock—I shudder—Dost hear how it draws me?*
> *It calls me "Machine" and it cries to me "Sew!"*

In November 1909, two New York garment manufacturers responded to strikes by unskilled women workers by hiring thugs and prostitutes to beat up pickets. The strikers won the support of the Women's Trade Union League, a group of sympathetic female reformers that included Lillian Wald, Mary Dreier, and prominent society figures. The Uprising of the 20,000, as it became known, swept through the city's garment district. The strikers demanded union recognition, better wages, and safer and more sanitary conditions. They drew support from thousands of suffragists, trade unionists, and sympathetic middle-class women as well. Hundreds of strikers were arrested, and many were beaten by police. After three cold months on the picket line, the strikers returned to work without union recognition. But the International Ladies Garment Workers Union (ILGWU), founded in 1900, did gain strength and negotiated contracts with some of the city's shirtwaist makers. The strike was an important breakthrough in the drive to organize unskilled workers into industrial unions.

On March 25, 1911, the issues raised by the strike took on new urgency when a fire raced through three

New York City police set up this makeshift morgue to help identify victims of the disastrous Triangle Shirtwaist Company fire, March 25, 1911. Unable to open the locked doors of the sweatshop and desperate to escape from smoke and flames, many of the 146 who died had leaped eight stories to their death.

floors of the Triangle Shirtwaist Company. As the flames spread, workers found themselves trapped by exit doors that had been locked from the outside. Fire escapes were too narrow and too weak to withstand the heat. Within half an hour, 146 people, mostly young Jewish women, had been killed by smoke or had leaped to their deaths. In the bitter aftermath, women progressives led by Florence Kelley and Frances Perkins of the National Consumers' League joined with Tammany Hall leaders Al Smith, Robert Wagner, and Big Tim Sullivan to create a New York State Factory Investigation Commission. Under Perkins's vigorous leadership, the commission conducted an unprecedented round of public hearings and on-site inspections, leading to a series of state laws that dramatically improved safety conditions and limited the hours for working women and children.

Company Towns

Immigrant industrial workers and their families often established their communities in a company town, where a single large corporation was dominant. Cities such as Lawrence, Massachusetts; Gary, Indiana; and Butte, Montana, revolved around the industrial enterprises of Pacific Woolen, U.S. Steel, and Anaconda Copper. Workers had little or no influence over the economic and political institutions of these cities. In the more isolated company towns, residents often had no alternative but to buy their food, clothing, and supplies at company stores, usually for exorbitantly high prices. They did maintain some community control in other ways. Family and kin networks, ethnic lodges, saloons, benefit societies, churches and synagogues, and musical groups affirmed traditional forms of community in a setting governed by individualism and private capital.

On the job, modern machinery and industrial discipline meant high rates of injury and death. A 1910 study of work accidents revealed that nearly a fourth of all new steelworkers were killed or injured each year. Mutual aid associations, organized around ethnic groups, offered some protection through cheap insurance and death benefits.

In steel and coal towns, women not only maintained the household and raised the children, but they also boosted the family income by taking in boarders, sewing, and laundry. Many women also tended gardens and raised chickens, rabbits, and goats. Their produce and income helped reduce dependence on the company store. Working-class women felt the burdens of housework more heavily than their middle-class sisters. Pump water, indoor plumbing, and sewage disposal were often available only on a pay-as-you-go basis. The daily drudgery endured by working-class women far outlasted the "man-killing" shifts worked by their husbands. Many women struggled with the effects of their husbands' excessive drinking and faced early widowhood.

The adjustment for immigrant workers was not so much a process of assimilation as adaptation and resistance. Work habits and Old World cultural traditions did not always mesh with factory discipline or Taylor's "scientific management." A Polish wedding celebration might last three or four days. A drinking bout following a Sunday funeral might cause workers to celebrate "St. Monday" and not show up for work. Most immigrants were far more concerned with job security than with upward mobility. As new immigrants became less transient and more permanently settled in company towns, they increased their involvement in local politics and union activity.

The power of large corporations in the life of company towns was most evident among the mining communities of the West, as was violent labor conflict. The Colorado Fuel and Iron Company (CFI) employed roughly half of the 8,000 coal miners who labored in that state's mines. In mining towns such as Ludlow and Trinidad, the CFI thoroughly dominated the lives of miners and their families. "The miner," one union official observed, "is in this land owned by the corporation that owns the homes, that owns the boarding houses, that owns every single thing there is there . . . not only the mines, but all the grounds, all the buildings, all the places of recreation, as well as the school and church buildings." By the early twentieth century, new immigrants, such as Italians, Greeks, Slavs, and Mexicans,

composed a majority of the population in these western mining communities.

In September 1913, the United Mine Workers led a strike in the Colorado coalfields, calling for improved safety, higher wages, and recognition of the union. Thousands of miners' families moved out of company housing and into makeshift tent colonies provided by the union. In October, Governor Elias Ammons ordered the Colorado National Guard into the tense strike region to keep order. The troops, supposedly neutral, proceeded to ally themselves with the mine operators. By spring, the strike had bankrupted the state, forcing the governor to remove most of the troops. The coal companies then brought in large numbers of private mine guards who were extremely hostile toward the strikers. On April 20, 1914, a combination of guardsmen and private guards surrounded the largest of the tent colonies at Ludlow, where more than a thousand mine families lived. A shot rang out (each side accused the other of firing), and a pitched battle ensued that lasted until the poorly armed miners ran out of ammunition. At dusk, the troops burned the tent village to the ground, routing the families and killing fourteen, eleven of them children. Enraged strikers attacked mines throughout southern Colorado in an armed rebellion that lasted ten days, until President Woodrow Wilson ordered the U.S. Army into the region. News of the Ludlow Massacre shocked millions and aroused widespread protests and demonstrations against the policies of Colorado Fuel and Iron and its owner, John D. Rockefeller Jr.

Competing Visions of Unionism: The AFL and the IWW

Following the depression of the 1890s, the American Federation of Labor (AFL) emerged as the strongest and most stable organization of workers. Samuel Gompers's strategy of recruiting skilled labor into unions organized by craft had paid off. Union membership climbed from under 500,000 in 1897 to 1.7 million by 1904. Most of this growth took place in AFL affiliates in coal mining, the building trades, transportation, and machine shops. The national unions—the United Mine Workers of America, the Brotherhood of Carpenters and Joiners, the International Association of Machinists—represented workers of specific occupations in collective bargaining. Trade autonomy and exclusive jurisdiction were the ruling principles within the AFL.

The strength of craft organization also gave rise to weakness. Each trade looked mainly to the welfare of its own, and many explicitly barred women and African Americans from membership. There were some important exceptions. The United Mine Workers of America

Read the Document

Samuel Gompers, The American Labor Movement (1914) at **www.myhistorylab.com**

(UMWA) followed a more inclusive policy, recruiting both skilled underground pitmen and the unskilled aboveground workers. The UMWA even tried to recruit strikebreakers brought in by coal operators. With 260,000 members in 1904, the UMWA became the largest AFL affiliate.

AFL unions had a difficult time holding on to their gains. Economic slumps, technological changes, and aggressive counterattacks by employer organizations could be devastating. Trade associations using management-controlled efficiency drives fought union efforts to regulate output and shop practices. The National Association of Manufacturers (NAM), a group of smaller industrialists founded in 1903, launched an "open shop" campaign to eradicate unions altogether. "Open shop" was simply a new name for a workplace where unions were not allowed. Unfriendly judicial decisions also hurt organizing efforts. Not until the 1930s and New Deal legislation would unions be able to count on legislative and legal protections for collective bargaining and the right to strike.

Some workers developed more radical visions of labor organizing. In the harsh and isolated company towns of Idaho, Montana, and Colorado, miners suffered from low wages, poor food, and primitive sanitation, as well as injuries and death from frequent cave-ins and explosions. The Western Federation of Miners (WFM) had gained strength in the metal mining regions of the West by leading several strikes marred by violence. In 1899, during a strike in the silver mining district of Coeur d'Alene, Idaho, the Bunker Hill and Sullivan Mining Company had enraged the miners by hiring armed detectives and firing all union members. Desperate miners retaliated by destroying a company mill with dynamite. Idaho's governor declared martial law and obtained federal troops to enforce it. In a pattern that would become familiar in western labor relations, the soldiers served as strikebreakers, rounding up hundreds of miners and imprisoning them for months in makeshift bullpens.

In response to the brutal realities of labor organizing in the West, most WFM leaders embraced socialism and industrial unionism. In 1905, leaders of the WFM, the Socialist Party, and various radical groups gathered in Chicago to found the Industrial Workers of the World (IWW). The IWW charter proclaimed bluntly, "The working class and the employing class have nothing in common. . . . Between these two classes a struggle must go on until the workers of the world unite as a class, take possession of the earth and the machinery of production, and abolish the wage system."

William D. "Big Bill" Haywood, an imposing, one-eyed, hard-rock miner, emerged as the most influential and flamboyant spokesman for the IWW, or Wobblies, as

they were called. Haywood, a charismatic speaker and effective organizer, regularly denounced the AFL for its conservative emphasis on organizing skilled workers by trade. He insisted that the IWW would exclude no one from its ranks. The Wobblies concentrated their efforts on miners, lumberjacks, sailors, "harvest stiffs," and other casual laborers.

The IWW briefly became a force among eastern industrial workers, tapping the rage and growing militance of immigrants and the unskilled. In 1909, an IWW-led steel strike at McKees Rocks, Pennsylvania, challenged the power of U.S. Steel. In the 1912 "Bread and Roses" strike in Lawrence, Massachusetts, IWW organizers turned a spontaneous walkout of textile workers into a successful struggle for union recognition. Wobbly leaders such as Haywood, Elizabeth Gurley Flynn, and Joseph Ettor used class-conscious rhetoric and multilingual appeals to forge unity among the ethnically diverse Lawrence workforce of 25,000.

The IWW failed to establish permanent organizations in the eastern cities, but it remained a force in the lumber camps, mines, and wheat fields of the West. In spite of its militant rhetoric, the IWW concerned itself with practical gains. "The final aim is revolution," said one Wobbly organizer, "but for the present let's see if we can get a bed to sleep in, water enough to take a bath in and decent food to eat." But when the United States entered World War I, the Justice Department used the IWW's anticapitalist rhetoric and antiwar stance to crush it.

Rebels in Bohemia

During the 1910s, a small but influential community of painters, journalists, poets, social workers, lawyers, and political activists coalesced in the New York City neighborhood of Greenwich Village. These cultural radicals, nearly all of middle-class backgrounds and hailing from provincial American towns, shared a deep sympathy toward the struggles of labor, a passion for modern art, and an affinity for socialism and anarchism. Unlike most progressives, however, especially those from small towns and the nation's hinterlands, the "Village bohemians," particularly the women among them, challenged accepted middle-class morality and assumptions. They rejected the double standard of Victorian sexual morality, challenged traditional marriage and sex roles, advocated birth control, and experimented with homosexual relations. They became a powerful national symbol for rebellion and the merger of political and cultural radicalism.

The term "bohemian" referred to anyone who had artistic or intellectual aspirations and who lived with disregard for conventional rules of behavior. Other American cities, notably Chicago at the turn of the

Publicity poster for the 1913 pageant, organized by John Reed and other Greenwich Village radicals, supporting the cause of striking silk workers in Paterson, New Jersey. This poster drew on aesthetic styles associated with the Industrial Workers of the World, typically including a heroic, larger-than-life image of a factory laborer.

like-minded artists and activists. Yet the Village bohemians were united in their search for a new sense of community. Intellectuals and artists, as well as workers, feeling alienated from the rest of society, sought shelter in the collective life and close-knit social relations of the Village community. The Village bohemia lasted only a few years, a flame snuffed out by the chill political winds accompanying America's entry into World War I. Yet for decades, Greenwich Village remained a mecca for young men and women searching for alternatives to conventional ways of living.

Women's Movements and Black Activism

Like working-class radicals, politically engaged women and African American activists often found themselves at odds with more moderate and mainstream progressive reformers. They contested both gender and racial assumptions inherited from the nineteenth century. Some progressives supported the challenges in one or both of these spheres. They helped shape an agenda for social justice that would echo throughout the rest of the twentieth century. Women were at the forefront of several campaigns, such as the settlement house movement, prohibition, suffrage, and birth control. Millions of others took an active role in new women's associations that combined self-help and social mission. These organizations gave women a place in public life, increased their influence in civic affairs, and nurtured a new generation of female leaders.

In fighting racial discrimination, African Americans had a more difficult task. As racism gained ground in the political and cultural spheres, black progressives fought defensively to prevent the rights they had secured during Reconstruction from being further undermined. Still, they managed to produce leaders, ideas, and organizations that would have a long-range impact on American race relations.

The New Woman

The settlement house movement discussed in the opening of this chapter was just one of the new avenues of opportunity opened to progressive-era women. A steady proliferation of women's organizations attracted growing numbers of educated, middle-class women. With more men working in offices, more children attending school, and family size declining, the middle-class home was emptier. At the same time, more middle-class women were graduating from high school and college. In 1870, only 1 percent of college-age Americans had attended college, about 20 percent of them

> Read the Document
> *Helen M. Todd, "Getting Out the Vote" (1911)* at **www.myhistorylab.com**

century, had supported bohemian communities. But the Village scene was unique, if fleeting. The neighborhood offered cheap rents, studio space, and good ethnic restaurants, and it was close to the exciting political and labor activism of Manhattan's Lower East Side. The worldview of the Village's bohemian community found expression in *The Masses*, a monthly magazine founded in 1911 by socialist critic Max Eastman, who was also its editor. "The broad purpose of *The Masses*," wrote John Reed, one of its leading writers, "is a social one— to everlastingly attack old systems, old morals, old prejudices—the whole weight of outworn thought that dead men have saddled upon us." For some, Greenwich Village offered a chance to experiment with sexual relationships or work arrangements. For others, it was an escape from small-town conformity, or a haven for women; by 1910, about 5 percent of college-age Americans attended college, but the proportion of women among them had doubled to 40 percent.

Single-sex clubs brought middle-class women into the public sphere by celebrating the distinctive strengths associated with women's culture: cooperation, uplift, service. The formation of the General Federation of Women's Clubs in 1890 brought together 200 local clubs representing 20,000 women. By 1900, the federation boasted 150,000 members, and by World War I, it claimed to represent over a million women. The women's club movement combined an earlier focus on self-improvement and intellectual pursuits with newer benevolent efforts on behalf of working women and children. The Buffalo Union, for example, sponsored art lectures for housewives and classes in typing, stenography, and bookkeeping for young working women. It also maintained a library, set up a "noon rest" downtown where women could eat lunch, and ran a school for training domestics.

For many middle-class women, the club movement provided a new kind of female-centered community. Club activity often led members to participate in other civic ventures, particularly "child-saving" reforms, such as child labor laws and mothers' pensions. Some took up the cause of working-class women, fighting for protective legislation and offering aid to trade unions. As wives and daughters of influential and well-off men in their communities, club women had access to funds and could generate support for projects they undertook.

Other women's associations made even more explicit efforts to bridge class lines between middle-class homemakers and working-class women. The National Consumers' League (NCL), started in 1898 by Maud Nathan and Josephine Lowell, sponsored a "white label" campaign in which manufacturers who met safety and sanitary standards could put NCL labels on their food and clothing. Under the dynamic leadership of Florence Kelley, the NCL took an even more aggressive stance by publicizing labor abuses in department stores and lobbying for maximum-hour and minimum-wage laws in state legislatures. In its efforts to protect home and housewife, worker and consumer, the NCL embodied the ideal of "social housekeeping."

Birth Control

The phrase "birth control," coined by Margaret Sanger around 1913, described her campaign to provide contraceptive information and devices for women. Sanger had

A supportive crowd surrounds birth control pioneer Margaret Sanger and her sister, Ethel Byrne, as they leave the Court of Special Services in New York City in 1917. Police had recently closed Sanger's first birth control clinic in the immigrant neighborhood of Brownsville, New York, and Sanger herself had spent a month in jail.

seen her own mother die at age forty-nine after bearing eleven children. In 1910, Sanger was a thirty-year-old nurse and housewife living with her husband and three children in a New York City suburb. Excited by a socialist lecture she had attended, she convinced her husband to move to the city, where she threw herself into the bohemian milieu. She became an organizer for the IWW, and in 1912, she wrote a series of articles on female sexuality for a socialist newspaper.

When postal officials confiscated the paper for violating obscenity laws, Sanger left for Europe to learn more about contraception. She returned to New York determined to challenge the obscenity statutes with her own magazine, the *Woman Rebel*. Sanger's journal celebrated female autonomy, including the right to sexual expression and control over one's body. When she distributed her pamphlet *Family Limitation*, postal inspectors confiscated copies and she found herself facing forty-five years in prison. In October 1914, she fled to Europe again. In her absence, anarchist agitator Emma Goldman and many women in the Socialist Party took up the cause.

An older generation of feminists had advocated "voluntary motherhood," or the right to say no to a husband's sexual demands. The new birth control advocates embraced contraception as a way of advancing sexual freedom for middle-class women, as well as responding to the misery of those working-class women who bore numerous children while living in poverty. Sanger returned to the United States in October 1915. After the government dropped the obscenity charges, she embarked on a national speaking tour. In 1916, she again defied the law by opening a birth control clinic in a working-class neighborhood in Brooklyn and offering birth control information without a physician present. Arrested and jailed, she gained more publicity for her crusade. Within a few years, birth control leagues and clinics could be found in every major city and most large towns in the country.

Read the Document

History Bookshelf: Margaret Sanger, Woman and the New Race *(1920)* at **www.myhistorylab.com**

Racism and Accommodation

At the turn of the century, four-fifths of the nation's 10 million African Americans still lived in the South, where most eked out a living working in agriculture. In the cities, most blacks were relegated to menial jobs, but a small African American middle class of entrepreneurs and professionals gained a foothold by selling services and products to the black community. They all confronted a racism that was growing in both intensity and influence in American politics and culture. White racism came in many variants and had evolved significantly since slavery days. The more virulent strains, influenced by Darwin's evolutionary theory, held that blacks were a "degenerate" race, genetically predisposed to vice, crime,

and disease and destined to lose the struggle for existence with whites.

African Americans also endured a deeply racist popular culture that made hateful stereotypes of black people a normal feature of political debate and everyday life. Benjamin Tillman, a U.S. senator from South Carolina, denounced the African American as "a fiend, a wild beast, seeking whom he may devour." In northern cities "coon songs," based on gross caricatures of black life, were extremely popular in theaters and as sheet music. As in the antebellum minstrel shows, these songs reduced African Americans to creatures of pure appetite—for food, sex, alcohol, and violence. Southern progressives articulated a more moderate racial philosophy. They also assumed the innate inferiority of blacks, but they believed that black progress was necessary to achieve the economic and political progress associated with a vision of the New South. Their solution to the "race problem" stressed paternalist uplift.

Amid this political and cultural climate, Booker T. Washington won recognition as the most influential black leader of the day. Born a slave in 1856, Washington was educated at Hampton Institute in Virginia, one of the first freedmen's schools devoted to industrial education. In 1881, he founded Tuskegee Institute, a black school in Alabama devoted to industrial and moral education. He became the leading spokesman for racial accommodation, urging blacks to focus on economic improvement and self-reliance, as opposed to political and civil rights. In an 1895 speech delivered at the Cotton States Exposition in Atlanta, Washington outlined the key themes of accommodationist philosophy. "Cast down your buckets where you are," Washington told black people, meaning they should focus on improving their vocational skills as industrial workers and farmers. "In all things that are purely social," he told attentive whites, "we can be as separate as the fingers, yet one as the hand in all things essential to mutual progress."

Washington's message won him the financial backing of leading white philanthropists and the respect of progressive whites. His widely read autobiography, *Up from Slavery* (1901), stands as a classic narrative of an American self-made man. Written with a shrewd eye toward

Read the Document

History Bookshelf: Booker T. Washington, Up From Slavery *(1901)* at **www.myhistorylab.com**

cementing his support among white Americans, it stressed the importance of learning values such as frugality, cleanliness, and personal morality. Washington also gained a large following among African Americans, especially those who aspired to business success. With the help of Andrew Carnegie, he founded the National Negro Business League to preach the virtue of black business development in black communities.

Washington also had a decisive influence on the flow of private funds to black schools in the South.

Publicly, he insisted that "agitation of questions of social equality is the extremest folly." Privately, Washington also spent money and worked behind the scenes trying to halt disfranchisement and segregation. He offered secret financial support, for example, for court cases that challenged Louisiana's grandfather clause, the exclusion of blacks from Alabama juries, and railroad segregation in Tennessee and Georgia.

Racial Justice, the NAACP, and Black Women's Activism

Washington's focus on economic self-help remained deeply influential in African American communities long after his death in 1915. But alternative black voices challenged his racial philosophy while he lived. In the early 1900s, scholar and activist W. E. B. Du Bois created a significant alternative to Washington's leadership. A product of the black middle class, Du Bois had been educated at Fisk University and Harvard, where in 1895, he became the first African American to receive a PhD. His book *The Philadelphia Negro* (1899) was a pioneering work of social science that refuted racist stereotypes by, for example, discussing black contributions to that city's political life and describing the wide range of black business activity. In *The Souls of Black Folk* (1903), Du Bois declared prophetically that "the problem of the twentieth century is the problem of the color line." Through essays on black history, culture, education, and politics, Du Bois explored the concept of "double consciousness." Black people, he argued, would always feel the tension between an African heritage and their desire to assimilate as Americans. *Souls* represented the first effort to embrace African American culture as a source of collective black strength and something worth preserving.

●●◄ Read the Document

History Bookshelf: W.E.B. DuBois, The Souls of Black Folk (1903) at **www.myhistorylab.com**

Du Bois criticized Booker T. Washington's philosophy for its acceptance of "the alleged inferiority of the Negro." The black community, he argued, must fight for the right to vote, for civic equality, and for higher education for the "talented tenth" of their youth. In 1905,

((●◄ Hear the Audio

The Crisis Magazine by W. E.B. DuBois at **www.myhistorylab.com**

Du Bois and editor William Monroe Trotter brought together a group of educated black men to oppose Washington's conciliatory views. Discrimination they encountered in Buffalo, New York, prompted the men to move their meeting to Niagara Falls, Ontario. "Any discrimination based simply on race or color is barbarous," they declared. "Persistent manly agitation is the way to liberty." The Niagara movement protested legal segregation, the exclusion of blacks from labor unions, and the curtailment of voting and other civil rights.

The Niagara movement failed to generate much change. But in 1909, many of its members, led by

In July 1905, a group of African American leaders met in Niagara Falls, Ontario, to protest legal segregation and the denial of civil rights to the nation's black population. This portrait was taken against a studio backdrop of the falls. In 1909, the leader of the Niagara movement, W. E. B. Du Bois (second from right, middle row), founded and edited *The Crisis*, the influential monthly journal of the National Association for the Advancement of Colored People.

SOURCE: Photographs and Prints Division, Schomburg Center for Research in Black Culture, The New York Public Library, Astor, Lenox and Tilden Foundations.

Du Bois, attended a National Negro Conference held at the Henry Street Settlement in New York. The group included a number of white progressives sympathetic to the idea of challenging Washington's philosophy. A new interracial organization emerged from this conference, the National Association for the Advancement of Colored People. Du Bois, the only black officer of the original NAACP, founded and edited *The Crisis*, the influential NAACP monthly journal. For the next several decades, the NAACP would lead struggles to overturn legal and economic barriers to equal opportunity.

((●◄ Hear the Audio

The Progress of Colored Women by Mary Church Terrell at **www.myhistorylab.com**

The disenfranchisement of black voters in the South severely curtailed African American political influence. In response, African American women created new strategies to challenge white supremacy and improve life in their communities. Founded in 1900, the Women's

Convention of the National Baptist Convention, the largest black denomination in the United States, offered African American women a new public space to pursue reform work and "racial uplift." They organized settlement houses and built playgrounds; they created daycare facilities and kindergartens; they campaigned for women's suffrage, temperance, and advances in public health. In effect, they transformed church missionary societies into quasi–social service agencies. Using the motto "Lifting as We Climb," the National Association of Colored Women Clubs by 1914 boasted 50,000 members in 1,000 clubs nationwide.

National Progressivism

The progressive impulse had begun at local levels and percolated up. Some state progressive leaders, such as Robert La Follette of Wisconsin and Hiram Johnson of California, achieved national influence as they pushed Progressive forces in both major political parties to take a more aggressive stance on the reform issues of the day. On the presidential level, both Republican Theodore Roosevelt and Democrat Woodrow Wilson laid claim to the progressive mantle—a good example of how on the national level, progressivism animated many perspectives. In their pursuit of reform agendas, both significantly reshaped the office of the president. As progressivism moved to Washington, nationally organized interest groups and public opinion began to rival the influence of the old political parties in shaping the political landscape.

Theodore Roosevelt and Presidential Activism

The assassination of William McKinley in 1901 made forty-two-year-old Theodore Roosevelt the youngest man to ever hold the office of president. Roosevelt viewed the presidency as a "bully pulpit"—a platform from which he could exhort Americans to reform their society—and he aimed to make the most of it. In New York, his friend Jacob Riis, the muckraking journalist, took him on tours of the city's tenement districts and converted Roosevelt to progressivism. In 1897, Roosevelt went to Washington as assistant secretary of the navy, and during the Spanish-American War he won national fame as leader of the Rough Rider regiment in Cuba. Upon his return, he was elected governor of New York, and then in 1900, vice president.

Roosevelt was a uniquely colorful figure, a shrewd publicist, and a creative politician. His three-year stint as a rancher in the Dakota Territory, his fondness for hunting and nature study, and his passion for scholarship, which resulted in ten books before he became president,

all set "T. R." apart from most of his upper-class peers. Roosevelt preached the virtues of "the strenuous life," and he believed that educated and wealthy Americans had a special responsibility to serve, guide, and inspire those less fortunate. He also believed the nation was at a crossroads that required the national state to play a more active role in curbing the power of wealthy industrialists.

Read the Document

Theodore Roosevelt, "The Strenuous Life" (1900) at **www.myhistorylab.com**

Roosevelt made key contributions to national progressivism and to changing the office of the president. He knew how to inspire and guide public opinion. He stimulated discussion and aroused curiosity like no one before him. In 1902, Roosevelt demonstrated his unique style of activism when he personally intervened in a bitter dispute in the anthracite coal industry. Using public calls for conciliation, a series of White House meetings, and private pressure on the mine owners, Roosevelt secured an arbitrated settlement that won better pay and working conditions for the miners but without recognition of their union. Roosevelt also pushed for efficient government as the solution to social problems. Unlike most nineteenth-century Republicans, who had largely ignored economic and social inequalities, Roosevelt frankly acknowledged them. Administrative agencies run by experts, he believed, could find rational solutions that would satisfy everyone.

Trust-Busting and Regulation

One of the first issues Roosevelt faced was growing public concern with the rapid business consolidations taking place in the American economy. In 1902, he directed the Justice Department to begin a series of prosecutions under the Sherman Antitrust Act. The first target was the Northern Securities Company, a huge merger of transcontinental railroads brought about by financier J. P. Morgan. The deal would have created a giant holding company controlling nearly all the long-distance rail lines from Chicago to California. The Justice Department fought the case all the way through a hearing before the Supreme Court. In *Northern Securities* v. *United States* (1904), the Court held that the stock transactions constituted an illegal combination in restraint of interstate commerce.

This case established Roosevelt's reputation as a "trustbuster." During his two terms, the Justice Department filed forty-three cases under the Sherman Antitrust Act to restrain or dissolve business monopolies. These included actions against the so-called tobacco and beef trusts and the Standard Oil Company. Roosevelt viewed these suits as necessary to publicize the issue and assert the federal government's ultimate authority over big business. But he did not really believe in the need to break up large corporations. "Trust-busting" might be

This 1909 cartoon by Clifton Berryman depicts President Theodore Roosevelt slaying those trusts he considered "bad" for the public interest, while restraining those whose business practices he considered "good" for the economy. The image also plays on T. R.'s well-publicized fondness for big-game hunting.

good politics, but unlike many progressives, who were nostalgic for smaller companies and freer competition, Roosevelt accepted centralization as a fact of modern economic life. Indeed, many of the legal cases against trusts were dropped after business executives met privately with Roosevelt in the White House. What was most important, in T. R.'s view, was to insist on the right and power of the federal government to reign in excessive corporate behavior.

After easily defeating Democrat Alton B. Parker in the 1904 election, Roosevelt felt more secure in pushing for regulatory legislation. In 1906, Roosevelt responded to public pressure for greater government intervention and, overcoming objections from a conservative Congress, signed three important measures into law. The Hepburn Act strengthened the Interstate Commerce Commission (ICC), established in 1887 as the first independent regulatory agency, by authorizing it to set maximum railroad rates and inspect financial records.

Two other laws passed in 1906 also expanded the regulatory power of the federal government. The battles surrounding these reforms demonstrate how progressive measures often attracted supporters with competing motives. The Pure Food and Drug Act established the Food and Drug Administration (FDA), which tested and approved drugs before they went on the market. The Meat Inspection Act (passed with help from the shocking publicity surrounding Upton Sinclair's muckraking novel, *The Jungle*) empowered the Department of Agriculture to inspect and label meat products. In both cases, supporters hailed the new laws as providing consumer protection against adulterated or fraudulently labeled food and drugs.

Regulatory legislation found advocates among American big business as well. Large meatpackers such as Swift and Armour strongly supported stricter federal regulation as a way to drive out smaller companies that could not meet tougher standards. The new laws also helped American packers compete more profitably in the European export market by giving their meat the official seal of federal inspectors. Large pharmaceutical manufacturers similarly supported new regulations that would eliminate competitors and patent medicine suppliers. Thus, these reforms won support from large corporate interests that viewed stronger federal regulation as a strategy for consolidating their economic power. Progressive-era expansion of the nation-state had its champions among—and benefits for—big business as well as American consumers.

The Birth of Environmentalism

As a naturalist and outdoorsman, Theodore Roosevelt also believed in the need for government regulation of the natural environment. He worried about the destruction of forests, prairies, streams, and the wilderness. The conservation of forest and water resources, he argued, was a national problem of vital import. In 1905, he created the U.S. Forest Service and named conservationist Gifford Pinchot to head it. Pinchot recruited a force of forest rangers to manage the reserves. By 1909, total timber and forest reserves had increased from 45 to 195 million acres, and more than 80 million acres of mineral lands had been withdrawn from public sale.

On the broad issue of managing America's natural resources, the Roosevelt administration took the middle ground between preservation and unrestricted commercial development. But other voices championed a more radical vision of conservation, emphasizing the preservation of wilderness lands against the encroachment of commercial exploitation. The most influential and committed of these was John Muir, an essayist and founder of the modern environmentalist movement.

Read the Document

History Bookshelf: Gifford Pinchot, The Fight for Conservation *(1910) at* **www.myhistorylab.com**

William Robinson Leigh painted this landscape, *Grand Canyon*, 1911, one of many western scenes he created. Like many of his contemporaries, Leigh expressed his frustration with trying to capture the sublime in nature: "It challenges man's utmost skill; it mocks and defies his puny efforts to grasp and perpetuate, through art, its inimitable grandeur."

SOURCE: Leigh, William Robinson (1866–1955), *Grand Canyon*, 1911. Oil on canvas, 66" × 99". Collection of The Newark Museum, Newark, New Jersey, Gift of Henry Wallington Wack, 1930. Inv.: 30.203. © The Newark Museum /Art Resource, New York.

Muir made a passionate and spiritual defense of the inherent value of the American wilderness. Wild country, he argued, had a mystical power to inspire and refresh. "Climb the mountains and get their good tidings," he advised. "Nature's peace will flow into you as the sunshine into the trees." Muir served as first president of the Sierra Club, founded in 1892 to preserve and protect the mountain regions of the West Coast as well as Yellowstone National Park in Wyoming, Montana, and Idaho.

A bitter, drawn-out struggle over new water sources for San Francisco revealed the deep conflicts between conservationists, represented by Pinchot, and preservationists, represented by Muir. After a devastating earthquake in 1906, San Francisco sought federal approval to dam and flood the spectacular Hetch Hetchy Valley, located 150 miles from the city in Yosemite National Park. The project promised to ease the city's chronic freshwater shortage and to generate hydroelectric power. Conservationists and their urban progressive allies argued that developing Hetch Hetchy would be a victory for the public good over greedy private developers, since the plan called for municipal control of the water supply. To John Muir and the Sierra Club, Hetch Hetchy was a "temple" threatened with destruction by the "devotees of ravaging commercialism." Congress finally approved the reservoir plan in 1913; utility and public development triumphed over the preservation of nature. Although they lost the battle for Hetch Hetchy, the preservationists gained much ground in the larger campaign of alerting the nation to the dangers of a vanishing wilderness. They began to use their own utilitarian rationales, arguing that national parks would encourage economic growth through tourism and provide Americans with a healthy escape from urban and industrial areas. In 1916, the preservationists obtained their own bureaucracy in Washington with the creation of the National Park Service.

The Newlands Reclamation Act of 1902 represented another important victory for the conservation strategy of Roosevelt and Pinchot. With the goal of turning arid land into productive family farms through irrigation, the act established the Reclamation Bureau within the Department of the Interior and provided federal funding for dam and canal projects. But in practice, the bureau did more to encourage the growth of large-scale agribusiness and western cities than small farming. The Roosevelt Dam on Arizona's Salt River, along with the forty-mile Arizona Canal, helped develop the Phoenix area. The Imperial Dam on the Colorado River diverted water to California's Imperial and Coachella Valleys. The Newlands Act thus established a growing federal presence in managing water resources, the critical issue in twentieth-century western development.

The Election of 1912: A Four-Way Race

In 1908, Roosevelt kept his promise to retire after a second term. He chose Secretary of War William Howard Taft as his successor. Taft easily defeated Democrat William Jennings Bryan in the 1908 election. During Taft's presidency, the gulf between "insurgent" progressives and the "stand pat" wing split the Republican Party wide open. To some degree, the battles were as much over style as substance. Compared with Roosevelt, the reflective and judicious Taft brought a much more restrained concept of the presidency to the White House. He supported some progressive measures, including the constitutional amendment legalizing a graduated income tax (ratified in 1913), safety codes for mines and railroads, and the creation of a federal Children's Bureau (1912). But in a series of bitter political fights involving tariff, antitrust, and conservation policies, Taft alienated Roosevelt and many other progressives.

After returning from an African safari and a triumphant European tour in 1910, Roosevelt threw himself back into national politics. He directly challenged

●●●[Read the Document

Theodore Roosevelt, "The New Nationalism" (1910) at **www.myhistorylab.com**

Taft for the Republican Party leadership. In a dozen bitter state presidential primaries (the first ever held), Taft and Roosevelt fought for the nomination. Although Roosevelt won most of these contests, the old guard still controlled the national convention and renominated Taft in June 1912. Roosevelt's supporters stormed out, and in August, the new Progressive Party nominated Roosevelt and Hiram Johnson of California as its presidential ticket. Roosevelt's "New Nationalism" presented a vision of a strong federal government, led by an activist president,

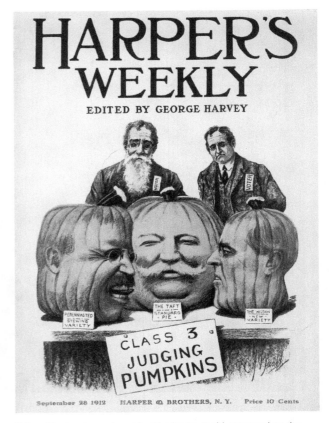

This political cartoon, drawn by Charles Jay Budd, appeared on the cover of *Harper's Weekly*, September 28, 1912. It employed the imagery of autumn county fairs to depict voters as unhappy with their three choices for president. Note that the artist did not include the fourth candidate, socialist Eugene V. Debs, who was often ignored by more conservative publications such as *Harper's*.

regulating and protecting the various interests in American society. The platform called for woman suffrage, the eight-hour day, prohibition of child labor, minimum-wage standards for working women, and stricter regulation of large corporations.

With the Republicans so badly divided, the Democrats sensed a chance for their first presidential victory in twenty years. They chose Governor Woodrow Wilson of New Jersey as their candidate. Although not nearly as well known nationally as Taft and Roosevelt, Wilson had built a strong reputation as a reformer. The son of a Virginia Presbyterian minister, Wilson spent most of his early career in academia. After teaching history and political science at several schools, he became president of Princeton University in 1902. In 1910, he won election as New Jersey's governor, running against the state Democratic machine. He won the Democratic nomination for president with the support of many of the party's progressives, including William Jennings Bryan.

Wilson declared himself and the Democratic Party to be the true progressives. Viewing Roosevelt rather than Taft as his main rival, Wilson contrasted his New Freedom campaign with Roosevelt's New Nationalism. Crafted largely by progressive lawyer Louis Brandeis, Wilson's platform was far more ambiguous than Roosevelt's. The New Freedom emphasized restoring conditions of free competition and equality of economic opportunity. Wilson did favor a variety of progressive reforms for workers, farmers, and consumers. But Wilson argued against allowing the federal government to become as large and paternalistic as Roosevelt advocated. "What this country needs above everything else," Wilson argued, "is a body of laws which will look after the men who are on the make rather than the men who are already made."

●●●⁃[Read the **Document**

Woodrow Wilson, "The New Freedom" (1913) at **www.myhistorylab.com**

Socialist Party nominee Eugene V. Debs offered the fourth and most radical choice to voters. The socialists had more than doubled their membership since 1908, to exceed 100,000. By 1912, more than a thousand socialists held elective office in thirty-three states and 160 cities, including fifty-six mayors and one congressman. The party's 1912 platform called for collective ownership of all large-scale industry and all means of transportation and communication. It demanded shorter working hours, an end to child labor, and the vote for women. An inspiring orator who drew large and sympathetic crowds wherever he spoke,

((●⁃[Hear the **Audio**

The Speech That Sent Debs to Jail at **www.myhistorylab.com**

Debs proved especially popular in areas with strong labor movements and populist traditions. He wrapped his socialist message in an apocalyptic vision. Socialists would "abolish this monstrous system and the misery and crime which flow from it." Debs and the socialists also took credit for pushing both Roosevelt and Wilson further toward the left. Both the Democratic and Progressive Party platforms contained proposals that had been considered extremely radical only ten years earlier.

In the end, the divisions in the Republican Party gave the election to Wilson (see Map 21.2). Even though he won with only 42 percent of the popular vote, Wilson swept the Electoral College with 435 votes to Roosevelt's 88 and Taft's 8, giving him the largest electoral majority up to that time. In several respects, the election of 1912 was the first "modern" presidential race. It featured the first direct primaries, challenges to traditional party loyalties, an issue-oriented campaign, and a high degree of interest-group activity.

Woodrow Wilson's First Term

As president, Wilson followed Roosevelt's lead in expanding the activist dimensions of the office. He became more responsive to pressure for a greater federal

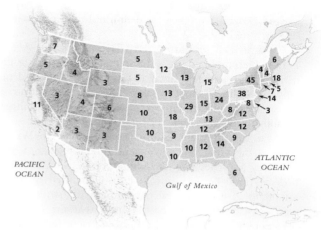

	Electoral Vote (%)	Popular Vote (%)
WOODROW WILSON (Democrat)	435 (82)	6,296,547 (42)
Theodore Roosevelt (Progressive)	88 (17)	4,118,571 (27)
William Taft (Republican)	8 (1)	3,486,720 (23)
Eugene Debs (Socialist)	—	900,672 (6)

MAP 21.2 The Election of 1912 The split within the Republican Party allowed Woodrow Wilson to become only the second Democrat since the Civil War to be elected president. Eugene Debs's votes were the highest ever polled by a socialist candidate.

role in regulating business and the economy. This increase in direct lobbying—from hundreds of local and national reform groups, Washington-based organizations, and the new Progressive Party—was itself a new and defining feature of the era's political life. With the help of a Democratic- controlled Congress, Wilson pushed through a significant battery of reform proposals.

The Underwood-Simmons Act of 1913 substantially reduced tariff duties on a variety of raw materials and manufactured goods, including wool, sugar, agricultural machinery, shoes, iron, and steel. Taking advantage of the newly ratified Sixteenth Amendment, which gave Congress the power to levy taxes on income, it also imposed the first graduated tax (up to 6 percent) on personal incomes. The Federal Reserve Act that same year restructured the nation's banking and currency system. It created twelve Federal Reserve Banks, regulated by a central board in Washington. Member banks were required to keep a portion of their cash reserves in the Federal Reserve Bank of their district. By raising or lowering the percentage of reserves required, "the Fed" could either discourage or encourage credit expansion by member banks.

By giving central direction to banking and monetary policy, the Federal Reserve Board diminished the power of large private banks.

Wilson also supported the Clayton Antitrust Act of 1914, which replaced the old Sherman Act of 1890 as the nation's basic antitrust law. The Clayton Act reflected the growing political clout of the American Federation of Labor. It exempted unions from being construed as illegal combinations in restraint of trade, and it forbade federal courts from issuing injunctions against strikers. But Wilson adopted the view that permanent federal regulation was necessary for checking the abuses of big business. The Federal Trade Commission (FTC), established in 1914, sought to give the federal government the same sort of regulatory control over corporations that the ICC had over railroads. Wilson believed a permanent federal body like the FTC would provide a method for corporate oversight superior to the erratic and time-consuming process of legal trust-busting.

On social issues, Wilson proved more cautious in his first two years. His initial failure to support federal child labor legislation and rural credits to farmers angered many progressives. A Southerner, Wilson also issued an executive order that instituted legal segregation in federal employment, requiring African Americans to work separately from white employees in government offices around Washington, DC. As the reelection campaign of 1916 approached, Wilson worried about defections from the labor and social justice wings of his party. He proceeded to support a rural credits act providing government capital to federal farm banks, as well as federal aid to agricultural extension programs in schools. He also came out in favor of a worker compensation bill for federal employees, and he signed the landmark Keating-Owen Act, which banned children under fourteen from working in enterprises engaged in interstate commerce. Although it covered less than 10 percent of the nation's 2 million working children, the new law established a minimum standard of protection and put the power of federal authority behind the principle of regulating child labor. But by 1916, the dark cloud of war in Europe had already begun to cast its long shadow over progressive reform.

Conclusion

In her memoirs, Lillian Wald summarized the growth of the Henry Street Settlement she founded in 1895 as a home health and visiting nurse service on New York's Lower East Side. "Our experience in one small East Side section," she recalled in 1934, "a block perhaps, has led to a next contact, and a next, in widening circles, until our community relationships have come to include the city, the state, the national government, and the world at large." Much the same could be said of the progressive movement. What had begun as a series of interlocking, sometimes contradictory, reform initiatives had come to redefine Americans' relationship to government itself. Cities and state legislatures routinely made active interventions to improve the lives of their citizens. Real advances had been made through a range of social legislation covering working conditions, child labor, minimum wages, and worker compensation. Social progressives, too, had discovered the power of organizing into extraparty lobbying groups, such as the National Consumers' League and the National American Woman Suffrage Association. The national government had become the focus of political power and reform energy. The president was expected to provide leadership in policymaking, and new federal bureaucracies exerted more influence over the day-to-day lives of Americans.

Yet many progressive reforms had uneven or unintended consequences. The tensions between fighting for social justice and the urge toward social control remained unresolved. The emphasis on efficiency, uplift, and rational administration often collided with humane impulses to aid the poor, the immigrant, the slum dweller. The large majority of African Americans, blue-collar workers, and urban poor remained untouched by federal assistance programs. The drive for a more open and democratic political process, in particular, had the effect of excluding some people from voting while including others. For African Americans, progressivism largely meant disenfranchisement from voting altogether. Stricter election laws made it more difficult for third parties to get on the ballot. Voting itself steadily declined after 1916. Overall, party voting became a less important form of political participation. Interest-group activity, congressional and statehouse lobbying, and direct appeals to public opinion gained currency as ways of influencing government. Business groups and individual trade associations were among the most active groups pressing their demands on government. Political action often shifted from legislatures to the new administrative agencies and commissions created to deal with social and economic problems. Popular magazines and journals grew significantly in both number and circulation, becoming more influential in shaping and appealing to national public opinion. America's entry into World War I effectively drained the energy out of progressive reform. The progressive movement, however, with all its contradictions and internal tensions, had profoundly changed the landscape of American political and social life.

CHRONOLOGY

1889	Jane Addams founds Hull House in Chicago	**1909**	Uprising of 20,000 garment workers in New York City's garment industries helps organize unskilled workers into unions
1890	Jacob Riis publishes *How the Other Half Lives*		National Association for the Advancement of Colored People (NAACP) is founded
1895	Booker T. Washington addresses Cotton States Exposition in Atlanta, emphasizing an accommodationist philosophy	**1911**	Triangle Shirtwaist Company fire kills 146 garment workers in New York City
	Lillian Wald establishes Henry Street Settlement in New York		Socialist critic Max Eastman begins publishing *The Masses*
1898	Florence Kelley becomes general secretary of the new National Consumers' League	**1912**	Democrat Woodrow Wilson wins presidency, defeating Republican William H. Taft, Progressive Theodore Roosevelt, and socialist Eugene V. Debs
1900	Robert M. La Follette is elected governor of Wisconsin		"Bread and Roses" strike involves 25,000 textile workers in Lawrence, Massachusetts
1901	Theodore Roosevelt succeeds the assassinated William McKinley as president		Margaret Sanger begins writing and speaking in support of birth control for women
1903	Lincoln Steffens publishes *The Shame of the Cities*	**1913**	Sixteenth Amendment, legalizing a graduated income tax, is ratified
1905	President Roosevelt creates U.S. Forest Service and names Gifford Pinchot head		Seventeenth Amendment, shifting the selection of U.S. senators to direct election by voters
	Industrial Workers of the World is founded in Chicago	**1914**	Clayton Antitrust Act exempts unions from being construed as illegal combinations in restraint of trade
1906	Upton Sinclair's *The Jungle* exposes conditions in the meatpacking industry		Federal Trade Commission is established
	Congress passes Pure Food and Drug Act and Meat Inspection Act and establishes Food and Drug Administration		Ludlow Massacre occurs
1908	In *Muller* v. *Oregon*, the Supreme Court upholds a state law limiting maximum hours for working women	**1916**	National Park Service is established

Review Questions

1. Discuss the tensions within progressivism between the ideals of social justice and the urge for social control. What concrete achievements are associated with each wing of the movement? What were the driving forces behind them?

2. Describe the different manifestations of progressivism at the local, state, and national levels. To what extent did progressives redefine the role of the state in American politics?

3. How did workers use their own values and communities to restrain the power of large corporations during the progressive era?

4. How did the era's new immigration reshape America's cities and workplaces? What connections can you draw between the new immigrant experience and progressive era politics?

5. Analyze the progressive era from the perspective of African Americans. What political and social developments were most crucial, and what legacies did they leave?

6. How do the goals, methods, and language of progressives still find voice in contemporary America?

Recommended Reading

James Chace, *1912: Wilson, Roosevelt, Taft & Debs—The Election That Changed the Country* (2004). Narrative account of this pivotal presidential election that revolved around competing visions of progressivism.

Alan Dawley, *Struggles for Justice: Social Responsibility and the Liberal State* (1991). Offers an important interpretation of progressivism that focuses on how the working class and women pushed the nation toward a more activist role in confronting social problems.

David von Drehle, *Triangle: The Fire That Changed America* (2003). Superb, deeply researched narrative of the disastrous Triangle Fire that re-creates the world of the victims and the reform movement that ensued from the tragedy.

Maureen Flanagan, *America Reformed: Progressives and Progressivisms, 1890s–1920s* (2007). An excellent new overview of progressive-era achievements, including a fine analysis of the contradictions within the movement.

Louise W. Knight, *Citizen: Jane Addams and the Struggle for Democracy* (2005). Beautifully written new biography of this key progressive figure, focusing on Addams's early life and the evolution of her political thought.

Michael McGerr, *A Fierce Discontent: The Rise and Fall of the Progressive Movement in America, 1870–1920* (2003). A new synthesis arguing that the heart of progressivism lay in the efforts of the urban middle class to reshape the behavior of both the poor and the wealthy.

Daniel Okrent, *Last Call: The Rise and Fall of Prohibition* (2010). A sweeping and colorful new account of the origins, impact, and repeal of the 18th Amendment. Okrent is especially strong on analyzing the disparate groups that forged the strange alliance dedicated to making America dry.

Daniel T. Rodgers, *Atlantic Crossings: Social Politics in a Progressive Age* (1998). A magisterial work of comparative history focusing on the transnational conversations that deeply influenced American progressive thinkers and reformers.

Cecelia Tichi, *Civic Passions: Seven Who Launched Progressive America* (2009). Uses the stories of seven influential activists as an introduction into key reform issues of the Progressive era.

PEARSON myhistorylab Connections

Reinforce what you learned in this chapter by studying the many documents, images, maps, review tools, and videos available at www.myhistorylab.com.

Read and Review

✓● Study and Review **Chapter 21**

●●● Read the Document

George W. Plunkitt, "Honest Graft" (1905)

Report of the Vice Commission, Louisville, Kentucky (1915)

Lee Chew, "Life of a Chinese Immigrant" (1903)

Letters to the Jewish Daily Forward (1906-1907)

Samuel Gompers, The American Labor Movement (1914)

Helen M. Todd, "Getting Out the Vote" (1911)

Theodore Roosevelt, "The Strenuous Life" (1900)

Theodore Roosevelt, "The New Nationalism" (1910)

Woodrow Wilson, "The New Freedom" (1913)

Research and Explore

●●● Read the Document

Exploring America: Hetch Hetchy

The Struggle for Women Suffrage

History Bookshelf
  Ida B. Wells-Barnett, The Red Record (1895)
  Booker T. Washington, Up From Slavery (1901)
  W.E.B. DuBois, The Souls of Black Folk (1903)
  Upton Sinclair, The Jungle (1906)
  Jane Addams, The Spirit of Youth and City Streets (1909)
  Jane Addams, Twenty Years at Hull House (1910)
  Margaret Sanger, Woman and the New Race (1920)
  Gifford Pinchot, The Fight for Conservation (1910)

Profiles
  John Muir
  Margaret Sanger

((●● Hear the Audio

The Crisis Magazine by W.E.B. Du Bois

The Progress of Colored Women by Mary Church Terrell

The Speech That Sent Debs to Jail

●● Watch the Video *What Was the Progressive Education Movement?*

((●● Hear the Audio

Hear the audio files for Chapter 21 at
www.myhistorylab.com.

Chapter 22 at www.myhistorylab.com
(((•)) Hear the Audio

A Global Power
The United States in the Era of the Great War
1901–1920

CHAPTER OUTLINE

American Communities 621
The American Expeditionary Force in France

Becoming a World Power **623**
Roosevelt: The Big Stick
Taft: Dollar Diplomacy
Wilson: Moralism and Intervention
 in Mexico

The Great War **628**
The Guns of August
American Neutrality
Preparedness and Peace
Safe for Democracy

American Mobilization **631**
Selling the War
Fading Opposition to War
"You're in the Army Now"
Racism in the Military
Americans in Battle
The Russian Revolution, the Fourteen
 Points, and Allied Victory

Over Here **635**
Organizing the Economy
The Government–Business Partnership
Labor and the War
Women at Work
Woman Suffrage

Prohibition
Public Health and the Influenza Pandemic

Repression and Reaction **641**
Muzzling Dissent: The Espionage and
 Sedition Acts
The Great Migration and Racial Tensions
Labor Strife

An Uneasy Peace **646**
Peacemaking and the Specter
 of Bolshevism
Wilson in Paris
The Treaty Fight
The Red Scare
The Election of 1920

Thomas Derrick (20th CE), *American Troops in Southhampton Embarking for France*, 1917. Imperial War Museum, London. Snark/Art Resource, NY.

The American Expeditionary Force in France

At 5:30 A.M. on September 26, 1918, some 600,000 soldiers of the American Expeditionary Force (AEF) pulled themselves out of the mud and headed into the dense gray fog on a twenty-mile front between the Meuse River and the Argonne Forest in northern France. The biggest and costliest American operation of World War I had begun. In sheer size and scale, the Meuse-Argonne offensive dwarfed anything an American army had ever attempted. The number of American soldiers involved exceeded the total of Union and Confederate soldiers who had fought at Gettysburg. American commander General John J. Pershing aimed to overwhelm the undermanned and dispirited German lines with massive numbers and swift movement and thereby force a German surrender. To be sure, elements of the AEF had seen action in several earlier battles, but in most of those engagements Americans had fought under British or French command. Pershing hoped to put a distinctively American stamp on ending the war with the Meuse-Argonne offensive.

The individual infantryman, however, had little time or use for grand strategy. Each man carried a rifle

AMERICAN Communities

621

and bayonet, steel helmet, and gas mask, along with 250 rounds of ammunition. His two days of "iron rations" consisted of two cans of corned beef, six boxes of hard crackers, and a quart canteen of water. The American thrust quickly stalled as the Germans put up fierce resistance with well-placed machine gun nests and artillery batteries, spread out amidst a ghostly landscape littered with abandoned trenches, tangled barbed-wire fences, water-filled craters, and dead and mangled bodies everywhere. The scene was nothing like the storybooks of war, recalled Lieutenant Maury Maverick. "There were no bugles, no flags, no drums, and as far as we knew, no heroes. . . . I have never read in any military history a description of the high explosives that break overhead. There is a great swishing scream, a smash-bang, and it seems to tear everything loose from you. The intensity of it simply enters your heart and brain and tears every nerve to pieces."

After America's entry into the European conflict in April 1917, millions of Americans traded their civilian clothes for a uniform, creating a new kind of community of soldiers in a modern mechanized army. The Wilson administration had acted swiftly to mobilize the nation's economy and civilian population. The Selective Service Act required the registration and classification for military service of all men between ages twenty-one and thirty-five, and by war's end in November 1918, some 24 million men had registered for the draft, and another 2 million had volunteered. The numbers were there, but the looming question remained: could the nation create a cohesive, efficient, and mass fighting force where none had existed before? The scale would be far greater than the Spanish-American conflict. And the nation's population was far more ethnically diverse than it had been at the time of the Civil War, America's only previous experience with mass mobilization of troops. In 1917, one out of five soldiers was born in another country and overall illiteracy rates ran as high as 25 percent. Nearly 400,000 African Americans would enter the armed forces, but they faced rigid segregation and deep prejudice against their fitness to fight.

Despite the extraordinary differences of region, class, education, and ethnicity, the "doughboys," as AEF members were affectionately called, shared a great deal of common experiences. For many, the journey to training camp represented their first substantial trip away from home. Many progressives saw the army as a field for continuing social reform and education. "The

military tent where they all sleep side by side," Theodore Roosevelt predicted, "will rank next to the public schools among the great agents of democratization." In training camps, the War Department mounted a vigorous campaign against venereal disease, and the scientific discussions of sex to which recruits were subjected in lectures, pamphlets, and films were surely a first for the vast majority. Accepting military discipline was new to most as well, and it often rubbed against traditional American notions of freedom and independence. As members of the AEF shipped off for the front, they also carried with them vague and often romantic notions of what to expect on the battlefield. By the summer of 1918, when most American soldiers traveled to France, the carnage across Europe was no secret; nor was the grim reality of death associated with machine guns, tanks, and trench warfare. The blizzard of posters, films, war bond drives, and other propaganda activities coordinated by the Committee on Public Information (CPI) mostly avoided this side of war. Instead, the CPI emphasized appeals to patriotism, manhood, heroism, and the fight for democracy. Many doughboys carried to France images of war shaped by their grandfathers' stories about the Civil War or romantic accounts of medieval knights.

Their experiences in the Meuse-Argonne offensive brought those doughboys face-to-face with the very different reality of mass mechanized killing. Rather than the swift victory General Pershing had hoped for, the campaign turned into a slow, sometimes chaotic slog. American combat units measured their gains in yards as they found their advances blunted by tough German defenders. Between September 25 and the Armistice ending the fighting on November 11, each day claimed an average of over 550 Americans dead, with a total of 26,000 Americans killed in the campaign. For many, the worst horror was artillery bombardment with unseen enemy guns lobbing high explosives that could instantly turn a group of men into unrecognizable piles of flesh. The men endured sleep deprivation, hunger, and lice, and they could never get dry. Behind the front, American inexperience with such a large-scale operation created enormous logistical problems. Huge traffic jams made it difficult to evacuate the wounded to hospitals and led to severe shortages of rations, water, and ammunition. Discipline frequently broke down with as many as 100,000 stragglers wandering in the rear areas, unable or unwilling to rejoin their units. Meanwhile, a

1. How and where did the United States expand its role on the international scene?

2. Why did the United States move from neutrality to participation in the Great War?

3. What methods and techniques did the federal government use to achieve wartime mobilization?

4. How did U.S. entry into the war alter the political landscape, especially with respect to dissent?

5. How can we explain Woodrow Wilson's failure to win the peace?

FOCUS Questions

1901–1920

lethal influenza outbreak, part of the worldwide pandemic that would claim over 20 million lives, swept through the AEF in France, afflicting 100,000 doughboys and killing about 10,000 of them.

Many AEF men would long remember their brief time in France as a life-changing high point of their lives, and for some it achieved a mythic significance. Revulsion at the horrors of warfare often coexisted with strong feelings of camaraderie, as expressed by one of the most celebrated doughboys, Sergeant Alvin York. A religious pacifist who had originally sought conscientious objector status, the Tennessee sharpshooter received the Medal of Honor for single-handedly eliminating an entire German machine gun battalion and taking 132 prisoners. War, York recalled, "turns you into a mad fightin' animal, but it also brings out something else, something I jes don't know how to describe, a sort of tenderness and love for the fellows fightin' with you."

America's emergence as a global power required mass mobilization of the armed forces and

Verdun

created a new community of veterans. In early 1919, encouraged by some senior officers, a group of AEF veterans founded the American Legion, "to preserve the memories and incidents of our association in the great war . . . to consecrate and sanctify our comradeship." American Legion halls soon became a familiar sight in communities across America. The Legion had a political mission as well, however, one that would play out during the postwar "Red Scare." Legion leaders saw their group as a way to counter radical ideas that might "infect" returning veterans, especially those who suffered from unemployment or had trouble readjusting to civilian life. The American Legion would commemorate the war, celebrate sacrifice, and honor the dead, all in the name of promoting "100 Per Cent Americanism" and fighting against "dangerous" socialists and other radical groups. As much a political lobby as a veterans' organization, the American Legion would extend the memory and life of the AEF community well into the twentieth century.

AMERICAN Communities

Becoming a World Power

In the first years of the new century, the United States pursued a more vigorous and aggressive foreign policy than it had in the past. In addition to its newfound imperial presence in Asia, the United States marked out the Western Hemisphere—especially the Caribbean, Mexico, and Central America—as a site for establishing American

hegemony. Presidents Theodore Roosevelt, William Howard Taft, and Woodrow Wilson all contributed to "progressive diplomacy," in which commercial expansion was backed by a growing military presence in the hemisphere. This policy reflected a view of world affairs that stressed the links between ensuring American commercial expansion and a foreign policy couched in terms of moralism, order, and a special, even God-given, role for the United States. By 1917, when the United States entered the Great War, the nation was just as complicit in building empire as were the European states and Japan.

Roosevelt: The Big Stick

Theodore Roosevelt left a strong imprint on the nation's foreign policy. Like many of his class and background, "T.R." took for granted the superiority of Protestant Anglo-American culture and the goal of spreading its values and influence. He believed that to maintain and increase its economic and political stature, America must be militarily strong. In 1900, Roosevelt summarized his activist views, declaring, "I have always been fond of the West African proverb, 'Speak softly and carry a big stick, you will go far.'"

Roosevelt brought the "big stick" approach to disputes in the Caribbean region. Since the 1880s, several British, French, and American companies had pursued plans for building a canal across the Isthmus of Panama, thereby connecting the Atlantic and Pacific Oceans. The canal was a top priority for Roosevelt, and he tried to negotiate a leasing agreement with Colombia, of which Panama was a province. When the Colombian Senate rejected a final American offer in the fall of 1903, Roosevelt invented a new strategy. A combination of native forces and foreign promoters associated with the canal project plotted a revolt against Colombia. Roosevelt kept in touch with at least one leader of the revolt, Philippe Bunau-Varilla, an engineer and agent for the New Panama Canal Company, and the president let him know that U.S. warships were steaming toward Panama.

On November 3, 1903, just as the USS *Nashville* arrived in Colón harbor, the province of Panama declared itself independent of Colombia. The United States immediately recognized the new Republic of Panama. Less than two weeks later, Bunau-Varilla, serving as a minister from Panama, signed a treaty granting the United States full sovereignty in perpetuity over a ten-mile-wide canal zone. America guaranteed Panama's independence and agreed to pay it $10 million initially and an additional $250,000 a year for the Canal Zone. Years after the canal was completed, the U.S. Senate voted another $25 million to Colombia as compensation.

THE WORLD'S CONSTABLE.

This 1905 cartoon portraying President Theodore Roosevelt, "The World's Constable," appeared in *Judge* magazine. In depicting the president as a strong but benevolent policeman bringing order in a contentious world, the artist Louis Dalrymple drew on familiar imagery from Roosevelt's earlier days as a New York City police commissioner.

The Panama Canal was a triumph of modern engineering and gave the United States a tremendous strategic and commercial advantage in the Western Hemisphere. It took eight years to build and cost hundreds of poorly paid manual workers their lives. Several earlier attempts to build a canal in the region had failed, but with better equipment and a vigorous campaign against disease, the United States succeeded. In 1914, after $720 million in construction costs, the first merchant ships sailed through the canal.

"The inevitable effect of our building the Canal," wrote Secretary of State Elihu Root in 1905, "must be to require us to police the surrounding premises." Roosevelt agreed. He was especially concerned that European powers might step in if America did not. In 1903, Great Britain, Germany, and Italy had imposed a blockade on Venezuela in a dispute over debt payments owed to private investors. To prevent armed intervention by the Europeans, in 1904 Roosevelt proclaimed what became known as the Roosevelt Corollary to the Monroe Doctrine. "Chronic wrongdoing, or an impotence which results in a general loosening of the ties of civilized society," the statement read, justified "the exercise of an international police power" anywhere in the hemisphere. Roosevelt invoked the corollary to justify U.S. intervention in the region, beginning with the Dominican Republic in 1905. Roosevelt and later presidents cited the corollary to justify armed intervention in the internal affairs of Cuba, Haiti, Nicaragua, and Mexico.

With the outbreak of the Russo-Japanese War in 1904, Roosevelt worried about the future of the Open Door policy in Asia (see Chapter 20). A total victory by Russia or Japan could upset the balance of power in East Asia and threaten American business enterprises there. He became especially concerned after the Japanese scored a series of military victories over Russia and began to loom as a dominant power in East Asia. Roosevelt mediated a settlement of the Russo-Japanese War at Portsmouth, New Hampshire, in 1905 (for which he was awarded the 1906 Nobel Peace Prize). In this settlement, Japan won recognition of its dominant position in Korea and consolidated its economic control over Manchuria. Yet repeated incidents of anti-Japanese racism in California kept American–Japanese relations strained. In 1906, for example, the San Francisco school board, responding to nativist fears of a "yellow peril," ordered the segregation of Japanese, Chinese, and Korean students. Japan angrily protested. In 1907, in the so-called Gentlemen's Agreement, Japan agreed not to issue passports to Japanese male laborers looking to emigrate to the United States, and Roosevelt promised to fight anti-Japanese discrimination. He then persuaded the San Francisco school board to exempt Japanese students from the segregation ordinance.

Roosevelt did not want these conciliatory moves to be interpreted as weakness. He thus built up American naval strength in the Pacific, and in 1908, he sent battleships to visit Japan in a muscle-flexing display of sea power. In that same year, the two burgeoning Pacific powers reached a reconciliation. The Root-Takahira Agreement affirmed the "existing status quo" in Asia, mutual respect for territorial possessions in the Pacific, and the Open Door trade policy in China. From the Japanese perspective, the agreement recognized Japan's colonial dominance in Korea and southern Manchuria.

Taft: Dollar Diplomacy

Roosevelt's successor, William Howard Taft, believed he could replace the militarism of the big stick with the more subtle and effective weapon of business investment. Taft and his secretary of state, corporate lawyer Philander C. Knox, followed a strategy (called "dollar diplomacy" by critics) in which they assumed that political influence would follow increased U.S. trade and investment. As Taft explained in 1910, he advocated "active intervention to secure for our merchandise and our capitalists opportunity for profitable investment."

Read the Document

William H. Taft, "Dollar Diplomacy" (1912) at **www.myhistorylab.com**

Overall American investment in Central America grew rapidly, from $41 million in 1908 to $93 million by 1914. Most of this money went into railroad construction, mining, and plantations. The United Fruit Company alone owned about 160,000 acres of land in the Caribbean by 1913. But dollar diplomacy ended up requiring military support. The Taft administration sent the navy and the marines to intervene in political disputes in Honduras and Nicaragua, propping up factions pledged to protect American business interests. A contingent of U.S. Marines remained in Nicaragua until 1933. The economic and political structures of Honduras and Nicaragua were controlled by both the dollar and the bullet (see Map 22.1).

In China, Taft and Knox pressed for a greater share of the pie for U.S. investors. They gained a place for U.S. bankers in the European consortium, building the massive new Hukuang Railway in southern and central China. But Knox blundered by attempting to "neutralize" the existing railroads in China. He tried to secure a huge international loan for the Chinese government that would allow it to buy up all the foreign railways and develop new ones. Both Russia and Japan, which had fought wars over their railroad interests in Manchuria, resisted this plan as a threat to the arrangements hammered out at Portsmouth with the help of Theodore Roosevelt. Knox's "neutralization" scheme, combined with U.S. support for the Chinese Nationalists in their 1911 revolt against the ruling Manchu dynasty, prompted Japan to sign a new friendship treaty with Russia. The Open Door to China was now effectively closed, and American relations with Japan began a slow deterioration that ended in war thirty years later.

Wilson: Moralism and Intervention in Mexico

Right after he took office in 1913, President Woodrow Wilson observed that "it would be the irony of fate if my administration had to deal chiefly with foreign affairs." His political life up to then had centered on achieving

United States and U.S. possessions
Countries influenced by U.S. activities
European possessions
■ U.S. military bases
✳ U.S. military actions

UNITED STATES

U.S. expeditionary force, 1916–17

●Santa Ysabel
●Parral

MEXICO

Gulf of Mexico

●Tampico

Mexico City ●

● Veracruz
U.S. seizure, 1914

Americans control 43% of Mexican property, 1910
U.S. exports to equal $1.3 billion by 1917

GUATEMALA   **HONDURAS**

United Fruit Co. organized 1899

EL SALVADOR

NICARAGUA
Financial supervision, 1911–24

COSTA RICA
Canal option, 1916

PANAMA
Acquired Canal Zone, 1903
Canal completed 1914

PACIFIC OCEAN

Sinking of Maine, 1898 ✳●Havana
CUBA
U.S. troops, 1898–1902, 1906–09, 1912, 1917–22

British Honduras (Br.)

U.S. troops, 1907, 1924–25

U.S. troops, 1909–10, 1912–25, 1926–33

Platt Amendment, 1903–34
U.S. exports to equal $1.6 billion by 1917

Bahama Islands **(Br.)**

Guantanamo, 1903 ■

HAITI   DOMINICAN REPUBLIC
U.S. troops, 1915–34
Jamaica **(Br.)**
Financial supervision, 1905–41

U.S. control of customs houses, 1905, U.S. troops, 1916–24

Virgin Islands **1917 (U.S.)**

Puerto Rico **1898 (U.S.)**

Guadeloupe **(Fr.)**

Martinique **(Fr.)**

Caribbean Sea

Trinidad **(Br.)**

Barbados **(Br.)**

●Caracas

VENEZUELA
Debt crisis, 1903–04

COLOMBIA

BRAZIL

ATLANTIC OCEAN

MAP 22.1 The United States in the Caribbean, 1865–1933 An overview of U.S. economic and military involvement in the Caribbean during the late nineteenth and early twentieth centuries. Victory in the Spanish-American War, the Panama Canal project, and rapid economic investment in Mexico and Cuba all contributed to a permanent and growing U.S. military presence in the region.

progressive reforms in the domestic arena. As it turned out, Wilson had to face international crises from his first day in office. He brought to foreign affairs a set of fundamental principles that combined a moralist's faith in American democracy with a realist's understanding of the power of international commerce. He believed that American economic expansion, accompanied by democratic principles and Christianity, was a civilizing force in the world.

Wilson, like most corporate and political leaders of the day, emphasized foreign investments and industrial exports as the keys to the nation's prosperity. He believed that the United States, with its superior industrial efficiency, could achieve supremacy in world commerce if artificial barriers to free trade were removed. He championed and extended

the Open Door principles of John Hay, advocating strong diplomatic and military measures "for making ourselves supreme in the world from an economic point of view." Wilson often couched his vision of a dynamic, expansive American capitalism in terms of a moral crusade. As he put it in a speech to a congress of salesmen, "[Since] you are Americans and are meant to carry liberty and justice and the principles of humanity wherever you go, go out and sell goods that will make the world more comfortable and more happy, and convert them to the principles of America." Yet he quickly found that the complex realities of power politics could interfere with moral vision.

Wilson's policies toward Mexico, which foreshadowed the problems he would encounter in World War I, best illustrate his difficulties. The 1911 Mexican Revolution had overthrown the brutally corrupt dictatorship of Porfirio Díaz, and popular leader Francisco Madero had won wide support by promising democracy and economic reform for millions of landless peasants. But the U.S. business community was nervous about the future of its investments which, in the previous generation, had come to dominate the Mexican economy. By 1910, American companies owned over one-quarter—130 million acres—of Mexico's land, including over half of its coastlines and border areas. A handful of American mining companies had led the way in exploiting Mexican natural resources, using high capitalization, advanced technology, and sophisticated marketing networks to win control of roughly four-fifths of the gold, silver, and copper extracted from Mexican mines.

Wilson at first gave his blessing to the revolutionary movement, expressed regret over the Mexican-American War of 1846–48, and disavowed any interest in another war. But right before he took office, Wilson was stunned when Madero was ousted and murdered by his chief lieutenant, General Victoriano Huerta. Other nations, including Great Britain and Japan, recognized the Huerta regime, but Wilson refused. He announced that the United States would support only governments that rested on the rule of law. An armed faction opposed to Huerta, known as the Constitutionalists and led by Venustiano Carranza, emerged in northern Mexico. Both sides rejected an effort by Wilson to broker a compromise between them. Carranza, an ardent nationalist, pressed for the right to buy U.S. arms, which he won in 1914. Wilson also isolated Huerta diplomatically by persuading the British to withdraw their support in exchange for American guarantees of English property interests in Mexico.

Huerta stubbornly remained in power. In April 1914, Wilson used a minor insult to U.S. sailors in Tampico as an excuse to invade Mexico. American naval forces bombarded and then occupied Veracruz, the main port through which Huerta received arms shipments. Nineteen Americans and 126 Mexicans died in the battle, which brought the United States and Mexico close to war, and provoked anti-American demonstrations in Mexico and throughout Latin America. Wilson accepted the offer of the ABC Powers—Argentina, Brazil, and Chile—to mediate the dispute. Huerta rejected a plan for him to step aside in favor of a provisional government. In August, however, Carranza managed to overthrow Huerta. Playing to nationalist sentiment, Carranza also denounced Wilson for his intervention.

As war loomed in Europe, Mexico's revolutionary politics continued to frustrate Wilson. For a brief period, Wilson threw his support behind Francisco "Pancho" Villa, Carranza's former ally, who led a rebel army of his own in northern Mexico. But Carranza's forces dealt Villa a major setback in April 1915. In October, when its

This 1914 political cartoon comments approvingly on the interventionist role adopted by the United States in Latin American countries. By depicting President Woodrow Wilson as a schoolteacher giving lessons to children, the image captures the paternalistic views that American policymakers held toward nations like Mexico, Venezuela, and Nicaragua.

attention was focused on the war in Europe, the Wilson administration recognized Carranza as Mexico's de facto president. Meanwhile, Pancho Villa, feeling betrayed, turned on the United States and tried to provoke a crisis that might draw the United States into war with Mexico. In 1916, Villa led several raids in Mexico and across the border into the United States that killed a few dozen Americans. The man once viewed by Wilson as a fighter for democracy was now dismissed as a dangerous bandit.

In March 1916, enraged by Villa's defiance, Wilson dispatched General John J. Pershing and an army that eventually numbered 15,000 to capture him. For a year, Pershing's troops chased Villa in vain, penetrating 300 miles into Mexico. The invasion made Villa a symbol of national resistance in Mexico, and his army grew from 500 men to 10,000 by the end of 1916. Villa's effective hit-and-run guerrilla tactics kept the U.S. forces at bay. A frustrated General Pershing complained that he felt "just a little bit like a man looking for a needle in a haystack."

Skirmishes between American forces and Carranza's army brought the two nations to the brink of war again in June 1916. Although Wilson prepared a message to Congress asking permission for American troops to occupy all of northern Mexico, he never delivered it. There was fierce opposition to war with Mexico throughout the United States. Perhaps more important, mounting tensions with Germany caused Wilson to hesitate. Wilson thus accepted negotiations by a face-saving international commission.

Wilson's attempt to guide the course of Mexico's revolution and protect U.S. interests left a bitter legacy of suspicion and distrust in Mexico. It also suggested the limits of a foreign policy tied to a moral vision rooted in the idea of American exceptionalism. Militarism and imperialism, Wilson had believed, were hallmarks of the old European way. American liberal values—rooted in capitalist development, democracy, and free trade—were the wave of the future. Wilson believed the United States could lead the world in establishing a new international system based on peaceful commerce and political stability. In both the 1914 invasion and the 1916 punitive expedition, Wilson declared that he had no desire to interfere with Mexican sovereignty. But in both cases, that is exactly what he did. The United States, he argued, must actively use its enormous moral and material power to create the new order. That principle would soon engage America in Europe's bloodiest war and its most momentous revolution.

The Great War

World War I, or the Great War as it was originally called, took an enormous human toll on an entire generation of Europeans. At the war's start in August 1914, both sides had confidently predicted a quick victory. Instead, the killing dragged on for more than four years, and in the end, transformed the old power relations and political map of Europe. The United States entered the war reluctantly, and American forces played a supportive, rather than a central, role in the military outcome.

The Guns of August

Only a complex and fragile system of alliances had kept the European powers at peace with each other since 1871. Two great competing camps had evolved by 1907: the Triple Alliance (also known as the Central Powers), which included Germany, Austria-Hungary, and Italy; and the Triple Entente (also known as the Allies), which included Great Britain, France, and Russia. At the heart of this division was the competition between Great Britain, long the world's dominant colonial and commercial power, and Germany, which had powerful aspirations for an empire of its own. The alliance system managed to keep small conflicts from escalating into larger ones for most of the late nineteenth and early twentieth centuries. But its inclusiveness was also its weakness: the alliance system threatened to entangle many nations in any war that did erupt. On June 28, 1914, Archduke Franz Ferdinand, heir to the throne of the unstable Austro-Hungarian Empire, was assassinated in Sarajevo, Bosnia. The archduke's killer was a

Serbian nationalist who believed the Austro-Hungarian province of Bosnia ought to be annexed to neighboring Serbia. Germany gave Austria-Hungary a blank check to stamp out the Serbian threat, and the Serbians in turn asked Russia for help.

That summer both sides began mobilizing their armies, and by early August they had exchanged declarations of war. Germany invaded Belgium and prepared to move across the French border. At the beginning, most Europeans supported the war effort, believing there would be quick and glorious victories. Appeals to nationalist sentiment and glory overcame even the antiwar socialists, who had long fought to transcend national boundaries in their political work. After the German armies were stopped at the River Marne in September, however, the war settled into a long, bloody stalemate. New and grimly efficient weapons, such as the machine gun and the tank, and the horrors of trench warfare, meant unprecedented casualties for all involved. In northern France, Poland, and on the Italian front, the fighting killed 5 million people over the next two and a half years. Allied campaigns waged against German colonies in Africa and against the Ottoman Empire in the Middle East reflected the global nature of the war, as did the British and French dependence on colonial troops from India and Africa.

American Neutrality

The outbreak of war in Europe shocked Americans. President Wilson issued a formal proclamation of neutrality and urged citizens to be "impartial in thought as well as in action." In practice, powerful cultural, political, and economic factors made the impartiality advocated by Wilson impossible. The U.S. population included many ethnic groups with close emotional ties to the Old World. Out of a total population of 92 million in 1914, about one-third were "hyphenated" Americans, either foreign-born or having one or both parents who were immigrants. Strong support for the Central Powers could be found among the 8 million German-Americans, as well as the 4 million Irish-Americans, who shared their ancestral homeland's historical hatred of English rule. On the other side, many Americans were at least mildly pro-Allies due to cultural and language bonds with Great Britain and the tradition of Franco-American friendship.

Both sides bombarded the United States with vigorous propaganda campaigns. The British effectively exploited their bonds of language and heritage with Americans. Reports of looting, raping, and the killing of innocent civilians by German troops circulated widely in the press. Many of these atrocity stories were exaggerated, but verified German actions—the invasion of neutral Belgium, submarine attacks on merchant ships, and the razing of towns—lent them credibility. Wartime propaganda highlighted the terrible human costs of the war and, thus, strengthened the conviction that America should stay out of it.

Economic ties between the United States and the Allies were perhaps the greatest barrier to true neutrality. Early in the war, Britain imposed a blockade on all shipping to Germany. The United States, as a neutral country, might have insisted on the right of nonbelligerents to trade with both sides, as required by international law. In practice, although Wilson protested the blockade, he wanted to avoid antagonizing Britain and disrupting trade between the United States and the Allies. Trade with Germany all but ended while trade with the Allies increased dramatically. As war orders poured in from Britain and France, the value of American trade with the Allies shot up from $824 million in 1914 to $3.2 billion in 1916. By 1917, loans to the Allies—primarily from private American banks—exceeded $2.5 billion, compared to loans to the Central Powers of only $27 million. As America's annual export trade jumped from $2 billion in 1913 to nearly $6 billion in 1916, the nation enjoyed a great economic boom and the United States became neutral in name only.

Preparedness and Peace

In February 1915, Germany declared the waters around the British Isles to be a war zone, a policy that it would enforce with unrestricted submarine warfare. All enemy shipping, despite the requirements of international law to the contrary, would be subject to surprise submarine attack. Neutral powers were warned that the problems of identification at sea put their ships at risk. The United States issued a sharp protest to this policy, calling it "an indefensible violation of neutral rights," and threatened to hold Germany accountable.

On May 7, 1915, a German U-boat sank the British liner *Lusitania* off the coast of Ireland. Among the 1,198 people who died were 128 American citizens. The *Lusitania* was, in fact, secretly carrying war materials, and passengers had been warned about a possible attack. Wilson nevertheless denounced the sinking as illegal and inhuman, and the American press loudly condemned the act as barbaric. An angry exchange of diplomatic notes led Secretary of State William Jennings Bryan to resign in protest against a policy he thought too warlike.

Tensions heated up again in March 1916 when a German U-boat torpedoed the *Sussex*, an unarmed French passenger ship, injuring four Americans. President Wilson threatened to break off diplomatic relations with Germany unless it abandoned its submarine warfare. He won a temporary diplomatic victory when Germany promised that all vessels

would be visited prior to attack. But the crisis also prompted Wilson to begin preparing for war. The National Security League, active in large eastern cities and bankrolled by conservative banking and commercial interests, helped push for a bigger army and navy and, most important, a system of universal military training. In June 1916, Congress passed the National Defense Act, which more than doubled the size of the regular army to 220,000 and integrated the state National Guards under federal control. In August, Congress passed a bill that dramatically increased spending for new battleships, cruisers, and destroyers.

Not all Americans supported these preparations for battle, and opposition to military buildup found expression in scores of American communities. As early as August 29, 1914, 1,500 women clad in black had marched down New York's Fifth Avenue in the Woman's Peace Parade. Out of this gathering evolved the American Union against Militarism, which lobbied against the preparedness campaign and against intervention in Mexico. Antiwar feeling was especially strong in the South and Midwest. A group of thirty to fifty House Democrats, led by majority leader Claude Kitchin of North Carolina, stubbornly opposed Wilson's military buildup. Jane Addams, Lillian D. Wald, and many other prominent progressive reformers spoke out for peace.

Wilson acknowledged the active opposition to involvement in the war by adopting the winning slogan

●●—[Read the Document

Eugene V. Debs, Critique of World War (1918) at **www.myhistorylab.com**

Patriotic marchers carry an over-sized American flag past spectators, as part of a "preparedness parade" in downtown Mobile Alabama, before American entry into World War I.

SOURCE: University of South Alabama Archives.

"He Kept Us Out of War" in the 1916 presidential campaign. He made a point of appealing to progressives of all kinds, stressing his support for the eight-hour day and his administration's efforts on behalf of farmers. The war-induced prosperity no doubt helped him to defeat conservative Republican Charles Evans Hughes.

Safe for Democracy

By the end of January 1917, Germany's leaders had decided against a negotiated peace settlement, placing their hopes instead in a final decisive offensive against the Allies. On February 1, 1917, with the aim of breaking the British blockade, Germany declared unlimited submarine warfare, with no warnings, against all neutral and belligerent shipping. This strategy went far beyond the earlier, more limited use of the U-boat. The decision was made with full knowledge that it might bring America into the conflict. In effect, German leaders were gambling that they could destroy the ability of the Allies to fight before the United States would be able to effectively mobilize manpower and resources.

Wilson was indignant and disappointed. He still hoped for peace, but Germany had made it impossible for him to preserve his twin goals of U.S. neutrality and freedom of the seas. Reluctantly, Wilson broke off diplomatic relations with Germany and called on Congress to approve the arming of U.S. merchant ships. On March 1, the White House shocked the country when it made public a recently intercepted coded message, sent by German foreign secretary Arthur Zimmermann to the German ambassador in Mexico. The Zimmermann note proposed that an alliance be made between Germany and Mexico if the United States entered the war. Zimmermann suggested that Mexico take up arms against the United States and receive in return the "lost territory in New Mexico, Texas, and Arizona." The note caused a sensation and became a very effective propaganda tool for those who favored U.S. entry into the war.

Revelation of the Zimmermann note stiffened Wilson's resolve. He issued an executive order in mid-March, authorizing the arming of all merchant ships and allowing them to shoot at submarines. In that month, German U-boats sank seven U.S. merchant ships, with a heavy death toll. Anti-German feeling increased, and thousands took part in prowar demonstrations in New York, Boston, Philadelphia, and other cities. Wilson finally called a special session of Congress to ask for a declaration of war.

On April 2, on a rainy night, before a packed and very quiet assembly, Wilson made his case. He reviewed the escalation of submarine warfare, which he called "warfare against mankind," and said that neutrality was no longer feasible or desirable. The conflict was not merely about U.S. shipping rights, Wilson argued. He employed highly idealistic language to make the case for war, reflecting his

James Montgomery Flagg's Navy recruiting poster from 1918 combined appeals to patriotism, the opportunity to "make history," and traditional images depicting liberty as a woman.

deeply held belief that America had a special mission as the world's most enlightened and advanced nation:

> It is a fearful thing to lead this great peaceful people into war, into the most terrible and disastrous of all wars, civilization itself seeming to be in the balance. But the right is more precious than peace, and we shall fight for the things which we have always carried nearest to our hearts—for democracy, for the right of those who submit to authority to have a voice in their own governments, for the rights and liberties of small nations, for a universal dominion of right by such a concert of free peoples as shall bring peace and safety to all nations and make the world itself at last free.

In effect, Wilson wrapped together American commercial and diplomatic interests in the language of universal principles like freedom of the seas and neutral rights. He expressed the realist ambition of making America a world power in terms of an absolute moral imperative. The Senate adopted the war resolution 82 to 6, the House 373 to 50. Wilson's eloquent speech won over not only the Congress, but also most of the press, and even his bitterest political critics, such as Theodore Roosevelt. On April 6, President Wilson signed the declaration of war. All that remained was to win over the American public.

American Mobilization

The overall public response to Wilson's war message was enthusiastic. Most newspapers, religious leaders, state legislatures, and prominent public figures endorsed the call to arms. The Wilson administration was less certain about the feelings of ordinary Americans and their willingness to fight in Europe. It therefore took immediate steps to strengthen public support for the war effort, to place a legal muzzle on antiwar dissenters, and to establish a universal military draft. War mobilization was, above all, a campaign to unify the country.

Selling the War

Just a week after signing the war declaration, Wilson created the Committee on Public Information (CPI) to organize public opinion. It was dominated by its civilian chairman, the journalist and reformer George Creel. He had become a personal friend of Wilson's while handling publicity for the 1916 Democratic campaign. Creel quickly transformed the CPI from its original function as coordinator of government news into a sophisticated and aggressive agency for promoting the war. To sell the war, Creel adapted techniques from the emerging field of public relations. He enlisted more than 150,000 people to work on a score of CPI committees. They produced more than 100 million pieces of literature—pamphlets, articles, books—that explained the causes and meaning of the war. Across the nation, a volunteer army of 75,000 "Four Minute Men" gave brief patriotic speeches before stage and movie shows. The CPI also created posters, slides, newspaper advertising, and films to promote the war. It called upon movie stars such as Charlie Chaplin, Mary Pickford, and Douglas Fairbanks to help sell war bonds at huge rallies. Famous journalists like the muckraker Ida Tarbell and well-known artists like Charles Dana Gibson were recruited. Many popular entertainers injected patriotic themes into their work as well, such as when Broadway composer George M. Cohan wrote the rousing prowar anthem "Over There," sung by the great opera tenor Enrico Caruso (see Seeing History).

The CPI led an aggressively negative campaign against all things German. Posters and advertisements

⬦⬦▶ [Read the Document

Joseph Buffington, "Friendly Words to the Foreign Born" (1917) at **www.myhistorylab.com**

depicted the Germans as Huns, bestial monsters outside the civilized world. German music and literature, indeed the German language itself, were suspect and were banished from the concert halls, schools, and libraries of many communities. Many restaurants offered "liberty

cabbage" and "liberty steaks" instead of sauerkraut and hamburgers. The CPI also urged ethnic Americans to abandon their Old World ties, to become "unhyphenated Americans." The CPI's push for conformity soon encouraged thousands of local, sometimes violent, campaigns of harassment against German-Americans, radicals, and peace activists.

Fading Opposition to War

By defining the call to war as a great moral crusade, President Wilson won over many Americans who had been reluctant to go to war. In particular, many liberals and progressives were attracted to the possibilities of war as a positive force for social change. Although some progressives—notably Senator Robert M. La Follette of Wisconsin—continued to oppose the war, many more identified with President Wilson's definition of the war as an idealistic crusade to defend democracy, spread liberal principles, and redeem European decadence and militarism.

The writer and cultural critic Randolph Bourne was an important, if lonely, voice of dissent among intellectuals. A former student of John Dewey's at Columbia University, Bourne wrote a series of antiwar essays warning of the disastrous consequences for reform movements of all kinds. He was particularly critical of "war intellectuals" such as Dewey, who were so eager to shift their energies to serving the war effort. "War is essentially the health of the State," Bourne wrote, and he accurately predicted sharp infringements on political and intellectual freedoms.

The Woman's Peace Party, founded in 1915 by feminists opposed to the preparedness campaign, dissolved. Most of its leading lights—Florence Kelley, Lillian D. Wald, and Carrie Chapman Catt—threw themselves into volunteer war work. Catt, leader of the huge National American Woman Suffrage Association (NAWSA), believed that supporting the war might help women win the right to vote. She joined the Women's Committee of the Council of National Defense and encouraged suffragists to mobilize women for war service of various kinds. A few lonely feminist voices, such as Jane Addams, continued steadfastly to oppose the war effort. But war work proved very popular among activist middle-class women. It gave them a leading role in their communities—selling bonds, coordinating food conservation drives, and working for hospitals and the Red Cross.

"You're in the Army Now"

The central military issue facing the administration was how to raise and deploy U.S. armed forces. When war was declared, there were only about 200,000 men in the army. Traditionally, the United States had relied on volunteer forces organized at the state level. But volunteer rates after April 6 were less than they had been for the Civil War or the Spanish-American War, reflecting the softness of prowar sentiment. The administration thus introduced the Selective Service Act,

Selling War

The Committee on Public Information (CPI), chaired by the progressive Denver journalist George Creel, oversaw the crucial task of mobilizing public opinion for war. Creel employed the most sophisticated sales and public relations techniques of the day to get Americans behind the war effort. The CPI created a flood of pamphlets, billboards, and news articles; sent volunteer "Four Minute Men" to make hundreds of thousands of patriotic speeches in movie theaters between reels; sponsored government-funded feature films depicting life on the front lines; and staged celebrity-studded rallies to promote the sale of war bonds. CPI writers and artists worked closely with government agencies such as the Food Administration and the Selective Service, as well as private organizations like the YMCA and the Red Cross, in creating patriotic campaigns in support of the war. The Division of Pictorial Publicity, headed by the popular artist Charles Dana Gibson, churned out posters and illustrations designed to encourage military enlistment, food conservation, war bond buying, and contributions for overseas victims of war.

The posters generally defined the war as a clear struggle between good and evil, in which American democracy and freedom opposed German militarism and despotism. Artists used a wide range of visual themes to illustrate these stark contrasts. World War I posters drew upon traditional ideas about gender differences (men as soldiers, women as nurturers), but they also illustrated the new wartime expectations of women working outside the home in support of the war effort. Appeals to American patriotism cutting across lines of ethnic and religious difference were common, as was the demonizing of the German enemy. And just as the wartime economy blurred the boundaries between public and private enterprises, businesses adapted patriotic appeals to their own advertising.

Creel aptly titled the memoir of his war experience *How We Advertised America.* These three images illustrate the range of World War I propaganda posters.

• **How would you contrast the different kind of patriotic appeals made by *Pershing's Crusaders, Americans All,* and *And They Thought We Couldn't Fight?* Which of these posters do you think makes the most compelling case for supporting the war? How do the artists portray gender differences as part of a visual strategy for winning the war?**

which provided for the registration and classification for military service of all men between ages twenty-one and thirty-five. On June 5, 1917, nearly 10 million men registered for the draft. There was scattered organized resistance, but overall, registration records offered evidence of national support. By the end of the war, some 24 million men had registered. Of the 2.8 million men eventually called up for service, about 340,000, or 12 percent, failed to show up.

The vast, polyglot army posed unprecedented challenges of organization and control. But progressive elements within the administration also saw opportunities for pressing reform measures, especially for the one-fifth of U.S. soldiers born in another country. Army psychologists gave the new Stanford-Binet intelligence test to all recruits and were shocked to find illiteracy rates as high as 25 percent. The low test scores among recent immigrants and rural African Americans undoubtedly reflected the cultural biases embedded in the tests and a lack of proficiency in English for many test takers. After the war, intelligence testing became a standard feature of America's educational system.

The recruits themselves took a more lighthearted view, while singing the army's praises:

> Oh, the army, the army, the democratic army,
> They clothe you and feed you because the army needs you
> Hash for breakfast, beans for dinner, stew for suppertime,
> Thirty dollars every month, deducting twenty-nine.
> Oh, the army, the army, the democratic army,
> The Jews, the Wops, and the Dutch and Irish Cops,
> They're all in the army now!

Racism in the Military

African Americans who served found severe limitations in the U.S. military. They were organized into totally segregated units, barred entirely from the marines and the Coast Guard, and largely relegated to working as cooks, laundrymen, stevedores, and the like in the army and navy. Thousands of black soldiers endured humiliating, sometimes violent, treatment, particularly from southern white officers. African American servicemen faced hostility from white civilians as well, North and South, and often were denied service in restaurants and admission to theaters near training camps. The ugliest incident occurred in Houston, Texas, in August 1917. Black infantrymen, incensed over continual insults and harassment by local whites, seized weapons from an armory and killed seventeen civilians. The army executed thirty black soldiers and imprisoned forty-one others for life, denying any of them a chance for appeal.

More than 200,000 African Americans eventually served in France, but only about one in five saw combat, as opposed to two out of three white soldiers. Black combat units served with distinction in various divisions of the French army. The French government awarded the Croix de Guerre to the all-black 369th U.S. Infantry regiment, and 171 officers and enlisted men were cited individually for exceptional bravery in action. African American soldiers by and large enjoyed a friendly reception from French civilians as well. The contrast with their

●◾─Read the Document
Statement to French Concerning Black American Troops (1918) at **www.myhistorylab.com**

African American officers of the 367th Infantry Regiment, 77th Division, pose with a girl in France, 1918. Nicknamed the "Buffalos," a reference to the black "buffalo soldiers" who had served in the U.S. Army during the late nineteenth century campaigns against Indians, this was one of only two army units that commissioned African American officers.

treatment at home would remain a sore point with these troops upon their return to the United States.

Americans in Battle

President Wilson appointed General John J. Pershing, recently returned from pursuing Pancho Villa in Mexico, as commander of the American Expeditionary Force (AEF). Pershing insisted that the AEF maintain its own identity, distinct from that of the French and British armies. He was also reluctant to send American troops into battle before they had received at least six months' training. The AEF's combat role would be brief but intense: not until early 1918 did AEF units reach the front in large numbers; eight months later, the war was over (see Map 22.2).

⊙ See the Map
World War I at
www.myhistorylab.com

By the time the guns went silent on November 11, some 2 million men had served in the AEF. Overall 60,000 Americans had died in battle with 206,000 wounded. Another 60,000 died from diseases, mainly influenza. These figures paled in comparison to the millions lost by the European nations. Yet the American contribution to winning the war was substantial, and both the Allies and the Germans attested to the bravery and enthusiasm that American soldiers displayed on the front. Still, the American impact in the Meuse-Argonne campaign was best understood not in terms of individual heroism or tactical brilliance. Rather, it was the prospect of facing seemingly unlimited quantities of American men and supplies that convinced the exhausted German army to surrender.

Read the Document
Eugene Kennedy, "A 'Doughboy' Describes the Fighting Front" (1918) at
www.myhistorylab.com

MAP 22.2 The Western Front, 1918 American units saw their first substantial action in late May, helping to stop the German offensive at the Battle of Cantigny. By September, more than 1 million American troops were fighting in a counteroffensive campaign at St. Mihiel, the largest single American engagement of the war.

The Russian Revolution, the Fourteen Points, and Allied Victory

Since early 1917, the turmoil of the Russian Revolution had changed the climate of both foreign affairs and domestic politics. The repressive and corrupt regime of Czar Nicholas II was overthrown in March 1917 by a coalition of forces demanding change. The new provisional government vowed to keep Russia in the fight against Germany. But the war had taken a terrible toll on Russian soldiers and civilians and had become very unpopular. The radical Bolsheviks, led by V. I. Lenin, gained a large following by promising "peace, land, and bread," and they began plotting to seize power. The Bolsheviks followed the teachings of German revolutionary Karl Marx, emphasizing the inevitability of class struggle and the replacement of capitalism by communism. In November 1917, the Bolsheviks took control of the Russian government.

Although sympathetic to the March revolution overthrowing the czar, President Wilson refused to recognize the authority of the Bolshevik regime. Bolshevism represented a threat to the liberal-capitalist values that Wilson believed to be the foundation of America's moral and material power. Thus, in January 1918, Wilson outlined American war aims, known as the Fourteen Points, in a speech before Congress. He wanted to counter a fierce Bolshevik campaign to discredit the war as a purely imperialist venture, their sensational publication of secret treaties that the czar had signed with the Allies, and their revelations about annexationist plans across Europe. In effect, Wilson's response to the Bolsheviks was the opening shot of the Soviet-American Cold War that would dominate so much of American domestic politics and foreign affairs for the remainder of the century.

As a blueprint for peace, the Fourteen Points contained three main elements. First, Wilson offered a series of specific proposals for setting postwar boundaries in Europe and creating new countries out of the collapsed Austro-Hungarian and Ottoman empires. The key idea here was the right of all peoples to "national self-determination." Second, Wilson listed general principles for governing international conduct, including freedom of the seas, free trade, open covenants instead of secret treaties, reduced armaments, and mediation for competing colonial claims. Third, and most important, Wilson called for a League of Nations to help implement these principles and resolve future disputes. The Fourteen Points offered a plan for world order deeply rooted in the liberal progressivism long associated with Wilson. The plan reflected a faith in efficient government and the rule of law as means for solving international problems. It advocated a dynamic democratic capitalism as a middle ground between Old World autocracy and revolutionary socialism.

•••—[Read the Document

Woodrow Wilson, "Fourteen Points" (1917) at **www.myhistorylab.com**

In March 1918, to the dismay of the Allies, the new Bolshevik government followed through on its promise and negotiated a separate peace with Germany, the Treaty of Brest-Litovsk. Russia was now lost as a military ally, and its defection made possible a massive shift of German troops to the western front. In the early spring of 1918, the Germans launched a major offensive that brought them within fifty miles of Paris. In early June, about 70,000 AEF soldiers helped the French stop the Germans in the battles of Château-Thierry and Belleau Wood. In July, Allied forces led by Marshal Ferdinand Foch of France began a counteroffensive designed to defeat Germany once and for all. American reinforcements began flooding the ports of Liverpool in England and Brest and Saint-Nazaire in France. The "doughboys" (a nickname for soldiers dating back to Civil War–era recruits who joined the army for the money) streamed in at a rate of over 250,000 a month. By September, General Pershing had more than a million Americans in his army.

In late September 1918, the AEF took over the southern part of a twenty-mile front in the Meuse-Argonne offensive. In seven weeks of fighting, most through terrible mud and rain, U.S. soldiers used more ammunition than the entire Union army had in the four years of the Civil War. The Germans, exhausted and badly outnumbered, began to fall back and look for a cease-fire. On November 11, 1918, the war ended with the signing of an armistice.

The massive influx of American troops and supplies no doubt hastened the end of the war. About two-thirds of the U.S. soldiers saw at least some fighting, but even they managed to avoid the horrors of the sustained trench warfare that had marked the earlier years of the war. For most Americans at the front, the war experience was a mixture of fear, exhaustion, and fatigue. Their time in France would remain a decisive moment in their lives. American casualty figures—120,000 dead and 200,000 wounded—awful as they were, paled against the estimated casualties (killed and wounded) suffered by the European nations: 9 million for Russia, more than 6 million for Germany, nearly 5 million for France, and over 2 million each for Great Britain and Italy.

Over Here

In one sense, World War I can be understood as the ultimate progressive crusade: an opportunity to expand the powers of the federal government in order to win the war. Nearly all the reform energy of the previous two decades turned toward that central goal. The federal government played a larger role than ever in managing and regulating the wartime economy. Planning, efficiency, scientific analysis, and cooperation were key principles for government agencies and large volunteer organizations. Although much of the regulatory spirit was temporary, the war experience started some important and lasting organizational trends in American life.

Organizing the Economy

In the summer of 1917, President Wilson established the War Industries Board (WIB) as a clearinghouse for industrial mobilization to support the war effort. Led by the successful Wall Street speculator Bernard M. Baruch, the WIB proved a major innovation in expanding the regulatory power of the federal government. Given broad authority over the conversion of industrial plants to wartime needs and the manufacture of war materials, the WIB had to balance price controls against war profits. Only by ensuring a fair rate of return on investment could it encourage stepped-up production. The WIB eventually handled 3,000 contracts worth $14.5 billion with various businesses.

In August 1917, Congress passed the Food and Fuel Act, authorizing the president to regulate the production and distribution of the food and fuel necessary for the war effort. To lead the Food Administration (FA), Wilson appointed Herbert Hoover, a millionaire engineer who had already won fame for directing a program of war relief for Belgium. He became one of the best-known figures of the war administration. Hoover imposed price controls on certain agricultural commodities, such as sugar, pork, and wheat. These were purchased by the government and then sold to the public through licensed dealers. The FA also raised the purchase price of grain, so that farmers would increase production. Hoover stopped short of imposing mandatory food rationing, preferring to rely on persuasion, high prices, and voluntary controls.

Hoover's success, like George Creel's at the CPI, depended on motivating hundreds of thousands of volunteers in thousands of American communities. The FA directed patriotic appeals for "Wheatless Mondays, Meatless Tuesdays, and Porkless Thursdays." These efforts resulted in a sharp cutback in the consumption of sugar and wheat as well as a boost in the supply of livestock. The resultant increase in food exports helped sustain the Allied war effort.

Large, unprecedented expenditures by the federal government were required to pay the enormous cost of fighting the war, about $33 billion. The tax structure shifted dramatically as a result. Taxes on incomes and profits replaced excise and customs levies as the major source of revenue. The minimum income subject to the graduated federal income tax, in effect only since 1913, was lowered to $1,000 from $3,000, increasing the number of Americans who paid income tax from 437,000 in 1916 to 4,425,000 in 1918. The bulk of war financing came from government borrowing, especially in the form of the popular Liberty Bonds sold to the American public. Bond drives became highly organized patriotic campaigns that ultimately raised a total of $23 billion for the war effort. The administration also used the new Federal Reserve Banks to expand the money supply, making borrowing easier. The federal debt jumped from $1 billion in 1915 to $20 billion in 1920.

A Food Administration poster blended a call for conservation of wheat with an imaginative patriotic appeal for recent immigrants to support the war effort.

The Government–Business Partnership

Overall, the war meant expansion and high profits for American business. Total capital expenditure in U.S. manufacturing jumped from $600 million in 1915 to $2.5 billion in 1918. Corporate profits as a whole nearly tripled between 1914 and 1919, and many large businesses did much better than that. Annual prewar profits for U.S. Steel, for example, had averaged $76 million; in 1917, they were $478 million. The total value of farm produce rose from $9.8 billion in 1914 to $21.3 billion by 1918. Expanded farm acreage and increased investment in farm machinery led to a jump of 20 to 30 percent in overall farm production.

The most important and long-lasting economic legacy of the war was the organizational shift toward corporatism in American business. The wartime need for efficient management, manufacturing, and distribution could be met only by a greater reliance on the productive and marketing power of large corporations. Never before had business and the federal government cooperated so closely. Under war administrators like Baruch and Hoover, entire

industries (such as radio manufacturing) and economic sectors (such as agriculture and energy) were organized, regulated, and subsidized. War agencies used both public and private power—legal authority and voluntarism—to hammer out and enforce agreements. Here was the genesis of the modern bureaucratic state.

Some Americans worried about the wartime trend toward a greater federal presence in their lives. As the *Saturday Evening Post* noted, "All this government activity will be called to account and reexamined in due time." Although many aspects of the government–business partnership proved temporary, some institutions and practices grew stronger in the postwar years. Among these were the Federal Reserve Board, the income tax system, the Chamber of Commerce, the Farm Bureau, and the growing horde of lobbying groups that pressed Washington for special interest legislation.

Labor and the War

Organized labor's power and prestige, though by no means equal to those of business or government, clearly grew during the war. The expansion of the economy, combined with army mobilization and a decline in immigration from Europe, caused a growing wartime labor shortage. As the demand for workers intensified, the federal government was forced to recognize that labor, like any other resource or commodity, would have to be more carefully tended to than in peacetime. For the war's duration, working people generally enjoyed higher wages and a better standard of living. Trade unions, especially those affiliated with the American Federation of Labor (AFL), experienced a sharp rise in membership. In effect, the government took in labor as a junior partner in the mobilization of the economy.

Samuel Gompers, president of the AFL, emerged as the leading spokesman for the nation's trade union movement. An English immigrant and cigar maker by trade, Gompers had rejected the socialism of his youth for a philosophy of "business unionism." Gompers pledged the AFL's patriotic support for the war effort, and in April 1918, President Wilson appointed him to the National War Labor Board (NWLB). During 1917, the nation had seen thousands of strikes involving more than a million workers. Wages were usually at issue, reflecting workers' concerns with spiraling inflation and higher prices. The NWLB, cochaired by labor attorney Frank Walsh and former president William H. Taft, acted as a kind of supreme court for labor, arbitrating disputes and working to prevent disruptions in production. The great majority of these interventions resulted in improved wages and reduced hours of work. Most important, the NWLB supported the right of workers to organize unions and furthered the acceptance of the eight-hour day for war workers—central aims of the labor movement. AFL unions gained more than a million new members during the war, and overall union membership rose from 2.7 million in 1914 to more than 5 million by 1920.

The war also brought widespread use of federal troops under the War Department's new "public utilities" doctrine, under which any private business remotely connected to war production was defined as a public utility. An influx of federal troops poured into lumber camps, coal districts, mining towns, and rail junctions across the nation, as employers requested help in guarding against threatened strikes or alleged "sabotage" by militant workers. Wartime conditions often meant severe disruptions and discomfort for America's workers as well. Overcrowding, rapid workforce turnover, and high inflation rates were typical in war-boom communities. In Bridgeport, Connecticut, a center for small-arms manufacturing, the population grew by 50,000 in less than a year.

In the Southwest, the demand for wartime labor temporarily eased restrictions against the movement of Mexicans into the United States. The Immigration Act of 1917, requiring a literacy test and an $8 head tax, had cut Mexican immigration nearly in half, down to about 25,000 per year. But employers complained of severe shortages of workers. Farmers in Arizona's Salt River Valley and in southern California needed hands to harvest grain, alfalfa, cotton, and fruit. El Paso's mining and smelting industries, Texas's border ranches, and southern Arizona's railroads and copper mines insisted they depended on unskilled Mexican labor as well.

Responding to these protests, in June 1917, the Department of Labor suspended the immigration law for the duration of the war and negotiated an agreement with the Mexican government permitting some 35,000 Mexican contract laborers to enter the United States. Mexicans let in through this program had to demonstrate they had a job waiting before they could cross the border. They received identification cards and transportation to their place of work from American labor contractors. Pressure from southwestern employers kept the exemptions in force until 1921, well after the end of the war, demonstrating the growing importance of cheap Mexican labor to the region's economy.

If the war boosted the fortunes of the AFL, it also spelled the end for more radical elements of the U.S. labor movement. The Industrial Workers of the World (IWW), unlike the AFL, had concentrated on organizing unskilled workers into all-inclusive industrial unions. The Wobblies denounced capitalism as an unreformable system based on exploitation, and they opposed U.S. entry into the war. IWW leaders advised their members to refuse induction for "the capitalists' war." The IWW had grown in 1916 and 1917, gaining strength among workers in several areas crucial to the war effort: copper mining, lumbering, and wheat harvesting. In September 1917, the Wilson administration responded to appeals from western business leaders for a crackdown on the Wobblies. Justice Department agents, acting under the broad authority of the recently passed Espionage Act, swooped down on IWW offices in more than sixty towns and cities, arresting over 300 people and confiscating files. The mass trials and convictions that followed broke the back of America's radical labor movement and marked the beginning of a powerful wave of political repression.

Women at Work

For many of the 8 million women already in the labor force, the war meant a chance to switch from low-paying jobs, such as domestic service, to higher-paying industrial employment. About a million women workers joined the labor force for the first time. Of the estimated 9.4 million workers directly engaged in war work, some 2.25 million were women. Female munitions plant workers, train engineers, drill press operators, streetcar conductors, and mail carriers became a common sight around the country. World War I also marked the first time that women were mobilized directly into the armed forces. Over 16,000 women served overseas with the AEF in France, where most worked as nurses, clerical workers, telephone operators, and canteen operators. Another 12,000 women served stateside in the navy and U.S. Marine Corps, and tens of thousands of civilian women were employed in army offices and hospitals. But the war's impact on women was greatest in the broader civilian economy.

In response to the widened range of female employment, the Labor Department created the Women in Industry Service (WIS). Directed by Mary Van Kleeck, the service advised employers on using female labor and formulated general standards for the treatment of women workers. The WIS represented the first attempt by the federal government to take a practical stand on improving working conditions for women. Its standards included the eight-hour day, equal pay for equal work, a minimum wage, the prohibition of night work, and the provision of rest periods, meal breaks, and restroom facilities. Although these standards had no legal force, they were accepted nonetheless as goals by nearly every group concerned with improving the conditions of working women.

At war's end, women lost nearly all their defense-related jobs. Wartime women railroad workers, for example, were replaced by returning servicemen, through the application of laws meant to protect women from hazardous conditions. But the war accelerated female employment in fields already dominated by women. By 1920, more women who worked outside the home did so in white-collar occupations—as telephone operators, secretaries, and clerks, for example—than in manufacturing or domestic service. The new awareness of women's work led Congress to create the Women's Bureau in the Labor Department, which continued the WIS wartime program of education and investigation through the postwar years.

Woman Suffrage

The presence of so many new women wageworkers, combined with the highly visible volunteer work of millions of middle-class women, helped finally to secure the vote for women. Volunteer war work—selling bonds, saving

Women workers at the Midvale Steel and Ordnance Company in Pennsylvania, 1918. Wartime labor shortages created new opportunities for over 1 million women to take high-wage manufacturing jobs like the women shown here. The opportunities proved temporary, however, and with the war's end, nearly all of these women lost their jobs. By 1920, the number of women employed in manufacturing was lower than it had been in 1910.

food, organizing benefits—was popular among house-wives and clubwomen. Until World War I, the fight for woman suffrage had been waged largely within individual states. Western states and territories had led the way. Various forms of woman suffrage became law in Wyoming in 1869, followed by Utah (1870), Colorado (1893), and Idaho (1896). Rocky Mountain and Pacific Coast states did not have the sharp ethnocultural divisions between Catholics and Protestants that hindered suffrage efforts in the East. For example, the close identification in the East between the suffrage and prohibition movements led many Catholic immigrants and German Lutherans to oppose the vote for women, because they feared it would lead to prohibition.

The U.S. entry into the war provided a unique opportunity for suffrage groups to shift their strategy to a national campaign for a constitutional amendment granting the vote to women. The most important of these groups was the National American Woman Suffrage Association (NAWSA). Before 1917, most American suffragists had opposed the war. Under the leadership of Carrie Chapman Catt, the NAWSA threw its support behind the war effort and doubled its membership to 2 million. Catt gambled that a strong show of patriotism would help clinch the century-old fight to win the vote for women. At the same time, more militant suffragists, led by the young Quaker activist Alice Paul, injected new energy and more radical tactics into the movement.

The confident bearing and direct gaze of this woman voter, depicted on a 1920 cover of *Leslie's Illustrated Weekly*, suggests how the historic achievement of woman suffrage reinforced images of the "New Woman."

Dissatisfied with the NAWSA's conservative strategy of quiet lobbying and orderly demonstrations, Paul left the organization in 1916. She joined forces with western women voters to form the National Woman's Party. Borrowing from English suffragists, this party pursued a more aggressive and dramatic strategy of agitation. Paul and her supporters picketed the White House, publicly burned President Wilson's speeches, and condemned the president and the Democrats for failing to produce an amendment. In one demonstration, they chained themselves to the White House fence, and after their arrest, went on a hunger strike in jail. The militants generated a great deal of publicity and sympathy.

Although some in the NAWSA objected to these tactics, Paul's radical approach helped make the NAWSA position more acceptable to Wilson. Carrie Chapman Catt used the president's war rhetoric as an argument for granting the vote to women. The fight for democracy, she argued, must begin at home, and she urged passage of the woman suffrage amendment as a "war measure." In 1917, the president urged Congress to pass a woman suffrage amendment as "vital to the winning of the war." The House did so in January 1918 and a more reluctant Senate approved it in June 1919. Another year of hard work was spent convincing the state legislatures. In August 1920, Tennessee gave the final vote needed to ratify the Nineteenth Amendment to the Constitution, finally making woman suffrage legal nationwide.

See the **Map**
Woman Suffrage before the Nineteenth Amendment at
www.myhistorylab.com

Prohibition

Another reform effort closely associated with women's groups triumphed at the same time. The movement to eliminate alcohol from American life had attracted many Americans, especially women, since before the Civil War. Temperance advocates saw drinking as the source of many of the worst problems faced by the working class, including family violence, unemployment, and poverty. By the early twentieth century, the Woman's Christian Temperance Union, with a quarter-million members, had become the single largest women's organization in American history.

The moral fervor that accompanied America's entry into the war provided a crucial boost to the cause. With so many breweries bearing German names, the movement benefited as well from the strong anti-German feeling of the war years. Outlawing beer and whiskey would also help to conserve precious grain, prohibitionists argued. In 1917, a coalition of progressives and rural fundamentalists in Congress pushed through a constitutional amendment providing for a national ban on alcoholic drinks. The Eighteenth Amendment was ratified by the

Read the **Document**
Eighteenth Amendment, Prohibition of Intoxicating Liquor (1919) at
www.myhistorylab.com

states in January 1919 and became the law of the land one year later. Although Prohibition would create a host of problems in the postwar years, especially as a stimulus for the growth of organized crime, many Americans, particularly native-born Protestants, considered it a worthy moral reform.

Public Health and the Influenza Pandemic

Wartime mobilization brought deeper government involvement with public health issues, especially in the realm of sex hygiene, child welfare, and disease prevention. The rate of venereal disease among draftees was as high as 6 percent in some states, presenting a potential manpower problem for the army. In April 1917, the War Department mounted a vigorous campaign against venereal disease, which attracted the energies of progressive-era sex reformers—social hygienists and antivice crusaders. Under the direction of Raymond Fosdick and the Commission on Training Camp Activities, the military educated troops on the dangers of contracting syphilis and gonorrhea. Venereal disease rates for soldiers declined by more than 300 percent during the war.

The wartime boost to government health work continued into the postwar years. The Children's Bureau, created in 1912 as a part of the Labor Department, undertook a series of reports on special problems growing out of the war: the increase in employment of married women, the finding of day care for children of working mothers, and the growth of both child labor and delinquency. In 1917, Julia C. Lathrop, chief of the bureau and a veteran of the settlement house movement, proposed a plan to institutionalize federal aid to the states for protection of mothers and children. Congress finally passed the Maternity and Infancy Act in 1921, appropriating over $1 million a year to be administered to the states by the Children's Bureau. In the postwar years, clinics for prenatal and obstetrical care grew out of these efforts and greatly reduced the rate of infant and maternal mortality and disease.

The disastrous influenza pandemic of 1918–19 offered the most serious challenge to national public health during the war years. It was part of a global scourge that originated in South China, then spread to the Philippines and moved across the United States, over to Europe, and then back with returning troops. Wartime conditions—large concentrations of people in military camps, on transport ships, and at the front—made its impact especially devastating. With no cure for the lethal combination of the "flu" and respiratory complications (mainly pneumonia), the pandemic killed over 21 million people worldwide. Few Americans paid attention to the disease until it swept through military camps and eastern cities in September 1918 and killed roughly 550,000 Americans in ten months. Most victims were young adults between the ages of twenty and forty. Congress appropriated a million dollars to the Public Health Service to combat and suppress

A nurse takes a patient's pulse in the influenza ward at Walter Reed Hospital, Washington, DC, November 1, 1918. Intensified by the crowded conditions on the battlefield, in training camps, and on troop ships, the influenza pandemic killed over half a million Americans and some 21 million people worldwide.

the epidemic, but it offered no money for research. Much of the care for the sick and dying came from Red Cross nurses and volunteers working in local communities across the nation. With a war on, and the nation focused on reports from the battlefront, even a public health crisis of this magnitude went relatively unnoticed.

Repression and Reaction

World War I exposed and intensified many of the deepest social tensions in American life. On the local level, vigilantes increasingly took the law into their own hands to punish those suspected of disloyalty. The push for national unity led the federal government to crack down on a wide spectrum of dissenters. The war inflamed racial hatred, and the worst race riots in the nation's history exploded in several cities. At war's end, a newly militant labor movement briefly asserted itself in mass strikes around the nation. Over each of these developments loomed the 1917 Bolshevik Revolution in Russia. Radicals around the world had drawn inspiration from what looked like the first successful revolution against a capitalist state. Many conservatives worried that similar revolutions were imminent. From 1918 through 1920, the federal government directed a repressive antiradical campaign that had crucial implications for the nation's future.

Muzzling Dissent: The Espionage and Sedition Acts

The Espionage Act of June 1917 became the government's key tool for the suppression of antiwar sentiment. It set severe penalties (up to twenty years' imprisonment

and a $10,000 fine) for anyone found guilty of aiding the enemy, obstructing recruitment, or causing insubordination in the armed forces. The act also empowered the postmaster general to exclude from the mails any newspapers or magazines he thought treasonous. Within a year, the mailing rights of forty-five newspapers had been revoked. These included several anti-British and pro-Irish publications, as well as such leading journals of American socialism as the Kansas-based *Appeal to Reason*, which had enjoyed a prewar circulation of half a million, and *The Masses*.

To enforce the Espionage Act, the government had to increase its overall police and surveillance machinery. Civilian intelligence was coordinated by the newly created Bureau of Investigation in the Justice Department. This agency was reorganized after the war as the Federal Bureau of Investigation (FBI). In May 1918, the Sedition Act, an amendment to the Espionage Act, outlawed "any disloyal, profane, scurrilous, or abusive language intended to cause contempt, scorn, contumely, or disrepute" to the government, Constitution, or flag.

These acts became a convenient vehicle for striking out at socialists, pacifists, radical labor activists, and others who resisted the patriotic tide. The most celebrated prosecution came in June 1918, when federal agents arrested Eugene V. Debs in Canton, Ohio, after he gave a speech defending antiwar protesters. Sentenced to ten years in prison, Debs defiantly told the court: "I have been accused of having obstructed the war. I admit it. Gentlemen, I abhor war. I would oppose the war if I stood alone." Debs served thirty-two months in federal prison before being pardoned by President Warren G. Harding on Christmas Day, 1921.

The Supreme Court upheld the constitutionality of the acts in several 1919 decisions. In *Schenck v. United States*, the Court unanimously agreed with Justice Oliver Wendell Holmes's claim that Congress could restrict speech if the words "are used in such circumstances and are of such a nature as to create a clear and present danger." The decision upheld the conviction of Charles Schenck for having mailed pamphlets urging potential army inductees to resist conscription. In *Debs v. United States*, the Court affirmed the guilt of Eugene V. Debs for his antiwar speech in Canton, even though he had not explicitly urged violation of the draft laws. Finally, in *Abrams v. United States*, the Court upheld Sedition Act convictions

> ◆●─ Read the Document
> *Abrams v. U.S.; Schenk v. U.S. (1919)* at
> **www.myhistorylab.com**

The War at Home in Wisconsin

America's entry into World War I provoked deep concerns about the loyalties of "hyphenated" Americans, and socialists immediately came under suspicion for their vocal opposition to an "imperialist" war. Pressure to conform was especially strong in Wisconsin, where German-Americans constituted a large fraction of the population and socialists played a leading political role in many cities and towns. In Milwaukee, nearly half the 500,000 residents were of German descent, and the city had many German newspapers, theaters, clubs, and music societies. Milwaukee's Loyalty League successfully pressured the school board to ban the teaching of German and shut down German theaters and music halls.

Extralegal and legal sanctions against allegedly disloyal Americans reinforced each other. The news story reproduced here, dated April 1, 1918, from the *Ashland* (Wisconsin) *Daily Press*, under the headline "Professor of Northland Tarred and Feathered; Taken From Room By A Mob; Masked Men Take Him Half Mile From the City, Give Him a Coat of Tar and Feathers and Let Him Walk Back Home," describes a vigilante action. It was one among many directed against allegedly disloyal Americans during World War I. In the Revolutionary Era, American Patriots sometimes used this very painful and dangerous form of punishment on Loyalists.

Socialists were also sanctioned: Victor Berger, editor of the *Milwaukee Leader,* a self-described "spokesman for evolutionary socialism" and a vigorous opponent of the war, wrote this angry editorial on October 19, 1918. In October 1917, Postmaster General Albert S. Burleson had banned the *Leader* from the mails under authority of the recently passed Espionage Act, which allowed him to prevent the postal system from handling reading matter "advocating or urging treason, insurrection, or forcible resistance to any law of the United States." In February 1918, the federal government indicted Berger and four other socialist leaders under the Espionage Act, and in December 1918 they were convicted of conspiracy to "willfully cause insubordination, disloyalty, and refusal of duty . . . by persistently dwelling upon the evils and horrors of war." Berger appealed his conviction and won election to Congress in 1918, but the House refused to seat him until 1923, when the Supreme Court finally overturned his conviction.

Professor E.A. Schimler Is Tarred and Feathered (April 1, 1918)

Professor E.A. Schimler, teacher of languages at Northland College, was taken from his room last night about midnight by nearly a dozen masked men, taken to a lonely spot about a half mile from the city, stripped of his clothing and given a substantial coat of tar and feathers.

After treating him to the coat of tar and feathers, the men in the party jumped into waiting automobiles and sped back to the city. They were very orderly. No one knew of the plot and it was carried out with such dispatch that hardly anyone in the city, except the parties interested, knew of the affair until everything was over.

Schimler, when left by the mob, found his undergarments and walked back to his boarding house. The police were then called and the police auto was sent at once to pick him up. He was taken to the city hall and later to the YMCA where he was given an opportunity to clean up.

> ". . . the mob was very liberal in the use of tar and also had on hand a lot of feathers."

When he arrived at the city hall, he was in such a condition that there was no question in any one's mind but that the mob were very liberal in the use of tar and also had on hand a lot of feathers.

Schimler could give absolutely no clue as to the parties who forcibly took him from his boarding house and the police have no clues to work on as they were not notified until the affair was all over. Chief of Police Blair stated that if the police had been called when the affair started that they would have prevented it and arrested the members of the mob. As they were not notified until the affair was all over and Schimler had time to walk back to the city, there was no way of apprehending them.

Schimler made claim to the police this morning that the mob not only treated him to a coat of tar and feathers but stole his coat and trousers and also his watch and other valuables from his person. He had not retired when the mob arrived at his boarding place but was sitting in his room, with his shoes off, reading.

Professor Schimler is an American citizen. He came to this country with his parents when he was fourteen years of age and received his

• **What does Professor Schimler's story tell us about local "vigilante justice" during World War I and its relationship to federal policies during the war?**

• **How does Victor Berger appeal to American historical traditions as part of his editorial against wartime government censorship? How might those who favored that censorship try to refute Berger's arguments?**

education in this country, being a graduate of the Boys' Latin School of Boston and of Dartmouth College. After leaving college he taught school in this country and then went to Germany where he taught for six years, returning to this country in 1913. He taught school in Carlisle, Pennsylvania, and Chicago and came to Northland last September to teach the languages. The college authorities say that Professor Schimler has been a very efficient teacher and that there is absolutely no evidence that he was disloyal in words or actions.

Mayor Dennis called at the *Daily Press* office this afternoon and stated that the city authorities would do all in their power to apprehend the guilty parties and in furtherance of this objective will give a reward of $100 for information that will lead to the arrest and conviction of any of the members of the mob that tarred and feathered Professor Schimler.

SOURCE: Wisconsin Historical Society, http://www.wisconsinhistory.org.

Victor Berger: "In the Land of the Free and the Home of the Brave" (October 19, 1918)

The following can not reach us by mail:

Money due on subscriptions.

Money for new subs.

Money for advertising.

Mail from our paid correspondents.

Mat and feature services.

Change of address and complaints.

Requests for advertising rates.

Mail from firms from which we buy material.

Price quotations.

But what's the use to go on? Any person with ordinary sense knows what the denial of the mail means to any concern, especially a newspaper. Since Oct. 3, 1917, when the mailing right of *The Leader* was revoked, we have LOST $70,000 IN SUBSCRIPTION MONEY AND $50,000 IN LOCAL AND NATIONAL ADVERTISING.

Now, mind you, no court has found us guilty of any crime. This tremendous loss of $120,000 was the result of the act of one man—the Postmaster General. The constitution says plainly: "No property shall be confiscated without due process of law." But a subjugated and "cowed congress" passed a law which violated, not only the constitution, but every principle of Americanism. This act gives to one man the power to ruin or confiscate the business of any citizen of this great democracy. This one man is prosecutor, judge, jury, and court of appeal. He may bankrupt the Standard Oil Company or the Steel Trust and snap his fingers at the sovereign people. Of course, there is no danger that the Postmaster General will exercise his Royal Prerogative on the Steel Trust or any other profiteering concern. Plutocracy is safe, but democracy is being murdered.

No republic can live without the freedom of press and speech. No republic can live without opposition and opposition parties. "Government is not eloquence, but force," as George Washington said. And men with unrestricted power—as we have them in the national capital now—become wolves and tyrants. We are not whining. We are not cringing. We are not cowed. We will not cry "enough!" We will fight on until the prison door clinks behind us or until the noose tightens around our necks. More precious than the freedom of the few, dearer than life itself, is Liberty. Too many have died that "government of the people, by the people, and

"Men with unrestricted power . . . become wolves and tyrants."

for the people" may not perish from this earth; too many great souls have breathed their last on fagot piles, amid dungeon walls and gallows ropes that Liberty may live. Go on, gentlemen, and do your worst! Someday a bruised and outraged people will rise in holy anger and cast you on the rubbish pile of history. Hiding behind the plea of making the "world safe for democracy" you are assassinating the freedom of the American people themselves. Go on! Do your damnedest and learn that all are not yet cowed "in the land of the free and the home of the brave."

SOURCE: http://www.marxisthistory.org.

of four Russian immigrants who had printed pamphlets denouncing American military intervention in the Russian Revolution. The nation's highest court thus endorsed the severe wartime restrictions on free speech.

In many western communities, local vigilantes used the superpatriotic mood to settle scores with labor organizers and radicals. In July 1917, for example, 2,000 armed vigilantes swept through the mining town of Bisbee, Arizona, acting on behalf of the Phelps-Dodge mining company and local businessmen. They wanted to break an IWW-led bitter strike that had crippled Bisbee's booming copper industry. The IWW's vocal opposition to the war made it vulnerable to charges of disloyalty. The vigilantes seized miners in their homes, on the street, and in restaurants and stores, delivering an ultimatum that any miner who refused to return to work would be deported. Some 1,400 miners refused to end their walkout; they were forced at gunpoint onto a freight train, which took them to Columbus, New Mexico, where they were dumped in the desert.

In thousands of other instances, government repression and local vigilantes reinforced each other. The American Protective League, founded with the blessing of the Justice Department, mobilized 250,000 self-appointed "operatives" in more than 600 towns and cities. Members of the league, mostly businessmen, bankers, and former policemen, spied on their neighbors and staged a series of well-publicized "slacker" raids on antiwar protesters and draft evaders. Many communities, inspired by Committee on Public Information campaigns, sought to ban the teaching of the German language in their schools or the performance of German music in concert halls (see Communities in Conflict).

The Great Migration and Racial Tensions

Economic opportunity brought on by war prosperity triggered a massive migration of rural black Southerners to northern cities. From 1914 to 1920, between 300,000 and 500,000 African Americans left the rural South for the North. Chicago's black population increased by 65,000, or 150 percent; Detroit's by 35,000, or 600 percent. Acute labor shortages led northern factory managers to recruit black migrants to the expanding industrial centers. The Pennsylvania Railroad alone drew 10,000 black workers from Florida and Georgia. Black workers eagerly left low-paying jobs as field hands and domestic servants for the chance at relatively high-paying work in meatpacking plants, shipyards, and steel mills (see Table 22.1).

Kinship and community networks were crucial in shaping what came to be called the Great Migration. The networks spread news about job openings, urban residential districts, and boardinghouses in northern cities. Black clubs, churches, and fraternal lodges in southern communities frequently sponsored the migration of their members, as well as return trips to the South. Single African American women often made the trip first, because they could more easily obtain steady work as maids, cooks, and laundresses. Relatively few African American men actually secured high-paying skilled jobs in industry or manufacturing. Most had to settle for such low-paying occupations as construction laborers, teamsters, janitors, or porters.

Read the Document
Letters from the Great Migration (1917) at www.myhistorylab.com

Rigid residential segregation of African Americans laid the foundation for the sprawling segregated ghettoes characteristic of twentieth-century northern cities. Shut out of white neighborhoods by a combination of custom and law (such as restrictive covenants forbidding homeowners to sell to nonwhites), African American migrants found themselves forced to squeeze into less desirable and all-black neighborhoods. In 1920, for example, approximately 85 percent of Chicago's 110,000 black citizens lived within a narrow strip roughly three miles long and a quarter mile wide. The city's South Side ghetto—surrounded on all sides by railroad tracks—had been born.

TABLE 22.1

The Great Migration: Black Population Growth in Selected Northern Cities, 1910–20

Northern Cities	1910		1920		
	No.	Percent	No.	Percent	Percent Increase
New York	91,709	1.9%	152,467	2.7%	66.3%
Chicago	44,103	2.0	109,458	4.1	148.2
Philadelphia	84,459	5.5	134,229	7.4	58.9
Detroit	5,741	1.2	40,838	4.1	611.3
St. Louis	43,960	6.4	69,854	9.0	58.9
Cleveland	8,448	1.5	34,451	4.3	307.8
Pittsburgh	25,623	4.8	37,725	6.4	47.2
Cincinnati	19,739	5.4	30,079	7.5	53.2

SOURCE: U.S. Department of Commerce.

This southern African American family is shown arriving in Chicago around 1910. Black migrants to northern cities often faced overcrowding, inferior housing, and a high death rate from disease. But the chance to earn daily wages of $6 to $8 (the equivalent of a week's wages in much of the South), as well as the desire to escape persistent racial violence, kept the migrants coming.

The persistence of lynching and other racial violence in the South no doubt contributed to the Great Migration, but racial violence was not limited to the South. On July 2, 1917, in East St. Louis, Illinois, a ferocious mob of whites

Read the Document
The Chicago Riot (1919)
at **www.myhistorylab.com**

attacked African Americans, killing at least 200. Before this riot, some of the city's manufacturers had steadily recruited black labor as a way to keep local union demands down. Unions had refused to allow black workers as members, and politicians had cynically exploited white racism in appealing for votes. In Chicago, on July 27, 1919, antiblack rioting broke out on a Lake Michigan beach. For two weeks, white gangs hunted African Americans in the streets and burned hundreds out of their homes. Twenty-three African Americans and fifteen whites died, and more than 500 were injured. In 1921, the bloodiest race riot of all took place in Greenwood, a thriving African American neighborhood in Tulsa, Oklahoma. A group of armed blacks, many of them army veterans, confronted a white mob intent on lynching a young African American accused of rape. The next day, whites invaded the Greenwood district, burned it to the ground, and murdered some 300 African Americans.

African Americans had supported the war effort as faithfully as any group. In 1917, despite a segregated army and discrimination in defense industries, most African Americans thought the war might improve their lot. Black disillusionment with the war grew quickly,

however, as did a newly militant spirit. A heightened sense of race consciousness and activism was evident among black veterans and the growing black communities of northern cities. Taking the lead in the fight against bigotry and injustice, in 1919 the NAACP held a national conference on lynching. By that time, membership in the NAACP had reached 60,000 and the circulation of its journal exceeded half a million.

Labor Strife

The relative labor peace of 1917 and 1918 dissolved after the armistice. In 1919 alone, more than 4 million American workers were involved in some 3,600 strikes. This unprecedented strike wave had several causes. Most of the modest wartime wage gains were wiped out by spiraling inflation and high prices for food, fuel, and housing. With the end of government controls on industry, many employers withdrew their recognition of unions. Difficult working conditions, such as the twelve-hour day in steel mills, were still routine in some industries.

Several of the postwar strikes received widespread national attention. They seemed to be more than simple economic conflicts, and they provoked deep fears about the larger social order. In February 1919, a strike in the shipyards of Seattle, Washington, over wages escalated into a general citywide strike involving 60,000 workers. The local press and Mayor Ole Hanson denounced the strikers as revolutionaries. Hanson effectively ended the strike by requesting federal troops to occupy the city. In September, Boston policemen went out on strike when the police commissioner rejected a citizens' commission study that recommended a pay raise. Massachusetts Governor Calvin Coolidge called in the National Guard to restore order and won a national reputation by crushing the strike. The entire police force was fired.

The biggest strike took place in the steel industry and involved some 350,000 steelworkers. Centered in several midwestern cities, this epic struggle lasted from September 1919 to January 1920. The AFL had hoped to build on wartime gains in an industry that had successfully resisted unionization before the war. The major demands were union recognition, the eight-hour day, and wage increases. The steel companies used black strikebreakers and armed guards to keep the mills running. Elbert Gary, president of U.S. Steel, directed a sophisticated propaganda campaign that branded the strikers as revolutionaries. Public opinion turned against the strike and condoned the use of state and federal troops to break it. The failed steel strike proved to be the era's most bitter and devastating defeat for organized labor.

An Uneasy Peace

The armistice of November 1918 ended the fighting on the battlefield, but the war continued at the peace conference. In the old royal Palace of Versailles near Paris, delegates from twenty-seven countries spent five months hammering out a settlement. Yet neither Germany nor Russia were represented. The proceedings were dominated by leaders of the "Big Four": David Lloyd George (Great Britain), Georges Clemenceau (France), Vittorio Orlando (Italy), and Woodrow Wilson (United States). President Wilson saw the peace conference as a historic opportunity to project his domestic liberalism onto the world stage. The stubborn realities of power politics would frustrate Wilson at Versailles and lead to his most crushing defeat at home.

Peacemaking and the Specter of Bolshevism

Even before November 1918, the Allies struggled with how to respond to the revolutionary developments in Russia. British and French leaders wanted to help counterrevolutionary forces overthrow the new Bolshevik regime. And President Wilson refused to recognize the authority of the Bolsheviks. Bolshevism represented a threat to the liberal-capitalist values that Wilson believed to be the foundation of America's moral and material power, and that provided the basis for the Fourteen Points. At the same time, however, Wilson at first resisted British and French pressure to intervene in Russia, citing his commitment to national self-determination and noninterference in other countries' internal affairs.

Woodrow Wilson, Georges Clemenceau, and David Lloyd George are among the central figures depicted in John Christen Johansen's *Signing of the Treaty of Versailles*. The gathered statesmen appear dwarfed by their surroundings.

SOURCE: John Christen Johansen (1876–1964), *Signing of the Treaty of Versailles*, 1919, oil on canvas, 249 cm × 224.5 cm (98-¹⁄₁₆ × 88-⅜"). Gift of an anonymous donor through Mrs. Elizabeth Rogerson, 1926. National Portrait Gallery, Smithsonian Institution, Washington, DC/Art Resource, New York.

By August 1918, as the Russian political and military situation became increasingly chaotic, Wilson agreed to British and French plans for sending troops to Siberia and northern Russia. Meanwhile, Japan poured troops into Siberia and northern Manchuria in a bid to control the commercially important Chinese Eastern and Trans-Siberian railways. After the Wilson administration negotiated an agreement that placed these strategic railways under international control, the restoration and protection of the railways became the primary concern of American military forces in Russia. Wilson's idealistic support for self-determination had succumbed to the demands of international power politics. Eventually, some 15,000 American troops served in northern and eastern Russia, with some remaining until 1920.

The Allied armed intervention widened the gulf between Russia and the West. In March 1919, Russian Communists established the Third International, or Comintern. Their call for a worldwide revolution deepened Allied mistrust, and the Paris Peace Conference essentially ignored the new political reality posed by the Russian Revolution.

Wilson in Paris

Wilson arrived in Paris with the United States delegation in January 1919. He believed the Great War revealed the bankruptcy of diplomacy based on alliances and the "balance of power." He believed that peacemaking, based on the framework put forward in his Fourteen Points, meant an opportunity for America to lead the rest of the world toward a new vision of international relations. The most controversial element, both at home and abroad, would prove to be the League of Nations. The heart of the League Covenant, Article X, called for collective security as the ultimate method of keeping the peace: "The members of the League undertake to respect and preserve as against external aggression the territorial integrity and existing political independence of all Members."

Despite Wilson's devotion to "open covenants," much of the negotiating in Paris was in fact done in secret among the Big Four. The ideal of self-determination found limited expression. The independent states of Austria, Hungary, Poland, Yugoslavia, and Czechoslovakia were carved out of the homelands of the defeated Central Powers. The Allies resisted Wilson's call for independence for the colonies of the defeated nations. A compromise mandate system of protectorates gave the French and British control of parts of the old German and Turkish empires in Africa and western Asia. Japan won control of former German colonies in China. Among those trying, but failing, to influence the treaty negotiations were the sixty-odd delegates to the first Pan African Congress, held in Paris at the same time as the peace talks. The group included Americans W. E. B. Du Bois and William Monroe Trotter as well as representatives from Africa and the West Indies. All were disappointed with the failure of the peace conference to grant self-determination to thousands of Africans living in former German colonies.

Another disappointment for Wilson came with the issue of war guilt. He had strongly opposed the extraction of harsh economic reparations from the Central Powers. But the French and British, with their awful war losses fresh in mind, insisted on making Germany pay. The final treaty contained a clause attributing the war to "the aggression of Germany," and a commission later set German war reparations at $33 billion. Bitter resentment in Germany over the punitive treaty helped sow the seeds for the Nazi rise to power in the 1930s.

The final treaty was signed on June 28, 1919, in the Hall of Mirrors at the Palace of Versailles. The Germans had no choice but to accept its harsh terms. President Wilson had been disappointed by the secret deals and the endless compromising of his ideals, no doubt underestimating the stubborn reality of power politics in the wake of Europe's most devastating war. He had nonetheless won a commitment to the League of Nations, the centerpiece of his plan, and he was confident that the American people would accept the treaty.

The Treaty Fight

Preoccupied with peace conference politics in Paris, Wilson had neglected politics at home. His troubles had started earlier when Republicans captured both the House and the Senate in the 1918 elections. Wilson then made a tactical error by including no prominent Republicans in the U.S. peace delegation. He therefore faced a variety of tough opponents to the treaty he brought home.

Wilson's most extreme enemies in the Senate were a group of about sixteen "irreconcilables" who were opposed to a treaty in any form. Some were isolationist progressives, such as Republicans Robert M. La Follette of Wisconsin and William Borah of Idaho, who opposed the League of Nations as steadfastly as they opposed American entry into the war. Others were racist xenophobes like Democrat James Reed of Missouri. He objected, he said, to submitting questions to a tribunal "on which a nigger from Liberia, a nigger from Honduras, a nigger from India, and an unlettered gentleman from Siam, each have votes equal to the great United States of America."

The less dogmatic, but more influential, opponents were led by Republican Henry Cabot Lodge of Massachusetts, powerful majority leader of the Senate. They had strong reservations about the League of Nations, especially the provisions for collective security should a member nation be attacked. Lodge argued that this provision impinged on congressional authority to declare war and placed unacceptable restraints on the nation's ability to pursue an independent foreign policy. Lodge proposed a series of amendments that would have weakened the League. Wilson refused to compromise, motivated in part by the long-standing hatred he and Lodge felt toward each other.

Read the Document

Henry Cabot Lodge, Objections to Treaty of Versailles (1919) at **www.myhistorylab.com**

In September, Wilson set out on a speaking tour across the country to drum up support for the League and the treaty. The strain took its toll. On September 25, after speaking in Pueblo, Colorado, the sixty-three-year-old Wilson collapsed from exhaustion. His doctor canceled the rest of the trip. A week later, back in Washington, the president suffered a stroke that left him partially paralyzed. With Wilson badly incapacitated, his wife and his doctor exercised significant decision-making authority, and they reinforced his refusal to agree to any amendments on the Treaty and the League Covenant. In November, Lodge brought the treaty out of committee for a vote, having appended to it fourteen reservations—that is, recommended changes. A bedridden Wilson stubbornly refused to compromise and instructed Democrats to vote against the Lodge version of the treaty. On November 19, Democrats joined with the "irreconcilables" to defeat the amended treaty, 39 to 55.

Wilson refused to budge. In January, he urged Democrats to either stand by the original treaty or vote it down. The 1920 election, he warned, would be "a great and solemn referendum" on the whole issue. In the final vote, on March 19, 1920, twenty-one Democrats broke with the president and voted for the Lodge version, giving it a majority of 49 to 35. But this was seven votes short of the two-thirds needed for ratification. As a result, the United States never signed the Versailles Treaty, nor did it join the League of Nations. The absence of the United States weakened the League and made it more difficult for the organization to realize Wilson's dream of a peaceful community of nations.

The Red Scare

Revolutionary changes taking place in Russia became an important backdrop for domestic politics. In the United States, it became common to blame socialism, the IWW, trade unionism in general, and even racial disturbances on foreign radicals and alien ideologies. The accusation of Bolshevism became a powerful weapon for turning public opinion against strikers and political dissenters of all kinds. In truth, by 1919, the American radicals were already weakened and badly split. In the spring of 1919, a few extremists mailed bombs to prominent business and political leaders. That June, simultaneous bombings in eight cities killed two people and damaged the residence of Attorney General A. Mitchell Palmer. With public alarm growing, state and federal officials began a coordinated campaign to root out subversives and their alleged Russian connections.

Read the Document

A. Mitchell Palmer, On the Menace of Communism (1920) at **www.myhistorylab.com**

Palmer used the broad authority of the 1918 Alien Act, which enabled the government to deport any immigrant found to be a member of a revolutionary organization prior to or after coming to the United States. In a series of raids in late 1919, Justice Department agents in eleven cities arrested and roughed up several hundred members of the IWW and the Union of Russian Workers. Little evidence of revolutionary intent was found, but 249 people were deported, including prominent anarchists Emma Goldman and Alexander Berkman. In early 1920, some 6,000 people in thirty-three cities, including many U.S. citizens and non-Communists, were arrested and herded into prisons and bullpens. Again, no evidence of a grand plot was found, but another 600 aliens were deported. The Palmer raids had a ripple effect around the nation, encouraging other repressive measures against radicals. In New York, the state assembly refused to seat five duly elected Socialist Party members.

Palmer's popularity had waned by the spring of 1920, when it became clear that his predictions of revolutionary uprisings were wildly exaggerated. A report prepared by a group of distinguished lawyers questioned the legality of the attorney general's tactics. As part of the resistance to Palmer's policies, a group of progressive activists formed the American Civil Liberties Union (ACLU) in 1920. Its founders included Clarence Darrow, Felix Frankfurter, Jane Addams, Helen Keller, and John Dewey. For progressives dispirited by the wartime political repression, the ACLU offered a new political front stressing the militant defense of civil liberties just when they seemed most fragile.

The Red Scare left an ugly legacy: wholesale violations of constitutional rights, deportations of hundreds of innocent people, fuel for the fires of nativism and intolerance. Business groups, such as the National Association of Manufacturers, found "Red-baiting" to be an effective tool in postwar efforts to keep unions out of their factories. Indeed, the government-sanctioned Red Scare reemerged later in the century as a powerful political force. In many communities, local vigilantes invoked the threat of Bolshevism and used the superpatriotic mood to settle scores with labor organizers and radicals.

The Red Scare took its toll on the women's movement as well. Before the war, many suffragists and feminists had maintained ties and shared platforms with socialist and labor groups. But the calls for "100 percent Americanism" during and after the war destroyed the fragile alliances that had made a group such as the National American Woman Suffrage Association so powerful. Hostility to radicalism marked the political climate of the 1920s, and this atmosphere narrowed the political spectrum for women activists.

The Election of 1920

Woodrow Wilson had wanted the 1920 election to be a "solemn referendum" on the League of Nations and his conduct of the war. Ill and exhausted, Wilson did not run for reelection. A badly divided Democratic Party compromised on Governor James M. Cox of Ohio as its candidate. A proven vote-getter, Cox distanced himself from Wilson's policies, which had come under withering attack from many quarters.

The Republicans nominated Senator Warren G. Harding of Ohio. A political hack, the handsome and genial Harding had virtually no qualifications to be president, except that he looked like one. Harding's campaign was vague and elusive about the Versailles Treaty and almost everything else. He struck a chord with the electorate in calling for a retreat from Wilsonian idealism. "America's present need," he said, "is not heroics but healing; not nostrums but normalcy; not revolution but restoration."

The notion of a "return to normalcy" proved very attractive to voters exhausted by the war, inflation, big government, and social dislocation. Harding won the greatest landslide in history to that date, carrying every state outside the South and taking the popular vote by 16 million to 9 million. Republicans retained their majorities in the House and Senate as well. Socialist Eugene V. Debs, still a powerful symbol of the dream of radical social change, managed to poll 900,000 votes from jail. But the

Read the Document
History Bookshelf: Walter Lippmann, Public Opinion (1922) at **www.myhistorylab.com**

CHRONOLOGY

1903	United States obtains Panama Canal rights
1905	President Theodore Roosevelt mediates peace treaty between Japan and Russia at Portsmouth Conference
1908	Root-Takahira Agreement with Japan affirms status quo in Asia and Open Door policy in China
1911	Mexican Revolution begins
1914	U.S. forces invade Mexico
	Panama Canal opens
	World War I begins in Europe
	President Woodrow Wilson issues proclamation of neutrality
1915	Germany declares war zone around Great Britain
	German U-boat sinks *Lusitania*
1916	Pancho Villa raids New Mexico and is pursued by General Pershing
	Wilson is reelected
	National Defense Act establishes preparedness program
1917	February: Germany resumes unrestricted submarine warfare
	March: Zimmermann note, suggesting a German-Mexican alliance, shocks Americans
	April: United States declares war on the Central Powers

	May: Selective Service Act is passed
	June: Espionage Act is passed
	November: Bolshevik Revolution begins in Russia
1918	January: Wilson unveils Fourteen Points
	May: Sedition Act is passed
	June: U.S. troops begin to see action in France
	September: Influenza outbreaks among AEF troops in France
	November: Armistice ends war
1919	January: Eighteenth Amendment (Prohibition) is ratified
	Wilson serves as chief U.S. negotiator at Paris Peace Conference
	June: Versailles Treaty is signed in Paris
	July: Race riot breaks out in Chicago
	Steel strike begins in several midwestern cities
	November: Palmer raids begin
1920	March: Senate finally votes down Versailles Treaty and League of Nations
	August: Nineteenth Amendment (woman suffrage) is ratified
	November: Warren G. Harding is elected president

overall vote repudiated Wilson and the progressive movement. Americans seemed eager to pull back from moralism in public and international controversies. Yet many of the economic, social, and cultural changes wrought by the war would accelerate during the 1920s. In truth, there could never be a "return to normalcy."

Conclusion

The global impact of the Great War, including the United States' place in relation to the rest of the world, was profound. Although the casualties and social upheavals endured by the European powers might seem to dwarf the price paid

by the United States, the war created economic, social, and political dislocations that helped reshape American life long after Armistice Day. The ability to raise and deploy the massive American Expeditionary Force overseas so quickly had proved decisive to ending the fighting. The government's direct intervention in every aspect of the wartime economy was unprecedented, and wartime production needs contributed to a "second industrial revolution" that transformed the economy in the decade following the war. Republican administrations invoked the wartime partnership between government and industry to justify an aggressive peacetime policy fostering cooperation between the state and business. Although the United States would not join the League of

Nations, the war turned the United States into a major global force: the world's new leading creditor nation would now also take its place as a powerful commercial and industrial engine in the global economy.

Patriotic fervor and the exaggerated threat of Bolshevism were used to repress radicalism, organized labor, feminism, and the entire legacy of progressive reform. The wartime measure of national prohibition evolved into perhaps the most contentious social issue of peacetime. Sophisticated use of sales techniques, psychology, and propaganda during the war helped define the newly powerful advertising and public relations industries of the 1920s. The growing visibility of immigrants and African Americans, especially in the nation's cities, provoked a xenophobic and racist backlash in the politics of the 1920s. More than anything else, the desire for "normalcy" reflected the deep anxieties evoked by America's wartime experience.

Review Questions

1. What central issues drew the United States deeper into international politics in the early years of the century? How did American presidents justify a more expansive role? What diplomatic and military policies did they exploit for these ends?

2. Compare the arguments for and against American participation in the Great War. Which Americans were most likely to support entry? Which were more likely to oppose it?

3. How did mobilizing for war change the economy and its relationship to government? Which of these changes, if any, spilled over to the postwar years?

4. How did the war affect political life in the United States? What techniques were used to stifle dissent? What was the war's political legacy?

5. Analyze the impact of the war on American workers. How did the conflict affect the lives of African Americans and women?

6. What principles guided Woodrow Wilson's Fourteen Points? How would you explain the United States' failure to ratify the Treaty of Versailles?

Recommended Reading

Christopher Cappozzola, *Uncle Sam Wants You: World War I and the Making of the Modern American Citizen* (2008). An excellent new account exploring how World War I expanded the powers of the state at the expense of citizens' rights and redefined the obligations of citizenship itself.

Alan Dawley, *Changing the World: American Progressives in War and Revolution* (2003). Thoughtful analysis that traces the interplay between progressive politics and America's involvement in the Great War.

James H. Hallas, *Doughboy War: The American Expeditionary Force in World War I* (2000). Excellent and wide-ranging account of the AEF told entirely from first-person accounts—letters, diaries, and interviews—of the doughboys themselves.

Robert Hannigan, *The New World Power: American Foreign Policy, 1898–1917* (2002). An ambitious analysis of how the American policy-making elite sought to impose political and economic order around the globe.

Adriane Lentz-Smith, *Freedom Struggles: African Americans and World War I* (2009). A new comprehensive account of the black experience during World War I, emphasizing how the war intersected with the fight for civil rights both at home and within the military.

Richard Slotkin, *Lost Battalions: The Great War and the Crisis of Nationality* (2006). A beautifully written and imaginative account of two AEF units: the African American 369th Infantry (the "Harlem Hellfighters") and the 77th Division (the "Melting Pot"). Slotkin explores the tensions inherent in the wartime mobilization that included large groups of citizens—in these cases blacks and immigrants—who were deemed inferior yet also promised the benefits of full citizenship rights.

Susan Zeiger, *In Uncle Sam's Service: Women Workers with the American Expeditionary Force, 1917–1919* (1999). The first in-depth study of American women's experiences with the armed forces overseas.

Robert H. Zieger, *America's Great War: World War I and the American Experience* (2000). The best recent one-volume synthesis on how the war transformed the United States and its role in the world.

PEARSON
myhistorylab Connections

Reinforce what you learned in this chapter by studying the many documents,
images, maps, review tools, and videos available at www.myhistorylab.com.

Read and Review

✓●─[Study and Review **Chapter 22**

●ᴣ●─[Read the Document

William H. Taft, "Dollar Diplomacy" (1912)

Eugene V. Debs, Critique of World War (1918)

*Joseph Buffington, "Friendly Words to the
Foreign Born" (1917)*

*Statement to French Concerning Black American
Troops (1918)*

*Eugene Kennedy, "A 'Doughboy' Describes the
Fighting Front" (1918)*

Woodrow Wilson, "Fourteen Points" (1917)

*Eighteenth Amendment, Prohibition of
Intoxicating Liquor (1919)*

Abrams v. U.S.; Schenk v. U.S. (1919)

Letters from the Great Migration (1917)

The Chicago Riot (1919)

*Henry Cabot Lodge, Objections to Treaty of
Versailles (1919)*

*A. Mitchell Palmer, On the Menace of
Communism (1920)*

👁●─[See the **Map**

World War I

*Woman Suffrage before the Nineteenth
Amendment*

Research and Explore

●ᴣ●─[Read the Document

Exploring America: Becoming American

Profiles
Alice Paul
General John J. Pershing

History Bookshelf: Walter Lippmann, Public
Opinion *(1922)*

((●─[Hear the Audio *Over There*

●─[Watch the Video

The Panama Canal

American Entry into WWI

The Outbreak of World War I

((●─[**Hear** the **Audio**

Hear the audio files for Chapter 22 at
www.myhistorylab.com.

Chapter 23 at www.myhistorylab.com

((•-[Hear the Audio

23

The Twenties
1920–1929

CHAPTER OUTLINE

American Communities 653
The Movie Audience and Hollywood: Mass Culture Creates a New National Community

Postwar Prosperity and Its Price 655
The Second Industrial Revolution
The Modern Corporation
Welfare Capitalism
The Auto Age
Cities and Suburbs

The State, the Economy, and Business 660
Harding and Coolidge

Herbert Hoover and the "Associative State"
War Debts, Reparations, Keeping the Peace
Global Commerce and U.S. Foreign Policy
Weakened Agriculture, Ailing Industries

The New Mass Culture 664
Movie-Made America
Radio Broadcasting
New Forms of Journalism
Advertising Modernity
The Phonograph and the Recording
   Industry
Sports and Celebrity
A New Morality?

Modernity and Traditionalism 672
Prohibition
Immigration Restriction
The Ku Klux Klan
Fundamentalism in Religion

Promises Postponed 675
Feminism in Transition
Mexican Immigration
The "New Negro"
Alienated Intellectuals
The Election of 1928

America Today: City Activities with Dance Hall, 1830 by Thomas Hart Benton (1889–1975). Distemper and egg tempera on gessoed linen with oil glaze, 92 × 134 ½ in.

The Movie Audience and Hollywood: Mass Culture Creates a New National Community

Inside midtown Manhattan's magnificent new Roxy Theater, a sellout crowd eagerly settled in for opening night. Outside, thousands of fans cheered wildly at the arrival of movie stars such as Charlie Chaplin, Gloria Swanson, and Harold Lloyd. A squadron of smartly uniformed ushers guided patrons under a five-story-tall rotunda to some 6,200 velvet-covered seats. The audience marveled at the huge gold- and rose-colored murals, classical statuary, plush carpeting, and Gothic-style windows. It was easy to believe newspaper reports that the theater had cost $10 million to build. Suddenly, light flooded the orchestra pit and 110 musicians began playing "The Star Spangled Banner." A troupe of 100 performers took the stage, dancing ballet numbers and singing old southern melodies such as "My Old Kentucky Home" and "Swanee River." Congratulatory telegrams from President Calvin Coolidge and other dignitaries flashed on the screen. Finally, the evening's feature presentation, *The Love of Sunya,* starring Gloria Swanson, began. Samuel L. "Roxy" Rothapfel, the theater's designer, had realized his grand dream—to build "the cathedral of the motion picture."

AMERICAN Communities

When Roxy's opened in March 1927, nearly 60 million Americans "worshiped" each week at movie theaters across the nation. The "movie palaces" of the 1920s were designed to transport patrons to exotic places and different times. As film pioneer Marcus Loew put it, "We sell tickets to theaters, not movies." Every large community boasted at least one opulent movie theater. Houston's Majestic was built to represent an ancient Italian garden; it had a ceiling made to look like an open sky, complete with stars and cloud formations. The Tivoli in Chicago featured French Renaissance decor; Grauman's Egyptian in Los Angeles re-created the look of a pharaoh's tomb; and Albuquerque's Kimo drew inspiration from Navajo art and religion.

The remarkable popularity of motion pictures, and later radio, forged a new kind of community. A huge national audience regularly went to the movies, and the same entertainment could be enjoyed anywhere in the country by just about everyone. People who may have had little in common in terms of ethnicity, background, or geographic location found themselves part of a virtual community of movie fans. Hollywood films also achieved a global popularity that represented the cultural side of America's newfound influence in the world. American films, especially slapstick comedies, had begun appearing regularly in European theaters during the Great War, as producers took advantage of wartime dislocation to penetrate foreign markets. The Webb-Pomerene Act of 1918 proved a boon for the global expansion of Hollywood film, as it exempted export associations from antitrust laws, allowing them to form cartels, fix prices, and engage in other trade practices that would have been barred at home. Hollywood movies soon emerged as among the most widely circulated American commodities in the world, second only to Gillette razor blades and Ford automobiles. Producers found strong allies in the federal government, which touted the connections between the export of Hollywood movies and the growth of American trade around the world. "Trade follows the film," as one Commerce Department report put it, with movies supplying "an animated catalogue for ideas of dress, living, and comfort."

Hollywood's emergence might be thought of as part of a broader "second industrial revolution" that modernized industrial production and greatly expanded the availability of consumer goods in the postwar years. The studios concentrated on producing big-budget feature films designed for mass audiences, with the "star system" providing the industry's version of product branding. The economies of large-scale production allowed studios to sign popular actors to long-term contracts and invest heavily in their salaries and promotion. The stars themselves had to be willing to sacrifice their privacy in order to promote their "celebrity" status. Movie stars like Charlie Chaplin, Mary Pickford, Rudolph Valentino, Gloria Swanson, and Douglas Fairbanks became popular idols as much for their highly publicized private lives as for their roles on-screen. Many accumulated great wealth, becoming the nation's experts on how to live well. They built luxurious mansions in a variety of architectural styles and outfitted them with swimming pools, tennis courts, golf courses, and lavish gardens. Americans embraced the culture of celebrity, voraciously consuming fan magazines, gossip columns, and news of the stars. Indeed, during the 1920s, there was a tight connection between celebrity and the rapid growth of new networks of mass culture—movies, radio, advertising, musical recordings, and big-time sports.

If the movies created a new kind of virtual community of fans in the 1920s, the town of Hollywood itself was also a new kind of American community. A suburb of Los Angeles that had barely existed in 1890, Hollywood was an alluring alternative to the East Coast cities where movies had been born. Its reliably sunny and dry climate was ideal for year-round filming. Its unique surroundings offered a perfect variety of scenic locations—mountains, desert, ocean—and downtown Los Angeles was only an hour away. Land was cheap and plentiful, and because Los Angeles was the leading nonunion, open-shop city in the country, so was labor. It lured the young and cosmopolitan with the promise of upward mobility and a new way of life.

Most of the top studio executives were Jewish immigrants from eastern and central Europe. In contrast to most Americans, who hailed from rural areas or small towns, more than half of Hollywood's writers, directors, editors, and actors were born in cities of over 100,000. Two-thirds of its performers were under thirty-five, and three-fourths of its actresses were under twenty-five. More than 90 percent of its writers (women made up one-third to one-half of this key group) had attended college or worked in journalism.

1. How did the "second industrial revolution" transform the American economy?

2. What were the promises and limits of prosperity in the 1920s?

3. How and why did the Republican Party dominate 1920s' politics?

4. How did the new mass media reshape American culture?

5. Which Americans were less likely to share in postwar prosperity and why?

6. What political and cultural movements opposed modern cultural trends?

FOCUS
Questions

1920–1929

Hollywood films celebrating the pleasures of leisure, consumption, and personal freedom redefined American cultural values in the 1920s. But the community that cranked them out was far from typically American.

Ordinary Americans found it easy to identify with movie stars despite their wealth and status. Unlike industrialists or politicians, stars had no social authority over large groups of employees or voters. They, too, had to answer to a boss, and most had risen from humble beginnings. But above all, Hollywood, like the movies it churned out, represented for millions of Americans new possibilities: freedom, material success, upward mobility, and the chance to remake one's very identity. By the end of the decade, the Hollywood "dream factory" had helped forge a national community whose collective aspirations and desires were increasingly defined by those possibilities, even if relatively few Americans realized them

Hollywood

during the 1920s. And around the world, Hollywood movies became the preeminent version of the American way of life.

Of course, Hollywood films offered nothing near an accurate reflection of the complexities of American society. As American culture became increasingly defined by an urban-based mass media that claimed the entire nation for its audience, resentment toward and resistance against the new popular culture was widespread. Movies celebrated prosperity, new technologies, and expanded consumerism, but these were by no means shared equally among Americans in the decade following World War I. While Hollywood films touted the promise of the modern, and the potential for people to remake themselves, tenacious belief in the old-fashioned verities of prewar America fueled some of the strongest political and cultural currents of the decade.

AMERICAN
Communities

Postwar Prosperity and Its Price

Republican Warren G. Harding won the presidency in 1920, largely thanks to his nostalgic call for a "return to normalcy." In the decade following the end of World War I, however, the American economy underwent profound structural changes that guaranteed life would never be "normal" again. The 1920s saw an enormous increase in the efficiency of production, a steady climb in real wages, a decline in the length of the average employee's workweek, and a boom in consumer-goods industries. Americans shared unevenly in

the postwar prosperity, and by the end of the decade, certain basic weaknesses in the economy helped to bring on the worst depression in American history. Yet overall, the nation experienced crucial transformations in how it organized its business, earned its living, and enjoyed its leisure time.

The Second Industrial Revolution

The prosperity of the 1920s rested on what historians have called the "second industrial revolution" in American manufacturing, in which technological innovations made it possible to increase industrial output without expanding the labor force. Electricity replaced steam as the main power source for industry in those years, making possible the replacement of older machinery with more efficient and flexible electric machinery. In 1914, only 30 percent of the nation's factories were electrified; by 1929, 70 percent relied on the electric motor rather than the steam engine.

Much of the newer, automatic machinery could be operated by unskilled and semiskilled workers, and it boosted the overall efficiency of American industry. Thus, in 1929, the average worker in manufacturing produced roughly three-quarters more per hour than he or she had in 1919. The machine industry itself, particularly the manufacture of electrical machinery, led in productivity gains, enjoying one of the fastest rates of expansion. It employed more workers than any other manufacturing sector—some 1.1 million in 1929—supplying not only a growing home market but 35 percent of the world market as well.

During the late nineteenth century, heavy industries such as machine tools, railroads, iron, and steel had pioneered mass-production techniques. These industries manufactured what economists call producer-durable goods. In the 1920s, modern mass-production techniques were increasingly applied to newer consumer-durable goods—automobiles, radios, washing machines, and telephones—permitting firms to make large profits while keeping prices affordable. Other consumer-based industries, such as canning, chemicals, synthetics, and plastics, began to change the everyday lives of millions of Americans. With more efficient management, greater mechanization, intensive product research, and ingenious sales and advertising methods, the consumer-based industries helped to nearly double industrial production in the 1920s.

The watchword for all this was efficiency, a virtue that progressives had emphasized in their prewar efforts to improve urban life and the mechanics of government itself. But efficiency became an obsession for American businessmen, who thought it defined modernity as well. American success in mechanization and the mass production of consumer goods evoked admiration and envy in much of the industrialized (and industrializing) world.

•••[Read the Document

Frederick W. Taylor, "Scientific Management" (1911) at **www.myhistorylab.com**

The Modern Corporation

In the late nineteenth century, individual entrepreneurs such as John D. Rockefeller in oil and Andrew Carnegie in steel had provided a model for success. They maintained both corporate control (ownership) and business leadership (management) in their enterprises. In the 1920s, a managerial revolution increasingly divorced ownership of corporate stock from the everyday control of businesses (see Figure 23.1). The new corporate ideal was to be found in men such as Alfred P. Sloan of General Motors and Owen D. Young of the Radio

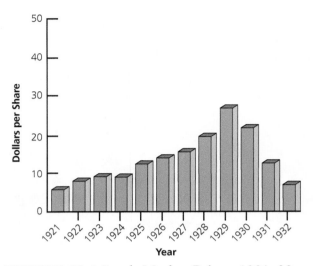

FIGURE 23.1 Stock Market Prices, 1921–32 Common stock prices rose steeply during the 1920s. Although only about 4 million Americans owned stocks during the period, "stock watching" became something of a national sport.

Corporation of America. A growing class of salaried executives, plant managers, and engineers formed a new elite, who made corporate policy without themselves having a controlling interest in the companies for which they worked. They stressed scientific management and the latest theories of behavioral psychology in their effort to make their workplaces more productive, stable, and profitable (see Figure 23.2). Modern managers also

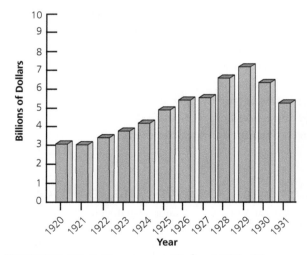

FIGURE 23.2 Consumer Debt, 1920–31 The expansion of consumer borrowing was a key component of the era's prosperity. These figures do not include mortgages or money borrowed to purchase stocks. They reveal the great increase in "installment buying" for such consumer durable goods as automobiles and household appliances.

brought a more sophisticated understanding of global markets to their management. Exploiting overseas markets, especially in Europe, became a key element in corporate strategy, especially for car manufacturers, chemical companies, and businesses engaged in the new world of modern mass media.

During the 1920s, the most successful corporations were those that led in three key areas: the integration of production and distribution, product diversification, and the expansion of industrial research. Until the end of World War I, for example, the chemical manufacturer Du Pont had specialized in explosives such as gunpowder. After the war, Du Pont moved aggressively into the consumer market with a diverse array of products. The company created separate but integrated divisions that produced and distributed new fabrics (such as rayon), paints, dyes, and celluloid products (such as artificial sponges). The great electrical manufacturers—General Electric and Westinghouse—similarly transformed themselves after the war. Previously concentrating on lighting and power equipment, they diversified into household appliances like radios, washing machines, and refrigerators.

By 1929, the 200 largest corporations owned nearly half the nation's corporate wealth—that is, physical plant, stock, and property. Half the total industrial income—revenue from sales of goods—was concentrated in 100 corporations. Oligopoly—the control of a market by a few

large producers—became the norm. Four companies packed almost three-quarters of all American meat. Another four rolled nine out of every ten cigarettes. National chain grocery stores, clothing shops, and pharmacies began squeezing out local neighborhood businesses. One grocery chain alone, the Great Atlantic and Pacific Tea Company (A&P), accounted for 10 percent of all retail food sales in America. A&P won out over thousands of older "mom and pop" grocery stores partly by selling its stores as "clean" and "modern," with no haggling over prices. These changes meant that Americans were increasingly members of national consumer communities, buying the same brands all over the country, as opposed to locally produced goods.

Welfare Capitalism

The wartime gains made by organized labor, and the active sympathy shown to trade unions by government agencies such as the National War Labor Board (NWLB), troubled most corporate leaders. Shortly after the war's end, largely as a result of pressure from business leaders, the Wilson administration dismantled the NWLB and other mechanisms aimed at mediation of labor disputes. To challenge the power and appeal of trade unions and collective bargaining, large employers aggressively promoted a variety of new programs designed to improve worker well-being and morale while also fending off unionization.

The A&P grocery chain expanded from 400 stores in 1912 to more than 15,000 by the end of the 1920s, making it a familiar sight in communities across America. A&P advertisements, like this one from 1927, emphasized cleanliness, order, and the availability of name-brand goods at discount prices.

These schemes, collectively known as welfare capitalism, became a key part of corporate strategy in the 1920s.

Large corporations mounted an effective antiunion campaign in the early 1920s called "the American plan" as an alternative to trade unionism and the class antagonism associated with European labor relations. Backed by powerful business lobbies such as the National Association of Manufacturers and the Chamber of Commerce, campaign leaders called for the open shop, in which no employee would be compelled to join a union. In effect, an "open shop" meant that no known union member would be hired. If a union existed, nonmembers would still get whatever wages and rights the union had won—a policy that put organizers at a disadvantage in signing up new members.

The open shop undercut the gains won in a union shop, where new employees had to join an existing union, or a closed shop, where employers agreed to hire only union members. As alternatives, large employers such as U.S. Steel and International Harvester began setting up company unions. Their intent was to substitute largely symbolic employee representation in management conferences for the more confrontational process of collective bargaining. These management strategies contributed to a sharp decline in the ranks of organized labor. Total union membership dropped from about 5 million in 1920 to 3.5 million in 1926. A large proportion of the remaining union members were concentrated in the skilled crafts of the building and printing trades. A conservative and timid union leadership was also responsible for the trend. William Green, who became president of the American Federation of Labor after the death of Samuel Gompers in 1924, showed no real interest in getting unorganized workers, such as those in the growing mass-production industries of automobiles, steel, and electrical goods, into unions.

Another approach encouraged workers to acquire property through stock-purchase plans or, less frequently, home-ownership plans. By 1927, 800,000 employees had more than $1 billion invested in more than 300 companies. Other programs offered workers insurance policies covering accidents, illness, old age, and death. By 1928, some 6 million workers had group insurance coverage valued at $7.5 billion. Many plant managers and personnel departments consciously worked to improve safety conditions, provide medical services, and establish sports and recreation programs for workers. Employers hoped such measures would encourage workers to identify personally with the company and discourage complaints on the job. To some extent they succeeded. But welfare capitalism could not solve the chronic problems faced by industrial workers: seasonal unemployment, low wages, long hours, and unhealthy factory conditions. Indeed, corporate policy reinforced economic insecurity for millions of workers and advanced growing income inequality. The failure of the 1920s' economy to distribute gains in productivity more equally would help set the stage for the Great Depression of the 1930s.

The Auto Age

In their classic community study *Middletown* (1929), sociologists Robert and Helen Lynd noted the dramatic impact of the car on the social life of residents of Muncie, Indiana. "Why on earth do you need to study what's changing this country?" asked one lifelong Muncie resident in 1924. "I can tell you what's happening in just four letters: A–U–T–O!" This remark hardly seems much of an exaggeration today. No other single development could match the impact of the postwar automobile explosion on the way Americans worked, lived, and played. The auto industry offered the clearest example of the rise to prominence of consumer durables. During the 1920s, America

Finished automobiles roll off the moving assembly line at the Ford Motor Company, Highland Park, Michigan, ca. 1920. During the 1920s, Henry Ford achieved the status of folk hero, as his name became synonymous with the techniques of mass production. Ford cultivated a public image of himself as the heroic genius of the auto industry, greatly exaggerating his personal achievements.

made approximately 85 percent of all the world's passenger cars. By 1929, the motor vehicle industry was the most productive in the United States in terms of value. In that year, the industry added 4.8 million new cars to the more than 26 million—roughly one for every five people—already on American roads.

This extraordinary new industry had mushroomed in less than a generation. Its great pioneer, Henry Ford, had shown how the use of a continuous assembly line could drastically reduce the number of worker hours required to produce a single vehicle. Ford revolutionized the factory shop floor with new, custom-built machinery, such as the engine-boring drill press and the pneumatic wrench, and a more efficient layout. "Every piece of work in the shop moves," Ford boasted. In 1913, it took thirteen hours to produce one automobile. In 1914, at his sprawling new Highland Park assembly plant just outside Detroit, Ford's system finished one car every ninety minutes. By 1925, cars were rolling off his assembly line at the rate of one every ten seconds.

In 1914, Ford startled American industry by inaugurating a new wage scale: $5 for an eight-hour day. This was roughly double the going pay rate for industrial labor, along with a shorter workday as well. In defying the conventional economic wisdom of the day, Ford acted less out of benevolence than out of shrewdness. He understood that workers were consumers as well as producers, and the new wage scale helped boost sales of Ford cars. It also reduced the high turnover rate in his labor force and increased worker efficiency. Roughly two-thirds of the labor force at Ford consisted of immigrants from southern and eastern Europe. By the early 1920s, Ford also employed about 5,000 African Americans, more than any other large American

Until 1924, Henry Ford had disdained national advertising for his cars. But as General Motors gained a competitive edge by making yearly changes in style and technology, Ford was forced to pay more attention to advertising. This ad was directed at "Mrs. Consumer," combining appeals to female independence and motherly duties.

corporation. Ford's mass-production system and economies of scale permitted him to progressively reduce the price of his cars, bringing them within the reach of millions of Americans. The famous Model T, thoroughly standardized and available only in black, cost just under $300 in 1924—about three months' wages for the best-paid factory workers.

By 1927, Ford had produced 15 million Model Ts. But by then, the company faced stiff competition from General Motors (GM), which had developed an effective new marketing strategy. Under the guidance of Alfred P. Sloan, GM organized into separate divisions, each of which appealed to a different market segment. Cadillac, for example, produced GM's most expensive car, which was targeted at the wealthy buyer; Chevrolet produced its least expensive model, which was targeted at working-class and lower-middle-class buyers. The GM business structure, along with its attempts to match production with demand through sophisticated market research and sales forecasting, became a widely copied model for other large American corporations. Both Ford and GM also pushed the idea of purchasing cars on credit, thus helping to make "installment buying" an underpinning of the new consumer culture.

The auto industry provided a large market for makers of steel, rubber, glass, and petroleum products. It stimulated public spending for good roads and extended the housing boom to new suburbs. Showrooms, repair shops, and gas stations appeared in thousands of communities. New small enterprises, from motels to billboard advertising to roadside diners, sprang up as motorists took to the highway. Automobiles widened the experience of millions of Americans. They made the exploration of the world outside the local community easier and more attractive. The automobile made leisure, in the sense of getting away from the routines of work and school, a more regular part of everyday life. It undoubtedly also changed the courtship practices of America's youth. Young people took advantage of the car to gain privacy and distance from their parents, and many had their first sexual experiences in automobiles.

Watch the Video

The Rise and Fall of the Automobile Economy at **www.myhistorylab.com**

Cities and Suburbs

Cars also promoted urban and suburban growth. The United States Census for 1920 was the first in American history in which the proportion of the population that lived in urban places (those with 2,500 or more people) exceeded the proportion of the population living in rural areas. More revealing of urban growth was the steady increase in the number of big cities. In 1910, there were sixty cities with more than 100,000 inhabitants; in 1920, there were sixty-eight; and by 1930, there were ninety-two. During the 1920s, New York grew by 20 percent, to

nearly 7 million, whereas Detroit, home of the auto industry, doubled its population, to nearly 2 million.

Cities promised business opportunity, good jobs, cultural richness, and personal freedom. They attracted millions of Americans, white and black, from small towns and farms, as well as immigrants from abroad. Immigrants were drawn to cities by the presence there of family and people of like background in already-established ethnic communities. In a continuation of the Great Migration that began during World War I, roughly 1.5 million African Americans from the rural South migrated to cities in search of economic opportunities during the 1920s, doubling the black populations of New York, Chicago, Detroit, and Houston.

Houston offers a good example of how the automobile shaped an urban community. In 1910, it was a sleepy railroad town with a population of about 75,000 that served the Texas Gulf coast and interior. The enormous demand for gasoline and other petroleum products helped transform the city into a busy center for oil refining. Its population soared to 300,000 by the end of the 1920s. Abundant cheap land and the absence of zoning ordinances, combined with the availability of the automobile, pushed Houston to expand horizontally rather than vertically. It became the archetypal decentralized, low-density city, sprawling miles in each direction from downtown and thoroughly dependent on automobiles and roads for its sense of community. Suburban communities grew at twice the rate of their core cities, also thanks largely to the automobile boom. Undeveloped land on the fringes of cities became valuable real estate. Grosse Pointe, near Detroit, and Elmwood Park, near Chicago, grew more than 700 percent in ten years. Long Island's Nassau County, just east of New York City, tripled in population. All the new "automobile suburbs" differed in important ways from earlier suburbs built along mass transit lines. The car allowed for a larger average lot size and, in turn, lower residential density.

The State, the Economy, and Business

Throughout the 1920s, a confident Republican Party dominated national politics, certain that it had ushered in a "new era" in American life. A new and closer relationship between the federal government and American business became the hallmark of Republican policy in both domestic and foreign affairs during the administrations of three successive Republican presidents: Warren Harding (1921–23), Calvin Coolidge (1923–29), and Herbert Hoover (1929–33). Republicans never tired of claiming that the business–government partnership their policies promoted was responsible for the nation's economic prosperity.

Harding and Coolidge

Handsome, genial, and well-spoken, Warren Harding may have looked the part of a president—but acting like one was another matter. Harding was a product of small-town Marion, Ohio, and the machine politics in his native state. Republican Party officials had made a point of keeping Senator Harding, a compromise choice, as removed from the public eye as possible in the 1920 election. They correctly saw that active campaigning could only hurt their candidate by exposing his shallowness and intellectual weakness. Harding understood his own limitations. He sadly told one visitor to the White House shortly after taking office, "I knew that this job would be too much for me."

Harding surrounded himself with a close circle of friends, the "Ohio gang," delegating to them a great deal of administrative power. The president often conducted business as if he were in the relaxed, convivial, and masculine confines of a small-town saloon. In the summer of 1923, Harding began to get wind of the scandals for which his administration is best remembered. Soon after Harding's death from a heart attack later that year, a series of congressional investigations revealed a deep pattern of corruption. Attorney General Harry M. Daugherty had received bribes from violators of the Prohibition statutes. He had also failed to investigate graft in the Veterans Bureau, where Charles R. Forbes had pocketed a large chunk of the $250 million spent on hospitals and supplies. The worst affair was the Teapot Dome scandal involving Interior Secretary Albert Fall. Fall received hundreds of thousands of dollars in payoffs when he secretly leased navy oil reserves in Teapot Dome, Wyoming, and Elk Hills, California, to two private oil developers. He eventually became the first cabinet officer ever to go to jail.

The Harding administration's legacy was not all scandal. Andrew Mellon, an influential Pittsburgh banker, served as secretary of the treasury under all three Republican presidents of the 1920s. One of the richest men in America, and a leading investor in the Aluminum Corporation of America and Gulf Oil, Mellon believed government ought to be run on the same conservative principles as a corporation. He was a leading voice for trimming the federal budget and cutting taxes on incomes, corporate profits, and inheritances. These cuts, he argued, would free up capital for new investment and, thus, promote general economic growth. Mellon's program sharply cut taxes both for higher-income brackets and for businesses. By 1926, a person with an income of a million a year paid less than a third of the income tax he or she had paid in 1921.

When Calvin Coolidge succeeded to the presidency, he seemed to most people the temperamental opposite of Harding. Born and raised in rural Vermont, elected governor of Massachusetts, and coming to national prominence only through the 1919 Boston police strike

(see Chapter 22), "Silent Cal" was the quintessential New England Yankee. Taciturn, genteel, and completely honest, Coolidge believed in the least amount of government possible. He spent only four hours a day at the office. His famous aphorism, "The business of America is business," perfectly captured the core philosophy of the Republican new era. He was in awe of wealthy men such as Andrew Mellon, and he thought them best suited to make society's key decisions.

Coolidge easily won election on his own in 1924. He benefited from the general prosperity and the contrast he provided with the disgraced Harding. Coolidge defeated little-known Democrat John W. Davis, the compromise choice of a party badly divided between its rural and urban wings. Also running was Progressive Party candidate Robert M. La Follette of Wisconsin, who mounted a reform campaign that attacked economic monopolies and called for government ownership of utilities. In his full term, Coolidge showed most interest in reducing federal spending, lowering taxes, and blocking congressional initiatives. He saw his primary function as clearing the way for American businessmen. They, after all, were the agents of the era's unprecedented prosperity.

Read the Document
Edward E. Purinton, "Big Ideas from Big Business" (1921) at **www.myhistorylab.com**

Herbert Hoover and the "Associative State"

The most influential figure of the Republican new era was Herbert Hoover, who as secretary of commerce dominated the cabinets of Harding and Coolidge before becoming president himself in 1929. A successful engineer, administrator, and politician, Hoover had earned an enviable reputation as wartime head of the U.S. Food Administration and director general of relief for Europe. He effectively embodied the belief that enlightened business, encouraged and informed by the government, would act in the public interest. In the modern industrial age, Hoover believed, the government needed only to advise private citizens' groups about what national or international polices to pursue. "Reactionaries and radicals," he wrote in *American Individualism* (1922), "would assume that all reform and human advance must come through government. They have forgotten that progress must come from the steady lift of the individual and that the measure of national idealism and progress is the quality of idealism in the individual."

Hoover thus fused a faith in old-fashioned individualism with a strong commitment to the progressive possibilities offered by efficiency and rationality. Unlike an earlier generation of Republicans, Hoover wanted not just to create a favorable climate for business but also to actively assist the business community. He spoke of creating an "associative state," in which the government would encourage voluntary cooperation among corporations, consumers, workers, farmers, and small businessmen. This became the central occupation of the Department of Commerce under Hoover's leadership. The Bureau of Standards became one of the nation's leading research centers, setting engineering standards for key American industries such as machine tools and automobiles. The bureau also helped standardize the styles, sizes, and designs of many consumer products, such as canned goods and refrigerators.

Hoover actively encouraged the creation and expansion of national trade associations. By 1929, there were about 2,000 of them. At industrial conferences called by the Commerce Department, government officials explained the advantages of mutual cooperation in figuring prices and costs and then publishing the information. The idea was to improve efficiency by reducing competition. To some, this practice violated the spirit of antitrust laws, but in the 1920s, the Justice Department's Antitrust Division took a very lax view of its responsibility. In addition, the Supreme Court consistently upheld the legality of trade associations. The government thus provided an ideal climate for the concentration of corporate wealth and power. The trend toward large corporate trusts and holding companies had been well under way since the late nineteenth century, but it accelerated in the 1920s. By 1929, the 200 largest American corporations owned almost half the total corporate wealth and about a fifth of the total national wealth. Concentration was particularly strong in manufacturing, retailing, mining, banking, and utilities.

War Debts, Reparations, Keeping the Peace

Rejection of the Treaty of Versailles and the League of Nations did not mean disengagement from the rest of the globe. The United States emerged from World War I as the strongest economic power in the world. The war transformed it from the world's leading debtor nation to its most important creditor. European governments owed the U.S. government about $10 billion in 1919. In the private sector, the war ushered in an era of expanding American investment abroad. As late as 1914, foreign investments in the United States were about $3 billion more than the total of American capital invested abroad. By 1919, that situation was reversed: America had $3 billion more invested abroad than foreigners had invested in the United States. By 1929, the surplus was $8 billion. New York replaced London as the center of international finance and capital markets. Yet America's postwar policies included a great contradiction: protectionism. The rest of the world owed the United States billions of dollars, but high tariffs on both farm products and manufactured goods made it much more difficult for debtor nations to repay by selling exports.

During the 1920s, war debts and reparations were the single most divisive issue in international economics. In France and Great Britain, which both owed the United States large amounts in war loans, many concluded that the Uncle Sam who had offered assistance during wartime was really a loan shark in disguise. In turn, many Americans viewed Europeans as ungrateful debtors. As President Coolidge acidly remarked, "They hired the money, didn't they?" In 1922, the U.S. Foreign Debt Commission negotiated an agreement with the debtor nations that called for them to repay $11.5 billion over a sixty-two-year period. But by the late 1920s, the European financial situation had become so desperate that the United States agreed to cancel a large part of these debts. Continued insistence by the United States that the Europeans pay at least a portion of the debt fed anti-American feeling in Europe and isolationism at home.

The Germans believed that war reparations, set at $33 billion by the Treaty of Versailles, not only unfairly punished the losers of the conflict but, by saddling their civilian economies with such massive debt, also deprived them of the very means to repay. In 1924, Herbert Hoover and Chicago banker Charles Dawes worked out a plan to aid the recovery of the German economy. The Dawes Plan reduced Germany's debt, stretched out the repayment period, and arranged for American bankers to lend funds to Germany. These measures helped stabilize Germany's currency and allowed it to make reparations payments to France and Great Britain. The Allies, in turn, were better able to pay their war debts to the United States.

In addition to the Dawes Plan and the American role in naval disarmament, the United States joined the league-sponsored World Court in 1926 and was represented at numerous league conferences. In 1928, with great fanfare, the United States and sixty-two other nations signed the Pact of Paris (better known as the Kellogg-Briand Pact, for the U.S. Secretary of State Frank B. Kellogg and French Foreign Minister Aristide Briand who initiated it), which grandly and naively renounced war in principle. Peace groups, such as the Woman's Peace Party and the Quaker-based Fellowship of Reconciliation, hailed the pact for formally outlawing war. Critics charged that the Kellogg-Briand Pact was essentially meaningless because it lacked powers of enforcement and relied solely on the moral force of world opinion. Within weeks of its ratification, the U.S. Congress had appropriated $250 million for new battleships.

Global Commerce and U.S. Foreign Policy

Throughout the 1920s, Secretary of State Charles Evans Hughes and other Republican leaders pursued policies designed to expand American economic activity abroad. They understood that capitalist economies must be dynamic; they must expand their markets if they were to thrive. The focus must be on friendly nations and investments that would help foreign citizens buy American goods. Toward this end, Republican leaders urged close cooperation between bankers and the government as a strategy for expanding American investment and economic influence abroad. Throughout the 1920s, investment bankers routinely submitted loan projects to Hughes and Secretary of Commerce Hoover for informal approval, thus reinforcing the close ties between business investment and foreign policy.

American oil, autos, farm machinery, and electrical equipment supplied a growing world market. Much of this expansion took place through the establishment of branch plants overseas by American companies. America's overall direct investment abroad increased from $3.8 billion in 1919 to $7.5 billion in 1929. Leading the American domination of the world market were General Electric, Ford, and Monsanto Chemical. American oil companies, with the support of the State Department, also challenged Great Britain's dominance in the oil fields of the Middle East and Latin America, forming powerful cartels with English firms.

The strategy of maximum freedom for private enterprise, backed by limited government advice and assistance, significantly boosted the power and profits of American overseas investors. But in Central and Latin America, in particular, aggressive U.S. investment also fostered chronically underdeveloped economies, dependent on a few staple crops (sugar, coffee, cocoa, bananas) grown for export. American investments in Latin America more than doubled between 1924 and 1929, from $1.5 billion to over $3.5 billion. A large part of this money went to taking over vital mineral resources, such as Chile's copper and Venezuela's oil. The growing wealth and power of U.S. companies made it more difficult for these nations to grow their own food or diversify their economies. U.S. economic dominance in the hemisphere also hampered the growth of democratic politics by favoring autocratic, military regimes that could be counted on to protect U.S. investments.

Weakened Agriculture, Ailing Industries

Amid prosperity and progress, there were large pockets of the country that lagged behind. Advances in real income and improvements in the standard of living for workers and farmers were uneven at best. In 1920, some 32 million Americans still lived on farms, out of a total population of 106 million. Yet during the 1920s, the farm sector failed to share in the general prosperity. The years 1914–19 had been a kind of golden age for the nation's farmers. Increased wartime demand, along with the devastation of much of European agriculture, had led to record-high prices for many crops. When the war ended, however, American farmers began to suffer from a chronic worldwide surplus of such farm staples as cotton, hogs, and corn.

In the South, farmers' dependency on "King Cotton" deepened, as the region lagged further behind the rest of the nation in both agricultural diversity and standard of living. Cotton acreage expanded, as large and heavily mechanized farms opened up new land in Oklahoma, west Texas, and the Mississippi-Yazoo delta. In most of the South, from North Carolina to east Texas, small one- and two-mule cotton farms, most under fifty acres, still dominated the countryside. With few large urban centers and inadequate transportation, even those southern farmers who had access to capital found it

extremely difficult to find reliable markets for vegetables, fruit, poultry, or dairy products. The number of white tenant farmers increased by 200,000 during the 1920s, while black tenantry declined slightly as a result of the Great Migration. Some 700,000 southern farmers, roughly half white and half black, still labored as sharecroppers. Modern conveniences such as electricity, indoor plumbing, automobiles, and phonographs remained far beyond the reach of the great majority of southern farmers. Widespread rural poverty, poor diet, and little access to capital meant the world of southern agriculture had changed very little since the days of the populist revolt in the 1890s.

The most important initiatives for federal farm relief were the McNary-Haugen bills, a series of complicated measures designed to prop up and stabilize farm prices. The basic idea, borrowed from the old populist proposals of the 1890s, was for the government to purchase farm surpluses and either store them until prices rose or sell them on the world market. President Calvin Coolidge viewed these measures as unwarranted federal interference in the economy and vetoed the McNary-Haugen Farm Relief bill of 1927 when it finally passed Congress. American farmers hoping to export produce abroad also suffered from the high tariffs imposed by European countries trying to protect their own devastated economies.

To be sure, some farmers thrived. Improved transportation and chain supermarkets allowed for a wider and more regular distribution of such foods as oranges, lemons, and fresh green vegetables. Citrus, dairy, and truck farmers in particular profited from the growing importance of national markets. Wheat production jumped more than 300 percent during the 1920s. Across the plains of Kansas, Nebraska, Colorado, Oklahoma, and Texas, wheat farmers brought the methods of industrial capitalism to the land. They hitched disc plows and combined harvester-threshers to gasoline-powered tractors, tearing up millions of acres of grassland to create a vast wheat factory. With prices averaging above $1 per bushel over the decade, mechanized farming created a new class of large-scale wheat entrepreneurs on the plains. But when the disastrous dust storms of the 1930s rolled across the grassless plains, the long-range environmental impact of destroying so much native vegetation became evident.

Overall, per capita farm income remained well below what it had been in 1919, and the gap between farm and nonfarm income widened. By 1929, the average income per person on farms was $223, compared with $870 for nonfarm workers. By the end of the decade, hundreds of thousands had quit farming altogether for jobs in mills and factories. And fewer farmers owned their land. In 1930, 42 percent of all farmers were tenants, compared with 37 percent in 1919.

Large sectors of American industry also failed to share in the decade's general prosperity. As oil and natural gas gained in importance, America's coal mines became a less important source of energy. A combination of shrinking demand, new mining technology, and a series of losing strikes reduced the coal labor force by one-quarter. The United Mine Workers, perhaps the strongest AFL union in 1920, with 500,000 members, had shrunk to 75,000 by 1928. Economic hardship was widespread in many mining communities dependent on coal, particularly Appalachia and the southern Midwest. Those miners who did work earned lower hourly wages.

In textiles, shrinking demand and overcapacity (too many factories) were chronic problems. The women's fashions of the 1920s generally required less material than had earlier fashions, and competition from synthetic fibers such as rayon depressed demand for cotton textiles. To improve profit margins, textile manufacturers in New England and other parts of the Northeast began a long-range shift of operations to the South, where nonunion shops and substandard wages became the rule. Older New England manufacturing centers such as Lawrence, Lowell, Nashua, Manchester, and Fall River were hard hit by this shift. The center of the American textile industry shifted permanently to the Piedmont region of North and South Carolina. By 1933, factories there employed nearly 70 percent of the workers in the industry.

The New Mass Culture

New communications media reshaped American culture in the 1920s, and much of the new mass culture was exported to the rest of the economically developed world. The phrase "Roaring Twenties" captures the explosion of image- and sound-making machinery that came to dominate so much of American life. Movies, radio, new kinds of journalism, the recording industry, and a more sophisticated advertising industry were deeply connected with the new culture of consumption. They also encouraged the parallel emergence of celebrity as a defining element in modern life. As technologies of mass impression, the media established national standards and norms for much of our culture—habit, dress, language, sounds, social behavior. Cultural traditionalists both in America and abroad found these new norms deeply disturbing, and the 1920s saw powerful collisions between newer and older values. To be sure, most working-class families had only limited access to the world of mass consumption—and many had only limited interest in it. But the new mass culture helped redefine the ideal of "the good life" and made the images, if not the substance, of it available to a national community.

Movie-Made America

The early movie industry, centered in New York and a few other big cities, had made moviegoing a regular habit for millions of Americans, especially immigrants and the working class. They flocked to cheap, storefront theaters, called nickelodeons, to watch short westerns, slapstick comedies, melodramas, and travelogues. By 1914, there were about 18,000 "movie houses" showing motion pictures, with more than 7 million daily admissions and $300 million in annual receipts. With the shift of the industry westward to Hollywood, movies entered a new phase of business expansion.

Large studios such as Paramount, Fox, Metro-Goldwyn-Mayer (MGM), Universal, and Warner Brothers dominated the business with longer and more expensively produced movies—feature films. These companies were founded and controlled by immigrants from Europe, all of whom had a talent for discovering and exploiting changes in popular tastes. Adolph Zukor, the Hungarian-born head of Paramount, had been a furrier in New York City. Warsaw-born Samuel Goldwyn, a founder of MGM, had been a glove salesman. William Fox, of Fox Pictures, born in Hungary and raised in New York, began as a garment cutter in Brooklyn. Most of the immigrant moguls had started in the business by buying or managing small movie theaters before beginning to produce films.

Each studio combined the three functions of production, distribution, and exhibition, and each controlled hundreds of movie theaters around the country. The era of silent films ended when Warner Brothers scored a huge hit in 1927 with *The Jazz Singer*, starring Al Jolson, which successfully introduced sound. New genres—musicals, gangster films, and screwball comedies—soon became popular. To maintain their hold on European markets, the major studios established production facilities abroad that used foreign actors for the "dubbing" of American films into other languages. The higher costs associated with "talkies" also increased the studios' reliance on Wall Street investors and banks for working capital.

At the heart of Hollywood's success was the star system and the accompanying cult of celebrity, both of which help define American popular culture to this day (see Seeing History). Stars became vital to the fantasy lives of millions of fans. For many in the audience, there was only a vague line separating the on-screen and off-screen adventures of the stars. Studio publicity, fan magazines, and gossip columns reinforced this ambiguity. Film idols, with their mansions, cars, parties, and private escapades, became the national experts on leisure and consumption. Their movies generally emphasized sexual themes and celebrated youth, athleticism, and the liberating power of consumer goods. Young Americans in particular looked to movies to learn how to dress, wear their hair, talk, or kiss.

Many Americans, however, particularly in rural areas and small towns, worried about Hollywood's impact on traditional sexual morality. They attacked the permissiveness associated with Hollywood life, and many states created censorship boards to screen movies before allowing them to be shown in theaters. To counter growing calls for government censorship, Hollywood's studios came up with a plan

Creating Celebrity

A common definition for "celebrity" is one who is famous for being famous. Although politics, the arts, science, and the military have produced famous people for centuries, the celebrity is a twentieth-century phenomenon, one closely linked to the emergence of modern forms of mass media. In the 1920s, Hollywood's "star system," along with tabloid newspapers and the new profession of public relations, created the modern celebrity. Film producers were at first wary of identifying screen actors by name, but they soon discovered that promoting popular leading actors would boost the box office for their movies. The use of "close-ups" in movies and the fact that screen images were literally larger than life distinguished the images of film actors from, say, stage performers or opera singers.

Fans identified with their favorites in contradictory ways. Stars like Charlie Chaplin and Mary Pickford were like royalty, somehow beyond the realm of ordinary mortals. Yet audiences were also curious about the stars' private lives. Film studios took advantage of this curiosity by carefully controlling the public image of their stars through press releases, planted stories in newspapers, and carefully managed interviews and public appearances. Theda Bara, for example, one of the biggest female stars of the 1920s, was best known for her "vamp" roles depicting sexually aggressive and exotic women. According to the publicity from Fox Pictures, she was of Egyptian background, offspring of "a sheik and a princess, given in mystic marriage to the Sphinx, fought over by nomadic tribesmen, clairvoyant, and insatiably lustful." In truth, Theodosia Goodman was born and raised in Cincinnati, the daughter of middle-class Jewish parents, and became a stage actress after two years of college. By the 1920s, film stars were essentially studio–owned-and-operated commodities, requiring enormous capital investment. And the new media universe of newspapers, magazines, radio, movies, and advertising was held together by the public fascination with, and the commercial power of, celebrities.

• **What visual themes strike you as most powerful in the accompanying images? How do they compare—in contrasts and parallels—to celebrity images of today?**

• **Why do you think male stars such as Valentino and Fairbanks were so often portrayed as exotic foreigners? How did these posters convey a more open and accepting attitude toward sexuality?**

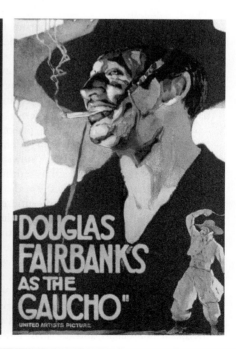

to censor themselves. In 1922, they hired Will Hays to head the Motion Picture Producers and Distributors of America. Hays was just what the immigrant moguls needed. An Indiana Republican, elder in the Presbyterian Church, and former postmaster general under President Harding, he personified midwestern Protestant respectability. As the movie industry's czar, Hays lobbied against censorship laws, wrote pamphlets defending the movie business, and began setting guidelines for what could and could not be depicted on the screen. He insisted that movies be treated like any other industrial enterprise, because he understood the relationship between Hollywood's success and the growth of the nation's consumer culture.

Radio Broadcasting

In the fall of 1920, Westinghouse executive Harry P. Davis noticed that amateur broadcasts from the garage of an employee had attracted attention in the local Pittsburgh press. A department store advertised radio sets capable of picking up these "wireless concerts." Davis converted this amateur station to a stronger one at the Westinghouse main plant. Beginning with the presidential election returns that November, station KDKA offered regular nightly broadcasts that were probably heard by only a few hundred people. Radio broadcasting, begun as a service for selling cheap radio sets left over from World War I, would soon sweep the nation.

Before KDKA, wireless technology had been of interest only to the military, the telephone industry, and a few thousand "ham" (amateur) operators who enjoyed communicating with each other. The "radio mania" of the early 1920s was a response to the new possibilities offered by broadcasting. By 1923, nearly 600 stations had been licensed by the Department of Commerce, and about 600,000 Americans had bought radios. Early programs included live popular music, the playing of phonograph records, talks by college professors, church services, and news and weather reports. For millions of Americans, especially in rural areas and small towns, radio provided a new and exciting link to the larger national community of consumption.

Who would pay for radio programs? In the early 1920s, owners and operators of radio stations included radio equipment manufacturers, newspapers, department stores, state universities, cities, ethnic societies, labor unions, and churches. But by the end of the decade, commercial (or "toll") broadcasting emerged as the answer. The dominant corporations in the industry—General Electric, Westinghouse, Radio Corporation of America (RCA), and American Telephone and Telegraph (AT&T)—settled on the idea that advertisers would foot the bill for radio. Millions of listeners might be the consumers of radio shows, but sponsors were to be the customers. Sponsors advertised directly or indirectly to the mass audience through such shows as the *Eveready Hour*, the *Ipana Troubadours*, and the *Taystee Loafers*. AT&T leased its nationwide system of telephone wires to allow the linking of many stations into powerful radio networks, such as the National Broadcasting Company (NBC) in 1926 and the Columbia Broadcasting System (CBS) in 1928. The rise of network radio squeezed out many of the stations and programs aimed at ethnic communities or broadcast in languages other than English, thus promoting a more homogenized culture.

NBC and CBS led the way in creating popular radio programs that relied heavily on older cultural forms. The variety show, hosted by vaudeville comedians, became network radio's first important format. Radio's first truly national hit, *The Amos 'n' Andy Show* (1928), was a direct descendant of nineteenth-century "blackface" minstrel entertainment. Radio did more than any previous medium to publicize and commercialize once-isolated forms of American music such as country-and-western, blues, and jazz. Broadcasts of baseball and college football games proved especially popular. In 1930, some 600 stations were broadcasting to more than 12 million homes with radios, or roughly 40 percent of American families. By that time, all the elements that characterize the present American system of broadcasting—regular daily programming paid for and produced by commercial advertisers, national networks carrying shows across the nation, and mass ownership of receiver sets in American homes—were in place.

Radio broadcasting created a national community of listeners, just as motion pictures created one of viewers. Like movies, it also transcended national boundaries. Broadcasting had a powerful hemispheric impact. In both Canada and Mexico, governments established national broadcasting systems to bolster cultural and political nationalism. Yet American shows—and advertising—continued to dominate Canadian airwaves. Large private Mexican radio stations were often started in partnership with American corporations such as RCA, as a way to create demand for receiving sets. Language barriers limited the direct impact of U.S. broadcasts, but American advertisers became the backbone of commercial radio in Mexico. Radio broadcasting thus significantly amplified the influence of American commercialism throughout the hemisphere.

New Forms of Journalism

A new kind of newspaper, the tabloid, became popular in the postwar years. The *New York Daily News*, founded in 1919 by Joseph M. Patterson, was the first to develop the tabloid style. Its folded-in-half page size made it convenient to read on buses or subways. The *Daily News* devoted much of its space to photographs and other illustrations. With a terse, lively reporting style that emphasized sex, scandal, and sports, *Daily News* circulation reached 400,000 in 1922 and 1.3 million by 1929. This success spawned a host of imitators in New York and elsewhere. New papers like the *Chicago Times* and the *Los Angeles Daily News* brought the tabloid style to cities across America, while some older papers, such as the *Denver*

Rocky Mountain News, also adopted the new format. The circulation of existing dailies was little affected. Tabloids had instead discovered an audience of millions who had never read newspapers before. Most of these new readers were poorly educated working-class city dwellers, many of whom were immigrants or children of immigrants.

The tabloid's most popular new feature was the gossip column, invented by Walter Winchell, an obscure former vaudevillian who began writing his column "Your Broadway and Mine" for the *New York Daily Graphic* in 1924. Winchell described the secret lives of public figures with a distinctive, rapid-fire, slangy style that made the reader feel like an insider. He chronicled the connections among high society, show business stars, powerful politicians, and the underworld. By the end of the decade, scores of newspapers "syndicated" Winchell's column, making him the most widely read—and imitated—journalist in America.

Journalism followed the larger economic trend toward consolidation and merger. Newspaper chains like Hearst, Gannett, and Scripps-Howard flourished during the 1920s, producing a more standardized kind of journalism that could be found anywhere in the country. There was a sizable increase in the number of these chains and in the percentage of total daily circulation that was chain-owned. By the early 1930s, the Hearst organization alone controlled twenty-six dailies in eighteen cities, accounting for 14 percent of the nation's newspaper circulation. One of every four Sunday papers sold in America was owned by the Hearst group.

Advertising Modernity

A thriving advertising industry both reflected and encouraged the growing importance of consumer goods in American life. Previously, advertising had been confined mostly to staid newspapers and magazines and offered little

A 1919 advertisement for Lucky Strike cigarettes featured the image of actress Billie Burke. Paid celebrity endorsements for consumer goods became a common practice in the post WWI years. Tobacco companies were among the most aggressive purveyors of this new advertising strategy.

more than basic product information. The most creative advertising
was usually for dubious products,
such as patent medicines. The suc-
cessful efforts of the government's Committee on Public
Information, set up to "sell" World War I to Americans, suggested that new techniques using modern communication
media could convince people to buy a wide range of goods
and services. As a profession, advertising reached a higher
level of respectability, sophistication, and economic power
in American life during the 1920s.

The larger ad agencies moved toward a more scientific approach by sponsoring market research and welcoming the language of psychology to their profession.
Behavioral psychologists like John B. Watson argued that
all human behavior could be shaped (or manipulated) by
careful study and application of stimulus and response.
Watson left his post at Harvard for an executive position
at the J. Walter Thompson advertising agency. The writings of Viennese psychoanalyst Sigmund Freud, especially his emphasis on the irrational in human behavior
and the power of the sex drive, were widely popularized
in American magazines and universities. Advertisers
began focusing on the needs, desires, and anxieties of the
consumer, rather than on the qualities of the product.
"There are certain things that most people believe,"
noted one ad agency executive in 1927. "The moment
your copy is linked to one of those beliefs, more than
half your battle is won."

Ad agencies and their clients invested extraordinary
amounts of time, energy, and money trying to discover
and, to some extent, shape those beliefs. Leading agencies
such as Lord and Thomas in Chicago and J. Walter
Thompson in New York combined knowledge gained
from market research and consumer surveys with carefully
prepared ad copy and graphics to sell their clients' wares.
High-powered ad campaigns made new products like
Fleischmann's Yeast, Kleenex, and Listerine household
words across the country. Above all, advertising celebrated
consumption itself as a positive good. In this sense, the
new advertising ethic was a therapeutic one, promising
that products would contribute to the buyer's physical,
psychic, or emotional well-being.

The Phonograph and the Recording Industry

Like radio and movies, the phonograph came into its
own in the 1920s as a popular entertainment medium.
Originally marketed in the 1890s, early phonographs
used wax cylinders that could both record and replay.
But the sound quality was poor, and the cylinders were
difficult to handle. The convenient permanently grooved
disc recordings introduced around World War I were
eagerly snapped up by the public, even though the discs
could not be used to make recordings at home. The success of records transformed the popular music business,
displacing both cylinders and sheet music as the major
source of music in the home.

Dance crazes such as the fox trot, tango, and grizzly
bear, done to complex ragtime and Latin rhythms,
boosted the record business tremendously. Dixieland
jazz, which recorded well, also captured the public's
fancy in the early 1920s, and records provided the music
for new popular dances like the Charleston and the
black bottom. In 1921, more than 200 companies produced some 2 million records, and annual record sales
exceeded $100 million.

Record sales declined toward the end of the decade,
due to competition from radio. But in a broader cultural
sense, records continued to transform American popular
culture. Record companies discovered lucrative regional
and ethnic markets for country music, which appealed
primarily to white Southerners, and blues and jazz,
which appealed primarily to African Americans. Country
musicians like the Carter Family and Jimmie Rodgers,
and blues singers like Blind Lemon Jefferson, Ma Rainey,
and Bessie Smith, had their performances put on records
for the first time. Their records sold mainly in specialized
"hillbilly" and "race" markets. Yet they were also played
over the radio, and millions of Americans began to hear
musical styles and performers who previously had been
isolated from the general population. Jazz records by such
African American artists as Louis Armstrong and Duke
Ellington found a wide audience overseas as well, and
jazz emerged as a uniquely American cultural form with
broad appeal around the globe. The combination of records
and radio started an extraordinary cross-fertilization of
American musical styles that continues to this day.

Sports and Celebrity

During the 1920s, spectator sports enjoyed an unprecedented growth in popularity and profitability. As radio,
newspapers, magazines, and newsreels exhaustively documented their exploits, athletes took their place alongside
movie stars in defining a new culture of celebrity. Big-
time sports, like the movies, entered a new corporate
phase. Yet it was the athletes themselves, performing extraordinary feats on the field and transcending their often-
humble origins, who attracted millions of new fans. The
image of the modern athlete—rich, famous, glamorous,
and often a rebel against social convention—came into its
own during the decade.

Major league baseball had more fans than any other
sport, and its greatest star, George Herman "Babe" Ruth,
embodied the new celebrity athlete. Aided by the new
"live ball," Ruth's prodigious home-run hitting completely changed baseball strategy and attracted legions of
new fans to the sport. Ruth was a larger-than-life character off the field as well. In New York, media capital of the
nation, newspapers and magazines chronicled his enormous appetites—for food, whiskey, expensive cars, and

This 1926 publicity photo shows Louis Armstrong and his Hot Five just after they made the historic recordings that established Armstrong as the most influential jazz soloist of the era. (L to R: Armstrong, Johnny St. Cyr, Johnny Dodds, Kid Ory, Lil Hardin Armstrong). Armstrong also had a huge impact as a singer, and his popularity extended to all racial groups.

big-city nightlife. He hobnobbed with politicians, movie stars, and gangsters, and he regularly visited sick children in hospitals. Ruth became the first athlete avidly sought by manufacturers for celebrity endorsement of their products. Ruth's impact helped the game recover from the serious public relations disaster of the "Black Sox" scandal. In 1919, eight members of the poorly paid Chicago White Sox had become involved in a scheme to "throw" the World Series in exchange for large sums of money from gamblers. Although they were acquitted in the courts, baseball commissioner Judge Kenesaw Mountain Landis, looking to remove any taint of gambling from the sport, banned the accused players for life.

Baseball attendance exploded during the 1920s, reaching a one-year total of 10 million in 1929. The attendance boom prompted urban newspapers to increase their baseball coverage, and the larger dailies featured separate sports sections. The best sportswriters, such as Grantland Rice, Heywood Broun, and Ring Lardner,

brought a poetic sensibility to descriptions of the games and their stars. William K. Wrigley, owner of the Chicago Cubs, discovered that by letting local radio stations broadcast his team's games, the club could win new fans, especially among housewives.

Among those excluded from major league baseball were African Americans, who had been banned from the game by an 1890s "gentleman's agreement" among owners. During the 1920s, black baseball players and entrepreneurs developed a world of their own, with several professional and semiprofessional leagues catering to expanding African American communities in cities. The largest of these was the Negro National League, organized in 1920 by Andrew "Rube" Foster. Black ballclubs also played exhibitions against, and frequently defeated, teams of white major leaguers. African Americans had their own baseball heroes, such as Josh Gibson and Satchel Paige, who no doubt would have been stars in the major leagues if not for racial exclusion.

Babe Ruth, baseball's biggest star, shakes hands with President Warren G. Harding at the opening day of the brand new Yankee Stadium, Bronx, New York, April 4, 1923. The new celebrity culture of the 1920s routinely brought together public figures from the worlds of politics, sports, show business, and even organized crime.

The new media configuration of the 1920s created heroes in other sports as well. Radio broadcasts and increased journalistic coverage made college football a big-time sport. Teams like Notre Dame, located in sleepy South Bend, Indiana, but coached by the colorful Knute Rockne, could gain a wide national following. The center of college football shifted from the old elite schools of the Ivy League to the big universities of the Midwest and Pacific Coast, where most of the players were second-generation Irish, Italians, and Slavs. Athletes such as boxers Jack Dempsey and Gene Tunney, tennis players Bill Tilden and Helen Wills, golfer Bobby Jones, and swimmers Gertrude Ederle and Johnny Weissmuller became household names who brought legions of new fans to their sports.

A New Morality?

Movie stars, radio personalities, sports heroes, and popular musicians became the elite figures in a new culture of celebrity defined by the mass media. They were the model for achievement in the new age. Great events and abstract issues were made real through movie close-ups, radio interviews, and tabloid photos. The new media relentlessly created and disseminated images that are still familiar

today: Babe Ruth trotting around the bases after hitting a home run; the wild celebrations that greeted Charles Lindbergh after he completed the first solo transatlantic airplane flight in 1927; the smiling gangster Al Capone, bantering with reporters who transformed his criminal exploits into important news events.

Images do not tell the whole story, however. Consider one of the most enduring images of the "Roaring Twenties," the flapper. She was usually portrayed on-screen, in novels, and in the press as a young, sexually aggressive woman with bobbed hair, rouged cheeks, and short skirt. She loved to dance to jazz music, enjoyed smoking cigarettes, and drank bootleg liquor in cabarets and dance halls. She could also be competitive, assertive, and a good pal. As writer Zelda Fitzgerald put it in 1924: "I think a woman gets more happiness out of being gay, light-hearted, unconventional, mistress of her own fate. . . . I want [my daughter] to be a flapper, because flappers are brave and gay and beautiful."

Was the flapper a genuine representative of the 1920s? Did she embody the "new morality" that was so widely discussed and chronicled in the media of the day? The flapper certainly did exist, but she was neither as new nor as widespread a phenomenon as the image would suggest.

A woman in a man's shirt and necktie wears a pair of Paul Jones knickers in this 1922 advertisement. Her boyish, almost androgynous look reflects one way that notions of the "new woman" intersected with the worlds of fashion and advertising.

The delight in sensuality, personal pleasure, and rhythmically complex dance and music had long been key elements of subcultures on the fringes of middle-class society: bohemian enclaves, communities of political radicals, African American ghettos, working-class dance halls. In the 1920s, these activities became normative for a growing number of white middle-class Americans, including women. Jazz, sexual experimentation, heavy makeup, and cigarette smoking spread to college campuses.

Several sources, most of them rooted in earlier years, can be found for the increased sexual openness of the 1920s. Troops in the armed forces during World War I had been exposed to government-sponsored sex education. New psychological and social theories like those of Havelock Ellis, Ellen Key, and Sigmund Freud stressed the central role of sexuality in human experience, maintaining that sex is a positive, healthy impulse that, if repressed, could damage mental and emotional health. The pioneering efforts of Margaret Sanger in educating women about birth control had begun before World War I (see Chapter 21). In the 1920s, Sanger campaigned vigorously—through her journal *Birth Control Review*, in books, and on speaking tours—to make contraception freely available to all women.

Read the Document

History Bookshelf: Margaret Sanger, Woman and the New Race (1920) at **www.myhistorylab.com**

Sociological surveys also suggested that genuine changes in sexual behavior began in the prewar years among both married and single women. Katherine Bement Davis's pioneering study of 2,200 middle-class women, carried out in 1918 and published in 1929, revealed that most used contraceptives and described sexual relations in positive terms. A 1938 survey of 777 middle-class females found that among those born between 1890 and 1900, 74 percent were virgins before marriage; for those born after 1910, the figure dropped to 32 percent. Women born after the turn of the century were twice as likely to have had premarital sex as those born before 1900. The critical change took place in the generation that came of age in the late teens and early twenties. By the 1920s, male and female "morals" were becoming more alike.

Read the Document

Eleanor R. Wembridge, "Petting and the Campus" (1925) at **www.myhistorylab.com**

The emergence of homosexual subcultures also reflected the newly permissive atmosphere of the postwar years. Although such subcultures had been a part of big city life since at least the 1890s, they had been largely confined to working-class saloons associated with the urban underworld. By the 1920s, the word "homosexual" had gained currency as a scientific term for describing romantic love between women or between men, and middle-class enclaves of self-identified homosexuals took root in cities like New York, Chicago, and San Francisco. Often organized around speakeasies, private clubs, tearooms, and masquerade balls, these venues also attracted heterosexual tourists and those looking to experiment with their sexuality, as well as homosexuals, for whom they served as important social centers. Even if these enclaves provided some sense of community and safety for homosexuals, the repressive shadow of the larger culture was never far away. Psychologists of the era, with Freud in the lead, condemned "perversion" as a mental illness and counseled the need for a "cure."

Modernity and Traditionalism

One measure of the profound cultural changes of the 1920s was the hostility and opposition expressed toward them by large sectors of the American public. Deep and persistent tensions, with ethnic, racial, and geographical overtones, characterized much of the decade's politics. The postwar Red Scare had given strength to the forces of antiradicalism in politics and traditionalism in culture. Resentments over the growing power of urban culture, on full display in Hollywood movies, modern advertising, and over the airwaves, were very strong in rural and small-town America. Several trends and mass movements reflected this anger and the longing for a less complicated past.

Prohibition

The Eighteenth Amendment, banning the manufacture, sale, and transportation of alcoholic beverages, took effect in January 1920. Prohibition was the culmination of a long campaign that associated drinking with the degradation of working-class family life and the worst evils of urban politics. Supporters, a coalition of women's temperance groups, middle-class progressives, and rural Protestants, hailed the new law as "a noble experiment." It became clear rather quickly that enforcing the new law would be extremely difficult. The Volstead Act of 1919 established a federal Prohibition Bureau to enforce the Eighteenth Amendment. Yet the bureau was severely understaffed with only about 1,500 agents to police the entire country.

The public demand for alcohol, especially in the big cities, led to widespread lawbreaking. Drinking was such a routine part of life for so many Americans that "bootlegging" quickly became a big business. Illegal stills and breweries, as well as liquor smuggled in from Canada, supplied the needs of those Americans who continued to drink. Nearly every town and city had at least one "speakeasy," where people could drink and enjoy music and other entertainment. Local law enforcement personnel, especially in the cities, were easily bribed to overlook these illegal establishments. By the early 1920s, many eastern states no longer made even a token effort at enforcing the law.

Liquor continued to be illegal, so Prohibition gave an enormous boost to violent organized crime. The profits to be made in the illegal liquor trade dwarfed the traditional sources of criminal income—gambling, prostitution, and

robbery. The pattern of organized crime in the 1920s closely resembled the larger trends in American business: smaller operations gave way to larger and more complex combinations. Successful organized crime figures, like Chicago's Al "Scarface" Capone, became celebrities in their own right and received heavy coverage in the mass media. Capone himself shrewdly used the rhetoric of the Republican new era to defend himself: "Everybody calls me a racketeer. I call myself a businessman. When I sell liquor it's bootlegging. When my patrons serve it on a silver tray on Lake Shore Drive, it's hospitality."

Organized crime, assisted by its huge profits from liquor, also made significant inroads into legitimate businesses, labor unions, and city government, especially in large cities. By the time Congress and the states ratified the Twenty-First Amendment in 1933, repealing Prohibition, organized crime was a permanent feature of American life. Prohibition did, in fact, significantly reduce per capita consumption of alcohol. In 1910, annual per capita consumption stood at 2.6 gallons; in 1934, the figure was less than a gallon. Yet among young people, especially college students, the excitement associated with speakeasies and lawbreaking contributed to increased drinking during Prohibition.

Immigration Restriction

Sentiment for restricting immigration, growing since the late nineteenth century, reached its peak immediately after World War I. Barriers against Asian immigrants were already in place with the Chinese Exclusion Act of 1882 and the so-called Gentleman's Agreement with Japan in 1907. The movement to curb European immigration reflected the growing preponderance after 1890 of "new immigrants"—those from southern and eastern Europe—over the immigrants from northern and western Europe, who had predominated before 1890. Between 1891 and 1920, roughly 10.5 million immigrants arrived from southern and eastern Europe. This was nearly twice as many as arrived during the same years from northern and western Europe (see Figure 23.3).

The "new immigrants" were mostly Catholic and Jewish, and they were darker-skinned than the "old immigrants." To many old-stock Americans, they seemed more exotic, more foreign, and less willing and able to assimilate the nation's political and cultural values. They were also relatively poorer, more physically isolated in the nation's cities, and less politically strong than earlier immigrants. In the 1890s, the anti-Catholic American Protective Association called for a curb on immigration, and by exploiting the economic depression of that decade, it reached a membership of 2.5 million. In 1894, a group of prominent Harvard graduates, including Senator Henry Cabot Lodge (R-Massachusetts) and John Fiske, founded the Immigration Restriction League, providing an influential forum for the fears of the nation's elite. The

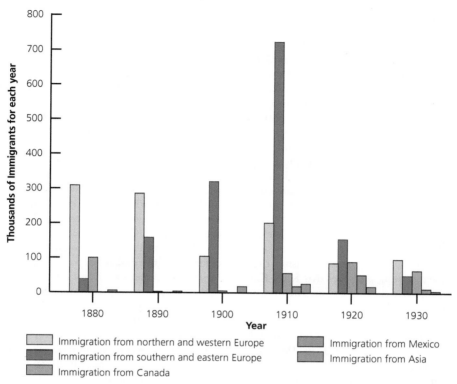

FIGURE 23.3 Immigration Trends to the United States by Continent/Region, 1880–1930

SOURCE: Reprinted with the permission of Cambridge University Press.

league used newer scientific arguments, based on a flawed application of Darwinian evolutionary theory and genetics, to support its call for immigration restriction. The new immigration, Lodge argued, "is bringing to the country people whom it is very difficult to assimilate and who do not promise well for the standard of civilization in the United States."

Theories of scientific racism, which had become more popular in the early 1900s, reinforced anti-immigrant bias and distorted genetic theory to argue that America was committing "race suicide." Eugenicists, who enjoyed considerable vogue in those years, held that heredity determined almost all of a person's capacities and that genetic inferiority predisposed people to crime and poverty. Such pseudoscientific thinking sought to explain historical and social development solely as a function of "racial" differences.

Against this background, the war and its aftermath provided the final push for the restriction of European immigration. The "100 percent American" fervor of the war years fueled nativist passions. So did the Red Scare of 1919–20, which linked foreigners with Bolshevism and radicalism of all kinds in the popular mindset. The postwar

depression coincided with the resumption of massive immigration, bringing much hostile comment on the relationship between rising unemployment and the new influx of foreigners. The American Federation of Labor proposed stopping all immigration for two years. Sensational press coverage of organized crime figures, many of them Italian or Jewish, also played a part.

In 1921, Congress passed the Immigration Act, setting a maximum of 357,000 new immigrants each year. Quotas limited annual immigration from any European country to 3 percent of the number of its natives counted in the 1910 U.S. Census. But restrictionists complained that the new law still allowed too many southern and eastern Europeans in, especially since the northern and western Europeans did not fill their quotas. The Reed-Johnson National Origins Act of 1924 revised the quotas to 2 percent of the number of foreign-born counted for each nationality in the census for 1890, when far fewer southern or eastern Europeans were present in the United States. The maximum total allowed each year was also cut to 164,000. A *Los Angeles Times* headline expressed both the fundamental premise

Read the Document

Immigration Law (1924) at **www.myhistorylab.com**

and flawed science of the new law: "Nordic Victory Is Seen in Drastic Restrictions."

The 1924 National Origins Act in effect limited immigration to white Europeans eligible for immigration by country of origin (nationality), while it divided the rest of the world into "colored races" (black, mulatto, Chinese, and Indian) who were ineligible for immigration. These new restrictions dovetailed with two recent Supreme Court decisions, *Ozawa* v. *U.S.* (1922) and *U.S.* v. *Thind* (1923), in which the Court held that Japanese and Asian Indians were unassimilable aliens and racially ineligible for U.S. citizenship. By the 1920s, American law had thus created the peculiar new racial category of "Asian" and codified the principle of racial exclusion in immigration and naturalization law.

The Ku Klux Klan

If immigration restriction was resurgent nativism's most significant legislative expression, a revived Ku Klux Klan (KKK) was its most effective mass movement. The original Klan had been formed in the Reconstruction South as an instrument of white racial terror against newly freed slaves (see Chapter 17). It had died out in the 1870s. The new Klan, born in Stone Mountain, Georgia, in 1915, was inspired by D. W. Griffith's racist spectacle *The Birth of a Nation*, a film released in that year depicting the original

KKK as a heroic organization. The new Klan patterned itself on the secret rituals and antiblack hostility of its predecessor and, until 1920, it was limited to a few local chapters in Georgia and Alabama.

When Hiram W. Evans, a dentist from Dallas, became imperial wizard of the Klan in 1922, he transformed the organization. Evans hired professional fund-raisers and publicists and directed an effective recruiting scheme that paid a commission to sponsors of new members. The Klan advocated "100 percent Americanism" and "the faithful maintenance of White Supremacy." It staunchly supported the enforcement of Prohibition, and it attacked birth control and Darwinism. The new Klan made a special target of the Roman Catholic Church, labeling it a hostile and dangerous alien power and claiming that their allegiance to the Pope made Catholics unfit for citizenship.

The new Klan also presented itself as the righteous defender of the embattled traditional values of small-town Protestant America. Ironically, to build its membership rolls, it relied heavily on the publicity, public relations, and business techniques associated with modern urban culture. By 1924, the new Klan counted more than 3 million members across the country. Its slogan, "Native, White, Protestant Supremacy," proved especially attractive in the Midwest and South, including

Read the Document "Creed of Klanswomen" (1924) at www.myhistorylab.com

Women members of the Ku Klux Klan in New Castle, Indiana, August 1, 1923. The revived Klan was a powerful presence in scores of American communities during the early 1920s, especially among native-born white Protestants, who feared cultural and political change. In addition to preaching "100 percent Americanism," local Klan chapters also served a social function for members and their families.

many cities. Klansmen boycotted businesses, threatened families, and sometimes resorted to violence—public whippings, arson, and lynching—against their chosen enemies. The Klan's targets sometimes included white Protestants accused of sexual promiscuity, blasphemy, or drunkenness, but most victims were African Americans, Catholics, and Jews. Support for Prohibition enforcement probably united Klansmen more than any single issue.

On another level, the Klan was a popular social movement, a defensive bastion against forces of modernity. Many members were more attracted by the Klan's spectacular social events and its efforts to reinvigorate community life than by its attacks on those considered outsiders. Perhaps a half-million women joined the Women of the Ku Klux Klan, and women constituted nearly half of the Klan membership in some states. Klanswomen drew on family and community traditions, such as church suppers, kin reunions, and gossip campaigns, to defend themselves and their families against what they saw as corruption and immorality. The Klan's power was strong in many communities precisely because it fit so comfortably into the everyday life of white Protestants.

At its height, the Klan also became a powerful force in Democratic Party politics, and it had a strong presence among delegates to the 1924 Democratic National Convention. The Klan began to fade in 1925, when its Indiana leader, Grand Dragon David C. Stephenson, became involved in a sordid personal affair. With one of its most famous leaders disgraced and in jail, the new Klan began to lose members and influence.

Fundamentalism in Religion

Paralleling political nativism in the 1920s was the growth of religious fundamentalism. In many eastern Protestant churches, congregations focused less on religious practice and worship than on progressive social and reform activities in the larger community. By the early 1920s, a fundamentalist revival had developed in reaction to these tendencies, particularly in the South and Midwest. The fundamentalists emphasized a literal reading of the Bible, and they rejected the tenets of modern science as inconsistent with the revealed word of God. Fundamentalist publications and Bible colleges flourished, particularly among southern Baptists.

One special target of the fundamentalists was the theory of evolution, first set forth by Charles Darwin in his landmark work *The Origin of Species* (1859). Using fossil evidence, evolutionary theory suggested that, over time, many species had become extinct and that new ones had emerged through the process of natural selection. These ideas directly contradicted the account of one fixed creation in the Book of Genesis. Although most Protestant clergymen had long since found ways of blending the scientific theory with their theology, fundamentalists launched an attack on the teaching of

Darwinism in schools and universities. By 1925, five southern state legislatures had passed laws restricting the teaching of evolution.

A young biology teacher, John T. Scopes, deliberately broke the Tennessee law prohibiting the teaching of Darwinism in 1925, in order to challenge it in court. The resulting trial that summer in Dayton, a small town near Chattanooga, drew international attention to the controversy. Scopes's defense team included attorneys from the American Civil Liberties Union and Clarence Darrow, the most famous trial lawyer in America. The prosecution was led by William Jennings Bryan, the old Democratic standard-bearer who had thrown himself into the fundamentalist and antievolutionist cause. Held in a circus atmosphere in sweltering heat, the trial attracted thousands of reporters and partisans to Dayton and was broadcast across the nation by the radio (see Communities in Conflict).

The Scopes "monkey trial"—so called because fundamentalists trivialized Darwin's theory into a claim that humans were descended from monkeys—became one of the most publicized and definitive moments of the decade. Scopes's guilt was never in question. The jury convicted him quickly, although the verdict was later thrown out on a technicality. The struggle over the teaching of evolution continued in an uneasy stalemate; state statutes were not repealed, but prosecutions for teaching evolution ceased. Fundamentalism, a religious creed and a cultural defense against the uncertainties of modern life, continued to have a strong appeal for millions of Americans.

Promises Postponed

The prosperity of the 1920s was unevenly distributed and enjoyed across America. Older progressive reform movements that had pointed out inequities faltered in the conservative political climate. But the new era did inspire a range of critics deeply troubled by unfulfilled promises in American life. Feminists sought to redefine their movement in the wake of the suffrage victory. Mexican immigration to the United States shot up, and in the burgeoning Mexican American communities of the Southwest and Midwest, economic and social conditions were very difficult. African Americans, bitterly disappointed by their treatment during and after the Great War, turned to new political and cultural strategies. Many American intellectuals found themselves deeply alienated from the temper and direction of modern American society.

Feminism in Transition

The achievement of the suffrage removed the central issue that had given cohesion to the disparate forces of female reform activism. In addition, female activists of all persuasions found themselves swimming against a national tide

The Scopes Trial in Dayton, Tennessee

The 1925 trial of John T. Scopes, a Tennessee high school science teacher arrested for teaching evolution, captured national attention. Scopes's guilt was never challenged, even by his defense team; the state's antievolution statute itself was on trial. Tennessee's case was argued by William Jennings Bryan, the aging stalwart of Populism, three-time Democratic presidential nominee, and hero to the growing legion of rural and small-town evangelical Christians. The defense, financed by the American Civil Liberties Union, was led by Chicago attorney Clarence Darrow, a religious skeptic and a labor and criminal defense lawyer long associated with radical causes.

The most electrifying moment of the trial came when Darrow put Bryan on the stand as an expert witness on the Bible. Although the judge expunged the testimony from the record, the wide press coverage proved embarrassing to Bryan and perhaps unfairly cemented his reputation as an antimodern rube. Bryan's criticism of Darwinian theory was in fact more sophisticated than his critics acknowledged. Bryan in particular objected to the use of evolutionary doctrine as scientific justification for social Darwinism, such as when eugenicists argued for selectively breeding human beings. After Bryan's testimony, Darrow, wanting to have the last word, asked the judge to instruct the jury to bring in a guilty verdict, thus making closing arguments unnecessary. The first excerpt is from the closing argument Bryan never had a chance to give. When he died three days after the trial, H. L. Mencken, the reporter for the *Baltimore Sun* and Bryan's most caustic critic, wrote a final assessment of "The Great Commoner," from which the second document is excerpted.

The clash between Bryan and Mencken embodied many of the profound cultural tensions that defined the 1920s. Today's conflicts over the teaching of "creationism" and "intelligent design," disputes over the authority of state and local boards to set curricula or choose textbooks, and the relevance of First Amendment protections in schools all echo the sharp clashes heard in 1925.

William Jennings Bryan's Undelivered Speech to the Jury

Science is a magnificent force, but it is not a teacher of morals. It can perfect machinery, but it adds no moral restraints to protect society from the misuse of the machine. It can also build gigantic intellectual ships, but it constructs no moral rudders for the control of storm tossed human vessels. It not only fails to supply the spiritual element needed but some of its unproven hypotheses rob the ship of its compass and thus endanger its cargo. In war, science has proven itself an evil genius; it has made war more terrible than it ever was before. Man used to be content to slaughter his fellowmen on a single plane—the earth's surface. Science has taught him to go down into the water and shoot up from below and to go up into the clouds and shoot down from above, thus making the battlefield three times as bloody as it was before; but science does not teach brotherly love. Science has made war so hellish that civilization was about to commit suicide; and now we are told that newly discovered instruments of destruction will make the cruelties of the late war

> "The case has [become] a battle-royal between unbelief . . . and the defenders of the Christian faith. . . ."

seem trivial in comparison with the cruelties of wars that may come in the future. If civilization is to be saved from the wreckage threatened by intelligence not consecrated by love, it must be saved by the moral code of the meek and lowly Nazarene. His teachings, and His teachings, alone, can solve the problems that vex the heart and perplex the world. . . .

It is for the jury to determine whether this attack upon the Christian religion shall be permitted in the public schools of Tennessee by teachers employed by the state and paid out of the public treasury. This case is no longer local, the defendant ceases to play an important part. The case has assumed the proportions of a battle-royal between unbelief that attempts to speak through so-called science and the defenders of the Christian faith, speaking through the legislators of Tennessee. It is again a choice between God and Baal; it is also a renewal of the issue in Pilate's court. . . .

Again force and love meet face to face, and the question, "What shall I do with Jesus?" must be answered. A bloody, brutal doctrine—Evolution—demands, as the rabble did nineteen hundred years ago, that

- **How does Bryan link his critique of science and scientific thinking to recent world events?**
- **Why, in Bryan's view, does public school education require a Christian component?**
- **From Mencken's perspective, how did Bryan exploit evangelical Christianity for political purposes?**
- **Do you think his view has merit?**

He be crucified. That cannot be the answer of this jury representing a Christian state and sworn to uphold the laws of Tennessee. Your answer will be heard throughout the world; it is eagerly awaited by a praying multitude. If the law is nullified, there will be rejoicing wherever God is repudiated, the savior scoffed at and the Bible ridiculed. Every unbeliever of every kind and degree will be happy. If, on the other hand, the law is upheld and the religion of the school children protected, millions of Christians will call you blessed and, with hearts full of gratitude to God, will sing again that grand old song of triumph: "Faith of our fathers, living still, In spite of dungeon, fire and sword; O how our hearts beat high with joy Whene'er we hear that glorious word—Faith of our fathers—Holy faith; We will be true to thee till death!"

SOURCE: *Bryan's Last Speech: Undelivered Speech to the Jury in the Scopes Trial.* Oklahoma City: Sunlight Publishing Society, 1925. http://www.law.umkc.edu/faculty/projects/ftrials/scopes/scopes.htm.

H. L. Mencken in the *Baltimore Evening Sun* (July 27, 1925)

One day it dawned on me that Bryan, after all, was an evangelical Christian only by sort of afterthought—that his career in this world, and the glories thereof, had actually come to an end before he ever began whooping for Genesis. So I came to this conclusion: that what really moved him was a lust for revenge. The men of the cities had destroyed him and made a mock of him; now he would lead the yokels against them. Various facts clicked into the theory, and I hold it still. The hatred in the old man's burning eyes was not for the enemies of God; it was for the enemies of Bryan.

Thus he fought his last fight, eager only for blood. It quickly became frenzied and preposterous, and after that pathetic. All sense departed from him. He bit right and left, like a dog with rabies. He descended to demagogy so dreadful that his very associates blushed. His one yearning was to keep his yokels heated up—to lead his forlorn mob against the foe. That foe, alas, refused to be alarmed. It insisted upon seeing the battle as a comedy. Even Darrow, who knew better, occasionally yielded to the prevailing spirit. Finally, he lured poor Bryan into a folly almost incredible.

I allude to his astounding argument against the notion that man is a mammal. I am glad I heard it, for otherwise I'd never believe it. There stood the man who had been thrice a candidate for the Presidency of the Republic—and once, I believe, elected—there he stood in the glare of the world, uttering stuff that a boy of eight would laugh at! The artful Darrow led him on: he repeated it, ranted for it, bellowed it in his cracked voice. A tragedy, indeed! He came into life a hero, a Galahad, in bright and shining armor. Now he was passing out a pathetic fool.

But what of his life? Did he accomplish any useful thing? Was he, in his day, of any dignity as a man, and of any value to his fellow-men? I doubt it. Bryan, at his best, was simply a magnificent job-seeker. The issues that he bawled about usually meant nothing to him. He was ready to abandon them whenever he could make votes by doing so, and to take up new ones at a moment's notice. For years he evaded Prohibition as dangerous; then he embraced it as profitable. At the Democratic National Convention last year he was on both sides, and distrusted by both. In his last great battle there was only a baleful and ridiculous malignancy. If he was pathetic, he was also disgusting.

Bryan was a vulgar and common man, a cad undiluted. He was ignorant, bigoted, self-seeking, blatant and dishonest. His career brought him into contact with the first men of his time; he preferred the company of rustic ignoramuses. It was hard to believe, watching him at Dayton, that he had traveled, that he had been received in civilized societies, that he had been a high officer of state. He seemed only a poor clod like those around him, deluded by a childish theology, full of an almost pathological hatred of all learning, all human dignity, all beauty, all fine and noble things. He was a peasant come home to the dung-pile. Imagine a gentleman, and you have imagined everything that he was not.

"The hatred in the old man's burning eyes was not for the enemies of God; it was for the enemies of Bryan."

SOURCE: http://www.etsu.edu/cas/history/docs/menckenken.htm.

of hostility to political idealism. During the 1920s, the women's movement split into two main wings over a fundamental disagreement about female identity. Should activists stress women's differences from men—their vulnerability and the double burden of work and family—and continue to press for protective legislation, such as laws that limited the length of the workweek for women? Or should they emphasize the ways that women were like men—sharing similar aspirations—and push for full legal and civil equality?

In 1920, the National American Woman Suffrage Association reorganized itself as the League of Women Voters. The league represented the historical mainstream of the suffrage movement, those who believed that the vote for women would bring a nurturing sensibility and a reform vision to American politics. This view was rooted in politicized domesticity, the notion that women had a special role to play in bettering society: improving conditions for working women, abolishing child labor, humanizing prisons and mental hospitals, and serving the urban poor. Most league members continued working in a variety of reform organizations, and the league itself concentrated on educating the new female electorate, encouraging women to run for office, and supporting laws for the protection of women and children.

A newer, smaller, and more militant group was the National Woman's Party (NWP), founded in 1916 by combative suffragist Alice Paul. The NWP downplayed the significance of suffrage and argued that women were still subordinate to men in every facet of life. The NWP opposed protective legislation for women, claiming that such laws reinforced sex stereotyping and prevented women from competing with men in many fields. Largely representing the interests of professional and business women, the NWP focused on passage of a brief Equal Rights Amendment (ERA) to the Constitution, introduced in Congress in 1923: "Men and women shall have equal rights throughout the United States and every place subject to its jurisdiction."

Many of the older generation of women reformers opposed the ERA as elitist, arguing that far more women benefited from protective laws than were injured by them. Mary Anderson, director of the Women's Bureau in the Department of Labor, argued that "women who are wage earners, with one job in the factory and another in the home, have little time and energy left to carry on the fight to better their economic status. They need the help of other women and they need labor laws." ERA supporters countered that maximum-hours laws or laws prohibiting women from night work prevented women from getting many lucrative jobs. M. Carey Thomas, president of Bryn Mawr College, defended the ERA with language reminiscent of laissez-faire: "How much better by one blow to do away with discriminating against women in work,

salaries, promotion and opportunities to compete with men in a fair field with no favour on either side!"

Most women's groups did not think there was a "fair field." Positions solidified. The League of Women Voters, the National Consumers' League, and the Women's Trade Union League opposed the ERA. ERA supporters generally stressed individualism, competition, and the abstract language of "equality" and "rights." ERA opponents emphasized the grim reality of industrial exploitation and the concentration of women workers in low-paying jobs in which they did not compete directly with men. ERA advocates dreamed of the labor market as it might be, one in which women might have the widest opportunity. Anti-ERA forces looked at the labor market as it was, insisting it was more important to protect women from existing exploitation. The NWP campaign failed to get the ERA passed by Congress, but the debates it sparked would be echoed during the feminist movement of the 1970s, when the ERA became a central political goal of a resurgent feminism.

A small number of professional women made real gains in the fields of real estate, banking, and journalism. The press regularly announced new "firsts" for women, such as Amelia Earhart's 1928 airplane flight across the Atlantic. Studies showed, however, that most women were clustered in the low-paying areas of typing, stenography, bookkeeping, cashiering, and sales clerking. Men still dominated in the higher-paid and managerial white-collar occupations.

The most significant, if limited, victory for feminist reformers was the 1921 Sheppard-Towner Act, which established the first federally funded health care program, providing matching funds for states to set up prenatal and child health care centers. These centers also provided public health nurses for house calls. Although hailed as a genuine reform breakthrough, especially for women in rural and isolated communities, the act aroused much opposition. Many Republicans, including President Harding, had supported it as a way to curry favor with newly enfranchised women voters. Their support faded when it became clear that there was little "gender gap" in voting patterns. The NWP disliked Sheppard-Towner for its assumption that all women were mothers. Birth control advocates such as Margaret Sanger complained that contraception was not part of the program. The American Medical Association (AMA) objected to government-sponsored health care and to nurses who functioned outside the supervision of physicians. By 1929, largely as a result of intense AMA lobbying, Congress cut off funds for the program.

Mexican Immigration

While immigration restriction sharply cut the flow of new arrivals from Europe, the 1920s also brought a dramatic influx of Mexicans to the United States. Mexican immigration, which was not included in the immigration laws of 1921 and 1924, had picked up substantially after the outbreak of the Mexican Revolution in 1911, when politically inspired violence and economic hardships provided incentives to cross the border to *El Norte*. According to the U.S. Immigration Service, an estimated 459,000 Mexicans entered the United States between 1921 and 1930, more than double the number for the previous decade (see Figure 23.4).

The primary pull was the tremendous agricultural expansion occurring in the American Southwest. Irrigation and large-scale agribusiness had begun transforming California's Imperial and San Joaquin Valleys from arid desert into lucrative fruit and vegetable fields. Cotton pickers were needed in the vast plantations of Lower Rio Grande Valley in Texas and the Salt River Valley in Arizona. The sugar beet fields of Michigan, Minnesota, and Colorado attracted many Mexican farmworkers. American industry had also begun recruiting Mexican workers, first to fill wartime needs and later to fill the gap left by the decline in European immigration.

The new Mexican immigration appeared more permanent than previous waves—that is, more and more newcomers stayed—and, like other immigrants, more were attracted to cities. This was partly the unintended consequence of new policies designed to make immigration more difficult. As the Border Patrol (established in 1924) made border crossing more difficult (through head taxes, visa fees, literacy tests, and document checks), what

had once been a two-way process for many Mexicans became a one-way migration. Permanent communities of Mexicans in the United States grew rapidly. By 1930, San Antonio's Mexican community accounted for roughly 80,000 people out of a total population of a quarter million. Around 100,000 Mexicans lived in central and east Los Angeles, including 55,000 who attended city schools. Substantial Mexican communities also flourished in midwestern cities such as Chicago, Detroit, Kansas City, and Gary. Many of the immigrants alternated between agricultural and factory jobs, depending on the seasonal availability of work.

Racism and local patterns of residential segregation confined most Mexicans to barrios. Housing conditions were generally poor, particularly for recent arrivals who were forced to live in rude shacks without running water or electricity. Disease and infant mortality rates were much higher than average, and most Mexicans worked at low-paying, unskilled jobs and received inadequate health care. Legal restrictions passed by states and cities made it difficult for Mexicans to enter teaching, legal, and other professions. Mexicans were routinely banned from local public works projects as well. Many felt a deep ambivalence about applying for American citizenship. Loyalty to the Old Country was strong, and many cherished dreams of returning to live out their days in Mexico.

Nativist efforts to limit Mexican immigration were thwarted by the lobbying of powerful agribusiness interests. The Los Angeles Chamber of Commerce typically employed racist stereotyping in its arguments to keep the borders open. Mexicans, it claimed, were naturally suited for agriculture, "due to their crouching and bending habits, . . . while the white is physically unable to adapt himself to them."

Mutual aid societies—*mutualistas*—became key social and political institutions in the Mexican communities of the Southwest and Midwest. They provided death benefits and widows' pensions for members and also served as centers of resistance to civil rights violations and discrimination. In 1928, the Federation of Mexican Workers Unions formed in response to a large farm labor strike in the Imperial Valley of California. A group of middle-class Mexican professionals in Texas organized the League of United Latin American Citizens (LULAC) in 1929. The founding of these organizations marked only the beginnings of a long struggle to bring economic, social, and racial equality to Mexican Americans.

The "New Negro"

The Great Migration spurred by World War I showed no signs of letting up during the 1920s, and African American communities in northern cities grew rapidly. By far the largest and most influential of these communities was New York City's Harlem. Previously a residential suburb,

FIGURE 23.4 Mexican Immigration to the United States in the 1920s Many Mexican migrants avoided official border-crossing stations so they would not have to pay visa fees. Thus, these official figures probably underestimated the true size of the decade's Mexican migration. As the economy contracted with the onset of the Great Depression, immigration from Mexico dropped off sharply.

Mexican workers gathered outside a San Antonio labor bureau in 1924. These employment agencies contracted Mexicans to work for Texas farmers, railroads, and construction companies. Note the three Anglo men in front (wearing suits and ties), who probably owned and operated this agency. During the 1920s, San Antonio's Mexican population doubled from roughly 40,000 to over 80,000, making it the second largest *colonia* in *El Norte* after Los Angeles.

Harlem began attracting middle-class African Americans in the prewar years. After the war, heavy black migration from the South and the Caribbean encouraged real estate speculators and landlords to remake Harlem as an exclusively black neighborhood (see Map 23.1).

Harlem emerged as the demographic and cultural capital of black America, but its appeal transcended national borders, as mass migration from the Caribbean helped reshape the community. Between 1900 and 1930, some 300,000 West Indians emigrated to the United States, roughly half of whom settled in New York City. By the late 1920s, about one-quarter of Harlem's population had been born in Jamaica, Barbados, Trinidad, the Bahamas, and other parts of the Caribbean. Some of the leading cultural, business, and political figures of the era—poet Claude McKay, newspaper publisher P. M. H. Savory, labor organizer Hubert Harrison, black nationalist Marcus Garvey—had roots in the West Indies. Most black Caribbean migrants came from societies where class differences mattered more than racial ones, and many refused to accept racial bigotry without protest. A large number also carried with them entrepreneurial experience that contributed to their success in running small businesses. Intraracial tensions and resentment between American-born blacks and an increasingly visible West Indian population were reflections of Harlem's transformation into a hemispheric center for black people.

Harlem was also headquarters to Marcus Garvey's Universal Negro Improvement Association. An ambitious Jamaican immigrant who had moved to Harlem in 1916, Garvey created a mass movement that stressed black economic self-determination and unity among the black communities of the United States, the Caribbean, and Africa. With colorful parades and rallies and a central message affirming pride in black identity, Garvey attracted as many as a million members worldwide. Garvey's best-publicized project was the Black Star Line, a black-owned and -operated fleet of ships that would link people of African descent around the world. But insufficient capital and serious financial mismanagement resulted in the spectacular failure of the enterprise. In 1923, Garvey was found guilty of mail fraud in his fund-raising efforts; he later went to jail and was subsequently deported to England. Despite the disgrace, Harlem's largest newspaper, the *Amsterdam News*, explained Garvey's continuing appeal to African Americans: "In a world where black is despised, he taught them that black is beautiful. He taught them to admire and praise black things and black people."

The demand for housing in this restricted geographical area led to skyrocketing rents, but most Harlemites

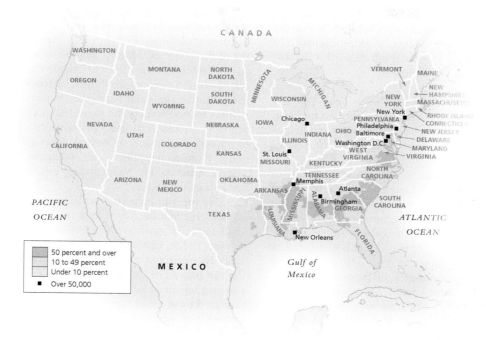

MAP 23.1 Black Population, 1920 Although the Great Migration had drawn hundreds of thousands of African Americans to the urban North, the southern states of the former Confederacy still remained the center of the African American population in 1920.

held low-wage jobs. This combination produced extremely overcrowded apartments, unsanitary conditions, and the rapid deterioration of housing stock. Disease and death rates were abnormally high. Harlem was well on its way to becoming a slum. Yet Harlem also boasted a large middle-class population and supported a wide array of churches, theaters, newspapers and journals, and black-owned businesses. It became a mecca, as poet and essayist James Weldon Johnson wrote, for "the curious, the adventurous, the enterprising, the ambitious, and the talented of the entire Negro world."

Harlem became the political and intellectual center for what writer Alain Locke called the "New Negro." Locke was referring to a new spirit in the work of black writers and intellectuals, an optimistic faith that encouraged African Americans to develop and celebrate their distinctive culture, firmly rooted in the history, folk culture, and experiences of African American people. This faith was the common denominator uniting the disparate figures associated with the Harlem Renaissance. The assertion of cultural independence resonated in the poetry of Langston Hughes and Claude McKay, the novels of Zora Neale Hurston and Jessie Fauset, the essays of Countee Cullen and James Weldon Johnson, the acting of Paul Robeson, and the blues singing of Bessie Smith.

There was a political side to the "New Negro" as well. The newly militant spirit that black veterans had brought home from World War I matured and found a variety of expressions in the Harlem of the 1920s. New leaders and movements began to appear alongside established organizations like the National Association for the Advancement of Colored People. A. Philip Randolph began a long career as a labor leader, socialist, and civil rights activist in these years, editing the *Messenger* and organizing the Brotherhood of Sleeping Car Porters.

Through the new mass media of radio and phonograph records, millions of Americans now listened and danced to a distinctively African American music, as jazz began to enter the cultural mainstream. Jazz found wildly enthusiastic fans in European capitals like Berlin and Paris, and noted classical composers such as Maurice Ravel and Igor Stravinsky treated it as a serious art form. The best jazz bands of the day, led by artists such as Duke Ellington, Fletcher Henderson, Cab Calloway, and Louis Armstrong, often had their performances broadcast live from such Harlem venues as the Cotton Club and Small's Paradise. These clubs themselves were rigidly segregated, however. Black dancers, singers, and musicians provided the entertainment, but no African Americans were allowed in the audience. Chronicled in novels and newspapers, Harlem became a potent symbol to white

America of the ultimate good time. Yet the average Harlemite never saw the inside of a nightclub. For the vast majority of Harlem residents, working menial jobs for low wages and forced to pay high rents, the day-to-day reality was depressingly different.

Alienated Intellectuals

War, Prohibition, growing corporate power, and the deep currents of cultural intolerance troubled many intellectuals in the 1920s. Some felt so alienated from the United States that they left to live abroad. In the early 1920s, Gertrude Stein, an American expatriate writer living in Paris, told the young novelist Ernest Hemingway: "All of you young people who served in the war, you are a lost generation." The phrase "a lost generation" was widely adopted as a label for American writers, artists, and intellectuals of the postwar era. Yet it is difficult to generalize about so diverse a community. For one thing, living abroad attracted only a handful of American writers. Alienation and disillusion with American life were prominent subjects in the literature and thought of the 1920s, but artists and thinkers developed these themes in very different ways.

The mass slaughter of World War I provoked revulsion and a deep cynicism about the heroic and moralistic portrayal of war so popular in the nineteenth century. Novelists Ernest Hemingway and John Dos Passos, who both served at the front as ambulance drivers, depicted the war and its aftermath in world-weary and unsentimental tones. The search for personal moral codes that would allow one to endure life with dignity and authenticity was at the center of Hemingway's fiction. In the taut, spare language of *The Sun Also Rises* (1926) and *A Farewell to Arms* (1929), he questioned idealism, abstractions, and large meanings. As Jake Barnes, the wounded war hero of *The Sun Also Rises* explained, "I did not care what it was all about. All I wanted to know was how to live it."

Hemingway and F. Scott Fitzgerald were the most influential novelists of the era. Fitzgerald joined the army during World War I but did not serve overseas. His

Read the Document

History Bookshelf: F. Scott Fitzgerald, This Side of Paradise *(1920)* at **www.myhistorylab.com**

work celebrated the youthful vitality of the "Jazz Age" (a phrase he coined) but was also deeply distrustful of the promises of American prosperity and politics. His first novel, *This Side of Paradise* (1920), won a wide readership around the country with its exuberant portrait of a "new generation," "dedicated more than the last to the fear of poverty and the worship of success; grown up to find all Gods dead, all wars fought, all faiths in man shaken." Fitzgerald's finest work, *The Great Gatsby* (1925), written in the south of France, depicted the glamorous parties of the wealthy, while evoking the tragic limits of material success.

At home, many American writers engaged in sharp attacks on small-town America and what they viewed as its provincial values. Essayist H. L. Mencken, caustic editor of the *American Mercury*, heaped scorn on fundamentalists, Prohibition, and nativists, while ridiculing what he called the "American booboisie." Mencken understood the power of the small town and despaired of reforming politics. Fiction writers also skewered small-town America, achieving commercial and critical success in the process. Sherwood Anderson's *Winesburg, Ohio* (1919) offered a spare, laconic, pessimistic, yet compassionate, view of Middle America. He had a lasting influence on younger novelists of the 1920s.

The most popular and acclaimed writer of the time was novelist Sinclair Lewis. In a series of novels satirizing small-town life, such as *Main Street* (1920) and especially *Babbitt* (1922), Lewis affectionately mocked his characters. His treatment of the central character in *Babbitt*—George Babbitt of Zenith—also had a strong element of self-mockery, because Lewis could offer no alternative set of values to Babbitt's crass self-promotion, hunger for success, and craving for social acceptance. In 1930, Lewis became the first American author to win the Nobel Prize for literature.

Read the Document

History Bookshelf: Sinclair Lewis, Babbitt *(1922)* at **www.myhistorylab.com**

In the aftermath of the postwar Red Scare, American radicalism found itself on the defensive throughout the 1920s. But one *cause célèbre* did attract a great deal of support from intellectuals. In 1921, two Italian American immigrants, Nicola Sacco and Bartolomeo Vanzetti, were tried and convicted for murder in the course of robbing a shoe factory in South Braintree, Massachusetts.

Read the Document

Nicola Sacco and Bartolomeo Vanzetti, "Court Statements" (1927) at **www.myhistorylab.com**

Neither Sacco, a shoemaker, nor Vanzetti, a fish peddler, had criminal records, but both had long been active in militant anarchist circles, labor organizing, and antiwar agitation. Their trial took place amidst an intense atmosphere of nativist and antiradical feeling, and both the judge and prosecuting attorney engaged in clearly prejudicial conduct toward the defendants. A six-year struggle to save Sacco and Vanzetti following the trial failed, despite attracting support from a broad range of liberal intellectuals, including Harvard law professor and future Supreme Court justice Felix Frankfurter. The two men were finally executed in 1927, and for many years, their case would remain a powerful symbol of how the criminal justice system could be tainted by political bias and anti-immigrant fervor.

Another side of intellectual alienation was expressed by writers critical of industrial progress and the new mass culture. The most important of these were a group of poets and scholars centered in Vanderbilt University in Nashville, Tennessee, collectively known as the Fugitives.

They included Allen Tate, John Crowe Ransom, Donald Davidson, and Robert Penn Warren, all of whom invoked traditional authority, respect for the past, and older agrarian ways as ideals to live by. The Fugitives attacked industrialism and materialism as modern-day ills. Self-conscious Southerners, they looked to the ante-bellum plantation-based society as a model for a community based on benevolence toward dependents (such as black people and women) and respect for the land. Their book of essays, *I'll Take My Stand* (1930), was a collective manifesto of their ideas.

The Election of 1928

The presidential election of 1928 served as a kind of national referendum on the Republican new era. It also revealed just how important ethnic and cultural differences had become in defining American politics. The contest reflected many of the deepest tensions and conflicts in American society in the 1920s: native-born versus immigrant; Protestant versus Catholic; Prohibition versus legal drinking; small-town life versus the cosmopolitan city; fundamentalism versus modernism; traditional sources of culture versus the new mass media (see Map 23.2).

See the Map

African American Population, 1910 and 1950 at www.myhistorylab.com

The 1928 campaign featured two politicians who represented profoundly different sides of American life. Al Smith, the Democratic nominee for president, was a pure product of New York City's Lower East Side. Smith came from a background that included Irish, German, and Italian ancestry, and he was raised as a Roman Catholic. He rose through the political ranks of New York's Tammany Hall machine. A personable man with a deep sympathy for poor and working-class people, Smith served four terms as governor of New York, pushing through an array of laws reforming factory conditions, housing, and welfare programs. Two of his closest advisers were the progressives Frances Perkins and Belle Moskowitz. Smith thus fused older-style machine politics with the newer reform emphasis on state intervention to solve social problems.

Herbert Hoover easily won the Republican nomination after Calvin Coolidge announced he would not run for reelection. Hoover epitomized the successful and forward-looking American. An engineer and self-made millionaire, he offered a unique combination of experience in humanitarian war relief, administrative efficiency, and probusiness policies. Above all, Hoover stood for a commitment to voluntarism and individualism as the best method for advancing the public welfare. He was one of the best-known men in America and promised to continue the Republican control of national politics.

Smith himself quickly became the central issue of the campaign. His sharp New York accent, jarring to many

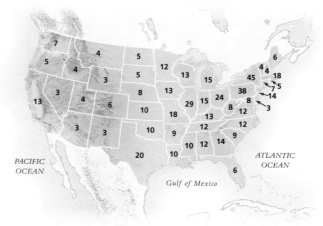

	Electoral Vote (%)	Popular Vote (%)
HERBERT HOOVER (Republican)	444 (82)	21,391,993 (58.2)
Alfred E. Smith (Democrat)	87 (17)	15,016,169 (40.9)
Norman Thomas (Socialist)	—	267,835 (0.7)
Other parties (Socialist Labor, Prohibition)	—	62,890 (0.2)

MAP 23.2 The Election of 1928 Although Al Smith managed to carry the nation's twelve largest cities, Herbert Hoover's victory in 1928 was one of the largest popular and electoral landslides in the nation's history.

Americans who heard it over the radio, marked him clearly as a man of the city. So did his brown derby and fashionable suits, as well as his promise to work for the repeal of Prohibition. As the first Roman Catholic nominee of a major party, Smith also drew a torrent of anti-Catholic bigotry, especially in the South and Midwest. Bishop James Cannon, head of the Southern Methodist Episcopal Church, insisted that "no subject of the Pope" should be permitted to occupy the White House. For his part, Smith ran a largely conservative race. He appointed John Raskob, a Republican vice president of General Motors, to manage his campaign and tried to outdo Hoover in his praise for business. He avoided economic issues such as the unevenness of the prosperity, the plight of farmers, or the growing unemployment. Democrats remained regionally divided over Prohibition, Smith's religion, and the widening split between rural and urban values. Hoover did not have to do much, other than take credit for the continued prosperity.

Hoover polled 21 million votes to Smith's 15 million, and swept the Electoral College 444 to 87, including New York State. Even the solid South, reliably Democratic since the Civil War, gave five states to Hoover—a clear reflection

Clifford K. Berryman's 1928 political cartoon interpreted that year's presidential contest along sectional lines. It depicted the two major presidential contenders as each setting off to campaign in the regions where their support was weakest. For Democrat Al Smith, that meant the West, and for Republican Herbert Hoover, the East.

of the ethnocultural split in the party. Yet the election offered important clues to the future of the Democrats. Smith was more successful in the big cities of the North and East than any Democrat in modern times. He outpolled Hoover in the aggregate vote of the nation's twelve largest cities and carried six of them, thus pointing the way to the Democrats' future dominance with urban, northeastern, and ethnic voters.

Conclusion

America's big cities, if not dominant politically, now defined the nation's cultural and economic life as never before. With Hollywood movies leading the way, the new mass media brought cosmopolitan entertainment and values to the remotest small communities. The culture of celebrity knew no geographic boundaries. New consumer durable goods associated with mass-production techniques—automobiles, radios, telephones, household appliances—were manufactured largely in cities. The advertising and public relations companies that sang their praises were also distinctly urban enterprises. Even with the curtailing of European immigration, big cities attracted a kaleidoscopic variety of migrants: white people from small towns and farms, African Americans from the rural South, Mexicans from across the border, and intellectuals and professionals looking to make their mark.

CHRONOLOGY

1920	Prohibition takes effect	**1925**	Scopes trial pits religious fundamentalism against modernity
	Warren G. Harding is elected president		
	Station KDKA in Pittsburgh goes on the air		F. Scott Fitzgerald publishes *The Great Gatsby*
	Census reports that urban population is greater than rural population for the first time	**1926**	National Broadcasting Company establishes first national radio network
1921	First immigration quotas are established by Congress	**1927**	McNary-Haugen Farm Relief bill finally passed by Congress but is vetoed by President Coolidge as unwarranted federal interference in the economy
	Sheppard-Towner Act establishes first federally funded health care program		Warner Brothers produces *The Jazz Singer*, the first feature-length motion picture with sound
1923	Equal Rights Amendment is first introduced in Congress		Charles Lindbergh makes first solo flight across the Atlantic Ocean
	Harding dies in office; Calvin Coolidge becomes president	**1928**	Kellogg-Briand Pact renounces war
1924	Ku Klux Klan is at height of its influence		Herbert Hoover defeats Al Smith for the presidency
	Dawes Plan for war reparations stabilizes European economies	**1929**	Robert and Helen Lynd publish their classic community study, *Middletown*
	Reed-Johnson Immigration Act tightens quotas established in 1921		

Many Americans, of course, remained deeply suspicious of postwar cultural and economic trends. Yet the partisans of Prohibition, members of the Ku Klux Klan, and religious fundamentalists usually found themselves on the defensive against what they viewed as alien cultural and economic forces centered in the cities. Large sectors of the population did not share in the era's prosperity. But the large numbers who did—or at least had a taste of good times—ensured Republican political dominance throughout the decade. Thus, America in the 1920s balanced dizzying change in the cultural and economic realms with conservative politics. The reform crusades that attracted millions during the progressive era were a distant memory. Political activism was no match for the new pleasures promised by technology and prosperity.

Review Questions

I. Describe the impact of the "second industrial revolution" on American business, workers, and consumers. Which technological and economic changes had the biggest impact on American society?

2. Analyze the uneven distribution of the 1920s' economic prosperity. Which Americans gained the most, and which were largely left out?

3. How did an expanding mass culture change the contours of everyday life in the decade following World War I? What role did new technologies of mass communication play in shaping these changes? What connections can you draw between the "culture of consumption" then and today?

4. What were the key policies and goals articulated by Republican political leaders of the 1920s? How did they apply these to both domestic and foreign affairs?

5. How did some Americans resist the rapid changes taking place in the post–World War I world? What cultural and political strategies did they employ?

6. Discuss the 1928 election as a mirror of the divisions in American society.

Recommended Reading

Roger Daniels, *Guarding the Golden Door: American Immigration Policy and Immigrants Since 1882* (2002). A comprehensive overview by a pioneering scholar in the field, with special emphasis on how racism and ethnocentrism have shaped American immigration policy.

Victoria De Grazia, *Irresistible Empire: America's Advance through Twentieth Century Europe* (2005). A sophisticated analysis of how and why American commercial culture made such strong inroads into postwar Europe.

Lynn Dumenil, *The Modern Temper: America in the 1920s* (1995). An excellent synthesis emphasizing the ambivalence that many Americans felt toward the emergence of modern society.

Colin Grant, *Negro With A Hat: The Rise and Fall of Marcus Garvey* (2008). This elegantly written new biography explores both the inner life and broader political impact of one of the most influential and controversial African American figures of the era.

Desmond King, *Making Americans: Immigration, Race, and the Origins of Diverse Democracy* (2000). Fine analysis of the shift of U.S. immigration policies in the 1920s, with special attention to the influence of eugenics, and the long-term consequences of the new restrictive legislation.

Michael A. Lerner, *Dry Manhattan: Prohibition in New York City* (2007). A sophisticated and well-written account, including excellent analysis of the political struggles both to establish and later repeal Prohibition.

William E. Leuchtenberg, *Herbert Hoover* (2009). A new critical biography of one of the era's most influential figures by a leading political historian.

Susan Smulyan, *Selling Radio: The Commercialization of American Broadcasting, 1920–1934* (1994). The best analysis of the rise of commercial radio broadcasting in the 1920s.

Joshua Zeitz, *Flapper* (2006). A lively and well-researched account of "the flapper" phenomenon, with emphasis on how a wide variety of women contributed to new cultural images for females.

PEARSON
myhistorylab Connections

Reinforce what you learned in this chapter by studying the many documents, images, maps, review tools, and videos available at www.myhistorylab.com.

Read and Review

✓● Study and Review **Chapter 23**

●●● Read the Document

Frederick W. Taylor, "Scientific Management" (1911)

Edward E. Purinton, "Big Ideas from Big Business" (1921)

Advertisements (1925, 1927)

Eleanor R. Wembridge, "Petting and the Campus" (1925)

Immigration Law (1924)

"Creed of Klanswomen" (1924)

Nicola Sacco and Bartolomeo Vanzetti, "Court Statements" (1927)

◉ See the Map *African American Population, 1910 and 1950*

Research and Explore

●●● Read the Document

Exploring America: Harlem Renaissance

Profiles
Mary Pickford
John B. Watson

History Bookshelf
W.E.B. DuBois, The Negro (1915)
Margaret Sanger, Woman and the New Race (1920)
F. Scott Fitzgerald, This Side of Paradise (1920)
Sinclair Lewis, Babbitt (1922)

((●● Hear the Audio *Prohibition is a Failure*

◉● Watch the Video

The Great Migration

The Rise and Fall of the Automobile Economy

The Harlem Renaissance

((●● Hear the Audio

Hear the audio files for Chapter 23 at
www.myhistorylab.com.

24

Chapter 24 at www.myhistorylab.com
((•─ Hear the Audio

The Great Depression and the New Deal 1929–1940

CHAPTER OUTLINE

American Communities 689
Sit-Down Strike at Flint: Automobile Workers Organize a New Union

Hard Times **691**
Underlying Weaknesses of the 1920s' Economy
The Bull Market and the Crash
Mass Unemployment
Hoover's Failure
A Global Crisis and the Election of 1932

FDR and the First New Deal **696**
FDR the Man

"The Only Thing We Have to Fear": Restoring Confidence
The Hundred Days
Roosevelt's Critics, Right and Left

Left Turn and the Second New Deal **700**
The Second Hundred Days
Labor's Upsurge: Rise of the CIO
The New Deal Coalition at High Tide

The New Deal in the South and West **702**
Modernizing Southern Farming and Landholding
An Environmental Disaster: The Dust Bowl
Water Policy

A New Deal for Indians

The Limits of Reform **709**
Court Packing
The Women's Network
A New Deal for Minorities?
The Roosevelt Recession and the Ebbing of the New Deal

Depression-Era Culture **711**
A New Deal for the Arts
The Documentary Impulse
Waiting for Lefty
Raising Spirits: Film, Radio, and the Swing Era

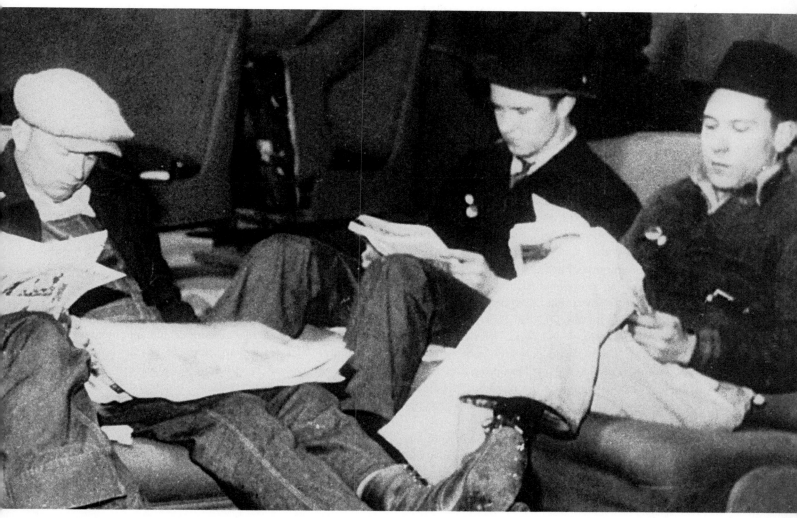

Workers in the GM Fisher body plant in Flint stage a sit-down strike, taking over the plant on December 30, 1936.

Sit-Down Strike at Flint: Automobile Workers Organize a New Union

In the gloomy evening of February 11, 1937, 400 tired, unshaven, but very happy strikers marched out of the sprawling automobile factory known as Fisher Body Number 1 in Flint, Michigan. Most carried American flags and small bundles of clothing. A makeshift banner on top of the plant announced "Victory Is Ours." A wildly cheering parade line of a thousand supporters greeted the strikers at the gates. Shouting with joy, honking horns, and singing songs, the celebrants marched to two other factories to greet other emerging strikers. After forty-four days, the great Flint sit-down strike was over.

Flint was the heart of production for General Motors, the largest

AMERICAN
Communities

corporation in the world. In 1936, GM's net profits had reached $285 million, and its total assets were $1.5 billion. Originally a center for lumbering and then carriage making, Flint had boomed with the auto industry during the 1920s. Thousands of migrants streamed into the city, attracted by assembly-line jobs averaging about $30 a week. By 1930, Flint's population had grown to about 150,000 people, 80 percent of whom depended on work at General Motors. A severe housing shortage made living conditions difficult. Parts of the city resembled a mining camp, with workers living in tar-paper shacks, tents, and even railroad cars.

The Great Depression hit Flint very hard. Employment at GM fell from a 1929 high of 56,000 to fewer than 17,000 in 1932. As late as 1938, close to half the city's families were receiving some kind of emergency relief. By that time, as in thousands of other American communities, Flint's private and county relief agencies had been overwhelmed by the needs of the unemployed and their families. Two new national agencies based in Washington, DC, the Federal Emergency Relief Administration and the Works Progress Administration, had replaced local sources of aid during the economic crisis. These New Deal programs embodied a new federal approach to providing relief and employment to American communities unable to cope with the enormity of mass unemployment.

The United Automobile Workers (UAW) came to Flint in 1936, seeking to organize GM workers into one industrial union. The previous year, Congress had passed the National Labor Relations Act (also known as the Wagner Act), which made union organizing easier by guaranteeing the right of workers to join unions and bargain collectively. The act established the National Labor Relations Board to oversee union elections and prohibit illegal antiunion activities by employers. But the obstacles to labor organizing were still enormous.

Unemployment was high, and GM had maintained a vigorous antiunion policy for years. By the fall of 1936, the UAW had signed up only a thousand members. The key moment came with the seizure of two Flint GM plants by a few hundred auto workers on December 30, 1936. The idea was to stay in the factories until strikers could achieve a collective bargaining agreement with General Motors. "We don't aim to keep the plants or try to run them," explained one sit-downer to a reporter, "but we want to see that nobody takes our jobs. We don't think we're breaking the law, or at least we don't think we're doing anything really bad."

A new and daring tactic—the sit-down strike—gained popularity among American industrial workers during the 1930s. In 1936, there were 48 sit-downs involving nearly 90,000 workers, and in 1937 some 400,000 workers participated in 477 sit-down strikes.

Sit-downs expressed the militant exuberance of the rank and file. As one union song of the day put it:

When they tie the can to a union man,
Sit down! Sit down!
When they give him the sack they'll take him back,
Sit down! Sit down!
When the speed up comes, just twiddle your thumbs,
Sit down! Sit down!
When the boss won't talk don't take a walk,
Sit down! Sit down!

The Flint strikers carefully organized themselves into what one historian called "the sit-down community." Each plant elected a strike committee and appointed its own police chief and sanitary engineer. No alcohol was allowed, and strikers were careful not to destroy company property. Committees were organized for food preparation, recreation, sanitation, education, and contact with the outside. A Women's Emergency Brigade—the strikers' wives, mothers, and daughters—provided crucial support preparing food and maintaining militant picket lines.

As the strike continued through January, support in Flint and around the nation grew. Overall production in the GM empire dropped from 53,000 vehicles per week to 1,500. Reporters and union supporters flocked to the plants. On January 11, in the so-called Battle of Running Bulls, strikers and their supporters clashed violently with Flint police and private GM guards. Michigan governor Frank Murphy, sympathetic to the strikers, brought in the National Guard to protect them. He refused to enforce an injunction obtained by GM to evict the strikers. In the face of determined unity by the sit-downers, GM gave in and recognized the UAW as the exclusive bargaining agent in all sixty of its factories.

The strike was perhaps the most important in American labor history, sparking a huge growth in union membership in the automobile and other mass-production industries. Out of the tight-knit, temporary community of the sit-down strike emerged a looser yet more permanent kind of community: a powerful, nationwide trade union of automobile workers. The UAW struggled successfully to win recognition and collective bargaining rights from other carmakers, such as Chrysler and Ford. The national UAW, like other new unions in the mass-production industries, was composed of locals around the country. The permanent

1. What were the causes of the Great Depression, and what were its consequences?

2. How did Hoover and Congress respond to the Great Depression?

3. What was the First New Deal, and how did it differ from the Second New Deal?

4. How did the New Deal expand the scope of the federal government in the South and West?

5. How did the Great Depression affect American cultural life during the 1930s?

6. What were the limits of the New Deal's reforms, and what legacy did they leave?

FOCUS
Questions

1929–1940

community of unionized auto workers won significant improvements in wages, working conditions, and benefits. Locals also became influential in the political and social lives of their larger communities—industrial cities such as Flint, Detroit, and Toledo.

More broadly, the Flint sit-down embodied the new political and economic dynamics of Depression-era America. Workers, farmers, and consumers hard hit by the worst economic catastrophe in U.S. history called for a more activist federal government to relieve suffering and offer greater economic security for Americans. In response, a rejuvenated Democratic Party, led by President Franklin D. Roosevelt and in solid control of Congress, created the New Deal, an ambitious collection of measures designed to promote relief, recovery, and reform. With the 1935 National Labor Relations Act, the New Deal encouraged labor organizing by legally assuring the right to

union membership for the first time in American history. A newly militant and aggressive labor movement in turn became a critical component of the "New Deal coalition" that kept Democrats in power. Organized labor provided crucial support for many of the social welfare initiatives associated with the New Deal throughout the 1930s and beyond: federal relief, a Social Security system, public works projects, new standards regulating minimum wages and maximum hours, and Washington-based efforts to improve the nation's housing. By the late 1930s, conservative resistance would limit the scope of New Deal reforms. But in communities around the nation, labor unions inspired by the Flint sit-down reached unprecedented levels of popularity and influence in economic and political life. Nationally, they would remain a crucial component of the New Deal political coalition, and a key power broker in the Democratic Party, for decades to come.

—Flint

AMERICAN
Communities

Hard Times

No twentieth-century event more profoundly affected American life than the Great Depression—the worst economic crisis in American history. Statistics tell only part of the story of a slumping economy, mass unemployment, and swelling relief rolls. Even today, the emotional and psychological toll of those years has left what one writer called an "invisible scar" on the lives and memories of millions of American families.

Underlying Weaknesses of the 1920s' Economy

It would be oversimple to say that the 1929 stock market collapse "caused" the Great Depression. Signs of deep economic weakness had already begun to surface amid the general prosperity of the 1920s. First, workers and consumers received too small a share of the enormous increases in labor productivity. Between 1923 and 1929, manufacturing output per worker-hour increased by 32 percent, while wages rose only 8 percent. Gains in wages and salaries were extremely uneven. While workers in newer industries such as automobiles and electrical manufacturing enjoyed pay increases, those in textiles and coal mining watched their wages fall. Moreover, the rise in productivity itself had encouraged overproduction in many industries, and the farm sector had never been able to regain the prosperity of the World War I years (see Chapter 23).

To be sure, Americans overall in the 1920s had more money to spend on cars, telephones, radios, washing machines, canned goods, and other consumer goods. Child labor was in decline, and more Americans than ever graduated from high school. But economic insecurity was still a brutal fact of life for millions of families, especially in rural communities. Most industrial workers endured regular bouts of unemployment and seasonal layoffs. The two-day weekend and paid vacations were largely unknown. Eighty percent of the nation's families had no savings at all, and an old age spent in poverty was far more likely for the average worker than "retirement." The most important weakness in the economy was the extremely unequal distribution of income, yielding the greatest concentration of wealth in the nation's history (see Table 24.1).

The Bull Market and the Crash

Stock trading in the late 1920s captured the imagination of the broad American public. The stock market resembled a sporting arena; millions followed stock prices as avidly as the exploits of Babe Ruth or Jack Dempsey. Business leaders and economists as much as told Americans that it was their duty to buy stocks. John J. Raskob, chairman of the board of General Motors, wrote an article for the *Ladies' Home Journal* titled "Everybody Ought to Be Rich." A person who saved $15 each month and invested it in good common stocks would, he claimed, have $80,000 within twenty years.

During the bull market of the 1920s, stock prices increased at roughly twice the rate of industrial production. By the end of the decade, stocks that once had been bought mainly on the basis of their earning power, which was passed on to stockholders in the form of dividends, came to be purchased only for the resale value after their prices rose. In 1928 alone, for example, the price of Radio Corporation of America stock shot up from $85 per share to $420; Chrysler stock more than doubled, from $63 to $132.

Yet only about 3 million Americans—out of a total population of 120 million—owned any stocks at all. Many of these stock buyers had been lured into the market through easy-credit margin accounts, which allowed investors to purchase stocks with a small down payment (as low as 10 percent), borrowing the rest from a broker and using the shares as collateral on the loan. Just as installment plans had stimulated the automobile and other industries, "buying on the margin" brought new customers to the stock market. Investment trusts, similar to today's mutual funds, attracted many new investors with promises of high returns. Corporations found that lending excess capital to stockbrokers was more profitable than investing in new technologies. All these factors fed an expansive and optimistic atmosphere on Wall Street.

Although often portrayed as a one- or two-day catastrophe, the Wall Street crash of 1929 was actually a steep slide. The bull market peaked in early September, and prices drifted downward. As expectations of an endless boom began to melt, the market had to decline. On Monday, October 28, the Dow lost 38 points—13 percent of its value. The next day—"Black Tuesday," October 29—the bottom fell out. Over 16 million shares, more than double the previous record, were traded as panic selling took hold. For many stocks, no buyers were available at any price.

The situation worsened. The market's fragile foundation of credit, based on the margin debt, quickly crumbled. Many investors with margin accounts had to sell when stock values fell. Since the shares themselves represented the security for their loans, more money had to be

TABLE 24.1

Distribution of Total Family Income Among Various Segments of the Population, 1929–44 (in Percentages)

Year	Poorest Fifth	Second-Poorest Fifth	Middle Fifth	Second-Wealthiest Fifth	Wealthiest Fifth	Wealthiest 5 Percent
1929		12.5	13.8	19.3	54.4	30.0
1935–36	4.1	9.2	14.1	20.9	51.7	26.5
1941	4.1	9.5	15.3	22.3	48.8	24.0
1944	4.9	10.9	16.2	22.2	45.8	20.7

SOURCE: Adapted from U.S. Bureau of the Census, *Historical Statistics of the United States, Colonial Times to 1970,* Bicentennial Edition (Washington, DC: U.S. Government Printing Office, 1975), 301.

Rollin Kirby's 1929 cartoon depicts an individual investor losing his money as he clings to a bear running down Wall Street. The bear symbolizes an atmosphere of panic selling and heavy losses, the opposite of a "bull" market in which investor confidence spurs buying and faith in the future.

9 percent of the labor force was out of work. By 1933, 12.6 million workers—over one-quarter of the labor force—were without jobs. (Other sources put the figure that year above 16 million, or nearly one out of every three workers.) No statistics tell us how long people were unemployed or how many Americans found only part-time work.

Many Americans, raised believing that they were responsible for their own fate, blamed themselves for their failure to find work. Journalists and social workers noted the common feelings of shame and guilt expressed by the unemployed. One jobless Houston woman told a relief caseworker, "I'm just no good, I guess. I've given up ever amounting to anything. It's no use." One despondent Pennsylvania man asked a state relief agency, "Can you be so kind as to advise me as to which would be the most human way to dispose of my self and family, as this is about the only thing that I see left to do."

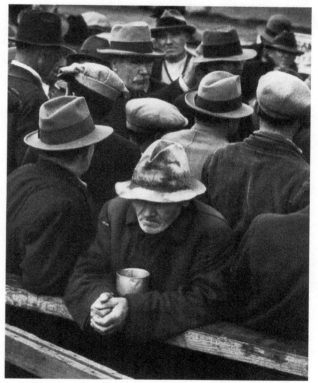

Dorothea Lange captured the lonely despair of unemployment in *White Angel Breadline, San Francisco, 1933*. During the 1920s, Lange had specialized in taking portraits of wealthy families, but by 1932, she could no longer stand the contradiction between her portrait business and "what was going on in the street." She said of this photograph: "There are moments such as these when time stands still and all you can do is hold your breath and hope it will wait for you."

SOURCE: Dorothea Lange, *White Angel Breadline, San Francisco, 1933*. Copyright the Dorothea Lange Collection, The Oakland Museum of California, City of Oakland. Gift of Paul S. Taylor.

put up to cover the loans when prices declined. By mid-November, about $30 billion in the market price of stocks had been wiped out. Half the value of the stocks listed in the *New York Times* index was lost in ten weeks.

The stock market crash undermined the confidence, investment, and spending of businesses and the well-to-do. Manufacturers cut production and began laying off workers, which brought further declines in consumer spending, and so another round of production cutbacks ensued. A spurt of consumer spending might have checked this downward spiral, but consumers had less to spend as industries laid off workers and reduced work hours. With a shrinking market for products, businesses feared to expand. A large proportion of the nation's banking funds had been tied to the speculative bubble. Many banks began to fail as anxious depositors withdrew their funds, which were uninsured, costing thousands of families all their savings. And an 86 percent plunge in agricultural prices between 1929 and 1933, compared to a decline in agricultural production of only 6 percent, brought terrible suffering to America's farmers.

Mass Unemployment

At a time when unemployment insurance did not exist and public relief was completely inadequate, the loss of a job could mean economic catastrophe for workers and their families. Massive unemployment across America became the most powerful sign of a deepening depression. In 1930, the Department of Labor estimated that roughly

Isaac Soyer's *Employment Agency*, a 1937 oil painting, offered one of the decade's most sensitive efforts at depicting the anxiety and sense of isolation felt by millions of depression-era job hunters.

SOURCE: Isaac Soyer, *Employment Agency*, 1937. Oil on canvas, 34 ½" × 45". Whitney Museum of American Art.

Unemployment upset the psychological balance in many families by undermining the traditional authority of the male breadwinner. Women, because their labor was cheaper than men's, found it easier to keep jobs. Female clerks, secretaries, maids, and waitresses earned much less than male factory workers, but their jobs were more likely to survive hard times. Pressures on those lucky enough to have a job increased as well. Anna Novak, a Chicago meat packer, recalled the degrading harassment at the hands of foremen: "You could get along swell if you let the boss slap you on the behind and feel you up. God, I hate that stuff, you don't know!" Men responded in a variety of ways to unemployment. Some withdrew emotionally; others became angry or took to drinking. A few committed suicide. In 1934, one Chicago social worker summed up the strains she found in families: "Fathers feel they have lost their prestige in the home; there is much nagging, mothers nag at the fathers, parents nag at the children. Children of working age who earn meager salaries find it hard to turn over all their earnings and deny themselves even the greatest necessities and as a result leave home." Fear of unemployment and a deep desire for security marked the Depression generation.

Hoover's Failure

The enormity of the Great Depression overwhelmed traditional—and meager—sources of relief. In most communities across America, these sources were a patchwork of private agencies and local government units, such as towns, cities, or counties. They simply lacked the money, resources, and staff to deal with the worsening situation. In large urban centers like Detroit and Chicago, unemployment approached 50 percent by 1932. Smaller communities could not cope either. For the year 1932, one West Virginia coal-mining county with 1,500 unemployed miners had only $9,000 to meet relief needs.

There was great irony, even tragedy, in President Hoover's failure to respond to human suffering. During World War I, he had effectively administered Belgian war relief abroad and won wide praise for his leadership of the Food Administration at home. As a leader of the progressive wing of the Republican Party, Hoover had long championed a kind of cooperative individualism that relied upon public-spirited citizens. Although he felt real personal anguish over the hardships people suffered, he lacked the political skill to demonstrate his compassion in public. Failing to face the facts of the depression, Hoover worried more about undermining individual initiative than providing actual relief for victims. He ignored all mounting evidence to the contrary when he claimed, in his 1931 State of the Union Address, "Our people are providing against distress from unemployment in true American fashion by magnificent response to public appeal and by action of the local governments."

Hoover's plan for recovery centered on restoring business confidence. His administration's most important institutional response to the depression was the Reconstruction Finance Corporation (RFC), established in early 1932 and based on the War Finance Corporation of the World War I years. The RFC was designed to make government credit available to ailing banks, railroads, insurance companies, and other businesses, thereby stimulating economic activity. The key assumption here was that the problem was one of supply (for businesses) rather than demand (from consumers). Given the public's low purchasing power, most businesses were not interested in obtaining loans for expansion. The RFC managed to save numerous banks and other businesses from going under, but its approach did not hasten recovery. Hoover was loath to use the RFC to make direct grants to states, cities, or individuals. In July 1932, congressional Democrats pushed through the Emergency Relief Act, which authorized the

RFC to lend $300 million to states that had exhausted their own relief funds. Hoover grudgingly signed the bill, but less than $30 million was actually given out by the end of 1933.

Two other federal actions—in each case, the opposite of what should have been done—worsened the situation. First, the Federal Reserve, whose policies of low interest rates and easy credit in the late 1920s helped fuel the speculative boom in stock buying, tightened credit sharply. That caused interest rates to spike, putting heavy pressure on the nation's banking system, especially the smaller banks on which farmers, merchants, and local businessmen relied. Without any state or federal insurance, more than 5,000 rural banks and ethnic-group-oriented savings and loans institutions failed between 1929 and 1932, and more than 9 million depositors lost their savings. Second, in 1930 Congress passed (and Hoover signed) the Smoot-Hawley Tariff, raising import duties to their highest levels in American history. Supporters, including the president, claimed that this would protect American farmers from global competition and raise farm prices. Other nations responded by raising their own tariffs, which caused world trade to decline steeply, thus exacerbating the economic collapse.

A Global Crisis and the Election of 1932

By 1931, the depression had spread not only across the United States but also throughout the world, a sign of how interdependent the global economy had become. The immediate problem was the highly unstable system of international finance. The 1919 peace settlement had saddled Germany with $33 billion in war reparations, owed largely to Great Britain and France. The United States loaned money to the British and French during the war, and American banks loaned large sums to Germany in the 1920s. Germany used these loans to pay reparations to the British and French, who in turn used these reparations to repay their American debts. The 1929 stock market crash put an end to American loans for Germany, thus removing a critical link in the international cash flow. When Germany then defaulted on its reparations, Great Britain and France in turn stopped paying what they owed to this country. As German banks collapsed and unemployment swelled, nervous European investors sold their American stocks, depressing the stock market even further. Great Britain and several other European nations also abandoned the gold standard and devalued (lowered) their currency relative to the dollar. This made American goods more difficult to sell abroad, further dampening production at home. With many nations also raising their tariffs to protect national industries, international trade slowed to a crawl. The total volume of global trade declined from about $36 billion in 1929 to roughly $12 billion by 1932. American banks, badly hurt by both domestic depositors

clamoring for their money and the foreign withdrawal of capital, began failing in record numbers. In 1931 alone, 2,294 U.S. banks failed, double the number that had collapsed in 1930.

By 1932, the desperate mood of many Americans was finding expression in direct, sometimes violent, protests that were widely covered in the press. On March 7, communist organizers led a march of several thousand Detroit auto workers and unemployed in Dearborn. Ford-controlled police fired tear gas and bullets, killing four demonstrators and seriously wounding fifty others. Desperate farmers in Iowa organized the Farmers' Holiday Association, aimed at raising prices by refusing to sell produce. In August, some 1,500 farmers dumped milk and other perishables into ditches.

The spring of 1932 also saw the "Bonus Army" begin descending on Washington, DC. This protest took its name from Congress's promise in 1924 to pay every veteran of World War I a $1,000 bonus—in the form of a bond that would not mature until 1945. The veterans who were gathering in Washington demanded immediate payment of the bonus in cash. By summer, they and their families numbered around 20,000 strong and were camping out all over the capital city. The House passed a bill for immediate payment, but when the Senate refused to agree, most of the downcast veterans left. At the end of July, U.S. Army troops, led by Chief of Staff General Douglas MacArthur, forcibly evicted the remaining 2,000 veterans. The spectacle of these unarmed and unemployed men, the heroes of 1918, being driven off by bayonets and bullets, provided the most disturbing evidence yet of the failure of Hoover's administration.

In 1932, Democrats nominated Franklin D. Roosevelt, governor of New York, for the presidency. Roosevelt's acceptance speech stressed the need for reconstructing the nation's economy. "I pledge you, I pledge myself," he said, "to a new deal for the American people." Roosevelt's plans for recovery were vague and contradictory. He frequently attacked Hoover for reckless and extravagant spending and accused him of concentrating too much power in Washington, but he also spoke of the need for government to meet "the problem of underconsumption" and to help in "distributing wealth and products more equitably." Above all, Roosevelt stressed, "the country demands bold, persistent experimentation." Hoover bitterly condemned Roosevelt's ideas as a "radical departure" from the American way of life. With the depression growing worse every day, probably any Democrat would have defeated Hoover. The Democratic victory was overwhelming. Roosevelt carried forty-two states, taking the Electoral College 472 to 59 and the popular vote by about 23 million to 16 million. Democrats won big majorities in both the House and the Senate. The stage was set for FDR's "new deal" (see Map 24.1).

•●•[Read the Document

Herbert Hoover, New York Campaign Speech (1932) at **www.myhistorylab.com**

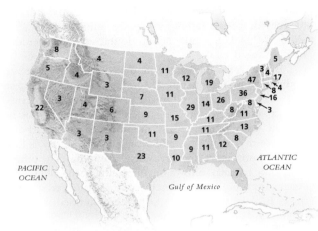

	Electoral Vote (%)	Popular Vote (%)
FRANKLIN D. ROOSEVELT (Democrat)	472 (89)	22,809,638 (57)
Herbert Hoover (Republican)	59 (11)	15,758,901 (40)
Minor parties	—	1,153,306 (3)

MAP 24.1 The Election of 1932 Democrats owed their overwhelming victory in 1932 to the popular identification of the depression with the Hoover administration. Roosevelt's popular vote was about the same as Hoover's in 1928, and FDR's Electoral College margin was even greater.

FDR and the First New Deal

No twentieth-century president had a greater impact on American life and politics than Franklin Delano Roosevelt (FDR). To a large degree, the New Deal was a product of his astute political skills and the sheer force of his personality. The only president ever elected to four terms, FDR would loom as the dominant personality in American political life through twelve years of depression and global war.

FDR the Man

Franklin Delano Roosevelt was born in 1882 in Dutchess County, New York, where he grew up an only child, secure and confident, on his family's vast estate. Roosevelt's education at private schools, Harvard, and Columbia Law School reinforced his aristocratic family's sense of civic duty. In 1905, he married his distant cousin, Anna Eleanor Roosevelt, a niece of President Theodore Roosevelt. He was elected as a Democrat to the New York State Senate in 1910, served as assistant secretary of the navy from 1913 to 1920, and was nominated for vice president by the Democrats in the losing 1920 campaign.

In the summer of 1921, Roosevelt was stricken with polio; he was never to walk again without support. His illness proved the turning point in his life. The wealthy aristocrat, for whom everything had come relatively easily, now personally understood the meaning of struggle and hardship. Elected governor of New York in 1928, Roosevelt served two terms and won a national reputation for reform. As governor, he instituted unemployment insurance, strengthened child labor laws, enacted tax relief for farmers, and provided pensions for the old. As the depression hit the state, he slowly increased public works.

"The Only Thing We Have to Fear": Restoring Confidence

In the first days of his administration, Roosevelt conveyed a sense of optimism and activism that helped restore the badly shaken confidence of the nation. "First of all," he told Americans in his Inaugural Address on March 4, 1933, "let me assert my firm belief that the only thing we have to fear is fear itself." The very next day, as people lined up to pull savings out of failing banks and hoarded cash under their mattresses, he issued an executive order calling for a four-day "bank holiday" to stop the collapse of the country's financial system.

●●●[Read the Document
Franklin D. Roosevelt, Fireside Chat (1933) at www.myhistorylab.com

The new Congress was not scheduled to convene until the end of 1933, but Roosevelt convened a special session to deal with the banking crisis, unemployment aid, and farm relief. On March 12, he broadcast his first "fireside chat" to explain the steps he had taken to meet the financial emergency. These radio broadcasts became a standard part of Roosevelt's political technique, and they proved enormously successful. They gave courage to ordinary Americans and communicated a genuine sense of compassion from the White House.

Congress immediately passed the Emergency Banking Act, which gave the president broad discretionary powers over all banking transactions and foreign exchange. It authorized healthy banks to reopen only under licenses from the Treasury Department and provided for greater federal authority in managing the affairs of failed banks. By the middle of March, about half the country's banks, holding about 90 percent of the nation's deposits, were open for business again. Banks began to attract new deposits from people who had been holding back their money. The bank crisis had passed.

Roosevelt assembled a group of key advisers, the "brains trust," to counsel him in the White House. They gave conflicting advice. Some advocated fiscal conservatism to restore confidence in the dollar; others pushed for central planning to manage the economy. But the "brain trusters" shared a basic belief in expert-directed government–business cooperation. Structural economic reform, they argued, must accept the modern reality of large corporate enterprise based on mass production and distribution.

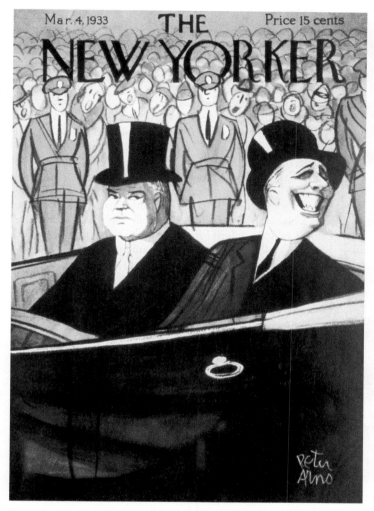

Mar. 4, 1933   THE NEW YORKER   Price 15 cents

This *New Yorker* magazine cover depicted an ebullient Franklin D. Roosevelt riding to his 1933 inauguration in the company of a glum Herbert Hoover. This drawing typified many mass media images of the day, contrasting the different moods and temperaments of the new president and the defeated incumbent.

The Hundred Days

From March to June 1933—"the Hundred Days"—FDR pushed through Congress an extraordinary amount of depression-fighting legislation. Roosevelt's enormous political skill—as a power broker, as a coalition builder, and as a communicator with the American public—was crucial. What came to be called the New Deal was no unified program to end the depression but rather an improvised series of reform and relief measures, some of which completely contradicted each other. Still, all the New Deal programs were united by the fundamental goals of relief, reform, and recovery.

Five measures were particularly important and innovative. The Civilian Conservation Corps (CCC), established in March as an unemployment relief effort, provided work for jobless young men in protecting and conserving the nation's natural resources. Road construction, reforestation, flood control, and national park improvements were some of the major projects performed in work camps across the country. CCC workers received room and board and $30 each month, up to $25 of which had to be sent home to dependents. By the time the program was phased out in 1942, more than 2.5 million youths had worked in some 1,500 CCC camps.

In May, Congress authorized $500 million for the Federal Emergency Relief Administration (FERA). Half the money went as direct relief to the states; the rest was distributed on the basis of a dollar of federal aid for every three dollars of state and local funds spent for relief. This system of outright federal grants differed significantly from Hoover's loans-only approach. Establishment of work relief projects, however, was left to state and local governments. To direct this massive undertaking, FDR tapped Harry Hopkins, a streetwise former New York City social worker driven by a deep moral passion to help the less fortunate and an impatience with bureaucracy. Hopkins would emerge as the key figure administering New Deal relief programs.

The Agricultural Adjustment Administration (AAA) was set up to provide immediate relief to the nation's farmers. The AAA established a new federal role in agricultural planning and price setting. It established parity prices for basic farm commodities, including corn, wheat, hogs, cotton, rice, and dairy products. The concept of parity pricing was based on the purchasing power that farmers had enjoyed during the prosperous years of 1909 to 1914. That period became the benchmark for setting the "floor," that is, minimum—prices for farm commodities. The AAA also incorporated the principle of subsidy, whereby farmers received benefit payments in return for reducing acreage or otherwise cutting production where surpluses existed. New taxes on food processing would pay for these programs.

The AAA raised total farm income and was especially successful in pushing up the prices of wheat, cotton, and corn. It had some troubling side effects, however. Landlords often failed to share their AAA payments with tenant farmers, and they frequently used benefits to buy tractors and other equipment that displaced sharecroppers. Many Americans were disturbed, too, by the sight of surplus crops, livestock, and milk being destroyed while millions went hungry.

The Tennessee Valley Authority (TVA) proved to be one of the most unique and controversial projects of the

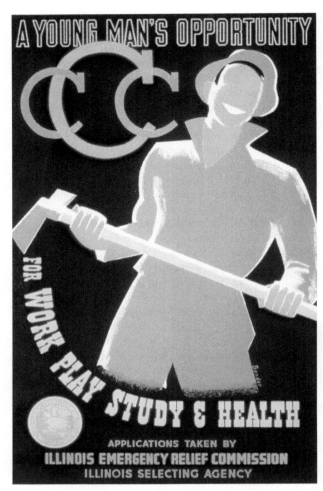

A recruitment poster represents the Civilian Conservation Corps (CCC) as much more than simply an emergency relief measure, stressing character building and the opportunity for self-improvement. By the time the CCC expired in 1942, it had become one of the most popular of all the New Deal programs.

New Deal era. The TVA, an independent public corporation, built dams and power plants, produced cheap fertilizer for farmers, and, most significantly, for the first time brought low-cost electricity to thousands of people in six southern states. Denounced by some as a dangerous step toward socialism, the TVA stood for decades as a model of how careful government planning could dramatically improve the social and economic welfare of an underdeveloped region.

See the Map
The Tennessee Valley Authority at
www.myhistorylab.com

On the very last of the Hundred Days, Congress passed the National Industrial Recovery Act, the closest attempt yet at a systematic plan for economic recovery. In theory, each industry would be self-governed by a code hammered out by representatives of business, labor, and consumers. Once approved by the National Recovery

Administration (NRA) in Washington, the codes would have the force of law. In practice, almost all the National Recovery Administration codes were written by the largest firms in any given industry; labor and consumers got short shrift. The sheer administrative complexities involved with code writing and compliance made a great many people unhappy with the NRA's operation.

Finally, the Public Works Administration (PWA), led by Secretary of the Interior Harold Ickes, authorized $3.3 billion for the construction of roads, public buildings, and other projects. The idea was to provide jobs and, through increased consumer spending, stimulate the economy. This strategy was called "priming the pump," borrowing a phrase from what an old-time farmer had to do to get his well pump going. Eventually the PWA spent over $4.2 billion building roads, schools, post offices, bridges, courthouses, and other public buildings, which in thousands of communities today remain tangible reminders of the New Deal era.

During the Hundred Days and the months immediately following, Congress passed other legislation that would have important long-range effects. The Glass-Steagall Act created the Federal Deposit Insurance Corporation (FDIC), which provided protection to individual depositors by guaranteeing accounts of up to $5,000 in case of bank failure. Congress also established the Securities and Exchange Commission (SEC) to regulate stock exchanges and brokers, require full financial disclosures, and curb the speculative practices that had contributed to the 1929 crash. The 1934 National Housing Act, aimed at stimulating residential construction and making home financing more affordable, set up the Federal Housing Administration (FHA). The FHA insured loans made by banks and other private lenders for home building and home buying.

Roosevelt's Critics, Right and Left

From the beginning, the New Deal had loud and powerful critics on the right who complained bitterly that FDR had overstepped the traditional boundaries of government action. From the left came angry cries that Roosevelt had not done nearly enough.

Pro-Republican newspapers and the American Liberty League, a group of conservative businessmen organized in 1934, vehemently attacked the administration for what they considered its attack on property rights, the growing welfare state, and the alleged decline of personal liberty. In the 1934 election, however, Democrats crushed their right-wing critics and—countering the losses that incumbent parties usually suffer at midterm—increased their majorities in both houses of Congress.

Father Charles E. Coughlin, a Catholic priest in suburban Detroit with a huge national radio audience of 40 million listeners, at first supported the New Deal. By 1934, however, frustrated by his limited influence on the president,

OVERVIEW | Key Legislation of the First New Deal ("Hundred Days," March 9–June 16, 1933)

Legislation	Purpose
Emergency Banking Relief Act	Enlarged federal authority over private banks
	Government loans to private banks
Civilian Conservation Corps	Unemployment relief
	Conservation of natural resources
Federal Emergency Relief Administration	Direct federal money for relief, funneled through state and local governments
Agricultural Adjustment Administration	Federal farm aid based on parity pricing and subsidy
Tennessee Valley Authority	Economic development and cheap electricity for Tennessee Valley
National Industrial Recovery Act	Self-regulating industrial codes to revive economic activity
Public Works Administration	Federal public works projects to increase employment and consumer spending

Read the Document
Father Charles E. Coughlin, "A Third Party" (1936) at
www.myhistorylab.com

"the radio priest" began attacking FDR in passionate broadcasts that also denounced Wall Street, international bankers, Jews, and "plutocratic capitalism." Roosevelt, he charged, wanted dictatorial powers, and New Deal policies were part of a communist conspiracy.

More troublesome for Roosevelt were the vocal and popular movements on the left. These found the New Deal too timid. In California, the well-known novelist and socialist Upton Sinclair entered the 1934 Democratic primary for governor by running on a program he called EPIC ("End Poverty in California"). He proposed a monthly pension of $50 for all poor people over age sixty and championed a government-run system of "production for use" (rather than profit) workshops for the unemployed. Sinclair shocked local and national Democrats by winning the primary easily. He lost a close general election only because the Republican candidate received heavy financial and tactical support from wealthy Hollywood studio executives and frightened regular Democrats. Another Californian, Francis E. Townsend, a retired dentist, won a large following among senior citizens with his Old Age Revolving Pension plan. He called for payments of $200 per month to all people over sixty, provided all the money was spent within thirty days. The pensions would be financed by a national 2 percent tax on commercial transactions.

Huey Long, Louisiana's flamboyant backcountry orator, posed the greatest potential threat to Roosevelt's leadership. Long had captured Louisiana's governorship in 1928 by attacking the state's entrenched oil industry and calling for a radical redistribution of wealth. In office, he significantly improved public education, roads, medical care, and other public services, winning the loyalty of the state's poor farmers and industrial workers. Elected to the U.S. Senate in 1930, Long came to Washington with national ambitions. He at first supported Roosevelt, but in 1934, his own presidential ambitions and his impatience with the pace of New Deal measures led to a break with FDR.

Long organized the Share Our Wealth Society. Its purpose, he thundered, "was to break up the swollen fortunes of America and to spread the wealth among all our people." Limiting the size of large fortunes, Long promised, would mean a homestead worth $5,000 and a $2,500 annual income for everyone. Although Long's economics were fuzzy, his "Every Man a King" slogan touched a deep popular

Read the Document
Huey Long, "Share Our Wealth" (1935) at
www.myhistorylab.com

nerve. A secret poll in the summer of 1935 stunned the Democratic National Committee by showing that Long might attract 3 or 4 million votes for president. Only his assassination that September by a political enemy of his corrupt political machine prevented Long's third-party candidacy, which might have proved disastrous for FDR.

A newly militant labor movement also loomed as a force to be reckoned with. Unemployed Councils, organized largely by the Communist Party in industrial cities, held marches and rallies demanding public works projects and relief payments. Section 7a of the National Industrial Recovery Act required that workers be allowed to bargain collectively with employers through representatives of their own choosing. Although this provision of the NIRA was not enforced, it did help raise expectations and sparked union organizing. Almost 1.5 million workers took part in some 1,800 strikes in 1934.

Employers continued to resist unionization, often with violence and the help of local and state police. In Minneapolis that year, a local of the International Brotherhood of Teamsters won a bloody strike against the combined opposition of the union's own national officials, vehemently antiunion employers, and a brutal city police force. Also in 1934, a San Francisco general strike in support of striking members of the International Longshoremen's Association (ILA) effectively shut down the city. Employer use of strikebreakers and violent intimidation prompted an outpouring of support for the ILA from the city's working class, as well as from many shopkeepers and middle-class professionals.

Left Turn and the Second New Deal

The popularity of Coughlin, Sinclair, Townsend, and Long suggested Roosevelt might be losing electoral support among workers, farmers, the aged, and the unemployed. In addition, FDR had to contend with a conservative Supreme Court that did not share the public's enthusiasm for the New Deal. In May 1935, in *Schecter* v. *United States*, the Court found the NRA unconstitutional in its entirety. In early 1936, ruling in *Butler* v. *United States*, the Court invalidated the AAA, declaring it an unconstitutional attempt at regulating agriculture. The Court was composed mostly of Republican appointees, six of them over seventy. Looking toward the 1936 election and eager for a popular mandate, Roosevelt and his closest advisers responded by turning left and offering new social-reform programs. These programs had three major goals: strengthening the national commitment to creating jobs; providing security against old age, unemployment, and illness; and improving housing conditions and cleaning slums. What came to be called "the Second Hundred Days," marked the high point of progressive lawmaking in the New Deal.

The Second Hundred Days

In April 1935, the administration pushed through Congress the Emergency Relief Appropriation Act, which allocated $5 billion for large-scale public works programs for the jobless. New Deal economists argued that each government dollar spent had a multiplier effect, pumping two or three dollars into the depressed gross domestic product. Over the next seven years, the WPA, under Harry Hopkins's leadership, oversaw the employment of more than 8 million Americans on a vast array of construction projects: roads, bridges, dams, airports, and sewers. Among the most innovative WPA programs were community service projects that employed thousands of jobless artists, musicians, actors, and writers.

The landmark Social Security Act of 1935 provided for old-age pensions and unemployment insurance. A payroll tax on workers and their employers created a fund from which retirees received monthly pensions after age sixty-five. The act's unemployment compensation plan established a minimum weekly payment and a minimum number of weeks during which those who lost jobs could collect. The old-age pensions were quite small at first, as little as $10 a month. The law originally excluded domestic and agricultural workers, primarily African Americans, reflecting the institutional racism entrenched in Congress and the Democratic Party. But Social Security, which has subsequently been amended many times, established the crucial principle of federal responsibility for America's most vulnerable citizens.

Read the Document
Frances Perkins, The Social Security Act, (1935; 1960) at **www.myhistorylab.com**

In July 1935, Congress passed the National Labor Relations Act, often called the Wagner Act for its chief sponsor, Democratic senator Robert F. Wagner of New York. For the first time, the federal government guaranteed the right of American workers to join, or form, independent labor unions and to bargain collectively for improved wages, benefits, and working conditions. The National Labor Relations Board would conduct secret-ballot elections in shops and factories to determine which union, if any, workers desired as their sole bargaining agent. The law also defined and prohibited unfair labor practices by employers, including firing workers for union activity. The Wagner Act, described as "the Magna Carta for labor," quickly proved a boon to union growth, especially in previously unorganized industries such as automobiles, steel, and textiles.

Finally, the Resettlement Administration (RA) produced one of the most utopian New Deal programs, designed to create new kinds of model communities. Established by executive order, and led by key brain truster Rexford G. Tugwell, the RA helped destitute farm families relocate to more productive areas. It granted loans for purchasing land and equipment, and it directed reforestation and soil erosion projects, particularly in the hard-hit Southwest. Due to lack of funds and poor administration, however, only about 1 percent of the projected 500,000 families were actually moved. Tugwell, one of the New Deal's most ardent believers in central planning, was more successful in his efforts at creating model

OVERVIEW | Key Legislation of the Second New Deal (1935–38)

Legislation	Purpose
Emergency Relief Appropriations Act (1935)	Large-scale public works program for the jobless (includes Works Progress Administration)
Social Security Act (1935)	Federal old-age pensions and unemployment insurance
National Labor Relations Act (1935)	Federal guarantee of right to organize trade unions and collective bargaining
Resettlement Administration (1935)	Relocation of poor rural families
	Reforestation and soil erosion projects
National Housing Act (1937)	Federal funding for public housing and slum clearance
Fair Labor Standards Act (1938)	Federal minimum wage and maximum hours

greenbelt communities, combining the best of urban and rural environments. As suburbs, a few of these communities still thrive.

Labor's Upsurge: Rise of the CIO

The Wagner Act greatly facilitated union organizing and galvanized the moribund labor movement. In 1932, only 2.8 million workers were union members, a half-million fewer than in 1929 and more than 2 million fewer than in 1920. Yet by 1942, unions claimed more than 10.5 million members, nearly a third of the total nonagricultural work force. This remarkable turnaround was one of the key events of the depression era. The growth in the size and power of the labor movement permanently changed the work lives and economic status of millions, as well as the national and local political landscapes.

At the core of this growth was a series of dramatic successes in the organization of workers in large-scale, mass-production industries such as automobiles, steel, rubber, electrical goods, and textiles. The conservative, craft-oriented unions that dominated the American Federation of Labor (AFL) had largely ignored workers in these industries. At the 1935 AFL convention, a group of more militant union officials led by John L. Lewis (of the United Mine Workers) and Sidney Hillman (of the Amalgamated Clothing Workers) formed the Committee for Industrial Organization (CIO) and set about organizing mass-production workers by industry—regardless of a worker's level of skill. They differed from nearly all old-line AFL unions by calling for the inclusion of black and women workers.

The gruff son of a Welsh miner, Lewis was articulate, ruthless, and very ambitious. He saw the new legal protection given by the Wagner Act as a historic opportunity. Lewis knew that establishing permanent unions in the mass-production industries would be a bruising battle. He committed the substantial resources of the United Mine Workers to a series of organizing drives, focusing first on the steel and auto industries. Many CIO organizers were communists or radicals of other kinds, and their dedication, commitment, and willingness to work within disciplined organizations proved invaluable in the often dangerous task of creating industrial unions. After the dramatic breakthrough in a 1937 sit-down strike against General Motors at Flint, Michigan, membership in CIO unions grew rapidly. In eight months, membership in the United Automobile Workers (UAW) alone soared from 88,000 to 400,000. CIO victories in the steel, rubber, and electrical industries followed, but often at a very high cost. One bloody example of the perils of union organizing was the 1937 Memorial Day Massacre in Chicago. In a field near the struck Republic Steel Mill in South Chicago, police fired into a crowd of union supporters, killing ten workers and wounding scores more.

In 1938, CIO unions, now boasting nearly 4 million members, withdrew from the AFL and reorganized themselves as the Congress of Industrial Organizations. For the first time ever, the labor movement had gained a permanent place in the nation's mass-production industries. Organized labor took its place as a key power broker in Roosevelt's New Deal and the national Democratic Party. Frances Perkins, FDR's secretary of labor and the nation's

Photographer Milton Brooks won the first Pulitzer Prize for photography with this 1941 image for the *Detroit News*. He captured a violent labor confrontation in front of the Ford Motor Company's River Rouge plant, as private armed guards, employed by Ford, assault and beat organizers for the United Automobile Workers.

first woman cabinet member, captured the close relationship between the new unionism and the New Deal: "Programs long thought of as merely labor welfare, such as shorter hours, higher wages, and a voice in the terms of conditions of work, are really essential economic factors for recovery."

The New Deal Coalition at High Tide

Both major political parties looked forward to the 1936 elections as a national referendum, and the campaign itself was exciting and hard fought. The Republicans nominated Governor Alfred M. Landon of Kansas, who had gained attention by surviving the Democratic landslide of 1934. His campaign served as a lightning rod for all those, including many conservative Democrats, who were dissatisfied with Roosevelt and the direction he had taken.

Roosevelt attacked the "economic royalists" who denied that government "could do anything to protect the citizen in his right to work and his right to live." At the same time, FDR was careful to distance himself from radicalism. "It was this administration," he declared, "which saved the system of private profit and free enterprise after it had been dragged to the brink of ruin." Huge and enthusiastic crowds greeted Roosevelt, especially in large cities. Still, the vast majority of the nation's newspapers endorsed Landon.

Election day erased all doubts: Roosevelt carried every state but Maine and Vermont, polling 61 percent of the popular vote. Democrats increased their substantial majorities in the House and Senate as well. In 1936, the Democrats drew millions of new voters into the political process, and at the same time, forged a new coalition of voters that would dominate national politics for two

◆◆─[Read the **Document**

Franklin D. Roosevelt, Second Inaugural Address (1937) at **www.myhistorylab.com**

generations. This "New Deal coalition," as it came to be known, included white Southern Democrats, ethnics who supported big-city political machines, unionized workers (including those being organized by the CIO), and many depression-hit farmers. Black voters in the North and West, long affiliated with the Republicans as "the party of Lincoln," went Democratic in record numbers. (Of course, blacks were largely barred from voting in the South.)

The Great Depression was by no means over. But the New Deal's active response to the nation's misery, particularly its bold initiatives in 1935, had obviously struck a powerful chord with the American electorate. Roosevelt was especially popular among first- and second-generation immigrants of Catholic and Jewish descent, and the New Deal drew enthusiastic support from millions who had never bothered with politics. The severity of the Great Depression had overwhelmed the ethnically based support networks—mutual benefit societies, immigrant banks, and religious charities—that had traditionally helped so many to survive hard times. Popular federal programs like Social Security, the WPA, and Home Owners Loan Corporation mortgages changed the consciousness of a generation of the ethnic working class. In exchange for their votes, they now looked to the state—especially the federal government—for relief, protection, and help in achieving the American dream.

The New Deal in the South and West

The New Deal had its profoundest impact in the South and the West. Federal farm programs moved southern agriculture away from its longtime dependence upon sharecropping and tenant farming and helped reorganize it around new patterns of wage labor and agribusiness. New Deal dam building and power projects introduced electricity to millions of rural Southerners, transforming their lives. New Deal programs reshaped western agriculture, created new sources of water and energy, and changed Indian policy. From Great Plains farming communities to Pacific Coast cities, federal subsidy and management became an integral part of western life. In the process, the New Deal helped propel both the South and the West into the modern era and laid the groundwork for the postwar "Sunbelt."

Modernizing Southern Farming and Landholding

In 1930, less than half of all southern farmers owned their own land; over three-quarters of the region's African American farmers and nearly half its white farmers were sharecroppers or tenants. Few of these earned any cash income at all; those who did averaged about $100 annually. The continued dominance of a few crops—mainly cotton and tobacco—had only intensified the depression by glutting the market and keeping crop prices at rock bottom. The Agricultural Adjustment Administration succeeded in boosting prices by paying farmers to "plow under"—take their land out of production. Particularly in the South, however, these federal subsidies went overwhelmingly to large landowners, who controlled local county committees charged with administering AAA programs. Most planters did not share these payments with sharecroppers and tenants, and individual protest was usually futile.

The Southern Tenant Farmers Union (STFU), founded in 1934, fought both landlords and AAA policies. Active in six southern states and composed of about thirty thousand tenant farmers (over half of them black), the STFU protested evictions, called strikes to raise farm labor wages, and challenged landlords to give tenants their fair share of subsidy payments. The STFU drew national attention to the plight of sharecroppers and tenant farmers, but it failed to influence national farm policy.

New Deal policies helped destroy the old sharecropping and tenant system largely by helping landowners prosper. Those farmers who had access to government funds were able to diversify their crops, consolidate holdings, and work their land more efficiently with laborsaving machinery, such as tractors and mechanical harvesters. Mechanized farming and government-subsidized reductions of cultivated land cut the demand for labor and increased evictions. Uprooted tenants, sharecroppers, and day laborers found themselves on the road in search of work; many thousands migrated to cities and towns.

No New Deal initiative had more impact on southern communities than electrification. In the early 1930s, only about 3 percent of rural Southerners had access to electric power and, hence, to household appliances and farm machinery. The Tennessee Valley Authority and the Rural Electrification Administration (REA) helped millions of southern households move into the modern era by making electricity available for the first time. The TVA built sixteen dams across some 800 miles of the Tennessee River basin, bringing flood control and electric power to hundreds of thousands of families in seven southern states. It also significantly reduced consumer electric rates in many cities and towns by providing a cheaper alternative to private utilities. By 1944, the TVA was the largest power producer in the United States. If rural life was still harsh, electrification allowed farm families to enjoy radio, electric lights, and conveniences that other Americans had long taken for granted.

An Environmental Disaster: The Dust Bowl

An ecological and economic catastrophe of unprecedented proportions struck the southern Great Plains in the mid-1930s. The region had suffered several drought years in the early 1930s. Such dry spells occurred regularly, in roughly twenty-year cycles. But this time, the parched earth became swept up in violent dust storms, the likes of which had never been seen before. The dust storms were largely the consequence of years of stripping the landscape of its natural vegetation. During World War I, wheat brought record-high prices on the world market, and for the next twenty years Great Plains farmers turned the region into a vast wheat factory.

The wide flatlands of the Great Plains were especially suited to mechanized farming, and gasoline-powered tractors, disc plows, and harvester-thresher combines increased productivity enormously. As wheat prices fell in the 1920s, farmers broke still more land to make up the difference with increased production. Great Plains farmers had created an ecological time bomb that exploded when drought returned in the early 1930s. With native grasses destroyed to grow wheat, there was nothing left to prevent soil erosion. Dust storms blew away tens of millions of acres of rich topsoil, and thousands of farm families left the region. Those who stayed suffered calamitous economic and psychological losses. The hardest-hit regions were western Kansas, eastern Colorado, western Oklahoma, the Texas Panhandle, and eastern New Mexico—areas that a Denver journalist named the "Dust Bowl" (see Map 24.2).

Black blizzards of dust a mile and a half high rolled across the landscape, darkening the sky and whipping the earth into great drifts that settled over hundreds of miles. Dust storms made it difficult for humans and livestock to breathe, and destroyed crops and trees over vast areas. "Dust pneumonia" and other respiratory infections afflicted thousands, and many travelers found themselves stranded in automobiles and trains unable to move.

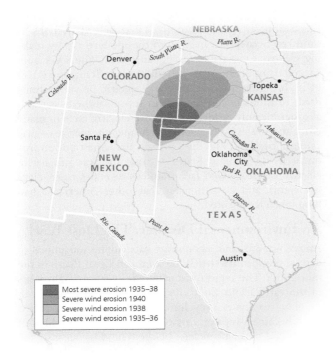

MAP 24.2 The Dust Bowl, 1935–40 This map shows the extent of the Dust Bowl in the southern Great Plains. Federal programs designed to improve soil conservation, water management, and farming practices could not prevent a mass exodus of hundreds of thousands out of the Great Plains.

While large landowners and ranchers were reaping sizable benefits from New Deal programs, thousands of tenant farmers and sharecropper families were being forced off the land in cotton-growing regions of Texas, Oklahoma, Missouri, and Arkansas. They became part of a stream of roughly 300,000 people, disparagingly called "Okies," who migrated to California in the 1930s. California migrants included victims of the Dust Bowl, but the majority were blue-collar workers and small businessmen hoping to improve their economic lot. California suffered from the depression along with the rest of the nation, but it still offered more jobs, higher wages, and higher relief payments than the southern plains. Most Okies could find work only as poorly paid agricultural laborers in the fertile San Joaquin and Imperial Valley districts, facing scorn as "poor white trash" while they struggled to create communities amid the squalor of migrant labor camps (see Communities in Conflict). Only the outbreak of World War II and the

In most Great Plains counties, from one-fifth to one-third of the families applied for relief; in the hardest-hit communities, as many as 90 percent of the families received direct government aid. Many thousands of Great Plains farm families were given direct emergency relief by the Resettlement Administration. Other federal assistance included crop and seed loans, moratoriums on loan payments, and temporary WPA jobs. The AAA paid wheat farmers millions of dollars not to grow what they could not sell and encouraged the diversion of acreage from soil-depleting crops like wheat to soil-enriching crops such as sorghum.

The federal government also pursued longer-range policies designed to alter land-use patterns, reverse soil erosion, and restore grasslands. The Department of Agriculture, under Secretary Henry A. Wallace, sought to change farming practices through the Soil Conservation Service (SCS), which conducted research into controlling wind and water erosion, set up demonstration projects, and offered technical assistance, supplies, and equipment to farmers engaged in conservation work on farms and ranches. By 1940, the acreage subject to dust storms in the Dust Bowl area of the southern plains had been reduced from roughly 50 million acres to fewer than 4 million acres.

Years of Dust. This 1936 poster by the artist and photographer Ben Shahn, served to publicize the work of the Resettlement Administration, which offered aid to destitute farm families hit hard by the Dust Bowl. Shahn's stark imagery here was typical of the documentary aesthetic associated with Depression-era art and photography.

pressing demand for labor allowed migrants to improve their situation significantly.

Mexican farm laborers faced stiff competition from Dust Bowl refugees. By the mid-1930s, they no longer dominated California's agricultural workforce. In 1936, an estimated 85 to 90 percent of the state's migratory workers were white Americans, as compared to less than 20 percent before the depression. Mexican farm worker families who managed to stay employed in California, Texas, and Colorado saw their wages plummet.

Southwestern communities, responding to racial hostility from unemployed whites and looking for ways to reduce their welfare burden, campaigned to deport Mexicans and Mexican Americans. Employers, private charities, and the Immigration and Naturalization Service joined in this effort. Authorities made little effort to distinguish citizens from aliens; most of the children they deported had been born in the United States and, hence, were citizens. Los Angeles County had the most aggressive campaign, using boxcars to ship out more than 13,000 Mexicans between 1931 and 1934. The hostile climate convinced thousands more to leave voluntarily. Approximately one-third of Los Angeles's 150,000 Mexican and Mexican American residents left the city in the early 1930s.

Water Policy

The New Deal ushered in the era of large-scale water projects, designed to provide irrigation and cheap power and to prevent floods. The long-range impact of these undertakings on western life was enormous. The key government agency in this realm was the Bureau of Reclamation of the Department of the Interior, established in 1902. The bureau's original responsibility had been to construct dams and irrigation works and thereby to encourage the growth of small farms throughout the arid regions of the West. Until the late 1920s, its efforts had been of little consequence. Its fortunes changed when its focus shifted to building huge multipurpose dams designed to control entire river systems (see Map 24.3).

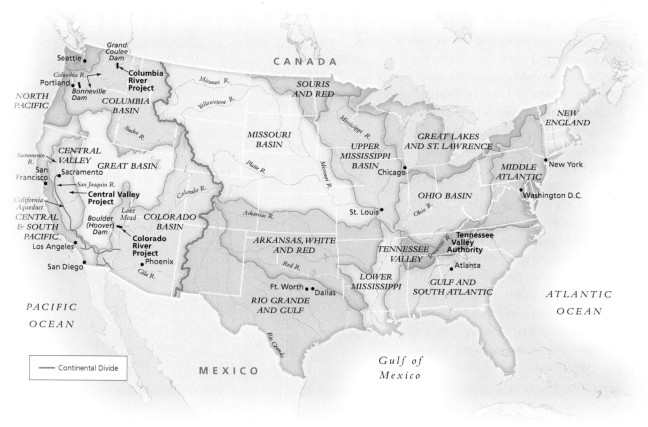

MAP 24.3 The New Deal and Water This map illustrates U.S. drainage areas and the major large-scale water projects begun or completed by federal agencies in them during the New Deal. By providing irrigation, cheap power, flood control, and recreation areas, these public works had a historically unprecedented impact on America's western communities.

Californians Face the Influx of "Dust Bowl" Migrants

During the 1930s, between 300,000 and 400,000 Americans left Oklahoma, Texas, Arkansas, and Missouri for a new life in California. Like westward pioneers of old they sought a better life. In the depths of the depression, however, most found only a shortage of work, low wages, and housing in tent camps or shacks. Many of these migrants were victims of the Dust Bowl disaster, but others were depression-hit town and city dwellers attracted by stories of opportunity in California. The new migration was most visible in rich agricultural areas, such as the San Joaquin Valley, about 100 miles from Los Angeles.

The state was largely hostile to poor newcomers. California's 1933 Indigent Act made it a crime to bring people with no visible means of support into the state, and dozens were prosecuted for helping relatives move to California. In 1936, the Los Angeles police department set up a border patrol, known as the "Bum Blockade," to turn back "undesirables" trying to enter the city limits. But the plight of the migrants also received widespread publicity and support in works like John Steinbeck's 1939 novel, *The Grapes of Wrath*, the evocative photographs of Dorothea Lange, and the reporting of journalists like Carey McWilliams and Paul Taylor. Most of this publicity focused on the problems faced by white families, who increasingly replaced the Mexicans, Filipinos, and single males who had traditionally worked the seasonal harvest.

A feature piece in the *Los Angeles Times* on July 21, 1937, offers a harrowing but sympathetic account of life among the roughly 50,000 migrant workers in the San Joaquin Valley. The focus is on the poor conditions endured by the migrants, as well as where they have come from. The opposing excerpt reflects the views of the California Citizens' Association, one of several conservative groups that saw the migrants as a growing peril to California's economy and social stability. In 1941, after a challenge to the Indigent Act by the American Civil Liberties Union, the U.S. Supreme Court ruled in *Edwards* v. *California* that states had no power to restrict migration by poor people or any other American citizens.

Los Angeles Times, July 21, 1937: "Squatter Army Wages Grim Battle for Life"

Human squalor—a picture of approximately 50,000 persons driven to California by dust storms, drought, ill health and debts—awaits the visitor looking beyond the roadside today in the San Joaquin Valley. A new chapter in American history is being written here. A battle for life, for food, health, homes and security is being waged by these hordes of transient indigents.

Within an hour the skeptic must admit he has seen disease, privation, filth and threats of epidemics. But he also must admit that he is seeing a fight for a home similar to that of the pioneers in the South and Middle West in the last century. These people are not hoboes. They are not tramps. They are not foreigners. They are men destroyed financially in the Middle West and Southwest. Many are the cotton belt "white trash" but they are Americans.

Whether one visits the Federal Resettlement Administration's camps at Shafter and Arvin or the huddles of migrant indigents beside the roads throughout Kern county, one almost is struck dumb with sympathy. Ranchers have provided eighty-six camps, ranging in size from a few dirty tents and tin shacks to the seventy-one bunkhouses, tents, trailer houses, railroad box and refrigerator cars on the Digiorgio farms near Alvin. The Digiorgio layout includes separate quarters for Americans, Filipinos, and Mexicans. But most camps throughout the county are populated by white Americans.

> "These people are not hoboes. They are not tramps."

• **How do these two accounts differ in their perceptions of who the migrants are and their motives for coming to California? How do they understand the meaning of "citizenship"?**

• **Do you find any correlations between these two documents and the contemporary debates over "illegal immigration" to the United States?**

There is no starvation—yet. Despite Works Progress Administration, State Relief Administration, and Kern County Welfare Department rules to care first for permanent residents, these transients do occasionally receive financial aid and hospitalization. But funds are almost totally lacking to aid them adequately. The men pick fruit and chop cotton. They earn an average of $2.75 to $3 a day. But they work, at the most, only half the days of the year. They must follow the crops throughout the San Joaquin Valley, and meantime their wives and children are falling prey to disease. Most camps have no baths, no showers, poor plumbing.

San Joaquin Valley growers welcome the indigents. Some have even advertised in the Southwestern States, inviting them, the workers say. As M.W. Skelton, Kern county welfare and county relief administration director, explains: "The growers prefer the migratory workers to permanent residents. The relief client may feel that if he doesn't like his job he can go back on the dole. The out-of-State workers must stay on the job."

What will happen next winter? Everyone is afraid to answer. Relief officials pray for Federal funds. Ranchers want more adequate camps. Police hope a crime wave will not break out. But no one can predict without a prayer.

SOURCE: From Ray Zeman, "Squatter Army Wages Grim Battle for Life," in the *Los Angeles Times*, July 21, 1937. Copyright © 1937 by The Los Angeles Times. Reprinted by permission.

Thomas McManus, California Citizens' Associations: California "Indigents Peril"

The Federal government is responsible for hundreds of thousands of indigents coming to this State. They stay here a year—then they are citizens, adding their burden of relief to the State.

The State Relief Administration relief fund is near exhaustion. If this keeps up it will break down entirely the security of citizens of this State.

It has been necessary for manufacturers and employers of the State to meet this influx. The result has been a breaking down of our wage standards. These indigents are willing to work for from one-third to one-sixth of the wage scale throughout the State—anything to get food and anything to stay here long enough to gain citizenship in the State.

We've kept the wage scales high here. As a result, indigents can come here, get on WPA, and make more than they ever made in their lives in their home sectors. Our wage scales in WPA are two or three times as large as they are where these people come from.

It is up to us to defend our legitimate California people—we can care for them with old age pensions and relief, but certainly we can't take care of the indigents of other states.

Our program is to save California jobs for Californians—if the Federal government is going to spend moneys for them let them spend where they live and keep them there. We have plenty of native youth in this State growing up who need the jobs there are here—we don't need relief chiselers from other States coming here chiseling the jobs of Californians.

SOURCE: "Indigents Peril" speech by Thomas McManus, Secretary, California Citizens' Association, *Los Angeles Times*, August 24, 1938. Copyright © 1938 The Los Angeles Times. Reprinted by permission.

"We don't need relief chiselers from other States."

The first of these projects, Boulder Dam (later renamed Hoover Dam), was designed to harness the Colorado River, the wildest and most isolated of the major western rivers. Completed in 1935 with the help of funds from the Public Works Administration, Boulder Dam's total cost was $114 million, to be offset by the sale of its hydroelectric power. Los Angeles and neighboring cities built a 259-mile aqueduct, costing $220 million, to channel water to their growing populations. Lake Mead, created by construction of the dam, became the world's largest artificial lake, extending 115 miles up the canyon and providing a popular new recreation area. The dam's irrigation water helped make the Imperial Valley, covering over 500,000 acres, one of the most productive agricultural districts in the world.

The success of Boulder Dam transformed the Bureau of Reclamation into a major federal agency commanding huge resources. In 1938, it completed the All-American Canal—an 80-mile channel connecting the Colorado River to the Imperial Valley and with a 130-mile branch to the Coachella Valley. This opened up more than a million acres of desert land to the cultivation of citrus fruits, melons, vegetables, and cotton. Irrigation districts receiving water promised to repay, without interest, the cost of the canal over a forty-year period.

In 1935, the bureau launched the giant Central Valley Project (CVP) in California's 500-mile-long interior watershed, designed to bring water from the Sacramento River in the north down to the arid San Joaquin Valley in the south. Costing $2.3 billion, the project was not completed until 1947. The CVP stored water and transferred it to the drier southern regions of the state. It also provided electricity, flood control, and municipal water.

The largest power and irrigation project of all was Grand Coulee Dam, northwest of Spokane, Washington. Completed in 1941, it was designed to convert the power of the Columbia River into cheap electricity and to irrigate previously uncultivated land, thereby stimulating economic development in the Pacific Northwest. Tens of thousands of workers built Grand Coulee, and the project pumped millions of dollars into the region's badly depressed economy. Between 1933 and 1940, Washington State ranked first in per-capita federal expenditures. In the longer run, Grand Coulee provided the cheapest electricity in the United States and helped attract new manufacturing to a region previously dependent on the export of lumber and ore.

These technological marvels and the new economic development they stimulated were not without an environmental and human cost. Grand Coulee and smaller dams nearby reduced the Columbia River, long a potent symbol of the western wilderness, to a string of lakes. Spawning salmon could no longer run the river above the dam. In California, the federal guarantee of river water made a relative handful of large farmers fabulously wealthy. But tens of thousands of farm workers, mostly of Mexican descent, labored in the newly fertile fields for very low wages, and pesticides undermined their health. The Colorado River, its flow into the sea drastically diminished, began to build up salt deposits, making its water increasingly unfit for drinking or irrigation. Water pollution in the form of high salinity continues to plague the 2,000-mile river.

A New Deal for Indians

The New Deal brought important changes and some limited improvements to the lives of Indians. In 1933, some 320,000 Indian people, belonging to about 200 tribes, lived on reservations, mostly in Oklahoma, Arizona, New Mexico, and South Dakota. Indians were the nation's poorest people with an infant mortality rate twice that of whites. Alcoholism, tuberculosis, and measles occurred at much higher rates on the reservation than off. Half of all those on reservations were landless. The Bureau of Indian Affairs (BIA) had a long history of corruption and mismanagement. For years, it had tried to assimilate Indians through education, in the process routinely interfering with Indian religious and tribal customs.

In 1933, Roosevelt appointed John Collier to bring change to the BIA. Collier had deep roots in progressive-era social work in eastern big-city slums. As the new BIA head, Collier pledged to "stop wronging the Indians and to rewrite the cruel and stupid laws that rob them and crush their family lives." Collier became the driving force behind the Indian Reorganization Act (IRA) of 1934. The IRA reversed the allotment provisions of the Dawes Severalty Act of 1887, which had weakened tribal sovereignty by shifting the distribution of land from tribes to individuals (see Chapter 18). The new legislation permitted the restoration of surplus reservation lands to tribal ownership, and it allocated funds to purchase additional lands and for economic development. At its heart, the IRA sought to restore tribal structures by making the tribes instruments of the federal government. Any tribe that ratified the IRA could then elect a tribal council that would enjoy federal recognition as the legal tribal government. Collier fought first to get the legislation through a reluctant Congress, uneasy with reversing the long-standing policy of Indian assimilation.

The more difficult battle involved winning approval by Indian peoples. Collier's efforts to win acceptance of the IRA met with mixed results on the reservations. Linguistic barriers made it nearly impossible for some tribes to fully assess the plan. In all, 181 tribes organized governments under the IRA, while 77 tribes rejected it.

Under Collier, the BIA became much more sensitive to Indian cultural and religious freedom. The number of Indian people employed by the BIA itself increased from a few hundred in 1933 to more than 4,600 in 1940. Collier trumpeted the principle of Indian political autonomy, a radical idea for the day. In practice, however, both the BIA and Congress regularly interfered with reservation governments, especially in money matters. For the long run, Collier's most important legacy was the reassertion of the status of Indian tribes as semisovereign nations. In 1934, a Department of the Interior lawyer, Nathan Margold, wrote a legal opinion that tribal governments retained all their original powers—their "internal sovereignty"—except when these were specifically limited by acts of Congress. Decades later, U.S. courts would uphold the Margold opinion, leading to a significant restoration of tribal rights and land to Indian peoples of the West.

The Limits of Reform

In his second Inaugural Address, Roosevelt emphasized that much remained to be done to remedy the effects of the depression. "I see one-third of a nation ill-housed, ill-clad, ill-nourished," the president said. With his stunning electoral victory, the future for further social reform seemed bright. Yet by 1937, the New Deal was in retreat. A rapid political turnaround over the next two years put continuing social reform efforts on the defensive.

Court Packing

After his landslide reelection, and still smarting from the Supreme Court having struck down the NRA and the AAA, Roosevelt wanted more friendly justices. In February 1937, he asked Congress to allow him to make new Supreme Court appointments whenever a justice failed to retire upon reaching age seventy. This would expand the Court from nine to a maximum of fifteen justices, the majority presumably sympathetic to the New Deal. Newspapers almost unanimously denounced FDR's "court-packing bill."

Even more damaging was the determined opposition from a congressional coalition of conservatives and outraged New Dealers. The president gamely fought on, disingenuously insisting that his purpose was simply to reduce the workload of elderly Supreme Court justices. As the battle dragged on through the spring and summer, FDR's claims weakened. Then a conservative justice retired, permitting Roosevelt to make his first Court appointment. More important, several justices began voting for rather than against Roosevelt's laws, so that the Court upheld the constitutionality of key measures from the second New Deal, including the Social Security Act and the National Labor Relations Act. At the end of August 1937, FDR backed off his court-packing scheme and accepted a compromise bill that reformed lower court procedures but left the Supreme Court untouched.

FDR lost the battle for his judiciary proposal, but he may have won the war for a more responsive Court. Still, the political price was very high. The Court fight badly weakened Roosevelt's relations with Congress. Many more conservative Democrats felt free to oppose further New Deal measures.

The Women's Network

The New Deal brought a measurable, if temporary, increase in women's political influence. For those women associated with social reform, the New Deal opened up possibilities to effect change. A "women's network," linked by personal friendships and professional connections, made its presence felt in national politics and government. Most of the women in this network had deep roots in progressive-era movements promoting suffrage, labor law reform, and welfare programs (see Chapter 21).

The center of the women's network, First Lady Eleanor Roosevelt, became a powerful political figure, using her prominence to fight for liberal causes. She revolutionized the role of the political wife by taking a position involving no institutional duties and turning it into a base for independent action. Privately, she enjoyed great influence with her husband, and behind the scenes she supported a wide network of women professionals and reformers whom she had come to know in the 1920s. As a strong supporter of protective labor legislation for women, she owed much to the social reform tradition of the women's movement. One of her first public acts as First Lady was to convene a White House Conference on the Emergency Needs of Women in November 1933.

Eleanor Roosevelt worked vigorously for antilynching legislation, compulsory health insurance, and child-labor reform, and she fought racial discrimination in New Deal relief programs. She saw herself as the guardian of "human values" within the administration, a buffer between depression victims and government bureaucracy. She frequently testified before legislative committees, lobbied her husband privately and the Congress publicly, and wrote a widely syndicated newspaper column.

Mrs. Roosevelt's closest political ally was Molly Dewson. A longtime social worker and suffragist, Dewson wielded great political clout as director of the Women's Division of the national Democratic Party. Under her leadership, women for the first time played a central role in shaping the party platform and running election campaigns. Dewson proved a tireless organizer, traveling to cities and towns around the country and educating women about Democratic policies and candidates. Her success impressed the president, and he relied on her judgment in recommending political appointments.

Perhaps Dewson's most important success came in persuading FDR to appoint Frances Perkins secretary of labor—the first woman cabinet member in U.S. history. A veteran activist for social welfare and reform, Perkins had served as FDR's industrial commissioner in New York before coming to Washington. As labor secretary, Perkins embodied the gains made by women in appointive offices. Her department was responsible for creating the Social Security Act and the Fair Labor Standards Act of 1938, both of which incorporated protective measures long advocated by women reformers. New Deal agencies opened up spaces for scores of women in the federal bureaucracy. These women were concentrated in Perkins's Labor Department, the FERA and WPA, and the Social Security Board. In addition, the social work profession, which remained roughly two-thirds female in the 1930s, grew enormously in response to the massive relief and welfare programs. By 1940, 25 percent of the workforce was female, as hard times increased the ranks of married working women. But sexual stereotyping still routinely forced most women into low-paying, low-status jobs. In sum, although the 1930s saw no radical challenges to existing male and female roles, working-class women and professional women held their own and managed to make some gains.

A New Deal for Minorities?

Long near the bottom of the American economic ladder, African Americans suffered disproportionately in the Great Depression. The old saying among black workers that they were "last hired, first fired" was never truer than during times of high unemployment. Out-of-work whites coveted even traditional "Negro jobs"—domestic service, cooking, janitorial work, and elevator operating.

Overall, the Roosevelt administration made little overt effort to combat the racism and segregation entrenched in American life. FDR was especially worried about offending the powerful Southern Democratic congressmen. Local administration of many federal programs meant that most early New Deal programs routinely accepted discrimination. The CCC established separate camps for African Americans. The NRA labor codes tolerated lower wages for black workers doing the same jobs as white workers. African Americans could not get jobs with the TVA. When local AAA committees in the South reduced acreage and production to boost prices, thousands of black sharecroppers and farm laborers were forced off the land. Racism was also embedded in the provisions of the Social Security Act and National Labor Relations Act, both of which explicitly excluded domestics and

farm laborers—whose ranks were disproportionately African American and Hispanic—from coverage.

Yet some limited gains were made. Roosevelt issued an executive order in 1935 banning discrimination in WPA projects. In cities, the WPA enabled thousands of jobless African Americans to survive, at minimum wages of $12 a week. Between 15 and 20 percent of all WPA employees were black people, although African Americans made up less than 10 percent of the nation's population. The Public Works Administration, under Harold Ickes, constructed a number of integrated housing complexes and employed more than its fair share of black workers in construction.

FDR appointed several African Americans to second-level positions in his administration. This group became known as "the Black Cabinet." Mary McLeod Bethune, an educator who rose from a sharecropping background to found Bethune-Cookman College, proved a superb leader of the Office of Minority Affairs in the National Youth Administration. Her most successful programs substantially reduced black illiteracy. Harvard-trained Robert Weaver advised the president on economic affairs, and in 1966, became the first black cabinet member when he was appointed secretary of housing and urban development.

Hard times were equally trying for Mexican Americans. As the Great Depression drastically reduced the demand for their labor, they faced massive layoffs, deepening poverty, and deportation. During the 1930s, more than 400,000 Mexican nationals and their children

First Lady Eleanor Roosevelt rides with miners in a flag-decorated car during a visit to the mining town of Bellaire, Ohio, in 1935. Mrs. Roosevelt was more outspoken than the president in championing the rights of labor and African Americans, and she actively used her prestige as First Lady in support of social justice causes.

returned to Mexico, often coerced by local officials unwilling to provide them with relief but happy to offer train fare to border towns. For those who stayed, the New Deal programs did little to help. The AAA benefited large growers, not laborers. Neither the National Labor Relations Act nor the Social Security Act made any provisions for farm laborers. After 1937, the WPA eliminated aliens from eligibility, causing great hardship for thousands of Mexican families.

The New Deal made no explicit attempt to attack the deeply rooted patterns of racism and discrimination in American life. The entrenched power of white Southern Democrats in the Congress and the exclusion of black voters from southern politics made such an assault unthinkable. There were, however, occasional symbolic victories for racial equality. In 1939, the conservative Daughters of the American Revolution (DAR) refused to permit the world-renowned African American classical singer Marian Anderson to perform in the DAR's Washington hall. Eleanor Roosevelt and Interior Secretary Harold Ickes intervened to arrange for Anderson to perform on Easter Sunday at the Lincoln Memorial before an integrated audience of 75,000. More broadly, African Americans, especially in the cities, benefited from New Deal relief and work programs, even though this assistance was not color-blind. Black industrial workers made inroads into labor unions affiliated with the CIO. By 1936, an important political shift had begun: for the first time, a majority of black voters abandoned "the party of Lincoln" and voted Democratic. Black voters and hardened white segregationists would coexist uneasily as partners in the New Deal coalition, a tension that would strain the Democratic Party for decades to come.

The Roosevelt Recession and the Ebbing of the New Deal

The nation's economy had improved significantly by 1937. Unemployment had declined to *only* 14 percent (9 million people), farm prices had improved to 1930 levels, and industrial production was slightly higher than the 1929 mark. Economic traditionalists, led by FDR's treasury secretary, called for reducing the federal deficit, which had grown to more than $4 billion in fiscal year 1936. Roosevelt, always uneasy about the growing national debt, called for large reductions in federal spending, and the Fed, worried about inflation, tightened credit policies.

This retrenchment caused a steep recession. The stock market plunged in August 1937, and industrial output and farm prices plummeted. Unemployment shot up alarmingly; by March 1938, it hovered around 20 percent, with more than 13 million people looking for work.

The blunt reality was that even after five years, the New Deal had not brought about economic recovery.

Throughout 1937 and 1938, the administration drifted. Roosevelt received conflicting advice on the economy. Some advisers, suspicious of the reluctance of business to make new investments, urged a massive antitrust campaign against monopolies. Others urged a return to the strategy of "priming the economic pump" with more federal spending. Emergency spending bills in the spring of 1938 put new life into the WPA and the PWA. But Republican gains in the 1938 congressional elections made it harder than ever to get new reform measures through. Conservative Southern Democrats increasingly allied themselves with Republicans in a coalition that would dominate Congress until the mid-1960s.

There were a couple of important exceptions. The 1938 Fair Labor Standards Act established the first federal minimum wage (twenty-five cents an hour) and set a maximum workweek of forty-four hours for all employees engaged in interstate commerce. The National Housing Act of 1937, also known as the Wagner-Steagall Act, funded public housing construction and slum clearance and provided rent subsidies for low-income families. But by and large, by 1938, the reform whirlwind of the New Deal was over.

Depression-Era Culture

The Great Depression profoundly affected American culture, as it did all other aspects of national life. Yet contradictory messages coexisted, sometimes within the same novel or movie. With American capitalism facing its worst crisis in history, radical expressions of protest and revolution became more frequent. But there were also strong celebrations of individualism, nostalgia for a simpler, rural past, and many attempts to define American core virtues.

A New Deal for the Arts

The depression hit America's writers, artists, and teachers just as hard as it did blue-collar workers. In 1935, the WPA allocated $300 million for the unemployed in these fields. Over the next four years, Federal Project No. 1, an umbrella agency covering writing, theater, music, and the visual arts, proved to be one of the most innovative and successful New Deal programs. "Federal One" offered work to desperate unemployed artists and intellectuals, enriched the cultural lives of millions, and left a substantial artistic and cultural legacy. Nearly all these works were informed by the "documentary impulse," a deep desire to record and communicate the experiences of ordinary Americans.

At its height, the Federal Writers Project employed 5,000 writers on a variety of programs. Most notably, it produced a popular (and still useful) series of state and city guidebooks. The 150-volume *Life in America* series included valuable oral histories of former slaves, studies of

Fletcher Martin painted *Mine Rescue* (1939) in the Kellogg, Idaho, post office. The work was part of a Treasury Department program that employed unemployed artists to beautify government buildings. The mural was eventually removed under pressure from local citizens who worried that it might upset those who had lost loved ones in mine accidents.

SOURCE: Fletcher Martin (1904–1979), *Mine Rescue*, 1939, mural study for Kellog, Idaho Post Office; tempera on panel, 15-¾ × 36-½ in (40.0 × 92.7 cm). Copyright Smithsonian American Art Museum, Washington, DC/Art Resource, NY.

ethnic and Indian cultures, and pioneering collections of American songs and folk tales. Work on the Writers Project helped many American writers to survive, to hone their craft, and later to achieve prominence—among them Ralph Ellison, Richard Wright, Margaret Walker, John Cheever, Saul Bellow, and Zora Neale Hurston. Novelist Anzia Yezierska recalled a strong spirit of camaraderie among the writers: "Each morning I walked to the Project as light-hearted as if I were going to a party." The Federal Theater Project (FTP) reached as many as 30 million Americans with its productions, expanding the audience for theater beyond the regular patrons of the commercial stage. Among its most successful productions were T. S. Eliot's *Murder in the Cathedral*, Maxwell Anderson's *Valley Forge*, and Orson Welles's version of *Macbeth* with an all-black cast. The parallel Federal Music Project, under Nikolai Sokoloff of the Cleveland Symphony Orchestra, employed 15,000 musicians and financed hundreds of thousands of low-priced public concerts by touring orchestras. The Composers' Forum Laboratory commissioned new works by important young American classical composers.

Among the struggling painters, later world famous, who received government assistance through the Federal Art Project (FAP) were Willem de Kooning, Jackson Pollock, and Louise Nevelson. The FAP employed painters and sculptors to teach studio skills and art history in schools, churches, and settlement houses. It also commissioned artists to paint hundreds of murals on the walls of post offices, meeting halls, courthouses, and other government buildings.

The Documentary Impulse

During the 1930s, an enormous number of artists, novelists, journalists, photographers, and filmmakers tried to document the devastation wrought by the depression in American communities. They also depicted people's struggles to cope with, and reverse, hard times. Mainstream mass media, such as *Life* magazine with its photo essays or "March of Time" newsreels, also adapted this stance.

The "documentary impulse" became a prominent style in 1930s' cultural expression. The most direct and influential expression of the documentary style was the photograph. In 1935, Roy Stryker, chief of the Historical Section of the Resettlement Administration, gathered a remarkable group of photographers to help document the work of the agency. Stryker encouraged them to photograph whatever caught their interest, even if the pictures had no direct connection with RA projects. These photographers, including Dorothea Lange and Walker Evans, left the single most significant visual record of the Great Depression. They traveled through rural areas, small towns, and migrant labor camps, and they produced powerful images of despair and resignation, of hope and resilience. Stryker believed that the faces of the subjects were most memorable. "You could look at the people," he wrote, "and see fear and sadness and desperation. But you saw something else, too. A determination that not even the depression could kill. The photographers saw it—documented it" (see Seeing History).

That double vision, combining a frank portrayal of pain and suffering with a faith in the possibility of overcoming disaster, could be found in many other cultural works of the period. John Steinbeck's *Grapes of Wrath* (1939), soon made into an acclaimed film, sympathetically portrayed the hardships of Oklahoma Dust Bowl migrants on their way to California. "We ain't gonna die out," Ma Joad asserts near the end of the book. "People is goin' on—changing' a little, maybe, but goin' right on." Many writers interrupted their work to travel around the country and discover the thoughts and feelings of ordinary people. "With real events looming larger than any imagined happenings," novelist Elizabeth Noble wrote, "documentary films and still photographs, reportage and the like have taken the place once held by the grand invention."

Waiting for Lefty

For some, capitalism itself was responsible for the Great Depression. Relatively few Americans became communists or socialists in the 1930s (at its height, the Communist Party of the United States had perhaps 100,000 members), and many of these remained active for only a brief time. Yet Marxist analysis, with its emphasis on class conflict and the failures of capitalism, had a wide influence on thought and writing.

Some writers joined the Communist Party, seeing in the Soviet Union an alternative to an American system mired in exploitation, racial inequality, and human misery. Communist writers sought to radicalize art and literature and celebrated collective struggle rather than individual achievement. Granville Hicks, an editor of the radical magazine the *New Masses*, flatly declared: "If there is any other working interpretation of the apparent chaos than that which presents itself in terms of the class struggle, it has not been revealed."

A more common pattern for intellectuals, especially young ones, was brief flirtation with communism. Many African American writers, attracted by the Communist Party's militant opposition to lynching, job discrimination, and segregation, briefly joined the party or found their first supportive audiences there. These included Richard Wright, Ralph Ellison, and Langston Hughes.

Watch the Video

Dorothea Lange and Migrant Mother at **www.myhistorylab.com**

Playwrights and actors associated with New York's influential Group Theater were often part of the Communist Party orbit in those years. One production of the group, Clifford Odets's *Waiting for Lefty* (1935), depicted a union-organizing drive among taxi drivers. At the climax, someone yells that the organizer Lefty (for whom everyone has been waiting) has been killed by the police, and the audience joins the actors in shouting "Strike!" A commercial and political success, it offered perhaps the most celebrated example of radical, politically engaged art.

Left-wing influence reached its height after 1935 during the "Popular Front" period. Alarmed by the rise of fascism in Europe (see Chapter 25), communists around the world followed the Soviet line of aligning with liberals and other antifascists. Some 3,000 American men and women volunteered for the Communist Party–organized by the Abraham Lincoln Brigade, which fought in the Spanish Civil War on the republican side against the fascists led by Francisco Franco. The Lincolns' sense of commitment and sacrifice appealed to millions of Americans sympathetic to the republican cause. At home, the American Communist Party adopted the slogan "Communism is Twentieth-Century Americanism," and Communists proclaimed strong support of Roosevelt's New Deal (which before they had denounced). Their influence became especially strong within the labor movement as Communists and other radicals, known for their dedication and effectiveness, played a leading role in the difficult CIO unionizing drives in the auto, steel, and electrical industries. The radical presence was also strong within certain WPA arts projects. A decade later, many young idealists who came into the Communist Party orbit, no matter how briefly, would pay a heavy price.

Raising Spirits: Film, Radio, and the Swing Era

Despite the depression, the mass-culture industry expanded enormously during the 1930s. If mass culture offered little in the way of direct responses to the economic and social problems of the day, it nonetheless played a more integral role than ever in shaping the rhythms and desires of the nation's everyday life.

Toward the end of the 1920s, the coming of "talking pictures" helped make movies the most popular entertainment form of the day. More than 60 percent of Americans attended one of the nation's 20,000 movie houses each week, and millions followed the lives and careers of movie stars more avidly than ever. At the same time, the movie studios themselves, responding to pressure from the Roman Catholic Church and other advocates of traditional morality, instituted a more stringent Production Code in 1933. For the next three decades, American filmmakers had to work within very narrow parameters of what was acceptable to depict on-screen. The code required unambiguous depictions of good triumphing over evil and a straight-laced treatment of sex.

With so many movies being churned out by Hollywood studios for so many fans, it is difficult to generalize about the cultural impact of individual films. Gangster films did very well in the early depression years, depicting violent criminals brought to justice by society—but along the way, they gave audiences a vicarious exposure to the pleasures of wealth, power, and

Documenting Hard Times in Black and White and Color

Between 1935 and 1942, photographers working for the Farm Security Administration (FSA) created a remarkable pictorial record of depression life. The photography project had a political goal as well: to prod New Deal agricultural policy into providing greater support for the poorest agricultural workers. The photographers thus took aim at social, economic, and racial inequalities within American agriculture. They worked under difficult conditions. On the road for months, they worked in harsh weather, often eating bad food and staying in primitive accommodations, trying to capture the lives of subjects suspicious of their motives. Their unexposed film had to be processed in Washington, so the photographers never knew what they had shot until they received prints weeks later.

Many FSA photographs were published in newspapers and popular magazines as part of the agency's campaign to win public support for a greater federal role in building more migrant worker camps. Some of these photographs, such as those by Dorothea Lange and Walker Evans, have become among the most widely circulated images in the history of the medium. Even though Lange's *Migrant Mother* became a kind of universal symbol of suffering, its context and social-science origins have been lost. Her original caption simply read, "Destitute pea pickers in California. Mother of seven children. Age thirty-two."

In 1939, some FSA photographers began using new 35-mm Kodachrome film to make color slides. Unlike black-and-white prints, color slides were neither easily made nor reproducible in newspapers and magazines. Black-and-white images also seemed to offer a starker, more "realistic" documentation of poverty; many thought color photos too cheery. FSA photographers produced some 164,000 black-and-white images and only about 1,600 in color. Photographs like Russell Lee's, however, remind us that people lived lives in color, even during the depression.

• **How does Lee's portrait of the homesteader couple compare to Lange's portrait of the *Migrant Mother* as a document of rural life in the Great Depression? Are there differences beyond black and white and color?**

lawbreaking. Social disorder could also be treated comically, as in such classic Marx Brothers films as *Duck Soup* (1933) and *A Night at the Opera* (1935). Mae West's popular comedies made people laugh by cleverly subverting expectations about sex roles. West was an independent woman, not afraid of pleasure. When asked on-screen (by Cary Grant), "Haven't you ever met a man who could make you happy?" she replied, "Sure, lots of times."

By and large, Hollywood avoided social or political controversy. Some 1930s' filmmakers expressed highly personal visions of core American values. Two who succeeded in capturing both popular and critical acclaim were Walt Disney and Frank Capra. By the mid-1930s, Disney's animated cartoons (including Mickey Mouse) had become moral tales that preached following the rules. Capra's comedies idealized a small-town America, with close families and comfortable homes. Although Capra's films dealt with contemporary problems more than most, he seemed to suggest that most of the country's ills could be solved if only its leaders learned the old-fashioned values of "common people"—kindness, loyalty, and charity.

Radio broadcasting emerged as the most powerful medium of communication in the home, profoundly changing the rhythms and routines of everyday life. In 1930, roughly 12 million American homes (40 percent of the total) had radio sets; by the end of the decade, 90 percent had them. Advertisers dominated the structure and content of American radio, forming a powerful alliance with the two large networks, the National Broadcasting Company (NBC) and the Columbia Broadcasting System (CBS). The Federal Communications Commission, established in 1934, continued long-standing policies that favored commercial broadcasting over other arrangements, such as municipal or university programming.

Reginald Marsh, *Twenty Cent Movie*, 1936. Marsh documented the urban landscape of the 1930s with great empathy, capturing the city's contradictory mix of commercialism, optimism, energy, and degradation. The popularity of Hollywood films and their stars reached new heights during the Great Depression.

SOURCE: Reginald Marsh, *Twenty Cent Movie*, 1936. Egg tempera on composition board. 40" × 40". Whitney Museum of American Art/Artists Rights Society, New York.

The depression actually helped radio expand. An influx of talent arrived from the weakened worlds of vaudeville, ethnic theater, and the recording industry. The well-financed networks offered an attractive outlet to advertisers seeking a national audience. Radio programming achieved a regularity and professionalism absent in the 1920s, making it much easier for a listener to identify a show with its sponsor. Much of network radio was based on older cultural forms. The variety show, hosted by comedians and singers, and based on the old vaudeville format, was the first important style. Its stars constantly plugged the sponsor's product. The use of an audible studio audience re-created the human interaction so necessary in vaudeville. The popular comedy show *Amos 'n' Andy* adapted the minstrel "blackface" tradition to the new medium. Its two white comedians used only their voices to invent a world of stereotyped African Americans for millions of listeners.

Daytime serials, dubbed "soap operas," dominated radio drama. Aimed at women working in the home, these serials alone constituted 60 percent of all daytime shows by 1940. Soaps revolved around strong, warm female characters who provided advice and strength to weak, indecisive friends and relatives. Action counted very little; the development of character and relationships was all-important. Thrillers such as *The Shadow* aired in the evening when whole families could listen; they emphasized crime and suspense and made clever use of music and sound effects.

Radio news arrived in the 1930s, showing the medium's potential for direct and immediate coverage of political events. Network news and commentary shows multiplied rapidly. Complex political and economic issues and the impending European crisis (see Chapter 25) fueled a news hunger among Americans. A 1939 survey found that 70 percent of Americans relied on the radio as their prime source of news. Yet commercial broadcasting, dominated by big sponsors and large radio manufacturers, failed to cover politically controversial events such as labor struggles.

One measure of radio's cultural impact was its role in popularizing jazz. Before the 1930s, jazz was heard largely among African Americans and a small coterie of white fans. Regular broadcasts of live performances exposed a broader public to the music. Bands led by black artists such as Duke Ellington and Count Basie began to enjoy reputations outside of traditional jazz centers like Chicago, Kansas City, and New York.

Benny Goodman became the key figure in the "swing era," largely through radio exposure. Goodman, a white, classically trained clarinetist, had been inspired by African American bandleaders who created big-band arrangements that combined harmonic call-and-response patterns with breaks for improvised solos. Goodman purchased a series of these arrangements, smoothing out the sound but keeping the strong dance beat. His band's late Saturday night broadcasts began to attract attention, and in 1935, at the Palomar Ballroom in Los Angeles, made the breakthrough that established his enormous popularity. When his band started playing, the young crowd, primed by radio broadcasts, roared its approval and began to dance wildly. Goodman's music was perfect for doing the jitterbug or lindy hop, dances borrowed from African American culture. As the "King of Swing," Goodman helped make big-band jazz a hit with millions of teenagers and young adults from all backgrounds. In the late 1930s, big-band music by artists like Goodman, Ellington, and Basie accounted for the majority of million-selling records.

Conclusion

Far from being the radical program its conservative critics charged, the New Deal did little to alter fundamental property relations or the distribution of wealth. Indeed, most of its programs largely failed to help the most powerless groups in America—migrant workers, tenant farmers and sharecroppers, African Americans, and other minorities. But the New Deal profoundly changed many areas of American life. Overall, it radically increased the role of the federal government in American lives and communities, creating a new kind of liberalism defined by an activist state. Social Security, unemployment insurance, and federal relief programs established at least the framework for a welfare state. The FDIC and the SEC established important new federal rules protecting individuals from financial ruin and unregulated stock markets. For the first time in American history, the national government took responsibility for assisting its needy citizens. And also for the first time, the federal government guaranteed the rights of workers to join trade unions, and it set standards for minimum wages and maximum hours. Western and southern communities in particular were transformed through federal intervention in water, power, and agricultural policies. In politics, the New Deal established the Democrats as the majority party. Some version of the Roosevelt New Deal coalition would dominate the nation's political life for another three decades.

The New Deal's efforts to end racial and gender discrimination were modest at best. Some of the more ambitious programs, such as subsidizing the arts or building model communities, enjoyed only brief success. Other reform proposals, such as national health insurance, never got off the ground. Conservative counterpressures, especially after 1937, limited what could be changed. Still, the New Deal did more than strengthen the presence of the national government in people's lives. It also fed expectations that the federal presence would intensify. Washington became a much greater center of economic regulation and political power, and the federal bureaucracy grew in size and influence. With the coming of World War II, the direct role

CHRONOLOGY

1929	Stock market crash
1930	Democrats regain control of the House of Representatives
1932	Reconstruction Finance Corporation established to make government credit available
	"Bonus Army" marches on Washington
	Franklin D. Roosevelt elected president
1933	Roughly 13 million workers unemployed
	The "Hundred Days" legislation of the First New Deal
	Twenty-First Amendment repeals Prohibition (Eighteenth Amendment)
1934	Indian Reorganization Act repeals Dawes Severalty Act and reasserts the status of Indian tribes as semisovereign nations
	Growing popularity of Father Charles E. Coughlin and Huey Long, critics of Roosevelt
1935	Second New Deal
	Committee for Industrial Organization (CIO) established

	Dust storms turn the southern Great Plains into the Dust Bowl
	Boulder Dam completed
1936	Roosevelt defeats Alfred M. Landon in reelection landslide
	Sit-down strike begins at General Motors plants in Flint, Michigan
1937	General Motors recognizes United Automobile Workers
	Roosevelt's "Court-packing" plan causes controversy
	Memorial Day Massacre in Chicago demonstrates the perils of union organizing
	"Roosevelt recession" begins
1938	CIO unions withdraw from the American Federation of Labor to form the Congress of Industrial Organizations
	Fair Labor Standards Act establishes the first federal minimum wage

of national government in shaping American communities would expand beyond the dreams of even the most ardent New Dealer.

Review Questions

1. What were the underlying causes of the Great Depression? What consequences did it have for ordinary Americans, and how did the Hoover administration attempt to deal with the crisis?

2. Analyze the key elements of Franklin D. Roosevelt's first New Deal program. To what degree did these succeed in getting the economy back on track and in providing relief to suffering Americans?

3. How did the so-called Second New Deal differ from the first? What political pressures did Roosevelt face that contributed to the new policies?

4. How did the New Deal reshape western communities and politics? What specific programs had the

greatest impact in the region? How are these changes still visible today?

5. Evaluate the impact of the labor movement and radicalism on the 1930s. How did they influence American political and cultural life?

6. To what extent were the grim realities of the depression reflected in popular culture? To what degree were they absent?

7. Discuss the long- and short-range effects of the New Deal on American political and economic life. What were its key successes and failures? What legacies of New Deal–era policies and political struggles can you find in contemporary America?

Recommended Reading

Anthony J. Badger, *The New Deal: The Depression Years, 1933–1940* (1989). Very useful overview that emphasizes the limited nature of New Deal reforms.

Alan Brinkley, *The End of Reform: New Deal Liberalism in Recession and War* (1995). A sophisticated analysis of the political and economic limits faced by New Deal reformers from 1937 through World War II.

Adam Cohen, *Nothing to Fear: FDR's Inner Circle and the Hundred Days That Created Modern America* (2009). A new history of the critical first few months of Franklin D. Roosevelt's presidency, focusing on FDR's achievements as chief executive and manager of an ambitious political agenda.

Stuart Cohen and Peter B. Hales, *The Likes of Us: America in the Eyes of the Farm Security Administration* (2008). The best new history of the extraordinary visual achievements of the FSA photographers, including scores of stunning pictures.

Michael Denning, *The Cultural Front: The Laboring of American Culture in the Twentieth Century* (1997). A provocative reinterpretation of 1930s' culture, emphasizing the impact of the Popular Front and its lasting influence on American modernism and mass culture.

Kristen Downey, *The Woman Behind the New Deal: The Life of Frances Perkins* (2009). A comprehensive new biography of one of the most influential architects of the New Deal.

Ronald Edsforth, *The New Deal: America's Response to the Great Depression* (2000). A concise political history of the 1930s, offering an excellent synthesis of the massive secondary literature.

Robert D. Leighinger, Jr., *Long Range Public Investment: The Forgotten Legacy of the New Deal* (2007). Demonstrates how, in addition to providing jobs and relief for victims of the Great Depression, the New Deal left a physical legacy of building across the nation.

Robert S. McElvaine, *The Great Depression: America, 1929–1941* (1984). The best one-volume overview of the Great Depression. It is especially strong on the origins and early years of the worst economic calamity in American history.

Jason Scott Smith, *Building New Deal Liberalism: The Political Economy of Public Works, 1935–1956* (2006). Argues for the centrality of public works programs such as the PWA and WPA for understanding how the New Deal transformed governmental priorities and remade the economy and landscape.

myhistorylab Connections

PEARSON

Reinforce what you learned in this chapter by studying the many documents, images, maps, review tools, and videos available at www.myhistorylab.com.

Read and Review

✓ Study and Review **Chapter 24**

Read the Document

Herbert Hoover, New York Campaign Speech (1932)

Franklin D. Roosevelt, Fireside Chat (1933)

Father Charles E. Coughlin, "A Third Party" (1936)

Huey Long, "Share Our Wealth" (1935)

Frances Perkins, The Social Security Act, (1935; 1960)

Franklin D. Roosevelt, Second Inaugural Address (1937)

See the Map

The Great Depression

The Tennessee Valley Authority

Research and Explore

Read the Document

Dealing with Hard Times: The Great Depression

Exploring America: The Dust Bowl

Profiles
John Lewis
Frances Perkins

Watch the Video

Responding to the Great Depression: Whose New Deal?

Dorothea Lange and Migrant Mother

The Plough that Broke the Plains

Hear the Audio

Hear the audio files for Chapter 24 at
www.myhistorylab.com.

World War II

1941–1945

Chapter 25 at www.myhistorylab.com

((•)) Hear the Audio

CHAPTER OUTLINE

American Communities 721
Los Alamos, New Mexico

The Coming of World War II 723
The Shadows of War Across the Globe
Roosevelt Readies for War
Pearl Harbor

The Great Arsenal of Democracy 726
Mobilizing for War
Organizing the War Economy
New Workers

The Home Front 730
Families in Wartime
The Internment of Japanese Americans
"Double V": Victory at Home and Abroad
Zoot Suit Riots
Popular Culture and "The Good War"

Men and Women in Uniform 735
Creating the Armed Forces
Women Enter the Military
Old Practices and New Horizons
The Medical Corps

The World at War 738
Soviets Halt Nazi Drive
Planning and Initiating the Allied
    Offensive
The Allied Invasion of Europe
The High Cost of European Victory
The War in Asia and the Pacific

The Last Stages of War 745
The Holocaust
The Yalta Conference
The Atomic Bomb

President Franklin Delano Roosevelt reviews helmeted soldiers standing at attention. Courtesy of the Library of Congress.

Los Alamos, New Mexico

On Monday, July 16, 1945, at 5:29:45 A.M., Mountain War Time, the first atomic bomb exploded in a brilliant flash visible in three states. Within just seven minutes, a huge, multicolored, bell-shaped cloud soared 38,000 feet into the atmosphere and threw back a blanket of smoke and soot to the earth below. The heat generated by the blast was four times the temperature at the center of the sun, and the light produced rivaled that of nearly twenty suns. Even ten miles away, people felt a strong surge of heat. The giant fireball ripped a crater a half-mile wide in the ground, fusing the desert sand into glass. The shock wave blew out windows in houses more than 200 miles away. The blast killed every living creature—squirrels, rabbits, snakes, plants, and insects—within a mile, and the smells of death lingered for nearly a month.

AMERICAN Communities

Very early that morning, Ruby Wilkening had driven to a nearby mountain ridge, where she joined several other women waiting for the blast. Wilkening worried about her husband, a physicist, who was already at the test site. No one knew exactly what to expect, not even the scientists who developed the bomb.

The Wilkenings were part of a unique community of scientists who had been marshaled for war. President Franklin D. Roosevelt, convinced by Albert Einstein and other physicists that the Nazis might successfully develop an atomic bomb, had inaugurated a small nuclear research program in 1939. Then, after the United States entered World War II in 1941, the president released resources to create the Manhattan Project and placed it under the direction of the Army Corps of Engineers. By December 1942, a team headed by Italian-born Nobel Prize winner Enrico Fermi had produced the first chain reaction in uranium under the University of Chicago's football stadium. Now the mission was to build a new formidable weapon, the atomic bomb.

In March 1943, the government moved the key researchers and their families to Los Alamos, New Mexico, a remote and sparsely populated region of soaring peaks, ancient Indian ruins, modern Pueblos, and villages occupied by the descendants of the earliest Spanish settlers. Some researchers and their families lived in a former boys' preparatory school until new houses could be built; others doubled up in rugged log cabins or at nearby ranches. Construction of new quarters proceeded slowly, causing nasty disputes between the "longhairs" (scientists) and the "plumbers" (army engineers) in charge of the grounds. Despite the chaos, outstanding American and European scientists eagerly signed up. Most were young, with an average age of twenty-seven, and quite a few were recently married. Many couples began their families at Los Alamos, producing a total of nearly a thousand babies between 1943 and 1949.

The scientists and their families formed an exceptionally close-knit community, united by the need for secrecy and their shared antagonism toward their army guardians. The military atmosphere was oppressive. Homes and laboratories were cordoned off by barbed wire and guarded by military police. Everything, from linens to food packages, was stamped "Government Issue." Security personnel followed the scientists whenever they left Los Alamos. Several scientists were reprimanded for discussing their work at home, although many of their wives worked forty-eight hours a week in the Technical Area. All outgoing mail was censored. Well-known scientists commonly worked under aliases—Fermi became "Eugene Farmer"—and code names were used for such terms as *atom, bomb,* and *uranium fission.* Los Alamos children were registered without surnames at nearby public schools. Even automobile accidents, weddings, and deaths went unreported. Only a group thoroughly committed to the war effort could accept such restrictions on personal liberty.

A profound urgency motivated the research team, which included refugees from Nazi Germany and Fascist Italy and a large proportion of Jews. The director of the project, California physicist J. Robert Oppenheimer, promoted a scientific élan that offset the military style of commanding general Leslie Groves. Just thirty-eight, slightly built, and deeply emotional, "Oppie" personified the idealism that helped the community of scientists overcome whatever moral reservations they held about placing such a potentially terrible weapon in the hands of the government.

In the Technical Area of Los Alamos, Oppenheimer directed research. At seven o'clock each workday morning, the siren dubbed "Oppie's Whistle" called the other scientists to their laboratories to wrestle with the theoretical and practical problems of building an atomic device. From May to November 1944, after the bomb had been designed, the key issue was testing it. Many scientists feared a test might fail, scattering the precious plutonium at the bomb's core and discrediting the entire project. Finally, with plutonium production increasing, the Los Alamos team agreed to test "the gadget" at a site 160 miles away.

The unprecedented scientific mobilization at Los Alamos mirrored changes occurring throughout American society as the nation rallied behind the war effort. Sixteen million men and women left home for military service and nearly as many moved to take advantage of wartime jobs. In becoming what President Franklin Roosevelt called "a great arsenal of democracy," the American economy quickly and fully recovered from the Great Depression. Several states in the South and Southwest experienced huge surges in population. California alone grew by 2 million people, a large proportion from Mexico. Many broad social changes with roots in earlier times—the economic expansion of the West, the erosion of farm tenancy among black people in the South and white people in Appalachia, and the increasing employment of married women—accelerated during the war. The events of the war eroded old communities, created new ones like Los Alamos, and transformed nearly all aspects of American society.

The transition to wartime was, however, far from smooth. Suspecting Japanese Americans of disloyalty,

1. What steps did Roosevelt take in the late 1930s to prepare the United States for war?

2. How did the government marshal the nation's resources to fight the war?

3. What major changes occurred in American society as a consequence of wartime mobilization?

4. What role did women play in the armed forces during World War II?

5. What were the main elements of the Allied war strategy?

6. What were the factors behind the decision to deploy the atomic bomb against Japan?

FOCUS Questions

1941–1945

President Roosevelt ordered the forced relocation of more than 112,000 men, women, and children to internment camps. Although African Americans won a promise of job equity in defense and government employment, hundreds of race riots broke out in the nation's cities. In Los Angeles, Mexican American youth, flaunting a new style of dress, provoked the ire of

Los Alamos

white sailors who proceeded to assault them, almost at random. And families of all kinds found themselves strained by wartime dislocations.

The United States nevertheless emerged from World War II far stronger than its European allies, who bore the brunt of the fighting. Indeed, the nation became strong enough to claim a new role as the world's leading superpower.

AMERICAN Communities

The Coming of World War II

The worldwide depression helped to undermine a political order that had been shaky since World War I. Political unrest spread across Europe and Asia as international trade dropped by as much as two-thirds and unemployment rose. Demagogues played on national and racial hatreds, fueled by old resentments and current despair, and offered solutions in the form of territorial expansion by military conquest.

Preoccupied with restoring the domestic economy, President Franklin D. Roosevelt had no specific plan to deal with growing conflict elsewhere in the world. Moreover, the majority of Americans strongly opposed foreign entanglements. As debate over diplomatic policy heated up, however, terrifying events overseas pulled the nation steadily toward war.

◉ Watch the Video
American Entry into WWI
at **www.myhistorylab.com**

The Shadows of War across the Globe

Two major threats to peace gathered force in the 1930s in East Asia and in Central Europe. In Japan, devastated by the depression, military leaders decided that imperialism

would make their nation the richest in the world, and in 1931 the Japanese army seized Manchuria from China. When the League of Nations objected, Japan simply quit the league. A full-scale Japanese invasion of China proper followed in 1937, and the world watched in horror the Rape of Nanking (today, Nanjing)—the destruction of what was then China's capital and the slaughter of as many as 300,000 Chinese men, women, and children. Within a year, Japan controlled most of coastal China.

In Europe, fanatical and tyrannical fascist leaders were taking power—first in Italy and later in Germany. "We have buried the putrid corpse of liberty," boasted Italy's fascist dictator Benito Mussolini in the 1920s. In Germany, nationalist resentment over the Treaty of Versailles fueled Adolf Hitler's National Socialist (Nazi) movement with its racist doctrine of "Aryan" supremacy that condemned nonwhites and Jews as "degenerate races." In January 1933, by political intrigue, Hitler became chancellor. He posed as the last bastion against Communism and had the backing of German industrialists, but only about one-third of the voters. With

 ◉ View the Image
Nazi Book Bonfire at
www.myhistorylab.com

his brown-shirted storm troopers ruling the streets, Hitler quickly destroyed opposition parties and made himself absolute dictator. Renouncing the disarmament provisions imposed by the Versailles peace treaty, he began to rebuild Germany's armed forces. No European powers opposed him.

Soon enough, Mussolini and Hitler began to act on their imperial visions. In 1935, Italy conquered Ethiopia and turned the African nation into a colony. In 1936, Hitler sent 35,000 troops to occupy the formerly demilitarized Rhineland region. In the Spanish Civil War that broke out later that year, Italy and Germany both supported General Francisco Franco's fascist rebels against the democratic republican regime. In November, Germany and Italy forged an alliance, the Rome–Berlin Axis.

Hitler was now nearly ready to put into operation his plan to secure *Lebensraum*—living space for the "Aryan" population—through territorial expansion. In 1938, he annexed Austria and then turned his attention to Czechoslovakia, the one remaining democracy in Central Europe, which Britain and France had pledged to assist. War seemed imminent. But Britain and France surprised the world by agreeing, at Munich on September 30, 1938, to allow Germany to annex the Sudetenland—the German-speaking parts of Czechoslovakia. "Appeasement," this was called: Hitler pledged that he would make no more territorial demands. Within six months, however, in March 1939, Germany seized the rest of the country.

By then, much of the world was aware of the horror of Hitler's racist regime. On the night of November 9, 1938, Nazi storm troopers rounded up Jews, beating them mercilessly and murdering an untold number. Reflecting the smashed windows of Jewish shops and burned synagogues, this attack came to be known as *Kristallnacht*, the "Night of Broken Glass." The Nazi government expropriated Jewish property and excluded Jews from all but the most menial jobs. Pressured by Hitler, his allies Hungary and Italy also enacted laws curtailing the civil rights of Jews.

On September 27, 1940, Germany, Italy, and Japan signed the anti-Communist Tripartite Pact and pledged to "stand by and co-operate with one another" for the next ten years.

Roosevelt Readies for War

FDR's instincts were to stand with other threatened democracies, but he knew that the American public and many members of Congress were strongly isolationist. In 1934, a committee headed by Republican senator Gerald P. Nye of North Dakota charged weapons manufacturers with driving the United States into World War I to make windfall profits. (Many, in fact, did.) In 1935, Congress passed the first of five Neutrality Acts to deter entanglements in future foreign wars. It required the president to embargo the sale and shipment of munitions to all belligerents. As late as 1937, nearly 70 percent of

Americans responding to a Gallup poll agreed that U.S. involvement in World War I had been a mistake.

Despite opposition, in October 1937, Roosevelt decided to call for international cooperation to "quarantine the aggressors." Although two-thirds of Congress opposed economic sanctions as a "backdoor to war," Roosevelt nevertheless managed to secure $1 billion in appropriations to enlarge the navy. Another less stringent Neutrality Act passed in 1939 permitted wartime arms sales to Great Britain, France, and China.

War broke out in Europe in the fall of 1939. In August, Germany and the Soviet Union, hitherto mortal enemies, stunned the world by signing a nonaggression pact. A week later, on September 1, Hitler invaded Poland. Within days, Poland's allies, Great Britain and France, declared war on Germany. On September 17, Soviet troops invaded Poland too. Warsaw capitulated, and Hitler and Stalin divided Poland between them. Fighting slowed to a near halt as French and German troops did not even exchange fire. Soviet forces, however, attacked Finland and seized the tiny Baltic republics.

Hitler began a crushing offensive against Western Europe in April 1940. In a *blitzkrieg* (lightning war), fast-moving columns of German tanks supported by air power struck first at Denmark and Norway and soon thereafter conquered Holland, Belgium, and Luxembourg. More than 338,000 British troops had to escape across the English Channel. Hitler's army, joined at the last minute by the Italians, then easily overran France in June 1940. When Britain refused to surrender, Hitler launched the Battle of Britain. Nazi bombers pounded cities while U-boats tried to cut off incoming supplies.

The American public desperately hoped to stay out of the war, but they also agreed with Roosevelt that the nation's security depended on both a strong defense and Hitler's defeat. Invoking the Neutrality Act of 1939, which permitted the sale of arms to Britain, France, and China, the president affirmed his position: "All aid to the Allies short of war." In May 1940, when France collapsed, he began to transfer surplus U.S. warships and equipment to Britain, in exchange for West Indies naval bases. In September, while the Battle of Britain raged, Roosevelt and Congress enacted the nation's first peacetime military draft, which sent 1.4 million young men to army training camps by July 1941.

FDR could not yet admit the inevitability of U.S. involvement—especially during an election year. His popularity had dropped with the 1937 "Roosevelt recession," and the Republicans had nominated a popular former Democrat turned anti–New Dealer, Wendell L. Willkie, from Indiana. Although isolationists who hated Roosevelt flocked to the folksy yet successful Wall Street industrialist, Wilkie pushed away many potential voters by supporting aid to Britain and rearming America and by waging a campaign enlivened primarily by his slurs on the

Roosevelt family. When FDR promised voters not to "send your boys to any foreign wars," he clinched an unprecedented third term.

Once reelected, Roosevelt moved more aggressively to aid hard-pressed Great Britain. In his annual message to Congress in early 1941, he proposed a bill allowing the president to sell, exchange, or lease arms to any country whose defense he judged vital to U.S. security. Passed in March 1941, the Lend-Lease Act made Great Britain the first beneficiary of massive aid. Congress also authorized the merchant marine to sail fully armed while conveying Lend-Lease supplies directly to Britain.

In August 1941, Roosevelt met on a warship off Newfoundland with Winston Churchill, the embattled British prime minister. Roosevelt evaded Churchill's pleas to enter the war—he knew that Congress and the American public still hoped to stay out—but the two leaders declared common goals for the postwar world in what was called the Atlantic Charter, a lofty proclamation calling for all peoples to live in freedom from fear, want, and tyranny.

The European war widened. Having conquered the Balkans, Hitler broke the Nazi–Soviet Pact and in June 1941 invaded the Soviet Union. Roosevelt sent Lend-Lease supplies to the Soviets and ordered U.S. warships to "sink on sight" any lurking German submarines. The result was an undeclared and unpublicized naval war between the United States and Nazi Germany on the North Atlantic.

Pearl Harbor

Throughout 1940 and 1941, Americans watched with dread the widening European struggle; meanwhile, war also escalated in East Asia. Anticipating trouble in the Pacific, in May 1940 Roosevelt transferred the Pacific fleet from its California bases to a forward position at Pearl Harbor in Hawai'i. Less than five months later, Japan formally joined Germany and Italy as a full Axis ally.

Both the United States and Japan were playing for time. Roosevelt wanted to bank resources to fight Germany (the greater danger, he thought); Japan's leaders gambled that America's preoccupation with Europe might allow them to conquer all Southeast Asia, including France's Indochinese colonies (today, Vietnam, Cambodia, and Laos), British outposts like Hong Kong and Singapore, and the oil-rich Dutch East Indies (today, Indonesia). Lacking petroleum, Japan was desperate to obtain a reliable source for oil; without that, its navy and huge land army in China could not fight. When Japan occupied French Indochina in July 1941, Roosevelt moved from economic sanctions, which had been in place for several months, to freezing Japanese assets in the United States and cutting off its oil supplies.

War with Japan looked more likely. The Japanese military decided to hit the Americans with a knock-out

On December 7, 1941, Japanese attack planes devastated the U.S. fleet stationed at Pearl Harbor, on the Hawaiian island of Oahu. This photograph shows the explosion of the USS *Shaw*, a drydocked destroyer, during the second wave of Japanese attack. The "sneak" attack on Pearl Harbor became a symbol of Japanese treachery and the necessity for U.S. revenge.

On the day after the attack on Pearl Harbor, President Franklin D. Roosevelt addressed a joint session of Congress and asked for an immediate declaration of war against Japan. The resolution passed with one dissenting vote, and the United States entered World War II.

blow that would give them time to seize Southeast Asia and the western Pacific; the United States, they hoped, would be too shaken to fight back. But American intelligence had broken the Japanese secret diplomatic code, and the president knew that Japan was preparing to strike somewhere, most likely the Philippines. By the end of November, all American Pacific forces were put on high alert.

Early on Sunday morning, December 7, 1941, carrier-borne Japanese bombers struck the Pacific fleet at Pearl Harbor. Americans were caught completely off guard. No one expected such a skillful attack. Within two hours, Japanese pilots destroyed nearly 200 American planes and badly damaged the fleet; more than 2,400 Americans were killed and nearly 1,200 wounded. (Fortunately, the U.S. carriers were spared, being out to sea on the morning of the attack.) That same day, Japan bombed U.S. bases on the Philippines, Guam, and Wake Island and attacked the British fleet and colonies in East Asia.

On December 8, declaring the attack on Pearl Harbor "a date which will live in infamy," Roosevelt asked Congress for a declaration of war against Japan. With only one dissenting vote—by pacifist Jeannette Rankin of Montana, who had voted against U.S. entry into World War I in 1917—Congress agreed. The United States did not declare war on Germany; it was Hitler who made that fateful decision when he ordered his puppet Reichstag on December 11 to proclaim war against "half Judaized and the half Negrified" America. Mussolini chimed in. World War II had begun for Americans.

●●●[Read the Document

Franklin Roosevelt, Date Which Will Live in Infamy (1941) at **www.myhistorylab.com**

The Great Arsenal of Democracy

As early as 1938, the American economy had begun to benefit from sales to the British and French when those countries started rearming. In 1940, Roosevelt told Americans in a radio "fireside chat" that the nation must become the "great arsenal of democracy," and by the time the United States entered the war, the U.S. economy had already geared up for military purposes. After Pearl Harbor, the federal government poured unprecedented energy and money into wartime production and assigned a huge army of experts to manage it. During the next three years, the economic machinery that had failed during the 1930s was running at full speed. Defense spending would spark the greatest economic boom in the history of any nation. Suddenly, it seemed, the Great Depression ended.

Mobilizing for War

A few days after the United States declared war, Congress passed the War Powers Act, establishing a precedent for executive authority that would endure long after the war's end. Under the new law, the president could reorganize the federal government and create new agencies, censor all news and information and abridge civil liberties, seize foreign-owned property, and even award government contracts without competitive bidding.

Roosevelt promptly used his authority to create special wartime agencies. At the top of his agenda was a massive reorientation and management of the economy, and to do that an alphabet soup of new agencies appeared. For example, the Supply Priorities and Allocation Board

(SPAB) oversaw the use of scarce materials and resources vital to the war, adjusting domestic consumption to military needs, even ending it for some products such as automobiles. The Office of Price Administration (OPA) used price controls to check inflation. The National War Labor Board (NWLB) mediated labor–management disputes. The War Manpower Commission (WMC) directed the mobilization of military and civilian services. And the Office of War Mobilization (OWM) coordinated operations among all these new agencies.

Several new agencies took on the responsibility of creating propaganda to promote a war that was being fought 3,000 miles away. Although Pearl Harbor brought an outpouring of rage against Japan, the government nevertheless fanned patriotic fires and tried to shape public opinion. In June 1942, the president created the Office of War Information (OWI) to engage the press, radio, and film industry in selling the war to the American people, as well as to publish leaflets for the armed services and to flood enemy ranks with subversive propaganda.

Domestic propaganda also fueled the selling of war bonds. Secretary of the Treasury Henry Morgenthau Jr., not only encouraged Americans to buy government bonds to finance the war but also planned the campaign "to use *bonds* to sell the war, rather than *vice versa*." Buying bonds would "mean bullets in the bellies of Hitler's hordes!" Discovering through market research that Americans felt more antagonism toward Japan than Germany, Morgenthau directed his staff to use more negative stereotypes of the Japanese in their advertising copy. Polls showed, however, that most depression-stung Americans bought war bonds— $185.7 billion by war's end—mainly to invest safely, to counter inflation, and to save for postwar purchases.

The federal government also sponsored various measures to prevent subversion. The attorney general authorized wiretapping in cases of espionage or sabotage, but the Federal Bureau of Investigation (FBI) also used it extensively—and illegally—for domestic surveillance. The Joint Chiefs of Staff created the Office of Strategic Services (OSS) to assess enemy military strength, gather intelligence, and conduct foreign espionage and engaged leading social scientists to plot psychological warfare.

In mid-1942, Roosevelt established an agency that would prove vital to the Allied victory and change the way science was conducted in the United States. The Office of Scientific Research and Development (OSRD) brought together government, business, and scientific leaders to coordinate military research. It developed better radar and early-warning systems, more effective medicines and pesticides, and improved weapons.

With the creation of these new agencies, the size of the federal government increased many times over its New Deal level. It cost about $250 million a day to fight the war, and the government spent twice as much during the war as it had during its entire history up to then. The number of federal employees nearly quadrupled, from a little over 1 million in 1940 to nearly 4 million by the war's end.

The New Deal itself, however, withered away. "Dr. New Deal" had been replaced by "Dr. Win the War," said Roosevelt in 1942. With the depression over and chronic unemployment giving way to acute labor shortages, FDR's administration directed all its resources toward securing the planes, ships, guns, and food—and the war workers—required for victory. Moreover, the 1942 elections weakened the New Deal coalition by unseating many liberal Democrats while sending fifty-five new and mostly conservative Republicans to Congress. Republicans quashed proposals to extend the social programs instituted during the 1930s, including the WPA and the CCC. One of the hallmarks of the New Deal, the Farm Security Administration, managed to hang on but only after severe cuts to its budget, as was the case with the Rural Electrification Administration, which the private power companies despised. One by one, New Deal agencies vanished.

Organizing the War Economy

Victory, many experts agreed, would ultimately depend less on military prowess and superior strategy than on the ability of the United States to outproduce its enemies. The nation enjoyed incomparable advantages: freedom from bombing and invasions, a huge industrial base, abundant natural resources, and a civilian population large enough to swell both its labor force and its armed forces. First, however, the entire civilian economy had to be both expanded and transformed for the production of arms and other military supplies.

Even before Pearl Harbor, by the summer of 1941, the federal government was pouring vast sums into defense production. Six months after the attack, allocations topped $100 billion for equipment and supplies, which exceeded what American firms had produced in all previous wars. Facing war orders too large to fill, American industries were primed for all-out production. Once-idled factories operated around-the-clock, seven days a week.

No wonder the actual volume of industrial output expanded at the fastest rate in American history. Military production alone grew from 2 percent of the 1939 gross national product (GNP) to 40 percent of the 1943 GNP. "Something is happening," announced *Time* magazine, "that Adolf Hitler does not understand . . . it is the miracle of production."

Defense production transformed entire regions. The impact was strongest in the West—the major staging area for the war in the Pacific—where the federal government spent nearly $40 billion for military and industrial expansion. California got 10 percent of all federal funds, and by 1944 Los Angeles was the nation's second largest manufacturing center, only slightly behind Detroit. The South benefited from having 60 of the army's 100 new military camps, and its textile factories hummed: the army alone required nearly 520 million pairs of socks and 230 million pairs of pants. Much of the South's sharecropping and tenant-farming population—already thinned by New Deal economic policies (see Chapter 24)—migrated into well-paid urban industrial jobs, and unprecedented profits poured into southern businesses.

Across the nation, the rural population decreased by almost 20 percent, and American farmers could not keep up with the rising international—or even the domestic—demand for milk, potatoes, fruits, and sugar. The Department of Agriculture reached its goals only in areas such as livestock production, thanks to skyrocketing wholesale meat prices. The war speeded the development of large-scale and mechanized crop production, including the first wide-spread use of chemical fertilizers and pesticides. By 1945, farm income had doubled, but thousands of small farms had disappeared.

Much like large-scale commercial agriculture, many big businesses did well during the war. Military contracts allowed huge profits. The government provided low-interest loans and even direct subsidies for the expansion of facilities, with generous tax write-offs for retooling. The 100 largest corporations, which manufactured 30 percent of all goods in 1940, garnered 70 percent of all war and civilian contracts and the bulk of war profits. On the other hand, many small businesses closed.

New Workers

The wartime economy required an unprecedented number of new workers. The *bracero* program, negotiated by the United States and Mexico in 1942, brought more than 200,000 Mexicans into the United States for short-term employment, mainly as farm and railroad workers. Sioux and Navajos were hired in large numbers to build ordnance depots and military training centers. African Americans secured in just four years a greater variety of jobs than in the seven decades since the outbreak of the Civil War. They joined white workers in defense industries—in iron and steel plants, shipyards and aircraft factories, and numerous government agencies. The number of black workers rose from 2.9 million to 3.8 million.

The war most dramatically altered the wage-earning patterns of women. The female labor force grew by more than 50 percent, reaching 19.5 million in 1945. The rate of growth proved especially high for white women over thirty-five, and for the first time married women became the majority of female wage earners. The employment rate changed comparatively little for African American women; fully 90 percent had been in the labor force in 1940. However, many black women left domestic service for higher-paying industrial jobs.

⊙ View the Image

Women Riveters in Navy Shipyard at www.myhistorylab.com

Neither government nor industry rushed to recruit women. Well into the summer of 1942, the Department of War advised businesses to hold back from hiring women "until all available male labor in the area had first been

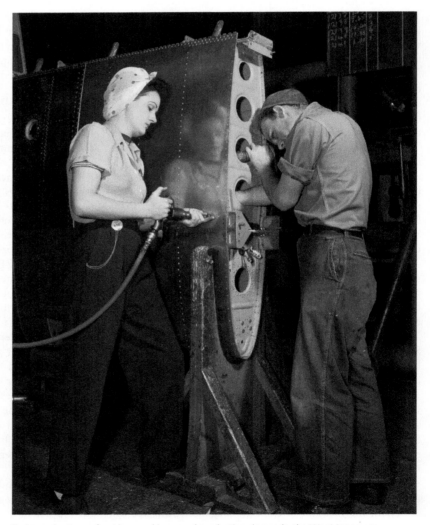

Facing a shortage of workers and increased production demands, the War Manpower Commission and the Office of War Information conducted a campaign to recruit women into the labor force. Women were encouraged to "take a job for your husband/son/brother" and to "keep the world safe for your children." Higher wages also enticed many women to take jobs in factories. In this photograph, a woman is shown riveting the wing of an airplane.

Norman Rockwell's "Rosie, the Riveter"

During his long career as an artist-illustrator, Norman Rockwell published forty-seven covers of the popular family magazine *The Saturday Evening Post*, all venerating various aspects of American life. "Rosie, the Riveter" appeared on the magazine's cover May 29, 1943, and virtually enshrined women's contributions to the war effort. The *Post* donated the original painting to the U.S. Treasury Department, which took "Rosie" on a national tour to get Americans to buy war bonds.

Now an iconic image, Rosie was modeled on a real-life woman, a telephone operator in Vermont. Rockwell took advantage of his artistic license by making Rosie older and more muscular than his slight nineteen-year-old model—who was quite surprised when she finally saw the portrait! There is no doubt, though, that Rockwell captured the spirit of wartime patriotism. The self-confident Rosie takes obvious pride in her work, keeping her riveter on her ample lap even during lunchtime. A halo encircles her head, the American flag waves in the background. To seal the message, Rockwell shows Rosie crushing Hitler's autobiography, *Mein Kampf*, under her penny loafer.

In calling attention to Rosie's impressive biceps, Rockwell nevertheless attended to the small details that assure viewers that his defense worker has lost none of her femininity. Like most other women in the 1940s, she wears lipstick and rouge and polishes her nails. She also keeps a lace hanky and compact in the pocket of her overalls and wears a necklace—albeit of merit buttons—around her neck. Moreover, Rockwell does not show Rosie riveting but instead eating a ham sandwich that she undoubtedly made at home.

Rockwell's painting, beloved during World War II, became even more popular with the rise of the women's liberation movement in the late 1960s and remains to this day an emblem of women's strength and determination. In May 2002, Sotheby's auctioned the original canvas for more than $4.9 million.

• **In what ways does Rockwell's painting convey ideals related to gender roles during the war?**

employed." Likewise, neither government nor industry expected women to stay in their jobs when the war ended. "Rosie the Riveter" appeared in posters and advertisements as the model female citizen, but only "for the duration" (see Seeing History). In Washington, DC, women bus drivers were given badges to wear on their uniforms that read: "I am taking the place of a man who went to war."

For the most part, recruiters used conventional gender stereotypes to make wartime jobs appealing to women. Posters and informational films depicted women's new industrial jobs as simple variations of domestic tasks. Where once housewives sewed curtains for their kitchens, they now produced silk parachutes. Their skill with a vacuum cleaner easily translated into riveting on huge ships. "Instead of cutting a cake," one male-narrated newsreel explained, "this woman [factory worker] cuts the pattern of aircraft parts."

Compared to the Great Depression, when married women were barred from many jobs, World War II opened up new fields. The number of women automobile workers jumped from 29,000 to 200,000, that of women electrical workers from 100,000 to 374,000. Polled near the end of the war, 75 percent of women workers said they wanted to keep working, preferably at the same jobs.

Although the war generated 17 million new jobs, the economic gains were not evenly distributed. Wages increased by as much as 50 percent, but never as fast as profits or prices. This widely reported disparity produced one of the most turbulent periods in American labor history (see Table 25.1). More workers went on strike in 1941, before the United States entered the war, than in any previous year except 1919. A militant union drive at Ford Motor Company's enormous River Rouge plant made the United Auto Workers (UAW) one of the most powerful labor organizations in the world. Total union membership increased from 10.5 million to 14.7 million, with the women's share alone rising from 11 to 23 percent. Unions also enrolled 1,250,000 African Americans, twice the prewar number.

Once the United States entered the war, the major unions patriotically agreed to no-strike pledges for the duration. Nevertheless, rank-and-file union members sporadically staged illegal "wildcat" strikes. The most dramatic, a walkout of more than a half-million coal miners in 1943 led by the rambunctious John L. Lewis, withstood the attacks of the government and the press. Roosevelt repeatedly ordered the mines seized, only to find, as Lewis retorted, that coal could not be mined with bayonets. The Democratic-majority Congress passed the first federal anti-strike bill, giving the president power to penalize or even draft strikers. And yet the strikes reached a level greater than in any other four-year period in American history.

Despite "no-strike" pledges, workers staged wildcat strikes in the war years. Union leaders negotiated shorter hours, higher wages, and seniority rules and helped to build union membership to a new height. When the war ended, nearly 30 percent of all nonagricultural workers were union members.

The Home Front

Alone among the major combatants, the homelands of the United States and Canada were neither invaded nor bombed, except for remote Pearl Harbor. On the U.S. mainland, most civilians—unless they had loved ones serving in the armed forces or relocated to distant parts—experienced the war mainly in terms of inconveniences: rationing, long workdays, and a sharp increase in income taxes. Nevertheless, Americans were not immune to the social upheavals that accompany war. Families were disrupted, and racial and ethnic hostilities flared repeatedly and sometimes violently.

Families in Wartime

"Economic conditions were ripe for a rush to the altar," quipped one social scientist. Men and women rushed into marriage, despite (or maybe because of) wartime uncertainties. The wartime boom sent personal incomes surging, allowing many young couples to set up separate households

TABLE 25.1

Strikes and Lockouts in the United States, 1940–45

	Number of Strikes	Number of Workers Involved	Number of Man-Days Idle	Percent of Total Employed
1940	2,508	576,988	6,700,872	2.3
1941	4,288	2,362,620	23,047,556	8.4
1942	2,968	839,961	4,182,557	2.8
1943	3,752	1,981,279	13,500,529	6.9
1944	4,956	2,115,637	8,721,079	7.0
1945	4,750	3,467,000	38,025,000	12.2

SOURCE: "Work Stoppages Caused by Labor–Management Disputes in 1945," *Monthly Labor Review*, May 1946, p. 720; and Martin Glaberman, *War Time Strikes* (Detroit: Bewick, 1980), p. 36.

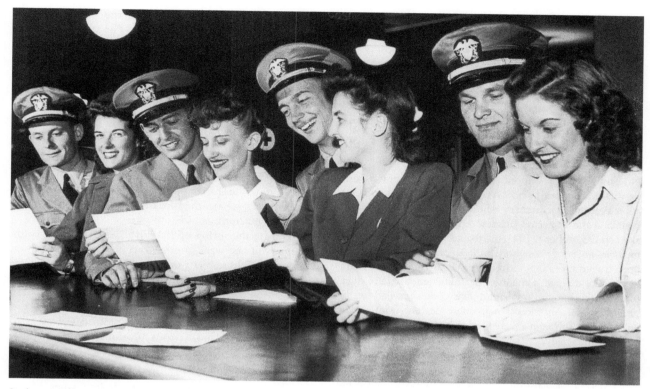

Students at Officers' Training School at Northwestern University, who were not allowed to marry until they were commissioned as ensigns, apply for marriage licenses in Chicago, August 20, 1943, shortly before graduation. These young couples helped the marriage rate skyrocket during World War II.

for the first time since the depression struck. The prospect of wartime separation pushed other couples into marriage. The marriage rate peaked in 1946—but by then divorces were also setting records.

Housing shortages were acute and rents were high. With apartments scarce, taxi drivers (for an extra fee) became up-to-the-minute guides to vacancies. Landlords were free to discriminate against families with children—and, even more so, against racial minorities.

Wartime wages made many Americans eager to stock up on consumer goods, including a few luxuries, but they soon discovered that even supplying a household was difficult. Shopping had to be squeezed in between long work hours. Rationing required extra planning for purchasing meat, cheese, sugar, milk, coffee, gasoline, and shoes, and such staples were often in short supply. One homemaker said she and her friends referred to butter as "twenty-four karat gold." Illegal black markets flourished despite the high prices charged for scarce or rationed goods.

Many women found it nearly impossible to manage both a demanding job and a household. This dual responsibility contributed to high turnover and absentee rates in factories. Caring for small children became a major problem. Wartime employment or military service often separated husbands and wives, leaving children in the care of

only one parent. Even when families stayed together, both adults often worked long hours, sometimes on different shifts. Although the War Manpower Commission estimated that as many as 2 million children needed some form of child care, federally funded day-care centers served less than 10 percent of defense workers' children. In most communities, the limited facilities sponsored by industry or municipal governments could not keep up with the growing number of "latchkey" children.

Juvenile delinquency rose. With employers relaxing minimum age requirements, many teenagers—too young for the draft—quit school for high-wage factory jobs. Runaways drifted from city to city, finding temporary work at wartime plants or military installations. Urban gangs spawned brawling, prostitution, and automobile thefts for joy rides. To curb this trend, the U.S. Office of Education and the Children's Bureau sponsored a back-to-school campaign and appealed to employers to hire only older workers.

Public health improved greatly. Forced to forgo medical care during the Great Depression, many Americans spent large portions of their wartime paychecks on doctors, dentists, and prescription drugs. Some families ate lots of healthy fresh vegetables raised in their backyard "victory gardens." Even more important were the medical benefits provided to the more than 16 million men inducted into the armed forces and their dependents. Nationally, incidences of such communicable diseases as typhoid fever, tuberculosis, and diphtheria dropped considerably, the infant death rate fell by more than a third, and life expectancy increased by three years. In the South and Southwest, however, racism and poverty combined to halt or even reverse these trends. These regions continued to have the nation's highest infant and maternal mortality rates.

The Internment of Japanese Americans

No families suffered more from wartime dislocations than Japanese Americans who were interned for the duration. After Pearl Harbor, military officials feared an invasion of the mainland and suspected Japanese Americans of secret disloyalty. On December 8, 1941, the federal government froze the financial assets of those born in Japan, called Issei, who had been barred from U.S. citizenship. Meanwhile, in the name of national defense, a coalition of politicians, patriotic organizations, business groups, and military officials called for the removal of all Americans of Japanese descent from Pacific coastal areas. Although a State Department intelligence report certified their loyalty, Japanese Americans—two-thirds of them American-born citizens—became the largest ethnic group singled out for legal sanctions.

Charges of sedition against the Japanese unleashed deep racial prejudices. Headlines freely blared the word

More than 110,000 Japanese Americans were interned during World War II, some for up to four years. This photograph, taken in May 1942 by Dorothea Lange (1895–1965), the famed photographer of depression-era migrant families, shows young boys waiting in the baggage-inspection line at the Assembly Center in Turlock, California.

Jap, while political cartoonists and the popular culture employed blatant racial stereotypes. "The very fact that no sabotage has taken place to date," an army report suggested, with twisted logic, "is a disturbing and confirming indication that action will be taken."

On February 19, 1942, Roosevelt signed Executive Order 9066, which banned more than 120,000 Japanese American men, women, and children from designated military areas, mainly in California, but also in Oregon, Washington, and southern Arizona. The army prepared for forced evacuation, rounding up and removing Japanese Americans from communities where they had lived and worked, sometimes for generations.

••—Read the Document
Executive Order 9066 (1942) at www.myhistorylab.com

During the spring of 1942, Japanese American families received one week's notice to close up their businesses and homes. Told to bring only what they could carry, they were then transported to one of the ten internment camps managed by the War Relocation Authority. The guarded camps were located as far away as Arkansas, although the majority had been set up in the remote desert areas of Utah, Colorado, Idaho, Arizona, Wyoming, and California. Karl G. Yoneda described his quarters at Manzanar in northern California:

> There were no lights, stoves, or window panes. My two cousins and I, together with seven others, were crowded into a 25 × 30 foot room. We slept on army cots with our clothes on. The next morning we discovered that there were no toilets or washrooms. . . . We saw GIs manning machine guns in the watchtowers. The barbed wire fence which surrounded the camp was visible against the background of the snow-covered Sierra mountain range. "So this is the American-style concentration camp," someone remarked.

By August, virtually every West Coast resident with at least one Japanese grandparent had been interned.

The Japanese American Citizens League charged that "racial animosity," not military necessity, motivated the internment policy. Despite the protest of the American Civil Liberties Union and several church groups, the Supreme Court in *Korematsu v. United States* (1944) upheld the constitutionality of relocation on grounds of national security. By this time a program of gradual release was in place, although the last center did not close until March 1946. In protest, nearly six thousand Japanese Americans renounced their U.S. citizenship. Japanese Americans had lost homes and businesses valued at $500 million in what many historians judge as being the worst violation of American civil liberties during the war. Not until 1988 did Congress vote to award each of the 60,000 surviving victims reparations of $20,000 and a public apology.

"Double V": Victory at Home and Abroad

Throughout the war, African American activists conducted a "Double V" campaign, mobilizing not only for Allied victory but also for their own rights as citizens. "The army is about to take me to fight for democracy," one Detroit resident said, "but I would as leave fight for democracy right here." Black militants demanded, at a minimum, fair housing and equal employment opportunities, laying the foundation for the postwar civil rights movement.

Even before the United States entered the war, the foremost black labor leader—A. Philip Randolph, president of both the Brotherhood of Sleeping Car Porters and the National Negro Congress—began to mobilize against discrimination. At a planning meeting in Chicago, a black woman proposed sending African Americans to Washington, DC, "from all over the country, in jalopies,

This painting is by Horace Pippin, a self-taught African American artist who began painting as therapy for an injury suffered while serving with the U.S. Army's 369th Colored Infantry Regiment during World War I. It is one of a series drawn during World War II illustrating the contradiction between the principles of liberty and justice, for which Americans were fighting abroad, and the reality of racial prejudice at home.

SOURCE: Horace Pippin (1888–1946), *Mr. Prejudice*, 1943. Oil on canvas, 18 × 14 inches. Philadelphia Museum of Art, Gift of Dr. and Mrs. Matthew T. Moore. Photo by Graydon Wood. 1984–108–1.

in trains, and any way they can get there until we get some action from the White House." African Americans across the country began to prepare for a "great rally" of no less than 100,000 people at the Lincoln Memorial on the Fourth of July.

Read the Document
A. Philip Randolph, Why Should We March (1942) at **www.myhistorylab.com**

Eager to stop the March on Washington movement, Roosevelt met with Randolph, who proposed an executive order "making it mandatory that Negroes be permitted to work in [defense] plants." Randolph reviewed several drafts before approving the text that became, on June 25, 1941, Executive Order 8802, banning discrimination in defense industries and government. The president later appointed a Fair Employment Practices Committee to hear complaints and redress grievances. Randolph called off the march but remained determined to "shake up white America."

Other civil rights organizations formed during wartime to fight discrimination and Jim Crow, including segregation in the armed forces. The interracial Congress of Racial Equality (CORE), formed by pacifists in 1942, staged sit-ins at Chicago, Detroit, and Denver restaurants that refused to serve African Americans. Membership in the NAACP, which fought discrimination in defense plants and the military, grew from 50,000 in 1940 to 450,000 in 1946. The Supreme Court ruling in *Smith* v. *Albright* (1944) overturning the legality of "white primaries" used in southern states to exclude black voters was a major victory paving the way for future civil rights struggles.

Despite these advances, racial conflict intensified during the war. Approximately 1.2 million African Americans left the rural South to take wartime jobs, and they faced not only serious housing shortages but also whites intent on keeping them out of their own jobs and neighborhoods. "Hate strikes" broke out in defense plants across the country when African Americans were hired or upgraded to "white" positions. In February 1942, when twenty black families attempted to move into new federally funded apartments adjacent to a Polish American community in Detroit, a mob of 700 armed white protesters halted the moving vans and burned a cross on the project's grounds. The police ignored the white rioters but arrested black youths. Finally, two months later, 1,000 state troopers supervised the move of these families into the Sojourner Truth Housing Project, named after the famous abolitionist and former slave.

Racial violence reached its wartime peak during the summer of 1943, when 274 conflicts broke out in nearly fifty cities. In Detroit, where the black population had grown by more than a third since the beginning of the war, twenty-five blacks and nine whites were killed and more than 700 were injured. The poet Langston Hughes, who supported U.S. involvement in the war, expressed the new militancy of many African Americans:

> *Looky here, America*
> *What you done done—*
> *Let things drift*
> *Until the riots come*
> *Yet you say we're fighting*
> *For democracy.*
> *Then why don't democracy*
> *Include me?*
> *I ask you this question*
> *Cause I want to know*
> *How long I got to fight*
> *BOTH HITLER—AND JIM CROW.*

Zoot Suit Riots

On the night of June 4, 1943, sailors poured into nearly 200 cars and taxis to drive through the streets of East Los Angeles in search of Mexican Americans dressed in "zoot suits." The sailors assaulted their victims at random, even chasing one youth into a movie theater and stripping him of his clothes while the audience cheered. Riots broke out and continued for five days.

Two communities had collided with tragic results. The sailors had only recently been uprooted from their hometowns and regrouped under the strict discipline of boot camp. Stationed in southern California while awaiting deployment overseas, they came face-to-face with Mexican American teenagers wearing long-draped coats, pegged pants, pocket watches with oversized chains, and big floppy hats. To the sailors, the zoot suit was not just a flamboyant fashion. Unlike the uniform the young sailors wore, the zoot suit signaled defiance and a lack of patriotism.

The zoot-suiters, however, represented less than 10 percent of the Hispanic community's youth. More than 300,000 Mexican Americans were serving in the armed forces (a number representing a greater proportion of their draft-age population than other Americans), often in the most hazardous branches, as paratroops and marines. Many others were employed in war industries in Los Angeles, which had become home to the nation's largest Mexican American community. For the first time, Mexican Americans were finding well-paying jobs, and like African Americans, they expected their government to protect them from discrimination.

Military and civilian authorities eventually contained the zoot suit riots by ruling several sections of Los Angeles off-limits to military personnel, and the city council passed legislation making the wearing of a zoot suit in public a criminal offense. Many Mexican Americans expressed concern about their personal safety; some feared that after the government rounded up the Japanese they would be the next group sent to internment camps.

Popular Culture and "The Good War"

Global events shaped the lives of American civilians but appeared to touch them only indirectly in their everyday activities. Food shortages, long hours in the factories, and even fears for loved ones abroad did not take away all the pleasures of full employment and prosperity. With money in their pockets, Americans spent freely at vacation resorts, country clubs, racetracks, nightclubs, dance halls, and movie theaters. Sales of books skyrocketed, and spectator sports attracted huge and diverse audiences.

Despite the sharpening racial divisions of the neighborhood and the workplace, popular music crossed racial lines. Transplanted southern musicians, black and white, brought their regional styles to northern cities. Played on jukeboxes in bars, bus stations, and cafés, "country" and "rhythm & blues" not only won new audiences but also inspired musicians to crisscross old boundaries. Musicians of the war years "made them steel guitars cry and whine," Ray Charles recalled. They also paved the way musically for the emergence of rock and roll a decade later.

War themes pervaded popular music. The plaintive "A Rainbow at Midnight" by country singer Ernest Tubb expressed the hope of a common "dogface" soldier looking beyond the misery and horror to the promise of a brighter tomorrow. The era's best-known tune, Irving Berlin's "White Christmas," evoked a lyrical nostalgia of past celebrations with family and friends close by. On the lighter side, novelty artist Spike Jones made his name with the "razz" or "Bronx cheer," in "We're Going to Ffft in the Fuehrer's Face."

Hollywood mobilized, as one screenwriters group explained, "to build morale" and to "stimulate . . . initiative and responsibility." Combat films such as *Action in the North Atlantic* made heroes of ordinary Americans under fire, depicting GIs of different races and ethnicities discovering their common humanity. With military cooperation, wartime movies encouraged Americans to think well of all the Allies—including the Soviet Union. Several films, such as *Tender Comrade*, plugged pro-Soviet views that would be abruptly reversed in the postwar years. Other films such as the Oscar-winning *Since You Went Away* portrayed the loyalty and resilience of American families with servicemen stationed overseas. Hollywood aided the war effort in additional ways. Frank Capra directed the government-sponsored *Why We Fight*, a series of documentaries to explain the war's aims to soldiers. Meanwhile, movie stars led the war bond campaign, selling nearly $1 billion worth in 1942 alone.

The wartime spirit infected even the juvenile world of comics. The climbing sales of nickel "books" spawned a proliferation of patriotic superheroes such as the Green Lantern, Captain Marvel, and Wonder Woman. Even Bugs Bunny put on a uniform and fought sinister-looking enemies.

The fashion industry also did its part. Production of nylon stockings was halted because the material was needed for parachutes; to save cotton and woolen fabric for the production of uniforms, women's skirts were shortened, while the War Production Board encouraged cuffless "Victory Suits" for men. Executive Order M-217 restricted the colors of shoes manufactured during the war to "black, white, navy blue, and three shades of brown." For many civilians, including civil defense volunteers and Red Cross workers, wearing a uniform demonstrated patriotism, and padded shoulders and straight lines became popular among fashion-conscious men and women. Women employed in defense plants wore slacks, often for the first time in their lives.

Much of this war fervor was spontaneous, but the government did all it could to encourage self-sacrificing patriotism. The Office of War Information screened all popular music, movies, radio programs, and advertisements to ensure that everyone got the message: only the collective effort of all Americans could preserve democracy at home and save the world from fascism. Washington tried to make sure that the public saw the daily inconveniences and shortages of wartime, and above all the drafting of young men to serve and die abroad, as sacrifices essential to victory. In the government's zeal to popularize sacrifice among the citizenry, no one was excluded and no action considered insignificant. The government even worried about war workers' casual conversations. People were told that snooping Nazi spies lurked everywhere; posters and advertisements warned "Loose Lips Sink Ships."

By the mid-1940s, popular culture had helped to shape a collective memory of World War II as "the good war," the standard by which the nation's subsequent wars would be judged. It also played an important part in bringing diverse and sometimes antagonistic communities together, not only in support of the war but also as steadfast consumers of mass entertainment.

Men and Women in Uniform

World War II mobilized 16.4 million Americans into the armed forces. Although only 34 percent of men who served in the army saw combat—the majority during the final year of the war—the experience had a powerful impact on nearly everyone. Whether working in the steno pool at Great Lakes Naval Training Center in northern Illinois or slogging through mud with rifle in hand in the Philippines, many men and women saw their lives reshaped in unpredictable ways. For those who survived, the war often proved to be the defining experience of their lives.

Hear the Audio
Soldier Boy Blues, 1943 at **www.myhistorylab.com**

Creating the Armed Forces

Neither the army nor the navy was prepared for the scale of combat World War II entailed. Before1939, when the European war broke out, most of the 200,000 men in the armed forces patrolled the Mexican border or occupied colonial possessions, such as the Philippines. Only the U.S. Marine Corps, which had been planning since the 1920s to seize the western Pacific from Japan in the event of war, were ready to fight.

On October 16, 1940, National Registration Day, all men between twenty-one and thirty-six had to register for military service. After the United States entered the war, the draft age was lowered to eighteen, and local boards were instructed to choose the youngest first.

The draft law exempted those "who by religious training or belief" opposed war, including members of a traditional "peace church" such as Quakers, Mennonites, and Seventh Day Adventists. About 25,000 conscientious objectors served in noncombatant roles in the military services; another 12,000 performed "alternative service." Approximately 6,000 men were jailed for refusing to register for the draft.

One-third of the men examined by the Selective Service were rejected. Surprising numbers were refused induction as physically unfit. For the first time, men were screened for "neuropsychiatric disorders or emotional problems," and approximately 1.6 million were rejected for that reason. At a time when only one American in four graduated from high school, many conscripts were turned away as functionally illiterate.

The officer corps, whose top ranks came from the Command and General Staff School at Fort Leavenworth, tended to be highly professional, politically conservative, and personally autocratic. General Douglas MacArthur, supreme commander in the Pacific, was said to admire the discipline of the German army and to disparage political democracy. General Dwight D. Eisenhower, however, who became the supreme commander of Allied forces in Europe, projected a new spirit. Mistrusted by MacArthur and many of the older brass, Eisenhower appeared to his troops a model of leadership.

The democratic rhetoric of the war and the sudden massive expansion of the armed forces contributed to this transformation of the officer corps. A shortage of officers during World War I had prompted a huge expansion of the Reserve Officer Training Corps (ROTC) on campuses, but it still could not meet the demand. Racing to make up for the deficiency, Army Chief of Staff George Marshall opened schools for officer candidates. In 1942, in seventeen-week training periods, these schools produced more than 54,000 platoon leaders. Closer in sensibility to the civilian population, these new officers were the kind of leaders Eisenhower sought.

Most GIs (short for "government issue"), who formed the vast majority of draftees, had little or no contact with high-ranking officers and instead forged bonds with the men in their own combat units and with their company commanders. "Everyone wants someone to look up to when he's scared," one GI explained. After undergoing basic and advanced training as members of a unit, once deployed, most soldiers depended on the loyalty of buddies to pull them through. Proud to serve in "the best-dressed, best-fed, best-equipped army in the world," the majority of these citizen-soldiers did not actually know why the world was at war. Antifascist zeal or democratic idealism, military leaders discovered, meant little to them. Most soldiers wanted foremost "to get the task done" and return soon to their families and communities.

Women Enter the Military

With the approach of World War II, Massachusetts Republican congresswoman Edith Nourse Rogers proposed legislation for the formation of a women's corps. The army instead drafted its own bill, which both Rogers and Eleanor Roosevelt supported, creating in May 1942 the Women's Army Auxiliary Corps (WAAC), later changed to Women's Army Corps (WAC). In 1942–43, other bills established a women's division of the navy (WAVES), the Women's Air Force Service Pilots, and the Marine Corps Women's Reserve.

Overall, more than 350,000 women served in World War II, two-thirds of them in the WACS and WAVES. As a group, they were better educated and more skilled—although paid less—than the average enlisted man. However, military policy prohibited women from supervising male workers, even in desk jobs.

New recruits to the Women's Army Corps (WAC) pick up their clothing "issue" (allotment). These volunteers served in many capacities, from nursing men in combat to performing clerical and communication duties "stateside" (within the United States). Approximately 140,000 women served in the WACS during World War II.

Barred from combat, women were not necessarily protected from danger. Nurses accompanied troops into combat, treated men under fire, and dug their own foxholes. More than 1,000 women flew planes, although not in combat missions. Others worked as photographers and cryptoanalysts. The vast majority remained far from battlefronts, however. Stationed mainly within the United States, most women worked in familiar jobs, serving in administration, communications, clerical, or health care facilities.

The WACS and WAVES were subject to both hostile commentary and bad publicity. The overwhelming majority of soldiers believed that most WACS were prostitutes; the War Department itself, fearing "immorality" among women in the armed forces, closely monitored their conduct and established much stricter rules for women than for men. The U.S. Marine Corps even used intelligence officers to ferret out suspected lesbians or women who showed "homosexual tendencies" (as opposed to homosexual acts), both causes for dishonorable discharge.

Old Practices and New Horizons

The Selective Service Act, in response to the demands of African American leaders, specified that "there shall be no discrimination against any person on account of race or color." The draft brought hundreds of thousands of young black men into the army, and African Americans enlisted at a rate 60 percent above their proportion of the general population. By 1944, black soldiers represented 10 percent of the army's troops, and overall approximately 1 million African Americans served in the armed forces during World War II. The army, however, channeled black recruits into segregated, poorly equipped units, commanded by white officers. Secretary of War Henry Stimson refused to challenge this policy, saying that the army could not be "a sociological laboratory." The majority of African Americans served mainly in construction or stevedore work.

Only toward the end of the war, when the shortage of infantry neared a crisis, were African Americans permitted to rise to combat status. The all-black 761st Tank Battalion, the first African American armored unit, served 183 days in action without relief. Despite the very small number of African Americans admitted to the Air Force, the 99th Pursuit Squadron, trained at the new base in Tuskegee, Alabama, earned high

The U.S. Marines recruited more than 400 Navajos to serve as code talkers by communicating in their own language. Deployed mainly to the Pacific Theater, they used radio and telegraph to transmit quickly vital information about battlefield activities, including troop movements. This photograph, taken in December 1943, shows Corporal Henry Bake, Jr., and Private First Class George H. Kirk operating a portable radio unit in a jungle clearing near the front lines.

Watch the Video

The Desegregation of the Military and Blacks in Combat at www.myhistorylab.com

marks in action against the feared German Luftwaffe. Even the Marine Corps and the Coast Guard agreed to end their historic exclusion of African Americans, although they recruited and promoted only a small number.

The ordinary black soldier, sailor, or marine experienced few benefits from these late-in-the-war gains. They encountered discrimination everywhere. Even the blood banks kept blood segregated by race (although a black physician, Dr. Charles Drew, had invented the process for storing plasma). The year 1943 marked the peak of unrest, with violent confrontations between blacks and whites breaking out at military installations, especially in the South, where the majority of African American soldiers were stationed. Toward the end of the war, to improve morale among black servicemen, the army relaxed its policy of segregation, mainly in recreational facilities.

The army also grouped Japanese Americans into segregated units, sending most to fight far from the Pacific Theater. Better educated than the average soldier, many Nisei soldiers who knew Japanese served stateside as interpreters and translators. When the army decided to create a Nisei regiment, more than 10,000 volunteers stepped forward, although only one in five was accepted. The Nisei 442nd fought heroically in Italy and France and became the most decorated regiment in the war.

Despite segregation, the armed forces ultimately pulled Americans of all varieties out of their separate communities. Many Jews and other second-generation

European immigrants, for example, described their military stint as an "Americanizing" experience. For the first time in their lives, many Indian peoples left reservations as approximately 25,000 served in the armed forces. In the Pacific war, Navajo "code talkers" used their native language (a complex, unwritten language unknown to the Japanese) to transmit information from the front lines and also improved their English in special classes. For many African Americans, military service provided a bridge to postwar civil rights agitation.

Many homosexuals also discovered a wider world in the service. Despite rules barring them from the military, most slipped through at the induction centers. Moreover, the emotional pressures of wartime, especially the fear of death, encouraged close friendships, and homosexuals in the military often found more room than in civilian life to express their sexual orientation openly. In army canteens, when there were no women present, even straight men often danced with one another. In civilian settings, such behavior would have brought ridicule or even arrest.

Most veterans looked back on World War II, with all its dangers and discomforts, as the greatest experience they ever knew. As *The New Republic* predicted in 1943, they met other Americans from every part of the country and recognized for the first time in their lives "the bigness and wholeness of the United States." "Hughie was a Georgia cracker, so he knew something about moonshine," remembered one soldier. Another fondly recalled "this fellow from Wisconsin we called 'Moose.'" The army itself promoted these expectations of new experience. *Twenty-Seven Soldiers* (1944), a government-produced film for the troops, showed Allied soldiers of several nationalities all working together in harmony.

The Medical Corps

By the time the war ended, nearly 500,000 Americans died in military actions. Although the European Theater produced the most casualties, the Pacific held grave dangers beyond enemy fire. For soldiers in humid jungles, malaria, typhus, diarrhea, or dengue fever posed the most common threat to their lives. For the 25th Infantry Division, which landed in Guadalcanal in 1943, the malaria-carrying mosquito proved an even more deadly enemy than the Japanese.

The prolonged stress of combat also took a toll in "battle fatigue"—the official army term for combat stress and what would today be called posttraumatic stress. Despite rigorous screening, more than 1 million soldiers suffered at one time or another from debilitating psychiatric symptoms, and the number of men discharged for neuropsychiatric reasons was 2.5 times greater than in previous wars. The cause, psychiatrists concluded, was not individual weakness but long stints in the front lines. In France, for example, where soldiers spent up to 200 days in the field without a break from fighting, thousands cracked, occasionally wounding themselves in order to be sent home. In 1944, the army concluded that eight months in combat was the maximum. When replacements were available, a rotation system relieved exhausted soldiers.

In basic training, soldiers received first-aid instruction, and they went into battle with bandages to treat minor wounds. For anything more serious, however, they needed physicians and medics. Army Medical Corps doctors went to the front lines. There, in makeshift tent hospitals, these physicians pioneered advanced surgical techniques and used new "wonder drugs" such as penicillin to save many wounded soldiers who in earlier wars would have died. Of the soldiers who underwent emergency field surgery, more than 85 percent survived. Overall, less than 4 percent of all soldiers who received medical care died of their injuries. Much of the success in treatment came from the use of blood plasma, which reduced the often lethal effect of shock from severe bleeding. By 1945, the American Red Cross Blood Bank, formed four years earlier, had collected more than 13 million units of blood from volunteers, converted most of it into dried plasma, and made it readily available throughout the European Theater.

Grateful for the care of skilled surgeons, many soldiers nevertheless named medics the true heroes of the battlefront. Thirty to forty medics were attached to each infantry battalion, and under fire they gave emergency first aid and transported the wounded to the aid station and, if necessary, the field hospital.

In the military hospitals, American nurses gave the bulk of care to recovering soldiers. Before World War II, the Army Nurse Corps, created in 1901, was scarcely a military organization; its recruits earned neither military pay nor held rank. To overcome the short supply of nurses, Congress extended military rank to nurses in 1944, although only for the duration plus six months. In 1945, Congress came close to passing a bill to draft nurses. Like medics, army nurses went first to training centers in the United States, learning how to dig foxholes and dodge bullets before being sent overseas. By 1945, approximately 56,000 women, including 500 African American women, were on active duty in the Army Nurse Corps, staffing medical facilities in every theater of the war.

The World at War

The Allies remained on the defensive almost until the end of 1942. During this time, from the Atlantic to deep in Russia, Hitler and his allies controlled most of continental Europe and continued to pound Great Britain from the air. A German army also swept across North Africa and almost took the Suez Canal from the British.

In the Pacific and East Asia, the situation was just as dire. Just two hours after the attack on Pearl Harbor, Japanese planes struck the main U.S. airbase in the Philippines and demolished half the warplanes commanded by General Douglas MacArthur. See the Map *World War II, European Theater* at www.myhistorylab.com Japanese troops soon conquered the entire Philippines. MacArthur retreated to the Bataan Peninsula and then fled by submarine to Australia. When his stranded troops on Bataan finally surrendered, they were subjected to a horrific "death march" into POW camps; there, they faced abuse, disease, and starvation until liberated. The Japanese easily overran Britain's Southeast Asian colonies, the Dutch East Indies, and the entire western Pacific. Although China officially joined the Allies, Japanese forces on the Chinese mainland remained on the offensive. Roosevelt called the news "all bad," and his military advisers predicted a long fight to victory (see Map 25.1).

The Allies did enjoy several important advantages: America's vast natural resources and a skilled workforce with sufficient reserves to accelerate the production of weapons and ammunitions; the determination of millions of antifascists throughout Europe and Asia; and the capacity of the Soviet people to endure immense losses. Slowly at first, but then with quickening speed, these advantages came into play.

Soviets Halt Nazi Drive

The weapons and tactics of World War II differed radically from those of World War I. Unlike that conflict, which was fought with poison gas and machine-gun fire by armies largely immobilized in trenches, World War II was a war of offensive maneuvers punctuated by surprise attacks. Its chief weapons—tanks and planes on land and aircraft carriers and submarines at sea—combined mobility and concentrated firepower. Also of major importance were artillery and explosives, which according to some estimates accounted for more than 30 percent of casualties. Major improvements in communication systems, mainly two-way radio transmission and radio-telephony that permitted commanders to stay in contact with division leaders, played a decisive role throughout the war.

From the beginning of the European war in 1939, Hitler had used these methods to seize the advantage, purposefully striking terror among stricken populations of Western Europe as he routed opposing armies. The Royal Air Force, however, fought the Luftwaffe to a standstill in the Battle of Britain, frustrating Hitler's hopes of invading England. By the spring of 1941, Hitler had turned his

MAP 25.1 The War in Europe The Allies remained on the defensive during the first years of the war, but by 1943 the British and Americans, with an almost endless supply of resources, had turned the tide.

attention eastward, planning to conquer the Soviet Union. But he had to delay the invasion to rescue Mussolini, whose weak army faced defeat in North Africa and Greece. Not until June 22, 1941, six weeks behind schedule, did Hitler invade the Soviet Union.

Hitler's forces initially devastated the Red Army, killing or capturing nearly 3 million soldiers and leaving thousands to die from exposure or starvation. But the brutality of the Nazis—from the beginning they intended to kill all the Jews and reduce the Russian population to slave laborers—kindled a desperate civilian resistance. The German army in Russia found its supply lines overextended and the brutal Russian winter just beginning, while Stalin was able to send every available resource to his troops concentrated just outside Moscow. The Red Army launched a massive counterattack, catching the frostbitten German troops off guard and driving them to retreat. For the first time, the Nazi war machine had suffered a major setback.

Hitler, however, remained stubbornly fixed on conquering Russia and then, with great resources at his disposal, turning on Britain and even the United States. In 1942, German troops had a new objective: occupying the rich oil fields of the Caucasus. But at Stalingrad (now Volgograd), a major Soviet industrial city on the Volga River, Hitler met his nemesis. In the battle for that city alone, the Soviets suffered more casualties than Americans did during the entire war. House-to-house fighting and a massive Red Army counterattack inflicted an even greater toll on the Nazis. Hitler ordered to his troops to die rather than surrender. In February 1943, the German Sixth Army, reduced to 100,000 starving men and overpowered by Soviet weaponry, at last gave up. Years later, only a handful would return from Soviet prison camps.

Already in retreat but plotting one last desperate attempt to halt the Red Army, the Germans threw most of their remaining armored vehicles into action at Kursk in July 1943. The clash quickly spiraled into the greatest tank battle in history, involving more than 2 million troops and 6,000 tanks. After another stunning defeat, the Germans had decisively lost the initiative. Their only option was to delay the advance of the Red Army toward their own homeland.

Meanwhile, the Soviet Union had begun to recover from its early losses, even as tens of millions of its people remained homeless and near starvation. Assisted by Lend-Lease, by 1942 the Soviets were outproducing Germany in many types of weapons and other supplies. Nazi officers and German civilians alike began to doubt that Hitler could win.

Soviet victories had turned the tide; the Soviet Union, not the Western Allies, bore by far the heaviest burden in stopping what had once seemed an unstoppable Nazi advance. The American and British people were grateful for this immense Soviet contribution (the full extent of which they did not know at the time), and the British and American governments found themselves under enormous pressure from Stalin to open a second front in the west. But to do so required complex strategic planning and the assembling of immense material and human resources.

Planning and Initiating the Allied Offensive

Despite the huge territories that Nazi Germany and Japan controlled in 1942, the Axis momentum was flagging. After Stalingrad, Hitler lost ground. In the Pacific that summer, Japan's plans to invade Hawai'i and Australia were stopped by the U.S. Navy. In the course of 1942 as well, American shipbuilding began to outpace the punishment Nazi U-boats could inflict on Allied shipping; that advance kept open the vital Lend-Lease supply lanes to Britain and Russia. Meanwhile, submarine-hunting destroyers greatly reduced the German undersea threat. The United States far outstripped Germany in building landing craft and amphibious vehicles, two of the most important innovations of the war. Now outnumbered by the Allies, the German Luftwaffe was increasingly limited to defensive action.

Against this backdrop, Roosevelt, Churchill, and their generals hammered out a strategy to defeat the Axis. They saw Japan as the lesser threat—one that for the moment should be contained rather than attacked all-out (although MacArthur, the U.S. Navy, and the American public all clamored for a "Japan-first" strategy of avenging Pearl Harbor). Germany, Roosevelt and Churchill agreed, must be beaten first, which meant eventually invading Europe and fighting Hitler's Reich from the west, while the Red Army advanced from the east.

But the Allies disagreed about where to attack Germany. Remembering the terrible bloodletting on the western front during World War I, the British dreaded another long, stalemated struggle in France. Churchill and his generals wanted to strike through what he called "Europe's soft underbelly," the Mediterranean. The American generals retorted that only a direct, though meticulously prepared, assault through France would bring down Nazi Germany.

In the end, Roosevelt and Churchill compromised: they would first send smaller armies into the Mediterranean, while gathering a huge Anglo-American invasion army in Britain. This strategy was set in motion in late 1942. On October 23–24, near El Alamein in the desert of western Egypt, the British Eighth Army halted a major offensive by the German Afrika Korps, headed by the famed "Desert Fox," General Erwin Rommel. Although suffering heavy losses, British forces destroyed the Italian North African Army and much of the Afrika Korps. Then, in November, American troops for the first time went into action in the European Theater by joining the British in Operation Torch, an invasion of Morocco and Algeria. While at the eastern end, the British drove Rommel back from El Alamein, from the west, a mostly American army, still inexperienced and mistake-prone, forced the Germans out of Tunisia. In six months, North Africa was cleared of Axis troops.

In January 1943, while the fighting raged in North Africa, Roosevelt and Churchill met at Casablanca in Morocco and announced that they would accept nothing less than the unconditional surrender of their enemies. There would be no negotiations with Hitler and Mussolini. Roosevelt's supporters hailed the policy as a clear statement of goals, a promise to the world that the scourge of fascism would be completely banished. Stalin, who did not attend, criticized the policy, predicting that it would only increase enemy determination to fight to the end. Western critics charged that the demand for total capitulation would prolong the war and swell the casualty list.

Allied aerial bombing was increasing the pressure on Germany. Some U.S. leaders believed that the B-17 Flying Fortress, "the mightiest bomber ever built," could win the war from the air without any western troops having to fight their way into Europe. The U.S. Army Air Corps (predecessor of the Air Force) described the B-17 as a "humane" weapon, capable of hitting specific military targets while sparing civilians. That claim was nonsense. Especially when weather or darkness required bombardiers to sight with radar, they could not distinguish between industrial, military, and civilian targets, and even with the best available targeting, bombs might land anywhere within a nearly two-mile radius. More often, bomber crews, who suffered awful losses from ground-based anti-aircraft fire, just wanted to dump their bombs fast and get away safely. American pilots preferred to bomb during daylight, while the British bombed at night, when they could see nothing at all of their blacked-out targets. Bombing missions over the Rhineland and the Ruhr did take out many German factories, while also costing tens of thousands of civilian lives, but the Germans successfully relocated many industrial plants to the countryside.

Determined to break German resistance, the Royal Air Force redirected its main attack away from military targets to cities, fuel dumps, and transportation lines. Indiscriminate bombing practically leveled the great city of Hamburg, killing between 60,000 and 100,000 people and destroying 300,000 buildings. Sixty other cities were hit hard, leaving 20 percent of Germany's total residential area in ruins. Americans joined in the very worst air raid of the war—650,000 incendiary bombs dropped on Dresden in 1945 destroying 8 square miles and killing perhaps 135,000 civilians (no one knows for sure, because the city sheltered uncounted refugees). Dresden, famous for its architecture and art galleries, had no military value. This was terror bombing. Hitler had started it, but the Allies more than repaid in kind.

Though the air war disappointed those who saw in it the means of a bloodless—to the attackers—victory, the Allied strategic air offensive did weaken the German economy and did terrorize (but also enrage) German civilians. Moreover, in trying to defend German cities and factories, the Luftwaffe sacrificed most of its remaining fighter planes and aircraft fuel. When the Allies finally invaded Western Europe in the summer of 1944, they would enjoy total air superiority.

The Allied Invasion of Europe

In the summer of 1943, the Allies continued their Mediterranean offensive by attacking southern Italy. On July 10, British and American troops stormed Sicily, and by mid-August conquered the island. King Vittorio Emmanuel fired Mussolini, calling him "the most despised man in Italy." After Allied troops landed near Naples, Italy surrendered to the Western Allies on September 8. Hitler, however, sent new divisions into northern and central Italy, stalling the Allied campaign. Almost until the end of

As part of the air war on Germany, Allied bombers launched a devastating attack on Dresden, a major economic center, in February 1945. Of the civilians who died, most from burns or smoke inhalation during the firestorm, a large number were women and children, refugees from the eastern front. The city was left in ruins.

D-Day landing, June 6, 1944, marked the greatest amphibious maneuver in military history. Troop ships ferried Allied soldiers from England to Normandy beaches. Within a month, nearly 1 million men had assembled in France, ready to retake western and central Europe from German forces.

the European war, a large Allied army was still bogged down on Italy's rugged terrain, battling a much smaller German force.

All across occupied Europe, resistance to the Nazis spread. Jews walled off in the Nazi-built Warsaw ghetto, realizing that they were marked for extermination, revolted in the summer of 1943 and fought to the death. Scattered revolts followed in the Nazi labor camps, where military prisoners of war and civilians were being worked on starvation rations. Underground fighters, known as partisans, resisted the Nazis from Norway to Greece and from Poland to France. Untrained and lightly armed, men, women, and children risked their lives to distribute antifascist propaganda, committed sabotage, rescued downed Allied bomber crews, and killed Nazi collaborators. They smuggled food and weapons to clandestine resistance groups and prepared the way for the offensive that, in shortwave radio broadcasts, the Allies promised.

Allied preparations for that offensive were thorough and time-consuming. As a huge American army gathered and trained in Britain, Churchill's objections to invading France gradually wore down, while Stalin ceaselessly demanded a second front. (To him, the stalled invasion of Italy was no substitute.) By early 1944, Anglo-American plans were being readied for Operation Overlord, a campaign to retake the Continent with a decisive counterattack through France. General Dwight D. Eisenhower, who was put in command, displayed great skill not only in strategizing but also in dealing with contentious British, Americans, and the prickly Free French leader, General Charles de Gaulle.

D-Day—the start of the Allied invasion—finally came on June 6, 1944. Much depended on surprise and even the right mix of tides, moonlight, and clear weather. After receiving a forecast of a short break in storms that otherwise might have doomed the operation, "Ike" made the courageous decision: "Go." Under heavy German machine-gun and mortar fire, wave after wave of American, British, Canadian, and Free French troops hit the Normandy beaches, the tides swelling with the dead and the wounded. Some 2,500 men died in the initial assault, many before they could fire a shot. Although the Germans responded slowly—they expected the invasion near Calais and at first thought Normandy a feint—at Omaha Beach they had prepared their defense almost perfectly, and the Americans who landed there had a particularly difficult time gaining a toehold. Within days, though, more than 175,000 Allied troops and 20,000 vehicles were battling the Germans—the largest landing operation in history. Over the next six weeks, nearly 1 million more Allied soldiers came ashore. Not until mid-July did this invasion army finally break out of Normandy and drive into the French interior.

All eyes now turned to Paris. Allied bombers pounded roads, bridges, rail lines, and factories that were producing German munitions all around the French capital. As demoralized German soldiers retreated, hoping only to survive, the French Resistance unfurled the French flag at impromptu demonstrations on Bastille Day, July 14. On August 10, railway workers staged one of the first successful strikes against Nazi occupiers, and three days later the Paris police defected to the Resistance, which distributed leaflets proclaiming that "the hour of liberation has come." With Free French and Allied troops, de Gaulle entered Paris on August 25 and announced a reconstituted French Republic. Belgium also fell swiftly to the liberators. But

Allied troops had only reached a resting place between bloody battles, their supply lines stretched thin and German resistance stiffening.

The High Cost of European Victory

By September 1944, Allied commanders were searching for a way to end the war quickly. Missing a spectacular chance to move through largely undefended territory and on to Berlin, they turned north instead, intending to strike through the Netherlands into Germany's industrial heartland. Faulty intelligence reports overlooked a well-armed German division at the Dutch town of Arnhem, waiting to cut Allied paratroops to pieces. The Germans captured 6,000 Americans.

That winter, making a final, desperate effort to break the Allied momentum, Hitler sent his last reserves, a quarter-million men, against American lines in Belgium's dense Ardennes forest. In this so-called Battle of the Bulge, the Germans surprised the Americans, driving them fifty miles back before literally running out of gas. This last effort—the bloodiest single campaign Americans had fought since Gettysburg—exhausted the German capacity for counterattack. After Christmas Day 1944, the Germans had to retreat into their own territory.

The end approached. In March 1945, discovery of a single intact bridge across the Rhine allowed the Allies to roll into the heart of Germany, taking the heavily industrialized Ruhr Valley.

By that time, Soviet offenses were crushing the German army in the east. The Red Army had reached Warsaw in the midsummer of 1944, but then stood by while the anti-Russian Polish resistance rose up—only to be destroyed (along with most of the city) by the Nazis. While that tragedy unfolded, the Soviets occupied the Balkans and battled the Germans in Hungary. Only in January 1945 did the Red Army sweep across Poland and by April besiege Berlin, where Hitler had holed up.

The defense of Germany, now hopeless, had fallen into the hands of teenagers, terrified elderly men, and a few desperate Nazis.

The War in Asia and the Pacific

Six months after Pearl Harbor, the United States began regaining naval superiority in the central Pacific. The Americans had been supremely lucky that their aircraft carriers were out at sea during the Pearl Harbor attack; that luck was spectacularly demonstrated in the great naval battle of the Coral Sea on May 7–8, 1942, in which carrier-based American aircraft blocked a Japanese thrust at Australia. A month later, on June 4, the Japanese fleet converged on Midway Island, an outpost vital to American communications and to the defense of Hawai'i. There, the Americans had another lucky break; intelligence officers had broken the Japanese codes and thus knew when and where the attack would fall. Still separated by hundreds of miles of open sea, the Japanese and American carrier fleets clashed at long distance. Descending from the clouds, American warplanes sank four Japanese carriers and destroyed hundreds of planes, ending Japan's offensive threat to Hawai'i and the West Coast. These two battles signaled a historic shift in naval warfare: aircraft carriers, not huge battleships, would rule the waves.

Even so, Japan controlled a vast arc of the western Pacific. That perimeter stretched from the outermost Aleutians (off Alaska) to northern New Guinea and the Solomon Islands (off Australia). Japan also dominated all of coastal China and the European colonies of Southeast Asia: Indochina, Malaya, present-day Indonesia, and Burma (see Map 25.2). In much of East Asia (except China), nationalistic and anticolonial sentiment played into Japanese hands at first. With only 200,000 troops, Japan easily overran Southeast Asia because so few people in the British, French, and Dutch colonies would fight for their imperial masters. Japan installed puppet governments in Burma and the Philippines, and independent Thailand became a Japanese ally. But the new Japanese empire proved terrifyingly cruel. Local nationalists from Indochina to the Philippines turned against the Japanese, forming guerrilla bands that harassed the invaders. In China, Japan's huge land army bogged down fighting both the Nationalist forces of Chiang Kai-shek and the Communist People's Liberation Army led by Mao Zedong.

See the Map
*World War II,
Pacific Theater* at
www.myhistorylab.com

Thus, in mid-1942, the war for the Pacific was still only beginning. Pulling back their offensive operations, the Japanese concentrated their remaining forces. Their commanders calculated that bitter fighting, with high casualties on both sides, would wear down the American military and public. The U.S. command, divided between MacArthur in the southwest Pacific and Admiral Chester Nimitz in the central Pacific, developed a strategy to strangle the Japanese import-dependent economy and to "island-hop" from one strategic outpost to another, closing in on the home islands.

In the Solomons and New Guinea, American and Australian ground troops began the counterattack. On Guadalcanal in the Solomons, American Marines struck at one Japanese stronghold, and during a six-month struggle endured tropical diseases, dangerous parasites, food and ammunition shortages, and very high casualty rates against Japanese defenders who fought to the death. The marines were reduced to eating roots and berries to stay alive. Amid these horrors, the vaunted American logistical system was not always effective: a week before Christmas, a shipment of winter coats arrived! Finally, with strong supply lines secured by a string of costly naval battles, in February 1943 the Americans finally prevailed, proving that they could defeat Japanese forces in brutal jungle combat.

For the next two years, the U.S. Navy and Marine Corps opened a path to Japan, capturing a series of important Pacific atolls but bypassing others, helplessly stranding

MAP 25.2 War in the Pacific Across an ocean battlefield utterly unlike the European Theater, Allies battled Japanese troops near their homeland.

well-armed Japanese defenders. Tarawa in the Gilbert Islands was first of these assaults in November 1943; it cost more than 1,000 U.S. Marine lives. In June 1944, simultaneously with the Normandy landings, the U.S. Navy inflicted crippling losses on the Japanese fleet in the Battle of the Philippine Sea. Then in August 1944, the Americans took Guam, Saipan, and Tinian in the Mariana Islands, for the first time bringing the Japanese home islands within bomber range. And in October of that year, MacArthur led an American force of 250,000 to retake the Philippines.

Trying to hold the islands, practically all that remained of the Japanese navy threw itself at the Americans in the Battle of Leyte Gulf, the largest naval battle in history. The Japanese lost eighteen capital ships, leaving the United States in control of the Pacific. While MacArthur mopped up operations in the Philippines—at a cost of 100,000 Filipino lives and leaving Manila devastated—the small but strategically important island of Iwo Jima, south of Japan, fell. Here too, the American death toll was high; casualties were estimated at nearly 27,000.

Even bloodier was the struggle for Okinawa, an island 350 miles southwest of the Japanese home islands and the site of vital airbases. The invasion—the largest American amphibious operation in the Pacific war—began on Easter Sunday, April 1, 1945. Waves of Japanese *kamikaze* ("divine wind") pilots, flying suicide missions with a 500-pound bomb and only enough fuel for a one-way flight, met the marines on the beaches. The U.S. troops who survived this onslaught used flame-throwers, each with 300 gallons of napalm, to incinerate dug-in Japanese defenders. On Okinawa, more Americans died or were wounded than at Normandy. At the end of June, when the ghastly struggle ended, 140,000 Japanese were dead, including 42,000 civilians.

The war was over in Europe, and the Allies could concentrate on Japan alone. Tokyo and other Japanese cities were targeted by B-17s and new B-29s flying from Guam with devastating results. Massive fire bombings burned thousands of civilians alive in their mostly wooden or bamboo houses, and hundreds of thousands were left homeless. Meanwhile, U.S. submarines cut off the home islands from supplies on the East Asian mainland.

Japan could not hold out forever. Without a navy or air force, critically important oil, tin, rubber, and grain could not be transported to maintain its soldiers or feed its people. Great Britain and particularly the United States, however, pressed for a quick and unconditional surrender. They had special reasons to hurry. Earlier they had sought a commitment from the Soviet Union to invade Japan, but now they looked beyond the war, determined to prevent the Red Army from taking any Japanese-held territories. These calculations, as well as chilling forecasts of the bloody cost of invading and subjugating the home islands, set the stage for unleashing the top-secret weapon that American scientists had been building: the atomic bomb (see Communities in Conflict).

The Last Stages of War

From the attack on Pearl Harbor until mid-1943, Roosevelt and his advisers had focused on military strategy rather than on postwar plans. Once the defeat of Nazi Germany appeared in sight, high government officials began to consider long-range objectives. Roosevelt wanted both to crush the Axis powers and to establish a system of collective security to prevent another world war. He knew he could not succeed without the cooperation of the other key leaders, Stalin and Churchill.

In 1944 and early 1945, these "Big Three" met several times to hammer out the shape of the postwar world. Although none of these nations expected to reach a final agreement, neither did they anticipate how quickly they would confront momentous global events, including the obvious fact that the only thing holding the "Grand Alliance" together was the mission of destroying the Axis.

The Holocaust

Another fact also became clear, at least to the American public, as the European war entered its final stages: the full horror of Nazi atrocities. As part of a comprehensive plan for achieving Aryan superiority and the "final solution of the Jewish question," Hitler had ordered the extermination of "racial enemies" and others deemed undesirable, including mentally retarded and crippled German children and adults. The toll included some 6 million Jews, 250,000 Romany (Gypsies), 60,000 homosexuals, members of other "inferior races" (such as Slavs), and indeed anyone else deemed an enemy of the German Reich and its "master race." Beginning in 1933, but accelerating from 1941 onward, the Nazis murdered millions of people in Germany and in all the European nations they conquered. Gruesome "medical experiments" were also performed on Jews and Soviet prisoners of war (POWs).

These policies had begun at the outset of the Hitler regime in 1933, and at the beginning of 1942 the Nazis initiated mass murder in death camps like Auschwitz in Poland. Very soon, word of what the Nazis were doing was leaking out of occupied Europe. Throughout almost the entire war, however, the U.S. government released little information about what came to be known as the Holocaust. Although liberal magazines such as *The Nation* and small committees of intellectuals tried to call attention to what was happening in the Nazi camps, major news media like the *New York Times* and *Time* magazine treated reports of genocide as minor news items. As late as 1943, only 43 percent of Americans polled believed that Hitler was systematically murdering European Jews.

Leaders of the American Jewish community, however, were better informed than the general population, and since the mid-1930s they had been petitioning the government to suspend immigration quotas that barred significant numbers of German Jews from taking refuge in the United States. Backed by public opinion (fixated on foreigners threatening American jobs), Roosevelt and Congress refused. Even after the United States entered the war, the president maintained that the liberation of European Jews and other oppressed peoples depended on a speedy and total Allied victory. Not until January 1944 did Roosevelt agree to change government policy. At that time, Secretary of the Treasury Henry Morgenthau, himself Jewish, reported to the president on "one of the greatest crimes in history, the slaughter of the Jewish people in Europe," and suggested that anti-Semitism in the State Department had stalled the development of an aggressive plan of action. Within a week, in part to avoid scandal, Roosevelt issued an executive order creating the War Refugee Board. However, when American Jews pleaded for bombing rail lines leading to the notorious death camp at Auschwitz, in occupied Poland, both Roosevelt and the War Department refused. Attempts to rescue civilians—such was the government's unshaken position—would divert resources from military operations.

On Deploying the Atomic Bomb

Although the scientists employed in the Manhattan Project embraced their assignment with fervor, they nevertheless thought deep and hard about the moral ramifications of their work. After the first test of the atomic bomb revealed its horrifying power, they began to discuss among themselves the necessary criteria for using a weapon of such deadly force. By May 1945, under Robert Oppenheimer's leadership, a "target committee" had outlined a list of conditions necessary to deploy the "gadget" (a code name for the atomic bomb) against Japan. A month later, small groups of scientists working on the Manhattan Project at the University of Chicago began to appeal to government officials, advising supreme caution in considering the use of the atomic bomb. They acknowledged "the military advantages and the saving of American lives" that deployment against Japan might bring, but warned that such gain "may be outweighed by the ensuing loss of confidence and wave of horror and repulsion, sweeping over the rest of the world, and perhaps dividing even the public opinion at home." They also recommended that, rather than immediately deploying the bomb, the United States invite nations to witness a demonstration on a barren island or desert. Oppenheimer and Fermi, however, both disagreed and held firm to the letter of their assignment: to produce the bomb for military use. In secret correspondence, which is now declassified, two of the top scientists of the Manhattan Project map the opposing positions.

Leo Szilard (1898–1964), a Hungarian-born scientist, is said to have conceived of the idea of nuclear chain reaction, the process that in uranium provides the power for nuclear energy. In a letter to President Truman in July 1945, he warns against using the atomic bomb against Japan. The physicist Edward Teller (1908–2003), also Hungarian-born, worked closely with Fermi and Oppenheimer at Los Alamos. After the war, he promoted the development of a "super bomb," the hydrogen bomb, and ultimately convinced President Truman to fund the project as a bulwark against the Soviet Union. In his letter, he replies to Szilard's request.

● **What arguments did the scientists pose for and against the deployment of the atomic bomb?**

July 3, 1945: A Petition to the President of the United States

Discoveries of which the people of the United States are not aware may affect the welfare of this nation in the near future. The liberation of atomic power which has been achieved places atomic bombs in the hands of the Army. It places in your hands, as Commander-in-Chief, the fateful decision whether or not to sanction the use of such bombs in the present phase of the war against Japan.

We, the undersigned scientists, have been working in the field of atomic power for a number of years. Until recently we have had to reckon with the possibility that the United States might be attacked by atomic bombs during this war and that her only defense might lie in a counterattack by the same means. Today with this danger averted we feel impelled to say what follows:

The war has to be brought speedily to a successful conclusion and the destruction of Japanese cities by means of atomic bombs may very well be an effective method of warfare. We feel, however, that such an attack on Japan could not be justified in the present circumstances. We believe that the United States ought not to resort to the use of atomic bombs in the present phase of the war, at least not unless the terms which will be imposed upon Japan after the war are publicly announced and subsequently Japan is given an opportunity to surrender.

If such public announcement gave assurance to the Japanese that they could look forward to a life devoted to peaceful pursuits in their homeland and if Japan still refused to surrender, our nation would then be faced with a situation which might require a re-examination of her position with respect to the use of atomic bombs in the war.

Atomic bombs are primarily a means for the ruthless annihilation of cities. Once they were introduced as an instrument of war it would be difficult to resist for long the temptation of putting them to such use.

> "Atomic bombs are primarily a means for the ruthless annihilation of cities."

The last few years show a marked tendency toward increasing ruthlessness. At present our Air Forces, striking at the Japanese cities, are using the same methods of warfare which were condemned by American public opinion only a few years ago when applied by the Germans to the cities of England. Our use of atomic bombs in this war would carry the world a long way further on this path of ruthlessness.

Atomic power will provide the nations with new means of destruction. The atomic bombs at our disposal represent only the first step in this direction and there is almost no limit to the destructive power which will become available in the course of this development. Thus a nation which sets the precedent of using these newly liberated forces of nature for purposes of destruction may have to bear the responsibility of opening the door to an era of devastation on an unimaginable scale.

In view of the foregoing, we, the undersigned, respectfully petition that you exercise your power as Commander-in-Chief to rule that the United States shall not, in the present phase of the war, resort to the use of atomic bombs.

Leo Szilard and 58 co-signers

SOURCE: Box 70, *J. Robert Oppenheimer Papers*, Manuscript Division, Library of Congress, Washington, D.C.

Teller's Response to Szilard

Dear Szilard:

Since our discussion I have spent some time thinking about your objections to an immediate military use of the weapon we may produce. I decided to do nothing; I should like to tell you my reasons.

First of all let me say that I have no hope of clearing my conscience. The things we are working on are so terrible that no amount of protesting or fiddling with politics will save our souls.

This much is true: I have not worked on the project for a very selfish reason and I have gotten mucsh (sic) more trouble than pleasure out of it. I worked because the problems interested me and I should have felt it a great restraint not to go ahead. I can not claim that I simply worked to do my duty. A sense of duty could keep me out of such work. It could not get me into the present kind of activity against my inclinations. If you should succeed in convincing me that your moral objections are valid, I should quit working. I hardly think that I should start protesting.

But I am not really convinced of your objections. I do not feel that there is any chance to outlaw any one weapon. If we have a slim chance of survival, it lies in the possibility to get rid of wars. The more decisive a weapon is the more surely it will be used in any real conflict and no agreements will help.

Our only hope is in getting the facts of our results before the people. This might help to convince everybody that the next war would be fatal. For this purpose actual combat use might even be the best thing.

And this brings me to the main point. The accident that we worked out this dreadful thing should not give us the responsibility of having a voice in how it is to be used. This responsibility must in the end be shifted to the people as a whole and that can be done only by making the facts known. This is the only cause for which I feel entitled in doing something: the necessity of lifting the secrecy at least as far as the broad issues of our work are concerned. My understanding is that this will be done as soon as the military situation permits it.

All this may seem to you quite wrong. I should be glad if you showed this letter to Eugene and to Franck who seem to agree with you rather than with me. I should like to have the advice of all of you whether you think it is a crime to continue to work. But I feel that I should do the wrong

"The more decisive a weapon is the more surely it will be used. . . ."

thing if I tried to say how to tie the little toe of the ghost to the bottle from which we just helped it to escape.

With best regards.

Yours,

E. Teller

SOURCE: Box 70, *J. Robert Oppenheimer Papers*, Manuscript Division, Library of Congress, Washington, D.C.

Belsen Camp: The Compound for Women, painted by American artist Leslie Cole, depicts Belsen as the Allied troops found it when they invaded Germany in 1945.

SOURCE: Leslie Cole, *Belsen Camp: The Compound for Women*. Imperial War Museum, London.

The extent of Nazi depravity was finally revealed to Americans when Allied troops invaded Germany and began liberating the Nazi camps. Touring Ohrdruf concentration camp in April 1945, Eisenhower found barracks crowded with corpses and crematories still reeking of burned flesh. "I want every American unit not actually in the front lines to see this place," Eisenhower ordered. "We are told that the American soldier does not know what he is fighting for. Now, at least, he will know what he is fighting against."

The Yalta Conference

Roosevelt was elected to a fourth term in November 1944, defeating the moderately liberal Republican governor of New York, Thomas E. Dewey. Many loyal Democrats looked forward to a revival of the New Deal after the war was won. Elected with FDR was a new vice president, a middle-of-the-road Missouri senator named Harry S. Truman, who replaced ultraliberal Henry Wallace. Unknown to the public, however, Roosevelt was now exhausted and gravely ill—though, as was his habit, he kept his vice president totally uninformed of his plans and of the most important wartime secrets.

In early 1945, with the end of the war in sight, Allied leaders began to reassess their goals. The Atlantic Charter of 1941 had stated noble objectives for the world after the defeat of fascism: national self-determination, no territorial aggrandizement, equal access of all peoples to raw materials and collaboration for the improvement of economic opportunities, freedom of the seas, disarmament, and "freedom from fear and want." Now, four years later, Roosevelt realized that neither Great Britain nor the Soviet Union intended to abide by any code of conduct that compromised their national security or conflicted with their economic interests. Stalin and Churchill soon reached a new agreement, one projecting their respective spheres of influence in Eastern Europe.

In early February 1945, Roosevelt held still another wartime meeting with Churchill and Stalin, this time at Yalta, a Crimean resort on the Black Sea. Seeking his partners' cooperation, the president recognized that prospects for postwar peace also depended on compromise. Although diplomats avoided the touchy phrase "spheres of influence," it was clear that this opportunistic principle guided all negotiations. Neither the United States nor Great Britain raised serious objections to Stalin's demand to retain the Baltic states and eastern Poland—booty from the time of the Nazi–Soviet pact—and to create an East European "buffer zone" protecting Russia against future German aggression. In return, Churchill insisted on restoring the British Empire in Asia, and the United States hoped to retain captured Pacific islands from which Japanese military resurgence could be checked. Roosevelt hoped to ease the harshness of these imperialistic goals by creating a global peacekeeping organization, the United Nations, and by using promises of postwar American economic aid to persuade Stalin to behave with restraint in countries, like Poland, that the Red Army was liberating and occupying.

The biggest and most controversial item on the agenda at Yalta was the Soviet entry into the Pacific war, which Roosevelt believed necessary for a timely Allied victory. After driving a hard bargain involving Soviet rights to territory in China, Stalin agreed to declare war against Japan within three months of

View the Image

Big Three at Yalta at **www.myhistorylab.com**

Germany's surrender. Roosevelt told Congress that the Yalta meeting had been a "great success," proof that the wartime alliance remained intact. Privately, however, the president concluded that the outcome of the conference revealed that the Atlantic Charter had been nothing more than "a beautiful idea."

The death of Franklin Roosevelt of a massive stroke on April 12, 1945, cast a dark shadow over all hopes for long-term, peaceful solutions to global problems. The president did not live to learn of Hitler's suicide in his Berlin bunker on April 30, 1945, or the unconditional surrender of Germany one week later, on May 8. Millions of Americans and people in other democratic nations deeply mourned the passing of the great pragmatic idealist, just as new and still greater challenges were looming.

The Atomic Bomb

Roosevelt's death made Allied cooperation even more difficult. Harry Truman, an honest and plainspoken product of Kansas City machine politics, made a national reputation as a U.S. senator investigating wartime corruption, but he lacked foreign-policy experience and had none of FDR's finesse and prestige.

The wartime Big Three—now Stalin, Truman, and Churchill (the latter soon replaced as prime minister by Clement Atlee when the British voted in a Labour Party government)—held their final conference at Potsdam, just outside Berlin, from July 17 to August 2, 1945. The meeting lacked the spirited give-and-take of the conferences in which Roosevelt and Churchill had participated. A huge agenda of thorny issues confronted the victorious leaders: the future of defeated and occupied Germany and other former Axis powers, the Soviet occupation of Eastern Europe, reparations and economic aid to rebuild a shattered Europe, and crucial details about organizing the new United Nations, on which the Americans set great store. The Big Three clashed sharply over most of these issues, but they held fast in demanding the unconditional surrender of reeling but still-defiant Japan.

It was while wrangling with Stalin at Potsdam that Truman learned a closely guarded secret: that on July 16 the United States had successfully tested an atomic bomb in New Mexico. As a senator and as vice president, Truman had not been informed of the existence of the Manhattan Project; he first heard about it upon Roosevelt's death. Until the moment of the test, Truman had been pressing Stalin to make good his Yalta promise to enter the Pacific war three months after Germany's surrender—a deadline that would fall on August 8. The president was eager to get Soviet participation in what everyone said would be a horrendously bloody U.S. invasion of Japan, and indeed he did extract Stalin's promise to attack Japan on schedule. But then Secretary of War Stimson received a cable: "Babies satisfactorily born."

Truman and his advisers concluded that Soviet assistance was no longer needed to end the war.

On August 3, 1945, Japan announced its refusal to surrender. Its military leaders still demanded a fight to the death, and Japanese civilian politicians wanted Allied guarantees that the emperor, considered sacred, would keep his throne. This response the Americans deemed unsatisfactory: they still demanded unconditional surrender, preferably before the Red Army moved against Japan. Three days later, the B-29 bomber nicknamed *Enola Gay* dropped the five-ton uranium bomb that destroyed the Japanese city of Hiroshima. Instantly, some 40,000 people died; in the following weeks, 100,000 more perished from radiation poisoning or burns. By 1950, the death toll reached 200,000.

"This is not war, this is not even murder; this is pure nihilism . . . a crime against God which strikes at the very basis of moral existence." So wrote the Japanese *Nippon Times*. In the United States, several leading religious publications echoed this view. The *Christian Century* judged the use of the bomb as a "moral earthquake" that by comparison made the long-denounced use of poison gas by Germany in World War I utterly insignificant. Albert Einstein, whose physics provided the foundation for the Manhattan Project (but in which he had taken no part), said that the atomic bomb had changed everything—except the nature of man.

Americans first heard of the atomic bomb on August 7, when the news reported the destruction and death it had brought to Hiroshima. But fears about the implications of the appalling new weapon were overwhelmed by an outpouring of relief: Japan surrendered—still not unconditionally—on August 14, several days after a second nuclear bomb destroyed Nagasaki, killing another 73,000. (On schedule between these cataclysmic events, the Soviet army invaded Japanese-occupied Manchuria.)

Allied insistence on unconditional surrender and the decision to atom-bomb Japan remain two of the most controversial political and moral questions about the conduct of World War II. Although Truman insisted in his memoirs (written years later) that he gave the order so as to save "a half a million American lives" in ground combat, no such official estimate exists. An intelligence document of April 30, 1946, stated that "the dropping of the bomb was the pretext seized upon by all [American] leaders as the reason for ending the war, but [even if the bomb had not been used] the Japanese would have capitulated upon the entry of Russia into the war." There is no question, however, that the use of nuclear weapons did strengthen U.S. policymakers' hand. It certainly did force caution upon Stalin, soon to emerge as America's primary adversary. Truman and his advisers knew that their nation's atomic monopoly would not last, but they hoped that in the meantime the United States could play the leading role in building the postwar world.

CHRONOLOGY

1931	September: Japan occupies Manchuria
1933	March: Adolf Hitler seizes power
	May: Japan quits League of Nations
1935	October: Italy invades Ethiopia
1935–1937	Neutrality Acts authorize the president to block the sale of munitions to belligerent nations
1936	July: Spanish Civil War begins
1937	August: Japan invades China
	October: Franklin D. Roosevelt calls for international cooperation against aggression
1938	March: Germany annexes Austria
	September: Munich Agreement lets Germany annex Sudetenland of Czechoslovakia
	November: *Kristallnacht*, Nazis attack Jews and destroy Jewish property
1939	March: Germany annexes remainder of Czechoslovakia
	August: Germany and the Soviet Union sign nonaggression pact
	September: Germany invades Poland; World War II begins
	November: Soviet Union invades Finland
1940	April–June: Germany's *bliztkrieg* sweeps over Western Europe
	September: Germany, Italy, and Japan—the Axis powers—conclude a military alliance
	First peacetime military draft in American history
	November: Roosevelt defeats Wendall Willkie and is elected to an unprecedented third term
1941	March: Lend–Lease Act extends aid to Great Britain
	May: German troops secure the Balkans
	A. Philip Randolph plans March on Washington movement for July
	June: Germany invades Soviet Union
	Fair Employment Practices Committee formed

	August: The United States and Great Britain agree to the Atlantic Charter
	December: Japanese attack Pearl Harbor; United States enters the war
1942	January: War mobilization begins
	February: Executive order mandates internment of Japanese Americans
	May–June: Battles of Coral Sea and Midway give the United States naval superiority in the Pacific
	August: Manhattan Project begins
	November: United States stages amphibious landing in North Africa; Operation Torch begins
1943	January: Casablanca Conference announces unconditional surrender policy
	February: Soviet victory over Germans at Stalingrad
	April–May: Coal miners strike
	May: German Afrika Korps troops surrender in Tunis
	July: Allied invasion of Italy
	Summer: Race riots break out in nearly fifty cities
1944	June–August: Operation Overlord and liberation of Paris
	November: Roosevelt elected to fourth term, defeating Thomas E. Dewey
1945	February: Yalta Conference renews American–Soviet alliance
	February–June: United States captures Iwo Jima and Okinawa in Pacific
	April: Roosevelt dies in office; Harry Truman becomes president
	May: Germany surrenders
	July–August: Potsdam Conference
	August: United States drops atomic bombs on Hiroshima and Nagasaki; Japan surrenders

Conclusion

The new tactics and weapons of World War II, such as massive air raids and the atomic bomb produced by the Los Alamos scientists, made warfare incomparably more deadly than before to both military and civilian populations. Between 40 and 50 million people died in World War II—four times the number in World War I—and half the casualties were women and children. More than 405,000 Americans died, and more than 670,000 were wounded. Although slight compared to the casualties suffered by other Allied nations—more than 20 million Soviets died during the war—the human cost of World War II for Americans was second only to that of the Civil War.

Coming at the end of two decades of resolutions to avoid military entanglements, the war pushed the nation's leaders to the center of global politics and into risky military and political alliances that would not outlive the war. The United States emerged the strongest nation in the world, but in a world where the prospects for lasting peace appeared increasingly remote. If World War II raised the nation's international commitments to a new height, its impact on ordinary Americans was not so easy to gauge. Many new communities formed as Americans migrated in mass numbers to new regions that were booming as a result of the wartime economy. Enjoying a rare moment of full employment, many workers new to well-paying industrial jobs anticipated further advances against discrimination. Exuberant at the Allies' victory over fascism and the return of the troops, the majority were optimistic as they looked ahead.

Review Questions

1. How did President Franklin D. Roosevelt ready the nation for war?

2. What role did the federal government, business, and labor play in gearing up the economy for wartime production?

3. How did the war affect the lives of American women?

4. Discuss the causes and consequences of the Japanese American internment program.

5. Describe the role of popular culture in promoting the war effort at home.

6. How did military service affect the lives of those who served in World War II?

7. What were the main points of Allied military strategy in both Europe and Asia?

8. How successful were diplomatic efforts in ending the war and in establishing the terms of peace?

Recommended Reading

Luis Alvarz, *The Power of the Zoot: Youth Culture and Resistance during World War II* (2008). Makes the quest for dignity a prime factor in the adoption of zoot suits by nonwhite working-class youth during World War II. Alvarez offers provocative insights on the emergence of jazz culture and its function as a site of racial tension.

Philip D. Beidler, *The Good War's Greatest Hits: World War II and American Remembering* (1998). Examines the popular culture produced about World War II, such as movies, photographs, cartoons, and books, to show how these sources created a lasting image of World War II as the "good war."

Linda Gordon and Gary Y. Okihiro, *Impounded: Dorothea Lange and the Censored Images of Japanese Internment* (2006). An anthology of 100 images from the relocation camps by the famed WPA photographer. Gordon and Okohiro provide essays discussing the production of the photographs and the impact of internment on the Japanese American community.

Laura Hein and Mark Selden, eds., *Living With the Bomb: American and Japanese Cultural Conflict in the Nuclear Age* (1997). Essays dealing with the ambiguous legacy of the atomic bomb in both the United States and Japan. Reviews the "official story" of the bomb as the symbol of U.S. triumph in the "good war" in light of the growing number of dissenting voices and the impact of both views on memorials and museum exhibits.

John W. Jeffries, *Wartime America: The World War II Homefront* (1996). Provides a useful synthesis of scholarship and assesses the major differences in the interpretations of leading historians.

David M. Kennedy, *The American People in World War II* (1999). The second volume in Kennedy's Pulitzer Prize–winning *Freedom from Fear*, this book examines U.S. strategy to win the war from the perspective of the nation's leader as well as its citizens. The narrative interweaves overseas military events and home front experiences.

Gerald F. Linderman, *The World within War: America's Combat Experience in World War II* (1997). Emphasizes the less glamorous aspects of war, mainly the strains placed on the combat soldiers on the front lines. Linderman examines in especially close detail the grim experiences of army infantrymen and the marine riflemen who fought in the Pacific campaign and provides a nuanced analysis of their complex responses to the horror of war.

Katrina R. Mason, *Children of Los Alamos: An Oral History of the Town Where the Atomic Age Began* (1995). Recollections of those who spent their childhood in Los Alamos. They describe their affection for the geographical setting as well as sense of safety growing up in a community so well protected. They also comment on the ethnic diversity of those who populated the town and on the pride they took in their parents' contribution to building the bomb and ending the war.

Evan Mawdsley, *World War II: A New History* (2009). A global history, covering Asia as well as Europe, with focus on military and strategy.

Neil R. McMillen, ed., *Remaking Dixie: The Impact of World War II on the American South* (1997). A collection of essays on the impact of World War II on the South that pay special attention to the experiences of African Americans and women. Several authors question the degree to which southern society was transformed by wartime mobilization.

Kenneth D. Rose, *Myth and the Greatest Generation: A Social History of Americans in World War II* (2008). A provocative argument designed to undermine the nostalgia encasing the historical memory of World War II. Rose deals with both domestic and military history to challenge one-dimensional depictions of World War II as "the good war."

Emily Rosenberg, *A Date Which Will Live: Pearl Harbor in American Memory* (2004). Examines the circulation of memories of Pearl Habor in American life and the media's role in shaping them. Rosenberg includes the impact of the fiftieth anniversary commemorations of Pearl Harbor.

Mark A. Stoler, *Allies in War; Britain and America Against the Axis Powers, 1940–1945* (2005). A compact overview of wartime military strategy and diplomatic missions. Stoler provides a useful synthesis of new scholarship on the war.

Ronald Takaki, *Double Victory: A Multicultural History of America in World War II* (2000). A history of the war years told from the perspective of ethnically diverse Americans. Takaki examines the tension between the "good war" and the treatment of people of color and the response to the Holocaust.

Kenneth William Townsend, *World War II and the American Indian* (2000). A close study of the policies developed by the Bureau of Indian Affairs to bring American Indians into the war effort.

Emily Yellin, *Our Mothers' War: American Women at Home and at the Front During World War II* (2004). Makes a convincing case, based on a wealth of primary courses, that the war greatly changed the expectations for many American women.

myhistorylab Connections

PEARSON

Reinforce what you learned in this chapter by studying the many documents, images, maps, review tools, and videos available at www.myhistorylab.com.

Read and Review

✓● Study and Review **Chapter 25**

●●● Read the Document

Franklin Roosevelt, Date Which Will Live in Infamy (1941)

Executive Order 9066 (1942)

A. Philip Randolph, Why Should We March (1942)

👁 See the Map

World War II, European Theater

World War II, Pacific Theater

⊙ View the Image

Nazi Book Bonfire

Women Riveters in Navy Shipyard

Big Three at Yalta

⊙ Watch the Video **American Entry into WWII**

Research and Explore

●●● Read the Document

Exploring America: Propaganda

Profiles
  Douglas MacArthur
  A. Philip Randolph

Whose History Is It?: Exhibiting the Enola Gay

((•● Hear the Audio

Soldier Boy Blues, 1943

Obey the Ration Laws

⊙ Watch the Video

Normandy Beach, June 6, 1944

The Desegregation of the Military and Blacks in Combat

((•● Hear the Audio

Hear the audio files for Chapter 25 at
www.myhistorylab.com.

The Cold War Begins
1945–1952

CHAPTER OUTLINE

American Communities 755
University of Washington, Seattle: Students and Faculty Face the Cold War

Global Insecurities at War's End 757
Financing the Future
The Division of Europe
The United Nations and Hopes for
    Collective Security

The Policy of Containment 760
The Truman Doctrine
The Marshall Plan

The Berlin Crisis and the Formation
    of NATO
Atomic Diplomacy

Cold War Liberalism 763
"To Err Is Truman"
The 1948 Election
The Fair Deal

The Cold War at Home 766
The National Security Act of 1947
The Loyalty-Security Program
The Second Red Scare
Spy Cases
McCarthyism

Cold War Culture 772
An Anxious Mood
The Family As Bulwark
Military-Industrial Communities in the
    American West
"The American Way"

Stalemate for the Democrats 777
Democratizing Japan and "Losing" China
The Korean War
The Price of National Security
"I Like Ike": The Election of 1952

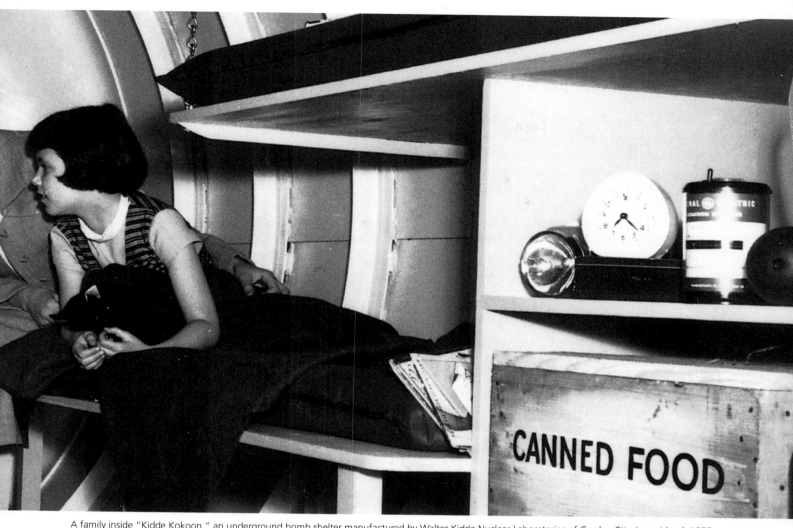

A family inside "Kidde Kokoon," an underground bomb shelter manufactured by Walter Kidde Nuclear Laboratories of Garden City, Long Island, 1955. Courtesy of the Library of Congress.

University of Washington, Seattle: Students and Faculty Face the Cold War

In May 1948, a philosophy professor at the University of Washington in Seattle answered a knock on his office door. Two state legislators, members of the state's Committee on Un-American Activities, entered. "Our information," they charged, "puts you in the center of a Communist conspiracy."

The accused professor, Melvin Rader, had never been a Communist. A self-described liberal, Rader drew fire because he had joined several organizations supported by Communists. During the 1930s, alarmed by the rise of fascism, Rader had become a prominent political activist in his community. At one point, he served as president of the University of Washington Teacher's Union, which had formed during the upsurge of labor organizing

AMERICAN Communities

during the New Deal. When invited to join the Communist Party, Rader bluntly refused. "The experience of teaching social philosophy had clarified my concepts of freedom and democracy," he later explained. "I was an American in search of a way—but it was not the Communist way."

Despite this disavowal, Rader was caught up in a second Red Scare—the first had been that of 1919–20 (see Chapter 22)—that curtailed free speech and political activity on campuses throughout the United States. At some universities, such as Yale, the FBI set up camp with the consent of the college administration, spying on students and faculty, screening the credentials of job or scholarship applicants, and enticing students to report on friends or roommates. The University of Washington administration turned down the Physics Department's recommendation to hire J. Robert Oppenheimer, the famed atomic scientist and former director of Los Alamos Scientific Laboratory who had become a vocal opponent of the arms race.

Although one state legislator claimed that "not less than 150 members" of the University of Washington faculty were subversives, the state's Committee on Un-American Activities turned up just six Communist Party members. These six were hauled before the university's Faculty Committee on Tenure and Academic Freedom, charged with violations ranging from neglect of duty to failing to inform the university administration of their party membership. Three were ultimately dismissed, while the other three were placed on probation.

What had provoked this paranoia? Instead of peace in the wake of World War II, "Cold War"— tense, icy relations but no outright fighting—prevailed between the United States and the Soviet Union. Uneasy wartime allies, the two superpowers now viewed each other as archenemies, and nearly all other nations lined up with one or the other. Within the United States, the Cold War demanded pledges of absolute loyalty from citizens in every institution, from universities to unions and from the media to government itself.

Without the Cold War, this era might have marked one of the most fruitful in the history of higher education. The Servicemen's Readjustment Act, popularly known as the G.I. Bill of Rights, passed by Congress in 1944, offered stipends covering tuition and living expenses to veterans attending vocational schools or college. By the 1947–48 academic year, the federal government was subsidizing nearly half of all male college students. Between 1945 and 1950, 2.3 million students benefited from the G.I. Bill, at a cost of more than $10 billion.

Seattle

At the University of Washington, the student population in 1946 had grown by 50 percent over its prewar peak of 10,000, and veterans represented two-thirds of the student body. A quickly expanded faculty taught into the evening to use classroom space efficiently. Meanwhile, the state legislature pumped in funds for the construction of new buildings, including dormitories and prefabricated units for married students.

The Cold War squelched much of that. FBI director J. Edgar Hoover testified that the college campuses were centers of "red propaganda," full of teachers "tearing down respect for agencies of government, belittling tradition and moral custom and . . . creating doubts in the validity of the American way of life." Due to "Communistic" teachers and "Communist-line textbooks," a senator wailed, thousands of parents sent "their sons and daughters to college as good Americans," only to see them return home "four years later as wild-eyed radicals."

These extravagant charges were far from true. The overwhelming majority of college graduates in the late 1940s and 1950s were conservative and conformist. Nevertheless, several states, including Washington, enacted or revived loyalty-security programs, obligating all state employees to swear in writing their loyalty to the United States and to disclaim membership in any subversive organization. Nationwide, approximately 200 "radical" faculty members were dismissed outright and many others were denied tenure. Thousands of students simply left school, dropped out of organizations, or changed friends after "visits" from FBI agents or interviews with administrators. The main effect on campus was the restraint of free speech generally and fear of criticizing U.S. racial, military, or diplomatic policies in particular.

This tense, gloomy mood reversed the wave of optimism that had swept through America only a few years earlier. V-J Day had escalated into two days of wild celebrations, ticker-tape parades, spontaneous dancing, and kisses for returning G.I.s. Americans, living in the richest and most powerful nation in the world, finally seemed to have gained the peace they had fought for and sacrificed to win. But peace proved fragile and elusive.

1. What steps did the Allies take to promote growth in the postwar global economy?

2. How did the Truman Doctrine shape U.S. postwar foreign policy?

3. How did the "Fair Deal" differ from the "New Deal"?

4. What factors contributed to the rise of McCarthyism?

5. What were the most important demographic trends in the 1950s?

6. What issues were at the center of the election of 1952?

FOCUS
Questions

1945–1952

Global Insecurities at War's End

The war that had engulfed the world from 1939 to 1945 created an international interdependence that no country could ignore. Legendary African American folksinger Leadbelly added fresh lyrics to an old spiritual: "We're in the same boat, brother. . . . And if you shake one end you're going to rock the other." Never before, not even at the end of World War I, had hopes been so strong for a genuine "community of nations." But, as a 1945 opinion poll indicated, most Americans believed that prospects for a durable peace rested to a large degree on one factor: Soviet–American harmony.

Financing the Future

In 1941, Henry Luce, the publisher of *Time, Life,* and *Fortune* magazines, forecast the dawn of "the American Century." During the darkest days of World War II, he wrote that Americans must "accept wholeheartedly our duty and our opportunity as the most powerful and vital nation in the world and in consequence to assert upon the world the full impact of our influence, for such means as we see fit." Immediately after the bombing of Hiroshima, President Truman pronounced the United States "the most powerful nation in the world—the most powerful nation, perhaps, in all history."

Americans had good reason to be confident about their prospects for setting the terms of reconstruction. Unlike Great Britain, France, and the Soviet Union, the United States had not only escaped the ravages of the war, but had actually prospered. By June 1945, the capital assets of manufacturing had increased 65 percent over prewar levels to equal in value approximately half the entire world's goods and services.

Yet many Americans recognized that massive wartime government spending, not the New Deal, had ended the

nightmare of the Great Depression. A stark question loomed: What would happen when wartime production slowed and millions of troops returned home to claim jobs?

"We need markets—big markets—in which to buy and sell," answered Assistant Secretary of State for Economic Affairs Will Clayton. Just to maintain the current level of growth, the United States needed to export—to a war-ravaged world—a staggering $14 billion in goods and services. During the war, many business leaders had looked to the Soviet Union as a future customer. With that prospect vanishing, with potential Eastern European markets threatened, and with the enormous European colonies closed to American enterprise, U.S. business and government leaders decided to integrate Western Europe, Latin America, and Asia into an international economy open to American trade and investment.

During the final stages of the war, President Roosevelt's advisers laid plans to establish U.S. primacy in the postwar global economy. In July 1944, representatives from forty-four Allied nations met at Bretton Woods, New Hampshire, and established the International Bank for Reconstruction and Development (the World Bank) and the International Monetary Fund (IMF). These institutions were expected to help rebuild war-torn Europe and Asia. By stabilizing exchange rates to permit the expansion of international trade, the IMF would deter currency conflicts and trade wars, two maladies of the 1930s that were blamed for the political instability and national rivalries leading to World War II. The United States was the principal supplier of funds for the IMF and the World Bank (more than $7 billion to each) and thus, by determining the allocation of loans, could unilaterally reshape the global economy.

The Soviet Union participated at Bretton Woods, but refused to ratify the agreements. From Stalin's perspective, the United States intended to rebuild the world economy along capitalist lines; accepting World Bank and IMF aid would, he believed, make the Soviet Union an economic colony of the capitalist West. By spurning this aid, the Soviet Union economically isolated itself and its East European satellites.

The Division of Europe

In the Atlantic Charter of 1941, the United States and Great Britain proclaimed the right of all nations to self-determination and renounced claims to new territories as spoils of war. Before the war ended, though, Churchill and Roosevelt violated the charter by dividing Europe into spheres of influence (see Chapter 25 and Map 26.1).

For Roosevelt, that strategy had seemed compatible with ensuring world peace. FDR balanced his internationalist idealism with a belief that the United States was entitled to extraordinary influence in Latin America and the Philippines and that other great powers might have similar privileges or responsibilities elsewhere. Roosevelt also recognized the diplomatic consequences of the brutal ground war that had been fought largely on Soviet territory: the Soviet Union's nonnegotiable demand for security along its western border. He hoped that American economic aid and the United Nations would serve, respectively, as carrot and stick in moderating Soviet domination in Eastern Europe.

From the earliest days of fighting Hitler, the Soviet Union was intent on reestablishing its 1941 borders. At the Potsdam Conference, held in the bombed-out Berlin suburb in July 1945, Stalin not only regained but also extended his territory, annexing eastern Poland with Western approval and the little Baltic nations without it. Soviet influence quickly became paramount in all East European countries that the Red Army had occupied. The question remained: Did Stalin aim to bring all of Europe into the Communist domain?

At the Potsdam Conference, when the wartime allies began to plan Germany's future, that question loomed over all deliberations. They decided to divide the conquered nation into four occupation zones, each temporarily ruled by one of the Allied nations. They could not agree on long-term plans, however. Having borne the brunt of German aggression, France and the Soviet Union both opposed reunification. Stalin, moreover, demanded heavy reparations and a limit on postwar German reindustrialization. Although Roosevelt had appeared to agree with the Soviets, after FDR's death Truman envisioned rebuilding Germany into a powerful counterweight to the Soviet Union and a strong market for U.S. and British exports.

After the war, continuing disagreements about the future of Germany darkened hopes for Soviet-American cooperation. By July 1946, Americans had begun to withhold reparations due to the Soviets from their occupation zone and began to grant amnesty to some former Nazis. Then, in December, the Americans and British merged their zones and invited France and the Soviet Union to join. France agreed; Stalin, fearing a resurgence of a united Germany, refused.

The United States and the Soviet Union were now at loggerheads. Twice in the twentieth century, Germany had invaded Russia, and the Soviet Union interpreted any moves toward German reunification as menacing. For their part, American policymakers, assuming Stalin to be aggressively expansionist, envisioned a united Germany as a bulwark against further Soviet encroachments.

Representatives of the "Big Three" nations—the Soviet Union, the United Kingdom, and the United States—gathered at Potsdam, Germany, near Berlin, July 17–August 2, 1945. This photograph shows Stalin, Truman, and Churchill as they begin to discuss the terms of peace and postwar arrangements. They concluded by issuing the "Potsdam Declaration," which demanded Japan's unconditional surrender.

MAP 26.1 Divided Europe During the Cold War, Europe was divided into opposing military alliances, the North American Treaty Organization (NATO) and the Warsaw Pact (Communist bloc).

The United Nations and Hopes for Collective Security

In 1944 at the Dumbarton Oaks Conference in Washington, and again in April 1945 at San Francisco, the Allies worked to shape the United Nations (UN) as a world organization that would arbitrate disputes among member nations and stop aggressors, by force if necessary.

The terms of membership, however, limited the UN's ability to mediate disputes. Although all fifty nations that signed the UN charter voted in the General Assembly, only five (the United States, Great Britain, the Soviet Union,

France, and China) served permanently on the Security Council, which had the "primary responsibility for the maintenance of international peace and security," and each had absolute veto power over the Council's decisions.

The UN achieved its greatest success with its humanitarian programs. Its relief agency gave war-torn European and Asian countries billions of dollars for medical supplies, food, and clothing. The UN also dedicated itself to protecting human rights. The high principles enunciated by its 1948 Universal Declaration of Human Rights owed much to lobbying by Eleanor Roosevelt, one of the first delegates from the United States.

On other issues, however, the UN operated strictly along lines dictated by the emerging Cold War. The Western nations allied with the United States held the balance of power and controlled the admission of new members. For example, in 1949 when the Communists won the Chinese civil war (discussed later), the Western powers would block the new People's Republic from claiming China's UN seat, held by the defeated Nationalists on Taiwan. East–West polarization made negotiated settlements virtually impossible.

The Policy of Containment

In March 1946, in a speech delivered in Fulton, Missouri, Winston Churchill spoke to the end of wartime coopera-

●◆[Read the Document

Churchill's "Iron Curtain" Speech (1946) at **www.myhistorylab.com**

tion. With President Truman at his side, the former British prime minister solemnly intoned: "An iron curtain has descended across the [European] continent." He called directly upon the United States, standing "at this time at the pinnacle of world power," to recognize its "awe-inspiring accountability to the future" and, in alliance with Great Britain, act vigorously to stop Soviet expansion.

Although Truman at first responded cautiously to Churchill's warning, his administration ultimately rose to the challenge. As a policy uniting military, economic, and diplomatic strategies, the "containment" of communism had a powerful ideological dimension—an "us versus them" division of the world into "freedom" and "slavery."

The Truman Doctrine

Many Americans believed that Franklin D. Roosevelt, had he lived, could have smoothed tensions between the Soviet Union and the United States. His successor sorely lacked FDR's diplomatic talent and experience. More comfortable with machine politicians than with polished New Dealers, Truman liked to talk tough and act defiantly. "I'm tired of babying the Soviets," he snapped.

Truman's attitude toward the Soviet Union was not always consistent; during the first years after the war, at times he attempted to be conciliatory. Among U.S. policymakers,

●◆[Read the Document

George F. Kennan, The Long Telegram (1946) at **www.myhistorylab.com**

however, an anti-Soviet consensus was growing, fed by perceptions that Stalin was taking a hard line. In February 1946, George F. Kennan, the nation's premier diplomat in dealing with the Soviet Union, sent an 8,000-word "long telegram" from Moscow to the State Department, insisting that Soviet fanaticism made cooperation impossible. The Soviet Union intended to extend its realm not by military means alone, he explained, but by "subversion" within "free" nations. Kennan warned that Stalin wanted to "destroy America and, therefore, tough-minded realism, not idealistic hopes, should govern America's relations with the Soviet Union. In the long run, Kennan predicted, the Soviet system would

collapse from within, but until that happened the West should pursue a policy of containment.

A perceived crisis in the Mediterranean marked the turning point. On February 21, 1947, amid a civil war in Greece, Great Britain informed the U.S. State Department that it could no longer afford to prop up the anti-Communist government there and announced its intention to withdraw all aid. Without U.S. intervention, Truman concluded, Greece, Turkey, and perhaps the entire oil-rich Middle East would fall under Soviet control. But, warned an influential Republican senator, Congress would not act unless the president "scare[d] hell out of the American people."

On March 12, 1947, the president made his case in a speech to Congress. Never naming the Soviet Union, he appealed for all-out resistance to a "certain ideology" wherever it appeared in the world. The preservation of peace and the freedom of all Americans depended, the president insisted, on containing communism.

Congress approved $400 million to aid Greece and Turkey, which helped conservative forces in those countries crush left-wing rebels. By dramatically opposing communism, Truman somewhat buoyed his sagging popularity and helped generate popular support for an anticommunist crusade at home and abroad.

The significance of what became known as the Truman Doctrine far outlasted events in the Mediterranean: the United States had declared its right to intervene to save other nations from communism. In advocating containment of the Soviet Union, Kennan called for political and economic, not military, countermeasures, although Truman and his advisers were willing to consider military responses, too. It was now the responsibility of the United States, the White House insisted, to safeguard what was coming to be called the Free World by any means necessary. They had fused anticommunism and internationalism into a strong foreign policy.

The Marshall Plan

The Truman Doctrine complemented the European Recovery Program, commonly known as the Marshall Plan. Introduced in a commencement speech at Harvard University on June 5, 1947, by Secretary of State George C. Marshall, the plan sought to reduce "hunger, poverty, desperation, and chaos" and to restore "the confidence of the European people in the economic future of their own countries and of Europe as a whole." Indirectly, the Marshall Plan aimed to turn back left-wing Socialist and Communist bids for votes in Western Europe. Not least, the plan was also designed to boost the U.S. economy by securing a European market for American goods.

Considered by many historians the most successful postwar U.S. diplomatic venture, the Marshall Plan improved the climate for a viable capitalist economy in Western Europe and, in effect, brought aid recipients into bilateral agreements with the United States. In addition,

OVERVIEW | Major Cold War Policies

Date	Policy	Provisions
1947	**Truman Doctrine**	Pledged the United States to the containment of communism in Europe and elsewhere. The doctrine was the foundation of Truman's foreign policy. It impelled the United States to support any nation whose stability was threatened by communism or the Soviet Union.
1947	**Federal Employees Loyalty and Security Program**	Established by Executive Order 9835, this barred Communists and fascists from federal employment and outlined procedures for investigating current and prospective federal employees.
1947	**Marshall Plan**	U.S. program to aid war-torn Europe, also known as the European Recovery Program. The Marshall Plan was a cornerstone in the U.S. use of economic policy to contain communism.
1947	**National Security Act**	Established Department of Defense (to coordinate the three armed services), the National Security Council (to advise the president on security issues), and the Central Intelligence Agency (to gather and evaluate intelligence data).
1948	**Smith-Mundt Act**	Launched an overseas campaign of anti-Communist propaganda.
1949	**North Atlantic Treaty Organization (NATO)**	A military alliance of twelve nations formed to deter possible aggression of the Soviet Union against Western Europe.
1950	**NSC-68**	National Security Council Paper calling for an expanded and aggressive U.S. defense policy, including greater military spending and higher taxes.
1950	**Internal Security Act (also known as the McCarran Act and the Subversive Activities Control Act)**	Legislation providing for the registration of all Communist and totalitarian groups and authorizing the arrest of suspect persons during a national emergency.
1951	**Psychological Strategy Board**	Created to coordinate anti–Communist propaganda campaigns.
1952	**Immigration and Nationality Act (also known as McCarran Walter Immigration Act)**	Reaffirmed the national origins quota system but tightened immigration controls, barring homosexuals and people considered subversive from entering the United States.

the United States and seventeen Western European nations ratified the tariff-cutting General Agreement on Tariffs and Trade pact, thus opening all to U.S. trade and investment. (Today, GATT has been renamed the World Trade Organization, or WTO.)

The Marshall Plan was costly to Americans. In its initial year, it accounted for 12 percent of the federal budget. But much of that aid was American-made goods, produced by American workers. In the European nations covered by the plan, industrial production increased by 35 percent between 1947 and 1952, living standards improved, and American consumer goods and the American lifestyle became familiar.

As Truman later acknowledged, the Marshall Plan and the Truman Doctrine were "two halves of the same

The Nazi occupation left Greece in economic ruins. Hunger and malnutrition were widespread. However, postwar foreign aid at first went mainly to fortify the military struggle against Communism. By 1949, after the civil war ended, government officials directed foreign aid to civilian needs. This photograph shows children lining up in Athens to receive bread made from wheat supplied by Marshall Plan.

walnut." The Marshall Plan drove a deeper wedge between the United States and the Soviet Union. Although invited to participate, Stalin denounced the plan for what it was—an American scheme to rebuild Germany and incorporate it into an anti-Soviet bloc. Soon after the announcement of the Marshall Plan, the Soviet Union tightened its grip in Eastern Europe. In February 1948, as the U.S. Congress formally approved the Marshall Plan, a Soviet-supported coup d' état established a communist government in Czechoslovakia.

The Berlin Crisis and the Formation of NATO

Within a year of the start of the Marshall Plan, the United States and Britain moved closer to the goal of economically integrating their occupation zones in Germany into the western sphere of influence. A common currency was established for these zones. Stalin reacted on June 24, 1948,

by halting all traffic to the western occupation zones of Berlin, deep within Soviet-occupied eastern Germany (see Map 26.1).

The Berlin blockade created both a crisis and an opportunity for the Truman administration. With help from the Royal Air Force, the United States began an unprecedented around-the-clock airlift. "Operation Vittles" delivered nearly 2 million tons of supplies (including food and coal) to West Berliners. Stalin finally lifted the blockade in May 1949, clearing the way for the western powers to merge their occupation zones into a single nation, the Federal Republic of Germany. The Soviet Union countered by turning its zone into the communist-dominated German Democratic Republic.

The Berlin Crisis had made a U.S.-led military alliance against the Soviet Union attractive to noncommunist Western Europeans. In April 1949, ten European nations, Canada, and the United States formed the North Atlantic Treaty Organization (NATO), a mutual-defense pact in which "an armed attack against one or more of them . . . shall be considered an attack against them all." NATO complemented the Marshall Plan, strengthening economic ties among the member nations. It also deepened divisions between Eastern and Western Europe, making a permanent military mobilization on both sides almost inevitable.

Global implications flowed from the forging of the North Atlantic alliance. Several Western European allies ruled valuable but restive colonial empires. During the war, FDR had urged British and French leaders to start dismantling their empires, a suggestion welcomed neither by Churchill nor by France's Charles de Gaulle. In 1947, a financially strapped Britain granted independence to India and Pakistan, and under U.S. pressure, the Dutch gave up Indonesia in 1949. The French, however, were determined to regain Indochina, lost to Japan before Pearl Harbor (see Chapter 25). Cold War anticommunism now trumped traditional American anticolonialism. Because the most important fighter against France's attempt to reconquer Indochina was Vietnamese communist Ho Chi Minh, Truman decided that France deserved American support and helped persuade France to join NATO. The first seeds had been planted of what would eventually become an American commitment to fight communism in Vietnam.

The Truman administration took Latin America for granted and was satisfied when the right-wing dictators ruling much of that region proclaimed themselves staunchly anticommunist. But Latin Americans complained that the United States' preoccupation with rebuilding Western Europe was depriving them of American investment capital desperately needed for economic development. The most positive gesture that the United States made toward Latin opinion was designating Puerto Rico a self-governing "commonwealth" in 1952. A rising Puerto Rican independence movement—extremist members of which attempted to assassinate Truman in 1950—prompted this move to make U.S. sovereignty over the island look less colonialist. Beneath the surface, though, trouble was brewing for the United States throughout the hemisphere.

Between 1947 and 1949, the Truman administration had defined the policies that would shape the Cold War for decades to come. The Truman Doctrine explained the ideological basis of containment, not just in Europe but also around the globe; the Marshall Plan put into place its economic underpinnings in Western Europe; and NATO created the mechanisms for military defense. When NATO extended membership to a rearmed West Germany in May 1955, the Soviet Union responded by creating a counterpart, the Warsaw Pact, including East Germany.

Atomic Diplomacy

The containment policy depended on the ability of the United States to back its commitments through military force, and Truman invested his faith in the U.S. monopoly of atomic weapons. After 1945, the United States began

to build an atomic stockpile and to conduct tests on remote Pacific islands. By 1950, as a scientific adviser subsequently observed, the United States "had a stockpile capable of somewhat more than reproducing World War II in a single day."

Despite warnings to the contrary by leading scientists, U.S. military analysts estimated it would take the Soviet Union three to ten years to produce an atomic bomb. In August 1949, the Soviet Union proved them wrong by testing its own atomic bomb. "There is only one thing worse than one nation having the atomic bomb," said Nobel Prize–winning scientist Harold C. Urey. "That's two nations having it."

The arms race that scientists had feared since 1945 was now under way. By the early 1950s, both the United States and the Soviet Union were testing hydrogen bombs a thousand times more powerful than the weapons dropped on Hiroshima and Nagasaki in 1945. By the late 1950s, stockpiles of nuclear bombs were being supplemented by nuclear-armed missiles.

The United States and the Soviet Union were firmly locked into the Cold War. The nuclear arms race risked global catastrophe, diverted economic resources, and fed public fears of impending doom. Despite the Allied victory in World War II, the world had again divided into hostile camps.

Cold War Liberalism

Truman's personality suited the confrontational mood of the early Cold War. He linked the Soviet threat abroad to the need for a strong presidency at home. Pressed to establish his own political identity, "Give 'em Hell" Harry cast himself as a fierce fighter against all challengers, yet loyal to Roosevelt's legacy.

Truman wanted to enlarge the New Deal, but settled on a modest domestic agenda to promote social welfare and an anti-isolationist, anti-Communist foreign policy. Fatefully, during his administration, domestic and foreign policy became increasingly entangled. Out of that entanglement emerged a distinctive brand of liberalism—Cold War liberalism.

"To Err Is Truman"

Within a year of assuming office, Harry Truman's poll ratings were among the lowest of any twentieth-century president. The responsibilities of reestablishing peacetime conditions seemed to overwhelm the new president. "To err is Truman," critics sneered.

The task of converting from a wartime to a peacetime economy was enormous. Truman faced millions of restless would-be consumers tired of rationing and eager to spend their wartime savings on shiny cars, new furniture, choice cuts of meat, and stylish clothing. The demand for consumer items rapidly outran supply, fueling inflation and a huge black market.

In 1945 and 1946, the country appeared ready to explode. While homemakers protested rising prices by boycotting neighborhood stores, industrial workers struck in unprecedented numbers. Employers, fearing a rapid decline to depression-level profits, determined to slash wages; workers wanted a bigger cut of the huge war profits they had heard about. With nearly 4.6 million workers on picket lines, the new president was alarmed. In May 1946, Truman proposed to draft striking railroad workers. The usually conservative Senate killed this plan.

Congress defeated most of Truman's proposals to revive the New Deal. One week after Japan's surrender, the president introduced a twenty-one-point program that included greater unemployment compensation, higher minimum wages, and housing assistance. Later he added national health insurance and atomic-energy legislation. Congress rejected most of these bills and passed the Employment Act of 1946, but only with substantial modification. The act created the Council of Economic Advisers, a panel of three experts who would counsel the president and formulate policies for maintaining employment, production, and purchasing power. But no funding mechanisms guaranteed the full employment to which the government committed itself. "Had enough?" Republicans, anticipating victory in the midterm elections, asked voters that simple question. The voters had.

They gave Republicans majorities in both houses of Congress and many state capitols. Symbolically repudiating FDR, Republican-dominated state legislatures ratified the Twenty-Second Amendment, limiting future presidents to two terms.

The Republicans, dominant in Congress for the first time since 1931, mounted a counterattack on the New Deal, beginning with organized labor. Unions had peaked in size and prestige; membership topped 15 million and encompassed nearly 40 percent of all wage earners. Claiming that "Big Labor" had gone too far, the Eightieth Congress aimed at abolishing many practices legalized by the Wagner Act of 1935 (see Chapter 24). The resultant Taft-Hartley Act of 1947, passed over Truman's veto: outlawed the closed shop, the secondary boycott, and the use of union dues for political activities; mandated an eighty-day cooling-off period in the case of strikes affecting "national safety or health"; and required all union officials to swear that they were not Communists—a Cold War mandate abridging First Amendment freedoms. Truman himself would later invoke the act against strikers.

The 1948 Election

Harry Truman had considered some of Roosevelt's advisers "crackpots and the lunatic fringe." By 1946, he forced out many of the remaining social planners who had staffed

Police and strikers confront each other in Los Angeles during one of many postwar strikes in 1946. Employers wanted to cut wages, and workers refused to give up the higher living standard achieved during the war.

the Washington bureaus for more than a decade. Truman also fired Roosevelt's secretary of commerce and former vice president, Henry Wallace, for advocating a more conciliatory policy toward the Soviet Union.

Wallace, refusing to fade away, vowed to run against Truman for president. He pledged to expand New Deal programs by moving boldly to establish full employment, racial equality, and stronger unions. He also promised peace with the Soviet Union. As the 1948 election neared, Wallace appeared a viable candidate on the new Progressive Party ticket.

Truman shrewdly repositioned himself. He deflated Wallace by branding him a tool of the Communists (who in fact were part of a coalition of ex–New Dealers who encouraged Wallace to run). Truman also attacked the conservative congressional Republicans, proposing federal funds for education, housing, and medical insurance. Summoning Congress back for a special session after the summertime political conventions of 1948, he dared it to enact the Republican platform—and when it predictably failed—lambasted the "do-nothing Congress."

Wallace and the Republican nominee, New York governor Thomas E. Dewey, had taken strong leads on civil rights, but Truman outflanked them. In July 1948, he issued executive decrees desegregating the armed forces and banning discrimination in the federal civil service. In response, some 300 southern delegates bolted from the Democratic National Convention and named a States' Rights ("Dixiecrat") ticket, headed by the staunchly segregationist governor of South Carolina, J. Strom Thurmond. With the South looking as good as lost, with Wallace threatening to siphon off left-leaning Democrats, and with soothing Dewey heading the Republicans, Truman appeared doomed.

But "Give 'em Hell Harry's" vigorous campaign slowly revived the New Deal coalition. Fear of Republicans who had passed Taft-Hartley won back the bulk of organized labor, and Truman's decision in May 1948 immediately to recognize the new State of Israel kept many liberal Jews loyally Democratic. The success of the Berlin airlift buoyed the president's popularity, and by Election Day growing anti-Communist sentiment among liberals was limiting the Wallace vote to the extreme left. Meanwhile, Dewey, who in 1944 had run a hard-hitting but unsuccessful campaign against Roosevelt, this time tried to coast to victory by appearing bland and "presidential."

Polls predicted a Dewey victory—but the pollsters stopped taking samples several weeks before Election Day and so missed a late Democratic surge. Truman won the popular vote by a 5 percent margin, trouncing Dewey 303 to 189 in electoral votes. Democrats regained majorities in both houses of Congress. But Truman had hit the apex of his popularity. A long downhill slide was about to begin (see Map 26.2).

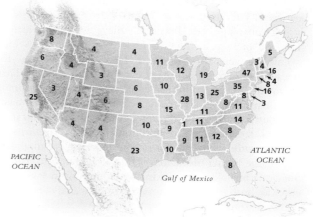

	Electoral Vote (%)	Popular Vote (%)
HARRY S. TRUMAN (Democrat)	303 (57)	24,105,812 (49.5)
Thomas E. Dewey (Republican)	189 (36)	21,970,065 (45.1)
Strom Thurmond (States' Rights)	39 (7)	1,169,063 (2.4)
Henry A. Wallace (Progressive)	—	1,157,172 (2.4)
Other candidates (Socialist, Prohibition, Socialist Labor, Socialist Workers)	—	272,713 (0.6)

MAP 26.2 The Election of 1948 Harry Truman holds up a copy of the *Chicago Daily Tribune* with headlines confidently and mistakenly predicting the victory of his opponent, Thomas E. Dewey. Initially an unpopular candidate, Truman made a whistle-stop tour of the country by train to win 49.5 percent of the popular vote to Dewey's 45.1 percent.

The Fair Deal

"Every segment of our population and every individual has a right," Truman announced in January 1949, "to expect from our Government a fair deal." Democratic congressional majorities would, he hoped, translate campaign promises into laws and expand the New Deal. But a powerful bloc of conservative southern Democrats and midwestern Republicans turned back his domestic agenda.

The National Housing Act of 1949 provided federally funded low-income housing. Congress also raised the minimum wage (from 40 to 75 cents per hour) and brought an additional 10 million people under Social Security coverage. Otherwise Truman made no headway. He and congressional liberals introduced a variety of bills to weaken southern racism, including a federal antilynching law, outlawing poll taxes, and banning discrimination in interstate transportation. Southern-led filibusters killed them all, while conservative-dominated congressional committees bottled up his initiatives for national health insurance, federal aid to education, and a repeal or modification of Taft-Hartley.

Truman's greatest domestic achievement was to articulate the basic principles of Cold War liberalism, which would remain the northern Democratic agenda for decades to come. Toning down visionary New Deal rhetoric about economic equality and reapportioning wealth and power, Truman's Fair Deal promoted bread-and-butter issues and economic growth. His administration insisted, therefore, on an ambitious program of expanded foreign trade, while relying on the federal government to encourage higher productivity. Equally important, Truman reshaped liberalism by making anticommunism a key element in both foreign policy and domestic affairs.

The Cold War at Home

"Communists . . . are everywhere—in factories, offices, butcher shops, on street corners, in private businesses," Attorney General J. Howard McGrath warned in 1949.

View the Image
How Communism Works (1938) at www.myhistorylab.com

"At this very moment [they are] busy at work—undermining your government, plotting to destroy the liberties of every citizen, and feverishly trying, in whatever way they can, to aid the Soviet Union." FBI director J. Edgar Hoover spoke darkly of "the diabolic machinations of sinister figures engaged in un-American activities."

By the late 1940s, the Communist Party, U.S.A., formed in 1919 and at the peak of its influence in the 1930s, was steadily losing ground. Nevertheless, anticommunism now held center stage in domestic politics. The federal government, with help from the media, led the crusade, using the threat of communism to reorder its operation and to quell dissent. Seeking absolute security, Americans permitted a greater concentration of power in government and, while promising to lead the Free World, allowed many of their own rights to be circumscribed.

The National Security Act of 1947

The imperative of national security destroyed old-fashioned isolation, forcing the United States into unprecedented alliances such as NATO and global leadership. "If we falter in our leadership," Truman warned, "we may endanger the peace of the world—and we shall surely endanger the welfare of this nation." Such responsibility required massive resources. Truman, therefore, demanded a substantial increase in the size of the federal government in both military forces and surveillance agencies. Security measures designed to keep the nation in a steady state of preparedness, readily justified during wartime, were now extended indefinitely into the very uneasy peacetime.

The sweeping National Security Act, passed by Congress in July 1947, established the Department of Defense and the National Security Council (NSC) to administer and coordinate defense policies and advise the president. The Department of Defense combined the old War and Navy Departments, bringing the Army, the Navy, and the new Air Force under a single cabinet-level secretary. Ties between the armed forces and the State Department grew closer as retired military officers routinely filled positions in the State Department and diplomatic corps; the highest-ranking World War II soldier, Five-Star General George C. Marshall, became secretary of state. The act also created the National Security Resources Board (NSRB) to coordinate plans throughout the government "in the event of war" and, for the first time in American history, to maintain military preparedness in peacetime.

The Department of Defense and the NSRB became the principal sponsor of scientific research during the first ten years of the Cold War. It was commonly recognized at the time that World War II had been the "physicists' war." Scientists had built the ultimate weapon, the atom bomb, and achieved major advances in military navigation and detection, strategic targeting, and communication. The National Science Foundation was created in 1950 for education and research, although the Office of Naval Research conducted basic research and development on a much larger budget. Federal agencies tied to military projects supplied well over 90 percent of the funding for research in the physical sciences, much of it in major universities.

The Central Intelligence Agency (CIA) was another product of the National Security Act. With roots in the wartime Office of Strategic Services (OSS), the new CIA became a permanent operation devoted to collecting political, military, and economic information for security purposes throughout the world. (It was barred from domestic intelligence gathering: that was the domain of its rival, the FBI.) Although information about the CIA was classified—that is, kept secret from both Congress and the public—historians have estimated that the agency soon dwarfed the State Department in number of employees and size of budget.

The national-security state required a huge workforce. Before World War II, approximately 900,000 civilians worked for the federal government, about 10 percent of them in security work; by the beginning of the Cold War, nearly 4 million people were on the government's payroll, 75 percent of them in national-security agencies.

National security absorbed increasingly large portions of the nation's resources. By the end of Truman's second term, defense allocations accounted for 10 percent of GNP, directly or indirectly employed hundreds of thousands of well-paid workers, and subsidized some of the nation's most profitable corporations. This vast financial outlay created the rationale for permanent, large-scale military spending and powerfully stimulated economic growth.

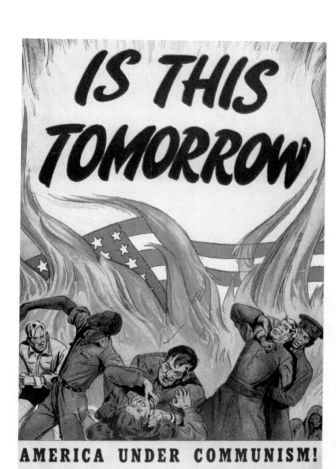

Published in 1947, this full-color comic book appeared as one of many sensationalistic illustrations of the threat of the "commie menace" to Americans at home. Approximately 4 million copies of *Is This Tomorrow?* were printed, the majority distributed to church groups or sold for ten cents a copy.

The Loyalty-Security Program

National security required increased surveillance at home. Within two weeks of proclaiming the Truman Doctrine, the president signed Executive Order 9835 on March 21, 1947, establishing a civilian loyalty program for all federal employees. The new Federal Employees Loyalty and Security Program, directed at members of the Communist Party—as well as fascists and anyone guilty of "sympathetic association" with either—in effect established a political test for federal employment. It also outlined procedures for investigating current and prospective federal employees. The loyalty review boards often asked employees about their opinions of the Soviet Union, the Marshall Plan, or NATO and whether they would report fellow workers if they found out they were Communists. Any employee could be dismissed merely on "reasonable grounds," including guilt by association (that is, knowing or being related to a "subversive" person), rather than on

proof of disloyalty. Later amendments added homosexuals as potential security risks on grounds that they might succumb to enemy blackmail.

Many state and municipal governments enacted loyalty programs and required public employees, including teachers at all levels, to sign loyalty oaths. In all, some 6.6 million people underwent loyalty and security checks. An estimated 500 government workers were fired, and perhaps as many as 6,000 more chose to resign. Numerous private employers and labor unions also instituted loyalty programs.

Attorney General Tom C. Clark aided this effort by publishing a list of hundreds of potentially subversive organizations selected by criteria so vague that any views "hostile or inimical to the American form of government" (as Clark's assistants noted in a memo) could make an organization liable for investigation and prosecution. There was no right of appeal for organizations so listed. The famous "Attorney General's List" effectively outlawed many political and social organizations, stigmatizing hundreds of thousands of individuals who had done nothing illegal. Church associations, civil rights organizations, musical groups, and even summer camps appeared on the list. Fraternal and social institutions, especially popular among aging Eastern European immigrants, were among the largest organizations destroyed. New York State, for example, legally dismantled the International Workers' Order, which had provided insurance to nearly 200,000 immigrants and their families. Only a handful of organizations had the funds to challenge legally "being on the List"; most simply closed their doors.

In 1950, Congress overrode the president's veto to pass a bill that Truman called "the greatest danger to freedom of press, speech, and assembly since the Sedition Act of 1798." The Internal Security (or McCarran) Act required Communist organizations to register with the Subversive Activities Control Board—if they did not register, they were prosecuted—and authorized the arrest of suspect persons during a national emergency. The Immigration and Nationality Act, also sponsored by Republican senator Pat McCarran of Nevada and adopted in 1952, again over Truman's veto, barred people deemed "subversive" or "homosexual" from becoming citizens or even visiting the United States. It also empowered the attorney general to deport immigrants who were members of Communist organizations, even if they had become citizens. Challenged repeatedly on constitutional grounds, the Subversive Activities Control Board remained in place until 1973, when it was terminated.

The Second Red Scare

Ultraconservative Democratic congressman Martin Dies of Texas, who had chaired a congressional committee on "un-American activities" since 1938, told reporters in 1944, that "Hollywood is the greatest source of revenue in this nation for the Communists and other subversive groups." Renamed and made a permanent standing committee in 1945, the House Committee on Un-American Activities (HUAC) had the power to subpoena witnesses and to compel them to answer all questions or face contempt of Congress charges. In well-publicized hearings held in Hollywood in October 1947, the mother of actress Ginger Rogers defended her daughter by saying that she had been duped into appearing in the 1943 pro-Soviet wartime film *Tender Comrade* and "had been forced" to read the subversive line "Share and share alike, that's democracy." HUAC encouraged such testimony by other "friendly witnesses," including actors Ronald Reagan and Gary Cooper. The committee intimidated many others, who feared loss of

●●─[Read the Document

Ronald Reagan, Testimony before HUAC (1947) at **www.myhistorylab.com**

their careers, into naming former friends and coworkers in order to be cleared for future work in Hollywood.

A small but prominent minority refused to cooperate with HUAC. By claiming the freedoms of speech and association guaranteed by the First and Sixth Amendments, they became known as "unfriendly witnesses," and a handful served prison sentences for refusing to "name names."

Hollywood studios would not employ any writer, director, or actor who refused to cooperate with HUAC. The resulting blacklist remained in effect until the 1960s and limited the production of films dealing with "controversial" social or political issues. Meanwhile, the privately published *Red Channels: The Report of Communist Influence in Radio and Television* (1950) persuaded advertisers to cancel their accounts with many programs considered friendly to the Soviet Union, the UN, or liberal causes.

In 1947, HUAC interviewed forty-one writers, directors, and actors and demanded they provide names of other workers in the Hollywood motion picture industry who were Communists. Claiming their rights under the First Amendment to the Constitution, a group known as the Hollywood Ten refused to answer any questions and were subsequently found guilty of contempt of Congress. This photograph shows a group of their supporters staging a protest demonstration.

The labor movement also became a victim of this second Red Scare. Like the Hollywood film industry, a sizable portion of its leaders and members had affiliated with the Communist Party or supported liberal causes in the 1930s, and they emerged from their wartime experiences even more deeply committed to social justice. The Food, Tobacco, Agricultural, and Allied Workers-Congress of Industrial Organizations (FTA-CIO) organized a postwar campaign against discriminatory practices within southern industry and allied with local civil rights activists to spearhead a major organizing drive. In 1947, the R. J. Reynolds Tobacco Company struck back by characterizing union organizers and supporters as Moscow's pawns. A year later, CIO president Philip Murray decided to rid his organization of all Communists. Soon, eleven unions representing more than a million workers were expelled. This "purge" succeeded in eliminating Communist influence and with it the commitment to industrial democracy that had buoyed the CIO since the 1930s.

Spy Cases

In August 1948, *Time* magazine editor Whittaker Chambers appeared before HUAC to name Alger Hiss as a fellow Communist in the Washington underground during the 1930s. Hiss, then president of the prestigious Carnegie Endowment for International Peace and a former member of FDR's State Department, denied the charges and sued his accuser for slander. Chambers then revealed his trump card, a cache of films of secret documents that had been hidden in a hollowed-out pumpkin on his Maryland farm. He claimed that Hiss had passed them to him for transmission to the Soviet Union. The statute of limitations for espionage having run out, a federal grand jury in January 1950 convicted Hiss of perjury for denying he knew Chambers. He received a five-year prison term. Hiss was released two years later proclaiming his innocence, a position he held throughout his life. Historians remain divided on the question of his spying.

Many Democrats, including Truman, dismissed the allegations against Hiss—conveniently publicized at the start of the 1948 election campaign—as a Republican slander. Nevertheless, the highly publicized allegations against Hiss hurt the Democrats, suggesting that FDR and Truman had allowed Communists to infiltrate the federal government.

The most dramatic spy case of the era involved Julius Rosenberg, a former government engineer, and his wife Ethel, who were accused of conveying atomic secrets to Soviet agents during World War II. The government had only a weak case against Ethel, but hoped that her conviction would "break" her husband, forcing him to name other spies. The Rosenberg case depended on testimony of alleged accomplices, some of them secretly coached by the FBI. Although the Rosenbergs maintained their innocence to the end, in March 1951 a jury found them both guilty. The American press showed them no sympathy, but the death sentence drew large protest demonstrations in the United States and abroad. Julius and Ethel Rosenberg died in the electric chair on June 19, 1953. Documents declassified in the 1990s provided evidence of Julius (but not Ethel) Rosenberg's guilt.

McCarthyism

In a sensational Lincoln Day speech to the Republican Women's Club of Wheeling, West Virginia, on February 9, 1950, Republican senator Joseph R. McCarthy of Wisconsin announced that the United States had been sold out by the "traitorous actions" of men holding important positions in the federal government. These acted as part of a conspiracy, he charged, of 205 card-carrying Communists in the State Department (see Communities in Conflict).

(•—[**Hear** the **Audio**
Joseph P. McCarthy Speech at **www.myhistorylab.com**

McCarthy refused to reveal names because, in reality, he had none. Nevertheless, a few days later, after a drinking bout, he told persistent reporters: "I'm not going to tell you anything. I just want you to know I've got a pailful [of dirt] . . . and I'm going to use it where it does the most good." Although investigations uncovered not a single Communist in the State Department, McCarthy launched a flamboyant offensive against New Deal Democrats and the Truman administration for failing to defend the nation's security. He gave his name to the era: McCarthyism.

Behind the blitz of publicity, the previously obscure junior senator from Wisconsin had struck a chord. Communism seemed to many Americans to be much more than a military threat; it was nothing less than a demonic force undermining all basic values. It compelled patriots to prepare Americans even for atomic warfare: "Better Dead Than Red."

Civil rights organizations faced the worst persecution since the 1920s. But attacks on women's organizations and homosexuals, which cloaked deep fears about changing sexual mores, also took a huge toll. Aided by FBI reports, the federal government fired up to sixty homosexuals per month in the early 1950s. Dishonorable discharges from the U.S. armed forces for homosexuality, an administrative procedure without appeal, also increased dramatically.

Joseph McCarthy and his fellow Red-hunters eventually burned themselves out. During nationally televised congressional hearings in 1954, not only did McCarthy fail to prove his wild charges of Communist infiltration of the Army, but also in the glare of television appeared deranged. Cowed for four years, the Senate finally censured him for "conduct unbecoming a member."

Congress and the Red Scare

Joseph McCarthy, the junior Republican senator from Wisconsin, stepped onto the national stage by pushing the Second Red Scare into the highest levels of government. On February 9, 1950, at a Lincoln's Day celebration in Wheeling, West Virginia, he took aim at President Truman's foreign policy. He charged Secretary of State Dean Acheson with harboring at least 205 "traitorous" Communists within his department. Two days later, McCarthy sent a letter to the president, revising downward the number of Communists employed by the State Department to fifty-seven. He nevertheless demanded a full investigation and predicted that hundreds more would turn up. He warned the president not to stall, for failure to act would "label the Democratic Party as being the bedfellow of international communism." He would give versions of his Wheeling speech, excerpted here, on many later occasions, never tiring of Red-baiting the Democrats. One of the first critics to challenge McCarthy was Senator Margaret Chase Smith, a member of his own party. Smith (1897–1995) had served eight years in the House of Representatives before being elected to the Senate in 1948. She was the first woman elected to serve in both houses of Congress. On June 1, 1950, Smith read to the Senate a "Declaration of Conscience," which she had composed. She reviled the leaders of both parties for "lack of effective leadership," deplored the atmosphere of suspicion, and strongly denounced the mudslinging anti-Communist campaign. Six additional Republican senators signed her Declaration, although Smith and her allies refused to endorse a report later prepared by Democrats that defended the State Department against McCarthy's "fraudulent" charges.

● **What is the basis of Joseph McCarthy's charges, and why is he targeting the State Department? What is the basis of Margaret Chase Smith's response to McCarthy, and why is she criticizing a fellow Republican?**

Senator Joseph McCarthy Charges That Communists Riddle the State Department, Wheeling, West Virginia (February 9, 1950)

Today we are engaged in a final, all-out battle between communistic atheism and Christianity. The modern champions of communism have selected this as the time, and ladies and gentlemen, the chips are down— they are truly down. . . .

Ladies and gentlemen, can there be anyone tonight who is so blind as to say that the war is not on? Can there be anyone who fails to realize that the Communist world has said the time is now? . . . that this is the time for the show-down between the democratic Christian world and the communistic atheistic world? . . .

As one of our outstanding historical figures once said, "When a great democracy is destroyed, it will not be from enemies from without, but rather because of enemies from within." . . .

> **"Today we are engaged in a final, all-out battle between communistic atheism and Christianity."**

The reason why we find ourselves in a position of impotency is not because our only powerful potential enemy has sent men to invade our shores . . . but rather because of the traitorous actions of those who have been treated so well by this Nation. It has not been the less fortunate, or members of minority groups who have been traitorous to this Nation, but rather those who have had all the benefits that the wealthiest Nation on earth has had to offer . . . the finest homes, the finest college education and the finest jobs in government we can give.

This is glaringly true in the State Department. There the bright young men who are born with silver spoons in their mouths are the ones who have been most traitorous. . . . I have here in my hand a list of 205 . . . a list of names that were made known to the Secretary of State as being members of the Communist Party and who nevertheless are still working and shaping policy in the State Department. . . .

As you know, very recently the Secretary of State proclaimed his loyalty to a man guilty of what has always been considered as the most abominable of all crimes—being a traitor to the people who gave him a position of great trust—high treason. . . .

He has lighted the spark which is resulting in a moral uprising and will end only when the whole sorry mess of twisted, warped thinkers are swept from the national scene so that we may have a new birth of honesty and decency in government.

SOURCE: Joseph McCarthy, "Speech at Wheeling, West Virginia, 9 February 1950." In Michael P. Johnson, ed. *Reading the American Past*, Vol. II (Boston: Bedford Books, 1998), 191–195. (The speech is also on several websites and freely available.)

Senator Margaret Chase Smith Announces Her Declaration of Conscience (June 1, 1950)

Mr. President, I would like to speak briefly and simply about a serious national condition. It is a national feeling of fear and frustration that could result in national suicide and the end of everything that we Americans hold dear. . . .

I speak as a Republican. I speak as a woman. I speak as a United States Senator. I speak as an American. . . .

I think that it is high time for the United States Senate and its Members to do some soul searching—for us to weigh our consciences—on the manner in which we are performing our duty to the people of America; on the manner in which we are using or abusing our individual powers and privileges.

I think that it is high time that we remembered that we have sworn to uphold and defend the Constitution. I think that it is high time that we remembered that the Constitution, as amended, speaks not only of the freedom of speech, but also of trial by jury instead of trial by accusation.

Whether it be a criminal prosecution in court or a character prosecution in the Senate, there is little practical distinction when the life of a person has been ruined.

Those of us who shout the loudest about Americanism in making character assassinations are all too frequently those who, by our own words and acts, ignore some of the basic principles of Americanism—

The right to criticize;
The right to hold unpopular beliefs;
The right to protest;
The right of independent thought.

The exercise of these rights should not cost one single American citizen his reputation or his right to a livelihood nor should he be in danger of losing his reputation or livelihood merely because he happens to know someone who holds unpopular beliefs. Who of us doesn't? Otherwise none of us could call our souls our own. Otherwise thought control would have set in.

The American people are sick and tired of being afraid to speak their minds lest they be politically smeared as "Communists" or "Fascists" by their opponents. Freedom of

"I am not proud of the way in which the Senate has been made a publicity platform for irresponsible sensationalism."

speech is not what it used to be in America. It has been so abused by some that it is not exercised by others. . . .

As a woman, I wonder how the mothers, wives, sisters, and daughters feel about the way in which members of their families have been politically mangled in Senate debate—and I use the word "debate" advisedly.

As a United States Senator, I am not proud of the way in which the Senate has been made a publicity platform for irresponsible sensationalism. . . .

I don't like the way the Senate has been made a rendezvous for vilification, for selfish political gain at the sacrifice of individual reputations and national unity. I am not proud of the way we smear outsiders from the floor of the Senate and hide behind the cloak of congressional immunity and still place ourselves beyond criticism on the floor of the Senate. . . .

SOURCE: Margaret Chase Smith (1972) *Declaration of Conscience*. (William C. Lewis, Jr., ed) Garden City NY: Doubleday & Company, Inc) (also on the website American Rhetoric: Top 100 Speeches).

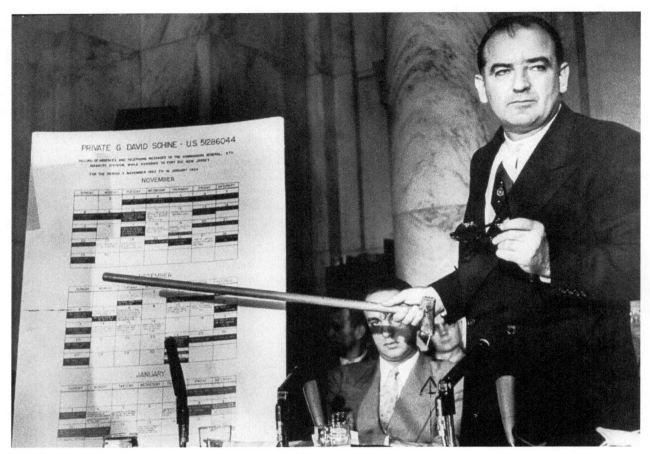

The tables turned on Senator Joseph McCarthy (1908–57) after he instigated an investigation of the U.S. Army for harboring Communists. A special congressional committee then investigated McCarthy for attempting to make the Army grant special privileges to his staff aide, Private David Schine. During the televised hearings, Senator McCarthy discredited himself. In December 1954, the Senate voted to censure him, thus robbing him of his power. He died three years later.

Cold War Culture

As the Truman Doctrine revealed, the Cold War did not necessarily mean military confrontation. Nor was it defined exclusively by a quest for economic supremacy. The Cold War embodied the struggle of one "way of life" against another. It was, in short, a contest of values. The president therefore, pledged the United States to "contain" communism within the parameters of the Soviet Union and its satellites and simultaneously called for fortifications at home. If Americans were to rebuild the world based on their own values, they must rededicate themselves to defending their birthright: freedom and democracy.

An Anxious Mood

"We have about 50 percent of the world's wealth," Kennan noted in 1948, "but only 3.6 percent of its population." However, many Americans feared an economic backslide.

If wartime production had ended the hardships of the Great Depression, how would the economy fare in peacetime? No one could say. Peace itself seemed precarious.

Anxieties surfaced as major themes in popular culture. *The Best Years of Our Lives* (1946), one of the most acclaimed Hollywood films of the era and winner of nine Academy Awards, showed three fictional veterans trying to readjust to civilian life. The former soldiers found that dreams of reunion with family and loved ones, which had sustained them through years of fighting, now seemed hollow. In some cases, their wives and children had become so self-reliant that the men had no clear function in the household; in other cases, the prospects for employment appeared dim. One veteran who had lost both arms was shunned by almost everyone. The feeling of community shared with wartime buddies dissipated, leaving only profound loneliness in a crass, selfish society.

The genre of *film noir* (French for "black film") deepened this postwar moodiness into a pessimistic aesthetic. American movies like *Out of the Past, Detour,* and *They Live by Night* told stories of relentless fate and ruthless betrayal. Their protagonists were loners running from a bad past, falsely accused of transgressions, or trapped into committing crimes. The high-contrast lighting of these black-and-white films accentuated the difficulty of distinguishing friend from foe.

Serious literature vividly captured a sense of anxious alienation. Playwright Arthur Miller in *Death of a Salesman* (1949) sketched an exacting portrait of self-destructive individualism. Willy Loman, the play's hero, is obsessively devoted to his career in sales, but is nevertheless a miserable failure. Worse, he taught his sons to excel in personal presentation and style—the very methods prescribed by standard American success manuals—making them both shallow and materialistic. J. D. Salinger's novel *Catcher in the Rye* (1951) explored the mental anguish of a teenage boy estranged by his parents' psychological distance and materialism. The novel was (and remains) very controversial: conservatives accused Salinger of encouraging disrespect for adults as "phonies," while for many young people he precisely articulated their alienation.

Cold War anxiety manifested itself in a flurry of unidentified flying object (UFO) sightings. Thousands of Americans imagined that a Communist-like invasion from outer space was already underway or hoped that superior creatures might arrive to show the way to world peace. The U.S. Air Force discounted "flying saucer" reports, but dozens of private researchers and faddists claimed to have been contacted by aliens. Hollywood fed these beliefs. In *The Invasion of the Body Snatchers* (1956), for example, a small town is captured by aliens who take over the minds of its inhabitants when they fall asleep, a subtle warning against apathy toward the threat of communist "subversion" (see Seeing History).

The Family As Bulwark

Postwar prosperity helped to strengthen the ideal of domesticity, although many Americans interpreted their rush toward marriage and parenthood, as one writer put it, as a "defense—an impregnable bulwark" against the era's anxieties.

Edward Hopper (1882–1967) was the most well-known realist painter in the United States at midcentury. Many of his paintings portray the starkness and often the loneliness of American life, with cityscapes depicting empty streets or all-night restaurants where the few patrons sit at a distance from each other. This painting, owned by the Metropolitan Museum of Art in New York, expresses the mood of alienation associated with Cold War culture.

SOURCE: Edward Hopper (1882–1967), *Office in a Small City*, 1953. Oil on canvas, H. 28 in. W. 40 in. Signed (lower left) Edward Hopper. The Metropolitan Museum of Art, George A. Hearn Fund, 1953. (53.183).

The Hollywood Film *Invasion, U.S.A*

Invasion, U.S.A. was the first of the genre of Red-scare films to do well at the box office. Shot in just seven days and released by Columbia Pictures in 1952, the film opens by depicting a group of well-off Americans, drinking casually in a New York bar and showing no particular concern about the imminent threat to their nation. Suddenly, they hear the news of horrific attacks by The Enemy. After atomic bombs fall and The Enemy approaches the nation's capital, they have all learned a potent lesson about complacency and begin to renounce their selfish ways. The group disperses, each character now understanding that freedom carries with it the price of vigilance.

The Enemy is never named, but Slavic accents and references to the "People's Government" that takes over Manhattan strongly suggest that the evildoers are Russian Communists.

The film's poster builds on the foundation of fear. Studio publicists also advised local movie theaters to promote the movie along the same line: "Dress a young man in full paratroop regalia and have him walk through the principal streets of town in advance of playdate with a sign on his back reading HERE'S HOW IT WOULD HAPPEN IF IT HAPPENED NOW! SEE COLUMBIA PICTURES' *INVASION, U.S.A.* AT THE STATE THEATER FRIDAY!" The studio also suggested that blasts by air raid sirens and the use of local Civil Defense workers would be good choices to advertise the film. Despite these fear-provoking messages, one reviewer pointed out that poor production quality–stock footages from World War II—and stilted dialogue unintentionally made *Invasion, U.S.A,* the first film to make audiences laugh at the atomic bomb.

• **How did Hollywood and other forms of mass media help to shape Cold War culture in the late 1940s and early 1950s?**

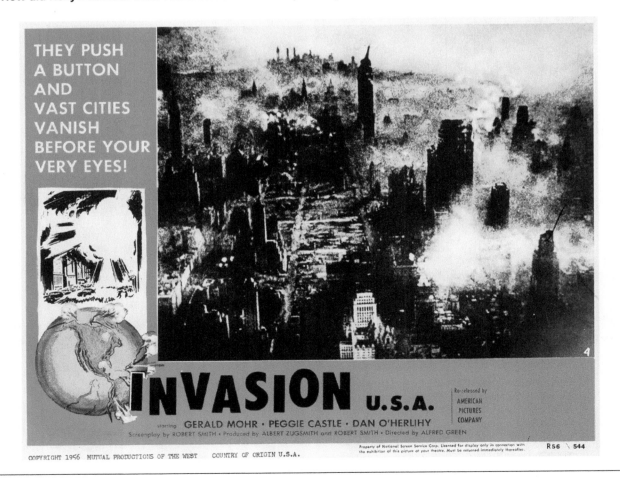

Young couples were marrying younger and producing more children than at any time in the past century. The Census Bureau predicted that the "baby boom" would be temporary. To everyone's surprise, the birthrate continued to grow at a record pace (see Figure 26.1).

The new families who enjoyed postwar prosperity inaugurated a spending spree of trailblazing proportions. "The year 1946," trumpeted *Life* magazine, "finds the U.S. on the threshold of marvels, ranging from runless stockings and shineless serge suits to jet-propelled airplanes that will flash across the country in just a little less than the speed of sound." By the time Truman left office, two-thirds of all American households claimed at least one television set.

View the Image
Cover Illustration for "The Desi-Lucy Love Story" (1956) at **www.myhistorylab.com**

These two trends—the baby boom and high rates of consumer spending—encouraged a major change in the middle-class family. Having worked during World War II, often in occupations traditionally closed to them, many women wished to continue in full-time employment. Reconversion to peacetime production forced the majority from their factory positions, but most women quickly returned, taking jobs at a faster rate than men and providing half the total growth of the labor force. By 1952, 2 million more wives worked than during the war. Gone, however, were the high-paying unionized jobs in manufacturing. Instead, most women found low-wage jobs in the expanding service sector: clerical work, health care and education, and restaurant, hotel, and retail services. Older women whose children were grown might work because they had come to value a job for its own sake. Younger women often worked out of "economic necessity" that is, to maintain a middle-class standard of living that now required more than one income. Indeed, mothers of young children were the most likely to be employed (see Table 26.1).

Even though most women sought employment primarily to support their families, they ran up against popular opinion and expert advice urging them to go home.

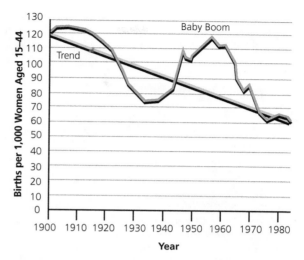

FIGURE 26.1 U.S. Birthrate, 1930–80 The bulge of the "baby boom," a leading demographic factor in the postwar economy, stands out for this fifty-year period.

SOURCE: National Archives and Records Administration.

Polls registered resounding disapproval—by 86 percent of those surveyed—of a married woman working if jobs were scarce and her husband could support her. Noting that most Soviet women worked outside the home, many commentators appealed for a return to an imaginary "traditional" American family where men alone were breadwinners and women were exclusively homemakers. FBI director J. Edgar Hoover exhorted the nation's women to fight "the twin enemies of freedom—crime and communism" by fulfilling their "natural" role as "homemakers and mothers."

Read the Document
Ladies Home Journal, "Young Mother" (1956) at **www.myhistorylab.com**

This campaign began on a shrill note. Ferdinand Lundberg and Marynia Farnham, in their best-selling *Modern Woman: The Lost Sex* (1947), attributed the "super-jittery age in which we live" to women's abandonment of

TABLE 26.1

Distribution of Total Personal Income among Various Segments of the Population, 1947–70 (in Percentages)*

Year	Poorest Fifth	Second Poorest Fifth	Middle Fifth	Second Wealthiest Fifth	Wealthiest Fifth	Wealthiest 5 Percent
1947	3.5	10.6	16.7	23.6	45.6	18.7
1950	3.1	10.5	17.3	24.1	45.0	18.2
1960	3.2	10.6	17.6	24.7	44.0	17.0
1970	3.6	10.3	17.2	24.7	44.1	16.9

Despite the general prosperity of the postwar era, the distribution of income remained essentially unchanged.
*Monetary income only.

SOURCE: Adapted from U.S. Bureau of the Census, *Historical Statistics of the United States, Colonial Times to 1970*, Bicentennial ed. (Washington, DC: U.S. Government Printing Office, 1975), p. 292.

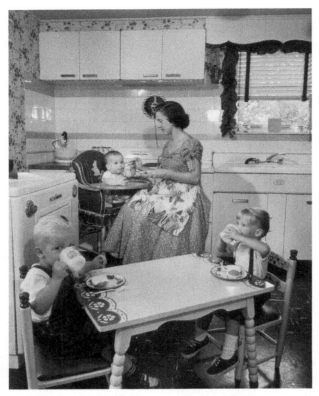

This photograph, taken in 1955, presents an ideal image of domestic life for American women during the Cold War. This young mother sits with her three small children in a well-equipped kitchen that depicts the high standard of living that symbolized the "American way of life."

encouraged a mass westward migration of people eager to find wartime jobs. Following the war, many cities successfully converted to peacetime production; Los Angeles, for example, attracted one-eighth of all new business in the nation during the late 1940s. It was the Cold War, however, that by reviving defense funding gave the western economy its most important boost.

So much defense money—nearly 10 percent of the entire military budget—was poured by the federal government into California that the state's rate of economic growth between 1949 and 1952 outpaced that of the nation as a whole; nearly 40 percent came from aircraft manufacturing alone. Ten years later, an estimated one-third of all Los Angeles workers were employed by defense industries, particularly aerospace, and the absolute number of defense workers far exceeded those of the peak production years in World War II. The concentration of defense workers was even greater in the Los Angeles suburbs. Orange Country, for example, grew quickly during the Cold War to become a major producer of communication equipment. The Bay Area also benefited economically from defense spending, and cities such as San Jose began their rise as home to the nation's budding high-technology industry.

The Cold War pumped new life into communities that had grown up during World War II. Hanford, Washington, and Los Alamos, New Mexico, both centers of the Manhattan Project, employed more people in the construction of the Cold War nuclear arsenal than in the development of the atom bomb. Once-rural Los Alamos mushroomed so fast that thirty years later its population density was second only in New Mexico to metropolitan Albuquerque. New communities accompanied the growth of the U.S. military bases and training camps in the West. Many of these installations, as well as hospitals and supply depots, not only survived but also expanded during the transition from the actual warfare of World War II to the threatened warfare of the Cold War. Between 1950 and 1953, approximately twenty western bases were reopened. California became at least a temporary home to more military personnel than any other state, and Texas was not far behind. The availability of public lands with areas of sparse population made western states especially attractive to military planners designing such dangerous and secretive installations as the White Sands Missile Range in the New Mexico desert.

Local politicians, real estate agents, and merchants usually welcomed these developments as sources of revenue and employment. There were, however, heavy costs for speedy and unplanned federally induced growth. To accommodate the new populations, the government poured money into new highway systems but did little for public transportation. Uncontrolled sprawl, traffic congestion, air pollution, and strains on limited water and energy resources all grew with the military-industrial communities in the West. For those populations living near nuclear

the home to pursue careers. To counter this danger, they proposed federally funded psychotherapy to readjust women to their housewifely roles and cash subsidies to encourage them to bear more children.

Articles in popular magazines, television shows, and high-profile experts chimed in with similar messages. In the first edition of his *Baby and Child Care* (1946), the child-rearing advice manual that soon outsold the Bible, Dr. Benjamin Spock advised women to devote themselves full time, if financially possible, to their maternal responsibilities.

Patterns of women's higher education reflected this conservative trend. Having made slight gains during World War II, when college-age men were serving in the armed forces or working in war industries, women lost ground after the G.I. Bill created a huge upsurge in male enrollment. Women represented 40 percent of all college graduates in 1940, but only 25 percent a decade later.

Military-Industrial Communities in the American West

All regions of the United States felt the impact of the Cold War, but none so directly as the West. World War II defense spending had stimulated the western economy and testing grounds, environmental degradation complemented the ultimate threat to their own physical well-being: over the next forty years, cancer rates soared.

"The American Way"

Following the massive and spontaneous V-J Day celebrations, Americans began to retreat from public displays of patriotism, but soon new organizations, like the Freedoms Foundation of Valley Forge and the American Heritage Foundation, were joining such stalwarts as the American Legion and the Chamber of Commerce in defining the "American way" in opposition to Soviet communism. These organizations sponsored events such as "freedom rallies" and "freedom fashion shows" to remind Americans of their nation's democratic values and commitment to free enterprise.

In Mosinee, Wisconsin, for example, the American Legion used political theater to inculcate the American way, orchestrating an imaginary Communist coup in the small community. In 1950, on May Day (the traditional left-wing holiday), "Communist agents," followed by more than sixty reporters, forced the mayor and the chief of police from their homes and announced that the Council of People's Commissars had taken over the local government. Roadblocks were put up to prevent residents from escaping to "free" territory. The restaurants served only Soviet fare: black bread, potato soup, and coffee. The local *Mosinee Times* printed a special edition on pink stock under its new "Red Star" masthead. Citizens discovered that all private property had been confiscated and all constitutional rights annulled. Every adult was required "to contribute to the State four extra hours of labor without compensation." That evening, after a full day of Communist indoctrination, the residents rallied in "Red Square" and declared an end to "Communist rule," and then raised the American flag and headed home singing "God Bless America." The national media all covered Mosinee's "Day under Communism."

Meanwhile, Attorney General Tom C. Clark, supported by Truman, by private donors, and by the American Heritage Foundation, was putting on the nation's rails the "Freedom Train." Carrying copies of the Bill of Rights, the Constitution, and the Emancipation Proclamation, the Freedom Train traveled to cities across the land. Local citizens got aboard to view various patriotic displays at the average rate of 8,500 people per day.

Patriotic messages also permeated public education. Following guidelines set down by the Truman administration, teachers were to "strengthen national security through education" by designing their lesson plans to illustrate the superiority of the American democratic system over Soviet communism. In 1947, the federal Office of Education launched a "Zeal for Democracy" program for implementation by school boards nationwide. The program veered toward propaganda, announcing its intention to "promote and strengthen democratic thinking and practice, just as the

schools of totalitarian states have so effectively promoted the ideals of their respective cultures." Meanwhile, in a national civil defense program, schoolchildren learned to "duck" under their desks and "cover" their heads in the event of a surprise Soviet nuclear attack.

Voices of protest were raised. The black poet Langston Hughes expressed his skepticism in verse, writing that he hoped the Freedom Train would carry no Jim Crow car. (The mayor of Memphis refused to allow the Freedom Train to stop in his city if whites and blacks were allowed to board together.) A brave minority of scholars protested infringements on academic freedom by refusing to sign loyalty oaths and by writing books pointing out the potential dangers of aggressively nationalistic foreign and domestic policies. But the chilling atmosphere, such as the political climate pervading the University of Washington, made many individuals reluctant to express contrary opinions or ideas.

Stalemate for the Democrats

With Cold War tensions festering in Europe, neither the United States nor the Soviet Union would have predicted that events in Asia would bring them to the brink of a new world war. Yet in China, the most populous land on earth, Communists completed their seizure of power in late 1949. A few months later, in June 1950, Communist armies threatened to conquer all of Korea.

Truman sent American forces to conduct a "police action" in Korea, which within a few years absorbed more than 1.8 million U.S. troops with no victory in sight. For Truman, the "loss" of China and the Korean stalemate proved political suicide, ending the twenty-year Democratic lock on the presidency and the greatest era of reform in U.S. history.

Democratizing Japan and "Losing" China

At the close of World War II, the United States acted deliberately to secure Japan firmly within its sphere of influence. General Douglas MacArthur directed an interim Japanese government in a modest reconstruction program that included land reform, creation of independent trade unions, abolition of contract marriages, granting of woman suffrage, sweeping demilitarization, and eventually a constitutional democracy that renounced war and barred Communists from all posts. American leaders worked to rebuild the nation's economy along capitalist lines and integrate Japan, like West Germany, into an anti-Soviet bloc. Japan also housed huge U.S. military bases, placing U.S. troops and weapons on the doorstep of the Soviet Union's Asian rim.

China could not be handled so easily. After years of civil war, the pro–Western Nationalist government of Jiang Jeishi (Chiang Kai-shek) collapsed. Since World War II, the United States had been aiding Jiang's unpopular and corrupt regime, while warning him that without major reforms and a coalition with his political opponents, the Nationalists were heading for defeat. Jiang refused any concessions, and in the late 1940s the Truman administration cut off virtually all aid and then watched as Nationalist troops surrendered to the Communists, led by Mao Zedong. Mao's Communists had the support of the Chinese countryside, where 85 percent of the population lived. Abandoning the entire mainland, the defeated Nationalists fled to the island of Taiwan. On October 1, 1949, Mao proclaimed the People's Republic of China, and in February 1950, the Soviet Union and the People's Republic of China signed an alliance.

China's "fall" to communism set off an uproar in the United States. The Asia First wing of the Republican Party, which saw the Far East rather than Europe as the primary target of U.S. trade and investment, blamed Truman for the "loss" of China. The president's adversaries, pointing to the growing menace of "international communism," called the Democrats the "party of treason."

The Korean War

At the end of World War II, the Allies had divided the Korean peninsula, surrendered by Japan, at the 38th Parallel. Although all Koreans hoped to reunite their nation under an independent government, the line between North and South hardened. While the United States backed the unpopular southern government of Syngman Rhee (the Republic of Korea), the Soviet Union sponsored a rival government in North Korea under Communist Kim Il-Sung (see Map 26.3).

On June 25, 1950, the U.S. State Department received a cablegram reporting an invasion of South Korea by the Communist North. "If we are tough enough now," President Truman pledged, "if we stand up to them like we did in Greece three years ago, they won't take any next steps." While the Soviet Union apparently regarded the invasion as Kim's affair, China supported and perhaps incited Kim to invade South Korea. Truman sought the Security Council's approval to send troops to defend South Korea under the UN's collective-security provisions. With the Soviet delegate withdrawn as an act to protest the exclusion of China, the Security Council backed the U.S. request for intervention. Two-thirds of Americans polled approved the president's decision to send troops under the command of General Douglas MacArthur.

Military events seemed at first to justify the president's decision. Seoul, the capital of South Korea, fell to North Korean troops within weeks, and Communist forces pushed

See the Map
The Korean War, 1950–1953 at www.myhistorylab.com

south, occupying most of the peninsula. The situation appeared grim until Truman authorized MacArthur to carry out an amphibious landing at Inchon, near Seoul, on September 15, 1950. With tactical brilliance and good fortune, the general's campaign not only halted the Communist drive, but also sent the North Koreans fleeing. By October, UN troops had retaken South Korea.

Basking in victory, the Truman administration could not resist the temptation to expand its war aims. Too prove that Democrats were not "soft on communism," the president decided to roll back the Communists beyond the 38th Parallel, uniting Korea as a showcase for democracy. China, not yet directly involved in the war, warned that crossing that dividing line would threaten its national security. Truman flew to Wake Island in the Pacific on October 15 to confer with MacArthur, who assured him of a speedy victory.

MacArthur had sorely miscalculated. Chinese troops massed along the Yalu River, the border between Korea and China. As the UN forces approached the Yalu, suddenly and without air support, a Chinese "human wave" attack began. MacArthur, who had foolishly divided his forces, suffered a crushing defeat. The Chinese drove the UN troops back into South Korea, where they regrouped south of the 38th Parallel. Finally, by the summer of 1951

Estimates runs as high as 6 million for the number of civilian refugees during the Korean War. This American news photograph, published in 1950, shows American soldiers heading toward battles sites while Korean refugees move in the opposite direction.

MAP 26.3 The Korean War The intensity of battles underscored the strategic importance of Korea in the Cold War.

a stalemate had been reached very near the old dividing line. Then, for the next eighteen months, negotiations for an armistice dragged out amid heavy fighting.

MacArthur tried to convince Truman to prepare for a new invasion of Communist territory. Encouraged by strong support at home, and defying the American tradition of civilian control over the military, MacArthur publicly criticized the president's policy, calling for bombing supply lines in China and blockading the Chinese coast. Such actions would certainly have led to a

Chinese-American war. Finally, on April 10, 1951, Truman fired MacArthur for insubordination.

The Price of National Security

The Korean conflict had profound implications for the use of executive power. By unilaterally instituting a peacetime draft in 1948 and in 1950 ordering American troops into Korea without a declaration of war, Truman had bypassed congressional authority. Republican Senator Robert Taft called the president's actions "evidence of an 'imperial presidency'" that was guilty of "a complete usurpation" of checks and balances. For a while, Truman sidestepped such criticisms and their constitutional implications by declaring a national emergency and by carefully referring to the military deployment not as a U.S. "war" but as a UN-sanctioned "police action."

The president was acting at the prompting of National Security Council Paper 68 (NSC-68), a sweeping declaration of Cold War policy. This lengthy document was submitted to Truman by the National Security Council in April 1950. NSC-68 declared it necessary and expedient

•●—[Read the Document]

National Security Council Memorandum Number 68 (1950) at **www.myhistorylab.com**

not only to repel Communist influence wherever it appeared but also to "foster the seeds of destruction within the Soviet Union." The document defined the struggle between

the United States and the Soviet Union as "permanent" and the era one of "total war." American citizens, it declared, must be willing to sacrifice—"to give up some of the benefits which they have come to associate with their freedom"—to defend their way of life. NSC-68 articulated the intellectual and psychological rationale behind U.S. national security policies for the next forty years.

Initially hesitant, after the outbreak of the Korean war, Truman accepted the policies outlined in NSC-68 and agreed to a rapid and permanent military buildup. By the time the Korean conflict subsided, the defense budget had quadrupled, from $13.5 billion to more than $52 billion in 1953. The U.S. Army had grown to 3.6 million—six times its size at the beginning of the "police action." At the same time, the federal government accelerated development of both conventional and nonconventional weapons. Its nuclear stockpile now included the thermonuclear hydrogen (or "H") bomb, first tested at full scale in November 1952. NCS-68 also proposed expensive "large-scale covert operations" for the "liberation" of Communist-dominated countries, particularly in Eastern Europe.

The Korean war also provided the rationale to expand anti-Communist propaganda. At the end of World War II, Truman had taken steps to transform the Office of War Information into a peacetime program with a much smaller budget. By 1948, however, Congress was ready to pass with bipartisan support the Smith-Mundt Act, designed "to promote the better understanding of the United States among the peoples of the world and to strengthen cooperative international relations." Within a year, Congress doubled the budget for such programming, granting $3 million to revive the Voice of America, the shortwave international radio program that had been established in 1942. The new legislation also funded films, print media, cultural exchange programs, and exhibitions, and it created a foundation to disseminate anti-Communist propaganda throughout the world.

By 1951, a massive "Campaign of Truth" was reaching 93 nations, and the Voice of America was broadcasting

anti-Communist programming in 45 languages. Project Troy, which was initially designed by professors from Harvard and MIT, aimed to penetrate the iron curtain by using balloons to drop leaflets and cheap American goods, such as playing cards and plastic chess sets. Army pilots joined the effort, showering leaflets on North Korean troops reading "ENJOY LIFE and plenty of cigarettes away from the war by coming over to the UN side. Escape. Save your life." In his annual message to Congress that year, President Truman requested $115 million to fund these programs, but as the war in Korea bogged down, he managed to get only $85 million. In the end, the Korean conflict did nothing to roll back communism, and it cost the United States approximately $100 billion, inaugurating an era of huge federal budget deficits.

In Korea, peace negotiations and fighting proceeded in tandem until the summer of 1953, when a settlement was reached returning North and South Korea to almost the same territory each had held at the start of the war. Approximately 54,000 Americans died in Korea; North Korea and China lost well over 2 million. The UN troops had employed both "carpet bombing" (an intense, destructive attack on a small area) and napalm (jellied gasoline bombs), destroying most of the housing and food supplies in both North and South Korea. True to patterns of modern warfare that emerged during World War II, the majority of civilians killed were women and children. Nearly a million Koreans were left homeless.

The Korean conflict enlarged the geographical range of the Cold War to include East Asia. "Red China" and the United States would be implacable enemies for the next twenty years. Moreover, Korea did much to establish an ominous tradition of "unwinnable" conflicts that left many Americans skeptical of official policy.

Decades later, the Korean war inspired the dark comedy *M★A★S★H*, adapted for television from the film written by Hollywood screenwriter Ring Lardner Jr., an "unfriendly witness" before HUAC, who was jailed during the Korean war for contempt of Congress. As late as 1990, members of Congress were still debating the terms of a Korean war memorial. "It ended on a sad note for Americans," one historian concluded, "and the war and its memories drifted off into a void."

"I like Ike": The Election of 1952

Korea dominated the election campaign of 1952. Truman's popularity had wavered continually since he took office in 1945, but it sank to an all-time low in the early 1950s shortly after he fired MacArthur. Thousands of letters and telegrams poured into Congress demanding Truman's impeachment, while MacArthur returned home to a hero's welcome. More than 7 million cheered him in New York City alone.

The case against Truman widened. The Asia First lobby argued that if in the late 1940s the president had aggressively turned back communism in China, there would have been no "limited war" in Korea. Large-scale corruption came to light in Truman's administration, with several agencies allegedly dealing in 5 percent kickbacks on government contracts. Business and organized labor complained about price and wage freezes during the Korean war. A late 1951 Gallup poll showed the president's approval rating at 23 percent. In March 1952, Truman announced he would not run for reelection, even though he was constitutionally permitted another term.

Accepting political defeat and disgrace, Truman endorsed the uncharismatic governor of Illinois, Adlai E. Stevenson Jr. Admired for his eloquence, wit, honesty, and intelligence, Stevenson offered no solutions to the conflict in Korea, the accelerating arms race, or the Cold War generally. Accepting the Democratic nomination, he candidly admitted that "the ordeal of the twentieth century is far from over."

The Republicans made the most of the Democrats' dilemma. Without proposing any sweeping answers of their own, they zeroed in on "K_1C_2"—Korea, Communism, and Corruption. When opinion polls showed retired General Dwight D. Eisenhower with an "unprecedented" 64 percent approval rating, they found in "Ike" the perfect candidate.

Eisenhower styled himself the voice of "modern Republicanism." He wisely avoided the negative impressions made in 1948 by Dewey, who had seemed as aggressive as Truman abroad and bent on repealing the New Deal at home. Eisenhower knew better: voters wanted peace and a limited welfare state. He called New Deal reforms "a solid floor that keeps all of us from falling into the pit of disaster," and without going into specifics promised "an early and honorable" peace in Korea. Whenever he was tempted to address questions of finance or the economy, his advisers warned him: "The chief reason that people want to vote for you is because they think you have more ability to keep us out of another war."

Richard Nixon, Eisenhower's vice presidential candidate, meanwhile waged a relentless and defamatory attack on "Adlai the Appeaser." Joe McCarthy chortled that with club in hand he might be able to make "a good American" of Stevenson. A month before the election, McCarthy went on network television with his requisite "exhibits" and "documents," purportedly showing that the Democratic presidential candidate had promoted communism at home and abroad. These outrageous charges kept the Stevenson campaign off balance.

The Republican campaign was itself not scandal-free: Nixon was caught accepting personal gifts from wealthy benefactors. On national television, he pathetically described his wife Pat's "good Republican cloth coat" and their struggling life, but then contritely admitted to indeed accepting one gift: a puppy named Checkers that his little daughters loved and that he refused to give back. "The Poor Richard Show," as critics called this masterfully maudlin "Checkers Speech," defused the scandal without answering the most important charges. The speech also underscored how important television was becoming in molding voters' perceptions.

Soaring above the scandal, Eisenhower inspired voters as the peace candidate. Ten days before the election, he dramatically announced: "I shall go to Korea." Eisenhower carried 55 percent of the vote and thirty-nine states, bringing an unusually large harvest of voters in normally Democratic areas, such as the South, and in New York, Chicago, Boston, and Cleveland. Riding his coattails, the Republicans regained narrow control of Congress. The New Deal coalition—ethnic minorities, northern blacks, unionized workers, liberals, Catholics, Jews, and white southern conservatives—no longer commanded a majority.

On September 23, 1952, Republican vice-presidential candidate Richard M. Nixon appeared on national television to defend himself against charges that he had taken illegal campaign contributions. This photograph shows him with one of those gifts, a black-and-white spotted cocker spaniel. He said: "And our little girl Tricia, the six year old, named it 'Checkers.' And you know, the kids, like all kids, love the dog, and I just want to say this, right now, that regardless of what they say about it, we're gonna keep it." This speech, which was simulcast on radio, won the hearts of many voters.

Conclusion

In his farewell address, in January 1953, Harry Truman reflected: "I suppose that history will remember my term in office as the years when the 'cold war' began to overshadow our lives. I have hardly had a day in office that has not been dominated by this all-embracing struggle."

The election of Dwight Eisenhower helped to diminish the intensity of the country's dour mood without actually bringing a halt to the conflict. The new president pledged himself to liberate the world from communism by peaceful means rather than force. "Our aim is more subtle," he announced during his campaign, "more pervasive, more complete. We are trying to get the world, by peaceful means, to believe the truth. . . ." Increasing the budget of the CIA, Eisenhower took the Cold War out of the public eye by relying to a far greater extent than Truman on psychological warfare and covert operations.

"The Eisenhower Movement," wrote journalist Walter Lippmann, was a "mission in American politics" to restore a sense of community among the American people. In a larger sense, many of the issues of the immediate post–World War II years seemed to have been settled or put off for a distant future. The international boundaries of communism were frozen with the Chinese Revolution, the Berlin Crisis, and now the Korean war. Meanwhile, at home, Cold War defense spending had become a permanent part of the national budget, an undeniable drain on tax revenues but an important element in the government contribution to economic prosperity. If the nuclear arms race remained a cause for anxiety, joined by more personal worries about the changing patterns of family life, a sense of relative security nevertheless spread. Prospects for world peace had dimmed, but the worst nightmares of the 1940s had eased as well.

Review Questions

I. Discuss the origins of the Cold War and the sources of growing tensions between the United States and the Soviet Union at the close of World War II.

2. Describe the basic elements of President Harry Truman's policy of containment. How did the threat of atomic warfare affect this policy?

3. Compare the presidencies of Franklin D. Roosevelt and Harry S. Truman, both Democrats.

4. Describe the impact of McCarthyism on American political life. How did the anti-Communist campaigns affect the media? What were the sources of Senator Joseph McCarthy's popularity? What brought about his downfall?

5. How did the Cold War shape mid-twentieth-century American culture?

6. Discuss the role of the United States in Korea in the decade after World War II. How did the Korean war affect the 1952 presidential election?

7. Why did Dwight D. Eisenhower win the 1952 presidential election?

Recommended Reading

Mary C. Brennan, *Wives, Mothers, and the Red Menace: Conservative Women and the Crusade against Communism* (2008). Argues that conservative women, in joining the crusade against communism, broke through the bounds of domesticity to challenge conventional gender roles during the 1950s. The author examines the rise of prominent conservatives such as Phyllis Schlafly and examines the race and class dimensions of their activism.

Mark S. Byrnes, *The Truman Years, 1945–1953* (2000). A concise history of the Truman administration and its role at the moment when the United States became the dominant economic power in the world. Byrnes covers this transformation with particular attention to the way the president helped to shape a view of the world that presented the United States and the Soviet Union as permanent enemies in a struggle for domination. Includes a set of twenty-one key documents and a detailed chronology of events.

Kevin J. Fernlund, ed., *The Cold War American West, 1945–1989* (1998). Ten essays illustrating the impact of the Cold War on the region of the United States that housed the bulk of military bases, airfields, nuclear testing grounds, and toxic waste dumps. Presenting a variety of interpretations, the contributors ask a common question: Was the West transformed or deformed by the policies of the growing national security state?

John Fousek, *To Lead the Free World: American Nationalism and the Cultural Roots of the Cold War* (2000). Examines the "public culture" of the Cold War through an innovative study of various responses to the official doctrines and declarations of the Truman administration. Fousek pays special attention to the publications of major civil rights organizations and the two largest labor unions of the period and argues that "a broad public consensus" supported Truman's nationalistic foreign policy.

Richard M. Fried, *The Russians Are Coming! The Russians Are Coming!: Pageantry and Patriotism in Cold-War America* (1998). Examines through vivid examples the creation of the fear of communism and its translation into patriotic zeal. Fried takes as his thesis that rallying the public to "fight" the Cold War required as much organization and energy as mobilizing Americans to defend the home front during World War II.

CHRONOLOGY

1941	Henry Luce forecasts the dawn of "the American Century"
1944	G.I. Bill of Rights benefits World War II veterans
	International Monetary Fund and World Bank founded
1945	Franklin D. Roosevelt dies in office; Harry S. Truman becomes president
	United Nations charter signed
	World War II ends
	Strike wave begins
	Truman proposes program of economic reforms
1946	Employment Act creates Council of Economic Advisers
	Churchill's Iron Curtain speech
	Atomic Energy Act establishes Atomic Energy Commission
	Republicans win control of Congress
	Benjamin Spock publishes *Baby and Child Care*
1947	Truman Doctrine announced; Congress appropriates $400 million in aid for Greece and Turkey
	Federal Employees Loyalty and Security Program established and attorney general's list of subversive organizations authorized
	Marshall Plan announced
	Taft-Hartley Act restricts union activities
	National Security Act establishes Department of Defense, the National Security Council, and the Central Intelligence Agency
	House Un-American Activities Committee hearings in Hollywood
1948	Smith-Mundt Act passed by Congress
	Ferdinand Lundberg and Marynia Farnham publish *Modern Woman: The Lost Sex*
	State of Israel founded; immediately recognized by the United States
	Berlin blockade begins
	Henry Wallace nominated for president on Progressive Party ticket

	Truman announces peacetime draft and desegregates U.S. armed forces and civil service
	Truman elected president, defeating Dewey, Wallace, and Thurmond; Democrats sweep both houses of Congress
1949	Truman announces Fair Deal
	North Atlantic Treaty Organization (NATO) created
	Communists, led by Mao Zedong, take power in China
	Berlin blockade ends
	Soviet Union detonates atomic bomb
1950	Alger Hiss convicted of perjury
	Senator Joseph McCarthy begins anti-Communist crusade
	Soviet Union and the People's Republic of China sign an alliance
	Adoption of NSC-68 consolidates presidential war powers
	Korean war begins
	Internal Security (McCarran) Act requires registration of Communist organizations and arrest of Communists during national emergencies
1951	Truman dismisses General Douglas MacArthur
	Psychological Strategy Board created
	Armistice talks begin in Korea
1952	Immigration and Nationality Act retains quota system, lifts ban on immigration of Asian and Pacific peoples, but bans "subversives" and homosexuals
	United States detonates first hydrogen bomb
	Dwight D. Eisenhower wins presidency, defeating Adlai Stevenson; Richard Nixon becomes vice president
1953	Julius and Ethel Rosenberg executed for atomic espionage
	Armistice ends fighting in Korea
1954	Army–McCarthy hearings end, discrediting McCarthy
1955	Warsaw Pact created

David Halberstam, *The Coldest Winter: America and the Korean War* (2007). The journalist David Halberstam conducted dozens of interviews with veterans to create a huge history of the Korean War that looks ahead to future U.S involvement in Southeast Asia and the Middle East.

David K. Johnson, *The Lavender Scare: The Cold War Persecution of Gays and Lesbians in the Federal Government* (2004). Goes beyond McCarthy and the persecution of Communists to examine the role of the national-security state in purging homosexuals from positions in the federal government. Johnson also covers the gay subculture of Washington, DC, which grew with the expansion of government during the New Deal and World War II.

Elaine Tyler May, *Homeward Bound: American Families in the Cold War Era* (1988). A lively account of the effects on family life and women's roles of the national mood of "containment." May argues that government policy became part of a popular culture that solidified the Cold War era's "feminine mystique."

Robert J. McMahon, *The Cold War: A Very Short Introduction* (2003). A compact history of the Cold War that emphasizes its global dimensions. McMahon traces its origins to the devastation of World War II and ends with the unification of Germany in 1990.

Ellen Schrecker, *The Age of McCarthyism: A Brief History with Documents,* 2nd ed. (2002). A useful collection of primary sources on internal security and anticommunism by one of the foremost scholars of the field.

Marc J. Selverstone, *Constructing the Monolith: The United States, Great Britain, and International Communism, 1945–1950* (2009). Examines the way fears of international communism as a monolith, dating to the Bolshevik Revolution and intensifying with the example of Nazi totalitarianism, led policymakers in the United States and Great Britain to ward off a perceived threat from the Kremlin that was more perceived than actual.

Naoko Shibusawa, *America's Geisha Ally: Reimagining the Japanese Enemy* (2006). With ample reference to American popular culture, this book examines the way the United States transformed Japan from a hated enemy into a bulwark against communism during the Cold War.

Judith E. Smith, *Visions of Belonging: Family Stories, Popular Culture, and Postwar Democracy, 1940–1960* (2004). Creatively uses literature, drama, and film to examine the ways public life and private experience were reshaped in the aftermath of World War II.

Stanley Weintraub, *MacArthur's War: Korea and the Undoing of an American Hero* (2000). Tells the story of the downfall of the commander of U.S. forces in the Far East, who was "senior to everyone but God" in the military services. The author additionally offers a detailed description of the horror and ruin accompanying the brutal ground war in Korea.

PEARSON myhistorylab Connections

Reinforce what you learned in this chapter by studying the many documents, images, maps, review tools, and videos available at www.myhistorylab.com.

Read and Review

✓• Study and Review **Chapter 26**

•••• Read the Document

Churchill's "Iron Curtain" Speech (1946)

George F. Kennan, The Long Telegram (1946)

Ronald Reagan, Testimony before HUAC (1947)

Ladies Home Journal, "Young Mother" (1956)

National Security Council Memorandum Number 68 (1950)

• View the Image

How Communism Works (1938)

Cover Illustration for "The Desi-Lucy Love Story" (1956)

• See the Map *The Korean War, 1950–1953*

Research and Explore

•••• Read the Document

Exploring America: The Truman Doctrine

Profiles
Julius and Ethel Rosenberg
Strom Thurmond

((•• Hear the Audio *Joseph P. McCarthy Speech*

((•• Hear the Audio

Hear the audio files for Chapter 26 at
www.myhistorylab.com.

America at Midcentury

1952–1963

CHAPTER OUTLINE

American Communities 787
Popular Music in Memphis

Under the Cold War's Shadow 789
The Eisenhower Presidency
The "New Look" in Foreign Affairs
Covert Action
Global Interventions

The Affluent Society 794
Subsidizing Prosperity
Suburban Life
Organized Labor and the AFL-CIO

Lonely Crowds and Organization Men
The Expansion of Higher Education
Health and Medicine

Youth Culture 801
The Youth Market
"Hail! Hail! Rock 'n' Roll!"
Almost Grown
Deviance and Delinquency

Mass Culture and Its Discontents 804
Television: Tube of Plenty
Television and Politics
Culture Critics

The Coming of the New Frontier 806
The Election of 1960
Ike's Warning: The Military-Industrial
    Complex
New Frontier Liberalism
Kennedy and the Cold War
The Cuban Revolution and the Bay
    of Pigs
The 1962 Missile Crisis
The Assassination of President Kennedy

Elvis Presley, the King of Rock and Roll, performs on an outdoor stage before a wildly enthusiastic audience during the Mississippi State Fair in the early 1950s. Getty Images, Inc./Hulton Archive Photos.

Popular Music in Memphis

The nineteen-year-old Mississippian peered nervously out over the large crowd at Overton Park, Memphis's outdoor amphitheater. He knew that people had come that hot, sticky July day in 1954 to hear the headliner, country music star Slim Whitman. Sun Records, a local Memphis label, had just released the unknown young man's first record, and it had begun to receive some airplay on local radio. He and his two bandmates had never played in a setting even remotely as large as this one. And their music defied categories: it wasn't black and it wasn't white; it wasn't pop and it wasn't country. But when he launched into his version of a black blues song called "That's All Right," the crowd went wild. "I came offstage," he later recalled, "and my manager told me that they was hollering because I was wiggling my legs. I went back out for an encore, and I did a little more, and the more I did, the wilder they went." Elvis Presley had arrived.

Elvis combined a hard-driving, rhythmic approach to blues and country music with a riveting performance style; as much as anyone, he defined the new music known as rock 'n' roll. An unprecedented cultural phenomenon, rock 'n' roll was made largely for and by

AMERICAN
Communities

teenagers. In communities all over America, rock 'n' roll brought teens together around jukeboxes, at sock hops, in cars, and at private parties. It also demonstrated the enormous consumer power of an emerging youth culture. Postwar teenagers would constitute the most affluent generation of young people in American history. Their ability and eagerness to buy records, phonograph players, transistor radios, clothing, makeup, and even cars forced businesses and advertisers to recognize a new teen market. Their buying power helped define the affluent society of the postwar era.

Elvis Presley's life and career also personified many of the themes and tensions of postwar American life. Elvis was born in Tupelo, Mississippi, in 1935, but like many thousands of other poor rural whites, the Presley family moved to Memphis in 1949. Elvis's father found work in a munitions plant. The Presleys were poor enough to qualify for an apartment in Lauderdale Courts, a Memphis public housing project built during the New Deal. Located halfway between St. Louis and New Orleans on the Mississippi River, Memphis enjoyed healthy growth during World War II, with lumber mills, furniture factories, and chemical manufacturing supplementing the cotton market as sources of jobs and prosperity. Memphis also boasted a remarkable diversity of popular theater and music, including a large opera house, numerous brass bands, vaudeville and burlesque, minstrel shows, jug bands, and blues clubs. Like the rest of the South, Memphis was a legally segregated city; whites and blacks lived, went to school, and worked apart. But music—in live clubs and on the radio—was an important means of breaking through the barriers of racial segregation.

As a boy, Elvis turned to music for emotional release and spiritual expression. He soaked up the wide range of musical styles available in Memphis. The all-white Assembly of God Church his family attended featured a renowned hundred-voice choir. Elvis and his friends went to marathon all-night "gospel singings" at Ellis Auditorium, where they enjoyed the tight harmonies and emotional style of white gospel quartets. Elvis also drew from the sounds he heard on Beale Street, the main black thoroughfare of Memphis and one of the nation's most influential centers of African American music. In the postwar years, local black rhythm and blues artists like B. B. King, Junior Parker, and Muddy Waters attracted legions of black and white

fans with their emotional power and exciting showmanship. Elvis himself performed along with black contestants in amateur shows at Beale Street's Palace Theater. Nat D. Williams, a prominent black Memphis disc jockey and music promoter, recalled how black audiences responded to Elvis's unique style. "He had a way of singing the blues that was distinctive. He could sing 'em not necessarily like a Negro, but he didn't sing 'em altogether like a typical white musician. . . . Always he had that certain humanness about him that Negroes like to put in their songs." Elvis himself understood his debt to black music and black performers. "The colored folks," he told an interviewer in 1956, "been singing and playing it just like I'm doing now, man, for more years than I know. They played it like that in the shanties and in their juke joints and nobody paid it no mind until I goosed it up. I got it from them."

Dissatisfied with the cloying pop music of the day, white teenagers across the nation were increasingly turning to the rhythmic drive and emotional intensity of black rhythm and blues. They quickly adopted rock 'n' roll (the term had long been African American slang for dancing and sexual intercourse) as their music. But it was more than just music: it was also an attitude, a celebration of being young, and a sense of having something that adult authority could not understand or control. For millions of young people, rock 'n' roll was an expression of revolt against the conformity and blandness found in so many new postwar suburbs. When Sun Records sold Presley's contract to RCA Records in 1956, Elvis became an international star. Records like "Heartbreak Hotel," "Don't Be Cruel," and "Jailhouse Rock" shot to the top of the charts and blurred the old boundaries between pop, country, and rhythm and blues. His appearances on network television shows contributed to his enormous popularity and demonstrated the extraordinary power of this new medium of communication. Television helped Elvis attract legions of new fans despite—and partly because of—the uproar over his overtly sexual performance style.

Yet in early 1958, at the height of his popularity, Elvis was drafted into the U.S. Army for a two-year hitch. The peacetime draft was a grim reminder for millions of American young men of the Cold War anxieties that hovered over the economic prosperity of the era. Even the most famous entertainer in the world could not escape them. Elvis did most of his service in

1. How did the Eisenhower administration's foreign policy respond to Cold War challenges?

2. On what foundations did the nation's post–World War II prosperity rest?

3. What ideals did America's suburban life evoke, and how did those ideals correspond to suburban realities?

4. What explains the emergence of a distinct youth culture in 1950s' America?

5. What criticisms did television and the 1950s' mass culture evoke?

6. Who was John F. Kennedy, and why did his New Frontier seem so promising to many Americans?

FOCUS Questions

1952–1963

Germany, a critical site of American and Soviet confrontation between 1948 and the early 1960s.

By helping to accustom white teenagers to the style and sound of black artists, Elvis helped establish rock 'n' roll as an interracial phenomenon. The considerable adult opposition to rock 'n' roll revolved largely around fears of race mixing. To a remarkable degree, the new music anticipated and contributed to the collapse of segregation, at least in the realm of popular culture. Institutional racism would continue to plague the music business—many black artists were routinely cheated out of royalties and severely underpaid—but the music of postwar Memphis at least pointed the way toward the exciting cultural possibilities that could emerge from breaking down the barriers of race. It also gave postwar American teenagers a newfound sense of community. In a broader sense, rock 'n' roll heralded a generational shift in American society. Just as Elvis's extraordinary popularity led the way for a new kind of music, in 1960 the nation elected John F. Kennedy, the youngest president in its history and a leader who came to symbolize youthful idealism. His assassination cut short the promise of the new frontier, but not before young people had established a crucial new presence in the nation's economy, culture, and political life.

Memphis

AMERICAN · ·
Communities

Under the Cold War's Shadow

By the time Dwight D. Eisenhower—universally called "Ike"—entered the White House in 1953, the confrontation with communism was already providing the framework for America's relations with the world. Eisenhower developed new strategies for the containment of what he called "international communism," including a greater reliance on nuclear deterrence and aggressively using the CIA for covert action. Yet Eisenhower also resolved to do everything possible to forestall an all-out nuclear conflict. Recognizing the limits of raw military power, he accepted a less-than-victorious end to the Korean conflict and avoided full military involvement in Indochina. Ironically, Eisenhower's promotion of high-tech strategic weaponry fostered what he called—disapprovingly—the military-industrial complex. By the time he left office in 1961, he felt compelled to warn the nation against excessive military spending. His Democratic successor, John F. Kennedy, would discover just how difficult it was to escape the Cold War framework in shaping American foreign policy.

The Eisenhower Presidency

Ike's landslide election victory in 1952 set the stage for the first full two-term Republican presidency since Ulysses S. Grant's presidency. Eisenhower's experience in foreign affairs had been one of his most attractive assets as a presidential candidate. As he had promised during his campaign, in December 1952 Eisenhower traveled to Korea just after his election and spent three days at the front. He returned home determined to end the fighting. The death of Soviet leader Joseph Stalin in March 1953, along with the exhaustion of Chinese and North Korean forces, created conditions favorable for a truce. In July 1953, a cease-fire agreement—not a peace settlement—brought the fighting to an uneasy end, freezing the division of North and South Korea near the 38th Parallel.

Eisenhower's success in ending the Korean fighting set the tone for his administration and increased his popularity. As president, Eisenhower kept up anti-Communist Cold War rhetoric while persuading Americans to accept the East–West stalemate as a more or less permanent fact. At home, Ike became the reassuring symbol of moderation and stability in a nation worried by threats ranging from communism and nuclear war to a new depression.

A conservative vision of community lay at the core of Eisenhower's political philosophy. He saw America as a corporate commonwealth, similar to Herbert Hoover's "associative state" of a generation earlier (see Chapter 23). Eisenhower believed the industrial strife, high inflation, and fierce partisan politics of the Truman years could be corrected only through cooperation, self-restraint, and disinterested public service. As president, Eisenhower sought to limit New Deal trends that had expanded federal power, and he encouraged a voluntary, as opposed to a regulatory, government–business partnership. To him, social harmony and "the good life" at home were closely linked to maintaining a stable, American-led international order abroad. He was fond of the phrase "middle of the road." As he told reporters, "I feel pretty good when I'm attacked from both sides. It makes me more certain I'm on the right track." The majority of the American public agreed with Eisenhower's seemingly easy-going approach.

In running his White House staff and his administration, Eisenhower adapted the staff system with which he had effectively managed unwieldy Allied forces during World War II. His "hidden hand presidency" relied on letting the states and corporate interests guide domestic policy and the economy. He appointed nine businessmen—three with ties to General Motors—to his first cabinet. Former GM chief Charles Wilson, his secretary of defense, epitomized the administration's economic views when he famously told Congress, "What was good for our country was good for General Motors, and vice versa." He appointed men congenial to the corporate interests they were supposed to regulate to the Federal Trade Commission, the Federal Communications Commission, and the Federal Power Commission. Forty billion dollars' worth of disputed offshore oil lands were transferred from the federal government to the Gulf states under the Submerged Lands Act of 1953, whose passage Eisenhower secured. This enhanced the presence of state governments and private companies in the oil business—and cost the Treasury billions in lost revenues.

At the same time, Eisenhower accepted the New Deal legacy of greater federal responsibility for social welfare. He rejected conservative Republican appeals to dismantle Social Security. His administration agreed to a modest expansion of Social Security and unemployment insurance and small increases in the minimum wage. Ike also created the Department of Health, Education and Welfare, appointing as its head the second woman in history to hold a cabinet position, Oveta Culp Hobby. In agriculture, Eisenhower continued to sustain farm prices—and the interests of agribusiness—by means of New Deal–style parity payments. Between 1952 and 1960, federal spending on agriculture jumped from about $1 billion to $7 billion, and government storage facilities bulged with surpluses.

Eisenhower, a fiscal conservative in Hoover's mold, hesitated to use fiscal policy (government spending) to pump up the economy when it twice went into recession: after the Korean war and again in 1958. In that year, though unemployment hit 7.5 percent, the administration refused to cut taxes or increase spending. Eisenhower feared inflation more than unemployment or poverty—and indeed, by the time he left office, he could boast that on his watch the average family's real wages (that is, factoring in inflation) had risen by 20 percent. With low inflation and steady, if modest, growth, the Eisenhower years were prosperous for most Americans. Long after he retired from public life, Ike liked to remember his major achievement as "an atmosphere of greater serenity and mutual confidence."

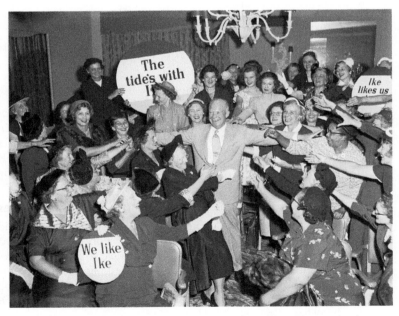

Presidential contender Dwight D. Eisenhower hosts a group of Republican National Committee women at his campaign headquarters in 1952. Ike's status as America's biggest war hero, along with his genial public persona, made him an extremely popular candidate with voters across party lines.

The "New Look" in Foreign Affairs

The death of Joseph Stalin in 1953, just two months after Eisenhower's inauguration, brought an internal power struggle in the Soviet Union. It also opened up the prospects for a thaw in the Cold War, giving Eisenhower hope for peaceful coexistence between the two superpowers. Although Eisenhower recognized that the United States was engaged in a long-term struggle with the Soviet Union, he feared that permanent Cold War mobilization might overburden the American economy and create a "garrison state." He therefore pursued a high-tech, capital-intensive defense policy that emphasized America's qualitative advantage in strategic weaponry and sought cuts in the military budget. As a percentage of the federal budget, military spending fell from 66 percent to 49 percent during Eisenhower's two terms. Much of this saving was gained through increased reliance on nuclear weapons and long-range delivery systems, which were relatively cheaper than conventional forces.

Secretary of State John Foster Dulles gave shape to the "new look" in American foreign policy in the 1950s. A devout Presbyterian lawyer, Dulles had been involved in diplomacy since World War I. He brought to the job a strong sense of righteousness, an almost missionary belief in America's responsibility to preserve the Free World from godless, immoral communism. Dulles called not simply for "containing" communism, but for a "rollback." The key would be greater reliance on America's nuclear superiority. As part of a new strategic doctrine, Dulles emphasized the capacity of the Strategic Air Command to inflict devastating destruction with thermonuclear H-bombs. This would be "massive retaliation . . . at times and places of our own choosing" to deter Soviet aggression.

The limits of a policy based on nuclear strategy became painfully clear when American leaders faced tense situations that offered no clear way to intervene without provoking full-scale war. When East Berliners rebelled against Communist rule in June 1953, Cold War hard-liners thought they saw the long-awaited moment for rollback. American agents had encouraged rebellion in East Berlin with implied promises of American support. It never came, and Soviet tanks crushed the uprising. But precisely how could the United States have responded? Bitter public sentiment about the still unresolved Korean conflict merged with Eisenhower's sense of restraint; in the end, the United States did nothing except protest angrily. U.S. leaders faced the same dilemma in 1956 when Hungary revolted against Communist rule. The United States opened its gates to thousands of Hungarian refugees, but despite desperate appeals on the rebel radio, it refused to intervene against Soviet tanks and troops. Eisenhower recognized that the Soviets would defend not just their own borders, but also their domination of Eastern Europe, by all-out war if necessary.

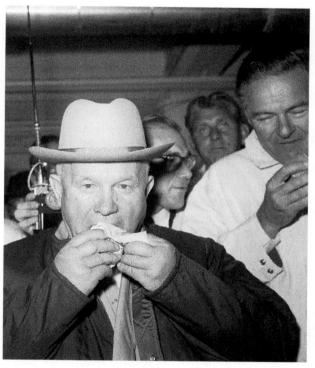

Soviet Premier Nikita Khrushchev enjoys a bite to eat during his tour of an Iowa farm in 1959. A colorful, earthy, and erratic man, Khrushchev loomed as the most visible human symbol of the Soviet Union for Americans. On this trip he called for Soviet–American friendship, yet he also boasted "We will bury you."

Nikita Khrushchev, who had emerged as Stalin's successor, in 1955 withdrew Soviet troops from eastern Austria in a conciliatory gesture. This first real rollback had been achieved by negotiation and a spirit of common hope, not by threats or force. In 1958, Khrushchev, probing American intentions and hoping to redirect the Soviet economy toward the production of more consumer goods, unilaterally suspended nuclear testing. Khrushchev made a twelve-day trip to America in 1959, visiting an Iowa farm, touring Hollywood, and conferring with Eisenhower at Camp David, the presidential retreat in Maryland. If nothing else, such "summit" diplomacy offered a psychological thaw in the Cold War. In early 1960, Khrushchev called for another summit in Paris, to discuss German reunification and nuclear disarmament. Eisenhower prepared for a friendship tour of the Soviet Union.

All that collapsed in May 1960. The Soviets shot down an American U-2 spy plane gathering intelligence on nuclear facilities. Secret American surveillance and probes of Soviet air defenses had been going on for years—justified in American officials' eyes by Moscow's refusal to allow international inspections as part of any disarmament agreement. A deeply embarrassed Eisenhower at first denied the existence of U-2 flights, but then the Soviets produced the

American pilot, who readily confessed. The summit collapsed when Eisenhower refused Khrushchev's demands for an apology and an end to spy flights. The U-2 incident demonstrated the limits of personal diplomacy in resolving the deep structural rivalry between the superpowers.

Eisenhower often provided a moderating voice on issues of defense spending and missile development. The Soviet Union's dramatic launch of *Sputnik,* the first Earth-orbiting satellite, in October 1957 upset Americans' precarious sense of security. This demonstration of Soviet technological prowess raised fears about Russian ability to deploy thermonuclear-tipped intercontinental ballistic missiles (ICBMs) against American cities. Critics attacked the Eisenhower administration for failure to keep up with the enemy. Senator Stuart Symington, a Missouri Democrat, bluntly warned, "Unless our defense policies are promptly changed, the Soviets will move from superiority to supremacy." In addition to huge increases in defense spending, some panic-stricken pundits urged a massive program to build fallout shelters for the entire population in case of nuclear attack.

Eisenhower rejected these radical responses. He knew from U-2 evidence that the Soviet Union in fact trailed far behind the United States in ICBM development, but he kept this knowledge secret so as not to reveal to the Soviets the sources of American intelligence. Instead of panicking before *Sputnik,* he held to a doctrine of "sufficiency": maintaining enough military strength to survive any attack and enough nuclear capability to deliver a massive counterattack. Two measures did emerge from Congress with Eisenhower's support: creation of the National Aeronautics and Space Agency (NASA) to coordinate space exploration and missile development, and the National Defense Education Act, which funneled more federal aid into science and foreign-language education. A bipartisan majority in Congress also voted to increase the military budget by another $8 billion, accelerating the arms race and bloating the defense sector of the economy.

Covert Action

A heavy reliance on covert CIA operations was the other side of Eisenhower's "New Look" defense policy of threatening massive retaliation on America's foreign enemies. He had been an enthusiastic supporter of covert operations during World War II, and during his presidency secret CIA-sponsored paramilitary operations became a key element of American foreign policy. With the American public wary of direct U.S. military interventions, the CIA promised a cheap, quick, and quiet way to depose hostile or unstable regimes, or to prop up conservative governments under siege by indigenous radicals, reformers, or revolutionaries.

Eisenhower's new CIA chief was Allen Dulles, John Foster's brother and an important figure in the OSS, the CIA's World War II precursor. Under Dulles's command, the CIA far exceeded its mandate to collect and analyze information. All over the world, thousands of covert agents

carried out operations that included making large, secret payments to friendly political parties (such as conservative Christian Democrats in Italy and Latin America) or to foreign trade unions that opposed the Communist Party.

Independence movements by now were shaking the European colonial empires throughout Asia and Africa, at the same time that dislike of U.S. hegemony was surging in Latin American. To the Eisenhower administration's alarm, the Soviet Union began winning influence in the "Third World," appealing to allegedly common anti-imperialist solidarity and by offering modest foreign aid. Communists played only small roles in most Third World independence movements. But widespread anti-Western feelings in these lands were fanned by publicity about America's racial problems and by resentment against foreign investors' control of natural resources, including oil and mineral wealth. If emerging nations questioned U.S. regional security arrangements by opting for neutrality—or, worse, expropriated American property—the Eisenhower administration was apt to try covert countermeasures and military intervention.

Global Interventions

In Iran in 1953, the CIA produced a swift, major victory. The popular Iranian prime minister, Mohammed Mossadegh, had nationalized Britain's Anglo-Iranian Oil Company, and the State Department worried that this might set a precedent throughout the oil-rich Middle East. Kermit Roosevelt, the CIA chief in Iran, organized and financed opposition to Mossadegh within the Iranian army and on the streets of Teheran. This CIA-sponsored movement drove Mossadegh from office and put in power an autocratic monarch (shah), Riza Pahlavi. The shah proved his loyalty to his American sponsors by renegotiating oil contracts, assuring American companies 40 percent of Iran's oil concessions. But U.S. identification with the shah's repressive regime in the long run created a groundswell of anti-Americanism among Iranians.

U.S. policy throughout the Middle East was complicated by the conflict between Israel and its Arab neighbors. Immediately after the United States and the Soviet Union recognized the newborn Jewish state in 1948, the Arab countries launched an all-out attack. Israel repulsed the attack, drove thousands of Palestinians from their homes, and seized territory considerably beyond the lines of the projected UN partition of Palestine into a Jewish and an Arab state. While the Arab world boycotted Israel economically and refused to recognize its right to exist, hundreds of thousands of Palestinians languished in squalid refugee camps. Yet most Americans supported the new Jewish state as a refuge for a people the Nazis had tried to exterminate in the Holocaust.

Israel became a reliable U.S. ally in an unstable region. Arab nationalism continued to vex American policymakers, culminating in the 1956 Suez Crisis. Egyptian president Gamal Abdel Nasser, a leading voice of Arab nationalism, dreamed of building the Aswan High Dam on the Nile to create more arable land and provide cheap electric power. To build the dam, he sought American and British economic aid. When negotiations broke down, Nasser turned to the Soviet Union for aid and announced he would nationalize the strategically vital—and British-controlled—Suez Canal. Eisenhower refused European appeals for help in forcibly returning the canal to the British. British, French, and Israeli forces then invaded Egypt in October 1956. The United States sponsored a UN cease-fire resolution demanding withdrawal of foreign forces. Yielding to this pressure and to Soviet threats, the British, French, and eventually Israeli forces withdrew. Eisenhower had won a major diplomatic battle through patience and pressure. But it brought no lasting peace to the troubled region. Arab nationalists continued to look primarily to the Soviet Union for support against Israel.

Guatemala saw the most publicized CIA intervention of the Eisenhower years (see Map 27.1). In that impoverished Central American country—where 2 percent of the population held 72 percent of all farmland and the

American-based United Fruit Company owned vast banana plantations—a fragile democracy took root in 1944. President Jácobo Arbenz Guzmán, elected in 1950, aggressively pursued land reform, encouraged the formation of trade unions, and tried to buy (at assessed value) enormous acreage that United Fruit owned but did not cultivate. The company demanded far more compensation for this land than Guatemala offered and, having powerful friends in the administration (CIA director Dulles had sat on United Fruit's board of directors), it began lobbying intensively for U.S. intervention, linking land-reform programs to international communism. The CIA spent $7 million training Guatemalan dissidents in neighboring Honduras.

U.S. intervention began when the Navy stopped Guatemala-bound ships and seized their cargoes, and on June 14, 1954, the U.S.-trained antigovernment force invaded from Honduras. Guatemalans resisted by seizing United Fruit buildings, but U.S. Air Force bombing gave the invaders cover. Guatemala appealed in vain to the United Nations for help, while Eisenhower publicly

MAP 27.1 The United States in the Caribbean, 1948–66 U.S. military intervention and economic presence grew steadily in the Caribbean following World War II. After 1960, opposition to the Cuban Revolution dominated U.S. Caribbean policies.

denied any knowledge of CIA involvement. A newly appointed Guatemalan leader, Carlos Castillo Armas, flew to the Guatemalan capital in a U.S. embassy plane. In the widespread terror that followed, unions were outlawed and thousands were arrested. United Fruit circulated photos of Guatemalans murdered by the invaders, mislabeling them "victims of communism." In 1957, Castillo Armas was assassinated, initiating a decades-long civil war between military factions and peasant guerrillas.

Vice President Nixon declared that the new Guatemalan government had earned "the overwhelming support of the Guatemalan people"—a boast belied by events in Guatemala and by the resentment that the United States aroused throughout Latin America. In 1958, while Nixon made a "goodwill" tour of the region, angry mobs stoned his limousine in Caracas, Venezuela. U.S. actions had in fact triggered an anti-American backlash.

The global anti-Communist strategy that the Truman and Eisenhower administrations embraced led to American backing of France's desperate attempt to maintain its colonial empire in Indochina (see Chapter 26).

Read the Document

Dwight D. Eisenhower, "Dien Bien Phu" (1954) at **www.myhistorylab.com**

From 1950 to 1954, the United States poured $2.6 billion in military aid (about three-quarters of the total French costs) and CIA assistance into the fight against the nationalist Vietminh movement, led by Communist Ho Chi Minh. When in March 1954, Vietminh forces surrounded 25,000 French troops at Dien Bien Phu, France pleaded for direct American intervention. Secretary of State Dulles and Vice President Nixon, among others, called for using tactical nuclear weapons and U.S. ground troops to rescue the French. But Eisenhower, remembering Korea, refused. "I can conceive of no greater tragedy," he said, "than for the United States to become engaged in all-out war in Indochina."

Still, Eisenhower feared that the loss of one country to communism would inevitably lead to the loss of others. "You have a row of dominoes set up," he said, "and you knock over the first one and what will happen to the last one is the certainty that it will go over quickly." This so-called domino theory meant that the "loss" of Vietnam would threaten other Southeast Asian nations (Laos, Thailand, and the Philippines) and perhaps even India and Australia. After the French surrender at Dien Bin Phu, an international conference in Geneva established a cease-fire and a "temporary" division into a Communist northern state and a non-Communist southern state. National elections and reunification were promised in 1956. But the United States refused to sign the accord. Instead, the Eisenhower administration created the Southeast Asia Treaty Organization (SEATO), a NATO-like and U.S.-dominated security pact including the United States, Great Britain, France, Australia, New Zealand, Thailand, the Philippines, and Pakistan.

Ngo Dinh Diem, who quickly emerged as South Vietnam's president, was a former Japanese collaborator and a Catholic in a 90 percent Buddhist country. Supported by Eisenhower, Diem refused to permit the promised 1956 elections, knowing that the popular hero Ho Chi Minh would easily win. American economic and military aid, along with covert CIA activity, kept the increasingly isolated Diem in power. His corrupt and repressive policies alienated many peasants. By 1959, his Saigon regime faced a civil war against the thousands of peasants who were joining guerrilla bands to drive him out. Eisenhower's commitment of military advisers and economic aid to South Vietnam, based on Cold War assumptions, had laid the foundation for the Vietnam war of the 1960s.

The Affluent Society

With the title of his influential book *The Affluent Society* (1958), economist John Kenneth Galbraith labeled postwar America. Galbraith observed that American capitalism had worked "quite brilliantly" in the years since World War II. But Americans, he argued, needed to spend less on personal consumption and devote more public funds to schools, medical care, culture, and social services. For most Americans, however, strong economic growth was the defining fact of the postwar period, and a fierce desire for consumer goods and the "good life" permeated American culture. The deeply held popular belief in the right to a continuously expanding economy and a steadily rising standard of living—even against the backdrop of global Cold War anxieties—shaped American social and political life.

Subsidizing Prosperity

During the Eisenhower years, the federal government played a crucial role in subsidizing programs that helped millions of Americans achieve middle-class status. Federal aid helped people to buy homes, attend colleges and technical schools, and live in new suburbs. Much of this assistance expanded on programs begun during the New Deal and World War II. The Federal Housing Administration (FHA), established in 1934, extended the government's role in subsidizing the housing industry by insuring long-term mortgage loans to private lenders for home building. By putting "the full faith and credit" of the federal government behind residential mortgages, the FHA attracted new private capital into home building and revolutionized the industry. A typical FHA mortgage required less than 10 percent for a down payment and spread low-interest monthly payments over thirty years. In addition, homeowners benefited from the provision in the Internal Revenue Code (dating back to 1913) that allowed the deduction of all forms of interest payments from taxes. The mortgage interest deduction was the most important middle-class tax benefit for millions of postwar home buyers.

Yet FHA policies had long-range drawbacks. FHA insurance went overwhelmingly to new residential developments. FHA policy favored the construction of single-family projects while discouraging multiunit housing,

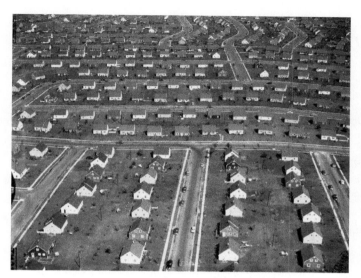

An aerial view of 1950s tract houses in the suburban development of Levittown, New York. Mass production techniques were key to providing affordable housing in the new postwar suburbs—but they required a "cookie cutter" approach to architecture, with little or no variation among the houses.

refused loans to repair older structures and rental units, and required for any loan guarantee an "unbiased professional estimate" rating of the property, the prospective borrower, and the neighborhood. In practice, these estimates resulted in blatant discrimination against racially mixed communities. Bluntly, the FHA's Underwriting Manual warned: "If a neighborhood is to retain stability, it is necessary that properties shall continue to be occupied by the same social and racial classes." Thus, the FHA reinforced racial and income segregation.

Most suburbs were built as planned communities. One of the first, Levittown, opened in 1947 in Hempstead, Long Island, on 1,500 acres of former potato fields. Developer William Levitt, who described his firm as "the General Motors of the housing industry," was the first entrepreneur to bring mass-production techniques to home building. All building materials were precut and prefabricated at a central factory, and then assembled on-site into houses by largely unskilled, nonunion labor. In this way, Levitt put up hundreds of identical houses each week. Eventually, Levittown encompassed more than 17,000 houses and 82,000 people. Yet in 1960 not one of Levittown's residents was African American, and owners who rented out their homes were told to specify that their houses would not be "used or occupied by any person other than members of the Caucasian race" (see Communities in Conflict).

The 1944 Servicemen's Readjustment Act—the G.I. Bill of Rights—made an unprecedented impact on American life. In addition to educational grants, the act gave returning veterans low-interest mortgages and business loans, thus subsidizing suburban growth as much as the postwar expansion of higher education. By 1956, of the roughly 15.4 million military veterans of World War II,

12.4 million, or 78 percent, received some form of benefits from the law. Over 2 million enrolled in colleges and universities, and nearly 6 million received vocational training. Another 3 million got loans to run businesses and farms.

Another key boost to postwar growth, especially in suburbs, came from the National Interstate and Defense Highways Act of 1956. It is significant that the program was sold to the country partly as a civil defense measure (supposedly to facilitate evacuating American cities in case of nuclear attack). The act originally authorized $32 billion to build a national interstate highway system. By 1972, the program had become the single largest public works program in American history, laying out 41,000 miles of highway at a cost of $76 billion. New taxes on gasoline, oil, tires, buses, and trucks paid for the program; the money was held in a Highway Trust Fund separately from general revenue. Federal subsidies for interstate highway construction stimulated both the automobile industry and suburb building and helped transform the American landscape with motels, fast-food outlets, and other businesses servicing road-tripping Americans. The interstate also accelerated the decline of American mass transit and of older cities. By 1970, the nation possessed the world's best roads—and one of the world's worst public transportation systems.

Cold War jitters also prompted the federal government to launch new initiatives to aid education. The Soviet launch of the *Sputnik* satellite in the fall of 1957 dealt a body-blow to Americans' confidence in the superiority of their technology and education; officials, pundits, and educators alike worried that the country might be lagging behind the Soviets in training scientists and engineers. With bipartisan congressional support, the administration pledged to strengthen support for educating American students in mathematics, science, and technology. The National Defense Education Act (NDEA) of 1958 allocated $280 million in grants—tied to matching grants from the states—for state universities to upgrade their science facilities. The NDEA also created low-interest loans for college students (who had to repay only half the amount if they went on to teach in elementary or secondary school after graduation), and fellowship support for graduate students planning to go into college and university teaching.

In a broader sense, the postwar economy floated on a sea of Cold War–justified military spending. At the height of the Korean war, defense expenditures swallowed up about half the federal budget, or 14 percent of GNP; after Korea, though military spending declined, by 1960 defense contracts still constituted about 10 percent of GNP. That spending provided an enormous boost to defense-industry employers like Boeing and Douglas Aircraft and created hundreds of thousands of new jobs.

●●─[Read the Document
National Defense Education Act (1958) at **www.myhistorylab.com**

COMMUNITIES in CONFLICT

Integrating Levittown, Pennsylvania

The construction of mass-produced suburban communities represented a crucial shift in the lives of millions of postwar American families. The opportunity to own a new home—one that often came with brand-new appliances such as refrigerators and ranges—proved enormously attractive. The availability of low-cost mortgages through the Federal Housing Administration (FHA) and the Veterans Administration (VA) provided a key boost into the middle-class world of home ownership. Builder William J. Levitt spearheaded this explosive expansion of suburbia by developing cheap prefabricated construction and creating Levittown, New York (with 17,500 homes on Long Island) and Levittown, Pennsylvania (with 15,500 homes just north of Philadelphia).

Most of the new postwar suburbs were racially segregated by a combination of local law and longstanding custom. Levitt was blunt about his belief in the business necessity for all-white communities. "As a Jew," he said, "I have no room in my mind or heart for racial prejudice. But I have come to know that if I sell to a Negro family, then 90 to 95 percent of our white customers will not buy into the community. That is their attitude, not ours."

Levitt and other builders had no say over the resale of houses. In August 1957, William Myers, an African American veteran of World War II, purchased a home in Levittown, Pennsylvania. When he and his wife and three small children moved in, they sparked an angry and violent response from some of their neighbors. Unlike the Deep South, northern communities did not live under the rules of legal segregation. The opposition to integration in places like Levittown revealed that racial prejudice was by no means limited to the South. In 1959, the New Jersey Appellate Court, considering a discrimination lawsuit brought by two African Americans, ruled that a third Levittown being built in that state could not bar African Americans from purchasing homes. Incidents like the one described here were fairly widespread in northern suburbs, and they foreshadowed the fierce political and legal battles over de facto segregation that would become an important element of the civil rights movement.

A news account describes the opposition faced by the Myers family as they moved into Levittown. A more in-depth feature on the incident includes a variety of views expressed by members of the community.

"Police Rout 400 at Negro's Home" (August 20, 1957)

Levittown, Pa.—State troopers armed with riot clubs broke up a disorderly crowd of 400 persons who had gathered here tonight to protest the purchase of a house by a Negro family.

The crowd, mostly teenagers, started to assemble at 6 P.M. near the home of Mr. and Mrs. William Myers Jr., the first Negroes to purchase a dwelling in this development. The Negro family moved into its home today in the Dogwood Hollow section of the 15,500 house development.

Despite an order barring the Dogwood Hollow section from all but residents and persons with business in the neighborhood, more people filtered into the area and the crowd numbered 400 at 9 P.M. There were derisive shouts and someone threw a stone, which struck a state trooper. Lieutenant M. J. Wicker [in charge of the state police contingent] announced over a loud speaker in a police car: "I will not tolerate this. I'll give you ten minutes to move out and go back to your homes."

> "Now we're here to stay."

The crowd refused to move and ten minutes later the police moved toward them. When the police used their clubs, poking and swinging, the crowd ran toward Haines Road, a block away. One man stopped to fight but was subdued and arrested. Some of the young girls in the group cried and there were shouts of "Gestapo" and "Is this Communist Russia?" The crowd thinned and at 10:30 o'clock there were only 150 left.

The incident tonight was the latest of several protest meetings by the residents of the community. The meetings had been forbidden as illegal assemblages.

Mr. Myers, an equipment tester for a refrigeration concern in nearby Trenton, N.J. moved some furniture into the $11,000 house a week ago. The next evening, shortly after the Myerses had left, two windows in the living room were smashed by persons in a crowd of more than 300.

Gov. George M. Leader denounced the stone throwing and assigned the state police at the request of C. Leroy Murray, sheriff of Bucks County. Today, a newly formed citizens' group, the Levittown Betterment Committee, declared that it would continue to hold protest meetings in defiance of Mr. Murray's edict.

Earlier today, when the Myerses walked into their home carrying some suitcases, towels and other small articles, Mr. Myers said: "Now we're here to stay."

- **What underlying assumptions about race relations do you find among white opponents to the integration of Levittown, Pennsylvania?**

- **How are economic arguments used to justify resistance to African Americans as neighbors?**

Reactions: "When a Negro Family Moved into a White Community" (August 30, 1957)

What happens when a Negro family buys a home and moves into a Northern community that has always had an all white population? This sprawling development of 16,000 homes just north of Philadelphia is finding out the hard way. It is a story of a peaceful community suddenly turned upside down by racial tension and unaccustomed turbulence.

Up till now, Levittown—with 55,000 residents—has been a quiet place. It was built between 1951 and 1955 by William J. Levitt, a real estate developer who also built the community of the same name on Long Island, N.Y.

No Negroes had ever lived in Levittown until August. Then William Myers, Jr., and his wife moved here from neighboring Bloomsdale Gardens, a racially integrated housing development. They are Negroes, parents of three small children.

Citizens committees—one favoring racial segregation for Levittown and another in favor of racial integration—quickly sprang up. The Levittown Betterment Association, formed among the Myerses' new neighbors, announced as its purpose the removal of the Negro family from the community by peaceful means. The Citizens' Committee for Levittown, composed of church and civic groups and backed by Quaker churchmen, appealed for an end to the violence and acceptance of the Myerses.

Almost overnight, Levittown residents whose principal concerns had been their homes and gardens and the cost of living found themselves on opposite sides of the fence in a king-sized row. Lewis Wechsler, who lives in the house next door, expresses one viewpoint. Of the Myerses he says: "They have a right to live here the same as any other American." Mr. Wechsler, a machinist, works in a plant across the Delaware River in Trenton, N.J.

James McDaniel, who lives on nearby Dogwood Drive, is one who doesn't like what has happened. A steelworker, he came north from Tennessee, and works in the big Fairless plant of U.S. Steel north of here. "We don't like Negroes living in the neighborhood," says Mr. McDaniel. "One family maybe is all right, but after one moves in others come. You hear a lot of talk among Negroes over at the plant that if the Myers family stays they'll move here, too. We don't like it, but there's nothing we can do about it legally."

George Bessam, a bachelor, also has a job at Fairless. What are his feelings on the racial storm that has struck Levittown? "I really don't have any objections to colored people, but I don't think they ought to live in white neighborhoods," he says. "A lot of people moved into Levittown from Philadelphia and other places for just one reason—to get away from colored people in their old neighborhoods. Now they're up against this—colored people moving into Levittown, too. I just don't think it ought to happen. And I

"Just say that I'm against it and I don't like it."

think all this police stuff is terrible—people getting hit over the head by police clubs when they're just trying to see that they get their rights," adds Mr. Bessam.

Champney Bernauer lives with his family in Levittown's Willowood section. He's a salesman, is against Negroes moving into the community. "I know how I feel about this thing," he says, "but you couldn't print what I would have to say. Just say that I'm against it and I don't like it. What anyone can do about it, I don't know."

On the opposite side of the fence are the civic groups like the Citizens' Committee for Levittown, headed by Rev. Ray Harwick of Levittown's Evangelical and Reformed Church of the Reformation. "An overwhelming majority of our neighbors," the committee reports, "have been calmly accepting the Myerses move, regardless of whether they personally support or oppose the Myerses decision."

On taking up residence in his new home, Mr. Myers is quoted as having said he would try to be "a good neighbor." After all the trouble began, he is reported to have decided to stay put "if at all possible" and to have voiced the hope that he would be allowed to bring up his children in the community. "Pressure can't be any greater than it is now," he reportedly said.

The Levittown Betterment Association, which opposes the settling of the Myerses in the community, has indicated that it would try to raise the money to buy out the Negro family.

Real estate men say privately that Negroes never will be allowed in Levittown in any numbers. They point out that this community is one of low and medium-priced homes occupied for the most part by young couples just getting a start as homeowners. Such people, it is held, are touchy about things like property values, which they believe will drop precipitously when Negroes move into a neighborhood.

SOURCE: *U.S. News & World Report*, August 30, 1957. Copyright © 1957 U.S. News & World Report. Reprinted by permission of Wrights Media, Inc.

New military bases, along with the growing aviation industry, spurred enormous economic and population growth across communities in southern California, around Seattle and Charleston, and on New York's Long Island. Military spending, which many associated with high-paying jobs and prosperous communities, thus acquired enormous local political support and powerful patrons in Congress, all devoted to keeping federal contracts flowing into their districts.

Suburban Life

For millions of Americans, the Great Depression and World War II had meant squeezing into cramped apartments or run-down houses, often sharing space with relatives and boarders. Suburban home owning was irresistibly alluring for them, especially when home builders threw into the deal new appliances—gas ranges, refrigerators, washers, and dryers. Unquestionably, suburban living meant a huge improvement in material conditions for many postwar American families, and the suburban boom strengthened the domestic ideal of the nuclear family as the model for American life. The image of the perfect suburban wife—efficient, patient, always charming—permeated television, movies, and magazines. Suburban domesticity was usually presented as women's only path to happiness and fulfillment.

That glowing image often masked a stifling existence defined by housework, child care, and boredom. In the late 1950s, Betty Friedan, a wife, mother, and journalist, began a systematic survey of her Smith College classmates. She found "a strange discrepancy between the reality of our lives as women and the image to which we were trying to conform." Extending her research, in 1963 Friedan published her landmark book *The Feminine Mystique,* which gave voice to the silent frustrations of suburban women and helped to launch a new feminist movement.

For millions of suburban families, only two incomes could yield the middle-class life. The expansion of the female labor force—from 17 million in 1946 to 22 million in 1958—was a central economic fact of the post–World War II years. By 1960, 40 percent of women were employed full-time or part-time, and 30 percent of married women looked to supplement the family income and ensure a solidly middle-class standard of living (see Figure 27.1).

The powerful postwar rebirth of American religion was strongly associated with suburban living. In 1940, less than half the American population belonged to institutional churches; by the mid-1950s, nearly three-quarters called themselves church members, and a church-building boom was part of the nation's suburban expansion. Best-selling religious authors like the Presbyterian pastor Norman Vincent Peale and the Roman Catholic bishop Fulton J. Sheen (who also appeared on TV) offered a shallow blend of spiritual reassurance and "the power of positive thinking," stressing individual solutions to problems and opposing social or political activism. Billy Graham's

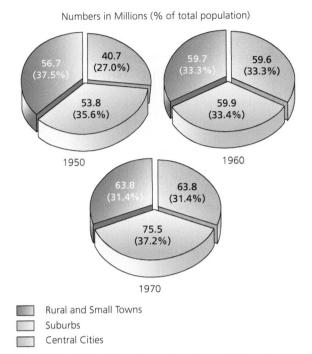

Numbers in Millions (% of total population)

Rural and Small Towns
Suburbs
Central Cities

FIGURE 27.1 The Growth of the Suburbs, 1950–70 Suburban growth, at the expense of older inner cities, was one of the key social trends in the twenty-five years following World War II. By 1970, more Americans lived in suburbs than in either inner cities or rural areas.

SOURCE: Adapted from U.S. Bureau of the Census, Current Censuses, 1930–1970 (Washington, DC: U.S. Government Printing Office, 1975).

hugely popular "Crusades for Christ" brought the religious revival to millions while warning of godless communism. Most popular religious writers emphasized the importance of belonging, of fitting in—an appeal that meshed perfectly with the conventional aspirations of suburban social life and with the ideal of family-centered domesticity.

California—so often the national trendsetter—came to embody postwar suburban life, centered on the automobile. Cars were a necessity for commuting to work. California led the nation in creating automobile-oriented facilities: motels ("motor hotels"), drive-in movies, drive-through fast-food eateries and banks, and parking-lot-encircled shopping malls. In Orange County, southeast of Los Angeles, the "centerless city" emerged as the dominant form of community. The experience of one woman resident there was typical: "I live in Garden Grove, work in Irvine, shop in Santa Ana, go to the dentist in Anaheim, my husband works in Long Beach, and I used to be the president of the League of Women Voters in Fullerton" (see Figure 27.2).

Contemporary journalists, novelists, and social scientists fed the popular image of suburban life as essentially dull, conformist, and peopled exclusively by the educated

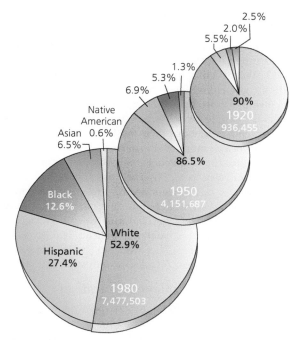

FIGURE 27.2 L.A. County Population 1920–80

middle class. John Cheever, for example, won the National Book Award for *The Wapshot Chronicle* (1957), a novel set in fictional Remsen Park, "a community of four thousand identical homes." Yet these writers (who were largely urban by birth and residence) tended to obscure the real class and ethnic differences among and between different suburban communities. Many new suburbs had a distinctively blue-collar cast. Milpitas, California, for example, grew up around a Ford auto plant about fifty miles outside San Jose. Its residents were blue-collar assembly-line workers and their families, not the stereotypical salaried, college-educated, white-collar employees. Self-segregation and zoning ordinances gave some new suburbs distinctively Italian, Jewish, or Irish ethnic identities, similar to older urban neighborhoods. For millions of new suburbanites, architectural and psychological conformity was an acceptable price to pay for the comforts of home ownership, a small plot of land, and a sense of security and status.

See the Map
Population Shifts, 1940–1950 at
www.myhistorylab.com

Organized Labor and the AFL-CIO

By the mid-1950s, American trade unions reached a historic high point in their penetration of the labor market, reflecting enormous gains made during the organizing drives in core mass-production industries during the New Deal era and World War II. Whereas only one in eight nonagricultural workers were union members on the eve of the Great Depression, twenty-five years later the figure

stood at one in three. Union influence in political life, especially within the Democratic Party, had also increased. Yet the Republican sweep to power in 1952 meant that for the first time in a generation organized labor was without an ally in the White House. New leaders in the nation's two major labor organizations, the American Federation of Labor (dominated by old-line construction and craft unions) and the Congress of Industrial Organizations (new unions in mass-production industry), pushed for a merger of the two rival groups as the way to protect and build on the movement's recent gains.

George Meany, the brusque, cigar-chomping head of the AFL, seemed the epitome of the modern labor boss. Originally a plumber, he had worked his way through the AFL bureaucracy and had played a leading role on the National War Labor Board during World War II. An outspoken anti-Communist, Meany pushed the AFL closer to the Democratic Party but took pride in never having been on a strike or a picket line. Unions, he believed, must focus on improving the economic well-being of their members. Meany's counterpart in the CIO was Walter Reuther, originally a tool-and-die maker in the auto shops of Detroit. Reuther had come to prominence as a leader of the United Automobile Workers during the tumultuous organizing drives of the 1930s and 1940s. Reuther believed strongly that American unions ought to stand for something beyond the bread-and-butter needs of their members. His support of a broader social vision, including racial equality, aggressive union organizing, and expansion of the welfare state, reflected the more militant tradition of the CIO unions. Despite their differences, both Meany and Reuther believed a merger of their two organizations offered the best strategy for the labor movement. In 1955, the newly combined AFL-CIO brought some 12.5 million union members under one banner, with Meany as president and Reuther as director of the Industrial Union Department.

The merger marked the apex of trade union membership, and after 1955 its share of the labor market began a slow but steady decline. For millions of workers and their families in well-paying manufacturing jobs, union membership helped bring the trappings of middle-class prosperity: home ownership, higher education for children, travel, and a comfortable retirement. But the AFL-CIO showed little commitment to bringing unorganized workers into the fold. Scandals involving union corruption and racketeering hurt the labor movement's public image. In 1959, after highly publicized hearings into union corruption, Congress passed the Landrum-Griffin Act, which widened government control over union affairs and further restricted union use of picketing and secondary boycotts during strikes.

While union membership as a percentage of the total workforce declined, important growth did take place in new areas, reflecting a broader shift in the American workplace from manufacturing to service jobs. During the 1950s and 1960s, union membership among public sector employees, especially at the state and local levels, increased dramatically as millions of civil servants, postal employees, teachers, police, and firefighters joined unions for the first time.

Lonely Crowds and Organization Men

Perhaps the most ambitious and controversial critique of postwar suburban America was sociologist David Riesman's *The Lonely Crowd* (1950). Riesman argued that modern America had given birth to a new kind of character type, the "other-directed" man. Previously the nation had cultivated "inner-directed" people—self-reliant individualists who from early in life had internalized self-discipline and moral standards. By contrast, the "other-directed" person typical of the modern era was peer-oriented. Morality and ideals came from the overarching desire to conform. Americans, Riesman thought, were now less likely to take risks or act independently. Their thinking and habits had come to be determined by cues they received from the mass media.

Similarly, William H. Whyte's *Organization Man* (1956), a study of the Chicago suburb of Park Forest, offered a picture of people obsessed with fitting into their communities and jobs. In place of the old Protestant ethic of hard work, thrift, and competitive struggle, Whyte believed, middle-class suburbanites now strove mainly for a comfortable, secure niche in the system. They held to a new social ethic, he argued: "a belief in the group as the source of creativity; a belief in 'belongingness' as the ultimate need of the individual."

The most radical critic of postwar society, and the one with the most enduring influence, was Texas-reared sociologist C. Wright Mills. In *White Collar* (1951), Mills analyzed the job culture that typified life for middle-class salaried employees, office workers, and bureaucrats. "When white collar people get jobs," he wrote, "they sell not only their time and energy, but their personalities as well. They sell by the week or month their smiles and their kindly gestures, and they must practice the prompt repression of resentment and aggression." In *The Power Elite* (1956), Mills argued that a small, interconnected group of corporate executives, military men, and political leaders had come to dominate American society. The arms race in particular, pursued in the name of Cold War policies, had given an unprecedented degree of power to what President Eisenhower later termed the military-industrial complex.

The Expansion of Higher Education

American higher education grew explosively after the war, creating the system of postsecondary training that still exists. This expansion both reflected and reinforced other postwar social trends. The number of students enrolled in colleges and universities climbed from 2.6 million in 1950 to 3.2 million in 1960, and then more than doubled—to 7.5 million—by 1970, as the baby boomers reached college

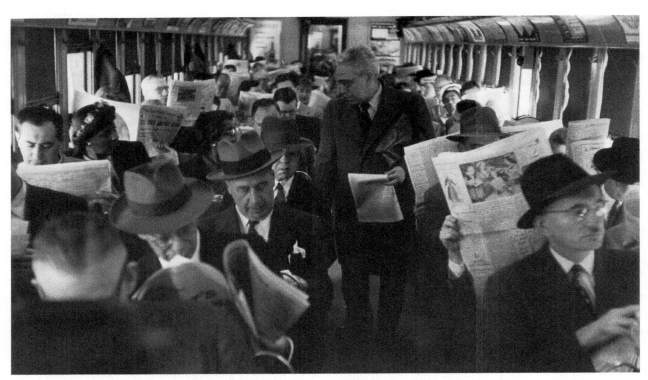

A crowded commuter train in Philadelphia, ca. 1955. The rapid growth of suburbs in the postwar era made commuting to work, either by mass transit or auto, a routine part of life for millions of Americans.

age. Most of these new students attended greatly enlarged state university systems.

College students enjoyed a deferment from the draft, which normally faced young men soon after they finished high school. (If college graduates married and became fathers, or entered graduate or professional school, they could usually count on being deferred until they were past draft age, at twenty-six.) In this sense, college marked an important class line in postwar America. Colleges and universities by and large accepted the values of postwar corporate culture. By the mid-1950s, 20 percent of all college graduates majored in business or similar fields.

A college degree opened a gateway to the middle class. It became a requirement for a whole range of expanding white-collar occupations in banking, insurance, real estate, advertising and marketing, and corporate management in general. Most administrators accommodated large business interests, which were well represented on university boards of trustees. Universities themselves were increasingly run like businesses, with administrators adopting the language of input-output, cost effectiveness, and quality control.

Health and Medicine

Dramatic improvements in medical care allowed many Americans to enjoy longer and healthier lives. New antibiotics such as penicillin, the "wonder drug" of World War II, became widely available to the general population. Federal support for research continued after the war with the reorganization of the National Institutes of Health in 1948.

Perhaps the most celebrated achievement of postwar medicine was the victory over poliomyelitis. Between 1947 and 1951, this disease, which usually crippled those it did not kill, struck an average of 39,000 Americans every year. In 1955, Jonas Salk pioneered the first effective vaccine against the disease, using a preparation of killed virus. A nationwide program of polio vaccination, later supplemented by the oral Sabin vaccine, virtually eliminated polio by the 1960s.

The Polio Epidemic and Polio Vaccine at **www.myhistorylab.com**

Yet access to "wonder drugs" and advanced medical techniques was not shared equally. More sophisticated treatments and expensive new hospital facilities sharply increased the costs of health care. Poor and many elderly Americans found themselves unable to afford modern medicine. Thousands of communities, especially in rural areas and small towns, lacked doctors or decent hospital facilities. The decline of the general practitioner—the family doctor—meant that fewer (and eventually no) physicians made house calls; for treatment, people went to hospital emergency rooms or outpatient clinics.

The American Medical Association (AMA), which certified medical schools, did nothing to increase the flow of new doctors. The number of physicians per 100,000 people actually declined between 1950 and 1960; doctors trained in other countries made up the shortfall. The AMA also lobbied hard against efforts to

expand government responsibility for the public's health. President Truman had proposed national health insurance, to be run along the lines of Social Security, and President Eisenhower later proposed a program that would offer government assistance to private health insurance companies. Both proposals were denounced as "socialized medicine" by the AMA. Until 1965, with the advent of Medicare (for the elderly) and Medicaid (for the poor)—both of which it also opposed—the AMA successfully fought any form of direct federal involvement in health care.

The growing prestige of science was not universally welcomed. In 1948, an Indiana University entomologist, Alfred Kinsey, published his landmark book on American sexuality, *Sexual Behavior in the Human Male,* followed five years later by *Sexual Behavior in the Human Female.* Based on personal interviews with thousands of subjects, Kinsey's books became best sellers—but offered a picture of American sexual behavior that many found shocking. He found, for example, that roughly half of American women had engaged in premarital sex and that some 10 percent of American men were homosexual. Overall Kinsey's work revealed that each new generation of young Americans was more sexually active than the preceding cohort, irrespective of class or gender. Many critics objected to what they saw as Kinsey's claim to objectivity and his reduction of sexual experience to statistics. Yet in the long run Kinsey's scientific approach helped to demystify sex and led to more openness about human sexuality.

Youth Culture

The term "teenager," describing someone between thirteen and nineteen, entered standard usage only at the end of World War II. According to the *Dictionary of American Slang,* the United States is the only country having a word for this age group and the only country to consider it "a separate entity whose influence, fads, and fashions are worthy of discussion apart from the adult world." During the fifteen years after World War II, unprecedented attention was paid to America's adolescents. Adults expressed deep fears about everything from teenage sexuality and juvenile delinquency to young people's driving habits, hairstyles, and choice of clothing. At the same time, advertisers and businesses pursued the disposable income of America's affluent youth with a vengeance.

The Youth Market

Birthrates had accelerated gradually during the late 1930s and more rapidly during the war years. The children born in those years had by the late 1950s grown into the original teenagers, the older siblings of the celebrated baby boomers of 1946–64. They came of age in a society that, compared with that of their parents and the rest of the world, was uniquely affluent. Converging, the demographic growth of teens and the postwar economic expansion created an explosive and profitable youth market.

Manufacturers and advertisers rushed to cash in on the special needs and desires of young consumers: cosmetics, clothing, radios and phonographs, and cars.

Life magazine summarized the new power of the youth market in 1959: "Counting only what is spent to satisfy their special teenage demands," the magazine reported, "the youngsters and their parents will shell out about $10 billion this year, a billion more than the total sales of GM." In addition, advertisers and market researchers found that teenagers often played a critical, if hard to measure, role as "secret persuaders" in a family's large purchase decisions. Specialized market research organizations, such as Eugene Gilbert & Company and Teen-Age Survey Incorporated, sprang up to serve business clients eager to attract teen consumers and instill brand loyalty.

To many parents, the emerging youth culture was a dangerous threat to their authority. One mother voiced this fear in a revealing, if slightly hysterical, letter to *Modern Teen* magazine:

> Don't you realize what you are doing? You are encouraging teenagers to write to each other, which keeps them from doing their school work and other chores. You are encouraging them to kiss and have physical contact before they're even engaged, which is morally wrong and you know it. You are encouraging them to have faith in the depraved individuals who make rock and roll records when it's common knowledge that ninety percent of these rock and roll singers are people with no morals or sense of values.

The special status of teenagers was also made apparent to the public by the increasing uniformity of public school education. In 1900, about one of every eight teenagers was in school; six out of eight were by the 1950s. Psychologists wrote guidebooks for parents, with titles like Dorothy Baruch's *How to Live with Your Teenager* (1953) and Paul Landis's *Understanding Teenagers* (1955). Traditional sources of adult authority and socialization— the marketplace, schools, child-rearing manuals, the mass media—all reinforced the notion of teenagers as a special community, united by age, rank, and status.

"Hail! Hail! Rock 'n' Roll!"

The demands of the new teen market, combined with structural changes in the postwar American mass media, reshaped the nation's popular music. As television broadcasting rapidly replaced radio as the center of family entertainment, people began using radios in new ways. There was a rapid rise in the production of car radios and portable transistor radios as listeners increasingly tuned them in for diversion

from or an accompaniment to other activities. By 1956, some 2,700 AM radio stations were on the air across the United States, with about 70 percent of their broadcast time devoted to record shows.

In the recording industry, change was in the air. Small independent record labels led the way in aggressively recording African American rhythm-and-blues artists. Atlantic Records, in New York, developed the most influential galaxy of artists, including Ray Charles, Ruth Brown, the Drifters, Joe Turner, LaVerne Baker, and the Clovers. Chess, in Chicago, had the blues-based, singer-songwriter-guitarists Chuck Berry and Bo Diddley, as well as the "doo-wop" group the Moonglows. In New Orleans, Imperial recorded the veteran pianist-singer Fats Domino, while Specialty unleashed on the world the outrageous Little Richard. On radio, over jukeboxes, and in record stores, all these African American artists "crossed over," adding millions of white teenagers to their solid base of black fans. In 1954, the music trade magazine *Billboard* noted a trend among white teenagers: "The present generation has not known the rhythmically exciting dance bands of the swing era. It therefore satisfies its hunger for 'music with a beat' in modern r&b (rhythm and blues) groups."

The older, more established record companies had largely ignored black music. They responded to the new trend with slick, toned-down "cover" versions of rhythm-and-blues originals by white pop singers. These were invariably pallid, artistically inferior imitations. While African American artists began to enjoy newfound mass acceptance, there were limits to how closely white kids could identify with black performers. Racism, especially in

The marquee at the Paramount Theater, New York City, advertises Alan Freed's "Holiday of Stars" rock 'n' roll show, 1957. Freed promoted live shows featuring both white and African American performers, attracting enthusiastic mixed race audiences.

so sexually charged an arena as musical performance, was a powerful force in American life. The major labels' superior promotional power, as well as institutional racism in the music business, ensured that white cover versions almost always outsold the black originals. At live shows, however, white and black teenagers often listened and danced together to the music of African American performers. Alan Freed, a white Cleveland DJ, popularized the term *rock 'n' roll* to describe the black rhythm and blues that he played on the air and promoted in live concerts before enthusiastic, racially mixed teen audiences.

The stage was thus set for the arrival of white rock 'n' roll artists who could exploit the new sounds and styles. As a rock 'n' roll performer and recording artist, Elvis Presley reinvented American popular music. His success challenged the old lines separating black music from white and pop from rhythm and blues or country. As a symbol of rebellious youth and as the embodiment of youthful sexuality, Elvis revitalized American popular culture. In his wake came a host of white rock 'n' rollers, many (like him) white Southerners: Jerry Lee Lewis, Buddy Holly, the Everly Brothers, Roy Orbison. The greatest songwriter and most influential guitarist to emerge from this first "golden age of rock 'n' roll" was Chuck Berry, an African American from St. Louis who worked part-time as a beautician and house painter. With humor, irony, and passion, Berry proved especially adept at capturing the teen spirit. Composing hits around the trials and tribulations of school ("School Days"), young love ("Memphis"), and cars ("Maybellene"), Berry created music that defined what it meant to be young in postwar America.

Almost Grown

Teenage consumers remade into their own turf the landscape of popular music. The dollar value of annual record sales nearly tripled between 1954 and 1959, from $213 million to $603 million. New magazines aimed exclusively at teens flourished in the postwar years, focusing on the rituals, pleasures, and sorrows surrounding teenage courtship. Paradoxically, behavior patterns among white middle-class teenagers in the 1950s and early 1960s exhibited a new kind of youth orientation and at the same time a more pronounced identification with adults.

While parents were worrying about the separate world inhabited by their teenage children, many teens seemed determined to become adults as quickly as possible. Postwar affluence multiplied the number of two-car families, making it easier for sixteen-year-olds to win driving privileges formerly reserved for eighteen-year-olds. Girls began dating, wearing brassieres and nylon stockings, and using cosmetics at an earlier age than before—twelve or thirteen rather than fifteen or sixteen. Several factors contributed to this trend, including a continuing decline in the age of menarche (first menstruation), the sharp drop in the age of marriage after World War II, and the precocious social climate of junior high schools (institutions that became widespread only after

1945). "Going steady," derived from the college custom of fraternity and sorority pinning, became commonplace among high schoolers. By the late 1950s, eighteen had become the most common age at which American females married. Teenagers often felt torn between their identification with youth culture and pressures to assume adult responsibilities. Many young people juggled part-time jobs with school and very active social lives—a dilemma for which teen-oriented magazines, music, and movies routinely dispensed advice and sympathy.

Deviance and Delinquency

Many adults blamed rock 'n' roll for the apparent decline of parental control over teens. Much of the opposition to rock 'n' roll, particularly in the South, played on longstanding racist fears of white females being attracted to black music and black performers. The undercurrent beneath all this opposition was a deep anxiety over the more open expression of sexual feelings by both performers and audiences.

Paralleling the rise of rock 'n' roll was a growing concern with an alleged increase in juvenile delinquency. An endless stream of magazine articles, books, and newspaper stories asserted that criminal behavior among the nation's young was chronic. Gang fights, drug and alcohol abuse, car theft, and sexual offenses drew the most attention. The U.S. Senate established a special subcommittee on juvenile delinquency. Highly publicized hearings in 1955 and 1956 convinced much of the public that youthful criminals were terrorizing the country. Although crime statistics do suggest an increase in juvenile crime during the 1950s, particularly in the suburbs, the public perception of the severity of the problem was surely exaggerated.

In retrospect, the juvenile delinquency controversy tells us more about anxieties over family life and the erosion of adult authority than about crime patterns. Teenagers seemed more defined by and loyal to their peer culture than to their parents. A great deal of their music, speech, dress, and style seemed alien and threatening. The growing importance of the mass media in defining youth culture brought efforts to regulate or censor media forms believed to cause juvenile delinquency. In 1954, for example, psychiatrist Fredric Wertham published *Seduction of the Innocent*, arguing that crime comic books incited youngsters to criminal acts. Mass culture, he believed, could overwhelm the traditional influences of family, school, and religion. He led a highly publicized crusade that forced the comic book industry to adopt a code strictly limiting the portrayal of violence and crime.

As reactions to two of the most influential "problem youth" movies of the postwar era indicate, teens and their parents frequently interpreted depictions of youthful deviance in the mass media in very different ways. In *The Wild One* (1954), Marlon Brando played the crude, moody leader of a vicious motorcycle gang. Most adults thought of the film as a critique of mindless gang violence, but many teenagers identified with the Brando character, who, when asked, "What are you rebelling against?" coolly replied, "Whattaya got?" In *Rebel Without a Cause* (1955), James Dean, Natalie Wood, and Sal Mineo played emotionally troubled youths in an affluent California suburb. The movie suggests that parents can cause delinquency when they fail to conform to conventional roles—Dean's father does housework wearing an apron, and his mother is domineering.

Elvis, Brando, and Dean (who died in a car crash at the height of his popularity) were probably the most popular and widely imitated teen idols of the era. For most parents, they were vaguely threatening figures whose sexual energy and lack of discipline placed them outside the bounds of middle-class respectability. For teens, however, they offered an irresistible combination of rough exterior and sensitive core. They embodied, as well, the contradiction of individual rebellion versus the attractions of a community defined by youth.

Mass Culture and Its Discontents

No mass medium ever achieved such power and popularity as rapidly as television. The basic technology for broadcasting visual images with sound had been developed by the late 1930s, but World War II and corporate competition postponed television's introduction to the public until 1946. By 1960, nearly nine in ten American families owned at least one set, which was turned on an average of more than five hours a day. Television reshaped leisure time and political life. It also helped create a new kind of

national community defined by the buying and selling of consumer goods.

Dissident voices challenged the economic trends and cultural conformity of the postwar years. Academics, journalists, novelists, and poets offered a variety of works criticizing the overall direction of American life. These critics of what was dubbed "mass society" were troubled by the premium American culture put on conformity, status, and material consumption. Although a distinct minority, these critics were persistent. Many of their ideas and prescriptions would reverberate throughout the political and cultural upheavals of the 1960s and 1970s, and even into the "culture wars" of the 1980s and beyond.

Television: Tube of Plenty

Television was a radical change from radio, and its development as a mass medium was quicker and less chaotic. The three main television networks—NBC, CBS, and ABC—grew directly from radio corporations. The networks led the industry from the start, rather than following individual stations, as radio had done. Nearly all TV stations were affiliated with one or more of the networks; only a handful of independent stations struggled for survival.

Television not only depended on advertising, but it also transformed the advertising industry. The television business, like radio, was based on the selling of time to advertisers who wanted to reach the mass audiences tuning into specific shows. Radio had offered entire shows produced by and for single sponsors, usually advertisers who wanted a close identification between their product and a star. But the higher costs of television production forced key changes. Sponsors left the production of programs to the networks, independent producers, and Hollywood studios.

Sponsors bought scattered time slots for spot advertisements instead of bankrolling an entire show. Ad agencies switched their creative energy to producing slick thirty-second commercials rather than entertainment programs. A shift from broadcasting live shows to filming them opened up lucrative opportunities for reruns and exports. The total net revenue of the TV networks and their affiliated stations in 1947 was about $2 million; by 1957 it was nearly $1 billion.

The staple of network radio, the comedy-variety show, was now produced visually. The first great national TV hit, *The Milton Berle Show,* followed this format when it premiered in 1948. Radio stars such

A 1950s' family watching *I Love Lucy*, one of the most popular situation comedies in the early days of television. Manufacturers designed and marketed TV sets as living room furniture and emphasized their role in fostering family togetherness.

Fess Parker, the actor who starred as Davy Crockett in Walt Disney's popular television series, greets young fans at New York's Idlewild Airport in 1955. The series generated enormous sales of coonskin caps and other Crockett-inspired merchandise, demonstrating the extraordinary selling power of the new medium of television.

as Jack Benny, Edgar Bergen, George Burns and Gracie Allen, and Eddie Cantor switched successfully to television. Boxing, wrestling, the roller derby, and other sporting events were also quite popular. For a brief time, original live drama flourished on writer-oriented shows such as *Goodyear Television Playhouse* and *Studio One.* In addition, early television featured an array of situation comedies with deep roots in radio and vaudeville.

Set largely among urban ethnic families, early shows like *I Remember Mama, The Goldbergs, The Life of Riley, Life with Luigi,* and *The Honeymooners* often featured working-class families struggling with the dilemmas posed by a consumer society. Most plots turned around comic tensions created and resolved by consumption: contemplating home ownership, going out on the town, moving to the suburbs, buying on credit, purchasing a new car. Generational discord and the loss of ethnic identity were also common themes. To some degree, these early shows mirrored and spoke to the real dilemmas facing families that had survived the Great Depression and World War II and were trying to find their place in a prosperous consumer culture.

By the late 1950s, all the urban ethnic comedy shows were off the air. A new breed of situation comedies presented nonethnic white, affluent, and insular suburban middle-class families. Shows like *Father Knows Best, Leave It to Beaver, The Adventures of Ozzie and Harriet,* and *The Donna Reed Show* epitomized the ideal suburban American family of the day. Their plots focused on genial crises, usually brought on by children's mischief or wives' inability to cope with money matters, but patiently resolved by kindly fathers. Shows aimed explicitly at children, such as *Howdy Doody,* pulled kids into the television orbit at an early age. In retrospect, what is most striking about these shows is what is absent: virtually unrepresented were politics, social issues, cities, white ethnic groups, African Americans, and Latinos.

Television also demonstrated a unique ability to create overnight fads and crazes across the nation. Elvis Presley's 1956 appearances on several network television variety shows, including those hosted by Milton Berle and Ed Sullivan, catapulted him from regional success to international stardom. A memorable example of TV's influence came in 1955 when Walt Disney produced a series of three one-hour shows on the life of frontier legend Davy Crockett. The tremendous success of the series instantly created a $300 million industry of Davy Crockett shirts, dolls, toys, and "coonskin" caps.

Television and Politics

Prime-time entertainment shows carefully avoided any references to the political issues of the day. Network executives bowed to the conformist climate created by the Cold War. Any hint of political controversy could scare off sponsors, ever wary of public protest. Anti-Communist crusaders set themselves up as private watchdogs, warning of alleged subversive influence in the broadcasting industry. Television and advertising executives responded by effectively blacklisting many talented individuals.

As in Hollywood, the Cold War chill severely restricted the range of political discussion on television. Any honest treatment of the conflicts in American society threatened the consensus mentality at the heart of the television business. Even public affairs and documentary programs were largely devoid of substantial political debate. An important exception was journalist Edward R. Murrow's *See It Now* on CBS—but that show was off the air by 1955. Television news did not come into its own until 1963, with the beginning of half-hour nightly network newscasts. Only then did television's extraordinary power to rivet the nation's attention during a crisis become clear.

Some of the ways that TV would alter the nation's political life were already emerging in the 1950s. Television made Democratic senator Estes Kefauver of Tennessee a national political figure through live coverage of his 1951 Senate investigation into organized crime. In 1952, Republican vice presidential candidate Nixon's rambling, emotionally manipulative television appeal to voters— the famous "Checkers" speech (see Chapter 26)—saved his career.

The 1952 election brought the first use of TV political advertising for presidential candidates. The Republican

Party hired a high-powered ad agency, Batten, Barton, Durstine & Osborn (BBD&O), to create a series of short, sophisticated advertisements touting Ike. The BBD&O campaign saturated TV with twenty-second Eisenhower spots for two weeks before Election Day. Ever since, television image-making has been the single most important element in American electoral politics.

Culture Critics

Critics argued that the audiences for the mass media were atomized, anonymous, and detached. The media themselves had become omnipotent, capable of manipulating the attitudes and behavior of the isolated individuals in the mass. Many of these critics achieved great popularity themselves, suggesting that the public was deeply ambivalent about mass culture. One of the best-selling authors of the day was Vance Packard, whose 1957 exposé *The Hidden Persuaders* showed how advertisers exploited motivational research into the irrational side of human behavior. These critics undoubtedly overestimated the media's power. They ignored the preponderance of research suggesting that most people watched and responded to mass media in family, peer group, and other social settings. The critics also missed the genuine vitality and creative brilliance to be found within mass culture: African American music; the films of Nicholas Ray, Elia Kazan, and Howard Hawks; the

Jack Kerouac, founding voice of the Beat literary movement, ca. 1957, the year he published *On the Road*. Kerouac's public readings, often accompanied by live jazz music, underlined the connections between his writing style and the rhythms and sensibilities of contemporary jazz musicians.

experimental television of Ernie Kovacs; even the madcap satire of teen-oriented *Mad* magazine.

Some of the sharpest dissents from the cultural conformity of the day came from a group of writers known collectively as the Beats. Led by the novelist Jack Kerouac and the poet Allen Ginsberg, the Beats shared a distrust of the American virtues of progress, power, and material gain. The Beats' sensibility celebrated spontaneity, friendship, jazz, open sexuality, drug use, and the outcasts of American society. Kerouac, born and raised in a working-class French Canadian family in Lowell, Massachusetts, coined the term *beat* in 1948. It meant for him "weariness with all the forms of the modern industrial state"—conformity, militarism, blind faith in technological progress. Kerouac's 1957 novel *On the Road,* chronicling the tumultuous adventures of Kerouac's circle of friends as they traveled by car back and forth across America, became the Beat manifesto.

Allen Ginsberg had grown up in New Jersey in an immigrant Jewish family. After being expelled from Columbia University, Ginsberg grew close to Kerouac and another writer, William Burroughs. At a 1955 poetry reading in San Francisco, Ginsberg read—actually, chanted—his epic poem *Howl* to a wildly enthusiastic audience. It began:

> *I saw the best minds of my generation destroyed*
> *by madness, starving hysterical naked,*
> *dragging themselves through the negro streets at dawn*
> *looking for an angry fix,*
> *angelheaded hipsters burning for the ancient heavenly*
> *connection*
> *to the starry dynamo in the machinery of night.*

Howl became one of the best-selling poetry books in the history of publishing, and it established Ginsberg as an important new voice in American literature.

Beat writers received a largely antagonistic, even virulent reception from the literary establishment, and the mass media soon trivialized them. A San Francisco journalist coined the word *beatnik,* which by the late 1950s had become popularly associated with scruffy, bearded men and promiscuous women, all dressed in black, sporting sunglasses and berets, and acting rebellious and alienated. By challenging America's official culture, however, Beat writers foreshadowed the mass youth rebellion and counterculture of the 1960s.

The Coming of the New Frontier

In personality, temperament, and public image, no one could have less resembled Dwight Eisenhower—or, for that matter, the beatniks—than John Fitzgerald Kennedy. The handsome son of a prominent, wealthy Irish American diplomat, husband of a fashionable, trendsetting heiress, forty-two-year-old JFK embodied youth, excitement, and sophistication. As only the second Catholic candidate for president—the first was Al Smith in 1928—Kennedy ran under the banner of his self-proclaimed "New Frontier." His liberalism inspired idealism and hope in millions of

young people at home and abroad, and his presidency seemed to embody the call for a new sense of national purpose beyond simply enjoying affluence. In foreign affairs, Kennedy generally followed, and in some respects deepened, the Cold War precepts that dominated postwar policymaking. But by the time of his assassination in 1963, he may have been veering away from the hard-line anti-Communist ideology he had earlier embraced.

The Election of 1960

John F. Kennedy's political career began in Massachusetts, which elected him to the House in 1946 and then the Senate in 1952. Kennedy won the Democratic nomination after a bruising series of primaries in which he defeated party stalwarts Hubert Humphrey of Minnesota and Lyndon B. Johnson of Texas. Vice President Richard M. Nixon, the Republican nominee, had faithfully served the Eisenhower administration for eight years and was far better known than his younger opponent. The Kennedy campaign stressed its candidate's youth and his war-hero image. During his World War II tour of duty in the Pacific, Kennedy had bravely rescued one of his crew after their PT boat had been sunk. Kennedy's supporters made much of his intellectual ability. JFK had won the Pulitzer Prize in 1957 for his book *Profiles in Courage*, which in fact had been written largely by his aides.

The 1960 election featured the first televised presidential debates. Political analysts have long argued over the impact of these four encounters, but agree that they moved television to the center of presidential politics, making image and appearance more critical than ever. Nixon, just recovering from illness, looked nervous, and heat from studio lights made his makeup run and his jowls look unshaven. Kennedy benefited from a confident manner, telegenic good looks, and less propensity to sweat. Both candidates emphasized foreign policy. Nixon defended the Republican record and stressed his maturity and experience. Kennedy hammered away at the alleged—but nonexistent—"missile gap" with the Soviet Union and promised executive leadership full of vigor. ("Vigah," he said in the Boston accent that became his trademark.)

Kennedy squeaked to victory (see Map 27.2), winning by a little more than 100,000 votes out of nearly 69 million cast. By solemnly promising to keep church and state separate, he had countered residual anti-Catholic prejudice among conservative Protestants and suspicious liberals. Although his margin of victory was tiny, Kennedy was a glorious winner. Surrounding himself with prestigious Ivy League academics, Hollywood movie stars, and talented artists and writers, he imbued the presidency with an aura of celebrity. The inauguration brought out a bevy of poets, musicians, and fashionably dressed politicians from around the world. The new administration promised to be exciting and stylish, a modern-day Camelot peopled by heroic young men and beautiful women. The new president's ringing inaugural address

Read the Document
John F. Kennedy, *"Inaugural Address" (1961)* at **www.myhistorylab.com**

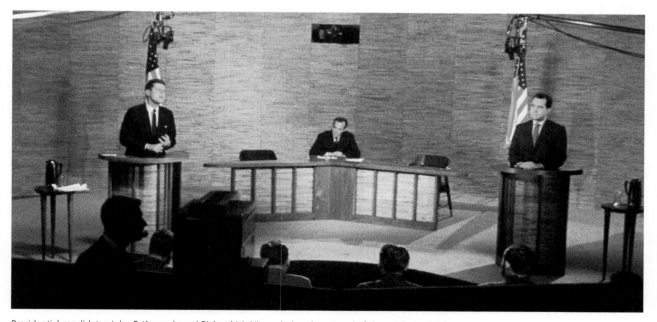

Presidential candidates John F. Kennedy and Richard M. Nixon during the second of three televised debates held during the 1960 election campaign. Moderator Frank McGee sits at a desk upstage, facing a panel of newsmen. Eighty-five million viewers watched at least one of the first-ever televised debates, which both reflected and increased the power of television in the electoral process.

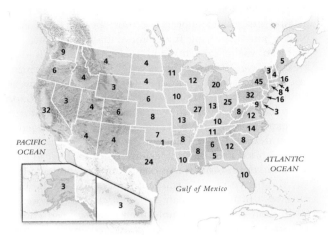

	Electoral Vote (%)	Popular Vote (%)
JOHN F. KENNEDY (Democrat)	303 (56)	34,227,096 (49.7)
Richard M. Nixon (Republican)	219 (41)	34,108,546 (49.5)
Harry F. Byrd (Independent)	15 (3)	501,643 (0.7)

MAP 27.2 The Election of 1960 Kennedy's popular vote margin over Nixon was only a little over 100,000 votes, making this one of the closest elections in American history.

("Ask not what your country can do for you—ask what you can do for your country") resonated through a whole generation of young Americans.

Just before Kennedy took office, President Eisenhower delivered a televised farewell address that included a stark and unexpected warning against what he called (coining a phrase) "the military-industrial complex." Throughout the 1950s, the small numbers of peace advocates in the United States had pointed to the ultimate illogic of Ike's "new look" in national-defense policy. Increasing reliance on nuclear weapons, they argued, did not strengthen national security—it threatened the entire planet with extinction. Peace advocates had demonstrated at military camps, nuclear-test sites, and missile-launching ranges, often getting arrested to make their point. Reports of radioactive fallout around the globe rallied a larger group of scientists and prominent intellectuals against further nuclear testing. Small but well-publicized actions protesting civil defense drills were led by groups such as National Committee for a Sane Nuclear Policy (SANE) and Women Strike for Peace in several big cities.

Eisenhower came to share some of the protesters' anxiety and doubts about the arms race, because he had found it difficult to rein in the "New Look" system he helped create. Frustrated—and disturbed by the incoming Democrats' demands for increased military spending to close the "missile gap"—he used his farewell address to express alarm at the growing influence of a large military and defense-industry establishment. "We annually spend on military security more than the net income of all United States corporations," Eisenhower warned the country. "This conjunction of an immense military establishment and a large arms industry is new in the American experience. The total influence—economic, political, even spiritual—is felt in every city, every State house, every office of the Federal government. . . . Our toil, resources and livelihood are all involved; so is the very structure of our society."

The old soldier understood better than most the dangers of raw military force, and in later years, critics of American foreign policy and budget priorities would adapt the sentiments behind this language. Eisenhower's public posture of restraint and caution in foreign affairs accompanied an enormous expansion of American economic, diplomatic, and military strength. Yet the Eisenhower years also demonstrated the limits of power and intervention in a world that did not always conform to the simple dualistic assumptions of Cold War ideology.

Read the Document
Dwight D. Eisenhower, "Farewell to the Nation" (1961) at **www.myhistorylab.com**

New Frontier Liberalism

As president, John F. Kennedy promised to revive the liberal domestic agenda, stalled since Truman's presidency. His New Frontier advocated such liberal programs as medical care for the elderly, greater federal aid for education and public housing, raising Social Security benefits and the minimum wage, and various antipoverty measures. Yet the thin margin of his victory and stubborn opposition by conservative southern Democrats in Congress made it difficult to achieve these goals. Congress blocked the administration's attempt to extend Social Security and unemployment benefits to millions of uncovered workers. Congress also failed to enact administration proposals for aid to public schools, mass-transit subsidies, and medical insurance for retired workers over sixty-five.

There were a few New Frontier achievements: modest increases in the minimum wage (to $1.25 per hour), Social Security benefits, and $5 billion appropriated for public housing. The Manpower Retraining Act provided $435 million to train the unemployed. The Area Redevelopment Act provided federal funds for rural, depressed Appalachia. The Higher Education Act of 1963 offered aid to colleges for constructing buildings and upgrading libraries.

The Peace Corps was the New Frontier's best-publicized initiative. It sent thousands of mostly young men and women overseas for two-year stints to provide technical and educational assistance to underdeveloped Third World countries. Volunteers set up health care programs, helped villagers modernize farm technology, and taught English. As a force for change, the Peace Corps produced modest results, but it epitomized Kennedy's promise to provide opportunities for service for a new generation of idealistic young people.

Kennedy's Presidential Commission on the Status of Women, led by Eleanor Roosevelt, helped revive attention to women's rights issues. The commission's 1963 report was the most comprehensive study of women's lives ever produced by the federal government. It documented the ongoing discrimination faced by American women in the workplace and in the legal system, as well as the inadequacy of social services such as day care. It called for federally supported day-care programs, continuing education programs for women, and an end to sex bias in Social Security and unemployment benefits. The Equal Pay Act of 1963, a direct result of the commission's work, mandated equal wages for men and women employed in industries engaged in interstate commerce. Kennedy also directed executive agencies to prohibit sex discrimination in hiring and promotion. The work of the commission contributed to a new generation of women's rights activism.

Kennedy took a more aggressive stance on stimulating economic growth and creating new jobs than had Eisenhower. The administration pushed lower business taxes through Congress, even at the cost of a higher federal deficit. The Revenue Act of 1962 encouraged new investment and plant renovation by easing tax depreciation schedules for business. Kennedy also gained approval for lower U.S. tariffs as a way to increase foreign trade. To help keep inflation down, he intervened in the steel industry in 1961 and 1962, pressuring labor to keep its wage demands low and management to curb price increases.

A wholly new realm of government spending also won Kennedy's enthusiastic backing: the space program. The National Aeronautics and Space Administration (NASA) had been established in reaction to *Sputnik*, and in 1961, Kennedy pushed through a greatly expanded space program. Dramatically, he announced the goal of landing an American on the moon by the end of the decade. NASA eventually spent $33 billion before reaching this objective in 1969. This program of manned space flight—the *Apollo* missions, with their science fiction aura—appealed to the public.

Kennedy's longest-lasting achievement as president may have been his strengthening of the executive branch itself. He insisted on direct presidential control of details that Eisenhower had left to advisers and appointees. Moreover, under Kennedy the White House staff assumed many of the decision-making and advisory functions previously held by cabinet members. This arrangement increased Kennedy's authority, since these appointees, unlike cabinet secretaries, escaped congressional oversight and confirmation proceedings. White House aides lacked independent constituencies; their power derived solely from their ties to the president. Kennedy's aides—"the best and the brightest," he called them—dominated policymaking. Kennedy intensified a pattern whereby American presidents increasingly operated through small groups of fiercely loyal aides, often in secret.

Kennedy and the Cold War

During Kennedy's three years as president, his approach to foreign policy shifted from aggressive containment to efforts at easing U.S.–Soviet tensions. Certainly when he first entered office, Kennedy and his chief aides saw their main task as confronting the Communist threat. In his first State of the Union Address, Kennedy told Congress that America must seize the initiative in the Cold War. The nation must "move outside the home fortress, and . . . challenge the enemy in fields of our own choosing." To head the State Department, Kennedy chose Dean Rusk, a conservative former assistant to Truman's secretary of state, Dean Acheson. Secretary of Defense Robert McNamara, a Republican and Ford executive, was determined to streamline military procedures and weapons buying; he typified the technical, cost-efficient, hyperrational approach to policymaking. These and other high officials believed, with Kennedy, that Eisenhower had timidly accepted stalemate when the Cold War could have been won.

Between 1960 and 1962, defense appropriations increased by nearly a third, from $43 billion to $56 billion. JFK expanded Eisenhower's policy of covert operations, deploying the Army's elite Special Forces to supplement covert CIA operations against Third World guerrillas. These soldiers, fighting under the direct orders of the president, could provide "rapid response" to "brush-fire" conflicts where Soviet influence threatened American interests. The Special Forces, authorized by Kennedy to wear the green berets that gave them their unofficial name, reflected the president's desire to acquire greater flexibility, secrecy, and independence in the conduct of foreign policy.

But incidents in Southeast Asia showed there were limits to advancing American interests with covert actions and Green Berets. In Laos, the United States had ignored the 1954 Geneva agreement and installed a friendly, CIA-backed military regime, but it could not defeat Soviet-supported Pathet Lao guerrillas. The president had to arrange with the Soviets to neutralize Laos. In neighboring South Vietnam, a more difficult situation developed when Communist Vietcong guerrillas launched an insurgency against the U.S.-supported Diem regime. Kennedy began sending hundreds of Green Berets and other military advisers to bolster Diem. In May 1961, in response to North Vietnamese aid to the Vietcong, Kennedy ordered a covert action against Ho Chi Minh's northern regime that included sabotage and intelligence gathering.

Kennedy's approach to Vietnam reflected an analysis of the situation in that country by two aides, General Maxwell Taylor and Walt Rostow, who saw things solely through Cold War spectacles. "The Communists are pursuing a clear and systematic strategy in Southeast Asia," Taylor and Rostow concluded, ignoring the inefficiency, corruption, and unpopularity of the Diem government. By 1963, with Diem's army unable to contain the Vietcong rebellion, Kennedy had sent nearly 16,000 support and combat troops to South Vietnam. At that time, a wide spectrum of South Vietnamese society had joined the revolt against the hated Diem, including highly respected Buddhist monks and their students. Americans watched in horror as evening newscasts showed Buddhists burning themselves to death on the streets of Saigon—the ultimate protest against Diem's repressive rule. American press and television also reported the mounting casualty lists of U.S. forces in Vietnam. The South Vietnamese army, bloated by U.S. aid and weakened by corruption, continued to disintegrate. In the fall of 1963, American military officers and CIA operatives stood aside with approval as a group of Vietnamese generals toppled Diem, killing him and his top advisers. It was the first of many coups that racked the South Vietnamese government over the next few years.

In Latin America, where millions of impoverished peasants were forced to relocate to already-overcrowded cities, various revolutionary movements were also gaining ground—and Kennedy looked for ways to forestall them. In 1961, he unveiled the "Alliance for Progress," a ten-year, $100 billion plan to spur economic development in Latin America. The United States committed $20 billion to the project with the Latin nations responsible for the rest. The main goals included greater industrial growth and agricultural productivity, a more equitable distribution of income, and improved health and housing.

Kennedy saw the Alliance for Progress as a Marshall Plan that would benefit Latin America's poor and middle classes. It did help raise growth rates in Latin American economies. But the expansion in export crops and in consumption by the tiny upper class did little to aid the poor or encourage democracy. The United States hesitated to challenge the dictators and extreme conservatives who were its staunchly anti-Communist allies. Thus, the alliance soon degenerated into just another foreign-aid program, incapable of generating genuine social change.

The Cuban Revolution and the Bay of Pigs

The direct impetus for the Alliance for Progress was the 1959 Cuban Revolution, which loomed over Latin America—inspiring the left and alarming the right. The U.S. economic domination of Cuba, beginning with the Spanish-American War (see Chapter 20), had continued through the 1950s. American-owned businesses controlled all of Cuba's oil production, 90 percent of its mines, and roughly half of its railroads and sugar and cattle industries. Havana, the island's capital, was an attractive tourist center for Americans, but U.S. crime syndicates shared control—with dictator Fulgencio Batista—of the island's lucrative gambling, prostitution, and drug trade. As a response, in the early 1950s a peasant-based revolutionary movement, led by a middle-class student named Fidel Castro, began gaining strength in the rural districts and mountains outside Havana.

On New Year's Day 1959, after years of guerrilla war, the rebels entered Havana and, amid great public rejoicing, seized power. For a brief time, Castro seemed a hero in North America as well. The *New York Times* had conducted sympathetic interviews with Castro in 1958, while he was still fighting in Cuba's mountains. The CIA and President Eisenhower shared none of this exuberance. Castro's land-reform program, involving the seizure of acreage from the tiny minority that controlled much of the fertile land, threatened to set an example for other Latin American countries. Although Castro had not yet joined the Cuban Communist Party, he turned to the Soviet Union after the United States withdrew economic aid. He began to sell sugar to the Soviets and soon nationalized American-owned oil companies and other enterprises. Eisenhower established an economic boycott of Cuba in 1960 and then severed diplomatic relations.

Kennedy inherited from Eisenhower plans for a U.S. invasion of Cuba, including the secret arming and training of Cuban exiles. The CIA drafted the invasion plan, which was based on the assumption that a U.S.-led invasion would trigger a popular uprising and bring down Castro. Kennedy went along with the plan, but at the last moment decided not to supply Air Force cover for the invaders. On April 17, 1961, a ragtag army of 1,400 counterrevolutionaries led by CIA operatives landed at the Bay of Pigs on Cuba's southern coast. Castro's efficient and loyal army easily subdued them.

The debacle revealed that the CIA, blinded by Cold War assumptions, had failed to understand the Cuban Revolution. There was no popular uprising against Castro. An embarrassed Kennedy reluctantly took the blame for the disaster, and his administration was censured time and again by Third World delegates in the United Nations. American liberals criticized Kennedy for plotting Castro's overthrow, while conservatives blamed him for not supporting the invasion. Despite the failure, Kennedy remained committed to getting rid of Castro.

The botched invasion had strengthened "Fidel's" standing among the urban poor and peasants, already attracted by his programs of universal literacy and medical care. As Castro stifled internal opposition, many Cuban intellectuals and professionals fled to the United States. These middle-class émigrés would transform Miami from a retirement resort into a bustling entrepreneurial center, but the growing Cuban presence in electoral-vote-rich Florida also created a powerful lobby for rigid anti-Castro U.S. policies. Even before the end of Kennedy's administration, the CIA's support for anti-Castro operations included at least eight attempts to assassinate Fidel, and the U.S. economic embargo against Cuba continues to this day.

The 1962 Missile Crisis

The aftermath of the Bay of Pigs led to the Cold War's most serious superpower confrontation: the Cuban missile crisis of October 1962. Frightened by U.S. belligerency,

Castro asked Soviet Premier Khrushchev for military help. Khrushchev responded in the summer of 1962 by shipping to Cuba a large amount of sophisticated weaponry, including intermediate-range nuclear missiles capable of hitting Washington, the Northeast, and the Midwest. In early October, American U-2 reconnaissance planes found camouflaged missile silos dotting the island. Several Kennedy aides and the Joint Chiefs of Staff demanded an immediate bombing of these missile sites, arguing that the Soviet move had decisively eroded the United States' strategic global advantage. The president and his advisers pondered their options in a series of tense meetings. Kennedy's aggressive attempts to exploit Cuba in the 1960 election and the Bay of Pigs disaster came back to haunt him: He worried that critics would accuse him of weakness in failing to stand up to the Soviets.

Shoppers in an appliance store watch President John F. Kennedy deliver an address to the nation during the Cuban missile crisis in October 1962. Kennedy's presidency coincided with the emergence of television as the nation's dominant mass medium.

Kennedy went on national television on October 22 to announce discovery of the missile sites. He publicly demanded the removal of all missiles and proclaimed a naval "quarantine" of offensive military equipment shipped to Cuba. (This was actually a blockade; Kennedy avoided the word because a blockade is an act of war.) Requesting an emergency meeting of the UN Security Council, he promised that any missiles launched from Cuba would bring "a full retaliatory response upon the Soviet Union." For a grim week, Americans wondered whether the long-dreaded nuclear Armageddon was imminent. Eyeball to eyeball, each superpower waited for the other to blink. On October 26 and 27, Khrushchev blinked, ordering twenty-five Soviet ships off their course to Cuba, thus avoiding a challenge to the U.S. Navy.

Read the **Document**

John F. Kennedy, Cuban Missile Crisis Address (1962) at
www.myhistorylab.com

Khrushchev offered to remove the missiles in return for a pledge from the United States not to invade Cuba and later added a demand for removal of American weapons from Turkey, which is as close to the Soviet Union as Cuba is to the United States. Secretly, Kennedy assured Khrushchev that the United States would dismantle its obsolete missiles in Turkey. On November 20, after weeks of delicate negotiations, Kennedy announced the withdrawal of Soviet missiles and bombers from Cuba. He also pledged to respect Cuban sovereignty and promised not to invade the island.

The crisis had passed. The Soviets, determined not to be intimidated again, began the largest weapons buildup in their history. For his part, Kennedy, perhaps chastened by this brush with nuclear disaster, made important gestures toward peaceful coexistence with the Soviets. In a June 1963 address at American University, Kennedy called for a rethinking of Cold War diplomacy. Both sides, he said, had been "caught up in a vicious and dangerous cycle in which suspicion on one side breeds suspicion on the other, and new weapons beget counterweaons."

Shortly after, Washington and Moscow set up a "hot line"—a direct phone connection to permit instant communication during times of crisis. More substantial was the Limited Nuclear Test-Ban Treaty, signed in August 1963 by the United States, the Soviet Union, and Great Britain. The treaty prohibited above-ground, outer-space, and underwater nuclear weapons tests, easing global anxieties about radioactive fallout. But underground testing continued to accelerate for years. The limited test ban was perhaps more symbolic than substantive, a psychological breakthrough in East–West relations after three particularly tense years.

By November 1963, the situation in South Vietnam was deteriorating; Diem's overthrow and murder in a U.S.-backed coup was symptomatic of U.S. failure to secure an anti-Communist alternative to Ho Chi Minh's revolutionary movement. Kennedy understood this. There are some indications that he was thinking of cutting losses, perhaps after winning reelection in 1964; there are other signs that he was preparing to escalate the U.S. commitment. Most likely, he meant to keep all options open. But we will never know what he would have done about Vietnam.

The Assassination of President Kennedy

The assassination of John F. Kennedy in Dallas on November 22, 1963, sent the entire nation into shock and mourning. Just forty-six years old and president for only three years, Kennedy quickly ascended to martyrdom in

Televising a National Tragedy

The assassination of President John F. Kennedy on Friday, November 22, 1963, marked the emerging power of television as a medium capable of focusing the entire nation's attention on an extraordinary news event.

Kennedy had traveled to Texas on November 21 to shore up popularity in a state crucial to his reelection hopes for 1964. Only local stations covered the presidential

arrival and motorcade. But once the president had been shot and declared dead, the networks cut into regular programming, combining live coverage with videotape from local stations. The hasty inauguration of Vice President Lyndon B. Johnson aboard *Air Force One* was not televised, but widespread dissemination of still photos showed Americans how the constitutional process of succession proceeded side by side with the personal grief of the president's widow, Jacqueline Kennedy.

The next day, Saturday, audiences watched television coverage of world leaders arriving in Washington for the presidential funeral. On Sunday, NBC offered live coverage of the accused assassin, Lee Harvey Oswald, being transferred from police custody to the county jail. Millions were stunned to suddenly see Jack Ruby, a shadowy Dallas underworld figure, emerge from the crowd and shoot Oswald himself to death—the first nationally televised murder.

On Monday, November 25, virtually the entire nation watched Kennedy's televised funeral: the ceremony at the National Cathedral and the procession to Arlington Cemetery. The images of the Kennedy family, especially five-year-old Caroline and three-year-old John Jr. saluting, lent a quiet dignity amid deep mourning. Critic Marya Mannes wrote of the four days of television coverage: "This was not viewing. This was total involvement. . . . I stayed before the set, knowing—as millions knew—that I must give myself over entirely to an appalling tragedy, and that to evade it was a treason of the spirit."

- **What strikes you as most powerful about these images from more than four decades ago?**

- **Can you think of any recent national events that have brought the nation together via television coverage?**

- **How has that coverage changed—or remained similar—in terms of both techniques and subjects covered?**

1950 David Riesman publishes *The Lonely Crowd*

1952 Dwight D. Eisenhower is elected president, defeating Adlai Stevenson

1953 CIA installs Riza Shah Pahlavi as monarch of Iran

1954 Vietminh force French surrender at Dien Bien Phu

CIA overthrows government of Jácobo Arbenz Guzmán in Guatemala

United States explodes first hydrogen bomb

1955 Jonas Salk pioneers vaccine for polio

James Dean stars in the movie *Rebel Without a Cause*

1956 Congress passes the National Interstate and Defense Highways Act

Elvis Presley signs with RCA

Eisenhower is reelected, defeating Stevenson a second time

Allen Ginsberg publishes *Howl*

1957 Soviet Union launches *Sputnik*, first space-orbiting satellite

Jack Kerouac publishes *On the Road*

1958 National Defense Education Act authorizes grants and loans to college students

1959 Nikita Khrushchev visits the United States

1960 Soviets shoot down U-2 spy plane and cancel planned summit meeting with Eisenhower

John F. Kennedy is elected president, defeating Richard Nixon

Almost 90 percent of American homes have television

1961 President Kennedy creates "Green Berets"

Bay of Pigs invasion of Cuba fails

1962 Cuban missile crisis brings the world to the brink of a superpower confrontation

1963 Report by the Presidential Commission on the Status of Women documents ongoing discrimination

Betty Friedan publishes *The Feminine Mystique*

Limited Nuclear Test-Ban Treaty is signed

President Kennedy is assassinated; Lyndon B. Johnson becomes president

---

the nation's consciousness. Millions had identified his strengths—intelligence, optimism, wit, charm, coolness under fire—as those of American society. In life, Kennedy had helped put television at the center of American politics. In the aftermath of his death, television riveted a badly shocked nation. One day after the assassination, the president's accused killer, an obscure misfit named Lee Harvey Oswald, was himself gunned down before television cameras covering his arraignment in Dallas. Two days later, tens of millions watched the televised spectacle of Kennedy's funeral, trying to make sense of the brutal murder (see Seeing History). Although a special commission headed by Chief Justice Earl Warren found the killing to be the work of Oswald acting alone, many Americans doubted this conclusion. Kennedy's death gave rise to a host of conspiracy theories, none of which seems provable.

We will never know, of course, what Kennedy might have achieved in a second term. In his 1,000 days

as president, he demonstrated a capacity to change and grow in office. Having gone to the brink during the missile crisis, he managed to launch new initiatives toward peaceful coexistence. At the time of his death, relations between the United States and the Soviet Union were more amicable than at any time since the end of World War II. Much of the domestic liberal agenda of the New Frontier would be finally implemented by Kennedy's successor, Lyndon B. Johnson, who dreamed of creating a Great Society.

Conclusion

America in 1963 still enjoyed its postwar economic boom. To be sure, millions of Americans, particularly African Americans and Latinos, did not share in the good times. But millions had managed to reach the middle class since the early 1950s. An expanding economy, cheap energy, government subsidies, and dominance in the global marketplace had made the "the good life" available to more Americans than ever. The postwar "American dream" promised home ownership, college education, secure employment at decent wages, affordable appliances, and the ability to travel—for one's children if not for one's self. The nation's public culture—its schools, mass media, politics, advertising—presented a powerful consensus based on the idea that the American dream was available to all who would work for it.

The presidential transition of 1961—from grandfatherly war hero Dwight Eisenhower to charismatic young war hero Jack Kennedy—symbolized for many a generational shift as well. By 1963, young people had more influence than ever before in shaping the nation's political life, its media images, and its burgeoning consumer culture. Kennedy himself inspired millions of young Americans to pursue public service and to express their idealism. But even by the time of Kennedy's death, the postwar consensus and the conditions that nurtured it were beginning to unravel.

Review Questions

1. How did Cold War politics and assumptions shape American foreign policy in these years? What were the key interventions the United States made in Europe and the Third World?

2. How did postwar economic prosperity change the lives of ordinary Americans? Which groups benefited most and which were largely excluded from "the affluent society"?

3. What role did federal programs play in expanding economic opportunities?

4. Analyze the origins of postwar youth culture. How was teenage life different in these years from previous eras? How did popular culture both reflect and distort the lives of American youth?

5. How did mass culture become even more central to American everyday life in the two decades following World War II? What problems did various cultural critics identify with this trend?

6. Evaluate the domestic and international policies associated with John F. Kennedy and the New Frontier. What continuities with Eisenhower-era politics do you find in the Kennedy administration? How did JFK break with past practices?

Recommended Reading

Glenn C. Altschuler, *All Shook Up: How Rock 'n' Roll Changed America* (2003). The best new social history of rock 'n' roll, with excellent coverage of the generational and racial controversies surrounding the new music.

Glenn C. Altschuler and Stuart M. Blumin, *The GI Bill: A New Deal for Veterans* (2009). A new and comprehensive history of the "GI Bill of Rights," demonstrating the enormous economic and social impact of this key postwar program.

James L. Baughman, *Same Time, Same Station: Creating American Television, 1948–1961* (2007). The best recent account of the emergence of television as the nation's dominant mass medium with emphasis on the influence of advertising.

Lizabeth Cohen, *A Consumers' Republic: The Politics of Mass Consumption in Postwar America* (2003). An ambitious, deeply researched overview of how postwar Americans negotiated the tensions between expanding opportunities for consumption and traditional ideals of citizenship and political activism.

Michael Dobbs, *One Minute to Midnight: Kennedy, Khrushchev, and Castro on the Brink of Nuclear War* (2008). A new narrative history of the 1962 Cuban missile crisis that focuses on how initial bellicosity on both sides quickly gave way to frantic efforts to prevent nuclear war.

Gary Donaldson, *The First Modern Campaign: Kennedy, Nixon, and the Election of 1960* (2007). Recent and deeply researched analysis of the 1960 election as the template for our media-dominated politics.

Lawrence Freedman, *Kennedy's Wars: Berlin, Cuba, Laos, and Vietnam* (2000). Analyzes JFK's foreign policy, emphasizing the context of Cold War liberalism.

David M. P. Freund, *Colored Property: State Policy and White Racial Politics in Suburban America* (2007). A recent detailed study demonstrating how legal policies and government regulations helped inscribe segregation in so many postwar American suburbs.

David E. Kaiser, *American Tragedy: Kennedy, Johnson, and the Origins of the Vietnam War* (2000). The most detailed account yet of how the contradictions of Cold War thinking pushed policymakers in three administrations toward an unnecessary and unwinnable war.

Elaine Tyler May, *Homeward Bound: American Families in the Cold War* (1988). A thoughtful social history linking family life of the 1950s with the political shadow of the Cold War.

PEARSON myhistorylab™ Connections

Reinforce what you learned in this chapter by studying the many documents,
images, maps, review tools, and videos available at www.myhistorylab.com.

Read and Review

✓● Study and Review Chapter 27

●●● Read the Document

Dwight D. Eisenhower, "Dien Bien Phu" (1954)

National Defense Education Act (1958)

John F. Kennedy, "Inaugural Address" (1961)

Dwight D. Eisenhower, "Farewell to the
   Nation" (1961)

John F. Kennedy, Cuban Missile Crisis
   Address (1962)

👁● See the Map Population Shifts, 1940–1950

Research and Explore

●●● Read the Document

Exploring America: How to Lie with Statistics

Profiles
   John Foster Dulles
   Jack Kerouac

Whose History Is It?: Any Old Way You Choose It:
   Rock and Roll as History, Myth, and Commerce

●● Watch the Video

Newsreel: JFK 1917-1963

The Polio Epidemic and Polio Vaccine

((●● Hear the Audio

Hear the audio files for Chapter 27 at
www.myhistorylab.com.

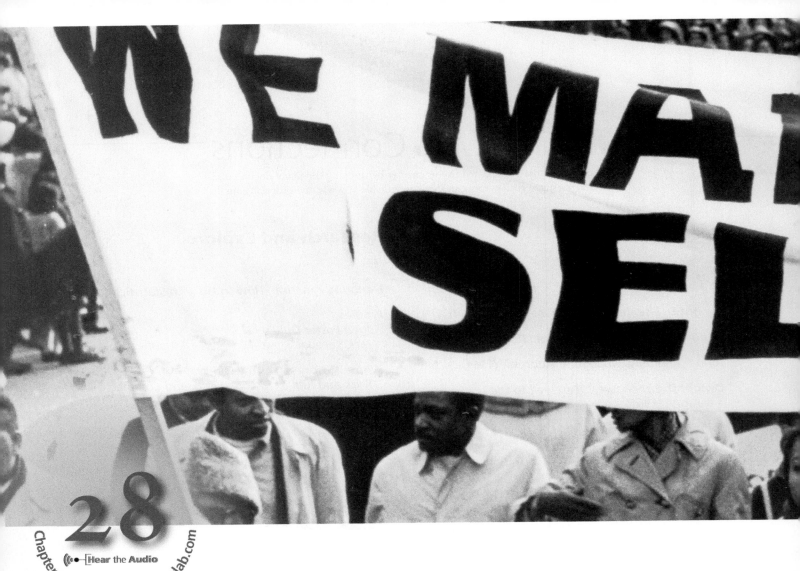

The Civil Rights Movement 1945–1966

CHAPTER OUTLINE

American Communities 817
The Montgomery Bus Boycott: An African American Community Challenges Segregation

Origins of the Movement 819
Civil Rights After World War II
The Segregated South
Brown v. Board of Education
Crisis in Little Rock

No Easy Road to Freedom, 1957–62 825
Martin Luther King Jr. and the SCLC
Sit-Ins: Greensboro, Nashville, Atlanta
SNCC and the "Beloved Community"
The Election of 1960 and Civil Rights
Freedom Rides
The Albany Movement: The Limits of Protest

The Movement at High Tide, 1963–65 831
Birmingham
JFK and the March on Washington
LBJ and the Civil Rights Act of 1964

Mississippi Freedom Summer
Malcolm X and Black Consciousness
Selma and the Voting Rights Act of 1965

Civil Rights Beyond Black and White 842
Mexican Americans and Mexican Immigrants
Puerto Ricans
Japanese Americans
Indian Peoples
Remaking the Golden Door: The Immigration and Nationality Act of 1965

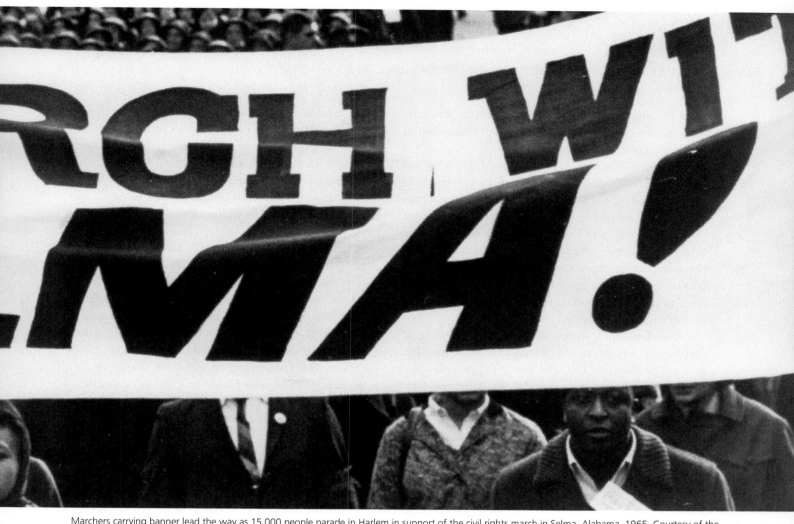

Marchers carrying banner lead the way as 15,000 people parade in Harlem in support of the civil rights march in Selma, Alabama, 1965. Courtesy of the Library of Congress.

The Montgomery Bus Boycott: An African American Community Challenges Segregation

On December 1, 1955, Rosa Parks, a seamstress and well-known activist in the African American community of Montgomery, Alabama, was taken from a bus, arrested, and jailed for refusing to give up her seat to a white passenger. Composing roughly half the city's 100,000 people, Montgomery's black community had long endured the humiliation of a strictly segregated bus system. Drivers could order a whole row of black passengers to stand for one white person. Black people had to pay their fares at the front of the bus, then step back outside and reenter through the rear door.

Protesting Mrs. Parks's arrest, more than 30,000 African Americans answered a hastily organized call to boycott the city's buses. On the day of the boycott, a steady stream of cars and pedestrians jammed the streets around Holt Street Baptist Church. By early evening, a patient, orderly, and determined crowd of more than 5,000 African Americans packed the church and spilled over onto the sidewalks. Loudspeakers had to be set up for the thousands who could not squeeze inside. After a brief prayer and a reading from scripture, all attention focused on the twenty-six-year-old minister, the Reverend Martin Luther King Jr., who rose to address the gathering. "We are here this evening," he began slowly, "for serious business. We are here in a general

AMERICAN Communities

817

sense because first and foremost we are American citizens, and we are determined to apply our citizenship to the fullness of its means."

Sensing the crowd's expectant mood, Dr. King got down to specifics and described Mrs. Parks's arrest. As he quickened his cadence and drew shouts of encouragement, he seemed to gather strength and confidence from the crowd. "You know, my friends, there comes a time when people get tired of being trampled over by the iron feet of oppression. There comes a time, my friends, when people get tired of being flung across the abyss of humiliation, when they experience the bleakness of nagging despair."

Even before Dr. King concluded, it was clear to all that the bus boycott would continue for more than just a day. The minister laid out the key principles that would guide the boycott—nonviolence, Christian love, unity. His brief but stirring address created a powerful sense of communion. "If we are wrong, justice is a lie," he told the clapping and shouting throng. "And we are determined here in Montgomery to work and fight until justice runs down like water and righteousness like a mighty stream." Dr. King made his way out of the church amid waves of applause and rows of hands reaching out to touch him.

Dr. King's prophetic speech catapulted him into leadership of the Montgomery bus boycott—but he had not started what would become known simply as the Movement. When Rosa Parks was arrested, local activists with deep roots in the black protest tradition galvanized the community with the idea of a boycott. Mrs. Parks herself had served for twelve years as secretary of the local NAACP chapter. She was a committed opponent of segregation and was thoroughly respected in the city's African American community. E. D. Nixon, president of the Alabama NAACP and head of the local Brotherhood of Sleeping Car Porters union, saw Mrs. Parks's arrest as the right case on which to make a stand. It was Nixon who brought Montgomery's black ministers together on December 5 to coordinate an extended boycott of city buses. They formed the Montgomery Improvement Association (MIA) and chose Dr. King as their leader. Significantly, Mrs. Parks's lawyer was Clifford Durr, a white liberal with a history of representing black clients. His politically active wife Virginia, for whom Mrs. Parks worked as a seamstress, had been a longtime crusader against the poll tax, which prevented many blacks from voting. And two

white ministers, Rev. Robert Graetz and Rev. Glenn Smiley, would offer important support to the MIA.

While Nixon organized black ministers, Jo Ann Robinson, an English teacher at Alabama State College, spread the word to the larger black community. Robinson led the Women's Political Council (WPC), an organization of black professional women founded in 1949. With her WPC allies, Robinson wrote, mimeographed, and distributed 50,000 copies of a leaflet telling the story of Mrs. Parks's arrest and urging all African Americans to stay off city buses on December 5. They did. Now the MIA faced the more difficult task of keeping the boycott going. Success depended on providing alternate transportation for the 30,000 to 40,000 maids, cooks, janitors, and other black working people who needed to get to work.

The MIA coordinated an elaborate system of car pools, using hundreds of private cars and volunteer drivers to provide as many as 20,000 rides each day. Many people walked. Local authorities, although shocked by the discipline and sense of purpose shown by Montgomery's African American community, refused to engage in serious negotiations. With the aid of the NAACP, the MIA brought suit in federal court against bus segregation in Montgomery. Police harassed boycotters with traffic tickets and arrests. White racists exploded bombs in the homes of Dr. King and E. D. Nixon. The days turned into weeks, then months, but still the boycott continued. All along, mass meetings in Montgomery's African American churches helped boost morale with singing, praying, and stories of individual sacrifice. The spontaneous remark of one elderly woman, refusing all suggestions that she drop out of the boycott on account of her age, became a classic refrain of the Movement: "My feets is tired, but my soul is rested."

The boycott reduced the bus company's revenues by two-thirds. In February 1956, city officials obtained indictments against King, Nixon, and 113 other boycotters under an old law forbidding hindrance to business without "just cause or legal excuse." A month later, King went on trial. A growing contingent of newspaper reporters and TV crews from around the country watched as the judge found King guilty, fined him $1,000, and released him on bond pending appeal. But on June 4, a panel of three federal judges struck down Montgomery's bus segregation ordinances as unconstitutional. On November 13, the Supreme Court affirmed the district court ruling. After eleven hard months and against all odds, the boycotters had won.

1. What were the legal and political origins of the African American civil rights struggle?

2. What accounts for Martin Luther King's rise to leadership?

3. How did student protesters and direct action shape the civil rights struggle in the South?

4. How did the civil rights movement intersect with national politics in the 1950s and 1960s?

5. What did the Civil Rights Act of 1964 and Voting Rights Act of 1965 accomplish?

6. How did America's other minorities respond to the African American struggle for civil rights?

FOCUS Questions

1945–1966

The boycotters' victory inspired a new mass movement for African American civil rights. A series of local struggles to dismantle segregation—in the schools of Little Rock, the department stores of Atlanta, the lunch counters of Greensboro, the streets of Birmingham—would coalesce into a broad-based national movement at the center of American politics. By 1963, the massive March on Washington would win the endorsement of President John F. Kennedy, and his successor, Lyndon B. Johnson, would push through the landmark Civil Rights Act and Voting Rights Act.

The struggle to end legal segregation took root in scores of southern cities and towns. African American communities led these fights, developing a variety of tactics, leaders, and ideologies. With white allies, they engaged in direct-action protests such as boycotts, sit-ins, and mass civil disobedience, as well as strategic legal battles in state and federal courts. The Movement was not without its inner conflicts. Tensions between local campaigns and national civil rights organizations flared up regularly. Within African American communities, long-simmering distrust between the working classes and rural folk on the one hand and middle-class ministers, teachers, and business people on the other sometimes threatened to destroy political unity. Generational conflicts pitted African American student activists against their elders. But overall, the civil rights movement created new social identities for African Americans, inspired a new "rights consciousness" among other minority groups, and profoundly changed American society.

Montgomery

AMERICAN·· Communities

Origins of the Movement

The civil rights movement arose out of the aspirations and community strength of African Americans. Its deepest roots lay in the historic injustices of slavery, racism, and segregation. African Americans' experiences during and immediately after World War II laid the foundation for the civil rights struggle of the 1950s and 1960s.

Watch the Video
The Civil Rights Movement at
www.myhistorylab.com

Civil Rights after World War II

Between 1939 and 1945, almost 1 million black men and women served in the armed forces. The discrepancy between fighting totalitarianism abroad while enduring segregation and racism in the military embittered many combat veterans and their families. Nearly 2 million African Americans worked in defense plants, and another 200,000 entered the federal civil service. Black union membership doubled, reaching more than 1.2 million. African American newspapers like the *Pittsburgh Courier* fought for the "Double V" campaign—victory over fascism abroad and over segregation at home. But wartime stress on national unity largely muted political protests. With the war's end, African Americans and their white allies determined to push ahead for full political and social equality.

The wartime boom spurred a mass northward migration of nearly a million black Southerners. Forty-three northern and western cities saw their black population double during the 1940s. Although racial discrimination in housing and employment was by no means absent in northern cities, greater economic opportunities and political freedom continued to attract rural African Americans after the war. With the growth of African American communities in cities like New York, Chicago, and Detroit, black people gained significant influence in urban political machines. Within industrial unions such as the United Automobile Workers and the United Steel Workers, white and black workers learned the power of biracial unity in fighting for better wages and working conditions.

After the war, civil rights issues returned to the national political stage for the first time since Reconstruction. Black voters had already begun to switch their allegiance from the Republicans to the Democrats during the New Deal. A series of symbolic and substantive acts by the Truman administration solidified that shift. In 1946, Truman created a President's Committee on Civil Rights. Its 1947 report, *To Secure These Rights*, set out an ambitious program to end racial inequality: creating a permanent civil rights division in the Justice Department, protecting voting rights, passing antilynching legislation, and challenging laws that permitted segregated housing. Although he publicly endorsed nearly all these proposals, Truman introduced no legislation to make them law.

Truman and his advisers walked a political tightrope on civil rights. They understood that black voters in several key northern states would be pivotal in the 1948 election. At the same time, they worried about the loyalty of white southern Democrats adamantly opposed to changing the racial status quo. In July 1948, the president made his boldest move on behalf of civil rights, issuing an executive order ending segregation in the armed forces. Later that summer, when liberals forced the Democratic National Convention to adopt a strong civil rights plank, outraged southern delegates walked out and nominated Governor Strom Thurmond of South Carolina for president on a States' Rights ticket. Thurmond carried four southern states in the election. But even with the help of more than 70 percent of the northern black vote, Truman barely managed to defeat Republican Thomas E. Dewey in November. The deep split over race issues would continue to wrack the national Democratic Party for a generation.

Electoral politics was not the only arena for civil rights work. During the war, membership in the National Association for the Advancement of Colored People had mushroomed from 50,000 to 500,000. Working- and middle-class urban black people provided the backbone of this new membership. The NAACP conducted voter registration drives and lobbied against discrimination in housing and employment. Its Legal Defense and Education Fund, vigorously led by special counsel Thurgood Marshall, mounted several significant legal challenges to segregation laws. In *Morgan* v. *Virginia* (1946), the Supreme Court used the interstate-commerce clause to declare segregation on interstate buses unconstitutional. Other Supreme Court decisions struck down all-white election primaries, racially restrictive housing covenants, and the exclusion of blacks from law and graduate schools.

The NAACP's legal work demonstrated the potential for using federal courts in attacking segregation. Courts were one place where black people, using the

Charlie Parker (alto sax) and Miles Davis (trumpet) with their group in 1947, at the Three Deuces Club in New York City. Parker and Davis were two creative leaders of the "bebop" movement of the 1940s. Working in northern cities, boppers reshaped jazz music and created a distinct language and style that were widely imitated by young people. They challenged older stereotypes of African American musicians by insisting that they be treated as serious artists.

constitutional language of rights, could make forceful arguments that could not be voiced in Congress or at political conventions. Federal enforcement of court decisions was often lacking, however. In 1947, a group of black and white activists tested compliance with the *Morgan* decision by traveling on a bus through the Upper South. This "Freedom Ride" was cosponsored by the Christian pacifist group Fellowship of Reconciliation (FOR) and its recent offshoot, the Congress of Racial Equality (CORE), which was devoted to interracial, nonviolent direct action. In North Carolina, several riders were arrested and sentenced to thirty days on a chain gang for refusing to leave the bus.

Two symbolic "firsts" raised black expectations and inspired pride. In 1947, Jackie Robinson broke the color barrier in major league baseball, winning rookie-of-the-year honors with the Brooklyn Dodgers. Robinson's courage in the face of racist taunts from fans and players paved the way for the other black ballplayers who soon followed him into the big leagues. In 1950, United Nations diplomat Ralph Bunche won the Nobel Peace Prize for arranging the 1948 Arab-Israeli truce. Bunche, however, later declined an appointment as undersecretary of state because he did not want to subject his family to Washington, DC's humiliating segregation laws.

Watch the Video
Jackie Robinson and the Integration of Baseball at **www.myhistorylab.com**

Cultural change could have political implications as well. In the 1940s, African American musicians created a new form of jazz that revolutionized American music and asserted a militant black consciousness. Although black musicians had pioneered swing and earlier styles of jazz, white bandleaders and musicians had reaped most of the recognition and money. Black artists such as Charlie Parker, Dizzy Gillespie, Thelonius Monk, Bud Powell, and Miles Davis revolted against the standard big-band format of swing, preferring small groups and competitive jam sessions to express their musical visions. The new music, dubbed "bebop," demanded a much more sophisticated knowledge of harmony and melody and featured more complex rhythms and extended improvisation than did previous jazz styles. The "boppers" insisted on independence from the white-defined norms of show business. Serious about both their music and the way it was presented, they refused to cater to white stereotypes of grinning, easygoing black performers.

The Segregated South

In the postwar South, still home to over half the nation's 15 million African Americans, the racial situation had changed little since the Supreme Court sanctioned "separate but equal" segregation in *Plessy* v. *Ferguson* (see Chapter 20). In practice, segregation meant separate but unequal. A tight web of state and local ordinances enforced strict separation of the races in schools, restaurants, hotels, movie theaters, libraries, restrooms, hospitals, and even cemeteries, and the facilities for black people were consistently inferior to those for whites. There were no black policemen in the Deep South and only a handful of black lawyers.

In the late 1940s, only about 10 percent of eligible southern black people voted, most of these in urban areas. A combination of legal and extralegal measures kept all but the most determined blacks disenfranchised. Poll taxes, all-white primaries, and discriminatory registration procedures reinforced the belief that voting was "the white man's business." African Americans who insisted on exercising their right to vote, especially in remote rural areas, faced physical violence—beatings, shootings, and lynchings. A former president of the Alabama Bar Association expressed a commonly held view when he declared, "No Negro is good enough and no Negro will ever be good enough to participate in making the law under which the white people of Alabama have to live."

Outsiders often noted that despite Jim Crow laws (see Chapter 20), contact between blacks and whites was ironically close. The majority of black Southerners worked on white-owned farms or in white households. One black preacher neatly summarized the nation's regional differences this way: "In the South, they don't care how close you get as long as you don't get too big; in the North, they don't care how big you get as long as you don't get too close." The South's racial code forced African Americans to accept, at least outwardly, social conventions that reinforced their low standing with whites. A black person did not shake hands with a white person, or enter a white home through the front door, or address a white person except formally. In these circumstances, survival and self-respect depended to a great degree on patience and stoicism. Black people learned to endure humiliation by keeping their thoughts and feelings hidden from white people.

Read the Document
Sterling A. Brown, "Out of Their Mouths" (1942) at **www.myhistorylab.com**

The consequences of violating the code could be fatal. In the summer of 1955, Emmett Till, a fourteen-year-old African American boy from Chicago, unaccustomed to local "folkways," was visiting relatives near Money, Mississippi. Leaving a store with some friends, Till spoke in an informal tone to the white wife of the store owner. Several days later, Till was kidnapped from his uncle's house in the middle of the night, and shortly thereafter his body was dragged out of the Tallahatchie River. Back in Chicago, Till's mother, Mamie Bradley, insisted on an open-casket funeral, and the photographs of his horribly mutilated body profoundly shocked African American readers of *Jet* magazine and other black publications around the country. No white publications carried these photos. Till's murderers were acquitted in a

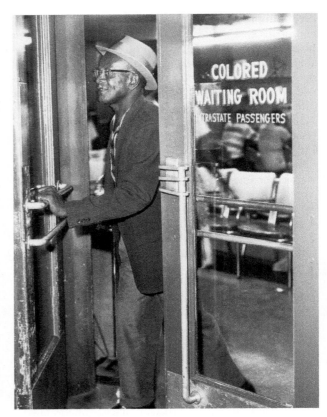

Signs designating "White" and "Colored" rest rooms, waiting rooms, entrances, benches, and even water fountains were a common sight in the segregated South. They were a constant reminder that legal separation of the races in public spaces was the law of the land.

trial that attracted national attention and underlined the stark realities of southern segregation. It also reminded northern blacks that racist violence could touch their lives as well. In Mamie Bradley's words, "Two months ago I had a nice apartment in Chicago. I had a good job. I had a son. When something happened to the Negroes in the South I said, 'That's their business, not mine.' Now I know how wrong I was. The murder of my son has shown me that what happens to any of us, anywhere in the world, had better be the business of us all."

Broad demographic and economic changes were also remaking the postwar South. On the eve of World War II, more than 40 percent of Southerners lived on farms; two-thirds of the South's 35 million people resided in places with fewer than 2,500 inhabitants. During the 1950s, tens of thousands of nonagricultural jobs were created in factories, mills, and office buildings across the region. More and more national corporations, attracted by the region's cheaper labor costs, began establishing a southern presence, and the region's towns and cities competed to lure them. A more highly mechanized agriculture and rapid industrialization pushed more Southerners, black and white, into cities and suburbs. By 1960, roughly half of all

Southerners inhabited metropolitan districts and only 15 percent lived on farms.

Brown v. *Board of Education*

Since the late 1930s, the NAACP had chipped away at the legal foundations of segregation. Rather than making a frontal assault on the *Plessy* separate-but-equal rule, civil rights attorneys launched a series of suits seeking complete equality in segregated facilities. Their strategy was to make segregation so prohibitively expensive that the South would be forced to dismantle it. In the 1939 case *Missouri v. ex rel. Gaines*, the Supreme Court ruled that the University of Missouri law school must either admit African Americans or build another, fully equal law school for them. NAACP lawyers pushed their arguments further, asserting that equality could not be measured simply by money or physical plant. In *McLaurin v. Oklahoma State Regents* (1950), the Court agreed with Thurgood Marshall's argument that regulations forcing a black law student to sit, eat, and study in areas apart from white students inevitably created a "badge of inferiority."

By 1951, Marshall had begun coordinating the NAACP's legal resources for a direct attack on the separate-but-equal doctrine, aiming to overturn *Plessy* and the constitutionality of segregation itself. For a test case, Marshall combined five lawsuits challenging segregation in public schools. One of these suits argued the case of Oliver Brown of Topeka, Kansas, who sought to overturn a state law permitting cities to maintain segregated schools. Topeka's ordinance, sanctioned by this law, forced Brown's eight-year-old daughter Linda to travel by bus to a black school even though she lived only three blocks from an all-white elementary school. The Supreme Court heard initial arguments on the cases, grouped together as *Brown* v. *Board of Education*, in December 1952. The *Brown* case offered an important reminder that segregation was not a purely southern phenomenon. Roughly 40 percent of America's 28 million schoolchildren attended legally segregated schools in the South and border states, while millions more were educated in northern communities where *de facto* segregation—created by housing patterns and school districting—was the norm.

In his argument before the Court, Thurgood Marshall argued that separate facilities, by definition, denied black people their full rights as American citizens. Marshall used sociological and psychological evidence that went beyond standard legal arguments. For example, he cited the research of African American psychologist Kenneth B. Clark, who had studied the self-esteem of black children in New York City and in segregated schools in the South. Using black and white dolls and asking the children which they preferred, Clark illustrated how black children educated in segregated schools developed a negative self-image. When Chief Justice Fred Vinson suddenly died in 1953, President Dwight Eisenhower appointed California Governor Earl Warren to fill the post. After hearing further arguments, the Court remained divided on the issue of overturning *Plessy*. Warren, eager for a unanimous decision, patiently worked at convincing two holdouts. Using his political skills to persuade and achieve compromise, Warren urged his colleagues to affirm a simple principle as the basis for the decision.

On May 17, 1954, Warren read aloud the Court's unanimous decision. "Does segregation of children in public schools solely on the basis of race . . . deprive the children of the minority

○●○─[**Read** the Document
Brown v. Board of Education of Topeka (1954) at
www.myhistorylab.com

group of equal educational opportunities?" The chief justice paused. "We believe that it does." Warren made a point of citing several of the psychological studies of segregation's effects. He ended by directly addressing the constitutional issue. Segregation deprived the plaintiffs of the equal protection of the laws guaranteed by the

Fourteenth Amendment. "We conclude that in the field of public education the doctrine of 'separate but equal' has no place. Separate educational facilities are inherently unequal . . . Any language in *Plessy* v. *Ferguson* contrary to this finding is rejected."

African Americans and their liberal allies around the country hailed the decision and the legal genius of Thurgood Marshall. Marshall himself predicted that all segregated schools would be abolished within five years. Black newspapers were full of stories on the imminent dismantling of segregation. The *Chicago Defender* called the decision "a second emancipation proclamation." But the issue of enforcement soon dampened this enthusiasm. To gain a unanimous decision, Warren had to agree to let the Court delay for one year its ruling on how to implement

◉─[Watch the Video

How Did the Civil Rights Movement Change American Schools? at
www.myhistorylab.com

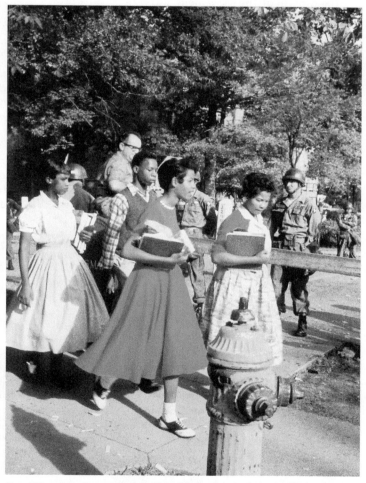

Four African American students walk swiftly past barricaded sidewalks as they integrate Central High School in Little Rock, Arkansas, in September 1957. Soldiers from the 101st Airborne Division, sent to Little Rock by President Eisenhower, protect the students during the tense racial confrontation.

Visualizing Civil Rights

Images from the front lines of the civil rights struggle were crucial to the evolution of "The Movement," and they could be used for very different purposes. They attracted local activists to the cause and helped to turn a regional battle into a national crusade. Photos of the racist violence that marked confrontations in Little Rock, the Freedom Rides, and in Birmingham circulated widely in foreign newspapers, complicating the freedom vs. tyranny narrative of Cold War era policymakers.

The growth of The Movement also converged with the emergence of television as the dominant mass medium in American life. By 1957, some eighty-five percent of American homes watched TV five hours each day. To the nascent world of television news, The Movement offered dramatic confrontations, compelling visuals, and a sharp distinction between good and evil that resembled familiar forms like Hollywood westerns or coverage of the Cold War. But images could also provide a more intimate and human sense of what was at stake.

When SCLC leaders planned the Birmingham campaign in the spring of 1963, they counted on a violent response from local authorities—and they got it. Images

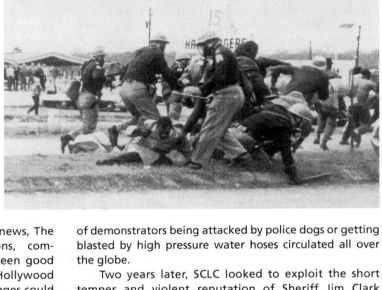

of demonstrators being attacked by police dogs or getting blasted by high pressure water hoses circulated all over the globe.

Two years later, SCLC looked to exploit the short temper and violent reputation of Sheriff Jim Clark when it brought its voting rights campaign to Selma, Alabama. As Andrew Young noted, "We're only saying to [Sheriff Clark] that if he still wants to beat heads he'll have to do it on Main Street, at noon, in front of CBS, NBC, and ABC television cameras." On March 7, 1965, when local police and Alabama state troopers attacked civil rights marchers on the Edmund Pettus Bridge, news cameras captured the searing moment. That night, ABC interrupted its premiere broadcast of the movie *Judgement at Nuremberg* with footage from Selma. The national outcry provided the final push for passage of the Voting Rights Act. As Selma's Mayor Joseph Smitherman later recalled, "I did not understand how big it was until I saw it on television."

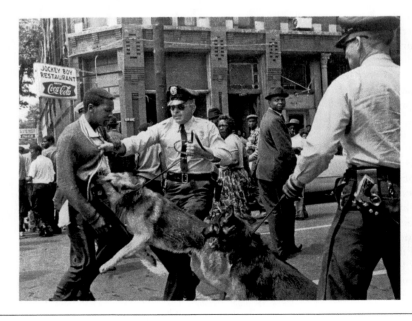

• How did compelling visual images help turn the civil rights movement from a regional struggle to a national one?

• Was the strategy of inciting violent reactions from its opponents hypocritical or cynical for a Movement devoted to non-violence?

desegregation. This second *Brown* ruling, handed down in May 1955, assigned responsibility for desegregation plans to local school boards. The Court left it to federal district judges to monitor compliance, requiring only that desegregation proceed "with all deliberate speed." Thus, although the Court had made a momentous and clear constitutional ruling, the need for compromise dictated gradual enforcement by unspecified means.

Crisis in Little Rock

Resistance to *Brown* took many forms. Most affected states passed laws transferring authority for pupil assignment to local school boards. This prevented the NAACP from bringing statewide suits against segregated school systems. Counties and towns created layers of administrative delays designed to stop implementation of *Brown*. Some school boards transferred public school property to new, all-white private "academies." State legislatures in Virginia, Alabama, Mississippi, and Georgia, resurrecting pre–Civil War doctrines, passed resolutions declaring their right to "interpose" themselves between the people and the federal government and to "nullify" federal laws. In 1956, 101 members of Congress from the former Confederate states signed the Southern Manifesto, urging their states to refuse compliance with desegregation. President Eisenhower declined to publicly endorse *Brown*, contributing to the southern resistance.

Read the Document

The Southern Manifesto (1956) at **www.myhistorylab.com**

In Little Rock, Arkansas, the tense controversy over school integration became a test case of state versus federal power. A federal court ordered public schools to begin desegregation in September 1957, and the local school board made plans to comply. But Governor Orval Faubus, facing a tough reelection fight, decided to make a campaign issue out of defying the court order. He dispatched Arkansas National Guard troops to Central High School to prevent nine black students from entering. For three weeks, armed troops stood guard at the school. Screaming crowds, encouraged by Faubus, menaced the black students, beat up two black reporters, and chanted "Two, four, six, eight, we ain't going to integrate." Moderate whites opposed Faubus, fearing that his controversial tactics would make it harder to attract new businesses and investment capital to the city. Indeed, Little Rock's industrial recruitment efforts declined with the integration crisis, suggesting to southern moderates that militant resistance to integration could be bad for business.

At first, Eisenhower tried to intervene quietly, gaining Faubus's assurance that he would protect the nine black children. But when Faubus suddenly withdrew his troops, leaving the black students at the mercy of the white mob, Eisenhower had to move. On September 24, he placed the Arkansas National Guard under federal command and ordered a thousand paratroopers of the 101st Airborne Division to Little Rock. The nine black students arrived in a U.S. Army car. With fixed bayonets, the soldiers protected the students as they finally integrated Central High School in Little Rock. Eisenhower, the veteran military commander, justified his actions on the basis of upholding federal authority and enforcing the law. He also defended his intervention as crucial to national prestige abroad, noting the propaganda victory Faubus was handing the Communist world. "Our enemies," the president argued, "are gloating over this incident and using it everywhere to misrepresent our whole nation." As the first president since Reconstruction to use armed federal troops in support of black rights, Eisenhower demonstrated that the federal government could, indeed, protect civil rights. Unfazed, Governor Faubus kept Little Rock high schools closed during the 1958–59 academic year to prevent what he called "violence and disorder."

No Easy Road to Freedom, 1957–62

The legal breakthrough represented by the *Brown* decision heartened opponents of segregation everywhere. Most important, *Brown* demonstrated the potential for using the federal court system as a weapon against discrimination and as a means of protecting the full rights of citizenship. Yet widespread opposition to *Brown* showed the limits of a strictly legal strategy. Although they welcomed Eisenhower's intervention in Little Rock, civil rights activists noted his reluctance to endorse desegregation, suggesting that they could not rely on federal help. As the Montgomery bus boycott had proved, black communities would have to help themselves first.

Martin Luther King Jr. and the SCLC

When it ended with the Supreme Court decision in November 1956, the 381-day Montgomery bus boycott had made Martin Luther King Jr. a national figure. In January 1957, *Time* magazine put King on its cover; he was only the second African American ever to appear on NBC's *Meet the Press*. Speaking invitations poured in from universities and organizations all over the country.

King himself was an extraordinary and complex man. Born in 1929 in Atlanta, he enjoyed a middle-class upbringing as the son of a prominent Baptist minister. After graduating from prestigious Morehouse College, an all-black school, King earned a divinity degree at Crozer Theological Seminary in Pennsylvania and a PhD. in theology from Boston University. In graduate school he was drawn to the Social Christianity of American theologian Walter Rauschenbusch, who insisted on connecting religious faith with struggles for social justice. Above all, King admired Mohandas Gandhi, a lawyer turned ascetic who had led a successful nonviolent resistance movement against British colonial rule in India. Gandhi taught his followers to confront authorities with a readiness to suffer in order to expose injustice and force those in power to end it. This tactic of nonviolent civil disobedience required discipline and sacrifice from its followers, who were sometimes called upon to lay their lives on the line against armed police and military forces. Crucially, King believed Gandhian nonviolence to be not merely a moral imperative but a potent political strategy. A unique blend of traditional African American folk preacher and erudite intellectual, King used his passion and intelligence to help transform a community's pain into a powerful moral force for change. Two northern pacifists, Bayard Rustin of the War Resisters' League and Glenn Smiley of the Fellowship of Reconciliation, helped deepen King's commitment to the Gandhian philosophy.

In a December 1956 address celebrating the Montgomery bus boycott victory, King laid out six key lessons from the yearlong struggle: "(1) We have discovered that we can stick together for a common cause; (2) our leaders do not have to sell out; (3) threats and violence do not necessarily intimidate those who are sufficiently aroused and nonviolent; (4) our church is becoming militant, stressing a social gospel as well as a gospel of personal salvation; (5) we have gained a new sense of dignity and destiny; (6) we have discovered a new and powerful weapon—nonviolent resistance."

King recognized the need to exploit the momentum of the Montgomery movement. In early 1957, with the help of Rustin and others, he brought together nearly 100 black ministers to found the Southern Christian Leadership Conference (SCLC). The clergymen elected King president and his close friend, the Reverend Ralph Abernathy, treasurer. The SCLC called upon black people "to understand that nonviolence is not a symbol of weakness or cowardice, but as Jesus demonstrated, nonviolent resistance transforms weakness into strength and breeds courage in the face of danger."

But King and other black leaders also understood that the white South was no monolith. They believed white Southerners could be divided roughly into three groups: first, a tiny minority—often with legal training, social connections, and money—that might be counted on to help overthrow segregation; second, extreme segregationists who were willing and able to use violence and terror in defense of white supremacy; and third, a broad middle group who favored and benefited from segregation but were unwilling to take personal risks to prevent its destruction. In the battles to come, civil rights leaders made this nuanced view of the white South central to their larger political strategy. Extreme segregationists could be counted on to over-react, often violently, to civil rights campaigns, and thereby help to win sympathy and support for the cause. White moderates, especially in the business community, might be reluctant to initiate change, but they would try to distance themselves from the desperate violence of extremists and present themselves as prag-matic supporters of order and peace.

The SCLC gained support among black ministers, and King vigorously spread his message in speeches and writings. But the organization failed to generate the kind of mass, direct-action movement that had made history in Montgomery. Instead, the next great spark to light the fire of protest came from what seemed at the time a most unlikely source: black college students.

Sit-Ins: Greensboro, Nashville, Atlanta

On Monday, February 1, 1960, four black freshmen from North Carolina Agricultural and Technical College in Greensboro sat down at the whites-only lunch counter in Woolworth's and politely ordered coffee and doughnuts. As the students had anticipated while planning the action in their dorm rooms, they were refused service. Although they could buy pencils or toothpaste, black people were not allowed to eat in Woolworth's. But the four students stayed at the counter until closing time. Word of their actions spread quickly, and the next day they returned with more than two dozen supporters. On the third day, students occupied sixty-three of the sixty-six lunch counter seats. By Thursday, they had been joined by three white students from the Women's College of the University of North Carolina in Greensboro. Scores of sympathizers overflowed Woolworth's and started a sit-in down the street in S. H. Kress. On Friday, hundreds of black students and a few white sympathizers jammed the lunch counters.

The week's events put Greensboro on the national news. City officials, looking to end the protest, offered to negotiate in exchange for an end to demonstrations. White business leaders and politicians proved unwilling to change the racial status quo, however, and the sit-ins resumed on April 1. In response to the April 21 arrest of forty-five students for trespassing, an outraged African American community organized a boycott of targeted stores that cut deeply into merchants' profits. Greensboro's leaders reluctantly gave in. On July 25, 1960, the first African American ate a meal at Woolworth's.

The Greensboro sit-in sent a shock wave through-out the South. During the next eighteen months, 70,000 people—most of them black students, a few of them white allies—participated in sit-ins against segre-gation in dozens of communities. More than 3,000 were arrested. African Americans had discovered a new form of direct-action protest, dignified and powerful, that white people could not ignore. The sit-in movement also transformed the participants' self-image, empower-ing them psychologically and emotionally. Franklin McCain, one of the original four Greensboro students, later recalled a great feeling of soul cleansing: "I proba-bly felt better on that day than I've ever felt in my life. Seems like a lot of feelings of guilt or what-have-you

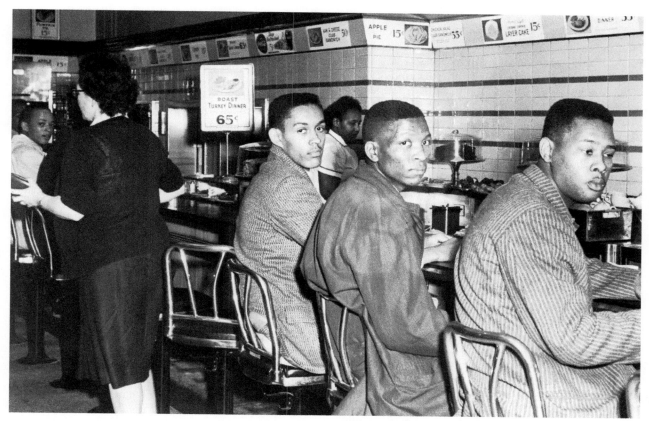

The second day of the sit-in at the Greensboro, North Carolina, Woolworth lunch counter, February 2, 1960. From left: Ronald Martin, Robert Patterson, and Mark Martin. The Greensboro protest sparked a wave of sit-ins across the South, mostly by college students, demanding an end to segregation in restaurants and other public places.

suddenly left me, and I felt as though I had gained my manhood, so to speak, and not only gained it, but had developed quite a lot of respect for it."

In Nashville, Reverend James Lawson, a northern-born black minister, had led workshops in nonviolent resistance since 1958. Lawson had served a jail term as a conscientious objector during the Korean war and had become active in the Fellowship of Reconciliation. He had also spent three years as a missionary in India, where he had learned close up the Gandhian methods of promoting social change. Lawson gathered around him a group of deeply committed black students from Fisk and Vanderbilt universities and other Nashville colleges. The psychological pressures were enormous. To be successful, practitioners of nonviolent resistance had to learn and practice strict self-control needed to resist lashing back at the angry crowds that would abuse them. Young activists there talked not only of ending segregation but also of creating a "Beloved Community" based on Christian idealism and Gandhian principles.

In the spring of 1960, more than 150 Nashville students were arrested in disciplined sit-ins aimed at desegregating downtown lunch counters. Lawson, who preached the need for sacrifice in the cause of justice, found himself expelled from the divinity school at Vanderbilt. Lawson and other veterans of the Nashville sit-ins, such as John Lewis, Diane Nash, and Marion Barry, would go on to play influential roles in the national civil rights movement. The Nashville group developed rules of conduct that became a model for protesters elsewhere: "Don't strike back or curse if abused. . . . Show yourself courteous and friendly at all times. . . . Report all serious incidents to your leader in a polite manner. Remember love and nonviolence."

The most ambitious sit-in campaign unfolded in Atlanta, the South's largest and wealthiest city, and home to the region's most powerful and prestigious black community. Students from Morehouse, Spelman, and the other all-black schools that made up Atlanta University took the lead. On March 15, 1960, 200 young black people staged a well-coordinated sit-in at restaurants in City Hall, the State Capitol, and other government offices. Police arrested and jailed seventy-six demonstrators that day, but the experience only strengthened the activists' resolve. Led by Julian

Bond and Lonnie King, two Morehouse undergraduates, the students formed the Committee on an Appeal for Human Rights. Over the summer they planned a fall campaign of large-scale sit-ins at major Atlanta department stores and a boycott of downtown merchants. In October 1960, Martin Luther King Jr. and thirty-six students were arrested when they sat down in the all-white Magnolia Room restaurant in Rich's Department Store. As in Greensboro and Montgomery, the larger African American community in Atlanta supported the continuing sit-ins, picketing, and boycotts. The campaign stretched on for months, and hundreds of protesters went to jail. The city's business leaders finally relented in September 1961, and desegregation came to Atlanta.

SNCC and the "Beloved Community"

The sit-in movement pumped fresh energy into the civil rights cause, creating a new generation of activists and leaders. Mass arrests, beatings, and vilification in the southern white press only strengthened the resolve of those in the Movement. Students also had to deal with the fears of their families, many of whom had made great sacrifices to send them to college. John Lewis, a seminary student in Nashville, remembered his mother in rural Alabama pleading with him to "get out of that mess, before you get hurt."

The new student militancy also caused discord within black communities. The authority of local African American elites had traditionally depended on their influence and cooperation with the white establishment. Black lawyers, school principals, and businessmen had to maintain regular and cordial relations with white judges, school boards, and politicians. Student calls for freedom disturbed many community leaders worried about upsetting traditional patronage networks. Some black college presidents, pressured by trustees and state legislators, sought to moderate or stop the Movement altogether. The president of Southern University in Baton Rouge, the nation's largest black college, suspended eighteen sit-in leaders in 1960 and forced the entire student body of 5,000 to reapply so that "agitators" could be screened out.

An April 1960 conference of 120 black student activists in Raleigh, North Carolina, underlined the generational and radical aspects of the new movement. The meeting had been called by Ella Baker, executive director of the SCLC, to help the students assess their experiences and plan future actions. Fifty-five at the time, Baker had for years played an important behind-the-scenes role in the civil rights cause, serving as a community organizer and field secretary for the NAACP before heading the staff of the SCLC. She counseled the student activists to resist affiliating with any of the national civil rights organizations, and she also encouraged the trend toward group-centered leadership among the students.

With Baker's encouragement, the conference voted to establish a new group, the Student Nonviolent Coordinating

Committee (SNCC, pronounced "Snick"). The strong influence of the Nashville students, led by James Lawson, could be found in the SNCC statement of purpose:

> We affirm the philosophical or religious ideal of nonviolence as the foundation of our purpose, the presupposition of our faith, and the manner of our action. Nonviolence as it grows from Judaic-Christian tradition seeks a social order of justice permeated by love. Integration of human endeavor represents the crucial first step towards such a society.

In the fall of 1960, SNCC established an organizational structure, a set of principles, and a new style of civil rights protest. The emphasis was on fighting segregation through direct confrontation, mass action, and civil disobedience. SNCC field-workers initiated and supported local, community-based activity. Three-quarters of the first field-workers were less than twenty-two years old. Leadership was vested in a nonhierarchical Coordinating Committee, but local groups were free to determine their own direction. SNCC people distrusted bureaucracy and structure; they stressed spontaneity and improvisation. A small but dedicated group of young white Southerners, inspired by SNCC's idealism and activism, joined the cause. Over the next few years SNCC was at the forefront of nearly every major civil rights battle.

Read the Document
Student Non-Violent Coordinating Committee, "Statement of Purpose" (1960) at
www.myhistorylab.com

The Election of 1960 and Civil Rights

The race issue was kept from center stage during the very close presidential campaign of 1960. As vice president, Richard Nixon had been a leading Republican voice for stronger civil rights legislation, whereas Democratic nominee Senator John F. Kennedy had played virtually no role in the 1950s' congressional battles over civil rights. During the campaign, however, their roles reversed. Kennedy praised the sit-in movement as part of a revival of national reform spirit. While the Republican platform contained a strong civil rights plank, Nixon, eager to court southern white voters, minimized his own identification with the Movement. Republican conservatives, believing that the GOP might pick up southern electoral votes, pushed a "states rights" position, thus planting seeds for a reborn conservative movement in the 1960s.

In October, Martin Luther King Jr. was jailed after leading a demonstration in Atlanta and faced the strong possibility of being sent to a notorious state prison. Kennedy telephoned King's wife, Coretta Scott King, to reassure her and express his personal support. Senator Kennedy's brother and campaign manager Robert telephoned the judge in the case and angrily warned him that he had violated King's civil rights and endangered the national Democratic ticket. The judge released King soon afterward. News of this intervention did not gain wide attention in the white South, much to the relief of the Kennedys. But the Kennedy campaign effectively played up the story among black voters all over the country, using black churches as a grapevine. Kennedy won 70 percent of the black vote, which helped put him over the top in such critical states as Illinois, Texas, Michigan, and Pennsylvania and secure his narrow victory over Nixon. Many civil rights activists optimistically looked forward to a new president who would have to acknowledge his political debt to the black vote.

The very closeness of his victory constrained Kennedy on race. Democrats had lost ground in the House and Senate, and Kennedy had to worry about alienating conservative Southern Democrats who chaired key congressional committees. Passage of major civil rights legislation would be virtually impossible. The president did appoint some forty African Americans to high federal positions, including Thurgood Marshall to a federal appellate court. He also established a Committee on Equal Employment Opportunity, chaired by Vice President Lyndon B. Johnson, to fight discrimination in the federal civil service and in corporations that received government contracts.

Most significantly, the Kennedy administration sought to invigorate the Civil Rights Division of the Justice Department. The division had been created by the Civil Rights Act of 1957, which authorized the attorney general to seek court injunctions to protect people denied their right to vote. But the Eisenhower administration had made little use of this new power. Robert Kennedy, the new attorney general, began assembling a staff of brilliant and committed attorneys, headed by Washington lawyer Burke Marshall. Kennedy encouraged them to get out of Washington and into the field wherever racial troubles arose. In early 1961, when Louisiana school officials balked at a school desegregation order, Robert Kennedy warned them that he would ask the federal court to hold them in contempt. When Marshall started court proceedings, the state officials gave in. The new, more aggressive mood at Justice could not solve the central political dilemma: how to move forward on civil rights without alienating southern Democrats. Pressure from the newly energized southern civil rights movement soon revealed the true difficulty of that problem. The movement would also provoke murderous outrage from white extremists determined to maintain the racial status quo (see Map 28.1).

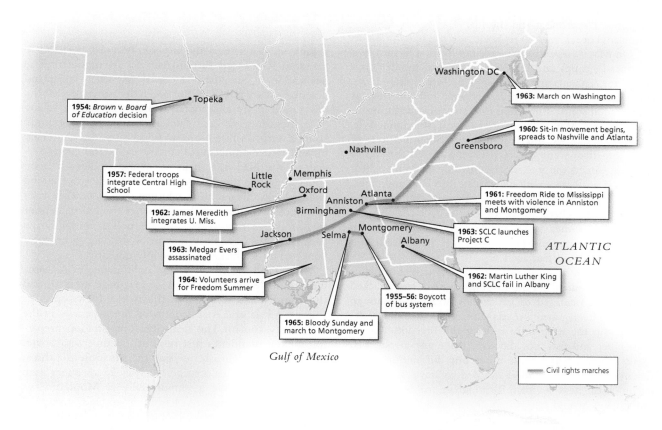

MAP 28.1 The Civil Rights Movement Key battlegrounds in the struggle for racial justice in communities across the South.

Freedom Rides

In the spring of 1961, James Farmer, national director of CORE, announced plans for an interracial Freedom Ride through the South. The goal was to test compliance with court orders banning segregation in interstate travel and terminal accommodations. One of the founders of CORE in 1942, Farmer had worked for various pacifist and socialist groups and served as program director for the NAACP. He designed the Freedom Ride to induce a crisis, in the spirit of the sit-ins. "Our intention," Farmer declared, "was to provoke the southern authorities into arresting us and thereby prod the Justice Department into enforcing the law of the land." CORE received financial and tactical support from the SCLC and several NAACP branches. It also informed the Justice Department and the FBI of its plans but received no reply.

A Freedom Riders' bus burns after being firebombed in Anniston, Alabama, May 14, 1961. After setting the bus afire, whites attacked the passengers fleeing the smoke and flames. Violent scenes like this one received extensive publicity in the mass media and helped compel the Justice Department to enforce court rulings banning segregation on interstate bus lines.

On May 4, seven blacks and six whites split into two interracial groups and left Washington on public buses bound for Alabama and Mississippi. At first the two buses encountered only isolated harassment and violence as they headed south. But when one bus entered Anniston, Alabama, on May 14, an angry mob surrounded it, smashing windows and slashing tires. Six miles out of town, the tires went flat. A firebomb tossed through a window forced the passengers out. The mob then beat the Freedom Riders with blackjacks, iron bars, and clubs, and the bus burst into flames. A caravan of cars organized by the Birmingham office of the SCLC rescued the wounded. Another mob attacked the second bus in Anniston, leaving one Freedom Rider near death and permanently brain damaged.

The violence escalated. In Birmingham, a mob of forty whites waited on the loading platform and attacked the bus that managed to get out of Anniston. Although police had been warned to expect trouble, they did nothing to stop the mob from beating the Freedom Riders with pipes and fists, nor did they make any arrests. FBI agents observed and took notes but did nothing. The remaining Freedom Riders decided to travel as a single group on the next lap, from Birmingham to Montgomery, but no bus would take them. Stranded and frightened, they reluctantly boarded a special flight to New Orleans arranged by the Justice Department. On May 17, the CORE-sponsored Freedom Ride disbanded.

That was not the end of the Freedom Rides. SNCC leaders in Atlanta and Nashville assembled a fresh group of volunteers to continue the trip. On May 20, twenty-one Freedom Riders left Birmingham for Montgomery. The bus station in the Alabama capital was eerily quiet and deserted as they pulled in. But when the passengers left the bus, a mob of several hundred whites rushed them, yelling "Get those niggers!" and clubbing people to the ground. James Zwerg, a white Freedom Rider from the University of Wisconsin, had his spinal cord severed. John Lewis, veteran of the Nashville sit-in movement, suffered a brain concussion. The mob indiscriminately beat journalists and clubbed John Siegenthaler, a Justice Department attorney sent to observe the scene. It took police more than an hour to halt the rioting. Montgomery's police commissioner later said, "We have no intention of standing guard for a bunch of troublemakers coming into our city."

The mob violence and the indifference of Alabama officials made the Freedom Ride first-page news around the country and throughout the world. Newspapers in Europe, Africa, and Asia denounced the hypocrisy of the federal government. The Kennedy administration, preparing for the president's first summit meeting with Soviet premier Nikita Khrushchev, saw the situation as a threat to the nation's global prestige. On May 21, an angry mob threatened to invade a support rally at Montgomery's First Baptist Church. A hastily assembled group of 400 U.S. marshals, sent by Robert Kennedy, barely managed to keep the peace. The attorney general called for a cooling-off period, but King, Farmer, and the SNCC leaders announced that the Freedom Ride would continue. A bandaged but spirited group of twenty-seven

Freedom Riders prepared to leave Montgomery for Jackson, Mississippi, on May 24. To avoid further violence, Robert Kennedy arranged a compromise through Mississippi's Senator James Eastland. In exchange for a guarantee of safe passage through Mississippi, the federal government promised not to interfere with the arrest of the Freedom Riders in Jackson. This Freedom Ride and several that followed thus escaped violence. But more than 300 people were arrested that summer in Jackson on charges of traveling "for the avowed purpose of inflaming public opinion." Sticking to a policy of "jail, no bail," Freedom Riders clogged the prison, where they endured beatings and intimidation by prison guards that went largely unreported in the press. Their jail experiences turned most of them into committed core leaders of the student movement.

The Freedom Rides exposed the ugly face of southern racism to the world and inspired grassroots activists around the South. But they also reinforced white resistance to desegregation and showed the limits of federal action against Jim Crow. Eventually the Justice Department did petition the Interstate Commerce Commission to issue clear rules prohibiting segregation on interstate carriers. At the end of 1962, CORE proclaimed victory in the battle against Jim Crow interstate travel. By creating a crisis, the Freedom Rides had forced the Kennedy administration to act. But they also revealed the unwillingness of the federal government to fully enforce the law of the land. The jailings and brutality experienced by Freedom Riders made clear to the civil rights community the limits of moral persuasion alone for effecting change.

The Albany Movement: The Limits of Protest

Where the federal government chose not to enforce the constitutional rights of black people, segregationist forces tenaciously held their ground, especially in the more remote areas of the Deep South. One such place was Albany, a small city in southwest Georgia, where activists from SNCC, the NAACP, and other local groups formed a coalition known as the Albany Movement. For more than a year, beginning in October 1961, thousands of Albany's black citizens marched, sat in, and boycotted as part of a citywide campaign to integrate public facilities and win voting rights. More than a thousand people spent time in jail. In December, the arrival of Martin Luther King Jr. and the SCLC transformed Albany into a national symbol of the struggle.

The gains at Albany proved minimal. Local SNCC workers opposed the more cautious approach of NAACP officials, even though the more established organization paid many of the campaign's expenses. Albany police chief Laurie Pritchett shrewdly deprived the movement of the kind of national sympathy won by the Freedom Riders.

Read the Document
Charles Sherrod, SNCC Memorandum (1961) at **www.myhistorylab.com**

Pritchett filled the jails with black demonstrators, kept their mistreatment to a minimum, and prevented white mobs from running wild. King himself was twice arrested in the summer of 1962, but Albany officials quickly freed him to avoid negative publicity. By late 1962, the Albany movement had collapsed, and Pritchett proudly declared the city "as segregated as ever." Albany showed that mass protest without violent white reaction and direct federal intervention could not end Jim Crow.

In contrast to the failure at Albany, a successful battle to integrate the University of Mississippi reinforced the importance of federal intervention for guaranteeing African American civil rights. In the fall of 1962, James Meredith, an Air Force veteran and a student at all-black Jackson State College, tried to register as the first black student at lily-white "Ole Miss." Defying a federal court order, Governor Ross Barnett personally blocked Meredith at the admissions office. When Barnett refused to assure Robert Kennedy that Meredith would be protected, the attorney general dispatched 500 federal marshals to the campus. Over the radio, Barnett encouraged resistance to the "oppressive power of the United States," and an enraged mob of several thousand whites, many of them armed, laid siege to the campus on September 30. A night of violence left two people dead and 160 marshals wounded, 28 from gunfire. President Kennedy ordered 5,000 Army troops onto the campus to stop the riot. A federal guard remained to protect Meredith, who graduated the following summer.

The Movement at High Tide, 1963–65

The tumultuous events of 1960–62 convinced civil rights strategists that segregation could not be dismantled merely through orderly protest and moral persuasion. Only comprehensive civil rights legislation, backed by federal power, could guarantee full citizenship rights for African Americans. To build the national consensus needed for new laws, civil rights activists looked for ways to gain broader support for their cause. By 1963, their sense of urgency had led them to plan dramatic confrontations that would expose the violence and terror routinely faced by southern blacks. With the whole country—indeed, the whole world—watching, the Movement reached the peak of its political and moral power.

Birmingham

At the end of 1962, Martin Luther King and his SCLC allies decided to launch a new campaign against segregation in Birmingham, Alabama. Having failed in Albany, King and his aides looked for a way to shore up his leadership and inject new momentum into the freedom struggle. They needed a major victory. Birmingham, the most segregated big city in America, had a deep history of racial violence. African Americans endured total segregation in schools, restaurants, city parks, and department store dressing rooms. Although black people constituted more than 40 percent of the city's population, fewer than 10,000 of Birmingham's 80,000 registered voters were black.

Working closely with local civil rights groups led by the longtime Birmingham activist Reverend Fred Shuttlesworth, the SCLC carefully planned its campaign. The strategy was to fill the city jails with protesters, boycott downtown department stores, and enrage Public Safety Commissioner Eugene "Bull" Connor, a die-hard segregationist. In April, King arrived with a manifesto demanding an end to racist hiring practices and segregated public accommodations and the creation of a biracial committee to oversee desegregation. Connor's police began jailing hundreds of demonstrators, including King himself, who defied a state court injunction against further protests. Held in solitary confinement for several days, King managed to write a response to a group of Birmingham clergy who had deplored the protests. King's "Letter from a Birmingham Jail" was soon widely reprinted and circulated as a pamphlet. It set out the key moral issues at stake, and scoffed at those who claimed the campaign was illegal and ill timed (see Communities in Conflict).

After King's release on bail, the campaign intensified. The SCLC kept up the pressure by recruiting thousands of Birmingham's young students for a "children's crusade." In early May, Connor unleashed high-powered water cannons, billy clubs, and snarling police dogs to break up demonstrations. Millions of Americans reacted with horror to the violent scenes from Birmingham shown on national television. Many younger black people, especially from the city's poor and working-class districts, began to fight back, hurling bottles and bricks at police. On May 10, mediators from the Justice Department negotiated an uneasy truce. The SCLC agreed to an immediate end to the protests. In exchange, businesses would desegregate and begin hiring African Americans over the next three months, and a biracial city committee would oversee desegregation of public facilities.

A few days after the announcement, more than a thousand robed Ku Klux Klansmen burned a cross in a park on the outskirts of Birmingham. When bombs rocked SCLC headquarters and the home of King's brother, a Birmingham minister, enraged blacks took to the streets and pelted police and firefighters with stones and bottles. President Kennedy ordered 3,000 Army troops into the city and prepared to nationalize the Alabama National Guard. The violence receded, and white businesspeople and politicians began to carry out the agreed-upon pact. But in September, a bomb killed four black girls in a Birmingham Baptist church, reminding the city and the world that racial harmony was still a long way off.

The Birmingham campaign and the other protests it sparked over the next seven months engaged more than 100,000 people and led to nearly 15,000 arrests. The civil rights community now drew support from millions of Americans, black and white, all inspired by the protesters and repelled by southern bigotry. At the same time, Birmingham changed the nature of black protest. The black unemployed and working poor who joined in the struggle brought a different perspective from that of the students, professionals, and members of the religious middle class who had dominated the Movement before Birmingham. They cared less about the philosophy of nonviolence and more about immediate gains in employment and housing and an end to police brutality.

JFK and the March on Washington

The growth of black activism and of white support convinced President Kennedy the moment had come to press for sweeping civil rights legislation. Continuing white resistance in the South also made clearer than ever the need for federal action. In June 1963, Governor George Wallace threatened to personally block the admission of two black students to the University of Alabama. Only the deployment of National Guard troops, placed under federal control by the president, ensured the students' safety and their peaceful admission into the university.

On June 11, the president went on national television and offered his personal endorsement of the Movement. Reviewing the racial situation, Kennedy told the nation: "We face . . . a moral crisis as a country and a people. It cannot be met by repressive police action." Even more than for Eisenhower at Little Rock, the realities of international Cold War politics pushed Kennedy toward support for civil rights. "Today we are committed to a worldwide struggle to promote and protect the rights of all who wish to be free. And when Americans are sent to Vietnam or West Berlin, we do not ask for whites only. . . . Are we to say to the rest of the world, and much more importantly, to each other, that this is a land of the free except for Negroes?" The next week, Kennedy asked Congress for a broad law that would ensure voting rights, outlaw segregation in public facilities, and bolster federal authority to deny funds for discriminatory programs. Knowing they would face a stiff fight from congressional conservatives, administration officials began an intense lobbying effort in support of the law. After three years of fence sitting, Kennedy finally committed his office and his political future to the civil rights cause.

Movement leaders lauded the president's initiative. Yet they understood that racial hatred still haunted the nation. Only hours after Kennedy's television speech, a gunman murdered Medgar Evers, leader of the Mississippi NAACP, outside his home in Jackson, Mississippi. To pressure Congress and demonstrate the urgency of their cause, a broad coalition of civil rights groups planned a massive, nonviolent March on Washington. The idea had deep roots in black protest. A. Philip Randolph, head of the

Brotherhood of Sleeping Car Porters, had originally proposed such a march in 1941 to protest discrimination against blacks in defense industries (see Chapter 25). More than twenty years later, Randolph, along with his aide Bayard Rustin, revived the concept and convinced leaders of the major civil rights groups to support it.

The Kennedy administration originally opposed the march, fearing it would jeopardize support for the president's civil rights bill in Congress. As plans for the rally solidified, Kennedy reluctantly gave his approval. Leaders from the SCLC, the NAACP, SNCC, the Urban League, and CORE—the leading organizations in the civil rights community—put aside their tactical differences to forge a broad consensus for the event. John Lewis, the young head of SNCC, who had endured numerous brutal assaults, planned a speech that denounced the Kennedys as hypocrites. Lewis's speech enraged Walter Reuther, the white liberal leader of the United Auto Workers union, which had helped finance the march. Reuther threatened to turn off the loudspeakers he was paying for, believing

Read the Document

John Lewis, Address at the March on Washington (1963) at **www.myhistorylab.com**

Lewis's speech would embarrass the Kennedys. At the last moment, Randolph, the Movement's acknowledged elder statesman, convinced Lewis to tone down his remarks. "We've come this far," he implored. "For the sake of unity, change it."

On August 28, 1963, more than a quarter of a million people, including 50,000 whites, gathered at the Lincoln Memorial to rally for "jobs and freedom." Union members, students, teachers, clergy, professionals, musicians, actors—Americans from all walks of life—joined the largest political assembly in the nation's history until then. The sight of all those people holding hands and singing "We Shall Overcome," led by white folksinger Joan Baez, would not be easily forgotten, either by participants or by millions of television viewers. At the end of a long, exhilarating day of speeches and freedom songs, Martin Luther King Jr. provided the emotional climax. Combining the democratic promise of the Declaration of Independence with the religious fervor of his Baptist heritage, King stirred the crowd and the nation with his dream for America.

Watch the Video

Civil Rights March on Washington (1963) at **www.myhistorylab.com**

Part of the huge throng of marchers at the historic March on Washington for "jobs and freedom," August 28, 1963. The size of the crowd, the stirring oratory and song, and the live network television coverage produced one of the most memorable political demonstrations in the nation's history.

Showdown at Oxford: Integrating Ole Miss, 1962

Born in 1933, raised and schooled in Mississippi, James Meredith served in the U.S. Air Force from 1951 to 1960. He attended Jackson State College for two years, but after being inspired by President John F. Kennedy's Inaugural Address, Meredith applied for admission to the all white University of Mississippi in Oxford. With legal help from the NAACP, he sued the university after his application was denied. A Federal district court ruled in June 1962 that the university must admit Meredith. Governor Ross Barnett vowed to prevent Meredith from registering for the fall 1962 semester, setting the stage for one of the most violent confrontations of the civil rights era. While negotiating with state officials, President Kennedy made a nationally televised address, appealing for law and order, and he sent 500 U.S. Marshals to protect Meredith.

By Sunday evening, September 30, 1962, a mob of several thousand white militants, many of them armed, had streamed into the Oxford campus to prevent Meredith from entering the university. Heckling and jeering soon escalated to throwing bricks and bottles, and the marshals responded with tear gas as a full-fledged riot enveloped the campus that night. To protect the besieged marshals, President Kennedy ordered in thousands of regular Army troops, and he federalized units of the Mississippi National Guard. By dawn, two men lay dead, 28 marshals had been wounded by gunfire, and some 160 soldiers were injured. After the federal military forces secured the campus Monday morning, Meredith registered and attended his first classes. Despite widespread harassment and ostracism from white students, Meredith completed his studies and graduated in June 1963 with a degree in political science. In later years, Meredith became an outspoken conservative who distanced himself from the civil rights struggle. But Oxford in the fall of 1962 had witnessed how the overwhelming force of the national government could confront massive white resistance in support of court ordered integration.

The first document is the letter that James Meredith wrote to Thurgood Marshall, head of the NAACP Legal Defense and Educational Fund, requesting legal assistance supporting his effort to attend the university. The second is from the address that Governor Ross Barnett delivered in September 1962 defending his refusal to allow Meredith admittance.

Document 1: Letter from James Meredith to Thurgood Marshall, NAACP Legal Defense and Educational Fund, January 29, 1961

Dear Sir:

I am submitting an application for admission to the University of Mississippi. I am seeking entrance for the second semester which begins the 6th of February, 1961. I anticipate encountering some type of difficulty with the various agencies here in the state which are against my gaining entrance in the school. I discussed this matter with Mr. Evers, the Mississippi Field Secretary for the NAACP, and he suggested that I contact you and request legal assistance from your organization in the event it is needed for I am not financially able to fight a legal battle against the state of Mississippi. I hope your decision on this request will be favorable. Below is a brief history of my background which might help you in reaching a decision.

I am a native Mississippian. All my elementary and secondary education was received in this state, except my last year of high school, which was completed in Florida. I spent nine years in the United States Air Force (1951-60), all of which were honorable. I have always been a "conscientious objector" to my "oppressed status" as long as I can remember. My long-cherished ambition has been to break the monopoly on rights and privileges held by the whites of the state of Mississippi.

My academic qualifications, I believe, are adequate. While in the Air Force, I successfully completed courses at four different schools conducting night classes. As an example, I completed 34 semester hours of work with the University of Maryland's Overseas Program. Of the twelve courses completed I made three A's and nine B's. I am presently enrolled at Jackson State College, here in Jackson. I have completed one quarter of work and I am now enrolled in a second quarter at Jackson. For the work completed I received one A, three B's and one C.

> "I have always been a 'conscientious objector' to my 'oppressed status' as long as I can remember."

• **How does Meredith make his case to the NAACP for legal help? What does the letter's tone convey about Meredith as an individual?**

• **What legal, historical, and moral arguments does Barnett use to defend segregation as state policy? To what extent do you think his words encouraged armed resistance to integration?**

Finally, I am making this move in what I consider the interest of and for the benefit of: (1) my country, (2) my race, (3) my family, and (4) myself. I am familiar with the probable difficulties involved in such a move as I am undertaking and I am fully prepared to pursue it all the way to a degree from the University of Mississippi.

Sincerely yours,
J H MEREDITH

Document 2: Governor Ross Barnett, Proclamation to the People of Mississippi, TV and Radio broadcast, September 12, 1962

"The powers not delegated to the United States by the Constitution nor prohibited by it to the States are reserved to the States respectively or to the people." These are not my words. This is the tenth amendment to the Constitution of the United States.

Ladies and gentlemen, my friends and fellow Mississippians: I speak to you as your Governor in a solemn hour in the history of our great state and in our nation's history. I speak to you now in the moment of our greatest crisis since the War Between the States.

In the absence of constitutional authority and without legislative action, an ambitious federal government, employing naked and arbitrary power, has decided to deny us the right of self-determination in the conduct of the affairs of our sovereign state. Having long since failed in their efforts to conquer the indomitable spirit of the people of Mississippi and their unshakable will to preserve the sovereignty and majesty of our commonwealth, they now seek to break us physically with the power of force.

Even now as I speak to you tonight, professional agitators and the unfriendly liberal press and other trouble makers are pouring across our borders intent upon instigating strife among our people. Paid propagandists are continually hammering away at us in the hope that they can succeed in bringing about a division among us. Every effort is being made to intimidate us into submission to the tyranny of judicial oppression. The Kennedy Administration is lending the power of the federal government to the ruthless demands of these agitators. Thus we see our own federal government teamed up with a motley array of un-American pressure groups against us. This is the crisis we face today.

Principle is a little word. It is easy to speak and to spell and in print is easily overlooked, but it is a word that is tremendous in its import and meaning denoting respect and obedience to those fundamental and eternal truths that should be respected and form the way of life of all honest and right-thinking people. Expediency is for the hour; principles are for the ages. Principles are a passion for truth and right and justice, and as long as the rains descend and the winds blow, it is but folly to build upon the shifting sands of political expediency. It is better for one's blood to be poisoned than for him to be poisoned in his principles. So deep and compelling were the convictions and principles of our forefathers that they risked even death to establish this now desecrated Constitution as the American way of life and handed it to us in trust as our sacred heritage and for our preservation.

The day of expediency is past. We must either submit to the unlawful dictates of the federal government or stand up like men and tell them no. The day of reckoning has been delayed as long as possible. It is now upon us. This is the day, and this is the hour. Knowing you as I do, there is

"In the absence of constitutional authority and without legislative action, an ambitious federal government . . . has decided to deny us the right of self-determination . . ."

no doubt in my mind what the overwhelming majority of loyal Mississippians will do. They will never submit to the moral degradation, to the shame and the ruin which have faced all others who have lacked the courage to defend their beliefs.

I have made my position in this matter crystal clear. I have said in every county in Mississippi that no school in our state will be integrated while I am your Governor. I shall do everything in my power to prevent integration in our schools. I assure you that the schools will not be closed if this can possibly be avoided, but they will not be integrated if I can prevent it. As your Governor and Chief Executive of the sovereign State of Mississippi, I now call on every public official and every private citizen of our great state to join me . . .

OVERVIEW | Landmark Civil Rights Legislation, Supreme Court Decisions, and Executive Orders

Year	Decision, Law, or Executive Order	Significance
1939	*Missouri v. ex. rel. Gaines*	Required University of Missouri Law School either to admit African Americans or build another fully equal law school
1941	Executive Order 8802 (by President Roosevelt)	Banned racial discrimination in defense industry and government offices; established Fair Employment Practices Committee to investigate violations
1946	*Morgan v. Virginia*	Ruled that segregation on interstate buses violated federal law and created an "undue burden" on interstate commerce
1948	Executive Order 9981 (by President Truman)	Desegregated the U.S. armed forces
1950	*McLaurin v. Oklahoma State Regents*	Ruled that forcing an African American student to sit, eat, and study in segregated facilities was unconstitutional because it inevitably created a "badge of inferiority"
1950	*Sweatt v. Painter*	Ruled that an inferior law school created by the University of Texas to serve African Americans violated their right to equal protection and ordered Herman Sweatt to be admitted to University of Texas Law School
1954	*Brown v. Board of Education of Topeka I*	Declared "separate educational facilities are inherently unequal," thus overturning *Plessy v. Ferguson* (1896) and the "separate but equal" doctrine as it applied to public schools
1955	*Brown v. Board of Education of Topeka II*	Ordered school desegregation to begin with "all deliberate speed," but offered no timetable
1957	Civil Rights Act	Created Civil Rights Division within the Justice Department
1964	Civil Rights Act	Prohibited discrimination in employment and most places of public accommodation on basis of race, color, religion, sex, or national origin; outlawed bias in federally assisted programs; created Equal Employment Opportunity Commission
1965	Voting Rights Act	Authorized federal supervision of voter registration in states and counties where fewer than half of voting age residents were registered; outlawed literacy and other discriminatory tests in voter registration

The following year, at age 35, King received the Nobel Peace Prize, which both solidified his reputation as the premier voice of the Movement and added greatly to his stature within mainstream American culture. The award also demonstrated the truly global impact of the Movement he led.

LBJ and the Civil Rights Act of 1964

An extraordinary demonstration of interracial unity, the March on Washington stood as the high-water mark in the struggle for civil rights. It buoyed the spirits of Movement leaders, as well as of liberals pushing the new civil rights bill through Congress. But the assassination of John F. Kennedy on November 22, 1963, in Dallas threw an ominous cloud over the whole nation and the civil rights movement in particular. Most African Americans probably shared the feelings of Coretta Scott King, who recalled her family's vigil: "We felt that President Kennedy had been a friend of the Cause and that with him as President we could continue to move forward. We watched and prayed for him."

Lyndon Baines Johnson (LBJ), Kennedy's successor, had never been much of a friend to civil rights. As a senator from Texas (1948–60, including six years as majority leader), Johnson had been one of the shrewdest and most powerful Democrats in Congress. Throughout the 1950s he had worked to obstruct the passage and enforcement of civil rights laws. But as vice president he had ably chaired Kennedy's working group on equal employment. Even so, civil rights activists looked upon Johnson warily as he took over the Oval Office.

As president, Johnson realized that he faced a new political reality, created by the civil rights movement. Eager to unite the Democratic Party and prove himself as a national leader, he seized on civil rights as a golden political opportunity. Throughout the early months of 1964, the new president let it be known publicly and privately that he would brook no compromise on civil rights. Johnson exploited all his skills as a political insider, cajoling, flattering, and threatening key members of the House and Senate. Working with the president, the fifteen-year-old Leadership Conference on Civil Rights coordinated a sophisticated lobbying effort in Congress. Groups such as the NAACP, the AFL-CIO, the National Council of Churches, and the American Jewish Congress made the case for a strong civil rights bill. The House passed the bill in February by a 290–130 vote. The more difficult fight would be in the Senate, where a southern filibuster promised to block or weaken the bill. By June, however, Johnson's persistence paid off. The southern filibuster collapsed.

On July 2, 1964, Johnson signed the Civil Rights Act of 1964. Every major provision had survived intact. This landmark law represented the most significant civil rights legislation since Reconstruction. It prohibited discrimination in most places of public accommodation; it banned discrimination in employment on the basis of race, color, religion, sex, or national origin; it outlawed bias in federally assisted programs; it authorized the Justice Department to institute suits to desegregate public schools and other facilities; and it provided technical and financial aid to communities desegregating their schools. The act also created the Equal Employment Opportunity Commission (EEOC) to investigate and litigate cases of job discrimination.

●•●━│Read the Document
*The Civil Rights Act
of 1964* at
**www.myhistory
lab.com**

There were important unintended consequences of this landmark legislation as well. It gave legal foundation to affirmative action policies and to the assertion of equal rights for women and nonblack minorities. The EEOC, for example, became an important site for contesting both gender and racial discrimination in the workplace, receiving over 100,000 complaints a year by the 1970s. And on a political level, LBJ was perhaps more prescient than he realized when he commented after signing the bill that the Civil Rights Act "delivered the South to the Republican Party." It took real political courage for Johnson, a Southern Democrat, to support the legislation as vigorously as he did, for the new law did indeed initiate a long-term political realignment that would transform the South from a solidly Democratic region to a solidly Republican one.

Mississippi Freedom Summer

While Johnson and his liberal allies won the congressional battle for the new civil rights bill, activists in Mississippi mounted a far more radical and dangerous campaign than any yet attempted in the South. In the spring of 1964, a coalition of workers led by SNCC launched the Freedom Summer project, an ambitious effort to register black voters and directly challenge the iron rule of segregation. Mississippi stood as the toughest test for the civil rights movement. It was the nation's poorest state and by most statistical measures the most backward, and it had remained largely untouched by the freedom struggle. African Americans constituted 42 percent of the state's population, but fewer than 5 percent could vote. A small white-planter elite controlled most of the state's wealth, and a long tradition of terror against black people maintained the racial caste system.

Bob Moses of SNCC and Dave Dennis of CORE planned Freedom Summer as a way of opening up this closed society. The project recruited over 900 volunteers, mostly white college students, to aid in voter registration, teach in "freedom schools," and help build a "Freedom Party" as an alternative to Mississippi's all-white Democratic Party. Organizers expected violence, which was precisely why they wanted white volunteers. Dave Dennis later explained their reasoning: "The death of a white college student would bring on more attention to what was going on than for a black college student getting it. That's cold, but that was also in another sense speaking the language of this country." Mississippi authorities prepared for the civil rights workers as if expecting a foreign army, beefing up state highway patrols and local police forces.

On June 21, while most project volunteers were still training in Ohio, three activists disappeared in Neshoba County, Mississippi, when they went to investigate the burning of a black church that was supposed to serve as a freedom school. Six weeks later, after a massive search belatedly ordered by President Johnson, FBI agents discovered the bodies of the three—northern white students Michael Schwerner and Andrew Goodman, and a local black activist, James Chaney—buried in an earthen dam. Over the summer, at least three other civil rights workers died violently. Project workers suffered 1,000 arrests, 80 beatings, 35 shooting incidents, and 30 bombings in homes, churches, and schools.

Within the project, simmering problems tested the ideal of the Beloved Community. Black veterans of SNCC resented the affluent white volunteers, many of whom had not come to terms with their own racial prejudices. White volunteers, staying only a short time in the state, often found it difficult to communicate in the

An interracial group of volunteers singing in front of a bus during the Freedom Summer Project in Mississippi, 1964. Images portraying black and white unity in the civil rights struggle reflected the powerful idealism that attracted many young people to "the Movement."

southern communities with local African Americans, wary of breaking old codes of deference. Sexual tensions between black male and white female volunteers also strained relations. A number of both black and white women, led by Ruby Doris Robinson, Mary King, and Casey Hayden, began to raise the issue of women's equality as a companion goal to racial equality. The day-to-day reality of violent reprisals, police harassment, and constant fear took a hard toll on everyone.

The project did manage to rivet national attention on Mississippi racism, and it won enormous sympathy from northern liberals. Among their concrete accomplishments, the volunteers could point with pride to more than forty freedom schools that brought classes in reading, arithmetic, politics, and African American history to thousands of black children. Some 60,000 black voters signed up to join the Mississippi Freedom Democratic Party (MFDP). In August 1964, the MFDP sent a slate of delegates to the Democratic National Convention looking to challenge the credentials of the all-white regular state delegation.

At the Democrats' Atlantic City convention, the idealism of Freedom Summer collided with the more cynical needs of the national Democratic Party. Concerned that Republicans might carry a number of southern states in November, President Johnson opposed seating the MFDP because he wanted to avoid a divisive floor fight. But before the convention opened, MFDP leaders and sympathizers gave dramatic testimony detailing the racism and brutality in Mississippi politics. "Is this America," asked Fannie Lou Hamer, "the land of the free and the home of the brave, where we are threatened daily because we want to live as decent human beings?" Led by Senator Hubert Humphrey, whom LBJ had already picked as his running mate, Johnson's forces offered a compromise that would have given the MFDP two token seats on the floor. Bitter over what they saw as a betrayal, the MFDP delegates turned the offer down. Within SNCC, the defeat of the MFDP intensified African American disillusionment with the Democratic Party and the liberal establishment.

Read the Document

Fannie Lou Hammer, Voting Rights in Mississippi (1962–1964) at www.myhistorylab.com

Malcolm X and Black Consciousness

Frustrated with the limits of nonviolent protest and electoral politics, younger activists within SNCC found themselves increasingly drawn to the militant rhetoric and vision of Malcolm X, who since 1950 had been the pre-eminent spokesman for the black nationalist religious sect, the Nation of Islam (NOI). Founded in depression-era Detroit by Elijah Muhammad, the NOI, like the followers of black-nationalist leader Marcus Garvey in the 1920s (see Chapter 23), aspired to create a self-reliant, highly disciplined, and proud community—a separate "nation" for black people. Elijah Muhammad preached a message of racial solidarity and self-help, criticized crime and drug use, and castigated whites as "blue-eyed devils" responsible for the world's evil. During the 1950s, the NOI (also called Black Muslims) successfully organized in northern black communities, appealing especially to criminals, drug addicts, and others on the margins of urban life. It operated restaurants, retail stores, and schools as models for black economic self-sufficiency.

The man known as Malcolm X had been born Malcolm Little in 1925 and raised in Lansing, Michigan. His father, a preacher and a follower of Marcus Garvey, was killed in a racist attack by local whites. In his youth, Malcolm led a life of petty crime, eventually serving a seven-year prison term for burglary. While in jail he educated himself and converted to the Nation of Islam. He took the surname "X" to symbolize his original African family name, lost through slavery. Emerging from jail in 1952, he became a dynamic organizer, editor, and speaker for the Nation of Islam. He spoke frequently on college campuses as well on the street corners of black neighborhoods like New York's Harlem. He encouraged his audiences to take pride in their African heritage and to consider armed self-defense rather than relying solely on nonviolence—in short, to break free of white domination "by any means necessary."

Malcolm ridiculed the integrationist goals of the civil rights movement. Black Muslims, he told audiences, do not want "to integrate into this corrupt society, but to separate from it, to a land of our own, where we can reform ourselves, lift up our moral standards, and try to be godly." In his best-selling *Autobiography of Malcolm X* (1965), he admitted that his position was extremist. "The black race here in North America is in extremely bad condition. You show me a black man who isn't an extremist," he argued, "and I'll show you one who needs psychiatric attention."

In 1964, troubled by Elijah Muhammad's personal scandals (he faced paternity suits brought by two young female employees) and eager to find a more politically effective approach to improving conditions for blacks, Malcolm X broke with the Nation of Islam. He made the pilgrimage to Mecca, the Muslim holy city, where he met Islamic peoples of all colors and underwent a "radical alteration in my whole outlook about 'white' men." He returned to the United States as El-Hajj Malik El-Shabazz, abandoned his black separatist views, and founded the Organization of Afro-American Unity. Malcolm now looked for common ground with the civil rights movement, addressing a Mississippi Freedom Democrats rally in

Born Malcolm Little, Malcolm X (1925–65) took the name "X" as a symbol of the stolen identity of African slaves. He emerged in the early 1960s as the foremost advocate of racial unity and black nationalism. The Black Power movement, initiated in 1966 by SNCC members, was strongly influenced by Malcolm X.

Harlem and meeting with SNCC activists. He stressed the international links between the civil rights struggle in America and the problems facing emerging African nations. On February 21, 1965, Malcolm X was assassinated while giving a speech at Harlem's Audubon Ballroom. His assailants were members of a New Jersey branch of the NOI, possibly infiltrated by the FBI.

SNCC leader John Lewis thought Malcolm X had been the most effective voice "to articulate the aspirations, bitterness, and frustrations of the Negro people," forming "a living link between Africa and the civil rights movement in this country." In his death, he became a martyr for the idea that soon became known as Black Power. As much as anyone, Malcolm X pointed the way to a new black consciousness that celebrated black history, black culture, African heritage, and black self-sufficiency.

Selma and the Voting Rights Act of 1965

Lyndon Johnson won reelection in 1964 by a landslide, capturing 61 percent of the popular vote. Of the 6 million black people who voted in the election—2 million more than in 1960—an overwhelming 94 percent cast their ballots for Johnson. Republican candidate Barry Goldwater managed to carry only his home state of Arizona and five Deep South states, where fewer than 45 percent of eligible black people could vote. With Democrats in firm control of both the Senate and the House, civil rights leaders believed the time was ripe for further legislative gains. There had already been some progress toward guaranteeing voting rights with the 1964 ratification of the Twenty-Fourth Amendment to the Constitution, outlawing the poll tax or any other tax as a condition of voting. Johnson and his staff began drafting a tough voting rights bill in late 1964, partly with an eye toward countering Republican gains among Deep South whites with newly registered black Democratic voters (see Map 28.2).

Once again, Movement leaders decided to create a crisis that would arouse national indignation, pressure Congress, and force federal action. King and his aides chose Selma, Alabama, as their target. Selma, a city of 27,000 some fifty miles west of Montgomery, had a notorious record of preventing black voting. Of the 15,000 eligible black voters in Selma's Dallas County, registered voters numbered only in the hundreds. In 1963, local activists had invited SNCC workers to aid voter registration efforts in the community. But they had met a violent reception from county sheriff Jim Clark. Sensing that

Clark might be another Bull Connor, King arrived in Selma in January 1965, just after accepting the Nobel Peace Prize in Oslo. "We are not asking, we are demanding the ballot," he declared. King, the SCLC staff, and SNCC workers led daily marches on the Dallas County Courthouse, where hundreds of black citizens tried to get their names added to voter lists. By early February, Clark had imprisoned more than 3,000 protesters.

Despite the brutal beating of Reverend James Bevel, a key SCLC strategist, and the killing of Jimmy Lee Jackson, a young black demonstrator in nearby Marion, the SCLC failed to arouse the level of national indignation it sought. Consequently, in early March SCLC staffers called on black activists to march from Selma to Montgomery, where they planned to deliver a list of grievances to Governor Wallace. On Sunday, March 7, while King preached to his church in Atlanta, a group of 600 marchers crossed the Pettus Bridge on the Alabama River, on their way to Montgomery. A group of mounted, heavily armed county and state lawmen blocked their path and ordered them to turn back. When the marchers did not move, the lawmen attacked with billy clubs and tear gas, driving the

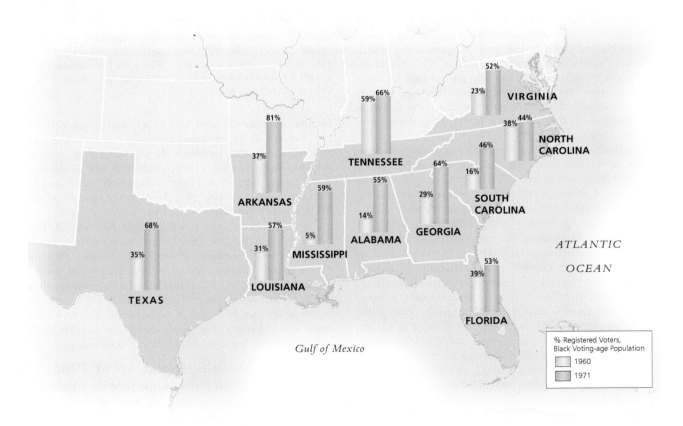

MAP 28.2 Impact of the Voting Rights Act of 1965 Voter registration among African Americans in the South increased significantly between 1960 and 1971.

protesters back over the bridge in a bloody rout. More than fifty marchers had to be treated in local hospitals.

The dramatic "Bloody Sunday" attack received extensive coverage on network television, prompting a national uproar. Demands for federal intervention poured into the White House from all over the country. King issued a public call for civil rights supporters to come to Selma for a second march on Montgomery. But a federal court temporarily enjoined the SCLC from proceeding with the march. King found himself trapped. He reluctantly accepted a face-saving compromise: in return for a promise from Alabama authorities not to harm marchers, King would lead his followers across the Pettus Bridge, stop, pray briefly, and then turn back. This plan outraged the more militant SNCC activists and sharpened their distrust of King and the SCLC.

Just when it seemed the Selma movement might die, white racist violence revived it. A gang of white toughs attacked four white Unitarian ministers who had come to Selma to participate in the march. One of them, Reverend James J. Reeb of Boston, died of multiple skull fractures. His death brought new calls for federal action. On March 15, President Johnson delivered a televised address to a joint session of Congress to request passage of a voting rights bill. In a stirring speech, the president fused the political power of his office with the moral power of the movement. "Their cause must be our cause, too. Because it is not just Negroes, but really all of us who must overcome the crippling legacy of bigotry and injustice. And," he concluded firmly, quoting the Movement's hymn, "we shall overcome." Johnson also prevailed upon federal judge Frank Johnson to issue a

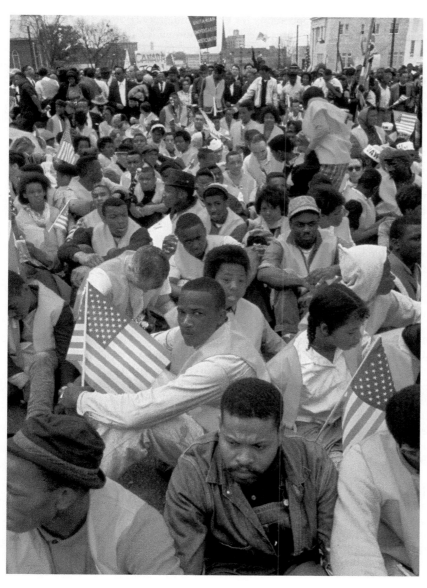

Voting rights demonstrators on the historic four-day, fifty-four mile trek from Selma to Montgomery Alabama, March 1965. Intensive media coverage helped swell the original 3,000 marchers to over 30,000 supporters at a climactic rally in front of the Alabama state capitol in Montgomery.

ruling allowing the march to proceed, and he warned Governor Wallace not to interfere.

On March 21, Martin Luther King Jr. led more than 3,000 black and white marchers out of Selma on the road to Montgomery, where the bus boycott that marked the beginning of his involvement had occurred nine years before. Four days later, they arrived at the Alabama statehouse. Their ranks had been swelled by more than 30,000 supporters, including hundreds of prominent politicians, entertainers, and black leaders. "I know some of you are asking today," King told the crowd, "'How long will it take?'" He went on in a rousing, rhythmic cadence:

> How long? Not long, because the arc of the moral universe is long but it bends toward justice. How long? Not long, because mine eyes have seen the glory of the coming of the Lord!

In August 1965, President Johnson signed the Voting Rights Act into law. It authorized federal supervision of registration in states and counties where fewer than half of voting-age residents were registered. It also outlawed literacy and other discriminatory tests that had been used to prevent blacks from registering to vote. Between 1964 and 1968, black registrants in Mississippi leaped from 7 percent to 59 percent of the statewide black population; in Alabama, from 24 percent to 57 percent. In those years, the number of southern black voters grew from 1 million to 3.1 million. For the first time in their lives, black Southerners in hundreds of small towns and rural communities could enjoy full participation in American politics. Ten years after the Montgomery bus boycott, the civil rights movement had reached a peak of national influence and interracial unity.

Yet even amid this triumph, the growing mood of desperation among African Americans in northern ghettoes suggested the limits of the Movement and interracial unity. There had been a violent uprising in New York's Harlem in the summer of 1964 and a far more widespread and destructive rebellion in the Watts section of Los Angeles in August 1965 (see Chapter 29). These marked the first of the "long, hot summer" uprisings that would alienate many white citizens who had been sympathetic to the nonviolent civil rights struggle. They served notice as well that the growing frustration and alienation of northern blacks, increasingly defined by a militant turn to the rhetoric of "black power," could not be addressed with the same principles, tactics, and solutions that had made the southern civil rights movement successful.

Civil Rights Beyond Black and White

Minorities other than African Americans also had long been denied their civil rights. After World War II, Latinos, Indian peoples, and Asian Americans began making their own halting efforts to improve their political, legal, and economic status. They faced strong opposition from institutional racism and various economic interests that benefited from keeping these groups in a subordinate position. At the same time, the civil rights struggle helped spur a movement to reform immigration policies. The largely unintended consequences of the 1965 Immigration and Nationality Act would radically increase and reshape the flow of new immigrants into the United States.

Mexican Americans and Mexican Immigrants

The Mexican American community in the West and Southwest included both longtime U.S. citizens—who found white authorities nonetheless unwilling to recognize their rights—and noncitizen immigrants from Mexico. After World War II, several Mexican American political organizations sought to secure equal rights and equal opportunity for their community by stressing its American identity. The most important of these groups were the League of United Latin American Citizens (LULAC), launched in Texas in 1928, and the GI Forum, founded in Texas in 1948 by Mexican American veterans of World War II. Both emphasized learning English, assimilating into American society, improving education, and voting to gain political power. LULAC successfully pursued two important legal cases that anticipated *Brown* v. *Board of Education*. In *Mendez* v. *Westminster*, a 1947 California case, and in the 1948 *Delgado* case in Texas, the Supreme Court upheld lower-court rulings that declared segregation of Mexican Americans unconstitutional. Like *Brown*, these two decisions did not immediately end segregation, but they offered pathbreaking legal and psychological victories to Mexican American activists. LULAC won another significant legal battle in the 1954 *Hernandez* decision, in which the Supreme Court ended the exclusion of Mexican Americans from Texas jury lists.

Mexican migration to the United States increased dramatically during and after World War II. The *bracero* program, a cooperative effort between the U.S. and Mexican governments, brought some 300,000 Mexicans to the United States during the war as temporary agricultural and railroad workers. American agribusiness came to depend on Mexicans as a key source of cheap farm labor, and the program continued after the war. Most *braceros* endured harsh work, poor food, and substandard housing in migratory labor camps. Some migrated into the newly emerging *barrios*—Hispanic neighborhoods—in cities such as San Antonio, Los Angeles, El Paso, and Denver. Many *braceros* and their children became American citizens, but most returned to Mexico. Another group of postwar Mexican immigrants were the *mojados*, or "wetbacks," so called because many swam the Rio Grande to enter the United States illegally.

This continued flow of immigrant workers into the Southwest heightened tensions within the Mexican

Delegates to the 1948 National Convention of the League of United Latin American Citizens met in Kingsville, Texas. After World War II, LULAC grew to about 15,000 members active in 200 local councils, mostly in Texas and California.

American community. LULAC and the GI Forum contended that Mexican American civil rights activists needed to focus their efforts on American citizens of Mexican descent. Thus, they lobbied to end the *bracero* program and enforce stricter limits on immigration from Mexico to help maintain strict boundaries between Mexican American citizens and Mexican immigrants. Yet within Mexican American communities, where citizens and noncitizens shared language and work experience and made families together, this distinction had always been blurry.

In 1954, trying to curb the flow of undocumented immigrants from Mexico, the Eisenhower administration launched the massive "Operation Wetback." For three years, Immigration and Naturalization Service (INS) agents rounded up some 3.7 million allegedly undocumented migrants and sent them back over the border. INS agents made little effort to distinguish so-called illegals from *braceros* and Mexican American citizens. Many families were broken up, and thousands who had lived in the United States for a decade or more found themselves deported. Many deportees were denied basic civil liberties, such as due process, and suffered physical abuse and intimidation. The breakup of families caused enormous resentment and anger, as did the contradictory policies of the federal government. As Ernesto Galarza, a leader of the National Agricultural Workers Union, put it, "while one agency of the United States government rounded up the illegal aliens and deported them to Mexico . . . another government agency was busily engaged in recruiting workers in Mexico to return them to U.S. farms."

The government campaign against aliens pushed LULAC, the GI Forum, and other activist groups to change their strategy in a critical way. The campaign to win full civil rights for American citizens of Mexican descent would increasingly be linked to improving the lives—and asserting the rights—of all Mexican immigrants, both documented and undocumented. If the government and the broader American public refused to distinguish between a Mexican national, a resident alien of the United States, a naturalized American citizen, or a native-born Spanish-speaking American, why should Mexican Americans cling to these distinctions? By the 1960s, a new civil rights movement emerged, *la raza*, based on the shared ethnicity and historical experiences of the broader Mexican American community.

Puerto Ricans

The United States seized Puerto Rico in 1898, during the final stages of the Spanish-American War. The Jones Act of 1917 made the island an unincorporated territory of the United States and granted U.S. citizenship to all Puerto Ricans. Over the next several decades, Puerto Rico's economic base shifted from a diversified, subsistence-oriented agriculture to a single export crop—sugar. U.S. absentee owners dominated the sugar industry, claiming most of the island's arable land, previously tilled by small farmers growing crops for local consumption. Puerto Rico's sugar industry grew enormously profitable, but few island residents benefited from this expansion. By the 1930s, unemployment and poverty were widespread and the island was forced to import its foodstuffs.

Small communities of Puerto Rican migrants had begun to form in New York City during the 1920s. The largest was on the Upper East Side of Manhattan—*el barrio* in East Harlem. During World War II, labor shortages led the federal government to sponsor the recruitment of Puerto Rican workers for industrial jobs in New Jersey, Philadelphia, and Chicago. But the "great migration" took place from 1945 to 1964. During these two decades, the number of Puerto Ricans living on the mainland jumped from fewer than 100,000 to roughly 1 million. Economic opportunity was the chief impetus for this migration, because the island suffered from high unemployment and low wages.

The advent of direct air service between Puerto Rico and New York in 1945 made the city easily accessible. The Puerto Rican community in East (or Spanish) Harlem mushroomed, and new communities in the South Bronx and Brooklyn began to emerge. By 1970, there were about 800,000 Puerto Ricans in New York—more than 10 percent of the city's population. New Puerto Rican communities also took root in Connecticut, Massachusetts, New Jersey, and the Midwest. Puerto Ricans frequently circulated between the island and the mainland, often returning home when economic conditions on the mainland were less favorable.

The experience of Puerto Rican migrants both resembled and differed from that of other immigrant groups in significant ways. Like Mexican immigrants, Puerto Ricans were foreign in language, culture, and experience; unlike Mexicans, they entered the continental United States as citizens. Many Puerto Ricans were also black. Racial and ethnic discrimination came as a double shock, since Puerto Ricans, as citizens, came to America with a sense of entitlement. In New York, Puerto Ricans found themselves barred from most craft unions, excluded from certain neighborhoods, and forced to take jobs largely in the low-paying garment industry and service trades. Puerto Rican children were not well served by a public school system insensitive to language differences and too willing to track Spanish-speaking students into obsolete vocational programs.

By the early 1970s, Puerto Rican families were substantially poorer on average than the total U.S. population, and they had the lowest median income of any Latino group. The steep decline in manufacturing jobs and in the garment industry in New York during the 1960s and 1970s hit the Puerto Rican community especially hard. The structural shift in the U.S. economy away from manufacturing and toward service and high-technology jobs reinforced the Puerto Rican community's goal of improving educational opportunities for its members. The struggle to establish and improve bilingual education in schools became an important part of this effort. Most Puerto Ricans, especially those who had succeeded in school and achieved middle-class status,

continued to identify strongly with their Puerto Rican heritage and Spanish language.

Japanese Americans

The harsh relocation program of World War II devastated the Japanese American community on the West Coast (see Chapter 25). But the war against Nazism also helped weaken older notions of white superiority and racism. During the war, the state of California had aggressively enforced an alien land law by confiscating property declared illegally held by Japanese. In November 1946, a proposition supporting the law appeared on the state ballot. Thanks in part to a campaign by the Japanese American Citizens League (JACL) reminding voters of the wartime contributions of Nisei (second-generation Japanese American) soldiers, voters overwhelmingly rejected the referendum. One JACL leader hailed the vote as proof that "the people of California will not approve discriminatory and prejudiced treatment of persons of Japanese ancestry." Two years later, the Supreme Court declared the law unconstitutional, calling it "nothing more than outright racial discrimination."

The 1952 Immigration and Nationality Act (see Chapter 26) removed the old ban against Japanese immigration and also made Issei (first-generation Japanese Americans) eligible for naturalized citizenship. Japanese Americans, who lobbied hard for the new law, greeted it with elation. "It gave the Japanese equality with all other immigrants," said JACL leader Harry Takagi, "and that was the principle we had been struggling for from the very beginning." By 1965, some 46,000 immigrant Japanese, most of them elderly Issei, had taken their citizenship oaths.

Indian Peoples

The postwar years also brought significant changes in the status and lives of Indian peoples. Congress reversed New Deal policies that had stressed Indian sovereignty and cultural independence. Responding to a variety of pressure groups, including mining and other economic interests wishing to exploit natural resources on reservations, Congress adopted a policy known as "termination," designed to cancel Indian treaties and terminate sovereignty rights. In 1953, Congress passed House Concurrent Resolution 108, which allowed Congress to terminate a tribe as a political entity by passing legislation specific to that tribe. Supporters of termination had varied motives, but the policy added up to the return of enforced assimilation for solving the "Indian problem."

Between 1954 and 1962, Congress passed twelve termination bills covering more than sixty tribes, nearly all in the West. Even when tribes consented to their own termination, they discovered that dissolution brought unforeseen problems. For example, members of the

Klamaths of Oregon and the Paiutes of Utah received large cash payments from the division of tribal assets. But after these one-time payments were spent, members had to take poorly paid, unskilled jobs to survive. Many Indian peoples became dependent on state social services and slipped into poverty and alcoholism.

Along with termination, the federal government gave greater emphasis to a relocation program aimed at speeding up assimilation. The Bureau of Indian Affairs encouraged reservation Indians to relocate to cities, where they were provided with housing and jobs. For some, relocation meant assimilation, intermarriage with whites, and loss of tribal identity. Others, homesick and unable to adjust to an alien culture and place, either returned to reservations or wound up on the margins of city life. Still others regularly traveled back and forth. In some respects, this urban migration paralleled the larger postwar shift of rural peoples to cities and suburbs.

Indians increasingly came to see termination as a policy geared mainly to exploiting resources on Indian lands. By the early 1960s, a new movement was emerging to defend Indian sovereignty. The National Congress of American Indians (NCAI) condemned termination, calling for a review of federal policies and a return to self-determination. The NCAI led a political and educational campaign that challenged the goal of assimilation and created a new awareness among white people that Indians had the right to remain Indians. When the termination policy ended in the early 1960s, it had affected only about 3 percent of federally recognized Indian peoples.

Taking their cue from the civil rights movement, Indian activists used the court system to reassert sovereign rights. Indian and white liberal lawyers, many with experience in civil rights cases, worked through the Native American Rights Fund, which became a powerful force in western politics. A series of Supreme Court decisions, culminating in *United States* v. *Wheeler* (1978), reasserted the principle of "unique and limited" sovereignty. The Court recognized tribal independence except where limited by treaty or Congress.

The Indian population had been growing since the early years of the century, but most reservations had trouble making room for a new generation. Indians suffered increased rates of poverty, chronic unemployment, alcoholism, and poor health. The average Indian family in the early 1960s earned only one-third of the average family income in the United States. Those who remained in the cities usually became "ethnic Indians," identifying themselves more as simply "Indians" than as members of specific tribes. By the late 1960s, ethnic Indians had begun emphasizing civil rights over tribal rights, making common cause with African Americans and other minorities. The National Indian Youth Council (NIYC), founded in 1960, tried to unite the two causes of equality for individual Indians and special status for tribes. But the organization faced difficult contradictions between a common Indian identity, emphasizing Indians as a single ethnic group, and tribal identity, stressing the citizenship of Indians in separate nations.

Remaking the Golden Door: The Immigration and Nationality Act of 1965

The egalitarian political climate created by the civil rights movement nurtured efforts to modernize and reform the country's immigration policies. In 1965, Congress passed a new Immigration and Nationality Act, abolishing the national origins quotas that had been in place since the

A Korean couple working behind the counter of their newly opened restaurant in Los Angeles, ca. 2000. In the thirty-five years after the Immigration and Nationality Act of 1965, the city's Asian American population had grown to over 1.2 million, including the largest Korean community outside of Korea.

1920s and substituting overall hemispheric limits: 120,000 visas annually for immigrants from the Western Hemisphere and 170,000 for those from the Eastern Hemisphere (with a 20,000 limit from any single country). The act was intended to redress the grievances of Eastern and Southern European ethnic groups who had been largely shut out since 1924. President Lyndon B. Johnson played down its importance. "It does not affect the lives of millions," he said when he signed the bill into law. "It will not reshape the structure of our daily lives, or really add importantly to our wealth or our power."

But the new law proved LBJ's prediction wrong. Exempted from numerical quotas were immigrants seeking family reunification with American citizens or resident aliens. In addition, preferences to those with specialized job skills and training, in fields like medicine and engineering, were extended to people from the nations of the Eastern Hemisphere. The high priority given family reunification created an unprecedented cycle of "chain immigration and sponsorship" of people seeking to join relatives already in the United States. As initial immigrants attained permanent resident or citizenship status, they would sponsor family members and relatives to come over. Once these family members and relatives arrived in the United States and became resident aliens or citizens, they in turn could sponsor their family members, and so on.

The consequences for Asian American communities in particular were profound. The number of Asian Americans soared from about 1 million in 1965 to 11 million by the end of the century. Immigrants from India and the Philippines included a high percentage of health care professionals, whereas many Chinese and Korean immigrants found work in professional and managerial occupations as well as their own small businesses. At the same time, low-skilled and impoverished Asians poured into the "Chinatowns" and "Koreatowns" of cities like New York and Los Angeles, taking jobs in restaurants, hotels, and garment manufacturing. Four times as many Asians settled in the United States in this period as in the entire previous history of the nation. This new wave also brought a strikingly different group of Asian immigrants to America. In 1960, the Asian American population was 52 percent Japanese, 27 percent Chinese, and 20 percent Filipino. In 1985, the composition had become 21 percent Chinese, 21 percent Filipino, 15 percent Japanese, 12 percent Vietnamese, 11 percent Korean, 10 percent Asian Indian, 4 percent Laotian, and 3 percent Cambodian.

The 1965 act also created conditions that increased undocumented immigration from Latin America. The new limits on Western Hemisphere migration, along with the simultaneous ending of the *bracero* program, tempted many thousands to enter the United States illegally. The Immigration and Naturalization Service arrested and deported 500,000 undocumented aliens each year in the decade following the act, most of them from Mexico, Central America, and the Caribbean. By the 1980s, more than 80 percent of all legal immigrants to the United States came from either Asia or Latin America; if one included illegal immigrants, the figure would surpass 90 percent.

Conclusion

The mass movement for civil rights was arguably the most important domestic event in twentieth-century American history. The struggle that began in Montgomery, Alabama, in December 1955 ultimately transformed race relations in thousands of American communities. By the early 1960s, this community-based movement had placed civil rights at the very center of national political life. It achieved its greatest successes by invoking the Constitution—the supreme law of the land—to destroy legal segregation and win individual freedom for African Americans. The Civil Rights Act of 1964 and the Voting Rights Act of 1965 testified to the power of an African American and white liberal coalition. Yet the persistence of racism, poverty, and ghetto slums challenged a central assumption of liberalism: that equal protection of constitutional rights would give all Americans equal opportunities in life. By the mid-1960s, many black people had begun to question the core values of liberalism, the benefits of alliance with whites, and the philosophy of nonviolence. At the same time, a conservative white backlash against the gains made by African Americans further weakened the liberal political consensus.

In challenging the persistence of widespread poverty and institutional racism, the civil rights movement called for deep structural changes in American life. By 1967, Martin Luther King Jr. was articulating a broad and radical vision linking the struggle against racial injustice to other defects in American society. "The black revolution," he argued, "is much more than a struggle for the rights of Negroes. It is forcing America to face all its interrelated flaws—racism, poverty, militarism, and materialism. It is exposing evils that are deeply rooted in the whole structure of our society." Curing these ills would prove far more difficult than ending legal segregation.

Review Questions

1. What were the key legal and political antecedents to the civil rights struggle in the 1940s and early 1950s? What organizations played the most central role? Which tactics continued to be used, and which were abandoned?

2. How did African American communities challenge legal segregation in the South? Compare the strategies of key organizations, such as the NAACP, SNCC, SCLC, and CORE.

CHRONOLOGY

1941	Executive Order 8802 forbids racial discrimination in defense industries and government
1946	In *Morgan* v. *Virginia*, U.S. Supreme Court rules that segregation on interstate buses is unconstitutional
	President Harry Truman creates the President's Committee on Civil Rights
1947	Jackie Robinson becomes the first African American on a major league baseball team
1948	President Truman issues executive order desegregating the armed forces
1954	In *Brown* v. *Board of Education*, Supreme Court rules segregated schools inherently unequal
1955	Supreme Court rules that school desegregation must proceed "with all deliberate speed"
	Montgomery bus boycott begins
1956	Montgomery bus boycott ends in victory as the Supreme Court affirms a district court ruling that segregation on buses is unconstitutional
1957	Southern Christian Leadership Conference (SCLC) is founded
	President Dwight Eisenhower sends in federal troops to protect African American students integrating Little Rock, Arkansas, high school
1960	Sit-in movement begins as four college students sit at a lunch counter in Greensboro, North Carolina, and ask to be served
	Student Nonviolent Coordinating Committee (SNCC) founded
	Board of Indian Commissioners is created

1961	Freedom Rides begin
1962	James Meredith integrates the University of Mississippi
	The Albany movement fails to end segregation in Albany, Georgia
1963	SCLC initiates campaign to desegregate Birmingham, Alabama
	Medgar Evers, leader of the Mississippi NAACP, is assassinated
	March on Washington; Martin Luther King Jr. delivers his historic "I Have a Dream" speech
1964	Mississippi Freedom Summer project brings students to Mississippi to teach and register voters
	President Johnson signs the Civil Rights Act of 1964
	Civil rights workers Michael Schwerner, James Chaney, and Andrew Goodman are found buried in Philadelphia, Mississippi
	Mississippi Freedom Democratic Party (MFDP) is denied seats at the 1964 Democratic Presidential Convention
1965	SCLC and SNCC begin voter registration campaign in Selma, Alabama
	Malcolm X is assassinated
	Civil rights marchers walk from Selma to Montgomery
	Voting Rights Act of 1965 is signed into law
	Immigration and Nationality Act

3. Discuss the varieties of white resistance to the civil rights movement. Which were most effective in slowing the drive for equality?

4. Analyze the civil rights movement's complex relationship with the national Democratic Party between 1948 and 1964. How was the party transformed by its association with the movement? What political gains and losses did that association entail?

5. What legal and institutional impact did the movement have on American life? How did it change American culture and politics? Where did it fail?

6. What relationship did the African Americans who struggled for civil rights have with other American minorities? How—if at all—did these minorities benefit? Did they build their own versions of the movement?

Recommended Reading

Raymond Arsenault, *Freedom Riders: 1961 and the Struggle for Racial Justice* (2006). A recent, definitive account of this pivotal moment in Movement history, Arsenault demonstrates how the Freedom Rides both galvanized national and international attention and inspired local activists around the South.

Taylor Branch, *Parting the Waters: America in the King Years, 1954–1963* (1988); *Pillar of Fire: America in the King Years, 1963–1965* (1998). Deeply researched and monumental narrative histories of the southern civil rights movement organized around the life and influence of Reverend Martin Luther King Jr.

Clayborne Carson et al., eds., *Reporting Civil Rights* (2003). A wide-ranging compilation of contemporary reportage on the movement and resistance to it.

Roger Daniels, *Guarding the Golden Door: American Immigration Policy and Immigrants Since 1882* (2004). A comprehensive history, including excellent coverage of the legislative and political battles behind post–World War II changes in immigration laws.

Mary L. Dudziak, *Cold War Civil Rights: Race and the Image of American Democracy* (2000). Pathbreaking analysis of the connections between the struggle for racial equality in America and the nation's contest with communism abroad.

Wesley C. Hogan, *Many Minds, One Heart: SNCC's Dream for a New America* (2007). The best recent history of this pivotal civil rights group, focusing on its internal political evolution from the idealism of the early sit-in movement through its declining influence by 1965.

Christopher B. Parker, *Fighting for Democracy: Black Veterans and the Struggle Against White Supremacy in the Postwar South* (2009). A deeply researched new history detailing how WW II military experiences inspired black veterans to play a vital role in the civil rights movement.

Howell Raines, *My Soul Is Rested: Movement Days in the Deep South Remembered* (1977). The best oral history of the civil rights movement, drawing from a wide range of participants and points of view. It is brilliantly edited by Raines, who covered the events as a journalist.

Jason Sokol, *There Goes My Everything: White Southerners in the Age of Civil Rights, 1945–1975* (2006). A sophisticated new study examining the range and complexity of white Southerners' encounters with the civil rights movement and the momentous changes it wrought.

PEARSON **myhistorylab** Connections

Reinforce what you learned in this chapter by studying the many documents, images, maps, review tools, and videos available at www.myhistorylab.com.

Read and Review

✓• Study and Review **Chapter 28**

•• Read the Document

Sterling A. Brown, "Out of Their Mouths" (1942)

Brown v. Board of Education of Topeka (1954)

The Southern Manifesto (1956)

Student Non-Violent Coordinating Committee, "Statement of Purpose" (1960)

Charles Sherrod, SNCC Memorandum (1961)

John Lewis, Address at the March on Washington (1963)

The Civil Rights Act of 1964

Fannie Lou Hammer, Voting Rights in Mississippi (1962–1964)

👁 See the Map **Impact of the Voting Rights Act of 1965**

Research and Explore

•• Read the Document

Exploring America: The American Indian Movement

The Civil Rights Movement

Profiles
Ella Baker
César Chávez

📹 Watch the Video

Malcolm X

The Civil Rights Movement

Civil Rights March on Washington (1963)

Jackie Robinson and the Integration of Baseball

Photographing the Civil Rights Movement: Birmingham, 1963

How Did the Civil Rights Movement Change American Schools?

(((•• Hear the Audio

Hear the audio files for Chapter 28 at **www.myhistorylab.com**.

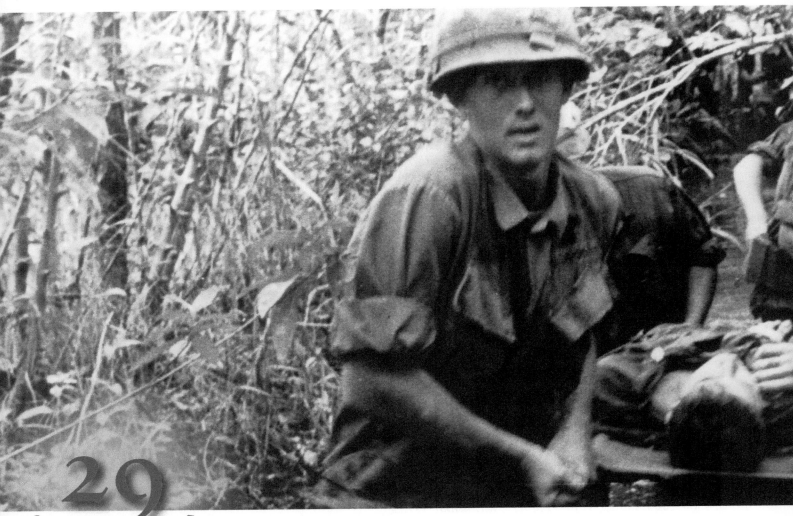

Chapter 29 at www.myhistorylab.com

(((•◦ Hear the Audio

War Abroad, War at Home 1965–1974

CHAPTER OUTLINE

American Communities 851

Uptown, Chicago, Illinois

The Vietnam War 853
Johnson's War
Deeper into the Quagmire
The Credibility Gap

A Generation in Conflict 855
"The Times They Are A-Changin'"
From Campus Protest to Mass
    Mobilization
Teenage Soldiers

Wars on Poverty 861
The Great Society
Crisis in the Cities
Urban Uprisings

1968: Year of Turmoil 865
The Tet Offensive
King, the War, and the Assassination
The Democrats in Disarray
"The Whole World Is Watching!"
The Republican Victory

The Politics of Identity 868
Black Power
Sisterhood Is Powerful
Gay Liberation
The Chicano Rebellion
Red Power
The Asian American Movement

The Nixon Presidency 874
Domestic Policy
Nixon's War
Nixon's Foreign Policy
Dirty Tricks and the 1972 Election
Watergate: Nixon's Downfall

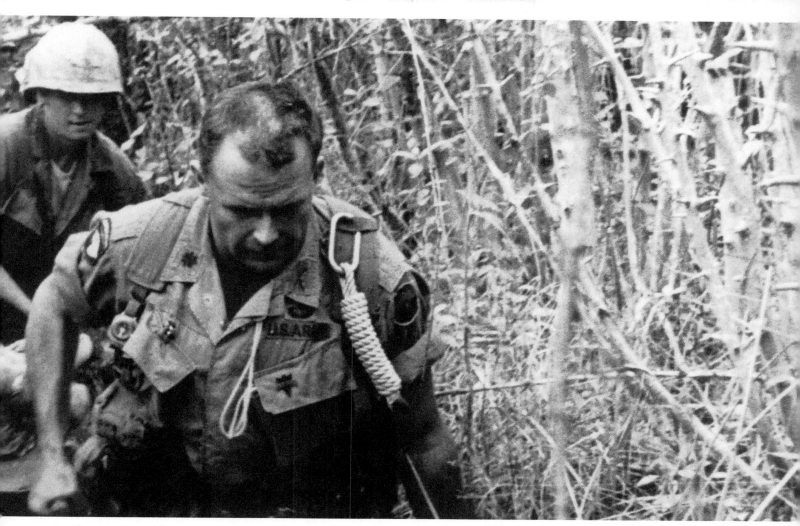

Three American soldiers carry a wounded comrade to safety on a stretcher. Vietnam. U.S. Army photo, Courtesy of the U.S. Military Academy.

Uptown, Chicago, Illinois

AMERICAN Communities

During the freedom summer of 1964, while teams of northern college students traveled south to join voter registration campaigns among African Americans, a small group moved to Chicago to help the city's poor people take control of their communities. They targeted a neighborhood known as Uptown, a one-mile-square section five miles north of the Loop, the city center. The residents, many transplanted from the poverty of the Appalachian South, lived in crowded tenements or in once-elegant mansions now subdivided into tiny, run-down apartments. The student organizers hoped to mobilize the community "so as to demand an end to poverty and the construction of a decent social order."

With the assistance of the Packinghouse Workers union, the students formed Jobs or Income Now (JOIN), opened a storefront office, and invited local residents to work with them to demand jobs and better living conditions. They spent hours listening to people, drawing out their ideas, and helping them

851

develop scores of programs. They campaigned against Mayor Richard Daley's policy of "police omnipresence" that had a fleet of squad cars and paddy wagons continually patrolling the neighborhood. They also helped establish new social clubs, a food-buying cooperative, a community theater, and a health clinic. Within a few years, Uptown street kids had formed the Young Patriots organization, put out a community newspaper, *Rising Up Angry*, and staffed free breakfast programs.

Chicago JOIN was one of ten similar projects sponsored by Students for a Democratic Society (SDS). Impatient with the nation's chronic poverty and Cold War politics, twenty-nine students from nine universities had met in June 1960 to form a new kind of campus-based political organization. SDS soon caught on with liberal students, encouraging them, as part of the nation's largest college population to date, to make their voices heard. By its peak in 1968, SDS had 350 chapters and between 60,000 and 100,000 members. Its principle of participatory democracy—with its promise to give people control over the decisions affecting their lives—appealed to a wider following of more than a million students.

In June 1962, in Port Huron, Michigan, SDS issued a declaration of principles, drafted mainly by graduate student Tom Hayden. "We are people ... bred in at least modest comfort, housed now in universities," *The Port Huron Statement* opened, "looking uncomfortably to the world we inherit." Poverty and social injustice, it continued, were not the only problems. A deeper ailment plagued American society. Everyone, including middle-class students with few material wants, suffered from a sense of "loneliness, estrangement, and alienation." *The Port Huron Statement* defined SDS as a new kind of political movement that would bring people "out of isolation and into community" so that not just the poor but all Americans could overcome their feelings of "powerlessness [and hence] resignation before the enormity of events."

SDS began with a campaign to reform the university, especially to disentangle the financial ties between campus-based research programs and the military-industrial complex. SDS also sent small groups of students to live and organize in the poor communities of Boston, Louisville, Cleveland, and Newark, as well as

Chicago. Ultimately, none of these projects recruited large numbers of people. Protests against local government did little to combat unemployment, and campaigns for better garbage collection or more playgrounds rarely evolved into lasting movements. Nevertheless, organizers did succeed, to some degree, in realizing the goal specified in its slogan: "Let the People Decide." By late 1967, SDS prepared to leave JOIN in the hands of the people it had organized, which was its intention from the beginning.

Initially, even Lyndon Baines Johnson promoted civic participation. The Great Society, as the president called his domestic program, promised more than the abolition of poverty and racial inequality. In May 1964, at the University of Michigan, the president described his goal as a society "where every child can find knowledge to enrich his mind and to enlarge his talents," where "the city of man serves not only the needs of the body and the demands of commerce but the desire for beauty and the hunger for community."

By 1967, the Vietnam War had pushed aside such ambitions. If SDSers had once believed they could work with liberal Democrats like Johnson, they now interpreted social injustice at home as the inevitable consequence of the president's dangerous and destructive foreign policies. SDS threw its energies into building a movement against the war in Vietnam. President Johnson, meanwhile, pursued a foreign policy that would swallow up the funding for his own plans for a war on poverty and would precipitate a very different war at home, Americans against Americans. As hawks and doves lined up on opposite sides, the Vietnam War created a huge and enduring rift. SDS member Richard Flacks had warned that the nation had to "choose between devoting its resources and energies to maintaining military superiority and international hegemony or rechanneling those resources and energies to meeting the desperate needs of its people." Ultimately, even President Johnson himself understood that the "bitch of a war" in Asia ruined "the woman I really loved— the Great Society."

The dream of community did not vanish, but consensus became increasingly remote by the late 1960s. By that time, parents and children were at odds over values and aspirations, urban uprisings were rocking the nation,

1. Why did President Johnson escalate the war in Vietnam?

2. How did campus protests shape national political debate?

3. What were the goals of Johnson's Great Society?

4. What divided the Democratic Party in 1968?

5. How did Richard Nixon win the presidential election in 1968?

6. What is meant by the "politics of identity"?

FOCUS Questions

1965–1974

and political leaders were struck down by assassins' bullets. New protest groups—Black Power, Women's Liberation, Gay Liberation, as well as Chicano, Native American, and Asian—were staking out a highly charged "politics of identity."

Chicago

Political conservatives managed to triumph in the election of Richard Nixon, who went on to disgrace the office. Meanwhile, the United States continued to fight—and eventually lost—the longest war in its history.

AMERICAN
Communities

The Vietnam War

The Vietnam War had its roots in the Truman Doctrine and its goal of containing communism (see Chapter 26). In 1954, after the Communist forces of Ho Chi Minh defeated the French colonialists and created a new government in the north, Vietnam emerged as a major zone of Cold War contention. President John Kennedy called it "the cornerstone of the Free World in Southeast Asia, the keystone in the arch, the finger in the dike," a barrier to the spread of communism throughout the region and perhaps the world. President Lyndon Johnson took office sounding a similar note, sharpened by Secretary of Defense Robert McNamara's warning that failure in Vietnam would result in "a complete shift of world power," with the "prestige and integrity" of the United States severely damaged. With the stakes so high, Johnson concluded that Americans had little choice but to fight for "the principle for which our ancestors fought in the valleys of Pennsylvania."

Vietnam was not Valley Forge, however, and the United States ultimately paid a huge price for its determination to turn back communism in Indochina. More

than 58,000 Americans died in an unwinnable overseas war that only deepened divisions at home.

▶ Watch the Video
Vietnam War at
www.myhistorylab.com

Johnson's War

Although President Kennedy had greatly increased the number of military advisers and Special Forces in South Vietnam (see Chapter 27), it was his successor, Lyndon B. Johnson, who made the decision to engage the United States in a major war there. At first, Johnson simply hoped to stay the course. Facing election in November 1964, he knew that a major military setback would cripple his campaign. But he was equally determined to avoid the fate of President Truman, who had been damaged politically after "losing" China to communism and producing a stalemate in Korea.

Throughout the winter and spring of 1964, as conditions worsened in South Vietnam, Johnson's advisers quietly laid the groundwork for a sustained bombing campaign against North Vietnam. In early August, they found a pretext to set this plan in motion. The National Security Agency—decades later admitting to faulty intelligence—reported two attacks against U.S. destroyers by North Vietnamese patrol boats in the Gulf of Tonkin, off the coast of North Vietnam. Although the second alleged attack never took place, the report prompted Johnson to order retaliatory air strikes against bases in North Vietnam.

Johnson appealed to Congress to give him the authority "to take all necessary measures" and "all necessary steps" to defend U.S. armed forces and "to prevent further aggression." The Gulf of Tonkin resolution moved unanimously through the House and passed the Senate on August 7 with only two dissenting votes. Wayne Morse, the Republican senator from Oregon, had denounced the resolution as a "pre-dated declaration of war."

Ironically, Johnson continued his presidential campaign in 1964 with a call for restraint in Vietnam. He assured voters that "we are not about to send American boys nine or ten thousand miles away from home to do what Asian boys ought to be doing for themselves." This strategy helped him win a landslide victory over conservative Republican Barry Goldwater of Arizona, who had advocated systematic bombing of North Vietnam as a prelude to invasion.

With the election behind him, Johnson faced a hard decision. U.S. forces failed to slow the Communist insurgency into South Vietnam. Meanwhile, the U.S.-backed government in Saigon, the capital city of South Vietnam, appeared near collapse. His advisors pressed him hard to chart a new course if he hoped to avoid, as National Security Advisor McGeorge Bundy put it, a "disastrous defeat."

Deeper into the Quagmire

In early February 1965, the Johnson Administration found a rationale to escalate the war. The Vietcong had dispatched a suicide bomb squad to the U.S. military base at Pleiku in the central highlands of Vietnam, killing seven and wounding more than 100 Americans. Waving the list of casualties, the president rushed into an emergency meeting of the National Security Council to announce that the time had passed for keeping "our guns over the mantel and our shells in the cupboard." He ordered immediate reprisal bombing and one week later, on February 13, authorized Operation Rolling Thunder, a campaign of gradually intensifying air attacks against North Vietnam.

Once Rolling Thunder began, President Johnson hesitated to speak frankly with the American public about his plan to widen the war by sending in more ground troops. Initially, he announced that only two battalions of Marines were being assigned to Danang to defend the airfields where bombing runs began. But six weeks later, 50,000 U.S. combat troops were in Vietnam. By November 1965, the total topped 165,000, and more troops were on the way.

The strategy pursued by the Johnson administration and implemented by General William Westmoreland—a war of attrition—was based on the premise that continuous

The massive bombing and ground combat created huge numbers of civilian casualties in Vietnam. The majority killed were women and children.

use of heavy artillery and air power would eventually exhaust North Vietnam's resources. Meanwhile, U.S. ground forces would defeat the Vietcong in South Vietnam and thereby restore political stability to South Vietnam's pro-Western government. As Johnson once boasted, the strongest military power in the world surely could crush a Communist rebellion in a "pissant" country of peasants.

●●─[Read the Document
Johnson's Defense of the U.S. Presence in Vietnam (1965) at **www.myhistorylab.com**

In practice, the United States wreaked havoc in South Vietnam, tearing apart its society and bringing ecological devastation to its land. Intending to eradicate the support network of the Vietcong, U.S. ground troops conducted search-and-destroy missions throughout the countryside. They attacked villagers and their homes. Seeking to ferret out Vietcong sympathizers, U.S. troops turned at any one time as many as 4 million people— approximately one-quarter of the population of South Vietnam—into refugees. By late 1968, the United States had dropped more than 3 million tons of bombs on Vietnam and eventually delivered more than three times the tonnage dropped by the Allies on all fronts during World War II.

◉ See the Map
The Vietnam War at **www.myhistorylab.com**

Using herbicides such as Agent Orange to defoliate forests, the United States also conducted the most destructive chemical warfare in history.

Several advisers urged the president to keep the American people informed about his decisions in Vietnam, even to declare a state of national emergency. But Johnson feared he would lose momentum on domestic reform if he drew attention to foreign policy. Seeking to avoid "undue excitement in the Congress and in domestic public opinion," he held to a course of intentional deceit.

The Credibility Gap

Johnson's popularity had surged at the time of the Gulf of Tonkin resolution, but it waned rapidly. To stem the tide, Johnson worked hard to control the news media. Despite his efforts, he found himself accused of lying to the American public.

During the early 1960s, network news had either ignored Vietnam or unquestioningly supported U.S. policy. Beginning with a CBS News report by Morley Safer in August 1965, however, the tenor changed. Although government officials described the U.S. operation in the South Vietnamese village Cam Ne as an attack on "fortified Vietcong bunkers," the *CBS Evening News* showed Marines setting fire to the thatched homes of civilians. President Johnson's sharp complaint to CBS did little to staunch the unfavorable news commentary that soon followed. By 1967, according to a noted media observer, "every subject tended to become Vietnam."

Scenes of human suffering and devastation, now broadcast daily, ultimately weakened the administration's moral justification of U.S. involvement as a defense of freedom and democracy in South Vietnam. Reporters described the varieties of American cluster bombs, which released up to 180,000 fiberglass shards, and showed photographs and film clips of the nightmarish effects of the defoliants used on South Vietnam's forests to uncover enemy strongholds. And every night, network television news tallied the soaring American body count, from 26 per week in 1965 to 180 in 1967.

Skeptics stepped forward in the U.S. Congress. Democratic Senator J. William Fulbright of Arkansas, who chaired the Senate Foreign Relations Committee and who had personally speeded the passage of Gulf of Tonkin resolution, became the most vocal critic of Johnson's war policy. A strong supporter of the Cold War, Fulbright had nevertheless concluded that the war in Vietnam was both unwinnable and destructive to domestic reform. In 1967, in his best-selling *Arrogance of Power*, he proposed a negotiated withdrawal from a neutralized Southeast Asia. He also persuaded prominent Democrats to put aside their personal loyalty to Johnson and push through Congress a nonbinding resolution appealing to the United Nations to help negotiate an end to hostilities.

Meanwhile, some of the nation's most trusted European allies called for restraint in Vietnam.

The impact of the war, which cost Americans $21 billion per year, was also felt by Americans at home. Johnson convinced Congress to levy a 10 percent surcharge on individual and corporate taxes. Later adjustments tapped the Social Security fund, heretofore safe from interference. Inflation raced upward, fed by spending on the war. Johnson promised that the end of the war was in sight and replaced advisers who questioned his policy. As casualties multiplied, however, more and more Americans began to question his credibility and to mistrust his handling of the war.

A Generation in Conflict

As the Vietnam war escalated, Americans from all walks of life began to doubt the wisdom of the administration's leadership. Between 1965 and 1971, much of this skepticism took on a distinctly generational character. At the forefront were the baby boomers just coming of age who broadened the definition of politics to encompass not only U.S. foreign policy but also everyday life.

This so-called sixties generation, the largest in American history, began to combine protest against the war in Vietnam with a broader, penetrating critique of American society. Through music, dress, and even hairstyle, they expressed a deep estrangement from the values and aspirations of their parents' generation. As early as 1967, when opposition to the war began to swell, "flower children" were putting daisies in the rifle barrels of troops sent to quash antiwar protests, providing a seemingly innocent counterpoint to the grim news of slaughter abroad. Meanwhile, campus organizations such as SDS called upon college students to demand an immediate and unconditional withdrawal of U.S. troops from Vietnam.

"The Times They Are A-Changin'"

The free speech movement at the University of California at Berkeley marked the beginning of a new kind of protest movement. In the fall of 1964, civil rights activists returned from Freedom Summer in Mississippi to the 27,000-student campus and decided to picket Bay Area stores that practiced discrimination in hiring. When the university administration tried to stop them from setting up information booths on campus, eighteen student groups objected, including the archconservative Students for Goldwater, claiming that their right to free speech had been abridged. The administration sent police to break up the protest rally and arrest participants. After university president Clark Kerr, under pressure from conservative regents, announced his intention to press charges against the free speech movement's leaders, a huge crowd gathered. Joining folk singer Joan Baez in singing "We Shall Overcome," nearly 1,000 people marched toward the university's administration building, where they planned to stage a sit-in until Kerr rescinded his order. The police moved in, detaining nearly 800 protestors in the largest mass arrest in California history.

Mario Savio, a Freedom Summer volunteer and philosophy student, explained that the free speech movement aspired to more than just the right to conduct political activity on campus. They wanted, in the phrase coined by SDS, participatory democracy. Across the country—and in many nations around the world—college students began to demand a say in their education. An activist at Columbia University, Mark Rudd enrolled to "search for truth in a world that desperately needed help. Instead, I found a huge corporation that made money from real estate, government research contracts, and student fees." Students also spoke out against campus rules that treated students as children instead of as adults. After a string of campus protests, most large universities, including the University of California, relinquished *in loco parents* (in the place of parents) policies and allowed students to live off-campus and to set their own hours.

Across the bay in San Francisco, other young adults staked out a new form of community—a counterculture. In 1967, the "Summer of Love," the population of the Haight-Ashbury district swelled by 75,000 as youthful adventurers from around the world gathered for a huge "be-in." Although the *San Francisco Chronicle* featured a headline reading "Mayor Warns Hippies to Stay Out of Town," masses of long-haired young men and women dressed in bell-bottoms and tie-dyed T-shirts congregated in "the Haight" to listen to music, take drugs, and "be" with each other. "If you're going to San Francisco," a popular rock group sang, "be sure to wear some flowers in your hair . . . you're going to meet some gentle people there." In the fall, the majority returned to their own communities, bringing with them the new hippie lifestyle.

The generational rebellion took many forms, including a revolution in sexual behavior that triggered countless quarrels between parents and their maturing sons and daughters. During the 1960s, more teenagers experienced premarital sex—by the decade's end, three-quarters of all college seniors had engaged in sexual intercourse—and far more talked about it openly than in previous eras. With birth control widely available, including the newly developed "pill," many young women were no longer deterred from sex by fear of pregnancy. "We've discarded the idea that the loss of virginity is related to degeneracy," one college student explained. "Sex doesn't mean the downfall of society, at least not the kind of society that we're going to build." Many heterosexual couples chose to live together outside marriage, a practice few parents condoned. A much smaller but significant number formed communes—approximately 4,000 by 1970—where members could share housekeeping and child care as well as sexual partners.

Mood-altering drugs played a large part in this counterculture. Soon-to-be-former Harvard professor Timothy Leary urged young people to "turn on, tune in, drop out" and also advocated the mass production and distribution of LSD (lysergic acid diethylamide), which was not criminalized until 1968. Marijuana, illegal yet readily available,

Folk and rock musician Henry Diltz was something of a hippie himself in the 1960s and took many photographs of the "alternative culture," including the famed event at Woodstock, New York. In this photograph, taken in Los Angeles in 1967, he captures a young hippie girl making a flower out of tissue paper.

was often paired with rock music in a collective ritual of love and laughter. Singer Bob Dylan taunted adults with the lyrics of his hit single, "Everybody must get stoned."

Music played a large part in defining the counterculture. With the emergence of rock 'n' roll in the 1950s, popular music had begun to express a deliberate generational identity (see Chapter 27), a trend that gained international momentum with the emergence of the British rock group the Beatles in 1964. Folk music, popular on campuses since the early 1960s, served as a voice of protest. Folk singer Bob Dylan issued a warning to parents:

> *Your sons and your daughters*
> *are beyond your command*
> *Your old road is*
> *rapidly agin'.*
> *Please get out of the new one*
> *If you can't lend your hand*
> *For the times they are a-changing'.*

By 1965, Dylan himself had turned to the electric guitar and rock, which triumphed as the musical emblem of a generation worldwide.

Many considered the Woodstock Music Festival the apotheosis of the counterculture. At a farm near Woodstock, New York, more than 400,000 people gathered in August 1969 for a three-day rock concert. Thousands took drugs while security officials and local police stood by, some stripped off their clothes to dance or swim, and a few even made love in the grass. "We were exhilarated," one reveler recalled. "We felt as though we were in liberated territory."

The Woodstock Nation, as the counterculture was mythologized, did not actually represent the sentiments of most young people. Nor would its good vibes persist. The attitudes and styles of the counterculture, especially the efforts to create a new community, did speak for the large minority seeking a peaceful alternative to the intensifying climate of war. The slogan "Make Love, Not War" linked generational rebellion and opposition to the U.S. war in Vietnam.

From Campus Protest to Mass Mobilization

Three weeks after the announcement of Operation Rolling Thunder in 1965, peace activists called for a daylong boycott of classes so that students and faculty might meet to discuss the war. At the University of Michigan in Ann Arbor, more than 3,000 students turned out. "Teach-ins" soon spread across the United States and to Europe and Japan. Meanwhile, SDS mobilized 20,000 people in an antiwar march on the nation's capital (see Communities in Conflict).

Students also protested against war-related research on their campuses. The expansion of higher education in the 1960s had depended largely on federally funded programs, including military research on counterinsurgency tactics and chemical weapons. Student protesters demanded an end to these programs and, receiving no response from university administrators, turned to civil disobedience. In October 1967, the Dow Chemical Company, manufacturers of napalm, a form of jellied gasoline that produces internal as well as external burns, sent job recruiters to the University of Wisconsin at Madison despite warnings that antiwar activists would try to disrupt interviews. A few hundred students sat-in at the building where the recruitment interviews were scheduled, and 2,000 onlookers gathered outside. Ordered by university administrators to disperse the crowd, the city's police broke glass doors, dragged students through the debris, and clubbed those who refused to move. Suddenly the campus erupted. Students chanted *Sieg Heil* at the police, who attempted to disperse them with tear gas and Mace. During the next three years, the momentum grew, and demonstrations took place on campuses in every region of the country.

Read the Document
The Report of the President's Commission on Campus Unrest (1970) at **www.myhistorylab.com**

The peace movement spread well beyond the campus. In April 1967, a daylong antiwar rally in Manhattan's Central Park drew more than 300,000 people. Meanwhile, 60,000 protesters turned out in San Francisco. By summer, Vietnam Veterans Against the War had begun to organize returning soldiers and sailors, encouraging them to cast off the medals and ribbons they had won in battle.

Watch the Video
Protests against the Vietnam War at **www.myhistorylab.com**

The steadily increasing size of antiwar demonstrations provoked conservatives and prowar Democrats to take a stronger stand, some calling for the arrest of antiwar leaders on charges of treason. Secretary of State Dean Rusk, appearing on NBC's *Meet the Press*, declared that "authorities in Hanoi" might conclude, incorrectly, that the majority of Americans did not back their president. He predicted that "the net effect of these demonstrations will be to prolong the war, not to shorten it."

Many demonstrators themselves, concluding that peaceful protest alone had little impact on U.S. policy, decided to change tactics—"from protest to resistance"—and serve as moral witnesses. Despite a 1965 congressional act providing for a five-year jail term and a $10,000 fine for destroying a draft card, thousands of young men burned their draft cards. Approximately a half-million more refused induction. Two Jesuit priests, Daniel and Philip Berrigan, raided the draft board offices in Catonsville, Maryland, in May 1968 and poured homemade napalm over records. Other activists determined to "bring the war home" went beyond civil disobedience. An estimated 40,000 bombing incidents or bomb threats took place from January 1969 to April 1970; more than $21 million of property was damaged, and forty-three people were killed.

The Prospects for Peace in Vietnam, April 1965

During the early months of 1965, President Johnson changed course in Vietnam by launching the "Rolling Thunder" campaign that sent massive bombing missions over North Vietnam and by introducing U.S. ground troops to fight the Vietcong in the South. In response, his opponents became yet more vocal in expressing their dissent. On college campuses, Students for a Democratic Society took the lead in organizing small, local demonstrations against the war and calling on peace activists throughout the United States to join a march in Washington on April 17 to protest the war.

In part to mollify critics of escalation, President Johnson decided to present the government of North Vietnam with an opportunity for "unconditional discussions" about a plan for peace. He also offered $1 billion in aid for a development project along the Mekong River, described by some in his administration as an extension of his Great Society policy abroad. He announced all this in a speech at the Johns Hopkins University on April 7, 1965, which was televised to 60 million viewers. Johnson's speech, called "Peace without Conquest," won approval from many Americans and briefly prompted optimism about prospects for peace.

But ten days later, the 20,000 to 25,000 peace activists who gathered in Washington, DC, were far from appeased by the president's offer. Paul Potter, the president of SDS and the final speaker at the rally, offered his own interpretation of the progress of the war and its significance for Americans. In his speech, titled "Naming the System," Potter directly answered Johnson's claims in the "Peace without Conquest" address. In speaking of "the system," the SDS president connected the injustices of war in Southeast Asia with the inequities borne by Americans in their own country. His speech inspired many, who then went home with renewed dedication to the peace movement and radical social change.

- **What are the main points of disagreement between President Johnson and Paul Potter?**

- **In connecting the war to social injustices at home, what political or social challenges stand out in Potter's critique of "the system"?**

President Lyndon Johnson Calls for "Peace without Conquest" (April 7, 1965)

Viet Nam is far away from this quiet campus. We have no territory there, nor do we seek any. The war is dirty and brutal and difficult. And some 400 young men, born into an America that is bursting with opportunity and promise, have ended their lives, on Viet-Nam's steaming soil.

Why must we take this painful road?

Why must this Nation hazard its ease, and its interest, and its power for the sake of a people so far away?

We fight because we must fight if we are to live in a world where every country can shape its own destiny. And only in such a world will our own freedom be finally secure . . .

The first reality is that North Viet-Nam has attacked the independent nation of South Viet-Nam. Its object is total conquest.

Of course, some of the people of South Viet-Nam are participating in attack on their own government. But trained men and supplies, orders and arms, flow in a constant stream from north to south . . .

> "Our objective is the independence of South Viet-Nam, and its freedom from attack."

Over this war and all Asia is another reality: the deepening shadow of Communist China. The rulers in Hanoi are urged on by Peking. This is a regime which has destroyed freedom in Tibet, which has attacked India, and has been condemned by the United Nations for aggression in Korea . . .

Why are these realities our concern? Why are we in South Vietnam?

We are there because we have a promise to keep. Since 1954 every American President has offered support to the people of South Viet-Nam. We have helped to build, and we have helped to defend. Thus, over many years, we have made a national pledge to help South Viet-Nam defend its independence. And I intend to keep that promise . . .

We are also there to strengthen world order. Around the globe, from Berlin to Thailand, are people whose well-being rests, in part, on the belief that they can count on us if they are attacked. To leave Viet-Nam to its fate would shake the confidence of all these people in the value of an American commitment and in the value of America's word. The result would be increased unrest and instability, and even wider war.

We are also there because there are great stakes in the balance. Let no one think for a moment that retreat from Viet-Nam would bring an end to conflict. The battle would be renewed in one country and then another. The central lesson of our time is that the appetite of aggression is never satisfied. To withdraw from one battlefield means only to prepare for the next. We must say in Southeast Asia as we did in Europe in the words of the Bible: "Hitherto shalt thou come, but no further." . . .

Our objective is the independence of South Viet-Nam, and its freedom from attack. We want nothing for ourselves, only that the people of South Viet-Nam be allowed to guide their own country in their own way. We will do everything necessary to reach that objective. And we will do only what is absolutely necessary.

In recent months attacks on South Viet Nam were stepped up. Thus, it became necessary for us to increase our response and to make attacks by air. This is not a change of purpose. It is a change in which we believe that purpose requires . . .

These countries of Southeast Asia are homes for millions of impoverished people. Each day these people rise at dawn and struggle through until the night to wrestle existence from the soil. They are often wracked by disease, plagued by hunger, and death comes at the early age of 40.

For our part I will ask the Congress to join in a billion dollar American investment in this effort as soon as it is underway.

The task is nothing less than to enrich the hopes and the existence of more than a hundred million people. And there is much to be done.

The vast Mekong River can provide food and water and power on a scale to dwarf even our own TVA . . .

SOURCE: Public Papers of the Presidents of the United States: Lyndon B. Johnson, 1965, pp. 394–397, as excerpted in "The Wars for Viet Nam," Vassar College website.

SDS President Paul Potter, "Naming the System" (April 17, 1965)

Not even the President can say that this is a war to defend the freedom of the Vietnamese people. Perhaps what the President means when he speaks of freedom is the freedom of the American people . . .

How much more of Mr. Johnson's freedom can we stand? How much freedom will be left in this country if there is a major war in Asia? By what weird logic can it be said that the freedom of one people can only be maintained by crushing another? . . .

What kind of system is it that allows good men to make those kinds of decisions? What kind of system is it that justifies the United States or any country seizing the destinies of the Vietnamese people and using them callously for its own purpose? What kind of system is it that disenfranchises people in the South, leaves millions upon millions of people throughout the country impoverished and excluded from the mainstream and promise of American society, that creates faceless and terrible bureaucracies and makes those the place where people spend their lives and do their work, that consistently puts material values before human values—and still persists in calling itself free and still persists in finding itself fit to police the world? What place is there for ordinary men in that system and how are they to control it, make it bend itself to their wills rather than bending them to its?

We must name that system. We must name it, describe it, analyze it, understand it and change it. For it is only when

that system is changed and brought under control that there can be any hope for stopping the forces that create a war in Vietnam today or a murder in the South tomorrow or all the incalculable, innumerable more subtle atrocities that are worked on people all over—all the time.

How do you stop a war then?

. . . If the people of this country are to end the war in Vietnam, and to change the institutions which create it, then the people of this country must create a massive social movement—and if that can be built around the issue of Vietnam then that is what we must do.

By a social movement I mean . . . people who are willing to change their lives, who are willing to challenge the system, to take the problem of change seriously. By a social movement I mean an effort that is powerful enough to make the country understand that our problems are not in Vietnam, or China or Brazil or outer space or at the bottom of the ocean, but are here in the United States. . . .

But that means that we build a movement that works not simply in Washington but in communities and with the problems that face people throughout the society. That means that we build a movement that understands Vietnam in all its horror as but a symptom of a deeper malaise, that we build a movement that makes possible the implementation of the values that would have prevented Vietnam, a movement based on the integrity of man and a belief in man's capacity to tolerate all the weird formulations of society that men may choose to strive

> "How much more of Mr. Johnson's freedom can we stand?"

for; a movement that will build on the new and creative forms of protest that are beginning to emerge, such as the teach-in, and extend their efforts and intensify them; that we will build a movement that will find ways to support the increasing numbers of young men who are unwilling to and will not fight in Vietnam; a movement that will not tolerate the escalation or prolongation of this war but will, if necessary, respond to the administration war effort with massive civil disobedience all over the country . . .

For in a strange way the people of Vietnam and the people on this demonstration are united in much more than a common concern that the war be ended. In both countries there are people struggling to build a movement that has the power to change their condition. The system that frustrates these movements is the same. All our lives, our destinies, our very hopes to live, depend on our ability to overcome that system.

SOURCE: SDS President Paul Potter, "Naming the System" (April 17, 1965). From the web site of Students for a Democratic Society, Document Library. Reprinted by permission.

On May 8, 1970, New York construction workers surged into Wall Street in Lower Manhattan, violently disrupting an antiwar rally and attacking the protesters with lead pipes and crowbars. Known as the "hard hat riots," the well-publicized event was followed later in the month by a march, 100,000 strong, of hard-hat workers unfurling American flags and chanting "All the way U.S.A."

Parallel wars were now being fought, one between two systems of government in Vietnam, another between the American government and masses of its citizens. Those Americans sent to Vietnam were caught in between.

Teenage Soldiers

The average age of soldiers who fought in Vietnam hovered around nineteen. Until late 1969, the Selective Service System—the draft—gave deferments to college students and to workers in selected occupations, while focusing intense recruiting in poor communities by advertising the armed forces as a provider of vocational training and social mobility. Working-class young men, disproportionately African American and Latino, signed up in large numbers under these inducements. They also bore the brunt of combat. Whereas college graduates constituted only 12 percent of the 2.5 million men who served in Vietnam and 9 percent of those who were killed in combat, high school dropouts were the most likely to serve in Vietnam and by far the most likely to die there. The casualty rate for African Americans during the early years of the war was disproportionately higher than the overall death rate for U.S. forces in Southeast Asia. These disparities created a rupture that would last well past the end of the war.

Yet the soldiers were not entirely isolated from the changes affecting their generation. Many G.I.s smoked marijuana, listened to rock music, hung psychedelic posters in their barracks, and participated in the sexual revolution, but most condemned antiwar protest as the self-indulgent behavior of their privileged peers who did not have to fight. As the war dragged on, however, some soldiers showed their frustration. By 1971, many G.I.s were putting peace symbols on their combat helmets,

joining antiwar demonstrations, and staging their own events such as "Armed Farces Day." Sometimes entire companies refused to carry out duty assignments or even to enter battle. A smaller number took revenge by intentionally wounding or killing—"fragging"—reckless commanding officers with grenades meant for the enemy. Some African American soldiers complained about fighting "a white man's war" and emblazoned their helmets with slogans like "No Gook Ever Called Me Nigger."

The war's course fed these feelings of disaffection. U.S. troops entering South Vietnam expected a warm welcome from the people whose homeland they had been sent to defend. Instead, they encountered anti-American demonstrations and placards with slogans like "End Foreign Dominance of Our Country." Moreover, despite their superior arms and air power, soldiers found themselves stumbling into booby traps as they chased an elusive guerrilla foe through deep, leech-infested swamps and dense jungles swarming with fire ants. They could never be sure who was friend and who was foe. Patently false U.S. government press releases that heralded glorious victories and extolled the gratitude of Vietnamese civilians deepened bitterness on the front lines.

Vietnam veterans returned to civilian life quietly and without fanfare, denied the glory earned by the combat veterans of previous wars. They reentered a society divided over the cause for which they had risked their lives. Tens of thousands suffered debilitating physical injuries. As many as 40 percent of the 8.6 million who served came back with drug dependencies or symptoms of posttraumatic stress disorder, haunted and depressed by troubling memories of atrocities. Moreover, finding and keeping a job proved to be particularly hard in the shrinking economy of the 1970s.

Wars on Poverty

During the early 1960s, the civil rights movement had spurred a new concern with poverty. What good was winning the right to sit at a lunch counter if one could not afford to buy a hamburger?

Hoping to build on Kennedy's legacy, President Johnson pledged to expand the antipoverty program that he had inherited. "That's my kind of program," he told his advisers. "It will help people. I want you to move full speed ahead on it." Over the next several years, he used the political momentum of the civil rights movement and the overwhelming Democratic majorities in the House and Senate to push through the most ambitious reform program since the New Deal. Ironically, violence at home as well as abroad ultimately undercut his aspiration to wage "an unconditional war on poverty" (see Figures 29.1 and 29.2).

The Great Society

The cornerstone of Johnson's plan for a Great Society was the Economic Opportunity Act, enacted in August 1964. The legislation established the Office of Economic Opportunity (OEO), which coordinated a network of community-based programs designed to help the poor help themselves by providing opportunities for education and employment. The results were mixed. The Job Corps provided vocational training mostly for urban black youth considered unemployable.

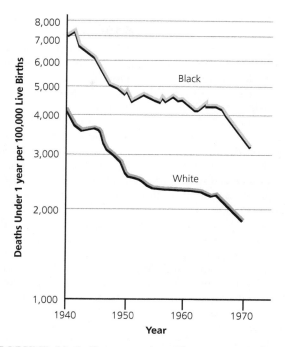

FIGURE 29.2 Comparative Figures on Infant Mortality by Race, 1940–70 The causes of infant mortality, such as inadequate maternal diets, prenatal care, and medical services, were all rooted in poverty, both rural and urban. Despite generally falling rates of infant mortality, nonwhite people continued to suffer the effects more than white people.

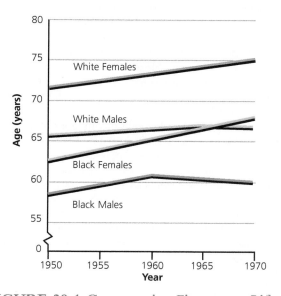

FIGURE 29.1 Comparative Figures on Life Expectancy at Birth by Race and Sex, 1950–70 Shifting mortality statistics suggested that the increased longevity of females increasingly cut across race lines, but did not diminish the difference between white people and black people as a whole.

Housed in dreary barracks-like camps far from home, trainees often found themselves learning factory skills that were already obsolete. The Neighborhood Youth Corps provided work for about 2 million young people aged sixteen to twenty-one, but nearly all the jobs were low paying and dead-end. Educational programs proved more successful. VISTA (Volunteers in Service to America), a kind of domestic Peace Corps, brought several thousand idealistic volunteers into poor communities for social service work.

The most innovative and controversial element of the OEO was the Community Action Program (CAP), which mandated "maximum feasible participation" of local residents. In theory, as the SDS organizers also believed, community action would empower the poor by giving them a direct say in mobilizing resources. What often resulted was a tug-of-war between local government officials and the poor over who should control funding and decision making. Such was the case in Chicago, where Mayor Richard Daley complained that letting the poor head antipoverty programs was "like telling the fellow who cleans up [at the newspaper] to be the city editor."

More successful and popular were the so-called national-emphasis programs, designed in Washington and administered according to federal guidelines. The Legal Services Program, staffed by attorneys, helped millions of poor people in legal battles with housing authorities, welfare departments, police, and slumlords. Head Start and Follow Through reached more than 2 million poor children and significantly improved the long-range educational achievement of participants. Comprehensive Community Health Centers provided basic medical services to patients who could not afford to see doctors. Upward Bound helped low-income teenagers develop the skills and confidence needed for college. Birth control programs dispensed contraceptive supplies and information to hundreds of thousands of poor women (see Figure 29.3).

But the root cause of poverty lay in the unequal distribution of power as well as of income. The Johnson administration never committed itself to reallocating income or wealth. Spending on social welfare jumped from 7.7 percent of the GNP in 1960 to 16 percent in 1974. But roughly three-quarters of social welfare payments went to the nonpoor. The largest sums went to Medicare, established by Congress in 1965 to provide basic health care for the aged, and to expanded Social Security payments and unemployment compensation.

The Great Society became a forgotten dream. "More than five years after the passage of the Economic Opportunity Act," a 1970 study concluded, "the war on poverty has barely scratched the surface. Most poor people have had no contact with it, except perhaps to hear the

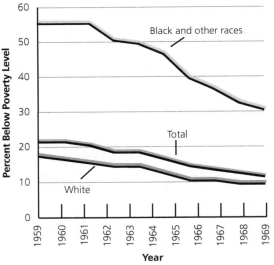

FIGURE 29.3 Percent of Population Below Poverty Level, by Race, 1959–69

NOTE: The poverty threshold for a nonfarm family of four was $3,743 in 1969 and $2,973 in 1959.

SOURCE: From *Congressional Quarterly, Civil Rights: A Progress Report*, 1971. Copyright 1971 by CQ-ROLL CALL GROUP. Reproduced with permission of CQ-ROLL CALL GROUP in the format Other book via Copyright Clearance Center.

promises of a better life to come." Having made the largest commitment to federal spending on social welfare since the New Deal, Johnson could take pride in the number of programs passed by Congress. At the same time, he had raised expectations higher than could be reached without a more drastic redistribution of economic and political power. Even in the short run, the president could not sustain the welfare programs and simultaneously fight a lengthy and expensive war abroad.

Crisis in the Cities

With funds for new construction limited during the Great Depression and World War II, and the postwar building boom taking place in the suburbs, the housing stock in the nation's cities declined. The Federal Housing Administration encouraged this trend by redlining poor urban neighborhoods (see Chapter 27). Slumlords took advantage of this situation, collecting high rents while allowing their properties to deteriorate. City officials meanwhile spearheaded civic revitalization programs that more often than not sliced up poor neighborhoods with new super highways, demolished them to build new office complexes, or, as in Chicago's Uptown, favored residential developments for the middle class rather than for the poor. In 1968, a federal survey showed that 80 percent of those displaced under these programs—dubbed "Negro removal" by former residents—were people of color.

Employment opportunities declined along with the housing stock. Nationwide, military spending for the Vietnam War brought the unemployment rate down from 6 percent, where it was in 1960, to 4 percent in 1966, where it remained until the end of the decade. Black unemployment, however, was nearly twice that of white unemployment. Moreover, the proportion working in the low-paying service sector continued to rise. In short, African Americans were steadily falling further behind whites.

Despite deteriorating conditions, millions of Americans continued to move to the cities, mainly African Americans from the Deep South, white people from the Appalachian Mountains, and Latinos from Puerto Rico. By the mid-1960s, African Americans had become near majorities in the nation's decaying inner cities. Many had fled rural poverty only to find themselves earning minimum wages at best and living in miserable, racially segregated neighborhoods. These conditions brought urban pressures to the boiling point.

Urban Uprisings

Just as the Vietnam War was heating up, more than 100 urban uprisings rocked the nation during the "long, hot summers" of 1964 to 1968. Unlike the race riots of the 1920s and 1940s, when angry whites assaulted blacks, masses of African Americans now took revenge for the

OVERVIEW | The Great Society

Major Legislation

Civil Rights

Civil Rights Act of 1964, forbidding segregation in public accommodations and banning job discrimination

Voting Rights Act of 1965, ensuring minority voter registration in places where patterns of past discrimination existed

Immigration and Nationality Services Act of 1965, abolishing national-origin quotas in immigration law

Civil Rights Act of 1968, banning discrimination in housing and extending constitutional protections to Native Americans on reservations

The War on Poverty

Economic Opportunity Act of 1964, establishing the Office of Economic Opportunity to oversee such community-based antipoverty programs as the **Job Corps**, the **Neighborhood Youth Corps, VISTA**, the **Model Cities Program, Upward Bound**, the **Community Action Program**, and **Project Head Start**

Education

Elementary and Secondary Education Act of 1965, providing federal funds for programs to schools in low-income areas

Bilingual Education Act of 1968, providing federal aid to school districts with large numbers of children needing to learn English as a second language

Health

Social Security Act of 1965, funding Medicare to help cover costs of health care for older Americans and Medicaid to provide funds for medical care of welfare recipients

Culture

National Foundation on the Arts and Humanities Act of 1965, creating the National Endowment for the Arts and the National Endowment for the Humanities

Public Broadcasting Act of 1967, chartering the Corporation for Public Broadcasting, which later established the Public Broadcasting Services (PBS) and National Public Radio (NPR)

Transportation

Urban Mass Transportation Act of 1964, funding large-scale urban public and private rail projects

National Traffic and Motor Vehicle Safety Act of 1966, laying the foundation for the National Highway Traffic Safety Administration to effect policy to reduce traffic injuries and fatalities

Highway Safety Act of 1966, permitting the federal government to set standards for motor vehicles and highways

Department of Transportation, established in 1966

Consumer Protection

Nine major enactments between 1965 and 1968, covering such areas as cigarette warning labels, motor safety, "fair packaging and labeling," child safety and flammable fabrics, meat and poultry packaging, "truth in lending," and radiation safety

Environment

Nine major enactments between 1964 and 1968, covering such areas as wilderness and endangered species protection, land and water conservation, solid waste disposal, air pollution, aircraft noise abatement, and historic preservation

National Environmental Policy Act of 1969, consolidating many of these gains, was passed in the first year of the Nixon administration

---

white domination of their communities and specifically for police abuse (see Map 29.1).

The first major uprising erupted in August 1965 in the Watts section of Los Angeles. There, one in three men was unemployed, and the nearest hospital was twelve miles away. It took only a minor arrest to set off the uprising, which quickly spread outward for fifty miles. Throwing rocks and bottles through store windows, participants reportedly shouted, "This is for Selma! This is for Birmingham!" and "Burn, baby, burn!" Nearly 50,000 people turned out, and 20,000 National Guard troops were sent in. After six days, 34 people lay

MAP 29.1 Urban Uprisings, 1965–1968 After World War II, urban uprisings precipitated by racial conflict increased in African American communities. In Watts in 1965 and in Detroit and Newark in 1967, rioters struck out at symbols of white control of their communities, such as white-owned businesses and residential properties.

dead, 900 were injured, and 4,000 more had been arrested. The Los Angeles police chief blamed civil rights agitators, the mayor accused Communists, and both feigned ignorance when the media reported that white police assigned to "charcoal alley," their name for the Watts district, had customarily called their night-sticks "nigger knockers."

"We are on a powder keg in a dozen places," President Johnson observed. The following summer, large-scale uprisings occurred in San Francisco, Milwaukee, Dayton, and Cleveland. On July 12, 1967, in Newark, New Jersey, a city with severe housing short-ages and the nation's highest black unemployment rate, the beating and arrest of a black taxi driver by a white police officer sparked a protest. Five days of looting and burning of buildings ended with 25 people dead. One week later, Detroit police raided a bar and arrested the after-hours patrons. Army tanks and paratroopers were

brought in to quell the disturbance, which lasted a week and left 34 people dead and 7,000 under arrest.

In July 1967, President Johnson created the National Advisory Commission on Civil Disorders to investigate the riots. Headed by Illinois Governor Otto Kerner, the eleven-member commission indicted "white racism" for creating an "explosive mixture" of poverty and police bru-tality. But the Johnson administration and Congress put aside the commission's warning that "our nation is moving toward two societies, one black, one white—separate and unequal" and disregarded its advice to direct funds into housing and jobs and to reduce segregation. By this time, the escalating costs of the Vietnam War left little federal money for antipoverty programs. Senator William Fulbright noted, "Each war feeds on the other, and, although the President assures us that we have the resources to win both wars, in fact we are not winning either of them."

1968: Year of Turmoil

The urban uprisings of the summer of 1967 marked the most drawn-out violence in the United States since the Civil War. Rather than offering a respite, however, 1968 proved to be even more turbulent. The bloodiest and most destructive fighting of the Vietnam War resulted in a hopeless stalemate that soured most Americans on the conflict and undermined their faith in U.S. invincibility in world affairs. Disillusionment deepened in the spring when two of the most revered political leaders were struck down by assassins' bullets. Once again, protesters and police clashed on the nation's campuses and city streets, and millions of Americans asked what was wrong with their country.

It was not just the United States that experienced 1968 as a year of turmoil. In May, hundreds of thousands of students and workers barricaded the streets of Paris in protest against their government. A sweeping series of liberal reforms in Czechoslovakia, known as the "Prague Spring," was followed in August by a massive invasion staged by Eastern-bloc countries. In October, an estimated 300 people were killed in the Tlatelolco section of Mexico City when government forces, using tanks and armored cars, broke up a student-led demonstration. And in China, Mao Zedong was deep into the "Cultural Revolution," a campaign to strengthen the Communist government against liberal reforms.

The Tet Offensive

On January 30, 1968, the North Vietnamese and their Vietcong allies launched the Tet Offensive (named for the Vietnamese lunar New Year holiday), stunning the U.S. military command in South Vietnam. The Vietcong pushed into the major cities and provincial capitals of the South, as far as the courtyard of the U.S. embassy in Saigon. U.S. troops ultimately halted the offensive, with comparatively modest casualties of 1,100 dead and 8,000 wounded. The North Vietnamese and Vietcong suffered more than 40,000 deaths, about one-fifth of their total forces. Civilian casualties ran to the tens of thousands. As many as 1 million South Vietnamese became refugees, their villages totally ruined (see Map 29.2).

The Tet Offensive, despite the U.S. success in stopping it, weakened the resolve of many Americans. News coverage—including scenes of U.S. personnel shooting from the embassy windows in Saigon—dismayed the nation. Television viewers saw the beautiful, ancient city of Hue devastated almost beyond recognition and heard a U.S. officer casually remark about a village in the Mekong Delta, "We had to destroy it, in order to save it."

The United States chalked up a major military victory, but lost the war at home. For the first time, polls showed strong opposition to the war, 49 percent concluding that the entire operation in Vietnam was a mistake. Meanwhile, in Rome, Berlin, Paris, and London, huge crowds protested U.S. involvement in Vietnam. President Johnson, facing the 1968 election campaign, watched his popularity plummet to an all-time low.

On March 31, the haggard-looking president appeared on television to declare a pullback in bombing over North Vietnam and the readiness of the United States to enter into comprehensive peace talks with Hanoi. He then shocked the nation: "I shall not seek, and I will not accept, the nomination of my party for another term as president." Like Truman almost thirty years earlier, and despite his determination not to repeat that bit of history, Johnson had lost his presidency in Asia.

King, the War, and the Assassination

By 1968, the civil rights leadership stood firmly against the war, and Martin Luther King Jr. had reached a turning point in his life. The FBI had been harassing King, tapping his telephones and spreading malicious rumors about him. Despite these threats (Bureau Chief J. Edgar Hoover had sworn to "destroy the burrhead"), King abandoned his customary caution in criticizing U.S. policy in Vietnam. As early as 1965, he had connected domestic unrest with the war abroad, calling the U.S. government the "greatest purveyor of violence in the world today." He became yet more outspoken in his opposition to the war, even if it meant losing the support of those liberal Democrats loyal to Johnson. King refused to compromise.

In the spring of 1968, King chose Memphis, Tennessee, home of striking sanitation workers, to launch a Poor People's Campaign for peace and justice. There he delivered, in what was to be his final speech, a message of hope. "I have a dream this afternoon that the brotherhood of man will become a reality," King told the crowd. "With this faith, I will go out and carve a tunnel of hope from a mountain of despair." The next evening, April 4, 1968, as he stood on the balcony of his motel, King was shot and killed.

Throughout the world, crowds turned out to mourn King's death. Former SNCC leader Stokely Carmichael stormed, "When white America killed Dr. King, she declared war on us." Riots broke out in more than a hundred cities, on college campuses, and on military bases in Vietnam. Chicago Mayor Richard Daley ordered his police to shoot to kill. In Washington, DC, U.S. Army units set up machine guns outside the Capitol and the White House. King's dream of the nation as a "Beloved Community" died with him.

The Democrats in Disarray

The dramatic events of the first part of the year had a direct impact on the presidential campaign. For those liberals dissatisfied with Johnson's conduct of the war, and especially for African Americans suffering the loss of their greatest leader, Senator Robert F. Kennedy of New York emerged as the candidate of choice. Kennedy enjoyed a strong record on civil rights, and, like King, he had begun to interpret the war as a mirror of injustice at

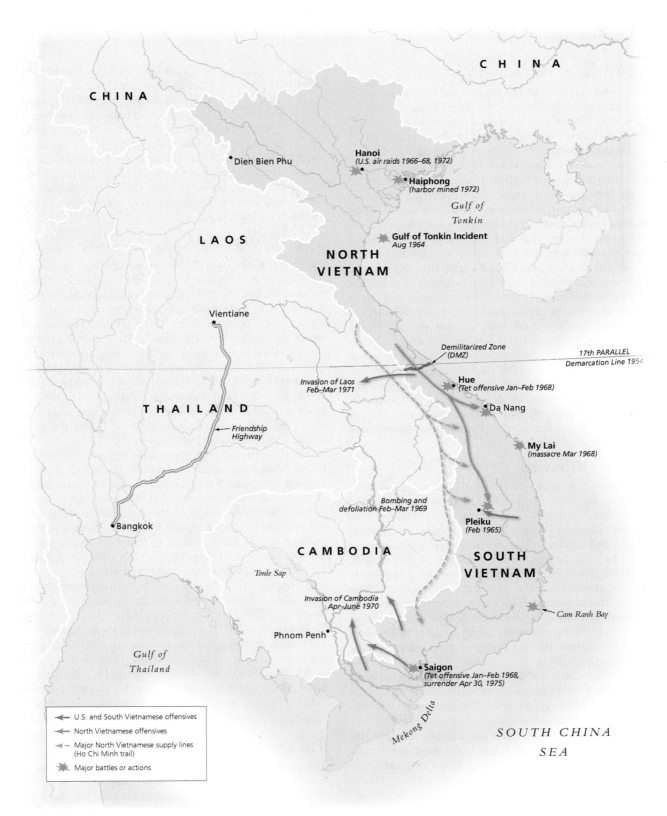

MAP 29.2 The Southeast Asian War The Indo-Chinese subcontinent, home to long-standing regional conflict, became the center of a prolonged war with the United States.

home. On these notes, he began to campaign for the Democratic nomination.

Ironically, Kennedy faced an opponent who agreed with him, Senator Eugene McCarthy of Minnesota. The race for the Democratic nomination positioned McCarthy, the witty philosopher, against Kennedy, the charismatic campaigner. McCarthy did well with liberal Democrats and white suburbanites. On college campuses, his popularity with antiwar students was so great that his campaign became known as the "children's crusade."

Kennedy captured the votes of African Americans and Latinos and emerged as the Democratic Party's strongest candidate. Having won all but the Oregon primary, he moved on to California. But on June 4, as the final tabulation of his victory came in just past midnight, Robert Kennedy was struck down by an assassin's bullet.

Vice President Hubert H. Humphrey, who had announced his candidacy in April, was now the sole Democrat with the credentials to succeed Johnson. He simultaneously courted Democrats who grimly supported the war and the King-Kennedy wing, which was sickened by it. He also skillfully cultivated the Democratic power brokers. Without entering a single state primary, he lined up delegates loyal to city bosses, labor leaders, and conservative southern Democrats. As the candidate least likely to rock the boat, he secured his party's nomination well before delegates met in convention.

"The Whole World Is Watching!"

The events surrounding the Democratic convention in Chicago, August 21–26, demonstrated how deep the divisions within the United States had become. Mayor Richard Daley, still reeling from the riots following King's assassination, refused to issue parade permits to the antiwar activists, who had called for a massive demonstration at the convention center. According to later accounts, he sent hundreds of undercover police into the crowds to encourage rock throwing and generally to incite violence so that retaliation would appear necessary and reasonable.

Daley's strategy boomeranged when his officers staged what a presidential commission later termed a "police riot," randomly assaulting demonstrators, casual passersby, and the television crews broadcasting the events. Angered by the embarrassing publicity, Daley sent his agents to raid McCarthy's campaign headquarters where antiwar Democrats had gathered.

Inside the convention hall, a raging debate over a peace resolution underscored the depth of the division within the party. Representative Wayne Hays of Ohio lashed out at those who substituted "beards for brains . . . [and] pot [for] patriotism." When the resolution failed, McCarthy delegates put on black armbands and sang "We Shall Overcome." Later, as tear gas used against the demonstrators outside turned the amphitheater air acrid, the beaming Humphrey praised Mayor Daley and Johnson's conduct of the Vietnam

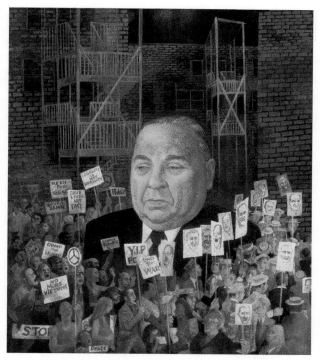

Bernard Perlin, *Mayor Daley, 1968*, Oil on canvas. In 1968, Richard J. Daley had been elected mayor of Chicago four times and held power as a traditional city boss. In December of that year, the National Commission on Violence released a report that concluded that Chicago police, acting under Mayor Daley's orders, had been "unrestrained and indiscriminate" in their attacks on demonstrators at the National Democratic Convention held the previous August. In response, Mayor Daley brazenly announced a 22 percent salary increase for members of the city's police and fire personnel.

War. When Senator Abraham Ribicoff of Connecticut protested the "Gestapo tactics" of the Chicago police, television cameras focused on Mayor Daley saying, "You Jew son of a bitch . . ., go home!" The crowd outside chanted, "The whole world is watching! The whole world is watching!" Indeed, through satellite transmission, it was.

Protest had spread worldwide. Across the United States the antiwar movement picked up steam. In Paris, students and workers scrawled on building walls such humorous and half-serious slogans as "Be Realistic, Demand the Impossible!" In Prague, Czechoslovakia, students wearing blue jeans and singing Beatles songs threw rocks at Soviet tanks. Meanwhile, demonstrations in Japan, Italy, Ireland, Germany, and England all brought young people into the streets to demand democratic reforms in their own countries and an end to the U.S. war in Vietnam.

The Republican Victory

The Republicans stepped into the breach. Presidential contender Richard Nixon deftly built on voter hostility toward youthful protesters and the counterculture. He wooed a growing constituency that he later termed the "silent majority"—those Americans who worked, paid taxes, and did not demonstrate or picket, "people who are not haters, people who love their country." Recovering from election defeats for president in 1960 and California governor in 1962, Nixon claimed to be the one candidate who could restore law and order. He chose as his running mate the governor of Maryland, Spiro T. Agnew, known for treating dissent as near treason (see Map 29.3).

After signing the landmark Civil Rights Act of 1964, President Johnson said privately, "I think we just delivered the South to the Republicans for a long time to come." Republican strategists moved quickly to make this prediction come true. They also recognized the growing electoral importance of the Sunbelt, where populations grew with the rise of high-tech industries and retirement communities. A powerful conservatism dominated this region, home to many military bases, defense plants, and an increasingly influential religious right. Although Johnson enjoyed a landslide

Watch the Video
LBJ Signing the Civil Rights Bill at **www.myhistorylab.com**

victory in 1964, his conservative Republican rival, Barry Goldwater, had trumped him in several states in the Deep South. Nixon took advantage of this trend.

The 1968 campaign exposed the increasing conservatism of white voters even outside the South. The most dramatic example was the relative success of Alabama governor George Wallace's third-party bid for the presidency. Wallace took state office in 1963 promising white Alabamans "Segregation now! Segregation tomorrow! Segregation forever!" In 1968, he waged a national campaign and won five southern states and nearly 14 percent of the popular vote nationwide.

The Nixon-Agnew team ushered in the greatest political realignment since Franklin Roosevelt's victory in 1932. They captured the popular vote by the slim margin of 43.4 percent to Democrat Hubert Humphrey and Maine senator Edmund Muskie's 42.7 percent, but they took nearly all the West's electoral votes. Bitterly divided by the campaign, the Democrats would remain out of presidential contention for more than two decades, except when the Republicans suffered scandal and disgrace. The Republicans in 1968 had paved the way for the conservative ascendancy.

Watch the Video
Richard Nixon Presidential Campaign Ad at **www.myhistorylab.com**

The Politics of Identity

Richard Nixon campaigned promising to "bring Americans together again." But, if anything, the divisions among Americans, especially among the young, grew sharper during his presidency. The tragic events of 1968 brought whole sectors of the counterculture to political activism. With great media fanfare, gay liberation and women's liberation movements took shape while young Latinos, Asian Americans, and Indian peoples pressed their own claims. In different ways, these groups drew their own lessons from Black Power, the nationalist movement that formed in the wake of Malcolm X's death. Soon, "Brown Power," "Yellow Power," and "Red Power" became the slogans of movements constituted distinctly as new communities of protest.

The politics of identity would continue to thrive through the next two decades of mainly conservative rule, broadening the content of literature, film, television, popular music, and even the curricula of the nation's schools. Collectively, the various movements pushed issues of race, gender, and sexual orientation to the forefront of American politics and simultaneously spotlighted the nation's cultural diversity as a major resource.

Black Power

Impatient with tactics based on voting rights and integration, many young activists spurned the civil disobedience of King's generation for direct action and militant self-defense. In 1966, Stokely Carmichael, who had helped

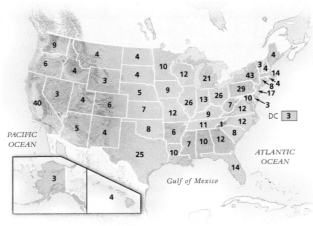

	Electoral Vote (%)	Popular Vote (%)
RICHARD M. NIXON (Republican)	301 (56)	31,785,480 (43.4)
Hubert H. Humphrey (Democrat)	191 (36)	31,275,165 (42.7)
George C. Wallace (American Independent)	46 (8)	9,906,473 (13.5)
Other candidates (Dick Gregory, Socialist Labor; Fred Halstead and Paul Boutelle, Socialist Workers; Eugene McCarthy, Peace and Freedom; E. Harold Munn and Rolland E. Fisher, Prohibition)	—	221,134 (0.3)

MAP 29.3 The Election of 1968 Although the Republican Nixon-Agnew team won the popular vote by only a small margin, the Democrats lost in most of the northern states that had voted Democratic since the days of FDR. Segregationist Governor George Wallace of Alabama polled more than 9 million votes.

The war in Vietnam contributed to the growing racial militancy in the United States. African Americans served on the front lines in Vietnam in disproportionate numbers, and many came to view the conflict as a "white man's war."

turn SNCC into an all-black organization, began to advocate Black Power as a means for African Americans to take control of their own communities.

The Black Panther Party, founded in Oakland, California, in 1966 by Huey P. Newton and Bobby Seale, demanded "land, bread, housing, education, clothing, and justice." They adopted a paramilitary style—black leather jackets, shoes, and berets and firearms—that infuriated the authorities. Monitoring local police was their major activity. In several communities, volunteers also ran free breakfast programs for schoolchildren, established medical clinics, and conducted educational classes. Persecuted by police and the FBI—there were more than thirty raids on Panther offices in eleven states during 1968 and 1969—their leaders were arrested, prosecuted, and sentenced to long terms in jail that effectively destroyed the organization.

Black Power nevertheless continued to grow into a multifaceted movement. The Reverend Jesse Jackson, for example, rallied African Americans in Chicago to boycott the A&P supermarket chain until the firm hired 700 black workers. A dynamic speaker and skillful organizer, Jackson encouraged African Americans to support their own businesses and services. His program, Operation Breadbasket, spread beyond Chicago to fifteen other cities.

Cultural nationalism became the most enduring component of Black Power. In their popular book *Black Power* (1967), Stokely Carmichael and Charles V. Hamilton urged African Americans "to assert their own definitions, to reclaim their history, their culture; to

Read the **Document**

Stokely Carmichael and Charles V. Hamilton, from Black Power: The Politics of Liberation in America *(1966)* at **www.myhistorylab.com**

create their own sense of community and togetherness." Thousands of college students responded by calling for more classes on African American history and culture. At San Francisco State University, students, with help from the Black Panthers, demanded a black studies department. After a series of failed negotiations with the administration, a campus-wide strike called by black students in December 1968 shut down the university. Strikes for "Third World studies" soon broke out on other campuses, including the University of Wisconsin at Madison, where the National Guard was brought in to quell the protest.

Meanwhile, trendsetters put aside Western dress for African-style dashikis and hairdos, and black parents gave their children African names. Many well-known activists and artists such as Imamu Amiri Baraka (formerly LeRoi Jones), Muhammad Ali (formerly Cassius Clay), and Kwame Touré (formerly Stokely Carmichael) rejected their "slave names." The new holiday Kwanzaa followed Christmas as a weeklong celebration of African heritage and culture. This deepening sense of racial pride was summed up in the popular slogan "Black Is Beautiful."

Sisterhood Is Powerful

In 1966, Betty Friedan's best-selling *Feminine Mystique* (see Chapter 27) sparked the formation of the National Organization for Women (NOW), which pledged "to take action to bring women into full participation in the mainstream of American society now." Members campaigned for the enforcement of laws banning sex discrimination in work and in education, for maternity leaves, and for government funding of day-care centers. NOW also backed the Equal Rights Amendment, first introduced in Congress in 1923, and demanded the repeal of legislation that prohibited abortion or restricted birth control.

Read the **Document**

Shirley Chisholm, Equal Rights for Women (1969) at **www.myhistorylab.com**

By the time Nixon took office, a different kind of movement had emerged: women's liberation. The women's liberation movement attracted young women who had been active in civil rights, SDS, and campus antiwar movements. Impatient with NOW's legislative agenda and angered by the sexism of male activists, these women organized separately under the slogan "Sisterhood Is Powerful."

The women's liberation movement issued a scathing critique of patriarchy—that is, the power of men to dominate all institutions, from the family to business and

OVERVIEW | Protest Movements of the 1960s

Year	Organization/Movement	Description
1962	*Students for a Democratic Society (SDS)*	Organization of college students that became the largest national organization of left-wing white students. Calling for "participatory democracy," SDS involved students in community-based campaigns against poverty and for citizens' control of neighborhoods. SDS played a prominent role in the campaign to end the war in Vietnam.
1964	*Free Speech Movement*	Formed at the University of California at Berkeley to protest the banning of on-campus political fundraising. Decried the bureaucratic character of the "multiuniversity" and advocated an expansion of student rights.
1965	*Anti–Vietnam War Movement*	Advocated grassroots opposition to U.S. involvement in Southeast Asia. By 1970, a national mobilization committee organized a demonstration of a half-million protesters in Washington, DC.
1965	La raza	A movement of Chicano youth to advance the cultural and political self-determination of Mexican Americans. *La raza* included the Brown Berets, which addressed community issues, and regional civil rights groups such as the Crusade for Social Justice, formed in 1965.
1966	*Black Power*	Militant movement that emerged from the civil rights campaigns to advocate independent institutions for African Americans and pride in black culture and African heritage. The idea of Black Power, a term coined by Stokely Carmichael, inspired the formation of the paramilitary Black Panthers.
1968	*American Indian Movement (AIM)*	Organization formed to advance the self-determination of Indian peoples and challenge the authority of the Bureau of Indian Affairs. Its most effective tactic was occupation. In February 1973, AIM insurgents protesting land and treaty violations occupied Wounded Knee, South Dakota, the location of an 1890 massacre, until the FBI and BIA agents drove them out.
1968	*Women's Liberation*	Movement of mainly young women that took shape following a protest at the Miss America Beauty Pageant. Impatient with the legislative reforms promoted by the National Organization for Women, founded in 1966, activists developed their own agenda shaped by the slogan "The Personal Is Political." Activities included the formation of "consciousness-raising" groups and the establishment of women's studies programs.
1968	Asian American *Political Alliance (AAPA)*	Formed at the University of California at Berkeley, the AAPA was one of the first pan-Asian political organizations to struggle against racial oppression. The AAPA encouraged Asian Americans to claim their own cultural identity and to protest the war against Asian peoples in Vietnam.
1969	*Gay Liberation*	Movement to protest discrimination against homosexuals and lesbians that emerged after the Stonewall Riots in New York City. Unlike earlier organizations such as the Mattachine Society, which focused on civil rights, gay liberationists sought to radically change American society and government, which they believed were corrupt.

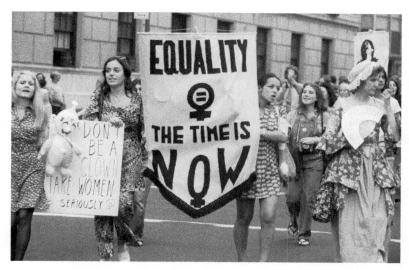

In 1971, Congress passed a joint resolution, introduced by Rep. Bella Abzug (D-NY), that designates August 26 each year as "Women's Equality Day" to commemorate the passage of the 19th Amendment to the Constitution granting women full voting rights. This photo shows a parade of women marking the first celebration of this day in 1971.

the family and marriage as well as the workforce and government.

Women's liberation activism ranged widely. Some feminists staged sit-ins at *Newsweek* to protest demeaning media depictions of women. Others established health clinics, day-care centers, rape crisis centers, and shelters for women fleeing abusive husbands or lovers. The movement also had a significant educational impact. Feminist bookstores and publishing companies, such as the Feminist Press, reached out to eager readers. In January 1972, *Ms. Magazine* hit the newsstands. Meanwhile, campus activists demanded women's studies programs and women's centers. Like black studies, women's studies programs included traditional academic goals, such as the generation of new scholarship, but also encouraged personal change and self-esteem. Between 1970 and 1975, as many as 150 women's studies programs were established; by 1980, nearly 30,000 women's studies courses were offered at colleges and universities throughout the United States. And the number of women in the workforce continued to increase (see Figure 29.4).

The women's liberation movement remained, however, a bastion of white middle-class women. The appeal to

government to the protest movements themselves. Outraged and sometimes outrageous, one New York group created a lot of publicity for the movement by storming the 1968 Miss America Beauty Pageant in Atlantic City. They crowned a live sheep as queen and threw "implements of female torture" (bras, girdles, curlers, and copies of the *Ladies' Home Journal*) into a "freedom trash can."

The media focused on such audacious acts and brazen pronouncements, but the majority of activists were less flamboyant women simply trying to rise above the limitations imposed on them because of their gender. They met more often outside the limelight in consciousness-raising groups, where they examined the relationship between public events and private lives. There, women shared their most intimate feelings toward men or other women and established the constituency for the movement's most important principle, expressed in the aphorism "The personal is political." Believing that no aspect of life lacked a political dimension, most emphatically including sexuality, consciousness-raising groups explored the power dynamics of

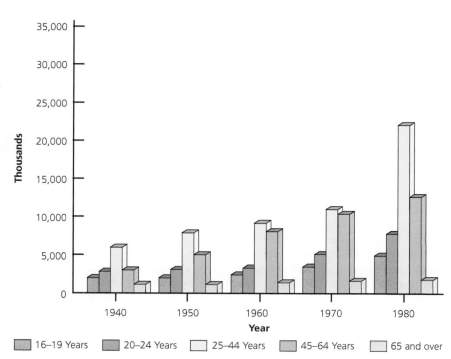

FIGURE 29.4 Women in the Workforce, 1940–80

SOURCE: U.S. Bureau of the Census.

sisterhood did not unite women across race or class or even sexual orientation. Lesbians, who charged the early NOW leaders with homophobia, found large pockets of "heterosexism" in the women's liberation movement and broke off to form their own organizations. Although some African American women were outraged at Stokely Carmichael's infelicitous joke that "the only position for women in SNCC is prone," the majority remained wary of white women's appeals to sisterhood. African American women formed their own "womanist" movement to address their distinct cultural and political concerns. Similarly, by 1970, a Latina feminist movement addressed issues uniquely relevant to women of color in an Anglo-dominated society.

Gay Liberation

The gay community had been generations in the making, but gained visibility only during World War II (see Chapter 25). In the mid-1950s, two pioneering homophile organizations, the Mattachine Society and the Daughters of Bilitis, campaigned against discrimination in employment, the armed forces, and all areas of social and cultural life. Other groups rooted themselves in New York's Greenwich Village, San Francisco's North Beach, and other centers of gay night life. But it was during the tumultuous late 1960s that a sizeable movement formed to encourage gays and lesbians to "come out": "Say It Loud, Gay Is Proud."

The major event prompting gays to organize followed repeated police raids of gay bars. On Friday, June 27, 1969, New York police raided the Stonewall Inn, a well-known gay bar in Greenwich Village, and provoked an uprising that lasted the entire night. The next day, "Gay Power" graffiti appeared throughout the neighborhood.

In New York City, the Gay Liberation Front (GLF) announced itself as "a revolutionary homosexual group of men and women . . . who reject society's attempt to impose sexual roles and definitions of our nature." Taking a stand against the war in Vietnam, the GLF quickly adopted the forms of public protest, such as street demonstrations and sit-ins, developed by civil rights activists and given new direction by antiwar protesters.

Read the Document
Gay Liberation Front (1970) at **www.myhistorylab.com**

Changes in public opinion and policies followed. Several churches opened their doors to gay activists; the San Francisco–based Council on Religion and Homosexuality established a network for clergy sympathetic to gay and lesbian parishioners. In 1973, the American Psychiatric Association, which since World War II had viewed homosexuality as a treatable mental illness, reclassified it as a normal sexual orientation. Meanwhile, a slow process of decriminalization of homosexual acts between consenting adults began. In 1975, the U.S. Civil Service Commission ended its ban on the employment of homosexuals.

The gay liberation movement encouraged more than legal and institutional changes. "Gay Is Good" (like "Black Is Beautiful" and "Sisterhood Is Powerful") called to a large hidden minority to demand public acceptance of their sexual identity. In 1970, to commemorate the first anniversary of the Stonewall raid, Gay Pride parades took place in at least eight American cities.

The Chicano Rebellion

To many Americans, the Chicano movement seemed to burst onto the scene in 1965, when the United Farm Workers (UFW), a union of mainly migrant workers, struck against grape growers of the San Joaquin Valley in California. By 1968, strike leaders César Chávez and Dolores Huerta were heading a nationwide boycott of non-union-picked grapes and lettuce.

Read the Document
Chávez, He Showed Us the Way (1978) at **www.myhistorylab.com**

While Chávez emerged as a national hero, many young Mexican Americans spearheaded an urban-based

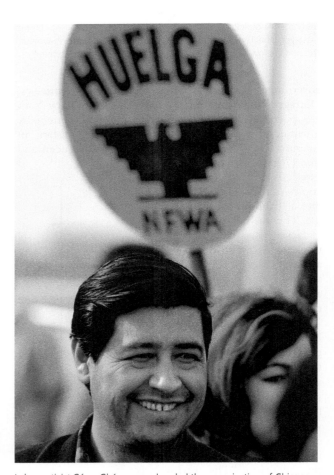

Labor activist César Chávez spearheaded the organization of Chicano agricultural workers into the United Farm Workers (UFW), the first successful union of migrant workers. In 1965, a strike of grape pickers in the fields around Delano, California, and a nationwide boycott of table grapes brought Chávez and the UFW into the media spotlight. Like Martin Luther King Jr., he advocated nonviolent methods for achieving justice and equality.

movement based on identity politics, which Chávez himself rejected. They adopted the slang term *Chicano*, in preference to Mexican American, to express a militant ethnic nationalism. Chicano militants demanded not only their full civil rights, but also recognition of their distinctive culture and history. Tracing their roots to the imperial Aztecs, they identified *la raza* (the race or people) as the source of a common language, religion, and heritage.

High school students were at the forefront of this new movement. In March 1968, the Brown Berets, a group modeled on the Black Panthers, helped to plan the "blow out" (walkout) that sent nearly 15,000 Chicano teenagers into the streets of East Los Angeles. The high school students demanded educational reform, including courses on the history, literature, art, and language of Mexican Americans. After the police arrested the protesters, students in San Antonio and Denver expressed their solidarity by conducting their own blow outs, holding placards reading "Teachers, Sí, Bigots, No!" Meanwhile, college students demanded Chicano studies programs.

The larger Chicano movement found vivid expression in the performing and visual arts and in literature. *Teatro*, comprising film and drama, flourished as an exploration of the political dimensions of Mexican American society. One of the most popular and visible media was the mural, often inspired by art of Mexican masters such as Diego Rivera. Chicano muralists painted an estimated 1,500 murals on public buildings throughout their communities, from the exteriors of retail shops to freeway overpasses, even to large drainage pipes. Artistic expression found its way into music and dance. The rock group Los Lobos, for example, dedicated its first recorded album to the UFW. One of the most important writers to capture the excitement of the Chicano movement was Oscar Zeta Acosta, whose *The Revolt of the Cockroach People*, published in 1973, renders into fiction some of the major events of the era.

Red Power

The phrase "Red Power," attributed to Vine Deloria Jr., commonly expressed a pan-Indian identity. At the forefront of this movement was the American Indian Movement (AIM). Founded in 1968, AIM represented mainly urban Indian communities. Like Black Panthers and Brown Berets, its young, militant leaders organized initially to monitor law enforcement practices. They soon built a network of urban centers, churches, and philanthropic organizations as well as the "powwow circuit" that publicized news of protest and educational activities across the country (see Map 29.4).

The movement's major catalyst was the occupation of the deserted federal prison on Alcatraz Island in San Francisco Bay. On November 20, 1969, a group of eighty-nine "Indians of All Tribes" claimed the island according to the terms of an 1868 Sioux treaty that gave Indians rights to unused federal property on Indian land. For the next nineteen months, around a hundred Indians, including about eighty UCLA students, occupied the island.

Although the protestors ultimately failed to achieve their specific goals, which included a deed to the land and federal funding for a cultural center, they rallied the larger Indian community. With the occupation at Alcatraz, a participant testified, "we got back our worth, our pride, our dignity, our humanity."

Another series of dramatic events began in 1972, when AIM sponsored the "Trail of Broken Treaties" caravan. First they went to Washington, DC, where they staged a weeklong occupation of the Bureau of Indian Affairs. AIM insurgents then headed west, to the Pine Ridge Reservation, the site of the 1890 massacre at Wounded Knee, South Dakota. There, in the spring of 1973, they demanded a restoration of treaty rights and began a siege that lasted ten weeks. Dozens of FBI agents with shoot-to-kill orders poured in, leaving two Indians dead and an unknown number of casualties on both sides.

The Red Power movement culminated in the "Longest Walk," a five-month march in 1978 from San Francisco to Washington, DC. Again, activists emphasized the history of the forced removal of Indians from their homelands and the U.S. government's repeated violations of treaty rights. By this time, several tribes had won in court, by legislation or by administrative fiat, small parts of what had been taken from them. Despite these victories, many tribal lands continued to suffer from industrial and government waste-dumping and other commercial uses. On reservations and in urban areas with heavy Indian concentrations, alcohol abuse and ill health remained serious problems.

The 1960s also marked the beginning of an "Indian Renaissance" in literature. Vine Deloria Jr.'s *Custer Died for Your Sins* (1969) reached numerous readers inside and outside Indian communities. A wide variety of Indian novelists, historians, and essayists, such as Pulitzer Prize–winning N. Scott Momaday and Leslie Silko, followed up these successes, and fiction and nonfiction works about Indian life and lore continued to attract a large audience. Inspired by these writers, many young Indians turned to their elders to learn tribal ways, including traditional dress and spiritual practices.

The Asian American Movement

In 1968, groups of Chinese, Japanese, and Filipino students began to identify for the first time as Asian Americans. Students at San Francisco State University formed the Asian American Political Alliance (AAPA), while UC-Berkeley students mobilized to "express Asian American solidarity in a predominantly white society." Within a short time, "Yellow Power" organizations spread throughout California and to the East Coast and Midwest.

These groups stood firmly against the Vietnam War, condemning it as a violation of the national sovereignty of the small Asian country. They also protested the racism directed against Southeast Asian peoples and proclaimed their solidarity with their "Asian brothers and sisters" in Vietnam.

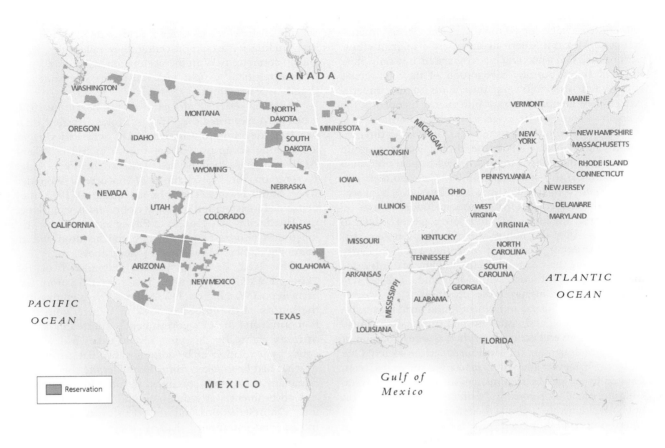

MAP 29.4 Major Indian Reservations, 1976 Although sizable areas, designated Indian reservations represented only a small portion of territory occupied in earlier times.

Throughout 1968 and 1969, Asian American college students boycotted classes and demanded the establishment of ethnic studies programs. By 1973, major universities introduced courses on Asian American studies, and a few set up interdisciplinary departments. Meanwhile, artists, writers, documentary filmmakers, oral historians, and anthropologists worked to recover the Asian American past. Maxine Hong Kingston's *Woman Warrior: A Memoir of a Girlhood among Ghosts* (1976) became a major best seller.

Looking to the example of the Black Panthers, Yellow Power activists also took their struggle into the community. In 1968, a group presented the San Francisco municipal government with a list of grievances about conditions in Chinatown, particularly the poor housing and medical facilities, and organized a protest march down the neighborhood's main street. The Redress and Reparations Movement, begun by Sansei (third-generation Japanese Americans) encouraged children to ask their parents about their wartime internment experiences and prompted older civil rights organizations, such as the Japanese American Citizens League, to raise the issue of reparations. Trade unionists organized new Asian workers, mainly in service

industries and garment trades. Other campaigns reflected the growing diversity of the Asian population. Filipinos, the fastest-growing group, demonstrated against the U.S.-backed Philippine dictator Ferdinand Marcos. Students from South Korea similarly denounced the repressive government in their homeland. Samoans publicized the damage caused by nuclear testing in the Pacific Islands. Ultimately, however, in blurring intergroup differences, the Asian American movement failed to reach the growing immigrant populations, especially the numerous Southeast Asians fleeing their devastated homeland.

The Nixon Presidency

Richard M. Nixon inherited not only an increasingly unpopular war but also a nation riven by internal discord. Without specifying his plans, he promised a "just and honorable peace" in Southeast Asia and the restoration of law and order at home. Yet, once in office, Nixon puzzled both friends and foes. He ordered unprecedented illegal government action against private citizens while agreeing with Congress to enhance several welfare programs and improve environmental protection. He widened and intensified the war in Vietnam, yet made stunning moves toward détente with the People's Republic of China. An architect of the Cold War in the 1950s, Nixon became the first president to foresee its end. Nixon worked hard in the White House, centralizing authority and reigning defiantly as an "Imperial President"—until he brought himself down.

Domestic Policy

Although Nixon showed comparatively little interest in domestic policy, he nevertheless promised to restore order in American society. "We live in a deeply troubled and profoundly unsettled time," he noted. "Drugs, crime, campus revolts, racial discord, draft resistance—on every hand we find old standards violated, old values discarded." Despite his efforts to dismantle many of Johnson's poverty programs, however, Nixon had some surprises for conservatives. Determined to win reelection in 1972, he supported new Social Security benefits and subsidized housing for the poor and oversaw the creation of the Environmental Protection Agency and the Occupational Safety and Health Administration. Most notable was his support, under the guidance of Democratic adviser Daniel P. Moynihan, for the Family Assistance Plan, which proposed a minimal income for the poor in place of welfare benefits. Conservatives judged the plan too generous, while liberals found it inadequate. Moreover, the plan was expensive. Bipartisan opposition ultimately killed the bill.

Nixon also embraced a policy of fiscal liberalism, even accepting the idea of deficit spending. Later that year, he ordered the dollar's value to float against other currencies on the world market rather than being tied to a fixed value of gold, thereby ending the international monetary policy established at Bretton Woods that allowed U.S. domination of the rest of the capitalist world. His ninety-day freeze on wages, rents, and prices, designed to halt the inflation caused by the massive spending on the Vietnam War, also closely resembled Democratic policies. Finally, Nixon's support of "black capitalism"—adjustments or quotas favoring minority contractors in construction projects—created an explosive precedent for "set-aside" programs later blamed on liberals.

Yet, for the most part, Nixon remained committed to the "Southern Strategy" that brought him into office. He lined up with conservatives on most civil rights issues and thus enlarged his southern Republican base. He slowed school desegregation and rejected the busing programs required to achieve racial balance. His nominees to the Supreme Court were far more conservative than those appointed by Eisenhower. Warren E. Burger, who replaced Chief Justice Earl Warren, steered the Court away from the liberal direction it had taken since the 1950s.

One of the few unifying events of Nixon's administration was a distant result of President Kennedy's determination to outshine the Soviets in outer space (see Chapter 27). On July 21, 1969, the lunar module *Apollo 11*

descended to the moon's Sea of Tranquility. As millions watched on television, astronauts Neil Armstrong and Buzz Aldrin stepped out to plant an American flag and to bear the message, "We came in peace for all mankind."

Nixon's War

Nixon promised to bring "peace with honor." Yet, despite this pledge, the Vietnam War raged for four more years before a peace settlement was reached (see Figure 29.5).

•●•⌐Read the Document
Richard Nixon, Peace with Honor at **www.myhistorylab.com**

Much of the responsibility for prolonging the war rested with Henry A. Kissinger, Nixon's national security adviser. A forceful personality, Kissinger insisted that the

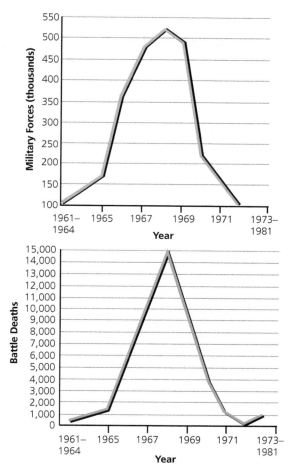

FIGURE 29.5 U.S. Military Forces in Vietnam and Casualties, 1961–81 The U.S. government estimated battle deaths between 1969 and 1973 for South Vietnamese troops at 107,504 and North Vietnamese and Vietcong at more than a half million. Although the United States suffered fewer deaths, the cost was enormous.

SOURCE: U.S. Department of Defense, *Selected Manpower Statistics*, annual and unpublished data; beginning 1981, National Archives and Records Service, "Combat Area Casualty File" (3-330-80-3).

United States could not retain its global leadership by appearing weak to either allies or enemies. After centralizing foreign policymaking in the White House, Kissinger and Nixon together overpowered those State Department members who had concluded that the majority of Americans no longer supported the war (see Figure 29.6).

In public, Nixon followed a policy of "Vietnamization." On May 14, 1969, he announced that the time was approaching "when the South Vietnamese . . . will be able to take over some of the fighting." During the next several months, he ordered the withdrawal of 60,000 U.S. troops. Hoping to placate public opinion, Nixon said he intended to "demonstrate to Hanoi that we were serious in seeking a diplomatic settlement." In private, Nixon mulled over the option of a "knockout blow" to the North Vietnamese.

On April 30, 1970, Nixon made one of the most controversial decisions of his presidency. Without seeking congressional approval, he ordered U.S. troops to invade the tiny nation of Cambodia. Nixon hoped in this way to end North Vietnamese infiltration into the South, but he also decided to live up to what he privately called his "wild man" or "mad bomber" reputation. "Let's go blow the hell out of them," he shouted. The enemy would be unable to anticipate the location or severity of the next U.S. strike, Nixon reasoned, and would thus feel compelled to negotiate.

Nixon could not have predicted what followed the invasion of Cambodia. The largest series of demonstrations and police–student confrontations in the nation's history erupted. At Kent State University in Ohio, the National

Guard shot into an unarmed crowd of students, killing four and wounding nine. Ten days later, on May 14, at Jackson State University, a black school in Mississippi, state troopers entered a campus dormitory and began shooting wildly, killing two students and wounding twelve others. Huge demonstrations took place on fifty campuses, and thirty-seven college and university presidents signed a letter calling on the president to end the war.

A few weeks later, the Senate adopted a bipartisan resolution outlawing the use of funds for U.S. military operations in Cambodia, starting July 1, 1970. Although the House rejected the resolution, Nixon saw the writing on the wall. He had planned to negotiate a simultaneous withdrawal of North Vietnamese and U.S. troops, but he could no longer afford to hold out for this condition.

The president did not accept defeat easily. In February 1971, Nixon directed the South Vietnamese army to invade Laos and cut supply lines, but the demoralized invading force suffered a quick and humiliating defeat. Faced with enemy occupation of more and more territory during a major offensive in April 1972, Nixon ordered the mining of North Vietnamese harbors and directed B-52s to conduct massively destructive bombing missions in Cambodia and North Vietnam (see Seeing History).

Nixon also sent Kissinger to Paris for secret negotiations with delegates from North Vietnam. They agreed to a cease-fire specifying the withdrawal of all U.S. troops and the return of all U.S. prisoners of war. Knowing these terms ensured defeat, South Vietnam's president refused to sign the agreement. On Christmas Day 1972, hoping for a better negotiating position, Nixon ordered one final wave of bomb attacks on North Vietnam's cities. To halt the bombing, the North Vietnamese resumed negotiations. But the terms of the Paris Peace Agreement, signed by North Vietnam and the United States in January 1973, differed little from the settlement Nixon could have procured in 1969.

The last U.S. troops withdrew from Vietnam in March 1973. Two years later, in April 1975, the North Vietnamese took over Saigon, and the Communist-led Democratic Republic of Vietnam soon united the small nation.

The war was finally over. It had cost the United States 58,000 lives and $150 billion. The nation had not only failed to achieve its stated war goal, but also had lost an important post in Southeast Asia. Equally important, the United States proved it could not sustain the policy of containment introduced by President Truman.

While Nixon was maneuvering to bring about "peace with honor," the chilling crimes of war had already begun to haunt Americans. In 1971, the army court-martialed a young lieutenant, William L. Calley Jr., for the murder of "at least" twenty-two Vietnamese civilians during a 1968 search-and-destroy mission subsequently known as the My Lai Massacre. Calley's platoon had destroyed a village and slaughtered more than 350 unarmed South

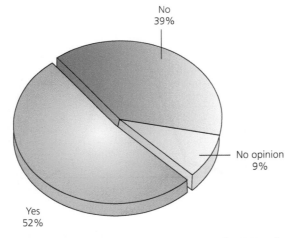

No
39%

No opinion
9%

Yes
52%

FIGURE 29.6 Public Opinion on the War in Vietnam By 1969, Americans were sharply divided in their assessments of the progress of the war and peace negotiations. The American Institute of Public Opinion, founded in 1935 by George Gallup, charted a growing dissatisfaction with the war in Vietnam.

Students at hundreds of colleges and universities turned out in mass demonstrations to protest widening the war in Southeast Asia and the increasing violence on campus. Following the Kent State "massacre," approximately 5 million students joined the national student strike, boycotting classes for the remainder of the week. This photograph, taken at George Washington University, shows a confrontation between Washington Metropolitan Police and an unidentified student.

Vietnamese, raping and beating many of the women before killing them. "My Lai was not an isolated incident," one veteran attested, but "only a minor step beyond the standard official United States policy in Indochina." The platoon commander at My Lai, Calley was first sentenced to life imprisonment before receiving a reduced term of ten years. The secretary of the army paroled Calley after three years of house arrest in his apartment.

Nixon's Foreign Policy

Apart from Vietnam, Nixon's foreign policy defied the expectations of liberals and conservatives alike. Actually, he followed traditions of previous Republican moderates such as Herbert Hoover and Dwight Eisenhower, who had so effectively "proved" their anticommunism that they could conciliate international foes without undermining their popularity at home. Nixon added a new page, however—a policy of détente that replaced U.S.–Soviet bipolarity with multilateral relations that included the People's Republic of China, a rising world power more rigidly Communist than the Soviet Union. Opponents of the Vietnam War accused Nixon of double-dealing, while conservatives howled at any compromise with Communist governments. But Nixon persisted in his plan to restore the prestige of the United States and secure global stability by improving U.S. relations with China and the Soviet Union.

Playing the "China card" was the most dramatic of the president's moves to reestablish the United States as a superpower. He and Kissinger understood that the People's Republic of China was too important to be isolated by the West and too obviously hostile to the Soviet Union to be discounted as a potential ally.

"Ping-Pong diplomacy" began in April 1971, when the Chinese hosted a table tennis team from the United States. Henry Kissinger embarked on a secret mission a few months later. Finally, in February 1972, Richard and First Lady Pat Nixon flew to Beijing, where foreign minister Zhou Enlai and a band playing "The Star-Spangled Banner" greeted them.

It was a momentous and surprising event, one that marked a new era in East-West diplomacy. Nixon claimed that he succeeded in bridging "16,000 miles and twenty-two years of hostility." The president's move successfully increased diplomatic pressure on the Soviet Union, but simultaneously weakened the Nationalist Chinese government in Taiwan, which now slipped into virtual diplomatic obscurity.

Next, the president went to Moscow to negotiate with Soviet leader Leonid Brezhnev, who was anxious about U.S. involvement with China and eager for economic assistance. Declaring, "There must be room in this world for two great nations with different systems to live together and work together," Nixon agreed to cooperate on science and technology, including a joint space mission. Nixon also completed negotiations of the Strategic Arms Limitation Treaty (SALT, known later as SALT I). A limited measure, SALT I represented the first success at strategic arms control since the start of the Cold War and a major public relations victory for the leaders of the two superpowers. After his return to Washington, Nixon announced to Congress "the end of that era which began in 1945."

Nixon's last major diplomatic foray was far less effective. The president sent Kissinger on a two-year mission of "shuttle diplomacy" to mediate Israeli-Arab disputes, to ensure the continued flow of oil, and to increase lucrative U.S. arms sales to Arab countries. The Egyptians and Israelis agreed to a cease-fire in their October 1973 Yom Kippur War, but little progress toward peace in the area was achieved.

Kim Phuc, Fleeing a Napalm Attack near Trang Bang

SEEING History

In 1972, during the phase of the war termed "Vietnamization," South Vietnamese aircraft bombed the village of Trang Bang, about twenty-five miles from Saigon. They were attacking North Vietnamese and Vietcong fighters, but mistakenly targeted a Buddhist pagoda. The incendiary bombs contained black, oily napalm that burned the villagers gathered there.

News photographer Nick Ut had been assigned to meet up with the South Vietnamese army at Trang Bang. "When we [the reporters] moved closer to the village we saw the first people running," he recalled in 1999. "I thought 'Oh my God' when I suddenly saw a woman with her left leg badly burned by napalm. Then came a woman carrying a baby, who died, then another woman carrying a small child with its skin coming off. When I took a picture of them I heard a child screaming and saw that young girl who had pulled off all her burning clothes. She yelled to her brother on her left. Just before the napalm was dropped soldiers [of the South Vietnamese Army] had yelled to the children to run but there wasn't enough time."

The Associated Press, which syndicates photographs to the media worldwide, at first refused to transmit the picture because of the nine-year-old girl's nudity but eventually concluded that the news value of the photograph was such that it could run, provided no-close up of the girl be transmitted. Ut, who took the severely burned girl to the hospital before delivering his film, won a Pulitzer Prize for the photograph.

In 1996, Phan Thi Kim Phuc, by then thirty-three, came to the United States, visited the Vietnam Veterans Memorial in Washington, DC, and resolved to form a foundation to help children victimized by war. She still wants the photograph to be seen: "Let the world see how horrible wars can be."

• **What does this photograph suggest about the role of the news media during the Vietnam war?**

• **In focusing on civilians, what does Nick Ut's photograph suggest about the course of the war?**

Although he had welcomed the publicity surrounding his historic moves toward détente with the Soviet Union and normalized relations with China, Nixon generally handled the nation's foreign affairs behind closed doors. But as opposition to the Vietnam War mounted in Congress, he began to face hard questions about this practice. In response, the president, the Department of State, and the CIA developed plans to tighten security even further.

At the time, apart from the highly publicized tour to China, Nixon revealed little about his policy for other parts of the globe. Unknown to most Americans, he accelerated the delivery of arms supplies to foreign dictators, including the shah of Iran, Ferdinand Marcos of the Philippines, and the white supremacist apartheid government in South Africa. His CIA assistants trained and aided SAVAK, the Iranian secret police force notorious for torturing political dissidents. They also stood behind the South African government in its effort to curtail the activities of the antiapartheid African National Congress. In Latin America, Nixon gave financial assistance and military aid to repressive regimes such as that of Anastasio Somoza of Nicaragua, notorious for its blatant corruption and repeated violations of human rights.

Still more controversial was Nixon's plan to overthrow the democratically elected socialist government of Salvador Allende in Chile. With the assistance of nongovernment agencies, such as the AFL-CIO's American Institute for Free Labor Development, the CIA destabilized the regime by funding right-wing parties, launching demonstrations, and preparing the Chilean army for a coup. In September 1973, a military junta killed President Allende and captured, tortured, or murdered thousands of his supporters. Nixon and Kissinger warmly welcomed the new ruler, General Augusto Pinochet, granting him financial assistance to restabilize the country.

Toward the end of Nixon's term, members of Congress who had been briefed on these policies began to break silence, and reports of clandestine operations flooded the media. Several former CIA agents issued anguished confessions of their activities in other countries. More troubling to Nixon, in spite of all his efforts, the United States continued to lose ground as a superpower.

Dirty Tricks and the 1972 Election

As Nixon approached the 1972 reelection campaign, he tightened his inner circle of White House staff who assisted him in withholding information from the public, discrediting critics, and engaging in assorted "dirty tricks." Staff members solicited illegal campaign contributions and laundered the money through Mexican bank accounts. They also formed a secret squad, "the plumbers," to halt the troublesome information leaks. This team, headed by former CIA agent E. Howard Hunt and former FBI agent G. Gordon Liddy, assisted in conspiracy at the highest levels of government.

The first person on the squad's "hit list" was Daniel Ellsberg, a former researcher with the Department of Defense, who in 1971 had turned over to the press secret documents outlining the history of U.S. involvement in Vietnam. The so-called Pentagon Papers exposed the role of presidents and military leaders in deceiving the public and Congress about the conduct of the United States in Southeast Asia. Nixon sought to bar publication by *The New York Times*, but the Supreme Court ruled in favor of the newspaper on the basis of the First Amendment. Within weeks, a complete version of the Pentagon Papers became a best-selling book, and in 1972 *The New York Times* won a Pulitzer Prize for the series of articles. Frustrated in his attempt to suppress the report, Nixon directed the Department of Justice to prosecute Ellsberg on charges of conspiracy, espionage, and theft. Meanwhile, Hunt and Liddy, seeking to discredit Ellsberg, broke into the office of his former psychiatrist. They found nothing that would make their target less heroic in the eyes of an increasingly skeptical public, and, by 1973, the charges against Ellsberg were dropped after the Nixon administration itself stood guilty of misconduct.

During the 1972 presidential campaign, the Committee to Re-Elect the President (CREEP) enjoyed a huge war chest and spent a good portion on dirty tricks designed to divide the Democrats and discredit them in the eyes of the voting public. They charged George McGovern, Nixon's liberal Democratic opponent, with advocating "abortion, acid [LSD], and amnesty" for draft resisters and deserters. They also informed the news media that McGovern's running mate, Senator Thomas Eagleton, had earlier undergone electric shock therapy for depression, thus forcing his resignation from the Democratic team.

In the short run, the Republicans tallied a monumental success. Nixon presented himself as the candidate of "middle Americans," the Great Silent Majority, and won reelection by a landslide, winning every state but Massachusetts. More important in the long run, the Republicans captured the once solidly Democratic South and the majority of blue-collar, Catholic, and urban voters.

As the carrier of conservatism, Nixon achieved the grandest moment of his long and complex political career. Nevertheless, even with this huge mandate from voters, the most audacious plan of his reelection committee—wiretapping the Democratic National Committee headquarters—ultimately backfired.

Watergate: Nixon's Downfall

On June 17, 1972, a security team had tripped up a group of intruders hired by CREEP to install listening devices in the Washington, DC, Watergate apartment and office complex where the Democrats were headquartered. The police arrested five men, who were later found guilty of conspiracy and burglary. Although Nixon disclaimed any knowledge of the plan, two *Washington Post* reporters, Bob Woodward and Carl Bernstein, followed a trail of evidence back to the nation's highest office.

Televised Senate hearings opened to public view more than a pattern of presidential wrongdoing: they showed an attempt to impede investigations of the Watergate case. Testifying before the committee, a former Nixon aide revealed evidence of secret tape recordings of conversations held in the Oval Office. After special prosecutor Archibald Cox refused to allow Nixon to claim executive privilege and withhold the tapes, the president ordered Cox fired. This "Saturday Night Massacre," as it came to be called, further tarnished Nixon's reputation and swelled curiosity about the tapes. On June 24, 1974, the Supreme Court voted unanimously that Nixon had to release the tapes to a new special prosecutor, Leon Jaworski.

Although incomplete, the Watergate tapes proved damning. They documented Nixon's ravings against his enemies, including anti-Semitic and racist slurs, and his conniving efforts to harass private citizens through federal agencies. The tapes also proved that Nixon had not only known about plans to cover up the Watergate break-in, but had in fact ordered it. The news media enjoyed a field day with the revelations of Nixon's role in a criminal conspiracy to obstruct justice. In July 1974, the House Judiciary Committee adopted three articles of impeachment, charging Nixon with obstructing justice, abusing the power of his office, and acting in contempt of Congress.

●●—Read the Document

House Judiciary Committee's Assessment of Nixon's Activities (1974) at **www.myhistorylab.com**

Charges of executive criminality had clouded the Nixon administration since his vice president left in disgrace. In 1972, Spiro Agnew admitted to accepting large kickbacks while serving as governor of Maryland. Pleading no contest to this and to charges of federal income tax evasion, Agnew resigned in October 1973. Gerald Ford, a moderate Republican representative from Michigan, replaced him and now stood in the wings while the president's drama unfolded.

A delegation from Congress, led by Senator Barry Goldwater, approached Nixon with the news that impeachment and conviction were certain. On August 8, 1974, in a speech underscoring his accomplishments and admitting only to "some errors in judgment," Nixon announced his intention to step down, becoming the first U.S. president to resign from office.

Conclusion

The resignations of Richard Nixon and Spiro Agnew did little to relieve the feeling of national exhaustion that followed the Vietnam War. U.S. troops pulled out of Vietnam in 1973 and the war officially ended in 1975, but bitterness lingered over the unprecedented—and, for many, humiliating—defeat. Moreover, confidence in the government's highest office was severely shaken. The passage of the War Powers Act in 1973, written to compel any future president to seek congressional approval for armed intervention abroad and passed over Nixon's veto, dramatized both the widespread suspicion of an "Imperial Presidency" and a yearning for peace. But the positive dream of community that had inspired Johnson, King, and a generation of student activists could not be revived. No other vision took its place.

In 1968, seven prominent antiwar protesters had been brought to trial for allegedly conspiring to disrupt the Democratic National Convention in Chicago. Just a few

Richard Nixon bid a final farewell to his White House staff as he left Washington, DC, on August 9, 1974. The first president to resign from office, Nixon had become so entangled in the Watergate scandal that his impeachment appeared certain. He was succeeded by Vice President Gerald Ford. After taking the oath of office later that day, President Ford remarked that the wounds of Watergate were "more painful and more poisonous than those of foreign wars."

CHRONOLOGY

1964   President Lyndon Johnson calls for "an unconditional war on poverty" in his state of the union address

Gulf of Tonkin resolution

The Economic Opportunity Act establishes the Office of Economic Opportunity

Free speech movement gets under way at University of California at Berkeley

Johnson defeats conservative Barry Goldwater for president

1965   President Johnson authorizes Operation Rolling Thunder, the bombing of North Vietnam

Teach-ins begin on college campuses

First major march on Washington for peace is organized

Watts uprising begins a wave of rebellions in black communities

1966   J. William Fulbright publishes *The Arrogance of Power*

Black Panther Party is formed

National Organization for Women (NOW) is formed

1967   Antiwar rally in New York City draws 300,000

Vietnam Veterans Against the War is formed

Uprisings in Newark, Detroit, and other cities

Hippie "Summer of Love"

1968   U.S. ground troop levels in Vietnam number 500,000

Tet Offensive in Vietnam, followed by international protests against U.S. policies

Martin Luther King Jr. is assassinated; riots break out in more than 100 cities

Vietnam peace talks begin in Paris

Robert Kennedy is assassinated

Democratic National Convention, held in Chicago, nominates Hubert Humphrey; "police riot" against protesters

Richard Nixon elected president

American Indian Movement (AIM) founded

1969   Woodstock music festival marks the high tide of the counterculture

Stonewall Riot in Greenwich Village sparks the gay liberation movement

Apollo 11 lands on the moon

1970   U.S. incursion into Cambodia sparks campus demonstrations; students killed at Kent State and Jackson State universities

1971   Lieutenant William Calley Jr. court-martialed for My Lai Massacre

The New York Times starts publishing the Pentagon Papers

1972   *Ms. Magazine* publishes first issue

Nixon visits China and Soviet Union

SALT I limits offensive intercontinental ballistic missiles

Intruders attempting to "bug" Democratic headquarters in the Watergate complex are arrested

Nixon is reelected in a landslide

Nixon orders Christmas Day bombing of North Vietnam

1973   Paris Peace Agreement ends war in Vietnam

FBI seizes Indian occupants of Wounded Knee, South Dakota

Watergate burglars tried; congressional hearings on Watergate

CIA destabilizes elected Chilean government, which is overthrown

Vice President Spiro T. Agnew resigns

1974   House Judiciary Committee adopts articles of impeachment against Nixon

Nixon resigns the presidency

years later, the majority of Americans had concluded that presidents Johnson and Nixon had conspired to do far worse. They had intentionally deceived the public about the nature and fortunes of the war. This moral failure signaled a collapse at the center of the American political system. Since Dwight Eisenhower left office warning of the potential danger embedded in the "military-industrial complex," no president had survived the presidency with his honor intact. Watergate, then, appeared to cap the politics of the Cold War, its revelations only reinforcing futility and cynicism. The United States was left psychologically at war with itself.

Review Questions

1. Discuss the events that led up to and contributed to U.S. involvement in Vietnam. How did U.S. involvement in the war affect domestic programs?

2. Discuss the reasons the protest movement against the Vietnam War started on college campuses. Describe how these movements were organized and how the opponents of the war differed from the supporters.

3. Discuss the programs sponsored by Johnson's plan for a Great Society. What was their impact on urban poverty in the late 1960s?

4. What was the impact of the assassinations of Martin Luther King Jr. and Robert Kennedy on the election of 1968? How were various communities affected?

5. How were the "politics of identity" movements different from earlier civil rights organizations? In what ways did the various movements resemble one another?

6. Why did Richard Nixon enjoy such a huge electoral victory in 1972? Discuss his foreign and domestic policies. What led to his sudden downfall?

Recommended Reading

John A. Andrew III, *Lyndon Johnson and the Great Society* (1998). An assessment of the Great Society, with special emphasis on the two major issues of civil rights and poverty. Andrew discusses Johnson's aspirations and the obstacles that kept them out of reach.

Alexander Bloom, ed., *Long Time Gone: Sixties America Then and Now* (2001). Ten essays covering various aspects of the social and political movements of the 1960s. The authors draw out the lasting significance of the "sixties" and dispel commonplace myths by providing accurate information and a sound context for interpretation.

Jane F. Gerhard, *Desiring Revolution: Second-Wave Feminism and the Rewriting of American Sexual Thought, 1920–1982* (2001). Discusses the background of the feminist side of the sexual revolution with special attention to popular versions of Freud's theories. Gerhard discusses disagreements among feminists on the meaning and experience of sexual liberation.

Michael H. Hunt, *Lyndon Johnson's War: America's Cold War Crusade in Vietnam, 1945–1968* (1996). Tracks Johnson's decisions to wage all-out war in Vietnam. Hunt interprets Johnson's actions as consistent with the Cold War foreign policy that had prevailed since the Truman administration and its pledge to "contain" communism.

Maurice Isserman and Michael Kazin, *America Divided: The Civil War of the 1960s*, 3rd ed. (2007). A survey and astute analysis of the Vietnam War and its impact on domestic politics, with close scrutiny of the youth movements that arose in the late 1960s.

Rebecca E. Klatch, *A Generation Divided: The New Left, the New Right, and the 1960s* (1999). Compares and contrasts the respective roles of Students for a Democratic Society and the conservative Young Americans for Freedom on college campuses. Klatch, a sociologist, presents lengthy oral interviews with former student activists in both camps.

Nancy MacLean, *The American Women's Movement, 1945–2000* (2009). A brief history of the rise of feminism with an emphasis on the role of grassroots activists in pressuring for social and political reform. MacLean provides excerpts from forty documents illustrating the breadth and diversity of the women's movement.

Joan Morrison and Robert K. Morrison, eds., *From Camelot to Kent State: The Sixties Experience in the Words of Those Who Lived It* (2001). A collection of fifty-nine oral histories of a range of people who lived through the 1960s. The volume includes stories of better-known activists, such as Eldridge Cleaver and Abbie Hoffman, as well as those who were soldiers in Vietnam or student activists. This edition also contains many photographs.

Rick Perlstein, *Nixonland: The Rise of a President and the Fracturing of America* (2008). A richly contextualized examination of the rise and fall of Richard Nixon. For Perlstein, Nixon's story is a vehicle for assessing large shifts in U.S. political culture.

Laura Pulido, *Black, Brown, Yellow, and Left: Radical Activism in Los Angeles* (2006). A well-documented survey of activism in communities of color since the 1960s. Pulido examines the role of women in dealing within minority men within various organizations and movements.

Melvin Small, *AntiWarriors: The Vietnam War and the Battle for America's Hearts and Minds* (2002). A readable, succinct study of the groundswell of opposition to the war in Vietnam. Small covers many facets of the antiwar movement, ranging from hippies to Vietnam Veterans Against the War.

James E. Westheider, *The African American Experience in Vietnam* (2008). Examines several facets of African American involvement in the Vietnam War, including antiwar protests and racial violence within the armed forces.

PEARSON myhistorylab Connections

Reinforce what you learned in this chapter by studying the many documents, images, maps, review tools, and videos available at www.myhistorylab.com.

Read and Review

✓● Study and Review **Chapter 29**

●●● Read the Document

Johnson's Defense of the U.S. Presence in Vietnam (1965)

The Report of the President's Commission on Campus Unrest (1970)

Stokely Carmichael and Charles V. Hamilton, from Black Power: The Politics of Liberation in America (1966)

Shirley Chisholm, Equal Rights for Women (1969)

Gay Liberation Front (1970)

Chávez, He Showed Us the Way (1978)

Richard Nixon, Peace with Honor (1973)

House Judiciary Committee's Assessment of Nixon's Activities (1974)

◉ See the Map *The Vietnam War*

Research and Explore

●●● Read the Document

Exploring America: Rachel Carson

Profiles
Janis Joplin
Eugene McCarthy

Whose History Is It? The Vietnam Memorial

◉ Watch the Video

Richard Nixon Presidential Campaign Ad: A Wavering Hubert Humphrey

Richard Nixon, "I am not a crook"

LBJ Signing the Civil Rights Bill

Protests against the Vietnam War

The Vietnam War

Newsreel: Peace March, Thousands Oppose Vietnam War

((●● Hear the **Audio**

Hear the audio files for Chapter 29 at
www.myhistorylab.com.

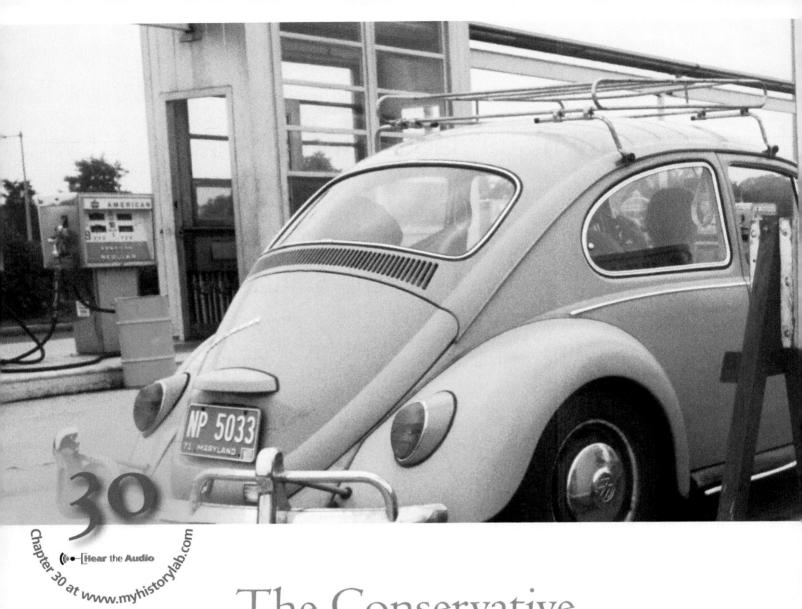

Chapter 30 at www.myhistorylab.com

((●—[Hear the Audio

The Conservative Ascendancy 1974–1991

CHAPTER OUTLINE

American Communities 885
Grassroots Conservatism in Orange County, California

The Overextended Society 887
A Troubled Economy
The Endangered Environment
"Lean Years Presidents": Ford and Carter
The Limits of Global Power
The Iran Hostage Crisis

The New Right 895
Neoconservatism
The Religious Right

The Pro-Family Movement
The 1980 Election

The Reagan Revolution 898
The Great Communicator
Reaganomics
The Election of 1984
Recession, Recovery, and Fiscal Crisis

Best of Times, Worst of Times 901
A Two-Tiered Society
The Feminization of Poverty
Sunbelt/Rustbelt Communities
Epidemics: Drugs, AIDS, Homelessness

Toward a New World Order 905
The Evil Empire
The Reagan Doctrine
The Middle East and the Iran-Contra Scandal
The Collapse of Communism

"A Kinder, Gentler Nation" 909
Reagan's Successor: George H. W. Bush
The Persian Gulf War
The Economy and the Election of 1992

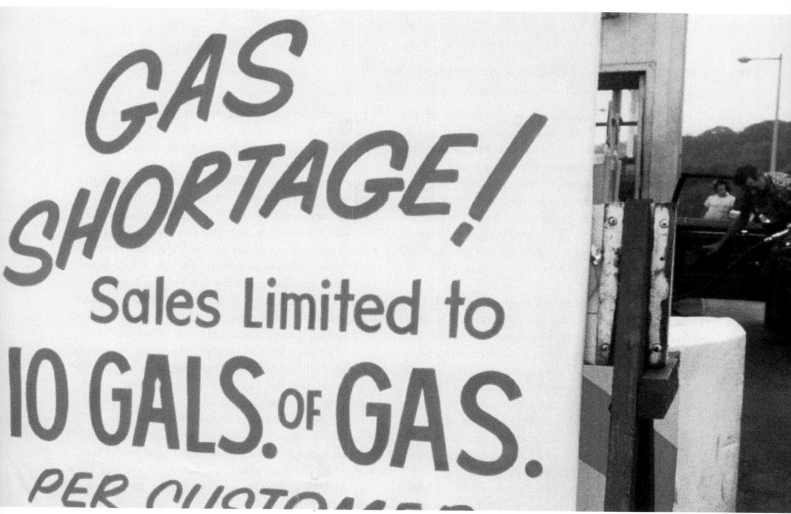

A gas station during the gasoline shortage and energy crisis of the 1970s rations gas to its customers.

Grassroots Conservatism in Orange County, California

In 1962, Bee Gathright, a Brownie leader and mother of three young girls, invited her neighbors to her suburban Garden Grove home to hear a political talk by a man from the nearby Knott's Berry Farm Freedom Center. "This is when I discovered that I was a conservative," she later recalled. She feared that "the Communists were going to bury us, were going to take over the world. . . ." She convinced her skeptical husband Neil, an aerospace engineer, to share her new conviction. They soon joined the California Republican Assembly, a volunteer organization committed to electing conservatives to office. In 1964, the Gathrights' home served as a local headquarters for the presidential campaign of conservative Arizona Senator Barry Goldwater.

In Orange County in the 1960s and 1970s, thousands of "kitchen table" activists like the Gathrights began a transformation of American conservatism and American politics that culminated in the presidential election of Ronald Reagan in 1980. Most of them were middle-class men and women, including large numbers of professionals and small business owners. Many, like the Gathrights, had moved to California to work in the burgeoning aerospace industry. Orange

AMERICAN Communities

County's 800 square miles lie at the center of the southern California basin, and large lemon and orange groves dominated the economy until the 1940s. World War II and Cold War defense-related spending accelerated the county's growth, creating thousands of new manufacturing jobs. A strong demand for housing spurred a construction boom and a roaring real estate market. By 1960, more than 700,000 people lived in Orange County, an increase of nearly 400 percent since 1940, and the population doubled again to top 2 million in the 1980s.

While Barry Goldwater's 1964 campaign ignited great enthusiasm in Orange County, his national defeat forced conservatives to consider ways to shed the "extremism" label. In 1966, they successfully backed the gubernatorial campaign of Ronald Reagan, a former Hollywood actor and New Deal liberal who had evolved in the 1950s into a prominent conservative and Republican Party activist. As governor, Reagan sought to limit state support for welfare and other social services, while expanding state power to enforce law and order.

Reagan's success in California, as well as Richard Nixon's election as president in 1968, signaled an important new turn for American conservatives. They still championed anticommunism but no longer engaged in the loose talk about using nuclear weapons that had hurt Goldwater. They attacked "big government," but no longer spoke openly about repealing popular New Deal programs like Social Security. Instead, they focused on the "social issues" that increasingly troubled and mobilized Orange County's grassroots activists. Their concerns, largely defined by a "backlash" against the antiwar movement, counterculture, women's liberation, and urban uprisings, emphasized so-called family issues, in which opposition to sex education, obscenity, abortion rights, gay liberation, and the Equal Rights Amendment were all linked. On the economic side, conservatives began to tap a deep well of resentment over rising property taxes and high inflation.

Two central themes of this new conservatism resonated with millions of Americans well beyond Orange County. One was the 1978 "revolt" of homeowners that led to

a sharp reduction in the property tax rate and soon spread to other states.

Orange County also helped form the second new force reshaping conservatism, "born-again" evangelical Christianity. Fundamentalist sects had long been associated with the rural poor of the South. But Orange County's religious revival featured educated professionals and middle-class suburbanites who turned to Christianity for spirituality and as a way to assert order amid rapid cultural and social change. "Born-again" Christians found community not only in Sunday services, but also in a wide range of tightly organized activities: Bible study groups, summer retreats, "singles' fellowships," prayer breakfasts, and "Christian" consumer culture, which allowed people to simultaneously embrace faith, modern business techniques, and worldly goods. The political implications of the new evangelicalism soon became clear.

President Jimmy Carter, who took office in 1976, was a "born-again" Christian, and his successor, Ronald Reagan, raced to victory in 1980 with the strong backing of newly politicized Christian voters. For Bee Gathright, Reagan's victory vindicated her years of grassroots activism and set the nation on a conservative political course that led into the twenty-first century.

Unlike Carter, who advised Americans to accept limits, Reagan promised to not only restore but also enhance American global supremacy. As president, Reagan introduced a new economic program—"Reaganomics"—that reduced income taxes for wealthy Americans and at the same time increased federal spending for the largest military buildup in American history. Abolishing the Great Society antipoverty programs, he fostered the growth of a two-tiered society characterized by a disproportionate number of women and children filling the ranks of the nation's poor. Meanwhile, the increases in military spending complemented Reagan's foreign policy, which included a revival of Cold War patriotism, interventions in the Caribbean and Central America, and labeling the Soviet Union an "Evil Empire." However, it was Reagan's successor, George H. W. Bush, who presided during one of the most dramatic events of the era: the dissolution of the Soviet Union.

Orange County

1. What explains the weakness in the U.S. economy in the 1970s?

2. What did Ford and Carter accomplish as presidents?

3. What were the factors behind the rise of the New Right?

4. What economic assumptions underlay "Reaganomics"?

5. Why did the gap between the rich and the poor grow in the 1980s?

6. How did the Cold War end?

FOCUS
Questions

1974–1991

The Overextended Society

The prosperity following World War II had helped keep conservatives at bay from the Eisenhower years through the 1960s. Then, in the 1970s, economic growth ground to a halt, and Americans saw their standard of living decline. In addition, the decade presented Americans with an unfamiliar combination of skyrocketing prices and rising unemployment. Economists termed this novel condition "stagflation." By the mid-1970s, the unemployment rate had reached nearly 9 percent, its highest level since the Great Depression, and it remained close to 7 percent for most of the rest of the decade. Inflation, meanwhile, reached double digits, rising to 13.5 percent by 1980.

The United States had come to an unhappy turning point in its economic history. Emerging from World War II as the world's richest nation and retaining this status through the 1960s, the country suddenly found itself falling behind Western Europe and Japan. Moreover, the proportion of families living in poverty, which had shrunk during the 1960s, grew at an alarming rate. Nixon's successors, presidents Gerald Ford and Jimmy Carter, hoped to restore integrity to the office that Nixon had tarnished, but when it came to the economy, they promised little and, as many voters concluded, delivered even less.

A Troubled Economy

The most vivid sign of the troubled economy, the energy crisis, seemed to appear suddenly in the fall of 1973, although it had been decades in the making. The United States, which used about 70 percent of all oil produced in the world, had a sufficient domestic supply until the mid-1950s. Rising demand began to outstrip national reserves, and by 1973 the nation was importing one-third of its crude oil, mainly from the Middle Eastern countries around the Persian Gulf. On October 17, the Arab members of the government-controlled Organization of Petroleum Exporting Countries (OPEC), in retaliation for U.S. support of Israel during the Yom Kippur War, announced an embargo on oil shipments to the United States and its Western European allies (see Map 30.1). As a result, Americans faced a severe oil shortage. OPEC ended the embargo five months later, but limited production to keep prices high.

President Nixon responded to the crisis by appointing an "energy czar" and paving the way for the creation of the Department of Energy in 1977. He ordered reductions in air travel and temperatures in public buildings. He also appealed to Congress to lower speed limits on interstate highways to 55 miles per hour and to extend daylight-saving time into the winter months. But the impact of these measures was slight, and the effects of the oil embargo rippled throughout the economy. While the cost of gasoline, oil, and electricity jumped to new heights, many other prices also rose, from apartment rents and telephone bills to restaurant checks. Meanwhile, Americans became yet more dependent on Middle East oil supplies (see Figure 30.1).

Despite the drama of the oil crisis, the economic downturn had deeper roots in the failure of the United States to keep up with the rising industrial efficiency of other nations. Manufacturers from Asia, Latin America, and Europe now produced cheaper and better products, including automobiles, long considered the monopoly of Detroit. U.S. automakers, determined to reduce costs, turned to "outsourcing"—that is, making cars and trucks from parts cheaply produced abroad and imported into the United States as semifinished materials (which were subject to a lower tariff than finished goods). In high-tech electronics, the United States could scarcely compete against Japanese-made televisions, radios, tape players, cameras, and computers. For the first time in the twentieth century, the balance of trade had tipped: Americans were importing more goods than exporting.

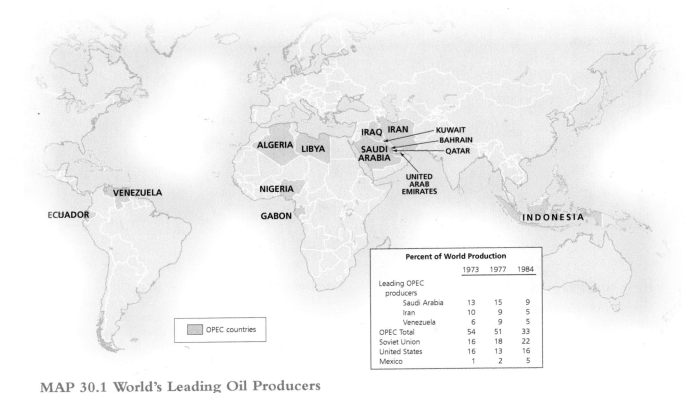

Percent of World Production			
	1973	1977	1984
Leading OPEC producers			
Saudi Arabia	13	15	9
Iran	10	9	5
Venezuela	6	9	5
OPEC Total	54	51	33
Soviet Union	16	18	22
United States	16	13	16
Mexico	1	2	5

MAP 30.1 World's Leading Oil Producers

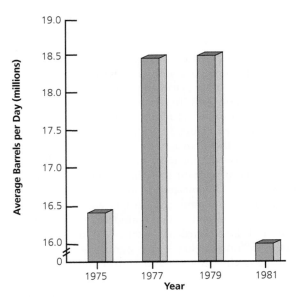

FIGURE 30.1 Decline of U.S. Oil Consumption, 1975–81 Boycotts causing shortages and high prices spurred the reduction in oil consumption. However, in the 1980s consumption once again began to rise to reach record highs.

SOURCE: Department of Energy, *Monthly Energy Review,* June 1982.

An AFL-CIO leader complained that the United States was becoming "a nation of hamburger stands . . . a country stripped of industrial capacity and meaningful work." Between 1970 and 1982 the AFL-CIO, since the early 1930s a leading source of support to the Democratic Party, lost nearly 30 percent of its membership (see Figure 30.2). The only real union growth took place among public employees, including teachers, civil service workers, and health professionals—all of them dependent on sagging public budgets.

Typical of hard times, an increasing number of women sought jobs to support their families. By 1980, more than half of all married women with children in their care were working outside the home. Yet despite their numerical gains, women lost ground relative to men. In 1955, women earned 64 percent of the average wages paid to men; in 1980, they earned only 59 percent. The growing service economy accounted for this dip: women clustered in occupations where the lowest wages prevailed.

African American women made some gains. Through Title VII of the Civil Rights Act, which outlawed workplace discrimination by sex or race, and the establishment of the Equal Employment Opportunity Commission to enforce it, they managed to climb the lower levels of the job ladder. By 1980, northern black women's median earnings were about 95 percent of white women's earnings.

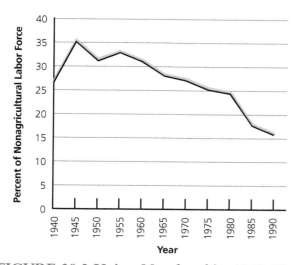

FIGURE 30.2 Union Membership, 1940–90
After reaching a peak during World War II, union membership steadily declined. In the 1980s, overseas production took an especially big toll on industrial unions.

SOURCE: Bureau of Labor Statistics, in Mary Kupiec et al., eds., *Encyclopedia of American Social History*, Vol. II. New York: Scribner's, 1993, p. 4188. Copyright © 1993 Scribner's. Reprinted by permission of Cengage Learning.

In contrast, Hispanic women, whose labor force participation leaped by 80 percent during the decade, were restricted to only a few occupations, mostly at or only slightly above the minimum wage. Puerto Ricans found jobs in the garment industry of the Northeast; Mexican Americans more typically worked as domestics or agricultural laborers in the Southwest.

The Endangered Environment

The roots of the modern environmentalist movement trace back to marine biologist Rachel Carson's best-seller, *Silent Spring,* which detailed the devastating effects of DDT and other pesticides. Following its publication in 1962, many Americans began to measure their high living standards against the damage done by industry to the nation's water, air, and soil. By the end of the decade, concerned citizens were advocating conservation practices such as recycling glass bottles and newspapers and providing popular support for the proclamation of Earth Day, first celebrated on April 22, 1970.

The oil embargo of 1973 and the high prices of energy that followed helped to underscore even more boldly the environmental downside of the post–World War II economic boom. Air and water pollution, climate change, and depletion of the ozone layer became major political issues. Long-standing organizations such as the Sierra Club, Audubon Society, Wilderness Society, and the National Wildlife Society picked up thousands of members. Newer groups, such as the Environmental Defense Fund, Natural Resources Defense Council, and Friends of the Earth, joined in to advocate the

development of renewable energy sources such as solar power and the conservation of renewable resources.

Cutting across nearly all population groups and regions, the growing environmental movement reached into conservative areas in the Deep South with warnings of the dangers of toxic wastes, the destruction of wetlands, and the ruin of fishing industries. Sometimes campaigns succeeded in blocking massive construction projects, such as nuclear energy plants; more often they halted small-scale destruction of a natural habitat or historic urban district. One of the most dramatic campaigns took place in Love Canal, near Buffalo, New York, following the discovery of high rates of cancer, miscarriages, and birth defects in the community. There, toxic wastes dumped by the Hooker Chemical Laboratory had oozed into basements and backyards, and homemaker Lois Gibbs organized her neighbors to draw national attention to the grim situation. In 1978, after a health emergency was declared, the state of New York bought their properties, fenced off the public school and 100 houses, and moved the residents to new homes.

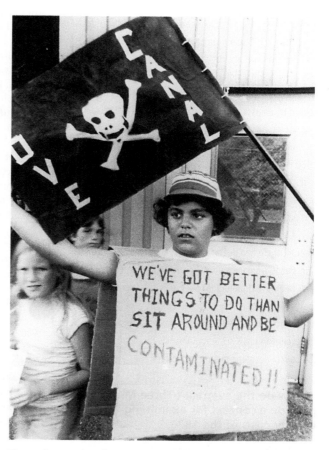

The media attention given to Love Canal residents, who reported high incidents of birth defects and rates of cancer, led to the passage of a new federal law in 1980 regulating toxic waste disposal. This photograph shows one of the endangered children demonstrating during a neighborhood meeting.

COMMUNITIES *in* CONFLICT

Three Mile Island, Pennsylvania

On March 28, 1979, mechanical failures and judgment errors at the nuclear generating facility at Three Mile Island (TMI), near Harrisburg, Pennsylvania, caused the breakdown of the plant's cooling system and risked a catastrophic core meltdown. Although the company that ran the facility denied that there was any danger, nearly 150,000 horrified residents fled their homes. What had seemed an isolated event had national repercussions. Elevated radioactivity was found in milk supplies several hundred miles away. Massive demonstrations against nuclear power culminated in a rally of more than 200,000 people in New York City.

The TMI accident climaxed in a debate that had been building throughout the 1970s. The OPEC oil embargo and energy crisis had encouraged communities to explore nuclear energy. But just four years before the TMI accident, more than 2,300 scientists petitioned Congress and the president to warn against rapid expansion.

Events surrounding the accident suggested at least two possible positions. One side insisted that the harm caused by the release of radiation during the TMI accident had not yet surfaced. This was the position of Jane Lee, an assistant manager of a dairy farm 3.5 miles from TMI. In a 1980 interview, she discussed her long-standing opposition to nuclear power. Lee became an environmental activist, served on the regional Environmental Quality Control Board, and opposed restarting Three Mile Island.

Others argued that the hazards had been exaggerated. After all, there had been neither a meltdown nor an explosion. Pennsylvania governor Richard Thornburgh twenty years later said: "I'm grateful that our prayers were answered and that the consensus view seems to be that there are no adverse long-term health or environmental consequences of the event." In his 2003 autobiography, Thornburgh spoke of the painful decisions that he had to face.

- **How do the events at Three Mile Island provide a context for examining the energy crisis of the 1970s?**

- **In view of today's fears of global warming, does the near-disaster at Three Mile Island take on new meaning?**

Environmental Activist Jane Lee Opposes Nuclear Power (1980)

I'm on pretty firm ground when I say that I know, over and above the accident, that we have been exposed to more than our share of radiation because of the total incompetency of the people who are operating that plant. There is no question about it. The [government-sponsored] Kemmeny Commission report, if you read it, proves beyond a shadow of a doubt that the people who were operating the plants down there simply do not know what they're doing. And the same people are still operating them. They want to bring Unit 1 on line. During the accident they kept telling us there was nothing to worry about, that everything was under control, and all the time *nothing* was under control. Most people don't know we still have an ongoing accident at TMI. . . .

> "[Radiation] is affecting all of us."

What I'm about to tell you is only the tip of the iceberg. Back in 1973 I began to log incidences of abortions, stillbirths, birth defects and abnormalities in farm animals and livestock. At first I logged just what was happening here on this farm. Then as I began to get reports, I began to find out that it wasn't just this farm that was having problems—it was most of the farms in approximately a five-mile radius of TMI. . . .

The radiation is striking at the reproductive system, the area most vulnerable to radiation. . . .

For two weeks just after the accident, there wasn't a sign of a bird anywhere . . .

Anywhere. When the farmers go out to plow their fields, the birds usually hover all over the fields. It was the weirdest thing to plow the ground without a sign of a bird. There wasn't a sign of a bird! York County, where I live, is notorious for its starlings, but this year the starlings never showed up. Now, starlings don't just come like average birds. They come by the hundreds of thousands in wave after wave and cloud after cloud. In fact, we were saying that something was going to have to be done abut the starlings because they were so bad. But they never showed up this year. . . .

We have a housing development near here which sits up real high. When those plants were operating, many times I could see the steam go over the top and settle right on that development. There are pockets of women up there who are having miscarriages. There's been two suits filed already in the area against Met. Ed. The women had stillborns. We don't know yet how far-ranging this is because in the Hershey Medical Center the cancer department is so secret that nobody can go into there and get the statistics. . . .

A lot of people here are developing pneumonia. I'm really surprised at how many. These days, you don't hear of pneumonia like you used to. This is part and parcel of radiation, it destroys the immunity system. . . .

[After the accident] we had a metallic taste in our mouths. It tasted like, you know, like when you're a kid and you put money in your mouth? That's what it tasted like. And we all had it. . . .

[Radiation] is affecting all of us. The radioactive materials are going from the waste into our environment. They're coming back to us through the food chain. So it doesn't make any difference how close you live or how far away you live from a nuclear plant. We're all going to be affected. And in five years, if we continue with the operation of nuclear power plants, the people in this country are not going to be strong enough to go out and work on a job, much less defend their nation. That is a fact. We are not going to be strong enough because it is going to destroy the immunity system. And it will affect all of us. Every last one of us, I don't care where we live.

It isn't going to go away by pretending it doesn't exist. And the longer it's postponed the greater the danger is. Now that's my feeling. Somebody has to speak out. I went for three years with people making fun of me, telling me I was crazy and I didn't know what I was talking about. Now we all live in fear. All of us. I'm not alone anymore.

SOURCE: Robert Leppzer, *Voices from Three Mile Island: The People Speak Out* (Trumansburg, NY: The Crossing Press, 1980), pp. 21, 23, 37, 44, 45, 48, 50. Copyright © 1980 The Crossing Press. Reprinted by permission of Random House, Inc.

Pennsylvania Governor Richard Thornburgh Recalls the Three Mile Island Accident (2003)

It later became clear that, while some of the reactor fuel heated to the point of melting, a disastrous "meltdown" was never close to occurring. Detectable amounts of radiation escaped into our air, water and even milk, but these amounts were limited enough that their impact, if any, on public health remains debatable to this day. And a massive evacuation of the up to 200,000 people residing in the area, with its potential for panic, injury and even loss of life, would have been far more dangerous and damaging than was the accident itself. But at 7:50 on that March morning, we knew none of this. The thought of issuing a general evacuation order entered my mind immediately and never left during the days to follow. . . .

Our first task was to find out exactly what was happening. This was to prove far more difficult than any of us could have imagined. The utility (Metropolitan Edison), its parent company (General Public Utilities), state and federal regulators, and other groups and institutions issued increasingly contradictory assessments, telling the public either more or less than they knew of the accident and its consequences. Self-appointed experts exaggerated either the danger or the

safety of the situation. The credibility of the utility, in particular, did not fare well. On that first day it sought to minimize the accident, assuring us, inaccurately, that "everything is under control" and that "all safety equipment functioned properly." When company technicians found that radiation levels in the surrounding area had climbed above normal, the company neglected to release that information to the public. It also vented some radioactive steam into the air for two and one-half hours at midday on Wednesday, without informing us or the public.

Thus it fell to Lieutenant Governor Scranton . . . to tell the people of central Pennsylvania that "this situation is more complex than the company first led us to believe" and that . . . further discharges were possible . . . but that off-site radioactivity levels had been decreasing during the afternoon and there was no evidence that they had ever reached a danger point. . . .

Shortly after noon on that third day of the crisis . . . I recommended that pregnant women and preschoolers leave the area within five miles of the plant until further notice, and that all schools within that zone be closed as well. I also ordered the opening of evacuation centers at various sites outside of the area to shelter those who had no place to go. "Current readings," I stated, "are no higher than they were yesterday [but] the continued presence of radioactivity in the area and the possibility of further emissions lead me to exercise the utmost of caution. . . ."

In general, reviews of our handling of TMI were favorable. . . . There were, of course, critics as well, mostly focusing upon my unwillingness to order a "precautionary" evacuation in light of all the uncertainty. In time, I was to be labeled both "antinuke" (by the industry) and "pronuke" (by environmentalists) for various positions taken after the accident. . . . In a

"Self-appointed experts exaggerated either the danger or the safety of the situation."

May 1979 address to the American Society of Newspaper Editors, I called for "a middle ground between those who would abandon [nuclear power] and those who would expand it tomorrow. . . . The question is not yes or no, but how best we can use it and keep it under control. . . . [If] we can't prepare ourselves to control it, then we must prepare ourselves to do without it."

SOURCE: Dick Thornburgh, *Where the Evidence Leads: An Autobiography* (Pittsburgh: University of Pittsburgh Press, 2003), pp. 112, 113, 114–115, 117, 123–24. Copyright © 2003 The University of Pittsburgh Press. Reprinted by permission.

Congress responded to growing pressure by passing during the1970s more than twenty new bills and amending earlier legislation to protect endangered species, reduce pollution caused by automobile emissions, limit and ban the use of some pesticides and fluorocarbon gases, and control strip-mining practices. The Environmental Protection Agency (EPA), established in 1970, grew to become the federal government's largest regulatory agency, employing more than 10,000 people by the end of the decade (see Communities in Conflict).

Business-based groups fought back and sometimes found unexpected allies. City officials, both Democratic and Republican, generally avoided congressional mandates for reduction in air pollution by requesting lengthy extensions of deadlines for compliance. Top labor officials such as George Meany, president of the AFL-CIO, denounced "tree hugger" environmentalists as enemies of economic growth, and United Auto Workers lobbyists joined auto makers in resisting compulsory gas mileage and tighter emissions controls in new models. Again and again, efforts at more environmentally attuned policies on energy met defeat. Environmentalists lost a key campaign in 1973 when Congress approved the Trans-Alaskan Pipeline, 800 miles of pipe often leaking into an endangered environment, connecting oil fields in Alaska's far north with refining facilities in the Lower 48. Despite the introduction of lead-free gasoline, the air in major metropolitan areas grew worse because automobile traffic increased.

"Lean Years Presidents": Ford and Carter

Gerald R. Ford and Jimmy Carter presided over not only a depressed economy but also a nation of disillusioned citizens, many of them wary of liberals and open to conservative appeals. The revelations of the Watergate break-in and Nixon's subsequent resignation as president had cast a pall over politics. Replacing Nixon in August 1974, Gerald Ford reassured the public that "our long national nightmare is over," but then quickly pardoned Nixon for all the federal crimes he may have committed while in office. At the time, the pardon reinforced public cynicism toward government and Ford in particular.

Ford annoyed the conservatives in his ranks by choosing New York Governor Nelson Rockefeller, a well-known liberal, as his vice president. He then annoyed Rockefeller by directing him to head his "Whip Inflation Now" campaign, which almost everyone ridiculed for asking people to help curb inflation by wearing red WIN lapel pins as reminders to hold back personal consumption. Even First Lady Betty Ford alienated conservative Republicans by breaking ranks to champion gun control, the Equal Rights Amendment, and abortion rights.

To many Americans, Ford seemed a pleasant person but an inept leader. Some members of Congress judged him more harshly and established special oversight committees to keep tabs on the executive branch. Ford nevertheless banked on his incumbency for the 1976 election,

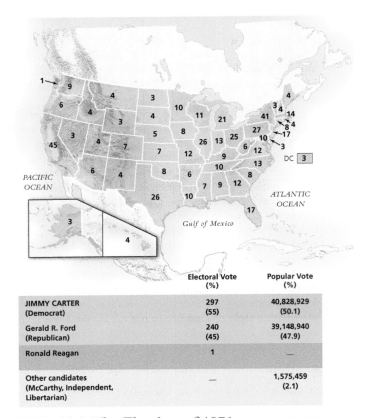

	Electoral Vote (%)	Popular Vote (%)
JIMMY CARTER (Democrat)	297 (55)	40,828,929 (50.1)
Gerald R. Ford (Republican)	240 (45)	39,148,940 (47.9)
Ronald Reagan	1	—
Other candidates (McCarthy, Independent, Libertarian)	—	1,575,459 (2.1)

MAP 30.2 The Election of 1976 Incumbent Gerald Ford could not prevail over the disgrace brought to the Republican Party by Richard Nixon. The lingering pall of the Watergate scandal, especially Ford's pardon of Nixon, worked to the advantage of Jimmy Carter, who campaigned as an outsider to national politics. Although Carter and his running mate Walter Mondale won by only a narrow margin, the Democrats gained control of both the White House and Congress.

dumped Rockefeller, and welcomed Senator Robert Dole of Kansas as his running mate, but only narrowly won nomination after holding off a challenge from Ronald Reagan. Democrats chose Jimmy Carter, a former navy officer and governor of Georgia, who presented himself as a political outsider. When Carter told his mother he was running for president, she reportedly asked, "president of what?"

A born-again Christian and successful southern politician, Carter was the first Democratic presidential candidate since the 1930s who declined to call himself a liberal, offering instead personal integrity as his chief qualification for the nation's highest office. "I will never lie to you," he promised the electorate. On domestic issues, Carter campaigned as a moderate. Counting on support from both conservative and southern voters who would ordinarily vote Republican, he defended existing entitlement programs while opposing Senator Edward Kennedy's call for comprehensive health coverage. He capitalized on Ford's unpopular Nixon pardon and, with his running mate Senator Walter Mondale of Minnesota, won with just over 50 percent of the popular vote and a 297-to-240 margin in the Electoral College. Carter won more than 90 percent of the black vote, which provided his margin of victory in Pennsylvania, Ohio, and seven southern states (see Map 30.2). But apathy proved the next most important factor. A record 46.7 percent of eligible voters did not bother to cast ballots.

If his outsider status helped win the election, Carter's lack of experience in national politics did little to prepare him to govern. And, as he later recalled, "the ghosts of Watergate still haunted the White House." Congress continued to pull tight on the reins of power, while the new president seemed to many observers enigmatic, even uninterested in the major issues. His most successful initiative, deregulation of the airlines, brought lower fares for millions of passengers. He also gained reforms in civil service, Social Security, and Medicare and created the Department of Education. Inflation proved to be his worst enemy. As older Americans could recognize, half of all the inflation since 1940 had occurred in just ten years. Interest rates rose, driving mortgages out of reach for many would-be home buyers. Rents in many locations doubled, sales of automobiles and other consumer products slumped, and many small businesses went under. Tuition costs skyrocketed along with unemployment, and many young men and women who could neither afford to go to college nor find a job moved back home.

An outspoken fiscal conservative, Carter could not deliver on his promise to turn the economy around or even to lower the federal deficit. By the time he left office in 1980, a majority of those polled agreed that "the people running the country don't really care what happens to you." He had managed to discredit the liberal tradition of the Democratic Party even while distancing himself from it, making his presidency the symbol of a larger political collapse.

Read the **Document**
Jimmy Carter, The "Crisis of Confidence" Speech (1979) at **www.myhistorylab.com**

The Limits of Global Power

In April 1975, the North Vietnamese captured Saigon while the South Vietnamese army, now without U.S. assistance, fell apart. All fighting stopped within a few weeks, and Vietnam was reunited under a government dominated by Communists. For many Americans, this outcome underscored the futility of U.S. involvement in the Vietnam War; for others, it suggested the limits of the global power of the United States.

President Carter pledged to inaugurate a new era in U.S. foreign policy, and, noting a shameful "loss of morality" in recent times, he placed international human rights at the top of his agenda. Carter condemned policies that allowed the United States to support "right-wing monarchs and military dictators" in the name of anticommunism. His secretary of state, Cyrus R. Vance, and the assistant secretary for human rights and humanitarian affairs, Pat Derrian, worked to punish or at least to censure repressive military regimes in Brazil, Argentina, and Chile. For the first time, leading U.S. diplomats spoke out against the South African apartheid regime. In line with this policy, Carter tried to reform operations at the CIA, particularly to halt covert interventions in the affairs of foreign governments.

Carter seemed within reach of a historic triumph in the Middle East. Early in his administration, he met privately with Israeli prime minister Menachem Begin to encourage conciliation with Egypt. When negotiations between the two countries stalled in 1978, Carter brought Begin together with Egyptian president Anwar el-Sadat for a thirteen-day retreat at Camp David, Maryland.

The Camp David Accords, signed in September 1978, set the formal terms for peace in the region. Egypt became the first Arab country to recognize Israel's right to exist, as the two nations established mutual diplomatic relations for the first time

President Carter signs the Middle East Peace Treaty with Egyptian President Anwar Sadat and Israeli Prime Minister Menachem Begin, in Washington, DC, March 1979. President Carter had invited both leaders to Camp David, the presidential retreat in Maryland, where for two weeks he mediated between them on territorial rights to the West Bank and Gaza Strip. Considered Carter's greatest achievement in foreign policy, the negotiations, known as the Camp David Peace Accords, resulted in not only the historic peace treaty but also the Nobel Peace Prize for Begin and Sadat.

since the founding of Israel in 1948. In return, Egypt regained control of the Sinai Peninsula, including important oil fields and airfields.

But disappointment lay ahead. Carter staked his hopes for regional peace on the final achievement of statehood, or at least political autonomy, for Palestinians in a portion of their former lands now occupied by the Israelis. The accords specified that Israel would eventually return to its approximate borders of 1967. However, although Begin agreed to dismantle some Israeli settlements in the Sinai, the Israeli government continued to sponsor more and more Jewish settlements, expropriating Palestinian holdings. The final status of the Palestinians remained in limbo.

Carter scored his biggest moral victory in foreign affairs by paving the way for Panama to assume the ownership, operation, and defense of the Panama Canal Zone. Negotiations with Panama had begun during Johnson's administration, following riots by Panamanians against U.S. territorial rule in their country. Carter pressured the Senate to ratify new treaties in 1978 that would turn the Panama Canal over to Panama by the year 2000.

Carter also succeeded in achieving full diplomatic relations with the Peoples Republic of China in January, 1979 and in paving the way for cultural and trade exchanges between the two nations. The agreement angered conservatives because it stipulated that the United States sever ties with its ally, the national regime on Taiwan.

Mired in problems inherited from his predecessors, however, Carter often found himself disoriented, and, despite his commitment to human rights, putting aside his principles. He chose to stabilize repressive regimes in nations considered vital to U.S. interests, such as South Korea and the Philippines. In Nicaragua, the overthrow in 1979 of the brutal dictator Anastasio Somoza Debayle, longtime U.S. ally, left Carter without a successor to support. When the new Sandinista revolutionary government pleaded for help, Congress turned down Carter's request for $75 million in aid to Nicaragua. Meanwhile, in El Salvador, the Carter administration continued to back a repressive government.

Carter's campaign for international human rights worsened the prospect for détente with the Soviet Union. Only after softening his criticism of the Soviet policy toward political dissidents did Carter achieve in June 1979 the SALT II agreement on arms control. But the thaw proved only temporary.

Carter's reaction to the Soviet occupation of Afghanistan produced a major setback. In December 1979, 30,000 Soviet troops invaded their neighbor to put down a revolt by Islamic insurgents against the weakening Soviet-backed government. The invasion succeeded mainly in heating up the civil war, which the American press quickly labeled the "Russian Vietnam." Noting that the Soviet occupation of Afghanistan posed "a grave threat to the free movement of Middle East oil," President Carter issued his own corollary to the Monroe Doctrine by affirming the right of the United States to use military force if necessary

to protect its interests in the Persian Gulf. He backed up his increasingly hard-line policies by halting exports of grain and high technology to the Soviet Union, by supporting Afghan resistance against the Russians, and by canceling American participation in the 1980 Moscow Olympics. Carter also called for ever-larger increases in the military budget. The prospect of détente dried up.

The Iran Hostage Crisis

Carter's downfall began just seven weeks before the Soviet Union invaded Afghanistan. On November 4, 1979, Iranian militants seized the U.S. embassy in Tehran and took nearly seventy American employees hostage.

For decades, U.S. foreign policy in the Middle East had depended on a friendly government in Iran. After the CIA had helped to overthrow the reformist, constitutional government and installed the Pahlavi royal family and the shah of Iran in 1953, millions of U.S. dollars had poured into the Iranian economy and the shah's armed forces. President Carter had toasted the shah for his "great leadership" and

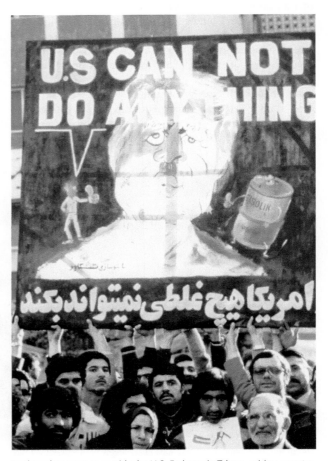

Iranians demonstrate outside the U.S. Embassy in Tehran, raising a poster with a caricature of President Carter. The Iran hostage crisis, which began November 8, 1979, when a mob of Iranians seized the U.S. embassy in Tehran, contributed to Carter's defeat at the polls the following year. Fifty-two embassy employees were held hostage for 444 days.

overlooked the rampant corruption in government and a well-organized opposition. By early 1979, however, a revolution led by the Islamic leader Ayatollah Ruhollah Khomeini overthrew the shah. After Carter had allowed the deposed Reza Shah Pahlavi to enter the United States for medical treatment, a group of Khomeini's followers retaliated, storming the U.S. embassy and demanding the return of the Shah to Iran to face a revolutionary tribunal for "crimes against the Iranian people."

Carter refused the militants' demands, and months passed without a resolution. Finally, after 444 days and caught up in a tight reelection campaign, the President ordered U.S. military forces to stage a nighttime helicopter rescue mission. But a sandstorm caused some of the aircrafts to crash and burn, leaving eight Americans dead, their charred corpses displayed by the enraged Iranians. Short of an all-out attack, which surely would have resulted in the hostages' deaths, Carter had used up his options.

The political and economic fallout was heavy. Cyrus Vance resigned, the first secretary of state in sixty-five years to leave office over a political difference with the president. The price of oil rose by 60 percent. Carter had failed in the one area he had proclaimed central to the future of the United States: energy. He had also violated his own human rights policy, which he had intended to be his distinctive mark on American foreign affairs.

The New Right

The failures in U.S. foreign policy, accompanied by the faltering economy, played a large part in mobilizing what one writer termed "the politics of resentment." Sizable numbers of white taxpayers begrudged the tax hikes required to fund the welfare programs that benefited minorities and expanded social services for the poor and, at the same time, slowed economic development. In 1978, California voters staged a "taxpayers' revolt," which cut property taxes and sharply reduced social programs and education. In other economically hard-pressed urban areas, conservative white voters who resented the gains made by African Americans, Latinos, and women formed a powerful backlash movement against liberalism.

Old-style conservatives lined up behind these initiatives, as did the New Right. But what distinguished the New Right from the old was an emphasis on "moral values" and its populist character. One element in this coalition comprised conservative ideologues, some of them former Democrats who had become disenchanted with liberalism. By far, the largest component comprised evangelical or born-again Protestants like the Gathrights who organized to become a powerful political force.

Neoconservatism

By the mid-1970s, a new variation of conservatism appeared on the political landscape: neoconservatism. Unlike earlier conservatives, such as Barry Goldwater, who had allied with the Republican Party, the most prestigious leaders of this new movement had been liberal Democrats, some even socialists, in the preceding decades. The unsettling social movements of the 1960s had prompted them to turn against New Deal–style liberalism and the welfare state. They continued to believe in equal opportunity, but forcefully rejected the goal of equality of outcome. "Neocons," as they were called, sought to repeal affirmative action programs and dismantle the antipoverty programs enacted during the Johnson administration.

The heart of the neoconservatism was, however, foreign policy. Angered over the failure to pursue victory in Vietnam, neoconservatives called for a stronger national defense against communism. They opposed Carter's move toward détente and accused the president of allowing Communists to advance in Third World countries. Carter's ineffective response to the Soviet occupation of Afghanistan, they charged, only underscored just how weak the United States had become in global affairs.

Neoconservatives played an important role in building the institutional foundation for the rightward turn in American politics. Richly funded by corporate donors, they established think tanks to engage scholars and intellectuals in policy-shaping discussions. The Heritage Foundation, founded by Coors in 1973, the American Enterprise Institute, and the Hoover Institution offered opportunities to individuals and institutions agreeable to their views. The growing intellectual prominence of neoconservatives smoothed the way for broader public support.

The Religious Right

Evangelical Protestants, more than 50 million Americans by the late 1970s, became the backbone of the new conservatism, serving as the chief fundraisers and recruiters for community-based organizations. The Religious Right typically endorsed neoconservative positions on foreign and domestic policy. They supported a balanced budget amendment to the Constitution, sought unsuccessfully to return prayer to the public schools, and endorsed the Supreme Court's reinstatement of the death penalty in 1976. As grassroots activists, they

Watch the Video
Evangelical Religion and Politics, Then and Now at www.myhistorylab.com

provided the political muscle that carried Bee Gathright's conservatism from the margins to the center of the Republican Party.

Finding huge audiences among the growing evangelical and Pentecostal congregations, Protestant ministers took to the airwaves. Televangelists such as Pat Robertson, Jimmy Swaggart, and Jim and Tammy Bakker frequently mixed conservative politics with appeals for both prayer and money. Jerry Falwell's *Old-Time Gospel Hour* was broadcast weekly over 200 television stations and 300 radio stations. By the late 1970s, more than 1,400 radio stations and 30 TV stations specialized in religious broadcasts that reached perhaps 20 million listeners weekly and became a major source of fundraising for conservative organizations and campaigns.

In 1979, the Reverend Jerry Falwell, a Bible Baptist, formed the Moral Majority following his U.S. tour to get evangelical Christians "saved, baptized, and registered" to vote. As a major political lobbying group, the Moral Majority, which claimed 2 to 3 million members, advocated tough laws against homosexuality and pornography and promoted a reduction of government services (especially welfare payments to single mothers) and increased spending for a stronger national defense. The Moral Majority also waged well-publicized campaigns against public school integration and especially the busing of schoolchildren.

The Pro-Family Movement

Most of all, the New Right embraced what they termed "traditional family values": defeating the Equal Rights Amendment (ERA) stood at the top of their political agenda. Approved by Congress in March 1972, nearly fifty years after its introduction (see Chapter 22), the ERA stated: "Equality of rights under the law shall not be denied or abridged by the United States or by any State on account of sex." Endorsed by many women's organizations, including the Girl Scouts of America, and by both the Democratic and Republican parties, the amendment appeared likely to be ratified by the individual states.

Cued by this groundswell of support in favor of the ERA, conservatives swung into action. Phyllis Schlafly, a self-described suburban housewife and popular lecturer, headed the STOP-ERA campaign, describing the amendment's supporters as "a bunch of bitter women seeking a constitutional cure for their personal problems." Under Schlafly's leadership, the New Right mounted large, expensive campaigns in each swing state and overwhelmed pro-ERA resources. Her supporters also built a strong,

religious-based coalition, with southern Protestants, western Mormons, northeastern Catholics, and Orthodox Jews temporarily putting aside differences to join forces to defeat the amendment that they believed was "against God's plan."

Although thirty-five states had ratified the ERA by 1979, the amendment remained three votes short of passage. Despite a three-year extension, the ERA died in Congress in 1982, with 85 percent of the Democrats and only 30 percent of the Republicans voting in its favor.

Meanwhile, the anti-ERA campaign had grown into a comprehensive "pro-family" movement that placed eliminating abortion rights at the top of its political agenda. In 1973, the Supreme Court had ruled in *Roe v. Wade* that state laws decreeing abortion a crime during the first two trimesters of pregnancy constituted a violation of a woman's right to privacy. Opponents of *Roe* rallied for a constitutional amendment defining conception as the beginning of life and then argued that the "rights of the unborn" supersede a woman's right to control her own body. The Roman Catholic Church organized the first antiabortion demonstrations and sponsored the formation of the National Right to Life Committee, which claimed 11 million members by 1980.

Read the Document
Roe v. Wade (1973) at **www.myhistorylab.com**

Antiabortion groups, such as the Orange County Pro-Life Political Action Committee, founded in 1973, also rallied against sex education programs in public schools. They picketed Planned Parenthood counseling centers, intimidating potential clients. A small minority turned to more extreme actions and bombed dozens of abortion clinics.

The 1980 Election

Despite the upsurge of the new right, Carter went into the 1980 presidential campaign determined to win a second term. His prospects, he knew, depended to a large extent on an uptick in the economy and a resolution to the hostage crisis in Iran. Ultimately, Carter's biggest advantage was his incumbency. Democrats unenthusiastically endorsed him along with his running mate, Walter Mondale.

On the Republican side, former California governor Ronald Reagan had been building his campaign since his near nomination in 1976. Former CIA director and Texas oil executive George H. W. Bush, more moderate than Reagan, became the Republican candidate for vice president.

Reagan rode the crest of the swelling conservative wave, repeatedly asking voters, "Are you better off now than you were four years ago?" While Carter implored Americans to tighten

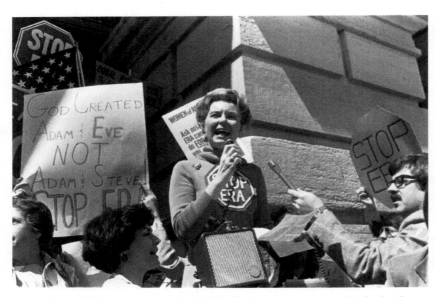

Phyllis Schlafly rallied her supporters in Springfield, Illinois, to demonstrate against the Equal Rights Amendment in March 1975. She also renamed her Stop ERA group the Eagle Forum, which would continue to serve, as she put it, as "the alternative to women's lib."

The Inaugurations of Carter and Reagan

Presidents-elect commonly plan their inauguration ceremonies to reflect symbolically their values and campaign pledges. In 1977, Jimmy Carter staged a "people's inaugural," and hoped to emphasize the unassuming style and frugality that would mark his presidency. He took the oath of office wearing a plain business suit and then broke tradition to walk hand-in-hand with his wife Rosalynn along the parade route. There were no flowers on display on the cold January day, and the White House reviewing stand was heated by solar energy.

Ronald Reagan hoped to convey a different message, not one of thrift but of wealth and security. On January 21, 1981, he became the nation's fortieth president wearing a formal black coat, striped pants, and black shoes and accompanied First Lady Nancy Reagan down the parade route in a limousine.

Everything about Reagan's inauguration, including eight formal balls spread across four days of festivities, reflected what Nancy Reagan described as her aspiration to put the White House "symbolically back up on a hill in people's minds, to have stature and loftiness." The Reagans hired a public relations expert to ensure that every event was telecast. All the inaugural balls, concerts, and receptions, including the opening evening event (an $800,000 light show and concert on the steps of the Lincoln Memorial), were planned to entertain and astound at-home audiences. Festivities at the Washington, DC, balls were also beamed through a $2 million satellite hookup to "mini-balls" held simultaneously across the nation. The Reagan inauguration cost nearly five times that of Carter.

Newspapers and magazines published many photographs of Nancy Reagan, noting that she had restored high style to the image of the First Lady. Whereas Rosalynn Carter had worn an old blue chiffon evening dress to the inaugural ball in 1977, Nancy Reagan had chosen a hand-beaded, crystal-studded gown designed by a leader in the fashion industry. Overall, her inaugural wardrobe was estimated to cost around $25,000. Unlike Rosalynn Carter, who appeared at the swearing-in ceremony in a modest cloth coat, Nancy Reagan chose a full-length mink.

Reagan's inauguration, touted by the press as the most expensive in U.S. history, showcased the theme the president-elect had chosen for his administration: "America—A New Beginning." Not the belt-tightening, "homespun ways" of the Carter presidency, noted one reporter, but an unabashed celebration of wealth would prevail.

- Why did the newly elected President Carter choose to celebrate thrift and humility?
- Why did his successor Ronald Reagan choose to celebrate wealth?
- What had happened in the United States between the mid-1970s and the beginning of the 1980s to make such a display of wealth and power acceptable to the public?

their belts, Reagan promised to cut their taxes. He assured them that "America's best days lay ahead." He also embraced the conservative heart of the GOP platform, condemning abortion rights, denouncing cumbersome government regulations, and calling for the restoration of "the family, the neighborhood, the community, and the workplace as vital alternatives in our national life to ever-expanding federal power." Although opponents questioned Reagan's competence, the attractive, soft-spoken actor shrugged off criticisms.

◉┤Watch the Video

Ronald Reagan Presidential Campaign Ad: A Bear in the Woods at **www.myhistorylab.com**

The Republicans cruised to victory. Carter won only 41.2 percent of the popular vote to Reagan's 50.9 percent, 49 votes in the Electoral College to Reagan's 489. The South voted strongly for Reagan, and Orange County gave the Republican ticket a whopping 68 percent of the vote. The Republicans won control of the Senate for the first time since 1952 and with the largest majority since 1928. White working people, the traditional supporters of the Democratic Party, had defected to the Republicans in large numbers, although women and African Americans voted for Reagan in far fewer numbers. And barely half of the eligible voters had turned out, bringing Ronald Reagan into office with a slim mandate of 25 percent. However, Reagan began on a high note: the Iranians released the American hostages on January 20, 1981, the day he took the oath of office (see Seeing History).

The Reagan Revolution

No other twentieth-century president except Franklin D. Roosevelt left as deep a personal imprint on American politics as Ronald Reagan. Ironically, Reagan himself began his political life as an ardent New Deal Democrat who considered Roosevelt an inspirational leader. But by the time he entered the White House in 1981, shortly before his seventieth birthday, Reagan had rejected the activist welfare state legacy of the New Deal era. "In the present crisis. . .," he declared, "government is not the solution to our problem, government is the problem." Reagan and his allies proceeded to reshape the political and social landscape of the nation along conservative lines (see Map 30.3).

The Great Communicator

Even as he took office, most Americans knew Ronald Reagan mainly from his Hollywood movies and television appearances. Although never a big star, on-screen he appeared tall, handsome, and affable. In later years, he credited his political success to his acting experience. He told one interviewer: "An actor knows two important things— to be honest in what he's doing and to be in touch with the audience. That's not bad advice for a politician either."

By midcentury, Reagan had emerged as one of the most prominent conservative politicians in the nation. While serving as president of the Screen Actors Guild from 1947 to

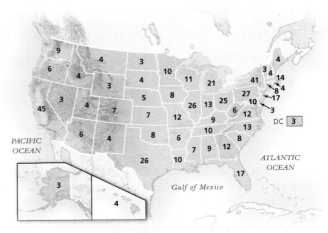

	Electoral Vote (%)	Popular Vote (%)
RONALD REAGAN (Republican)	489 (91)	43,201,220 (50.9)
Jimmy Carter (Democrat)	49 (9)	34,913,332 (41.2)
John B. Anderson (Independent)	—	5,581,379 (6.6)
Other candidates (Libertarian)	—	921,299 (1.1)

MAP 30.3 The Election of 1980 Ronald Reagan won a landslide victory over incumbent Jimmy Carter, who managed to carry only six states and the District of Columbia. Reagan attracted millions of traditionally Democratic voters to the Republican camp.

1952, he distanced himself from other New Deal Democrats by leading the anti-Communist forces in Hollywood. In 1954, he hosted a new national television program, *General Electric Theater,* and began a long stint as a national promoter for GE. In this role, he repeatedly celebrated the achievements of corporate America and emphasized the dangers of excessive liberalism and radical trade unions.

Reagan switched his party affiliation and became a successful fundraiser and popular speaker for the California Republican Party. After playing a leading role in Barry Goldwater's 1964 presidential campaign, and with the financial backing of some wealthy conservatives, he won the 1966 race for California governor, securing 72 percent of the Orange County vote. He won reelection in 1970. As governor, Reagan cut the state welfare rolls, reduced the number of state employees, and funneled a large share of state tax revenues back to local governments. He vigorously attacked student protesters and black militants, thereby tapping into the conservative backlash against the 1960s' activism.

When Reagan entered the White House in January 1981, his supporters interpreted his election as a popular mandate for the

●●┤Read the Document

Ronald Reagan, First Inaugural Address (1981) at **www.myhistorylab.com**

Ronald Reagan, the fortieth president of the United States, was known for his ability to articulate broad principles of government in a clear fashion. The most popular president since Dwight Eisenhower, he built a strong coalition of supporters from long-term Republicans, disillusioned Democrats, and evangelical Protestants.

conservatism that had been growing since Nixon took office. The "Reagan Revolution," they confidently predicted, would usher in a new age in American political life.

Reaganomics

Supply-side theory, dubbed "Reaganomics" by the media, dominated the Reagan administration's economic planning and helped redirect the American economy. Supply-side theorists urged a sharp break with the Keynesian policies that had prevailed since the New Deal era (see Chapter 24). During recessions, Keynesians traditionally favored moderate tax cuts and increases in government spending to stimulate the economy and reduce unemployment. By putting more money in people's pockets, they argued, greater consumer demand would lead to economic expansion.

By contrast, supply-siders called for simultaneous tax cuts and reductions in public spending. This combination—which Reagan himself described as simple "common sense"—would give private entrepreneurs and investors greater incentives to start businesses, take risks, invest capital, and thereby create new wealth and jobs. Whatever revenues were lost in lower tax rates would be offset by revenue from new economic growth. At the same time, spending cuts would keep the federal deficit under control and thereby keep interest rates down.

George Gilder, conservative author of the best-selling *Wealth and Poverty* (1981), summarized the supply-side view: "A successful economy depends on the proliferation of the rich." On the political level, supply-siders looked to reward the most loyal Republican constituencies: the

●◆● Read the Document

Paul Craig Robert, The Supply-Side Revolution (1984) at **www.myhistorylab.com**

affluent and the business community. At the same time, they hoped to reduce the flow of federal dollars to two core Democratic constituencies: the recipients and professional providers of health and welfare programs.

Reagan quickly won bipartisan approval for two key bills that culminated in the largest tax cut in the nation's history. The Economic Recovery Tax Act of 1981 brought across-the-board cuts for corporations and individuals. The new legislation also reduced the maximum tax on all income from 70 percent to 50 percent, lowered the maximum capital gains tax—the tax paid on profitable investments—from 28 percent to 20 percent, and eliminated the distinction between earned and unearned income. This last measure proved a boon to the smallest although richest fraction of the population that derives most of its income from rent, dividends, and interest instead of from wages.

With the help of conservative southern and western Democrats in the House, the administration also pushed through a comprehensive program of spending cuts, awkwardly known as the Omnibus Reconciliation Act of 1981. This bill mandated huge cuts affecting more than 200 social and cultural programs. The hardest-hit areas included education, the environment, health, housing, urban aid, food stamps, research on synthetic fuels, and the arts. The conservative coalition in the House allowed only one vote on the entire package of spending cuts, a strategy that allowed conservatives to slash appropriations for a wide variety of domestic programs in one fell swoop.

While reducing spending on domestic programs, the Reagan administration greatly increased the defense budget, a trend already under way during Carter's final two years as president. Overall, the military buildup indicated a significant shift in federal budget priorities.

Meanwhile, the Reagan administration created a chilly atmosphere for organized labor. In the summer of 1981, some 13,000 federal employees, all members of the Professional Air Traffic Controllers Organization (PATCO), went on strike. The president retaliated by firing all the strikers, and a crash course started by the Federal Aviation Administration permanently replaced them. Conservative appointees to the National Labor Relations Board and the federal courts toughened their antiunion position. By 1990, fewer than 15 percent of American workers belonged to a labor union, the lowest proportion since before World War II.

Deregulation also served as a key element in Reaganomics. The president's appointments to head the Environmental Protection Agency, the Occupational Safety and Health Administration, and the Consumer Product Safety Commission abolished or weakened hundreds of rules governing environmental protection, workplace safety, and consumer protection, all to increase the efficiency and productivity of business. The deregulatory fever dominated cabinet departments as well. Secretary of the Interior James Watt opened up formerly protected wilderness areas and wetlands to private developers. Secretary of Transportation Andrew L. "Drew" Lewis Jr. eliminated regulations passed in the 1970s aimed at reducing air pollution and improving fuel efficiency in cars and trucks.

Following supply-side theory, the Reagan administration weakened the Justice Department's Antitrust Division, the Securities and Exchange Commission, and the Federal Home Loan Bank Board. Large corporations, Wall Street stock brokerages, investment banking houses, and the savings and loan industry were all allowed to operate with a much freer hand than ever before. The appointment of Alan Greenspan in 1983, to succeed Carter appointee Paul Volker, greatly encouraged trends toward speculation in market trading. By the late 1980s, the unfortunate consequences of this freedom would become apparent in a series of unprecedented scandals in the nation's financial and banking industries.

The Election of 1984

Hoping to win back disgruntled voters, Democrats chose Carter's vice president, Walter F. Mondale, as their nominee. A former senator from Minnesota, Mondale had close ties with the party's liberal establishment, but also the support of its more military-minded wing. At the Democratic National Convention, Mondale named New York Representative Geraldine Ferraro as his running mate, a first for women in American politics.

Opinion polls showed Mondale for a time running even with Reagan, but the president's enormous personal popularity, along with the booming economy, overwhelmed the Democratic ticket. While Mondale emphasized the growing deficit, called attention to Americans who were left out of prosperity, and promised to raise taxes, Reagan cruised above it all. He offered the voters a choice between a Democratic "government of pessimism, fear, and limits" or his own, based on "hope, confidence, and growth."

"It's morning again in America," Reagan's campaign ads promised, and in one of the biggest landslides in American history, Reagan won 59 percent of the popular vote—nearly 75 percent in Orange County—and carried every state but Minnesota and the District of Columbia. A majority of blue-collar voters cast their ballots for the president, as did 54 percent of women, despite Ferraro's presence on the Democratic ticket. Even a quarter of all Democrats voted for Reagan.

Recession, Recovery, and Fiscal Crisis

Reagan's supply-side policies produced a mixed record but a highly favorable outcome for the wealthiest Americans. In 1982, a severe recession, the worst since the 1930s, gripped the nation. The official unemployment rate reached nearly 11 percent, or more than 11.5 million people. Another 3 million were out of work so long they no longer actively looked for jobs and, therefore, were not counted in official statistics. But by 1983, the economy recovered and headed into one of the longest periods of growth and expansion in American history. Unemployment dropped to about 8 percent while inflation fell below 5 percent. The stock market boomed, pushing the Dow Jones industrial average from 776 in August 1982 to an all-time high of 2,722 in August 1987. The administration took credit for the turnaround, hailing the supply-side policies that had drastically cut taxes and domestic spending. But critics pointed to other factors: the Federal Reserve Board's tight-money policies, an energy resource glut and a consequent sharp drop in energy prices, and the billions of dollars pumped into the economy for defense spending.

Most financial experts, however, believed that the supply-side formula intensified a significant fiscal crisis. Although Reagan had promised to balance the federal budget, his policies had the opposite effect. The national debt tripled, growing from $914 billion in 1980 to over $2.7 trillion in 1989, more than the federal government had accumulated in its entire previous history. Expenditures for paying just the interest on the national debt reached 14 percent of the annual budget in 1988, double the percentage set aside for that purpose in 1974.

During the Reagan presidency, the fiscal crisis became a structural problem with profound and long-lasting implications for the American economy. Big deficits kept

After the Dow Jones reached an all-time high at the end of August, stocks began to slide and then crashed. On October 19, 1987—"Black Monday"—traders at the New York Stock Exchange panicked, selling off stocks at such a rate that the market lost almost 23 percent of its value, marking the end of a five-year bull market. The market soon bounced back, and by September 1989 the Dow Jones had made up all its losses.

interest rates high, as the government drove up the cost of borrowing the money it needed to pay its own bills. Foreign investors, attracted by high interest rates on government securities, pushed up the value of the dollar in relation to foreign currencies. The overvalued dollar made it difficult for foreigners to buy American products, while making overseas goods cheaper to American consumers. Basic American industries—steel, autos, textiles—thus found it difficult to compete abroad and at home. In 1980, the United States still enjoyed a trade surplus of $166 billion. By 1987, the nation was indebted to foreigners to the tune of $340 billion. Since World War I, the United States had been the world's leading creditor; in the mid-1980s, it became its biggest debtor (see Figure 30.3).

On Wall Street, the bull market ended abruptly in the fall of 1987.

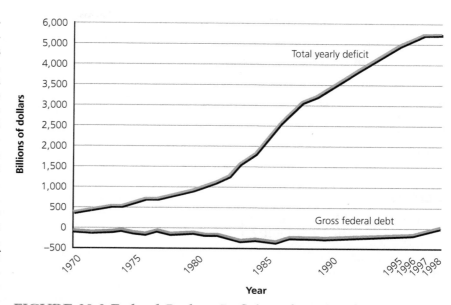

FIGURE 30.3 Federal Budget Deficit and National Debt, 1970–98 Tax cuts combined with huge increases in defense spending created a sharp increase in the budget deficit during the Republican administrations.

SOURCE: *Statistical abstract of the United States,* in Nash et al., *The American People,* 5th ed., p. 988.

After reaching its new high, the Dow Jones average of thirty leading industrial stocks began to slide downward and then crashed. On October 19, "Black Monday," the Dow lost almost one-quarter of its value. Although the causes for the panic remain uncertain, at the time many commentators pointed to anxiety spurred by the raging federal deficit.

Best of Times, Worst of Times

President Reagan set the tone for the era when he responded to a reporter's question asking him what was best about America. "What I want to see above all," Reagan replied, "is that this remains a country where someone can always get rich." The celebration of wealth, moneymaking, and entrepreneurship dominated much of popular culture, politics, and intellectual life in the 1980s, establishing a pattern that would persist into the twenty-first century. The dapper stock speculator Ivan Boesky, who was later indicted for criminal insider trading, echoed Reagan's philosophy and boasted of making more than $100 million on just two deals. "I think greed is healthy," he told cheering business students in 1986: "You can be greedy and still feel good about yourself." However, few Americans in the 1980s could actually live by these principles.

Various data indicated that the nation was moving toward greater inequality, that while income soared for the wealthiest Americans, poverty was also on the rise. Analysts disagreed over the causes of these trends. However, after eight years of tax cuts, defense buildup, growing budget deficits, and record trade imbalances, many Americans feared that the future looked uncertain at best. Two of their most cherished beliefs—that life would improve for most people and their children, and that membership in the comfortable middle class was possible for all who worked for it—looked shaky by the end of the decade (see Tables 30.1, 30.2, and 30.3).

A Two-Tiered Society

Until the mid-1970s, the rise in income had been fairly evenly distributed among Americans. During the Reagan presidency, in contrast, affluent Americans gained the most, with the top 1 percent way out in front. Before Reagan took office, a CEO of a major corporation earned about forty times that of a typical blue-collar worker; at

TABLE 30.1

Percentage Share of Aggregate Family Income, 1980–92

	1980	1992
Top 5 Percent	15.3%	17.6%
Highest Fifth	41.6	44.6
Fourth Fifth	24.3	24.0
Third Fifth	17.5	16.5
Second Fifth	11.6	10.5
Lowest Fifth	5.1	4.4

SOURCE: U.S. Bureau of the Census, *Current Population Reports: Consumer Incomes,* Series P-60, Nos. 167 and 184, 1990, 1993. U.S. federal data compiled by Ed Royce, Rollins College.

TABLE 30.2

Share of Total Net Worth of American Families

	1983	1989
Richest 1 percent of families	31%	37%
Next richest 9 percent	35	31
Remaining 90 percent	33	32

SOURCE: *The New York Times*, April 21, 1992, from Federal Reserve Survey of Consumer Finances. Copyright © 1992 The New York Times. Reprinted by permission.

TABLE 30.3

Measures of Average Earnings, 1980–92 (In 1990 Dollars)

Year	Average Weekly Earnings	Average Hourly Earnings
1980	$373.81	$10.59
1985	363.30	10.41
1992	339.37	9.87

SOURCE: U.S. House of Representatives, Committee on Ways and Means, *Overview of Entitlement Programs* (Washington, DC: GPO, 1993), table 35, p. 557. U.S. federal data compiled by Ed Royce, Rollins College.

the end of his second term, the typical CEO made ninety-three times as much. Poverty grew at an alarming rate. The number of fully employed workers earning below poverty-level incomes increased by 50 percent. Nearly one-quarter of all children lived in poverty.

The gains for African Americans achieved by the civil rights movement were steadily eroded. In 1954, the year of the *Brown* v. *Board of Education* decision, black families earned about 53 percent of the income of white families. This figure rose to 60 percent in 1969, peaked at 62 percent in 1975, and steadily dropped during the next decade. By 1992, 33 percent of all African Americans lived in poverty, as did 29 percent of Hispanics (the rate was especially high among Puerto Ricans, yet low among Cuban Americans).

The majority of African Americans, six out of ten, lived in central cities with high unemployment rates, and the bleak prospects took a toll especially on the young. A black child was twice as likely as a white child to die before reaching their first birthday and four times more likely to be killed between the ages of one and four. Among black teenagers, the unemployment rate topped 40 percent; the few jobs available to them were among the lowest paid in the economy. Meanwhile, the high school dropout rate skyrocketed, and the number of serious crimes, such as burglary, car theft, and murder, perpetrated by black teenagers increased at an alarming rate.

Moreover, opportunities for advancement into the middle class were dwindling. By 1980, fewer black students attended integrated schools

than in 1954, except in the South, where about half the black students did. The turnabout resulted in part from increasing opposition by white parents to court-ordered school busing, which had served since *Brown* v. *Board of Education* as the principal means of achieving racial balance in urban school systems. In 1975, a major clash between local white residents and black parents and their children occurred in Boston when a federally mandated busing plan was put into operation. During the 1980s, the busing controversy nearly disappeared because federal judges hesitated to mandate such programs. But more important was the change in the racial composition of American cities. As a consequence of "white flight" to the suburbs, big-city school systems were serving mainly African American and Latino children, making the issue of integration moot (see Tables 30.4, 30.5, and 30.6).

New legal rulings closed off important routes to employment in the professions. A 1978 U.S. Supreme Court decision dealt a sharp blow to affirmative action. To ensure acceptance of a minimum number of minority students, the University of California at Davis Medical School had established a quota system under affirmative action guidelines. In 1973 and 1974, the school denied admission to Allan Bakke, a white student. Bakke sued the university for "reverse discrimination," claiming his academic record was better than that of the sixteen minority students who were admitted. The U.S. Supreme Court handed down a five-to-four decision on June 18, 1978,

TABLE 30.4

Number of Poor, Rate of Poverty, and Poverty Line, 1979–92

	1979	1992
Millions of poor	26.1	36.9
Rate of poverty	11.7%	14.5%
Poverty line (family of four)	$7,412	$14,335

SOURCE: U.S. Bureau of the Census, *Current Population Reports: Consumer Income*, Series P-60, Nos. 161 and 185, 1988, 1993. U.S. federal data compiled by Ed Royce, Rollins College.

TABLE 30.5

Net New Job Creation by Wage Level, 1979–87

	Number of Net New Jobs Created	Percentage of Net New Jobs Created
Low-wage jobs (less than $11,611)	5,955,000	50.4%
Middle-wage jobs ($11,612 to $46,444)	4,448,000	31.7%
High-wage jobs ($46,445 and above)	1,405,000	11.9%

SOURCE: U.S. Senate, Committee on the Budget, *Wages of American Workers in the 1980s* (Washington, DC: U.S. Government Printing Office, 1988). U.S. federal data compiled by Ed Royce, Rollins College.

TABLE 30.6

Median Family Income and Ratio to White, by Race, and Hispanic Origin, 1980–92 (in 1992 Dollars)

Year	All Races	White	Black	Hispanic
1980	$35,839	$37,341	$21,606 (58%)	$25,087 (67%)
1985	36,164	38,011	21,887 (58%)	25,596 (67%)
1992	36,812	38,909	21,161 (54%)	23,901 (61%)

SOURCE: U.S. Bureau of the Census, *Current Population Reports,* Series P-60, No. 184, 1993. U.S. federal data compiled by Ed Royce, Rollins College.

stating that the use of an "explicit racial classification" in situations where no earlier discrimination had been demonstrated violated the equal protection clause of the Fourteenth Amendment. The Court ordered the University of California to admit Bakke to its medical school. During the 1980s, therefore, affirmative action programs could operate only when "a legacy of unequal treatment" could be proved.

The Feminization of Poverty

While the gap between the rich and poor was growing to its widest point since 1945, the experience of poverty became the lot of primarily women and children. Throughout the era, women with young children continued to enter the labor force at a fast pace, but the majority of jobs available to them paid too little to support their children. It took the financial support of an adult male breadwinner to keep a family out of poverty.

The rising rate of divorce and desertion paralleled the increasing number of women and children in poverty. Most women usually lost ground following a divorce, which now affected nearly half of all new marriages. New no-fault divorce laws lowered or eradicated alimony, pushing even many middle-class women into poverty. Moreover, the majority of men defaulted on child-support payments within one year after separation. Whereas divorced men enjoyed a sizable increase in their standard of living, divorced women and their children suffered a formidable decline.

A sharp rise in teenage pregnancy reinforced this trend. Nearly one in four babies was born to unmarried mothers. Many of these mothers were too young to have gained either the education or skills to secure jobs that paid enough to support themselves and their children. Even with Aid to Families with Dependent Children (AFDC) payments and food stamps, unemployed single mothers could rarely keep their families above the poverty line. By 1992, female-headed households, comprising 13.7 million people, accounted for 37 percent of the nation's poor. Among black women, the number of female-headed families increased in just one decade from 30 percent in 1970 to 47 percent in

1980. More than half of all black babies were now born to unmarried mothers. With few jobs for black men, especially for teenagers, the prospects for two-parent families were dim. Even in prosperous Orange County, by 1990 more than one in ten families was headed by a female householder with no husband present.

Sunbelt/Rustbelt Communities

A distinctive pattern of poverty and prosperity mirrored changes in the nation's political tenor.

The bastion of prosperity as well as the bulwark of political conservatism was the Sunbelt, which extended from Florida to Orange County, California. This region boasted a gross product greater than many nations and more cars, television sets, houses, and even miles of paved roads than the rest of the United States, along with a growing number of Republicans.

Much of the Sunbelt's growth depended on a huge outlay of federal funds, including defense spending and the allocation of Social Security benefits. The number of residents over age sixty-five increased by 30 percent during the 1970s, reaching 26 million by the time President Reagan took office. Armed with retirement packages won decades earlier, huge "golden age" migrations created new communities in Florida, Arizona, and southern California. Immigrants from Latin America, the Caribbean, and Asia joined Americans fleeing the depressed Northeast to boost the region's population (see Map 30.4).

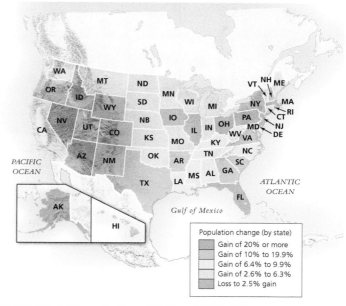

MAP 30.4 Population Shifts, 1970–80 Industrial decline in the Northeast coincided with an economic boom in the Sunbelt, encouraging millions of Americans to head for warmer climates and better jobs.

The Sunbelt witnessed a dramatic turnaround in demographic and economic trends. Southern cities reversed the century-long trend of out-migration among African Americans. The Southwest and West changed yet more dramatically. Aided by air conditioning, water diversions, public improvements, and large-scale development and subsidies to agribusiness, California became the nation's most populous state; Texas moved to third, behind New York. Former farms and deserts were turned almost overnight into huge metropolitan areas ringed by new automobile-dependent suburbs. Phoenix grew from 664,000 in 1960 to 1,509,000 in 1980, Las Vegas from 127,000 to 463,000 (see Figure 30.4).

Much Sunbelt wealth tended to be temporary or sharply cyclical, producing a boom-and-bust economy. Corporate office buildings in cities such as Houston emptied almost as fast as they filled. Income was also distributed unevenly. Older Hispanic populations made only modest gains, while recent Mexican immigrants and Indian peoples suffered from a combination of low wages and poor public services. The Sunbelt states directed their tax and federal dollars to strengthening police forces, building roads or sanitation systems for the expanding suburbs, and creating budget surpluses, in contrast to eastern and midwestern states, which continued to spend significantly on public housing, education, and mass transit.

The "Rustbelt" states, longtime centers of voting strength for the Democratic Party, meanwhile suffered severe population losses accompanying the sharp decline of manufacturing. The production of steel, automobiles, and heavy machinery suffered from foreign competition and from new, more efficient factories that opened in the South. Of the nineteen metropolitan areas that lost population, all were old manufacturing centers, topped by New York, Cleveland, Pittsburgh, Boston, Philadelphia, and Buffalo. The rural areas of the Midwest and Plains States also lost population, as farmers abandoned land that no longer produced a decent livelihood. By the time Reagan began his second term, the rural poverty rate was twice that of metropolitan areas.

Epidemics: Drugs, AIDS, Homelessness

Illegal drug addiction and drug trafficking took on frightening new dimensions in the early 1980s. Even the urban poor could afford the new arrival, "crack," a cheap, smokable, and highly addictive form of cocaine. The crack trade spawned a new generation of young drug dealers who were willing to risk jail and death for enormous profits. In city after city, drug wars over turf took the lives of dealers and innocents, both caught in the escalating violence.

In 1982, the Reagan administration declared a highly publicized "war on drugs," a multibillion-dollar paramilitary

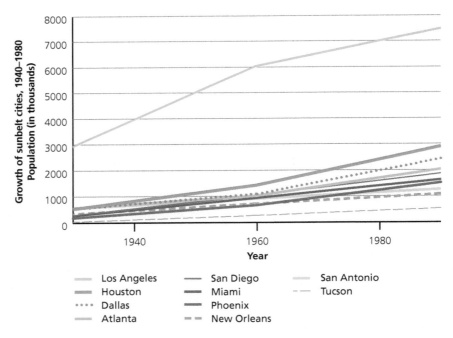

FIGURE 30.4 Growth of Sunbelt Cities, 1940–80 The old industrial cities in the Northeast and Midwest steadily lost population to the southern and western decentralized cities and their surrounding suburbs.

SOURCE: From Statistical abstract of the United States, in Nash et al., *The American People*, 5th ed., p. 988. Reprinted by permission of Longman Publishing Group, a division of Pearson Education.

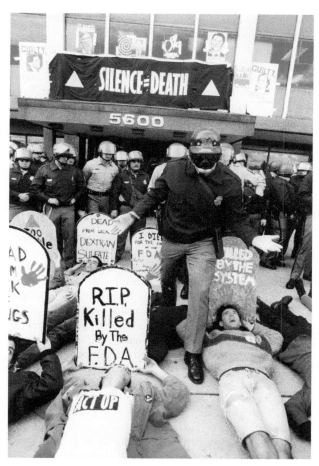

In May 1987, members of the Lesbian and Gay Community Services in downtown Manhattan organized ACT-UP. Protesting what they perceived to be the Reagan administration's mismanagement of the AIDS crisis, they used nonviolent direct action, which often took the form of dramatic acts of civil disobedience. ACT-UP grew to more than seventy chapters in the United States and around the world.

operation to halt drug trafficking. Critics charged that the war on drugs focused on supply from abroad when it needed to look at demand here at home. They urged more federal money for drug education, treatment, and rehabilitation, dismissing as insufficient First Lady Nancy Reagan's "Just Say No" campaign aimed at children. Drug addiction and drug use, they argued, were primarily health problems, not law enforcement issues. The Reagan administration held firm in its policy and, moreover, named drug trafficking a major threat to national security.

Also new to the 1980s was the outbreak of the AIDS epidemic. In 1981, doctors began encountering a puzzling new medical phenomenon. Young homosexual men were dying suddenly from opportunistic infections such as pneumonia and cancer caused by a mysterious viral disease that damaged the body's immune system. Researchers at the Centers for Disease Control (CDC) in Atlanta called

the new disease Acquired Immune Deficiency Syndrome (AIDS) and identified the means of transmission as the exchange of bodily fluids, such as semen and blood. Because the majority of early victims were homosexual men who acquired AIDS through sexual contact, many Americans perceived AIDS as a disease of homosexuals. But other victims became infected through intravenous drug use, blood transfusions, heterosexual transmission, or birth from AIDS-carrying mothers.

AIDS provoked fear, anguish, and anger. It also brought an upsurge of organization and political involvement. In city after city, the gay community responded to the AIDS crisis with energy and determination. Most gay men changed their sexual habits, practicing "safe sex" to lessen the chances of infection. President Reagan, playing to antigay prejudices, had largely ignored the epidemic. By the time he left office, the CDC had confirmed 82,764 AIDS cases and 46,344 deaths.

Homelessness emerged as a chronic social problem during the 1980s. Often disoriented, shoeless, and forlorn, street people in growing numbers slept over heating grates, on subways, and in parks. Homeless people wandered city sidewalks panhandling and struggling to find scraps of food. In the early 1980s, the Department of Housing and Urban Development placed the number of the nation's homeless at between 250,000 and 350,000. Advocates for the homeless estimated that the number was as high as 3 million.

Who were the homeless? Analysts agreed that at least a third were mental patients who had been discharged from psychiatric hospitals amid the deinstitutionalization trend of the 1970s. Many more were alcoholics and drug addicts unable to hold jobs. But the ranks of the homeless also included female-headed families, battered women, Vietnam veterans, AIDS victims, and elderly people with no place to go. Some critics pointed to the decline in decent housing for poor people and the deterioration of the nation's health care system as the major causes.

Toward a New World Order

Throughout his presidency, Reagan campaigned to restore American leadership in world affairs. He revived Cold War patriotism and championed U.S. intervention in the Third World, especially in the Caribbean and Central America. His infusion of funds into national security programs had enormous consequences for the domestic economy as well as for the nation's status as a global power. Yet along with hard-line exhortations against the Soviet Union and international terrorism, the Reagan administration also pursued a less ideological, more pragmatic approach in key foreign policy decisions. Most important, sweeping and unanticipated internal changes within the Soviet Union made the entire Cold War framework of international affairs largely irrelevant by the late 1980s.

The Evil Empire

In the early 1980s, the Reagan administration made vigorous anticommunism the centerpiece of its foreign policy. In a sharp turn from President Ford's pursuit of détente and President Carter's focus on human rights, Reagan described the Soviet Union as "an evil empire. . . the focus of evil in the modern world."

Read the Document

Ronald Reagan, Address to the National Association of Evangelicals (1983) at **www.myhistorylab.com**

Administration officials argued that during the 1970s the nation's military strength had fallen dangerously behind that of the Soviet Union. Critics disputed this assertion, pointing out that the Soviet advantage in intercontinental ballistic missiles (ICBMs) was offset by U.S. superiority in submarine-based forces and strategic aircraft. Polls showed that more than 70 percent of Americans favored not an escalation of the arms race but instead a nuclear freeze with the Soviet Union. Nonetheless, the administration proceeded with plans to secure global military supremacy, including enlarging America's nuclear strike force. U.S. defense spending jumped by 50 percent to reach $1.5 trillion to accomplish the largest military buildup in peacetime.

In 1983, President Reagan introduced an unsettling new element into superpower relations when he presented his Strategic Defense Initiative (SDI), the plan for a space-based ballistic-missile defense system that journalists dubbed "Star Wars," after the popular Hollywood film series. This proposal for a five-year, $26 billion program promised to give the United States the capacity to shoot down incoming missiles with laser beams and homing rockets. As critics pointed out, this plan was unworkable, impossibly expensive, and likely to destabilize existing arms treaties. The Reagan administration pressed ahead, but without achieving any convincing results. The prospect of meaningful arms control dimmed in this atmosphere, and U.S.-Soviet relations deteriorated.

The Reagan Doctrine

Declaring the "Vietnam syndrome" over, the president moved beyond President Truman's "containment" policy and confidently promised to "roll back" communism. He reasserted America's right to intervene anywhere in the world and pledged to supply overt and covert aid to anti-Communist resistance movements, including those led by right-wing dictators. The so-called Reagan Doctrine assumed that all political instability in the Third World resulted not from indigenous factors such as poverty or corruption but from the pernicious influence of the Soviet Union.

One of Reagan's most successful interventions took place in Afghanistan, which the Soviet Union had invaded in 1979. Reagan greatly expanded the U.S. aid initiated by President Carter to include supplies of weapons and antiaircraft missiles. During the course of his administration, the CIA also sent billions of U.S. dollars to the mujahedeen. These fundamentalist Islamic "holy warriors" managed to drive out the Soviet Union but also eventually gave rise to the Taliban and Osama bin Laden's al-Qaeda, which would emerge in the 1990s as major agent of global terrorism.

The Reagan doctrine found its most important expression in Central America, where the United States hoped to reestablish its historical control over the Caribbean basin (see Map 30.5). Claiming that all problems throughout the Western Hemisphere stemmed from a "Moscow-Havana" alliance, the administration worked to support anti-Communist groups in Cuba and elsewhere in Latin America. Between 1980 and 1983, the United States poured more military aid into the region than it had during the previous thirty years.

In October 1983, the administration directed U.S. Marines to invade Grenada, claiming that the tiny island governed by Marxists since 1979 had become a Cuban military base and, therefore, would soon serve as "an outpost of communism" and terrorism. Condemned by the United Nations General Assembly as "a flagrant violation of International law," the triumphant invasion proved popular with most Grenadans and Americans. "We got there just in time," Reagan announced in justifying the first major U.S. military operation since the war in Vietnam.

In other nations such as El Salvador, this sort of unilateral military action proved politically and strategically more difficult to carry out. But the Reagan administration directed nearly $5 billion to shore up El Salvador's pro-American yet highly repressive regime. By 1983, right-wing death squads had tortured and assassinated thousands of opposition leaders. The election of centrist president José Napoleón Duarte in 1984 failed to end the bloody civil war that took the life of more than one in every hundred Salvadorans.

In Nicaragua, the Reagan administration claimed that the revolutionary Sandinista government posed "an unusual and extraordinary threat to the national security." U.S. officials accused the Sandinistas of shipping arms to antigovernment rebels in El Salvador. In December 1981, Reagan approved a CIA plan to arm and organize Nicaraguan exiles, known as Contras, to fight against the Sandinista government. As Reagan escalated this undeclared war, the aim became not merely the cutting off of Nicaraguan aid to Salvadoran rebels but also the overthrow of the Sandinista regime itself.

In 1984, the CIA secretly mined Nicaraguan harbors. When Nicaragua won a judgment against the United States in the World Court over this violation of its sovereignty, the Reagan administration refused to recognize the court's jurisdiction in the case and ignored the verdict. Predictably, the U.S. covert war pushed the Sandinistas

MAP 30.5 The United States in Central America, 1978–90 U.S. intervention in Central America reached a new level of intensity with the so-called Reagan Doctrine. The bulk of U.S. aid came in the form of military support for the government of El Salvador and the Contra rebels in Nicaragua.

closer to Cuba and the Soviet bloc. Meanwhile, American grassroots opposition to Contra aid grew more vocal and widespread. A number of American communities set up sister-city projects offering humanitarian and technical assistance to Nicaraguan communities. Scores of American churches offered sanctuary to political refugees from Central America.

In 1984, Congress sought to rein in the covert war by passing the Boland Amendment, introduced by Democratic Representative Edward Boland of Massachusetts. It forbade government agencies from supporting "directly or indirectly military or paramilitary operations" in Nicaragua. Denied funding by Congress, President Reagan turned to the National Security Council (NSC) to find a way to keep the Contra war going. Between 1984 and 1986, the NSC staff secretly assisted the Contras, raising enough

money privately to support the largest mercenary army in hemispheric history. In 1987, the revelation of this unconstitutional scheme exploded before the public as part of the Iran-Contra affair, the most damaging political scandal of the Reagan years.

The Middle East and the Iran-Contra Scandal

In 1987, the revelations of what became known as the Iran-Contra scandal laid bare the contradictions in Reagan's foreign policy. The scandal also revealed how overzealous and secretive government officials subverted the Constitution and compromised presidential authority under the guise of patriotism.

Terrorist acts, including the seizing of Western hostages and the bombing of commercial airplanes and cruise ships, continued to redefine the politics of the

Middle East. Many of these attacks were desperate acts of retaliation by small pro-Palestinian sects or Islamic extremists opposed to U.S. support of Israel. However, the Reagan administration insisted that behind international terrorism lay the sinister influence of the Soviet bloc, the Ayatollah Khomeini of Iran, and Libyan leader Muammar el-Qaddafi. In the spring of 1986, the president, eager to demonstrate his antiterrorist resolve, ordered the bombing of Tripoli in a failed effort to kill Qaddafi, whom he called "the mad dog of the Middle East."

As a fierce war between Iran and Iraq escalated, the administration tilted publicly toward Iraq to please the Arab states around the Persian Gulf. Iraq's dictator, Saddam Hussein, was treated as an ally and provided much sophisticated weaponry. But in 1986, Reagan's advisers changed course and began secret negotiations with the revolutionary Iranian government. They eventually offered to supply Iran with weapons for use against Iraq in exchange for help in securing the release of

Americans who were being held hostage by radical Islamic groups in Lebanon (see Map 30.6).

Subsequent disclosures elevated the arms-for-hostages deal into a major scandal. The American public soon learned the sordid details from investigative journalists and through televised congressional hearings held during the summer of 1987. They learned that the NSC had sold weapons and missiles to the Iranians, using Israel as a go-between. The public also found out that millions of dollars from the weapons sale had been secretly diverted into covert aid of the Nicaraguan Contras in blatant and illegal disregard of the Boland Amendment.

In the televised congressional hearings, NSC staffer and Marine Lieutenant Colonel Oliver North took center stage and defended his grossly illegal actions in the name of patriotism. Some Americans saw the dashing North as a hero; most were appalled by his and Admiral John Poindexter's blithe admissions that they had lied to Congress, shredded evidence, and refused to keep the

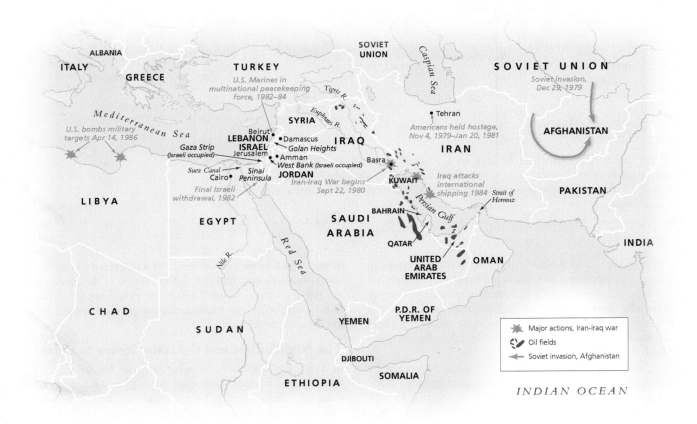

MAP 30.6 The United States in the Middle East in the 1980s The volatile combination of ancient religious and ethnic rivalries, oil, and emerging Islamic fundamentalism made peace and stability elusive in the Middle East.

Lt. Col. Oliver North, who once described the scheme to sell arms to Iran to help the Contras as a "neat idea," is shown testifying in July 1987 before a joint Congressional committee formed to investigate the Iran-Contra affair.

president fully informed in order to guarantee his "plausible deniability."

Ultimately, the Iran-Contra investigation raised more questions than it answered. The full role of CIA Director William Casey, who died in 1987, particularly his relationships with North and the president, remained murky. The role of Vice President George H. W. Bush remained mysterious as well. Both North and Poindexter were convicted of felonies, but higher courts overturned their convictions on technical grounds. Reagan held fast to a plea of ignorance. When pressed on what had happened, he repeatedly claimed, "I'm still trying to find out."

The Collapse of Communism

Meanwhile, momentous political changes within the Soviet Union ultimately led to the end of the Cold War. In 1985, a reform-minded leader, Mikhail Gorbachev, took over as Soviet leader. Although a lifelong Communist, Gorbachev represented a new generation of disenchanted party members who wanted both major economic reforms and an end of the dangerous superpower rivalry. He encouraged open political discussion and released longtime dissidents from prison. His government also took the first halting steps toward a profit-based market economy.

In Gorbachev's view, improving the economic performance of the Soviet system depended first on halting the arms race. Over 10 percent of the Soviet GNP went to defense spending, while the majority of its citizens could not find even the most basic consumer items in shops. Fully aware that the Soviet Union could not compete with Reagan's Star Wars program, Gorbachev took the lead to end the arms race with the United States. The historical ironies were stunning. Reagan had made militant anticommunism the centerpiece of his administration, but between 1985 and 1988 he had four separate summit meetings with the new Soviet leader. Culminating in a modest treaty allowing comprehensive, mutual, on-site inspections, the meetings also provided an important psychological breakthrough. At one of the summits, a Soviet leader humorously announced, "We are going to do something terrible to you Americans—we are going to deprive you of an enemy."

Indeed, the reforms initiated by Gorbachev—and, more immediately, the failed Soviet war in Afghanistan—led to the dissolution of the Soviet Union and to the end of Communist rule throughout Eastern Europe. In March 1989, the Soviet Union held its first open elections since 1917, and Gorbachev announced that he would not use force to keep the satellite nations in line. In June 1989, when Poland held its first free elections since the close of World War II in 1945, prodemocracy demonstrations forced out longtime Communist leaders in Hungary, Czechoslovakia, Bulgaria, and Romania. Most dramatic of all were the events in East Germany. The Berlin Wall, for thirty years the ultimate symbol of Cold War division, came down on November 9, 1989. Hundreds of thousands of East Germans immediately rushed into West Berlin, paving the way for German reunification the following year. On Christmas Day 1991, Gorbachev signed a decree officially dissolving the Soviet Union and then resigned as president.

The Soviet Union's dissolution marked the end of the great superpower rivalry that had shaped American foreign policy and domestic politics for nearly a half century. Reagan's successor, President George H. W. Bush, proclaimed the end of the Cold War as an event of "biblical proportions."

"A Kinder, Gentler Nation"

During the 1988 presidential campaign, moderate Republican George Herbert Walker Bush, hoped to ride on Reagan's conservative coattails. He made a clear-cut pledge to voters: "Read my lips: no new taxes." He also promised to energize the war against drugs and back initiatives to allow prayer in public schools. Bush won the general election handily over Massachusetts governor George Dukakis in forty states and with 56 percent of the popular vote and did especially well among evangelical Christians. After winning such widespread support, he concluded that he could set his own agenda. President Bush began to distance himself from Reagan and infuriate

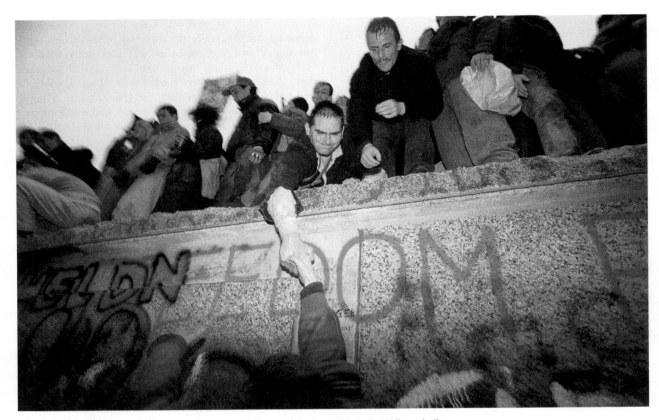

In August 1961, the border between East and West Berlin was closed, and the Berlin Wall was built to divide the city into two sections. After twenty-eight years, on November 9, 1989, the government in East Germany lifted travel restrictions. This photograph shows demonstrators defiantly tearing down the Berlin Wall, which for three decades had embodied the political divisions of the Cold War.

conservatives, promising in his inaugural address to deliver a "kinder and gentler nation."

In international affairs, President Bush had prepared well to provide leadership in a dramatically changing world. Before serving as Reagan's vice president, he held several major appointive offices that involved him directly in foreign policy—UN ambassador, envoy to China, and director of the CIA. However, as president, he soon found himself facing a host of problems complicated rather than resolved by the end of the Cold War. Somewhat belatedly, President Bush announced that it was "time to move beyond containment to a new policy for the 1990s," without specifying what that new policy would be. He also faced a Congress with a Democratic majority.

Reagan's Successor: George H. W. Bush

President Bush carried over several policies from the Reagan administration, such as the war on illegal drugs. He appointed William Bennett as the new "drug czar" and outlined a plan to increase funding for more police and prisons. He also fortified the border patrols in an attempt to stem the flow of drugs from Latin America. In December 1989, President Bush sent U.S. troops to Panama on a mission to capture General Manuel Noriega, an international drug dealer who at one time had been on the CIA payroll. Thousands of Panamanians died before Noriega was taken into custody and brought to the United States to stand trial on drug trafficking and racketeering charges. During the Bush presidency, the federal budget for drug control tripled.

As a self-proclaimed "compassionate" Republican, President Bush endorsed the Americans with Disabilities Act, which had been introduced during the Reagan administration and now passed through Congress. The act penalized employers who discriminated against qualified workers with disabilities and required employers and local governments to provide access to their facilities. Against the opposition of many business leaders, President Bush signed the bill in July 1990. Showing less compassion, he vetoed a family-leave bill that would have provided up to six months of unpaid leave to workers with new children or with family emergencies.

Bush also endorsed several bills to enhance environmental legislation, including revisions to the Clean Water and the Clean Air Act passed during the 1970s. He also approved federal initiatives to raise local educational standards. But Bush thoroughly angered conservative Republicans when he broke his "no new taxes" promise and allowed Congress to impose a small hike on wealthy taxpayers.

The Persian Gulf War

President Bush soon saw that the end of the Cold War did not bring world peace but instead let loose a multitude of furies in the form of renewed nationalism, ethnic and religious conflict, and widening divisions between the world's rich and poor. Just as dramatically, as the old geopolitical order disappeared, ideological rivalry shifted to the Middle East and other areas in the world where Islamic militants had forcefully turned against the West.

On August 2, 1990, Iraqi troops swept into neighboring Kuwait and quickly seized control of its rich oil fields. The motives of Saddam Hussein, Iraq's military dictator, were mixed. Like most Iraqis, Hussein believed that oil-rich Kuwait was actually an ancient province of Iraq that had been illegally carved away by British imperial agents in the 1920s as part of the dismemberment of the Ottoman Empire. Control of Kuwait would give Saddam Hussein control of its huge oil reserves, as well as major Persian Gulf ports for his almost landlocked country. Just emerging from an exhausting and inconclusive eight-year war with Iran, Iraqis also bitterly resented Kuwait's production of oil beyond OPEC quotas, which had helped send the world price of oil plummeting from the highs of the 1970s and early 1980s.

The United States responded swiftly to news of the invasion. Its first concern was that Saddam Hussein might also attack Saudi Arabia, which the United States had defined as vital to its interests as far back as 1943. On August 15, President Bush ordered U.S. forces to Saudi Arabia and the Persian Gulf, calling the action Operation Desert Shield. The United States also led a broad coalition in the United Nations, including the Soviet Union, that condemned the Iraqi invasion of Kuwait and declared strict economic sanctions against Iraq if it did not withdraw.

In early November, President Bush announced a change in policy to what he called "an offensive military option." Administration officials now demonized Saddam Hussein as another Adolf Hitler. The UN sanctions failed to budge Hussein from Kuwait, and the drift to war looked inevitable. In January 1991, Congress narrowly passed a joint resolution authorizing the president to use military force.

After a last-minute UN peace mission failed to break the deadlock, President Bush announced, on January 16,

Read the Document
George H. W. Bush, Gulf War Address (1990) at **www.myhistorylab.com**

1991, the start of Operation Desert Storm. U.S.-led air strikes began forty-two days of massive bombing of Iraqi positions in Kuwait, as well as Baghdad and other Iraqi cities. The ground war, which began on February 24, took only 100 hours to force Saddam Hussein's troops out of Kuwait. Hussein's vaunted military machine—the fourth largest army in the world—turned out to be surprisingly weak. U.S. forces lost only 184 dead, compared to nearly 100,000 Iraqi deaths, mostly from the bombing.

Victory in the Gulf War rekindled national pride, and many Americans declared the end of the "Vietnam syndrome." But for the 18 million people of Iraq, it produced the worst possible outcome. The ecological damage in the Gulf region was extensive and long-lasting. Oil fires burned out of control. Human rights groups reported an appalling death toll among civilians.

The limits of military power to solve complex political and economic disputes became clear in the aftermath of victory. The Persian Gulf War failed to dislodge Saddam Hussein, who remained in power despite CIA attempts to overthrow him and repeated bombings of Iraqi military positions. Iraqi Kurds, who had supported the U.S. invasion in hopes it would topple Saddam, faced violent reprisals, including gassing and chemical weapons, from the Iraqi army. Trade sanctions did little to weaken his rule, although the economic boycott, which brought increasing hardship to the civilian population, eventually divided the Western powers, leaving the United States and Great Britain isolated in their sanctions against Iraq.

The repercussions of the Gulf War were long-lasting. The leading U.S. ally in the region, the oil-rich kingdom of Saudi Arabia, had served as the launching pad for the invasion of Iraq, and following the war the Saudis had allowed the continuing presence of U.S. troops and weapons. This occupation of Saudi territory, which included Islamic holy sites, intensified the hatred of Americans among many Muslims and prompted appeals for revenge.

Among those actively opposed to the U.S. role in the region was Saudi millionaire Osama bin Laden, just a few years earlier a close ally of the United States during the Soviet invasion of Afghanistan. He now turned squarely against his former arms suppliers and CIA contacts. Using his own funds and a vast tribal network, bin Laden built his shadowy Al Qaeda organization, training small groups in terror tactics to be used against Western interests, particularly to force U.S. troops out of the Middle East.

See the Map
The Middle East in the 1980s and 1990s at **www.myhistorylab.com**

The Economy and the Election of 1992

Politically, the Persian Gulf War marked the high point of Bush's popularity. Claiming that the United States had finally "kicked the Vietnam Syndrome," Bush watched his approval rating jump to nearly 90 percent, higher than

President Roosevelt's during World War II. Basking in his success, the president proclaimed the United States the leader in the creation of a "new world order" that would be "freer from the threat of terror, stronger in the pursuit of justice, and more secure in the quest for peace, an era in which the nations of the world, East and West, North and South, can prosper and live in harmony."

However, it was the economy rather than foreign affairs that fueled the 1992 presidential election campaign. Republicans took credit for forcing the fall of communism and reviving America's military strength. But they had also promised to cut government spending and balance the budget. Just as Bush was about to take office in 1989, many of the nation's savings and loan institutions, which had been deregulated by Reagan, collapsed. Then, on Friday, October 13, 1989, the stock market took its worst nosedive since 1987, signaling a major recession. With the national debt reaching $4 trillion, the paradoxes of the Reagan-Bush years became readily apparent.

American consumers had been spending extravagantly, many falling deep into debt, and now, with the prospect of a recession, they pulled back. Real estate prices plummeted, unemployment hovered at 7 percent, and many businesses filed for bankruptcy. Eventually, Bush reneged on his campaign promise and worked with Democrats in Congress to raise taxes. By the end of 1991, the president's performance rating had dropped to just 51 percent.

As the 1992 campaign heated up, President Bush found himself facing a formidable opponent, William Jefferson Clinton. Personable, articulate, and highly intelligent, Bill Clinton won the Democratic nomination on the first ballot and chose Tennessee senator Albert Gore as his running mate. In the Democrats' campaign headquarters a sign humorously reminded the staff: "It's the economy, stupid." Candidate Clinton promised economic leadership. While promising deficit reduction and a tax cut for the middle class, he also took advantage of Bush's betrayal of his own campaign promise not to raise taxes.

Clinton effectively adopted many of the conservative themes that proved so advantageous to Republicans over the past twelve years. He called for "responsibility" on the part of recipients of social programs and spoke of the importance of stable families, promised to be tough on crime and to reduce the bureaucracy, and stressed the need for encouraging private investment to create new jobs. Economic issues also fueled the independent campaign of Texas billionaire H. Ross Perot, who with his folksy East Texas twang argued that someone as successful in business as himself was better qualified to solve the nation's economic woes than Washington insiders.

At the polls in November, Orange County and the nation came in together, each giving Clinton 43 percent of the popular vote. He also carried thirty-two states. Although failing to carry a single state, Perot scored 19 percent of the popular vote. The newly elected Clinton interpreted Perot's relative success at the polls as a mandate to focus, as he put it, "like a laser beam on the economy."

Conclusion

The success of conservatives to halt and in some cases actually reverse key trends in American politics, from Franklin Roosevelt's New Deal to Lyndon Johnson's Great Society, was made possible by the legacy of the Cold War and the trauma of defeat in Vietnam. But that success also owed a great deal to a deepening anxiety about cultural changes and a growing pessimism about the ability of politicians to offer solutions, especially at the national level. Those community activists struggling to broaden the 1960s' protest movements into an updated, comprehensive reformism encompassing such issues as feminism, ecology, and affirmative action readily recognized that the liberal era had ended.

President Ronald Reagan, a charismatic figure who sometimes invented his own past and seemed to believe in it, offered remedies for a weary and nostalgic nation. By insisting that the rebellious 1960s had been a terrible mistake, lowering national self-confidence along with public morals and faith in the power of economic individualism, he successfully wedded the conservatism of Christian fundamentalists, many suburbanites, and Sunbelt voters with the more traditional conservatism of corporate leaders. In many respects, the Reagan administration actually continued and added ideological fervor to the downscaling of government services and upscaling of military spending already evident under President Jimmy Carter, while offering supporters the hope of a sweeping conservative revolution.

In the end, critics suggested, supporters of Ronald Reagan and Reaganism could not go back to the 1950s—just as the erstwhile rebels of the 1960s could not go back to their favorite era. Economically, conservatives achieved many of their goals, including widespread acceptance of sharper economic divisions within society and fewer restraints on corporations and investments. But socially and culturally, their grasp was much less secure.

Review Questions

1. Evaluate the significance of the major population shifts in the United States from the 1940s through the 1970s. What was their impact on local and national politics?

2. Discuss the connections between the energy crisis and the rise of the environmental movement.

3. Interpret the decline of liberalism and the rise of conservative political groups. How did these changes affect the outcome of presidential elections?

CHRONOLOGY

1973	*Roe* v. *Wade* legalizes abortion
	Arab embargo sparks oil crisis in the United States
1974	Richard Nixon resigns presidency; Gerald Ford takes office
	President Ford pardons Nixon and introduces anti-inflation program
1975	Unemployment rate reaches nearly 9 percent
	South Vietnamese government falls to communists
	Antibusing protests break out in Boston
1976	Percentage of African Americans attending college peaks at 9.3 percent and begins a decline
	Democrat Jimmy Carter defeats incumbent Gerald Ford in presidential election
1977	President Carter announces human rights as major tenet in foreign policy
1978	*Bakke* v. *University of California* decision places new limits on affirmative action programs
	Camp David meeting sets terms for Middle East peace
	California passes Proposition 13, cutting taxes and government social programs
1979	Three Mile Island nuclear accident threatens a meltdown
	Nicaraguan Revolution overthrows Anastasio Somoza
	Iranian fundamentalists seize the U.S. embassy in Tehran and hold U.S. citizens hostage for 444 days
	Soviets invade Afghanistan

1980	Inflation reaches 13.5 percent
	Republican Ronald Reagan defeats incumbent Jimmy Carter in presidential election
1981	Reagan administration initiates major cuts in taxes and domestic spending
	Military buildup accelerates
	AIDS is recognized and named
1982	Economic recession grips the nation
1983	Reagan announces the Strategic Defense Initiative, labeled "Star Wars" by the media
	241 U.S. Marines killed in Beirut terrorist bombing
1985	Mikhail Gorbachev initiates reforms in the Soviet Union
1986	Iran-Contra hearings before Congress reveal arms-for-hostages deal and funds secretly and illegally diverted to Nicaraguan rebels
1988	Republican George H. W. Bush defeats Michael Dukakis in presidential election
	Communist authority collapses in Eastern Europe
1990	Iraqi invasion of Kuwait leads to massive U.S. military presence in the Persian Gulf
1991	Operation Desert Storm forces Iraq out of Kuwait
	Soviet Union dissolves into Commonwealth of Independent States
1992	Democrat Bill Clinton defeats incumbent George H. W. Bush and independent candidate Ross Perot in the presidential election

4. Was the Iran hostage crisis a turning point in American politics or only a thorn in Carter's reelection campaign? How did the Iran-Contra scandal affect the Republicans?

5. Describe the central philosophical assumptions behind Reaganomics. What were the key policies by which it was implemented? To what extent were these policies a break with previous economic approaches?

6. Evaluate Reagan's foreign policy. How did it differ from Carter's approach to foreign affairs?

7. Analyze the key structural factors underlying recent changes in American economic and cultural life. Do you see any political solutions for the growth of poverty and inequality?

Recommended Reading

Donald T. Critchlow, *The Conservative Ascendancy: How the GOP Right Made Political History* (2007). Examines the way conservatives gained control of the Republican party, but often floundered in their attempts to unseat the liberal legacy of the New Deal and the Great Society. As a result, Critchlow argues, the opposition between liberals and conservatives widened and heated up politics in the last quarter of the twentieth century.

David Farber, *Taken Hostage: The Iran Hostage Crisis and America's First Encounter with Radical Islam* (2004). Examines the events of November 1979, emphasizing the larger context of a decade of uncertainty and anxiety. Farber also considers the meaning of Carter's hostage crisis for the larger war on terrorism at the turn of the century.

Frances FitzGerald, *Way Out There in the Blue: Reagan, Star Wars, and the End of the Cold War* (2000). A well-documented study of the conservative mood that made Star Wars both credible and popular among conservatives. FitzGerald provides a sweeping historical context for Star Wars with special attention given to the impact of the Cold War on traditional isolationism.

John Karaagac, *Between Promise and Policy: Ronald Reagan and Conservative Reformism* (2000). Assesses Reagan's major polities, such as increased funding for federal government and regulatory reform, in light of his professed conservative ideals. Karaagac argues that Reagan wielded ideology as a political weapon to gain support for his programs while acting pragmatically and with a good deal of flexibility on particular issues.

Melani McAlister, *Epic Encounters: Culture, Media, and U.S. Interests in the Middle East, 1945–2000* (2001). A close reading of American popular culture, including films, television news broadcasts, museum exhibits, and fiction, representing relationships between the Middle East and the United States. McAlister considers the importance of the abundance of oil and the Islamic religion of the Middle East as factors shaping U.S. foreign policy.

Lisa McGirr, *Suburban Warriors: The Origins of the New American Right* (2001). Traces the resurgence of American conservatism by analyzing issues that galvanized grassroots middle-class activism in southern California in the 1960s and 1970s.

Michael Schaller, *Right Turn: American Life in the Reagan-Bush Era, 1980–1992* (2007). A succinct overview of the rise of conservatism and its impact on national and foreign policies, with ample attention paid to major developments in American society and culture during the era.

Bruce J. Schulman, *The Seventies: The Great Shift in American Culture, Society, and Politics* (2001). Examines the move away from the public-spirited universalism that characterized the New Deal and civil rights movement toward the sovereignty of the free market and celebration of private life. With a geopolitical twist that emphasizes the increasing importance of the Sunbelt, Schulman argues that the conservative 1980s actually began a decade earlier.

Judith Stein, *Running Steel, Running America: Race, Economic Policy, and the Decline of Liberalism* (1998). Discusses the impact of the decline of the U.S. steel industry on its large African American labor force. Stein analyzes trade policy, especially under Carter, that benefited foreign steel producers and led to the closing of American plants.

Robert A. Strong, *Working in the World: Jimmy Carter and the Making of American Foreign Policy* (2000). A collection of nine case studies of international affairs covering Carter's presidency. Strong's goal is not to provide new insight into the central crises of the era but to open a window to the range of presidential responsibilities in the diplomatic arena.

Andrew Szasz, *EcoPopulism: Toxic Waste and the Movement for Environmental Justice* (1994). A careful analysis of a turning point in federal regulation of toxic waste. Szasz shows how the prevention of pollution, previously considered a local issue, through strengthened state and federal regulations became a national issue and a springboard for the environmental movement.

J. Samuel Walker, *Three Mile Island: A Nuclear Crisis in Historical Perspective* (2004). Sponsored by the United States Nuclear Regulatory Commission, this book provides a detailed description of the "accident" at Three Mile Island and a broad historical context, including the growth of commercial nuclear power and the emergence of forces in opposition to this source of energy.

Sean Wilentz, *The Age of Reagan: A History 1974–2008* (2008). Examines the rise of the conservative movement, its consolidation during the Reagan administration, and its continuing impact on national politics. Wilentz places Reagan at the center of this unfolding drama, identifying his heroic stature in the pantheon of conservatives.

Natasha Zaretsky, *No Direction Home: The American Family and the Fear of National Decline, 1868–1980* (2007). Studies the fears American faced in the aftermath of the Vietnam War, a sense of imperiled national identity fatefully linked to images of a family similarly endangered.

PEARSON myhistorylab Connections

Reinforce what you learned in this chapter by studying the many documents, images, maps, review tools, and videos available at www.myhistorylab.com.

READ AND REVIEW

✓• Study and Review **Chapter 30**

•••• Read the Document

Jimmy Carter, The "Crisis of Confidence" Speech (1979)

Roe v. Wade (1973)

Ronald Reagan, First Inaugural Address (1981)

Paul Craig Robert, The Supply-Side Revolution (1984)

Ronald Reagan, Address to the National Association of Evangelicals (1983)

George H. W. Bush, Gulf War Address (1990)

The Middle East in the 1980s and 1990s

RESEARCH AND EXPLORE

•••• Read the Document

Exploring America: Growing Inequality

Profiles
Jimmy Carter
Jerry Falwell

•••• Watch the Video

Evangelical Religion and Politics, Then and Now

Ronald Reagan Presidential Campaign Ad: A Bear in the Woods

Ronald Reagan on the Wisdom of Tax Cuts

•••• Read the Document

The Berlin Wall

President George Bush's Early Response in the Persian Gulf War

President Bush on the Gulf War

((•• Hear the Audio

Hear the audio files for Chapter 30 at
www.myhistorylab.com.

The United States in a Global Age 1992–2010

CHAPTER OUTLINE

American Communities 917
Transnational Communities in San Diego and Tijuana

The Presidency of Bill Clinton 919
A "New Democrat" in the White House
The "Globalization" President
Presiding Over the Boom
High Crimes and Misdemeanors

Changing American Communities 923
Silicon Valley
New Media and Virtual Communities
The New Immigrants
Growing Social Disparities
Culture Wars

President George W. Bush and the War on
Terror 930
The Election of 2000
Terrorist Attack on America

Reshaping U.S. Foreign Policy
Invasion of Iraq
Bush's "Compassionate Conservatism"
Divided Government, Divided Nation

Barack Obama and the Audacity
of Hope 938
The Election of 2008
The Great Recession
Obama in Office

Washington DC, 2009. The inauguration of President-Elect Barack Obama.

Transnational Communities in San Diego and Tijuana

As the new millennium began, Norma Ojeida crossed the U.S.-Mexico border on a daily basis, leaving for work in the morning and returning home at night. She held a position at a high-powered research institute in Rosarito, a suburb of the booming city of Tijuana in Baja, California, Mexico, and made her home in suburban San Diego, in the border community of Chula Vista, where nearly half the population was Hispanic. The second-largest city in San Diego County was known locally as "Chulajuana" because it was just as much a suburb of Tijuana as of San Diego. Ojeida therefore had plenty of company in making the daily journey across the busiest border crossing in North America. Thousands of other affluent, educated professionals made the same trip southward, while a steady stream of 40,000 Mexicans left Tijuana to work on the U.S. side of the border.

AMERICAN Communities

Many of these "fonterizos" or "borderlanders" enjoyed some of the best of both nations. Often fluent in both Spanish and English, they could choose between upward mobility in Mexico and a rewarding life in San Diego County. Their children, growing up bilingual, often crossed the border to attend school or to go on dates. This transnational lifestyle, Ojeida

917

explained, gave the residents of this growing region "the luxury of living where you want, working where you want, having the identity you want," a luxury, however, that only a minority of residents on either side was fortunate enough to enjoy.

Tijuana, hardly more than a small, poor town of 60,000 in 1950, had depended on a lucrative tourist trade since at least 1919, when a transnational railroad connected it with San Diego. Since midcentury, Tijuana served as a mecca not only for a growing number of American tourists, but also for Mexicans looking for better jobs. Poor people from distant regions of Mexico were migrating to the rich agricultural valleys and hills surrounding Tijuana, often to prepare for *El Norte*, the trip north to the United States.

Meanwhile, San Diego, which grew from a Spanish mission and fishing village to a Navy boomtown during World War II, developed into a major center of defense-industry manufacturing and research. In the 1950s, the aircraft industry dominated the local economy. Three decades later, the city supported a thriving high-tech industry and the famed San Diego Zoo. Tourism, upscale retirement communities, and a major research branch of the University of California helped to make San Diego the second-largest city in California and the seventh in the United States, with mainly Hispanics and Asians accounting for the major share of population growth since 1985.

For better or worse, the fates of these two border communities had become increasingly intertwined. In 1961, the Border Industrialization Program paved the way for a closer economic relationship between Tijuana and San Diego. The program fostered the creation of *maquiladoras*, assembly plants for such American-owned firms as Ford Motors and General Electric; in the 1990s, the adoption of the North American Free Trade Agreement (NAFTA) helped to secure these economic structures. By the end of the twentieth century, Tijuana, the fourth-largest city in Mexico and home to 1.5 million people, had become the only Mexican border city where the size of the middle class most nearly approached that of the impoverished population. Well-heeled shoppers from Tijuana were able to pour about $2.8 billion a year into the San Diego economy, $120 million from sales tax revenue alone.

San Diego and Tijuana, one of eight transnational metropolitan regions on the 2,000-mile U.S.-Mexico border, had come to share not only people but also problems that flout political boundaries. For example, unregulated growth on both sides of the border threatened ecological disaster, created bumper-to-bumper traffic on highways, and encouraged the kind of suburban sprawl that surrounded most large American cities. The Tijuana River, which flows into the San Diego Bay, by the 1990s was carrying 1.5 million gallons of untreated sewage per day, threatening to overwhelm the saltwater marsh that is home to some 370 species of birds and the estuaries that serve ocean fish and mammals. The virtually unregulated airborne pollution of the *maquiladoras* posed additional threats to the region. The continuous cross-border traffic in goods and people also caused substantial amounts of native vegetation to succumb to exotic weedy grasses.

By the end of the century, the Californian and Mexican governments began to catch up with problems festering for decades. A joint feasibility study was funded by the California legislature for the construction of an aqueduct to the Colorado River to bring more water into the region. Other plans included mass transit on the San Diego side and airport expansion on the Tijuana side to relieve congestion at San Diego's overtaxed international airport. To foster such projects and to bring them to the highest level of government, President Vicente Fox of Mexico created the Commission for Northern Border Affairs soon after he took office in December 2000, and he urged the new president of the United States, George W. Bush, to make the region a priority for Americans. The bright promise of the transnational San Diego/Tijuana community was held in check, however, by the dark shadows of world recession and environmental exhaustion that gathered in the first decade of the twenty-first century.

The governments of Mexico and the United States continued to explore scores of binational projects, while San Diego and Tijuana invested in a major border initiative to promote sustainable development and effective public health programs on both sides of the border. In 2006, the governors from the border states of the United States and Mexico met to affirm once again their "common values and . . . vision for the prosperity of the border region." It seemed clear to everyone that the accelerating diffusion of information technologies,

FOCUS Questions

1. As a "New Democrat," what changes in public policy did Bill Clinton promote during his presidency?
2. What factors contributed to the economic boom of the 1990s?
3. What major demographic shifts did the 2000 U.S. Census reveal?
4. How did the presidency of George W. Bush rekindle conservatism in the early years of the twenty-first century?
5. Is globalization a meaningful term and, if so, how did it affect U.S. policies at home and abroad?
6. How did the threat of global terrorism transform the American political landscape in the first decade of the twenty-first century?

1992–2008

such as television, film, and the Internet, continued to create sources of community where none had previously existed. The key word of the new era, "globalization," however, held together

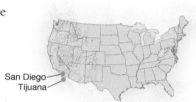

San Diego
Tijuana

many contradictory tendencies. For one, international terrorism offered dramatic and unwelcome proof that no part of the world was far removed—or safe—from the conflicts of any other part.

AMERICAN Communities

The Presidency of Bill Clinton

During his campaign, Bill Clinton promised to bring a new kind of Democratic leadership to the presidency. Since 1985, he had been active in the Democratic Leadership Council (DLC), a group of Democrats serving in Congress or as governors who feared for the fate of their party after the Reagan Republicans won forty-nine of fifty states during the 1984 election. Responding to the conservative challenge, they sought to distance the Democratic Party even further from the liberal tradition established by Franklin D. Roosevelt and revived by Lyndon Johnson in the 1960s. They sought to recapture the blue-collar and white southern defectors "by redefining and reclaiming the political center."

Youthful and energetic, Clinton carried this mission to the White House. He presented a bold agenda that included balancing the federal budget, reforming welfare, reducing crime, promoting economic growth, and ensuring a strong national defense. Trimming the federal government and promoting free markets worldwide became hallmarks of his administration.

A "New Democrat" in the White House

Despite his remarkable powers of persuasion, President Clinton got off to a rocky start. As a candidate, he had promised to end the ban on gays and bisexuals in the armed forces. Congress refused, however. He ultimately settled for a compromise and issued an executive order that satisfied virtually no one: "Don't ask, don't tell."

Clinton's biggest stumbling block during his first term was health care reform. Nearly 40 million Americans had no health insurance. Many simply could not afford it; others were denied coverage by private insurers because of preexisting conditions ranging from cancer, cardiovascular disease, and diabetes to AIDS. For millions of others, health insurance was tied to the workplace and a loss or change of jobs threatened their coverage. Private spending on health care had skyrocketed from $246 billion in 1980 to more than $880 billion during the year Clinton took office.

In a controversial move, President Clinton appointed First Lady Hillary Rodham Clinton, an accomplished attorney, to head a task force charged with preparing a sweeping legislative overhaul of health care. The task force, in trying to find a political middle ground, ultimately produced an impossibly complicated compromise. Opposed by such powerful forces as the Chamber of Commerce, the National Association of Manufacturers, the Health Insurance Association of America, and most Republicans, the plan died in Congress in August, 1994, just as the midterm election campaign moved into its final phase.

> Read the Document
> *Statements of the Clinton Health Care Plan (1993)*
> at **www.myhistorylab.com**

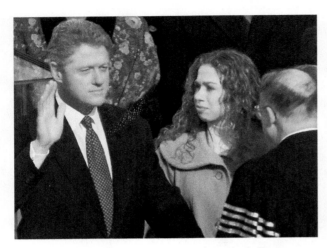

Chief Justice William Rehnquist administers the oath of office to President William Jefferson Clinton on January 20, 1993. Daughter Chelsea and wife Hillary Rodham Clinton stand by his side. In his Inaugural Address as the nation's 42nd president, Clinton invited his fellow citizens to "celebrate the mystery of the American renewal" and to help him "revitalize our democracy."

In the 1994 midterm elections, Clinton's defeat on health care reform helped the Republicans gain control of both the House and Senate for the first time in forty years—a disaster of historic proportions for Clinton and the Democratic Party. Congress was now dominated by conservative Republicans led by the new House Speaker, Newt Gingrich of Georgia. With his scathing denunciations of big government and celebration of entrepreneurship, the formidable polemicist Gingrich challenged Clinton's leadership by presenting his own set of proposals labeled the "Contract with America." The House did indeed pass much of the "Contract," including a large tax cut, an increase in military spending, cutbacks in federal regulatory power in the environment and at the workplace, a tough anticrime bill, and a sharp reduction in federal welfare programs.

Meanwhile, Clinton undercut the Republicans by adapting many of their proposals to his own. He endorsed the goal of a balanced federal budget and declared, in his January 1996 State of the Union message, that "the era of big government is over." Clinton opposed his own party's efforts to block a Republican plan to dismantle the federal welfare system in place since the New Deal and instead backed new legislation—the Welfare Reform Act—that abolished the sixty-year-old Aid to Families with Dependent Children program (AFDC). Poor mothers with dependent children would now have access to aid for only a limited period and only if they were preparing for or seeking work. After Congress passed the act in August 1996, Clinton held a public signing ceremony and declared "an end to welfare as we know it."

With such deft maneuvers, Clinton set the theme for his 1996 reelection campaign against Robert Dole of Kansas, the Republican majority leader of the Senate. By staking out the political center, the president won a resounding reelection victory in November, confounding the predictions of the media pundits who had pronounced his political death. It was a victory without coattails, however: the Republicans retained control of both houses of Congress.

The Republican majority worked with Clinton to achieve a sweeping deregulation of the banking industry that would allow corporate mergers resulting in huge, multipurpose financial institutions such as Citibank. The Republicans managed to get sufficient bipartisan support for this initiative, and Congress passed the controversial Financial Services Modernization Act of 1999. The bill, signed by President Clinton in November, repealed sections of the Glass-Steagall Act of 1933 and allowed banking, securities, and insurance companies to consolidate services and to combine (see Chapter 24).

The "Globalization" President

"Everything from the strength of our economy, to the safety of our cities, to the health of our people," Clinton declared, "depends on events not only within our border but half a world away." Following in the footsteps of his Democratic predecessor, Jimmy Carter, he insisted that U.S. foreign policy reflect "the moral principles most Americans share" and promote humanitarian goals. But even more central to his vision was the goal of enlarging "the world's free community of market democracies" under the leadership of the United States. The editors of *Foreign Affairs* dubbed Clinton the "globalization" president.

These principles drove Clinton's policy toward the People's Republic of China (PRC). During the spring of 1989, Chinese government forces had brutally attacked prodemocracy demonstrators in Beijing's Tiananmen Square, resulting in the death of some 3,000 protestors and the wounding of 10,000 more. During the 1992 election campaign, Clinton criticized Bush for continuing "to coddle" China in light of such gross human rights violations. Then, after taking office, he modified his position and, looking for "hopeful seeds of change," recommended restoring Most Favored Nation (MFN) status with the PRC. Clinton acknowledged that serious human rights abuses continued, but he pointed out that China, the world's most populous nation, had the world's fastest-growing economy—as well as a nuclear arsenal and veto in the Security Council of the UN. He promoted free enterprise as a principal means to advance democracy in not only the PRC but also in other nations, such as Turkey, Saudi Arabia, and Indonesia.

During his first term, President Clinton pushed through Congress two major trade agreements to expand markets and encourage "free trade," both building on the earlier efforts of the Reagan and Bush administrations. Approved in November 1993, the North American Free Trade Agreement (NAFTA) eased the international flow

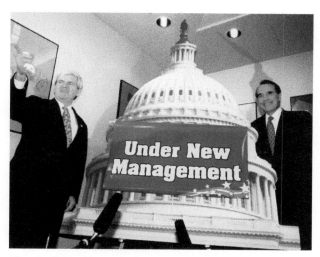

After the 1994 midterm election gave Republicans control of the House of Representatives for the first time in forty years, the new Speaker, Newt Gingrich of Georgia, presented a list of legislative initiatives to be completed within the first one hundred days of the new session. On April 7, 1995, he appeared at a rally on Capitol Hill to celebrate the success of the Republicans' "Contract with America."

of goods, services, and investments among the United States, Mexico, and Canada by eliminating tariffs and other trade barriers. The second trade agreement, which led to the establishment of the World Trade Organization (WTO) in 1995, continued the GATT policy of keeping tariffs low on thousands of goods throughout the world and phased out many import quotas imposed by the United States and other industrialized nations—except in agriculture, where the United States and Europe maintained quotas to the detriment of the developing peasant-based Third World economies.

Critics and supporters argued over whether these trade agreements would encourage global competition, thereby boosting American export industries and creating new high-wage jobs for American workers, or simply erode the U.S. industrial base and accelerate environmental degradation. Cities on the U.S.-Mexico border, such as Tijuana and San Diego, were clear beneficiaries, but the downside was considerable. New *maquiladoras* (factories and assembly plants) lacked pollution controls and spewed tons of toxic wastes into the air and groundwater. Despite the boost from NAFTA, the Mexican peso collapsed, and only a $20 billion bailout of the Mexican economy directed by executive order from the White House on January 31, 1995, prevented a serious depression there.

On humanitarian grounds, Clinton's accomplishments fell short of his lofty goals. During his first year in office, in October 1993, the United States took part in a UN mission to restore civil order in Somalia in East Africa. Eighteen ill-equipped American soldiers were killed in battle, while several thousand Somalian fighters and civilians died in the ill-fated attack. The president

aborted the military mission and adopted a more cautious policy of intervention for humanitarian reasons.

In 1995, acting reluctantly, Clinton committed U.S. troops to a multinational effort in Bosnia where, following the collapse of communism and the dissolution of Yugoslavia, ethnic and religious rivalry among Serbs, Croats, and Muslims had erupted into a civil war. President Bush, seeing no threat to American interests, had opposed U.S. military intervention. As reports of "ethnic cleansing"—forced removal and murder of Croats and Muslims by Bosnian Serbs—increased, and as the numbers of refugees grew, Clinton, with congressional support, joined NATO in bombing Serbian strongholds in Bosnia. After negotiating with Yugoslav president Slobodan Milosevic, on November 27, Clinton announced a peace accord that called for a federated, multiethnic state of Bosnia.

Clinton's worst foreign crisis erupted in Kosovo, Yugoslavia, where intensifying clashes between Serbs and Albanians spread to neighboring Macedonia and to Albania itself. He once again tried to negotiate, but failed to resolve the problems through diplomacy. After NATO authorized air strikes, Clinton informed Americans in March 1999 that U.S. armed forces were joining the attack on Serbian forces in Kosovo.

The so-called Clinton Doctrine, articulated in 1999 to justify the dispatch of U.S. troops to Yugoslavia, departed sharply from Cold War policies that sanctioned intervention primarily on the grounds of strategic interest and national security. In a later statement, Clinton insisted that "genocide is in and of itself a national interest where we should act." In 1998, he acknowledged that the United States, as part of the global community, must share the blame for failing to intervene in Rwanda in 1994, where a struggle for power led to genocide in the killing of up to 1 million Tutsis and moderate Hutu by Hutu extremists. This tragedy, Clinton declared, represented "the most intensive slaughter in this blood-filled century we are about to leave." At the time it occurred, however, the Clinton administration had known about the genocide and had chosen not to act.

Nor did Clinton's understanding of the global community extend to include the most important international environmental issue of the 1990s: climate change. During the late 1970s, scientists had presented data indicating that the earth was warming, causing polar ice caps to melt, oceans to rise, and ultimately marine life to die, and they pointed to the emission of "greenhouse gases," the by-products of the fossil fuels burned to run factories and automobiles, as the main cause. Delegates from various nations began to work on ways to limit greenhouse gas emissions, but the United States, responsible for an estimated 25 percent of the total worldwide, refused to make a commitment. The controversy came to a head at the world summit held in 1997 in Kyoto, Japan, where delegates outlined a protocol that included targets and timetables for the reduction of greenhouse gases and required the richer, industrialized countries to take the lead. Although the fifteen-member nations of the European Union endorsed the terms of the treaty, both Japan and the United States held out.

Presiding Over the Boom

By any number of measures, Bill Clinton presided over one of the strongest and longest economic booms in American history. Between 1992 and 2000, the economy produced more than 20 million new jobs, and by 2000 the unemployment rate fell below 4 percent, the lowest in more than thirty years. With government spending down and economic growth increasing tax revenues, the largest federal budget deficit in American history (a quarter trillion dollars) became a surplus nearly as large by the time Clinton left office.

A soaring stock market, with "tech stocks" leading the way, provided a great boost to Clinton's second term as president. The record highs of the Bush years, when the Dow Jones index of thirty industrials approached 4,000, paled by comparison to the leap in 1999 when the Dow hit 10,000 in March and then peaked above 11,000 in May. Throughout the decade, the market remained volatile, but profits were extraordinarily high.

Equally remarkable was the involvement of ordinary citizens "in the market." By the end of the century, Americans had 60 percent of their investments and savings in stocks, more than double the proportion in 1982. An estimated 78.7 million people held stocks, often through mutual funds or in retirement fund portfolios managed by their employers or unions.

The downside of the economic boom was nearly invisible. Productivity had risen sharply since the 1970s while labor costs had actually declined, hoisting profits to new levels. Critics observed, however, that while a corporate official had earned around twenty or thirty times the pay of a blue-collar worker at the same company a few decades earlier, corporate executive income was now more than two hundred times greater than that of a blue-collar employee. In the blue-collar sector, industrial jobs continued to disappear as factories closed or companies moved production across borders or overseas.

High Crimes and Misdemeanors

During his second term as president, Clinton had to answer many questions about his moral conduct. Real estate deals involving both him and Hillary Rodham Clinton blew up into a scandal known as Whitewater. A former Arkansas state employee, Paula Jones, charged Clinton with sexual assault during his gubernatorial term. Attorney General Janet Reno appointed an independent counsel, former judge Kenneth Starr, to investigate these allegations. In the summer of 1998, Starr instead delivered to the House Judiciary Committee a report focusing on an extramarital affair with a young White House intern, Monica Lewinsky. Starr's report outlined several potential

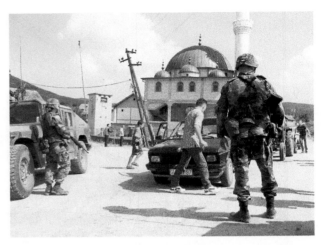

U.S. Army Military Police stop and search vehicles for weapons and explosives at this checkpoint near Vitina, Kosovo in Yugoslavia, 1999. They were part of the NATO led international force sent to attack Serbian forces in Kosovo.

impeachable offenses allegedly committed by the president to keep secret his relationship with Lewinsky.

The Congress and the American people at large fiercely debated the nature of the charges against the president: Were they truly impeachable—"high crimes and misdemeanors" as the Constitution put it—or merely part of a partisan political effort to overturn the election of 1996? For only the third time in history, in October 1998, the House of Representatives voted to open an inquiry into possible grounds for impeachment.

Republicans hoping to reap a wholesale victory from the scandal in the midterm elections were bitterly disappointed. Contrary to predictions, the president's party added seats, trimming the Republican majority in the 105th Congress. Voters evidently had more on their minds than President Clinton's sex life. The election also brought a shakeup in the Republican leadership. Newt Gingrich, under pressure from Republican colleagues angry about a campaign strategy that had narrowly focused on Clinton's impeachment problem, announced his resignation as Speaker of the House and from his seat in Congress.

In the aftermath of the 1998 midterm election, most politicians and analysts, and indeed most Americans, believed the impeachment inquiry to be at a dead end. They were proved wrong when the House Judiciary Committee voted to bring four articles of impeachment— charging President Clinton with perjury, obstruction of justice, witness tampering, and abuse of power—to the full House. Unlike the bipartisan case the Judiciary Committee brought against Richard Nixon in 1974 (see Chapter 29), this time the votes were strictly along party lines. On February 12, 1999, the Senate trial concluded with the president's acquittal. When Clinton left office, he enjoyed the highest approval rating of any president since Dwight Eisenhower.

Changing American Communities

During the Clinton administration, economists coined the phrase "the new economy" to underscore the increasing importance of globalization and corporate restructuring as well as the growing service sector. This included all those workers not directly involved in producing or processing a physical product: from highly paid lawyers, financial analysts, and software designers to poorly paid fast food employees. In 1965, an estimated 50 percent of all jobs were in the service sector; by 2000, the figure had grown to about 70 percent.

The new economy helped to change American society in significant ways. It depended on a global workforce and attracted millions of immigrants, documented and undocumented, who were forming new communities throughout the United States. It created new forms of social relationships and communication based on electronic media. It also helped to widen the fissures in American society by reshaping manners and morals.

Silicon Valley

The real and symbolic capital of the new economy was a thirty-by-ten-mile strip of Santa Clara County, California. As late as 1960, this region was the major processor of fruits and vegetables in the world; forty years later, high-tech companies employed one-third of the valley's workforce.

Dubbed "Silicon Valley" in 1971 after the material used in semiconductor chips, the region flourished thanks to its unique combination of research facilities, investment capital, attractive environment, and a large pool of highly educated people. At first, military contracts predominated, but the consumer electronics revolution of the 1970s fueled an explosive new wave of growth. Silicon Valley firms gave birth to pocket calculators, video games, home computers, cordless telephones, digital watches, and almost every other new development in electronics. It became home to thousands of high-tech firms that specialized in gathering, processing, or distributing information or in manufacturing information technology. Silicon Valley boasted the greatest concentration of new wealth in the United States.

By the end of the twentieth century, Silicon Valley had become the home and workplace of a diverse population. The managers and engineers, nearly all of whom were white males, had settled in affluent communities such as Palo Alto, Mountain View, and Sunnyvale. Manual workers on assembly lines and in low-paying service jobs clustered in San Jose and Gilroy. Most of these were immigrants or temporary workers—Mexican, Southeast Asian, Iranian, Vietnamese, Cambodian, and Filipino men and women who constituted a cheap, nonunionized labor pool with an extremely high turnover rate.

The prime example of the new economy, Silicon Valley was part of a global enterprise. Its firms were closely linked to the microelectronics industry of the greater Pacific Rim. American companies competed on the world market

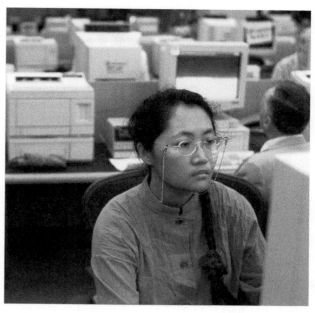

Yi Li, a graduate student from Taiwan, uses a computer terminal at the New York Public Library to gain access to the Internet. By the 1990s banks of personal computers had become a familiar sight in American offices, businesses, schools, and libraries. Millions of Americans made connecting with the new world of cyberspace a part of their daily routines.

against similar companies in Japan, Korea, China, and Malaysia or protected themselves against such competition by owning a large share of the plants in those countries.

By the end of Clinton's administration, the rate of growth slowed, dramatized by a sharp plunge of technology stocks. In the aftermath of this burst of the so-called dot-com bubble in March 2000, entrepreneurs throughout the Pacific Rim found it more difficult to start new companies and to make the leap from a small, start-up company to a large corporation. By this time, high prices in housing, traffic jams, inflated cost of living, and unemployment were already highlighting the downside to the new economy.

New Media and Virtual Communities

The technological developments produced in Silicon Valley helped reconfigure cultural life in the United States and the world. Revolutions in computers and telecommunications merged telephones, televisions, computers, cable, and satellites into a global system of information exchange.

The new technologies changed the way people worked, played, and conducted business and politics. The twin arrivals of pay cable services and videocassette recorders (VCR) expanded and redefined the power of television and by the early 1990s had penetrated roughly two-thirds of American homes. Cable and satellite in the 1990s offered television viewers not just four or five channels but also scores of new programming choices, especially sports events and movies. The rental and sale of movies for home viewing quickly outstripped ticket sales at theaters as the main profit source for filmmakers.

New digital technologies continued to reshape American culture. Compact discs (CDs) and digital video discs (DVDs) emerged as the dominant media for popular music and movies, replacing tape-based technologies. Millions of Americans now used digital cameras to document their vacations and everyday lives. Digital telephones—"cell phones"—became ubiquitous in the streets, malls, campuses, cars, and workplaces of American communities.

Perhaps no aspect of the electronic culture was more revolutionary than the creation of cyberspace, the conceptual region occupied by people linked through computers and communications networks. It began with ARPANET, the first computer network, which the Department of Defense developed in the early 1970s. Computer enthusiasts known as "hackers" created unexpected grassroots spinoffs from ARPANET, including electronic mail, computer conferencing, and computer bulletin board systems. In the mid-1980s, alongside the launch of Microsoft Word and Windows operating programs, the boom in cheap personal computers capable of linking individuals to the worldwide telecommunications network began a population explosion in cyberspace. By then, tens of thousands of researchers and scholars at universities and in private industry were linked to the Internet, the U.S. government–sponsored successor to ARPANET. The establishment of the World Wide Web and easy-to-use browser software such as Netscape, introduced in 1994, made the "information highway" accessible to millions of Americans with few computer skills and created a popular communications medium with global dimensions.

By the beginning of the new century, more than half of all households had at least one computer and more than 40 percent were connected to the Internet. Nearly 85 percent of classrooms in public schools were online. At work, Americans spent an average of 21 hours per week online. At home, they spent an average of 9.5 hours per week online. By 2010, surveys indicated that children and teenagers spent 7.5 hours per day using an electronic device, such as a computer or smart phone. Americans used their computers to play games, access information and entertainment, and purchase a huge array of goods and services, ranging from books and airline tickets to automobiles and psychotherapy sessions.

Through these electronic media, Americans created "virtual" communities, widening their base of friends and acquaintances through social networking sites accessed through their computers and smart phones. They sent electronic mail, discussed issues in public forums, posted opinions in "blogs." Text messaging–the sending of short messages—became by the first decade of the twenty-first

century the most form of communication by mobile phone users. Facebook, invented by Harvard University sophomore student Mark Zuckerman in 2003, became in just six years the most used on-line social network in the world.

These new information technologies gave birth to "virtual" communities that transcended national boundaries. During the 1980s, exports from Hollywood to the rest of the world doubled in value. The number of hours of television watched throughout the world nearly tripled: MTV was broadcast to an estimated 250 million households. By the mid-1990s, there were more television sets in China than in the United States. Americans, however, owned a disproportionate share of the largest media corporations in the world, with Time Warner, Disney, and Bertlesman in the lead. More than 40 percent of television programs in the world originated in the United States.

The New Immigrants

During the 1990s, the nation's population grew by 32.7 million, a number greater than that of any other decade in U.S. history. In October 2006, the U.S. population hit 300 million.

More than a third of the nation's population growth came from the influx of new immigrants (see Figure 31.1). Although three-quarters of the newcomers joined many other Americans in flocking to the Sunbelt states, headed by California, Texas, and Florida, they also helped to reverse population loss in such major urban centers as New York and Chicago and slow the decline in Rustbelt cities like Cleveland, Detroit, and Milwaukee. For the first time, they also played a major role in the population increase in all fifty states. Nationally, at the turn of the century the percentage of Americans born outside the United

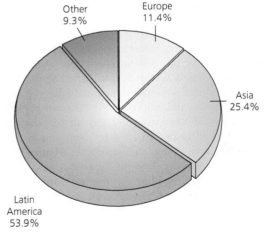

FIGURE 31.1 Continent of Birth for Immigrants, 1990–2000 By 2000, the number of foreign-born residents and their children—56 million according to the U.S. Census Bureau—had reached the highest level in U.S. history.

States was 11.2 percent, its highest point since 1930; in California, the percentage of foreign-born approached 26 percent.

The Immigration Act of 1965 had revolutionary, if largely unintended, consequences (see Chapter 28). The act abolished the discriminatory national origins quotas that had been in place since the 1920s. It also for the first time limited immigration from the Western Hemisphere, while giving preference to people from the nations of the Eastern Hemisphere who had specialized job skills and training. This provision created the conditions for Asian immigrants to become the fastest-growing ethnic group in the United States. With a steady flow of professionals and workers skilled in technology into their communities, Chinese Americans remained the largest Asian ethnicity in the United States. However, other groups grew at faster rates, particularly Indo Americans (from the subcontinent of India), whose numbers doubled during the 1990s to become the third-largest Asian group. Meanwhile, Japanese Americans, once the largest and most influential members of the pan-Asian community, declined.

Hispanics also benefited from the changes in immigration law. By 1990, Hispanics had already formed over a third of the population of New Mexico, a quarter of the population of Texas, and over 10 percent of the populations of California, Arizona, and Colorado. Nearly a million Mexican Americans lived in Los Angeles alone. Demographers predicted that Hispanics, who had grown from 22.4 million in 1990 to 35.3 million in 2000, according to U.S. Census data, would replace African Americans as the nation's largest minority group by the middle of the twenty-first century.

Mexicans were the largest Hispanic group in the United States at 20.6 million, representing nearly 60 percent of the total Hispanic population. The boom of the U.S. economy in the 1990s provided a significant "pull" for these newcomers. But other factors encouraged many Mexicans to make an often difficult and dangerous sojourn to the United States. First, a drop in worldwide oil prices followed by the deflation of the Mexican national currency dramatically lowered living standards in Mexico in the mid-1990s. NAFTA and the greater integration of the U.S. and Mexican economies brought new jobs but often with increasingly expensive living conditions. Tens and perhaps hundreds of thousands of Mexicans worked in the United States temporarily while planning a permanent move north—with or without legal documentation.

The cultural implications of immigration were far-reaching. Children born to the new immigrants of the 1980s and 1990s, despite increasing neighborhood segregation by race, played on the streets together, attended the same schools, and often married outside their racial groups. In the 2000 U.S. Census, 6.8 million Americans nationwide listed themselves as multiracial. Identities blurred as popular entertainment created new mixes of traditions and styles. "World beat" music (heavily influenced by "Afro-Pop"), *Alternalatino* (alternative Latin music—a mixture of salsa and merengue), *bhangra* (a fusion of Punjabi music and African American hip-hop), and other musical mixtures became as common to Manhattan, Atlanta, or Los Angeles as to Mexico City, Rio, or Karachi.

At the same time, many native-born Americans became increasingly concerned about the impact of "illegal aliens" on their communities, particularly in California and throughout the Southwest. The Immigration Reform and Control Act of 1986 marked a break with the previous

Read the Document
Illegal Immigration Reform and Immigrant Responsibility Act at **www.myhistorylab.com**

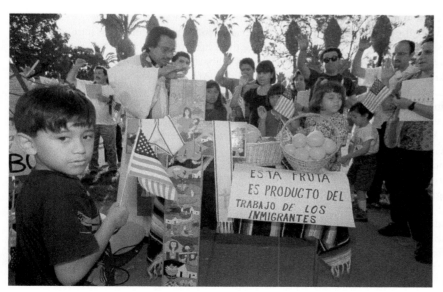

The sign at this 1996 vigil in Echo Park, Los Angeles, reads, "This fruit is the product of immigrants' labor." Members of the city's Latino community bless fruit baskets as they protest a state crackdown on illegal immigration and the increase of border patrol guards.

attempts to address this problem. Instead of mass deportation programs, the law strengthened the patrols along the border with Mexico and simultaneously offered amnesty to all undocumented workers who had entered the country since 1982. Four years later, additional revisions of this act enlarged the quota of immigrants, once again giving priority to skilled and professional workers. In many communities, however, opposition mounted. For example, in 1994, a California ballot initiative, Proposition 187, called for denying social services, public schooling, and health care to undocumented immigrants. In 1997, a federal judge ruled the law unconstitutional.

Growing Social Disparities

The prosperity of the 1990s, which encouraged immigration, did little to alleviate inequality. Although at the turn of the twenty-first century the poverty rate had dropped to 11.3 percent of the population, near the lowest level ever recorded, more than 31 million people still lived below the poverty level. Among other wealthy industrialized nations, the United States had the highest poverty rate by the end of the decade.

By 2000, the United States outstripped sixteen other developed countries in terms of income inequality. Roughly one in every eight Americans lived below the poverty line; the figure for children was one in five. Median family income was just below $40,000 per year. And the new economy had done little to close the gap between the highest and lowest income earners. To the contrary, while the poorest fifth of households saw their income decrease since 1990, the wealthiest fifth saw their income grow nearly 30 percent. In 1989, the average American CEO earned 89 times the pay of the average worker; by 2005, the ratio had soared to 262:1. Women as a group made few gains, earning 73 cents to each dollar earned by men. With African Americans and Latinos continuing to earn, on average, far less than non-Hispanic whites, race relations benefited little from the economic boom of the 1990s.

In the spring of 1992, an upheaval in Los Angeles offered the starkest evidence that racial tensions had not eased. Outrage over police brutality ignited the worst riot of the century. A year earlier, Rodney King, a black motorist, had been pulled from his vehicle and severely beaten by four white police officers. When, despite the graphic evidence of an amateur videotape of the incident, a jury acquitted the officers of all but one of eleven counts of assault, South Central Los Angeles erupted, with crowds looting and burning businesses throughout the community and into Koreatown. More than fifty people were killed, and 500 buildings were destroyed before L.A. police and National Guard troops restored order.

More than a quarter century after the uprising in Watts, the situation in South Central Los Angeles in 1992 seemed more desperate than ever to most African Americans. The poverty rate was 30.3 percent, more than twice the national average. The unemployment rate for adult black males hovered around 40 percent, and a quarter of the population was on welfare. Drug dealing and gang warfare had escalated, reflecting the sense of despair among young people.

The events in Los Angeles exposed the deep animosity among various groups—so much so that the observers referred to the event as a "multicultural riot." Almost 2,000 Korean businesses were destroyed, and Koreans angrily accused the police of making no effort to defend their stores. The division was sharpest, though, between whites and the minority populations. "We are all quite isolated in our own communities," a resident of Westwood, a mostly white upper-middle-class neighborhood, explained. "We don't know and don't care about the problems in the inner cities. Driving to work every day most of us don't even know where South Central is—except many of us saw the fires from that direction when we were stuck in traffic."

The situation in Los Angeles was not unique. Segregation was on the rise, not only in many large cities, but also in their surrounding suburbs. For example, in the Atlanta region, which claimed the largest share of black suburbanites in the nation (26 percent), the percentage living separately from whites had increased from 52 percent in 1990 to nearly 60 percent by 2000. Similarly, in the nation's schools, the gains from the civil rights era diminished and, in some communities, disappeared altogether. Despite the increasing racial and ethnic diversity of the nation's youth, segregation was more pronounced in grades K–12.

The U.S. criminal justice system reflected these disparities. Despite a drop in violent crime in the past twenty years, the prison population in the United States grew to be the largest prison population in the world. By 2009, one in 100 American adults were imprisoned, with ethnic and racial minorities accounting for the majority. The Bureau of Justice estimated that nearly one-third of African American men would enter a state or federal prison during their lifetimes.

Various civil liberties groups reviewed these statistics and concluded that African Americans were not necessarily more prone to criminal activity but were far more likely to be stopped, searched, arrested, convicted, and given harsher penalties than white Americans. Critics singled out the practice of "racial profiling," whereby police disproportionately stopped people of color as likely offenders. "Driving while black" headlined in all the major media, leading to the introduction of a bill in the U.S. Senate in 1999 to collect statistics on traffic stops.

The Culture Wars

At the 1992 Republican National Convention, the conservative Patrick Buchanan gave the opening speech. "There is a religious war going on in our country for the soul of America," he declared. "It is a cultural war, as critical to the

The California ballot initiative Proposition 187 was designed to deny basic social services, including health and education, to undocumented immigrants. To express their opposition to the legislation, as many as 250,000 people took the streets in downtown Los Angeles. This photograph shows Grace Lee and a group of fellow students demonstrating in the Westwood section of the city shortly after voters approved the bill known as "the last gasp of White America in California" on November 8, 1994.

kind of nation we will one day be as was the Cold War itself." Into the twenty-first century, politics focused on issues like reproductive rights and reproductive technology, homosexuality and gay rights, the curriculum in public schools, codes of speech and standards in the arts, gun control, and scientific developments such as cloning, genetic alteration, and fetal tissue research, and even the validity of Darwin's theory of evolution.

The growing racial and ethnic diversity of American society, as well as the expansion of rights for groups such as women and gays, had sparked a broad and controversial movement known as "multiculturalism." Unlike earlier descriptions of America as a "melting pot," new metaphors such as "salad bowl" or "mosaic" became popular expressions to call attention to the unique attributes and achievements of formerly marginal groups and recent immigrants. On college campuses, multiculturalism marked the high point of the curricular reform that had been ongoing since the late 1960s and early 1970s, when women's and ethnic studies programs were launched (see Chapter 29).

Similar controversies surrounded gay rights, particularly around a push for the legal recognition of civil unions and marriage for same-sex couples. In 1996, President Clinton responded to these challenges by signing the Defense of Marriage Act, which specified that gay couples would be ineligible for spousal benefits provided by federal law and that no state would be required to recognize

such marriages even if legally recognized in another state. In 2000, Vermont became the first state to recognize civil unions, allowing same-sex couples to receive many, although not all, of the legal benefits of marriage. Several other states passed versions of civil union or domestic partner laws. By 2010, five states, either by legislation or court ruling, had recognized the right of same sex couples to marry and receive state benefits. Meanwhile, thirty states passed constitutional amendments prohibiting same sex marriage. In June 2008, the California Supreme Court allowed the state to grant marriage licenses to same-sex couples, but a ballot initiative, Proposition 8, eliminated this right. In 2010 a federal district judge ruled the Proposition 8 initiative to be unconstitutional. The future of gay marriage remained unclear, but it would continue to be a powerful symbolic issue.

Women's reproductive rights also remained a prime "hot button" issue, with extreme opponents targeting providers of abortion services. Although the ratio of abortions to live pregnancies had declined since 1979, some antiabortion groups became more belligerent. Operation Rescue launched a well-publicized and illegal blockade of three abortion clinics in Wichita, Kansas, in September 1991. Although the "war in Wichita" ended peacefully after forty-six days, antiabortion protests became increasingly violent in its wake. Several medical providers were murdered outside their clinics. In 1994, with the support of President Clinton, Congress enacted the Freedom of Access to Clinic Entrance Act, which provides protection to any abortion clinic requesting it. The number of violent incidents declined from the peak of thirty-two bombings, arsons, or attempted attacks in 1992 and twelve murders or attempted murders in 1994. After the turn of the century, the attacks continued to diminish but did not stop. In May 2009, Dr. George Tiller, a Wichita physician who provided late-term abortions, was shot and killed at Sunday church services by antiabortion activist.

Nearly as volatile was the controversy sparked by government financing of an area of scientific research of growing importance since the birth of the first test-tube baby in 1981—human embryonic stem cell research. These microscopic clusters of cells have the potential to grow into any tissue in the body, so embryonic stem cells hold promise, scientists believe, for refurbishing or replacing damaged tissues or organs and, therefore, might prove useful in treating or perhaps even curing diseases such as diabetes, Parkinson's, and Alzheimer's. Religious

Illegal Immigrants and the Border Fence

In 2005, the House of Representatives initiated legislation to reform U.S. immigration policy, particularly to stem a flow of illegal immigrants now thought to have brought in 12 million people, more than half from Mexico. Opinions clashed, often along party lines, on proposals for amnesty programs, "guest worker" provisions, and the sanctioning and deportation of illegal migrants. One proposal proved especially divisive: a plan to construct a huge, high-tech, double-layered fence along the 2,000-mile U.S.-Mexico border, including powerful lighting, radar, cameras, and even unmanned aircraft. The Border Patrol would also be augmented by 1,500 new troops.

Politicians and experts on immigration reform heatedly debated these issues. The House ultimately passed the Border Protection, Antiterrorism, and Illegal Immigration Act of 2005, but the Senate initially refused to provide funding; only in September 2006 did the upper chamber vote $1.2 billion to construct a 700-mile fence, extending along just one-third of the 2,000-mile border separating the United States from Mexico. Senator Edward Kennedy (D-MA) voiced strong opposition, calling the new legislation "just a bumper sticker solution for a complex problem." Although most Republicans supported the measure, President Bush and some legislators feared that stringent measures would stem the flow of needed workers.

The most extreme opposition came from ultraconservatives, such as the superpatriotic organization Let Freedom Ring, which organized a petition and fund-raising campaign to support construction of the entire fence. Meanwhile, a paramilitary anti-immigration group, the Minutemen, illegally started patrolling the border and constructing a ten-mile-long iron and steel fence. In response, the Mexican government garnered support from twenty-seven other nations to express "deep concern regarding the decision adopted by the United States of America to build and extend a wall on its border with Mexico, considering it to be a unilateral measure that goes against the spirit of understanding."

Bill Richardson, who served in Congress for seventeen years and became governor of New Mexico in 2002, spoke for many Democrats, criticizing the proposed border fence and advocating comprehensive immigration reform that would address illegal immigration from Mexico. Richardson is of Hispanic American ancestry. Another viewpoint emerges in the statement of Jan C. Ting, a professor of law at Temple University and a former assistant commissioner of the U.S. Immigration and Naturalization Service, who in 2005 called for enhanced border security. Of Chinese American ancestry, Ting ran unsuccessfully for the U.S. Senate in Delaware.

Governor Bill Richardson Urges Comprehensive Immigration Reform (December 7, 2006)

Today, there are over 11 million illegal immigrants in the United States. Most are law abiding, except for the fact that they have entered this country illegally. And almost all have come here to work—to build a better life for themselves and their families, just as previous generations of immigrants have done.

Eleven million people living in the shadows is a huge problem, and we need to address it intelligently and thoughtfully—and urgently. If Congress fails to do so, it will only get worse, and the demagoguery about it which we have heard so much of recently will only get louder.

As the California-born son of an American father and a Mexican mother, I have known immigrants all my life and I know why they come to America. And as Governor of New Mexico I have known the problem of illegal immigration all too well—we live with this issue every day in my state.

> "No fence ever built has stopped history and this one wouldn't either."

Like it or not, these people have become part of the fabric of our economy and our culture. They have broken the law to enter our country, but they are here—there are millions of them building and cleaning our homes and offices, picking and cooking our food, caring for our children. These men and women are here illegally, but they work hard, pay taxes, and contribute to the communities they live in.

America needs to SOLVE this problem, not tear itself apart over it. . . .

Governors must promote public safety and ensure that all residents of the state—welcome or unwelcome, legally here or not—are productive, self-supporting, and law-abiding contributors to our community. But treating illegal immigrants like human beings won't make the problem go away. We also need to face up to the problem, and that begins with better border security.

Securing the border must come first—but we must understand that building a fence will not in any way accomplish that objective. No fence ever built has stopped history and this one wouldn't either. The Congress should abandon the fence, lock, stock, and barrel. It flies in the face of America as a symbol of freedom.

This is what we should do: immediately put enough National Guard troops at the border to keep it covered until we can secure it with Border Patrol officers. That should take no longer than three years. If it takes another year, let's do it.

Second, we must hire and train enough Border Guards to actually cover the entire border. I have spent a lot of time at the border and I

- **How do the writers of these documents employ different perspectives on American history to help make their case?**
- **Do you find contrasting ideals of American patriotism and national interest here as well?**

know we cannot secure it with a fence, but we can secure it with enough trained Border Patrol officers. I propose doubling the number of Border Patrol agents from approximately 12 thousand to 24 thousand. That would secure the border. And you could more than pay for it with the funding for the first segment of that ill-advised fence between Mexico and the United States. Real security, real results, at a fraction of the financial or political cost.

Third, we should give the Border Patrol the benefit of the best surveillance equipment available to our military. And, as suggested by Texas Congresswoman Sheila Jackson Lee, a leader on immigration issues, we should implement a system of "informant visas" and cash rewards for aliens who provide law enforcement with information on human traffickers and document forgers.

We should establish a "fraudulent documents task force" to constantly update law enforcement and border officials on the latest fraudulent documents being marketed for entry into the United States.

Finally, we have to work closely with the Mexican government. Illegal immigration is, at its root, primarily an economic problem: Mexicans need jobs and incomes, and Mexico benefits greatly from illegal immigration to the United States. It is a safety valve for their unemployed, and a major source of revenue in their economy, from the money illegal workers here send home.

Under present conditions, the Mexicans just don't have enough incentive to give us the help we need at the border. Mexico needs to do more to stem the flow. But if we create a reasonable guest worker program and provide a path to legalization for illegal immigrants already here . . . there is every reason to expect Mexico to do its part to create more jobs in Mexico and to help us with border security. . . .

SOURCE: Gov. Bill Richardson, "Speech on Comprehensive Immigration Reform at Georgetown University," Dec. 7, 2006. http://www.richardsonforpresident .com/issues/immigration.

Law Professor Jan C. Ting Considers "Immigration, National Security, and the Need for a Border Fence" (2005)

[I]t is supremely ironic that four years after 9/11 our national borders remain open and uncontrolled, and our government seems unconcerned. The simple reality is that tonight, four years after 9/11, and every night of the year, thousands of foreigners covertly enter the United States, and we have no idea who they are. Every night. Thousands. Who are they?

It's perhaps an overstatement to say we have no idea, because we do have some idea. We do catch some of them, and that provides us with a kind of sample of who is covertly crossing our borders into the U.S. in violation of our laws. But how big of a sample is it? The official estimate is that the Border Patrol catches 1 out of every 4 illegal border crossers, and this is typically the estimate public officials use in discussing the problem. Three get in for every one caught. But Border Patrol officers speaking off the record, and retired Border Patrol officials speaking for the record, say that the ratio of those getting in to those caught is much higher. . . .

Apprehensions along the southern border make up about 97–98% of the total apprehensions. Most of those apprehended near the southern border are Mexicans. . . .

Even though the number of Border Patrol apprehensions nationally and along the southern border has been fluctuating, the number of OTM's [Other Than Mexicans] apprehended near the southern border has been clearly and dramatically increasing from 28,598 in 2000 to 65,814 in 2004, despite a lower number of overall apprehensions in 2004. And we already have 100,142 OTM apprehensions for the first eight months of 2005. So the word is out to the rest of the world what the Mexicans have known for years. The border is wide open, and it's easy for anyone who wants to get into the United States covertly. . . .

Can it possibly be true that, although we can put a man on the moon, although we can put a rover on Mars and hit a comet in outer space with rockets, there's nothing we can do to stop people from walking across our borders into the United States? I think there's plenty that we could do if only we had the political will to do so. And I think it's remarkable that four years after 9/11 we still don't have the political will to do so. Are we not capable of building a fence like the one the Israelis have found effective in preventing terrorists from entering Israel? We can do it. We are in fact fortifying the westernmost 14 miles of our southern border. That leaves only 2,000 miles left on our southern border to go!

The fence is the essential element in any plan to limit illegal immigration across our border. The southern border is the first priority because of the large numbers of illegal entrants compared to our northern border. But we have already had at least one terrorist enter from Canada, so we must also address northern border security once the southern border fence is complete. The fence is essential. . . . Without the fence to control illegal immigration, no reform of immigration is possible. Any reform will fail under the rising tide of illegal immigration and the dangers that accompany it.

SOURCE: Jan C. Ting "Immigration, National Security, and the Need for a Border Fence" Sept. 9, 2005. http://www.letfreedomringusa.com/Fileuploads/.

"The fence is the essential element in any plan to limit illegal immigration. . . ."

Rescue workers carried an injured man from the rubble of the U.S. Embassy in Nairobi, Kenya. A terrorist bomb killed more than 100 people and injured more than 1,600 on August 8, 1998.

conservatives opposed this research because it may involve the destruction of human embryos, usually derived from the excess products of *in vitro* fertilization processes and scheduled for disposal by fertility clinics. In 1995, in response to pressure from conservative groups such as the National Right to Life Committee, Congress enacted legislation banning the use of federal funds for research that involves the destruction of human embryos. However, in his last year in office, President Clinton loosened the ban and thereby generated another round of controversy. Most Christian conservative groups remained firm in their opposition, agreeing with the United States Conference of Catholic Bishops, which insisted "that the government must not treat any living human being as research material, as a mere means for benefit to others."

President George W. Bush and the War on Terror

The end of the Cold War had reconfigured global politics, ending the bilateralism that had dominated international affairs since the end of World War II. The United States alone held fast to its superpower status, but this achievement did not necessarily make Americans more secure or safe. The old enemy, Soviet communism, was succeeded by more-fanatic, less-predictable foes.

On September 11, 2001, a devastating attack on the World Trade Center in New York City and other targets proved critical for Clinton's successor, who had taken office just nine months earlier. George W. Bush, the forty-third president, speedily reconfigured U.S. foreign policy around the strategy of a "war on terror." As a part of that strategy, in 2003 he ordered an invasion of Iraq, which he

and his advisors warned harbored not only terrorists but also stockpiles of weapons of mass destruction. The prolonged war that resulted defined the Bush presidency more than any other issue.

The Election of 2000

George W. Bush's election campaign played out as high drama. Voters went to the polls as usual on election day, watched as late-night television newscasters projected a victory for the Democratic candidate, Clinton's vice president Al Gore, and then woke up the next morning to learn that perhaps the winner was not the vice president but his Republican opponent, Governor George W. Bush of Texas, son of former president George H. W. Bush. It was clear that Gore and his running mate, Connecticut Senator Joseph Lieberman, had won the popular vote, although by the closest margin since John F. Kennedy defeated Richard Nixon in 1961. In doubt was the number of votes in the Electoral College. The cliffhanger ended early the next morning when Florida earmarked the state's decisive twenty-five electoral votes for the Republicans. Gore called Bush to concede. Bush's margin of victory in Florida was only a few hundred votes, however, so narrow that Florida law mandated a machine recount in all sixty-seven counties. Gore soon retracted his concession (see Map 31.1).

The 2000 campaign resulted in the first disputed presidential election since 1876, when Democrat Samuel J. Tilden won the popular vote. His Republican opponent, Rutherford B. Hayes, assumed the presidency only after a special Congressional committee, split along partisan lines, awarded him the electoral vote (see Chapter 17). A similar question of legitimacy hung over the 2000 election. After

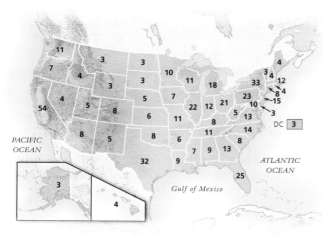

	Electoral Vote (%)	Popular Vote (%)
GEORGE W. BUSH (Republican)	271 (50.5)	50,456,169 (48.0)
Al Gore (Democrat)	266 (49.5)	50,996,116 (48.0)

MAP 31.1 The Election of 2000 The 2000 presidential election was the closest one in U.S. history and the first one to be decided by a decision of the Supreme Court.

Florida completed its machine recount of votes, the Democrats requested a hand tally in selected counties where the ballots were in dispute. The Republicans responded by suing in the Miami district court to prohibit the manual recounting. Meanwhile, Florida election officials, mainly Republicans, set November 14 as the date to certify the election results, thereby disallowing the returns on overseas ballots that might favor Al Gore. In turn, Democrats sued to extend the deadline. Eventually, appeals by both parties reached the Florida Supreme Court and finally the U.S. Supreme Court, which voted five to four along partisan lines to halt the counting. Time had run out, and on December 12, Gore conceded defeat, despite having received over 500,000 more votes than Bush. With less fanfare than usual, George W. Bush took the oath of office in January 2001.

Terrorist Attack on America

On September 11, 2001, hijackers, armed only with knives and box cutters, crashed two jetliners into New York's World Trade Center towers, while a third jetliner slammed into the Pentagon in Virginia. A fourth plane, diverted from its terrorist mission by courageous passengers, hurtled to the ground near Pittsburgh. In all,

246 people perished in the four planes. At the sites of the attack, the damage was devastating. At the Pentagon, the death toll soon reached 184, including 59 people who had been on board the hijacked airliner. In New York City, the collapse of the twin towers killed 2,752 people, including hundreds of police and rescue workers who had run into the buildings to help. The stark images of the second plane hitting the World Trade Center, the dramatic collapse of the buildings, and the fear on the faces of thousands fleeing the sites were replayed over and over again on televisions throughout the world (see Seeing History).

The terrorist attacks on September 11, 2001 shocked most Americans, although anxiety about terrorism and random violence had escalated during the 1990s. A small group of Arab Islamist terrorists had bombed the World Trade Center on February 26, 1993, killing six people and injuring more than a thousand others. Undertaken in retaliation for U.S. intervention in the Middle East, the attack was the most destructive act of foreign terrorism committed within the United States to that time. It spurred the Antiterrorism and Effective Death Penalty Act of 1996, which greatly expanded the budget and powers of federal authorities to monitor likely terrorists. Despite increased surveillance, terrorists struck another lethal blow. On August 7, 1998, car bombings of U.S. embassies in Kenya and Tanzania injured more than 4,000 people and killed 220. And on October 12, 2000, terrorists bombed the USS *Cole*, anchored in Aden, Yemen, killing seventeen American sailors.

The September 11, 2001 attacks, however, sparked a massive response. While the media recalled Pearl Harbor, President Bush declared the deadly attacks an act of war and vowed to hunt down those responsible for the "evil,

More than 5,000 activists gathered in Seattle in November 1999 to demonstrate against the meeting of the World Trade Organization. The event, which was marked by a violent clash with police and the arrest of dozens of protestors, marked the beginning of a movement for global economic justice.

The 9/11 Attacks

SEEING History

The first plane hit at 8:48 A.M.; the second, at 9:03 A.M. Then, as millions of disbelieving television viewers watched, the 110-story Twin Towers collapsed. Already, many Americans were saying that they would forever remember where they were and what they were doing when they heard the news.

Journalists and ordinary Americans alike repeatedly invoked two twentieth-century catastrophes as parallels to 9/11: the Japanese attack at Pearl Harbor on December 7, 1941, and the assassination of John F. Kennedy on November 22, 1963. Neither of the earlier disasters played out in real time over modern media, however.

The World Trade Center attack occurred virtually before the eyes of millions. Video cameras caught the image of the second plane hitting the South Tower, panic on the faces of those fleeing, smoke billowing from the towers, and their collapse. Reporters were soon pulling comments from traumatized survivors. The networks immediately preempted regular programming and allowed millions of horrified Americans to watch endless replays. Newscasters drew out the Pearl Harbor analogy as another "Day of Infamy." Within days, programmers edited the videotapes to enhance the drama—adding images of cell phones (to remind viewers of the final calls many of the victims made), overlaying images of the collapsing towers with an unfurling American flag, and piping in patriotic music. To enhance the emotional impact, they borrowed such cinematic techniques as slowing the pace and using jump cuts that fast-timed images of the burning towers with close-ups of anguished observers' faces.

Some seventy history-oriented institutions created an Internet site, 911history.net, to collect oral histories and artifacts. Said Diane Kresh of the Library of Congress, "The Internet has become for many the public commons, a place where they can come together and talk." Importance of the Internet aside, the searing pictures of the burning towers will likely remain the preeminent image for 9/11.

• **What role did the media play in shaping our understanding of the events of September 11, 2001?**

• **How does the ability of modern media to dramatize the horror and immediacy of such events enhance their "value" to terrorists launching attacks?**

• **In what ways did the 9/11 attacks facilitate the Bush administration's decision to go to war in Iraq?**

despicable acts of terror." Congress, with only one dissenting vote, granted him power to take whatever steps necessary. For the first time ever, NATO invoked the mutual defense clause in its founding treaty, which in effect supported any U.S. military action.

Observers described Bush's response as the defining moment of his presidency, as it was for many Americans. Millions rushed to donate blood, and thousands traveled to New York to assist rescue efforts. Prayer vigils were held in churches, synagogues, mosques, public buildings, and parks, and flags were displayed on homes and cars. Millions of dollars were soon raised for the relief effort and to assist the families of those who perished. Perhaps most dramatic was the unprecedented shutdown of all airports in the United States, stranding thousands around the world. Service returned several days later at greatly reduced levels and with enhanced security. Fear had chilled most Americans' spirit. Two-thirds of those polled believed the worst might still come.

The day following the highly coordinated terrorist attack, President Bush identified the Saudi Arabian Osama bin Laden as the prime suspect and linked the airline hijackers, all presumed to be Islamic fundamentalists, to his Al Qaeda network. In 1998, bin Laden had issued a decree that granted religious legitimacy to all efforts to expel the United States from the lands of Islam in the Middle East. He had based Al Qaeda's operations in Afghanistan, where he enjoyed the protection of a government run by the Taliban, a radical Islamist group. Although a communiqué from bin Laden denied involvement, U.S. intelligence sources insisted that only bin Laden had the resources to carry out such a sophisticated operation and sufficient motivation. His network of terrorist cells, which reportedly operated in sixty countries, had directed rage at what they believe to be the global arrogance of the United States.

Reshaping U.S. Foreign Policy

At a memorial service for victims, President Bush warned: "Our responsibility to history is already clear: to answer these attacks and rid the world of evil." He then outlined a new approach to U.S. foreign policy. "From this day forward," he announced, "any nation that continues to harbor or support terrorists will be regarded by the United States as a hostile regime." The first theater of the campaign against terrorism would be Afghanistan. With the support of a United Nations Security Council resolution, the United States delivered an ultimatum to the Taliban-dominated government of Afghanistan: hand over Osama bin Laden and other Al Qaeda leaders presumed to be responsible, and close all terrorist training camps immediately and unconditionally.

On October 7, after the Taliban had refused to comply, President Bush announced the beginning of Operation

•◦•–Read the Document

George W. Bush, Address to Congress (2001) at
www.myhistorylab.com

Enduring Freedom, a joint American-British military campaign aimed at capturing bin Laden and overthrowing the Taliban regime that had sheltered him. An aerial bombing campaign targeted Taliban and Al Qaeda forces, while U.S. Special Forces launched a raid deep into the Taliban stronghold of Kandahar, in southeastern Afghanistan. Fierce fighting continued through December as U.S.-led coalition troops grew to a force of over 10,000. The Taliban government toppled, but bin Laden and much of the Al Qaeda leadership escaped, presumably into a mountainous region of Pakistan. Despite a massive manhunt and the aid of Pakistan's government, American forces proved unable to capture him.

In his January 2002 State of the Union address, President Bush expanded on his vision of a global war on terrorism. He argued that America now faced a grave and unprecedented danger not merely from Al Qaeda terrorists but also from nation-states seeking chemical, biological, or nuclear weapons of mass destruction. He denounced the regimes of North Korea, Iran, and Iraq as an "axis of evil, arming to threaten the peace of the world." The United States, the president promised, "will not permit the world's most dangerous regimes to threaten us with the world's most destructive weapons."

The new focus on the threat of weapons of mass destruction formed a central part of a sweeping reformulation of American foreign policy. In the fall of 2002, the Bush administration released a new National Security Strategy Report that offered the most radical revision of American foreign policy since the Truman administration in the early days of the Cold War (see Chapter 26). It argued that "the struggle against global terrorism is different from any other war in our history," requiring the United States to "deter and defend against the threat before it is unleashed," acting preemptively and alone if necessary.

•◦•–Read the Document

George W. Bush, From National Security Strategy of the U.S. (2002) at
www.myhistorylab.com

The war on terrorism had a domestic front as well. The partisan bitterness of the 2000 election largely dissolved amid post–9/11 calls for national unity, making it easier for the Bush administration to push new legislation through Congress. Signed into law in the fall of 2001, the USA Patriot Act gave federal officials greater authority to track and intercept communications for law-enforcement and intelligence-gathering purposes, new powers to curb foreign money laundering, and broader discretion in tightening borders against suspected foreign terrorists. It created new crimes and penalties against suspected domestic and international terrorists. In the months after the 9/11 attacks, more than a thousand Muslims, some of them U.S. citizens, were arrested and detained, the largest such roundup since the Palmer Raids following World War I (see Chapter 22). Only a few of these suspects were actually charged with crimes related to terrorism. Congress passed the USA

Patriot Act II in 2003, further expanding the ability of law-enforcement and intelligence-gathering authorities to perform surveillance and authorize secret arrests.

The Bush administration also created a new cabinet-level Department of Homeland Security (DHS), consolidating twenty-two different domestic agencies to coordinate the nation's defense against military threats. Its components included the Immigration and Naturalization Service, the U.S. Customs Service, the Secret Service, the Coast Guard, and the Federal Emergency Management Agency. It was no surprise that it proved quite difficult to combine so many huge federal bureaucracies into one effective whole. Critics of the new department worried especially about the continued vulnerability of the nation's ports, rail system, chemical facilities, and nuclear plants to terrorist attacks.

Many questions remained unanswered about the events and circumstances surrounding the 9/11 attacks, particularly the multiple failures within the U.S. intelligence community. The Bush administration at first resisted efforts to mount a full-scale inquiry. Pressure from the families of 9/11 victims, as well as widespread calls for a bipartisan investigation, forced the administration to reverse its opposition, and in November 2002, Congress established the National Commission on Terrorist Attacks upon the United States. In July 2004, the panel of five Democrats and five Republicans issued its final report—which became an instant best seller—concluding that the government "failed to protect the American people" because it did not understand the "gravity of the threat." The report underscored the bureaucratic rivalry between the CIA and FBI, which made it difficult to act despite clear evidence that "Islamist terrorists mean to kill Americans in high numbers."

Invasion of Iraq

The president's pledge to confront threats to security before they reached American shores—a policy of "preemptive defense"—became known as the Bush Doctrine, and its first major test was Iraq. Planning for a U.S.-led invasion and the overthrow of Saddam Hussein had actually begun in the first weeks after the September 11 attacks. President Bush himself had come to believe that "regime change" was necessary, and several major figures in his administration focused their attention on making that case to the nation and the world. Vice President Dick Cheney, Secretary of Defense Donald Rumsfeld, and his deputy secretary, Paul Wolfowitz, had all worked for Bush's father, President George H. W. Bush, and they viewed removal of Saddam as the unfinished business of the Persian Gulf War of 1991. Along with National Security Adviser Condoleeza Rice and a more reluctant Secretary of State Colin Powell, these aides began to plan for war in early 2002.

Proponents of war reiterated three central arguments in various public speeches, in testimony before Congress,

and finally at the United Nations. First, Saddam Hussein must be removed by force because he possessed biological and chemical weapons—weapons of mass destruction—and was planning to develop nuclear weapons. Second, they argued that Saddam's intelligence services had direct connections to the September 11 hijackers and to Al Qaeda operatives around the world. Third, toppling Saddam would make possible a democratic Iraq that could then serve as a herald of political change throughout the Middle East and Muslim world. The majority of the Iraqi people, they asserted, would welcome and support a U.S.-led campaign to oust the brutal dictator, ensuring a swift and fairly painless victory.

Throughout late 2002 and early 2003, while U.S. military planners prepared for battle, opponents of war refuted the arguments of the Bush administration. Many political analysts and veteran diplomats doubted that Saddam had the weapon capability credited to him. They charged that Vice President Cheney and Secretary Rumsfeld had manipulated Pentagon intelligence estimates to make their case. Others doubted Saddam's links

President George W. Bush announces the end of major combat operations in Iraq, May 1, 2003, speaking on the deck of the aircraft carrier USS *Abraham Lincoln*, anchored near San Diego. A banner proclaimed "Mission Accomplished," but American troops would continue to face stiff opposition and endure thousands of casualties battling Iraqi insurgents.

to Al Qaeda and argued that war with Iraq would sideline the hunt for bin Laden. A growing number of Americans questioned the assumption that removing Saddam would make America safer, envisioning an invasion instead as a boost to the recruitment efforts of Al Qaeda and other terrorist organizations. Millions of citizens began organizing against the push for war via Internet organizations such as MoveOn.org and in vigils and gatherings in their local communities.

The antiwar movement went global. On February 15, 2003, millions of demonstrators turned out in more than 300 cities, including 500,000 in New York, 2 million in London, and 1 million in Rome. This was the single largest expression of antiwar sentiment in history.

Meanwhile, Secretary of State Powell tried but failed to gain support for war from the UN Security Council. Facing staunch opposition from France, Russia, and Germany, the Bush administration decided to invade Iraq with what it called a "coalition of the willing," with Great Britain as its major partner. On March 19, President Bush announced

the beginning of war, claiming the United States "has the sovereign authority to use force in assuring its own national security." He also told Iraqis "the tyrant will soon be gone; the day of your liberation is near" (see Map 31.2).

Some 150,000 U.S. troops, along with a smaller British force, began a thrust toward Baghdad, while a "shock and awe" campaign of massive aerial bombing targeted several major Iraqi cities. The American and British forces overwhelmed the regular Iraqi army fairly easily and secured Baghdad and several other major cities. On May 1, 2003, on the flight deck of the USS *Abraham Lincoln*, anchored off the San Diego coast, President Bush appeared before a cheering throng of American sailors and a live television audience. Standing beneath a large banner reading "Mission Accomplished," Bush announced the official end of combat operations. "In the battle of Iraq," the president declared, "the United States and our allies have prevailed."

The purely military act of removing Saddam's regime from power proved far simpler than bringing peace and

MAP 31.2 Invasion in Iraq On March 20, 2003, American and British troops poured into Iraq from bases in Kuwait, crossing the Iraqi border to the east near Safwan. The American Third Infantry Division used armored bulldozers to create wide gaps in the Iraqi defensive line.

stability to Iraq. The invasion turned into an occupation, and the plight of ordinary Iraqis and American soldiers worsened quickly. Amid widespread civil disorder and massive looting, millions of Iraqis had their electricity, water, and basic food supplies disrupted. Well-organized resistance movements fought back and also fought among themselves. Tensions between major religious groups fueled the insurgency, as Sunni Muslims feared the loss of their traditional power to the majority Shiites. While UN relief workers, journalists, and private American contractors poured into the country to help with reconstruction efforts, a violent campaign of suicide bombings, shootings, roadside ambushes, and kidnappings spread across Iraq. The American invasion created about 4.5 million refugees in Iraq, roughly half of whom fled the country. Rather than weaken terrorists, the U.S. occupation instead strengthened a new generation of terror networks now drawn to do battle with U.S. forces in Iraq.

In early 2004, the well-coordinated, heavily armed, and well-financed resistance to the American occupation gained strength. Badly stretched U.S. forces, which included a high percentage of National Guard and Army Reserve units, were forced back into combat. A year after President Bush had confidently declared the fighting over, American troops engaged in the toughest fighting since the Vietnam War.

Troubling new questions about the decision to invade and the conduct of the war emerged. In early 2004, David Kay, the Bush administration's former chief weapons inspector, told Congress that any stockpiles of weapons of mass destruction Saddam might have possessed in the early 1990s had been destroyed by UN inspections and Iraq's own actions. Nor was there any nuclear weapons program. In the spring of 2004, graphic images and descriptions of Iraqi detainees abused and tortured by American guards in the Abu Ghraib prison were broadcast around the world, inciting international outrage and protest. In public, President Bush expressed "a deep disgust that those prisoners were treated the way they were treated." White House memos, however, revealed that the president's legal counsel Alberto Gonzales had urged Bush to declare the war on terror and the treatment of Al Qaeda and Taliban prisoners exempt from the provisions of the Geneva Convention.

In January 2005, Iraq conducted its first national elections for an assembly charged with writing a new constitution by 2006. Amidst enormous media coverage, the Bush administration hailed the elections as a historic step toward democracy. Saddam Hussein was finally captured in a U.S. military operation in December 2003 and executed three years later after an Iraqi Special Tribunal found him guilty of crimes against humanity.

The occupation continued to take a heavy toll on U.S. forces. Military commanders found themselves strapped for replacement troops. Tens of thousands of National Guard and Army Reserve soldiers were forced to stay in Iraq beyond their regular tour of duty, subject in effect to a "backdoor draft." When they finally returned home, nearly one-third of troops presented signs of mental illness. By 2005, over 1,500 Americans had been killed in Iraq and nearly 12,000 wounded, many of them severely. Estimates of Iraqi civilian deaths ranged as high as 100,000. The Iraq War also put a heavy strain on the federal budget. The cost of deploying one soldier for one year neared $400,000 and total expenditures pushed toward $800 billion. Military spending on the war on terrorism during Bush's administration helped push the deficit to a record high.

Bush's "Compassionate Conservatism"

National security and the war on terrorism became the keynotes in Bush's 2004 reelection campaign. With Iraq dominating the news, he described himself as a "wartime president" and appealed to patriotism and national unity.

Democrats, although still smarting from the disputed 2000 election, believed their chances for retaking the White House were strong and nominated the Vietnam War hero Senator John Kerry of Massachusetts as their presidential candidate. However, their campaign quickly faltered. Republicans attacked Kerry's war record, claiming that his Purple Hearts and other citations had been undeserved. Moreover, Kerry's patrician background, distant personality, and cool manner made it difficult for many voters to warm up to him. Perhaps most damaging, Kerry waffled on his position on the Iraq war.

President Bush won reelection with 51 percent of the popular vote to Kerry's 48 percent, a 3-million-vote margin. The results could be interpreted in a variety of ways. Bush polled the first popular vote majority in twenty years and the overall turnout of 60 percent was the highest since 1968. Republicans fielded a formidable grassroots get-out-the-vote operation, especially in small-town and rural America, where they appealed effectively to many voters on so-called "moral values" issues: opposition to gay marriage and abortion rights. Republicans also increased their majorities in both the House and the Senate. However, Bush's victory margin was also the smallest for reelection in a century. Though not as close as the 2000 election, few would dispute that the 2004 election revealed a nation that was as politically divided as any time since the Civil War. President Bush himself interpreted the 2004 election results as support for the Iraq war and as a mandate for the "compassionate conservatism" that marked his first administration. On the domestic front, he promised to spend his "political capital" by advancing the Republican agenda that President Reagan had shaped: tax cuts, strong military defense, and the overhaul of Social Security and Medicare.

Lowering federal income taxes became an important signature of the Bush presidency. During his first term, Bush promoted the Economic Growth and Tax Relief

Reconciliation Act, which had squeaked through Congress with bipartisan support in 2001. The act lowered tax rates, disproportionately for the wealthy, and gave most Americans a small rebate from the IRS as "reconciliation" for paying too much in taxes. While many Americans did see a decline in their income tax payments, many found that increases in local property taxes, college tuitions, and other fees more than made up for the savings.

Domestically, Bush's earliest Congressional victory came with the No Child Left Behind Act, a response to data indicating that more than one-third of Americans were "functionally illiterate," that is, unable to read well enough to get along. Among developed nations, the American educational system, once the envy of the world, now ranked near the bottom. In 2001, Congress, with support by Democratic Senator Edward Kennedy, mobilized to pass a sweeping educational reform bill. The act provided for the implementation of standards and assessments for math and reading skills for children in grades three to eight and allowed parents to transfer their children out of schools that did not reach these goals. Bush also promoted abstinence-based sex education in the public schools, a program initiated during Clinton's administration, even though it failed to prevent teenage birthrates from rising.

Bush won a decisive victory in gaining approval for the addition of a prescription drug benefit to Medicare. This bill, which included a $400 billion price tag, helped older Americans cover the skyrocketing costs of prescription medicine while providing huge subsidies to drug manufacturers and private insurers. The bill passed Congress in 2003 as the most extensive expansion of Medicare since its creation in 1965. However, Bush failed in his persistent efforts to "reinvent Social Security." Congress refused to heed Bush's call for a major overhaul of the popular New Deal–era social insurance program by substituting private investment accounts. Moreover, national statistics indicated that the typical American family made no economic gains since he took office; adjusted for inflation, the median household income had sunk since Clinton's final year in office. During his second term, President Bush saw the post–9/11 political consensus largely dissolve as victory in Iraq, as well as the larger "war on terror," proved elusive and increasingly difficult to define.

The Bush administration endured a heated and prolonged controversy sparked by its response to one of the most cataclysmic events of the new century—Hurricane Katrina. On August 25, the third strongest hurricane to make landfall in the United States made its way through Florida, killing six people, destroying homes, and uprooting trees before heading into the Gulf of Mexico. Local officials called for the evacuation of New Orleans, a city below sea level, and opened the Superdome "as a refuge of last resort." President Bush directed the Federal

A U.S. Coast Guard helicopter rescues flood-stranded victims of Hurricane Katrina from their homes in New Orleans, September 2005. Images like this one received wide circulation in the news media, prompting criticism of the government's failures to offer more and swifter help to Katrina's victims.

Emergency Management Agency (FEMA) to coordinate federal assistance to state and local governments in the case of disaster.

Hurricane Katrina struck New Orleans on August 31 and destroyed several parishes, including the Lower Ninth Ward, the home to an African American population already steeped in poverty. Canal levees failed, submerging 80 percent of the city. President Bush, who had been vacationing at his ranch in Crawford, Texas, did not rush to the area but instead four days later flew over in *Air Force One* on his early return to the White House. Meanwhile, the rescue operations stalled amid bureaucratic mishaps. Conditions at the Superdome deteriorated to a point that newscasters described a reign of anarchy. Shortages of food, water, blankets, sanitary facilities, and medical supplies put the lives of the 5,000 refugees at risk. Only slowly did FEMA relocate staff to the area and, worse, actually hampered private relief efforts. Television crews captured scenes of people stranded on rooftops, waiting rescue while the waters continued to rise, and bodies floating in the streets.

The press largely vilified President Bush, labeling his response to this disaster as "a national disgrace." Much of the shame resulted from the way unfolding events underscored the race and class dimensions of the tragedy. The population of New Orleans, with a poverty rate 76 percent higher than the national average, was two-thirds African American, and more than a quarter of those black citizens of New Orleans lacked access to an automobile. When the mandatory evacuation order came, the majority of white residents drove away from the city, while many black residents had no choice but to board the special buses headed for the ill-equipped Superdome. A news poll indicated that 60 percent of African Americans believed that race was a major factor in the government's slow and inefficient rescue efforts.

More than 1,600 people had died in New Orleans alone, and nearly a million had fled the greater region. Only very slowly did business activity—especially tourism in the French Quarter—revive. President Bush was left with the legacy of having one of the nation's most important cities nearly destroyed during his administration.

Divided Government, Divided Nation

The 2006 midterm elections, occurring in the aftermath of Hurricane Katrina, brought a return of the divided government that had characterized the Clinton years. This time, however, the parties and players were reversed. Democrats took control of both the House (233–202) and the Senate (51–49) for the first time since 1992. A record-breaking number of women were elected to Congress, and Nancy Pelosi (D-CA) became the first woman to serve as Speaker of the House.

The new Congress tried to put limits on the president's requests for war funding. Although a large number of Democrats had originally supported the invasion, many had since changed their minds and now believed that a military "victory" was both impossible and an illusion. Democrats tried to attach deadlines for withdrawal to the president's funding bills, but enjoying only a narrow majority, they could not override President Bush's vetoes.

Rather than scaling back, President Bush asked for yet greater funding, a total of $170 billion for 2007, for the war. In January, he unveiled his new and costly plan, a "surge" of some 30,000 additional American troops to Iraq. The goal was to clamp down on sectarian violence and thereby create space for the shaky Iraqi political system to govern more effectively. The Bush administration touted the success of its new strategy, pointing to a substantial decline in both political violence and attacks on U.S. forces throughout 2007–8. In September 2008, the president announced a plan to withdraw about 4,500 troops, with a little more than half deployed to Afghanistan.

Even though the "surge" represented a tactical success, the larger picture in Iraq remained grim. The Iraqi government proved unable to provide basic security and services in many parts of the country. A poll conducted in September 2007 indicated that 80 percent of Iraqis believed that conditions had worsened since the escalation began. Some 2 million Iraqis, including much of the nation's educated middle class and professionals, fled the country to nearby nations such as Syria, Jordan, and Egypt. Another 2 million Iraqis, forced to leave their neighborhoods and towns, found themselves refugees within their own country. Moreover, violence continued. Total Iraqi deaths from the war were hard to calculate, and estimates

ranged from 100,000 to over 600,000. Although the number of American casualties dropped from their peak in 2007, by the time President Bush left office in 2009, nearly 4,400 American troops had been killed in Iraq and more than 31,600 wounded, many of them gravely.

By the end of his second term, President Bush faced growing disillusionment with the Iraq War, the single issue that most clearly defined his presidency. He continued to defend the war as part of a broader, long-term struggle against global terrorism carried out by well-armed Islamic extremists. By this time, the argument had lost credibility. Newly released classified documents showed no direct link between Al Qaeda and Saddam Hussein and, moreover, no weapons of mass destruction in Iraq, as Bush had charged. While the president blamed "false intelligence," the Senate Intelligence Committee concluded in 2008 that the Bush administration had knowingly "misrepresented the intelligence and the threat from Iraq." Although the Iraq war remained a distant reality for the vast majority of Americans, intensive television and press coverage kept the bloody stalemate front and center in the nation's consciousness. The financial cost of the Iraq war, moreover, affected everyone.

To fund the wars in Afghanistan and Iraq and the open-ended war on terror, Bush pushed the deficit to record levels. When he left office, the federal debt had reached an estimated $1.3 trillion. Moreover, whereas in the previous decades, the federal debt was held by Americans in the form of government securities, about 45 percent was now held mainly by foreign governments, with Japan and China the largest creditors. This situation prompted the International Monetary Fund to issue a report stating that the "large U.S. fiscal deficits posed a significant risk for the rest of the world." President Bush left office with nearly three-quarters of Americans disapproving of the way he had governed during his two terms. Approximately two-thirds of those polled had also come to oppose the Iraq war.

Barack Obama and the Audacity of Hope

The 2008 election followed one of the most dramatic election campaigns in modern U.S. history and brought the first African American to the presidency of the United States. Running on a platform promising change, Barack Obama inspired many Americans, especially young people and first-time voters, to get involved in his quest for the White House. The nation's worst economic downturn since the Great Depression of the 1930s also loomed over the political landscape, raising fundamental questions about the strength and the future of the nation's economy.

Watch the Video
The Historical Significance of the 2008 Presidential Election at **www.myhistorylab.com**

The Election of 2008

On January 20, 2009, 143 years after the end of slavery, Barack Hussein Obama took the oath as the nation's first African American president. The nation and the world were mesmerized by the deep symbolism of this truly historic moment. Only a year earlier, such a prospect seemed highly unlikely, even impossible in the eyes of most Americans. How did a young, black, largely unknown, first-term Democratic U.S. Senator produce such a stunning breakthrough in the 2008 election? The winds of political change had already started blowing with the Democrats taking back control of both the House and Senate in 2006. They focused on the Bush Administration's poor performance after Hurricane Katrina, the persistent unpopularity of the Iraq war, and growing fears over a stalled economy. The Republicans looked vulnerable—and for the first time since 1928, neither party had a sitting president or vice president who would be a natural front-runner for the nomination, leaving a wide-open field for both parties.

When Senator Obama announced his candidacy for president in January 2007, he was relatively unknown outside Illinois. The vast majority of the nation's political class—office holders, pollsters, campaign operatives, and pundits—believed his unconventional background and life story made him an improbable and unelectable nominee. Born in 1961, the mixed-race child of a Kenyan father and a white Kansan mother who had met in Hawaii, Obama

((•—[Hear the **Audio**

Barack Obama, Excerpt from The Audacity of Hope at **www.myhistorylab.com**

had grown up in an extended multiracial family. After his father abandoned the family when he was two years old, Obama spent portions of his boyhood in Hawaii and Indonesia, shuttling between his anthropologist mother and his white grandparents. After graduating from New York's Columbia University in 1983, Obama moved to Chicago where he worked for five years as a community organizer among low-income residents whose neighborhoods had been devastated by the loss of manufacturing jobs. The goal was to help empower poor people to gain more influence in city politics. He then moved on to Harvard Law School, graduating in 1991 as the first African American editor of the prestigious law review. He returned to Chicago, working as a civil rights attorney and lecturer at the University of Chicago Law School and organizing voter registration drives for Bill Clinton's 1992 presidential campaign.

Obama made the leap into electoral politics in 1996, and won election to the Illinois State Senate. After an unsuccessful campaign for Congress, he set his sights on the U.S. Senate. In 2002, while still a state senator, he began to attract national attention for his vocal opposition to the American invasion of Iraq. After winning the Democratic Senate nomination, Obama was invited to give the keynote address at the 2004 National Democratic convention, where he impressed the national audience with his unique blend of cool demeanor and passionate oratory, and his emphasis on what united, rather than what divided, Americans. That fall, Obama became only the third African-American elected to the U.S. Senate since Reconstruction.

Obama launched his campaign for the presidency barely two years later. Unlike his main rival for the nomination, Sen. Hillary Rodham Clinton (D-NY), he had no political machine, no fund-raising apparatus, and little national reputation. He did have a carefully thought-out electoral strategy that relied heavily on his experiences as a community organizer. He focused on registering new voters, especially among the young and people of color. He defined himself as an outsider, looking to shake up Washington's "politics as usual." Although his policy positions largely reflected those of mainstream liberal Democrats—reform of health care, more funding for education, new public investment in infrastructure, for example—he carefully framed his appeals to attract independent voters and even Republicans disgruntled with the Bush presidency. His surprise victory in the January 2008 Iowa caucuses vindicated his strategy, proved his appeal to white voters, and revealed his campaign's fund-raising prowess.

Hillary Clinton emerged as Obama's main rival, and their battle for the Democratic nomination continued into the spring and across a string of primary states. An accomplished attorney, former First Lady, a savvy campaigner and fund-raiser, and influential U.S. Senator, her status as a pioneer for women in politics added a special dimension to her appeal. Millions of Democrats, including most African American elected officials, believed Hillary Clinton would make the strongest candidate to take back the White House. Throughout their primary battles, the fundamental issue of race simmered in media coverage and soured the increasingly tense relations between the campaigns—could a black candidate actually get elected? The issue boiled over in March 2008 when highly controversial videos of Rev. Jeremiah Wright, the longtime pastor of Obama's church in Chicago, surfaced. Wright's militant oratory, fusing Black Nationalist rhetoric and anti-American epithets, received endless replay on television and the Internet. The uproar raised questions about why Obama had not left the church, jeopardized his carefully crafted message of racial unity, and threatened to sink the campaign.

In response, Obama took on Rev. Wright and the broader issue of race in American history in a speech delivered at the National Constitution Center in Philadelphia. He offered a condensed review of the nation's racial history, acknowledging the racial resentments of both African Americans and working-class whites. He invoked his own multiracial background and family experiences, "a story that has seared into my genetic makeup the idea that this nation is more than the sum of its parts—that out of many, we are truly one." Obama stressed the progress the nation had made against racism. "What we have already achieved,' he declared, "gives us hope—the audacity to hope—for what we can and must achieve tomorrow." Most commentators judged Obama's presentation as the most thoughtful, nuanced, and historically grounded speech on race relations ever delivered by a political candidate.

Obama clinched the Democratic nomination in June, and then he and his running mate, Sen. Joseph Biden (D-DE) took to the campaign trail. Obama's network of organizers helped register hundreds of thousands of new voters, especially among minorities, and turned out huge crowds wherever Obama appeared. Avoiding public financing, organizers raised record-breaking sums, mainly from individual donors. They also made use of the Internet, including social networking sites such as Facebook, to direct their message to prospective voters among the population under age thirty. The campaign slogans "Change we can believe in" and "Yes we can" reaffirmed Obama's basic message of hope and created what many observers believed was a genuine political movement that would persist past election day.

The Republican campaign generated no less excitement. The Republicans nominated Sen. John McCain (R-AZ), who had lost his 2000 bid for the presidency to George W. Bush. McCain first came to national prominence as a fighter pilot shot down over Vietnam, where he was held as a prisoner of war for five years. McCain supporters stressed his national security and military credentials, and compared his long experience to Obama's thin resume. Yet McCain's judgment came under fire when he announced his surprise pick for vice-president, Governor Sarah Palin (R-AL). Palin, a mother of five and a social conservative with working-class roots, excited the Republican base, and she instantly became a national celebrity. A series of national media interviews exposed her uninformed, at times embarrassing, views on foreign policy and raised serious doubts among many, including some high-level Republicans. Was she ready to be president if the 72-year-old McCain, a cancer survivor, became indisposed? The Palin choice also weakened the "lack of experience" argument against Obama.

In November, Obama won the election with the biggest margin by any candidate in twenty years. He took the Electoral College by 365–173 and the popular vote by nearly 10 million. Observers noted Obama's reversal of some long-standing trends. He was the first Democratic candidate since Lyndon B. Johnson in 1964 to receive more than 50% of the popular vote. This reflected large gains made for his party among young voters, Latinos, and suburbanites. He attracted a higher percentage of white voters than either John Kerry in 2004 or Al Gore in 2000, helping him to carry several states, such as Virginia and North Carolina, that had not gone Democratic in decades. Although the broken economy no doubt contributed to Obama's victory, his election also reflected the changing demography of the twenty-first century: the electorate was younger, more nonwhite, and less divided by racial polarization. To drive home the symbolism, Obama chose to celebrate on election night in Chicago's Grant Park, site of the police attack on peace demonstrators at the 1968 Democratic convention (see Chapter 29). Hundreds of thousands, black and white, old and young alike, turned out to cheer his victory and weep with joy.

The Great Recession

Much of the final phase of Obama's election campaign had focused on the economic crisis facing the nation—and much of the world—and helped to give him an edge over his Republican opponent. While McCain remained aloof from the tense, high-stakes negotiations going on in Washington, Obama dived into the public debates over how to rescue the economy. By the time he took office in January 2009, however, there was no time for basking in his victory. Wall Street's woes had quickly spread to Main Street, and the recession was deepening to become the worst economic crisis since the Great Depression.

The immediate cause of the recession was the abrupt burst of the "real estate bubble" that had artificially inflated the value of houses for years. Approximately 80 percent of mortgages recently contracted had been in the hands of risky borrowers, homeowners who had been encouraged by the banks to buy with little or no money down and take subprime or adjustable-rate mortgages. When housing prices slid downward and interest rates moved up, many of these new homeowners could not make their payments or realized that the money they still owed on their mortgages far exceeded the market value of their homes, putting them "underwater." Hundreds of thousands defaulted on their loans and let the lending agencies take over their property. Hundreds of billions of dollars in mortgage-backed stocks and bonds that were owned and traded by large financial institutions became worthless when the real estate market collapsed. As a result, leading banks, investment houses, and insurance companies suddenly faced imminent failure. In the fall of 2008, the bankruptcy of Bear Stearns and Lehman Brothers, two of Wall Street's wealthiest investment banks that had securitized many subprime mortgages, shocked the international financial markets. So did the near-collapse of American International Group, one of the world's biggest insurers.

In its final months, the Bush Administration worked frantically to stabilize the financial system, eventually pushing through Congress an unprecedented bailout package. The Troubled Asset Relief Program (TARP) allowed the Department of Treasury to buy or insure up to $700 billion in bad loans and other "toxic" assets held by financial institutions. A recalcitrant Congress agreed to pass TARP only after the Dow Jones industrial average dropped nearly 800 points, wiping out $1.2 trillion from the stock market in the biggest one-day decline since the crash of 1987. Despite the infusion of funds, banks continued to collapse. By early 2010, the Federal Deposit Insurance Corporation had taken over nearly 200 banks and many more were assigned to the federal government's secret list of "troubled" banks.

Obama in Office

President Obama pushed through Congress in February 2009 the largest stimulus package in U.S. history. While Bush's TARP program made capital available to big financial institutions, the $787 billion American Recovery and Reinvestment Act targeted ordinary Americans. It combined tax breaks with spending on infrastructure projects, extensions of welfare and unemployment benefits, and education. While the Obama administration hoped to jump-start recovery, as well as create or save 3.5 million jobs by 2011, many economists warned that the funds allocated were too small.

Recovery proved hard to measure. By early 2010, nearly one in four American homeowners found themselves "underwater," owing more on their mortgages than their property was worth. Millions could not make payments and faced foreclosure on their houses. The stock market crash, the most severe since 1974, had wiped out large portions of retirement savings that were invested in equities rather than tied to employer-sponsored pensions, and many older Americans put off retirement. Many colleges and universities, their endowments cut by one-third or more, raised tuition, putting higher education out of reach for many Americans. Whole industries, such as automaking, continued to teeter on the brink of bankruptcy. The unemployment rate topped 10 percent, 15.3 million Americans had joined the rolls of those looking for jobs, and the sense that most lost jobs might never return reinforced a deep sense insecurity and frustration. The future remained uncertain and the consensus continued to hold that America was in the grip of the worst economic crisis since the Great Depression.

President Obama signing the Health Care and Education Reconciliation Act in March 2010. It represented the most ambitious overhaul of America's healthcare system since the enactment of Medicare in 1965.

Beyond the economy, Obama faced many hurdles during his first year in office. His two biggest issues were foreign policy and health care reform, both key elements in his election campaign. He swiftly set to work on these two issues. Opposition would be strong and steady. Obama's stimulus bill had passed without a single Republican vote in the House and only three in the Senate and previewed the difficulty of realizing his oft-stated goal of bringing a more bipartisan, even "post-partisan" tone to Washington. Such opposition also forecast the resistance the ambitious president would face in passing legislation that would fulfill his campaign promises.

In foreign policy, Obama had campaigned promising to end the unilateral actions that had made President Bush unpopular with many other heads of state. To help reach this goal, as well as demonstrate his political savvy, he named his toughest rival, Hillary Clinton, as secretary of state. Clinton agreed with Obama that there was "a lot of damage to repair" from the Bush administration. She also supported Obama's boldest moves in foreign policy that, surprisingly to some observers, made less of a break with Bush-era policies than anticipated.

Within days of taking office, Obama ordered the closing of the notorious Guantanamo Bay Naval Camp prison, relocation of its 250 terror suspects to the United States, and trials by American courts. This policy provoked enormous opposition and proved slow to implement; in early 2010, plans for the removal of the prisoners had stalled.

Obama also began the difficult process of repairing America's standing and prestige on the global stage. In June 2009, he traveled to Cairo, Egypt where he called for "a new beginning between the United States and Muslims around the world; one based upon mutual interest and mutual respect; and one based upon the truth that America and Islam are not exclusive, and need not be in competition." It would take more than a speech to undo the damage wrought by the Iraq War and the legacy of Islamist terrorism. The speech, however, and the largely positive reaction to it, at least temporarily, placed the United States in a new diplomatic light.

Renewing his campaign promise, President Obama announced a process for a gradual troop drawdown from Iraq. By summer 2010 Obama had removed all combat troops, leaving roughly 50,000 military personnel as training forces scheduled to leave by the end of 2011. At the same time, he pledged to expand the war in Afghanistan. The failure to capture Osama bin Laden and the revival of the Taliban had once again made that country a haven for al Qaeda and other terrorist groups. In December 2009, the president announced a plan to deploy 30,000 additional troops to Afghanistan. This announcement came as he prepared to accept the Nobel Peace Prize. "Let us reach for the world that ought to be," he said to the Oslo audience in justifying his leadership in the conduct of two wars: "Clear-eyed, we can understand that there will be war and still strive for peace."

On several domestic issues, Obama signaled new directions. The first bill he signed into law, the Lilly Ledbetter Fair Pay Act, allowed workers more time to sue employers over unequal pay. He issued an executive order lifting Bush-era restrictions on funding for international aid groups that provided abortions. He overturned a ban on federal funding for stem cell research, and ramped up public spending for research into curing Parkinson's and other diseases. He supported some $30 billion in bridge loans to help automakers General Motors and Chrysler emerge from bankruptcy. For his first Supreme Court nomination, Obama chose Sandra Sotomayor, a federal court judge with Puerto Rican roots who became the first-ever Latino Supreme Court justice in 2009. His second appointment, former Harvard law School dean Elena Kagan, was sworn in the next year.

On the domestic front, Obama's biggest challenge was health care reform. Health care represented more than 17 percent of the nation's GDP. Yet the recession made health care less and less affordable, and roughly one in seven Americans lacked health insurance and access to regular medical care. Throughout the first year of his term, deep partisan divisions in Congress stalled Obama's effort to create a comprehensive universal system of health insurance. The bill that finally emerged from the House and Senate, and that Obama signed into law in March 2010, included a series of reforms to be fully implemented by 2014. Some 32 million uninsured Americans would gain coverage, many with the help of government subsidies. Insurers would be forbidden from denying coverage to people with pre-existing medical conditions or from placing lifetime dollar limits on policies. But with no government run "public option" to compete with private insurers, the legislation itself was more focused on reforming insurance industry practices than on overhauling how patient care was delivered and paid for.

President Obama and Democrats in Congress hailed the new law as an historic achievement in social legislation, on a par with Social Security (1935) or Medicare (1965). Yet not a single Republican in either the House or Senate had supported it. In their eyes, it represented an unwarranted expansion of federal power. The political fallout remained unclear, but the extremely contentious debate over health care reform epitomized how sharply the two parties, and Americans, were divided. The fundamental split centered on the role of the federal government in American life. Should it be seen as an active agent for improving the lives of ordinary people, or had it become a bloated and wasteful barrier to progress and prosperity?

CHRONOLOGY

1981	MTV and CNN start broadcasting as cable channels
1986	Immigration Reform and Control Act addresses concerns about undocumented aliens
1988	George H. W. Bush is elected president
1989	Tiananmen Square demonstration in China
1990	Iraqi invasion of Kuwait leads to massive U.S. military presence in the Persian Gulf
1991	Operation Desert Storm forces Iraq out of Kuwait
	Operation Rescue launched in Wichita, Kansas
1992	Rodney King verdict sparks rioting in Los Angeles
	Bill Clinton is elected president
1993	Terrorist bombing of World Trade Center kills six people
	Clinton administration introduces comprehensive health care reform, but it fails to win passage in Congress
	Congress approves the North American Free Trade Agreement (NAFTA)
1994	Republicans win control of Senate and House for first time in forty years
	Congress approves the General Agreement on Tariffs and Trade (GATT)
	Congress passes the Comprehensive AIDS Revenue Emergency Act
	Congress passes Defense of Marriage Act
	California voters approve Proposition 187
1995	Bombing of Alfred P. Murrah Federal Building in Oklahoma City kills 168 people
1996	Congress passes Welfare Reform Act
	Congress enacts the Antiterrorism and Effective Death Penalty Act
	President Bill Clinton is reelected
1997	Kyoto Protocol endorsed by European Union but not United States
1998	U.S. embassies in Kenya and Tanzania bombed by terrorists
	House of Representatives votes to impeach President Clinton, but vote fails in Senate
1999	U.S. joins NATO forces in Kosovo
	Protesters disrupt meetings of the World Trade Organization in Seattle
2000	USS *Cole* bombed by terrorists
2001	George W. Bush becomes president after contested election
	Terrorists attack World Trade Center and Pentagon
	U.S. begins military campaign in Afghanistan
	Homeland Security Department established
	USA Patriot Act passed
2003	Invasion of Iraq and occupation
	USA Patriot Act II passed
2004	Release of *The 9/11 Commission Report*
	Reelection of George W. Bush
2005	Elections in Iraq
	Hurricane Katrina devastates New Orleans and the Gulf Coast

Review Questions

I. How is the "new economy" different from the old economy? How has it reshaped American business and financial practices? Explain the relationship between the new economy and electronic media, such as the Internet and cable television.

2. Evaluate the presidency of Bill Clinton. Compare his domestic and foreign policies to those of the Republican presidents who preceded and followed him in office. What was the impact of the scandals that plagued his presidency?

3. Describe the major demographic trends revealed by the 2000 U. S. Census. Identify the racial and ethnic

groups with the greatest gains in population. How have various legislative acts since 1965 affected immigration to the United States? How have communities changed as a result of the influx of new immigrants?

4. The concept of globalization is highly controversial. Are borders between nations "melting away" as some scholars contend? How does this concept square with the description of the United States as the single superpower in the world? Does this concept apply primarily to economics, or is it useful for discussing issues related to culture, media, the environment, and population trends?

5. How has the "war on terror" differed from other wars in this century? How and why did the 9/11 attacks lead to fundamental changes in the conduct of U.S. foreign policy? What arguments for the American invasion of Iraq in 2003 do you find most and least persuasive?

Recommended Reading

Jonathan Alter, *The Promise: President Obama, Year One* (2010). A candid inside look at Obama's first year in office, based on over 200 interviews with the president, his aides, and friends.

William C. Berman, *From the Center to the Edge: The Politics and Policies of the Clinton Presidency* (2001). A highly readable assessment of Clinton's accomplishments as president. Although focusing on domestic issues, including the impact of Clinton's impeachment trial, Berman also considers major foreign policy developments in the context of globalization.

Douglas Brinkley, *The Great Deluge: Hurricane Katrina, New Orleans, and the Mississippi Gulf Coast* (2006). The first comprehensive narrative history of Hurricane Katrina, the government response, and the aftermath.

Stephen Coll, *Ghost Wars: The Secret History of the CIA, Afghanistan, and Bin Laden from the Soviet Invasion to September 10, 2001* (2004). Deeply researched examination of the CIA's influence in Afghanistan and its support for Islamic fundamentalists resisting Soviet occupation.

Thomas Frank, *What's the Matter with Kansas? How Conservatives Won the Heart of America* (2004). A provocative look at how political conservatives have successfully recast themselves as the voice of populism and ordinary Americans over the last thirty years.

National Commission on Terrorist Attacks upon the United States, *The 9/11 Commission Report* (2004). The best-selling final report of the independent bipartisan inquiry into the events surrounding the 9/11 attacks, including recommendations for reorganizing American intelligence to more effectively meet terrorist threats.

Todd S. Purdum, *A Time of Our Choosing: America's War in Iraq* (2004). An excellent narrative account of how the Bush administration made the decision to invade Iraq.

Sam Roberts, *Who We Are Now: The Changing Face of America in the Twenty-First Century* (2004). Using the 2000 U.S. Census, Roberts focuses on the changes in American society that occurred between 1990 and 2000. He discusses population growth, the largest decadal increase in American history, as well as shifts in ethnic composition, family structure, and inequality.

Joseph Stiglitz, *Freefall: America, Free Markets, and the Sinking of the World Economy* (2010). A critical assessment of how Wall Street, the financial sector, and government regulators contributed to the great recession. Stiglitz, a Nobel laureate in economics, explains how the "financialization" of the American economy has weakened the nation in recent decades.

Eric G. Swedin and David L. Ferro, *Computers: The Life Story of a Technology* (2005). A very clearly written overview of the development of mechanical aids for computing and the research scientists and entrepreneurs who brought them into the electronic age.

Richard Wolffe, *Renegade: The Making of a President* (2009). A lively, gracefully written account by a journalist who covered the Obama campaign for *Newsweek* magazine.

PEARSON
myhistorylab Connections

Reinforce what you learned in this chapter by studying the many documents, images, maps, review tools, and videos available at www.myhistorylab.com.

Read and Review

✓•—[Study and Review **Chapter 31**

•◆•—[Read the Document

Statements of the Clinton Health Care Plan (1993)

Illegal Immigration Reform and Immigrant Responsibility Act

George W. Bush, Address to Congress (2001)

George W. Bush, From National Security Strategy of the U.S. (2002)

((•●—[Hear the Audio *Barack Obama, Excerpt from The Audacity of Hope*

👁—[See the Map *Immigration to the United States, 1945–1990*

Research and Explore

•◆•—[Read the Document

Exploring America: Globalization

Profiles
  Bill Gates
  Jesse Jackson

◉—[Watch the Video

Bill Clinton Sells Himself to America: Presidential Campaign Ad, 1992

Bill Clinton First Inauguration

The Historical Significance of the 2008 Presidential Election

The Connection between Obama and Lincoln

((•●—[**Hear** the **Audio**

Hear the audio files for Chapter 31 at
www.myhistorylab.com.

THE DECLARATION OF INDEPENDENCE

When in the course of human events it becomes necessary for one people to dissolve the political bands which have connected them with another and to assume, among the powers of the earth, the separate and equal station to which the laws of nature and of nature's God entitle them, a decent respect to the opinions of mankind requires that they should declare the causes which impel them to the separation.

We hold these truths to be self-evident, that all men are created equal; that they are endowed by their Creator with certain unalienable rights; that among these are life, liberty, and the pursuit of happiness. That, to secure these rights, governments are instituted among men, deriving their just powers from the consent of the governed; that, whenever any form of government becomes destructive of these ends, it is the right of the people to alter or to abolish it, and to institute a new government, laying its foundation on such principles, and organizing its powers in such form, as to them shall seem most likely to effect their safety and happiness. Prudence, indeed, will dictate that governments long established should not be changed for light and transient causes; and, accordingly, all experience hath shown that mankind are more disposed to suffer, while evils are sufferable, than to right themselves by abolishing the forms to which they are accustomed. But when a long train of abuses and usurpations, pursuing invariably the same object, evinces a design to reduce them under absolute despotism, it is their right, it is their duty, to throw off such government and to provide new guards for their future security. Such has been the patient sufferance of these colonies, and such is now the necessity which constrains them to alter their former systems of government. The history of the present King of Great Britain is a history of repeated injuries and usurpations, all having, in direct object, the establishment of an absolute tyranny over these States. To prove this, let facts be submitted to a candid world:

He has refused his assent to laws the most wholesome and necessary for the public good.

He has forbidden his governors to pass laws of immediate and pressing importance, unless suspended in their operation till his assent should be obtained; and, when so suspended, he has utterly neglected to attend to them.

He has refused to pass other laws for the accommodation of large districts of people, unless those people would relinquish the right of representation in the legislature, a right inestimable to them and formidable to tyrants only.

He has called together legislative bodies at places unusual, uncomfortable, and distant from the depository of their public records, for the sole purpose of fatiguing them into compliance with his measures.

He has dissolved representative houses, repeatedly for opposing, with manly firmness, his invasions on the rights of the people.

He has refused, for a long time after such dissolutions, to cause others to be elected; whereby the legislative powers, incapable of annihilation, have returned to the people at large for their exercise; the state remaining, in the meantime, exposed to all the danger of invasion from without and convulsions within.

He has endeavored to prevent the population of these States; for that purpose, obstructing the laws for naturalization of foreigners, refusing to pass others to encourage their migration hither, and raising the conditions of new appropriations of lands.

He has obstructed the administration of justice by refusing his assent to laws for establishing judiciary powers.

He has made judges dependent on his will alone for the tenure of their offices and the amount and payment of their salaries.

He has erected a multitude of new offices and sent hither swarms of officers to harass our people and eat out their substance.

He has kept among us, in time of peace, standing armies, without the consent of our legislatures.

He has affected to render the military independent of, and superior to, the civil power.

He has combined with others to subject us to a jurisdiction foreign to our Constitution and unacknowledged by our laws, giving his assent to their acts of pretended legislation—

For quartering large bodies of armed troops among us;

For protecting them by mock trial, from punishment for any murders which they should commit on the inhabitants of these States;

For cutting off our trade with all parts of the world;

For imposing taxes on us without our consent;

For depriving us, in many cases, of the benefit of trial by jury;

For transporting us beyond seas to be tried for pretended offences;

For abolishing the free system of English laws in a neighboring province, establishing therein an arbitrary government, and enlarging its boundaries, so as to render it at once an example and fit instrument for introducing the same absolute rule into these colonies;

For taking away our charters, abolishing our most valuable laws, and altering, fundamentally, the powers of our governments.

For suspending our own legislatures and declaring themselves invested with power to legislate for us in all cases whatsoever.

He has abdicated government here by declaring us out of his protection and waging war against us.

He has plundered our seas, ravaged our coasts, burnt our towns, and destroyed the lives of our people.

He is, at this time, transporting large armies of foreign mercenaries to complete the works of death, desolation, and tyranny already begun with circumstances of cruelty and perfidy scarcely paralleled in the most barbarous ages, and totally unworthy the head of a civilized nation.

He has constrained our fellow citizens, taken captive on the high seas, to bear arms against their country, to become the executioners of their friends and brethren, or to fall themselves by their hands.

He has excited domestic insurrections amongst us and has endeavored to bring on the inhabitants of our frontiers, the merciless Indian savages, whose known rule of warfare is an undistinguished destruction of all ages, sexes, and conditions.

In every stage of these oppressions, we have petitioned for redress in the most humble terms; our repeated petitions have been answered only by repeated injury. A prince whose character is thus marked by every act which may define a tyrant is unfit to be the ruler of a free people.

Nor have we been wanting in attention to our British brethren. We have warned them, from time to time, of attempts made by their legislature to extend an unwarrantable jurisdiction over us. We have reminded them of the circumstances of our emigration and settlement here. We have appealed to their native justice and magnanimity, and we have conjured them, by the ties of our common kindred, to disavow these usurpations, which would inevitably interrupt our connections and correspondence. They, too, have been deaf to the voice of justice and consanguinity. We must, therefore, acquiesce in the necessity which denounces our separation, and hold them, as we hold the rest of mankind, enemies in war, in peace, friends.

We, therefore, the representatives of the United States of America, in general Congress assembled, appealing to the Supreme Judge of the world for the rectitude of our intentions, do, in the name and by the authority of the good people of these colonies, solemnly publish and declare, that these united colonies are, and of right ought to be, free and independent states: that they are absolved from all allegiance to the British Crown, and that all political connection between them and the state of Great Britain is, and ought to be, totally dissolved; and that, as free and independent states, they have full power to levy war, conclude peace, contract alliances, establish commerce, and to do all other acts and things which independent states may of right do. And, for the support of this declaration, with a firm reliance on the protection of Divine Providence, we mutually pledge to each other our lives, our fortunes, and our sacred honor.

THE ARTICLES OF CONFEDERATION AND PERPETUAL UNION*

Between the states of New Hampshire, Massachusetts-bay Rhode Island and Providence Plantations, Connecticut, New York, New Jersey, Pennsylvania, Delaware, Maryland, Virginia, North Carolina, South Carolina, and Georgia.

Article 1

The Stile of this Confederacy shall be "The United States of America."

Article 2

Each state retains its sovereignty, freedom, and independence, and every power, jurisdiction, and right, which is not by this Confederation expressly delegated to the United States, in Congress assembled.

Article 3

The said States hereby severally enter into a firm league of friendship with each other, for their common defense, the security of their liberties, and their mutual and general welfare, binding themselves to assist each other, against all force offered to, or attacks made upon them, or any of them, on account of religion, sovereignty, trade, or any other pretense whatever.

Article 4

The better to secure and perpetuate mutual friendship and intercourse among the people of the different States in this Union, the free inhabitants of each of these States, paupers, vagabonds, and fugitives from justice excepted, shall be entitled to all privileges and immunities of free citizens in the several States; and the people of each State shall have free ingress and regress to and from any other State, and shall enjoy therein all the privileges of trade and commerce, subject to the same duties, impositions, and restrictions as the inhabitants thereof respectively, provided that such restrictions shall not extend so far as to prevent the removal of property imported into any State, to any other State of which the owner is an inhabitant; provided also that no imposition, duties or restriction shall be laid by any State, on the property of the United States, or either of them.

If any person guilty of, or charged with, treason, felony, or other high misdemeanor in any State, shall flee from justice, and be found in any of the United States, he shall, upon demand of the Governor or executive power of the State from which he fled, be delivered up and removed to the State having jurisdiction of his offense.

Full faith and credit shall be given in each of these States to the records, acts, and judicial proceedings of the courts and magistrates of every other State.

Article 5

For the most convenient management of the general interests of the United States, delegates shall be annually appointed in such manner as the legislatures of each State shall direct, to meet in Congress on the first Monday in November, in every year, with a power reserved to each State to recall its delegates, or any of them, at any time within the year, and to send others in their stead for the remainder of the year.

No State shall be represented in Congress by less than two, nor by more than seven members; and no person

---

*Agreed to in Congress November 15, 1777; ratified March 1781.

shall be capable of being a delegate for more than three years in any term of six years; nor shall any person, being a delegate, be capable of holding any office under the United States, for which he, or another for his benefit, receives any salary, fees or emolument of any kind.

Each State shall maintain its own delegates in a meeting of the States, and while they act as members of the committee of the States.

In determining questions in the United States in Congress assembled, each State shall have one vote.

Freedom of speech and debate in Congress shall not be impeached or questioned in any court or place out of Congress, and the members of Congress shall be protected in their persons from arrests or imprisonments, during the time of their going to and from, and attendence on Congress, except for treason, felony, or breach of the peace.

Article 6

No State, without the consent of the United States in Congress assembled, shall send any embassy to, or receive any embassy from, or enter into any conference, agreement, alliance or treaty with any King, Prince or State; nor shall any person holding any office of profit or trust under the United States, or any of them, accept any present, emolument, office or title of any kind whatever from any King, Prince or foreign State; nor shall the United States in Congress assembled, or any of them, grant any title of nobility.

No two or more States shall enter into any treaty, confederation or alliance whatever between them, without the consent of the United States in Congress assembled, specifying accurately the purposes for which the same is to be entered into, and how long it shall continue.

No State shall lay any imposts or duties, which may interfere with any stipulations in treaties, entered into by the United States in Congress assembled, with any King, Prince or State, in pursuance of any treaties already proposed by Congress, to the courts of France and Spain.

No vessel of war shall be kept up in time of peace by any State, except such number only, as shall be deemed necessary by the United States in Congress assembled, for the defense of such State, or its trade; nor shall any body of forces be kept up by any State in time of peace, except such number only, as in the judgement of the United States in Congress assembled, shall be deemed requisite to garrison the forts necessary for the defense of such State; but every State shall always keep up a well-regulated and disciplined militia, sufficiently armed and accoutered, and shall provide and constantly have ready for use, in public stores, a due number of filed pieces and tents, and a proper quantity of arms, ammunition and camp equipage.

No State shall engage in any war without the consent of the United States in Congress assembled, unless such State be actually invaded by enemies, or shall have received certain advice of a resolution being formed by some nation of Indians to invade such State, and the danger is so imminent as not to admit of a delay, till the United States in Congress assembled can be consulted; nor shall any State grant commissions to any ships or vessels of war, nor letters of marque or reprisal, except it be after a declaration of war by the United States in Congress assembled, and then only against the King-dom or State and the subjects thereof, against which war has been so declared, and under such regulations as shall be established by the United States in Congress assembled, unless such State be infested by pirates, in which case vessels of war may be fitted out for that occasion, and kept so long as the danger shall continue, or until the United States in Congress assembled shall determine otherwise.

Article 7

When land forces are raised by any State for the common defense, all officers of or under the rank of colonel, shall be appointed by the legislature of each State respectively, by whom such forces shall be raised, or in such manner as such State shall direct, and all vacancies shall be filled up by the State which first made the appointment.

Article 8

All charges of war, and all other expenses that shall be incurred for the common defense or general welfare, and allowed by the United States in Congress assembled, shall be defrayed out of a common treasury, which shall be supplied by the several States in proportion to the value of all land within each State, granted to or surveyed for any person, as such land and the buildings and improvements thereon shall be estimated according to such mode as the United States in Congress assembled, shall from time to time direct and appoint.

The taxes for paying that proportion shall be laid and levied by the authority and direction of the legislatures of the several States within the time agreed upon by the United States in Congress assembled.

Article 9

The United States in Congress assembled, shall have the sole and exclusive right and power of determining on peace and war, except in the cases mentioned in the sixth article; of sending and receiving ambassadors; entering into treaties and alliances, provided that no treaty of commerce shall be made whereby the legislative power of the respective States shall be restrained from imposing such imposts and duties on foreigners, as their own people are subjected to, or from prohibiting the exportation or importation of any species of goods or commodities whatsoever; of establishing rules for deciding in all cases, what captures on land or water shall be legal, and in what manner prizes taken by land or naval forces in the service of the United States shall be divided or appropriated; of granting letters of marque and reprisal in times of peace; appointing courts for the trial of piracies and felonies committed on the high seas and establishing courts for receiving and determining finally appeals in all cases of captures, provided that no member of Congress shall be appointed a judge of any of the said courts.

The United States in Congress assembled shall also be the last resort on appeal in all disputes and differences now subsisting or that hereafter may arise between two or more States concerning boundary, jurisdiction or any other causes whatever; which authority shall always be exercised in the manner following. Whenever the legislative or executive authority or lawful agent of any State in controversy with another shall present a petition to Congress stating the matter in question and praying for a hearing, notice thereof shall be given by order of Congress to the legislative or executive authority of the other State in controversy, and a day assigned for the appearance of the parties by their lawful agents, who shall then be directed to appoint by joint consent, commissioners or judges to constitute a court for hearing and determining the matter in question: but if they cannot agree, Congress shall name three persons out of each of the United States, and from the list of such persons each party shall alternately strike out one, the petitioners beginning, until the number shall be reduced to thirteen; and from that number not less than seven, nor more than nine names as Congress shall direct, shall in the presence of Congress be drawn out by lot, and the persons whose names shall be so drawn or any five of them, shall be commissioners or judges, to hear and finally determine the controversy, so always as a major part of the judges who shall hear the cause shall agree in the determination: and if either party shall neglect to attend at the day appointed, without showing reasons, which Congress shall judge sufficient, or being present shall refuse to strike, the Congress shall proceed to nominate three persons out of each State, and the secretary of Congress shall strike in behalf of such party absent or refusing; and the judgement and sentence of the court to be appointed, in the manner before prescribed, shall be final and conclusive; and if any of the parties shall refuse to submit to the authority of such court, or to appear or defend their claim or cause, the court shall nevertheless proceed to pronounce sentence, or judgement, which shall in like manner be final and decisive, the judgement or sentence and other proceedings being in either case transmitted to Congress, and lodged among the acts of Congress for the security of the parties concerned: provided that every commissioner, before he sits in judgement, shall take an oath to be administered by one of the judges of the supreme or superior court of the State, where the cause shall be tried, "well and truly to hear and determine the matter in question, according to the best of his judgement, without favor, affection or hope of reward:" provided also, that no State shall be deprived of territory for the benefit of the United States.

All controversies concerning the private right of soil claimed under different grants of two or more States, whose jurisdictions as they may respect such lands, and the States which passed such grants are adjusted, the said grants or either of them being at the same time claimed to have originated antecedent to such settlement of jurisdiction, shall on the petition of either party to the Congress of the United States, be finally determined as near as may be in the same manner as is before prescribed for deciding disputes respecting territorial jurisdiction between different States.

The United States in Congress assembled shall also have the sole and exclusive right and power of regulating the alloy and value of coin struck by their own authority, or by that of the respective States; fixing the standards of weights and measures throughout the United States; regulating the trade and managing all affairs with the Indians not members of any of the States; provided that the legislative right of any State within its own limits be not infringed or violated; establishing or regulating post offices from one State to another, throughout all the United States, and exacting such postage on the papers passing through the same as may be requisite to defray the expenses of the said office; appointing all officers of the land forces in the service of the United States, excepting regimental officers; appointing all the officers of the naval forces, and commissioning all officers whatever in the service of the United States; making rules for the government and regulation of the said land and naval forces, and directing their operations.

The United States in Congress assembled shall have authority to appoint a committee, to sit in the recess of Congress, to be denominated "A Committee of the States," and to consist of one delegate from each State; and to appoint such other committees and civil officers as may be necessary for managing the general affairs of the United States under their direction; to appoint one of their members to preside, provided that no person be allowed to serve in the office of president more than one year in any term of three years; to ascertain the necessary sums of money to be raised for the service of the United States, and to appropriate and apply the same for defraying the public expenses; to borrow money, or emit bills on the credit of the United States, transmitting every half year to the respective States an account of the sums of money so borrowed or emitted; to build and equip a navy; to agree upon the number of land forces, and to make requisitions from each State for its quota, in proportion to the number of white inhabitants in such State; which requisition shall be binding, and thereupon the legislature of each State shall appoint the regimental officers, raise the men and cloath, arm and equip them in a soldierlike manner, at the expense of the United States; and the officers and men so cloathed, armed and equipped shall march to the place appointed, and within the time agreed on by the United States in Congress assembled; but if the United States in Congress assembled shall, on consideration of circumstances judge proper that any State should not raise men, or should raise a smaller number of men than the quota thereof, such extra number shall be raised, officered, cloathed, armed and equipped in the same manner as the quota of each State, unless the legislature of such State shall judge that such extra number cannot be safely spared out in the same, in which case they shall raise, officer, cloath, arm and equip as many of such extra number as they judge can be safely spared. And the officers and men so cloathed, armed, and equipped, shall march to the place appointed, and within the time agreed on by the United States in Congress assembled.

The United States in Congress assembled shall never engage in a war, nor grant letters of marque or reprisal in time of peace, nor enter into any treaties or alliances, nor coin money, nor regulate the value thereof, nor ascertain the sums and expenses necessary for the defense and welfare of the United States, or any of them, nor emit bills, nor borrow money on the credit of the United States, nor appropriate money, nor agree upon the number of vessels of war, to be built or purchased, or the number of land or sea forces to be raised, nor appoint a commander in chief of the army or navy, unless nine States assent to the same: nor shall a question on any other point, except for adjourning from day to day be determined, unless by the votes of the majority of the United States in Congress assembled.

The Congress of the United States shall have power to adjourn to any time within the year, and to any place within the United States, so that no period of adjournment be for a longer duration than the space of six months, and shall publish the journal of their proceedings monthly, except such parts thereof relating to treaties, alliances or military operations, as in their judge-ment require secrecy; and the yeas and nays of the delegates of each State on any question shall be entered on the journal, when it is desired by any delegates of a State, or any of them, at his or their request shall be furnished with a transcript of the said journal, except such parts as are above excepted, to lay before the legislatures of the several States.

Article 10

The Committee of the States, or any nine of them, shall be authorized to execute, in the recess of Congress, such of the powers of Congress as the United States in Congress assembled, by the consent of the nine States, shall from time to time think expedient to vest them with; provided that no power be delegated to the said Committee, for the exercise of which, by the Articles of Confederation, the voice of nine States in the Congress of the United States assembled is requisite.

Article 11

Canada acceding to this confederation, and adjoining in the measures of the United States, shall be admitted into, and entitled to all the advantages of this Union; but no other colony shall be admitted into the same, unless such admission be agreed to by nine States.

Article 12

All bills of credit emitted, monies borrowed, and debts contracted by, or under the authority of Congress, before the assembling of the United States, in pursuance of the present confederation, shall be deemed and considered as a charge against the United States, for payment and satisfaction whereof the said United States, and the public faith are hereby solemnly pledged.

Article 13

Every State shall abide by the determination of the United States in Congress assembled, on all questions which by this confederation are submitted to them. And the Articles of this Confederation shall be inviolably observed by every State, and the Union shall be perpetual; nor shall any alteration at any time hereafter be made in any of them; unless such alteration be agreed to in a Congress of the United States, and be afterwards confirmed by the legislatures of every State.

These articles shall be proposed to the legislatures of all the United States, to be considered, and if approved of by them, they are advised to authorize their delegates to ratify the same in the Congress of the United States; which being done, the same shall become conclusive.

THE CONSTITUTION OF THE UNITED STATES OF AMERICA

We the people of the United States, in order to form a more perfect union, establish justice, insure domestic tranquillity, provide for the common defense, promote the general welfare, and secure the blessings of liberty to ourselves and our posterity, do ordain and establish this Constitution for the United States of America.

Article I

Section 1. All legislative powers herein granted shall be vested in a Congress of the United States, which shall consist of a Senate and House of Representatives.

Section 2. 1. The House of Representatives shall be composed of members chosen every second year by the people of the several States, and the electors in each State shall have the qualifications requisite for electors of the most numerous branch of the State legislature.

2. No person shall be a representative who shall not have attained to the age of twenty-five years, and been seven years a citizen of the United States, and who shall not, when elected, be an inhabitant of that State in which he shall be chosen.

3. Representatives and direct taxes[1] shall be apportioned among the several States which may be included within this Union, according to their respective numbers, which shall be determined by adding to the whole number of free persons, including those bound to service for a term

of years, and excluding Indians not taxed, three fifths of all other persons.[2] The actual enumeration shall be made within three years after the first meeting of the Congress of the United States, and within every subsequent term of ten years, in such manner as they shall by law direct. The number of representatives shall not exceed one for every thirty thousand, but each State shall have at least one representative; and until such enumeration shall be made, the State of New Hampshire shall be entitled to choose three, Massachusetts eight, Rhode Island and Providence Plantations one, Connecticut five, New York six, New Jersey four, Pennsylvania eight, Delaware one, Maryland six, Virginia ten, North Carolina five, South Carolina five, and Georgia three.

4. When vacancies happen in the representation from any State, the executive authority thereof shall issue writs of election to fill such vacancies.

5. The House of Representatives shall choose their speaker and other officers; and shall have the sole power of impeachment.

Section 3. 1. The Senate of the United States shall be composed of two senators from each State, chosen by the legislature thereof,[3] for six years; and each senator shall have one vote.

2. Immediately after they shall be assembled in consequence of the first election, they shall be divided as equally as may be into three classes. The seats of the senators of the first class shall be vacated at the expiration of the second year,

---

[1]See the Sixteenth Amendment.

[2]See the Fourteenth Amendment.
[3]See the Seventeenth Amendment.

of the second class at the expiration of the fourth year, and of the third class at the expiration of the sixth year, so that one third may be chosen every second year; and if vacancies happen by resignation, or otherwise, during the recess of the legislature of any State, the executive thereof may make temporary appointments until the next meeting of the legislature, which shall then fill such vacancies.[4]

3. No person shall be a senator who shall not have attained to the age of thirty years, and been nine years a citizen of the United States, and who shall not, when elected, be an inhabitant of that State for which he shall be chosen.

4. The Vice President of the United States shall be President of the Senate, but shall have no vote, unless they be equally divided.

5. The Senate shall choose their other officers, and also a president pro tempore, in the absence of the Vice President, or when he shall exercise the office of the President of the United States.

6. The Senate shall have the sole power to try all impeachments. When sitting for that purpose, they shall be on oath or affirmation. When the President of the United States is tried, the chief justice shall preside: and no person shall be convicted without the concurrence of two thirds of the members present.

7. Judgment in cases of impeachment shall not extend further than to removal from office, and disqualification to hold and enjoy any office of honor, trust or profit under the United States: but the party convicted shall nevertheless be liable and subject to indictment, trial, judgment and punishment, according to law.

Section 4. 1. The times, places, and manner of holding elections for senators and representatives, shall be prescribed in each State by the legislature thereof; but the Congress may at any time by law make or alter such regulations, except as to the places of choosing senators.

2. The Congress shall assemble at least once in every year, and such meeting shall be on the first Monday in December, unless they shall by law appoint a different day.

Section 5. 1. Each House shall be the judge of the elections, returns and qualifications of its own members, and a majority of each shall constitute a quorum to do business; but a smaller number may adjourn from day to day, and may be authorized to compel the attendance of absent members, in such manner, and under such penalties as each House may provide.

2. Each House may determine the rules of its proceedings, punish its members for disorderly behavior, and, with the concurrence of two thirds, expel a member.

3. Each House shall keep a journal of its proceedings, and from time to time publish the same, excepting such parts as may in their judgment require secrecy; and the yeas and nays of the members of either House on any question shall, at the desire of one fifth of those present, be entered on the journal.

4. Neither House, during the session of Congress, shall, without the consent of the other, adjourn for more than three days, nor to any other place than that in which the two Houses shall be sitting.

Section 6. 1. The senators and representatives shall receive a compensation for their services, to be ascertained by

---

[4]See the Seventeenth Amendment.

law, and paid out of the Treasury of the United States. They shall in all cases, except treason, felony, and breach of the peace, be privileged from arrest during their attendance at the session of their respective Houses, and in going to and returning from the same; and for any speech or debate in either House, they shall not be questioned in any other place.

2. No senator or representative shall, during the time for which he was elected, be appointed to any civil office under the authority of the United States, which shall have been created, or the emoluments whereof shall have been increased, during such time; and no person holding any office under the United States shall be a member of either House during his continuance in office.

Section 7. 1. All bills for raising revenue shall originate in the House of Representatives; but the Senate may propose or concur with amendments as on other bills.

2. Every bill which shall have passed the House of Representatives and the Senate, shall, before it become a law, be presented to the President of the United States; If he approves he shall sign it, but if not he shall return it, with his objections, to that House in which it shall have originated, who shall enter the objections at large on their journal, and proceed to reconsider it. If after such reconsideration two thirds of that House shall agree to pass the bill, it shall be sent, together with the objections, to the other House, by which it shall likewise be reconsidered, and if approved by two thirds of that House, it shall become a law. But in all such cases the votes of both Houses shall be determined by yeas and nays, and the names of the persons voting for and against the bill shall be entered on the journal of each House respectively. If any bill shall not be returned by the President within ten days (Sundays excepted) after it shall have been presented to him, the same shall be a law, in like manner as if he had signed it, unless the Congress by their adjournment prevent its return, in which case it shall not be a law.

3. Every order, resolution, or vote to which the concurrence of the Senate and the House of Representatives may be necessary (except on a question of adjournment) shall be presented to the President of the United States; and before the same shall take effect, shall be approved by him, or being disapproved by him, shall be repassed by two thirds of the Senate and House of Representatives, according to the rules and limitations prescribed in the case of a bill.

Section 8. The Congress shall have the power

1. To lay and collect taxes, duties, imposts, and excises, to pay the debts and provide for the common defense and general welfare of the United States; but all duties, imposts, and excises shall be uniform throughout the United States.

2. To borrow money on the credit of the United States;

3. To regulate commerce with foreign nations, and among the several States, and with the Indian tribes;

4. To establish a uniform rule of naturalization, and uniform laws on the subject of bankruptcies throughout the United States;

5. To coin money, regulate the value thereof, and of foreign coin, and fix the standard of weights and measures;

6. To provide for the punishment of counterfeiting the securities and current coin of the United States;

7. To establish post offices and post roads;

8. To promote the progress of science and useful arts, by securing for limited times to authors and inventors the exclusive right to their respective writings and discoveries;

9. To constitute tribunals inferior to the Supreme Court;

10. To define and punish piracies and felonies committed on the high seas, and offenses against the law of nations;

11. To declare war, grant letters of marque and reprisal, and make rules concerning captures on land and water;

12. To raise and support armies, but no appropriation of money to that use shall be for a longer term than two years;

13. To provide and maintain a navy;

14. To make rules for the government and regulation of the land and naval forces;

15. To provide for calling forth the militia to execute the laws of the Union, suppress insurrections and repel invasions;

16. To provide for organizing, arming, and disciplining the militia, and for governing such part of them as may be employed in the service of the United States, reserving to the States respectively, the appointment of the officers, and the authority of training the militia according to the discipline prescribed by Congress;

17. To exercise exclusive legislation in all cases whatsoever, over such district (not exceeding ten miles square) as may, by cession of particular States, and the acceptance of Congress, become the seat of the government of the United States, and to exercise like authority over all places purchased by the consent of the legislature of the State in which the same shall be, for the erection of forts, magazines, arsenals, dockyards, and other needful buildings; and

18. To make all laws which shall be necessary and proper for carrying into execution the foregoing powers, and all other powers vested by this Constitution in the government of the United States, or any department or officer thereof.

Section 9. 1. The migration or importation of such persons as any of the States now existing shall think proper to admit, shall not be prohibited by the Congress prior to the year one thousand eight hundred and eight, but a tax or duty may be imposed on such importation, not exceeding ten dollars for each person.

2. The privilege of the writ of habeas corpus shall not be suspended, unless when in cases of rebellion or invasion the public safety may require it.

3. No bill of attainder or ex post facto law shall be passed.

4. No capitation, or other direct, tax shall be laid, unless in proportion to the census or enumeration hereinbefore directed to be taken.[5]

5. No tax or duty shall be laid on articles exported from any State.

6. No preference shall be given by any regulation of commerce or revenue to the ports of one State over those of another: nor shall vessels bound to, or from, one State be obliged to enter, clear, or pay duties in another.

7. No money shall be drawn from the treasury, but in consequence of appropriations made by law; and a regular statement and account of the receipts and expenditures of all public money shall be published from time to time.

---

[5]See the Sixteenth Amendment.

8. No title of nobility shall be granted by the United States: and no person holding any office of profit or trust under them, shall, without the consent of the Congress, accept of any present, emolument, office, or title, of any kind whatever, from any king, prince, or foreign State.

Section 10. 1. No State shall enter into any treaty, alliance, or confederation; grant letters of marque and reprisal; coin money; emit bills of credit; make any thing but gold and silver coin a tender in payment of debts; pass any bill of attainder, ex post facto law, or law impairing the obligation of contracts, or grant, any title of nobility.

2. No State shall, without the consent of the Congress, lay any imposts or duties on imports or exports, except what may be absolutely necessary for executing its inspection laws: and the net produce of all duties and imposts laid by any State on imports or exports, shall be for the use of the treasury of the United States; and all such laws shall be subject to the revision and control of the Congress.

3. No State shall, without the consent of Congress, lay any duty of tonnage, keep troops, or ships of war in time of peace, enter into any agreement or compact with another State, or with a foreign power, or engage in war, unless actually invaded, or in such imminent danger as will not admit of delay.

Article II

Section 1. 1. The executive power shall be vested in a President of the United States of America. He shall hold his office during the term of four years, and, together with the Vice President, chosen for the same term, be elected, as follows:

2. Each State shall appoint, in such manner as the legislature thereof may direct, a number of electors, equal to the whole number of senators and representatives to which the State may be entitled in the Congress: but no senator or representative, or person holding any office of trust or profit under the United States, shall be appointed an elector.

The electors shall meet in their respective States, and vote by ballot for two persons, of whom one at least shall not be an inhabitant of the same State with themselves. And they shall make a list of all the persons voted for, and of the number of votes for each; which list they shall sign and certify, and transmit sealed to the seat of the government of the United States, directed to the president of the Senate. The president of the Senate shall, in the presence of the Senate and House of Representatives, open all the certificates, and the votes shall then be counted. The person having the greatest number of votes shall be the President, if such number be a majority of the whole number of electors appointed; and if there be more than one who have such majority, and have an equal number of votes, then the House of Representatives shall immediately choose by ballot one of them for President; and if no person have a majority, then from the five highest on the list the said House shall in like manner choose the President. But in choosing the President, the votes shall be taken by States, the representation from each State having one vote; a quorum for this purpose shall consist of a member or members from two thirds of the States, and a majority of all the States shall be necessary to a choice. In every case after the choice of the President, the person having the greatest number of votes of the electors shall be the Vice President. But if there should remain two or more who have equal votes, the Senate shall choose from them by ballot the Vice President.[6]

3. The Congress may determine the time of choosing the electors, and the day on which they shall give their votes; which day shall be the same throughout the United States.

4. No person except a natural born citizen, or a citizen of the United States, at the time of the adoption of this Constitution, shall be eligible to the office of President; neither shall any person be eligible to the office who shall not have attained to the age of thirty-five years, and been fourteen years a resident within the United States.

5. In case of the removal of the President from office, or of his death, resignation, or inability to discharge the powers and duties of the said office, the same shall devolve on the Vice President, and the congress may by law provide for the case of removal, death, resignation or inability, both of the President and Vice President, declaring what officer shall then act as President, and such officer shall act accordingly until the disability be removed, or a President shall be elected.

6. The President shall, at stated times, receive for his services a compensation which shall neither be increased nor diminished during the period for which he shall have been elected, and he shall not receive within that period any other emolument from the United States, or any of them.

7. Before he enter on the execution of his office, he shall take the following oath or affirmation:—"I do solemnly swear (or affirm) that I will faithfully execute the office of President of the United States, and will to the best of my ability, preserve, protect and defend the Constitution of the United States."

Section 2. 1. The President shall be commander in chief of the army and navy of the United States, and of the militia of the several States, when called into the actual service of the United States; he may require the opinion in writing, of the principal officer in each of the executive departments, upon any subject relating to the duties of their respective offices, and he shall have power to grant reprieves and pardons for offenses against the United States, except in cases of impeachment.

2. He shall have power, by and with the advice and consent of the Senate, to make treaties, provided two thirds of the senators present concur; and he shall nominate, and by and with the advice and consent of the Senate, shall appoint ambassadors, other public ministers and consuls, judges of the Supreme Court, and all other officers of the United States, whose appointments are not herein otherwise provided for, and which shall be established by law; but the Congress may by law vest the appointment of such inferior officers, as they think proper, in the President alone, in the courts of laws, or in the heads of departments.

3. The President shall have power to fill up all vacancies that may happen during the recess of the Senate, by granting commissions which shall expire at the end of their next session.

Section 3. He shall from time to time give to the Congress information of the state of the Union, and recommend to their consideration such measures as he shall judge necessary and expedient; he may, on extraordinary occasions, convene both Houses, or either of them, and in case of disagreement between them with respect to the time of adjournment, he may adjourn them to such time as he shall think proper; he shall receive ambassadors and other public ministers; he shall take care that the laws be faithfully executed, and shall commission all the officers of the United States.

Section 4. The President, Vice President, and all civil officers of the United States, shall be removed from office on impeachment for, and conviction of, treason, bribery, or other high crimes and misdemeanors.

Article III

Section 1. The judicial power of the United States shall be vested in one Supreme Court, and in such inferior courts as the Congress may from time to time ordain and establish. The judges, both of the Supreme and inferior courts, shall hold their offices during good behavior, and shall, at stated times, receive for their services, a compensation, which shall not be diminished during their continuance in office.

Section 2. 1. The judicial power shall extend to all cases, in law and equity, arising under this Constitution, the laws of the United States, and treaties made, or which shall be made, under their authority;—to all cases of admiralty and maritime jurisdiction;—to controversies to which the United States shall be a party;[7]—to controversies between two or more States;—between a State and citizens of another State;—between citizens of different States;—between citizens of the same State claiming lands under grants of different States, and between a State, or the citizens thereof, and foreign States, citizens or subjects.

2. In all cases affecting ambassadors, other public ministers and consuls, and those in which a State shall be party, the Supreme Court shall have original jurisdiction. In all the other cases before mentioned, the Supreme Court shall have appellate jurisdiction, both as to law and fact, with such exceptions, and under such regulations as the Congress shall make.

3. The trial of all crimes, except in cases of impeachment, shall be by jury; and such trial shall be held in the State where the said crimes shall have been committed; but when not committed within any State, the trial shall be such place or places as the congress may by law have directed.

Section 3. 1. Treason against the United States shall consist only in levying war against them, or in adhering to their enemies, giving them aid and comfort. No person shall be convicted of treason unless on the testimony of two witnesses to the same overt act, or on confession in open court.

2. The Congress shall have power to declare the punishment of treason, but no attainder of treason shall work corruption of blood, or forfeiture except during the life of the person attained.

---

[6]Superseded by the Twelfth Amendment.

[7]See the Eleventh Amendment.

Article IV

Section 1. Full faith and credit shall be given in each State to the public acts, records, and judicial proceedings of every other State. And the Congress may by general laws prescribe the manner in which such acts, records and proceedings shall be proved, and the effect thereof.

Section 2. 1. The citizens of each State shall be entitled to all privileges and immunities of citizens in the several States.[8]

2. A person charged in any State with treason, felony, or other crime, who shall flee from justice, and be found in another State, shall on demand of the executive authority of the State from which he fled, be delivered up to be removed to the State having jurisdiction of the crime.

3. No person held to service or labor in one State under the laws thereof, escaping into another, shall, in consequence of any law or regulation therein, be discharged from such service or labor, but shall be delivered up on claim of the party to whom such service or labor may be due.[9]

Section 3. 1. New States may be admitted by the Congress into this Union; but no new State shall be formed or erected within the jurisdiction of any other State, nor any State be formed by the junction of two or more States, or parts of States, without the consent of the legislatures of the States concerned as well as of the Congress.

2. The Congress shall have power to dispose of and make all needful rules and regulations respecting the territory or other property belonging to the United States; and nothing in this Constitution shall be so construed as to prejudice any claims of the United States, or of any particular State.

Section 4. The United States shall guarantee to every State in this Union a republican form of government, and shall protect each of them against invasion; and on application of the legislature, or of the executive (when the legislature cannot be convened) against domestic violence.

Article V

The Congress, whenever two thirds of both Houses shall deem it necessary, shall propose amendments to this Constitution, or, on the application of the legislatures of two thirds of the several States, shall call a convention for proposing amendments, which in either case shall be valid to all intents and purposes, as part of this Constitution, when ratified by the legislatures of three fourths of the several States, or by conventions in three fourths thereof, as the one or the other mode of ratification may be proposed by the Congress; Provided that no amendment which may be made prior to the year one thousand eight hundred and eight shall in any manner affect the first and fourth clauses in the ninth section of the first article; and that no State, without its consent, shall be deprived of its equal suffrage in the Senate.

Article VI

1. All debts contracted and engagements entered into, before the adoption of this Constitution, shall be as valid against the United States under this Constitution, as under the Confederation.[10]

2. This Constitution, and the laws of the United States which shall be made in pursuance thereof; and all treaties made, or which shall be made, under the authority of the United States, shall be the supreme law of the land; and the judges in every State shall be bound thereby, any thing in the Constitution or laws of any State to the contrary notwithstanding.

3. The senators and representatives before mentioned, and the members of the several State legislatures, and all executive and judicial officers, both of the United States and of the several States, shall be bound by oath or affirmation to support this Constitution; but no religious test shall ever be required as a qualification to any office or public trust under the United States.

Article VII

The ratification of the conventions of nine States shall be sufficient for the establishment of this Constitution between the States so ratifying the same.

Done in Convention by the unanimous consent of the States present the seventeenth day of September in the year of our Lord one thousand seven hundred and eighty-seven, and of the independence of the United States of America the twelfth. In witness whereof we have hereunto subscribed our names.

[Signatories' names omitted]
★ ★ ★

Articles in addition to, and amendment of, the Constitution of the United States of America, proposed by Congress, and ratified by the legislatures of the several States, pursuant to the fifth article of the original Constitution.

Amendment I [First ten amendments ratified December 15, 1791]

Congress shall make no law respecting an establishment of religion, or prohibiting the free exercise thereof; or abridging the freedom of speech, or of the press; or the right of the people peaceably to assemble, and to petition the government for a redress of grievances.

Amendment II

A well regulated militia, being necessary to the security of a free State, the right of the people to keep and bear arms, shall not be infringed.

Amendment III

No soldier shall, in time of peace be quartered in any house, without the consent of the owner, nor in time of war, but in a manner to be prescribed by law.

Amendment IV

The right of the people to be secure in their persons, houses, papers, and effects, against unreasonable searches

---

[8]See the Fourteenth Amendment, Sec. 1.
[9]See the Thirteenth Amendment.

[10]See the Fourteenth Amendment, Sec. 4.

and seizures, shall not be violated, and no warrants shall issue, but upon probable cause, supported by oath or affirmation, and particularly describing the place to be searched, and the persons or things to be seized.

Amendment V

No person shall be held to answer for a capital or otherwise infamous crime, unless on a presentment or indictment of a grand jury, except in cases arising in the land or naval forces, or in the militia, when in actual service in time of war or public danger; nor shall any person be subject for the same offense to be twice put in jeopardy of life or limb; nor shall be compelled in any criminal case to be a witness against himself, nor be deprived of life, liberty, or property, without due process of law; nor shall private property be taken for public use, without just compensation.

Amendment VI

In all criminal prosecutions, the accused shall enjoy the right to a speedy and public trial, by an impartial jury of the State and district wherein the crime shall have been committed, which district shall have been previously ascertained by law, and to be informed of the nature and cause of the accusation; to be confronted with the witnesses against him; to have compulsory process for obtaining witnesses in his favor, and to have the assistance of counsel for his defense.

Amendment VII

In suits at common law, where the value in controversy shall exceed twenty dollars, the right of trial by jury shall be preserved, and no fact tried by a jury shall be otherwise reexamined in any court of the United States, than according to the rules of the common law.

Amendment VIII

Excessive bail shall not be required, nor excessive fines imposed, nor cruel and unusual punishments inflicted.

Amendment IX

The enumeration in the Constitution of certain rights shall not be construed to deny or disparage others retained by the people.

Amendment X

The powers not delegated to the United States by the Constitution, nor prohibited by it to the States, are reserved to the States respectively, or to the people.

Amendment XI [January 8, 1798]

The judicial power of the United States shall not be construed to extend to any suit in law or equity, commenced or prosecuted against one of the United States by citizens of another State, or by citizens or subjects of any foreign State.

Amendment XII [September 25, 1804]

The electors shall meet in their respective States, and vote by ballot for President and Vice President, one of whom, at least, shall not be an inhabitant of the same State with themselves; they shall name in their ballots the person voted for as President, and in distinct ballots the person voted for as Vice President, and they shall make distinct lists of all persons voted for as President and of all persons voted for as Vice President, and of the number of votes for each, which lists they shall sign and certify, and transmit sealed to the seat of the government of the United States, directed to the President of the Senate;—The President of the Senate shall, in the presence of the Senate and House of Representatives, open all the certificates and the votes shall then be counted;—The person having the greatest number of votes for President, shall be the President, if such number be a majority of the whole number of electors appointed; and if no person have such majority, then from the persons having the highest numbers not exceeding three on the list of those voted for as President, the House of Representatives shall choose immediately, by ballot, the President. But in choosing the President, the votes shall be taken by States, the representation from each State having one vote; a quorum for this purpose shall consist of a member or members from two thirds of the States, and a majority of all the States shall be necessary to a choice. And if the House of Representatives shall not choose a President whenever the right of choice shall devolve upon them, before the fourth day of March next following, then the Vice President shall act as President, as in the case of the death or other constitutional disability of the President. The person having the greatest number of votes as Vice President shall be the Vice President, if such number be a majority of the whole number of electors appointed, and if no person have a majority, then from the two highest numbers on the list, the Senate shall choose the Vice President; a quorum for the purpose shall consist of two thirds of the whole number of Senators, and a majority of the whole number shall be necessary to a choice. But no person constitutionally ineligible to the office of President shall be eligible to that of Vice President of the United States.

Amendment XIII [December 18, 1865]

Section 1. Neither slavery nor involuntary servitude, except as a punishment for crime whereof the party shall have been duly convicted, shall exist within the United States, or any place subject to their jurisdiction.

Section 2. Congress shall have power to enforce this article by appropriate legislation.

Amendment XIV [July 28, 1868]

Section 1. All persons born or naturalized in the United States, and subject to the jurisdiction thereof, are citizens of the United States and of the State wherein they reside. No State shall make or enforce any law which shall abridge the privileges or immunities of citizens of the United States; nor shall any State deprive any person of life, liberty, or property, without due process of law; nor deny to any person within its jurisdiction the equal protection of the laws.

Section 2. Representatives shall be apportioned among the several States according to their respective numbers, counting the whole number of persons in each State, excluding Indians not taxed. But when the right to vote at any election for the choice of electors for President and Vice President of the United States, representatives in Congress, the executive and judicial officers of a State, or the members of the legislature thereof, is denied to any of the male inhabitants of such State, being twenty-one years of age, and citizens of the United States, or in any way abridged, except for participating in rebellion, or other crime, the basis of representation there shall be reduced in the proportion which the number of such male citizens shall bear to the whole number of male citizens twenty-one years of age in such State.

Section 3. No person shall be a senator or representative in Congress, or elector of President and Vice President, or hold any office, civil or military, under the United States, or under any State, who having previously taken an oath, as a member of Congress, or as an officer of the United States, or as a member of any State legislature, or as an executive or judicial officer of any State, to support the Constitution of the United States, shall have engaged in insurrection or rebellion against the same, or given aid or comfort to the enemies thereof. But Congress may by a vote of two thirds of each House, remove such disability.

Section 4. The validity of the public debt of the United States, authorized by law, including debts incurred for payment of pensions and bounties for services in suppressing insurrection or rebellion; shall not be questioned. But neither the United States nor any State shall assume or pay any debt or obligation incurred in aid of insurrection or rebellion against the United States, or any claim for the loss or emancipation of any slave; but all such debts, obligations, and claims shall be held illegal and void.

Section 5. The Congress shall have the power to enforce, by appropriate legislation, the provisions of this article.

Amendment XV [March 30, 1870]

Section 1. The right of citizens of the United States to vote shall not be denied or abridged by the United States or by any State on account of race, color, or previous condition of servitude.

Section 2. The Congress shall have power to enforce this article by appropriate legislation.

Amendment XVI [February 25, 1913]

The Congress shall have power to lay and collect taxes on incomes, from whatever source derived, without apportionment among the several States, and without regard to any census or enumeration.

Amendment XVII [May 31, 1913]

The Senate of the United States shall be composed of two senators from each State, elected by the people thereof, for six years; and each senator shall have one vote. The electors in each State shall have the qualifications requisite for electors of the most numerous branch of the State legislature.

When vacancies happen in the representation of any State in the Senate, the executive authority of such State shall issue writs of election to fill such vacancies: Provided, That the legislature of any State may empower the executive thereof to make temporary appointments until the people fill the vacancies by election as the legislature may direct.

This amendment shall not be so construed as to affect the election or term of any senator chosen before it becomes valid as part of the Constitution.

Amendment XVIII[11] [January 29, 1919]

After one year from the ratification of this article, the manufacture, sale, or transportation of intoxicating liquors within, the importation thereof into, or the exportation thereof from the United States and all territory subject to the jurisdiction thereof for beverage purposes is thereby prohibited.

The Congress and the several States shall have concurrent power to enforce this article by appropriate legislation.

This article shall be inoperative unless it shall have been ratified as an amendment to the Constitution by the legislatures of the several States, as provided in the constitution, within seven years from the date of the submission hereof to the States by Congress.

Amendment XIX [August 26, 1920]

The right of citizens of the United States to vote shall not be denied or abridged by the United States or by any State on account of sex.

Congress shall have the power to enforce this article by appropriate legislation.

Amendment XX [January 23, 1933]

Section 1. The terms of the President and Vice President shall end at noon on the 20th day of January and the terms of Senators and Representatives at noon on the 3d day of January, of the years in which such terms would have ended if this article had not been ratified; and the terms of their successors shall then begin.

Section 2. The Congress shall assemble at least once in every year, and such meeting shall begin at noon on the 3d day of January, unless they shall by law appoint a different day.

Section 3. If, at the time fixed for the beginning of the term of President, the President-elect shall have died, the Vice President-elect shall become President. If a President shall not have been chosen before the time fixed for the beginning of his term, or if the President-elect shall have failed to qualify, then the Vice President-elect shall act as President until a President shall have qualified; and the Congress may by law provide for the case wherein neither a President-elect nor a Vice President-elect shall have qualified, declaring who shall then act as President, or the manner in which one who is to act shall be selected, and such person shall act accordingly. until a President or Vice President shall have qualified.

Section 4. The Congress may by law provide for the case of the death of any of the persons from whom, the

---

[11]Repealed by the Twenty-first Amendment

House of Representatives may choose a President whenever the right of choice shall have devolved upon them, and for the case of the death of any of the persons from whom the Senate may choose a Vice President whenever the right of choice shall have devolved upon them.

Section 5. Sections 1 and 2 shall take effect on the 15th day of October following the ratification of this article.

Section 6. This article shall be inoperative unless it shall have been ratified as an amendment to the Constitution by the legislatures of three-fourths of the several States within seven years from the date of its submission.

Amendment XXI [December 5, 1933]

Section 1. The Eighteenth Article of amendment to the Constitution of the United States is hereby repealed.

Section 2. The transportation or importation into any State, Territory, or possession of the United States for delivery or use therein of intoxicating liquors in violation of the laws thereof, is hereby prohibited.

Section 3. This article shall be inoperative unless it shall have been ratified as an amendment to the Constitution by conventions in the several States, as provided in the Constitution, within seven years from the date of the submission thereof to the States by the Congress.

Amendment XXII [March 1, 1951]

No person shall be elected to the office of the President more than twice, and no person who has held the office of President, or acted as President, for more than two years of a term to which some other person was elected President shall be elected to the office of the President more than once.

But this article shall not apply to any person holding the office of President when this article was proposed by the Congress, and shall not prevent any person who may be holding the office of President, or acting as President, during the term within which this article becomes operative from holding the office of President or acting as President during the remainder of such term.

This article shall be inoperative unless it shall have been ratified as an amendment to the Constitution by the legislatures of three-fourths of the several States within seven years from the date of its submission to the States by the Congress.

Amendment XXIII [March 29, 1961]

Section 1. The District constituting the seat of Government of the United States shall appoint in such manner as the Congress may direct.

A number of electors of President and Vice President equal to the whole number of Senators and Representa-tives in Congress to which the District would be entitled if it were a State, but in no event more than the least populous State; they shall be in addition to those appointed by the States, but they shall be considered, for the purposes of the election of President and Vice President, to be electors appointed by a State; and they shall meet in the District and perform such duties as provided by the twelfth article of amendment.

Section 2. The Congress shall have power to enforce this article by appropriate legislation.

Amendment XXIV [January 23, 1964]

Section 1. The right of citizens of the United States to vote in any primary or other election for President or Vice President, for electors for President or Vice President, or for Senator or Representative in Congress, shall not be denied or abridged by the United States or any State by reason of failure to pay any poll tax or other tax.

Section 2. The Congress shall have power to enforce this article by appropriate legislation.

Amendment XXV [February 10, 1967]

Section 1. In case of the removal of the President from office or of his death or resignation, the Vice President shall become President.

Section 2. Whenever there is a vacancy in the office of the Vice President, the President shall nominate a Vice President who shall take office upon confirmation by a majority of both Houses of Congress.

Section 3. Whenever the President transmits to the President pro tempore of the Senate and the Speaker of the House of Representatives his written declaration that he is unable to discharge the powers and duties of his office, and until he transmits to them a written declaration to the contrary, such powers and duties shall be discharged by the Vice President as Acting President.

Section 4. Whenever the Vice President and a majority of either the principal officers of the executive departments or of such other body as Congress may by law provide, transmit to the President pro tempore of the Senate and the Speaker of the House of Representatives their written declaration that the President is unable to discharge the powers and duties of his office, the Vice President shall immediately assume the powers and duties of the office as Acting President.

Thereafter, when the President transmits to the President pro tempore of the Senate and the Speaker of the House of Representatives his written declaration that no inability exists, he shall resume the powers and duties of his office unless the Vice President and a majority of either the principal officers of the executive departments or of such other body as Congress may by law provide, transmit within four days to the President pro tempore of the Senate and the Speaker of the House of Representatives their written declaration that the President is unable to discharge the powers and duties of his office. Thereupon Congress shall decide the issue, assembling within forty-eight hours for that purpose if not in session. If the Congress, within twenty-one days after receipt of the latter written declaration, or, if Congress is not in session, within twenty-one days after Congress is required to assemble, determines by two-thirds vote of both Houses that the President is unable to discharge the powers and duties of his office, the Vice President shall continue to discharge the same as Acting President; otherwise, the President shall resume the powers and duties of his office.

Amendment XXVI [June 30, 1971]

Section 1. The right of citizens of the United States who are eighteen years of age or older to vote shall not be denied or abridged by the United States or by any State on account of age.

   Section 2. The Congress shall have power to enforce this article by appropriate legislation.

Amendment XXVII[12] *[May 7, 1992]*

   No law, varying the compensation for services of the Senators and Representatives, shall take effect until an election of Representatives shall have intervened.

.

[12]James Madison proposed this amendment in 1789 together with the ten amendments that were adopted as the Bill of Rights, but it failed to win ratification at the time. Congress, however, had set no deadline for its ratification, and over the years—particularly in the 1980s and 1990s—many states voted to add it to the Constitution. With the ratification of Michigan in 1992 it passed the threshold of 3/4ths of the states required for adoption, but because the process took more than 200 years, its validity remains in doubt.

●♦●┤Read the Document

Admission of States to the Union
Demographics of the United States

PRESIDENTS AND VICE PRESIDENTS

1. George Washington (1789)
    John Adams (1789)

2. John Adams (1797)
    Thomas Jefferson (1797)

3. Thomas Jefferson (1801)
    Aaron Burr (1801)
    George Clinton (1805)

4. James Madison (1809)
    George Clinton (1809)
    Elbridge Gerry (1813)

5. James Monroe (1817)
    Daniel D. Thompkins (1817)

6. John Quincy Adams (1825)
    John C. Calhoun (1825)

7. Andrew Jackson (1829)
    John C. Calhoun (1829)
    Martin Van Buren (1833)

8. Martin Van Buren (1837)
    Richard M. Johnson (1837)

9. William H. Harrison (1841)
    John Tyler (1841)

10. John Tyler (1841)

11. James K. Polk (1845)
    George M. Dallas (1845)

12. Zachary Taylor (1849)
    Millard Fillmore (1849)

13. Millard Fillmore (1850)

14. Franklin Pierce (1853)
    William R. King (1853)

15. James Buchanan (1857)
    John C. Breckinridge (1857)

16. Abraham Lincoln (1861)
    Hannibal Hamlin (1861)
    Andrew Johnson (1865)

17. Andrew Johnson (1865)

18. Ulysses S. Grant (1869)
    Schuyler Colfax (1869)
    Henry Wilson (1873)

19. Rutherford B. Hayes (1877)
    William A. Wheeler (1877)

20. James A. Garfield (1881)
    Chester A. Arthur (1881)

21. Chester A. Arthur (1881)

22. Grover Cleveland (1885)
    T. A. Hendricks (1885)

23. Benjamin Harrison (1889)
    Levi P. Morgan (1889)

24. Grover Cleveland (1893)
    Adlai E. Stevenson (1893)

25. William McKinley (1897)
    Garret A. Hobart (1897)
    Theodore Roosevelt (1901)

26. Theodore Roosevelt (1901)
    Charles Fairbanks (1905)

27. William H. Taft (1909)
    James S. Sherman (1909)

28. Woodrow Wilson (1913)
    Thomas R. Marshall (1913)

29. Warren G. Harding (1921)
    Calvin Coolidge (1921)

30. Calvin Coolidge (1923)
    Charles G. Dawes (1925)

31. Herbert C. Hoover (1929)
    Charles Curtis (1929)

32. Franklin D. Roosevelt (1933)
    John Nance Garner (1933)
    Henry A. Wallace (1941)
    Harry S. Truman (1945)

33. Harry S. Truman (1945)
    Alben W. Barkley (1949)

34. Dwight D. Eisenhower (1953)
    Richard M. Nixon (1953)

35. John F. Kennedy (1961)
    Lyndon B. Johnson (1961)

36. Lyndon B. Johnson (1963)
    Hubert H. Humphrey (1965)

37. Richard M. Nixon (1969)
    Spiro T. Agnew (1969)
    Gerald R. Ford (1973)

38. Gerald R. Ford (1974)
    Nelson A. Rockefeller (1974)

39. James E. Carter Jr. (1977)
    Walter F. Mondale (1977)

40. Ronald W. Reagan (1981)
    George H. Bush (1981)

41. George H. Bush (1989)
    James D. Quayle III (1989)

42. William J. Clinton (1993)
    Albert Gore (1993)

43. George W. Bush (2001)
    Richard Cheney (2001)

44. Barack H. Obama (2009)
    Joseph Biden (2009)

PRESIDENTIAL ELECTIONS

Year	Number of States	Candidates	Party	Popular Vote*	Electoral Vote[†]	Percentage of Popular Vote*
1789	11	GEORGE WASHINGTON	No party designations		69	
		John Adams			34	
		Other Candidates			35	
1792	15	GEORGE WASHINGTON	No party designations		132	
		John Adams			77	
		George Clinton			50	
		Other Candidates			5	
1796	16	JOHN ADAMS	Federalist		71	
		Thomas Jefferson	Democratic-Republican		68	
		Thomas Pinckney	Federalist		59	
		Aaron Burr	Democratic-Republican		30	
		Other Candidates			48	
1800	16	THOMAS JEFFERSON	Democratic-Republican		73	
		Aaron Burr	Democratic-Republican		73	
		John Adams	Federalist		65	
		Charles C. Pinckney	Federalist		64	
		John Jay	Federalist		1	
1804	17	THOMAS JEFFERSON	Democratic-Republican		162	
		Charles C. Pinckney	Federalist		14	
1808	17	JAMES MADISON	Democratic-Republican		122	
		Charles C. Pinckney	Federalist		47	
		George Clinton	Democratic-Republican		6	
1812	18	JAMES MADISON	Democratic-Republican		128	
		DeWitt Clinton	Federalist		89	
1816	19	JAMES MONROE	Democratic-Republican		183	
		Rufus King	Federalist		34	
1820	24	JAMES MONROE	Democratic-Republican		231	
		John Quincy Adams	Independent-Republican		1	
1824	24	JOHN QUINCY ADAMS	Democratic-Republican	108,740	84	30.5
		Andrew Jackson	Democratic-Republican	153,544	99	43.1
		William H. Crawford	Democratic-Republican	46,618	41	13.1
		Henry Clay	Democratic-Republican	47,136	37	13.2
1828	24	ANDREW JACKSON	Democrat	647,286	178	56.0
		John Quincy Adams	National-Republican	508,064	83	44.0
1832	24	ANDREW JACKSON	Democrat	687,502	219	55.0
		Henry Clay	National-Republican	530,189	49	42.4
		William Wirt	Anti-Masonic	33,108	7	
		John Floyd	National-Republican		11	2.6

*Percentage of popular vote given for any election year may not total 100 percent because candidates receiving less than 1 percent of the popular vote have been omitted.

[†]Prior to the passage of the Twelfth Amendment in 1904, the electoral college voted for two presidential candidates; the runner-up became Vice-President. Data from *Historical Statistics of the United States, Colonial Times to 1957* (1961), pp. 682–683, and *The World Almanac*.

PRESIDENTIAL ELECTIONS (continued)

Year	Number of States	Candidates	Party	Popular Vote	Electoral Vote	Percentage of Popular Vote
1836	26	MARTIN VAN BUREN	Democrat	765,483	170	50.9
		William H. Harrison	Whig		73	
		Hugh L. White	Whig		26	
		Daniel Webster	Whig	739,795	14	49.1
		W. P. Mangum	Whig		11	
1840	26	WILLIAM H. HARRISON	Whig	1,274,624	234	53.1
		Martin Van Buren	Democrat	1,127,781	60	46.9
1844	26	JAMES K. POLK	Democrat	1,338,464	170	49.6
		Henry Clay	Whig	1,300,097	105	48.1
		James G. Birney	Liberty	62,300		2.3
1848	30	ZACHARY TAYLOR	Whig	1,360,967	163	47.4
		Lewis Cass	Democrat	1,222,342	127	42.5
		Martin Van Buren	Free-Soil	291,263		10.1
1852	31	FRANKLIN PIERCE	Democrat	1,601,117	254	50.9
		Winfield Scott	Whig	1,385,453	42	44.1
		John P. Hale	Free-Soil	155,825		5.0
1856	31	JAMES BUCHANAN	Democrat	1,832,955	174	45.3
		John C. Frémont	Republican	1,339,932	114	33.1
		Millard Fillmore	American ("Know Nothing")	871,731	8	21.6
1860	33	ABRAHAM LINCOLN	Republican	1,865,593	180	39.8
		Stephen A. Douglas	Democrat	1,382,713	12	29.5
		John C. Breckinridge	Democrat	848,356	72	18.1
		John Bell	Constitutional Union	592,906	39	12.6
1864	36	ABRAHAM LINCOLN	Republican	2,206,938	212	55.0
		George B. McClellan	Democrat	1,803,787	21	45.0
1868	37	ULYSSES S. GRANT	Republican	3,013,421	214	52.7
		Horatio Seymour	Democrat	2,706,829	80	47.3
1872	37	ULYSSES S. GRANT	Republican	3,596,745	286	55.6
		Horace Greeley	Democrat	2,843,446		★43.9
1876	38	RUTHERFORD B. HAYES	Republican	4,036,572	185	48.0
		Samuel J. Tilden	Democrat	4,284,020	184	51.0
1880	38	JAMES A. GARFIELD	Republican	4,453,295	214	48.5
		Winfield S. Hancock	Democrat	4,414,082	155	48.1
		James B. Weaver	Greenback-Labor	308,578		3.4
1884	38	GROVER CLEVELAND	Democrat	4,879,507	219	48.5
		James G. Blaine	Republican	4,850,293	182	48.2
		Benjamin F. Butler	Greenback-Labor	175,370		1.8
		John P. St. John	Prohibition	150,369		1.5

★Because of the death of Greeley, Democratic electors scattered their votes.

PRESIDENTIAL ELECTIONS (continued)

Year	Number of States	Candidates	Party	Popular Vote	Electoral Vote	Percentage of Popular Vote
1888	38	BENJAMIN HARRISON	Republican	5,447,129	233	47.9
		Grover Cleveland	Democrat	5,537,857	168	48.6
		Clinton B. Fisk	Prohibition	249,506		2.2
		Anson J. Streeter	Union Labor	146,935		1.3
1892	44	GROVER CLEVELAND	Democrat	5,555,426	277	46.1
		Benjamin Harrison	Republican	5,182,690	145	43.0
		James B. Weaver	People's	1,029,846	22	8.5
		John Bidwell	Prohibition	264,133		2.2
1896	45	WILLIAM MCKINLEY	Republican	7,102,246	271	51.1
		William J. Bryan	Democrat	6,492,559	176	47.7
1900	45	WILLIAM MCKINLEY	Republican	7,218,491	292	51.7
		William J. Bryan	Democrat; Populist	6,356,734	155	45.5
		John C. Woolley	Prohibition	208,914		1.5
1904	45	THEODORE ROOSEVELT	Republican	7,628,461	336	57.4
		Alton B. Parker	Democrat	5,084,223	140	37.6
		Eugene V. Debs	Socialist	402,283		3.0
		Silas C. Swallow	Prohibition	258,536		1.9
1908	46	WILLIAM H. TAFT	Republican	7,675,320	321	51.6
		William J. Bryan	Democrat	6,412,294	162	43.1
		Eugene V. Debs	Socialist	420,793		2.8
		Eugene W. Chafin	Prohibition	253,840		1.7
1912	48	WOODROW WILSON	Democrat	6,296,547	435	41.9
		Theodore Roosevelt	Progressive	4,118,571	88	27.4
		William H. Taft	Republican	3,486,720	8	23.2
		Eugene V. Debs	Socialist	900,672		6.0
		Eugene W. Chafin	Prohibition	206,275		1.4
1916	48	WOODROW WILSON	Democrat	9,127,695	277	49.4
		Charles E. Hughes	Republican	8,533,507	254	46.2
		A. L. Benson	Socialist	585,113		3.2
		J. Frank Hanly	Prohibition	220,506		1.2
1920	48	WARREN G. HARDING	Republican	16,143,407	404	60.4
		James M. Cox	Democrat	9,130,328	127	34.2
		Eugene V. Debs	Socialist	919,799		3.4
		P. P. Christensen	Farmer-Labor	265,411		1.0
1924	48	CALVIN COOLIDGE	Republican	15,718,211	382	54.0
		John W. Davis	Democrat	8,385,283	136	28.8
		Robert M. La Follette	Progressive	4,831,289	13	16.6
1928	48	HERBERT C. HOOVER	Republican	21,391,993	444	58.2
		Alfred E. Smith	Democrat	15,016,169	87	40.9
1932	48	FRANKLIN D. ROOSEVELT	Democrat	22,809,638	472	57.4
		Herbert C. Hoover	Republican	15,758,901	59	39.7
		Norman Thomas	Socialist	881,951		2.2

PRESIDENTIAL ELECTIONS (continued)

Year	Number of States	Candidates	Party	Popular Vote	Electoral Vote	Percentage of Popular Vote
1936	48	FRANKLIN D. ROOSEVELT	Democrat	27,752,869	523	60.8
		Alfred M. Landon	Republican	16,674,665	8	36.5
		William Lemke	Union	882,479		1.9
1940	48	FRANKLIN D. ROOSEVELT	Democrat	27,307,819	449	54.8
		Wendell L. Willkie	Republican	22,321,018	82	44.8
1944	48	FRANKLIN D. ROOSEVELT	Democrat	25,606,585	432	53.5
		Thomas E. Dewey	Republican	22,014,745	99	46.0
1948	48	HARRY S TRUMAN	Democrat	24,105,812	303	49.5
		Thomas E. Dewey	Republican	21,970,065	189	45.1
		J. Strom Thurmond	States' Rights	1,169,063	39	2.4
		Henry A. Wallace	Progressive	1,157,172		2.4
1952	48	DWIGHT D. EISENHOWER	Republican	33,936,234	442	55.1
		Adlai E. Stevenson	Democrat	27,314,992	89	44.4
1956	48	DWIGHT D. EISENHOWER	Republican	35,590,472	457 ★	57.6
		Adlai E. Stevenson	Democrat	26,022,752	73	42.1
1960	50	JOHN F. KENNEDY	Democrat	34,227,096	303 †	49.9
		Richard M. Nixon	Republican	34,108,546	219	49.6
1964	50	LYNDON B. JOHNSON	Democrat	42,676,220	486	61.3
		Barry M. Goldwater	Republican	26,860,314	52	38.5
1968	50	RICHARD M. NIXON	Republican	31,785,480	301	43.4
		Hubert H. Humphrey	Democrat	31,275,165	191	42.7
		George C. Wallace	American Independent	9,906,473	46	13.5
1972	50	RICHARD M. NIXON‡	Republican	47,165,234	520	60.6
		George S. McGovern	Democrat	29,168,110	17	37.5
1976	50	JAMES E. CARTER JR.	Democrat	40,828,929	297	50.1
		Gerald R. Ford	Republican	39,148,940	240	47.9
		Eugene McCarthy	Independent	739,256		
1980	50	RONALD W. REAGAN	Republican	43,201,220	489	50.9
		James E. Carter Jr.	Democrat	34,913,332	49	41.2
		John B. Anderson	Independent	5,581,379		
1984	50	RONALD W. REAGAN	Republican	53,428,357	525	59.0
		Walter F. Mondale	Democrat	36,930,923	13	41.0
1988	50	GEORGE H. W. BUSH	Republican	48,901,046	426	53.4
		Michael Dukakis	Democrat	41,809,030	111	45.6
1992	50	WILLIAM J. CLINTON	Democrat	43,728,275	370	43.2
		George H. W. Bush	Republican	38,167,416	168	37.7
		H. Ross Perot	United We Stand, America	19,237,247		19.0

★Walter B. Jones received 1 electoral vote.

†Harry F. Byrd received 15 electoral votes.

‡Resigned August 9, 1974: Vice President Gerald R. Ford became President.

PRESIDENTIAL ELECTIONS (continued)

Year	Number of States	Candidates	Party	Popular Vote	Electoral Vote	Percentage of Popular Vote
1996	50	WILLIAM J. CLINTON	Democrat	45,590,703	379	49.0
		Robert Dole	Republican	37,816,307	159	41.0
		H. Ross Perot	Reform	7,874,283		8.0
2000	50	GEORGE W. BUSH	Republican	50,459,624	271	47.9
		Albert Gore	Democrat	51,003,328	266	49.4
		Ralph Nader	Green	2,882,985	0	2.7
2004	50	GEORGE W. BUSH	Republican	59,117,523	286	51.1
		John Kerry	Democrat	55,557,584	252	48.0
		Ralph Nader	Green	405,623	0	0.3
2008	50	BARACK H. OBAMA	Democrat	69,456,897	365	52.9
		John McCain	Republican	59,934,814	173	45.7

BIBLIOGRAPHY

CHAPTER 17

The Politics of Reconstruction

Richard H. Abbott, *The Republican Party and the South, 1855–1877* (1986)

Bruce E. Baker, *What Reconstruction Meant: Historical Memory in the American South* (2008)

Herman Belz, *Emancipation and Equal Rights* (1978)

Michael Les Benedict, *A Compromise of Principle: Congressional Republicans and Reconstruction* (1974)

———, *The Impeachment and Trial of Andrew Johnson* (1973)

Michael Kent Curtis, *No State Shall Abridge: The Fourteenth Amendment and the Bill of Rights* (1990)

Ellen Carol DuBois, *Feminism and Suffrage* (1978)

Laura F. Edwards, *Gendered Strife & Confusion: The Political Culture of Reconstruction* (1997)

William C. Harris, *With Charity for All: Lincoln and the Restoration of the Union* (1997)

Robert Kaczorowski, *The Politics of Judicial Interpretation: The Federal Courts, Department of Justice, and Civil Rights, 1866–1876* (1985)

James McPherson, *Ordeal by Fire: The Civil War and Reconstruction* (1982)

Michael Perman, *Emancipation and Reconstruction, 1862–1879* (1987)

Brooks D. Simpson, *The Reconstruction Presidents* (1998)

Kenneth M. Stampp, *The Era of Reconstruction, 1865–1877* (1965)

The Meaning of Freedom

Ira Berlin et al., eds., *Freedom: A Documentary History*, 3 vols. (1985–1991)

Paul A Cimbala and Randall M. Miller, eds., *The Freedmen's Bureau and Reconstruction.* (1999)

W. E. B. DuBois, *Black Reconstruction* (1935)

Carol Faulkner, *Women's Radical Reconstruction: The Freedmen's Aid Movement* (2004)

Barbara J. Fields, *Slavery and Freedom on the Middle Ground* (1985)

Eric Foner, *Freedom's Lawmakers: A Directory of Black Officeholders during Reconstruction* (1996)

Noralee Frankel, *Freedom's Women: Black Women and Families in Civil War Era Mississippi* (1999)

Herbert G. Gutman, *The Black Family in Slavery and Freedom* (1976)

Sharon Ann Holt, *Making Freedom Pay: North Carolina Freedpeople Working for Themselves, 1865–1900* (2000)

Richard Hume and Jerry Gough, *Black Carpetbaggers and Scalawags: The Constitutional Conventions of Radical Reconstruction* (2008)

Leon Litwack, *Been in the Storm So Long: The Aftermath of Slavery* (1975)

Lynda J. Morgan, *Emancipation in Virginia's Tobacco Belt* (1992)

Nell Irvin Painter, *Exodusters* (1977)

Howard N. Rabinowitz, *Race Relations in the Urban South, 1865–1890* (1978)

Roger L. Ransom and Richard Sutch, *One Kind of Freedom: The Economic Consequences of Emancipation* (1977)

Edward Royce, *The Origins of Southern Sharecropping* (1993)

Leslie A. Schwalm, *A Hard Fight for We: Women's Transition from Slavery to Freedom in South Carolina* (1997)

Southern Politics and Society

James A. Baggett, *The Scalawags: Southern Dissenters in the Civil War and Reconstruction* (2003)

Nancy Bercaw, *Gendered Freedoms: Race, Rights, and the Politics of the Household in the Delta, 1861–1875* (2003)

Pamela Brandwein, *Reconstructing Reconstruction: The Supreme Court and the Production of Historical Truth* (1999)

Charles W. Calhoun, *Conceiving a New Republic: The Republican Party and the Southern Question, 1869–1900* (2006)

Dan T. Carter, *When the War Was Over: The Failure of Self Reconstruction in the South, 1865–1877* (1985)

Richard N. Current, *Those Terrible Carpetbaggers* (1988)

Michael W. Fitzgerald, *The Union League Movement in the Deep South* (1989)

Stephen Hahn, *The Roots of Southern Populism* (1983)

Sally McMillen, *To Raise Up the South: Sunday Schools in Black and White Churches, 1865–1915* (2001)

Scott Reynolds Nelson, *Iron Confederacies: Southern Railroads, Klan Violence, and Reconstruction* (1999)

Michael S. Perman, *The Road to Redemption: Southern Politics, 1868–1979* (1984)

Daniel W. Stowell, *Rebuilding Zion: The Religious Reconstruction of the South, 1863–1877* (1998)

Allen W. Trelease, *White Terror: The Ku Klux Klan Conspiracy and Southern Reconstruction* (1971)

Richard Valelly, *The Two Reconstructions: The Struggle for Black Enfranchisement* (2004)

Jonathan M. Wiener, *Social Origins of the New South* (1978)

Reconstructing the North

Stephen Buechler, *The Transformation of the Woman Suffrage Movement* (1986)

Morton Keller, *Affairs of State* (1977)

David Montgomery, *Beyond Equality: Labor and the Radical Republicans, 1862–1872* (1967)

Keith I. Polakoff, *The Politics of Inertia: The Election of 1876 and the End of Reconstruction* (1973)

Heather Cox Richardson, *The Death of Reconstruction: Race, Labor, and Politics in the Post Civil War North, 1865–1901* (2001)

———, *West From Appomattox: The Reconstruction of America After the Civil War* (2007)

Andrew Slap, *The Doom of Reconstruction: The Liberal Republicans in the Civil War Era* (2006)

Amy Dru Stanley, *From Bondage to Contract: Wage Labor, Marriage, and the Market in the Age of Slave Emancipation* (1998)

Mark W. Summers, *Railroads, Reconstruction, and the Gospel of Prosperity* (1984)

———, *The Era of Good Stealings* (1993)

Xi Wang, *The Trial of Democracy: Black Suffrage and Northern Republicans, 1860–1910* (1997)

C. Vann Woodward, *Reunion and Reaction: The Compromise of 1877 and the End of Reconstruction* (1956)

Biography

Kenneth D. Ackerman, *Boss Tweed* (2005)

Philip Dray, *Capitol Men: The Epic Story of Reconstruction Through the Lives of the First Black Congressmen* (2008)

Stephen Kantrowitz, *Ben Tillman and the Reconstruction of White Supremacy* (2000)

William S. McFeely, *Frederick Douglass* (1989)

———, *Grant: A Biography* (1981)

———, *Yankee Stepfather: General O. O. Howard and the Freedmen* (1968)

Hans L. Trefousse, *Andrew Johnson* (1989)

———, *Thaddeus Stevens: Nineteenth Century Egalitarian* (1997)

CHAPTER 18

Indian Peoples and Indian–White Relations

David Wallace Adams, *Education for Extinction: American Indians and the Boarding School Experience, 1875–1928* (1995)

Henrik Andersson, *The Lakota Ghost Dance of 1890* (2008)

Jacqueline Fear-Segal, *White Man's Club: Schools, Race, and the Sturggle of Indian Acculturation* (2007)

Ian Frazier, *Great Plains* (2001)

Lisbeth Haas, *Conquests and Historical Identities in California, 1769–1936* (1995)

Shelley Bowen Hatfield, *Chasing Shadows: Indians along the United States–Mexico Border, 1876–1911* (1998)

Frederick E. Hoxie, *A Final Promise: The Campaign to Assimilate the Indians, 1880–1920* (1984, 2001)

Albert L. Hurtado, *Indian Survival on the California Frontier* (1988)

Alvin M. Josephy Jr., *Nez Perce Country* (2007)

Patricia Nelson Limerick, *The Legacy of Conquest: The Unbroken Past of the American West* (1987)

John D. McDermott, *A Guide to the Indian Wars of the West* (1998)

Joseph M. Marshall III, *The Day the World Ended at Little Bighorn* (2007)

Valerie Sherer Mathes and Richard Lowitt, *The Standing Bear Controversy: Prelude to Indian Reform* (2003)

Devon Abbott Mihesuah, *Cultivating the Rosebuds: The Education of Women at the Cherokee Female Seminary, 1851–1909* (1993)

J. Diane Pearson, *The Nez Perces in the Indian Territory: Nimiipuu Survival* (2008)

Theda Perdue, ed., *Sifters: Native American Women's Lives* (2001)

Catherine Price, *The Oglala People, 1841–1879* (1996)

Glenda Riley, *Women and Indians on the Frontier, 1825–1915* (1984)

Clifford E. Trafzer, Jean A. Keller, and Lorene Sisquoc, *Boarding School Blues: Revisiting American Indian Educational Experiences* (2006)

Elliott West, *The Last Indian War: The Nez Perce Story* (2009)

Richard White, *The Roots of Dependency: Subsistence, Environment, and Social Change among the Choctaws, Pawnees, and Navajos* (1983)

Murray R. Wickett, *Contested Territory: Whites, Native Americans, and African Americans in Oklahoma, 1865–1907* (2000)

Internal Empire

Armando C. Alonzo, *Tejano Legacy: Rancheros and Settlers in South Texas, 1734–1900* (1998)

Susan Armitage and Elizabeth Jameson, eds., *The Women's West* (1987)

Susan Armitage, Ruth B. Moynihan, and Christiane Fischer Dichamp, eds., *So Much to Be Done: Women Settlers on the Mining and Ranching Frontier* (1990)

Anne M. Butler and Michael J. Lansing, *The American West: A Concise History* (2008)

Arnoldo De Leon, *Racial Frontiers: Africans, Chinese, and Mexicans in Western America, 1848–1890* (2002)

Sarah Deutsch, *No Separate Refuge: Culture, Class and Gender on an Anglo-Hispanic Frontier in the American Southwest, 1880–1940* (1987)

David M. Emmons, *The Butte Irish: Class and Ethnicity in an American Mining Town, 1875–1925* (1989)

Sarah Barringer Gordon, *The Mormon Question: Polygamy and Constitutional Conflict in Nineteenth-Century America* (2002)

Eugene P. Moehring, *Urbanism and Empire in the Far West, 1840–1890* (2004)

Douglas Monroy, *Thrown among Strangers: The Making of Mexican Culture in Frontier California* (1990)

Jeffrey Nichols, *Prostitution, Polygamy, and Power: Salt Lake City, 1847–1918* (2002)

Gunter Peck, *Reinventing Free Labor: Padrones and Immigrant Workers in the North American West, 1880–1930* (2000)

William G. Robbins, *Colony and Empire: The Capitalist Transformation of the American West* (1994)

Carlos A. Schwantes and James P. Ronda, *The West the Railroads Made* (2008)

Quintard Taylor, *In Search of the Racial Frontier: African Americans in the American West, 1528–1990* (1998)

Samuel Truett, *Fugitive Landscapes: The Forgotten History of U.S.-Mexico Borderlands* (2006)

Sally Zanjani, *A Mine of Her Own: Women Prospectors in the American West, 1850–1950* (1997)

Ranching and Farming

Allan G. Bogue, *From Prairie to Corn Belt: Farming on the Illinois and Iowa Prairies in the Nineteenth Century* (1963)

Sucheng Chan, *This Bitter-Sweet Soil: The Chinese in California Agriculture, 1860–1910* (1986)

Philip Durham and Everett L. Jones, *The Negro Cowboys* (1965)

Mark Fiege, *Irrigated Eden: the Making of an Agricultural Landscape in the American West* (1999)

Dee Garceau, *The Important Things of Life: Women, Work, and Family in Sweetwater County, Wyoming, 1880–1929* (1997)

C. Robert Haywood, *Victorian West: Class and Culture in Kansas Cattle Towns* (1991)

Stan Hoig, *The Oklahoma Land Rush of 1889* (1984)

Frederick C. Luebke, ed., *European Immigrants in the American West: Community Histories* (1998)

Jaqueline M. Moore, *Cow Boys and Cattle Men: Class and Masculinities on the Texas Frontier, 1865–1900* (2009)

Pamela Riney-Kehrberg, *Childhood on the Farm: Work, Play, and Coming of Age in the Midwest* (2005)

David Vaught, *Cultivating California: Growers, Specialty Crops, and Labor, 1875–1920* (1999)

Paul I. Wellman, *The Trampling Herd: The Story of the Cattle Range in America* (1939, 1988)

Donald E. Worcester, *The Chisholm Trail* (1980)

The Western Landscape

Alfred L. Bush and Lee Clark Mitchell, *The Photograph and the American Indian* (1994)

William Cronon, George Miles, and Jay Gitlin, eds., *Under an Open Sky: Rethinking America's Western Past* (1992)

William H. Goetzmann and William N. Goetzmann, *The West of the Imagination* (1986)

Don Gulbrandsen, *Edward Sheriff Curtis: Visions of the First Americans* (2006)

Joy S. Kasson, *Buffalo Bill's Wild West: Celebrity, Memory, and Popular History* (2000)

Karl Jacoby, *Crimes Against Nature: Squatters, Poachers, Thieves, and the Hidden History of American Conservation* (2001)

Chris J. Magoc, *Yellowstone: The Creation and Selling of an American Landscape, 1870–1903* (1999)

Walter Nugent and Martin Ridge, eds., *The American West: The Reader* (1999)

Paige Raibmon, *Authentic Indians: Episodes of Encounter from the Late-Nineteenth-Century Northwest Coast* (2005)

Martha A. Sandweiss, *Print the Legend: Photography and the American West* (2002)

Richard Slotkin, *Gunfighter Nation: The Myth of the Frontier in 20th-Century America* (1992)

Mark David Spence, *Dispossessing the Wilderness: Indian Removal and the Making of the National Parks* (1999)

Margaret Walsh, *The American West: Visions and Revisions* (2005)

Richard White, *"It's Your Misfortune and None of My Own": A History of the American West* (1991)

Richard White and Patricia Nelson Limerick, *The Frontier in American Culture* (1994)

Donald Worster, *An Unsettled Country: Changing Landscapes of the American West* (1994)

David M. Wrobel, *Promised Lands: Promotion, Memory, and the Creation of the American West* (2002)

Biography

Gordon Morris Bakken, ed., *Icons of the American West, Vo. 1* (2008)

Matthew Baigell, *Albert Bierstadt* (1981)

Louise Barnett, *Touched by Fire: The Life, Death, and Mythic Afterlife of George Armstrong Custer* (1996)

Thom Hatch, *Black Kettle: The Cheyenne Chief Who Sought Peace but Found War* (2004)

Robert W. Larson, *Red Cloud: Warrior-Statesman of the Lakota Sioux* (1997)

James D. McLaird, *Calamity Jane* (2005)

Joan T. Mark, *A Stranger in Her Native Land: Alice Fletcher and the American Indians* (1988)

Joseph M. Marshall, *The Journey of Crazy Horse* (2004)

Sara R. Massey, ed., *Black Cowboys of Texas* (2000)

Valerie Mathes, *Helen Hunt Jackson and Her Indian Reform Legacy* (1990)

Kent Nerburn, *Chief Joseph and the Flight of the Nez Perce* (2005)

Elinore Pruitt Stewart, *Letters of a Woman Homesteader* (1914, 1989)

Jerry D. Thompson, *Cortina: Defending the Mexican Name in Texas* (2007)

Benson Tong, *Susan La Flesche Picotte, M.D.: Omaha Indian Leader and Reformer* (1999)

Robert M. Utley, *The Lance and the Shield: The Life and Times of Sitting Bull* (1993)

Donald Worster, *A River Running West: The Life of John Wesley Powell* (2001)

Donald Worster, *A Passion for Nature: The Life of John Muir* (2008)

Sally Zanjani, *Sarah Winnemucca* (2001)

CHAPTER 19

Science, Technology, and Industry

Alfred D. Chandler Jr., *The Visible Hand: The Managerial Revolution in American Business* (1977)

David A. Hounshell, *From the American System to Mass Production, 1800–1932* (1984)

Walter Licht, *Industrializing America: The Nineteenth Century* (1995)

A. J. Millard, *Edison and the Business of Innovation* (1990)

David F. Noble, *America by Design: Science, Technology and the Rise of Corporate Capitalism* (1977)

William S. Pretzer, ed., *Working at Inventing: Thomas A. Edison and the Menlo Park Experience* (2001)

Leonard S. Reich, *The Making of American Industrial Research: Science and Business at G.E. and Bell, 1876–1926* (1985)

Business and the Economy

Jack Beatty, *Age of Betrayal: The Triumph of Money in America, 1865–1900* (2007)

Wendy Gamber, *The Female Economy: The Millinery and Dressmaking Trades, 1860–1930* (1997)

Pamela Walker Laird, *Advertising Progress: American Business and the Rise of Consumer Marketing* (1998)

Naomi R. Lamoreaux, *The Great Merger Movement in American Business, 1895–1904* (1985)

Daniel Nelson, *Managers and Workers: Origins of the Factory System in the United States, 1880–1920* (1975)

William G. Roy, *Socializing Capital: The Rise of the Large Industrial Corporation in America* (1997)

Sarah Lyons Watts, *Order against Chaos: Business Culture and Labor Ideology in America, 1800–1915* (1991)

Olivier Zunz, *Making America Corporate, 1870–1920* (1990)

Working Class and Labor

Eric Arnesen, *Waterfront Workers of New Orleans: Race, Class, and Politics, 1863–1923* (1991)

James R. Barrett, *Work and Community in the Jungle* (1987)

John Bodnar, *Immigration and Industrialization: Ethnicity in an American Mill Town* (1977)

Ileen A. Devault, *United Apart: Gender and the Rise of Craft Unionism* (2004)

Lisa M. Fine, *The Souls of the Skyscraper: Female Clerical Workers in Chicago, 1870–1930* (1990)

Herbert G. Gutman, *Work, Culture and Society in Industrializing America: Essays in American Working-Class and Social History* (1977)

David M. Katzman, *Seven Days a Week: Women and Domestic Service in Industrializing America* (1978)

Joanne Meyerowitz, *Women Adrift: Industrial Wage Earners in Chicago, 1880–1930* (1988)

David Montgomery, *The Fall of the House of Labor: The Workplace, the State, and American Labor Activism, 1865–1925* (1987)

Daniel T. Rodgers, *The Work Ethic in Industrial America, 1850–1920* (1978)

Dave Roediger and Franklin Rosemont, eds., *Haymarket Scrapbook* (1986)

Roy Rosenzweig, *Eight Hours for What We Will: Workers and Leisure in an Industrial City, 1870–1920* (1983)

Lara Vapnek, *Breadwinners: Working Women and Economic Independence, 1865–1920* (2009)

Robert E. Weir, *Beyond Labor's Veil: The Culture of the Knights of Labor* (1996)

The Industrial City

Perry R. Duis, *Challenging Chicago: Coping with Everyday Life, 1837–1920* (1998)

Robert M. Fogelson, *Bouregeois Nightmares: Suburbia 1870–1930* (2005)

John S. Garner, ed., *The Midwest in American Architecture* (1991)

Dolores Hayden, *The Grand Domestic Revolution: A History of Feminist Designs for American Homes, Neighborhoods, and Cities* (1981)

Julie Husband and Jim O'Loughlin, *Daily Life in the Industrial United States, 1870–1900* (2004)

Scott Molloy, *Trolley Wars: Streetcar Workers on the Line* (1996)

Christopher Robert Reed, *Black Chicago's First Century: Vol. 1: 1833–1900* (2005)

Mark H. Rose, *Cities of Light and Heat: Domesticating Gas and Electricity in Urban America* (1995)

Carl Smith, *Urban Disorder and the Shape of Belief: The Great Chicago Fire, the Haymarket Bomb, and the Model Town of Pullman* (1995)

John R. Stilgoe, *Borderland: Origins of the American Suburb, 1820–1939* (1988)

The New South

Edward L. Ayers, *The Promise of the New South* (1992)

Don Doyle, *New Men, New Cities, New South* (1990)

Jacquelyn Dowd Hall, et al., *Like a Family: The Making of a Southern Cotton Mill World* (1987, 2000)

Gerald D. Jaynes, *Branches without Roots: Genesis of the Black Working Class in the American South, 1862–1882* (1986)

Lawrence H. Larsen, *The Rise of the Urban South* (1985)

Cathy McHugh, *Mill Family: The Labor System in the Southern Textile Industry, 1880–1915* (1988)

Karin A. Shapiro, *A New South Rebellion: The Battle Against Convict Labor in the Tennessee Coalfields, 1871–1896* (1998)

Rise of Consumer Society

Elaine S. Abelson, *When Ladies Go A-Thieving* (1989)

Stuart Blumin, *The Emergence of the Middle Class* (1989)

Joshua Brown, *Beyond the Lines: Pictorial Reporting, Everyday Life, and the Crisis of Gilded Age America* (2003)

Sarah Burns, *Inventing the Modern Artist: Art and Culture in Gilded Age America* (1996)

Yong Chen, *Chinese San Francisco, 1850–1943* (2000)

Priscilla Ferguson Clement, *Growing Pains: Children in the Industrial Age, 1850–1890* (1997)

Steven Conn, *Museums and American Intellectual Life, 1876–1926* (1998)

Perry Duis, *Challenging Chicago: Coping with Everyday Life, 1837–1920* (1998)

Robert M. Fogelson, *Bourgeois Nightmares: Suburbia, 1870–1930* (2005)

Warren Goldstein, *Playing for Keeps: A History of Early Baseball* (1989)

Katherine C. Grier, *Culture and Comfort: Parlor Making and Middle-Class Identity, 1850–1930* (1988, 1997)

Judy Hilkey, *Character Is Capital: Success Manuals and Manhood in Gilded Age America* (1997)

John F. Kasson, *Amusing the Millions: Coney Island at the Turn of the Century* (1978)

Lawrence W. Levine, *Highbrow/Lowbrow: The Emergence of Cultural Hierarchy in America* (1988)

Patricia Marks, *Bicycles, Bangs, and Bloomers: The New Woman in the Popular Press* (1990)

Steven A. Riess, *City Games: The Evolution of American Urban Society and the Rise of Sports* (1989)

Roy Rosenzweig and Elizabeth Blackmar, *The Park and the People: A History of Central Park* (1992)

Leigh Eric Schmidt, *Consumer Rites: The Buying and Selling of American Holidays* (1995)

Biography

David Cannadine, *Mellon: An American Life* (2006)

Ron Chernow, *Titan: The Life of John D. Rockefeller, Sr.* (1998)

Bruce J. Evensen, *God's Man for the Gilded Age: D. L. Moody and the Rise of Modern Mass Evangelism* (2003)

Helen Lefkowitz Horowitz, *The Power and Passion of M. Carey Thomas* (1994)

Paul Israel, *Edison: A Life of Invention* (1998)

J. Paul Jeffers, *Diamond Jim Brady* (2001)

David Nasaw, *Andrew Carnegie* (2006)

Craig Phelan, *Grand Master Workman: Terence Powderly and the Knights of Labor* (2000)

Stiles, T.J., *The First Tycoon: The Epic Life of Cornelius Vanderbilt* (2009)

Jean Strouse, *Morgan: American Financier* (1999)

Robert C. Twombly, *Louis Sullivan* (1986)

Michael Zuckerman, *Almost Chosen People: Oblique Biographies in the American Grain* (1993)

CHAPTER 20

The Nation and Politics

Paula C. Baker, *The Moral Frameworks of Public Life: Gender, Politics and the State in Rural New York, 1870–1930* (1991)

Jack Beatty, *Age of Betrayal: The Triumph of Money in America, 1865–1900* (2007)

Michael Lewis Goldberg, *An Army of Women: Gender and Politics in Gilded Age Kansas* (1997)

J. William Harris, *Deep Souths: Delta, Piedmont, and Sea Island Society in the Age of Segregation* (2001)

Michael F. Holt, *By One Vote: The Disputed Presidential Election of 1876* (2008)

Erika Lee, *At America's Gates: Chinese Immigration during the Exclusion Era, 1882–1943* (2003)

Gwendolyn Mink, *Old Labor and New Immigrants in American Political Development* (1986)

Nell Irvin Painter, *Standing at Armageddon: The United States, 1877–1919* (1987)

Douglas Steeples and David O. Whitten, *Democracy in Desperation: The Depression of 1893* (1998)

Mark. W. Summers, *Party Games: Getting, Keeping, and Using Power in Gilded Age Politics* (2004)

Brook Thomas, *Plessy v. Ferguson: A Brief History with Documents* (1997)

David Traxel, *1898: The Birth of the American Century* (1998)

C. Vann Woodward, *The Strange Career of Jim Crow*, 3rd rev. ed. (1974)

Populism

Peter Argersinger, *The Limits of Agrarian Radicalism: Western Populism and American Politics* (1995)

Lawrence Goodwyn, *Democratic Promise: The Populist Moment in America* (1976)

Steven Hahn, *The Roots of Southern Populism* (1983)

Matthew Hild, *Greenbackers, Knights of Labor, and Populists* (2007)

Michael Kazin, *The Populist Persuasion: An American History* (1995, rev. ed., 1998)

Robert C. McMath, *American Populism: A Social History* (1993)

Scott G. McNall, *The Road to Rebellion: Class Formation and Kansas Populism 1865–1900* (1988)

Norman Pollack, *The Humane Economy: Populism, Capitalism and Democracy* (1990)

Protest and Reform Movements

Ruth Bordin, *Woman and Temperance: The Quest for Power and Liberty, 1873–1900* (1981)

Kathleen Ann Clark, *Defining Moments: African American Commemoration and Political Culture in the South, 1863–1913* (2005)

Susan Curtis, *A Consuming Faith: The Social Gospel and Modern American Culture* (1991)

William D. Harpine, *From the Front Porch to the Front Page: McKinley and Bryan in the 1896 Presidential Campaign* (2005)

Paul Krause, *The Battle for Homestead, 1880–1892* (1992)

Ralph E. Luker, *The Social Gospel in Black and White* (1991)

Alison M. Parker, *Purifying America: Women, Cultural Reform, and Pro-Censorship Activism, 1873–1933* (1997)

Gretchen Ritter, *Goldbugs and Greenbacks: The Antimonopoly Tradition and the Politics of Finance in America, 1865–1896* (1997)

Richard Schneirov, Shelton Stromquist, and Nick Salvatore, eds., *The Pullman Strike and the Crisis of the 1890s: Essays on Labor and Politics* (1999)

Carlos A. Schwantes, *Coxey's Army* (1985)

Gary Scott Smith, *The Search for Social Salvation: Social Christianity and America, 1880–1925* (2000)

David O. Stowell, ed., *The Great Strikes of 1877* (2008)

Imperialism and Empire

Tunde Adeleke, *Unafrican Americans: Nineteenth-Century Black Nationalists and the Civilizing Mission* (1998)

Nupur Chaudhuri and Margaret Strobel, eds., *Western Women and Imperialism* (1992)

Willard B. Gatewood, Jr., *Black Americans and the White Man's Burden* (1975)

Patricia Hill, *The World Their Household: The American Women's Foreign Mission Movement and Cultural Transformation, 1870–1920* (1985)

Amy Kaplan and Donald E. Pease, eds., *Cultures of United States Imperialism* (1993)

Paul A. Kramer, *The Blood of Government: Race, Empire, the United States, and the Philippines* (2007)

Paul T. McCartney, *Power and Progress: American National Identity, the War of 1898, and the Rise of American Imperialism* (2006)

Walter Nugent, *Habits of Empire: A History of American Expansion* (2008)

Emily S. Rosenberg, *Spreading the American Dream: American Economic and Cultural Expansion, 1890–1945* (1982)

Robert W. Rydell, *All the World's a Fair: Vision of Empire at the American International Expositions, 1876–1916* (1984)

Anders Stephanson, *Manifest Destiny: American Expansion and the Empire of Right* (1995)

Spanish–American War and the Philippines

Virginia M. Bouvier, ed., *Whose America? The War of 1898 and the Battles to Define the Nation* (2001)

Julian Go and Anne L. Foster, eds., *The American Colonial State in the Philippines: Global Perspectives* (2003)

Kenneth E. Hendrickson, *The Spanish-American War* (2003)

Kristin L. Hoganson, *Fighting for American Manhood: How Gender Politics Provoked the Spanish-American and Philippine-American Wars* (1998)

Paul A. Kramer, *The Blood of Government: Race, Empire, the United States, and the Philippines* (2006)

Brian McAllister Linn, *The Philippine War, 1899–1902* (2000)

Ivan Musicant, *Empire By Default: The Spanish-American War and the Dawn of the American Century* (1998)

Louis A. Perez, Jr., *The War of 1898: The United States and Cuba in History and Historiography* (1998)

Harvey Rosenfeld, *Diary of a Dirty Little War: The Spanish-American War of 1898* (2000)

Thomas David Schoonover, *Uncle Sam's War of 1898 and the Origins of Globalism* (2003)

David J. Silbey, *A War of Frontier and Empire: The Philippine-American War, 1899-1902* (2007)

Angel Smith and Emma Davila-Cox, eds., *The Crisis of 1898: Colonial Redistribution and Nationalist Mobilization* (1999)

John Lawrence Tone, *War and Genocide in Cuba, 1895–1898* (2006)

Biography
Ruth Bordin, *Frances Willard: A Biography* (1986)

Mari Jo Buhle, Paul Buhle, and Harvey J. Kaye, eds., *The American Radical* (1995)

Edward P. Crapol, *James G. Blaine: Architect of Empire* (2000)

Bruce J. Evensen, *God's Man for the Gilded Age: D. L. Moody and the Rise of Modern Mass Evangelism* (2003)

Jane Taylor Nelsen, *A Prairie Populist: The Memoirs of Luna Kellie* (1992)

Allan Peskin, *Garfield: A Biography* (1978)

Ben Procter, *William Randolph Hearst: The Early Years, 1863–1910* (1998)

Nick Salvatore, *Eugene V. Debs* (1982)

Peggy Samuels and Harold Samuels, *Teddy Roosevelt at San Juan: The Making of a President* (1997)

Patricia A. Schechter, *Ida B. Wells-Barnett and American Reform, 1880–1930* (2001)

C. Van Woodward, *Tom Watson* (1963)

CHAPTER 21

The Currents of Progressivism
Walter M. Brasch, *Forerunners of Revolution: Muckrakers and the American Social Conscience* (1990)

John D. Buenker, *Urban Liberalism and Progressive Reform* (1973)

Mina Carson, *Settlement Folk: Social Thought and the American Settlement Movement, 1885–1930* (1990)

Nancy Cohen, *Reconstruction of American Liberalism, 1865–1914* (2002)

Leon Fink, *Progressive Intellectuals and the Dilemmas of Democratic Commitment* (1997)

Richard Hofstadter, *The Age of Reform: From Bryan to FDR* (1955)

Robert D. Johnston, *The Radical Middle Class: Populist Democracy and the Question of Capitalism in Progressive Era Portland, Oregon* (2003)

James T. Kloppenberg, *Uncertain Victory: Social Democracy and Progressivism in European and American Thought, 1870–1920* (1986)

William A. Link, *The Paradox of Southern Progressivism, 1880–1930* (1992)

Richard McCormick, *The Party Period and Public Policy* (1986)

Michael Perman, *Struggle for Mastery: Disfranchisement in the South, 1888–1908* (2001)

Robert Wiebe, *The Search for Order, 1877–1920* (1967)

Social Control and Its Limits
Paul M. Boyer, *Urban Masses and Moral Order in America, 1820–1920* (1978)

Eldon J. Eisenach, *The Lost Promise of Progressivism* (1994)

Randy D. McBee, *Dance Hall Days: Intimacy and Leisure Among Working-Class Immigrants in the United States* (2000)

Ruth Rosen, *The Lost Sisterhood: Prostitutes in America, 1900–1918* (1982)

Andrea Tone, *The Business of Benevolence: Industrial Paternalism in Progressive America* (1997)

Working-Class Communities and Protest
John Bodnar, *The Transplanted* (1985)

Susan A. Glenn, *Daughters of the Shtetl: Life and Labor in the Immigrant Generation* (1990)

James R. Green, *The World of the Worker: Labor in Twentieth-Century America* (1980)

Alice Kessler-Harris, *Out to Work: A History of Wage-Earning Women in the United States* (1982)

David Montgomery, *The Fall of the House of Labor* (1987)

Kathy Peiss, *Cheap Amusements: Working Women and Leisure in Turn-of-the-Century New York* (1986)

Roy Rosenzweig, *Eight Hours for What We Will* (1983)

Ronald Takaki, *Strangers from a Different Shore: A History of Asian Americans* (1989)

Women's Movements and Black Awakening
Paula Baker, *The Moral Frameworks of Public Life* (1991)

Mari Jo Buhle, *Women and American Socialism* (1983)

Rebecca Edwards, *Angels in the Machinery: Gender in American Party Politics from the Civil War to the Progressive Era* (1997)

Linda Gordon, *Woman's Body, Woman's Right: A Social History of Birth Control* (1976)

Molly Ladd-Taylor, *Mother Work: Women, Child Welfare, and the State, 1890–1930* (1994)

National Progressivism
Kendrick A. Clements, *The Presidency of Woodrow Wilson* (1992)

John M. Cooper Jr., *The Warrior and the Priest: Theodore Roosevelt and Woodrow Wilson* (1983)

Lewis L. Gould, *The Presidency of Theodore Roosevelt* (1991)

Biography
Ellen Chesler, *Woman of Valor: Margaret Sanger and the Birth Control Movement in America* (1992)

Louis R. Harlan, *Booker T. Washington: Wizard of Tuskegee, 1901–1915* (1983)

J. Joseph Huthmacher, *Senator Robert F. Wagner and the Rise of Urban Liberalism* (1971)

Stephen Kantrowitz, *Ben Tillman and the Reconstruction of White Supremacy* (2000)

David Levering Lewis, *W.E.B. Du Bois: Biography of a Race, 1868–1919* (1993)

Nick Salvatore, *Eugene V. Debs: Citizen and Socialist* (1982)

Patricia A. Schechter, *Ida B. Wells-Barnett and American Reform, 1880–1930* (2001)

Kathryn Kish Sklar, *Florence Kelley and the Nation's Work* (1995)

Melvin I. Urofsky, *Louis D. Brandeis: A Life* (2009)

Bernard A. Weisberger, *The LaFollettes of Wisconsin* (1994)

Robert Westbrook, *John Dewey and American Democracy* (1991)

CHAPTER 22

Becoming a World Power

Richard H. Collin, *Theodore Roosevelt's Caribbean* (1990)

John M. Hart, *Empire and Revolution: The Americans in Mexico since the Civil War* (2002)

Walter LaFeber, *The Panama Canal* (1978)

Lester E. Langley, *The Banana Wars: An Inner History of American Empire, 1900–1934* (1983)

Mary A. Renda, *Taking Haiti: Military Occupation and the Culture of U.S. Imperialism, 1915–1940* (2001)

William Tilchin and Charles E. Neu, eds., *Artists of Power: Theodore Roosevelt, Woodrow Wilson, and Their Enduring Impact on U.S. Foreign Policy* (2006)

The Great War

Lloyd E. Ambrosius, *Woodrow Wilson and the American Diplomatic Tradition* (1987)

Paul Fussell, *The Great War and Modern Memory* (1973)

Martin Gilbert, *The First World War: A Complete History* (1994)

Ross A. Kennedy, *The Will to Believe: Woodrow Wilson, World War I, and America's Strategy for Peace and Security* (2009)

American Mobilization

Alan Axelrod, *Selling the Great War: The Making of American Propaganda* (2009)

Carol R. Byerly, *Fever of War: The Influenza Epidemic in the U.S. Army during World War I* (2005)

John W. Chambers, *To Raise an Army: The Draft in Modern America* (1987)

Nancy Gentile Ford, *Americans All! Foreign Born Soldiers in World War I* (2001)

Mark E. Grotelueschen, *The AEF Way of War* (2007)

Jeanette Keith, *Rich Man's War, Poor Man's Fight: Race, Class, and Power in the Rural South during the First World War* (2004)

Gerald E. Shenk, *"Work or Fight": Race, Gender, and the Draft in World War I* (2006)

Robert W. Tucker, *Woodrow Wilson and the Great War* (2007)

Stephen Vaughn, *Holding Fast the Inner Lines: Democracy, Nationalism, and the Committee on Public Information* (1980)

Over Here

Allen J. Brandt, *No Magic Bullet: A Social History of Venereal Disease in the United States since 1880* (1985)

Leslie M. DeBauche, *Reel Patriotism: The Movies and World War I* (1997)

Frances R. Early, *A World Without War: How U.S. Feminists and Pacifists Resisted World War I* (1997)

Margaret Mary Finnegan, *Selling Suffrage: Consumer Culture and Votes for Women* (1999)

Maureen Greenwald, *Women, War, and Work* (1980)

Ellis W. Hawley, *The Great War and the Search for Modern Order*, 2nd ed. (1992)

Jeffrey Haydu, *Making American Industries Safe for Democracy* (1997)

David M. Kennedy, *Over Here* (1980)

Ronald Schaffer, *America in the Great War: The Rise of the War Welfare State* (1991)

Neil A. Wynn, *From Progressivism to Prosperity: World War I and American Society* (1986)

Repression and Reaction

Beverly Gage, *The Day Wall Street Exploded* (2009)

James P. Grossman, *Land of Hope: Chicago, Black Southerners, and the Great Migration* (1989)

Tim Madigan, *The Burning: Massacre, Destruction, and the Tulsa Race Riot of 1921* (2001)

Paul L. Murphy, *World War I and the Origin of Civil Liberties* (1979)

Regin Schmidt, *Red Scare: The FBI and the Origins of Anticommunism in the United States, 1919–1943* (2000)

Mark Robert Schneider, *"We Return Fighting": The Civil Rights Movement in the Jazz Age* (2002)

William H. Thomas, *Unsafe for Democracy: WW I and the US Justice Department's Covert Campaign to Suppress Dissent* (2008)

Joe William Trotter Jr., ed., *The Great Migration in Historical Perspective* (1991)

An Uneasy Peace

Dana Frank, *Purchasing Power: Consumer Organizing, Gender, and the Seattle Labor Movement, 1919–1929* (1994)

Lloyd Gardner, *Safe for Democracy: The Anglo-American Response to Revolution, 1913–1923* (1984)

Robert D. Johnson, *The Peace Progressives and American Foreign Relations* (1995)

Carol Wilcox Melton, *Between War and Peace: Woodrow Wilson and the American Expeditionary Force in Siberia, 1918–1921* (2002)

Richard Polenberg, *Fighting Faiths: The Abrams Case, the Supreme Court, and Free Speech* (1987)

Daniel D. Stid, *The President As Statesman: Woodrow Wilson and the Constitution* (1998)

Biography

John M. Cooper, *Woodrow Wilson: A Biography* (2009)

Ellen Carol DuBois, *Harriot Stanton Blatch and the Winning of Woman Suffrage* (1997)

Godfrey Hodgson, *Woodrow Wilson's Right Hand: The Life of Colonel Edward M. House* (2006)

Jim Lacey, *Pershing* (2008)

Jacqueline van Voris, *Carrie Chapman Catt* (1987)

Warren Zimmerman, *First Great Triumph: How Five Americans Made Their Country a World Power* (2002)

CHAPTER 23

Postwar Prosperity and Its Price

David Brody, *Workers in Industrial America* (1980)

Gilbert C. Fite, *Cotton Fields No More: Southern Agriculture, 1865–1980* (1984)

Greg Grandin, *Fordlandia: The Rise and Fall of Henry Ford's Forgotten Jungle City* (2009)

Ellis W. Hawley, *The Great War and the Search for Modern Order* (1979)

Kenneth T. Jackson, *Crabgrass Frontier* (1985)

William Leuchtenberg, *The Perils of Prosperity, 1914–1932* (1958)

Clay McShane, *Down the Asphalt Path* (1994)

Gwendolyn Wright, *Building the American Dream* (1981)

Gerald Zahavi, *Workers, Managers, and Welfare Capitalism* (1988)

The State, the Economy, and Business

Kendrick A. Clements, *Hoover, Conservation, and Consumerism: Engineering the Good Life* (2000)

Warren I. Cohen, *Empire without Tears* (1987)

Louis Galambos and Joseph Pratt, *The Rise of the Corporate Commonwealth* (1988)

John Earl Haynes, ed., *Calvin Coolidge and the Coolidge Era* (1998)

Roland Marchand, *Creating the Corporate Soul: The Rise of Public Relations and Corporate Imagery in American Big Business* (1998)

Charles L. Mee, *The Ohio Gang: The World of Warren G. Harding* (1981)

Emily S. Rosenberg, *Spreading the American Dream* (1982)

The New Mass Culture

Beth A. Bailey, *From Front Porch to Back Seat: Courtship in Twentieth-Century America* (1988)

Court Carney, *Cuttin' Up: How Early Jazz Got America's Ear* (2009)

Douglas B. Craig, *Fireside Politics: Radio and Political Culture in the United States, 1920–1940* (2000)

Daniel J. Czitrom, *Media and the American Mind* (1982)

Susan Currell, *American Culture in the 1920s* (2009)

John D'Emilio and Estelle B. Freedman, *Intimate Matters: A History of Sexuality in America* (1988)

Clifford J. Doerksen, *American Babel: Rogue Radio Broadcasters of the Jazz Age* (2005)

Susan J. Douglas, *Listening In: Radio and the American Imagination* (1999)

Pamela Walker Laird, *Advertising Progress: American Business and the Rise of Consumer Marketing* (1998)

Jackson Lears, *Fables of Abundance: A Cultural History of Advertising in America* (1994)

Roland Marchand, *Advertising the American Dream: Making Way for Modernity, 1920–1940* (1985)

Andre Millard, *America On Record: A History of Recorded Sound* (1999)

Charles L. Ponce de Leon, *Self Exposure: Human Interest Journalism and the Emergence of Celebrity in America, 1890–1940* (2002)

Steven J. Ross, *Working Class Hollywood: Silent Film and the Shaping of Class in America* (1998)

Robert Sklar, *Movie Made America*, rev. ed. (1995)

Modernity and Traditionalism

Katherine M. Blee, *Women and the Klan: Racism and Gender in the 1920s* (1991)

David Critchley, *The Origins of Organized Crime in America* (2009)

David J. Goldberg, *Discontented America: The United States in the 1920s* (1999)

John Higham, *Strangers in the Land: Patterns of American Nativism, 1860–1925* (1955)

Edward J. Larson, *Summer of the Gods: The Scopes Trial and America's Continuing Debate over Science* (1997)

Mae M. Ngai, *Impossible Subjects: Illegal Aliens and the Making of Modern America* (2004)

Thomas R. Pegram, *Battling Demon Rum: The Struggle for a Dry America, 1800–1933* (1998)

Robert Oglesbee, *'Prohibition is Here to Stay': Rev. Edward S. Schumaker and the Dry Crusade in America* (2009)

Daniel J. Tichenor, *Dividing Lines: Immigration Control in America* (2002)

Promises Postponed

Nancy F. Cott, *The Grounding of American Feminism* (1987)

Ann Douglas, *Terrible Honesty: Mongrel Manhattan in the 1920s* (1995)

Patrick Ettinger, *Imaginary Lives : Border Enforcement and the Origins of Undocumented Immigration* (2009)

Nathan I. Huggins, *Harlem Renaissance* (1971)

Cary D. Mintz, *Black Culture and the Harlem Renaissance* (1988)

George J. Sanchez, *Becoming Mexican American* (1993)

Mark Robert Schneider, *"We Return Fighting": The Civil Rights Movement in the Jazz Age* (2002)

Judith Stein, *The World of Marcus Garvey* (1985)

Bruce Watson, *Sacco and Vanzetti* (2007)

Daphne M. Lamothe, *Inventing the New Negro* (2008)

Biography

Katharine H. Adams and Michael L. Keene, *Alice Paul and the American Suffrage Campaign* (2008)

Edith L. Blumhofer, *Aimee Semple McPherson* (1993)

David Cannadine, *Mellon: An American Life* (2006)

Neal Gabler, *Winchell: Gossip, Power, and the Culture of Celebrity* (1994)

David Greenberg, *Calvin Coolidge* (2006)

David Levering Lewis, *W. E. B. DuBois: The Fight for Equality and the American Century, 1919–1963* (2000)

David Nasaw, *The Chief: The Life of William Randolph Hearst* (2000)

Arnold Rampersad, *The Life of Langston Hughes*, 2 vols. (1986–1988)

Terry Teachout, *Pops: A Life of Louis Armstrong* (2009)

CHAPTER 24

Hard Times

Michael A. Bernstein, *The Great Depression* (1987)

Michael D. Bordo, et al., eds., *The Defining Moment: The Great Depression and the American Economy in the Twentieth Century* (1998)

Robert S. McElvaine, ed., *Down and Out in the Great Depression* (1983)

Janet Poppendieck, *Breadlines Knee-Deep in Wheat* (1986)

Amity Shlaes, *The Forgotten Man: A New History of the Great Depression* (2008)

Jeff Singleton, *The American Dole: Unemployment Relief and the Welfare State in the Great Depression* (2000)

Studs Terkel, *Hard Times* (1970)

T.H. Watkins, *The Hungry Years: A Narrative History of the Great Depression in America* (1999)

Elmos Wicker, *The Banking Panics of the Great Depression* (1996)

FDR and the First New Deal

Jonathan Alter, *The Defining Moment: FDR's Hundred Days and the Triumph of Hope* (2006)

Anthony Badger, *FDR: The First Hundred Days* (2008)

Steve Fraser and Gary Gerstle, eds., *The Rise and Fall of the New Deal Order* (1988)

David M. Kennedy, *Freedom From Fear: The American People in Depression and War* (1999)

R. Alan Lawson, *A Commonwealth of Hope: The New Deal Responds to Crisis* (2006)

William Leuchtenberg, *The FDR Years* (1995)

Neil M. Maher, *Nature's New Deal: The Civilian Conservation Corps and the Roots of the American Environmental Movement* (2008)

George McJimsey, *The Presidency of Franklin Delano Roosevelt* (2000)

James S. Olson, *Saving Capitalism* (1988)

Donald Ritchie, *Electing FDR: The New Deal Campaign of 1932* (2007)

Elliot Rosen, *Roosevelt, the Great Depression, and the Economics of Recovery* (2005)

Theodore M. Saloutos, *The American Farmer and the New Deal* (1982)

Left Turn and the Second New Deal

Irving Bernstein, *The Turbulent Years: A History of the American Worker, 1933–1941* (1970)

John Braeman et al., eds., *The New Deal: The State and Local Levels* (1975)

Alan Brinkley, *Voices of Protest: Huey Long, Father Coughlin, and the New Deal* (1982)

Lizabeth Cohen, *Making a New Deal: Industrial Workers in Chicago, 1919–1939* (1990)

Peter Friedlander, *The Emergence of a UAW Local* (1975)

Gary Gerstle, *Working Class Americanism* (1989)

Kenneth J. Heineman, *A Catholic New Deal: Religion and Reform in Depression Pittsburgh* (1999)

Robin D. G. Kelley, *Hammer and Hoe: Alabama Communists during the Great Depression* (1990)

Joseph P. Lash, *Dealers and Dreamers* (1988)

Fraser Ottanelli, *The Communist Party of the United States: From the Depression to World War II* (1991)

Mary Poole, *The Segregated Origins of Social Security: African Americans and the Welfare State* (2006)

Mary E. Triece, *On the Picket Line: Strategies of Working Class Women During the Depression* (2007)

Robert H. Zieger, *The CIO, 1935–1955* (1995)

The New Deal and the West

James M. Gregory, *American Exodus: The Dust Bowl Migration and Okie Culture in California* (1989)

Norris Hundley Jr., *The Great Thirst: California and Water, 1770s–1990s* (1992)

Laurence Kelly, *The Assault on Assimilation: John Collier and the Origins of Indian Policy Reform, 1920–1954* (1983)

Richard Lowitt, *The New Deal and the West* (1984)

Sarah T. Phillips, *This Land, This Nation: Conservation, Rural America, and the New Deal* (2007)

Vicki Ruiz, *Cannery Women / Cannery Lives: Mexican Women, Unionization, and the California Food Processing Industry, 1930–1950* (1987)

Charles J. Shindo, *Dust Bowl Migrants in the American Imagination* (1997)

Kevin Starr, *Endangered Dreams: The Great Depression in California* (1996)

Donald Worster, *Dust Bowl* (1979)

The Limits of Reform

Raymond Arsenault, *The Sound of Freedom: Marian Anderson, the Lincoln Memorial, and the Concert that Awakened America* (2009)

Francisco E. Balderrama, *Decade of Betrayal: Mexican Repatriation in the 1930s* (1995)

Suzanne Mettler, *Dividing Citizens: Gender and Federalism in New Deal Public Works* (1998)

Mary Poole, *The Segregated Origins of Social Security* (2006)

Robert Shogan, *Backlash: The Killing of the New Deal* (2006)

Lauren Sklaroff, *Black Culture and the New Deal: The Quest for Civil Rights in the Roosevelt Era* (2009)

Burt Solomon, *FDR v. The Constitution: The Court Packing Fight and the Triumph of Democracy* (2009)

Landon R.Y. Storrs, *Civilizing Capitalism: The National Consumers' League, Women's Activism, and Labor Standards in the New Deal Era* (2000)

Patricia Sullivan, *Days of Hope: Race and Democracy in the New Deal Era* (1996)

Susan Ware, *Beyond Suffrage: Women in the New Deal* (1981)

———, *Partner and I: Molly Dewson, Feminism, and New Deal Politics* (1987)

Nancy J. Weiss, *Farewell to the Party of Lincoln: Black Politics in the Age of FDR* (1983)

G. Edward White, *The Constitution and the New Deal* (2000)

Robert L. Zangrando, *The NAACP Crusade against Lynching* (1980)

Depression-Era Culture

Peter Carroll, *The Odyssey of the Abraham Lincoln Brigade* (1990)

Thomas P. Doherty, *Pre-Code Hollywood: Sex, Immorality, and Insurrection in American Cinema, 1930–1934* (1999)

Lewis A. Erenberg, *Swingin' the Dream: Big Band Jazz and the Rebirth of American Culture* (1998)

Vivian Gornick, *The Romance of American Communism* (1976)

Harvey Klehr, *The Heyday of American Communism* (1984)

Anthony W. Lee, *Painting on the Left* (1999)

Bruce Lenthall, *Radio's America: The Great Depression and the Rise of Modern Mass Culture* (2007)

J. Fred MacDonald, *Don't Touch That Dial* (1979)

Barbara Melosh, *Engendering Culture: Manhood and Womanhood in New Deal Public Art and Theater* (1991)

Mark Naison, *Communists in Harlem During the Depression* (1983)

David P. Peeler, *Hope among Us Yet* (1987)

Richard H. Pells, *Radical Visions and American Dreams: Culture and Social Thought in the Depression Years* (1973)

Thomas Schatz, *The Genius of the System: Hollywood Filmmaking in the Studio Era* (1988)

William Stott, *Documentary Expression and Thirties America* (1973)

William H. Young and Nancy K. Young, *The Great Depression in America: A Cultural Encyclopedia* (2007)

Biography

Blanche W. Cook, *Eleanor Roosevelt: A Life* (1992)

John C. Culver and John Hyde, *American Dreamer: The Life and Times of Henry A. Wallace* (2001)

Steven Fraser, *Labor Will Rule: Sidney Hillman and the Rise of American Labor* (1991)

Neil Gabler, *Walt Disney* (2006)

Linda Gordon, *Dorothea Lange: A Life Beyond Limits* (2009)

Dorothy Healey and Maurice Isserman, *California Red: A Life in the American Communist Party* (1990)

June Hopkins, *Harry Hopkins: Sudden Hero, Brash Reformer* (1999)

Nelson Lichtenstein, *The Most Dangerous Man in Detroit: Walter Reuther and the Fate of American Labor* (1995)

Lois Scharf, *Eleanor Roosevelt* (1987)

Jean Edward Smith, *FDR* (2007)

Robert Zieger, *John L. Lewis* (1988)

CHAPTER 25

Coming of World War II

Justus D. Doenecke, *Storm on the Horizon: The Challenge to American Intervention, 1939–1941* (2000)

Akira Iriye, *The Origins of the Second World War in Asia and the Pacific* (1987)

Deborah Lipstadt, *Beyond Belief: The American Press and the Coming of the Holocaust, 1933–1945* (1986)

Emily Rosenberg, *A Date Which Will Live: Pearl Harbor in American Memory* (2004)

Geoffrey S. Smith, *To Save a Nation* (1992)

Robert B. Stinnett, *Day of Deceit: The Truth about FDR and Pearl Harbor* (2000)

Arsenal of Democracy and the Home Front

Karen Anderson, *Wartime Women* (1981)

Amy Bentley, *Eating for Victory: Food Rationing and the Politics of Domesticity* (1998)

Alison R. Bernstein, *American Indians and World War II* (1991)

Allan Berube, *Coming Out under Fire: The History of Gay Men and Women in World War II* (1990)

Dominic J. Capeci and Martha Wilkerson, *Layered Violence: The Detroit Rioters of 1943* (1991)

Paul D. Casdorph, *Let the Good Times Roll: Life at Home in America during World War II* (1989)

Charles D. Chamberlain, *Victory at Home: Manpower and Race in the American South during World War II* (2003)

Roger Daniels, *Concentration Camps USA: Japanese Americans and World War II* (1971)

Thomas Doherty, *Projections of War: Hollywood, American Culture and World War II* (1993)

Lewis A. Erenberg and Susan E. Hirsch, eds., *The War in American Culture: Society and Consciousness during World War II* (1996)

Sherna Berger Gluck, *Rosie the Riveter Revisited: Women, the War, and Social Change* (1987)

Rachel Waltner Goosen, *Women against the Good War: Conscientious Objection and Gender on the American Home Front, 1941–1947* (1997)

Marilyn E. Hegarty, *Victory Girls, Khaki-Wackies, and Patriotutes: The Regulation of Female Sexuality during World War II* (2008)

Maureen Honey, *Bitter Fruit: African American Women in World War II* (1999)

John Howard, *Concentration Camps on the Home Front: Japanese Americans in the House of Jim Crow* (2008)

James J. Kimble, *Mobilizing the Home Front: War Bonds and Domestic Propaganda* (2006)

Andrew E. Kersten, *Labor's Home Front: The American Federation of Labor during World War II* (2006)

Paul A. C. Koistinen, *Arsenal of World War II: The Political Economy of American Warfare, 1940–1945* (2004)

Daniel Kryder, *Divided Arsenal: Race and the American State during World War II* (2000)

Roger W. Lotchin, *The Bad City in the Good War: San Francisco, Los Angeles, Oakland, and San Diego* (2003)

Franklin Odo, *No Sword to Bury: Japanese Americans in Hawai'i during World War II* (2004)

Gary Y. Okihiro, *Whispered Silences: Japanese Americans and World War II* (1996)

Eduardo Obregón Pagán, *Murder at the Sleepy Lagoon: Zoot Suits, Race, and Riot in Wartime L.A.* (2003)

Greg Robinson, *By Order of the President: FDR and the Internment of Japanese Americans* (2001)

George H. Roeder, *The Censored War: American Visual Experience during World War II* (1993)

Lawrence R. Samuel, *Pledging Allegiance: American Identity and the Bond Drive of World War II* (1997)

William M. Tuttle Jr., *"Daddy's Gone to War": The Second World War in the Lives of America's Children* (1993)

Meghan K. Winchell, *Good Girls, Good Food, Good Fun: The Story of USO Hostesses during World War II* (2008)

K. Scott Wong, *Americans First: Chinese Americans and the Second World War* (2005)

World at War

Antony Beevor, *D-Day: The Battle for Normandy* (2009)

Alison Bernstein, *American Indians and World War II* (1991)

Conrad C. Crane, *Bombs, Cities, and Civilians* (1993)

John W. Dower, *War without Mercy* (1986)

Max Hastings, *Retribution: The Battle for Japan, 1944–45* (2008)

Akira Iriye, *Power and Culture: The Japanese-American War, 1941–1945* (1981)

Lee Kennett, *G.I.: The American Soldier in World War II* (1987)

Eric Markusen and David Kopf, *The Holocaust and Strategic Bombing: Genocide and Total War in the Twentieth Century* (1995)

Peter Maslowski, *Armed with Cameras: The American Military Photographers of World War II* (1993)

Evan Mawdsley, *World War II: A New History* (2009)

Brenda L. Moore, *Serving Our Country: Japanese American Women in the Military during World War II* (2003)

Williamson Murray and Allan R. Millett, *A War to be Won: Fighting the Second World War* (2000)

Barbara Brooks Tomblin, *G.I. Nightingales: The Army Nurse Corps in World War II* (1996)

Edward W. Wood Jr., *Worshipping the Myths of World War II* (2006)

David S. Wyman, *The Abandonment of the Jews: America and the Holocaust, 1941–1945* (1984)

Last Stages of War

John D. Chappell, *Before the Bomb: How America Approached the End of the Pacific War* (1997)

David P. Colley, *Blood for Dignity: The Story of the First Integrated Combat Unit in the U.S. Army* (2003)

Paul Fussell, *The Boy's Crusade: The American Infantry in Northwestern Europe, 1944–1945* (2003)

Lloyd C. Gardner, *Spheres of Influence: The Great Powers Partition Europe, from Munich to Yalta* (1993)

J. Robert Moskin, *Mr. Truman's War: The Final Victories of World War II and the Birth of the Postwar World* (1996)

Peter Schrijvers, *The Crash of Ruin: American Combat Soldiers in Europe during World War II* (1998)

Michael S. Sherry, *The Rise of American Air Power* (1987)

Atomic Bomb

Gar Alperovitz, *The Decision to Use the Atomic Bomb and the Architecture of an American Myth* (1995)

Michael D. Gordon, *Five Days in August: How World War II Became a Nuclear War* (2007)

Peter Bacon Hales, *Atomic Spaces: Living on the Manhattan Project* (1997)

Ruth H. Howes, *Their Day in the Sun: Women of the Manhattan Project* (1999)

Andrew J. Rotter, *Hiroshima: The World's Bomb* (2008)

J. Samuel Walker, *Prompt and Utter Destruction: Truman and the Use of Atomic Bombs against Japan* (1997)

Biography/Memoir

Mark M. Anderson, ed., *Hitler's Exiles: Personal Stories of the Flight from Nazi Germany to America* (1998)

Jeremy Bernstein, *Oppenheimer: Portrait of an Enigma* (2004)

Terry Brighton, *Patton, Montgomery, Rommel: Masters of War* (2008)

Kenneth S. Davis, *FDR, the War President, 1940–1943* (2000)

Preston John Hubbard, *Apocalypse Undone: My Survival of Japanese Imprisonment during World War II* (1990)

Andrew E. Kersten, *A Philip Randolph* (2007)

Michael Korda, *Ike: An American Hero* (2007)

Don Malarky and Bob Welch, *Easy Company Soldier* (2009)

Robert Underhill, *FDR and Harry: Unparalleled Lives* (1996)

CHAPTER 26

Global Insecurities and the Policy of Containment

Christian G. Appy, ed., *Cold War Constructions: The Political Culture of United States Imperialism, 1945–1966* (2000)

Elizabeth Borgwardt, *A New Deal for the World: America's Vision for Human Rights* (2005)

H. W. Brands Jr., *The Devil We Knew: Americans and the Cold War* (1993)

Warren I. Cohen, *America in the Age of Soviet Power, 1945–1991* (1993)

John Gaddis, *The Cold War: A New History* (2006)

Walter Hixson, *Parting the Curtain: Propaganda, Culture, and the Cold War, 1945–1961* (1997)

Townsend Hoopes and Douglas Brinkley, *FDR and the Creation of the U.N.* (1997)

William Inboden, *Religion and American Foreign Policy, 1945–1960* (2008)

Walter LaFeber, *America, Russia, and the Cold War, 1945–1992,* 7th ed. (1993)

Arnold A. Offner, *Another Such Victory: President Truman and the Cold War* (2002)

Arch Puddington, *Broadcasting Freedom: The Cold War Triumph of Radio Free Europe and Radio Liberty* (2000)

Richard Rhodes, *Dark Sun: The Making of the Hydrogen Bomb* (1995)

David F. Rudgers, *Creating the Secret State: The Origins of the Central Intelligence Angency, 1943–1947* (2000)

Michael Schaller, *American Occupation of Japan: The Origins of the Cold War in Asia* (1985)

The Truman Presidency

Jonathan Bell, *The Liberal State on Trial: The Cold War and American Politics in the Truman Years* (2004)

Gary A. Donaldson, *Truman Defeats Dewey* (1999)

Michael R. Gardner, *Harry Truman and Civil Rights* (2002)

Zachary Karabell, *The Last Campaign: How Harry Truman Won the 1948 Election* (2000)

Robert David Johnson, *Congress and the Cold War* (2006)

Melvyn P. Leffler, *A Preponderance of Power: National Security, the Truman Administration, and the Cold War* (1992)

Michael D. Pearlman, *Truman and MacArthur: Policy, Politics, and the Hunger for Honor and Renown* (2008)

Sean J. Savage, *Truman and the Democratic Party* (1997)

Elizabeth Edwards Spalding, *The First Cold Warrior: Harry Truman, Containment, and the Remaking of Liberal Internationalism* (2006)

The Cold War at Home

Larrry Ceplair and Steven Englund, *The Inquisition in Hollywood: Politics in the Film Community, 1930–1960* (1980)

Robert W. Cherny, William Issel, Kieran Walsh Taylor, eds., *American Labor and the Cold War* (2004)

Noam Chomsky, ed., *The Cold War and the University: Toward an Intellectual History of the Postwar Years* (1997)

K.A. Cuordileone, *Manhood and American Political Culture in the Cold War* (2005)

Sigmund Diamond, *Compromised Campus: The Collaboration of Universities with the Intelligence Community, 1945–1995* (1992)

Andrew D. Grossman, *Neither Dead Nor Red: Civilian Defense and American Political Development during the Early Cold War* (2001)

Michael J. Hogan, *A Cross of Iron: Harry S Truman and the Origins of the National Security State, 1945–1954* (1998)

Michael Kackman, *Citizen Spy: Television, Espionage, and Cold War Culture* (2005)

Scott Lucas, *Freedom's War: The American Crusade against the Soviet Union* (1999)

Patrick McGilligan and Paul Buhle, *Tender Comrades: A Backstory of the Hollywood Blacklist* (1997)

Lisle A. Rose, *The Cold War Comes to Main Street: America in 1950* (1999)

Ellen Schrecker, *Many Are the Crimes: McCarthyism in America* (1998)

———, *No Ivory Tower: McCarthyism and the Universities* (1986)

Wendy L. Wall, *Inventing the "American Way": The Politics of Consensus from the New Deal to the Civil Rights Movement* (2008)

Jeff Woods, *Black Struggle, Red Scare: Segregation and Anti-Communism in the South, 1948–1968* (2004)

Cold War Culture

Michael Barson, *"Better Dead Than Red!" A Nostalgic Look at the Golden Years of Russiaphobia, Red-Baiting, and Other Commie Madness* (1992)

Paul Buhle and Dave Wagner, *Radical Hollywood* (2002)

Michael L. Krenn, *Fall-out Shelters for the Human Spirit: American Art and the Cold War* (2005)

George Lipsitz, *A Rainbow at Midnight: Labor and Culture in the 1940s* (1994)

Lary May, ed., *Recasting America: Culture and Politics in the Age of the Cold War* (1989)

Elaine McClarnand and Steve Goodson, eds., *The Impact of the Cold War on American Popular Culture* (1999)

Julia L. Mickenberg, *Learning from the Left: Children's Literature, the Cold War, and Radical Politics in the United States* (2006)

John L. Rudolph, *Scientists in the Classroom: The Cold War Reconstruction of American Science Education* (2002)

David Seed, *American Science Fiction and the Cold War* (1999)

Joanne P. Sharp, *Condensing the Cold War:* Reader's Digest *and American Identity* (2000)

Jessica Wang, *American Science in an Age of Anxiety: Scientists, Anticommunism, and the Cold War* (1999)

Scott C. Zeman, ed. *Atomic Culture: How We Learned to Stop Worrying and Love the Bomb* (2004)

Korean War

Bevin Alexander, *Korea: The First War We Lost,* rev. ed., (2000)

William T. Bowers, William M. Hammond, George L. MacGarrigle, *Black Soldier, White Army: The 24th Infantry Regiment in Korea* (1996)

Steven Casey, *Selling the Korean War: Propaganda, Politics, and Public Opinion in the United States, 1950–1953* (2008)

Albert E. Cowdrey, *The Medics' War* (1987)

Stephen Endicott and Edward Hagerman, *The United States and Biological Warfare: Secrets from the Early Cold War and Korea* (1998)

Paul G. Pierpaoli Jr., *Truman and Korea: The Political Culture of the Early Cold War* (1999)

Ron Robin, *The Making of the Cold War Enemy* (2001)

Stanley Sandler, *The Korean War: No Victors, No Vanquished* (1999)

Biography

Robert L. Beisner, *Dean Acheson: A Life in the Cold War* (2006)

Kai Bird and Margin J. Sherwin, *American Prometheus: The Triumph and Tragedy of J. Robert Oppenheimer* (2005)

Allida M. Black, *Casting Her Own Shadow: Eleanor Roosevelt and the Shaping of Postwar Liberalism* (1996)

John C. Culver, *American Dreamer: The Life and Times of Henry A. Wallace* (2000)

Martin Bauml Duberman, *Paul Robeson* (1988)

Curt Gentry, *J. Edgar Hoover: The Man and the Secrets* (1991)

Alonzo L. Hamby, *Man of the People: A Life of Harry S Truman* (1995)

Arthur Herman, *Joseph McCarthy: Reexamining the Life and Legacy of America's Most Hated Senator* (1999)

Robert M. Lichtman, *Deadly Farce: Harvey Matusow and the Informer System in the McCarthy Era* (2004)

George Lukacs, *George Kennan: A Study of Character* (2007)

David G. McCullough, *Truman* (1992)

Geoffrey Perret, *Old Soldiers Never Die: The Life of Douglas MacArthur* (1996)

Jeremi Suri, *Henry Kissinger and the American Century* (2007)

CHAPTER 27

Under the Cold War's Shadow

James G. Blight and Peter Kornbluh, eds., *Politics of Illusion: The Bay of Pigs Invasion Reexamined* (1999)

Robert R. Bowie, *Waging Peace: How Eisenhower Shaped an Enduring Cold War Strategy* (1998)

James Carroll, House of War: *The Pentagon and the Disastrous Rise of American Power* (2006)

Nick Cullather, *Secret History: The CIA's Classified Account of its Operations in Guatemala, 1952–1954* (2nd ed., 2006)

Paul Dickson, *Sputnik: The Shock of the Century* (2001)

Piero Gleijeses, *Shattered Hope: The Guatemalan Revolution and the United States, 1944–1954* (1991)

William Inboden, *Religion and American Foreign Policy, 1945–60: The Soul of Containment* (2008)

Howard Jones, *The Bay of Pigs* (2008)

Zachary Karabell, *Architects of Intervention: The United States, the Third World, and the Cold War, 1946–1962* (1999)

Kenneth Osgood, *Total Cold War: Eisenhower's Secret Propaganda Battle at Home and Abroad* (2006)

Kathryn Statler and Andrew Johnson, eds., *The Eisenhower Administration, the Third World, and the Globalization of the Cold War* (2006)

Odd Arne Westad, *The Global Cold War: Third World Interventions and the Making of Our Times* (2005)

The Affluent Society

Roslyn Fraad Baxandall and Elizabeth Ewen, *Picture Windows: How the Suburbs Happened* (2000)

Robert A. Beauregard, *When America Became Suburban* (2006)

Stephanie Coontz, *The Way We Never Were* (1992)

Edward Humes, *Over Here: How the GI Bill Transformed the American Dream* (2006)

Kenneth T. Jackson, *Crabgrass Frontier* (1985)

James T. Patterson, *Grand Expectations: Postwar America, 1945–1974* (1996)

Adam Ward Rome, *The Bulldozer in the Countryside: Suburban Sprawl and the Rise of American Environmentalism* (2001)

Stephen Wagner, *Eisenhower Republicanism: Pursuing the Middle Way* (2006)

Jessica Weiss, *To Have and to Hold: Marriage, the Baby Boom and Social Change* (2000)

Youth Culture

Wini Breines, *Young, White, and Miserable: Growing Up Female in the Fifties* (1992)

Thomas Doherty, *Teen Pics* (1994)

Marc Fisher, *Something in the Air: Radio, Rock, and the Revolution that Shaped a Generation* (2007)

Nelson George, *The Death of Rhythm and Blues* (1988)

James B. Gilbert, *A Cycle of Outrage: America's Reaction to the Juvenile Delinquent in the 1950s* (1986)

Jim Miller, *Flowers in the Dustbin: The Rise of Rock and Roll, 1947–1977* (1999)

Grace Palladino, *Teenagers: An American History* (1996)

Mass Culture and Its Discontents

Erik Barnouw, *Tube of Plenty* (1982)

Nancy E. Bernhard, *U.S. Television News and Cold War Propaganda, 1947–1960* (1999)

Joel Foreman, ed., *The Other Fifties: Interrogating Midcentury American Icons* (1997)

John Leland, *Why Kerouac Matters* (2007)

George Lipsitz, *Time Passages* (1990)

J. Fred MacDonald, *Television and the Red Menace* (1985)

David Marc, *Demographic Vistas: Television and American Culture* (1984)

James Schwoch, *Global TV: New Media and the Cold War, 1946–69* (2009)

Lynn Spigel, *Make Room for TV* (1992)

Stephen J. Whitfield, *The Culture of the Cold War* (2nd ed., 1996)

The Coming of the New Frontier

Vincent Bugliosi, *Reclaiming History: The Assassination of President John F. Kennedy* (2007)

Shaun Casey, *The Making of a Catholic President: Kennedy vs. Nixon, 1960* (2009)

James N. Giglio, *The Presidency of John F. Kennedy* (2006)

Trumbull Higgins, *The Perfect Failure: Kennedy, Eisenhower, and the CIA at the Bay of Pigs* (1988)

Walter LaFeber, *Inevitable Revolutions* (1983)

Thomas G. Paterson, ed., *Kennedy's Quest for Victory* (1989)

Sheldon M. Stern, *Averting "The Final Failure": John F. Kennedy and the Secret Cuban Missile Crisis Meetings* (2003)

David Talbot, *Brothers: The Hidden History of the Kennedy Years* (2007)

Richard E. Welch Jr., *Response to Revolution: The United States and Cuba, 1959–1961* (1985)

Mark J. White, ed., *Kennedy: The New Frontier Revisited* (1998)

Garry Wills, *The Kennedy Imprisonment* (1983)

Biography

David Aikman, *Billy Graham: His Life and Influence* (2007)

Chuck Berry, *Chuck Berry: The Autobiography* (1987)

Rick Coleman, *Blue Monday: Fats Domino and the Lost Dawn of Rock' n'Roll* (2007)

Robert Dallek, *An Unfinished Life: John F. Kennedy, 1917–1963* (2003)

Carol George, *God's Salesman: Norman Vincent Peale and the Power of Positive Thinking* (1993)

Peter Guralnick, *Last Train to Memphis: The Rise of Elvis Presley* (1994)

Daniel Horowitz, *Betty Friedan and the Making of the Feminine Mystique* (1998)

David Kirby, *Little Richard and the Birth of Rock'n'Roll* (2009)

Bill Morgan, *I Celebrate Myself: The Somewhat Private Life of Allen Ginsberg* (2006)

Gerald Nicosia, *Memory Babe: A Critical Biography of Jack Kerouac* (1983)

Michael O'Brien, *Rethinking Kennedy: An Interpretive Biography* (2009)

Geoffrey Perret, *Eisenhower* (1999)

CHAPTER 28

Origins of the Movements

Michael R. Belknap, *Federal Law and Southern Order* (1987)

Scott DeVeaux, *The Birth of BeBop* (1998)

Glenda Gilmore, *Defying Dixie: The Radical Origins of Civil Rights, 1919–1950* (2008)

Grace Elizabeth Hale, *Making Whiteness: The Culture of Segregation in the South, 1890–1940* (1998)

Charles P. Henry, *Ralph Bunche: Model Negro or American Other* (1999)

Aldon D. Morris, *The Origins of the Civil Rights Movement: Black Communities Organizing for Change* (1984)

Grace Williams O'Brien, *The Color of the Law: Race, Violence, and Justice in the Post–World War II South* (1999)

James T. Patterson, Brown *v.* Board of Education: *A Civil Rights Milestone and Its Troubled Legacy* (2001)

Harriet Pollack and Christopher Metress, *Emmett Till in Literary Memory and Imagination* (2008)

Bernard Schwartz, *The NAACP's Legal Strategy against Segregated Education* (1987)

Mark Tushnet, *Making Civil Rights Law: Thurgood Marshall and the Supreme Court, 1936–1961* (1994)

No Easy Road to Freedom, 1957–1962

Karen Anderson, *Little Rock: Race and Resistance at Central High School* (2010)

Clayborne Carson, *In Struggle: SNCC and the Black Awakening of the 1960s* (1981)

William Chafe, *Civilities and Civil Rights: Greensboro, North Carolina, and the Black Struggle for Equality* (1980)

David Chappell, *A Stone of Hope: Prophetic Religion and the Death of Jim Crow* (2004)

Constance Curry, et al., *Deep In Our Hearts: Nine White Women in the Freedom Movement* (2000)

John Dittmer, *Local People: The Struggle for Civil Rights in Mississippi* (1994)

David J. Garrow, *The FBI and Martin Luther King, Jr.* (1983)

Keith M. Finley, *Denying the Dream: Southern Senators and the Fight Against Civil Rights, 1938–65* (2008)

Frank Lambert, *The Battle of Ole Miss: Civil Rights v. States' Rights* (2010)

Charles M. Payne, *I've Got the Light of Freedom: The Organizing Tradition and the Mississippi Freedom Struggle* (1995)

J. Mills Thornton, *Dividing Lines: Municipal Politics and the Struggle for Civil Rights in Montgomery, Birmingham, and Selma* (2002)

The Movement at High Tide, 1963–1965

Thomas Borstelmann, *The Cold War and the Color Line: American Race Relations in the Global Arena* (2001)

Nick Bryant, *The Bystander: John F. Kennedy and the Struggle for Black Equality* (2006)

Emilye Crosby, *A Little Taste of Freedom: The Black Freedom Struggle in Claiborne County, Mississippi* (2005)

Sara Evans, *Personal Politics: The Roots of Women's Liberation in the Civil Rights Movement and the New Left* (1979)

Henry Hampton and Steve Fayer, *Voices of Freedom: An Oral History of the Civil Rights Movement* (1990)

Davis W. Houck and David E. Dixon, eds., *Women and the Civil Rights Movement, 1954–65* (2009)

Peniel E. Joseph, *Waiting 'Til the Midnight Hour: A Narrative History of Black Power in America* (2006)

Doug McAdam, *Freedom Summer* (1988)

Diane McWhorter, *Carry Me Home: Birmingham, Alabama: The Climax of the Civil Rights Revolution* (2001)

Belinda Robnett, *How Long? How Long? African American Women in the Struggle for Civil Rights* (1997)

Renee C. Romano and Leigh Raiford, eds., *The Civil Rights Movement in American Memory* (2006)

Sasha Torres, *Black, White, and in Color: Television and Black Civil Rights* (2003)

Clive Webb, *Fight against Fear: Southern Jews and Black Civil Rights* (2001)

Robert Weisbrot, *Freedom Bound: A History of America's Civil Rights Movement* (1990)

Civil Rights Beyond Black and White

Elizabeth Aranda, *Emotional Bridges to Puerto Rico: Migration, Return Migration, and the Struggles of Incorporation* (2007)

Donald Fixico, *Termination and Relocation: Federal Indian Policy, 1945–1960* (1986)

Manuel G. Gonzalez, *Mexicanos: A History of Mexicans in the United States* (1999)

David G. Gutierrez, *Walls and Mirrors: Mexican Americans, Mexican Immigrants, and the Politics of Ethnicity* (1998)

Gabriel Haslip-Viera, et al., eds, *Boricuans in Gotham: Puerto Ricans and the Making of New York City* (2004)

Mae M. Ngai, *Impossible Subjects: Illegal Aliens and the Making of Modern America* (2004)

Cynthia Orozco, *No Mexicans, Women, or Dogs Allowed: The Rise of the Mexican-American Civil Rights Movement* (2009)

David Palumbo-Liu, *Asian Americans: Historical Crossings of a Racial Frontier* (1999)

Maria E. Perez y Gonzalez, *Puerto Ricans in the United States* (2000)

Kenneth R. Philp, *Termination Revisited: American Indians on the Trail to Self-Determination, 1933–1953* (1999)

Zaragosa Vargas, *Labor Rights Are Civil Rights: Mexican American Workers in Twentieth Century America* (2005)

Biography

Katharine M. Charron, *Freedom'e Teacher: The Life of Septima Clark* (2009)

Robert Dallek, *Flawed Giant: Lyndon B. Johnson and His Times, 1961–1973* (1998)

John D'Emilio, *Lost Prophet: The Life and Times of Bayard Rustin* (2003)

David J. Garrow, *Bearing the Cross: Martin Luther King, Jr., and the Southern Christian Leadership Conference* (1986)

Alex Haley and Malcolm X, *The Autobiography of Malcolm X* (1965)

Chana Kai Lee, *For Freedom's Sake: The Life of Fannie Lou Hamer* (1999)

John Lewis, *Walking With the Wind: A Memoir of the Movement* (1998)

Manning Marable, *Malcolm X: A Life of Reinvention* (2011)

Laura T. McCarty, *Coretta Scott King* (2009)

Barbara Ramsey, *Ella Baker and the Black Freedom Movement* (2003)

Jerald E. Podair, *Bayard Rustin: American Dreamer* (2009)

Jo Ann Gibson Robinson, *The Montgomery Bus Boycott and the Women Who Started It* (1987)

Harvard Sitkoff, *King: Pilgrimage to the Mountaintop* (2009)

Dennis D. Wainstock, *Malcolm X: African American Revolutionary* (2008)

CHAPTER 29

Vietnam: America's Longest War

David L. Anderson, *The Columbia Guide to the Vietnam War* (2002)

David L. Anderson and John Ernst, eds., *The War That Never Ends: New Perspectives on the Vietnam War* (2007)

Christian G. Appy, *Working-Class War: American Combat Soldiers in Vietnam* (1993)

Larry Berman, *No Peace, No Honor: Nixon, Kissinger, and Betrayal in Vietnam* (2001)

Robert Buzzanco, *Vietnam and the Transformation of American Life* (1999)

Kenton J. Clymer, *The Vietnam War: Its History, Literature and Music* (1998)

Michael S. Foley, *Confronting the War Machine: Draft Resistance during the Vietnam War* (2003)

Herman Graham III, *The Brothers' War: Black Power, Manhood, and the Military Experience* (2003)

William M. Hammond, *Reporting Vietnam: Media and Military at War* (1998)

George C. Herring, *America's Longest War: The United States and Vietnam, 1950–1975*, 3rd ed. (1996)

———, ed., *The Pentagon Papers*, abridged ed. (1993)

Andrew E. Hunt, *The Turning: A History of Vietnam Veterans Against the War* (1999)

David Kaiser, *American Tragedy: Kennedy, Johnson, and the Origins of the Vietnam War* (2000)

Jeffrey Kimball, *Nixon's Vietnam War* (1998)

Fredrik Logevall, *Choosing War: The Lost Chance for Peace and the Escalation of War in Vietnam* (1999)

Robert Mann, *A Grand Illusion: America's Descent into Vietnam* (2001)

James S. Olson and Randy Roberts, *My Lai: A Brief History with Documents* (1998)

Randy Shilts, *Conduct Unbecoming: Lesbians and Gays in the U.S. Military, Vietnam to the Persian Gulf* (1993)

Fred Turner, *Echoes of Combat: The Vietnam War in American Memory* (1996)

James E. Westheider, *Fighting on Two Fronts: African Americans and the Vietnam War* (1997)

Marilyn B. Young, *The Vietnam Wars, 1945–1990* (1991)

A Generation in Conflict

David Allyn, *Make Love, Not War: The Sexual Revolution, Unfettered History* (2000)

Beth Bailey, *Sex in the Heartland* (1999)

Alexander Bloom and Wini Breines, eds., *Takin' It to the Streets: A Sixties Reader* (1995)

Aniko Bodroghkozy, *Groove Tube: Sixties Television and the Youth Rebellion* (2001)

Peter Braunstein and Michael William Doyle, eds., *Imagine Nation: The American Counterculture of the 1960s and '70s* (2002)

Howard Brick, *Age of Contradiction: American Thought and Culture in the 1960s* (1998)

Paul Buhle and John McMillian, eds., *The New Left Revisited* (2003)

David Farber, *The Age of Great Dreams: America in the 1960s* (1994)

James J. Farrell, *The Spirit of the Sixties: The Making of Postwar Radicalism* (1997)

Jennifer Frost, *"An Interracial Movement of the Poor": Community Organizing and the New Left in the 1960s* (2001)

Gretchen Lemke-Santagelo, *Daughters of Aquarius: Women of the Sixties* Counterculture (2009)

Robbie Lieberman, *Prairie Power: Voices of 1960s Midwestern Student Protest* (2004)

Paul Lyons, *New Left, New Right, and the Legacy of the Sixties* (1996)

Mark Hamilton Lytle, *America's Civil Wars: The Sixties Era from Elvis to the Fall of Richard Nixon* (2005)

John C. McWilliams, *The 1960s Cultural Revolution* (2000)

Sidney M. Milkis and Jerome M. Mileur, eds. *The Great Society and the High Tide of Liberalism* (2005)

Timothy Miller, *The 60s Communes: Hippies and Beyond* (1999)

Mark Oppenheimer, *Knocking on Heaven's Door: American Religion in the Age of Counterculture* (2003)

George Rising, *Clean for Gene: Eugene McCarthy's 1968 Presidential Campaign* (1997)

William L. Van Deburg, *New Day in Babylon: The Black Power Movement and American Culture, 1965–1975* (1992)

Mary Ann Wynkoop, *Dissent in the Heartland: The Sixties at Indiana University* (2002)

The Politics of Identity

Kathleen C. Berkeley, *The Women's Liberation Movement in America* (1999)

Winifred Breines, *The Trouble Between Us: An Uneasy History of White and Black Women in the Feminist Movement* (2006)

Dudley Clendinen and Adam Nagourney, *Out for Good: The Struggle to Build a Gay Rights Movement in America* (1999)

Rachel Blau De Plessis and Ann Snitow, *The Feminist Memoir Project: Voices from Women's Liberation* (1998)

Susan J. Douglas, *Where the Girls Are: Growing Up Female with the Mass Media* (1994)

Martin Duberman, *Stonewall* (1993)

Gerald Horne, *Fire This Time: The Watts Uprising and the 1960s* (1995)

Matthew Frye Jacobson, *Roots, Too: White Ethnic Revival in Post–Civil Rights America* (2006)

Blance Linden-Ward and Carol Hurd Green, *American Women in the 1960s* (1993)

Marguerite V. Marin, *Social Protest in an Urban Barrio: A Study of the Chicano Movement, 1966–1974* (1991)

George Mariscal, *Brown-eyed Children of the Sun: Lessons from the Chicano Movement, 1965–1975* (1991)

Peter Matthiessen, *In the Spirit of Crazy Horse* (1992)

Joane Nagel, *American Indian Ethnic Renewal: Red Power and the Resurgence of Identity and Culture* (1996)

Armando Navarro, *Mexican American Youth Organization: Avant-Garde of the Chicano Movement in Texas* (1995)

Jeffrey Ogbonna Green Ogbar, *Black Power: Radical Politics and African American Identity* (2005)

Ruth Rosen, *The World Split Open: How the Modern Women's Movement Changed America* (2000)

Kimberly Springer, *Living for the Revolution: Black Feminist Organizations, 1968–1980* (2005)

Joy Ann Williamson, *Black Power on Campus* (2003)

The Nixon Presidency and Watergate

Mary C. Brennan, *Turning Right in the Sixties: The Conservative Capture of the GOP* (1995)

Robert Dallek, *Nixon and Kissinger: Partners in Power* (2007)

J. Brooks Flippen, *Nixon and the Environment* (2000)

Daniel E. Frick, *Reinventing Richard Nixon: A Cultural History of an American Obsession* (2008)

Lewis L. Gould, *1968: The Election That Changed America* (1993)

Dean J. Kotlowski, *Nixon's Civil Rights: Politics, Principle, and Policy* (2001)

Frank Kusch, *Battleground Chicago: The Police and the 1968 Democratic National Convention* (2004)

Margaret MacMillan, *Nixon and Mao: The Week That Changed the World* (2007)

Allen J. Matusow, *Nixon's Economy: Booms, Busts, Dollars and Votes* (1998)

Keith W. Olson, *Watergate: The Presidential Scandal that Shook America* (2003)

Asaf Siniver, *Nixon, Kissinger, and U.S. Foreign Policy Making: The Machinery of Crisis* (2008)

Biography

David L. Anderson, ed., *The Human Tradition in the Vietnam Era* (2000)

Avital H. Bloch and Lauri Umansky, eds., *Impossible to Hold: Women and Culture in the 1960s* (2005)

Elaine Brown, *A Taste of Power: A Black Woman's Story* (1992)

Dan T. Carter, *The Politics of Rage: George Wallace, the Origins of the New Conservatism, and the Transformation of Politics* (2000)

Robert Cohen, *Freedom's Orator: Mario Savio and the Radical Legacy of the 1960s* (2009)

Robert Dallek, *Flawed Giant: Lyndon Johnson and His Times, 1961–1973* (1998)

Adam Fortunate Eagle, *Heart of the Rock: The Indian Invasion of Alcatraz* (2002)

Elliot Gorn, ed., *Muhammed Ali: The People's Champ* (1996)

Joan Hoff, *Nixon Reconsidered* (1994)

Daniel Horowitz, *Betty Friedan and the Making of the Feminine Mystique: The American Left, the Cold War, and Modern Feminism* (1998)

Maurice Isserman, *The Other American: The Life of Michael Harrington* (2000)

Joseph A. Palermo, *In His Own Right: The Political Odyssey of Senator Robert F. Kennedy* (2001)

Rick Perlstein, *Before the Storm: Barry Goldwater and the Unmaking of the American Consensus* (2001)

Jonah Raskin, *For the Hell of It: The Life and Times of Abbie Hoffman* (1996)

Dominic Sandbrook, *Eugene McCarthy* (2004)

Kenneth S. Stern, *Loud Hawk: The United States versus the American Indian Movement* (1994)

Evan Thomas, *Robert Kennedy: His Life* (2000)

Jack Todd, *Desertion: In the Time of Vietnam* (2001)

Irwin Unger and Debi Unger, *LBJ: A Life* (1999)

CHAPTER 30

The Overextended Society

Edward D. Berkowitz, *Something Happened: A Political and Cultural Overview of the Seventies* (2006)

Michael A. Bernstein and David E. Adler, eds., *Understanding American Economic Decline* (1994)

W. Carl Biven, *Jimmy Carter's Economy: Policy in an Age of Limits* (2002)

Jefferson Cowie and Joseph Heathcott, eds., *Beyond the Ruins: The Meanings of Deindustrialization* (2003)

Claudia Goldin, *Understanding the Gender Gap: An Economic History of American Women* (1990)

Burton I. Kaufman, *The Arab Middle East and the United States: Inter-Arab Rivalry and Superpower Diplomacy* (1996)

Paul Krugman, *Peddling Prosperity: Economic Sense and Nonsense in the Age of Diminished Expectations* (1994)

Bonnie A. Osif, Anthony J. Baratta, and Thomas W. Conkling, *TMI 25 Years Later* (2004)

Bruce J. Schulman, *From Cotton Belt to Sunbelt* (1991)

Jon Teaford, *Cities of the Heartland: The Rise and Fall of the Industrial Midwest* (1993)

J. Samuel Walker, *Three Mile Island: A Nuclear Crisis in Historical Perspective* (2004)

Daniel Yergin, *The Prize: The Epic Quest for Oil, Money, and Power* (1990)

"Lean Year" Presidents

Gary M. Fink and Hugh Davis Graham, eds., *The Carter Presidency: Policy Choices in the Post–New Deal Era* (1998)

John Robert Greene, *The Presidency of Gerald R. Ford* (1995)

Kevin Mattson, *What the Heck Are you Up To, Mr. President? Jimmy Carter, America's 'Malaise,' and the Speech That Should Have Changed the Country* (2009)

Yanek Mieczkowski, *Gerald Ford and the Challenges of the 1970s* (2005)

Gary Sick, *October Surprise: America's Hostages in Iran and the Election of Ronald Reagan* (1991)

The New Conservatism

William C. Berman, *America's Right Turn: From Nixon to Clinton* (1998)

Joel A. Carpenter, *Revive Us Again: The Reawakening of American Fundamentalism* (1997)

Dan T. Carter, *From George Wallace to Newt Gingrich: Race in the Conservative Counterrevolution, 1963–1994* (1996)

Marisa Chappell, *The War on Welfare: Family, Poverty, and Politics in Modern America* (2009)

Joseph Crespino, *In Search of Another Country: Mississippi and the Conservative Counterrevolution* (2007)

Lee Edwards, *The Conservative Revolution: The Movement That Remade America* (1999)

Susan Faludi, *Backlash: The Undeclared War Against American Women* (1991)

Angela Howard and Sasha Ranae Adams Tarrant, eds., *Reaction to the Modern Women's Movement, 1963 to the present* (1997)

Kevin M. Kruse, *White Flight: Atlanta and the Making of Modern Conservatism* (2005)

Matthew D. Lassiter, *The Silent Majority: Suburban Politics in the Sunbelt South* (2005)

William Martin, *With God on Our Side: The Rise of the Religious Right in America* (1996)

Kim Phillips-Fein, *Invisible Hands: The Making of the Conservative Movement from the New Deal to Reagan* (2009)

Catherine E. Rymph, *Republic Women: Feminism and Conservatism from Suffrage through the Rise of the New Right* (2006)

Bryon E. Shafer and Richard Johnston, *The End of Southern Exceptionalism: Class, Race, and Partisan Change in the Postwar South* (2006)

Grass-Roots Politics

Henry F. Bedford, *Seabrook Station: Citizen Politics and Nuclear Power* (1990)

Nicholas Dagen Bloom, *Suburban Alchemy: 1960s New Towns and the Transformation of the American Dream* (2001)

Elizabeth D. Blum, *Love Canal Revisited: Race, Class, and Gender in Environmental Activism* (2008)

Craig Cox, *Storefront Revolution: Food Co-ops and the Counterculture* (1994)

David Frum, *How We Got Here: The 70s, The Decade That Brought You Modern Life (For Better or Worse)* (2000)

Gerald Markowitz and David Rosner, *Deceit and Denial: The Deadly Politics of Industrial Pollution* (2002)

Donald G. Mathews and Jane S. De Hart, *Sex, Gender, and the Politics of ERA* (1990)

Stephen Paul Miller, *The Seventies Now: Culture as Surveillance* (1999)

Gordana Rabrenovic, *Community Builders: A Tale of Neighborhood Mobilization in Two Cities* (1996)

David Brian Robertson, ed., *Loss of Confidence: Politics and Policy in the 1970s* (1998)

Suzanne Staggenborg, *The Pro-Choice Movement: Organization and Activism in the Abortion Conflict* (1991)

Winifred D. Wandersee, *On the Move: American Women in the 1970s* (1988)

Foreign Policy

Christopher Hemmer, *Which Lessons Matter? American Foreign Policy Decision Making in the Middle East, 1979–1987* (2000)

David E. Hoffman, *The Dead Hand: The Untold Story of the Cold War Arms Race and Its Dangerous Legacy* (2009)

William M. LeoGrande, *Our Own Backyard: The United States in Central America, 1977–1992* (1998)

Timothy P. Maga, *The World of Jimmy Carter: U.S. Foreign Policy, 1977–1981* (1994)

James Mann, *The Rebellion of Ronald Reagan* (2009)

Jack F. Matlock Jr., *Reagan and Gorbachev: How the Cold War Ended* (2004)

Morris H. Morley, *Washington, Somoza, and the Sandinistas: State and Regime in U.S. Policy toward Nicaragua, 1969–1981* (1994)

The Reagan Revolution

Dean Baker, *The United States since 1980* (2007)

Robert M. Collins, *More: The Politics of Economic Growth in Postwar America* (2000)

Matthew Dallek, *The Right Moment: Ronald Reagan's First Victory and the Decisive Turning Point in American Politics* (2000, 2004)

John Ehrman, *The Eighties: America in the Eighties* (2005)

Nicholas Laham, *Ronald Reagan and the Politics of Immigration Reform* (2000)

Kyle Longley, Jeremy Mayer, Michael Schaller, and John Sloan, *Deconstructing Reagan: Conservative Mythology and America's Fortieth President* (2007)

John W. Sloan, *The Reagan Effect: Economics and Presidential Leadership* (1999)

Itai Nartzizenfield Sneh, *The Future Almost Arrived: How Jimmy Carter Failed to Changed U.S. Foreign Policy* (2008)

Gil Troy, *Morning in America: How Ronald Reagan Invented the 1980s* (2005)

Best of Times, Worst of Times

John-Manuel Andriote, *Victory Deferred: How AIDS Changed Gay Life in America* (1999)

James D. Cockcroft, *Outlaws in the Promised Land: Mexican Immigrant Workers and America's Future* (1986)

Robert M. Collins, *Transforming America: Politics and Culture During the Reagan Years* (2006)

Barbara Ehrenreich, *Fear of Falling: The Inner Life of the Middle Class* (1989)

Elizabeth Fee and Daniel M. Fox, eds., *AIDS: The Making of a Chronic Disease* (1992)

Jacqueline Jones, *The Dispossessed: America's Underclasses from the Civil War to the Present* (1992)

Michael B. Katz, ed., *The "Underclass" Debate* (1993)

Hilda Scott, *Working Your Way to the Bottom: The Feminization of Poverty* (1985)

Randy Shilts, *And the Band Played On: Politics, People, and the AIDS Epidemic* (1987)

Ruth Sidel, *Women and Children Last: The Plight of Poor Women in Affluent America* (1986)

Lenore J. Weitzman, *The Divorce Revolution: The Unexpected Social and Economic Consequences for Women and Children in America* (1985)

Richard White, *Rude Awakenings: What the Homeless Crisis Tells Us* (1992)

"A Kinder, Gentler Nation"

Meena Bose and Rosanna Perotti, eds., *From Cold War to New World Order: The Foreign Policy of George H. W. Bush* (2002)

Stephen F. Cohen, *Failed Crusade: America and the Tragedy of Post-Communist Russia* (2000)

David Halberstam, *War in a Time of Peace: Bush, Clinton, and the Generals* (2001)

William G. Hyland, *Clinton's World: Remaking American Foreign Policy* (1999)

Robert D. Kaplan, *The Coming Anarchy: Shattering the Dreams of the Post–Cold War* (2000)

Tomas W. Lippman, *Madeleine Albright and the New American Diplomacy* (2000)

Robert Litwak, *Rogue States and U.S. Foreign Policy: Containment after the Cold War* (2000)

Christopher Maynard, *Out of the Shadow: Geroge H.W. Bush and the End of the Cold War* (2008)

David Mosler and Bob Catley, *Global America: Imposing Liberalism on a Recalcitrant World* (2000)

Micah L. Sifry and Christopher Cerf, eds., *The Gulf War Reader* (1991)

Jeff Wheelwright, *The Irritable Heart: The Medical Mystery of the Gulf War* (2001)

Biography

Peter G. Bourne, *Jimmy Carter: A Comprehensive Biography from Plains to Postpresidency* (1997)

Jimmy Carter, *Keeping Faith: Memoirs of a President* (1982, 1995)

Rosalynn Carter, *First Lady from Plains* (1984)

Adam Clymer, *Edward M. Kennedy: A Biography* (1999)

Donald T. Critchlow, *Phyllis Schlafly and Grassroots Conservatism* (2005)

Jim Cullen, *Born in the U.S.A.: Bruce Springsteen and the American Tradition* (1997, 2005)

John Patrick Diggins, *Ronald Reagan: Fate, Freedom, and the Making of History* (2007)

Betty Ford, with Chris Chase, *Betty, A Glad Awakening* (1987)

Marshall Frady, *Jesse: The Life and Pilgrimage of Jesse Jackson* (1996)

Ernest B. Furgurson, *The Hard Right: The Rise of Jesse Helms* (1986)

Steven M. Gillon, *The Democrats' Dilemma: Walter F. Mondale and the Legacy of Liberalism* (1992)

Kitty Kelley, *Nancy Reagan* (1991)

Linda J. Lear, *Rachel Carson* (1997)

Peter Meyer, *Defiant Patriot: The Life and Exploits of Lt. Colonel Oliver L. North* (1987)

Edmund Morris, *Dutch: A Memoir of Ronald Reagan* (1999)

Timothy Naftali, *Geroge H.W. Bush* (2007)

William E. Pemberton, *Exit with Honor: The Life and Presidency of Ronald Reagan* (1997)

Ronald Reagan, *The Reagan Diaries* (2007)

Tom Wicker, *George Herbert Walker Bush* (2004)

CHAPTER 31

The Clinton Presidency

Sidney Blumenthal, *The Clinton Wars* (2003)

Steven J. Gillon, *The Pact: Bill Clinton, Newt Gingrich, and the Rivalry that Defined a Generation* (2008)

Nigel Hamilton, *Bill Clinton: Mastering the Presidency* (2007)

Richard A. Posner, *An Affair of State: The Investigation, Impeachment, and Trial of President Clinton* (1999)

Alvin Z. Rubinstein, Albina Shayevich, and Boris Zlotnikov, eds., *The Clinton Foreign Policy Reader: Presidential Speeches with Commentary* (2000)

Steven E. Schier, ed., *The Postmodern Presidency: Bill Clinton's Legacy in U.S. Politics* (2000)

Hanes Walton Jr., *Reelection: William Jefferson Clinton as a Native-Son Presidential Candidate* (2000)

Alex Waddan, *Clinton's Legacy: A New Democrat in Governance* (2001)

Changing American Communities

David Brooks, *Bobos in Paradise: The New Upper Class and How They Got There* (2000)

Jorge G. Castaneda, *Ex Mex: From Migrants to Immigrants* (2008)

John D'Emilio, William B. Turner, Urbashi Vaid, eds., *Creating Damage: Sexuality, Public Politicy and Civil Rights* (2000)

Sara M. Evans, *Tidal Wave: How Women Changed America at Century's End* (2003)

Chester Hartman, ed., *Double Exposure: Poverty and Race in America* (1997)

Edward S. Herman and Robert W. McChesney, *The Global Media: The New Missionaries of Corporate Capitalism* (1997)

Denis Lynn Daly Heyck, ed., *Barrios and Borderlands: Cultures of Latinos and Latinas in the United States* (1994)

Bill Ong Hing, *Making and Remaking Asian America through Immigration Policy, 1850–1990* (1993)

Godfrey Hodgson, *More Equal Than Others: America from Nixon to the New Century* (2004)

Randall Kennedy, *Race, Crime, and the Law* (1997)

Ted G. Lewis, *Microsoft Rising: . . . and Other Tales of Silicon Valley* (1999)

Mae M. Ngai, *Impossible Subjects: Illegal Aliens and the Making of Modern America* (2005)

J. Eric Oliver, *Democracy in Suburbia* (2001)

Christian Parenti, *Lockdown America: Police and Prisons in the Age of Crisis* (1999)

Daniel R. Pinello, *America's Struggle for Same-Sex marriage* (2006)

Howard Rheingold, *The Virtual Community* (1994)

Adam Ward Rome, *The Bulldozer in the Countryside: Suburban Sprawl and the Rise of American Environmentalism* (2001)

Reed Ueda, *Postwar Immigrant America* (1994)

Bernard P. Wong, *The Chinese in Silicon Valley: Globalization, Social Networks, and Ethnic identity* (2006)

Stuart A. Wright, *Patriots, Politics, and the Oklahoma City Bombing* (2007)

The Bush Presidency

Rajiv Chandrasekaran, *Imperial Life in the Emerald City: Inside Iraq's Green Zone* (2006)

Richard Clarke, *Against All Enemies: Inside America's War on Terror* (2004)

Alexander Cockburn, Jeffrey St. Clair, and Alan Sekula, *Five Days That Shook the World: Seattle and Beyond* (2000)

William Crotty, ed., *A Defining Moment: The Presidential Election of 2004* (2005)

David Finkel, *The Good Soldiers* (2009)

Peter W. Galbraith, *Unintended Consequences: How War in Iraw Strengthened America's Enemies* (2008)

Lloyd C. Gardner, *The Long Road to Baghdad: A History of U.S. Foreign Policy from the 1970s to the Present* (2008)

James Glanz and Eric Lipton, *City in the Sky: The Rise and Fall of the World Trade Center* (2003)

Joshua Karliner, *The Corporate Planet: Ecology and Politics in the Age of Globalization* (1997)

Margaret Keck and Kathryn Sikkink, *Activists beyond Borders: Advocacy Networks in International Politics* (1998)

Michael T. Klare, *Blood and Oil: The Dangers and Consequences of America's Growing Dependecy* (2004)

Joanne Meyerowitz, ed. *History and September 11th* (2003)

Thomas E. Ricks, *Fiasco: The American Military Adventure in Iraq* (2006)

Roger Simon, *Divided We Stand: How Al Gore Beat George Bush and Lost the Presidency* (2001)

Amory Starr, *Naming the Enemy: Anti-Corporate Movements Confront Globalization* (2000)

Marita Sturken, *Tourists of History: Memory, Kitsch, and Consumerism from Oklahoma City to Ground Zero* (2007)

Laurence Wright, *The Looming Tower: Al-Qaeda and the Road to 9/11* (2006)

John D. Wirth, *Smelter Smoke in North America: The Politics of Transborder Pollution* (2000)

The 2008 Campaign and the Obama Presidency

Dan Balz and Haynes Johnson, *The Battle for America 2008* (2009)

John Heilemann and Mark Halperin, *Game Change: Obama and the Clintons, McCain and Palin, and the Race of a Lifetime* (2010)

David Plouffe, *The Audacity to Win: The Inside Story and Lessons of Barack Obama's Historic Victory* (2009)

Sam Tanenhaus, *The Death of Conservatism* (2009)

Adia Harvey Wingfield and Joe R. Feagin, eds., *Yes We Can?: White Racial Framing and the 2008 Presidential Campaign* (2010)

Biography

Andrew Kirtzman, *Betrayal: The Life and Lies of Bernie Madoff* (2009)

George W. Bush, *Decision Points* (2010)

Bill Clinton, *My Life* (2004)

Karlene Faith, *Madonna, Brawdy & Soul* (1997)

Nigel Hamilton, *Bill Clinton: An American Journey* (2003)

John F. Harris, *Survivor: Bill Clinton in the White House* (2005)

Molly Ivins and Lou Dubose Shrub: *The Short but Happy Political Life of George W. Bush* (2000)

Joyce Milton, *The First Partner: Hillary Rodham Clinton* (1999)

Christopher D. O'Sullivan, *Colin Powell: American Power and Intervention from Vietnam to Iraq* (2009)

Kevin Phillips, *American Dynasty* (2004)

Gerald L. Posner, *Citizen Perot: His Life and Times* (1996)

Richard A. Serrano, *One of Ours: Timothy McVeigh and the Oklahoma City Bombing* (1998)

Mel Steely, *The Gentleman from Georgia: The Biography of Newt Gingrich* (2000)

CREDITS

Text, Tables, Maps and Figures

Chapter 17 Page 480: Reprinted with permission from the Alabama Department of Archives and History, Montgomery, Alabama **Page 481:** "Affairs in Insurrectionary States: Report and Minority Reviews, Alabama, vol. 2," *Senate Reports*, 42nd Congress, 2nd Session, vol. 2, pt. 9, no. 41.

Chapter 18 Page 516: Excerpt from *Battlefield and Classroom: Four Decades with the American Indian*. By Pratt and Utley. pp. 232–234. Copyright 2003 University of Oklahoma Press. Reprinted by permission. **Page 517:** Reproduced from *Land of the Spotted Eagle* by Luther Standing Bear by permission of the University of Nebraska Press. Copyright 1933 by Luther Standing Bear. Copyright renewed 1960 by May Jones. **Map 18.1:** From *The Historical Atlas of Oklahoma* by Morris, Goins, McReynolds. Copyright 1965 University of Oklahoma Press. Reprinted by permission. **Map 18.4:** "THE MORMON CULTURE REGION: STRATEGIES AND PATTERNS IN THE GEOGRAPHY OF THE AMERICAN WEST, 1847-1964" by Donald W. Meinig, from *The Annals of the Association of American Geographers* 55, no. 2, June 1965., reprinted by permission of the publisher (Taylor & Francis Group, http://www.informaworld.com).

Chapter 19 Table 19.1: From THE GILDED AGE edited by Charles W. Calhoun. © 1996. Reprinted by permission of Rowman & Littlefield. **Map 19.2:** From LORD. *Historical Atlas of the United States*, 1E. © 1962 Wadsworth, a part of Cengage Learning, Inc. Reproduced by permission. www.cengage.com/permissions.

Chapter 20 Map 20.1: From *Geographical Inquiry and American Historical Problems*, edited by Earl Carville. (Stanford, CA: Stanford University Press, 1992). Originally published in the *Third Annual Report of the Commissioner of Labor*, 1887.

Chapter 23 Figure 23.3: Reprinted with the permission of Cambridge University Press.

Chapter 24 Page 690: From the Maurice Sugar Papers, Archives of Labor History and Urban Affairs, Wayne State University. Reprinted by permission. **Page 706:** From Ray Zeman, "Squatter Army Wages Grim Battle for Life," in the *Los Angeles Times*, July 21, 1937. Copyright © 1937 by The Los Angeles Times. Reprinted by permission. **Page 707:** "Indigents Peril" speech by Thomas McManus, Secretary, California Citizens' Association, *Los Angeles Times*, August 24, 1938. Copyright © 1938 The Los Angeles Times. Reprinted by permission.

Chapter 25 Page 732: "Beaumont to Detroit: 1943." From The Collected Poems of Langston Hughes, by Langston Hughes, edited by Arnold Rampersad with David Roessel, Associate Editor, copyright © 1994 by the Estate of Langston Hughes. Reprinted by permission of Harold Ober Associates, and Alfred A. Knopf, a division of Random House. **Page 746:** Box 70, *J. Robert Oppenheimer Papers*, Manuscript Division, Library of Congress, Washington, D.C. **Page 747:** Box 70, *J. Robert Oppenheimer Papers*, Manuscript Division, Library of Congress, Washington, D.C.

Chapter 27 Page 796: From *The New York Times*, August 20, 1957 © 1957 The New York Times. All rights reserved. Used by permission and protected by the Copyright Laws of the United States. The printing, copying, redistribution, or retransmission of the Material without express written permission is prohibited. **Page 797:** From *U.S. News & World Report*, August 30, 1957. Copyright © 1957 U.S. News & World Report. Reprinted by permission of Wrights Media, Inc **Page 806:** From Howl and Other Poems, by Allen Ginsberg. City Lights Books. Reprinted by permission.

Chapter 28 Page 828: The SNCC Statement of Purpose, by James Lawson. Reprinted by permission of the author. **Page 834:** John F. Kennedy Library, http://www.jfklibrary.org/meredith/jmfr.html **Page 835:** John F. Kennedy Library, http://www.jfklibrary.org/meredith/jmfr.html.

Chapter 29 Page 857: Copyright © 1963, 1964 by Warner Bros Inc., renewed 1991, 1992 by Special Rider Music. All Rights Reserved. International copyright secured. Reprinted by permission. **Page 859:** SDS President Paul Potter, "Naming the System" (April 17, 1965). From the web site of Students for a Democratic Society, Document Library. Reprinted by permission. **Figure 29.3:** From Congressional Quarterly, *Civil Rights: A Progress Report*, 1971. Copyright 1971 by CQ-ROLL CALL GROUP. Reproduced with permission of CQ-ROLL CALL GROUP in the format Other book via Copyright Clearance Center. From THE GALLUP POLL 1835–1971 by George Gallup. Copyright © 1972 The Gallup Organization. All rights reserved. Reprinted by permission.

Chapter 30 Figure 30.2: From Bureau of Labor Statistics, in Mary Kupiec et al., eds., *Encyclopedia of American Social History*, Vol. II. New York: Scribner's, 1993, p. 4188. Copyright © 1993 Scribner's. Reprinted by permission of Cengage Learning. **Page 890:** Robert Leppzer, *Voices from Three Mile Island: The People Speak Out* (Trumansburg, NY: The Crossing Press, 1980), pp. 21, 23, 37, 44, 45, 48, 50. Copyright © 1980 The Crossing Press. Reprinted by permission of Random House, Inc. **Page 891:** From Dick Thornburgh, *Where the Evidence Leads: An Autobiography* (Pittsburgh: University of Pittsburgh Press, 2003), pp. 112, 113, 114–115, 117, 123–24. Copyright © 2003 The University of Pittsburgh Press. Reprinted by permission. **Table 30.2:** From *The New York Times*, April 21, 1992, from Federal Reserve Survey of Consumer Finances. Copyright © 1992 The New York Times. Reprinted by permission. **Figure 30.4:** From Statistical abstract of the United States, in Nash et al., *The American People*, 5th ed., p. 988. Reprinted by permission of Longman Publishing Group, a division of Pearson Education. "Listen to the original public radio documentary, VOICES FROM THREE MILE ISLAND, featuring Jane Lee: www.turningtide.com/voicesfromtmi.htm <http://www.turningtide.com/voicesfromtmi.htm>".

Chapter 31 Page 928: Gov. Bill Richardson, "Speech on Comprehensive Immigration Reform at Georgetown University," Dec. 7, 2006. http://www.richardsonforpresident.com/issues/immigration. Reprinted by permission of Governor Bill Richardson. **Page 929:** From Jan C. Ting, "Immigration, National Security, and the Need for a Border Fence" Sept 9, 2005. http://www.letfreedomringusa.com/Fileuploads/. Copyright © 2005 Jan C. Ting. Reprinted by permission.

Photos

Chapter 17 Chapter Opener: Theodor Kaufmann (1814–1896), *On to Liberty*, 1867. Oil on canvas, 36 × 56 in (91.4 × 142.2 cm). Runaway slaves escaping through the woods. Art Resource/Metropolitan Museum of Art. **Page 462:** The Granger Collection, New York. **Page 463:** CORBIS- NY **Page 465:** Library of Congress **Page 467:** Courtesy of the Library of Congress **Page 468:** The Granger Collection, New York. **Page 471:** The Granger Collection **Page 475:** The Granger Collection, New York. **Page 477:** From The Henry Clay Warmoth Papers # 752, Southern Historical Collection, Wilson Library, University of North Carolina at Chapel Hill.

Chapter 18 Chapter Opener: Getty Images Inc. - Hulton Archive Photos **Page 496:** Colorado Historical Society **Page 497:** Silverhorn (Native American), "Kiowa Preparing for a War Expedition." From "Sketchbook," 1887. Graphite, ink and crayon on paper. Collection of the McNay Art Museum, Gift of Mrs. Terrell Bartlett. **Page 499:** CORBIS- NY **Page 501:** Thomas Allen, "Market Plaza," 1878–1879. Oil on canvas, 26 × 39 ½ inches. Witte Museum, San Antonio, Texas. **Page 504:** Denver Public Library **Page 507;** Nebraska State Historical Society, Solomon D. Butcher Collection **Page 508:** Library of Congress **Page 509:** Thomas Hill, "Irrigating at Strawberry Farm, Santa Clara," 1888. Courtesy of The Bancroft Library, University of California, Berkeley **Page 512:** Albert Bierstadt (1830–1902), "Among the Sierra Nevada Mountains, California," 1868. Oil on canvas, 71 × 120 in. (183 × 305 cm). © Smithsonian American Art Museum, Washington, DC/Art Resource, NY **Page 513:** The Granger Collection **Page 518:** U.S. Department of the Interior Geological Survey.

Chapter 19 Chapter Opener: Courtesy of the Library of Congress **Page 528:** Courtesy of the Library of Congress **Page 530:** Carson, Pirie, Scott & Co. **Page 531:** Courtesy of the Library of Congress **Page 532:** The Granger Collection, New York **Page 534:** North Wind Picture Archives **Page 535:** © Bettmann/CORBIS. **Page 537:** Cook Collection, Valentine Richmond History Center **Page 543:** "The Bowery at Night," 1885. Watercolor. Museum of the City of New York **Page 544:** Courtesy of the Library of Congress. **Page 546:** The Granger Collection **Page 548:** The Granger Collection, New York **Page 550:** Courtesy of the Library of Congress.

Chapter 20 Chapter Opener: ICHi-08428; Destruction of the battleship Maine in Havana harbor; in the Spanish-American war; Havana (Cuba) 1898 Feb. 15; Creator-Kurz & Allison/Chicago Historical Society **Page 559:** The Granger Collection, New York **Page 560:** Library of Congress. **Page 563:** The Granger Collection, New York **Page 564:** Courtesy of the Library of Congress **Page 565:** Courtesy of the Library of Congress **Page 566:** Courtesy of the Library of Congress **Page 568:** The Granger Collection, New York **Page 572:** North

INDEX

A

A&P, 657

AAA. *See* Agricultural Adjustment Administration (AAA)

Abortion, 896, 927

Abrams v. *United States*, 641, 644

Abu Ghraib prison, 936

Accommodation, 609–610

Acheson, Dean, 770, 809

ACLU. *See* American Civil Liberties Union (ACLU)

Addams, Jane, 586, 589, 591, 592

Advertising, 529, 667–668

Affirmative action, 902–903

Affluent society, 794–801

The Affluent Society (Galbraith), 794

Afghanistan
  Soviets in, 894, 906
  U.S. war in, 933
  war in, 942

AFL. *See* American Federation of Labor

AFL-CIO. *See* American Federation of Labor-Congress of Industrual Organizations (AFL-CIO)

Africa, World War II in, 740–741

African Americans. *See also* Civil rights movement
  activism by, 607, 609–611
  black power movement and, 868–869
  churches of, 470–471
  in Congress, 1867-1900, 570
  crime and, 926
  culture of, 681–682, 716, 821
  education of, 548, 596
  families, 470–471
  gender roles and, 470
  Harlem Renaissance and, 679–682
  Jim Crow laws and, 569–571
  New Deal and, 710–711
  northern migration of, 644–645

politics of, 473, 475

poverty of, 902

in Reconstruction era, 463, 464–466, 469–475

schools of, 471–472

segregation and, 477, 569–571, 596, 644, 821–825

sharecroppers, 472–473

sports and, 669

unions and, 537

violence against, 468, 477–478, 570, 645, 674–675

voting rights for, 475, 478–479

in West, 502

westward migration of, 492

women, 470, 610–611, 872, 888

in workforce, 534

during World War I, 633–634, 728

during World War II, 733–734, 736–737

Afrika Korps, 740

Agent Orange, 855

Agnew, Spiro, 880

Agricultural Adjustment Administration (AAA), 697, 699, 703

Agriculture. *See also* Farmers/farming
  in 1920s, 663
  in California, 509–510
  commercial, 507–510
  falling prices in, 561
  irrigation and, 510
  prices, 697, 728
  technological innovations in, 507–509
  toll on environment from, 510

Aguinaldo, Emilio, 577

AIDS epidemic, 904–905

Aid to Families with Dependent Children (AFDC), 903, 920

AIM. *See* American Indian Movement (AIM)

Alaska, 574

Albany Movement, 831

Alcohol consumption
  during Prohibition, 672
  in public, 549
  temperance movement and, 596–597

Aldrin, Buzz, 875

Alger, Horatio, 533

Ali, Muhammad, 869

Alien Act, 648

All-American Canal, 708

Allende, Salvador, 879

Alliance for Progress, 810

Allies
  in World War I, 628
  in World War II, 738, 740–743

Al Qaeda, 933, 936, 938

Amalgamated Iron, Steel and Tin Workers, 566

American Civil Liberties Union (ACLU), 648

American Expeditionary Force (AEF), 621–623, 635

American Federation of Labor (AFL), 535–536, 564–565, 605–606, 616, 637, 701

American Federation of Labor-Congress of Industrial Organizations (AFL-CIO), 799–800, 888

American Heritage Foundation, 777

American Historical Association, 513

American Indian Movement (AIM), 870, 873

American Legion, 777

American Liberty League, 698

American Medical Association (AMA), 678, 801

American Missionary Association (AMA), 472

American Protective Association, 569

American Protective League, 644

American Railway Union (ARU), 566–567

American Recovery and Reinvestment Act, 941

Americans with Disabilities Act, 910

American way, 777

American Woman Suffrage Association (AWSA), 469

Amos 'n' Andy, 716

Anaconda Copper Mining Company, 499

Ancient Society (Morgan), 514

Anderson, Marian, 711

Anderson, Sherwood, 682

Andreae, Percy, 598–599

Anglo-Iranian Oil Company, 792

Animals, extinction of, 510

Animated cartoons, 715

Anthony, Susan B., 468, 469

Anti-imperialism, 578–579, 580

Anti-Saloon League, 596, 598

Anti-Semitism, 724

Antiterrorism and Effective Death Penalty Act, 931

Antitrust laws, 530, 569, 611–612, 616

Antiwar protests, 855–860, 870, 935

Apache Indians, 496, 519

Apollo mission, 809, 875

Apprenticeships, 548

Architecture, 530, 541–542

Area Redevelopment Act, 808

Arizona Canal, 614

Armas, Carlos Castillo, 794

Armstrong, Louis, 668, 669

Army nurses, in WWII, 738

ARPANET, 924

Art/artists
   documentary impulse, 712–713
   New Deal and, 711–712
   of West, 510–511, 513–514

Arthur, Chester A., 558

Asia. *See also specific countries*

Asian American movement, 873–874

Asian American Political Alliance (AAPA), 870, 873–874

Asian Americans, 846

Assembly lines, 528

Aswan High Dam, 792–793

Atlanta sit-in, 827–828

Atlantic Charter, 725, 758

Atomic bomb, 721–723, 746–747, 749

Atomic diplomacy, 763

Attorney General's List, 767

Auto industry, 658–660, 887

Automobiles, 798

Axis powers, 740

B

Babbitt (Lewis), 682

Babcokc, Orville E., 485

Baby and Child Care (Spock), 776

Baby boom, 775

Baby boomers, 855–860

Baez, Joan, 855

Bakke, Allan, 902–903

Bakker, Jim and Tammy, 895

Banks and banking, Federal Reserve, 615–616

Baptist churches, 471

Baraka, Imamu Amiri, 869

Barnard, Evan G., 491

Barnett, Ross, 831

Barry, Marion, 827

Baruch, Dorothy, 802

Baseball, 549–551, 668–670

Bataan death march, 738

Battle fatigue, 737–738

Battle of Britain, 724

Bay of Pigs, 810

Bayonet Constitution, 556

Beatles, 857

Beats, 806

Bebop music, 820, 821

Belknap, William W., 485

Bell, Alexander, 527

Beloved Community, 837–838

Bennett, William, 910

Berger, Victor, 642–643

Berkman, Alexander, 648

Berlin, Irving, 734

Berlin crisis, 762–763

Berlin Wall, 909, 910

Best Years of Our Lives (film), 772

Bethune, Mary McLeod, 710

Bevel, James, 840

Beveridge, Albert J., 556

Bicycles, 545

Biden, Joseph, 940

Bierstadt, Albert, 512

Bilingual Education Act, 863

Bin Laden, Osama, 933

Birmingham, Alabama, 831–832, 834–835

Birth control, 608–609, 671

Birth control pill, 856

Birthrate, 775, 801

Black activism, 607

Black capitalism, 875

Black codes, 464–465

Black consciousness, 838–839

Black Kettle, chief, 494

Black Panther Party, 869

Black power movement, 868–869, 870

Black Star Line, 680

Black Tuesday, 692

Blaine, James G., 556, 574

Bloody Sunday, 841

Blues, 668

Board of Indian Commissioners, 515

Bohemians, 606–607

Bolsheviks, 635, 641, 646

Bonanza farming, 509

Bond, Julian, 827–828

Bonus Army, 695

Boomers, 492

Boomtowns, 499

Booth, John Wilkes, 463

Borderlands, 500–502

Bosnia, 921

Boston, Massachusetts, Back Bay neighborhood, 542

Boulder Dam, 708

Bourne, Randolph, 631

Boycotts, civil rights movement and, 817–819

Bozeman Trail, 495

Braceros, 842–843, 846

Brandeis, Louis, 591, 592, 615

Brando, Marlon, 803–804

Bretton Woods system, 757, 875

Brezhnev, Leonid, 877

Broadway, 546–547

Brooklyn Bridge, 542

Brooks, Milton, 702

Brotherhood of Sleeping Car Porters, 733, 833

Brown, Henry Billings, 570

Brown v. *Board of Education*, 822–823, 825, 836, 902

Bryan, William Jennings, 568, 569, 614–615, 675, 676–677

Buchanan, Patrick, 926–927

Budget deficit, 901

Buffalo, 494, 510

Buffalo Bill, 512

Bunche, Ralph, 821

Bureaucracy, growth of government, 557–558

Bureau of Indian Affairs (BIA), 494, 708–709, 844

Bureau of Reclamation, 705, 708

Burger, Warren E., 875

Burlingame Treaty, 483

Burroughs, William, 806

Bush, George H.W., 886
  economy during, 911–912
  election of 1988 and, 909–910
  election of 1992 and, 911–912
  Persian Gulf War and, 911
  presidency of, 910–911
  as vice president, 896

Bush, George W.
  compassionate conservatism of, 936–938
  Democratic congress and, 938
  election of 2000 and, 930–931
  election of 2004 and, 936
  foreign policy of, 933–934
  Iraq war and, 934–936, 938
  war on terror and, 930, 931–934

Bush Doctrine, 933–934

Business. *See also* Industry
  age of capital and, 482–484
  integration and merger in, 529–530

labor and big, 533–536

post–WWI, 656–657

railroad, 482–484

rise of big, 527–533

during World War I, 636–637

Butler, Benjamin F., 463

Butler v. *United States*, 700

C

Cable, 923–924

California
  agribusiness in, 509–510
  Dust Bowl migrants in, 706–707
  irrigation districts, 510
  suburbs of, 798

Calley, William L., Jr., 876

Cambodia, 876

Caminetti Act, 500

Camp David Accords, 893–894

Camping, 545

Canada, 574
  foreign policy of, 893–895
  immigrants from, 603

Canal Ring, 485

Canals, 614
  All-American Canal, 708
  Panama Canal, 624–625
  Suez Canal, 793

Canal Zone, 624–625

Capital, age of, 482–484

Capitalism, 713
  black, 875
  welfare, 657–658

Capone, Al, 672

Capra, Frank, 715

Caribbean, U.S. involvement in, 626, 793–794

Caribbean immigrants, 603, 680

Carlisle Indian Industrial School, 516–517

Carmichael, Stokely, 865, 868–869, 872

Carnegie, Andrew, 532–533, 578–579

Carpetbaggers, 476

Carranza, Venustiano, 627

Carson, Rachel, 889

Carter, Jimmy, 886
  election of 1976 and, 892–893
  election of 1980 and, 896, 898
  inauguration of, 897
  Iran hostage crisis and, 894–895
  presidency of, 893

Carver, George Washington, 548

Castro, Fidel, 810

Catcher in the Rye (Salinger), 773

Catholic Church, Mexican borderland communities and, 502

Catholics, immigrants, 672–673

Cattle industry, 502–504, 505

Cattle trails, 498

Celebrity, 665, 668–670

Central America
  dollar diplomacy and, 625
  U.S. involvement in, 663, 906–907

Central bank, 615–616

Central Intelligence Agency (CIA), 766, 792, 793–794, 809, 810, 879

Central Pacific Railroad, 482–483

Central Park, 548

Central Powers, 628

Central Valley Project (CVP), 708

A Century of Dishonor (Jackson), 515

Chain stores, 528

Chamber of Commerce, 777

Chambers, Whittaker, 769

Chaney, James, 837

Chavez, Cesar, 872–873

"Checkers Speech" (Nixon), 781, 805

Cheever, John, 799

Chemical warfare, 855

Cherokee Indians, 491

Cherokee Nation v. *Georgia*, 493–494

Cheyenne Indians, 494–495, 519–520

Chiang Kai-shek, 743, 777–778

Chicago, Illinois, 548, 606–607, 644
  Haymarket Square riots, 525–526
  Uptown, 851–853

Chicago World's Fair, 571

Chicano rebellion, 872–873

Chickasaw Indians, 491

Child labor, 588, 595–596, 616

Childrearing, 776
Children
    in late nineteenth century, 545
    during World War II, 731
Children's Bureau, 614, 640, 731
Chile, 879
China
    Carter and, 894
    communism in, 777–778
    Cultural Revolution in, 865
    dollar diplomacy and, 625
    Japanese aggression in, 723
    Nixon and, 877
    Open Door policy and, 626
    trade with, 920
Chinese Exclusion Act, 483, 534, 672
Chinese immigrants
    agribusiness and, 509–510
    discrimination against, 534
    railroads and, 482–483
Choctaw Indians, 491
Chrisman, Lizzie, 507
Christianity, fundamentalism in, 886
Christian missionaries, 573–574
Churches. See also Religion
    African American, 470–471
Churchill, Winston, 725, 740, 745,
    748–749, 758
CIA. See Central Intelligence
    Agency (CIA)
Cigarette-making machine, 528
Cities
    architecture of, 541–542
    crisis in, 862
    diseases in, 542
    ethnic neighborhoods in, 545, 546
    ghettos in, 603–604
    growth of, 540–541, 660
    immigrants in, 540–541, 545–546
    impact on environment of, 542–543
    industrial, 540–543
    post–WWI, 660
    public spaces, 548–549
    racial tensions in, 644–645
    tenement houses in, 542
    uprisings in, 862–864

City Beautiful movement, 542
City bosses, 558–559, 593–594
City parks, 548–549
Civilian Conservation Corps (CCC),
    697, 698, 699
Civil liberties, during World War I, 641
Civil rights, after World War II,
    819–821
Civil Rights Act (1866), 460, 465, 477
Civil Rights Act (1875), 478
Civil Rights Act (1957), 836
Civil Rights Act (1964), 836–837, 863
Civil Rights Act (1968), 863
Civil Rights Cases, 478–479, 570
Civil rights movement, 816–847
    Albany Movement, 831
    election of 1960 and, 828–829
    Freedom Rides, 830–831
    Indian peoples and, 843–844
    Japanese Americans and, 843
    Johnson and, 836–837, 841–842
    Kennedy and, 832–833
    landmark legislation and Supreme
        Court decisions, 836
    Malcolm X and, 838–839
    March on Washington, 832–833
    Martin Luther King and, 825–826,
        831–836, 840–842
    Mexican Americans and, 842–843
    Mississippi Freedom Summer,
        837–838
    Montgomery bus boycott and,
        817–819
    origins of, 819–825
    Puerto Ricans and, 843–844
    Selma, Alabama and, 839–842
    sit-ins, 826–828
    Student Nonviolent Coordinating
        Committee and, 828
    television and, 824
Civil rights organizations, 733
Civil service reform, 559–560
Civil Service Reform Association, 560
Civil War, casualties in, 461
Clark, Jim, 824
Clark, Tom C., 767, 777
Clayton Antitrust Act, 616

Clean Air Act, 911
Clean Water Act, 911
Clemenceau, Georges, 646
Cleveland, Grover, 510, 556, 558,
    567–568
Climate change, 921–922
Clinton, Bill
    economy of, 922
    election of 1992 and, 911–912
    foreign policy of, 920–922
    impeachment of, 922
    inauguration of, 920
    presidency of, 919–922
    Republicans and, 920
    scandals of, 922
Clinton, Hillary Rodham, 919, 922,
    939, 942
Clinton Doctrine, 921
Club movement, 608
Coal industry, 664
Cody, William F., 512–513
Coeur d'Alene strike, 565
Coinage Act, 567
Cold War, 754–782
    affluence during, 794–801
    anxiety, 772–773
    beginning of, 757–760
    Berlin crisis, 762–763
    containment policy and, 760–763
    covert actions during, 792,
        793–794, 809
    culture of, 772–777
    defense spending in, 776, 795, 798
    Eisenhower administration and,
        789–794
    end of, 909
    espionage during, 769
    families in, 773, 775–776
    at home, 766–772
    House Committee on Un-
        American Activities and,
        767–769
    Kennedy and, 809–810
    Korean War and, 778–780
    liberalism during, 763–766
    major policies of, 761
    McCarthyism and, 769–772

patriotism, 777
propaganda during, 780
Reagan and, 905–906
Colfax, Schulyer, 484
Collective security, 759–760
College football, 670
Colleges and universities
in Cold War era, 776, 800–801
land-grant, 508
in late nineteenth century, 547–548
student activism on, 855–857
women's, 547–548
Collier, John, 708–709
Collins, Elizabeth, 504
Colorado Volunteers, 494
Comanche Indians, 493–494, 496
Comic books, 734
Commerce, in 1920s, 662–663
Commercial agriculture, 507–510
Committee for Industrial
Organization (CIO), 701–702
Committee on Public Information
(CPI), 631, 632
Committee to Re-Elect the President
(CREEP), 879
Commons, John R., 591
Communes, 856
Communism
in China, 777–778
collapse of, 909
Red Scare and, 648
Communist Party, 700, 713, 755, 769
Community Action Program
(CAP), 861
Community health centers, 862
Company towns, 604–605
Compassionate conservatism, 936–938
Compromise of 1877, 486
Concentration camps, 745, 748
Congress of Racial Equality (CORE),
733, 821, 830
Conservation movement, 612–614
Conservatism, 885–886, 895–896,
936–938
Conspicuous consumption, 543–544
Consumer debt, 656

Consumer goods, 545–546
Consumerism, 528–529
Consumer protection legislation, 863
Consumer society, 543–546
Consumer spending, in Cold War
era, 775
Consumption, 543–544
Containment policy, 760–763
Contraception, 608–609, 671, 856
Contract with America, 920
Convict labor, 537
Coolidge, Calvin, 661
Corporations, 656–657
antiunionism and, 658
company towns and, 604–605
Corruption, in city governments,
593–594
Cotton
in Reconstruction era, 479, 482
in South, 536, 663
Coughlin, Charles E., 698–699
Counterculture movement, 856–857
Cowoys, 502–503
Cox, Archibald, 880
Cox, James M., 648
Coxey, Jacob Sechler, 565
Crater Lake, 511
Creek Indians, 491–492
Creel, George, 636
Crime
in 1990s, 926
organized, 672, 673
Crook, George, 496
Crop lien system, 479, 482
Cuba
Bay of Pigs and, 810
Spanish-American War and,
575–577
Cuban-American Treaty, 577
Cuban immigrants, 541
Cuban Missile Crisis, 810–811
Cuban Revolution, 810
Culture wars, 926–927
Cumming v. *Richmond County Board of
Education*, 570

Currency, silver, 567–568
Curtis, Edward Sheriff, 513
Curtis Act, 492
Custer, George Armstrong,
495–496, 513

D

Daley, Richard, 852, 861, 865, 867
Dams, 614, 708
Dance, 668
Darrow, Clarence, 675, 676
Darwin, Charles, 533, 609, 675
Daughters of the American
Revolution (DAR), 711
Davis, Henry W., 463
Davis, Miles, 820
Dawes Plan, 662
Dawes Severalty Act, 515, 519, 708
D-Day, 742
Deadwood Dick (Wheeler), 503
Dean, James, 804
Death of a Salesman (Miller), 773
Debayle, Anastasio Somoza, 894
Debs, Eugene V., 566–567, 615,
641, 648
Deere, John, 507
Defense of Marriage Act, 927
Defense spending, 776, 795, 798,
808, 906
Deloria, Vine, Jr., 873
Democratic Convention, 1968, 867
Democratic Leadership Council
(DLC), 919
Democratic Party
black voters and, 711
in Cold War era, 777–780
in late nineteenth century, 558
in South, 476, 478
Department of Agriculture, 508, 510
Department of Defense, 766
Department of Energy, 887
Department of Health, Education and
Welfare, 790
Department of Homeland Security, 934
Department of the Interior, 510,
558, 614

Department of the Treasury, 558
Department of Transportation, 863
Department stores, 526, 529
Depression(s). *See also* Great
        Depression
    of 1873, 484–485
    of 1890s, 564–565
    in late nineteenth century, 534, 561
Deregulation, 899–900
Derrian, Pat, 893
Derrick, Thomas, 621
Detroit, Michigan, 644
Dewey, George, 577
Dewey, John, 591, 592
Dewey, Thomas E., 765, 820
Dewson, Molly, 709
Díaz, Porfirio, 627
Dies, Martin, 767
Digital technologies, 924
Dime novels, 512
Diplomacy. *See also* Foreign policy
    atomic, 763
        dollar, 625
        Ping-Pong, 877
        progressive, 623–624
Direct primary, 595, 596
Discrimination
    against African Americans, 569–571
    against Chinese laborers, 534
Diseases
    in cities, 542
    influenza epidemic, 640–641
    venereal, 640
Disenfranchisement, of African
        Americans, 478–479, 570, 596,
        610–611
Disney, Walt, 715
Dissent, during Cold War era, 806
Doctors, 801
Documentary impulse, 712–713
Dole, Robert, 892
Dollar diplomacy, 625
"Don't ask, don't tell" policy, 919
Dorr, Rheta Childe, 593
Dos Passos, John, 682

Double V campaign, 733–734, 819
Douglass, Frederick, 469
Dow Chemical Company, 857
Draft
    during Vietnam War, 860
    during World War II, 735
Dreier, Mary, 604
Dresden, Germany, 741
Drew, Charles, 737
Du Bois, W.E.B., 610
Dulles, Allen, 792
Dulles, John Foster, 791
Du Pont, 657
Dust Bowl, 703–709
Dylan, Bob, 857

E

Earp, Wyatt, 504
East Harlem, 843
Eastland, James, 831
Eastman, Max, 607
Economic crises. *See also* Great
        Depression
    of 1890s, 564–567
    in 1980s, 900–901
    Panic of 1837, 484–485
    under Roosevelt, 711
Economic Opportunity Act, 863
Economy
    in 1920s, 660–664
    of 1920s, 691–692
    in 1950s, 794–798
    in 1970s, 887–889
    in 1990s, 911–912, 922
    in 2000s, 940–941
    market, 528–529
    post–WWII, 757–758
    during Reagan years, 900–903
    of South, 536
    during World War I, 636
    during World War II, 727–728
Edison, Thomas Alva, 527, 528
Edmunds Act, 500
Edmunds-Tucker Act, 500

Education
    of African Americans, 471–472,
        548, 596
    in Cold War era, 795
    in late nineteenth century, 547–548
    of Native Americans, 515–517
    No Child Left Behind Act and, 937
    reform, 597, 600–601
    in South, 596
    for women, 547–548
Egypt, 792–793, 877
Eighteenth Amendment, 640, 672
Eight-hour workday, 593
Einstein, Albert, 721
Eisenhower, Dwight D.
    civil rights movement and, 825
    election of 1952 and, 780–781
    foreign policy of, 791–794
    military-industrial complex
        and, 808
    presidency of, 789–794
    during World War II, 735, 742
Electricity, 527
Elementary and Secondary Education
        Act, 863
Eliot, T.S., 712
Ellison, Ralph, 713
Ellsberg, Daniel, 879
El Salvador, 894, 906
Ely, Richard, 591
Embryonic stem cell research,
        927, 930
Emergency Banking Act, 696
Emergency Banking Relief Act, 699
Emergency Relief Act, 694–695
Emergency Relief Appropriation Act,
        700, 701
Employee Act, 764
Enforcement Acts, 478
Environmentalism, 612–614
Environmental movement, 889
Environmental problems, 889–892,
        921–922
Environmental Protection Agency
        (EPA), 875, 892

Environmental protection legislation, 863

EPIC, 699

Equal Employment Opportunity Commission (EEOC), 837

Equal Rights Amendment (ERA), 678, 896

Erdman Act, 569

Erie Railroad, 532

Espionage, 769

Espionage Act, 638, 641

Ethnic diversity, in U.S., 927

Ethnic neighborhoods, 545, 546

Eugenics, 673

Europe. *See also specific countries*
    division of, after World War II, 758–759
    fascism in, 723–724
    Marshall Plan in, 760–762
    post–WWII, 758–760
    World War II in, 723–725
    World War I in, 628

European immigrants
    in early twentieth century, 601–603
    in late nineteenth century, 540–541

Evagelism, 573

Evans, John, 494

Evans, Walker, 712

Evers, Medgar, 832

Evolutionary theory, 609, 673, 675

Executive Order 8802, 836

Executive Order 9066, 732

Executive Order 9981, 836

Expansion, U.S., overseas, 571–581

Expatriates, 682–683

Exports, in nineteenth century, 574

Extinction, animal, 510

F

Factories, 541–542
    assembly lines and, 528

Factory system, 482

Factory workers, 533–534, 537

Fair Deal, 765–766

Fair Labor Standards Act, 701, 711

Falwell, Jerry, 896

Families
    African American, 470–471
    in Cold War era, 773, 775–776
    middle class, 544–545
    suburban, 798–799
    traditional, 775–776
    during World War II, 730–732

Family Assistance Plan, 875

Farmer, James, 830

Farmers' Alliance, 561–564

Farmers' organization, 560–562

Farming/Farmers
    bonanza, 509
    on Great Plains, 505–507
    sharecroppers, 472–473, 479, 663
    in South, 703
    tenant, 482

Farm Security Administration (FSA), 714, 727

Fascism, 723–724

Fashion industry, 734–735

Faubus, Orval, 825

FBI. *See* Federal Bureau of Investigation (FBI)

Federal Art Project (FAP), 712

Federal Bureau of Investigation (FBI), 641, 727, 756, 865

Federal Communications Commission, 790

Federal Deposit Insurance Corporation (FDIC), 698

Federal Emergency Management Agency (FEMA), 937

Federal Emergency Relief Administration (FERA), 697, 699

Federal Employees Loyalty and Security Program, 761, 767

Federal Housing Administration (FHA), 698, 794–795, 796

Federal Music Project, 712

Federal Power Commission, 790

Federal Reserve, 695

Federal Reserve Act, 615

Federal Reserve Banks, 615–616

Federal Theater Project (FTP), 712

Federal Trade Commission (FTC), 616, 790

Federal Writers Project, 711–712

The Feminine Mystique (Friedan), 798, 869

Feminism
    in 1920s, 675, 678
    in 1960s, 869, 871–872

Ferdinand, Franz, 628

Field, Stephen J., 591

Fielden, Samuel, 525

Fifteenth Amendment, 467, 468, 469, 478–479, 486

Filene's, 529

Film industry, 597, 653–655, 664–666, 713, 715, 734, 774

Film noir, 773

Financial crises. *See* Economic crises

Fireside chats, 696

First African Baptist Church, 471

First Reconstruction Act, 473

Fiscal policy
    of Nixon, 875
    of Reagan, 899–900

Fitzgerald, F. Scott, 682

Five Civilized Tribes, 491–492

Flacks, Richard, 852

Flappers, 670–671

Flathead Indians, 519

Fletcher, Alice Cunningham, 514

Flint, Michigan, strike in, 689–691

Follow Through, 862

Food Administration, 636

Food and Drug Administration (FDA), 612

Food and Fuel Act, 636

Football, 670

Ford, Betty, 892

Ford, Gerald, 880, 892

Ford, Henry, 659–660

Ford Motor Company, 658–660, 702, 730

Foreign-born residents. *See also* Immigrants
    by region, 1880, 541

Foreign missionaries, 573–574

Foreign policy
  in 1920s, 662–663
  under Bush, Jr., 933–934
  under Carter, 893–895
  under Clinton, 920–922
  containment policy, 760–763
  under Eisenhower, 791–794
  under FDR, 724–725
  Good Neighbor policy, 574
  under Kennedy, 809–810
  in Middle East, 792
  under Nixon, 877–879
  under Obama, 942
  progressive diplomacy, 623–624
  under Reagan, 905–909
  under Roosevelt, 624–625
  under Taft, 625
  under Truman, 760–762, 777
  under Wilson, 625–628

Forest Management Act, 510

Forest Reserve, 510, 612

Fort Laramie, Treaty of, 495

"Forty acres and a mule," 463

Fourteen Points, 635, 646

Fourteenth Amendment, 466, 469, 478, 479, 486, 591

France
  American Expeditionary Force in, 621–623
  Indochina and, 794
  during World War II, 724, 742

Franco, Francisco, 724

Frankfurter, Felix, 682

Freedmen's Bureau, 463, 465, 471–472

Freedom Foundation of Valley Forge, 777

Freedom Ride, 821

Freedom Rides, 830–831

Freedom Summer project, 837–838

Freedom Train, 777

Free labor, 464–466

Free silver issue, 567–568

Free speech movement, 870

Free trade agreements, 920–921

Frick, Henry C., 565–566

Friedan, Betty, 798, 869

Frontier. *See also* West
  violence on, 504–505

Frontier thesis, 513

Fugitives, 682–683

Fulbright, J. William, 855, 864

Fundamentalism, 675, 886

G

Galarza, Ernesto, 843

Galbraith, John Kenneth, 794

Gambling, 504

Gandhi, Mohandas, 825–826

Garfield, James A., 558, 559

Garment industry, 533, 604

Garvey, Marcus, 603, 839

Gathright, Bee, 885

Gay Liberation Front (GLF), 872

Gay liberation movement, 870, 872

Gay marriage, 927

General Agreement on Tariffs and Trade (GATT), 761, 921

General Electric, 657

General Land Revision Act, 510

General Motors, 689–691

Gentleman's Agreement, 672

George, David Lloyd, 646

George, Henry, 562

Germany
  division of, 758–759
  Holocaust and, 745, 748
  Nazi, 723–724, 745, 748
  war reparations and, 647, 662
  World War I and, 628, 630
  World War II and, 724–725, 738, 740

Geronimo, 496

Gerraro, Geraldine, 900

Ghettos, 603–604

Ghost Dance, 518–519

G.I. Bill of Rights, 756, 776, 795

Gibson, Charles Dana, 632

Gingrich, Newt, 920

Ginsberg, Allen, 806

Gladden, Washington, 567

Glass-Steagall Act, 698, 920

Global economy, post–WWII, 757–758

Globalization, 920–922

Global warming, 921–922

Goldman, Emma, 648

Gold rush, 498

Gold Standard Act, 569

Goldwater, Barry, 839–840, 854, 868, 885–886

Gompers, Samuel, 535–536, 564–565, 605, 637

Goodman, Andrew, 837

Goodman, Benny, 716

Good Neighbor policy, 574

Gorbachev, Mikhail, 909

Gore, Al, 930–931

Gossip columns, 667

Gould, Jay, 483, 532

Government
  civil service reform and, 559–560
  growth of, 557–558
  municipal, 558–559, 593–594
  regulation by, 612

Grady, Henry W., 569–570

Grady, Henry Woodfin, 536

Graham, Billy, 798

Grand Canyon (Leigh), 613

Grand Coulee Dam, 708

Grandfather clauses, 570, 596

Granger movement, 560–561, 563

Grant, Ulysses S., 466
  election of 1868 and, 467–468
  election of 1872 and, 484

Grapes, 509

The Grapes of Wrath (Steinbeck), 706, 712–713

Grassroots conservatism, 885–886

Great Britain, World War II and, 724–725

Great Depression, 691–695. *See also* New Deal
  causes of, 691–692
  culture during, 711–716
  documenting, 714

Hoover's response to, 694–695
unemployment during, 693–694
worldwide effects of, 695
The Great Gatsby (Fitzgerald), 682
Great Migration, 644–645, 681
Great Plains
commercial agriculture in, 507–509
Dust Bowl, 703–709
farming communities on, 505–507
Indian Territory and, 493–494
Great Recession, 940–941
Great Sioux War, 495
Great Society, 852, 861–862, 863
Great Uprising of 1877, 563
Great War. *See* World War I
Greece, 762
Greeley, Horace, 484, 505
Green, James K., 460
Green Berets, 809
Greensboro sit-in, 826–827
Greenwich Village, 606–607
Grenada, 906
Grizzly bear, 510
Group Theater, 713
Guadalupe Hidalgo, Treaty of, 500–501
Guam, 580
Guantanamo Bay, 577
Guatemala, 793–794
Gulf of Tonkin resolution, 854

H

Hale County, Alabama, 459–461
Hamilton, Charles V., 869
Hanford, Washington, 776
Harding, Warren G., 648–649, 661
Harlem Renaissance, 603, 679–682
Harrison, Benjamin, 510, 558
Harvester, 507
Harvey, Marcus, 680
Hatch Act, 508
Hawai'i, annexation of, 555–557, 574–575
Hay, John, 626
Hayden, Casey, 838

Hayes, Rutherford B., 485–486, 558
Haymarket Square riot, 525–526
Hays, Wayne, 867
Haywood, William D., 606
Head Start, 862
Health care reform, 919, 942
Hearst, William Randolph, 576
Helldorados, 499
Hemingway, Ernest, 682
Henry Street Settlement House, 585–586, 592–593, 616
Hepburn Act, 612
Heritage Foundation, 895
Hernandez decision, 842
Hetch Hetchy Valley, 613
Hickok, James Butler, 504
Hicks, Granville, 713
The Hidden Persuaders (Packard), 806
Higher education, 547–548, 776, 800–801
Higher Education Act, 808
High schools, 547, 600–661, 803
Highways, 776, 795
Highway Safety Act, 863
Highway Trust Fund, 795
Hiking, 545
Hill, James J., 483
Hill, Thomas, 509
Hillman, Sidney, 701
Hines, Lewis, 588
Hippies, 856–857
Hiroshima, 749, 763
Hiss, Alger, 769
Hitler, Adolf, 723–724, 725, 738, 740, 745, 749
Hobby, Oveta Culp, 790
Ho Chi Minh, 763, 794, 809
Hollywood, 653–655, 664–666, 713, 715, 734, 767–768, 774
Holmes, Oliver Wendell, Jr., 591, 641
Holocaust, 745, 748
Homelessness, 904–905
Homestead Act, 505
Homestead strike, 565–566
Homosexuality, 671–672

Homosexuals, 737, 801
Honduras, 625
Hoover, Herbert, 865
election of 1928 and, 683–684
election of 1932 and, 695
at Food Administration, 636
Great Depression and, 694–695
presidency of, 661–662
Hoover, J. Edgar, 756, 775
Hoover Dam, 708
Hopi Indians, 520
Hopkins, Harry, 697, 700
Hopper, Edward, 775
Horizontal combination, of business, 530
House Committee on Un-American Activities (HUAC), 767–769
Houston, George, 480–481
Houston, Texas, 660
Howe, Frederic C., 592, 594
Howl (Ginsber), 806
How the Other Have Lives (Riis), 588
Huerta, Victoriano, 627
Hughes, Charles Evans, 662
Hughes, Langston, 713, 733–734, 777
Hull House, 589, 592, 593
Humphrey, Hubert, 838, 867
Hunt, E. Howard, 879
Huntington, Collis P., 483
Hurricane Katrina, 937–938
Hussein, Saddam, 911, 934, 936, 938
Hydrogen bomb, 780

I

Ice-skating, 545
Ickes, Harold, 698, 711
Identity politics, 868–874
Illegal immigrants, 842–843, 846, 928–929
Illinois Factor Investigation Act, 536
I Love Lucy (TV show), 804
Immigrants/immigration
in 1920s, 672–674, 678–679
in 1990s, 924–926
Asian, 846

Caribbean, 603, 680
Chinese, 482–483, 534
in cities, 540–541, 545–546
in early twentieth century, 601–603
on Great Plains, 505–506
illegal, 842–843, 846, 928–929
Japanese, 603
Jewish, 540–541, 604
Mexican, 603, 678–679
Immigration Act (1917), 637
Immigration Act (1921), 673
Immigration and Nationality Act, 761, 767, 845–846, 863
Immigration and Naturalization Service (INS), 705, 843
Imperial Dam, 614
Imperialism, 571–581
critics of, 578–580
Philippines and, 577
of righteousness, 571, 573–574
Spanish-American War and, 575–577
Imports, 887
Incandescent lamp, 527
Indian peoples. See also specific tribes
assimilation of, 515, 519
civil rights movement and, 843–844
endurance and rejuvenation of, 519–520
Ghost Dance and, 518–519
New Deal and, 708–709
Oklahoma land rush and, 491–493
reservation policy and, 494, 495, 515
schools for, 515–517
slaughter of buffalo and, 494
transformation of Indian societies, 514–520
treaties with, 494, 514
U.S. policy toward, 492–494, 515
Indian Reorganization Act (IRA), 708
Indian reservations, 494, 495, 515, 874
Indian Territory, 491–494
Indian wars, 494–496
Indochina, 794
Industrial cities, 540–543

Industrial technology, 527–528
Industrialization
in North, 482–484
second industrial revolution, 527, 655–656
in South, 536–540
Industrial Workers of the World (IWW), 606, 637–638
Industry
in 1920s, 663–664
in late nineteenth century, 527–533
mechanization and, 527–528
military and, 776–777
patterns of, 1900, 529
during World War I, 636–637
during World War II, 727–728
Infant mortality, 861
The Influence of Sea Power upon History (Mahan), 574
Influenza, 640–641
Initiatives, 595
Intellectuals, alienation of, 682–683
Intercontinental ballistic missiles (ICBMs), 792, 906
Internal Security Act, 761, 767
International Brotherhood of Teamsters, 700
International Ladies Garment Workers Union (ILGWU), 604
International Longshoremen's Association (ILA), 700
International Monetary Fund (IMF), 757–758
Internet, 924
Interstate Commerce Commission (ICC), 558, 612
Invasion, U.S.A. (film), 774
Invasion of the Body Snatchers (film), 773
Iran, 792
Iran-Contra scandal, 907–909
Iran hostage crisis, 894–895
Iranian Revolution, 894–895
Iraq
Persian Gulf War and, 911
U.S. invasion of, 934–936, 938
Irrigation systems, 510, 705, 708
Isolationism, 724–725

Israel, 792–793, 877, 893–894, 908
Italy, fascism in, 723

J
Jackson, Helen Hunt, 515
Jackson, Jesse, 869
Jackson, Jimmy Lee, 840
Jackson State University, 876
Japan
atomic bomb and, 749
post–World War II, 777
seizure of Manchuria by, 723
World War II and, 743–745
Japanese American Citizens League (JACL), 843
Japanese Americans
civil rights movement and, 843
internment of, 732, 874
Japanese immigrants, 603
Jazz, 668, 681, 716, 820, 821
Jenckes, Thomas A., 559
Jewish immigrants, 540–541, 604
Jews
German, 724
Holocaust and, 745, 748
Jiang Jeishi, 777–778
Jim Crow laws, 569–571, 821
Jobs or Income Now (JOIN), 851–852
John Hopkins University, 547
Johnson, Andrew
impeachment of, 466–467
presidential reconstruction and, 464
Radical Republicans and, 464–466
Johnson, Hiram, 592, 595, 611
Johnson, Lyndon B.
civil rights movement and, 836–837, 841–842
election of 1964 and, 839–840
Great Society of, 852, 861–862
inauguration of, 812
Vietnam War and, 853–854, 855, 858–859
Jones, Samuel, 592
Jones, Spike, 734
Jones Act, 843

Joseph, Chief, 497
Journalism
  muckraking, 588–589
  tabloid, 666–667
Judson, Edward Zane Carroll, 512
The Jungle (Sinclair), 589, 612
Junior high, 803
Juvenile delinquency, 803–804

K

Kansas, 506
Keating-Owen Act, 616
Kefauver, Estes, 805
Kelley, Florence, 538–539, 586, 592, 593, 604
Kelley, Oliver H., 560
Kellogg-Briand Pact, 662
Kenna, Michael, 558
Kennan, George F., 760
Kennedy, Edward, 892–893, 937
Kennedy, John F., 831
  assassination of, 811–813
  Bay of Pigs and, 810
  civil rights movement and, 829, 832–833
  Cold War and, 809–810
  Cuban Missile Crisis and, 810–811
  election of 1960 and, 807–808, 828–829
  foreign policy of, 809–810
  New Frontier and, 806–809
  Vietnam and, 809–810
Kennedy, Robert, 830, 865, 867
Ken State University, 876
Kerner, Otto, 864
Kerouac, Jack, 806
Kerr, Clark, 855–856
Kerry, John, 936
Kindergartens, 600
King, Coretta Scott, 836
King, Lonnie, 828
King, Martin Luther, Jr.
  assassination of, 865
  civil rights movement and, 825–826, 831–832, 840–842
  election of 1960 and, 828–829

"Letter from Birmingham Jail," 832, 835
  Montgomery bus boycott and, 817–819
  Southern Christian Leadership Conference and, 826
King, Mary, 838
King, Rodney, 926
King Cotton. *See* Cotton
Kingston, Maxine Hong, 874
Kinsey, Alfred, 801
Kiowa Indians, 496, 497
Kipling, Rudyard, 572
Kissinger, Henry A., 875–877
Knights of Labor, 534–535, 537
Knox, Pilander C., 625
Kooning, Willem de, 712
Korean War, 778–780, 789–790
Korematsu v. *United States*, 732
Kosovo, 921
Krushchev, Nikita, 791–792, 811
Ku Klux Klan, 460, 468, 477–478, 480–481, 674–675, 832
Kuwait, 911
Kwanzaa, 869
Kyoto protocol, 921–922

L

Labor
  in age of big business, 533–536
  child, 588, 595–596, 616
  convict, 537
  free, 464–466
  IWW, 606
  machine, on farm, 508
  post–WWI, 645–646
  in South, 536–537
  wage, 482, 533–534
  during World War I, 637–638
  during World War II, 728–730
Labor laws, 593, 595–596, 616
Labor movement, 526
  in 1930s, 700, 701–702
  in late nineteenth century, 562–563
  second Red Scare and, 769
  work hours and, 538–539

Labor Party, 562–563
Labor unions
  AFL-CIO, 799–800
  African Americans and, 537
  American Federation of Labor (AFL), 535–536, 605–606
  Committee for Industrial Organization (CIO), 701–702
  in early twentieth century, 605–606
  International Brotherhood of Teamsters, 700
  Knights of Labor, 534–535
  membership, 1940-90, 889
  post–WWI, 658
  rise of, 701–702
  women and, 535
  during World War I, 637–638
  during World War II, 730
La Follette, Robert, 592, 595, 611
Land
  for former slaves, 472–473
  Oklahoma land rush, 491–493
Land-grant colleges, 508
Landis, Paul, 802
Landon, Alfred M., 702
Land speculation, 505
Lange, Dorothea, 693, 712
La raza, 870, 872–873
Las Gorras Blancas, 502
Lathrop, Julia, 593, 640
Latin America
  Good Neighbor policy, 574
  U.S. involvement in, 663, 810
Lawson, James, 827, 828
Leadville, Colorado, 504
League of Nations, 647, 723
League of United Latin American Citizens (LULAC), 842, 843
League of Women Voters, 678
Leary, Timothy, 856
Lease, Mary E., 563
Lee, Russell, 714
Legal Services Program, 862
Legal theory, 591
Leigh, William Robinson, 613
Leisure time, 545, 546, 548–549, 597

Lend-Lease Act, 725

"Letter from Birmingham Jail" (King), 832, 835

Levitt, William, 795

Levittown, New York, 795–797

Lewinsky, Monica, 922

Lewis, John L., 701, 827, 828, 833, 839

Lewis, Sinclair, 682

Liberal Republicans, 484

Liberty Bonds, 636

Liddy, G. Gordon, 879

Lieberman, Joseph, 930

Life expectancy, 732, 861

Lili'uokalani, Queen, 555–557, 577

Lilly Ledbetter Fair Pay Act, 942

Lincoln, Abraham, 482
  amnesty proclamation of, 462–464
  assassination of, 463
  plan of, for Reconstruction, 462–464

Literacy tests, 596

Literature
  of 1920s, 682
  of Cold War era, 773, 799
  of Harlem Renaissance, 681
  Indian, 873

Little Rock, Arkansas, 825

Lochner v. *New York*, 591

Locke, Alain, 681

Lodge, Henry Cabot, 647–648, 672

The Lonely Crowd (Riesman), 800

Long, Huey, 699

Longest Walk, 873

Los Alamos, New Mexico, 721–723, 776

Los Angeles, California, 545, 799, 926

Lost generation, 682

Love, Nat, 503

Love Canal, 889

Lowell, Josephine Shaw, 578–579

Lower South. *See* South

LSD, 856

Luce, Henry, 757

Lusitania, 629

Lynchings, 504, 570, 645

M

MacArthur, Douglas, 695, 735, 738, 743–744, 778–779

Macy's, 529

Mahan, Alfred Thayer, 574

Mail-order houses, 528

Main Street (Lewis), 682

Malcolm X, 838–839

Manchuria, 723

Manhattan Project, 722, 746–747, 749

Manpower Retraining Act, 808

Manufacturing. *See also* Industry
  decline in, 887–888
  post–WWI, 655–656
  during World War I, 636–637
  during World War II, 727–728

Mao Zedong, 743, 778, 865

March on Washington, 832–833

Marcos, Ferdinand, 874, 879

Margold, Nathan, 709

Marijuana, 856–857

Market economy, 528–529

Market revolution. *See also* Industrialization

Marriage
  in Cold War era, 775
  same-sex, 927

Marsh, Reginald, 715

Marshall, George C., 735, 760, 766

Marshall, Thurgood, 822–823

Marshall Field & Company, 526, 529

Marshall Plan, 760–762

Martí, José, 575

Martin, Fletcher, 712

Marx Brothers, 715

Marxism, 713

Mass culture
  in 1920s, 664–672
  in 1950s, 804–806

Mass production, 527, 528, 656

Mass transit, 800

McCain, John, 940

McCarran, Pat, 767

McCarran Act, 761, 767

McCarran Walter Immigration Act, 761

McCarthy, Eugene, 867

McCarthy, Joseph, 769–772

McCarthyism, 769–772

McClure, S.S., 588–589, 592

McClure's, 588–589

McCormick, Cyrus, 507

McCormick Reaper Works, 526

McCoy, Joseph G., 502, 512

McGovern, George, 879

McKinley, William
  annexation of Hawaii and, 556, 574–575
  assassination of, 611
  election of 1896 and, 568–569
  foreign policy of, 574–575
  Philippines and, 577
  presidency of, 569
  Spanish-American War and, 576–577

McKinley Tariff, 558, 567

McLaurin v. *Oklahoma State Regents*, 822, 836

McManus, Thomas, 707

McNamara, Robert, 809

McNary-Haugen Farm Relief bill, 663

Meany, George, 799, 892

Meat Inspection Act, 612

Meatpacking industry, 612

Mechanization, 527–528

Medical advances, 801

Medical corps, 737–738

Medicare, 862, 937

Medicine Lodge Treaty of 1867, 494

Men, African American, 470

Mencken, H.L., 677, 682

Mendez v. *Westminster*, 842

Menlo Park, New Jersey, 527

Meredith, James, 831

Mexican Americans
  in California, 705
  civil rights movement and, 842–843

New Deal and, 710–711
in Southwest, 500–502
zoot suit riots and, 734
Mexican borderland communities, 500–502
Mexican farm workers, 705, 708
Mexican immigrants, 678–679
in 1990s, 925
civil rights movement and, 842–843
immigrants and, 603
Mexicanos, 500–502
Mexican Revolution, 626–627
Mexico
border with, 921, 928–929
U.S. involvement in, 626–628
Middle class
leisure activities of, 545
self-improvement and, 544–545
women, 544–545, 607–608
Middle East
oil interests in, 792, 888
U.S. policy toward, 792, 907–909
Midway Island, 743
Migration, of African Americans to North, 644–645
Military, U.S.
African Americans in, 736–737
"don't ask, don't tell" policy, 919
medical corps, 737–738
racism in, 633–634
women in, 736
during World War II, 735–738
Military-industrial complex, 776–777, 808
Mill communities, 537–540
Miller, Arthur, 773
Mills, C. Wright, 800
Mine Rescue (Martin), 712
Minimum wage, 701
Mining industry, 565, 605, 606, 664
Mining towns, 497–500
Missionaries, foreign, 573–574
Mississippi Freedom Democratic Party (MFDP), 838
Mississippi Freedom Summer, 837–838

Missouri v. ex rel. Gaines, 822, 836
Model T, 660
Momaday, N. Scott, 873
Mondale, Walter, 893, 900
Monroe Doctrine, 625, 894
Montgomery bus boycott, 817–819
Montgomery Improvement Association (MIA), 818
Montgomery Ward, 526, 528
Mood-altering drugs, 856–857
Moon landing, 875
Moralism, 625–628
Morality, 670–672
Morgan, Albert, 476
Morgan, J.P., 611
Morgan, Lewis Henry, 514
Morgan v. Virginia, 820, 836
Morgenthau, Henry, Jr., 727
Mormon settlements, 500
Morrill Act, 508
Moscow Olympics, 894
Moses, Bob, 837
Mossadegh, Mohammed, 792
Motherhood, 776
Mount Rainier, 511
Movies, 597, 600, 653–655, 664–666, 713, 715, 734, 774, 803–804
Movies (Sloan), 600
Movie stars, 664
Moynihan, Daniel P., 875
Muckraking journalism, 588–589
Muhammad, Elijah, 839
Muir, John, 612–613
Muller v. Oregon, 591
Multiculturalism, 927
Municipal government, 558–559, 593–594
Munn v. Illinois, 561
Murray, Philip, 769
Music
African American, 681, 716, 802–803, 821
bebop, 820, 821
jazz, 668, 716, 820, 821
rock, 787–789, 802–804, 857
during World War II, 734

Music industry, 668, 802–803
Muskie, Edward, 868
Mussolini, Benito, 723, 724
Mutual aid societies, 679
Myers, William, 796–797
My Lai Massacre, 876–877

N

NAFTA. *See* North American Free Trade Agreement (NAFTA)
Nagasaki, 749, 763
Napalm, 857, 878
Nash, Diane, 827
Nashville sit-in, 827
Nasser, Gamal Abdel, 792–793
Nast, Thomas, 474, 534
National Advisory Committee on Civil Disorders, 864
National Aeronautics and Space Agency (NASA), 792, 809
National American Woman Suffrage Association (NAWSA), 570–571, 631, 639–640, 678
National Association for the Advancement of Colored People (NAACP), 593, 610, 681, 818, 820
National Association of Manufacturers (NAM), 606
National Board of Censorship (NBC), 597
National Committee for a Sane Nuclear Policy (SANE), 808
National Congress of American Indians (NCAI), 844
National Consumer's League (NCL), 608
National debt, 901
National Defense Education Act (NDEA), 795
National-emphasis programs, 861–862
National Environmental Policy Act, 863
National forests, 510, 511
National Foundation on the Arts and Humanities Act, 863
National Housing Act, 701, 765–766

National Indian Youth Council (NIYC), 844
National Industrial Recovery Act, 698, 699
National Institutes of Health, 801
National Interstate and Defense Highways Act, 795
National Labor Relations Act, 700, 709
National Labor Relations Board, 700
National Mineral Act, 484
National Negro Congress, 733
National Organization for Women (NOW), 869
National Origins Act, 673–674
National parks, 511
National Park Service, 614
National pastimes, 549–550
National Reclamation Act, 510
National Recovery Administration (NRA), 698, 700
National Registration Day, 735
National Science Foundation, 766
National security, during Cold War, 766–767, 779–780
National Security Act, 766–767
National Security Council (NSC), 766, 780
National Security Resources Board (NSRB), 766
National trade associations, 662
National Traffic and Motor Vehicle Safety Act, 863
National War Labor Board (NWLB), 637, 657, 727
National Woman's Party (NWP), 640, 678
National Woman Suffrage Association (NWSA), 469
Nation of Islam (NOI), 839
Native American Rights Fund, 844
Native Americans. See Indian peoples
Nativism, 569, 679
NATO. See North Atlantic Treaty Organization (NATO)
Navajo code talkers, 737
Navajo Indians, 520
Naval War College, 574

Navy, U.S., 574
Nazi Germany, 723–724, 738, 745, 748
Nazi-Soviet Pact, 725
Nebraska, 506
Neoconservatism, 895
Nevelson, Louise, 712
New Deal
    arts and, 711–712
    ebbing of, 711
    end of, 727
    First Hundred Days, 696–698, 699
    Indians and, 708–709
    key legislation, 699, 701
    limits of, 709–711
    minorities and, 710–711
    in South, 702–703
    water policy and, 705, 708
    in West, 703–709
    women and, 709–710
New England colonies, second, 700–702
New Freedom, 615
New Frontier, 806–809
Newlands Reclamation Act, 614
New Masses (magazine), 713
New media, 923–924
New Nationalism, 614, 615
"New Negro," 681
New Orleans, Louisiana, 937–938
New Right, 895–898
New South, 536–540
Newspapers, tabloid, 666–667
Newton, Huey P., 869
New Woman, 607–608
New York City, 604
    Central Park, 548
    Greenwich Village, 606–607
    Harlem, 679–682
    slums of, 590
Nez Perce Indians, 496–497
Ngo Dinh Diem, 794
Niagara movement, 610
Nicaragua, 625, 894, 906–907
Nicolas II, 635

9/11 Commission, 934
Nixon, Richard
    "Checkers Speech," 781, 805
    domestic policy of, 875
    election of 1960 and, 807–808, 828–829
    election of 1968 and, 867–868
    election of 1972 and, 879
    foreign policy of, 877–879
    Guatemala and, 794
    presidency of, 874–880
    resignation of, 880
    as vice president, 781
    Vietnam War and, 875–877
    Watergate scandal and, 879–880
No Child Left Behind Act, 937
No Man's Land, 492
Nonviolent civil disobedience, 825–826
Normal schools, 548
North
    industry in, 482–484
    migration of African Americans to, 644–645
    reconstruction in, 482–486
North, Oliver, 908–909
North American Free Trade Agreement (NAFTA), 920–921
North Atlantic Treaty Organization (NATO), 761, 762–763
North Dakota, 506
Northern Securities v. North America, 611
North Vietnam, 809, 853–854. See also Vietnam War
Novels, dime, 512
NOW. See National Organization for Women (NOW)
NSC-68, 761, 780
Nuclear arms race, 763, 808, 906

O

Oakley, Annie, 512, 513
Obama, Barack
    election of 2008 and, 938–940
    foreign policy of, 942
    presidency of, 941–942

Occupational Safety and Health Administration, 875

Odet, Clifford, 713

Office buildings, 542

Office of Economic Opportunity (OEO), 861

Office of Indian Affairs (OIA), 519

Office of Price Administration (OPA), 727

Office of Scientific Research and Development (OSRD), 727

Office of Strategic Services (OSS), 727

Office of War Information, 735

Office of War Mobilization (OWM), 727

Oil consumption, 888

Oil crisis, 887

Oil embargo, 889

Oil interests, in Middle East, 792

Oil refining, 484

Okies, 704–705, 706–707

Okinawa, 745

Oklahoma land rush, 491–493

Old age pensions, 699, 700

Olney, Richard C., 566

Omaha Act, 514

OPEC. *See* Organization of Petroleum Exporting Countries (OPEC)

Open Door policy, 626

Open shop campaign, 606

Operation Desert Storm, 911

Operation Rolling Thunder, 854–855, 857, 858

Operation Wetback, 843

Oppenheimer, J. Robert, 722, 746, 756

Orange County, California, 885–886

Oranges, 509

Organization Man (Whyte), 800

Organization of Petroleum Exporting Countries (OPEC), 887

Organized crime, 672, 673

Organized labor. *See* Labor unions

The Origin of the Species (Darwin), 675

Orlando, Vittorio, 646

Orrick, John, 459

O'Sullivan, Timothy, 463

Oswald, Lee Harvey, 812, 813

Outsourcing, 887

Ozawa v. U.S., 674

P

Pacific Railway Act, 482

Packard, Vance, 806

Pact of Paris, 662

Pahlavi, Riza (shah), 792

Palestine, 792, 893–894

Palin, Sarah, 940

Palmer, A. Mitchell, 648

Palmer, Potter, 543

Pan African Congress, 647

Panama Canal, 624–625, 894

Panama Canal Company, 624

Pan-American Conference, 574

Paramount Theater, 802

Parker, Alton B., 612

Parker, Charlie, 820

Parker, Fess, 805

Parks, Rosa, 817–819

Partisan politics, 558

Patent medicines, 546

Patriotism, 777

Patronage, 558, 559, 560

Paul, Alice, 639–640

Peace Corps, 808–809

Peale, Norman Vincent, 798

Pearl Harbor, 725–726

Pears' Soap, 572

Pendleton Civil Service Reform Act, 560

Penicillin, 801

Pennsylvania Railroad, 483

Pension Office, 558

Pentagon Papers, 879

People's Party, 563–564

Perkins, Frances, 604, 701–702, 709–710

Perlin, Bernard, 867

Pershing, John J., 621, 627, 634

Persian Gulf War, 911

Personal income, 775

Philippines
   war in, 577
   during World War II, 744

Phonographs, 668

Photography, 513–514, 590, 712–713, 714

Piedmont communities, 537–540

Pillips, David Graham, 589

Pima Indians, 519

Pinchot, Gifford, 612, 613, 614

Ping-Pong diplomacy, 877

Pinochet, Augusto, 879

Pinzer, Maimie, 597

Pippin, Horace, 733

Plains Indians, 493–494

Planned communities, 795–797

Platt Amendment, 577

Playgrounds Movement, 597

Plessy v. *Ferguson*, 821, 823

Plows, 507

Plunkitt, George Washington, 593

Polio, 801

Political cartoons, 614, 627

Political machines, 593–594

Political parties, during Reconstruction, 476–478

Political reforms, 595

Politics
   African American, 475
   city, 593–594
   of identity, 868–874
   machinery of, 558–559
   partisan, 558
   of Reconstruction, 461–469, 476–482
   of reform, 567–568
   television and, 805–806

Pollock, Jackson, 712

Poll taxes, 596

Pollution, 542–543, 889

Polygamy, 500

Popular culture, in World War II, 734–735

Popular Front, 713

Populism, 560–564, 568

Port Huron Statement, 852
Potsdam Conference, 758
Potter, Paul, 858–859
Poverty
    in 1980s, 902
    feminization of, 903
    war on, 861–864
Powell, Colin, 934, 935
Powell, John Wesley, 509, 518
The Power Elite (Mills), 800
Pratt, Richard Henry, 516–517
Presidential elections
    of 1868, 467–468
    of 1872, 484
    of 1876, 485–486
    of 1896, 568–569
    of 1904, 612
    of 1912, 614–615
    of 1920, 648–649
    of 1928, 683–684
    of 1932, 695–696
    of 1936, 702
    of 1940, 724–725
    of 1948, 764–765
    of 1952, 780–781, 805–806
    of 1960, 807–808, 828–829
    of 1964, 839–840
    of 1968, 865, 867–868
    of 1972, 879
    of 1976, 892
    of 1980, 896, 898
    of 1984, 900
    of 1988, 909–910
    of 1992, 911–912
    of 2000, 930–931
    of 2004, 936
    of 2008, 938–940
President's Committee on Civil
    Rights, 820
Presley, Elvis, 787–789, 803
Prison population, 926
Pritchett, Laurie, 831
Pro-family movement, 896
Professional sports, 549–550, 668–670
Progressive diplomacy, 623–624

Progressive Party, 614–615, 765
Progressivism
    challenges to, 601–607
    national, 611–616
    origins of, 587–595
    social control and, 596–601
    state level, 595–596
    unifying themes in, 588
    urban reform and, 593–595
    women's movements and, 607–611
Prohibition, 596–599, 640, 672
Project Troy, 780
Pro-life movement, 896
Promontory Point, 483
Propaganda
    anti-Communist, 780
    World War I, 631, 632
    World War II, 727
Property taxes, 886
Proposition 187, 927
Prostitution, 504, 597
Protestant work ethic, 532
Protest movements, 855–860, 870
Psychological Strategy Board, 761
Public Broadcasting Act, 863
Public education. *See* Education
Public health, 542–543, 640–641,
    731–732, 801
Public spaces, 548–549
Public Works Administration (PWA),
    698, 699, 708
Puerto Ricans, 843–844
Puerto Rico, 577, 843
Pulitzer, John, 576
Pullman strike, 566
Pure Food and Drug Act, 612

R

Race riots, 570, 733–734, 842
Racial diversity, 927
Racial justice, 610–611
Racial pride, 869
Racism, 462, 569–571, 609–610, 711
    black music and, 802–803
    eugenics and, 673

against Mexican immigrants, 679
    in military, 633–634
    during World War II, 733–734
Rader, Melvin, 755–756
Radical Republicans, 464–466
Radio broadcasting, 666, 715–716
Railroads, 492
    business and, 483–484
    Chinese labor and, 482–483
    Gould and, 532
    industrial growth and, 527–528
    industry and, 499
    regulation of, 595
    routes, 1860-1900, 498
    settlement of West and, 505–506
    strikes, 563, 566
    transcontinental, 482–483, 527–528
Raisins, 509
Randolph, A. Philip, 733, 832–833
Range wars, 505
Rape of Nanking, 723
Raskob, John J., 692
Rationing, during World War II, 731
Reagan, Nancy, 905
Reagan, Ronald, 885–886
    economy during, 900–903
    election of 1980 and, 896, 898
    election of 1984 and, 900
    foreign policy of, 905–909
    inauguration of, 897
    Iran-Contra scandal and, 907–909
    presidency of, 898–901
    social problems under, 904–905
Reagan Doctrine, 906–907
Reaganomics, 886, 899–900
Reaper, 507
Rebel Without a Cause (film), 804
Recalls, 595
Recession
    in 1980s, 900–901
    of 2008-2009, 940–941
    under Roosevelt, 711
Reconstruction Acts, 466–467,
    469, 473
Reconstruction era, 458–487

black political activism in, 473, 475

congressional reconstruction, 466–467

election of 1868, 467–468

end of, 486

free slaves in, 469–475

Lincoln's plan for, 462–464

in North, 482–486

politics and society during, 476–482

politics of, 461–469

presidential reconstruction, 464

radical reconstruction, 464–466

southern economy during, 479, 482

white resistance during, 477–479

woman suffrage and, 468–469

Reconstruction Finance Corporation (RFC), 694–695

Recording industry, 668, 802–803

Red Cloud, 495

Red Power, 873

Red River War, 496

Red Scare, 648, 673, 767–769

Reeb, James J., 841

Reed, John, 607

Reed-Johnson National Origins Act, 673–674

Reese, Brister, 460

Referendums, 595

Reform and reform movements. *See also* New Deal; Progressivism

civil service reform, 559–560

education reform, 597, 600–601

intellectual trends promoting, 589, 591

settlement house movement, 591–593

temperance movement, 596–599

urban, 593–595

women and, 591–593

women's rights, 607–611

Regulatory agencies, 558, 612

Reid, Whitelaw, 536

Reisman, David, 800

Religion

in Cold War era, 798

evangelical, 573

fundamentalism in, 675, 886

social gospel, 567

televangelists, 895–896

Religious right, 895–896

Remington, Frederic, 513

Reno, Janet, 922

Reproductive rights, 927

Republican Party

African Americans and, 475

Contract with America and, 920

election of 1872 and, 484

election of 1896 and, 568–569

in late nineteenth century, 558

New Right and, 895–898

in South, 476, 868

Southern Strategy of, 875

Reservation policy, 494, 495

Reserve Officer Training Corps (ROTC), 735

Resettlement Administration (RA), 700–701

Retail industry, 528–529

Reuther, Walter, 799, 833

Revenue Acts, 809

Rice, Condoleezza, 934

Richardson, Bill, 928–929

Riis, Jacob, 588, 590, 592, 611

Riots

race, 570, 733–734, 842

urban, 525–526, 862–864

zoot suit, 734

Rivera, Diego, 873

On the Road (Kerouac), 806

Roads, 776, 795

Robertson, Pat, 895

Robinson, Jackie, 821

Robinson, Jo Ann, 818

Robinson, Ruby Doris, 838

Rockefeller, John D., 484, 530, 531, 589, 656

Rockefeller, Nelson, 892

Rock music, 787–789, 802–803

Rock 'n' roll music, 803–804, 857

Rockwell, Norman, 729

Rocky Mountains, 511

Roe v. *Wade*, 896

Roller-skating, 545

Rommel, Erwin, 740

Roosevelt, Eleanor, 709, 710, 711, 809

Roosevelt, Franklin D.. *See also* New Deal

court-packing plan of, 709

critics of, 698–700

death of, 749

election of 1932 and, 695–696

election of 1936 and, 702

election of 1940 and, 724–725

fireside chats of, 696

First Hundred Days, 696–698

Japanese American interment and, 732

life of soldier on, 696

recession of, 711

Second Hundred Days, 700–702

World War II and, 724–727, 740, 745

at Yalta Conference, 748–749

Roosevelt, Theodore, 512, 592

conservation and, 612–614

election of 1912 and, 614–615

foreign policy of, 624–625

as governor of New York, 595

presidency of, 611–614

progressivism and, 611

Spanish-American War and, 576

trust-busting by, 611–612

Roosevelt Corollary, 625

Roosevelt Dam, 614

Root, Elihu, 625

Rosenberg, Julius and Ethel, 769

Rosie the Riveter, 729

Ross, Edward A., 596

Ross, Edwin A., 592

Rostow, Walt, 809–810

Rough Riders, 576

Ruby, Jack, 812

Rudd, Mark, 856

Rumsfeld, Donald, 934

Rural Electrification Administration (REA), 703

Rusk, Dean, 857
Russell, Charles, 513
Russian Revolution, 635, 641,
    644, 646
Russo-Japanese War, 625
Rustbelt communities, 903–904
Ruth, Babe, 668, 670

S

Sacco, Nicola, 682
Safer, Morley, 855
Salawags, 476
Salinger, J.D., 773
Salk, Jonas, 801
Saloons, 504
Same-sex marriage, 927
Sand Creek Massacre, 494–495
San Diego, California, 917–919
Sandinistas, 906–907
San Francisco, California, 545,
    856–857
Sanger, Margaret, 608–609, 671
Savio, Mario, 856
Schecter v. *United States*, 700
Schenck v. *United States*, 641
Schimler, E.A., 642–643
Schlafly, Phyllis, 896
Schomburg, Arturo, 603
Schools, 600–661. *See also* Education
    African American, 471–472
    desegregation, 822–823, 825
    high schools, 547, 600–661, 803
    Indian, 515–517
    normal, 548
Schreyvogel, Charles, 513
Schwerner, Michael, 837
Science, 801
Scientific management, 533, 656
Scopes trial, 675, 676–677
Seale, Bobby, 869
Sears, Roebuck and Company, 528
SEATO. *See* Southeast Asia Treaty
    Organization (SEATO)
Second industrial revolution, 527,
    655–656
Second Red Scare, 767–769

Sedition Act, 641
Segregation, 569–571, 644
    constitutionality of, 822–823
    in military, 736–737
    in South, 477, 596, 821–825
Selective Service, 735
Selective Service Act, 736
Self-improvement, 544–545
Selma, Alabama, 839–842
Seminoles, 491
Separate but equal doctrine, 570
September 11, 2001, 930, 931–933
Servicemen's Readjustment Act,
    756, 795
Settlement houses, 585–587, 591–593
Seventeenth Amendment, 595
Seward, William Henry, 574
Sewer systems, 542
Sex education, 671
Sexuality
    in 1920s, 671
    studies of, 801
Sexual revolution, 856
Seymour, Horatio, 467–468
Shahn, Ben, 704
The Shame of the Cities (Steffens), 589
Sharecropping, 472–473, 479, 663
Share Our Wealth Society, 699
Sheen, Fulton J., 798
Sheldon, Charles M., 567
Sheppard-Towner Act, 678
Sherman, William Tecumseh, 463
Sherman Antitrust Act, 530, 611–612
Shuttlesworth, Fred, 832
Sierra Club, 613
Silent Spring (Carson), 889
Silicon Valley, 923
Silko, Leslie, 873
Silver Democrats, 568
Silver issue, 567–568
Silver rush, 498
Sinclair, Upton, 589, 592, 612, 699
Singing plows, 507
Sioux Indians, 493–495, 518–519
Sit-ins, 826–828
Sitting Bull, 496, 512

Sixteenth Amendment, 469, 615
Sixties generation, 855–860
Slaughterhouse cases, 478
Slaves/slavery, freedom for, 469–475
Sloan, John, 600
Slums, 590
Smith, Al, 592, 683, 806
Smith, Hoke, 592
Smith, Margaret Chase, 770–771
Smith, Perry H., 543
Smith-Mundt Act, 761
Smith v. *Albright*, 733
Smoot-Hawley Tariff, 695
Soap operas, 716
Social Control (Ross), 596
Social Darwinism, 533, 589, 673
Social disparities, 926
Social gospel, 567
Socialism, 567, 648
Socialist Party, 615
Social reform movements
    prostitution and, 597
    temperance movement, 596–597,
        598–599
Social sciences, 589
Social Security, 790
Social Security Act, 700, 701, 709, 863
Sociology, 589
Soil Conservation Service (SCS), 704
Sokoloff, Nikolai, 712
Sokoza, Anastasio, 879
Somalia, 921
Sotomayor, Sandra, 942
South
    black codes in, 464–465
    destruction of, following Civil War,
        461–462
    economy of, 479, 482, 536
    farming in, 703
    industry in, 536–540
    Jim Crow laws in, 569–571, 821
    labor in, 536–537
    "new," 536–540
    New Deal in, 702–703
    Piedmont communities of, 537–540
    progressivism in, 595–596

Reconstruction era in, 458–487

segregation in, 477, 569–571, 596, 821–825

South Africa, 879

Southeast Asia Treaty Organization (SEATO), 794

Southern Christian Leadership Conference (SCLC), 826, 831–832, 840

Southern Strategy, 875

Southern Tenant Farmers Union (STFU), 703

South Korea, 874

South Vietnam, 794, 809, 853, 854–855. *See also* Vietnam War

Southwest

during Dust Bowl, 705

Mexican borderland communities, 500–502

Soviet Union, 713

Afghanistan and, 894

Carter and, 894

Cold War and, 789–790, 791–794

collapse of, 909

division of Europe and, 758–759

as "evil empire," 906

following World War II, 757–758

Nixon and, 877

Reagan and, 905–906

Sputnik, 792, 795, 809

World War II and, 724, 725, 738, 740, 743

Soyer, Isaac, 694

Space race, 792, 809

Spain, Cuba and, 575–577

Spalding, Albert, 550

Spanish-American War, 575–577

Spanish Civil War, 724

Spencer, Herbert, 589

Spock, Benjamin, 776

Spoil system, 558, 559–560

Sports, 549–550, 668–670

Sputnik, 792, 795, 809

Spy cases, 769

Stalin, Joseph, 745, 748–749, 757–758, 760, 762, 789–790

Stalingrad, Battle of, 740

Standard Oil Company, 484, 530–531, 589

Standard Oil Trust, 530–531

Standing Bear, Luther, 516–517

Stanford, Leland, 483

Stanton, Edwin M., 466

Stanton, Elizabeth Cady, 468, 469

Starr, Kenneth, 922

State government, progressivism and, 595–596

Stead, W. T., 567

Steel industry, 646

Steffens, Lincoln, 589, 592

Steinbeck, John, 706, 712–713

Stevens, Thaddeus, 464

Stevenson, Adlai E., 781

Stewart, William M., 484

Stock market

in 1980s, 900, 901

crash of 1929, 692–693

in twenties, 656, 692

Stone, Lucy, 468, 469

Stonewall riot, 872

Strategic Arms Limitation Treaty (SALT), 877

Strategic Defense Initiative (SDI), 906

Streetcars, 542

Strikes, 526, 700

in 1890s, 565–567

auto industry, 689–691

garment industry, 604

mining, 605, 606

post–WWI, 645–646

railroad, 563, 566

by state, 1880, 562

during World War II, 730

Strong, Josiah, 571, 573, 580

Stryker, Roy, 712

Student activism, 855–857

Student Nonviolent Coordinating Committee (SNCC), 828, 837–838, 840

Students for a Democratic Society (SDS), 852, 870

Submerged Lands Act, 790

Subprime mortgage crisis, 940–941

Suburbs

growth of, 660, 798, 800

life in, 798–799

planned communities in, 795–797

Subversive Activities Control Act, 761

Subway systems, 542

Suez Canal, 793

Suez Crisis, 792–793

Suffrage, women's, 468–469, 563, 638–640

Sullivan, Louis, 530

Sullivan, Timothy D., 593–594

Summer, William Graham, 533

Summer of Love, 856–857

Sumner, William Graham, 589

The Sun Also Rises (Hemingway), 682

Sunbelt communities, 903–904

Supply-side economics, 899–900

Supreme Court, U.S.. *See also specific cases*

Civil Rights Cases, 478–479, 570

court-packing plan and, 709

Slaughterhouse cases, 478

Swaggart, Jimmy, 895

Sweatt v. *Palmer*, 836

Syminton, Stuart, 792

Szilard, Leo, 746–747

T

Tabloids, 666–667

Taft, Robert, 779–780

Taft, William Howard, 577, 614–615, 625

Takagi, Harry, 843

Taliban, 933, 936

Tammany Hall, 558, 562, 593, 594

Tarbell, Ida, 531, 589, 592

Tariffs, 558, 809

McKinley Tariff, 558, 567

Smoot-Hawley Tariff, 695

TARP. *See* Troubled Asset Relief Program (TARP)

Tax cuts

under Bush, Jr., 936–937

under Reagan, 899

Taxes, property, 886

Taylor, Frederick Winslow, 533
Taylor, Maxwell, 809–810
Teapot Dome scandal, 661
Technological innovations
    in 1990s, 923–924
    in late nineteenth century, 527–528
Teenage pregnancy, 903
Teenagers, 801–804
Telephone, 527
Televangelists, 895–896
Television, 804–806, 824
Teller, Edward, 746–747
Teller, Henry, 576
Temperance movement, 596–597,
    598–599
Tenant farming, 482
Tenement houses, 542
Tennessee Valley Authority (TVA),
    697–698, 699, 703
Ten Percent Plan, 463
Tenure of Office Act, 466
Terrorism, 930, 931–933
Tet Offensive, 865
Textile mills, 536, 537, 664
Theaters, 546–547
Thirteenth Amendment, 469
Three Mile Island, 890–891
Thurman, Allen G., 559
Tijuana, Mexico, 917–919
Tilden, Samuel J., 485, 486
Till, Emmett, 821–822
Tillman, Benjamin, 609
Ting, Jan C., 928–929
Townsend, Francis E., 699
Toynbee Hall, 589
Trade, free, 920–921
Trade imbalance, 887
Tramps, 485
Transcontinental railroad, 482–483,
    527–528
Transnational communities, 917–919
Transportation. *See also* Railroads
    mass transit, 800
    roads, 776, 795
Triangle Shirtwaist Company, 604

Triple Alliance, 628
Trolleys, 542
Troubled Asset Relief Program
    (TARP), 940–941
Truman, Harry
    atomic bomb and, 749
    civil rights and, 820
    election of 1948 and, 764–765
    election of 1952 and, 780–781
    Fair Deal and, 765–766
    foreign policy of, 760–762, 777
    Korean War and, 778–780
    at Potsdam Conference, 758
    presidency of, 763–766
Truman Doctrine, 760–762
Trust-busting, 611–612
Trusts, 530
Tubb, Ernest, 734
Tugwell, Rexford G., 700–701
Turner, Frederick Jackson, 513, 571
Tuskegee Institute, 548
Tweed, William Marcy, 558
Tweed Ring, 485
Twenties, 652–685
    economy of, 660–664, 691–692
    immigration during, 672–674,
        678–679
    intellectuals during, 682–683
    mass culture in, 664–672
    morality in, 670–672
    Prohibition during, 672
    prosperity during, 655–660
    women in, 675, 678
Twenty Cent Movie (Marsh), 715
Twenty-first Amendment, 672
Twenty-second Amendment, 764

U

U-boats, 629
Underwood-Simmons Act, 615
Unemployed Councils, 700
Unemployment
    in 1890s, 564–565
    during Great Depression, 693–694
Unemployment Agency (Soyer), 694

Unemployment insurance, 700
Unidentified flying objects
    (UFOs), 773
Union League, 475
Unions. *See* Labor unions
United Automobile Workers (UAW),
    690–691, 701, 730, 799
United Farm Workers (UFW),
    872–873
United Fruit Company, 530, 625, 793
United Mine Workers, 605–606, 664
United Nations, 759–760
United States, as world power,
    623–628
United States v. *Cruikshank*, 478–479
United States v. *Reese*, 478–479
United States v. *Reynolds*, 500
United States v. *Wheeler*, 844
Universal Negro Improvement
    Association, 680
University of California, Berkeley,
    855–860
University of Washington, 755–756
Up from Slavery (Washington), 609
Uptown, Chicago, 851–853
Urbanization. *See also* Cities
    industry and, 540–543
Urban machine, 593–594
Urban Mass Transportation Act, 863
Urban reform, 593–595
Urban riots, 525–526, 862–864
Urey, Harold C., 763
USA Patriot Act, 933–934
U.S. dollar, 875
U.S. Forest Service, 612
U.S.-Mexico border, 921, 928–929
USS *Maine*, 576
U.S. v. *Thind*, 674
Utah, 500
Ute Indians, 519

V

Vance, Cyrus R., 893
Vanderbilt, Cornelius, 483
Van Kleeck, Mary, 638

Vanzetti, Bartolomeo, 682

Vaqueros, 502

Vardaman, James K., 592

Vaudeville, 549

Veblen, Thorstein, 543

Venereal disease, 640

Versailles, Treaty of, 647–648, 662

Vertical integration, of business, 529–530

Veterans, Vietnam War, 860

Victory Suits, 735

Vietcong, 854–855, 865

Vietminh, 794

Vietnamization policy, 876, 878

Vietnam veterans, 860

Vietnam War, 852, 853–860

  casualties in, 875

  end of, 876

  escalation of, 854–855

  Gulf of Tonkin resolution and, 854

  impact of, 855

  Johnson and, 853–854, 855, 858–859

  Kennedy and, 809–810

  map of, 866

  My Lai Massacre, 876–877

  Nixon and, 875–877

  protests against, 855–860

  public opinion on, 876

  soldiers in, 860

  Tet Offensive in, 865

Vinson, Fred, 823

Violence. *See also* Riots

  against African Americans, 468, 477–478, 570, 645, 674–675

  frontier, 504–505

Virgin Islands, 580

Virtual communities, 923–924

VISTA (Volunteers in Service of America), 861

Vocational schools, 548

Voice of America, 780

Volstead Act, 672

Voter turnout, in late nineteenth century, 558

Voting rights

  for African Americans, 475, 478–479

  for women, 468–469

Voting Rights Act, 836, 839–842, 863

W

Wade, Benjamin F., 463

Wade-Davis Bill, 463

Wage labor, 482, 533–534

Wages, 537

  gender gap in, 888

  during World War II, 731

Wagner Act, 700, 701

Waiting for Lefty (Odet), 713

Wald, Lillian, 585–586, 592–593, 604, 616

Walker, Moses, 550

Wallace, George, 868

Wallace, Henry A., 704, 765

The Wapshot Chronicle (Cheever), 799

War bonds, 727

Ward, Lester Frank, 589

War Democrats, 464

War Department, 637

Warehouse Act, 561

War Industries Board, 636

War Manpower Commission (WMC), 727

War on drugs, 904–905

War on poverty, 852, 861–864

War on terror, 930–934

War Production Board, 735

Warren, Earl, 813, 823, 875

War reparations, 647, 662

Washington, Booker T., 548, 609–610

Watergate scandal, 879–880

Water policy, in West, 705, 708

Water systems, 542

Watson, Henry, 460

Watson, Tom, 568

Watts riots, 842, 863–864

WAVES, 736

Wealth, gospel of, 532–533

Wealth distribution

  in 1980s, 901–903

  in 1990s, 926

Wealthy, conspicuous consumption by, 543–544

Weapons of mass destruction (WMDs), 934

Webb, Alex, 459, 475

Welfare capitalism, 657–658

Welfare Reform Act, 920

Welfare system, 903

Welles, Orson, 712

Wells, Ida B., 570, 589

West

  crime in, 504–505

  landscape of, 510–514

  legend of Wild West, 512–513

  military-industrial communities in, 776–777

  New Deal in, 703–709

  settlement of, 505–506

  water policy in, 705, 708

West, Mae, 715

Western Federation of Miners (WFM), 606

Western novels, 512

Westinghouse, 657

Westmoreland, William, 854

Weyler, Valeriano, 575–576

Wheat, 561, 663

Wheeler, Edward, 503

Whiskey Ring, 485

White, James A., 598–599

White Collar (Mills), 800

White man's burden, 572

White settlers

  on Great Plains, 505–506

  in Indian Country, 492–494

White supremacy, 569–571

Whitewater, 922

Whyte, William H., 800

The Wild One (film), 803–804

Wild West, 512–513

Wild West shows, 512–513

Wilkening, Ruby, 721

Willard, Frances E., 563, 564

Willkie, Wendel L., 724

Wilson, Charles, 790

Wilson, Woodrow, 592
    election of 1912 and, 614–615
    first term of, 615–616
    foreign policy of, 625–628
    Fourteen Points of, 635, 646
    League of Nations and, 647
    New Freedom of, 615
    Treaty of Versailles and, 647–648
    World War I and, 629–631

Winchell, Walter, 667

Wisconsin Idea, 595

Wives, suburban, 798

Wobblies, 606, 637–638

Wolfowitz, Paul, 934

Woman's Christian Temperance
    Union (WCTU), 563

Woman's Peace Party, 631

Woman suffrage, 638–640

Women
    in 1920s, 670–671, 675, 678
    activism by, 563
    African American, 470, 610–611,
        872, 888
    in Cold War era, 775–776
    education of, 776
    labor unions and, 535
    in late nineteenth century, 544–545
    middle class, 544–545, 607–608
    in military, 736
    New Deal and, 709–710
    in poverty, 903
    social gospel movement and, 567
    voting rights for, 468–469
    in workforce, 533, 537, 775,
        871, 888
    working class, 545
    during World War I, 638–640
    during World War II, 728–730,
        731, 736

Women in Industry Service
    (WIS), 638

Women's Army Auxiliary Corps
    (WAAC), 736

Women's Army Corp (WAC), 736

Women's Christian Temperance
    Union (WCTU), 596, 598

Women's clubs, 608

Women's colleges, 547–548

Women's Educational and Industrial
    Union, 548

Women's liberation movement, 869,
    870, 871–872

Women's National Indian Association
    (WNIA), 515

Women's network, 709–710

Women's Political Council (WPC), 818

Women's rights movement, 563
    in 1920s, 675, 678
    black women and, 610–611
    in early twentieth century, 607–611
    suffrage movement, 638–640

Women's Trade Union League, 604

Woodstock Music Festival, 857

Woolworth, Charles, 528

Workers
    African American, 534, 536–537
    factory, 533–534, 537
    welfare capitalism and, 657–658
    women, 533, 537, 775, 871, 888
    in World War II, 728–730

Work hours, 538–539, 591, 593

Working class
    in late nineteenth century, 545–546
    leisure activities of, 546

World Bank, 757–758

World's Columbian Exposition,
    512–513, 571

World Trade Center, 931

World Trade Organization (WTO),
    761, 921

World War I
    African American soldiers in,
        633–634
    Allied victory in, 635
    Allies in, 628
    America neutrality at beginning of,
        629–630
    American Expeditionary Force in,
        621–623

Central Powers in, 628
    debts from, 662
    dissent during, 641, 644
    economy during, 636
    in Europe, 628
    fighting of, 634
    financing of, 636
    homefront during, 635–641
    labor during, 637–638
    Lusitania and, 629
    mobilization for, 631–635
    opposition to, 630, 631
    peacemaking following, 646–648
    preparations for, 629–630
    racism during, 633–634
    recruitment for, 631, 633
    U.S. entrance into, 630–631
    wartime propaganda, 631, 632
    western front in, 634
    women in, 638–640

World War II, 720–751
    African Americans during, 728,
        733–734, 736–737
    Allied offensive in, 740–743
    in Asia and Pacific, 743–745
    atomic bomb and, 746–747, 749
    civil rights after, 819–821
    D-Day, 742
    division of Europe after, 758–759
    Double V campaign in, 733–734,
        819
    draft in, 735
    economy during, 727–728
    end of, 749
    in Europe, 739
    events leading to, 723–724
    fighting of, 738–745
    Holocaust and, 745, 748
    homefront during, 730–735
    Japanese American interment in, 732
    military in, 735–738
    mobilization for, 726–730
    Pearl Harbor and, 725–726
    popular culture during, 734–735
    preparations for, 724–725

propaganda during, 727
Soviet and, 738, 740
U.S. entrance into, 726
victory in Europe, 743
women during, 728–730, 731, 736
workers during, 728–730
Yalta Conference, 748–749
Wright, Jeremiah, 939
Wright, Richard, 713

Y

Yalta Conference, 748–749
Yana Indians, 519
Yellow Power, 874
Yellowstone National Park, 510, 511
Yezierska, Anzia, 712
Yom Kippur War, 877
Yosemite Act, 511
Yosemite National Park, 613
Young, Andrew, 824

Young, Brigham, 500
Young Women's Christian Association
(YWCA), 567
Youth culture, 801–804
Youth market, 801–802

Z

Zimmermann, Arthur, 630
Zoot suit riots, 734
Zwerg, James, 830

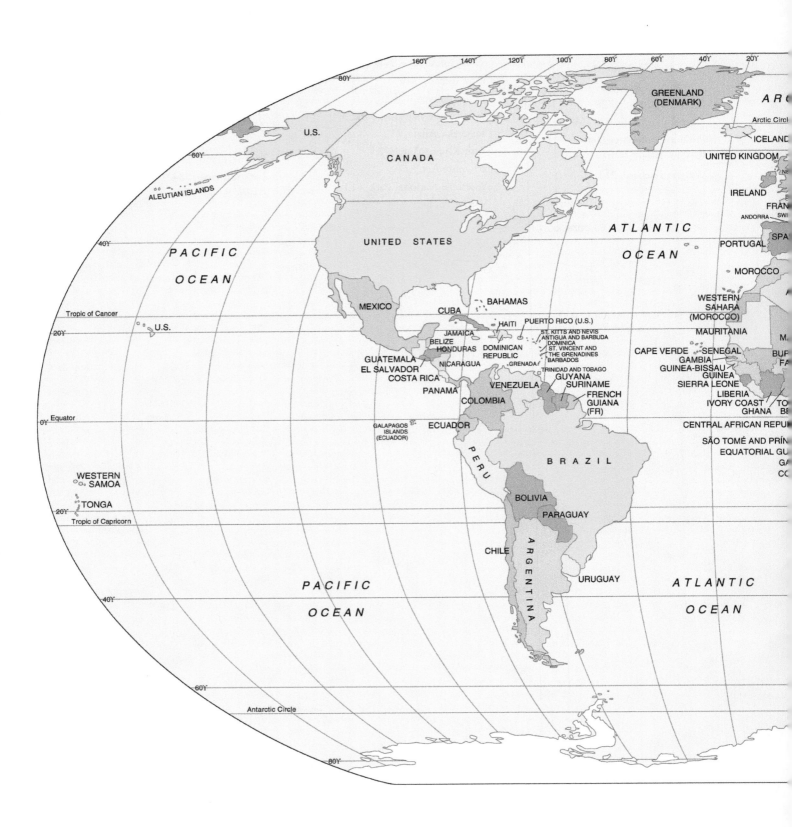

160Y 140Y 120Y 100Y 80Y 60Y 40Y 20Y

80Y

GREENLAND
(DENMARK)

AR C

Arctic Circl

ICELAND

U.S.

CANADA

60Y

UNITED KINGDOM

ALEUTIAN ISLANDS

IRELAND

FRAN

ANDORRA

SWI

40Y

PACIFIC

UNITED STATES

ATLANTIC

OCEAN

PORTUGAL

SPA

OCEAN

MOROCCO

Tropic of Cancer

MEXICO

BAHAMAS

WESTERN
SAHARA
(MOROCCO)

U.S.

CUBA

20Y

PUERTO RICO (U.S.)

MAURITANIA

M

HAITI

JAMAICA

ST. KITTS AND NEVIS
ANTIGUA AND BARBUDA
DOMINICA
ST. VINCENT AND
THE GRENADINES
BARBADOS

CAPE VERDE

SENEGAL

BUF

BELIZE

GUINEA-BISSAU

GAMBIA

FA

HONDURAS

DOMINICAN
REPUBLIC

GUINEA

GUATEMALA

NICARAGUA

GRENADA

SIERRA LEONE

EL SALVADOR

TRINIDAD AND TOBAGO

LIBERIA

COSTA RICA

GUYANA

IVORY COAST

TO

PANAMA

VENEZUELA

SURINAME

GHANA

BI

FRENCH
GUIANA
(FR)

COLOMBIA

Equator

CENTRAL AFRICAN REPU

0Y

GALAPAGOS
ISLANDS
(ECUADOR)

ECUADOR

SÃO TOMÉ AND PRÍN

EQUATORIAL GU

GA

PERU

CO

BRAZIL

WESTERN
SAMOA

BOLIVIA

TONGA

20Y

PARAGUAY

Tropic of Capricorn

A
R
G
E
N
T
I
N
A

CHILE

PACIFIC

URUGUAY

ATLANTIC

40Y

OCEAN

OCEAN

60Y

Antarctic Circle

80Y

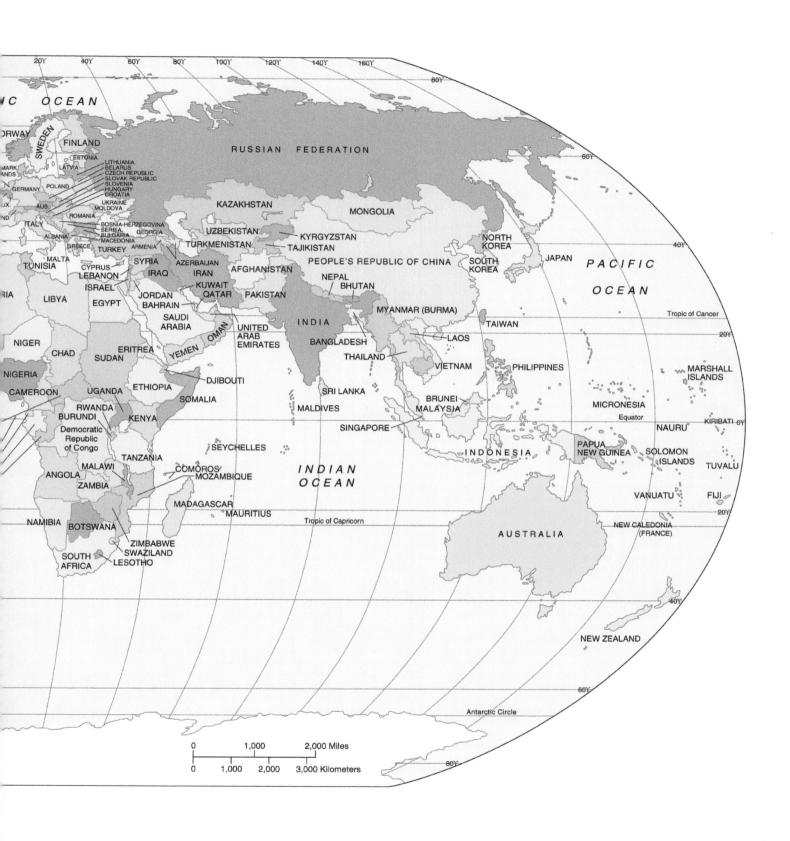

NC OCEAN

ORWAY
SWEDEN
FINLAND
ESTONIA
MARK)
ANDS
LITHUANIA
LATVIA
BELARUS
CZECH REPUBLIC
SLOVAK REPUBLIC
SLOVENIA
HUNGARY
CROATIA
GERMANY
POLAND
UKRAINE
MOLDOVA
LUX.
AUS.
ND
ROMANIA
ITALY
BOSNIA-HERZEGOVINA
SERBIA
BULGARIA
MACEDONIA
ALBANIA
GEORGIA
GREECE
TURKEY
ARMENIA
RIA
TUNISIA
MALTA
CYPRUS
LEBANON
SYRIA
AZERBAIJAN
ISRAEL
IRAQ
IRAN
LIBYA
EGYPT
JORDAN
BAHRAIN
KUWAIT
QATAR
SAUDI
ARABIA
OMAN
UNITED
ARAB
EMIRATES
YEMEN

RUSSIAN FEDERATION

KAZAKHSTAN
MONGOLIA
UZBEKISTAN
KYRGYZSTAN
TURKMENISTAN
TAJIKISTAN
AFGHANISTAN
PEOPLE'S REPUBLIC OF CHINA
NORTH
KOREA
SOUTH
KOREA
JAPAN
PACIFIC

OCEAN

NEPAL
BHUTAN
PAKISTAN
INDIA
MYANMAR (BURMA)
TAIWAN
Tropic of Cancer
BANGLADESH
LAOS
THAILAND
VIETNAM
PHILIPPINES
MARSHALL
ISLANDS

NIGER
CHAD
SUDAN
ERITREA
DJIBOUTI
SRI LANKA
MALDIVES
MICRONESIA
Equator
NAURU
KIRIBATI OY
NIGERIA
CAMEROON
UGANDA
ETHIOPIA
SOMALIA
BRUNEI
MALAYSIA
RWANDA
BURUNDI
KENYA
SINGAPORE
Democratic
Republic
of Congo
SEYCHELLES
INDONESIA
PAPUA
NEW GUINEA
SOLOMON
ISLANDS
TUVALU
TANZANIA
ANGOLA
MALAWI
COMOROS
MOZAMBIQUE
INDIAN
OCEAN
VANUATU
FIJI
ZAMBIA
MADAGASCAR
MAURITIUS
Tropic of Capricorn
NAMIBIA
BOTSWANA
ZIMBABWE
SWAZILAND
LESOTHO
AUSTRALIA
NEW CALEDONIA
(FRANCE)
SOUTH
AFRICA

NEW ZEALAND

Antarctic Circle

0   1,000   2,000 Miles
0   1,000   2,000   3,000 Kilometers